THE ASHGATE RESEARCH COMPANION TO MODERN IMPERIAL HISTORIES

'*The Ashgate Research Companion to Modern Imperial Histories* is a fluidly written, comprehensive, and authoritative approach to the current state of the knowledge and conceptions of empire that will be an essential tool for students and researchers alike.... A colossal subject has been effectively tackled here and we are left with a volume that is strikingly unique in it geographical and temporal scope, its empirical fortitude, and its analytical depth.'

Michael Charney, School of Oriental and African Studies,
University of London, UK

'Neither Eurocentric nor restricted to a single privileged historiographical approach, the essays that Levine and Marriot have brought together systematically introduce readers to the breadth – chronological, geographic, and thematic – of modern imperial studies.'

Andrew Zimmerman, The George Washington University, USA

ASHGATE
RESEARCH
COMPANION

The *Ashgate Research Companions* are designed to offer scholars and graduate students a comprehensive and authoritative state-of-the-art review of current research in a particular area. The Companions' editors bring together a team of respected and experienced experts to write chapters on the key issues in their speciality, providing a comprehensive reference to the field.

The Ashgate Research Companion to Modern Imperial Histories

Edited by

PHILIPPA LEVINE

University of Texas at Austin, USA

and

JOHN MARRIOTT

University of East London, UK

ASHGATE

Published by
Ashgate Publishing Limited
Wey Court East
Union Road
Farnham
Surrey GU9 7PT
England

Ashgate Publishing Company
Suite 420
101 Cherry Street
Burlington,
VT 05401-4405
USA

www.ashgate.com

British Library Cataloguing in Publication Data
The Ashgate research companion to modern imperial histories.
  1. Imperialism–History. 2. History, Modern.
  I. Research companion to modern imperial histories
  II. Levine, Philippa. III. Marriott, John, 1944–
  325.3'2'09-dc23

Library of Congress Cataloging-in-Publication Data
The Ashgate research companion to modern imperial histories / [edited by]
Philippa Levine and John Marriott.
    p. cm.
  Includes bibliographical references and index.
  ISBN 978-0-7546-6415-4 (hardcover : alk. paper) 1. Imperialism–History.
I. Levine, Philippa. II. Marriott, John, 1944– III. Title: Research
companion to modern imperial histories.
  JC359.A72 2012
  325'.3209–dc23

                     2011044087

ISBN 9780754664154 (hbk)
ISBN 9781409445906 (ebk)

Printed and bound in Great Britain by
MPG Books Group, UK

Contents

List of Figures and Tables

Figures

Tables

List of Maps

Acknowledgements

This volume owes much to Tom Gray, our editor at Ashgate, who, in late 2006 suggested we consider tackling this project. His encouragement and enthusiasm helped us tremendously along the way. More recently, Alexis Harasemovitch-Truax has patiently put into practice our sometimes-changing ideas about bringing this large and complex project to fruition. She has remained cheerful even as we were dilatory, and she has made sense of the mountain of files that have flown across oceans in the past year. Jack Loveridge tackled the enormous task of the index with grace, good humour and ferocious intelligence. We owe all three of them a great deal. We would also like to acknowledge the generous support of the Mary Helen Thompson Centennial Professorship in the Humanities at the University of Texas at Austin.

Philippa Levine, Austin, Texas, USA
John Marriott, Howden, Yorkshire, UK

Notes on Contributors

Michael Adas is the Abraham E. Voorhees Professor and Board of Governors' Chair at Rutgers University at New Brunswick. His works on European and American colonialism include *Machines as the Measure of Men: Science, Technology and Ideologies of European Dominance* (1989), which won the Dexter Prize in 1992, and *Dominance by Design: Technological Imperatives and America's Civilizing Mission* (2006).

Virginia H. Aksan is Professor of History at McMaster University, Hamilton, Ontario, Canada. Her current interest focuses on transcultural intellectual encounters, and the circulation of knowledge in the early modern world. She is working on a manuscript entitled *Friends, Foes and Ideologues of the Ottomans 1700–1850*. Prior work on Ottoman intellectual history, and Ottoman and Russian warfare, includes *Ottoman Wars 1700–1870: An Empire Besieged* (2007), and *The Early Modern Ottomans: Remapping the Empire*, edited with Daniel Goffman (2007).

Kenneth J. Andrien is Humanities Distinguished Professor in History at Ohio State University. He has written *Crisis and Decline: The Viceroyalty of Peru in the Seventeenth Century* (1985), *The Kingdom of Quito, 1690–1830: The State and Regional Development* (1995) and *Andean Worlds: Indigenous History, Culture, and Consciousness Under Spanish Rule, 1532–1825* (2001), and edited *The Human Tradition in Colonial Latin America* (2003). He has also co-edited (with Rolena Adorno) *Transatlantic Encounters: Europeans and Andeans in the Sixteenth Century* (1991) and (with Lyman L. Johnson) *The Political Economy of Spanish America in the Age of Revolution, 1750–1850* (1994).

Lauren Benton is Professor of History and Affiliate Professor of Law at New York University. Her research focuses on the comparative legal history of empires. Recent publications include *A Search for Sovereignty: Law and Geography in European Empires, 1400–1900* (2010) and *Law and Colonial Cultures: Legal Regimes in World History, 1400–1900* (2002), which won the J. Willard Hurst and the World History Association Book Prizes. She is currently Dean for the Humanities at New York University.

Hugh Glenn Cagle is Assistant Professor of History at the University of Utah. He specialises in the study of Brazil and the Portuguese empire, and in the history of science. His work has been supported by the Andrew W. Mellon Foundation, the Society for the Social History of Medicine, Portugal's Fundação Luso-Americano, Rutgers University, and the University of Texas at Austin. He is currently revising a book manuscript titled *Dead Reckonings: Disease, Medicine, and Early Modern Empire, 1450–1700*.

Vinita Damodaran is Senior Lecturer in History at the School of History, Art History and Philosophy at the University of Sussex. She is also the Director of the Centre for World Environmental History. She has published numerous articles and books. Her recent publications include the co-edited volume *The British Empire and the Natural World: Environmental Encounters in South Asia* (2010).

Natasha Eaton is Lecturer in the History of Art at University College London. Her research interests include the role of the museum in Britain and South Asia – a project sponsored by a Philip Leverhulme Prize; colour, colonialism and postcoloniality (Clark Art Institute Fellowship awarded); and mimesis as the lens through which to view and misconstrue cultural exchange. She has published widely in international journals including *Cultural Critique, Eighteenth-Century Studies*, the *Journal of Material Culture* and *Comparative Studies in Society and History*. Her next book will be entitled *Nomadism of Colour: Art, Empire and Redemption*.

Michael H. Fisher holds the Danforth Chair in History at Oberlin College. He has published many books and articles about the social, cultural and political interactions between Indians and Europeans, in India and in Europe from the sixteenth century onward. His most recent book, *The Inordinately Strange Life of Dyce Sombre: Victorian Anglo Indian MP and Chancery 'Lunatic'* (2010), traces the life of a subject of the late Mughal Empire who emigrated to Britain, married into the English aristocracy, became the first Asian in the British Parliament and fought in British courts for the last eight years of his life to prove that he was sane.

Richard Grove is the author of *Green Imperialism: Colonial Expansion, Tropical Island Edens and the Origins of Environmentalism 1600–1860* (1996) and *Ecology, Climate and Empire: Colonialism and Global Environmental History 1400–1940* (1997). He has also edited *Nature and the Orient: The Environmental History of South and South East Asia* with V. Damodaran and S. Sangwan (1998) and *El Nino: History and Crisis* (2000) with John Chappell.

Ryūta Itagaki is an anthropologist and historian of modern and contemporary Korea. He teaches at Doshisha University, Kyoto, Japan, and was a 2009–10 Visiting Scholar at Harvard-Yenching Institute. In his award-winning book *Historical Ethnography of Modern Korea* (2008), he explored multiple dimensions of social change in Sangju, Kyŏngbuk Province, under Japanese colonialism. He is also a co-editor of *Lieux de Mémoire of East Asia* (2011), *Japan-Korea: 20 Chapters for New Beginnings* (2007), and *Right to Privacy and Surveillance Society in the World* (2003).

Lara Kriegel is a cultural historian of modern Britain and its empire and teaches in the Departments of History and English at Indiana University, Bloomington. She published her first book *Grand Designs: Labor, Empire, and the Museum in Victorian*

Culture in 2007. A pre-history of the Victoria and Albert Museum, *Grand Designs* placed the market and the empire at the centre of nineteenth-century cultural formation. She has also published on Victorian imperialism, design and museums in anthologies and journals, including the *Journal of British Studies*, *Victorian Studies* and *Victorian Review*. Kriegel is currently working on a cultural history of the Crimean War, and especially its implications for army reform, war reportage, gender practice and heroic recognition in Britain and the British world.

Christopher J. Lee is Assistant Professor of History at the University of North Carolina at Chapel Hill. He is the editor of *Making a World After Empire: The Bandung Moment and Its Political Afterlives* (2010). He is currently completing a political history of British Central Africa.

Philippa Levine is the Mary Helen Thompson Centennial Professor in the Humanities at the University of Texas at Austin and Co-Director of the University's Program in British Studies. Her recent books include *Prostitution, Race and Politics: Policing Venereal Disease in the British Empire* (2003) and *The British Empire, Sunrise to Sunset* (2007). Her *Oxford Handbook of the History of Eugenics*, co-edited with Alison Bashford, was published in 2010. She is writing a book on colonial nakedness.

Elsbeth Locher-Scholten is Senior Researcher at the Research Institute for History and Culture of Utrecht University and a retired associate professor at the same university. Specialising in the history of colonial Indonesia in the nineteenth and twentieth century, she has published *Women and the Colonial State: Essays on Gender and Modernity in the Netherlands Indies 1900–1942* (2000), and *Sumatran Sultanate and the Colonial State: Jambi and the Rise of Dutch Imperialism 1830–1907* (2004). She has also co-edited two volumes on women in Indonesia: *Indonesian Women in Focus: Past and Present Notions* (1992) and *Women and Mediation in Indonesia* (1992).

Michael Mann was Assistant Professor at the FernUniversität in Hagen (Germany's open university) from 1992 to 2005, before joining several research projects, one on historiographical representations of South Asia in modern times and the second on telegraphy and the public sphere in British India. He has been a Professor of Modern History and Culture of South Asia at Berlin's Humboldt University since April 2010. He is author of *Sinnvolle Geschichte: Historische Repräsentationen im neuzeitlichen Südasien* (2009) and *British Rule on Indian Soil: North India in the First Half of the Nineteenth Century* (1999).

John Marriott is Professor of History at the Raphael Samuel History Centre, University of East London. His particular research interests are in London and empire, and he has published *The Other Empire: Metropolis, India and Progress in the Colonial Imagination* (2003) and co-edited the six-volume collection *Britain in India, 1765–1905* (2006). His *Beyond the Tower: A History of East London* was published by Yale University Press in 2011, and with Philippa Levine he co-edits the Ashgate series 'Empires and the Making of the Modern World'. He has recently emigrated to Yorkshire where he is struggling to renovate an early Georgian townhouse.

Søren Mentz is Senior Researcher and Curator at The Museum of National History at Frederiksborg Castle, which is a part of The Carlsberg Foundation. He has written on various topics concerning Danish history. Among his English publications are *The English Gentleman Merchant at Work: Madras and the City of London, 1660–1740* (2005), 'Cultural Interaction between the British Diaspora in Madras and the Host Community, 1650–1790' in H. Masashi (ed.), *Asian Port Cities 1600–1800* (2009), and 'European Private Trade in the Indian Ocean, 1500–1800', in Om Prakash (ed.), *Trading World of the Indian Ocean 1500–1800* (2012).

Satoshi Mizutani specialises in the social history of the British Empire with a focus on colonial India. He is the author of *The Meaning of White: Race, Class and India's 'Domiciled Community', 1858–1930* (2011). His current research examines the 'imperial politics of comparison' engaged by Japanese colonial rulers in Taiwan, exploring how their comparative studies assessed Britain's experience of colonial education in India. He teaches at Doshisha University (Kyoto, Japan), and in 2006 with Ryūta Itagaki co-founded DOSC (Doshisha Studies in Colonialism), an interdisciplinary research group devoted to studies on European and Japanese colonialisms.

Peter C. Perdue is Professor of History at Yale University. He focuses on East Asian environmental and frontier history. He is the author of *Exhausting the Earth: State and Peasant in Hunan, 1500–1850 AD* (1987) and *China Marches West: The Qing Conquest of Central Eurasia* (2005), and co-editor of two books on empires: *Imperial Formations* (2007) and *Shared Histories of Modernity: China, India, and the Ottoman Empire* (2008). His new projects include a comparative study of Chinese frontiers, and a global history of tea.

Derek R. Peterson teaches African history at the University of Michigan. He is the author of *Creative Writing: Translation, Bookkeeping, and the Work of Imagination in Colonial Kenya* (2004), and editor of several books, including *Recasting the Past: History Writing and Political Work in Modern Africa* (2009), *Abolitionism and Imperialism in Britain, Africa and the Atlantic* (2010) and *The Invention of Religion: Rethinking Belief in Politics and History* (2002). He was formerly Director of African Studies at the University of Cambridge. In 2007 he was awarded the Philip Leverhulme Prize, given to scholars based in Britain for their accomplishments in research.

Erika Rappaport is Associate Professor of History at the University of California, Santa Barbara, where she teaches European women's history, modern British and European history. She has published *Shopping for Pleasure: Women in the Making of London's West End* (2000), and articles on gender and consumer culture in such journals as the *Journal of British Studies*, *Victorian Studies* and *Gender and History*. She is currently writing a global history of the tea trade, *Tea Parties: Britishness, Global Cultures and Imperial Legacies*. A chapter, 'Packaging China: Foreign Articles and Dangerous Tastes in the Mid-Victorian Tea Party', was published in Frank Trentmann (ed.), *The Making of the Consumer: Knowledge, Power and Identity in the Modern World* (2006).

Mary A. Renda is Associate Professor of History at Mount Holyoke College. She is the author of *Taking Haiti: Military Occupation and the Culture of US Imperialism, 1915–1940* (2001); 'Practical Sovereignty: The Caribbean Region and the Rise of US Empire', in Thomas Holloway (ed.), *The Blackwell Companion to Latin American History* (2007); and 'Doing Everything: Religion, Race, and Empire in US Protestant Women's Missionary Enterprise, 1812–1960', in Barbara Reeves Ellington, Connie Shemo and Kathryn Kish Sklar (eds), *Competing Kingdoms: Women, Mission, Nation, and American Empire, 1812–1938* (2010). She is currently working on a study of the relationship between nation-building and empire-building in nineteenth and early twentieth-century US history.

Damon Salesa is Associate Professor of Pacific Studies at the University of Auckland, New Zealand. He is a historian of the British and American empires, as well as a scholar of the indigenous Pacific Islands, especially Polynesia. He is the author of *Racial Crossings: Victorian Race, Intermarriage and the Victorian British Empire* (2011) as well as of a number of articles and chapters, including those in Giselle Byrnes (ed.), *New Oxford History of New Zealand* (2009) and Anne Laura Stoler (ed.), *Haunted by Empire* (2006). His next book focuses on the complex of encounters between four nineteenth-century empires and the peoples of Samoa.

Ben Silverstein (La Trobe University) has published articles on sovereignty and settler colonialism, and has conducted research in the areas of native title, decolonisation and subjectivation. His recent PhD dissertation addressed the influence of indirect rule on Australia's government of Indigenous peoples in the interwar period.

Sujit Sivasundaram is University Lecturer in World and Imperial History since 1500 at the University of Cambridge, and Fellow, College Lecturer and Tutor at Gonville and Caius College, Cambridge. He is the author of *Nature and the Godly Empire: Science and Evangelical Mission in the Pacific, 1795–1850* (2005) and is currently completing a book on the transition to British colonialism in South Asia by considering the maritime placement of Sri Lanka in the expanding empire. His essays have appeared in *American Historical Review*, *Past and Present*, *Isis*, *Historical Journal* and *Modern Asian Studies*, and examine themes across the cultural, scientific, environmental and intellectual history of modern empire.

Richard Smith works in the Department of Media and Communications, Goldsmiths, University of London. He specialises in the race and gender implications of military service and has written widely on the experience of West Indians and black Britons in the First World War. His book *Jamaican Volunteers in the First World War* (2004) has recently been reissued and he is currently researching imperial propaganda in the British West Indies during the First World War, postwar radicalism among West Indian veterans and moving-image representations of colonial troops.

Willard Sunderland is Associate Professor and Chair of the Department of History at the University of Cincinnati. He is the author of *Taming the Wild Field: Colonization and Empire on the Russian Steppe* (2004).

Hideaki Tobe teaches at Tokyo Keizai University. He is a historian of modern and contemporary Japan with a special focus on the post/colonial situation of Okinawa under Japanese and US imperialism. His current research concerns the relationship between schoolteachers and nationalism in the context of social movements in postwar Okinawa under US military occupation. While publishing his historical studies, he has also contributed journal articles and book chapters on the historiographical questions of Japanese colonial studies.

Eve M. Troutt Powell teaches the history of the modern Middle East at the University of Pennsylvania. She is the author of *A Different Shade of Colonialism: Egypt, Great Britain and the Mastery of the Sudan* (2003). She has received fellowships from the American Research Center in Egypt and the Social Science Research Council, and has been a fellow at the Institute for Advanced Study in Princeton and at the Radcliffe Institute for Advanced Study. In 2003 she was named a MacArthur Foundation Fellow. Troutt Powell is now working on a book about the memory of slavery in the Nile valley, which examines how slaves and slave owners narrated the experience of servitude and its meaning in their societies.

Jon E. Wilson is a historian of modern South Asia and Senior Lecturer in the Department of History as well as India Institute at King's College London. Trained in both history and anthropology in Oxford and New York, his work focuses on the emergence and consequences of modern governance in South Asia. He is particularly concerned to trace the relationship between political ideas and the everyday world of political practice. His first book, *The Domination of Strangers: Modern Governance in Eastern India, 1785–1835* (2008), will be followed by a study of the British conquest of India, and a history of land reform in postcolonial South Asia.

Patrick Wolfe is a freelance historian associated with La Trobe University. He is the Freeman Spogli Institute International Visiting Scholar for 2012 in the Humanities Center at Stanford University. In 2008, the Organization of American Historians appointed him to their Distinguished Lectureship Program. Wolfe has taught, published and lectured on race, colonialism, Aboriginal histories, theories of imperialism, genocide and the history of anthropology. He is currently working on a comparative history of colonial regimes of race in Australia, the US, Brazil and Palestine.

Introduction

Philippa Levine and John Marriott

I

What is a modern empire? Beneath this seemingly innocuous question lie some troublesome currents. Becky Conekin, Frank Mort and Chris Waters,[1] writing together, have pointed out that 'there is no historical or sociological agreement about the meaning of the term' modernity. Slippery though the term is, it has nonetheless been in constant use among historians, and has fuelled valuable debates in the imperial field. The idea of colonial modernity has often been criticised for its tendency to highlight either western achievements (the positive view) or western impositions (the negative view), but this volume contends that while the term 'colonial modernity' needs to be scrutinised critically, we are by no means ready to abandon it. In his chapter in this volume John Marriott points out that the very idea of modernity derived in part from the processes of imperialism, but since it was not a uniform, consistent or uncontested phenomenon, the modern empire remains difficult to define with any precision. A modern empire, we might say, is an empire of the modern era. Tautology apart, this tends to raise as many questions as it answers. If, for the sake of argument, we agree with Chris Bayly that the modern era began around 1780 does it necessarily follow that modern empires also began at that time?[2] The British perspective gives some weight to this argument, for Britain had just lost the thirteen colonies and was in the process of consolidating its hold over India, thereby laying the foundation for an empire of unprecedented scale and power. At a wider level, we might argue that this moment also signalled the ascent of European imperial might. This rather linear narrative of imperial ascent, however, marginalises imperial formations outside Europe, of which there were no small number. The Chinese, Ottoman and to a lesser extent Mughal empires were still powerful when European imperialism was growing in the eighteenth century. If, on the other hand, we define a modern empire as one displaying 'modern'

---

1   Becky Conekin, Frank Mort and Chris Waters, 'Introduction', in their *Moments of Modernity: Reconstructing Britain 1945–1964* (London, 1999), p. 1.

2   C.A. Bayly, *The Birth of the Modern World, 1780–1914: Global Connections and Comparisons* (Oxford, 2004).

characteristics, then we have to decide what these characteristics are, and identify their manifestations in various imperial experiences at different times. This almost inevitably complicates any notion of a linear narrative of the creation of a universal modern era, and also undoes a wholly Eurocentric reading of both modernity and empire. Tani Barlow has argued, for example, that 'the modernity of non-European colonies is as indisputable as the colonial core of European modernity'.[3] China was motivated by profit very early. The eighteenth-century Ottoman Empire was visibly consumer-oriented and the Mughal economy was monetised, also by the eighteenth century, all characteristics often associated with modernity. In thus moving the frame of modernity beyond and outside Europe as we have attempted to do in this volume, a broader reading of the contours and boundaries of colonial modernity both widens and deepens our scope.

In an attempt to untangle the arguments over the nature of colonial modernity, it is worth briefly reviewing the record of modern imperial expansion. That of Europe itself long predated the so-called modern era. As early as the thirteenth century, galleys from Genoa and Venice brought Italian merchants to the Netherlands and England who came to dominate the markets 'as if in conquered lands'.[4] The wealth created brought life to the Iberian Peninsula, thereby preparing the way for the so-called 'age of discovery'. In the remarkable final two decades of the fifteenth century, Europeans showed an interest in the goods to be gleaned from Africa, the Americas and India, and although the opportunities thus opened up were slow to be exploited fully these discoveries heralded an age of European global dominance.

The putative simultaneity of Europe's imperial ascent, globalisation and the birth of the modern world has led many to see an intimate interconnectedness. According to this logic, because European powers made possible for the first time a truly global and modern ecumene, modernisation was distinctively European – that is, it was through European intervention that the non-European world was able to enter into the modern age. The trouble here is that not only did Europe (or the west if we include the Americas) continue to display significant characteristics that might be regarded as pre-modern, but many of the features identified as modern were to be found equally in societies beyond and often unconnected to Europe. China, for example, had developed a 'modern' bureaucracy based on merit, and a technologically sophisticated economy long before the rise of the west, and which continued to provide a standard of living for its people comparable to Europe at least until 1800. India and the Ottoman lands pioneered scientific advances in navigation, mathematics and manufacturing technology upon which the west would come to depend. The Ottoman and Russian were both broad and diverse empires. Meanwhile, Britain clung to a long-standing hierarchy in which a landed aristocracy pulled many of the strings of financial and political power while the majority of the population lived in poverty and without the franchise. The slave trade not only enriched many western nations but persisted into the twentieth

---

3   Tani E. Barlow (ed.), *Formations of Colonial Modernity in East Asia* (Durham, NC, 1997), p. 1.
4   Fernand Braudel, *The Mediterranean and the Mediterranean World in the Age of Philip II*, vol. 1 (London, 1972), p. 227.

century, and its divisive legacy of the 'colour line' dogs United States politics even now. And it was largely those countries regarded as the most advanced which, in the twentieth century, waged wars of monumental slaughter and destruction, and committed acts of genocide unprecedented in their scale and ferocity.[5]

What this evidence suggests is that the modern was neither exclusively western, nor definitive of a particular moment. Does this mean that we cannot legitimately distinguish modern empires from their predecessors? Was there nothing about the modern imperial experience which set it apart? Not entirely. One of the most striking features of the modern imperial formation was its spatial ordering. Previous empires had been extensive, and possessed vaulting ambitions comparable to any western power in the modern age, but even at the height of their power they mostly remained regionally based. Extant technology, communications, financial structures and strategies of rule placed real and physical limits on the geography of imperial endeavour. Furthermore, power in the ancient world was shared among empires in such a way that expansionist empires such as Rome and Greece inevitably came into conflict with one another, testing their imperial ambitions and perhaps speeding their decline.

In spatial terms, the modern imperial experience contrasted sharply with its ancient predecessors. In 1760, Europe colonised 18 per cent of the world's land area, 3 per cent of its population. After the American Revolution the colonised land area fell, but then climbed dramatically in the nineteenth century as the combined imperial endeavours of Europe, the United States and Japan extended its reach to virtually every part of the globe. By 1938, at the height of western imperial ambition, 42 per cent of the world was colonised, 32 per cent of the population.[6] This was facilitated by a welter of technological advances which conferred decisive advantages on the colonising powers. The supersession of wood and sail by iron and steam ensured supremacy over the world's oceans, and provided unprecedented ease and speed of conveying human and commodity cargoes. Medical treatments to combat diseases such as malaria, which had taken a heavy toll on the lives of Europeans, enabled them to penetrate into and claim previously uncharted territories, which they could defend with the newly acquired Maxim machine gun and its ilk. Telegraphy, unreliable and expensive though it may have been in the early stages, was nothing short of a revolution in communication. The transmission of messages between the metropole and colony, or within a colony such as India, which had previously taken months by sea and land, now took seconds.

The technologies emerging in the eighteenth and nineteenth centuries around transport, communications, commercial production and medicine, in particular, also exercised a tremendous influence on the identity of modern empires. Colonialism was frequently trumpeted as a beneficial exercise in scientific

---

5   John Darwin, *After Tamerlane: The Rise and Fall of Global Empires, 1400–2000* (Harmondsworth, 2008), p. 26.

6   Bouda Etemad, *La Possession du monde: poids et mesures de la colonisation*, quoted in Jane Burbank and Frederick Cooper, *Empires in World History: Power and the Politics of Difference* (Princeton, NJ, 2010), p. 288.

progress bringing everything – from railways to vaccination, from electricity to the production line – to those unschooled in modern technology. It was not just doctors and engineers who could harness such sentiments, but missionaries, too, whose often pioneering efforts in health care afforded them some degree of entry into local communities. However, science, technology and medicine were often divisive forms of knowledge, working to strengthen the idea that it was from the west that all such innovation emerged.[7]

The beneficence of science and technology was perhaps most visible in the era of public health; as the European empires expanded ever further into the tropics, there was increasing emphasis on protecting the health of whites, whether settlers or not. What Alison Bashford has dubbed 'lines of hygiene' demarcated the boundaries of colonial rule, separating safe and unsafe, clean and unclean areas and constructing borders to segregate these, designed with the safety of Europeans in mind.[8] Not infrequently these sanitary states overlapped with political ones, and areas that were unsafe medically were often coterminous with those regarded as unsafe politically. Medical improvement, then, more often than not benefited the colonisers more than the colonised, and was occasionally the leading edge of increasingly interventionist colonisation. Furthermore, proclamations of sanitary danger illuminated the neutral ground science often claimed for itself. The growing insistence that the empirical method produced value-free knowledge of colonial dirt, lack of reason or lower intellectual capacity, formed one more justification for imperial rule, this one made in the name of scientific progress.

Advantages such as these empowered western imperial ambition to the extent that it could now take on other great empires, shifting the balance of world power decisively in its favour. The story is a familiar one. Late in the eighteenth century, the Chinese and Ottoman empires could still act as counterweights to, and place limits on, European imperial ambition, and, despite the weakened state of the Mughal Empire, European powers in India were forced to acknowledge its sovereignty and symbolic power.[9] In the nineteenth century, however, China's ability to police its trade with foreign powers by restricting them to commercial enclaves on the coast was breached by the two Opium Wars from which the British, with superior military technology, emerged victorious. British merchants after the 1840s could sell opium and other commodities freely. The Ottoman Empire, meanwhile, was vulnerable at its North African boundary. Ottoman governors in Egypt had already begun to assert a degree of independence from Istanbul when the pasha Mehemet Ali set about the modernisation of the country in the first half of the nineteenth century. He relied on European expertise and knowledge, providing British and French merchants with opportunities to exploit Egyptian trade, and later construct the Suez Canal. A threat to its interests in the canal provided the British with a pretext to put in place a protectorate in Egypt in 1882. Simultaneously, the French

---

7   See the chapter by Sujit Sivasundaram on science and technology in this volume.
8   Alison Bashford, *Imperial Hygiene: A Critical History of Colonialism, Nationalism and Public Health* (Basingstoke, 2004), p. 1.
9   See Michael Fisher's chapter on the Mughal Empire in this volume.

asserted their interest in Algeria, another region of the Ottoman Empire vulnerable to incursion from foreign powers.

By the time France declared itself a republic in 1871, it had effective control of Algerian institutions. In the Balkans a series of nationalist struggles forced the Ottomans to cede further territory to Greece, Serbia and Bulgaria, so that on the eve of the First World War the empire was greatly reduced in size, and could do little to resist the devastation which followed. Britain occupied Istanbul in 1920, and the League of Nations formalised the parcelling out of former Ottoman lands to the European victors in the war, declaring the Ottoman Empire defunct in 1922.[10] By the early twentieth century Japanese territorial expansion represented the major exception to European imperial dominance, albeit one which the Europeans regarded as a serious threat to their pre-eminence. The Japanese were just as mindful of European expansion in the region, and wary of its effect on East Asian power formations. The spread of Japanese imperialism in the 1940s, and its easy conquests over a number of European overseas territories, did much to undermine European claims of supremacy.

Superior technology was not the entire story underpinning changing imperial power structures. Radical new visions of the nature of imperial expansion and rule were also important. Changing concepts of labour, in particular, were crucial in determining the success of new empires. One of the key transitions from older forms of empire to a characteristically modern mode inhered in the Atlantic slave trade. The buying and selling of African bodies, available not as the spoils of war but by routine commercial transaction, signalled a market-driven approach to labour in which older understandings of mutual obligation between worker and owner were obliterated. Slave labour produced goods bound for the broader market places, and as the free-trade lobby grew the unmistakably coercive form of slavery came under increasing political, judicial and philosophical scrutiny. The liberty of the subject – the freeborn Englishman, the new American, the non-aristocratic Frenchman, figures always depicted as male – which was the clarion call of late eighteenth-century Europe cast a long shadow on the unfree labour of slavery, and lent abolitionism a helpful and powerful rhetoric.

Many factors beyond the humanitarian helped in the fight against slavery for, as Philip Morgan has argued, abolitionism was 'a mix of moral and material motives'.[11] The slave trade, however, did not suddenly or quickly disappear in the colonies it had done so much to enrich.[12] Its dismantling was slow and uneven; at the end of the nineteenth century there was still a need for the Brussels Conference Act (1890), a collection of anti-slavery measures aimed at ending what it called the 'Negro slave trade'. Moreover, as a recent collection demonstrates, the rhetoric

---

10   See Virginia Aksan's chapter on the Ottoman Empire in this volume.

11   Philip D. Morgan, 'Ending the Slave Trade: A Caribbean and Atlantic Context', in Derek R. Peterson (ed.), *Abolitionism and Imperialism in Britain, Africa, and the Atlantic* (Athens, OH, 2010), p. 103.

12   In this volume Philippa Levine's chapter on the European empires and Eve Troutt Powell's chapter on slavery in late nineteenth-century Sudan both demonstrate this.

around slavery and abolition lived on well into the twentieth century.[13] The effect of colonialism was to move the Atlantic world which had dominated eighteenth-century European imperialism from what Ira Berlin called 'societies with slaves' to 'slave societies'.[14] In the former, slaves worked alongside other types of labourers – free and indentured – as was the case in the Spanish and British colonies in the Americas. Over the course of the century a tighter and more rigid separation of these categories of labour cohered around racial difference.

The property-in-person which underpinned the condition of slavery was only one of the new forms of property right associated with modern empires. From the seventeenth century, labour in the Americas became increasingly migratory as indigenous workers were replaced by a mix of enslaved and indentured migrants with no local connections to the land. Far more than in earlier imperial formations, modern empires thus frequently involved the dispossession of indigenous peoples and the alienation of their individual and collectively owned lands in favour of absolute ownership imposed by colonising forces. Even after slavery began to ebb, the relationship between labour and property remained important, forming the basis of class difference in a variety of locations. Forced from the land, many former slaves found a livelihood as landless labourers under various forms of contract.

In general, modern imperial rule fostered a growing distance between coloniser and colonised, visible in property, occupation and other material ways as well as in culture and religion. This fed the growing interest characteristic, particularly of (but not exclusive to) modern European empires, in naming and emphasising points of difference that in turn both shaped and justified the uneven power relations at the heart of imperialism. Other empires – the Japanese and the Russian are powerful examples – also embraced difference as a rationale for the inequities enshrined in their imperial rule, increasingly contemptuous of those they successfully colonised. Racial exclusion marked the course of twentieth-century Japanese imperialism as much as it defined European imperial rule.

From the late eighteenth century, especially as slavery acquired a racial base, the articulation of difference came to revolve increasingly around race as both a descriptive and prescriptive category. Scientists from the late eighteenth century on explored the possibility that race was biologically grounded – another mode in which science served imperial ends even while trumpeting its political neutrality. One of the key precepts to emerge from the growing attachment of imperial ideologies to racial difference was the fear of miscegenation. Notwithstanding the growing numbers of slave children whose fathers were European and whose mothers were African, and the liaisons between European traders and indigenous women in many areas, colonial states often actively prohibited what they regarded as mixed-race marriages in the nineteenth and twentieth centuries. The responsibility of racial purity lay not surprisingly with women, who were charged with policing their own reproductive capacities in ways that would enhance imperial rule. This was

---

13   Peterson, *Abolitionism and Imperialism*.
14   Ira Berlin, *Many Thousands Gone: The First Two Centuries of Slavery in North America* (Cambridge, MA, 1998), p. 8.

by no means the only way in which sexual difference, alongside racial difference, shaped colonial rule.[15] Imperialism was 'never gender-neutral'.[16] Men and women were accorded roles and tasks which shifted as readings of gender responsibilities changed over time and in different locations.

These ideas of difference were not confined to the social categories of race and gender, however. In the adoption of an ideology of free trade (which, by the early nineteenth century, had largely supplanted mercantilism) empires found their rationale not only for new labour practices but for new class identities. Burgeoning trade networks produced a new class of traders and merchants and business communities on a hitherto unknown scale.[17]

These changes ushered in new economic formations. Although the Ottomans had long rejected the mercantilism favoured by European nations by allowing foreign merchants to assume part control of its trade networks, there was a decisive shift early in the nineteenth century, perhaps not uncoincidentally at a time when slavery was in decline and indentured labour became increasingly associated with non-western peoples. Under the banner of free trade, the major European colonial powers embarked on determined campaigns to dominate the world's markets. The underlying premises were deceptively simple and had great appeal for the more advanced nations of Europe. If foreign lands could, through the promotion of free, reciprocal trade, be made into 'informal' colonies providing profitable sources of income for imperial powers, then why assume the onerous and costly responsibility of governing them?[18] Armed with the advantages conferred by the Industrial Revolution, European powers took control of markets previously controlled by foreign manufacturers. In India, for example, indigenous manufacturers of fine cotton cloth, reduced to producers of raw materials, were unable to compete with the steam-driven mills of Lancashire. With commercialisation came a growing emphasis on consumerism. Foreign and domestic markets were assiduously cultivated in order to stimulate demand for commodities in ways which strengthened the hold of imperial economies.[19] In the climate of intense imperial rivalry that characterised Europe at the end of the nineteenth century, the chimera of free trade was abandoned and European powers turned increasingly to neo-mercantilist forms of direct rule resulting in the imperial plunder of countries in Africa, Asia and Latin America which had previously been relatively immune to foreign incursion.

---

15   See Damon Salesa's chapter on race in this volume.

16   See Elsbeth Locher-Scholten's chapter on gender in this volume.

17   In the British context, this has cohered largely around the debate initiated by P.J. Cain and A.G. Hopkins over what they dubbed 'gentlemanly capitalism'. There is now an extensive literature on this idea. For a helpful overview, see Raymond E. Dumett (ed.), *Gentlemanly Capitalism and British Imperialism: The New Debate on Empire* (London, 1999).

18   Bernard Semmel, *The Rise of Free Trade Imperialism: Classical Political Economy and the Empire of Free Trade Imperialism, 1750–1850* (Cambridge, 1970), p. 8.

19   See the chapter on consumption by Erika Rappaport in this volume.

This new wave of European expansion is often seen to have heralded what is sometimes unhelpfully referred to as the classic imperial age. The description does, however, touch on a matter of some import, for one of the defining features of this phase of imperial endeavour was precisely that it was imperial rather than colonial; that is, it moved away from earlier settler ideals, thereby exercising authority without direct colonisation. Historically, since imperialism and colonisation overlapped, it was never possible to segregate them with precision – indeed, the terms are often used interchangeably – but from the time Britain put in place the Egyptian protectorate in 1882, 'purer' forms of imperial rule emerged. In South America, for example, the economies of Peru and Argentina were controlled by the European metropolis before ceding power to the United States which had embarked on its own imperial endeavours. In the longer term, imperialism or neo-colonialism survived the granting of independence to European colonies.[20]

Explanations for this phase of imperial expansion may differ but they do tend to shed light on some of the motives behind modern imperial rule. Take the example of the so-called scramble for Africa, which has come to define this phase of expansion. The seeming paradox is that European powers displayed an unprecedented pace and ferocity in grabbing independent territories that were of limited economic value, and at the risk of provoking yet more intense interimperial rivalries.[21] And yet precisely who were these powers? Governments, initially at least, seemed reluctant to get involved directly in Africa, and therefore responded tardily and grudgingly to demands for more active intervention. The revival among the European imperial powers of the early modern trading company in the late nineteenth century gave the impression that it was private interests alone which governed commerce in colonised lands, as if the state was uninvolved. And when states acknowledged their stake in such enterprises, control was exercised according to what, in the 1920s, the British colonial administrator Lord Lugard would describe as the 'dual mandate' system, in which a thinly spread corpus of administrators relied heavily on African intermediaries. Economic arguments have stressed the role of capitalist multinational firms which, having exhausted the potential of Europe, sought new territories to exploit, or of financiers who attempted to make the world a more secure place for investment by extending European influence. Traders who had already worked in these territories to establish profitable concerns in mining, cotton and palm oil actively lobbied their governments with varying degrees of success to intervene as a means of providing propitious conditions for further exploitation of indigenous resources. In contrast, the well-known theory associated with Ronald Robinson and Jack Gallagher denied that imperialism in the widest sense was the principal motive for British intervention in Africa.[22]

Even when the reluctance of the British state gave way to more direct involvement in African affairs, territorial claims were neither part of a grand strategy to build

---

20   Marco Ferro, *Colonization: A Global History* (London, 1997), p. 19.
21   Bayly, *Birth of the Modern World*, pp. 228–33.
22   Ronald Robinson and John Gallagher, *Africa and the Victorians: The Official Mind of Imperialism* (London, 1961).

a new empire there nor a means of promoting commerce, but were a political response at a regional level to perceived threats to its empire, particularly in India and the Mediterranean. Thus Egypt was first occupied because the unresolved internal political crisis provided opportunities for a hostile France to occupy the Suez Canal. And in southern Africa the war waged against Afrikaner nationalism was designed to restore the prospects of Cape colonial expansion upon which the whole of the region was seen to depend.

Yet these motives were hardly unique to European empire-building. Japanese imperialism was centrally motivated by the emergence and growth there of a capitalist ethos and economy, while the Russian Empire resembled, in its often opportunistic expansion, the British model where local and contingent events and needs drove the acquisition of new territory rather more than a grand imperial vision emanating from the centre.

Overall, what this suggests is that imperial policy was often a pragmatic response to economic, commercial and political threats and opportunities. It was driven by industrial and financial capital, an often hesitant state, powerful entrepreneurs, and a small body of colonial administrators.[23] This does not mean that, once they had colonised, states did not seek to protect and often to extend their territories, but simply registers the complex and multiple imperatives – economic as well as political – of modern imperial formations. Such a policy continued well into the twentieth century when in the aftermath of the First World War new opportunities opened up for some of the European powers, and even framed responses to the increasingly urgent demands of colonised peoples for independence from foreign rule. But by then, Europe faced a new imperial power from across the Atlantic.[24]

II

This collection aims to provide a comprehensive overview of modern empires and modern colonialism from a wide variety of perspectives. Three broad general chapters temporally divided, and which constitute Part I of the text, provide a chronological framework which posits three main eras for modern imperialism. The first was that in which the ideal and the practice were dominated by the settlement impulse, with migrants – many voluntarily and many more by force – making new lives in the colonies. This impulse gave way, most especially in the nineteenth century, to a period of busy and rapid expansion which was less likely to promote new settlement, and in which colonists more frequently saw their sojourn in colonial lands as temporary and related to the business mostly of governance and trade. Lastly, in the twentieth century in particular, empires began to fail

---

23 For an interesting recent discussion of these factors in the British context, see Gary B. Magee and Andrew S. Thompson, *Empire and Globalisation: Networks of People, Goods and Capital in the British World, c.1850–1914* (Cambridge, 2010).

24 See the chapter by Mary Renda on North American empire in this volume.

and to fall. By the last quarter of the century the Ottoman, Habsburg, Russian, Chinese, Japanese and the various European empires had begun or were in the process of being dismantled, and imperial possessions no longer denoted global political power or garnered national pride. This narrative may seem at first glance a Eurocentric one, but this basic temporal thread has a broader, if not exclusive, purchase which may be applied in other contexts as well. The European empires may have been the last to dissolve, but they were also, on the whole, more recent phenomena than those which had been disbanded earlier in the twentieth century. The Ottoman Empire, after all, survived for some 600 years, in part because of its capacity to adapt and to draw on a variety of political cultures. What these chapters offer, then, is a strong sense of the interactions between the different empires over time, the ebb and flow of different power zones at various moments, not always focused on European dominance nor assuming Europe as the *locus classicus* of modern imperial formation.

Part II of the volume offers studies of each of the major empires extant in the eighteenth century, including some, such as China, not routinely included in discussions of modern imperialism. The individual chapters survey the broad dynamics of change both within the empires themselves and in their relationships with other imperial formations, and reflect critically on the ways in which they have been approached in the literature. In the case of the Ottoman, Mughal and Chinese empires, in particular, our contributors also bring the seventeenth century into their discussions disrupting an avowedly western reading of modernity as emerging only towards the late eighteenth century when liberalism, nationalism and new economic philosophies began to circulate widely. But correcting for an overly western reading must not be allowed to become an excuse for ignoring the west; by the eighteenth century, and indeed in the Atlantic even earlier, European colonial activity was burgeoning and, as Michael Fisher and Peter Perdue point out in their chapters in this volume, the Eurasian continental empires which predated Europe's empires faced increasing pressure from western expansion. Britain, for example, was kept as busy by Mughal hostilities in India as by its rivalries with the French in the late eighteenth- and early nineteenth-century Caribbean and Atlantic.

It will be clear from the range of empires covered here that we reject the distinction typically drawn between maritime and land-based empires, incorporating considerations of both into our framework. Defining the modern empire as a definitionally maritime enterprise introduces a tautology, one which forces the focus of modern imperialism onto Europe. Indeed, there has been debate over the years as to whether empires such as the Russian and Chinese should even be called empires, since their principal activities involved lands close by, and not typically overseas. As Michael Adas and Hugh Cagle show in their chapter, the early Ming dynasty established extensive trading networks around the Indian Ocean, but this did not encourage colonial settlement; rather, by the mid-fifteenth century it was evident that attempts to extend its maritime influence had been abandoned, the dynasty choosing instead to increase its control of nomadic pastoral populations in the macroregions which comprised the empire. When the Qing dynasty assumed power in the seventeenth century, it advanced further into the vast regions of Central Eurasia. By the mid-eighteenth century, when what can legitimately be described as the empire was at its height, the Qing controlled territory approximately three times the size of that of its predecessor. We therefore find the division based on maritime endeavour unhelpful, preferring rather to understand empire as a practice that does not necessarily rely on naval prowess. The modern empires, we contend, are varied phenomena utilising a broad range of politics and rule for multiple ends.

In Part III we invited researchers to think critically about some of the key features of modern empires. Here we did not wish to be too prescriptive, but rather encouraged contributors to draw upon their own work to identify issues and concerns which have attracted their attention. All these chapters are brief, many provocative, but they reflect the current state of the field, and suggest new lines of inquiry which may follow from more comparative perspectives on empire. There are doubtless many other themes we might have chosen to explore; we opted for a broad range of topics we believe reflect the vitality and diversity of contemporary scholarship on questions of empire and colonialism. These encompass political, economic and cultural processes central to the formation and maintenance of empires as well as institutions, ideologies and social categories that shaped the lives of both those implementing and those experiencing the force of empire. In these pages the reader will find the slave and the criminal, the merchant and the maid, the scientist and the artist alongside the structures which sustained their lives and their livelihoods.

Overall, we would choose to emphasise the diversity of imperial experience and process which we hope these chapters illuminate. Frederick Cooper has argued that reading 'the story of European colonial empires ... alongside the histories of the continental empires with which they shared time and space ... and those empires that lay outside Europe, notably the Japanese and the Chinese' can only enrich our understanding.[25] We would add that a volume such as this, comprehensive in its scope, also allows us to emphasise the particularities of individual empires, rather than over-generalising as if all empires, at all times, and in all places, behaved in a similar manner. It is this contingent and historical specificity that allows us to explore in expansive ways precisely what constituted the modern empire.

---

25 Frederick Cooper, *Colonialism in Question: Theory, Knowledge, History* (Berkeley, CA, 2005), p. 22.

PART I
Times

Age of Exploration, c. 1500–1650

Kenneth J. Andrien

Spain and Portugal dominated European overseas enterprises in the age of exploration. These activities began slowly with Iberian incursions into the Atlantic Islands and Africa, and then expanded rapidly into the Americas following the first voyage of Christopher Columbus in 1492. Even before this historic Atlantic crossing, the Portuguese had made landfalls on the Atlantic islands of Madeira (1419), the Azores (1427) and the Cape Verdes (1456). Spaniards also had begun conquering the Canary Islands (between 1478 and 1493). Portuguese explorers made their way along the coast of Africa, founding an outpost in Ceuta (1415), and between 1450 and 1505 they established at least fourteen trading posts in Guinea, where they exchanged European goods with local African polities for slaves, gold, ivory and other products. Portuguese merchants also explored the coast of Africa, and in 1488 Bartolomeu Dias rounded the Cape of Good Hope on the southern tip of Africa, demonstrating that sea-going vessels could gain entry into the Indian Ocean. Vasco de Gama took this same route in 1497 when he sailed around the Cape to reach Calcutta in 1498, initiating a rapid expansion of Portuguese economic penetration into Asian markets. The Brazilian landfall of Pedro Álvares Cabral two years later seemed dwarfed by these immensely profitable African and eastern trading outposts. After Portuguese control over the far-eastern spice trade weakened a century later, however, Portuguese settlements in Brazil would become the 'jewel' of Portugal's overseas possessions.

After 1492 Spain's possessions expanded from the small Caribbean islands of Puerto Rico (1493), Santo Domingo (1498) and Cuba (1511) to include Mexico, as the army of Fernando Cortés and his Amerindian allies defeated the Aztec (Mexica) Empire by 1521 and later moved southward to conquer Maya city states in southern Mexico and Central America. Within a decade the small invading force commanded by Francisco Pizarro and Diego de Almagro brought down the Inca Empire (Tawantinsuyu) in 1533, giving the Spaniards control over extensive human and mineral resources in the Andean region of South America. Over the course of the sixteenth century new groups of conquistadors, followed by crown bureaucrats and Catholic clergymen, slowly but firmly consolidated Spanish control over the central regions of Mexico and Peru. By 1565 Spain had gained a foothold in Asia by conquering the Philippine Islands, which later became a trading centre for illicit commerce with China, even though the modest Spanish settlements were only maintained with an annual subsidy (*situado*) from Mexico.

The Spanish and Portuguese overseas exploits represented the first great wave of European expansion across the Atlantic Ocean. The Dutch, English and French would follow these Iberian powers in establishing permanent settlements across the globe over a century later, but their overseas colonies were shaped by a set of European cultural values and customs that had changed markedly since the voyages of Columbus. These later European enterprises would utilise new forms of political and economic organisation – such as joint-stock companies, proprietary agreements and monopoly trading contracts – that reflected the evolution of European political, cultural and economic institutions over the century since the first Spanish and Portuguese settlements had taken place. Nonetheless, Dutch, English and French overseas enterprises remained in their infancy when the first age of exploration and empire ended around 1650.

European Composite Monarchies in the Age of Exploration

Europe in the period of exploration and colonisation was governed largely by 'composite monarchies', consisting of distinct provinces or kingdoms united by a common monarch.[1] These decentralised European political structures formed just under 500 independent polities by 1500, each with its own distinct political culture. This motley group of different states contained dynastic polities that resulted from war or strategic family unions, such as Spain, united in 1469 by the marriage of Ferdinand of Aragon and Isabella of Castile. Composite monarchies held together because of a compact between the monarch and the ruling classes of the different provinces. As a result, they could also be brittle; the union of Castile and Aragon nearly splintered with the death of Queen Isabella in 1504, and it only took on a more permanent form when Charles, the grandson of the 'Catholic Monarchs', inherited both crowns in 1516 (as Charles I of Spain and Charles V of the Holy Roman Empire). Other polities were united tenuously, such as the 'ideal of universal Christian monarchy' that brought together the polyglot of kingdoms, principalities and city states of the Holy Roman Empire. Indeed, as late as 1789 Europe still counted nearly 350 independent political entities, while by 1900 the number of European states had shrunk to only 25.[2] It was not until the nineteenth century that

---

1   This view of the political organisation of early modern European states is presented in two path-breaking articles: J.H. Elliott, 'A Europe of Composite Monarchies', *Past and Present* 137 (1992): pp. 48–71; and H.G. Koenigsberger, 'Dominium Regale or Dominium Politicum et Regale', in H.G. Koenigsberger, *Politicians and Virtuosi: Essays in Early Modern History* (London, 1986), pp. 1–25.

2   Jack P. Greene, 'Negotiated Authorities: The Problem of Governance in the Extended

large, centralised nation states dominated the use of force and commanded the loyalty of subjects in Europe.[3]

The structure of the composite monarchy in each European nation and local conditions in the colonies exercised considerable influence over the type of colonial state implanted in overseas territories. The Spaniards encountered dense Amerindian populations, organised into highly sophisticated polities, and they found vast deposits of precious metals, particularly gold and silver. Using the more extensive legal powers of the monarch in Castile, the crown set up a large bureaucracy to govern and supervise the extraction of wealth from America. Spaniards also imposed rigid Roman Catholic orthodoxy, justifying their conquest as a moral crusade to convert Amerindians. The Portuguese lacked the human, administrative and military resources to establish large settler colonies, except in Brazil, and they favoured founding only small fortresses and warehouses. The Portuguese enforced their commercial prominence with superior naval power. The decentralised Dutch Republic established two joint-stock companies, the Dutch East India Company (Vereenigde Oost-Indische Compagnie or VOC) in 1602 and the Dutch West India Company (Geoctroyeerde Westindische Compagnie or WIC) in 1621 to prey on Spanish and Portuguese shipping, to gain control over the sugar trade in Brazil, to participate in the slave trade in Africa and to take over the spice trade in Asia. The English established their colonies in the seventeenth century, and their flexible approach to governing in the British Isles encouraged the monarchy to use multiple forms of government in its overseas possessions, depending on local circumstances. The French impulse to centralise state power in Europe also influenced the pattern of French overseas expansion: the crown tried to maintain strict central control, while in practice the colonies retained a great deal of flexibility in responding to crown initiatives.[4]

Scholarship on the Age of Exploration

Older studies of European overseas empires tend to focus on the formal institutions of the colonial state (and in many cases a state-supported church).[5] This gave the impression that authority flowed from a unified metropolitan centre through

---

Polities of the Early Modern Atlantic World', in Jack P. Greene (ed.), *Negotiated Authorities: Essays in Colonial Political and Constitutional History* (Charlottesville, VA and London, 1994), p. 5.

3   Charles Tilly, *Coercion, Capital, and European States, AD 990–1990* (Cambridge, MA, 1990), pp. 43–4.

4   Greene, 'Negotiated Authorities', pp. 8–11.

5   Edward Gaylord Bourne, *Spain in America, 1450–1580* (New York, 1904); C.H. Haring, *The Spanish Empire in America* (New York, 1947); C.R. Boxer, *Four Centuries of Portuguese Expansion, 1415–1825: A Succinct Survey* (Johannesburg, 1965); Charles McLean Andrews, *The Colonial Period in American History* (New Haven, CT, 1934); and W.J. Eccles, *France in America* (New York, 1972).

colonial bureaucracies and local institutions of government. This was particularly true for Spanish America, which had well-developed systems of governance that included viceroys or governors, bureaucracies and a military that embodied the metropolitan state's coercive power in the overseas colonies. While this picture of metropolitan state power might have been true of the late nineteenth- and twentieth-century European empires in Asia and Africa, it fails to capture the complex patterns of negotiation, resistance, collaboration and cooptation that scholars have uncovered for European colonial empires in the first age of exploration from 1500 to 1650.[6] Despite these institutions of colonial government and the large corpus of colonial laws, the politics of maintaining an empire required both authority and flexibility from colonial states, which were themselves often deceptively decentralised polities. Moreover, even in large Spanish, Portuguese and English settler colonies, relations among the crown, local colonists and Amerindian, African and Asian populations never blindly followed patterns of administrative hierarchy and centralisation embodied in colonial law and institutions. Early modern composite monarchies were patrimonial, and human relationships helped define how they functioned.[7] Moreover, there was always a gap between the law and its observance.

Since the 1960s, influential scholarly works on European empires dealt with problems of colonialism, imperialism and later economic underdevelopment, and much of this literature was influenced by the neo-Marxist dependency paradigm. Advocates of the dependency paradigm postulated that the expansion of capitalism from Europe led to economic subordination and underdevelopment in colonised regions during the age of exploration. In their influential 1970 study, Stanley J. and Barbara H. Stein claimed that Spain was an economic dependency of Northern Europe from as early as 1492, and the Spaniards incorporated the Americas into a pre-existing web of economic subordination, domestic inequalities and structural underdevelopment. The spread of capitalist commercial transactions over the course of the sixteenth century simply promoted the widespread underdevelopment and subordination of Spanish America to the economic core nations in Northern Europe – the Netherlands, France and finally England.[8] Immanuel Wallerstein and Fernand Braudel have altered the dependency paradigm by taking as their unit of analysis a single world system that linked the expansion of European capitalism in the fifteenth century with the exploitation of European overseas colonies.[9] According to Wallerstein and Braudel, mercantile capitalism spread from the

---

6   Greene, 'Negotiated Authorities', pp. 2–8.
7   I use 'patrimonial' as defined in Max Weber, *The Theory of Social and Economic Organization*, trans. Talcott Parsons (New York, 1964), pp. 352–8.
8   Stanley J. Stein and Barbara H. Stein, *The Colonial Heritage of Latin America: Essays on Economic Dependence in Perspective* (Oxford, 1970), p. 4.
9   Immanuel Wallerstein, *The Modern World System*, vol. 1: *Capitalist Agriculture and the Origins of the World-Economy in the Sixteenth Century* (New York, 1974); and Fernand Braudel, *Civilization and Capitalism, 15th–18th Century*, vol. 3: *The Perspective of the World*, trans. Sian Reynolds (New York, 1984).

European core regions – first Spain and Portugal, then the Netherlands – from the late fifteenth century to incorporate 'peripheral zones' in the Americas and other parts of the globe. Semi-peripheral zones, such as Spain (after it fell from core status by the seventeenth century), occupied an intermediary role as a conveyor belt, transferring resources (particularly American silver) from the peripheries to the core zones. Trade was the mechanism for this expansion of the European-centred world system, with the core draining resources from peripheries and semi-peripheries, which fuelled the expansion of capitalism and led to the historical underdevelopment of peripheral zones in Europe's overseas possessions.

Despite linking Europe and its empires in a single capitalist commercial system, most historians are now quite critical of (or even ignore) both the dependency paradigm and world-system theory. Some leftist critics fault *dependencia* for overemphasising the importance of international market forces and ignoring class structures or modes of production. Other economic historians argue that the framework is based on an inadequate empirical or statistical substructure, which does not measure unequal commercial exchanges from the peripheries to the core. Nowadays, most historians also focus on a central paradox of *dependencia*: it is not a theory to be proven but a paradigm that cannot be verified by the empirical research that underpins most academic histories. Scholars unwilling to embrace the basic methodological and theoretical parameters of the dependency and world-system's paradigms have downplayed or ignored their importance as an organising framework for understanding empires.[10]

Instead of concentrating on colonial institutions or unequal commercial exchanges, more recent studies examine more closely how early modern states actually functioned in Europe and its overseas colonies.[11] In his influential article in *Past and Present*, for example, J.H. Elliott advanced the concept of early modern European states as 'composite monarchies', built on a mutual compact between the crown and the ruling classes.[12] Such a compact involved a great deal of negotiation, political bargaining and the liberal use of patronage to govern effectively. Despite crown efforts to centralise authority in Europe and its overseas possessions, extending royal sovereignty involved great risk of upheaval in the various provinces of Europe and its colonies. Moreover, early European empires established small and often fragmentary European states over a broader substratum of indigenous and African cultures. European trading centres in Africa and Asia depended on the support of more powerful local indigenous polities. Changes in

---

10   For a summary of the dependency literature and its critics, see Kenneth J. Andrien, *The Kingdom of Quito, 1690–1830: The State and Regional Development* (Cambridge, 1985), pp. 4–7.

11   There is a large social science literature on comparative histories of early modern empires. Some examples are: Susan Reynolds, 'Empires: A Problem of Comparative History', *Historical Research* 79/204 (2006): pp. 151–65; Tilly, *Coercion, Capital, and European States*; David B. Abernethy, *The Dynamics of Global Dominance: European Overseas Empires, 1415–1980* (New Haven, CT, 2000).

12   Elliott, 'A Europe of Composite Monarchies', pp. 52–3, 57, 69.

both the metropolis and the overseas settlements over time affected the political, social, economic and religious configuration of the whole empire. As a result, works dealing with empires in the era of exploration now study a whole range of political, social, economic and cultural issues, well beyond examining formal legal and institutional issues or the expansion of mercantile capitalism.

Despite a number of important macro-studies of empire, most historians of early modern European overseas enterprises have written local or regional studies of urban and rural groups (such as merchants, artisans, women and slaves), elite political contestation, indigenous communities and their resistance to colonial oppression and the operation of agricultural holdings (particularly large landed estates). These studies also tend to eschew a Eurocentric approach to Spanish, Portuguese, Dutch, English and French colonial possessions. Such works have devised innovative methods to examine and analyse an array of sources, drawing inspiration from anthropology, cultural studies, art history and philology. Nonetheless, this scholarship seldom attempts to connect local or regional communities to the wider imperial world. Likewise, scholars studying ordinary people – artisans, petty traders, inn-keepers, small farmers, Amerindian miners, slaves and poor European or mixed-race peoples – have found it difficult linking everyday lived experiences to broader structural changes occurring in the whole Empire.

Apart from such local or regional studies, some scholars (past and present) have taken a broad imperial perspective: C.R. Boxer and J.H. Parry have emphasised the maritime dimensions of the Portuguese and Spanish empires, and Annales historians Pierre and Huguette Chaunu have presented a massive compilation of Spanish imperial trade statistics for the Philippines and the Spanish Indies.[13] Frédéric Mauro performed a similar study for the Portuguese Atlantic trade.[14] The highly successful works of John Lynch and Henry Kamen also present Spanish expansion from an imperial perspective, viewing the linkages and mutual influences of events in Spain and its overseas possessions.[15] More recently, scholars such as Anthony Pagden, John Robert McNeil and Patricia Seed have written bold comparative studies.[16] The most ambitious of these comparative works, however,

---

13 Boxer, *Four Centuries of Portuguese Expansion*; Boxer, *The Dutch Seaborne Empire, 1600–1800* (London, 1973); Boxer, *The Dutch in Brazil, 1624–1654* (Oxford, 1957); J.H. Parry, *The Spanish Seaborne Empire* (New York, 1966); Huguette Chaunu and Pierre Chaunu, *Seville et l'Atlantique, 1504–1650*, 8 vols (Paris, 1955–59); Chaunu, *Les Philippines et le Pacifique des Ibériques (XVIe, XVIIe, XVIIIe siècles): introduction méthodologique et indices d'activité* (Paris, 1960).

14 Frédéric Mauro, *Le Portugal et l'Atlantique au XVIIe siècle, 1570–1670: étude économique* (Paris, 1960).

15 John Lynch, *Spain under the Habsburgs*, 2 vols (Oxford, 1968); Henry Kamen, *Empire: How Spain Became a World Power, 1492–1763* (New York, 2003).

16 Anthony Pagden, *Lords of All the World: Ideologies of Empire in Spain, Britain, and France c. 1500–c. 1800* (New Haven, CT, 1995); John Robert McNeil, *Atlantic Empires of France and Spain: Louisbourg and Havana* (Baltimore, MD, 1985); Patricia Seed, *Ceremonies of Possession: Europe's Conquest of the New World, 1492–1640* (Cambridge, 1995); Seed,

is the magisterial synthesis by J.H. Elliott, *Empires of the Atlantic World: Britain and Spain in the Americas, 1492–1830*.[17] Another important new addition to this growing scholarly literature on European empires in the Atlantic World is an encyclopaedic study by Thomas Benjamin, *The Atlantic World: Europeans, Africans, Indians and their Shared History, 1400–1900*.[18] Studies of migration across the Atlantic and the spread of diseases have also made substantial contributions.[19] Histories of the transatlantic slave trade, as early as Philip Curtin's seminal study in 1969, examined the role of Africa and slavery in European expansion.[20] Intellectual and cultural approaches have appeared, most notably with D.A. Brading's ambitious *The First America: The Spanish Monarchy, Creole Patriots and the Liberal State, 1492–1867*.[21] Stuart B. Schwartz has also published a recent study of popular religious beliefs in the Iberian Atlantic world.[22] Nonetheless, much remains to be done; since the decline of the dependency paradigm, scholars of early European empires are only now defining and giving greater direction to studies with a wider imperial focus.[23]

American Pentimento: The Invention of Indians and the Pursuit of Riches (Minneapolis, MN, 2001).

17   J.H. Elliott, *Empires of the Atlantic World: Britain and Spain in America, 1492–1830* (New Haven, CT, 2006).

18   Thomas Benjamin, *The Atlantic World: Europeans, Africans, Indians and their Shared History, 1400–1900* (Cambridge, 2009).

19   Peter Boyd-Bowman, *Índice geobiográfico de cuarenta mil pobladores españoles de América en el siglo XVI*, 2 vols (Bogotá, 1964); Ida Altman, *Transatlantic Ties in the Spanish Empire: Brihuega, Spain, and Puebla Mexico, 1560–1620* (Stanford, CA, 2000); Altman, *Emigrants and Society: Extremadura and America in the Sixteenth Century* (Berkeley and Los Angeles, CA, 1989); Alfred Crosby, *Ecological Imperialism: The Biological Expansion of Europe, 900–1900* (Cambridge, 1986); Noble David Cook, *Born to Die: Disease and New World Conquest, 1492–1650* (Cambridge, 1998).

20   Philip Curtin, *The Atlantic Slave Trade: A Census* (Madison, WI, 1969) is the seminal work, but the literature on the Atlantic slave trade is immense. The most recent overviews are David Eltis, *The Rise of African Slavery in the Americas* (Cambridge, 2000); Gwendolyn Midlo Hall, *Slavery and African Ethnicities in the Americas: Restoring the Links* (Chapel Hill, NC, 2005); and Herbert S. Klein and Ben Vinson III, *African Slavery in the Caribbean and Latin America* (New York, 2007). See also Stuart Schwartz (ed.), *Tropical Babylons: Sugar and the Making of the Atlantic World, 1450–1680* (Chapel Hill, NC, 2004).

21   D.A. Brading, *The First America: The Spanish Monarchy, Creole Patriots, and the Liberal State, 1492–1867* (Cambridge, 1991).

22   Stuart B. Schwartz, *All Can Be Saved: Religious Tolerance and Salvation in the Iberian Atlantic World* (New Haven, CT, 2008).

23   Some recent examples of work that is reshaping methodological perspectives about European colonial expansion in the emerging field of Atlantic History are Jack P. Greene and Philip D. Morgan (eds), *Atlantic History: A Critical Appraisal* (New York, 2008); David Armitage and Michael J. Braddick (eds), *The British Atlantic World, 1500–1800* (London, 2002), pp. 11–27; Alison Games, 'Atlantic History: Definitions, Challenges, and Opportunities', *American Historical Review* 113/3 (2006): pp. 741–56; Rafe Blaufarb, 'The Western Question: The Geopolitics of Latin American Independence', *American Historical Review* 112/3 (2007): pp. 742–63; Eliga H. Gould, 'Entangled Worlds: The

Studying early modern overseas expansion has the potential to allow historians of the Spanish, Portuguese, Dutch and British empires to emphasise the interconnections among global, regional and local processes.[24] Such a perspective also permits historians to examine important historical changes without regard to modern political borders, and it encourages comparisons among the European empires. It also highlights differences between densely populated central regions and the more sparsely settled frontier zones within empires – where European rule was more insecure as various indigenous groups challenged their control, along with competing powers. Studying frontier zones such as Florida or New Mexico has led to renewed scholarly interchanges among specialists of Spanish, Portuguese, Dutch, French and English America. Moreover, an imperial perspective emphasises the world of merchants and maritime commercial exchanges, including marginal people – sailors, pirates, inn-keepers and prostitutes – who played a role in this trade, particularly in the Caribbean. Empires were also the site of gendered relationships, where men and women of very different cultures interacted, often leading to generations of mixed-race children. Wars connected European overseas possessions as conflicts in Europe spread to America and beyond, while the commerce in slaves sometimes prompted wars among African polities. An imperial perspective places renewed emphasis on movement, particularly migration back and forth across oceans. In addition, it brings greater scholarly attention to the role of Africa, demonstrating the centrality of the slave trade and the lives of enslaved and free Africans living in European overseas empires. In short, an imperial perspective encourages scholars of Europe and its overseas possessions to explore a wide range of topics and relationships and to see old problems from different viewpoints.

Apart from the advantages of using an imperial perspective in analysing early European overseas expansion, there are also potential pitfalls. Imperial histories run the risk of Euro-centrism. Studies focusing on imperial government, official ideologies, the political disputes and power relationships between colonies and metropoles too often present a largely European meta-narrative of empire. Such studies also can ignore the life experiences of subaltern groups – Amerindians, Africans, subjected peoples in Asia and women living in an empire. This approach can even lead to nostalgic views of empire which fail to examine the oppression,

---

English-Speaking Atlantic as a Spanish Periphery', *American Historical Review* 112/3 (2007): pp. 764–86; Jorge Cañizares-Esguerra, 'Entangled Histories: Borderland Historiographies in New Clothes', *American Historical Review* 112/3 (2007): pp. 787–99; Sanjay Subrahmanyam, 'Holding the World in the Balance: The Connected Histories of the Iberian Overseas Empires, 1500–1640', *American Historical Review* 112/5 (2007): pp. 1329–58; Eliga H. Gould, 'Entangled Atlantic Histories: A Response from the Anglo-American Periphery', *American Historical Review* 112/5 (2007): pp. 1415–22; Jorge Cañizares-Esguerra, 'The Core and Peripheries of Our National Narratives: A Response from IH-35', *American Historical Review* 112/5 (2007): pp. 1423–33.

24   Kathleen Wilson, *A New Imperial History: Culture, Identity, and Modernity in Britain and its Empire, 1660–1840* (Cambridge, 2004), pp. 1–26, provides some important directions for imperial history, even though it covers a later period.

violence and injustices that accompanied early European imperial expansion. In part, these problems are related to extant archival sources, which often reflect the needs of metropolitan and colonial authorities rather than marginalised groups – such as pirates, prostitutes, illiterate poor farmers or labourers, African slaves and Amerindians. All of these subaltern groups do appear in archival sources, however, and scholars must look carefully to find their unique stories. Studies of European overseas expansion have to examine how the reciprocal influences of Europeans and various indigenous groups in Africa, Asia and the Americas shaped their enjoined histories. To accomplish this goal, new imperial histories benefit from perspectives drawn from other disciplines, such as literary studies, anthropology and archaeology, and gender studies. Methods drawn from ethno-history and cultural studies, for example, have been particularly influential in allowing scholars to examine how contacts between Europeans and native peoples shaped new societies, with different political, cultural, economic and social trajectories after the period of contact. This is particularly true for studying the complex human interactions, and political, economic, social and cultural exchanges that accompanied the foundation of European overseas empires.

The First Phase of European Expansion: Portugal

The Portuguese global diaspora began in 1415 with the successful conquest of Ceuta, giving Portugal a foothold in Africa. At the outset of Portugal's expansion, its monarch presided over a small state, more consolidated than most European counterparts. The Christian re-conquest of Portugal from the Muslims had ended by the fourteenth century, allowing the crown time to accrue lands and levy taxes. These the king distributed judiciously to the nobles, buying their loyalty. King John II (r.1481–95) made great strides in curtailing the traditional powers of the nobility and towns, causing considerable unrest in the kingdom. With the advent of overseas expansion, however, the crown had access to growing commercial revenues – 68 per cent of crown income came from this maritime trade by 1515.[25] These new revenue sources allowed King John's successor, Manuel I (r.1495–1521), to reverse the policy of confrontation by restoring lands confiscated from the nobility and the towns and by granting favoured nobles concessions to participate in this lucrative overseas trade. Such patronage won the loyalty of noble families, but it did not allow the crown to consolidate the Portuguese state.[26] As a result, Portugal remained a composite monarchy, with the nobles and the towns retaining many of their traditional rights, privileges and protective institutions.

Over the course of the fifteenth century, the Portuguese sent ships to explore in the Atlantic, leading to the discovery and settlement of the Madeira, Azores and

---

25   James Lang, *Portuguese Brazil: The King's Plantation* (New York, 1979), p. 6.
26   Greene, 'Negotiated Authorities', p. 9.

Cape Verde Islands and also São Tomé and Príncipe off the coast of West Africa.[27] Portuguese ships also extended their explorations along the coast of Africa, establishing forts and smaller outposts to engage in the slave trade. The voyages of Bartolomeu Dias (1487) and Vasco de Gama (1497) came after more than seventy years of experience with the currents and winds of the Central and South Central Atlantic. After capturing footholds in Hormuz in the Persian Gulf (1515), Goa in India (1510), Malacca in Southeast Asia (1511) and Macau in the China Sea (1535–57), the Portuguese dominated sea lanes from West and East Africa to the Indian and Pacific Oceans, giving them control over most of the Asian spice trade to Europe. The crown established only small overseas fortresses and warehouses and enforced its commercial prominence with its navy, seldom attempting to establish settler colonies, like its later rival, Spain. The only crown agency supervising the empire was the India House, established in Lisbon in 1503.[28]

The Portuguese Asian Empire was based on a system of trading posts (*feitorias*) established at key ports from the east coast of Africa to Macau and as far as Nagasaki in Japan. The lynchpin of these *feitorias* was the Portuguese settlement of Goa in India. By 1515 the crown received over 39 per cent of royal revenues from levies on the Asian spice trade alone.[29] By 1550, however, private merchant houses, often run by Portuguese Jewish converts to Christianity, dominated the Asian trade.[30] The merchants organised trade in local commodities for European wares, gold procured in Africa and goods secured from the carrying trade from one East African or Asian port to another. From their strategic *feitorias*, the Portuguese controlled the sea lanes and dominated international, regional and local trade in Asian silks, porcelains and spices. Portuguese governors established favourable commercial relations with local polities, and in many cases their *feitorias* existed only with the support of local East African and Asian rulers. Their fortified port cities were populated by a small military force, ruled by a crown-appointed governor and populated by small mercantile and religious communities. Portuguese authorities in the east exerted a great deal of authority independent of far-away Lisbon, and their armies sometimes served as mercenaries, aiding Asian allies in conflicts with their enemies. In a few cases, such as in Ceylon, Portuguese settlers tried to extend their control from a series of coastal settlements to a significant portion of the island's interior, but most often their authority was confined to port cities and their immediate hinterlands.[31]

---

27 For a discussion of Portuguese colonisation of the Atlantic Islands, see T. Bentley Duncan, *Atlantic Islands: Madeira, the Azores, and the Cape Verdes in Seventeenth Century Commerce and Navigation* (Chicago, IL, 1972). Robert Garfield, *A History of São Tomé Island, 1470–1655: The Key to Guinea* (San Francisco, CA, 1992); Tony Hodges and Malyn Newitt, *São Tomé and Príncipe: From Plantation Colony to Microstate* (Boulder, CO, 1988).

28 Francisco Bethencourt and Diogo Ramada Curto, *Portuguese Oceanic Expansion, 1400–1800* (Cambridge, 2007), p. 3.

29 Lang, *Portuguese Brazil*, p. 16.

30 James C. Boyajian, *Portuguese Trade in Asia under the Habsburgs, 1580–1640* (Baltimore, MD, 1993), pp. 1–52.

31 Joseph C. Miller, *Way of Death: Merchant Capitalism and the Angolan Slave Trade, 1730–1830* (Madison, WI, 1988), passim.

The Portuguese extended their control in Asia by sending missionaries to evangelise local populations, and they enjoyed some successes in Southern India and Japan. Portuguese settlers frequently intermarried with local families, producing racially mixed colonies. Miscegenation and missionary activities together produced culturally hybrid societies, which differed in each of the Portuguese *feitorias*. Despite their successes, Portuguese influence in Asia rested on fragile foundations: military control of the sea lanes and an extensive network of strategic port cities. When the Dutch and later the English made inroads into Southeast Asia, the Persian Gulf, the Malabar coast and India during the seventeenth century, local leaders allied with these European interlopers to expel the Portuguese from parts of East Africa, India, Ceylon and Japan, which vastly reduced their commercial profits over the course of the century.[32]

In Africa, the Portuguese established several settlements on the Upper Guinea coast or on offshore islands to engage in trading European products – metals, weapons, alcohol and tobacco – for a variety of African products, particularly gold and slaves by the late fifteenth century. Like Portuguese settlements in Asia, these early outposts were primarily small *feitorias*, except on the archipelago of São Tomé and Príncipe, which attracted Portuguese settlers who brought slave labourers to work on prosperous sugar plantations. Bondsmen were shipped from Guinea either to São Tomé or to Portuguese settlements in the Cape Verde Islands and then sent to Portugal, which served as the centre for the growing European slave trade. At the same time, Portuguese settlers and their African bondsmen transformed the Madeira Islands into prosperous producers of sugar cane, sold throughout the Mediterranean and northern Europe.

Portuguese traders moved southwards to West Central Africa, encountering the Kingdom of Kongo in 1483. Under the influence of Portuguese missionaries, the ruler, Nzinga a Nkuwu, converted to Christianity (baptised as João I) in 1491. The Kongolese royal family promoted evangelisation efforts by Portuguese clergymen, and in 1595 the papacy named the kingdom an Episcopal see. The church in the capital of São Salvador became West Central Africa's first official cathedral.[33] Despite this auspicious reception, the Kongolese rulers did not permit permanent Portuguese settlements, although the region traded ivory, gold and other local products, particularly slaves, to Portuguese merchants who sold them primarily to planters in Brazil or to Spanish America.[34] The Portuguese established settlements farther south in the Kingdom of Ndongo, where they ultimately founded the town of São Paulo de Luanda in 1576. As noted for Asia, many settlers engaged in casual unions or married local African women, leading to a growing number of

---

32   Boyajian, *Portuguese Trade in Asia*, pp. 146–65.

33   Linda M. Heywood and John K. Thornton, *Central Africans, Atlantic Creoles, and the Foundation of the Americas, 1585–1660* (New York, 2007), pp. 49–108; Anne Hilton, *The Kingdom of Kongo* (Oxford, 1985).

34   For a recent study of the slave trade to Spanish America, see: Linda A. Newson and Susie Minchin, *From Capture to Sale: The Portuguese Slave Trade to Spanish America in the Early Seventeenth Century* (Leiden and Boston, MA, 2007).

mixed-race inhabitants.[35] The large number of Christianised Africans, particularly in the Kongo, gave rise to an Atlantic Creole culture, as many of the slaves sold by Europeans knew the Portuguese language and were related by blood to the inhabitants of Portuguese settlements.[36]

During the seventeenth century, rising demands for slave labour in the Americas led the Portuguese to move from relying on trade to promoting war and political instability as a means for procuring slaves. The Portuguese exploited local rivalries in Ndongo, often in alliance with Imbangala mercenaries (independent armies that lived in fortified camps of several thousand and survived on war and rapine) to promote chaos and disorder as a means to obtain abundant, cheap supplies of slaves. Political disorder spread northward, destabilising the Kongo, as the formerly strong monarchy lapsed into factionalism and political instability. The Dutch invasion of Luanda in 1641 only exacerbated the disorder, although a relief expedition from Brazil under the command of Salvador de Sá eventually expelled the invaders in 1648.[37] The Portuguese then continued their strategy of using war, diplomacy and trade to gain access to a steady supply of slave labourers, exporting approximately 9,000–12,000 slaves from West Central Africa to the Atlantic World each year between 1607 and 1660.[38]

Portuguese exploration and settlement of Brazil in South America proceeded more slowly, since the local indigenous peoples formed no densely populated, organised polities capable of funnelling trade goods to Portuguese coastal outposts. After the initial explorations of Cabral, the crown licensed a few small coastal dyewood trading posts to barter with the indigenous Tupi-Guarani peoples for brazilwood. Within a few decades this barter system began to break down as many Amerindian groups, who had no tradition of trading their labour for trade goods, balked at cutting dyewoods for the Portuguese. The inroads of French traders also placed increased demands on the semi-sedentary Tupi-Guarani peoples, which emboldened them to demand more valuable goods (including firearms) to cut and haul dyewoods. In response, Portuguese settlers began systematically enslaving the native Brazilians, leading to periodic wars.[39]

The Portuguese monarchy later promoted full-scale colonisation in Brazil by granting charters to wealthy notables, called *donatarios* (proprietors) who bankrolled and governed the first settlements. The crown gave these proprietors authority to control the distribution of land, dispense justice, grant town charters, oversee

---

35   Peter Mark, *Portuguese Style and Luso-African Identity: Precolonial Senegambia, Sixteenth–Nineteenth Centuries* (Bloomington, IN, 2002); George Brooks, *Eurafricans in Western Africa: Commerce, Social Status, Gender, and Religious Observance from the Sixteenth to the Eighteenth Century* (Athens, OH, 2003).

36   John Thornton, *Africa and Africans in the Making of the Atlantic World, 1400–1800* (Cambridge, 1998).

37   The standard work on the Brazilian expedition to recapture Luanda is C.R. Boxer, *Salvador de Sá and the Struggle for Brazil and Angola, 1602–1688* (London, 1952).

38   Heywood and Thornton, *Central Africans, Atlantic Creoles*, p. 159.

39   John Heming, *Red Gold: The Conquest of the Brazilian Indians, 1500–1760* (Cambridge, MA, 1978).

commerce with Amerindians and force indigenous people to work for the colony.[40] The crown also granted the proprietors large personal tracts of land. Although he authorised the trade in dyewoods, the king made the business a royal monopoly, ensuring the monarchy a large share of the profits. Nonetheless, only the colonies at Pernambuco, Bahia, Rio de Janeiro and Saõ Vicente managed to survive and prosper by 1650. Hostile relations with the indigenous peoples, chronic shortages of capital and hostility between settlers and proprietors led other settlements to wither.[41]

In 1549 the crown dispatched the first governor-general of Brazil, Tomé de Sousa, to expel the French and subdue hostile Amerindian groups. Sousa founded the city of Salvador da Bahia de Todo os Santos as the capital of Brazil (1549). The economic success of Portuguese Brazil was not ensured, however, until profitable sugar plantations emerged in the northeast around Olinda and Salvador. The Portuguese colonists continued exploiting and enslaving Tupi-Guarani peoples until their near extinction from disease and overwork in some coastal regions. The demographic collapse of the Amerindian population encouraged the importation of African slaves to work on Brazilian sugar plantations.[42] The colonial enterprise in Brazil required permanent settlements, ongoing relations with indigenous peoples and commercial agriculture, costing the Portuguese more resources than they had expended to build trading outposts in Africa and Asia.

The institutional influence of the Roman Catholic Church in Brazil remained small in the first half of the sixteenth century, and the first bishopric in Salvador da Bahia was not established until 1551. Most of the evangelisation of the indigenous peoples fell to the Society of Jesus, whose first representatives arrived in 1549. Although Jesuits were influential in educational, spiritual and economic affairs, they engaged in conflicts with settlers over the welfare of Amerindians. The colonists viewed the missions as an impediment to enslaving indigenous workers for sugar plantations. The Jesuits argued that many Portuguese settlers acted as immoral, abusive aggressors in dealings with Amerindians. The Jesuits even ran afoul of the first Bishop of Bahia, Pedro Fernandes Sardinha, who argued that the Society's first responsibility lay in ministering to Portuguese settlers, not converting Amerindians.[43] Divisions within the Church, and between the Jesuits

---

40 Lang, *Portuguese Brazil*, pp. 27–31; Alida Metcalf, *Go Betweens and the Colonization of Brazil* (Austin, TX, 2005).

41 For an overview of the scholarly literature on the Portuguese Atlantic Empire, see A.J.R. Russell-Wood, 'The Portuguese Atlantic, 1415–1808', in Greene and Morgan (eds), *Atlantic History*, pp. 81–109; and Russell-Wood, 'Centers and Peripheries in the Luso-Brazilian World, 1500–1808', in Christine Daniels and Michael V. Kennedy (eds), *Negotiated Empires: Centers and Peripheries in the Americas, 1500–1820* (New York and London, 2002), pp. 105–142.

42 Stuart B. Schwartz, *Sugar Plantations in the Formation of Brazilian Society: Bahia, 1550–1835* (Cambridge, 1985), passim.

43 C.R. Boxer, *The Church Militant and Iberian Expansion, 1440–1770* (Baltimore, MD and London, 1978); Dauril Alden, *The Making of an Enterprise: The Society of Jesus in Portugal, Its Empire, and Beyond, 1540–1750* (Stanford, CA, 1996).

and civil society, limited the influence in Brazil that the Catholic Church attained in Spanish America.

The First Phase of Expansion: Spain

During its era of exploration, the Spanish monarchy presided over a patchwork of different kingdoms and provinces, united primarily through dynastic inheritance. Spanish kings ruled over Castile, Aragon, Navarre, Catalonia, Valencia and (between 1580 and 1640) Portugal, but each province retained its own laws, currency and political institutions. The king also appointed a series of councils to assist in ruling these diverse polities, but only the Holy Office of the Inquisition had jurisdiction over all the monarch's domains.[44] Provinces also had representative assemblies or *Cortes*, which voted the crown subsidies, drawn from taxes levied on towns and individual taxpayers (*pecheros*). Before granting these subsidies, however, each *Cortes* usually exacted concessions from the monarch. As a result, the crown came to rely on a series of royal taxes, levied on the citizenry of Castile, and on borrowing from foreign and domestic bankers to support the diplomatic and military ventures of the royal family (rather than calling regular meetings of the *Cortes*). When King Philip IV and his chief minister (*válido*), the Count-Duke of Olivares, tried to impose new levies to support a standing army, the monarchy nearly collapsed. Portugal rebelled in 1640, eventually winning its independence, and a simultaneous revolt of the Catalans was only subdued with great cost and loss of life.[45] The monarch controlled vast resources in Spain and its overseas possessions, but, as the revolts of 1640 demonstrated, the king had neither the resources nor the administrative means to consolidate his various kingdoms and provinces into a single state apparatus.

The Spanish invasion of the New World (which the Spaniards called the Indies) proceeded from the Caribbean islands first to Mexico and Central America and then to Peru, as expeditions spread across North and South America to incorporate new lands into the crown's domain. The famous expeditions of Cortés in Mexico and Pizarro in Peru both benefited from having large numbers of Amerindian allies, and their victories resulted from leading small, highly mobile and technologically superior Spanish forces, which headed indigenous uprisings against the unpopular and divided Aztec and Inca states. As a small minority in each area, the position of the conquistadors was insecure after the overthrow of the major indigenous polities. As a result, Spanish invaders consolidated their newly acquired wealth,

---

44 Two important overviews of the Spanish Inquisition are Henry Kamen, *Inquisition and Society in Spain: Sixteenth and Seventeenth Centuries* (London, 1985) and Stephen Haliczer, *Inquisition and Society in the Kingdom of Valencia* (Berkeley, CA, 1990).

45 J.H. Elliott, *The Revolt of the Catalans: A Study in the Decline of Spain, 1580–1640* (Cambridge, 1963).

status and power by making strategic alliances with powerful indigenous ethnic groups, often marrying or taking as concubines the daughters of local elites.

Spanish conquistadors came from the middle sectors of Spanish society, and they travelled to the Indies in search of the wealth, status and power denied them in Europe.[46] Some had military experience in Europe or the Indies, but most did not. Like the Puritans of New England, they were religious men with a strong entrepreneurial spirit, filled with an innate sense of their destiny to win new lands for the king and to enrich themselves. The conquistadors engaged in all types of economic activity – investing in mines, landed estates and commerce. To divide the spoils of conquest and ensure their wealth and status, the conquistadors allocated grants of *encomienda*, which allowed them to collect taxes and labour services from a designated group of indigenous towns in return for military protection and religious instruction. These were not grants of land, but they gave the Spanish holder (called an *encomendero*) social status and economic wealth – a source of capital and labour to buy property, engage in mining or pursue commercial opportunities. The *encomienda* allowed the conquistadors to drain resources from the already existing Amerindian economies and invest them in emerging colonial enterprises.

By the middle of the sixteenth century the crown slowly phased out the *encomienda* in wealthy, densely populated central areas of Mexico and Peru, although it persisted along the frontiers of the empire. Crown officials had to suppress squabbles among the quarrelsome conquistadors, particularly in Peru, and the onset of European epidemic diseases dramatically reduced the Amerindian population in central zones of the Spanish Indies. In Mexico, for example, the indigenous population declined from 20–25 million before the European invasion in 1519 to under 1.5 million a century later.[47] Moreover, crown authorities had no desire to create a New World nobility of independent-minded *encomenderos*, and churchmen wanted control over evangelising the indigenous peoples. Moreover, the rise of new colonial cities and the discovery of rich gold and especially silver mines – such as Zacatecas, Guanajuato and Sombrete in current-day Mexico, and Carabaya, Oruro and Potosí in current-day Peru and Bolivia – attracted a new influx of migrants from Spain who resented the political, social and economic dominance of those first conquistadors who monopolised *encomiendas*.

As the power of the *encomenderos* declined, the crown sent bureaucrats, churchmen and other settlers to rule, convert and populate the new lands. In Spain, the crown established the Board of Trade (1503) to control colonial commerce and

---

46 James Lockhart, 'Trunk Lines and Feeder Lines: The Spanish Reaction to American Resources', in Kenneth J. Andrien and Rolena Adorno (eds), *Transatlantic Encounters: Europeans and Andeans in the Sixteenth Century* (Berkeley, CA, 1991), pp. 90–120. Some other more detailed works on the social composition of the Spanish conquistadors are James Lockhart, *Men of Cajamarca: A Social and Biographical Study of the First Conquistadors of Peru* (Austin, TX, 1972) and José Ignacio Avellaneda, *The Conquerors of the New Kingdom of Granada* (Albuquerque, NM, 1996).

47 Woodrow Borah and Sherburne Cook, *The Aboriginal Population of Mexico on the Eve of the Spanish Conquest* (Berkeley, CA, 1963), passim.

the Council of the Indies (1524) to advise the king on policies for the Indies. In America, the crown set up an extensive bureaucracy to rule the newly conquered lands, headed by a viceroy in each of the two major political units, the Viceroyalties of New Spain and Peru. New Spain encompassed all the lands in southern portions of what are now the United States, the Caribbean, Mexico and Central America to the borders of current-day Panama. The Viceroyalty of Peru included all the territory from Panama to the southern tip of South America, except for Brazil, which fell under Portuguese control. Within these two massive territorial units, the metropolitan government founded a series of high courts, called *audiencias* (six in Peru and four in New Spain), to hear civil and criminal cases. The justices of these courts worked with the viceroys to enforce legislation sent from Spain and to issue any necessary laws dealing with local matters. To limit the regional power of *encomenderos*, authorities in Spain created a network of rural magistrates (*corregidores de indios*) to regulate contact between Spaniards and Amerindians, to collect the head tax or tribute and to assign forced (*corvée*) labour service for state projects. Magistrates (*corregidores de españoles*) also served in municipalities to hear court cases and to preside over civic affairs with the city council (*cabildo*).

Roman Catholic clergymen took responsibility for converting the Amerindians to Catholicism. At first the religious orders – primarily the Franciscans, Dominicans, Augustinians, Mercedarians and Jesuits – played a leading role in evangelising the indigenous peoples.[48] Over time, members of the secular clergy established parishes under the overall supervision of a series of bishops appointed by the crown (seven in New Spain and eight in Peru).[49] The regular orders maintained a number of rural parishes and kept missions in the frontier zones of the empire. The crown increasingly tended to favour the secular clergy, because the Pope gave the king control over appointments to the high ranks of the secular clergy and a share of the tithes paid to the Church.[50] The regulars, responsible only to the heads of their order and the Pope, always remained more independent of royal authority.

As colonial trade grew, the crown issued regulations on commerce with the Indies. All trade was funnelled through Spain's Atlantic port of Seville and a series of licensed ports in the Indies.[51] From 1561 all trade crossed the Atlantic in legally

---

48 The orders were called 'regular clergy' because they lived according to the rules or *regula* established by the founder of the order. In Europe the religious orders most commonly lived communally in religious houses. Charles Gibson, *Spain in America* (New York, 1966), p. 77.

49 Ibid. In contrast to the religious orders the secular clergy ministered directly to the laity or *saeculum* and they were subject to the authority of the local bishop. The secular clergy comprised the hierarchy of bishops, the cathedral chapters and the parish clergy. The Archbishoprics of Lima in Peru and Mexico City in New Spain were the central seat of clerical power in the New World.

50 The Pope granted these privileges in two concessions, one in 1501 and the second in 1503. Haring, *Spanish Empire in America*, pp. 167–70.

51 By the early eighteenth century the build-up of silt in the Guadalquivir River at Seville made it difficult for larger ocean-going vessels to reach the port, so the crown gave

sanctioned annual convoys (*flotas y galeones*) dispatched from Seville to designated locations, where trade fairs (at Veracruz, Cartagena and Portobelo) were held to exchange European wares for colonial products, particularly silver from mines in New Spain and Peru. Merchant guilds (*consulados*) in Seville, Mexico City and Lima regulated commerce in the transatlantic trade between Spain and the Indies.

As war and defeat in Europe preoccupied the Spanish crown, the crown bureaucracy in the Indies underwent significant changes. The fiscally strapped Spanish crown began selling appointments systematically for most key bureaucratic posts, which allowed creoles (people of European descent born in the Indies) to purchase key posts, even in their own cities and towns, giving locals the opportunity to gain unprecedented political clout.[52] Corruption, graft and influence peddling abounded, as the new venal officeholders enriched themselves and their allies at the expense of the embattled European metropolis. Nonetheless, empowering creole elites did little to better the lives of most Amerindians, Africans and mixed-blood peoples in the Indies, who occupied the lowest positions in the colonial socioeconomic order.

By 1650 the Spanish and Portuguese empires spanned the globe, and they brought together an immensely varied group of landscapes, climates, disease environments, cultures, languages and customs. Despite their diversity, these empires also had unifying networks of political, economic and social cohesion. The encounters between the Spanish and Portuguese and the indigenous peoples of Asia, America and Africa altered (in varying degrees) pre-existing modes of production, technology, commerce, politics and social hierarchies, and patterns of disease, diet and religion. At the same time, Asian, African and Amerindian peoples managed to incorporate these changes into their own political, social and religious practices, producing a constantly evolving mixture that was neither entirely European, indigenous, nor African, particularly in the Americas. Spanish and Portuguese notions of wealth, for example, led to intensive mining of precious metals, commercial agriculture and the introduction of new foodstuffs and animals. These economic activities set in motion changes that transformed Africa, Brazil and the Indies in significant ways. At the same time, indigenous food products (such as chocolate, potatoes, manioc and tobacco) and cultural practices reshaped European ways of life.

Cadiz the right to monopolise Atlantic trade with the Indies. The merchant guild moved from Seville to Cadiz. Haring, *Spanish Empire in America*, p. 302.

52   Kenneth J. Andrien, *Crisis and Decline: The Viceroyalty of Peru in the Seventeenth Century* (Albuquerque, NM, 1985), pp. 103–129 and Mark A. Burkholder and D.S. Chandler, *From Impotence to Authority: The Spanish Crown and the American Audiencias, 1687–1808* (Columbia, MO, 1977), passim.

The Second Phase of European Expansion:
The Dutch, the English and the French

The Dutch, English and French began challenging the commercial and settlement rights of Iberian powers in Asia, Africa and the Americas by the sixteenth century. The papacy had divided the non-European world in 1493, awarding control over Asia, Africa and Brazil to Portugal, and the bulk of the Americas to Spain. This papal bull was verified in 1494 by the Treaty of Tordesillas between the two Iberian monarchies.[53] As a result of these agreements, the Spanish and Portuguese claimed complete sovereignty over the lands and sea lanes outside of Europe. The other European powers challenged these claims by supporting voyages of exploration, followed by licensing privateers to prey on Iberian shipping and finally by dispatching their own colonial enterprises. Spanish and Portuguese diplomats in Amsterdam, London and Paris repeatedly protested against such infringements on their claims to sovereignty over these waters and lands, but to no avail. By the 1550s these other European powers argued instead for freedom of the seas and for their own claims to lands in Africa, Asia and the Americas.[54] All three nations had a seafaring history, lively ship-building industries, sea ports on the Atlantic and vibrant merchant communities capable of promoting and financing overseas expansion. In short, these three powers had all the necessary prerequisites to intrude on prosperous Iberian overseas enterprises.

The Dutch were the first of the European powers to make serious challenges to Spanish and Portuguese imperial supremacy early in the seventeenth century. Dutch hostility to Spain (and after the union of 1580 with Portugal) stemmed from their revolt against the Spanish Habsburgs in 1566. The spread of Calvinism in the Netherlands by the 1560s, conflicts over the powers granted by the Spanish crown to the Inquisition and fears over efforts to centralise the Spanish crown's fiscal controls prompted the Dutch revolt against the Habsburg monarchy. The Union of Utrecht in 1579 created the Republic of the Seven United Netherlands (not recognised by Spain until 1609) as a decentralised union of highly independent provinces. The institutions of the Dutch Republic remained weak, and its formal rulers exercised little authority over the Republic's constituent provinces. The strongest economic partners in the federation, Holland (centred on the merchant community in Amsterdam) and Zeeland, largely controlled the principal governing body, the States General, but any joint policies required constant negotiation among the Dutch provinces.[55] Holland and Zeeland also dominated the Republic's overseas expansion by gaining a controlling interest in the two state-licensed joint-stock companies, the Dutch East India Company (VOC) and the Dutch West India Company (WIC). The East and West India companies took over Dutch overseas

---

53   Elizabeth Mancke, 'Negotiating an Empire: Britain and its Overseas Possessions', in Daniels and Kennedy, *Negotiated Empires*, pp. 235–8.
54   Ibid.
55   Greene, 'Negotiated Authorities', p. 10.

trade and settlement, dividing commercial opportunities into separate Pacific and Atlantic spheres.[56]

The Dutch began challenging Portuguese dominance in the Asian spice trade in the late sixteenth century. Inefficient Portuguese trading enterprises could not meet the rising demand in Europe for pepper, cloves, nutmeg and cinnamon, leading to rising prices for these Asian commodities. Price rises and inelastic demand for spices in Europe encouraged Dutch trading voyages to wrest a share of the Asian spice trade. Moreover, the political union of Portugal and Spain (from 1580 to 1640) gave the Dutch the perfect excuse to challenge Portuguese commercial supremacy in Asia. In 1602 the States General chartered the VOC, giving it monopoly control over trade and political power in any Dutch-controlled territories in the far east. Following the fort-factory model pioneered by the Portuguese, the Dutch established their first trading post at Banten in West Java in 1603, and by 1611 founded another settlement at Batavia (Jakarta), which became the centre of their East Indian empire. In 1610 the VOC created the post of governor-general to rule over the company's Asian fortresses, and afterwards company holdings in Asia expanded to include trading settlements in Persia, Malacca and Thailand; in mainland China at Canton; Formosa; and Bengal, the Malabar Coast and the Coromandel Coast in India. They also set up a settler colony in southern Africa. The VOC gradually gained control of the sea from the Portuguese and expelled these rivals from most strategic trading areas, except Goa, by the 1640s. Gaining control over the spice trade made the VOC one of the most profitable joint-stock companies in the early modern world, with its own private army, fleet of merchant ships and warships and thousands of employees.[57]

The States General founded the West India Company in 1621, with the same structure and powers of the highly successful VOC, except that the new company could not carry out military operations without approval from the Dutch government.[58] The WIC mounted a number of maritime expeditions to prey on Spanish shipping in the Caribbean, and in 1628 company warships commanded by Piet Heyn captured the entire Spanish silver fleet at Matanzas, off the coast from Cuba. The company also established a North American colony at New Netherland in 1609 to exploit the fur trade with Native Americans, but Dutch settlers arrived

---

56   Wim Klooster, 'Other Netherlands Beyond the Sea: Dutch America between Metropolitan Control and Divergence, 1600–1795', in Daniels and Kennedy, *Negotiated Empires*, pp. 171–5.

57   The classic work on the Dutch rise to primacy in the far east is Niels Steensgaard, *The Asian Trade Revolution of the Seventeenth Century: The East India Companies and the Decline of the Caravan Trade* (Chicago, IL and London, 1973), pp. 344–67.

58   Klooster, 'Other Netherlands Beyond the Sea', pp. 171–4; Klooster, 'The Dutch Atlantic, 1600–1800: Expansion Without Empire', *Itinerario* 23 (1999): pp. 48–69; Jan de Vries, 'The Dutch Atlantic Economies', in Peter Coclanis (ed.), *The Atlantic Economy During the Seventeenth and Eighteenth Centuries: Organization, Operation, Practice and Personnel* (Columbia, SC, 2005), pp. 1–29; Benjamin Schmidt, 'The Dutch Atlantic: From Provincialism to Globalism', in Greene and Morgan, *Atlantic History*, pp. 166–71.

slowly in the region, until it fell to the English in 1664.[59] Dutch settlers in New Netherland and other WIC possessions were either employees of the company or free settlers. Wealthier settlers were often given large landholdings as *patrons* (proprietors of manorial estates), provided that they brought 50 additional colonists to the colony over three years. The WIC also sponsored settlements in the Caribbean at St Martin, St Eustatius, Tobago and Saba in the 1630s.[60]

During this period the company devoted considerable resources to gaining footholds in Africa to exploit the slave trade and in Portuguese Brazil to control the sugar industry. The WIC mounted a large fleet of 26 ships and 3,300 soldiers in 1624, which captured the Brazilian capital of Salvador da Bahia, but a joint Spanish–Portuguese expedition recaptured the city and province the next year. The Dutch returned to Brazil in 1630, recapturing the Portuguese city of Recife in Pernambuco. The WIC wanted Pernambuco as a permanent Dutch colony, which they called New Holland, so that the Dutch could dominate sugar production in Brazil. When the company named the supremely able Johan Maurits of Nassau-Siegen the royal governor, he established alliances with local Portuguese planters, expanded the sugar trade, and even mounted a successful expedition to Africa, capturing Luanda, on Africa's Atlantic coast in modern-day Angola, in 1641. This gave the WIC a firm foothold to participate in the slave trade, providing a steady supply of bondsmen for sugar plantations in New Holland.[61]

After their successful rebellion against the Spanish monarchy, however, the Portuguese directed more attention to combating the WIC in Africa and Brazil. An expedition led by Salvador de Sá, scion of a wealthy donatary family in Brazil, led an expedition from Brazil that recaptured Luanda in 1648. That same year at the Battle of Guararapes the Portuguese in Pernambuco defeated the Dutch, restricting their control to the capital of Recife and its immediate environs. Finally, in 1653 a major Portuguese fleet of 77 ships sailed from Lisbon to recapture Recife, and the Dutch surrendered in 1654.[62] Although the company retained its important sugar-producing colony in Suriname, these reverses in Africa and Brazil ultimately undermined the solvency of the WIC, which folded in 1674.

While Spain and Portugal consolidated their overseas empires, the English remained preoccupied with European affairs, particularly in the British Isles. England formed the core of a robust composite monarchy, which had built a strong state structure centred in London, with a functioning court system and an effective royal treasury.[63] Nonetheless, the English state relied heavily on local elites, particularly the nobility and gentry, even after the early Tudor monarchs effectively curbed the independent military power of great noble houses following the Wars

---

59   Jaap Jacobs, *New Netherland: A Dutch Colony in Seventeenth-Century America* (Leiden, 2005); Joyce Goodfriend (ed.), *Revisiting New Netherland: Perspectives on Early Dutch America* (Leiden, 2005).

60   Klooster, 'Other Netherlands Beyond the Sea', p. 173.

61   The classic work on the Dutch in Brazil is Boxer, *The Dutch in Brazil*.

62   Boxer, *Salvador de Sá*.

63   Greene, 'Negotiated Authorities', p. 9.

of the Roses (c. 1455–87). The Acts of Union of 1536 and 1543 legally incorporated Wales into the monarchy.[64] The English pursed a more militant strategy in Ireland, however, subduing that largely Roman Catholic island by 1603 and granting large tracts of land to English landlords. Poynings Law of 1494 had subordinated the Irish Parliament to the English Privy Council, and the monarchy maintained order in Ireland by keeping a large standing army there.[65] Scotland was slowly brought into a political union with England and Wales after King James VI of Scotland inherited the English throne (as James I) in 1603. Nonetheless, the formal political institutions of the two kingdoms remained separate until 1707.[66]

While extending political control in Wales and Ireland, the English confined overseas ventures to commercial fishing enterprises in Newfoundland and the dramatic exploits of privateers such as Sir Francis Drake, who raided shipping and plundered coastal settlements in the Spanish Caribbean.[67] The Tudor monarchs spent more attention and treasure aiding the Dutch Protestants in their revolt against the Spanish Habsburgs and in the conquest of Ireland than on supporting more distant overseas enterprises. Indeed, some scholars argue that Ireland was England's 'laboratory for empire'.[68] Nonetheless, like the Dutch, the English had a well-developed merchant community in several ports, particularly London, Southampton, Dartmouth and Plymouth on the English Channel, and Bristol and Barnstaple facing the Atlantic, with a substantial commercial fleet.

After the defeat of the Spanish Armada in 1588, which removed the threat of a Spanish invasion of the British Isles, a group of London merchants petitioned Queen Elizabeth I to trade in Asia. In 1600 she chartered the East India Company, granting it a fifteen-year monopoly to trade with all countries to the east of the Cape of Good Hope and west of the Straits of Magellan.[69] Although the Company struggled to compete in the spice trade with more established Portuguese and Dutch trading ventures, it did establish a trading post at Bantam (1603) in Java and at Machilipatnam (1611) on the Bay of Bengal. King James I extended the company's charter indefinitely in 1609, and with the support of the Mughal Emperor, it gained permanent bases in Surat (1612), Madras (1638) and Bombay (1668). By 1647 the company had a network of 23 factories and nearly 100 employees.[70] Its profits did

---

64   Elliott, 'A Europe of Composite Monarchy', p. 52.

65   Jane Ohlmeyer, 'Seventeenth-Century Ireland and the New British and Atlantic Histories', *American Historical Review* 104/2 (1999): p. 450.

66   Elliott, 'A Europe of Composite Monarchies', p. 55.

67   Trevor Burnard, 'The British Atlantic', in Greene and Morgan, *Atlantic History*, p. 112; Gillian T. Cell, *English Enterprise in Newfoundland, 1577–1660* (Toronto, ON, 1969).

68   Ohlmeyer, 'Seventeenth-Century Ireland', p. 460. For the role of English activities in Ireland see Nicholas Canny, *Kingdom and Colony: Ireland in the Atlantic World, 1560–1800* (Baltimore, MD, 1988); and Canny, *Making Ireland British, 1580–1650* (Oxford, 2001).

69   Mancke, 'Negotiating an Empire', p. 243.

70   Philip Lawson, *The East India Company: A History* (London, 1993), pp. 24–48. For a recent historiographical overview of the East India Company, see Philip J. Stern, 'History and Historiography of the English East India Company: Past, Present, and Future', *History Compass* 7/4 (2009): pp. 1146–80.

not outstrip the vast holdings of the VOC in Asia, but by 1650 the British East India Company had passed the Portuguese as the second largest European trader in Asia.

At the same time, English explorers searched for a northwest passage to Asia and the English nobleman, Sir Walter Raleigh, launched an unsuccessful overseas colonisation effort in Roanoke in Virginia.[71] Despite this setback, the British established a small colony in Bermuda in 1600, which largely served as a base for privateers. Colonisation began in earnest in 1606 when a group of London merchants formed the joint-stock London Company, with a charter to set up a settlement in the Americas. After a gruelling five-month sea voyage, the settlers established a colony at Jamestown in Virginia (named after King James I). Although the colony struggled, the importation of indentured servants (and later African slaves) and the successful cultivation of tobacco by 1620 ensured its ultimate survival.[72] The English colony in Jamestown was followed by other settlements. In 1620 religious separatists, known as Pilgrims, established Plymouth in New England, followed by a Puritan colony in nearby Massachusetts Bay a decade later. The growth of the British Empire in the Atlantic was then hindered by the English Civil War (1641–51), but this conflict allowed fledgling North American colonies to develop their own institutions of government virtually independent of the Parliament in London.[73] After the end of the Civil War, English colonisation expanded anew, with the establishment of settlements in Barbados and the Leeward Islands, and the seizure of Jamaica from the Spanish in 1654. By the end of the seventeenth century, English colonies dotted the coast of North America, and over 300,000 settlers had left for the Americas and Ireland.[74] British missionary efforts to convert Amerindians and Asians remained much more limited than in Spanish America (or even French America) and there was also less intermarriage and miscegenation in England's Asian and American colonies.[75] Moreover, the establishment of successful English colonies in North America eventually led merchants from the colonies and from England to engage in the West African slave trade.[76] Indeed, by 1650 England had successful and growing commercial enterprises in the Atlantic and in Asia.

The French were relative latecomers to founding overseas colonies, largely because warfare in Europe and political and religious divisions at home impeded

---

71   David B. Quinn, *Set Fair for Roanoke: Voyages and Colonies, 1584–1606* (Chapel Hill, NC, 1985); Alison Games, *The Web of Empire: English Cosmopolitans in an Age of Expansion, 1560–1660* (Cambridge, MA, 2008).

72   Edmund S. Morgan, *American Slavery, American Freedom: The Ordeal of Colonial Virginia* (New York, 1975); April Lee Hatfield, *Atlantic Virginia: Intercolonial Relations in the Seventeenth Century* (Philadelphia, PA, 2007).

73   Carla Gardina Pestana, *The English Atlantic in an Age of Revolution, 1640–1661* (Cambridge, MA, 2004), p. 9.

74   Burnard, 'The British Atlantic', p. 118.

75   The classic work on English missionary activities in North America is James Axtell, *The Invasion Within: The Contest of Cultures in Colonial North America* (Oxford, 1985).

76   Ira Berlin, *Many Thousands Gone: The First Two Centuries of Slavery in North America* (Cambridge, MA, 1998).

overseas commercial and colonisation ventures. The French state evolved piecemeal during the late medieval and early modern eras by incorporating a diverse array of provinces and feudal principalities. Each of these provinces maintained their own legal and political relationships with the monarchy. To enhance royal power, crown ministers such as Cardinal Richelieu (1624–42) and Cardinal Mazarin (1642–61) created a large bureaucracy and a standing army to integrate the various regions into a more centralised state apparatus. Many of these bureaucratic posts were sold, however, leading to a great deal of local influence over the affairs of government, inhibiting the consolidation of royal power. Moreover, Mazarin's efforts at raising taxes to pay for French involvement in the Thirty Years' War (1618–48) led to friction with the French Parliament, culminating in the revolt of the Fronde in 1648. This destructive civil war threatened to reverse the consolidation of royal power in France before it ended in 1653. As a result, France remained a composite monarchy, despite the efforts of the French crown to create an aggressive centralising state capable of controlling powerful local vested-interest groups in France.

French overseas activities began with privateering off the African coast and in the Caribbean. Merchants from Brittany and Normandy outfitted ships to trade for ivory, gold and slaves in West Africa, and to raid Portuguese shipping. French traders also established small settlements on the coast of Brazil to trade in dyewoods, but the Portuguese eventually expelled them by 1550. French corsairs also plied the Caribbean, raiding Spanish settlements and briefly capturing Havana (1555), the lynchpin of Spanish defences in the region. The French also established a small settlement in Florida, which the Spanish destroyed in 1565.[77] It was only in 1603 that King Henry IV gave permission for Pierre du Gua, Sieur de Monts to found a company with merchants from La Rochelle, which received a ten-year trade monopoly to colonise Acadia and other territories of New France in North America. De Monts and his lieutenant, Samuel de Champlain, founded a colony at Port Royal in Acadia in 1605 to trade fish and furs, and later to grow wheat. Champlain used this base to explore the Saint Lawrence River, building a fort at Quebec in 1608 to oversee the fur trade with local Algonquin and Huron tribesmen.[78] Although French traders had explored the region and traded with local Amerindians since the 1580s, Quebec was the first permanent French settlement in the region. French settlers engaging in the fur trade often lived among their Amerindian partners, marrying indigenous women and fathering mixed-race children.[79] Jesuit missionaries attempted to convert the indigenous peoples, but they were never as successful as their counterparts in the Spanish Indies.[80]

In 1627 the king's chief minister, Cardinal Richelieu, established the Company of the 100 Associates, bringing French state support for establishing strategic and

---

77   John T. McGrath, *The French in Early Florida: In the Eye of the Hurricane* (Gainesville, FL, 2000).

78   Benjamin, *The Atlantic World*, pp. 242–7.

79   Gilles Havard and Cécil Vidal, *Histoire de l'Amerique française* (Paris, 2003), p. 12.

80   Marie-Christine Pioffet, *La Tentation de l'épopée dans les Relations des Jésuites* (Sillery, 1997); Allan Greer, *Mohawk Saint: Catherine Tekakwitha and the Jesuits* (Oxford, 2005).

economic footholds in the Americas. Even by the 1640s, however, New France had a population of barely 400 inhabitants. Likewise, French colonisation efforts in the Caribbean in the first half of the seventeenth century have been characterised as a 'pioneering frontier'.[81] The French incursions into St Christopher, Guadalupe and Martinique met stern resistance from local indigenous groups, and the small French settlements produced modest quantities of foodstuffs, cotton, indigo and sugar. By the 1650s, the numbers of French settlers and imported African slave labourers in the Antilles may have numbered 10–15,000 of each race.[82] These modest French settlements would grow significantly only in the eighteenth century. Indeed, some modern scholars contend that France's overseas possessions never constituted a cohesive overseas empire, even at its zenith.[83]

The Spanish and Portuguese monopoly of overseas expansion into Asia, Africa and the Americas had ended around 1650. The Dutch, British and French had succeeded in overturning the Papal division and the Treaty of Tordesillas, which had allowed the Iberian powers to claim sovereignty over the oceans and territories outside of Europe. These three newcomers to empire all began with modest privateering ventures, raiding Spanish and Portuguese shipping. These activities expanded when the Dutch and the English founded joint stock companies to establish commercial settlements in Asia and Africa, followed by successful efforts to found colonies in the Americas. The Dutch made huge profits by taking over Portuguese trade routes in Asia, although their ventures in the Atlantic, after some early successes, ultimately proved disappointing. The English and French efforts to trade and found colonies were modest successes that would mature and prosper well after 1650. The seventeenth century produced a world contested by five European overseas powers, as their wars and dynastic rivalries expanded into Asia and the Atlantic world. This second phase of European exploration and overseas expansion introduced new rivalries and conflicts, but it also led to greater colonisation and trade.

Despite this rapid expansion of European power and influence, the actions of other powerful empires often shaped the course of Europe's overseas enterprises. The growth of the Ottoman Empire into North Africa and the Balkans (to the gates of Vienna in 1529) threatened to destabilise Eastern Europe, but Turkish domination of traditional overland trade routes to the east actually encouraged European powers to explore sea lanes to the far east. These routes were only open to Portuguese, Spanish, Dutch and, later, English penetration, however, because

---

81   Philip Boucher, 'The 'Frontier Era' of the French Caribbean, 1620s–1690s', in Daniels and Kennedy, *Negotiated Empires*, pp. 207–234.

82   Ibid., p. 218.

83   See, for example, Kenneth Banks, *Chasing Empire Across the Sea: Communications and the State in the French Atlantic, 1713–1763* (Montreal, QC, 2002); James Pritchard, *In Search of Empire: The French in the Americas, 1670–1730* (Cambridge, 2004); Gail Bossenga, *The Politics of Privilege: Old Regime and Revolution in Lille* (Cambridge, 1991); and David Bell, 'The Unbearable Lightness of Being French: Law, Republicanism and National Identity at the End of the Old Regime', *American Historical Review* 106/4 (2001): pp. 1215–35.

the Ming dynasty in China turned away from sponsoring long-distance sea-going ventures in the fifteenth century and failed to maintain and replace their vast navy of large ships. At the same time, China remained a large market for furs, supplied by Russia and the British East India Company, and for silver, which the Spanish and Portuguese provided from their New World possessions. Moreover, European trading enclaves such as Luanda, Hormuz, Goa and Nagasaki only existed with the cooperation and support of local African and Asian rulers, who recognised benefits from trading with European powers. The European nations may have enjoyed naval superiority in many places, but powerful local empires, such as the Kingdom of Kongo in Africa, the Safavid Empire in Persia, the Mughal Empire in India and the Ming Emperors in China, all possessed the military might on land to impose clear limits on European overseas expansion. Even in the Americas, where the conquest of the Aztec and Inca empires brought Spain great riches, geographical barriers and powerful local indigenous groups blocked or slowed European territorial ambitions. In short, the age of exploration promoted commercial, religious, social and political interactions on a global scale, but Europeans did not always dictate the terms of these relationships.

Scholars of early modern European empires take a broad perspective that unites immensely varied landscapes, climates, disease environments, cultures, languages and customs. After the first violent encounters between European invaders and Amerindian peoples, for example, a series of profound changes altered indigenous modes of production, technology, commerce, politics, social hierarchies, patterns of disease, diet and religion. The forced migration of African slaves only added to the ethnic and cultural complexity prompted by European explorations. Europeans also promoted significant political changes in African polities, as they encouraged an expansion of warfare to capture slaves needed in Europe and on New World plantations. At the same time, Asian, African and Amerindian peoples managed to incorporate these changes into their own political, social and religious practices, producing a constantly evolving cultural mixture. Wherever Europeans established settler colonies, these changes were profound and permanent, while change was less extensive in smaller trading enclaves, such as Portuguese Goa. Differing notions of wealth, for example, led to intensive mining of precious metals in the Spanish Indies, the introduction of commercial agriculture and the introduction of new foodstuffs and animals, which transformed the world in significant ways over the period from c. 1500 to 1650. At the same time, indigenous food products (such as chocolate, potatoes and tobacco) and cultural practices reshaped settler and European ways of life. In short, European overseas expansion led to functional imperial systems that produced religious, cultural, political, social and economic interchanges by 1650, which dramatically and permanently transformed large segments of the world. Indeed, the first voyages of the age of exploration began the process, today called globalisation, which has so influenced the world from the late fifteenth century to the present.

Age of Settlement and Colonisation

Michael Adas and Hugh Glenn Cagle

European Underdevelopment and the Imperative of Overseas Expansionism

The dramatic burst of European overseas expansion that began in the fifteenth century and peaked in the first century of the industrial era generated a profound and lasting Eurocentrism that has dominated historical explanations of the geopolitics and global cross-cultural exchanges of the last half-millennium. Eurocentric perspectives remain pervasive. They underwrite the early modern and modern labels we use for the periodisation of recent centuries in global history. And they have sustained a conceptual framework that encapsulates widely held convictions regarding the exceptional nature of the socioeconomic and political transformations that led to Europe's rise to unprecedented affluence and global hegemony.[1] But research in recent decades has made it clear that Europe was but one of a number of highly dynamic, expansive core regions in the fourteenth and fifteenth centuries.[2] In terms of its population, the extent of its urbanisation, the size of its armies, the productivity of its agriculture and other indices of socioeconomic and political development, Europe lagged well behind societies in China, the Islamic world and Mesoamerica. In short, Europe was an underdeveloped region. And the reports of European merchants, missionaries and other travellers to the Middle East and Asia devoted considerable time and attention to this fact. Their accounts, which by the late fifteenth century had begun to accumulate throughout

---

1   Notions that persist in both academic scholarship and popular attitudes to the present day. For prominent, recent exemplars of the former, see David S. Landes, *The Wealth and Poverty of Nations: Why Some are So Wealthy and Some So Poor* (New York, 1998); and E.L. Jones, *The European Miracle: Environments, Economies and Geopolitics in the History of Europe and Asia* (Cambridge, 1981).

2   These are surveyed in rather different ways in David Ringrose, *Expansion and Global Interaction, 1200–1700* (New York, 2001); and John Darwin, *After Tamerlane: The Rise and Fall of Global Empires, 1400–2000* (Harmondsworth, 2008).

Europe, did much to arouse the fears and needs that were among the forces driving early European overseas projects.[3]

The geographic expanse and diversity of cultures conquered by several non-western empires were often a match for those of the Iberian vanguard, despite the much greater global reach of Spanish *conquistadores* and Portuguese *fidalgos*. Between the second half of the fifteenth century and the end of the sixteenth, Muscovy on the eastern fringes of Europe expanded deep into Central Asia and towards the Pacific Ocean and the borderlands of China. In roughly the same century and a half, the Ottoman Turks extended their imperial sway over the Balkans, portions of central Europe, North Africa, and the Arab heartlands in the eastern Mediterranean. Rival Muslim dynasties built smaller gunpowder empires. The Safavid domain was centred on the Iranian plateau and hemmed in by the Ottomans in the west and by the Mughals in the east who, from their base in north-central India, had conquered all but the southern cone of the South Asian subcontinent by the end of the sixteenth century.

By 1400, the African Sahel was home to a number of powerful and growing land-bound empires. In the fourteenth century Islam had spread to this region and was widely adopted by rulers of the Sudanic kingdoms. The rulers and merchants of the empire of Mali, whose power was already underwritten by its strategic location between the gold fields to the south and the Saharan salt deposits to the north, found in the Islamic religion diplomatic and commercial links to trade networks that spanned much of the known world. Cities such as Timbuktu were key centres of exchange. Based in the fertile lands of the Niger River basin, Mali projected its power – albeit tenuously – all the way to present-day Gambia on the West African coast. When Mali declined in the latter half of the fifteenth century, several other trade-oriented, urban-based polities, including Songhai and the kingdom of Kanem-Bornu, emerged to take its place.[4]

In roughly the same period as these Sudanic empires flourished, the Aztecs and Incas were establishing the largest, wealthiest and most centrally administered polities that had ever arisen in the Americas. The heart of the Aztec Empire was the island city of Tenochtitlan in the valley of Mexico, which had steadily extended its influence over a cluster of tributary states that had reached the rainforest remnants of the Maya kingdoms by the time of the Spanish invasion in 1519. The Inca Empire, which was more centralised and better integrated than the Aztec, expanded from a nucleus around Cuzco in present-day Peru across the length of the Andes mountains and beyond from contemporary Colombia well into northern Chile. Both societies practised intensive agriculture. But, facilitated by an extensive network of roads and way stations, Inca authority extended more broadly up and down the Andes. This in turn allowed the Incas, much more than the Aztecs, to

---

3   Margaret Hodgen, *Early Anthropology in the Sixteenth and Seventeenth Centuries* (Philadelphia, PA, 1964); and Michael Adas, *Machines as the Measure of Men: Science, Technology and Ideologies of Western Dominance* (Ithaca, NY, 1989).

4   Christopher Ehret, 'Sudanic Civilizations', in Michael Adas (ed.), *Agricultural and Pastoral Societies in Classical History* (Philadelphia, PA, 2001), pp. 224–74.

coordinate the circulation of crops and trade goods throughout their realm. The Aztecs, relying on a military hierarchy and incessant warfare, focused their control on the richest markets of the central valley, which were located in and around the lake region that was dominated by Tenochtitlan.[5]

Only one of the great empires that the Europeans encountered in the first phase of exploration and colonisation could rival their capacity to harness sea power.[6] The early rulers of the Ming dynasty, which had wrested control of China from the Mongols in the late fourteenth century, had invested heavily in massive war and commercial ships and launched a series of impressive naval expeditions that had traversed most of the vast Indian Ocean trading network between 1405 and 1433.[7] But the Ming voyages led neither to the establishment of an overseas trading network nor to settlement colonies, and by the mid-fifteenth century the Chinese navy was much reduced in size and confined mainly to patrolling the coasts of China. The Ming retreat from the sea was paralleled by the end of sustained efforts to control the nomadic peoples of inner Asia, and growing restrictions on trading contacts with both China's Japanese and Korean neighbours as well as merchant and missionary intruders from the far west of Eurasia. Though Chinese war fleets proved able to hold their own against their Portuguese counterparts in the early 1500s, the Ming dynasty's abandonment of attempts to project its power and influence by sea left no Asian rival that was capable of countering the Portuguese resort to force and extortion when they found that they had little to exchange in the peaceful commerce that had dominated the Indian Ocean trading system for millennia.

Advances in sailing ships proved to be only one of a number of key advantages the Europeans possessed in their efforts to break out by sea from the Muslim encirclement that had for centuries menaced Christendom from North Africa to Asia Minor. Though it has become fashionable to dispute or play down the ways in which Europe's political, socioeconomic and cultural development diverged significantly from other colonising societies,[8] the macro-approach which seeks

---

5   For a thorough discussion of the history of development of both of these major pre-Columbian civilisations, see Friedrich Katz, *Ancient American Civilizations* (New York, 1972).

6   Even though the Ottomans had a very large navy, their galleys were unsuitable for extended voyages on the high seas and lacked the cannon that the Portuguese used to good effect in battles, such as that against a combined Ottoman–Indian fleet off the port of Diu in 1507, to establish their hegemony in the Indian Ocean.

7   The most readable and comprehensive account of these remarkable achievements is Edward Dreyer's *Zheng He: China and the Oceans in the Early Ming Dynasty, 1405–1433* (New York, 2007).

8   For differing perspectives on what has in effect become a debate over the extent to which Europe's historical trajectory from the early modern centuries onward has been exceptional, see Landes and Jones for the most extreme formulations affirming of this position. For those who seek to contest it, see Andre Gunder Frank, *ReOrient: The Silver Age in Asia and the World Economy* (Berkeley, CA, 1998) and Kenneth Pomeranz, *The Great Divergence: China, Europe, and the Making of the Modern World Economy* (Princeton, NJ, 2000), who argue that Europe's achievements were either matched (Pomeranz) or

to tally up the strengths and weaknesses of whole culture areas (Europe, China, Sudanic Africa, and so on) or empires (for example, the Ottoman or Inca) is at best misdirected. As we have suggested, in the fifteenth century western Europe was at parity with, or lagged behind, other societies and empires in key sectors of societal development. But as recent research and ongoing debates have shown, the level of development of whole societies is very difficult to measure with any precision. Rather than an overall advantage relative to other expansive empires, the Europeans' ability to engage in diverse overseas enterprises hinged on the interplay among a select and often quite specific cluster of innovations and endeavours in which it had forged ahead of most or all of its potential global rivals. European expansionism was also facilitated by factors – such as its geographical position and resource endowment – over which its inhabitants had little control, but which would again and again prove critical to the success of its overseas endeavours.

Because Europe was geophysically a collection of peninsulas on the far west of Eurasia,[9] its geography, which also featured extensive and navigable river systems and ample harbours, had long favoured water-borne travel and trade. The fact that the more developed western portions of the continent projected into the Atlantic and had ready access to the Baltic and Mediterranean served to enhance the Europeans' maritime orientation. The initial overseas probes of the Portuguese and Spanish rivals were favoured by the winds and currents off the Iberian Peninsula as well as the fact that they could draw on instruments, maps, navigation techniques, ship designs and sailors from both the north Atlantic and Mediterranean. Millennia of contacts across the Mediterranean Sea, which the spread of Islam often enhanced rather than disrupted, also meant that the Italians and Iberians in particular were aware of, and able to adopt, key elements of the seafaring traditions of non-European societies, most critically the Arabs' fine maps and navigational instruments, and the *lateen* sails and narrow hulls of their highly navigable *dhows*. The steady growth of water-borne transport and the challenges of deep-sea fishing also meant that Europe had disproportionate numbers of sailors and skilled navigators relative to its population, which was smaller than that of most of the expansive empires that would soon be encountered overseas. Early explorers, traders and adventurers could also draw on time-tested skills in shipbuilding and instrument-making. And from ancient times in the Mediterranean and in the centuries of Viking raids from the Baltic Sea to Sicily from the eighth to eleventh centuries CE, the sea had been a major arena for intra-continental warfare. The growing deployment of handguns, and later small cannon in combat at sea, coincided with the very centuries when the Portuguese mounted their successive expeditions into the Atlantic and down the coast of Africa. This convergence made possible the development of the

---

exceeded by (Frank) those attained by the Chinese. For thoughtful assessments of the arguments on each side, see the essays by Joseph M. Bryant, especially 'The West and the Rest Revisited: Debating Capitalist Origins, European Colonialism, and the Advent of Modernity', *Canadian Journal of Sociology/Cahiers canadiens de sociologie* 31/4 (2006): pp. 403–444.

9   For an elaboration on this notion, see Darwin, *After Tamerlane*, pp. 95–6.

superb *caravels*, which in their combination of seaworthiness, manoeuvrability and firepower – if not in size – had no match anywhere in the world from the late fifteenth to the early seventeenth century.[10]

Innovations in the design and construction of armed, long-distance sailing ships provided the most decisive technological advantage Europeans were able to deploy as they ventured overseas. But a number of late medieval and early modern improvements in agrarian production, machines, commercial transactions and instrumentation proved critical to their ability to increase domestic productivity and labour efficiency, and to integrate the bullion, handicraft goods and foodstuffs imported from Asia, Africa and the Americas into a steadily growing continental economy. The introduction of the horse collar, iron ploughs capable of turning the heavy north European soils, long field cultivation and crop rotation raised agrarian productivity – though still not to the levels per hectare achieved by Asian wet-rice cultivators. They also facilitated the introduction of new foods from the Americas, particularly beans, maize and potatoes, into the European diet.[11] In the centuries before the age of expansion, wind and water mills greatly enhanced the non-animate power available to millers and metal workers as well as to the Dutch and other peoples who sought to reclaim new agricultural lands from the sea. Increasingly sophisticated combinations of gears, cogs and trip-hammers ground grain, worked metals and inflated bellows. According to one estimate, by 1500 Europe as a whole enjoyed a 5:1 advantage in the ability to extract energy from animal and machine power over China, which had been the world leader in technological innovation and transfer for millennia.[12]

Although few observers recognised it at the time, Iberian empire builders and their north European successors possessed a range of colonising options that exceeded those of any of their expansionist rivals. Would-be European empire builders could refer to a range of classical and medieval precedents in organising their overseas enterprises. Greek, Roman and, more recently, Islamic empires and Italian city states had generated and refined several time-tested modes of expansion and colonisation that, although historically intertwined, were fundamentally distinct. Urban-based tribute systems, export-oriented plantation enclaves, trade diasporas, trading post empires and settlement colonies provided a broad repertoire of models for colonisation.[13]

---

10 J.H. Parry, *The Discovery of the Sea* (Berkeley, CA, 1981), chap. 1 and pp. 102–144, 193–7; Pierre Chaunu, *L'expansion Européenne du XIIIe au XVe siècle* (Paris, 1969), pp. 141–60 and passim; and Carlo Cipolla, *Guns, Sails, and Empires: Technological Innovation and the Early Phases of European Expansion 1400–1700* (New York, 1965), esp. pp. 78–83.

11 Lynn White, Jr, *Medieval Technology and Social Change* (London, 1962); Jean Gimple, *The Medieval Machine* (New York, 1983); J.U. Nef, *The Conquest of the Material World* (Chicago, IL, 1964); and Joel Mokyr, *The Lever of Riches: Technological Creativity and Economic Progress* (New York, 1990).

12 Chaunu, *L'expansion Européenne*, pp. 335–6.

13 A thoughtful and thorough exploration of these early Mediterranean models for expansion and domination is central to Ben Kiernan's *Blood and Soil: A World History of Genocide and Extermination from Sparta to Darfur* (New Haven, CT, 2007), especially

Roman imperial expansion and colonisation depended on the creation of urban centres to exploit the neighbouring hinterland and its inhabitants. Tribute arrangements with local populations, which involved a combination of agricultural products and labour, formed the basis of the Roman presence. An even more widely deployed institution for extracting agricultural products and organising a labour force was the plantation enclave. These export-oriented, large-scale, labour- and capital-intensive sources of commercial produce became a persisting feature of European history from the time of the Crusades. Although both the consumption of sugar (the premier plantation crop) and its intensive cultivation were Indian in origin and disseminated to the Mediterranean by the Arabs, Italian families with financial backing from German and Iberian moneylenders spearheaded the growth and development of plantation-based sugar cultivation, which spread across the Mediterranean to Iberia and into the Atlantic between the twelfth and fifteenth centuries.[14]

Long before the Iberians made their way overseas, trade diasporas, or networks of interconnected merchant communities and their agents, were found across most of the Americas and Eurasia.[15] Traders from diverse regions migrated over land and the oceans to establish new operations in receptive foreign societies. Concentrated in urban settlements and linked by religious, kinship and ethnic ties, the primary purpose of these expatriate merchant communities was to forge links with local traders and producers in host societies, and establish or maintain inter-cultural exchanges in exotic cultivars, manufactures and other items that might prove to be mutually profitable. Trade diasporas often became important channels for cross-cultural contact in other ways as well, such as the transfer of religious ideas, technologies and pathogens. From the Silk Road and the far-flung Indian Ocean system to the African Sahel and rainforests of Mesoamerica, these diasporas had been a key component of cross-cultural interaction and exchange since ancient times. The seaborne trading networks forged by the Venetians and the Genoese provided the expansionist commercial models with which the Iberians, and later the northern Europeans, would first experiment with as they ventured across the Atlantic and into the Indian Ocean.[16] A kindred mode of expansionism, also inspired by the example of the Venetians and Genoese, was the trading-post empire. These networks consisted of centrally controlled but widely dispersed trading settlements that were often fortified and dominated by 'factories' or warehouses for the storage of local products to be exported, and imported goods

---

chaps 1, 2 and 5–7.

14   See Charles Verlinden's excellent discussion of the relevant features of Roman expansion in *The Beginnings of Modern Colonization* (Ithaca, NY, 1970).

15   Philip D. Curtin, *Cross-Cultural Trade in World History* (New York, 1984); Janet L. Abu-Lughod, *Before European Hegemony: The World System AD 1250–1350* (New York, 1991).

16   French and Belgian historians of the Annales School crafted the pioneering accounts of these influences. See, especially, Chaunu, *L'expansion Européenne*, part 2, chap. 2, III and IV, and part 3, chap. 2, IV; and Verlinden, *Beginnings of Modern Colonization*, part 1, chap. 1 and part 2.

to be offered in exchange. Forts and heavily armed ships deployed to control high-priced commodities, particularly spices in the first centuries of Iberian expansion, enabled small numbers of Portuguese to build an 'empire' in the Indian Ocean with stunning rapidity in the early decades of the sixteenth century.

The most immediate precedent for settler colonies was that forged during the seven centuries of the Spanish *Reconquista*. The competition between Christian and Muslim forces for control of the Iberian peninsula had at times depopulated whole towns and villages. Sparsely settled territory yielded little in the way of rent or agricultural produce, and was notoriously difficult to defend. As Christian leaders advanced southward, they needed Spanish peasants and herders to move into newly conquered lands to generate both surplus produce and, later, local conscripts for their armies. Several factors drew commoners to settle in these borderland regions. Spanish law provided mechanisms that allowed squatters in such situations to become landholders, which elevated their status among the local population. In return for protection in these frontier areas by lesser noblemen, the peasant migrants exchanged labour and produce.[17]

In a carefully researched analysis, one historian has recently argued that Spain, Portugal, England, France and the Netherlands deployed distinctive and culturally rooted rituals to signify their possession of, and authority over, peoples and lands in the Americas.[18] And certainly early modern imperial strategists and overseas colonisers operated within a framework inflected by culture. But the interplay between local circumstances and the immediate concerns of indigenous and European agents, more than particular historical experiences and precise cultural differences, determined the form and substance of individual colonial projects, and thus better explain the divergent manifestations of empire.[19]

The most important local variables in determining European mode(s) of colonisation included the existence, size and degree of political unity of the

---

17 Angus McKay, *Spain in the Middle Ages: From Frontier to Empire, 1000–1500* (New York, 1977); Anthony M. Stevens Arroyo, 'The Inter-Atlantic Paradigm: The Failure of Spanish Medieval Colonization of the Canary and Caribbean Islands', *Comparative Studies in Society and History* 35/3 (1993): pp. 515–43; Miguel Angel Ladero Quesada, 'Spain, circa 1492: Social Values and Structures', in Stuart B. Schwartz (ed.), *Implicit Understandings: Observing, Reporting, and Reflecting on the Encounters between Europeans and Other Peoples in the Early Modern Era* (New York, 1994), pp. 96–133. In situations where repopulation proved difficult, the region was left to armed Christian raiders who sought to extract tribute from – or to plunder – local Muslim communities. The famed eleventh-century leader Rodrigo Díaz de Vivar – 'El Cid' – was one such figure. But the popularity of his and similar stories, combined with the subsequent and systematic repression of Muslims and Jews in the fifteenth century, tends to obscure the earlier settlement aspect of the *Reconquista*.

18 Patricia Seed, *Ceremonies of Possession in Europe's Conquest of the New World, 1492–1640* (Cambridge, 1995).

19 Sanjay Subrahmanyam offers a similar analysis in 'Holding the World in Balance: The Connected Histories of the Iberian Overseas Empires, 1500–1640', *American Historical Review* 112/5 (2007): pp. 1359–85.

indigenous population, the nature of the local economy, the extent of bureaucratic centralisation, and the effectiveness of local military forces. But perhaps the most pivotal factors were the nature of the local climate, the environment and the virulence of prevalent diseases. Europeans shared with their distant neighbours in the densely populated regions of the Middle East, Central Asia, China, India and Africa recurring exposure to such Old World diseases as the plague and smallpox. But the distinctive disease environments of Africa's Atlantic and Indian Ocean coasts, as well as the tropical regions of the Indian subcontinent and much of Southeast Asia, meant that death resulting from dysentery, yellow fever, malaria and other maladies was a regular occurrence for newly arrived Europeans that limited their colonising options in those regions. In a disease environment free of pathogens lethal to the Europeans, and where climate and soil conditions were conducive to animal husbandry and the cultivation of crops (including those for export) familiar to Europeans, overland expansion and large-scale permanent settlement became more tenable.[20]

Phase I (c. 1350–1580): Conquest, Trading Empires and the Beginnings of Settlement

European overseas expansion began in the waters that stretched from the Straits of Gibraltar west to the Azores and south to the Canary Islands. Much of this region was steeped in European mythology – the Canaries as exotic isles known to the ancients and the West African littoral as a land laden with gold. The Azores and Madeira were entirely unknown to Europeans. Expansion and colonisation therefore began in unfamiliar settings and were characterised by experimentation and improvisation. The same would apply to Asia and the Americas; they too were either steeped in mythology or entirely unknown and demanded a great deal of improvisation by the first groups of European colonisers. What occurred in this small region of the Atlantic – in the development of administrative institutions, economic relationships and cross-cultural interaction – would prove to be a microcosm of the dynamics that characterised European expansion more generally from the fourteenth to the late sixteenth century.[21]

Madeira and the Azores were uninhabited when the Portuguese began colonising them in the early fifteenth century. With rich soils, no indigenous resistance and Italian financial backing, Iberian colonists soon experimented with two prominent European cultivars. Wheat and sugar competed for land and the labour of poor migrants and slaves who arrived either from Iberia or directly from West Africa. Portugal was a reliable market for wheat, since its frequent low crop yields forced

20 Crosby, *Ecological Imperialism: The Biological Expansion of Europe, 900–1900* (Cambridge, 1986).
21 Useful guides to the major issues include Verlinden, *The Beginnings of Modern Colonization*; and Schwartz (ed.), *Implicit Understandings*.

it to buy from foreign markets. Sugar had proved a lucrative cash crop in markets throughout Europe and the Mediterranean. Under the auspices of Prince Henry, Portuguese settlers first arrived on the islands in the 1420s, some with titles to land, others merely to till it.[22] Though the variable climate of the Azores made them less suited to sugar cultivation, on Madeira despite its mountainous interior, plantations worked by a mixed labour force (slave and free) had spread across the island by the 1450s. Madeira was thus transformed into a sugar monoculture that dominated the European and Mediterranean markets before its precipitous decline in the early 1500s.[23]

By contrast, the colonisation of the Canary Islands was far more varied and complex. These islands were home to peoples who shared cultural ties with the Berbers of mainland North Africa, and their diverse societies were built on a combination of pastoralism and sedentary agriculture. The Canary islanders did not practise metallurgy and did not build watercraft; they neither maintained contact with the mainland nor journeyed between the islands. As a result, they lacked immunity to mainland pathogens and were ill equipped to prevent European encroachment. Two of the largest islands, Tenerife and Grand Canary, contained the best soils and supported the largest and most highly structured societies. These became the focus of Franciscan missionary activity in 1351, when a string of European trading posts was established on the islands. When Jean de Béthencourt and Gadifer de La Salle began a period of seignorial conquest of the more peripheral islands fifty years later, these earlier commercial and religious contacts helped them forge alliances with indigenous leaders. The noblemen's efforts brought only the most limited territorial control or local authority, but such alliances proved useful when in the late fifteenth century a unified Spain sought more thorough consolidation of royal power and territorial control on Grand Canary, La Palma and Tenerife. Plantations were established in the Canaries by the end of the century. As in Madeira, they depended upon a mixed labour force, which included Portuguese and Spanish immigrants, to grow the sugarcane and operate the mills. Slaves from Africa and Iberia (often *moriscos*, Muslim converts to Christianity) and those captured in the Canaries themselves provided most of the labour.[24]

Iberian undertakings in the Atlantic also included the coast of Africa, where they were lured by the longstanding belief that rich gold fields lay just beyond the coast. The Portuguese launched a series of exploratory probes of the trade-and-

---

22 Peter Russell provides a thorough discussion of the role of Prince Henry, the Portuguese Duke of Viseu, in the process of Iberian expansion in *Prince Henry 'the Navigator': A Life* (New Haven, CT, 2000).

23 Verlinden, *TheBeginnings of Modern Colonization*, pp. 14–22; Felipe Fernández-Armesto, *Before Columbus: Exploration and Colonization from the Mediterranean to the Atlantic, 1229–1492* (Philadelphia, PA, 1987), pp. 185–202; and Alberto Vieira, "Sugar Islands: The Sugar Economy of Madeira and the Canaries, 1450 to 1650," in Stuart B. Schwartz (ed.), *Tropical Babylons: Sugar and the Making of the Atlantic World, 1450-1680* (Chapel Hill, NC, 2004), pp. 42-84.

24 Fernández-Armesto, *Before Columbus*, pp. 151–202; Eduardo Aznar Vallejo, 'The Conquest of the Canary Islands', in Schwartz (ed.), *Implicit Understandings*, pp. 134–56.

raid variety, and were able to procure small numbers of slaves in this fashion. But initial clashes demonstrated that West African *pirogues* (water craft) outmatched Portuguese caravels on the calm estuaries that might otherwise have allowed the Portuguese greater access to the interior. All along Africa's Atlantic coast, the Portuguese were forced to consent to formal trade agreements with local leaders if they wanted reliable access to the gold and slave markets of the interior. Here, as in the Canaries, trade pacts almost invariably embroiled the Portuguese in domestic politics. But, unlike the Canaries, they were confronted with fiercely inhospitable disease environments and large, stratified and well-organised indigenous societies. These peoples possessed a range of immunities that surpassed those of the Europeans in the tropical disease environment of the African littoral. Moreover, these West African kingdoms were themselves already engaged in territorial conquest and were home to large contingents of experienced warriors backed by communities which were readily mobilised for combat. Trade-and-raid tactics quickly gave way to formal diplomatic relations between the kingdoms of Portugal and the Kongo, as well as the creation of an African Catholic Church in 1491. These connections facilitated Portugal's overland expansion in west Central Africa. But rulers in the Kongo were careful to curtail the power and influence of Portugal's secular and ecclesiastical officials. All along Africa's Atlantic littoral, the Portuguese were generally confined to their coastal trading posts. And here, coastal Africa's distinctive disease environment, more lethal than any Europeans had previously encountered, rendered their presence even more tenuous. This was an arrangement that persisted for nearly four centuries: the rate of survival – so often aided by contacts with local peoples – was sufficient to sustain forts and factories, but even when the Portuguese, Dutch, French or English achieved some degree of authority along the coast, their control weakened in proportion to the distance they travelled inland.[25]

Both of the Iberian powers moved beyond this initial zone of expansion in the late fifteenth century with the objective of establishing direct connections to the Asian sources of the lucrative spice trade. By 1498 the Portuguese had succeeded in finding a sea route linking them to the Indian Ocean trading network, where they sought in the first decades of the sixteenth century to establish a trading-post empire. But here again the strength of local rulers and the effectiveness of their military forces, combined with immunological factors, put more ambitious colonising efforts out of reach. Goa, the capital of Portugal's trading-post empire in the Indian Ocean, provides a superb illustration of these limitations. It was both the heart of Portuguese imperial power and the base from which it sought to dominate

---

25 John Thornton, *Africa and Africans in the Making of the Atlantic World, 1400–1800* (Cambridge, 1998), 13-125. On West African epidemiology and Europeans' limited survival see Kenneth F. Kiple, *The Caribbean Slave: A Biological History* (New York, 1984), 3-50; Judith A. Carney and Richard Nicholas Rosomoff, *In the Shadow of Slavery: Africa's Botanical Legacy in the Atlantic World* (Berkeley, CA, 2009), 46-64; and Philip D. Curtin, *Death by Migration: Europe's Encounter with the Tropical World in the Nineteenth Century* (New York, 1989).

the Asian trade in pepper and cinnamon. But Goa was always hemmed in by the more powerful Hindu kingdom of Vijayanagara to its east and by expansive Muslim sultanates of the Deccan to its north. Using force, the Portuguese could piece together a trading empire in the Indian Ocean but little more. Their partial monopoly of the spice trade and broader, peaceful participation in the long-established Asian trade system generated enough wealth that, for a few decades at least, there was little incentive to expand Portuguese activities in Brazil, even though expansion there was a possibility.[26]

The Portuguese did manage to gain control over an existing tribute system for cinnamon production and export that had long been a major source of revenue for the rulers of the Kotte kingdom, founded centuries earlier in the tropical rainforest regions of southwest Ceylon. After seizing power from the Kotte rulers, the Portuguese compelled the *chalias*, a caste that had traditionally harvested the bark from the cinnamon trees, to meet compulsory quotas and transport the cinnamon to special warehouses in Colombo on the western coast of the island. The peelers and carters continued to live in the village communities that their forebears had inhabited under Sinhalese rulers. Their labours were monitored by Portuguese officials, and overseen by several layers of Sinhalese notables who staffed the lower rungs of the special government department charged with enforcing the government's monopoly control over the groves of cinnamon trees, and the harvest and export of the spice. Whether in bark or ground form, the bulk of the crop, which was the highest quality cinnamon then available, was exported to Europe, the Middle East and North Africa.[27]

At roughly the same time that the Portuguese landed in India, the Spanish moved into the Caribbean. Early contacts with the Taíno peoples on Hispaniola gave way to tentative trade relations. But, unlike the Portuguese-Asian networks, these early Caribbean trade contacts were not sufficient to sustain the commercial ties desired by Iberian merchants and traders. Immunological factors, combined with the military strength of the Spanish, meant they could experiment with other options in their imperial arsenal. A settlement colony linked to placer gold mining and an embryonic plantation enclave grew up on Hispaniola. The potential for greater riches on the mainland soon drew the Spanish to Mesoamerica and the Andes, where once again immunological factors proved decisive.[28] In Mesoamerica the Aztec capital, Tenochtitlan, fell to a coalition of Spanish and Amerindian

---

26   Although their interpretations differ, Michael N. Pearson, *The New Cambridge History of India: The Portuguese in India* (New York, 1987) and Sanjay Subrahmanyam, *The Political Economy of Commerce: Southern India, 1500–1650* (New York, 1990) both highlight the limited extent of Portuguese territorial expansion.

27   For the fullest description of the cinnamon tribute system in the Portuguese period, see Tikiri Abeyasinghe, *Portuguese Rule in Ceylon* (Colombo, 1964); for changes under the Dutch, see Sinnappah Arasaratnam, *Dutch Power in Ceylon, 1658–87* (Amsterdam, 1958).

28   Mervyn Ratekin, 'The Early Sugar Industry in Española', *Hispanic American Historical Review* 34/1 (1954): pp. 1–19; Frank Pons, *Después de Colón: Trabajo, sociedad, y política en la economía del oro* (Madrid, 1987); and Noble David Cook, 'Sickness, Starvation, and Death in Early Hispaniola', *Journal of Interdisciplinary History* 32/3 (2002): pp. 349–86.

forces in 1521; just over a decade later the Spanish defeated the Incas as well. From Mexico to the Andes, European invaders introduced diseases to which the native peoples had no prior exposure. Scarlet fever, measles and – most lethally – smallpox were transmitted with catastrophic consequences for the native peoples. Losses may have reached as high as 90 per cent in heavily populated regions such as central and southern Mexico.[29] The consequences were far ranging because disease did more than eliminate the Spaniards' primary competitors for economic, political and military power. With fewer hands to till the fields, even the richest Amerindian lands remained only partly cultivated. As agricultural shortages grew, starvation compounded the loss to disease. Fertility plummeted, further stalling an indigenous recovery. The emptying of the countryside and the development of pastoral agriculture gave Europeans control of lands formerly inhabited by wealthy and powerful indigenous societies.[30]

The Spanish presence in the Americas expanded steadily, if unevenly. Although colonisation was initially concentrated in centres of pre-Columbian civilisation – central Mexico and the Andes – by 1600, Spanish-dominated cities and towns could be found from north-central Mexico to Buenos Aires far to the south. Spain's Charles I (and Holy Roman Emperor Charles V) strengthened royal authority on the mainland with the creation of viceroyalties in Mexico City, formerly Tenochtitlan, in 1535 and in the new city of Lima on Peru's coastal plain in 1544. Colonisation also entailed the introduction of non-native plants and animals. Spanish settlements thrived as their plants and animals out-competed indigenous flora and fauna. The convergence of foreign plants, animals, pathogens and cultivation techniques transformed and often devastated the native ecology. Whole stretches of central Mexico were deforested, leading to the slow desiccation of the surrounding lands. The land itself would ultimately be conquered and colonised.[31]

In roughly the same time period, but on the other side of the Atlantic, Ireland became a target for increased English and Welsh migration and settlement. The 'Pale' region west of Dublin along the Boyne and Liffey river valleys had begun to be occupied by Anglo-Norman invaders in the twelfth century. Beginning in the mid-sixteenth century, this bridgehead served as a base for the conquest of much of the island. Initially, the 'old English' community was augmented by discharged soldiers who chose to remain in Ireland. Over time, nobles and gentry, traders and artisans, clergymen, farmers and herders migrated to claim and settle what were viewed as scantily inhabited and poorly developed lands throughout much of the island. By one well-informed estimate, there were 100,000 English and

---

29 For an in-depth discussion of the data and the controversy surrounding the estimates see Robert McCaa, 'Spanish and Nahuatl Views on Smallpox and Demographic Catastrophe in the Conquest of Mexico', *Journal of Interdisciplinary History* 25/3 (1995): pp. 397–431; Noble David Cook provides a comprehensive overview in *Born to Die: Disease and New World Conquest, 1492–1650* (Cambridge, 1998).

30 Crosby, *Ecological Imperialism*, especially pp. 145-216; and Elinor G. K. Melville, *A Plague of Sheep: Environmental Consequences of the Conquest of Mexico* (New York, 1994).

31 Melville, *A Plague of Sheep*.

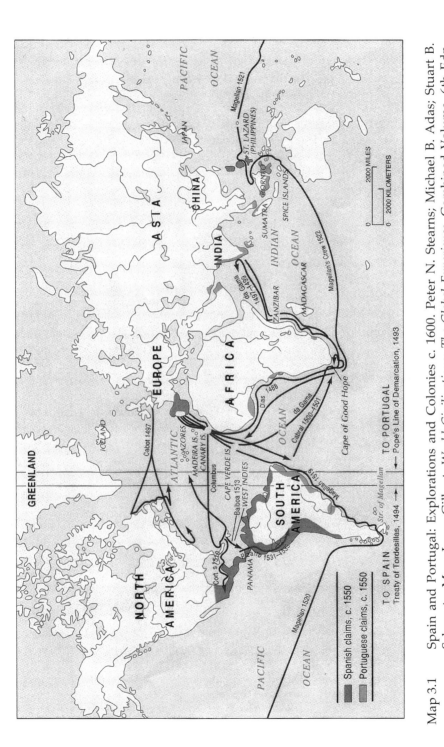

Map 3.1   Spain and Portugal: Explorations and Colonies c. 1600. Peter N. Stearns; Michael B. Adas; Stuart B. Schwartz; Marc Jason Gilbert: *World Civilizations: The Global Experience*, Combined Volume, 6th Edn, © 2011. Reprinted by permission of Pearson Education, Inc., Upper Saddle River, NJ, USA

Welsh settlers in Ireland by the mid-seventeenth century, and the island was the wealthiest and most favoured settlement colony established by English migrants.[32] In some areas the indigenous population, which was actually much denser and more highly developed than the invaders allowed, was displaced as English lords and settlers claimed large tracts of lands. Irish farmers frequently became tenants on English estates or the lands of local Irish notables who, through collaboration with the colonisers or by demonstrating that they had sufficient retainers and resources to forcibly resist displacement, managed to maintain possession of their ancestral holdings. Though some advocates of colonisation sought to establish crown authority and English legal precedents, and to assimilate the Irish elite, most settlers as well as officials and potential migrants in the British Isles viewed the Irish as barbaric and dangerous heathens.[33]

Phase II (c. 1580–1790): A Predominance of Plantation Enclaves and Settlement Colonies

The Spanish conquests in the Americas and the fort and factory network of the Portuguese laid the foundations for the settlement colonies and the slave plantations that proved to be the main modes of European overseas expansion in the two centuries that followed. In the seventeenth century the Dutch and English vied for supremacy in the Indian Ocean, and fought for control of the lucrative spice trade that the Portuguese had struggled in vain to monopolise throughout the 1500s. Port cities and trading posts on both sides of the Atlantic were also key components of the slave plantation system. But in the seventeenth and eighteenth centuries the locus of European colonial political consolidation, society formation and economic enterprise shifted from coasts and sea lanes to overland frontiers in the Americas, southern Africa and central Asia as well as to the building or consolidation of formal empires in the Americas, and South and Southeast Asia. The strength and timing of the forward movement in each of these areas varied considerably, and in many cases the advance of settlers and the acquisition of territory were preceded by the infiltration of European transfrontier groups ranging from trappers, traders and explorers to missionaries and market-oriented pastoralists.

By 1540, Spain's conquest and colonisation of indigenous peoples and their vast, fertile lands had expanded beyond the core areas of pre-Columbian settlement in central Mexico and the Andean highlands. And as they grew the

---

32   Nicholas Canny, *Kingdom and Colony: Ireland in the Atlantic World, 1560–1800* (Baltimore, MD, 1988), p. 96.

33   Nicholas Canny's many books and articles are consistently among the best histories we have on the English colonisation of Ireland. See *Kingdom and Colony* and his monumental *Making Ireland British, 1580–1650* (Oxford, 2001). Also informative on the early decades of colonisation is John McGurk's study of *The Elizabethan Conquest of Ireland* (Manchester, 1997).

new colonies acquired the characteristics of both a settler society and a tribute empire. Colonial society was formally conceived as two large and interrelated but distinct and viable communities – one Indian, the other Spanish, and each with its own privileges and obligations as expressed in the division between the *república de los indios* and the *república de los españoles*. The former consisted of indigenous peoples living within the remaining networks of Indian communities, the latter of Iberian immigrants, Creoles, and peoples of African descent, as well as the mixed-descent *castas* ('castes'), who included mestizos and mulattoes. The *encomienda* system helped establish and perpetuate this framework, and constituted part of the tributary character of colonial society. The *encomienda* was an enforceable claim to a portion of the labour of a specified Indian community or municipality. The Spanish did not exercise direct control over Indian communities; rather, because the surviving Indian communities retained much of their internal political and economic organisation – including mechanisms for the periodic allocation of communal labour – the institution of *encomienda* allowed the Spanish to ally with Indian leaders to exploit pre-Columbian indigenous labour practices.[34]

Although grants of *encomienda* were prizes awarded only to prominent conquistadors or other colonists, any settler could apply for grants of land. The landed estate – or *hacienda* – was the institution through which settlers accumulated, made use of and controlled access to land. Disease and depopulation of the countryside, combined with continued Spanish immigration and the proliferation of Old World plants and animals, contributed to the multiplication of *haciendas*. They initially formed in the rural areas that surrounded cities and towns but quickly expanded outward, extending the frontiers of Spanish influence. *Encomenderos* or their descendants could and did possess *haciendas*, but the two were distinct if complementary institutions of colonisation. Both were linked to the silver mining industry, which by the mid-sixteenth century was a mainstay of the colonial economy and a cornerstone of the all-important export sector. The first substantial veins mined were those of Zacatecas in Mexico and Potosí in Bolivia (referred to as Upper Peru during the colonial era), both of which started to bear silver in the late 1540s. Interregional markets emerged, supplied by local manufactories and craft workers, both of which were in the hands of the growing number of *castas* and poorer Creoles.[35] Religious institutions – cathedrals, churches, chapels, monasteries, nunneries and missions – as well as secular and regular ecclesiastical posts also proliferated; these too were increasingly filled by Creoles

---

34 The divergent characteristics of pre-Columbian society in Mesoamerica and the Andes meant that the impact of Spanish colonisation would have distinct repercussions in each region. For a concise discussion, see James Lockhart and Stuart B. Schwartz, *Early Latin America: A History of Colonial Spanish America and Brazil* (New York, 1983), pp. 164–77.

35 Conceptualisations of the economy of colonial Latin America have been heavily influenced by both dependency and world-systems theory. For an illuminating consideration and critique of such approaches, see the debate between Immanuel Wallerstein and Steve Stern that appeared in the *American Historical Review* 93/4 (1988): pp. 829–97.

and *castas*. The political, economic and religious institutions of Spanish colonial society were thus all increasingly tied to local or regional – as opposed to imperial – affairs and interests.

Although in principle a stringent social hierarchy placed peninsular Spaniards at the top and Indians and Africans at the bottom, in practice these distinctions became increasingly difficult to maintain. Indian leaders used their wealth and influence to take advantage of the new economic opportunities created by the Spanish presence, even as their authority within native communities tended to diminish. There also emerged a growing population of *castas* and of Indian labourers affiliated less with an indigenous community than with the affairs of an expanding settler society. Increasing numbers of indigenous residents left their communities to seek either permanent or temporary wage labour on *haciendas*. The power of estate owners grew in turn – a tendency that the Spanish crown sought to curb with the formal abolition of *encomienda* in 1542. Nevertheless, not only did Indian labour remain a cornerstone of the mining and agricultural sectors of colonial society, but the roles of Indians and individuals of mixed descent also became more diverse, allowing some to gain a measure of power and influence in colonial society that defied any formal hierarchy imagined by Spanish colonial authorities.[36]

The frontiers of colonial Latin America were vast and included the Amazon, the American Southwest, the Rio de La Plata region and most of Chile and Argentina. In these areas transfrontier groups – including missionaries, slavers and traders – often represented the first wave of a growing European presence. Nonetheless, these regions tended to remain borderlands, often beyond the effective reach of European authorities throughout the colonial era.[37] Raiding across the borderlands was common practice among both Europeans and indigenous peoples. One striking example is the case of the *bandeirantes* of Portuguese America. Based in the frontier plateau of modern São Paulo, this collection of poor Portuguese and mixed-race colonists would plunge into the vast forests of the Brazilian interior on slaving and pillaging expeditions that often lasted a year or more. Plunder was distributed among the members of the raiding party, but the primary aim of these ventures was often to capture Indians who could be sold into slavery along the coast where, by the late sixteenth century, sugar plantations proliferated.[38] Another sort of transfrontier adaptation, based on semi-sedentary pastoralism, developed on the northern and southern borderlands of Spain's American empire. The proliferation of wild cattle, horses and other ungulates gave rise to roving groups of herders. There were also pathways to power on the edge of European empires. The Comanche became skilled equestrians and capitalised on their access

---

36   R. Douglas Cope provides a very brief but trenchant analysis in *The Limits of Racial Domination: Plebeian Society in Colonial Mexico City, 1660–1720* (Madison, WI, 1994).

37   Donna J. Guy and Thomas E. Sheridan (eds), *Contested Ground: Comparative Frontiers on the Northern and Southern Edges of the Spanish Empire* (Tucson, AZ, 1998)); and Paul W. Mapp, *The Elusive West and the Contest for Empire, 1713-1763* (Chapel Hill, NC, 2011).

38   A classic discussion is Richard M. Morse, *The Bandeirantes: The Historical Role of the Brazilian Pathfinders* (New York, 1965).

to firearms (often through French traders) to create an empire centred on the plains of the American Southwest. Confronted with an emergent and expansive indigenous empire, both the British and the Spanish were compelled to reckon with the Comanche. On frontiers, indigenous societies could leverage their own shifting access to varied resources in order to transform themselves and effectively challenge European powers.[39]

Missionary orders – the Jesuits and Franciscans foremost among them – often established outposts along and beyond the frontiers of European settlement, where they sought to convert indigenous peoples. They lived in surviving villages or in settlements newly created specifically for the purpose of proselytising. Missionary settlements often proved to be the leading edge of further European encroachment. They facilitated colonial expansion through the introduction of European languages, values, rituals, crops and modes of production. But missionary settlements could also, and perhaps inadvertently did, aid indigenous resistance and cultural survival. For example, in the early 1750s Guarani leaders from the Jesuits' expansive and populous Paraguayan missions used their knowledge of European languages and legal practices to petition Spanish authorities to reverse their decision, forcing the Indians to resettle west of the Uruguay River. And, in northern Mexico, Jesuit administration afforded the Yaquí Indians protection from the encroachment of Spanish miners, thereby allowing them to maintain not only community solidarity, but aspects of their language, religion and material culture as well.[40]

In Portuguese America and in the scattered Caribbean island colonies of England and France, the plantation enclave became an effective and durable mode of early modern territorial expansion. The Portuguese had already experimented with territorial conquest in the 1530s in India, with the acquisition of coastal territories north of Goa, and in Brazil, where the development of donatary captaincies (grants of land) was meant to foster settlement. But Portugal's empire retained a largely seaborne character until the last decades of the sixteenth century. Beginning in the 1570s, a combination of factors drove Portugal towards inland expansion. The Dutch offered increasing seaborne competition in the Atlantic and Indian Ocean theatres. Safavid expansion in Persia under Shah Abbas led to the capture of Portugal's fort at Hormuz, further eroding Portuguese seaborne power in Asia. Mughal expansion into southern India under Shah Jahan ultimately made inland expansion in Asia an even more untenable option than it had previously been. At the same time, the aging state of its poorly maintained fleet contributed to Portugal's losses at sea. And royal profits as a percentage of the total returns from the spice trade began to fall. After mid-century the example of Spain's rich American silver mines prompted the Portuguese to renew their own brand of prospecting and looting in Africa and Asia. But the disastrous Barreto–Homem

---

39   Richard W. Slatta, *Comparing Cowboys and Frontiers: New Perspectives on the History of the Americas* (Norman, OK, 1997); and Pekka Hämäläinen, *The Comanche Empire* (New Haven, CT, 2008).

40   Erick Langer and Robert H. Jackson (eds), *The New Latin American Mission History* (Lincoln, NE, 1995).

expedition to gain control of the gold producing region far up the Zambezi River testified to the difficulties of securing territorial control anywhere in Indian Ocean Asia.[41] So it was in the Atlantic that the late-sixteenth-century development of sugar plantations in Brazil gave Portugal's empire the territorial aspect that would define both it and the Caribbean for centuries.

The plantation enclaves of the Americas varied greatly in terms of their location, development and organisation. At the outset, plantations in Brazil and the Caribbean drew their organisation and technology and even some of their specialised personnel directly from their Atlantic predecessors. Genoese capital helped to deliver the first water- and oxen-powered mills in the sixteenth century. The system of hereditary land grants and attendant privileges – designed to lure settlers to the Atlantic – found their parallels in the sixteenth-century Americas as well. And skilled technicians and sugar masters arrived from Madeira and the Canaries. In the Americas, they oversaw the work of Amerindian and, increasingly, African slaves.

For all the plantation enclaves, large inputs of manual labour were essential at nearly every stage of cultivation and production. The technology required for refining sugar was costly and required constant upkeep. The substantial financial and human resources already coursing through Portugal's global exchange networks were crucial for making sugar plantations viable in Brazil. Financing continued to come from various parts of Europe, while labour came increasingly from West and sub-Saharan Africa. As Amerindians died in large numbers from disease, malnutrition and overwork, European slavers, traders and shippers increased the numbers of Africans sent to Brazil. Africans began to outnumber Amerindians on the plantations of Brazil's eastern littoral by 1580. From that point forward, African slavery became inextricably bound to American plantation agriculture. Before the demise of slavery in the Americas in the nineteenth century, approximately 12.5 million Africans would face the Middle Passage, where mortality ranged between 12 and 13 per cent.[42]

In the seventeenth century, the Americas increasingly became a theatre of international competition for commercial, human and natural resources. The initial English and French ventures in the Caribbean began not as plantation enclaves but as colonies of settlement and trade. England's early presence in the Caribbean combined the settlement features of its Irish colonies with a trading-post model similar to that deployed later by the East India Company. In Barbados, where settlement began in the 1620s, indentured labourers grew food for local consumption and cultivated tobacco for export. Contraband trade with the Spanish mainland provided additional commercial opportunities. These island outposts could defend English interests in North America from Spanish incursions, while

41 Sanjay Subrahmanyam, *The Portuguese Empire in Asia, 1500-1700: A Political and Economic History* (New York, 1993); and Ernst van Veen, *Decay or Defeat: An Inquiry into the Portuguese Decline in Asia, 1580-1645* (Leiden, 2000).
42 See the website *Voyages: The Trans-Atlantic Slave Trade Database*, www.slavevoyages.org/tast/index.faces.

supporting English raiding activities aimed at capturing the bullion shipped from Spanish mines. The French began trading with the Caribs of the Lesser Antilles, but like the English were quick to expand their commerce with the mainland Spanish colonies. In 1635 the French Crown began to award special privileges to joint-stock companies that would undertake Caribbean settlement. Initial efforts focused heavily on Guadeloupe and Martinique. Company stockholders often enjoyed a monopoly over not only trade but all lands they could make productive. At first this meant the settlement of thousands of French Catholics, many of whom worked as indentured servants. Here, too, the crown and colonial planners intended settlement both in the form of trading posts and immigrant communities that could support armed attacks on Spain's silver fleet.

Neither sugar plantations nor African slavery figured significantly in the initial English and French Caribbean colonisation schemes. But geography, disease and the profitability of sugar combined with the availability of capital, know-how and abundant forced labour to foster plantation development. Sugar plantation reached new heights in terms of ecological devastation, human violence and the centralisation of both ownership and oversight. The Dutch played an important role in the development of Caribbean sugar plantations. After a short-lived occupation of the Brazilian Northeast (1630–54), the Dutch continued in their pivotal role as Atlantic shippers, bringing sugarcane, milling technology and African slaves to the English and French Caribbean. African slaves appeared to survive the imported tropical diseases, especially malaria and yellow fever, better than European settlers and, as in Brazil, became the principal source of manual labour. The Dutch also shared their knowledge of cultivation techniques and sold milling equipment. As ever larger tracts of the most fertile land were needed to capitalise on advances in milling technology, slave populations had to increase as well. The whole process accelerated as improvements in shipping and navigation technologies meant that both sugar and slaves could be transported more cheaply.

The successful growth of the plantation as a form of territorial settlement in the Caribbean occurred first on Barbados, then in the English Leeward Islands and finally in the French Antilles. The distribution of wealth and power was radically skewed in favour of a dwindling white minority that often comprised no more than 25 per cent of the total population. Virtually all the best agricultural lands were planted with sugarcane, making these fertile islands food importers. Atlantic economies by the eighteenth century were characterised by intensified regional specialisation: Caribbean sugar and rum, tobacco and rice from the North American Southeast, slaves from Africa, capital and technology from Europe. Free white settlers often left the Caribbean for the North American mainland, feeding European expansion there. Meanwhile, the explosive tensions engendered by the maw of Caribbean plantation enclaves of the seventeenth and eighteenth centuries would culminate in the Haitian Revolution (c. 1790–1804). In the same period, the political shifts in Europe, and especially the process of industrialisation in England, were about to transform the configuration and nature of European empires in the nineteenth century.[43]

---

43 Franklin W. Knight, *The Caribbean: The Genesis of a Fragmented Nationalism*, 2nd ed.

Although early voyages of exploration led by the Genoese John Cabot (1497) and Jacques Cartier (1534–42) established the basis for later English and French claims to North America, the north European pursuit of overseas empire began in earnest nearly a century after the Columbian voyages and the Spanish occupation of the Caribbean. Attempts to found English settlements on the mid-Atlantic coast in the last decades of the sixteenth century failed. But Samuel de Champlain's 1603 expedition up the St Lawrence River opened the way for French penetration of what later became eastern Canada and eventually expansion into the Great Lakes region, the Ohio valley and down the Mississippi River into the territory that comprised Louisiana. Though towns were soon established at Quebec and Montreal, the French presence in North America was slight and transient well into the eighteenth century. Fur trappers and traders and small bands of Catholic missionaries formed the vanguard of a sparse and sporadic French population. The trappers or *coureurs des bois* (forest rovers) had begun to exploit the seemingly inexhaustible beaver population of North America even before Champlain's arrival in the early 1600s. The warm, water-repellent fur pelts of these industrious animals were in great demand in Europe, where the indigenous beaver population had been driven to extinction in many areas by excessive trapping and hunting. Close behind the *coureurs des bois* came French, and later Dutch, traders, who built overland networks of forts and warehouses, where the furs could be marketed and prepared for transport across the Atlantic. In many ways the fur trading networks were overland versions of the trading-post empires established in the Atlantic and Indian Oceans, and these fortified market nodes often developed into the earliest European towns in North America.[44]

French, and later English and Dutch, trappers readily adopted the techniques, traps and other tools that the Amerindian peoples had long used in pursuit of beaver, mink, otter and other animal pelts. From clothing fashioned from animal hides and canoes to snowshoes and moccasins, trappers also assimilated more broadly to the formidable Indian cultures they encountered as they traversed the woods and lakes of North America in pursuit of furs for the market. Trappers often took Indian women as spouses, and they in turn provided critical ties to indigenous communities, local knowledge and hunting and foraging skills essential for survival in the wilderness, particularly during the winter months, when most of the trapping took place. But the cultural exchange was by no means one-sided. Trappers and traders introduced iron kettles, fishhooks and steel knives as well as muskets, woollen blankets and a variety of other European goods into

---

(New York, 1990), pp. 27–119; Robin Blackburn, *The Making of New World Slavery: From the Baroque to the Modern, 1492–1800* (London, 1997).

44   Harold Innis's account of *The Fur Trade in Canada* (Toronto, 1956) has long been the standard work on the fur trade in New France. But in recent decades new research and publications, particularly the pioneering articles of Ann M. Carlos and Frank D. Lewis, have taken the history of the trade to new levels of analysis and understanding. For a superb summary of their many essays, see 'The Economic History of the Fur Trade', at http://eh.net/encyclopedia/article/carlos.lewis.furtrade.

Amerindian cultures. And both as allies and competitors, Indian peoples became engaged in the trans-Atlantic commercial network. In areas controlled by the French, Indian hunters supplied most of the fur pelts that were bartered mainly for European manufactured goods – but rarely alcohol and the trinkets that have long been featured in popular accounts of the trade. The Indians themselves delivered the furs to trading posts that chartered French companies, such as the *Compagnie d'Occident*, leased to individual merchants, who were in charge of transporting the pelts and marketing them in Europe.[45]

The Catholic missionary orders that advanced in tandem with, or at times ahead of, the trappers into transfrontier regions introduced Christian rituals and beliefs into Indian societies. Though enduring conversions were usually few, and the woodlands of North America yielded a disproportionate number of martyrs, some Indian communities, particularly among the Hurons, welcomed the French missionary presence, either to cement alliances with the French or connections with the fur trading network.[46] Trading networks and missionary stations, as well as the mapping of the new territories by French explorers, facilitated the immigration and settlement of French farmers and artisans who sought to make permanent homes in North America. Unwittingly, these transfrontier agents were also the carriers of diseases, such as measles and smallpox, which proved as lethal for the North American Indians, who had no immunity, as they had for the Aztecs and Incas. The depletion and demoralisation of the Indian population left sparsely peopled and weakly defended frontiers for Europeans to settle. But for a variety of demographic and cultural reasons, the number of French migrants who intended to settle permanently in North America remained minuscule well into the eighteenth century. At the outset of the Seven Years' War (or the French and Indian War, as it was known in North America) in 1756, scarcely 70,000 French nationals were spread in several urban clusters, small communities and tiny bands across the extent of the Bourbons' possessions. This discrepancy between bloated French territorial claims and their failure to settle more than a small fraction of the lands at issue would prove a major factor in France's loss of Canada in the war.[47]

Fishermen and merchants, rather than trappers, provided the entering wedge of Dutch and English colonisation and settlement in North America. And missionaries were conspicuously absent from the early English and Dutch exploratory expeditions and trading parties. As had been the case with the French, Dutch and English fishermen working the cod-abundant waters off the eastern seaboard came into contact with local Indian peoples, who were quite willing to barter fur pelts for fish hooks and copper kettles. The 1609 expedition led by the English explorer

---

45   Innis, *The Fur Trade* (Toronto, 1974).

46   Carole Blackburn, *Harvest of Souls: The Jesuit Missions and Colonization in North America, 1632–1650* (Montreal, QC, and Kingston, ON, 2000); and F. Gabriel Sagard Theodat, *Le grand voyage du pays des Hurons* (Paris, 1865).

47   Frank McLynn, *1759: The Year that Made Great Britain the Master of the World* (New York, 2004), Introduction.

Henry Hudson opened the river and adjoining valley lands that were given his name to settlement by the Dutch, who had commissioned his probes. Initially they concentrated on establishing trading posts that provided new channels for the fur trade with the Iroquois nations, the Mohegans and other Indian peoples in what later became eastern New York and New Jersey. Soon thereafter the town of New Amsterdam was established on Manhattan Island as a more diversified entrepôt at the mouth of the Hudson River. To encourage permanent migration by Dutch farmers, the West India Company (Westindische Compagnie) made extensive land grants to wealthy burghers and noblemen on the condition that they recruit and provide transport for at least fifty settlers to clear and cultivate estates in the fertile Hudson valley. But largely owing to the excessive powers that the charters granted under what was known as the *patroon* system to the estate holders, few of the lands leased under these feudal-style arrangements were able to attract sufficient numbers of Dutch cultivators to make them viable.

The Dutch managed to drive out their Swedish rivals, who had founded a colony in the Delaware River basin in the 1630s. Nonetheless, their investment in North America never matched that expended in the Caribbean or Brazil, much less their commitment to winning control of the Indian Ocean spice trade. One gauge of the low priority the Dutch gave to North America was the paucity of their long-term migration, even in the decades when their presence peaked. Despite a proliferation of promotional literature and material incentives, there were at best a few thousand Dutch settlers by the 1640s as compared to at least 60,000 from the British Isles. Not surprisingly, when trading and expansionist rivalries between the Dutch and English led to a series of global Anglo-Dutch wars in the middle decades of the seventeenth century, the Dutch concentrated on protecting their trading empire in Asia and plantation colonies in the Caribbean and Brazil rather than the underpopulated colony of New Netherlands centred on the Hudson River valley. By the Treaty of Westminster, which ended the Third Anglo-Dutch War in 1667, the Dutch ceded New Amsterdam (renamed New York) to the English in exchange for retaining Suriname on the northern coast of South America.[48]

Fishermen, trappers and fur traders were as pivotal to the beginnings of English colonisation in North America as they were for the French and Dutch. But the much larger volume of English settlers migrating to the New World beginning in the early 1600s meant that through much of the century these transfrontier agents and their enterprises would play a less important role than in rival colonies. Religious dissidents figured prominently in early immigration to New England, while the lesser gentry, second sons of noble lineage and their body servants, and indentured labourers sought to make their fortunes in the Chesapeake region and further south. The enclosure movement in England, which displaced large numbers of smallholders, tenants and agricultural labourers, as well as persisting inflation, swelled the number of migrants through much of the century. Farmers and foresters dominated production both for domestic and overseas trade, and

---

48   Jaap Jacobs, *New Netherland: A Dutch Colony in Seventeenth-Century America* (Leiden, 2005), and Russell Shorto, *The Island at the Center of the World* (New York, 2004).

by the last decades of the seventeenth century a substantial merchant class had developed in port cities along the eastern seaboard. Forest products, including timber, pitch and tar, were the main exports from the colonies, though tobacco proved the key to survival for settlements in Virginia and the upper south. Having ousted their Swedish and Dutch rivals and held the French at bay or driven them towards the western wilderness, the English began to settle further and further inland from New England to the Carolinas.[49]

The ever-increasing settler population soon proved a far more formidable and enduring threat to the indigenous peoples of North America than that posed by the French or Dutch. Old World diseases ravaged the coastal Indian peoples, whose abandoned fields and hunting grounds were eagerly claimed by incoming migrants. English settlers surmised that the appalling mortality rates among indigenous peoples were part of a larger divine plan. The Indians were given little credit for supplying the food that, in the early stages of colonisation, proved critical to the survival of English settlements. Perversely, the cultivating practices that provided sustenance for the settlers were either ignored or disparaged, in large part because agriculture was largely women's work in Indian societies. They were also frequently cited as evidence of the fact that the Indians had proved incapable of making productive use of the abundance of the land and resources of the New World. These assessments appeared to justify the consensus of all but a few dissidents that Indian cultures had little to offer more advanced Europeans and ought to be supplanted by western ways. This belief was only belatedly matched by efforts at conversion, education and assimilation.[50] The settlers' determination to dispossess and remove through war or forced migration the Indians who were regarded by both early colonisers (and later pioneers who opened up the American West) as obstacles to the advance of civilisation and material increase, and to erase the cultural heritage of the indigenous peoples, calls into question Frederick Jackson Turner's iconic characterisation of the American frontier as a locus of freedom.

In roughly the same decades as the Puritans and Virginians were struggling to establish viable settlements in eastern North America, their Dutch counterparts, beginning in 1652, developed a small outpost in southwest Africa. Intended initially as a fortified way station, where Dutch merchant and warships making the long voyage around the Cape of Good Hope to the East Indies could take on fresh water and other provisions, Cape Town soon became the base for the slow, but steady, colonisation of the interior of southern Africa. The temperate

49   Edmund S. Morgan, *American Slavery, American Freedom: The Ordeal of Colonial Virginia* (New York, 1975); Timothy Silver, *A New Face on the Countryside: Indians, Colonists, and Slaves in the South Atlantic Forests* (Cambridge, 1990); and Jack P. Greene, *Pursuits of Happiness: The Social Development of Early Modern British Colonies and the Formation of American Culture* (Chapel Hill, NC, 1988).
50   Karen Ordahl Kupperman, *Settling with the Indians: The Meeting of English and Indian Cultures in America, 1580–1640* (Totowa, NJ, 1980); Bernard W. Sheehan, *Savagism and Civility: Indians and Englishmen in Colonial Virginia* (Cambridge, 1980); and James Axtel, *The Invasion Within: The Contest of Cultures in Colonial North America* (Oxford, 1985).

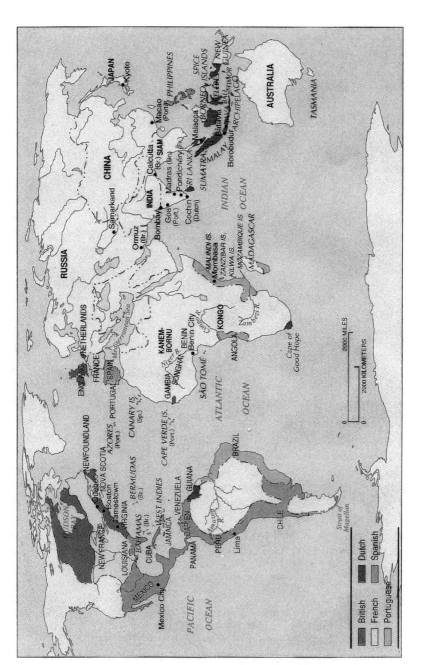

Map 3.2   French, British and Dutch Holdings, c. 1700. Peter N. Stearns; Michael B. Adas; Stuart B. Schwartz; Marc Jason Gilbert: *World Civilizations: The Global Experience*, Combined Volume, 6th Edn, © 2011. Reprinted by permission of Pearson Education, Inc., Upper Saddle River, NJ, USA

climate, and the adequate rainfall in areas adjacent to and directly east of Cape Town, made it possible to farm crops such as tobacco and wheat and to breed livestock for sale to passing ships. The sparse population of Khoikhoi pastoralists and San hunter-gatherers in these areas, which was ever more scant in the arid regions to the northeast, made it possible for *Boers* (Dutch farmers) to settle in the interior and to carve out extensive cattle- and sheep-raising estates. The advance of these transfrontier settlers, who came to be known as *trekboers* (migrating farmers), provided the impetus for the creation of a larger European settlement colony across the southern cone of Africa. The *trekboer* ranchers established large, extended families on their widely separated holdings, and warred, traded, enslaved and procreated with the San and especially the Khoikhoi, who both resisted and cohabited with the Europeans. The offspring of such liaisons formed the basis for the large, mixed-racial or 'coloured' population of present-day South Africa.

Phase III: Industrialisation, Tropical Dependencies and New Frontiers of Settlement in Oceania and Africa

Between 1776 and 1810 a series of upheavals – in British North America, France and its Caribbean colonies, and later in Spanish and Portuguese America – radically altered the European imperial landscape. Revolution and independence were by no means inevitable outcomes of these conflicts. Especially in British North America, French Saint Domingue and throughout Spanish America, deep class, ethnic, racial and regional divisions meant that within each imperial sphere settlers shared little in the way of an overarching identity that might underwrite a unified sense of revolutionary purpose or concerted action. Interregional trade within colonies may have served to forge broader inter-empire ties, but communication, transportation and commercial networks oriented to the export of foodstuffs and raw materials often linked colonised regions to European metropoles rather than with each other. Throughout the colonial Americas, the most clearly discernible loyalties were those linking colonists to their locality or region and then to their home country. Over the course of the late eighteenth century, however, a number of factors coalesced to spark revolutionary activity and strengthen the appeal of formal political independence.

By the late 1700s, discontent with colonial rule had spread beyond political and intellectual dissidents to formerly loyal expatriate European elites, and had begun to influence urban and rural residents alike. The timing in different colonial regions varied, as did the specific economic and political issues at stake. But there were nevertheless broad similarities and parallels across the Americas. One of these was the embrace of republican ideology, which had emerged from decades of intellectual ferment in eighteenth-century western Europe. The appeal to settlers and mestizo or mulatto social groups of a government that more thoroughly represented their interests and addressed their concerns was further strengthened when European imperial regimes sought to impose tighter strictures on economic and political activities in their American territories. Often the tightening of metropolitan control followed periods of relative autonomy in the colonies, during which settlers had gained greater influence in economic, political and religious life. Britain's increased taxes and tighter restrictions on the trade and migration of its nationals in North America in the 1760s, the successive Bourbon reforms in the far-flung Spanish Empire during the eighteenth century and state intervention in the agricultural, commercial and manufacturing sectors of Portugal in the mid-1700s were all seen by settler social groups as assaults on their constricted political influence and economic well-being. Metropolitan interests increasingly appeared at odds with those of the colonies. Settlers found themselves subjected to greater regulation and stiffer limitations at the same time that greater numbers of wealthy – and often Creole or mixed-race – planters, merchants and professionals sought trading opportunities and political inclusion.[51]

Of all the anti-colonial struggles, the upheavals in French Saint Domingue provide the best example of a complete social revolution. Civil war broke out in 1790 between the white and mulatto residents of this French plantation colony. In 1791, the colony's slaves seized the opportunity provided by the quarrels among local elites to foment a general rebellion that ultimately came under the leadership of Toussaint L'Ouverture. By 1804, when Jean Jacques Dessalines finally proclaimed the independence of the nation of Haiti, the revolution had proven so violent and protracted that the island's productive capacity was severely crippled. The French and Haitian revolutions had profound and far-reaching consequences throughout the Caribbean and the Americas.[52] The Haitian Revolution signalled the death of the plantation as a mode of formal imperial expansion (though not of slave-based sugar production).

Such upheavals – with some important exceptions – made the Americas no longer formally a part of Europe's imperial domain.[53] Instead, the third phase of colonisation was dominated by a shift to territorial conquest and the creation of tropical dependencies and settler colonies throughout Africa and South and Southeast Asia. Here too, the last decades of the eighteenth century were pivotal. Two fundamentally transformative processes that began in the late 1700s significantly reconfigured the nature of colonisation and settlement worldwide in the nineteenth century. Watershed advances in science and technology, which were even more concentrated in Europe than in the early modern era, greatly increased the advantages the expansive powers of the west enjoyed relative to all other societies in extracting resources, manufacturing, building commercial

---

51 Jaime E.. Rodríguez O, *The Independence of Spanish America* (New York, 1998); Knight, *The Caribbean*, pp. 159–92. The case of Brazil is an exception: independence was achieved with little violence, and for a time it remained a monarchy. See Emilia Viotti da Costa, *The Brazilian Empire: Myths and Histories*, 2nd ed. (Chapel Hill, NC, 2000), pp. 1–23.

52 David Barry Gaspar and David Patrick Geggus (eds.), *A Turbulent Time: The French Revolution and the Greater Caribbean* (Bloomington, IN, 1997).

53 Britain and Spain, for example, held onto their Caribbean colonies, and Britain and France still controlled vast domains in North America.

networks and waging war. These innovations, and the late nineteenth-century medical breakthroughs that made it possible to control or mollify the effects of such tropical diseases as malaria and yellow fever, allowed expansive European nations to establish formal colonial control over much of Africa, Asia and the Pacific by the early 1900s. From the 1870s the surge in European empire building was accompanied by an intensification of globalisation that by the end of the century left Europeans and increasingly Americans and Japanese in control of much of the world's trade, communications networks, manufacturing and finance. The improvements in transportation and expanded commercial linkages also ushered in an unprecedented wave of emigration from Europe to temperate regions in Oceania, the southern cone of South America and Africa, where the influx of migrants gave great impetus to frontier expansionism and the displacement of indigenous peoples. Even late-industrialising empires, particularly Tsarist Russia and to a lesser extent Manchu China, made use of railroads, telegraph lines and breech-loading rifles both to ward off western rivals and to extend and tighten their control, often through substantial settlement, over the eastern and central Asian frontier lands that both sought to colonise, and which consequently soon became major points of contention between them.[54]

Nations, most notably Spain and Portugal, that had been major overseas colonisers in the first centuries of expansion but participated only marginally in the later scientific and early industrial revolutions, experienced a steady diminution of their influence and ability to project their power overseas. As we have seen, Portugal had lost most of its trading empire in Asia to the Dutch in the seventeenth century, but still managed in the nineteenth century to enlarge its holdings in parts of Africa, in large part by playing the northern European powers against one another. The rise of extensive formal colonies in the eastern hemisphere originated on the island of Java. The Dutch established a fortified trading base, similar to those that served as nodes for the Portuguese trading-post empire, at Batavia in 1619. The need to protect Batavia from periodic assaults launched by uneasy monarchs in central Java as well as pirates based on Sumatra embroiled the Dutch in the politics of neighbouring kingdoms in Java and south Sumatra. In addition to their military forays into the districts surrounding Batavia, Dutch interventions in quarrels over succession and inter-state conflicts resulted in steady accretions of territory and subjects. In the early stages of what would become the conquest of the entire island of Java, the Dutch relied on the long-standing practice of divide-and-conquer that, aside from advances in their war fleet, owed little to either scientific or technological advances in Europe. Small, but disciplined and well-organised, mixed forces of European and local soldiers usually proved a match for the larger armies of the Sultans of Mataram or other local rulers. And the Dutch skilfully entered into alliances with deposed or disgruntled claimants to overthrow strong monarchs who sought to resist their dominance on Java or nearby

---

54   W.C. Fuller, *Strategy and Power in Russia, 1600–1914* (New York, 1992); Marc Raeff, *Understanding Imperial Russia* (New York, 1984); and Peter Perdue, *China Marches West: The Qing Conquest of Central Eurasia* (Cambridge, MA, 2005).

islands. Following the brief occupation of Java by the British in the Napoleonic Wars, the Dutch used the island, with its large population and highly productive rice and sugar economy, as the base for the conquest of the 'outer islands' of what is today the archipelago that constitutes the nation of Indonesia. Throughout the Netherlands Indies, they ruled mainly through indigenous officials, drawn at the higher levels from the well-entrenched Javanese nobility (*priyayi*). These regents were supervised by Dutch counterparts, or residents, who in turn answered to a governor-general and an increasingly elaborate European bureaucratic hierarchy residing mainly in Batavia and its environs.[55]

Perhaps because it began well over a century later and was carried out by the first industrial nation, the rise of British power on the Indian subcontinent is usually linked to the technological advances so pivotal for the age of high imperialism in the later nineteenth century. But the first stages in the building of the British Raj from the 1740s onward bore strong similarities to the Dutch conquest of Java. Like the Dutch, the British were drawn into the rivalries of regional rulers, Hindu, Muslim and Sikh. Their backing for one prince against others was often prompted by alliances that adversary potentates had struck with the French, whose series of global wars with the British were fought in India as well as the Caribbean, North America and Europe itself.

From the late eighteenth until the mid-twentieth century the Indian empire served as one of the largest and most lucrative markets for Britain's manufactured products from textiles to locomotives, a major source of raw materials essential for its factories, and by far the most favoured of Britain's tropical dependencies for its surplus investment capital. India also generated a massive migrant flow to British-ruled colonies. Though perhaps the majority of these immigrants were seasonal workers, thousands made up non-European strata of permanent settlers who, together with their Chinese and Japanese counterparts, far surpassed the prodigious levels of emigration from Europe in the nineteenth century.

The changes engendered in Europe by the Industrial Revolution had profound consequences for imperial expansion in Africa. Imperial policymakers viewed colonies both as suppliers of raw materials and sources of cheap labour, as well as potential markets for cheap manufactured goods. Colonial policies through much of the nineteenth century reflected these priorities. In coastal Africa trading settlements remained points of intersection between expansive inland trading networks and global seaborne traffic, and served as points from which European colonisers established other coastal settlements. Industrialisation transformed and deepened the economic, social, political and cultural repercussions of colonial expansion. New technologies in communication, medicine, firearms and transportation made it difficult, if not impossible, for indigenous leaders throughout Africa to hold the intruders at bay. European incursions were now far more successful than they would have been a century earlier. African peoples, even in more remote areas, now came face to face with Europeans.

---

55   M.C. Ricklefs, *A History of Modern Indonesia* (Bloomington, IN, 1981), chaps 3, 6 and 9.

The process of colonisation varied among European powers and from region to region. But it consisted of a combination of territorial control by chartered companies, land grants to individual settlers and direct rule. The construction of railroads, the implementation of scientific farming and plantation agriculture, rapid increases in mining and the shift from food crops to the cultivation of exportable cash crops all exemplify the reorganisation of local economies to serve the needs of industrial Europe. Colonial officials drew increasingly sharp distinctions between European and native populations. Through control of such institutions as governance, the military, law, the police, science, education, religion and health, colonial regimes reconfigured social, political, economic, ethnic and cultural relationships between Europeans and non-Europeans and among local peoples. This extension of power entailed the accommodation of indigenous secular and religious leaders. Local agents were vital partners in the overland trade networks that stretched ever farther into the African interior.[56]

In the nineteenth century, extensive areas throughout Africa became sites for the expansion and development of new settler societies. The genesis of two of the largest and richest of these settler societies, South Africa and Algeria, preceded the late-nineteenth-century scramble and owed little to the industrial competition and great power rivalries that spurred colonisation elsewhere. As we have seen, extensive Dutch settlement in South Africa had begun in the coastal areas around Table Bay in the middle decades of the seventeenth century and spread over much of the southwestern interior regions by the late 1700s. As early as 1702, the first contacts were made between *trekboer* settlers on the transfrontier and the Xhosa and other Bantu peoples near the Great Fish River. By the last years of the century, the interaction between the Boers and the Bantus became one of the defining processes of South African history. Another was the arrival of the British in this era of revolution and interstate warfare in Europe. Seeking to preempt efforts by republican France to increase its influence in the region, the British ousted the feeble Dutch regime in 1795 after the French had occupied the Netherlands. In the following decades British efforts to control the Boer settlers, and especially attempts to regulate settlers' relations with the indigenous peoples (including a campaign to free Khoikhoi and San slaves), gave great impetus to Boer migration into the interior. Culminating in the 'great trek', which began in 1836, the mass migration of the Boer settlers led to more than a half-century of wars with ever shifting alliances.

Initially, the British were more or less content to let the pastoralist Boer trekkers take refuge and establish a patchwork of 'republics' in what later became the Orange Free State and Transvaal. But a seemingly endless succession of wars with powerful African kingdoms, most famously the Zulu, and fears that the Boers might ally themselves with imperial Germany or other European rivals forced the British to secure the southern and eastern coast and to intervene repeatedly in conflicts in the interior. Missionary pressures, and especially the discovery of rich diamond and gold deposits in the Orange Free State in 1867 and the Transvaal

---

56 See for example David Robinson, *Paths of Accommodation: Muslim Societies and French Colonial Authorities in Senegal and Mauritania, 1880–1920* (Athens, OH, 2000).

in 1886, led to an influx of British migrants. The threats these changes posed for the Boer republics led to violent clashes with the increasingly assertive British and ultimately to the Anglo-Boer War of 1899–1902, which resulted in the absorption of the Orange Free State and Transvaal into the Union of South Africa in 1910.[57]

Excepting perhaps South Africa, none of Britain's settler colonies in Africa matched French Algeria in strategic importance, in the number of European settlers who chose to make it a permanent home, or the extent to which French prestige depended on its domination. France's colonisation of Algeria, beginning in the 1830s, had little to do with resources or great power rivalries. Cynically manipulating an insult to the French ambassador in Algiers, Charles X and his advisors sought to deflect rising dissent against an inept Bourbon monarchy by sending an expeditionary force into the Maghreb. A deceptively easy conquest of the city of Algiers opened the way for a violent, forty-year struggle against the overwhelmingly Muslim Berber and Arab population in the farmlands, mountains and deserts of the colony the French would forcibly carve out of North Africa. Nonetheless, within a decade of the capture of Algiers, significant numbers of French immigrants began to occupy the towns and lands on the Mediterranean coast, where the climate was temperate. The French applied a *razzia* or scorched-earth policy, which led to the destruction of villages, livestock and woodlands, and the indiscriminate slaughter of the indigenous inhabitants.

In the following decades, successive waves of mainly Italian and Spanish migrants – very often enticed by special incentives offered by the colonial regime – swelled the European population from roughly 140,000 in the 1850s to over 700,000 just before the First World War. As was the case in South Africa, the indigenous population, who unlike those in the Americas and Oceania had long shared and built up similar immunities to the diseases that afflicted the European intruders, continued to far outnumber the *colons* or settlers. But most of the Arabs and Berbers were dispossessed and driven into areas where the soil was infertile and often lacking in sufficient rainfall for cultivation. Some went hungry or starved, many became landless labourers or poorly paid workers on the margins of society, and all but a handful of Algerian *assimiles* were deprived of political power and the civil liberties that the French republic proclaimed the set piece of its *mission civilisatrice*. These conditions of inequality and oppression intensified throughout the first half of the twentieth century, and gave rise to sporadic resistance and eventually the violent revolutionary movement that led to the forced repatriation of the *colons* and gave birth to the Algerian nation in the 1960s.[58]

Although the 'scramble' of the great powers of Europe for colonies at the end of the nineteenth century also encompassed the Pacific Islands or Oceania, the

---

57 Leonard Thompson, *A History of South Africa* (New Haven, CT, 1990), and Freda Troup, *South Africa: An Historical Introduction* (Harrmondsworth, 1975).

58 The standard accounts of the rise and fall of settler colonialism in Algeria include Charles-André Julien, *L'Histoire de l'Algérie contemporaine*, vol. 1 (Paris, 1964); Charles-Robert Ageron, *Histoire de l'Algérie contemporaine, 1830–1970* (Paris, 1970); and David Gordon, *The Passing of French Algeria* (London, 1966), chaps 3–4.

basis for the largest settlement colonies outside of the Americas and Africa was established a century earlier in the late 1700s. The migration of English colonists who intended to settle permanently in both Australia and New Zealand was roughly contemporaneous, but the outcome of their arrival and advance diverged significantly. Both Australia and New Zealand contained extensive temperate regions with adequate rainfall for agriculture, but the Australian interior was semi-arid and suitable mainly for ranching, while much of the South Island of New Zealand was too cold for more than herding. As a result, pastoralism, especially sheep raising, became an economic mainstay in both colonies. The transfrontier pioneers who provided the entering wedge for the early colonisation of Australia were convicts transported to relieve the overcrowded prisons of Great Britain. In New Zealand whalers, as well as merchants seeking to exploit the *kauri* timber of the North Island, were the first Europeans to establish ongoing relations with the Maori population.

In contrast to the indigenous peoples or Aborigines whom the English settlers encountered in Australia, the Maori were more densely settled (there were as many as 125–130,000 on the eve of European colonisation, living mostly on the North Island), and lived in cohesive and well-organised tribal and clan groups. Competition and intermittent warfare among the clans made the Maori formidable adversaries. They adapted more easily than Australian Aboriginals to the European influx, both by transforming their traditional ways of farming and actively participating in international trading networks. The dynamics of contact and contestation were radically different in the Australian colonies. Though colonial officials sought to promote agriculture, most of the early settlers preferred to herd sheep and hunt. Both in the coastal areas and interior they clashed with the Aboriginal peoples. Living and moving about in small bands, the Aborigines were generally despised by the Europeans for the low level of their material culture as well as their physical appearance and vagabond ways. While the Maori population had begun to stabilise by the late nineteenth century, the assault of the colonisers on the much more dispersed Australian aboriginal population was a good deal more brutal. In Van Diemen's Land (Tasmania), most egregiously, the indigenous peoples had been all but eliminated by the 1870s, often through systematic massacres amounting to ethnic cleansing, including the infamous 'Black Line' campaign in the early 1830s.

As the indigenous populations declined precipitously, ceded the best farming and pasture lands to colonisers and were driven to the margins of society or increasingly relegated to mainly subordinate positions within the colonial system, the settlers of Australia and New Zealand followed the lead of the Canadians in asserting political autonomy within the broader framework of the British Empire. Largely peacefully but inexorably, first Canada and then several decades later Australia and New Zealand won dominion status between the late 1860s and 1907. Having brought the indigenous peoples under control, the leaders of the new dominions set about putting exclusionary 'whites only' immigration laws in place that were intended to insure settler dominance for an indefinite future.[59]

The Dynamics of European Expansion, Colonisation and Settlement

Europe was in many respects the least likely of the prominent expansionist societies of the fourteenth and fifteenth centuries to emerge as the progenitor of transoceanic discovery, intercontinental empires and an incipient global commercial network. As we have argued, by most of the commonly cited indices of development – including level of urbanisation, sophistication of handicraft production, population and capacity to sustain large military forces – Europe lagged far behind the empires of Asia, the Middle East, Sudanic Africa and the Americas. But as they began to probe, however tentatively, into the largely unknown Atlantic Ocean, Europeans soon found that they had a number of select advantages – above all highly navigable and relatively well-armed warships – that allowed them to sustain more direct contacts abroad, to exploit rather constricted but often lucrative commercial and political openings, and to achieve dominance in parts of Asia, the Americas and (to a far lesser extent) sub-Saharan Africa.

The success or failure of what were often highly improvised expansionist schemes depended both upon forces within Europe and, almost invariably a good deal more, on the nature of the societies and situations the Europeans encountered overseas. European deficiencies – such as grain shortages, limited commercial linkages and especially what proved to be a narrow range of exportable commodities – spurred expansion and motivated Europeans to take advantage of borrowed technologies in novel ways. Remarkably rapid European advances in metal working, scientific instrumentation, the harnessing of inanimate power and military discipline and weaponry proved essential to their successes overseas. But internal circumstances could impede expansion. Political and geographic fragmentation, for example, spurred competition, and hence economic and technological development, but it also meant that throughout the more than four centuries under consideration Europeans remained engaged in incessant internal wars that often extended overseas. These conflicts not only consumed their rather limited resources, including human lives, but they were also manipulated by peoples seeking to fend off western colonisation and settlement.

Long before they began to break out across the Atlantic, Europeans were familiar with a range of models for overseas expansion that facilitated adaptation to the very diverse societies and circumstances they encountered as they moved

---

59   Perhaps the best general survey of the settlement of Australia and the resistance and oppression of the indigenous peoples can be found in Kiernan *Blood and Soil*, chap. 7. For New Zealand, see Harrison M. Wright, *New Zealand, 1769–1840: Early Years of Western Contact* (Cambridge, MA, 1959); and Alan D. Ward, *A Show of Justice* (Canberra, 1974).

into different regions across the globe. Whether trading-post empires, plantation enclaves, tribute systems, formal colonisation or extensive overseas settlement, the mode Europeans deployed in a given contact zone was determined in part by cultural proclivities and the priorities of rulers and social groups committed to expansion in the metropoles. But at least until well into the nineteenth century, the slow pace of communication and transportation relative to the often vast distances travelled and the small numbers of Europeans who ventured overseas meant that local exigencies, opportunities, disease environments and the strengths and weaknesses of host societies were the most critical factors shaping the nature and impact of western overseas enterprises. From the momentous decision of the Chinese to abandon their overseas voyages and neglect their war and merchant fleet, for example, to the dynastic conflict between Atahualpa and Huáscar that divided the Incas on the eve of Spanish arrival, Europeans benefited from circumstances not of their making as they sought to establish themselves overseas. Foremost among these was disease. The pathogens carried by Europeans and the millions of Africans whom they forcibly transported across the Atlantic proved devastating for such peoples as those of the Americas and Oceania, thereby facilitating settlement. By contrast, until the late nineteenth century diseases for which westerners had little or no immunity greatly limited their capacity to settle further inland throughout most of sub-Saharan Africa. For Europeans everywhere in both the pre- and post-industrial eras, their ability to trade, build empires, extract resources and settle the land hinged also on the degree of collaboration or resistance of local elites and their subjects. And much like the Europeans whose encroachment they sought to fend off, conquered, enslaved and displaced non-western peoples fought back using borrowed technologies, learning and modes of organisation in circumstances not of their choosing.

Age of Imperial Crisis

Philippa Levine

The twentieth century began with the Europeans at their possessive peak, confident in their power and in their wealth. But their supremacy was far from stable, always vulnerable to indigenous resistance, to intra-European strife and to economic unpredictability. By the end of the twentieth century, Europe's political and economic supremacy would be successfully challenged and its colonial era all but over.

Before then, however, the boundaries of the European empires would expand even further than they had in the nineteenth century. The collapse of the Ottoman Empire burnished their holdings, as the mandate system devised by the new League of Nations after the First World War parcelled out former Ottoman territories to the two largest European empires, France and Britain, who were also the victors in that war.

The fate of the Ottomans had since the eighteenth century been connected with the emergence of another imperial power that straddled Europe and the east, that of Russia.[1] A series of Russo-Ottoman wars, in which the Russians invaded Ottoman territories in the Balkans and the Caucasus, had weakened Ottoman power over the course of the nineteenth century, and led to the loss of a number of Ottoman territories such as Serbia, Greece, Romania and Bulgaria. Alongside the incursions of the Russian Empire, the nineteenth century had seen western European powers make inroads into the Ottoman Empire. The 'capitulations' gave Europeans legal and fiscal privileges, and Ottoman Christians were accorded protection by the European Christian powers. Furthermore, economic concessions to Europeans in major ports and trading centres meant they had economic and commercial as well as religious and political footholds in the Ottoman lands.

The weaknesses which had long been apparent were not easy to control, and in the 1870s it became increasingly apparent that the centre could not hold. The Ottoman treasury went bankrupt, Christian rebellions in the Balkan provinces as well as a coup distracted the emperor, and a protracted war with Russia resulted in a considerable loss of Ottoman territory in 1878. Sultan Abdülhamid II (r. 1876–1909) responded by dissolving parliament and asserting an increasingly

---

1   For a detailed history of the Ottoman empire, see Virginia Aksan in this volume.

authoritarian rule as well as courting Germany as an ally and attempting to make peace with the Russians. The 1908 uprising by the Young Turks, Abdülhamid's most capable opponents, inaugurated a brief era of secular democracy.[2] But the nationalist uprisings in the European Ottoman lands that quickly followed, and the inroads made by the newly formed Balkan League in 1911 and 1912, resulted in yet another coup in 1913. By the summer of 1913, the Ottoman Empire had lost almost all of its European territory.[3] Italy, for example, had taken the colonies of Cyrenaica and Tripolitania in 1912 at the close of the Italo-Turkish War; they would be folded into the colony of Italian Libya in 1934.

The First World War brought no relief, as the Ottomans faced hostilities in Europe from the Russians and from the British and the French in the Middle East. Even during the war, the Allies were privately discussing how to partition the Ottoman Empire when the conflict ended. And though Russia's abrupt withdrawal from the war after the Revolution in 1917 annulled their share of the spoils, France and Britain would gain control of considerable territory in the Middle East in 1920.[4] In that year the Treaty of Sèvres stripped the Ottoman Empire of all its Arab provinces, as well as creating an independent Armenian state. With the establishment of the Turkish Republic in Anatolia and eastern Thrace, the Ottoman Empire officially came to an end in 1922.

The re-allocation of former Ottoman territories, which also heralded the final phase of European overseas expansion, ushered in a new level of global political attention to the Middle East.[5] Arab nationalism, already a force in French North Africa, and in Egypt and the Sudan where Britain dominated, gained new supporters, although it was by no means a unified movement. The area was vital to the British because it helped secure their growing oil interests in Persia, and because the Suez Canal provided a key route to their Asian and African empire.[6]

The Middle East, though increasingly important, was not the only new factor in colonial politics in the early twentieth century. Japan successfully took on first the Chinese in 1894 and then the Russians in 1904, acquiring new territories after each victory, as well as securing an alliance with the British in 1902 aimed largely at preventing further Russian expansion. By 1910 Taiwan and Korea were both under Japanese control, and the Japanese Empire was a globally significant power when war broke out in 1914.

Alongside the emergence of Japan as a colonising power, another major feature of the early years of the century was the massive political change that overtook

---

2   Hasan Kayali, *Arabs and Young Turks: Ottomanism, Arabism, and Islamism in the Ottoman Empire, 1908–1918* (Berkeley, CA, 1997).

3   F. Adanir, *The Ottomans and the Balkans: A Discussion of Historiography* (Leiden, 2002).

4   M. Şükrü Hanioğlu, *A Brief History of the Late Ottoman Empire* (Princeton, NJ, 2008).

5   Jukka Nevakivi, *Britain, France and the Arab Middle East 1914–1920* (London, 1969).

6   John Darwin, *Britain, Egypt, and the Middle East: Imperial Policy in the Aftermath of War, 1918–1922* (Basingstoke, 1981); D.K. Fieldhouse, *Western Imperialism in the Middle East 1914–1958* (Oxford, 2006); Priya Satia, *Spies in Arabia: The Great War and the Cultural Foundations of Britain's Covert Empire in the Middle East* (Oxford, 2008); Ann Williams, *Britain and France in the Middle East and North Africa, 1914–1967* (London, 1968).

the Russian Empire in 1917. By the war's end the Russian Empire was no more, but it exerted considerable political influence until 1917.[7] Like its neighbour, the Habsburg Empire, the Russian Empire was wholly a land empire, and one which, like other European empires, had expanded rapidly and considerably in the nineteenth century. After Russia's defeat in the Crimean War in 1856 its pace of colonisation stepped up, a response in some respects to the imperial activities of the western European powers with whom it perceived itself in competition.

Russia expanded into Eastern Europe, Asia and the Kazhaks, creating a multi-ethnic empire that stretched from Finland and the Baltic states, across Belarus and east past the Caspian Sea into western and northern Asia. In Asia, expansion southward into the Hindu Kush precipitated diplomatic manoeuvring with the British. Fearing that the Russians saw Afghanistan as a staging post from which to enter British India, the British conducted tense negotiations – as well as a few skirmishes – with the Russians over these borderlands in the last quarter of the nineteenth century.[8] The Pamir Agreement of 1895 settled the definition of the southern Afghan border, while the 1907 Anglo-Russian Entente did the same for Persia and Tibet, as well as making Afghanistan a British protectorate off limits to the Russians.

Russian expansion drew sizeable protests from the many non-Russian constituencies within the empire. There was a major anti-Russian rebellion in Poland in 1863, and even before the 1905 Revolution peasant movements began to gel in the early twentieth century in many non-Russian areas of the empire. In Muslim territories, the Ottoman authorities encouraged disaffection with colonial rule. Though many Muslims living under Russian rule had emigrated to Ottoman lands after the Crimean War, those who stayed in Russia were irked by the growing emphasis on assimilation to Russian culture and often turned to Muslim nationalism.

By the time Russia withdrew from the First World War, much of its western empire had already been lost, and the 1918 Treaty of Brest-Litovsk erased the rest of its western holdings, along with most of the southern empire. The new Bolshevik regime was critical of imperialism, but rapidly recognised that without a clear set of imperialist frontier policies its own fragile power would be severely compromised; its critique of colonialism was thus reserved for the capitalist variant, and the Bolshevik's own march, especially eastward over the course of the twentieth century, was justified on revolutionary grounds.

---

7   See Martin Aust, 'Writing the Empire: Russia and the Soviet Union in Twentieth-Century Historiography', *European Review of History* 10/2 (2003): pp. 375–91; Boris Kagarlitsky, *Empire of the Periphery: Russia and the World System* (London, 2007); Andreas Kappeler, *The Russian Empire: A Multiethnic History* (Harlow, 2001); Dominic Lieven, *Empire: The Russian Empire and its Rivals* (London, 2000); William G. Rosenberg, 'The Problems of Empire in Imperial Russia', *Ab Imperio* 3 (2005): pp. 453–69, and especially Willard Sunderland in this volume.

8   Susash Chakravarty, *Afghanistan and the Great Game* (Delhi, 2002); Karl Meyer, *Tournament of Shadows: The Great Game and the Race for Empire in Central Asia* (Washington, DC, 1999).

War and Its Aftermath

Tension between empires was among the major factors which led to the First World War, and a good deal of the war was fought on colonial territory, including the first military encounter between Britain and Germany in early August 1914, which took place in West Africa. Within a matter of weeks much of southern Africa was embroiled in the war, and before hostilities ended in 1918 the Pacific and the Middle East would also experience the disruptions of war.

The contributions of colonial troops were critical to the war effort, although imperial expectations of support did not meet with universal enthusiasm. The Russian Empire faced a revolt in Middle Asia in 1916, catalysed in the first instance by demands for military service. In Canada, the introduction of conscription in 1917 generated riots while the Australians twice rejected compulsory military service. Some 3 million colonial soldiers from every part of the British Empire fought in the war, and the French conscripted over 800,000 men from their colonies. More than 200,000 workers from French colonies faced discrimination in France on the factory floor and assaults by co-workers. The British, meanwhile, fearful of nationalist sentiments, rigorously censored the letters of Indian soldiers.[9]

The consequences of the war for the European empires were substantial. Colonial peoples were resentful of the way the war drained their resources, human and otherwise. The brutality and senseless violence that came to characterise the conflict shattered Europe's self-image as a progressive and civilised global leader. Promises made to colonial populations in exchange for wartime support created postwar political crises, as nationalists anticipated political gains for their wartime sacrifices.[10] 40,000 Malagasy, for example, fought for the French. Jean Ralaimongo was among them, and campaigned for French citizenship for Madagascans, believing that the wartime evidence of their allegiance deserved political recognition. His beliefs cost him dearly; he was convicted of sedition in 1922 and placed under house arrest in 1930, a palpable symbol of the unequal relations between coloniser and colonised that characterised European imperialism well into the twentieth century.[11]

In Ireland, where the power-sharing Home Rule Act of 1914 had been suspended as a result of the war, nationalists took advantage of wartime conditions to advance the Irish nationalist cause. Roger Casement, an Irish poet and activist who worked

---

9   Richard S. Fogarty, *Race and War in France: Colonial Subjects in the French Army, 1914–1918* (Baltimore, MD, 2008); David Omissi, *Indian Voices of the Great War: Soldiers' Letters, 1914–18* (Basingstoke, 1999); Tyler Stovall, 'Colour-blind France? Colonial Workers During the First World War', *Race and Class* 35/2 (1993): pp. 35–55.

10   Bill Nasson, 'War Opinion in South Africa, 1914', *Journal of Imperial and Commonwealth History* 23/2 (1995): pp. 248–76.

11   A. Adu Boahen, *Africa Under Colonial Domination, 1880–1935* (Berkeley, CA, 1990); Jonathan Derrick, *Africa's 'Agitators': Militant Anti-Colonialism in Africa and the West, 1918–1939* (New York, 2008); Dominic Thomas, *Black France: Colonialism, Immigration, and Transnationalism* (Bloomington, IN, 2007); Virginia Thompson and Richard Adloff, *The Malagasy Republic: Madagascar Today* (Stanford, CA, 1965).

for the British consular service, sought German help against the British. Casement raised a German–Irish Brigade but, intercepted on his return to Ireland, was executed for treason in 1916, just a few months after the Easter Rebellion in Dublin. Though that uprising was quickly quashed, the harsh British response to it swelled the nationalist ranks. Factional fighting intensified when a previously minor nationalist organisation, Sinn Féin, swept the board at the elections in 1918. The British bisected Ireland into the six predominantly Protestant counties of Northern Ireland and the Catholic remainder of the country, an uneasy compromise which resulted in civil war. In 1922 southern Ireland became a Dominion of the Empire while Northern Ireland remained within Britain, albeit with a degree of self-government.

Britain faced nationalist protests elsewhere during the war. In 1915 there was rioting in Ceylon; four years later the Ceylon National Congress was founded to seek greater independence from Britain. In Burma the Young Men's Buddhist Association led an anti-British campaign in 1916.[12] Activists in India, disappointed by the limited concessions granted by the 1919 Government of India Act, led non-cooperation campaigns in the early 1920s, and dissatisfaction with the British presence would remain a steady drumbeat in Indian politics until independence and partition in 1947.

Inter-War Conflict

Even before 1914 anti-colonial protest had been mounting.[13] A mutiny of African troops in German Cameroon in 1893 was brutally quashed by the Germans. The French faced constant guerilla warfare in French Indochina in the 1890s, and in 1907 thirteen activists were executed for attempting to poison French military officers at the Hanoi Garrison. The following year saw an attempted bombing of a British judge in Calcutta. The years before 1914 were tumultuous ones all over British India, but especially in eastern India where the partition of Bengal in 1905 met with boycotts and protests, especially amongst Hindus. In 1912 John Dube and Tshekisho (Sol) Plaatje founded the South African Native National Congress (SANNC), later renamed the African National Congress.[14] In the Dutch East Indies, a peasant movement in central Java led by Surontiko Samin alarmed the authorities sufficiently that they exiled him 1907, although this failed to stem the passive

---

12   A.J. Stockwell, 'Imperialism and Nationalism in South-East Asia', in Judith M. Brown and Wm. Roger Louis (eds), *The Oxford History of the British Empire*, vol. 4: *The Twentieth Century* (Oxford, 1999), p. 467.

13   Shula Marks, *Reluctant Rebellion: The 1906–8 Disturbances in Natal* (Oxford, 1970); David Marr, *Vietnamese Anticolonialism, 1885–1925* (Berkeley, CA, 1971).

14   Heidi Holland, *The Struggle: A History of the African National Congress* (London, 1989); Maureen Rall, *Peaceable Warrior: The Life and Times of Sol T. Plaatje* (Kimberley, 2003); Brian Willan, *Sol Plaatje, South African Nationalist, 1876–1932* (Berkeley, CA, 1984).

resistance he had inspired.[15] Islamist organisations, trades unions and student groups in Indonesia all began demanding self-government. In the Dutch colonies a radical literature dubbed *batjaan liar* (wild publications) spread rapidly in the 1910s and 1920s.[16] The Egyptian National Party was founded in 1892, and across Africa protests against colonial governments erupted – in Sierra Leone in 1898, on the Gold Coast (Asante) in 1900, in Angola in 1902, in German South West Africa in 1904.

The Herero War (1904–1907) in German South West Africa left at least 60,000 Africans dead, and those who survived were rounded up into labour camps. The labour camp was also deployed by the British in the South African War (1899–1902; also known as the Anglo-Boer or Boer War) which, although waged against another colonial force (the Boer settlers), left at least 15,000 black Africans dead. These were both serious and lengthy conflicts in which colonial powers did not hesitate to use methods of considerable cruelty and brutality. The death toll in both these conflicts was crushing. In the Congo, Leopold faced both civilian resistance and mutinies within his own army. Even after the Belgian state acquired the Congo in 1908, rebellions remained commonplace. By the 1930s the Belgian Congo was one of the cornerstones of African rural radicalism.[17]

The fractures of the 1914–18 war only added fuel to the fire of anti-colonial resistance. In 1920 Winston Churchill remarked in the House of Commons that 'collisions between troops and native populations have been painfully frequent in the melancholy aftermath of the Great War'.[18] His comments came during Parliamentary discussions of the Amritsar Massacre in which, a year earlier, British officer Reginald Dyer's order to fire on Indian protesters left not only almost 400 dead and another 1,500 wounded, but also an enduring anti-British bitterness.[19] The French, meanwhile, faced insurrections in their African, Indochinese and Middle East holdings during the 1920s and 1930s, protests they swiftly and mercilessly repressed.

The colonial yoke had been around long enough to make itself widely and broadly felt, and while there were remote areas where the sight of a European

---

15 Robert Aarsse, 'Le Saminisme ou le refus non-violent de révoltés', in Pierre Brocheux and Robert Aarsse (eds), *Histoire de l'Asie du Sud-Est: revoltes, reformes, revolutions* (Lille, 1981); George Kahin, *Nationalism and Revolution in Indonesia* (Ithaca, NY, 2003), pp. 43–4; Norman G. Owen, *The Emergence of Modern Southeast Asia: A New History* (Honolulu, HI, 2005), p. 254; Merle Ricklefs, *A History of Modern Indonesia since c. 1200* (Stanford, CA, 2001), p. 211; Takashi Shiraishi, *An Age in Motion: Popular Radicalism in Java, 1912–1926* (Ithaca, NY, 1990).

16 Hilmar Farid and Razif, '*Batjaan liar* in the Dutch East Indies: A Colonial Antipode', *Postcolonial Studies* 11/3 (2008): pp. 277–92.

17 Neal Ascherson, *The King Incorporated: Leopold II in the Age of Trusts* (London, 1963).

18 Hansard, House of Commons, 8 July 1920, p. 1725.

19 Richard Cavendish, 'The Amritsar Massacre', *History Today* 59/4 (2009): p. 13; Nigel Collett, *The Butcher of Amritsar: Brigadier-General Reginald Dyer* (London, 2005); Vinay Lal, 'The Incident of the 'Crawling Lane': Women in the Punjab Disturbances of 1919', *Genders* 16 (1993): pp. 35–60; Derek Sayer, 'British Reaction to the Amritsar Massacre 1919–1920', *Past and Present* 131/1 (1991): pp. 130–64.

was rare, in most places local peoples recognised the effect of colonialism on the physical, economic and cultural landscape. In many instances it worsened conditions through the imposition of new and often dangerous forms of manual labour such as gold and diamond mining, through famines induced by the effect of the market on agriculture and through radical changes in the lifestyles of those affected. European information technologies, however, often helped to further the nationalist cause. For the literate, newspapers and broadsheets (often closely monitored by colonial officials) publicised both the deeds of colonists and the messages of their opponents.[20] Faster travel, and to regions hitherto difficult to reach, brought news and ideas to fresh populations, and new recruits to the nationalist cause. After the First World War, Europe seemed less undefeatable, though continued exploitation of its colonies in the years between the world wars should not be underestimated. In 1918 famine in the Middle East and bubonic plague in parts of Africa exacerbated the miseries of war and colonialism. In that same year, the influenza epidemic reached deep into the colonial world: French North Africa, Sierra Leone, New Zealand, many Pacific island communities, Hong Kong and India.

The League of Nations, created after the war to promote collective security and prevent further conflict, took on a kind of international colonial responsibility, especially in its devising of the mandate system.[21] It was the League which appointed 'trustees' to administer colonies that had been part of the now defunct German and Ottoman empires. At the end of the war France acquired Syria and Lebanon, and Britain gained Iraq (Mesopotamia) and Palestine. Japan and Belgium, as well as Britain, its Pacific Dominions and France, were given responsibility for former German colonies. But in relying principally on the European victors for implementation, the League helped to stabilise European imperialism, which would survive, after all, well into the last third of the twentieth century. The use of the European colonial powers to administer the mandate system revealed an acceptance in powerful political circles that the world was divided into capable 'advanced' nations and those needing their guidance.

The new mandate system, however, provoked intractable inter-war problems, and this was nowhere more apparent than in Palestine. European Jews, who had moved to what they regarded as their spiritual homeland, encountered an indigenous population disinclined to move aside. It fell to the British as the trustees of the mandate to adjudicate between the settlers and the Palestinians, a task about which they were at best ambivalent.[22] Politicians and officials in Britain and on the ground in Palestine were deeply divided between pro-Arab and pro-

---

20   C.A. Bayly, *Empire and Information: Intelligence Gathering and Social Communication in India, 1780–1870* (Cambridge, 1996); Zoë Laidlaw, *Colonial Connections, 1815–45: Patronage, the Information Revolution and Colonial Government* (Manchester, 2005).

21   Erez Manela, *The Wilsonian Moment: Self-Determination and the International Origins of Anticolonial Nationalism* (Oxford, 2007).

22   Jonathan Schneer, *The Balfour Declaration: The Origins of the Arab-Israeli Conflict* (New York, 2010).

Jewish factions, and the presence in Britain of a growing Jewish population further complicated the situation. Conflicting guarantees to the Palestinians and Jews did nothing to ease tensions that repeatedly erupted in violent confrontations during the 1920s and 1930s.

The British ran their mandate territories largely as they had Egypt since 1882 – that is, through the intervention of British advisers. Even after nominal independence, a continuing military presence secured for them a good deal of influence. The French were less actively engaged in their mandate areas, despite long-held plans for a larger French presence in the Middle East. One French official outlined the need for 'an indigenous facade ... behind which we can operate without direct responsibility and in the way and under the circumstances which we judge useful'.[23] A Druze revolt in 1925 forced the French to hold elections in Syria for the first time, but there was no serious move towards independence, as provided for in the mandate, until the 1930s.

Little further European expansion ensued after the division in 1920 of Germany's colonies and the break-up of the Ottoman Empire. In the 1920s Spain extended its hold on Morocco, and in 1934 Mussolini established the colony of Italian North Africa (Africa Settentrionale Italiana) after crushing Libyan resistance movements with considerable ferocity.[24] In 1935 he invaded Ethiopia, creating the short-lived colony of Italian East Africa (Africa Orientale Italiana), a move that highlighted the weakness of the League of Nations and the collusion of other colonial powers.[25] Though it was Italy's fascist allies (Japan and Germany) who first offered official recognition to this new imperial possession, France and Britain followed suit in 1938. Italy, likewise, recognised Japan's claims to Manchuria, which the Japanese had invaded in 1931, establishing a puppet government. Both Italy and Japan withdrew from the League of Nations, whose opposition to their actions was limited to mild censure and, in the case of Italy, short-lived and ineffective sanctions. Britain's last territorial acquisition came in 1934, as part of a treaty to define the frontier between the existing British protectorate of Aden and the Yemen.

Reform and Critique

Where nineteenth-century opposition to imperialism had often centred on cost rather than on the ethics of colonial practice, there was a growing moral distaste for colonialism in the twentieth century, especially on the Left. One of the earliest theoretical critiques of European imperialism in the west was that of J.A. Hobson,

---

23 Quoted in Fieldhouse, *Western Imperialism*, p. 254.
24 Claudio Segrè, *Fourth Shore: The Italian Colonization of Libya* (Chicago, IL, 1974).
25 Christopher Hollis, *Italy in Africa* (London, 1941); Patrizia Palumbo (ed.), *A Place in the Sun: Africa in Italian Colonial Culture from Post-Unification to the Present* (Berkeley, CA, 2003); Esmonde Robertson, *Mussolini as Empire-Builder: Europe and Africa, 1932–36* (London, 1977).

whose 1902 book, *Imperialism*, explicitly linked imperialism to capitalist economics.[26] This new 'morality' did have some effect on the ground. It helped precipitate the Dutch Ethical Policy of 1901 (which, though it stressed material improvement in Dutch colonies, had minimal effect), and British concessions to Indian nationalists in the 1920s and 1930s.

Inter-war European colonialism was characterised by new experimental economic policies (what the French called *mise en valeur*), although the need to curb colonial rebellions was always also prominent.[27] These new interventions turned specifically on the principle of improving colonial infrastructure, and, in keeping with political developments in Europe itself, presaged a greater degree of state involvement than had characterised nineteenth-century colonial rule. Public works, education and medical access formed the largest areas of activity. In British Africa, the government encouraged new educational ventures, working in tandem with existing missionary enterprises and attempting to unify policy in disparate areas. Frederick Lugard's enormously influential 1922 tome on colonial trusteeship, *The Dual Mandate in British Tropical Africa*, saw education as the key to 'improving' Africa.[28] In Rwanda and Burundi, *foyers sociaux* taught modern domestic skills to urban women in preparation for marriage.[29] Basic and practical education along these lines was seen as safer than higher education, which ran the risk of schooling potential radicals. As in earlier periods, a tiny elite continued to receive a western education in European institutions, but for the most part the colonial powers chose to implement cautious changes designed principally to stabilise their own position and standing.[30]

Although agriculture was often targeted as a development initiative, the middle years of the twentieth century were also years of substantial colonial urbanisation.[31] Cities in South Africa, Indochina, India and elsewhere grew denser. Family and kin

---

26   P.J. Cain, *Hobson and Imperialism: Radicalism, New Liberalism, and Finance 1887–1938* (Oxford, 2002). See too Stephen Howe, *Anticolonialism in British Politics: The Left and the End of Empire, 1918–1964* (Oxford, 1993); Nicholas Owen, *The British Left and India Metropolitan Anti-Imperialism, 1885–1947* (Oxford, 2007); Neelam Srivastava, 'Anti-colonialism and the Italian Left', *Interventions: The International Journal of Postcolonial Studies* 8/3 (2006): pp. 413–29; John Cunningham Wood, 'J.A. Hobson and British Imperialism', *American Journal of Economics and Sociology* 42/4 (1983): pp. 483–500.

27   Stephen Constantine, *The Making of British Colonial Development Policy, 1914–1940* (London, 1984); Michael Havinden, *Colonialism and Development: Britain and its Tropical Colonies, 1850–1960* (London, 1993); Joanna Lewis, *Empire State-Building: War and Welfare in Kenya, 1925–52* (London, 2001).

28   John Anderson, *The Struggle for the School: The Interaction of Missionary, Colonial Government and Nationalist Enterprise in the Development of Formal Education in Kenya* (London, 1970).

29   Nancy Rose Hunt, 'Domesticity and Colonialism in Belgian Africa: Usumbura's *Foyer Social*, 1946–1960', *Signs* 15/3 (1990): pp. 447–74.

30   See, for example, Hibba Abugideiri, *Gender and the Making of Modern Medicine in Colonial Egypt* (Farnham, 2010).

31   Mia Fuller, *Moderns Abroad: Architecture, Cities and Italian Imperialism* (London, 2007); Gwendolyn Wright, *The Politics of Design in French Colonial Urbanism* (Chicago, IL, 1991).

networks were disrupted as first men and then women sought work in the cities, forging new kinds of relationships. Women offered men alone in the city a mixture of domestic and sexual services for a fee.[32] In many places both were subject to pass laws which restricted mobility, often severely. Marriages of convenience which allowed freer travel to both parties were common. The anonymity offered by city living cloaked these hitherto unconventional arrangements.

Colonial cities were already deeply segregated along racial lines. White neighbourhoods were less densely populated, often suburban in form. Commerce was usually kept at a distance reinforcing western distinctions between private family spaces and public commercial spaces. It was also in the cities that a growing anti-colonial nationalism fomented the most rapidly, certainly in its more organised forms. There were rural protests aplenty, but cohesive nationalist movements began to cluster around educated and urbanised leaders. Few areas escaped unrest.

In the period immediately after the First World War, African delegations arrived in the colonial capitals of Europe to present demands for independence, though they rarely achieved much.[33] Such deputations did, however, feed the Pan-African movement. The first Pan-African Congress was held in Paris in 1919, reviving a movement begun in the 1890s among American and Caribbean blacks. The new movement hoped to influence the deliberations of the 1919 Versailles Peace Conference, but despite their cogent resolutions – which included better protection from exploitation, the abolition of slavery and capital punishment, and the right to education – European and American delegates, more concerned with the allocation of the former Ottoman and German territories, sidestepped these issues. The Pan-African Congress lived on, reconvening in London in 1921 and thereafter another three times until 1945, when their final and most radical meeting took place in Manchester.

The Pan-African Congress was not alone in seeing the Peace Conference as an appropriate forum. Vietnamese activist Nguyễn Ái Quốc (who would later become better known as Hồ Chí Minh), also petitioned for independence from colonial rule, though no more successfully than the Africans. It was thus in the 1920s and 1930s that protest and the desire for independence escalated and in increasingly organised fora. The Bolsheviks carefully cultivated ties with anti-colonial nationalists in many colonial arenas, and, as in Europe, the 1920s saw the establishment of Communist parties dedicated to the overthrow of colonial regimes. The Indonesian Communist Party was founded in 1923, the first Marxist organisation in India in 1920 and the Vietnamese Communist Party in 1930.

Anti-colonial nationalism, however, ran a wide gamut of political opinion from Marxist critiques to the spiritualist non-violence espoused by Gandhi after his return to India in 1915. Rebellions across the colonised world signalled growing dissatisfaction with European rule and, though they were sometimes easily suppressed, their frequency expressed a growing instability of, and antipathy to, colonial rule.

32   Luise White, *The Comforts of Home: Prostitution in Colonial Nairobi* (Chicago, IL, 1990).
33   Derrick, *Africa's 'Agitators'*, p. 21.

Throughout the colonised world Islam became associated increasingly with opposition to colonialism.[34] The jihad in Somaliland that followed the conquest of the Sudan in the late 1890s prompted many Africans to convert to Islam as a declaration of anti-colonialism. Alongside the predominantly Hindu Indian National Congress, the Muslim League in India joined the non-cooperation movement which spread mass civil disobedience across the land in the early 1920s. In Portuguese India (Goa in the southwest) activists were disappointed when the 1910 republican revolution in Portugal did not bring to an end the colonial era. The Goa National Congress, founded in 1928, had links to the Indian National Congress, but the 1930s brought increasing restrictions to the area. The Vietnamese Nationalist Party (Việt Nam Quốc Dân Đảng) assassinated French officials as well as indigenous collaborators, but the quick French reaction to the 1930 Yen Bai uprising, and the disturbances that followed, scattered the militants. Serious unrest also broke out sporadically in Africa: the British faced protests in Nigeria in 1929, in Sierra Leone in 1931 and in Northern Rhodesia in 1935. The black trades union movement grew rapidly in parts of Africa in the 1920s. The Southern Rhodesian African National Congress was founded in 1938, and urban nationalism became increasingly radical with boycotts of European shops as well as strikes and stoppages. Chad resisted French rule constantly and often violently. The Kongo Wara uprising of 1928 in the Ubangi-Shari region of central Africa protested the French state's indifference to labour conditions in privately owned European companies. News of the rebellion was suppressed in France while in Africa it led to forcible relocations. In 1926 France backed Spain's extension of its Moroccan territory, bringing to a close the bloody Rif War.

Throughout Africa, resistance was persistent but sporadic. Retributions followed indigenous protest: houses were burned and destroyed as were crops and livestock. Whippings, incarceration and even capital punishment, public in some places into the 1930s, were common.[35] But to no avail. The tight suppression of radicalism in Algeria failed to prevent either new nationalist bodies or protests. Muslim organisations constantly called for reform in voting rights. New organisations such as the Étoile Nord Africaine (1926), the Parti du Peuple Algérien (1937) and the Union Populaire Algérien (1938) championed self-government and advocated equal rights. In 1924 the assassination of the British commander of the Egyptian army in the Sudan precipitated a mutiny among Sudanese troops. The British quickly removed influential Egyptians with nationalist leanings from office, but the incident revealed the widespread dissatisfactions in the region.

These, then, were decades in which rebellion and revolt was commonplace and in which new nationalist organisations took root across the colonial world.[36] In

---

34   The 1930s also saw an Islamist revival in Algeria.

35   David Killingray, 'The Maintenance of Law and Order in British Colonial Africa', *African Affairs* 85/340 (1986): pp. 434–5. Contrast Britain, where public hangings ended in the 1860s.

36   In this respect, I depart from John Darwin's claim that India was alone in the British Empire in the inter-war years in having "a recognisably mass nationalism." See *The*

Europe new forms of anti-imperialism also gathered pace through the combined efforts of political activists, journalists and writers. In France the novelist André Gide wrote critically of colonial labour conditions after he travelled in the 1920s to French Africa; among the places he visited was the Ubangi-Shari region, where the Kongo Wara conflict erupted in 1928. Louis-Ferdinand Céline offered a searing portrait of colonial life in his 1932 novel, *Voyage au bout de la nuit*. William Plomer's novel *Turbott Wolfe* (1925) caused a stir in his native South Africa for its subject matter of interracial love and its criticisms of the South African government. It was published in London by Leonard and Virginia Woolf's Hogarth Press. Joseph Conrad's *Heart of Darkness* (1902) was a thinly disguised narrative of conditions in Leopold's Congo territories. Conrad befriended Roger Casement, who, with Edmund Morel, spearheaded the early twentieth-century campaigns against the atrocities in the Belgian Congo.[37]

The literary and the political came together not only among Europeans who opposed colonialism but in the colonies too. The unauthorised anti-Dutch literature that the authorities had tried so hard to suppress in the East Indies was banned after an uprising in 1926, but an important new literature emerged among black activists. The Négritude of the 1930s embraced both a pride in black identity and a critique of colonialism. Associated initially with a group of Francophone Marxists, including the Senegalese poet and politician, Léopold Sédar Senghor and the Martinican poet, Aimé Césaire, it quickly spread to the new black awareness movements in the United States, influencing in particular the Harlem Renaissance.[38]

The years between the two world wars also saw a great increase in explicitly anti-colonial activity among women. In the late nineteenth and early twentieth century, women's moral critiques of empire were not always anti-imperialist, as is evident in the activities of social reform and feminist pressure groups who wanted to Christianise but not dismantle empire. Their position was that effective imperialism was a principled mission and that imperialism had strayed from its true Christian aims. The twentieth century, however, saw a growing articulation of anti-colonial nationalism on the part of colonised women. South African women had demonstrated against the pass laws in 1913, and the threat of their reintroduction galvanised the formation in 1918 of the Bantu Women's League led by Charlotte Maxeke and closely aligned with the SANNC.[39] The All-India Women's Conference

Empire Project: The Rise and Fall of the British World-system, 1830-1970 (Cambridge, 2009), p. 462.

37 Catherine Cline, *E.D. Morel, 1873–1924: The Strategies of Protest* (Belfast, 1980); Jordan Goodman, *The Devil and Mr Casement: One Man's Battle for Human Rights in South America's Heart of Darkness* (New York, 2010); Adam Hochschild, *King Leopold's Ghost: A Story of Greed, Terror, and Heroism in Colonial Africa* (Boston, MA, 1998).

38 Brent Edwards, *The Practice of Diaspora: Literature, Translation, and the Rise of Black Internationalism* (Cambridge, MA, 2003); Michael C. Lambert, 'From Citizenship to Negritude: "Making a Difference" in Elite Ideologies of Colonized Francophone West Africa', *Comparative Studies in Society and History* 35/2 (April 1993): pp. 239–62.

39 Judy Kimble and Elaine Unterhalter, '"We Opened the Road for You, You Must Go Forward": ANC Women's Struggles, 1912–1982', *Feminist Review* 12 (1982): pp. 11–35.

was founded in 1927, the National Council of African Women a decade later and the Congress of Indonesian Women in 1928.

Western women likewise began to join the chorus of anti-colonial protest, though they sometimes encountered resentment from indigenous women anxious that their voices not be drowned out by the more privileged women who took up their cause.[40] Doreen Wickremasinghe (née Young) left the United States in 1930 for what was then Ceylon, where she was deeply involved in girls' education as well as left-wing politics.[41] A small group of women Members of Parliament regularly raised questions about conditions in British Africa.[42] Margery Perham, who would become a highly influential voice in the Colonial Office, was one of Britain's leading experts on Africa, and, while not an anti-colonialist, she was sensitive to African opinion.[43] More radical in her views, and a foe of Perham's, was the socialist feminist Sylvia Pankhurst, who was involved in some of the earliest anti-racist organisations in Britain. After Italy's invasion of Ethiopia in 1935 Pankhurst launched a campaign for the restoration of Ethiopian independence.[44]

Women involved in nationalist struggles often found that their male colleagues regarded the claims of women as secondary, employing a rhetoric of nationalism which bound women to their status as mothers and care-givers.[45] This gendered rhetoric (the 'motherland', the 'birth of the nation') sometimes turned women into the guardians of a pre-colonial history and tradition as well as functionaries of population supply.[46] Just as colonialists had envisioned their own activities as masculine and the conquered colonies as feminised, nationalists found the metaphors of traditional gender useful in their own war of words. Javanese intellectuals invoked the idea of Europe as a cruel and thus unnatural mother to her

40   Antoinette Burton, *Burdens of History: British Feminists, Indian Women, and Imperial Culture, 1865–1915* (Chapel Hill, NC, 1994).
41   Kumari Jayawardena, *The White Woman's Other Burden: Western Women and South Asia During British Colonial Rule* (New York, 1995).
42   Barbara Bush, 'Britain's Conscience on Africa: White Women, Race and Imperial Politics in Inter-war Britain', in Clare Midgley (ed.), *Gender and Imperialism* (Manchester, 1998), pp. 200–223; Susan Pedersen, 'National Bodies, Unspeakable Acts: The Sexual Politics of Colonial Policy-making', *Journal of Modern History* 63/4 (1991): pp. 647–80; Pedersen, 'The Maternalist Moment in British Colonial Policy: The Controversy over "Child Slavery" in Hong Kong 1917–1941', *Past and Present* 171/1 (2001): pp. 161–202.
43   Alison Smith and Mary Bull (eds), *Margery Perham and British Rule in Africa* (London, 1991).
44   Mary Davis, *Sylvia Pankhurst: A Life in Radical Politics* (Sterling, VA, 1999); Patricia Romero, *E. Sylvia Pankhurst: Portrait of a Radical* (New Haven, CT, 1987). Pankhurst lived the last four years of her life in Ethiopia, dying there in 1960.
45   Joyce M. Chadya, 'Mother Politics: Anti-colonial Nationalism and the Woman Question in Africa', *Journal of Women's History* 15/3 (2003): pp. 153–7.
46   Kumari Jayawardena, *Feminism and Nationalism in the Third World* (New Delhi, 1986), p. 14.

colonial children.[47] Hindu nationalists portrayed women as selfless and spiritual, subordinating their own needs to the cause.[48]

The Second World War

The Second World War further loosened the colonial knot, already unravelling after the conflict of 1914–18. Although the French Empire survived for a further three decades, Martin Thomas sees its demise as all but inevitable by the time the war began.[49] The war years also precipitated a protracted process of decolonisation in the British Empire, which began very soon after the end of the war and continued into the 1980s.[50]

As occupied countries, France, Belgium and the Netherlands were cut off wholly from their overseas colonies. In 1942 the Japanese overran a good number of Europe's eastern colonies, which they held for the remainder of the war, including Hong Kong, Macao, Singapore and the Malay Peninsula, Burma, the Philippines and, after a treaty with Vichy France, Cambodia, cutting a swath across southeast Asia.[51] Though their presence seldom improved conditions for the inhabitants, the significance of an Asian force subduing the European imperium was profound. That fact resonated even in areas which did not fall to Japan and where colonial governance was uninterrupted. Nationalists once more extracted guarantees of postwar self-rule.

Loyalties were often strained or unclear during the war. The presence of a pro-Japanese Indian military faction in Burma was a reminder to the British of just how deep resentment against them could run. The Azad Hind Fauj (Indian National Army), led first by Mohan Singh and then Subhas Chandra Bose, fought alongside the Japanese in Burma.[52] Altogether the INA probably numbered no more than 25,000, but its very existence symbolised a growing and radical rejection

---

47 Frances Gouda, 'The Gendered Rhetoric of Colonialism and Anti-Colonialism in Twentieth-Century Indonesia', *Indonesia* 55 (1993): pp. 7–9.

48 Uma Chakravarti, 'Whatever Happened to the Vedic Dasi? Orientalism, Nationalism, and a Script for the Past', in Kumkum Sangari and Sudesh Vaid (eds), *Recasting Women: Essays in Indian Colonial History* (New Delhi, 1989), pp. 27–87; Anirban Das and Ritu Sen Chaudhuri, 'The Desired "One": Thinking the Woman in the Nation', *History Compass* 5 (2007): pp. 1483–99; Tanika Sarkar, *Hindu Wife, Hindu Nation: Community, Religion, and Cultural Nationalism* (London, 2001).

49 www.h-net.org/~diplo/roundtables/PDF/Thomas-FrenchEmpire.pdf, accessed 28 May 2010.

50 R.T. Kerslake, *Time and the Hour: Nigeria, East Africa and the Second World War* (London, 1997).

51 C.A. Bayly and Tim Harper, *Forgotten Armies: The Fall of British Asia, 1941–1945* (Cambridge, MA, 2005).

52 Peter Ward Fay, *The Forgotten Army: India's Armed Struggle for Independence, 1942–1945* (Ann Arbor, MI, 1993). A women's regiment established in 1943 had some 300 members by the end of the year.

of colonialism. Many French African colonies sided with the Vichy regime during the occupation of France, though Cameroon and most of French Equatorial Africa joined de Gaulle and the Free French in their fight against the Axis powers.[53]

As had been the case in 1914–18, many colonial soldiers fought with the Allies. In 1943 many colonial units shifted their alliance to the Free French offering invaluable support; it was troops from Chad who led the critical battles against Italy and Libya at the end of 1943. The Belgians, French and British all employed colonial soldiers in combat and in auxiliary tasks.[54] The colour bar in the British military was suspended for the duration of the war, although non-whites were routinely refused commissions. In the various theatres of war there were Maori and Senegalese soldiers, *askaris* from East Africa, Moroccans and Algerians, Hondurans and South Africans, West Indians and Nepali Gurkhas alongside large contingents from white settler colonies. Merchant ships continued their long tradition of being crewed by colonial seamen. More than 2 million Indians fought in the Middle East, North Africa, Italy, Burma and Malaya, often alongside African soldiers. West Indians staffed prisoner of war camps in the Caribbean. Subjects of the European colonies, in short, served in every theatre of the war.

Yet, as Indian nationalists angrily noted after Britain declared war in 1939, the colonial power entered the war (as it had in 1914) without consultation, and on behalf not only of the metropole but the colonies. That action had spurred indignation in 1914 from Dominion leaders who wanted a greater say in defence decisions. In 1939 the Dominions had the right to determine for themselves whether their armies would participate, but despite the limited power-sharing ushered in by the 1919 and 1935 Government of India Acts, that privilege was not extended to Indian politicians. On the declaration of war, the Congress Party, which had won so decisively in the elections in 1937, resigned *en masse* from the Indian government in protest. In 1942, following the failure of negotiations with the Indian National Congress, the Quit India movement, reviving mass civil disobedience, created havoc for colonial authorities. The nationalist leaders were swiftly jailed and remained incarcerated until the war ended. Their confinement escalated violence in the cities and countryside alike. In the Belgian Congo, a mutiny in 1944 was only one of many anti-colonial protests that constantly erupted throughout the war. In the Middle East, Lebanon declared its independence in 1941, and the French honoured this in 1943. The war, then, in no way put the demands of nationalists in the colonies on hold.

---

53   Ruth Ginio, *French Colonialism Unmasked: The Vichy Years in French West Africa* (Lincoln, NE, 2006); J. Kim Munholland, *Rock of Contention: Free French and Americans at War in New Caledonia, 1940–1945* (New York, 2005).

54   Rita Headrick, 'African Soldiers in World War II', *Armed Forces and Society* 4/3 (1978): pp. 501–526; Michael S. Healy, 'Colour, Climate, and Combat: The Caribbean Regiment in the Second World War', *International History Review* 22/1 (2000): pp. 65–85; Adrienne M. Israel, 'Measuring the War Experience: Ghanaian Soldiers in World War II', *Journal of Modern African Studies* 25/1 (1987): pp. 159–68.

European colonialism took a further bashing when in 1942 the US State Department released an official paper backing independence for colonies under European control. In the early years of the 1940s there was a good deal of anti-colonialism in the higher echelons of the US government which would, after the war, be tempered considerably by Cold War strategies.[55] The actions of the Axis powers as empire-builders did little to enhance the reputation of colonialism. By war's end many factors contributed to a new political climate in which the justifications for colonial control were rapidly shrinking.

The Quickening Pace

With the end of the war in 1945, Europe regained those colonies which the Japanese had occupied since 1942. It was not, in many cases, easy for them to re-establish the level of control they had previously enjoyed. Nationalist fervour had grown and Europe no longer seemed indomitable. The two new super-powers of the US and the Soviet Union both expressed – although did not always pursue – an antagonism to colonialism.

In the years immediately following the war a considerable number of colonies gained independence, the first chapter in the protracted process of decolonisation which proved one of the most characteristic features of the late twentieth century. Indonesia won recognition of its independence from the Netherlands in 1949, and the Philippines from the United States in 1946. France formally recognised independent sovereignty in Laos and Cambodia in 1949. Both remained, however, within the French Union, which gave France a significant say in key political arenas such as the judicial system and finances. The French also maintained military bases there. In Vietnam, French attempts to restore colonial rule in 1946 pitted them against Hồ Chí Minh in what the Vietnamese now call the Anti-French Resistance War (also known as the First Indochina War), which saw the French, though not their American allies, finally ousted in 1954. Despite a serious Malagasy rebellion in 1947, the French held on to Madagascar (*République malagache*) until 1960, using North African regiments to quell the rebellion.[56]

For Britain, the late 1940s brought considerable losses. They gave up the mandate in Transjordan in 1946, and in 1947 rather hastily exited India, leaving behind a divided country and years of bloodshed. The partition of India, in which the northernmost and easternmost territories of British India became the new Muslim nation of Pakistan, would cost thousands of lives and create a tension still extant between India and its new neighbour. Burma and Ceylon (now Sri Lanka) became independent in 1948, also the year in which Israel declared itself a state following terrorist attacks on the mandate authorities by the Zionist Irgun group.

---

55   Wm. Roger Louis, 'American Anti-Colonialism and the Dissolution of the British Empire', *International Affairs* 61/3 (1985): pp. 395–420.

56   Eugène-Jean Duval, *La Révolte des sagaies: Madagascar 1947* (Paris, 2002).

Britain had withdrawn from the Palestinian mandate in 1947 and the new United Nations proposed to partition the country into separate Arab and Jewish states. Arab nationalists opposed the plan and civil war erupted. On 14 May, the day before the mandate was due to expire, Israel declared its sovereignty and was immediately attacked by the combined forces of Egypt, Syria, Jordan, Lebanon and Iraq. Like partition in India, this would prove a political trouble-spot with a lengthy history, but one which for strategic reasons it was impossible for the west to ignore.

Malaya also erupted in the closing weeks of 1945. Local unease about Britain's postwar plans for the future were complicated by the perceived Communist threat there. British officials feared losing Malay support in this multi-ethnic region, but in reaching out to native Malays alienated the considerable Straits Chinese population of the area. Communist-organised rural guerilla activity severely disrupted the local economy, and the state of emergency declared in 1948 lasted until 1960. Ultimately successful in its aim of contesting Communism and continuing to keep open the flow of rubber and tin that made this so important a territory, the fight was nonetheless very costly. Independence (but not the end of the emergency) came to the colony in 1957.

What might with hindsight now seem obvious, that the power of European colonialism was unsustainable certainly in its more formal guise, was not always apparent to those invested in the system. Indeed, John Darwin argues that Britain, Belgium, the Netherlands and France sought from the colonies a postwar solution to their damaged economies: for the raw materials colonies offered they 'could be forced to accept payment at below the world price, and in Europe's soft currencies not hard American dollars'.[57] The plan was to continue a policy of expropriation and exploitation for the benefit of the home country. Such an explanation helps make sense of the protracted, costly and bloody struggles of the 1950s and 1960s – in Algeria and Indochina for the French, in Kenya, Cyprus and Malaya for the British, and in Angola, Mozambique and Guinea for the Portuguese. Ultimately, and in every case, the colonial power withdrew but not without significant costs, both human and economic. The French, in particular, embroiled first in Indochina (1945–54) and then in Algeria (1954–62) were at war in their colonies for almost twenty years after the close of the Second World War.[58] These were lengthy and bitter wars, and in both instances the French ultimately withdrew, although in

---

57   John Darwin, *After Tamerlane: The Rise and Fall of Global Empires, 1400–2000* (Harmondsworth, 2008), p. 436.

58   Martin Evans, *The Memory of Resistance: French Opposition to the Algerian War (1954–1962)* (Oxford, 1997); Ellen Hammer, *The Struggle for Indochina* (Stanford, CA, 1954); Mohammed Harbi and Benjamin Stora, *La Guerre d'Algérie* (Paris, 2005); Alistair Horne, *A Savage War of Peace: Algeria 1954–1962* (London: Macmillan, 1977); Todd Shepard, *The Invention of Decolonization: The Algerian War and the Remaking of France* (Ithaca, NY, 2006); Maurice Vaïsse, *L'Armée française dans la guerre d'Indochine, 1946–1954: Adaptation ou inadaptation* (Paris, 2000). For an economic explanation of French colonialism, see Jacques Marseille, *L'Âge d'or de la France coloniale* (Paris, 1986); Marseille, *Empire colonial et capitalisme français: histoire d'un divorce* (Paris, 1989).

Vietnam they were replaced by the United States bent on curbing the influence of Communism in Southeast Asia.

The second phase of the decolonisation process began in 1954 when Kwame Nkrumah, the West African leader of the Gold Coast nationalist movement, issued his stirring 'Declaration to the Colonial Peoples of the World'. Three years later the Gold Coast was the first British African colony to win independence as Ghana, after which a steady stream of new nations carved from former colonial territories emerged virtually annually in the late 1950s and 1960s. These were also the years in which the Cold War was at its height, producing the McCarthy trials in the United States, the Korean War (1950–53) and the Cuban missile crisis (1962). The 1960s also saw Britain's first unsuccessful attempt to join the European Economic Community, a move suggesting that it recognised the weakening of its colonial economic ties and was seeking different markets and new partners. In 1951 Britain's oil refinery in Iran was nationalised, but without UN and US support – neither of which was forthcoming – there was little that could be done. More was at stake than just money. The capacity of Muhammad Musaddiq, the Iranian Prime Minister, to expel the British indicated their weakened hold on an area in which they had previously exercised considerable control.

The year after the refinery incident, a nationalist revolution brought Gamal Abdel Nasser to power in Egypt. Within three years his military alliance with the Soviet bloc made the region a key focus of Cold War anxieties, and Nasser actively promoted Arab nationalist politics in the region. Though Iraq had been nominally independent since the expiration of the League of Nations mandate in 1932, with Nasser's backing a republican coup in 1958 overthrew the Hāshimite monarchy favoured (indeed installed) by the British. Coming on top of Britain's international humiliation at Suez in 1956, this made it clear that colonialism in the region was under fire. The failure of Britain's assault on Egypt in 1956, in the wake of the nationalisation of the Suez Canal, demonstrated Britain's reduced global and imperial power; the debacle at Suez made abundantly clear that Britain was no longer able to take unilateral action without the support of the US.[59] The French had withdrawn from Syria during the war and from Lebanon in 1946; with the diminishing British influence of the 1950s, the Middle East entered a radically new phase in its political history, bolstered, of course, by the promise of oil.

The Middle East was not the only region where this new phase of decolonisation would have a profound effect. The year after Nkrumah's Declaration, the Bandung conference brought together newly independent African and Asian countries to promote cooperation.[60] The participants issued a ringing condemnation of

---

59   Anthony Gorst, *The Suez Crisis* (London, 1997); Jonathan Pearson, *Sir Anthony Eden and the Suez Crisis: Reluctant Gamble* (New York, 2003); Simon C. Smith, *Reassessing Suez 1956* (Farnham, 2008).

60   Odette Guitard, *Bandoung et le réveil des peuples colonisés* (Paris, 1976); I. Kovalenko, 'Bandung: Past and Present', *Far Eastern Affairs* 3 (1980): pp. 17–28; Christopher J. Lee (ed.), *Making a World after Empire: The Bandung Moment and its Political Afterlives* (Athens, OH, 2010); J.A.C. Mackie, *Bandung 1955: Non-Alignment and Afro-Asian*

colonialism but not of Communism, a significant absence in this era of heightened political tension between the US and the USSR. As Roger Louis has noted, 'in the American mind anti-Communism always prevailed over anti-imperialism'.[61] Thus the Americans, had, for example, prevented the Dutch from re-imposing colonial rule in Indonesia, believing that the nationalist leadership did not embrace Communism. Sukarno moved increasingly into the Soviet ambit in the 1950s, when the US aided groups trying to oust him, but in 1949 he was still favoured. (It was, of course, also Sukarno who hosted the Bandung conference, increasingly confident of his power in the new anti-colonial world.)

The Europeans faced as many challenges to their overseas rule in Africa in 1950s as they did in Asia and the Middle East.[62] Independence came to the Sudan and to Morocco and Tunisia in 1956, and the floodgates opened in sub-Saharan Africa with Ghana's independence in 1957. But it was 1960 that would prove a landmark year. The UN – following the lead of Nkrumah and Bandung – passed a 'Declaration on the Granting of Independence to Colonial Countries and People'. Sixteen newly independent African nations became members of the organisation. Both the Belgians and the French chose in that same year to withdraw from Africa, the Belgians from the Congo, and the French from West and Central Africa.[63] This left the British and the Portuguese as the two principal powers in Africa. Britain speeded up the process of withdrawal in many of its colonies. In an attempt to hold on to Kenya, where there were almost 70,000 white settlers mostly of British origin, the British offered concessions to the nationalists in order to end the Mau Mau uprising (1952–60), which had cost thousands of pounds and thousands of lives, and which had sullied Britain's reputation as a rational and reasonable power.[64]

Solidarity (Singapore, 2005); see Seng Tan and Amitav Acharya (eds), *Bandung Revisited: The Legacy of the 1955 Asian-African Conference for International Order* (Singapore, 2008); Nicholas Tarling, '"Ah-Ah": Britain and the Bandung Conference of 1955', *Journal of Southeast Asian Studies* 23/1 (1992): pp. 74–111.

61   Wm. Roger Louis, 'The Dissolution of the British Empire', in Brown and Louis, *Oxford History of the British Empire: The Twentieth Century*, p. 330.

62   On the activities of women in these struggles, see for example, Susan Geiger, *TANU Women: Gender and Culture in the Making of Tanganyikan Nationalism, 1955–1965* (Portsmouth, NH, 1997); Nina Emma Mba, *Nigerian Women Mobilized: Women's Political Activity in Southern Nigeria, 1900–1965* (Berkeley, CA, 1982); Josephine Nhongo-Simbanegavi, *For Better or Worse? Women and ZANLA in Zimbabwe's Liberation Struggle* (Harare, 2000).

63   Tony Chafer, *The End of Empire in French West Africa: France's Successful Decolonization?* (Oxford, 2002); Frederick Cooper, *Decolonization and African Society: The Labor Question in French and British Africa* (Cambridge, 1996).

64   S.M. Shamsul Alam, *Rethinking the Mau Mau in Colonial Kenya* (New York, 2007); David Anderson, *Histories of the Hanged: The Dirty War in Kenya and the End of Empire* (New York, 2005); Daniel Branch, *Defeating Mau Mau, Creating Kenya: Counterinsurgency, Civil War, and Decolonization* (Cambridge, 2009); Caroline Elkins, *Imperial Reckoning: The Untold Story of Britain's Gulag in Kenya* (New York, 2005); E.S. Atieno Odhiambo and John Lonsdale (eds), *Mau Mau and Nationhood: Ams, Authority & Narration* (Athens, OH, 2003).

Incarceration, forced repatriation, the uprooting of communities and torture were widespread and more than a thousand Kenyans were executed, more than double the number executed by the French in the Algerian War.[65] Yet independence would follow in 1963, and was preceded in British Africa by Nigeria (1960), Tanganyika and Sierra Leone (1961) and Uganda (1962).

The Portuguese left Goa in 1961, but held on to their African territories. In that same year the Angolan War of Independence against their rule flared. It would end only when a coup in 1974 forced a change in leadership in Portugal.[66] One of the smallest of the modern empires was, thus, the last with major African territory. With the exception of Portuguese Angola and Guinea-Bissau, what was left of European colonialism by the mid-1960s was overwhelmingly British, and with every year British overseas holdings diminished.[67]

Caribbean independence began with Jamaica and Trinidad/Tobago in 1962, although many of the West Indian islands became independent only in the 1980s. Throughout the 1960s and 1970s there were very few years in which a handful of former British colonies did not establish their sovereignty; in many instances the transition was relatively peaceful and uneventful, in others Britain was responding to increasingly vociferous and sometimes violent demands. Britain faced an odd situation in southern Africa in 1965 when white settlers declared their independence from Britain, fearful of a majority black rule that they felt would disadvantage them. The pace of independence slowed considerably in the 1980s but the politics of empire were not over when Margaret Thatcher came to power as Britain's first woman Prime Minister. Four areas would continue to be at issue: Northern Ireland, the South Atlantic, Southern Rhodesia and Hong Kong. The future of all but Northern Ireland would be resolved by the time she resigned in 1990, and only the Islas Malvinas (Falkland Islands) would remain in the now tiny British Empire. In 1980 Southern Rhodesia became independent as Zimbabwe, and in 1984 Britain agreed to abide by the terms of the 99-year lease of Hong Kong and to return the colony to China in 1997. Three years after Thatcher came to power, and only a few months after the withdrawal of the naval garrison stationed on the remote Falkland Islands in the South Atlantic, the British sent a fleet to protect British rights there when the Argentinians, who had long sought possession, invaded. Britain shifted rapidly from regarding the islands as an unnecessary expense at a time of rigorous cost-cutting to a willingness to deploy considerable troops to defend this tiny bastion of European colonialism. The British naval presence was quickly restored and the islands remain British overseas territory even into the second decade of the twenty-first century.

The situation in Ireland proved the most intractable of these final few imperial issues, for there was a vocal and militant pro-British lobby in Northern Ireland as

---

65 Anderson, *Histories of the Hanged*, p. 7.
66 Norrie Macqueen, *The Decolonization of Portuguese Africa: Metropolitan Revolution and the Dissolution of Empire* (London, 1997).
67 For a discussion of French decolonisation, see Robert Aldrich, *The Last Colonies* (Cambridge, 1998).

well as a strong republican tradition. By the late 1960s civil rights had become a major arena of conflict in Northern Ireland and the violence that had scarred the 1920s reappeared, first in Ireland itself and later in England.[68] The British Army, mobilised in 1969, was regarded by the republican movement as an invading army. The Parliament of Northern Ireland was dissolved in 1973 amid rising violence, but finding a solution proved a tough business for many years. Finally in 1998 the Belfast Agreement established a Northern Ireland Assembly with power-sharing between unionists and nationalists. The agreement repealed the 1920 Government of Ireland Act, maintained Northern Ireland as part of the United Kingdom but allowed citizens to choose British, Irish or dual citizenship.

At the start of the twenty-first century a few former colonial powers still have a smattering of overseas dependent territories. Most British overseas territories are in the West Indies, where the French also still retain interests, including French Guiana, Guadeloupe and Martinique. The Dutch territories of Aruba and the Antilles have full internal autonomy, as do the Danish Faroe Islands and Greenland. Australia and New Zealand still administer a few Commonwealth territories in the Pacific where France also retains parts of Polynesia and Melanesia (New Caledonia). The United States claims considerable territory in the Pacific and some, including Puerto Rico, in the Caribbean. Many more previously colonised areas remain dependent on western aid, and a good deal of contemporary political debate turns on the idea especially of a US neo-imperialism.[69] An equal amount of debate has been generated over the benefits or ills of the colonial period, and whether some colonial powers acted more responsibly than others. The continued and striking inequality between those parts of Europe which spearheaded the modern era of colonialism (and which continue to enjoy considerable prosperity for the most part) and the struggles which largely characterise former dependencies are a key index of that assessment: few former colonies, and most especially those where there was no significant white settler presence, have emerged as economic powerhouses.[70] The legacy of colonial underdevelopment, the disintegration of cultural networks, and divide-and-rule strategies bring alive even now the vivid and complex history of European colonialism whether in the form of railways, manufacturing plants and modern cities, on the one hand, or the continued poverty and inequality which continues to mark those countries which experienced the exigencies of the European colonial years.

This long and chaotic history of new sovereignty and the loss of colonial power demonstrates the essential incoherence of decolonisation. In the decades after the First World War, the European powers were at best ambivalent about their colonial interests, at times seeing them as an economic panacea for the depredations of war, at times moving, albeit far from systematically, between

---

68   Irish militants operated a 'hands-off' policy in Scotland and Wales, and their bombing campaign was waged only in England.
69   See Mary Renda in this volume.
70   There are, of course, exceptions such as Singapore and Hong Kong.

seeing decolonisation as inevitable or colonial rule as worth fighting for. One thing, though, was certain: the distinctive era of European imperialism was essentially over by the last quarter of the twentieth century.

PART II
Spaces

Late Imperial China (c. 1500–1911)

Peter C. Perdue

The late Chinese imperial era comprised two empires, the Ming (1368–1644) and Qing (1644 –1911), which together lasted over five hundred years. These imperial formations were only the last two of a series of dynasties beginning with the first emperor of the Qin dynasty in the third century BCE. Chinese historians have described a continuous imperial tradition going back even further to prehistoric and mythical times, by producing 26 official histories establishing a continuous lineage of orthodox structures of imperial rule. Modern historians have questioned the adequacy of this stereotyped scheme, but it still persists strongly in Chinese understanding of imperial history.[1] The Republic of China wrote a draft history of the Qing dynasty, and in 2002 the government of the People's Republic of China launched a very large-scale project to write another official history of the Qing. Although the PRC calls itself a nation-state, not an empire, it still relies heavily on the invocation of the imperial legacy.

Many Chinese and western historians have tried to free themselves from the straitjacket of the official dynastic histories by investigating new periodisations and new themes of research. Although the ruling political structures changed at the points of dynastic transition in 1368 and 1644, social and economic processes often followed different tempos, and many regions of the empire did not change at the same rate as the centre. Furthermore, the Qing imperial realm was much larger than the Ming, so those regions beyond Ming rule had substantially different orientations during the fourteenth to eighteenth centuries until Qing armies conquered them. This volume begins in the sixteenth century because of its focus on the modern. A significant transformation also took place in China at this time, when the Ming Empire became part of the global economy. After a brief introduction to Ming structures of rule in the fifteenth century, I will therefore concentrate here on the sixteenth to nineteenth centuries.[2]

---

1   On the modern historiography of China, see Paul A. Cohen, *Discovering History in China: American Historical Writing on the Recent Chinese Past* (New York, 1984); Prasenjit Duara, *Rescuing History from the Nation: Questioning Narratives of Modern China* (Chicago, IL, 1995).

2   For a general overview of this period, see Jonathan D. Spence, *The Search for Modern China* (New York, 1999).

Structures of the Ming State

The Ming dynasty ruled a territory of nearly 4 million square kilometres, corresponding closely to what we now call China Proper, or the 'Inner Territories' (*neidi*), occupied almost exclusively by ethnically Han Chinese.[3] Since the Ming was a native Han-ruled dynasty, like its predecessors the Song of the tenth to thirteenth centuries, it never controlled the nomadic pastoral regions (see Map 5.1). Its geography was extraordinarily diverse and its population huge, amounting to 60 million at its beginning and reaching up to 150 million people at its peak in the sixteenth century. It was by far the largest political unit on the planet in 1500.

Eight large 'physiographic macroregions' formed the economic geography of the empire. Two of these, the core regions of Jiangnan (the lower Yangzi river valley) and north China, undergirded the Ming state. Each of them contained an imperial capital. The first emperor of the Ming dynasty, Zhu Yuanzhang (also known as Ming Taizu) (r. 1368–98) began life in a poor peasant family in south China, spent time as a beggar and Buddhist monk, and joined one of many rebel armies that drove out the remnant Mongols of the Yuan dynasty in the late fourteenth century. He founded his new capital in Nanjing ('Southern Capital') near his home town. Zhu Yunwen, or the Yongle Emperor (r. 1402–1424), overthrew his nephew, the weak successor to Taizu, and crowned himself the third ruler of the Ming in 1402. This emperor was a prince from northwestern China who conducted aggressive campaigns against the Mongolian pastoralists and founded the dynasty's second capital in Beijing ('Northern Capital'). The dynasty continued to have two capitals until its end, but Beijing rose to become the primary political centre.

The two capital regions accumulated more wealth and political power than the other six. In the region of Jiangnan, along the Lower Yangzi River, Nanjing and other nearby cities, with their hinterlands, provided most of the agrarian and commercial wealth of the empire. The rich rice paddy fields produced a substantial surplus, enough to support farming households, urban populations, officials and soldiers at a reasonably comfortable standard of living. North China, a dry-field area, grew mainly millet, wheat and sorghum, and its population suffered frequent droughts and floods. Northwest China was even poorer and more arid. The Middle and Upper basins of the Yangzi River held much sparser populations living along banks of the tributaries, while non-Han populations occupied the hills. Further south, around the delta of the Pearl River, a dense lowland population produced several crops per year in a subtropical environment, but malaria and uninhabitable marshlands limited their development. Along the southeast coast, Chinese farmers occupied small scraps of land and attempted to clear fields in the remote hill

---

3   For a succinct summary of Ming administration, see Charles O. Hucker, *The Traditional Chinese State in Ming Times (1368–1644)* (Tucson, AZ, 1961). There are extensive details in Frederick Mote and Denis Twitchett (eds), *The Cambridge History of China*, vol. 7: *The Ming Dynasty, 1368–1644*, part 1 (Cambridge, 1988); Denis Twitchett and Frederick W. Mote (eds), *The Cambridge History of China*, vol. 8: *The Ming Dynasty, 1368–1644*, part 2 (Cambridge, 1998).

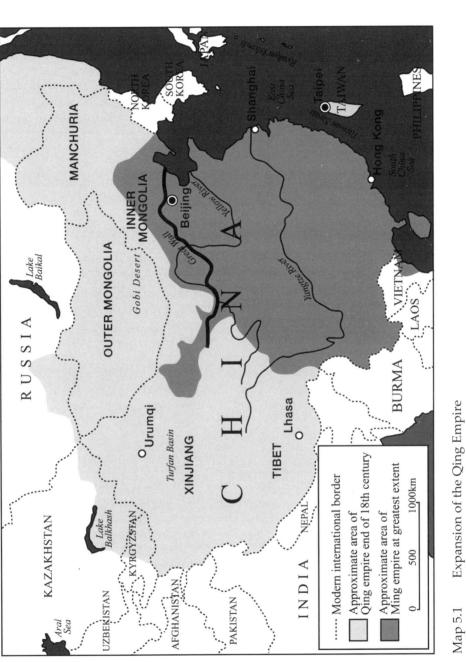

Map 5.1   Expansion of the Qing Empire

country, but many others headed out to sea to settle Southeast Asia, while keeping contact with their homelands. The eighth region, the plateau of Guizhou and Yunnan, mainly a non-Han hill population, did not come under Ming control until the late sixteenth century, and only after a series of bloody campaigns.

The Ming rulers, following the Yuan model, divided the empire into fifteen provinces, each ruled by a provincial governor. Below the provinces were about 150 prefectures, and under the prefectures were about 1,500 counties or districts, each under a district magistrate. China had the oldest bureaucracy in the world, but the entire salaried officialdom numbered at its maximum only 24,000, including capital and military officials. It was very a small number for such a large population. The rulers limited the size of the bureaucracy in order to avoid the need to increase tax burdens and to limit its independence from the centre.

The military had a separate structure from the civil administration, but the provincial governors controlled both military and civil officials. (The Qing added the rank of governor-general, who also combined military and civil functions in several provinces.) Ming rulers assigned a small percentage of the population to hereditary military households, whose male members owed lifetime military service. They spent their lives in far-flung garrisons on defensive duty or in military campaigns on the edges of the empire. They were also called on to repress local uprisings, combining the functions of imperial defence and policing. For such a large population, again, the military was initially rather small, numbering only about one million, rising to four million in the late Ming. The Qing conquerors, who had partly nomadic origins, added a second military organisation, the banners, to this classically Han Chinese military administration.

At the centre, the emperors surrounded themselves with non-bureaucratic associates, a dependent class of servitors, many of whom were eunuchs. In addition, members of the imperial clan grew to become a large group dependent on stipends from the state. The tension between this 'inner court' of imperial dependents and the 'outer court' of bureaucratic officials marked much of the politics of the Ming and Qing empires.

The bureaucrats attained their positions by achieving top marks in a gruelling series of examinations, designed to select the elite of society in meritocratic fashion. In principle, access to power was open to any male adult regardless of family connections or wealth. In practice, since there was no national education system, it took support from private funds to hire the tutors who taught the principles of the Chinese classics. On the other hand, promising young men received fellowships from their lineages and wealthy patrons to support their studies. There were three basic levels of examinations, from the district to provincial to metropolitan. Every year, hundreds of thousands of aspiring students took the lowest-level examinations to qualify for the provincial examinations. One could also purchase the lowest-level degree. About 4,000 scholars in each province then competed for 25 to 50 degrees every three years. Attaining this rank gave one considerable local status, but did not qualify the degree holder for a post. Only the several hundred top degree holders, including those who passed the metropolitan examination in Beijing and some others, had any chance of getting an official position. The vast majority of degree holders never held any official posts, but they could keep taking examinations for decades in the hopes of attaining higher degrees.

The examination system had been the predominant method of selecting officials since the tenth century; the Yuan abolished it, but later restored it. The Ming had removed the hereditary privileges that dominated the Song system, making it more meritocratic, but wealth still retained some privileges. By late Ming times, mobility in and out of the official positions was quite high, although attaining a post was no guarantee of passing it on to the next generation. Still, the combination of high competition, the potential to rise from poverty to a high official post, partial subsidies from relatives and the prestige of scholarship made the imperial examination system an extremely effective tool of imperial integration.

Even those degree holders without official posts retained considerable prestige in their local communities. As local 'gentry', they performed some functions analogous to English local elites, although they did not formally judge legal cases or ride horses around their estates. The itinerant district magistrate, who stayed in one post for about three to five years, was the only salaried official in charge of over 300,000 people. He could not rule effectively without gentry assistance. Some of the gentry were aspiring scholars who continued to study for higher-level degrees; some were merchants who had purchased lower-level degrees; some were retired officials returning home, or officials on leave to conduct mourning rituals for their families. All of them shared a common interest in maintaining a social order that preserved their positions: they would help the official track down thieves, bandits or unruly peasants who resisted tax and rent payments; they might help prosecute heterodox religious believers or drive out foreign intruders; they would also contribute to charities and famine relief campaigns. On the other hand, they concealed much of their landholding from the state, dodged tax payments and corvée labour services wherever possible and pursued the interests of their families by currying favour with whomever they knew. The wise local official knew that he should not prosecute miscreants from prominent families of the locality, while even the most upright official could do little about the miseries inflicted on commoners by abusive gentry.

Some parts of the empire lay beyond the civil administration. In the southwest, especially, the Ming delegated authority to local chieftains of the hill tribes, in the interests of convenience. Most of this poor and remote region had few Han settlers, and there was no need to intervene extensively. The local people could settle their disputes according to customary law, and they only needed to provide stipulated amounts of tax and corvée service. On the northwest borders, military garrisons created military farms under their own administrative structure to support themselves while conducting static defence.

Fiscal Structures

The first Ming emperor distrusted and detested the wealthy elites. He confiscated much of their property, deported them to Nanjing to build his capital and imposed extra burdens on the rich properties of the lower Yangzi. The fiscal system reflected his vision of an idealised agrarian economy based on self-sufficient villages. The land tax, paid in kind in grain or cloth by peasant farmers, was the dominant support of the imperial structure. Farmers also owed corvée labour services to build public works or support the military. In principle, every peasant household should hold sufficient land to support itself and pay the exactions required by the state. Tenant farmers and the landless paid no taxes. No one should need to leave his home village; trade was discouraged, and stability had the highest value. The emperor's static vision echoed the ideals of classical texts, and he was able to pronounce in his Grand Declaration, a major statement of the principles of his rule, issued in 1385, the realisation of the Golden Age.

But even the autocratic emperor could not prevent social change. Song and Yuan China had already developed a high degree of commercial activity, including mobility and large cities. The turmoil of the dynastic transition disrupted trade, but by the sixteenth century parts of China had become a dynamic, mobile, cash-rich society based as much on the pursuit of monetary profit as on stable agriculture.

The fiscal system was not designed for this kind of society. Tax revenues did not go to one central place, and there was no central budget. Instead, individual tax items, paid in dribs and drabs throughout the year, were allocated to individual expense throughout the empire. The fiscal system, a 'telephone switchboard without an operator', in the words of Ray Huang, was a marvellously complex engineered structure, utterly inadequate to the needs of a changing society.[4] The transformation of this structure from the sixteenth to the end of the eighteenth centuries was a remarkable feat. From a decentralised, unmonetised, tangled and unsystematised assortment of separate levies, it gradually turned into a mainly monetised set of regular payments under local official control. This transformation, known as the Single Whip Reform, was one of the few reform efforts in China conducted almost entirely from the bottom up, as many local officials enacted gradual changes which the centre later approved. They consolidated the local levies, turned grain and corvée levies into cash equivalents, collected them twice a year and attempted, with mixed success, to uncover concealed landholdings and tax inequalities. The Qing dynasty built on the achievements of these Ming officials and systematised collection even further. Although undramatic and inconspicuous, this fiscal reform formed the keystone that ensured the survival of the imperial regime until the twentieth century.

---

4   Ray Huang, *Taxation and Governmental Finance in Sixteenth Century Ming China* (Cambridge, 1974).

Imperial Autocracy?

The first emperor led the armies that overthrew the last of the Yuan dynasty rulers. Primarily a military leader, he had little use for the carefully balanced structure of the Chinese bureaucracy. Since the Song dynasty, civil officials had run the administrative machinery based on legal codes and precedent, and on philosophical principles derived from Confucian texts. At the top of the apparatus, emperors in principle had complete power, but in the Song they consulted with a council chaired by a Prime Minister, and in fact ruled by consensus or passivity. The first Ming emperor abolished the Prime Minister's post, and replaced him with a weaker Grand Secretary, resolving to give commands directly to all of his subordinates.

Some scholars have described the Ming as the most 'despotic' dynasty because of this act.[5] But, even without a Prime Minister, the bureaucracy operated much as it did before. Later emperors did not have nearly as much personal dynamism or resentment of the bureaucrats. Most of their actions were controlled by the dictates of ritual observance. In the mid-fifteenth century, when Mongols captured the emperor after a bungled expedition, the officials in the capital put a replacement on the throne and carried on business as usual until his return four years later. By the mid-sixteenth century, when the Wanli emperor (r. 1573–1620) had retired to his palace, refusing to appoint officials or approve documents handed to him, the Grand Secretary in effect ran the government.[6] The Ming dynasty lasted for nearly three hundred years not because of autocratic rulership, but because of the routine activities of thousands of dedicated civil servants.

Local Government

At the local level, one district magistrate ruled each county, with a small staff of salaried officials. He had no regular police force. He was the sole judicial official. Military forces under the control of provincial officials had garrisons in some counties in strategic regions, but few forces in the typical county. The crucial element in ensuring stability were the local literati, often called 'gentry'. These men had obtained degrees in the examination system, and either stayed in their home areas as teachers and landowners, or retired there after an official career. Unlike the magistrates, who rotated positions every few years, the local literati stayed put and knew the local dialect and local news. Every magistrate relied heavily on them to facilitate his administration. They had some fiscal and legal privileges, such as immunity from corporal punishment and corvée, but in principle they paid taxes

---

5   Frederick Mote, 'The Growth of Chinese Despotism: A Critique of Wittfogel's Theory of Oriental Despotism as Applied to China', *Oriens Extremus* 8/1 (1961): pp. 1–41.

6   Ray Huang, *1587: A Year of No Significance* (New Haven, CT, 1981).

like everyone else. Since they could not formally transmit their elite status to their sons and their descendants had to obtain degrees in order to keep their privileges, they thus were not an hereditary nobility in the European sense. And yet the local elites did maintain their power over many generations, and they expanded their authority beyond their formal privileges. Lineages – families sharing a common surname and claiming common descent in genealogies – linked together many elite families in large corporate units. Even if one family's sons did not get high degrees, other members of the lineage would take care of them. Lineages also provided scholarship support for promising young men to study with tutors to train them in the classic texts. China appeared to have a high amount of upward and downward social mobility if we look only at nuclear family units, since many high degree holders did not have sons with equal status. But if we include lineages mobility seemed much less since the same families dominated many localities for generations.

The tenacious hold of lineages on local society limited the authority of officials from the top down. Again, in practice, Ming and Qing China were much less autocratic than they appeared. Elite lineages had extensive land holdings, invested in trade and cultivated patronage networks with other lineages and influential powerholders in the capital. They kept their taxes low by concealing land from the state, by bribing local clerks and by manipulating exchanges of grain for silver. They could also offer tax shelters to other landholders, protecting their lands from confiscation in return for personal services. Many smallholding farmers, on the other hand, had little independence socially or economically from the dominant lineages. In lawsuits, they could not get equal justice, since the magistrate would generally follow the preferences of the dominant elites. In this sense, the local elites did resemble British gentry, since they enjoyed relatively permanent judicial and economic privileges, and controlled local justice and local society in collaboration with the local official.[7]

Buddhist institutions also had significant local power in some parts of the empire. The Chinese mixed together many religious beliefs and practices in daily life. Buddhists in monasteries were only a small part of the population, but monasteries had extensive landholdings, especially in southeast China. Monasteries had to register with the state, but they kept much of their administration beyond local control. Still, they never controlled large landed properties on the scale of the clergy in Europe.[8]

---

7   Michael Szonyi, *Practicing Kinship: Lineage and Descent in Late Imperial China* (Stanford, CA, 2002).

8   Timothy Brook, *Praying for Power: Buddhism and the Formation of Gentry Society in Late-Ming China* (Cambridge, MA, 1993).

Commercialisation, Social Change and Military Defence

The first Ming emperor had attempted to impose an agrarian ideal on a society that contained the largest cities in the world. The chaotic destruction following the collapse of the Yuan made some of his policies possible, but domestic and foreign commerce eventually revived. The government had banned nearly all foreign trade in the fifteenth century, but China's position in a world of actively competing commercial states made this policy untenable in the sixteenth century. All across maritime Southeast and East Asia a variety of traders and state representatives tried to gain access to China's markets, and many Chinese on the coast also longed for the profits from trade. These Chinese and their counterparts from Malaya, Java and Japan joined oceangoing ships and raided the coast, smuggled goods and bought off compliant local officials. The Ming government, giving these traders the misleading name of 'dwarf [Japanese] pirates' attempted to suppress the trade, without success. Only in 1567, when a new emperor less hostile to foreigners came to power and pragmatic officials negotiated the reopening of China's ports, did the pirate menace abate.

At approximately the same time, the Ming attempted a similar policy of sealing off the northwestern frontier. Here, it had somewhat greater success. Mongols had repeatedly raided the northwestern frontier, but the raids generally came only after Ming officials refused repeated requests for trade. The Mongols wanted China's luxury manufactured goods in exchange for horses, sheep and animal products. Again, it was the Ming trade ban that caused the raids, and military efforts to drive out the Mongols repeatedly failed. Finally, in the 1570s, the emperor allowed the 'surrender' of Altan Khan, the Mongol leader, offering him access to trade along the frontier. Mongols then competed for trading licences from the Ming, and the threat of raids decreased somewhat. At the same time, however, the Ming undertook the renovation and completion of their massive defence bulwark, the Great Wall. They joined together pieces of old walls, added signal towers and garrison forts and invested heavily in support of military garrisons along the frontier. But these forces also needed to be fed and clothed and paid in silver. The construction of the Great Wall thus depended heavily on the domestic commercial economy of the core of Ming China.[9]

On both its northwestern and southeastern frontiers, the Ming dynasty adopted a defensive stance, allowing limited amounts of trade under official supervision, in order to keep foreigners from penetrating deeply into the interior. But even under these constraints Ming China, through its commercial links in Central Eurasia and the southern seas, tied itself inextricably to a global economy. As commerce expanded throughout the world in the sixteenth century, Ming China became the world's richest source of luxury consumer goods and the greatest attractor of silver bullion.

---

9   Arthur Waldron, *The Great Wall of China: From History to Myth* (Cambridge, 1990); Peter C. Perdue, 'Commerce and Coercion on Two Chinese Frontiers', in Nicola Di Cosmo (ed.), *Military Culture in China* (Cambridge, MA, 2009), pp. 317–38.

The main forces promoting the revival of commerce everywhere were population growth and contacts with the New World. In China, the population grew steadily, reaching a peak of 100 to 150 million by the late sixteenth century. (We do not know the exact number, because the fiscal system did not count individual taxpayers accurately.) The growing population generated a larger demand for basic subsistence goods, but also for new consumer items like silk clothing, jade, inkstones, gardens and tobacco.[10] Conservatives denounced the decline of the simpler ways of the past, but the pressure of fashion in urban centres was irresistible. Farmers learnt that specialising in products for urban markets would earn them more profits, so different regions of the country focused on specific crops, exchanging them for cash in order to buy supplies for daily needs. The growing division of labour in the countryside meant an increased demand for cash currency. The standard copper cash coins, tied together in strings of up to 1,000 coins, served well enough for local needs, but they were too bulky and insecure for long-distance trade. Ming China needed silver, but Chinese mines produced inadequate amounts of precious metal. Fortunately for the Chinese, Japan became a large exporter of silver during the late sixteenth century, exporting from 40,000 to 100,000 kilograms per year over the last half of the century in return for Chinese raw silk, porcelain and textiles. Japanese supplies, however, ran out in the early seventeenth century when the Tokugawa regime imposed a ban on currency exports.

The Portuguese arrived on the southeast coast of China with their armed ships just as the Ming were fighting the coastal pirates. In return for aid in suppressing piracy, the Portuguese were granted a lease of the island of Macao in 1557. After the Spanish arrived in the Philippines in 1521, Chinese merchants eager to open trade soon followed them. The silver mines in Bolivia opened in the 1570s. Soon a river of silver flowed from the mines of Bolivia and later Mexico across the Pacific through the Philippines and Macao into China, providing the essential fuel for the commercialising economy. The Chinese exported their classic products of tea, silk and porcelain in exchange for silver. The silver circulated generally in unminted form, valued by its weight and fineness. With silver, merchants could carry supplies from one large city to another to serve the growing urban demand for luxury products from distant regions. The drive for profit by merchants and the drive for luxuries supported each other. The conservative scholar Zhang Han denounced the pervasiveness of the profit motive strikingly reminiscent of a modern capitalist society:

> Human disposition is such that people pursue what is profitable to them, and with profit in mind they will go up against disaster. They gallop in pursuit of it day and night, never satisfied with what they have, though it wears down their spirits and exhausts them physically. Since profit is what all people covet, they rush after it like torrents pouring into a valley: coming and going without end, never resting

---

10   Timothy Brook, *The Confusions of Pleasure: Commerce and Culture in Ming China* (Berkeley, CA, 1998); Craig Clunas, *Superfluous Things: Material Culture and Social Status in Early Modern China* (Urbana, IL, 1991).

day or night, never reaching the point at which the raging floods within them subside.[11]

The imperial officials faced these economic changes with ambivalent attitudes. In principle, they regarded commerce as a disruptive and morally suspect activity, which would encourage selfishness, stimulate mobility and undermine the ideal self-sufficient village structure. But they also believed that the purpose of government was to ensure prosperity for the people, and recognised that the new commerce was definitely raising living standards. They themselves, as gentry landlords, profited from the new opportunities for trade, and many collaborated with merchants in lucrative joint ventures. As noted above, the gradual transformation of the imperial fiscal system also responded to the increasing prevalence of silver, and imposing taxes in silver forced even more taxpayers into the market. The government had to accommodate and promote economic change in its own interest.

Use of the Grand Canal, the major transportation artery linking north and south China, also responded to the new market growth. Originally built in the seventh century CE, the Grand Canal had served as a vital source of grain for the population of the capital cities of north China. The Ming developed the Grand Canal into a very large military logistical operation, supporting the movement of thousands of barges escorted by soldiers carrying tons of grain from the productive south to support the soldiers and officials of Beijing.[12] One barge could carry 30,000 kilograms of grain. But the Canal also served private merchant transport, and the volume of private traffic competed with the military transports. People used the canal for delivering letters, personal travel and shipment of many luxury goods, crowding official transportations. Eventually, the government found it easier to allow merchants to ship much of the grain along with their other goods, as it reduced the dominance of the military over the economy. By the time of the Qing dynasty, the Canal had been transformed from a military supply route to a private trade route.

Commercialisation had broader effects beyond economic growth. It also encouraged physical and social mobility, and changed the intellectual culture of the empire. More people travelled than ever before, from large-scale long-distance merchants to local traders. Families could send some of their sons to faraway cities to carry on a branch of the business, and private postal services helped them communicate with each other. Women could break out of the close confines of their homes, particularly to go on pilgrimages to sacred mountains and temples.[13] These pilgrimage sites became major commercial centres in their own right, and along with them there grew inns, travel guides, route books and services to assist the

---

11   Zhang Han (1511–93), in Brook, *Confusions of Pleasure*.
12   Mark Elvin, *The Pattern of the Chinese Past* (Stanford, CA, 1973); Hoshi Ayao, *The Ming Tribute Grain System* (Ann Arbor, MI, 1969).
13   Susan Naquin and Chün-fang Yü (eds), *Pilgrims and Sacred Sites in China* (Berkeley, CA, 1992).

pilgrims. New religious sects with popular leaders also attracted large crowds of believers to particularly renowned sites.

The printing and book publishing industries also flourished in this period, dramatically changing intellectual life. Chinese had pioneered the technology of woodblock printing since the eighth century CE, and there had always been an active market for printed literature to serve the needs of the literati class. Sixteenth-century publishers expanded their markets significantly to meet the demands of newly literate urban populations. They sold not only manuals to prepare for examinations, but almanacs, encyclopaedias, travel guides, erotica, popular religious literature and stories written in the vernacular language. They created elaborate distribution networks to bring cheap editions to the major cities of the empire, and they kept testing the market to find new ways to sell both classical and vernacular texts.[14]

In the higher realms of Confucian classical thought, activist scholars made efforts to connect the ancient texts with popular daily life.[15] Instead of confining scholarship to schools and academies, some scholars gave outdoor lectures to large assemblies. They believed that classical learning should directly affect the practice of daily life. At the same time, academies flourished, gathering students around popular teachers not only to prepare for the examinations but to engage in discussions of current affairs. In this sense, a restricted public sphere grew in the late sixteenth century within the academies, where concerned intellectuals could discuss solutions based on classical learning to critical policy issues.

Policy Questions of the Late Ming

There was no lack of critical questions to discuss. Under the long reign of the Wanli emperor (1573–1620), many of the deep tensions of the imperial regime had grown to crisis proportions. The emperor himself nearly abdicated his role in ruling, secluding himself in his palace and refusing to make major appointments. His main concern was the building of his own tomb, which cost millions of silver taels and diverted large amounts of labour and supplies from the defence of the state. Corruption spread widely through the bureaucracy, but no single group could take charge. The forceful Grand Secretary Zhang Juzheng did make strenuous efforts to crack down on tax evasion and bribery: he carried out the most accurate land survey done in imperial China for several hundred years in order to raise land revenue. But eventually, undermined by opposition and lacking the emperor's support, his efforts generally petered out.

The twelve thousand eunuchs in the imperial palace formed a powerful faction within the court. They were close to the emperor and his harem of women, so

---

14   Cynthia Joanne Brokaw, *Commerce in Culture: The Sibao Book Trade in the Qing and Republican Periods* (Cambridge, MA, 2007).
15   William Theodore De Bary (ed.), *Self and Society in Ming Thought* (New York, 1970).

they had intimate access to policy discussions, but because they did not obtain examination degrees the literati detested them. Eunuchs have taken most of the blame for the decline of the Ming in the official sources written by the scholars, but the causes of Ming decline are more complex. Eunuchs did impose extra burdens on certain regions of the empire, when they demanded precious jewels from one site for the emperor's household, for example, and many of them were corrupt. But literate officials could be equally corrupt and demanding. The structural deficiencies of the Ming rather than particular personalities accounted for the fundamental difficulties of the end of the empire.[16]

A conflict between gentry leaders in the academies and eunuchs in the inner court brought about near paralysis of the Ming government in the early seventeenth century. A group of scholars called the Eastern Forest Faction organised themselves to protest against the declining moral character of the government and call for significant reforms, but eunuch leaders repressed their protest brutally. A second, even more activist group of scholars, the Restoration Society, also tried to exert influence on government policy, but they too were repressed. The late emperors of the Ming, caught between powerful interests on different sides, could not exert much influence, and vacillated over critical decisions on military and fiscal policies.

End of the Ming

As court disputes escalated, famine and drought struck northwest China, rebel groups contested imperial control and a new, powerful state formed in the northeast. The poor farmers of the northwest had faced heavy tax levies and poor harvests for many decades, and the unpaid soldiers nearby at the Great Wall deserted their posts. One of these former soldiers, Li Zicheng (c. 1605–45), organised the discontented peasantry of the region, raising a major rebellion that soon took over the provinces of the northwest. In 1644, he captured the capital in Beijing and proclaimed a new dynasty, while the last Ming emperor, Chongzhen, hung himself in the palace compound. In Sichuan, also, another peasant leader, Zhang Xianzhong, organised bands of paramilitary groups to attack local government offices, leading to a collapse of government control.

Famines and epidemics across north China indicated the deep ineffectiveness of local government responses to major calamities. Climatic change, marked by lower global temperatures, reduced agricultural output, while disruptions in the global flow of silver in the early seventeenth century, from both Latin America and Japan, altered the balance of copper and silver currency in China, inflicting heavier burdens on peasants, merchants and urban residents.[17] The Ming intervened in Korea in

---

16   David Robinson, *Bandits, Eunuchs, and the Son of Heaven: Rebellion and the Economy of Violence in Mid-Ming China* (Honolulu, HI, 2001).

17   Jonathan D. Spence and John E. Wills, Jr (eds), *From Ming to Ch'ing: Conquest, Region and Continuity in Seventeenth-Century China* (New Haven, CT, 1979); William S. Atwell,

1592 with a large military force to drive out the Japanese invader, Hideyoshi. They earned the gratitude of the Koreans, but the expedition greatly strained the Ming military budget. Most ominous of all, northeast of the Great Wall, in Manchuria, a series of tribal leaders created a powerful military challenge to the Ming armies.

The Rise of the Manchus

The Mongols had been the primary threat to the Ming frontier ever since its founding, but the Mongols, except for several abortive episodes of centralisation, had remained fragmented. They mounted numerous raids, but never constituted a threat to the empire as a whole. The Manchus had begun as a group of tribes similar to the Mongols, in an equally decentralised society in the forests of the northeast. Then, Nurhaci (1559–1626), the founder of the Manchu state, defeated his fellow tribesmen and made himself the pre-eminent leader of the region. His successor, Hung Taiji (1592–1643), named his people Manchus, declared the new Qing dynasty, and established the banner system, which cut across tribal loyalties and united his subjects in a tightly coordinated military and administrative structure. Chinese settlers in southern Manchuria also submitted to the Manchu banner system in order to escape Ming impositions and benefit from Manchu relief programmes.

By the 1630s, the Manchus had created a powerful military and administrative machine that dominated the northeast, but the logistical support for this new state was precarious. The peasantry of southern Manchuria had only limited supplies for the new troops and officials, and famines threatened the Manchu state. Li Zicheng's capture of Beijing in 1644 gave the Manchus the opportunity they were waiting for. When a Chinese general guarding the pass decided to give them access to the capital, Manchu forces drove out Li Zicheng and established the capital of the Qing dynasty in Beijing. Then they marched south, driving Ming forces beyond the southern frontier. It was on the whole an extraordinarily rapid and unusually disciplined conquest.[18]

The Manchu forces did inflict severe damage on certain areas, most notably in the Yangzhou 'massacre' of 1645. The conquest of this major commercial city was a very disorderly affair, in which defenders of the Ming dynasty, refugees, bandits, opportunists and Manchu troops engaged in a confused melee, leading to many deaths both from battle and disease. At the end of the dynasty, anti-Manchu nationalists revived the memory of the Yangzhou conquest and recast it as evidence

---

'Volcanism and Short-Term Climatic Change in East Asian and World History, c. 1200–1699', *Journal of World History* 12/1 (2001): 29–98.

18   For the general history of this period, see Willard J. Peterson (ed.), *The Cambridge History of China*: vol. 9, *The Ch'ing Empire to 1800*, part 1 (Cambridge, 2002).

of vicious slaughter of Han people by Manchu barbarians, but conditions during the conquest were much more fluid than this myth indicates.[19]

By the end of the seventeenth century, under the vigorous young Kangxi emperor (r. 1662–1722), the Qing rulers had restored order, promoted the revival of agriculture and commerce and proclaimed themselves the legitimate inheritors of the Mandate of Heaven. (In classical Chinese thought, dynasties collapsed because of misrule, and impersonal Heavenly forces caused the mandate for legitimate rule to be transferred to new conquerors.) They had taken over the island of Taiwan from a merchant-pirate who made it the base for raids on the mainland. They left local elites in place with the same privileges, while removing the hated Ming surtaxes and enforcing more equitable tax collection. They did not, however, threaten the landed elite by conducting a thorough land survey, but left most other Ming levies in place. They continued the conversion of tax levies to silver, merging the corvée labour levy with the land tax, and fixing the tax level permanently. They revived the examination system, allowing Ming loyalists to join the new regime. Most scholars and officials, with some misgivings, gladly accepted the chance to renew their careers.

But Qing expansion did not stop with the recovery of Ming territory. Because of their Central Eurasian heritage, the Manchus knew well how to handle nomads and settlers in the steppes and oases. Their greatest rival was the Zunghar confederation led by Galdan (r. 1671–97), a Mongol who returned from seminary in Tibet to create a powerful military and administrative machine that dominated western Mongolia and Xinjiang. The Kangxi emperor was determined to eliminate this challenger; like his counterpart, Peter the Great of Russia, he enjoyed military campaigning and shared the rugged life of his soldiers. He personally led several partially successful campaigns far into Mongolia against Galdan. He succeeded in winning over the eastern Mongols to his side, but he did not destroy the Zunghar state. Galdan's successors continued to exert power over Central Eurasia, leaving a geopolitical challenge for Kangxi's successors.[20]

In the late seventeenth and early eighteenth century, the arrival of Russian forces in eastern Siberia altered the balance of power to the advantage of the Qing. The Russians, led by mobile Cossack forces, extracted furs as tribute from native peoples of the north, and sought markets for them in China. The Qing, for their part, needed to ensure Russian neutrality in their conflict with the Zunghars. These balanced interests produced the first treaties of a Chinese dynasty with a western power, negotiated with the help of Jesuit intermediaries at the border towns of Nerchinsk in 1687 and Kiakhta in 1727. Through several sharp military actions, Qing forces made the Russians destroy several fortresses in the region, in return for offering the Russians opportunities to sell their furs on markets in Beijing.

---

19   Antonia Finnane, *Speaking of Yangzhou: A Chinese City, 1550–1850* (Cambridge, MA, 2004); Lynn A. Struve, *Voices from the Ming-Qing Cataclysm: China in Tigers' Jaws* (New Haven, CT, 1993).

20   Peter C. Perdue, *China Marches West: The Qing Conquest of Central Eurasia* (Cambridge, MA, 2005).

Having neutralised the Russian threat, the Qing rulers could pursue their project of eliminating the Mongolian rival state. The Russians kept their word, refusing desperate Mongol appeals for aid, allowing Qing forces to advance further into Central Eurasia. By the mid-eighteenth century, the Qing took advantage of divisions among the Zunghars to eradicate the state and eliminate the Zunghar people. The conquest of Xinjiang's oases followed soon after. Along with paramount Qing influence in Tibet, the new empire had expanded its territory into vast new regions, larger than any other empire in Asia since the short-lived Yuan dynasty of the thirteenth century. The Qing controlled nearly 12 million square kilometres, three times the size of the Ming, and 20 per cent larger than the modern People's Republic of China.

The growth of the domestic economy supported external expansion.[21] Populations grew nearly everywhere during the eighteenth century, but China grew faster than average, reaching over 300 million by 1800. The availability of newly opened land encouraged settlers to create new families, and crops from the New World like maize, sweet potatoes and tobacco supported farming on steep hillsides. At tens of thousands of rural markets, farmers sold their produce for cash and purchased manufactured goods. The rural markets were connected in an intricate hierarchical system to higher-level markets reaching up to local cities and provincial capitals. Although China was still 80 per cent rural, the elaborate urban hierarchy tied the rural producers to urban dwellers and fostered the growth of commerce. The state in turn tapped the prosperous farmers for its tax revenue. Building on the trends of the sixteenth century, the eighteenth century witnessed even larger-scale mobility and integration. Regions connected by water transport, like the lower Yangzi valley or the Pearl River delta, had the highest levels of integration, but even landlocked provinces of the interior participated in general economic growth. The Qing state stabilised the agrarian system by establishing an empire-wide network of 'evernormal' granaries, which bought grain for storage at harvest time when prices were low and sold grain in the times of dearth in early spring. By timing purchases and sales appropriately, competent local officials kept the granaries stocked and levelled prices so that rural producers and urban consumers faced stable markets.[22] In times of extreme drought or flood, the officials shipped grain along the Grand Canal or major rivers to relieve suffering farmers. By shipping in grain, or encouraging merchants to sell grain, or hiring those who had lost their farms to work on dykes, the Qing state ensured that the poor gained entitlements to relief, preventing them from wandering the roads and becoming beggars or bandits. In the private sector, local elites also sponsored charitable activity, by giving aid to orphans, the widowed, the elderly and the sick. When the Qing relief system worked, the state maintained a huge population at a reasonably

---

21   Susan Naquin and Evelyn Rawski, *Chinese Society in the Eighteenth Century* (New Haven, CT, 1987).
22   Pierre-Étienne Will, R. Bin Wong, et al., *Nourish the People: The State Civilian Granary System in China, 1650–1850* (Ann Arbor, MI, 1991); Pierre-Étienne Will, *Bureaucracy and Famine in Eighteenth-Century China* (Stanford, CA, 1990).

high level of secure subsistence. Economic estimates have shown that in 1800 the standard of living and life expectancy of the average Chinese was roughly equivalent to that of Europe.[23]

This growing commercial economy also needed increased supplies of currency, and China once again obtained its silver from abroad. This time it was the British who supplied the bulk of the silver, when the East India Company arrived in Canton in the early eighteenth century. England's demand for tea skyrocketed in the eighteenth century, and China still held the world's monopoly. Under the Canton system, British and other foreign merchants could only trade in the city of Canton, and the East India Company's monopoly was matched by a monopoly guild of licensed Chinese merchants called the Cohong.[24] Taxes on the trade went directly to the Imperial Household department, serving the emperor's personal needs. The British tried and failed to find a product besides silver that the Chinese would accept in exchange for tea, silk and porcelain. Still, despite the constraints on trade, during the eighteenth century British merchants and their Chinese counterparts profited mutually from trade, as did the emperor himself. The Chinese also exported tea by land to Russia, in exchange for silver and Russian furs. Tea was just as important to the Russians as it was to the British. Revenue from Russian fur exports to China supported an important fraction of the Russian state budget.[25] Tea, China's ancient herbal monopoly, thus linked together the three great empires of the world in a network of profitable exchange.

During this 'flourishing age' of the eighteenth century, however, ominous social tensions increased. The Kangxi emperor had fixed the level of tax collection, arguing that 'wealth should be stored among the people'. He believed that a fixed tax levied in money would encourage farmers to increase their output, sell crops on the market and keep extra income for themselves. The low level of formal levies, however, left local governments underfunded, forcing local officials to add informal levies to the regular collections. These levies could easily balloon out of proportion, encouraging corruption. Kangxi's successor, the Yongzheng emperor (r. 1723–35), tried to solve this problem by giving officials large 'nourishing virtue' bonuses to discourage informal taxation.[26] His solution, however, only had a temporary effect. Canny officials found many ways to gain personal profit under the guise of local administration. A policy to increase famine relief funds by selling examination degrees, for example, allowed a cabal of officials in Gansu to accumulate large amounts of money which never went into the granary system at all. An imperial

---

23 Kenneth Pomeranz, *The Great Divergence: China, Europe, and the Making of the Modern World Economy* (Princeton, NJ, 2000).

24 Michael Greenberg, *British Trade and the Opening of China* (Cambridge, 1951); Paul A. van Dyke, *The Canton Trade: Life and Enterprise on the China Coast, 1700–1845* (Hong Kong, 2005).

25 Clifford M. Foust, *Muscovite and Mandarin: Russia's Trade with China and its Setting, 1727–1805* (Chapel Hill, NC, 1969).

26 Madeleine Zelin, *The Magistrate's Tael: Rationalizing Fiscal Reform in Eighteenth-Century Ch'ing China* (Berkeley, CA, 1984).

investigation uncovered a widespread conspiracy in which hundreds of officials had peculated the funds. At the end of the eighteenth century, the rot continued at the top, when the Qianlong emperor (r. 1736–96) allowed a beautiful young guardsman to take charge of many branches of the bureaucracy. He collected huge amounts from his patronage network, siphoning off a large percentage of the imperial treasury. On the central and local level, the corruption problem derived from structural as well as personal factors. The Qing state by 1800 tried to govern an enormous population with a bureaucracy not much larger than the Ming bureaucracy of the fifteenth century. But China's population had multiplied by five since that time, commercial interests had penetrated the entire society, and the complexity of social transactions far exceeded what officials could directly manage. The state had to subcontract many of its important functions to non-official actors who had interests that might diverge from those of the state itself.

The dilution of the Manchu military regime also undermined the state's direct control. The early Manchu state relied on the powerful bannermen for military and administrative functions. These men acted under tight control from the emperor and his close companions. By the eighteenth century, the banner institutions worked together with the Han Chinese bureaucracy to manage a large administrative machine, very different from the glorious years of the early conquest. One bureaucratic innovation, the Grand Council, gave the emperor close personal contact with his top policy advisors, and a secret palace memorial system provided rapid information from provincial officials.[27] But the sheer volume of traffic in information overwhelmed this system too, turning the emperor himself into a passive ratifier of decisions made by bureaucratic interest groups.

Emperors vainly tried to restore the military virtues of the Manchu elite, by insisting on study of the Manchu language, military drill and large-scale hunts. They also staged lavish imperial tours to demonstrate their power to prosperous southerners. The Qianlong emperor in particular indulged in these large-scale cultural exercises, which exhibited publicly the multiple cultures joined together in the sovereign's person. Mongols, Manchus, Han Chinese, Tibetans and other peoples all participated in these rituals of sovereignty, by accompanying the emperor on his travels to the south and north beyond the Great Wall, and by delivering tribute to his court. One incident from the Yongzheng reign, however, illustrated the nervousness of Qing rulers about their cultural impact on the large Han society beneath them. When an obscure student named Zeng Jing, inspired by early Ming loyalist writings, attacked the Manchus as barbarians who did not deserve imperial power, and proposed a rebellion to a high-ranking Han official, the emperor reacted with paranoid fury. He forced a confession out of Zeng Jing and wrote a vitriolic response, and made his writings required reading in the schools. The Yongzheng emperor could have easily ignored Zeng Jing, but his touchiness

---

27 Beatrice S. Bartlett, *Monarchs and Ministers: The Grand Council in Mid-Ch'ing China, 1723–1820* (Berkeley, CA, 1991).

about this lone critic indicated plausible suspicions of the loyalty of many others in the Han elite towards Manchu culture.[28]

The 'soulstealers' incident of 1768 also revealed substantial Manchu anxieties about the loyalty of their subjects.[29] When rumours spread that rebels were secretly cutting off the queues of some local people, the emperor launched a full-scale investigation. The Manchus had imposed the wearing of the queue on all male Han Chinese in the early years of the conquest, in order to imprint physically their authority on Chinese bodies. Cutting off one's queue was an act of treason. The emperor feared that these queue-cutters planned a major revolt, while many people regarded the loss of one's hair as the loss of one's soul. Although widespread fear swept through the countryside, the Qing dragnet failed to find any genuine queue-cutting rebels. The campaign degenerated into opportunistic scheming by local informers carrying out grudges against their neighbours. The incident demonstrates severe insecurity at the top of the Qing government and the lack of connection between the court and the vast society it ruled.

Other intellectual trends of the period showed, however, deeper signs of collaboration between Han and Manchus, joined to lingering distrust. The Manchus never really 'assimilated' to Han culture, nor did they want to. They kept themselves apart as a conquering minority, but they enjoyed much of the culture of the people they had subdued. Han scholars, for their part, gained greatly from participating in the stable, prosperous order of the Qing. The 'empirical research' and 'statecraft' schools of scholarship turned away from abstract speculation on metaphysics and towards practical policies of improving local administration and a highly scientific philological approach to the classics. These were China's equivalent of Enlightenment reformers, content to work within the privileges granted them by the state.[30]

The great scholarly public works project, the *Complete Records of the Four Treasuries*, gathered thousands of scholars together to produce the most philologically precise editions of tens of thousands of volumes of texts in the classical tradition. It still represents the largest, most accurate study of these texts, a culmination of centuries of accumulated cultural knowledge.[31] At the same time, a Literary Inquisition purged from the canon a limited number of works which implied criticism of Manchu legitimacy.

---

28   Pamela Kyle Crossley, *A Translucent Mirror: History and Identity in Qing Imperial Ideology* (Berkeley, CA, 1999); Mark C. Elliott, *The Manchu Way: The Eight Banners and Ethnic Identity in Late Imperial China* (Stanford, CA, 2001); Michael Chang, *A Court on Horseback: Imperial Touring and the Construction of Qing Rule, 1680–1785* (Cambridge, MA, 2007); Jonathan D. Spence, *Treason by the Book* (New York, 2001); Pamela Kyle Crossley, Helen F. Siu and Donald S. Sutton (eds), *Empire at the Margins: Culture, Ethnicity, and Frontier in Early Modern China* (Berkeley, CA, 2006).

29   Philip A. Kuhn, *Soulstealers: The Chinese Sorcery Scare of 1768* (Cambridge, MA, 1990).

30   Benjamin Elman, *From Philosophy to Philology: Intellectual and Social Aspects of Change in Late Imperial China* (Cambridge, MA, 1984).

31   R. Kent Guy, *The Emperor's Four Treasuries: Scholars and the State in the Late Ch'ien-Lung Era* (Cambridge, MA, 1987).

The greatest vernacular novel in Chinese literature, still a favourite for all Chinese readers, also came from this period. *The Dream of the Red Chamber*, or *Story of the Stone*, by Cao Xueqin, portrays the life of a wealthy family in south China who gained great privilege and wealth as bondservants to the Qing elite.[32] The novel contains detailed discussions of household relations and elegant descriptions of poetry contests and parties, but the most emotionally impressive parts describe the life of a young man, Bao Yu, who is deeply disillusioned about the prospects of an official career. Despite beatings by his father to force him to study, he much prefers the company of young women, and the novel describes a personal life far removed from the strict orthodoxy of Confucian scholarship. After the death of his true love, Bao Yu leaves the secular world to become a Buddhist monk. In his novel, Cao describes the intimate emotional life of the scholar class while also advocating detachment from the repression, compromise and discipline that success in the world of examinations and officials required.

Signs of Decline

The late eighteenth century exhibited ominous signs of decay in the administrative structures of the dynasty and evidence of deep social conflict.[33] Population growth over the course of the century had increased ecological pressures everywhere. In north China, farmers struggled to increase output from shrinking supplies of land per capita. In the south, extra effort on rice paddy cultivation could squeeze out increasing yields from tiny fields, and specialisation in cash crops like mulberry trees or silk cultivation could increase cash income, but these improvements required intensive labour. Others left their microplots for more open fields in frontier regions. The earliest migrants found relatively large amounts of land, but later arrivals clashed with those who had taken the best fields. A series of conflicts in these border regions, beyond effective control by the state, led to major rebellions around the empire. In Gansu in 1780 Muslim Chinese fought each other over sectarian differences and resisted imperial troops who tried to restore order. During the early nineteenth century, feuding between lineages spread across south China, Turkic Muslims rebelled in Xinjiang, and a popular religious sect raised tens of thousands of followers who attempted to storm the palace in Beijing.[34]

But the most threatening uprising came from adherents of the White Lotus, a millenarian Buddhist sect, which flourished in the uplands of a tributary of the Yangzi river in central China. Gaining support from frontier settlers desperate for land, they

---

32   Xueqin Cao, *The Story of the Stone* (New York, 1973).
33   John K. Fairbank (ed.), *The Cambridge History of China*: vol. 10, *Late Ch'ing, 1800–1911*, Part 1 (Cambridge, 1978); John K. Fairbank and Kwang-Chih Liu (eds), *The Cambridge History of China*: vol. 11, *Late Ch'ing, 1800–1911*, Part 2 (Cambridge, 1980).
34   Susan Naquin, *Millenarian Rebellion in China: The Eight Trigrams Uprising of 1813* (New Haven, CT, 1976).

attacked local government offices and took control of a large area on the border of Hupei, Henan, Shaanxi and Sichuan. Meanwhile, bandits preyed on commercial trade along the Yangzi river from Sichuan to Hunan. Suppressing the rebellion in this region took over a decade and cost over 200 million taels, or ounces of silver, far more than previous military campaigns. By comparison, Qianlong's vast expeditions against the Zunghars had only cost 33 million taels. After the suppression of the late eighteenth-century rebellions, the treasury suffered permanent deficits.

The most serious economic threat to the empire, however, came from growing illegal opium imports on the south coast. The Canton trade system restricted Western European traders to the single city of Canton and allowed them to reside there for only a few months of the year. The British, followed by Americans, French and others, established 'factories' or warehouses outside the city walls to conduct trade with the monopoly guild, the Cohong. Faced with insatiable demands for Chinese tea, but unable to sell very much of value to the Chinese, the British needed a saleable good to offset their silver drain. They found it in opium, which they cultivated in large quantities on plantations in the newly acquired possession of Bengal. The Chinese had consumed opium as a medical herb for many centuries, and, since the sixteenth century, opium mixed with tobacco imported from Southeast Asia had become a very popular product. Wealthy merchants and scholars also enjoyed smoking opium in 'flower boats', or floating brothels, on the rivers of the lower Yangzi valley.[35] Chinese consumption of pure opium rose during the eighteenth century; in this respect, China shared in the boom in consumption of tropical addictive crops – tea, sugar, tobacco, coffee, cocoa – which spanned the world. (Further north, Americans likewise intoxicated themselves with apple cider and Russians increased vodka consumption during the same period.) Imperial edicts prohibited opium distribution and consumption repeatedly during the eighteenth century, but Chinese smugglers in collaboration with foreign ships found many ways to deliver the drug. The dubious British contribution to the opium trade was to lower the price of the drug and develop multiple channels for delivering it to the Chinese interior. East India Company merchants were not supposed to trade in opium, but acting as private merchants, or 'country traders', many British sailors made a fortune in the trade. Unconstrained by a chartered monopoly, Americans also entered the trade in large numbers, relying on the newly designed fast clipper ships to bring opium to coastal ports and fresh tea back to America. The abolition of the East India Company China monopoly in 1834 led to a frenzy of competition to bring even more opium to China in exchange for tea.

The critical conflict broke out when the emperor, after a vigorous debate in the court, sent the uncompromising official Lin Zexu to Canton to stamp out the opium trade in 1839.[36] Lin publicly destroyed the entire year's supply of opium in front of the foreign factories and executed Chinese opium dealers, causing the

---

35 Yangwen Zheng, *The Social Life of Opium in China* (Cambridge, 2005).

36 Hsin-Pao Chang, *Commissioner Lin and the Opium War* (Cambridge, MA, 1964); James M. Polachek, *The Inner Opium War* (Cambridge, MA, 1992); Man-houng Lin, *China Upside Down: Currency, Society, and Ideologies, 1808–1856* (Cambridge, MA, 2006).

merchant community to clamour for recompense for their losses. British troops and ships arrived in Canton, and bombarded and destroyed Chinese forts in south China, the lower Yangzi and near Tianjin, while troops invaded the countryside in the hills around Canton. The imperial armies, with outdated cannon and firearms, could put up no effective resistance. Thousands of peasant militia troops, however, incensed by desecration of tombs and rapes of local women, gained a brief victory when they repelled a small patrol of British and Indian troops near the village of Sanyuanli. Sanyuanli became a powerful myth of the potential of mobilised Chinese masses to defeat well-armed foreign forces.[37] But in the actual treaty settlement at Nanjing in 1842, China had to open five of its ports to trade, cede the island of Hong Kong and pay compensation for the confiscated opium and the costs of the military expedition.

In this first major confrontation with a western empire since the battles with the Russians in 1689, China had clearly failed to keep up with European advances in military technology. Europeans, engaged in an incessant tournament of competition with each other in the seventeenth and eighteenth centuries, had mounted powerful artillery pieces on ships which could bombard coastal forces from a distance, and they had drilled their troops effectively for limited incursions into the Asian mainland. Chinese armies could mount major expeditions into Xinjiang, Nepal, Burma and Vietnam through the eighteenth century, but they failed to modernise their equipment and organisation, which remained nearly the same as in the early seventeenth century. Chinese military advances were in logistics instead of weaponry. They excelled in supporting long marches of large armies to distant frontiers, but they neglected investments in new artillery and coastal defence.

Despite the defeat and the humiliating treaty, the court still did not take major steps to strengthen its military forces, as internal rebellions and disagreements at court diverted resources from naval and coastal defence. In the Second Opium War of 1856–60, the British and French joined to force further trade on the weakened empire.[38] The new treaties signed after this war opened more ports, specifically legalised opium and allowed access by foreign missionaries to the interior. When the court rejected the treaty agreement, the allied armies looted and burned the emperor's Summer Palace to force him to come to terms.[39] Meanwhile, the Russians took advantage of imperial defeat to inflict a treaty of their own giving them substantial territorial concessions on the northern frontier.

---

37 Frederic Wakeman Jr, *Strangers at the Gate: Social Disorder in South China 1839–61* (Berkeley, CA, 1966).
38 J.Y. Wong, *Deadly Dreams: Opium and the Arrow War in China* (Cambridge, 1998).
39 James L. Hevia, *English Lessons: The Pedagogy of Imperialism in Nineteenth-Century China* (Durham, NC, 2003).

Internal Rebellions

Internal rebellions during the mid-nineteenth century, far more pervasive than in the late eighteenth century, challenged the empire so severely that they nearly brought it down. The Taiping movement (1850–64), a Christian sectarian movement which grew in the hills of southwest China in the 1850s, formed an army which marched northward to the Yangzi River and occupied Nanjing from 1853 to 1864.[40] The Taiping constructed a radical new regime, announcing the redistribution of land, the abolition of family hierarchies, the replacement of Confucian classics with Christian religious texts and an all-out attack on the Manchu ruling authority and local elites. At the same time, dispersed groups of salt smugglers, bandits and uprooted peasants called the Nian established fortresses and independent territories in the region between the Yangzi and Yellow rivers. In western Hunan and Guizhou, a disparate collection of rebel groups, including Miao minority peoples, religious sectarians, refugees, bandits and military adventurers, resisted imperial authority in the remote highlands. Muslim Chinese reacted to an attempted pogrom against them by Han migrants to Yunnan by expelling local authorities, and created an independent kingdom. In the northwest, Turkic and Chinese Muslims joined forces with a military adventurer from central Asia called Yakub Beg, who promoted 'holy war' against a variety of contending forces.[41]

Despite these multiple challenges, the Qing dynasty survived. The imperial armies, especially the Manchu bannermen, proved impotent against most of these local uprisings, but provincial and local elites, facing a death struggle for the fate of classical civilisation, mobilised militia troops to defend their local areas.[42] Several charismatic provincial governors melded militia groups and personal supporters into powerful regional armies, which tenaciously resisted the rebel movements. Zuo Zongtang (1812–85), who came from Hunan, took his army first against the Taiping in the middle Yangzi, and then engaged in brutal fighting in northwest China and Xinjiang to suppress the Muslim uprisings. He also drove the Russians out of the strategically important Ili valley. Li Hongzhang (1823–1901) from Anhui led his army to fight in Shanghai, and Zeng Guofan (1811–72), another Hunanese, led his troops against the Taiping and others. Even the foreigners in Shanghai, who

---

40   Jonathan D. Spence, *God's Chinese Son: The Taiping Heavenly Kingdom of Hong Xiuchuan* (New York, 1996); Philip A. Kuhn, 'The Taiping Rebellion', in John K. Fairbank (ed.), *The Cambridge History of China*: vol. 10, *Late Ch'ing, 1800–1911*, Part 1 (Cambridge, 1978), pp. 264–317.

41   Elizabeth J. Perry, *Rebels and Revolutionaries in North China, 1845–1945* (Stanford, CA, 1980); Robert Darrah Jenks, *Insurgency and Social Disorder in Guizhou: The 'Miao' Rebellion, 1854–1873* (Honolulu, HI, 1994); David G. Atwill, *The Chinese Sultanate: Islam, Ethnicity, and the Panthay Rebellion in Southwest China, 1856–1873* (Stanford, CA, 2005); Hodong Kim, *Holy War in China: The Muslim Rebellion and State in Chinese Central Asia, 1864–1877* (Stanford, CA, 2004).

42   Philip A. Kuhn, *Rebellion and Its Enemies in Late Imperial China: Militarization and Social Structure* (Cambridge, MA, 1970).

initially supported the Christian Taiping, turned against the rebels and contributed military forces to save the dynasty.

Reform Programmes

Other empires during the mid-century had faced major challenges and launched reform programmes to regenerate imperial strength. The Ottoman Tanzimat, Japan's Meiji Restoration, Russian reforms after the loss in the Crimean War, including the abolition of serfdom, and even the aftermath of the American Civil War represent radical programmes to preserve state power by abolishing critical institutions – slavery, serfdom, service militaries based on land – that held back economic and technological growth. China came late to these reform efforts, but did participate in them under the name of the 'self-strengthening movements' of the late nineteenth century.[43] The activist provincial governors, like Zeng, Zuo and Li, knew that China needed advanced military technology and industrial growth if the empire were to survive. Although they were Han Chinese, they identified their interest and those of their subjects with the Manchu imperial court. They launched expensive projects, like arsenals, dockyards, textile mills and railroad building campaigns, and the court supported their proposals to finance these programmes with a new tax on commerce, the *lijin*. They translated foreign texts on international law, and they set up China's first real Foreign Ministry, the Zongli Yamen, to consolidate policy on foreign affairs. Until recently, scholars generally regarded these programmes as failures, but now, seeing parallels with China's modern reforms, they treat the self-strengthening movement with considerable respect.[44] China's reform movement only lagged behind those of other empires by a few decades, and it modelled itself on Japan's Meiji restoration of 1868, when activist reformers in Japan had seized control of the state and centred their modernisation project around the Meiji emperor. Chinese reformers likewise attempted to preserve the imperial institution as a central focus of loyalty, while introducing the technology for useful purposes, under the slogan 'Western learning for useful purposes, Chinese learning as the foundation'.

Ultimately, however, the reforms could not save the dynasty, because they were not effective enough to respond to the enormous external and internal pressures on the regime. Foreigners, while propping up the Qing dynasty for geopolitical purposes, continued to exert pressures that compromised its sovereignty and economic independence. They took over control of the customs revenue in order

---

43   Mary C. Wright, *The Last Stand of Chinese Conservatism: The T'ung-Chih Restoration, 1862–1874* (Stanford, CA, 1962).

44   Jennifer Rudolph, *Negotiated Power in Late Imperial China: The Zongli Yamen and the Politics of Reform* (Ithaca, NY, 2008); Richard S. Horowitz, 'International Law and State Transformation in China, Siam, and the Ottoman Empire in the Nineteenth Century', *Journal of World History* 15/4 (2004): pp. 445–86.

to ensure repayment of the indemnities imposed by the Opium Wars. Foreign missionaries penetrated the interior backed by imperialist diplomacy, attracting significant numbers of poor people with their philanthropic activities, but sabotaging the influence of gentry elites in village communities. Steamships brought foreign goods up the Yangzi river, acquainting millions of Chinese consumers with industrially manufactured cheap foreign products. The Russians, French, Germans and British established footholds on Chinese territory in the form of leaseholds and special zones of influence. Japan soon followed with claims to the Ryukyu islands and intervention in Korea.

Attacks on Chinese and foreign Christians provoked by a belligerent French missionary (the Tianjin massacre of 1870), Russian intervention in Xinjiang, French incursions in Vietnam and Japanese moves in the northeast instigated a serious debate over China's geopolitical priorities, splitting the major modernisers. Zuo Zongtang argued strongly for bolstering land forces in order to drive the Russians out of Central Eurasia (China's traditional source of threats since the third century BCE), while Li Hongzhang promoted the development of naval forces to resist the threats along the southern coasts. At the same time, however, one of the worst famines in China's long history of harvest failures raged in north China, leading to the deaths of tens of millions of people. In its famine experience, too, China was one of a number of other regions, including India, Brazil and Africa, which suffered the catastrophes inflicted by the combination of climatic anomaly (the El Niño Southern Oscillation [ENSO]) and imperial disregard for poor native populations. The debate over allocating limited imperial resources ended with putting most of the funds into the continental military, a smaller amount into naval expenditures, and a more limited amount into famine relief in north China. The greatest failing of the Qing in this critical period was the lack of investment in rural infrastructure, particularly rural roads on the dry north China plains and the decay of dyke works and irrigation canals across the empire.[45]

Japan's victory over China in the Sino-Japanese war of 1895 brutally exposed the internal contradictions of the empire to a global audience. The war was fought over Korea, China's most loyal tributary state, when pro-Chinese and pro-Japanese factions within the Korean elite invited supporters of rival modernisation programmes. Nearly all observers expected the much larger modernised Chinese military to win, but Japanese troops and naval forces gained a quick and stunning victory. Japan imposed an indemnity of 200 million taels, took over Taiwan and proceeded to make Korea into a colony. Japanese propagandists celebrated violent

---

45   Immanuel C.Y. Hsu, 'The Great Policy Debate in China 1874: Maritime Defense vs. Frontier Defense', *Harvard Journal of Asiatic Studies* 25 (1964–65): pp. 212–28; Mike Davis, *Late Victorian Holocausts: El Niño Famines and the Making of the Third World* (New York, 2001); Kathryn Edgerton-Tarpley, *Tears from Iron: Cultural Responses to Famine in Nineteenth-Century China* (Berkeley, CA, 2008); Kenneth Pomeranz, *The Making of a Hinterland: State, Society, and Economy in Inland North China, 1853–1937* (Berkeley, CA, 1993); Lillian M. Li, *Fighting Famine in North China: State, Market, and Environmental Decline, 1690s–1990s* (Stanford, CA, 2007).

conquest, including atrocities, as evidence of Japan's arrival in the ranks of a modern nation. Japan had escaped from stagnant and backward Asia, while Chinese feared the end of the entire classical civilisation.[46]

Events moved fast and furiously over the next fifteen years toward the dynasty's collapse. China sent tens of thousands of students to Japan to learn the secrets of success from the 'dwarf barbarians'. A young emperor attempted, with the support of radical reformers, a crash reform programme in 1898, which lasted for only 100 days before his grandmother suppressed it. When a coalition of anti-Christian gentry, martial arts practitioners and desperate peasantry uprooted by severe famine attacked Chinese Christians and foreigners across north China in 1900, the court conservatives decided to back these 'Righteous Fists' (or Boxers) to drive out the foreign imperialists with mass militia attacks.[47] This episode ended with a siege of the foreign legations in Beijing, an invasion by eight foreign armies, the burning and looting once again of the summer palace and the imposition of a colossal indemnity of 450 million taels of silver. A final effort at reform by the Manchu elite in 1905 attempted to save the dynasty by abolishing the examination system, drastically modernising the army and administration and promoting foreign loans to invest in railroads and industries. Meanwhile, however, nationalist activists in exile in Japan and Southeast Asia organised campaigns to expel the barbarian Manchus in order to create a nation for the Han race alone. They gained support not only among overseas student groups, but among overseas merchants, young soldiers recruited to the modern armies and urban citizens who resented the heavy foreign imperial presence. Sun Yat-sen (1866–1925), a Cantonese educated in Hawaii, tirelessly mobilised support for anti-Manchu activities, including assassination attempts from underground brotherhoods, overseas merchants and New Army soldiers. When a military revolt broke out in Wuhan on 10 October 1911, military support for the dynasty quickly collapsed and the emperor abdicated; Sun Yat-sen was declared President of the new Republic of China on 1 January 1912. The Qing dynasty was gone.[48]

The Ming and Qing in World Perspective

The Ming and Qing dynasties spanned the entire period from the opening of the New World to the first decade of the twentieth century. In its tenacious preservation of classical traditions of rule while constantly interacting with other empires,

---

46   For graphic imagery of Japanese celebration of victory in the Sino-Japanese war, see http://visualizingcultures.mit.edu 'Throwing off Asia'.

47   Joseph W. Esherick, *The Origins of the Boxer Uprising* (Berkeley, CA, 1987); Paul A. Cohen, *History in Three Keys: The Boxers as Event, Experience, and Myth* (New York, 1997).

48   Mary C. Wright, *China in Revolution: The First Phase, 1900–13* (New Haven, CT, 1968); Joseph W. Esherick, *Reform and Revolution in China: The 1911 Revolution in Hunan and Hubei* (Berkeley, CA, 1976).

China resembled most closely the Ottoman and Muscovite/Russian empires, with some similarities to the Mughals. China was the wealthiest and most populated of them all in 1500, and remained so in 1800. The four empires had in common their dependence on a large territory of peasant cultivators, who financed the state with taxes and provided the mass of soldiers. The ruling elites were conquerors from central Eurasia, inheriting steppe traditions of personal loyalty, mobile cavalry, rapid expansion and substantial internecine conflict. (Even the Muscovite state absorbed substantial amounts of Tatar elites.) China moved towards greater commercial and administrative integration in the sixteenth century, as did the Mughals and Russians, even though the late Ming did not expand its territory. It faced a relatively brief seventeenth-century crisis compared to the turmoil of Western Europe or Russia's Time of Troubles. The Manchus quickly re-established order and promoted expansion into central Eurasia, in parallel with Russian expansion into Siberia. When the two empires met each other, they negotiated treaties implicitly recognising the other's comparable status, driven by a common interest in trade and in the elimination of their Mongol rival.

In the eighteenth century, all the empires faced concurrent challenges from western European expansion and internal pressure for regional autonomy. Peter the Great in Russia responded first, with a radical reform imposing Western European military and cultural norms on a resisting population. Catherine continued Peter's western orientation, making Russia one of the great European powers while tightening Russia's grip on its peasant population. China in the eighteenth century greeted the Europeans with curiosity and suspicion, allowing trade on both maritime and continental frontiers, embracing European painters, astronomers and, to a limited extent, Jesuit missionaries. It did not, however, substantially transform its institutions on a European model of nobilities and parliaments. While the Mughal and Ottoman central authorities yielded power to regional leaders, allowing the penetration of European traders and colonialists. China and Russia successfully maintained centralised power and held off foreign challenges.

Until 1800, China's economy at least equalled that of Western Europe in standard of living, commercialisation, life expectancy, mobility of labour and capital, security of property rights and other indicators of economic modernity. The most advanced region of China, the lower Yangzi, looked similar to advanced areas of Europe like the Netherlands and England. The industrial revolution beginning in England looks from this perspective like a sudden, contingent process, not one deeply rooted in western cultural superiority. By 1850, however, as industrialisation spread to the rest of Europe and the US, China clearly lagged behind in technology and creativity. The giant empire faced such serious challenges from internal upheaval and external attack that even the most perceptive reformers could not stimulate a rapid response.

Nineteenth-century industrialisation, European imperial expansion and mass mobilisation challenged all the Eurasian continental empires, which responded with various waves of reform and resistance, staging a tenacious fight for survival. Seen comparatively, China faced larger threats from a more numerous set of rivals than its peers, and the endurance of the empire in the face of massive disturbances seems quite impressive. Only China among the great empires faced the simultaneous onslaught of the British, French, Germans, Russians and Japanese combined. Within Asia, only China, Siam and Japan escaped becoming colonies. China's mid-century self-strengthening programme did achieve significant results, like the reforms in the Ottoman Empire and Russia. Even if the reforms were too little too late, the Japanese victory in 1895 was by no means inevitable. China also faced internal upheavals whose frequency and scale were found nowhere else in the world, from a bewildering variety of groups including ethnic minorities, uprooted peasants, mobile merchants, religious sectarians and lineage feuds, among others. Very little of this resistance fits very well with orthodox Marxist explanations as class struggle, or with conservative explanations as mere 'disorder'.

The republican revolutionaries, who first radically rejected the Manchu presence in favour of a racially defined Han nation, soon found themselves compelled to reconstruct the Qing Empire in a new way, as a 'multinational nation-state' including Manchus, Mongols, Muslims, Tibetans and Han Chinese. As in the Soviet Union, Sun Yat-sen developed a nationality-based justification of the new nation that derived its principles from the Qing efforts to accommodate multiple identities within a single regime. Instead of deriving legitimacy from the top down, in the emperor's bestowal of benevolent grace, however, nationalists had to derive legitimacy from the bottom up, as an expression of the people's inborn loyalties to their ancestral genealogy and place. The imperial legacy survived awkwardly in the new nation, but it still haunts the three states (Mongolia, People's Republic of China and Taiwan) which now occupy Qing imperial space.[49] Their efforts to invoke, ignore or reject the Qing imperial period reflect unresolved contradictions created by the long endurance of the dynastic regimes.

---

49   Uradyn Erden Bulag, *The Mongols at China's Edge: History and the Politics of National Unity* (Lanham, MD, 2002); Emma Jinhua Teng, *Taiwan's Imagined Geography: Chinese Colonial Travel Writing and Pictures, 1683–1895* (Cambridge, MA, 2004).

Ottoman Empire

Virginia H. Aksan

The Ottoman Empire, the largest of the pre-modern Muslim empires, survived six hundred years from c. 1300 to 1923, and at it greatest extent encompassed the majority of the geopolitical space of the present-day Middle East and the Balkans: Hungary, Albania, Bosnia, Romania, Greece, Bulgaria, large parts of North Africa, especially Egypt and Libya and the Hijaz in Saudi Arabia. The Ottomans first appeared in Anatolia (present-day Turkey) in the thirteenth century. Their arrival there was part of an immense shift in the geopolitical and cultural parameters of civilisations in the Middle East in the post-Mongolian age. Arab geographers recorded the settlement of tens of thousands of tents in the mountain valleys and plateaus of Anatolia, signalling the arrival of nomadic, pastoral (and largely Turkish) tribes, who had converted to Islam by contact with itinerant preachers and Sufis since the ninth century. One of the eight to ten significant such tribes was that of Osman I (r. 1281–1324), who gave his name to the dynasty.[1]

Osman's victory over the Byzantine army near Iznik in 1301 is our first record of this new force, which appears to have included Christians as well as Muslims. Furthermore, Osman and his immediate successors established Byzantine Bursa as the first Ottoman capital (1326) after a long siege, built the first mosque and madrasa there, and allied themselves with Byzantine and Balkan daughters and sisters. The next century and a half was taken up with a gradual spread of Ottoman influence, and the collapse of Bulgaria, Thrace and ultimately Serbia by the early 1400s. Repeated calls in Rome for crusades against the Muslim invaders resulted in significant campaigns by the allied forces of Rome, Venice, Hungary and Byzantium at Nicopolis in 1396 and at Varna in 1444. Both failed to dislodge the new power in the Balkans. Under Murad I (r. 1362–89) and Bayezid I (r. 1389–1402), the Ottomans created the Janissary army, a formidable standing infantry drawn from Balkan Christian communities as part of their submission, and known as *devşirme* (round-up). The Janissaries were sent to join the sultan's entourage, were circumcised, steeped in Muslim culture and given the best education of the time. The Janissary corps has entered the annals of the Balkan successor states as the

---

1   Europeans derived Ottoman from the Arabic form of Osman's name, 'Uthman (the third caliph of early Islam), signifying the dynasty's attachment to Islam from the beginning.

most feared and most hated institution of Ottoman rule. From the elite of the new troops were chosen the grand viziers and governors of provinces of the empire for over two hundred years.

When Mehmed II (known as Fatih, the Conqueror, briefly on the throne at age twelve, 1444–46, and again 1451–81) occupied the walled city of Constantinople in 1453, he inaugurated the true imperial age of the Ottomans. It was during his rule that the Ottomans also became known as a 'gunpowder empire', credited with making adroit use of the new weapons technology emerging in Europe. It was Ottoman artillery-fire, from enormous cannons cast with intelligence from Hungarian sources, which breached the reputedly impregnable walls of Constantinople.

Mehmed II organised the basis of the Ottoman legal system, and established a pattern of administration which allowed him and his successors to govern a multi-ethnic and multi-religious landscape through the astute combination of sharia Islamic law, customary law and sultanic decrees, called *kanun*. Constantinople (or Konstantiniye, hereafter Istanbul), which was renamed Istanbul only in the twentieth century, became the capital of a cosmopolitan civilisation, and was then (c. 1550) and now the largest city of Europe.

Much of the character of the present-day Middle East and the Balkans was determined by Ottoman rule. The Ottomans dominated the eastern Mediterranean Sea, and Red and Arabian Seas from 1500 to 1700, when Sultan Süleyman the Magnificent (r. 1520–66) and his successors contested the power of the Habsburgs of Spain and Austria on land and on sea. Under Selim I (r. 1512–20), a series of remarkable victories had brought Syria, Egypt and the Hijaz (Arabia) under Ottoman hegemony. This meant that the Ottomans assumed the status of protectors of the most sacred cities of Islam: Jerusalem, Mecca and Medina, and could command the nominal allegiance (and occasional tribute) of much of the Muslim commonwealth stretching from West Africa to Bali in Indonesia.

By the reign of Süleyman, the Ottoman system was largely in place in the central Ottoman lands (Anatolia and the Balkans, and thinly spread to the peripheries). Süleyman's victories at Belgrade in 1521 and Mohacs in 1526 signalled the beginning of the submission of the proud Hungarian kingdom to Ottoman dominion until 1699. Client peripheries included Libya, Algeria and Tunisia on the coast of Africa; Ragusa in the Adriatic; Transylvania, Wallachia and Moldavia on the Danubian frontier; and the Tatar Khanate in the Crimea. Süleyman ruled as the shadow of God on earth, and as Caliph of the Muslim populations of the world, making the Ottomans a truly global phenomenon. Europeans were stunned, some dazzled, by an empire that welcomed all, renegades and aristocrats, by a simple matter of conversion. The benefits for those who styled themselves Ottomans were enormous. Others scorned a system built on slavery and lack of inherited status,[2] but the Ottoman style embraced the notion of a political household, the largest

---

2 Lucette Valensi, *The Birth of the Despot: Venice and the Sublime Porte* (Ithaca, NY, 1993); David Blanks (ed.), *Images of the Other: Europe and the Muslim World Before 1700* (Cairo, 1997); Kaiser Thomas, 'The Evil Empire? The Debate on Turkish Despotism in Eighteenth-Century French Political Culture', *Journal of Modern History* 72/1 (2000): pp. 6–34.

being that of the sultan himself, whose beneficence began with his loyal sons, the Janissaries, and extended to the smallest peasant, who had the right of appeal to sultanic justice, as embodied in sharia and customary law.

The spread of gunpowder expertise from Istanbul to the east had enabled the rise to prominence of two other rival Muslim empires of the pre-modern age, Safavid Persia and Moghul India. The three so-called gunpowder empires occupied the world stage in the early modern era (1500–1800). All originated as Mongol–Turkic dynasties, heirs to the brilliant Timurid traditions of Samarqand and Bukhara, whose courts were renowned for their splendour and patronage, sharia-based orthodoxy, nomadic warrior iconography and forbearance of religious heterodoxy, but which could vary enormously according to the policies of individual rulers and territories.

Ottoman connections with the Mughals were sporadic and largely inconsequential, especially once the Portuguese and English trading colonies had penetrated the Indian Ocean in the sixteenth century. The Ottoman eastern frontier, however, remained paradoxically undefined but constant in exemplifying the Turco-Persian, Sunni–Shi'ite confrontation. The reluctance of latter-day Janissaries to fight fellow Muslims proved problematic for successive sultans, and the continued nomadic impulse of an unfixed border resisted central control until the nineteenth century. Safavid rulers, such as Shah Abbas (d. 1629), presented themselves as allies of western powers in their struggles with the Ottomans in Europe, and facilitated much of the early penetration of western traders into the Persian Gulf. In 1639, Murad IV's major campaign to the east ended in the Ottoman–Safavid Treaty of Zuhab, which restored Baghdad to Ottoman territories essentially until 1918.

Safavid hegemony – always tenuous – was broken up by Afghan warriors in the 1720s, inaugurating another round of Ottoman–Persian confrontations, only this time Russian interests in the Caucasus had begun to complicate the picture. Nadir Shah, errant outsider, and later usurper of power in Iran, put an end to the brief Ghalzay Afghan period of rule in Iran. He then had himself crowned as Shah in 1736, invaded India, and in 1739 sacked Moghul Delhi, probably contributing to the ease with which the British defeated the Moghuls some two decades later. Nadir Shah's campaigns in Azerbaijan and eastern Anatolia caused ripple effects and uprisings among the semi-independent warlords of the eastern frontier. War between the Ottomans and Nadir Shah broke out in 1742, leading to the latter's lengthy siege of Mosul the following year. To confront and defeat Nadir Shah, the Ottomans were forced to rely on a regional Kurdish/Arab army, which had important consequences for later events in the region. The treaty of Kurdan was finally agreed upon in 1746, by which the Ottomans recognised the Shi'ites as religious equals rather than as the schismatics of past such negotiations.

Similarly, as the Russo-British rivalry over Afghanistan heated up in the nineteenth century, the Ottoman–Persian border became rife with nomadic predations and fluid military associations. In the mid-nineteenth century, the Ottomans expended considerable resources to settle Kurds and Bedouin Arab tribes, partly because they wished to counter Britain's colonial aspirations in the Gulf, but also because they needed manpower for the new conscript armies, and because the tribal predations on pilgrimage caravans were a source of embarrassment to a dynasty reputedly protecting the Muslim routes to Mecca. In 1847, the Treaty of Erzurum reaffirmed and drew the Turco-Persian border after negotiations with the Qajar dynasty, successors to both Nadir Shah and the Zand dynasty in Iran until their own collapse at the turn of the twentieth century. Iran by that time had come largely under the influence of Britain in the south and Russia to the north, as part of the colonial encirclement and contestation of Ottoman rule that continued throughout the century.

But it was the northern and western borders with Europe which eventually challenged Ottoman expansionism seriously and permanently. Generally acknowledged as masters of three continents, the Ottomans styled themselves lords of the universe, and held their own on European borderlands until the 1750s, after which Ottoman sovereignty was largely checked and reduced to semi-colonial status by the superior military and economic power of Europe.

The Ottoman Middle Period

In the early seventeenth century, Istanbul had become the centre of an empire wracked by instability and an identity crisis. The transition from one Ottoman sultan to another was never easy, and the practice of fratricide almost completely eliminated heirs to the throne in the early 1600s. Succession was settled on the oldest surviving member of the house, a move which seemed to provide a certain stability of ascent to the throne by the eighteenth century. The upheaval at the centre, however, which was once blamed on the 'rule of the [royal] women', has led some recent historians to draw the Ottomans into the general crisis historiography of seventeenth-century Europe, and to contrast it with France's regency of Louis XIII and XIV, and England's regicide of Charles I.[3]

Regencies and palace bureaucrats governed the empire in an era marked by significant rebellions, financial shortages and the sustained, lengthy and expensive siege of Venetian Crete, which took 22 years to complete, ending in 1669. The latter half of the seventeenth century was convulsed by a decades-long, intermittent war (called the Long War) not just with Venice, but with the Habsburgs. The period 1683–99 altered the status of the Ottomans in Europe, a fact reflected in the Treaty of Karlowitz in 1699, which is consistently (and legitimately) argued as the marker for the beginning of the end of Ottoman expansion. To reach peace, Ottoman representatives negotiated for four months with those of the Austrians, Poles, Muscovites and Venetians, as well as Dutch and English mediators. The Ottomans lost Hungary and Transylvania to Austria, and returned Podolia to the Polish; the Venetians acquired the Peloponnesus, and the Russian tsar was recognised as

---

3   Geoffrey Parker, 'Crisis and Catastrophe: The Global Crisis of the Seventeenth Century', *American Historical Review* 113/4 (2008): pp. 1053–1079.

an equal to the sultan. The new Habsburg–Ottoman–Romanov imperial triangle sketched by the treaty ushered in a more or less sustained peace with the Austrians, a new era of fixed borders and reciprocal diplomacy.

Fixed borders had financial implications for an Ottoman ideology based on ever expanding boundaries and redistributive military systems. The Janissaries stationed in the countryside had long melted into provincial economies, joining and competing with agrarian-based elites such as the timariots (who were traditional cavalrymen and fief holders) and a new emerging class of tax farmers. Lax discipline and repeated debasement of coinage combined to create a military force better known for rebellion and thuggery than military valour. What prevented Ottoman administrators from recognising this long decline of martial capabilities was not just the resilience of mobile warriors, who could be repeatedly mobilised in large numbers with consistency and effectiveness, and of a rural population willing to support the logistics system, but also similar weaknesses in their traditional enemies, the Habsburgs and the Venetians. The failure of Ottoman leadership at the siege of Vienna in 1683, and the subsequent evaporation of Ottoman forces as they fled down the Danube, leaving behind all the future military artefacts for Viennese museums, should have served as a significant indicator of serious trouble ahead.[4]

In 1703, a major revolt in Istanbul broke out, largely as a consequence of the two decades of war, and the concessions of the Karlowitz treaty (kept from the Ottoman public long after it was signed), as well as the perceived abuse of power exercised by Mustafa II's chief religious officer, Feyzullah Efendi. This was one of the seminal moments of the empire, because the *ulema* (religious classes), the merchants of the city *and* the Janissaries presented a united voice against the sultan, who had withdrawn to Edirne. A brief period of troubled governance ensued but when Mustafa II was replaced by Ahmed III (r. 1703–30) order was restored in such a way as to allow the domination of the new, emerging bureaucracy. The handful of astute statesmen, well aware of the state of the Janissaries who had failed so miserably on the battlefields of the Danube, endeavoured to keep the Ottomans out of further European entanglements.

The era of Ahmed III is also called 'the Tulip Age' as the rage for the bulbs spread to Istanbul, and pleasure kiosks, palaces and gardens sprouted up all along the Bosphorus.[5] A revived economy, stimulated by the creation of a new system of lifetime tax farming, redistributed wealth among a larger group of grandees, which had the effect of restricting professional careers in the bureaucracy and the religious class to a small, select number of families. The period was characterised by an immense interest in consumer culture and European goods, remarkably like Versailles or Petrograd. It was an era of extravagance and spectacle.

---

4   Rhoads Murphey, *Ottoman Warfare 1500–1700* (London, 1999) is particularly good on the persistence and the commonality of small frontier wars as a cultural phenomenon of the Ottoman–Austro-Hungarian frontier.

5   It has been argued that the 'Tulip Age' historiography was a later historical construction to locate the origins of 'westernisation' in the early eighteenth century: Can Erimtan, *The Origins of the Tulip Age and its Development in Modern Turkey* (London, 2008).

The grand opening to Europe ended abruptly in 1730, when Ahmed III's rule was challenged by a city-wide revolt led by disgruntled Janissaries, artisans and merchants, all of whom opposed the mobilisation and taxes for war against the Afghans after they toppled the Safavids in Isfahan. Another Janissary revolt in Izmir was engendered by much the same disgruntlement and dissatisfaction of plain folk, hinting at the breakdown of Ottoman ideological cohesion. It was a time of masterless men, and the growth of provincial armies, without whom the sultan could no longer go to war. Unrest was often engendered by mobile, undisciplined and easily manipulated manpower.[6] War finally broke out again in 1736–39, with Russia and Austria allied against the Ottomans. It was a disastrous series of campaigns for both the Austrians and the Ottomans, and exhausted both sides, but the extraordinary return of Austrian-occupied Belgrade to Ottoman territory by the treaty of 1740 masked the true state of affairs in Istanbul, even as the sultan and his advisors embarked on an extended era of non-involvement in European wars.

Sitting out the Seven Years' War (1756–63), the Ottomans fell further behind European military developments, especially battlefield formations, drill and arms; the demobilised army fell into desuetude. Thus, when the Ottomans declared war on Russia in 1768 they were completely unprepared for campaigning on the Danube again. The 1774 treaty of Küçük Kaynarca, signed in just a few days on Ottoman terrain below the Danube, signalled to all of Europe that Russia was on the march to Istanbul. Another round of ferocious confrontations between the Russians and Ottomans in 1787–92, along the great chain of fortresses that studded the Danube, ended in the complete collapse of the Ottoman forces.

Ottoman Modernity

Reform was no longer an option: it was imperative. The reform period began as a truly radical enterprise with the destruction of the imperial army, the Janissaries, in 1826, by Mahmud II (r. 1808–39), although the seeds were planted in the reign of his predecessor, Sultan Selim III (r. 1789–1807). Selim III, after suffering the single most devastating set of defeats of any sultan, sought the advice of his entourage and embarked on a wholesale revision of the Ottoman system, beginning with the treasury. Piecemeal in the past, such reforms usually consisted of cleaning up neglected tax registers, and thereby restoring some revenues, and applying vigilance to bloated military muster rolls, but this time the sultan envisioned introducing new systems of finance and new European-style military regiments.[7] Called the 'New Order' (*Nizam-ı Cedid*), the sultan's reform agenda was understood

---

6   See particularly Reşat Kasaba, *A Moveable Empire: Ottoman Nomads, Migrants and Refugees* (Seattle, WA, 2009).

7   One estimate for the eighteenth century claims that 400,000 were entitled to Janissary salaries, but only 20,000 were combat-ready. See Virginia H. Aksan, *Ottoman Wars 1700–1873: An Empire Besieged* (Harlow, 2007).

as transformative and engendered much dispute between those who favoured restoration and those committed to complete overhaul.

Facing divisive rivalry from provincial magnates whose power and wealth had increased because of their responsibility in raising regional armies and collecting taxes, Selim III understood that he needed to establish direct communications with European states to preserve power, and in order to reassert Ottoman suzerainty. He ordered the first permanent Ottoman embassies to European capitals in 1793. Had Selim's reforms taken root, the Ottoman recovery might have taken a different turn, but in 1798 Napoleon Bonaparte invaded Alexandria, and the modern age of the Middle East (or the Eastern Question as some prefer) began in earnest. Selim III's Francophilia (he admired Napoleon and consistently tried to stay allied to France), and his reform programmes went up in flames in a huge rebellion in Istanbul in 1807.[8]

To Sultan Mahmud II, referred to as the 'infidel sultan', was left the task of manoeuvring great power diplomacy to prevent the dissolution of the empire; of facing the shocking disloyalty of his Serbian and Greek subjects as the age of nationalism unfolded; of ruthlessly engineering a centralisation drive which eliminated regional rivalries; of curbing the power of the religious classes; and of introducing the Napoleonic regimental system, conscription, and education to an outmoded military. Mahmud II mowed down the remnants of the Janissaries on the streets of Istanbul in 1826, in response to their final rebellion, and started over with a brand new army. For the first time in more than a century, a sultan left Istanbul to visit the fortresses on the Danube and talk to his subjects. Mahmud II made five separate trips into the countryside in his final decade of rule in an effort to call his subjects to arms, and convince them of the imperative of the transformation he had under way. His model of defensive modernisation, triggered by the need for state security and survival, involved a massive, undoubtedly brutal, structural transformation affecting internal and external relations alike.

Just as significantly, the political and social chaos which Bonaparte encountered and exacerbated in Egypt resulted in the creation of the fourth 'frontier' for the Ottomans in the rise of Mehmed Ali, Albanian thug, Ottoman Governor, military reformer and then challenger to the Ottoman right to rule Syria from 1831 to 1841. Mehmed Ali was responsible for the remarkable and rapid transformation of Egyptian society, but at great cost once he sent his army into Syria. Mobilising Egyptian resources into monopoly export crops such as cotton, Mehmed Ali rebuilt both army and navy, and had conscripted more than 10 per cent (an army of 100,000) of his peasant population when his armies defeated Mahmud II's new forces at Nizib on the plains of Anatolia in 1839, a defeat which reputedly hastened the sultan's death.[9]

Risking the complete collapse of the empire, Mahmud II's successors continued his concessions to Britain in return for naval support, which had resulted in the 1838 Anglo-Ottoman Trade Agreement, and the pacification of Mehmed Ali by

---

8   Ibid., chaps 5–6; Juan Cole, *Napoleon's Egypt: Invading the Middle East* (London, 2007).
9   Khaled Fahmy, *Mehmed Ali: From Ottoman Governor to Ruler of Egypt* (Oxford, 2009).

combined British and Ottoman forces. The 1840 Convention of London reduced Mehmed Ali's forces to 18,000, but also recognised a hereditary governorship in Egypt called the Khedive, nominally still part of the empire, which lasted until King Farouk I was overthrown by revolutionary forces in 1952. The 1841 Treaty of London (or London Straits Convention) closed the Bosphorus and Dardanelles to foreign warships. The Ottoman economy had its fate sealed by the 1838 document which essentially opened all domestic markets to British trade with minimal tariffs. It marked the beginning of Ottoman and Egyptian indebtedness, especially once Mahmud II's successors sought foreign loans to underwrite the continued modernisation of the army and navy (as described below).

The era now generally known as the *Tanzimat* (Reorganisation, or Constitutional period) began in 1839 as well, and culminated in the first Ottoman constitution of 1876. Two great reform documents were crafted and promulgated by the new civilian bureaucratic class of the Sublime Porte (*Bab-ı Ali*) in that period. The Gülhane edict of 1839 promised equality before the law, a regular system of assessing taxes (in other words, the elimination of tax farming) and a modern conscription system for mobilisation and service in the army. The Hatt-ı Hümayun edict following the Crimean War in 1856 reiterated equality of citizenship; proclaimed freedom of religion, freedom of access to the bureaucracy and the military, mixed tribunals for Muslim–Christian disputes, and codification of penal and commercial laws; and promised once more to introduce direct taxation. Closer inspection of the 1856 document indicates that recognition of the equalisation of Muslim and non-Muslim citizens – that is, unrestricted religious practice – in effect codified for the first time the confessional (*millet*) system of religious communities, which heretofore had been largely ad hoc. Where there had been three basic *millets*, the Greek Orthodox, Armenian and Jewish, there were now some seventeen, including the new Protestant *millet*, forced on the Ottomans by British Ambassador Stratford Canning in 1847. Scores of Christian missionaries (largely Protestant) poured into the empire in the mid-nineteenth century, exacerbating an already bifurcated Muslim/non-Muslim society.

In other words, the face of the transformative period was contradictory. Muslims continued to dominate in government and were the backbone of the conscript army, in spite of repeated efforts by the *Tanzimat* bureaucrats to regulate the participation of non-Muslims in the new army. Even when required by law to enlist, non-Muslims found ways to buy out of conscription, so much so that the old *cizye* or non-Muslim poll (head) tax was converted into a tax in lieu of military service (*bedel*). Muslims were generally prohibited from buying out of military service, but massive exemptions, such as for young religious scholars, forced the burden of defending the empire onto the peasantry of the Anatolian countryside. Ottoman subjects in Istanbul and the empire's major cities were divided by conflicting loyalties to an elite, increasingly impoverished Muslim class, which ran the government as its officers, administrators and provincial officials, and to a wealthy commercial class made up of Greeks, Armenians and Jews with extraterritorial privileges from the major powers, exemption from military service and familial networks all over the Mediterranean and Black Sea coasts.[10]

Thus, the legal turn to constitutionalism engendered social forces which did indeed challenge the Ottoman system. By the end of the *Tanzimat* period, generally dated to the accession to the throne of autocrat Sultan Abdülhamid II (r. 1876–1909), a small and mostly Muslim elite group dominated an increasingly powerful bureaucracy that had emerged to rule over a largely disaffected empire. The new bureaucrats were graduates of secularised schools and the military academy. It was a government without teeth, however, as the financial management of the late empire gradually moved into foreign hands, and international and domestic events brought absolutist Sultan Abdülhamid II to the throne.

The Road to Indebtedness

As with all pre-modern empires, military expenditures consumed a majority of the Ottoman expenses, and the increasing inability of the state to support the major campaigns became all too evident in the long engagements with the Habsburgs in the 1680s. Ottoman bureaucrats made efforts to reform some traditional taxation policies, which included equalising *cizye* payments, minting a new silver coin, the *kuruş*, which became the stable coinage of the eighteenth century, and introducing the widespread use of lifeterm tax-farming (*malikane*) after 1695, for all transactions of the state: agriculture, customs and excise taxes. Those who possessed *malikanes*, largely the wealthy elites of Istanbul and their local agents, were given a set income against the revenues expected of their holdings, and obligated to pay up to three years advance to the state. In 1722, such sales netted 1.45 million *kuruş*; by 1768, this had risen to 9.78 million; by 1787, 13.16 million, approximating the annual revenue of the period which in times of general stability ran 15–16,000,000 million *kuruş* in the eighteenth century. The system 'constituted a form of long-term borrowing by the state, secured against tax revenues'.[11] A further development was the diversification of such investments as shares, creating private wealth of extraordinary degree, with an urban class, as Linda Darling notes, involved largely in 'debt patronage' rather than agricultural or industrial development. Janissaries and central state elites were the main beneficiaries.[12] Non-Muslims were excluded from the system, but themselves profited as bankers and money-lenders, and, increasingly, as liaisons and partners with the foreign trading communities of the

---

10   Fatma Müge Göçek is particularly good on this trend: *Social Constructions of Nationalism in the Middle East* (Albany, NY, 2002).

11   Linda Darling, 'Public Finances: The Role of the Ottoman Centre', in Suraiya Faroqhi (ed.), *Cambridge History of Turkey*: vol. 3, *The Later Ottoman Empire 1603–1839* (Cambridge, 2006), pp. 124–8. Figures are on p. 127, and drawn from the work of Mehmet Genç and Ariel Salzmann.

12   Ibid., pp. 124–8.

empire. Here, again, revenue was generated by the selling of patronage certificates (*berat*) by the foreign consuls, first granted from the Ottoman government – often in cash, as were most of the transactions of the eighteenth century.[13] Local merchants, largely non-Muslim Ottoman subjects, thus acquired the privilege and protection of foreign nations, alienating both citizen and investment capital from the Ottoman dynasty.

In 1789, Selim III ascended the throne of an empire with empty coffers. His efforts to re-establish solvency are evident in his reformed treasury. The main problem continued to be the inability to eliminate outdated agricultural systems and the practice of tax farming. In one estimate, by the mid-nineteenth century, only about 12 per cent of the revenues owed to the Ottomans ever made it into state coffers.[14] Karen Barkey puts it best: 'The Ottoman state, unlike England and France, was never able to centralize tax farms into one large, bureaucratic entity with increasingly refined modes of collection and control.'[15] As with many other policies, the Ottomans preferred negotiation to coercion, something that could be said generally about their reforms in the nineteenth century. Reforms related to tax farming had the net effect of reducing the burden on the peasant and, consequently, state revenues. Initially abolished by the Gülhane document, tax farming was reinstated in 1840 willy-nilly because the reformers could not find (or were unwilling to impose) another way to convert agricultural revenues into an equalised tax system. Taxation amounted to 20–25 per cent of rural income, not any more oppressive than tax regimes in Europe, but it forced the indebtedness of Ottoman taxpayers, many of whom operated at marginal subsistence, to money-lenders.

Mahmud II used drastic measures to finance his reform agenda: confiscation of the estates of wealthy Ottoman subjects (bankers and bureaucrats), which was later prohibited by *Tanzimat* legislation, was one way; devaluation of the coinage was another. The latter had devastating consequences, leading Şevket Pamuk to describe it as the most extreme period of devaluation in the entire existence of the empire.[16] One problem lay in the profligate spending of the dynasty itself, especially the construction of the Dolmabahçe Palace on the Bosphorus, arguably one of the most egregious examples of baroque Orientalism, yet a much-studied imitation of European absolutist court architecture.[17] Builder Sultan Abdülaziz (r. 1839–61)

---

13   Edhem Eldem, 'Capitulations and Western Trade', in Faroqhi, *Cambridge History of Turkey*: vol. 3, *Later Ottoman Empire 1603–1839*, p. 321.

14   Dominic Lieven, *Empire: The Russian Empire and Its Rivals* (New Haven, CT, 2000).

15   Karen Barkey, *Empire of Difference: The Ottomans in Comparative Perspective* (Cambridge, 2008), p. 271.

16   Christopher Clay, *Gold for the Sultan* (London, 2000); Şevket Pamuk, *A Monetary History of the Ottoman Empire* (Cambridge, 2000); also his 'Institutional Change and the Longevity of the Ottoman Empire, 1600–1800', *Journal of Interdisciplinary History* 35/2 (2004): pp. 225–47.

17   Ottoman dynastic models for reform were, it should be remembered, probably derived from contemporaries Metternich, Bismarck, Romanov Nicholas I and Kaiser Wilhelm II of Germany.

was also committed to improving both navy and army, and simply ordered new military equipment without consideration of budgetary restrictions or consultation with his advisors. In the years between 1841 and 1876, there were only two years of surpluses. By 1876, the Ottoman state had a deficit of 505 million *kuruş*.[18]

Ottoman manufacturing, or lack of it, is often simply dismissed as one further piece of evidence of the Ottoman failure to deal with the world markets of the late nineteenth century. Certain goods, such as British imports of wool and cotton yarn, did have an enormously deleterious impact on local textile production, but today one of the most robust industries in republican Turkey is textiles. Similarly, olive oil and its by-products such as soap (as produced in Nablus in the nineteenth century) have become a truly globalised economy, with Turkish oil frequently bottled and labelled as virgin Italian oil. Generally, small-scale enterprises survived in preference to larger entrepreneurial manufactures. In the late empire, mass wage labour was as difficult to mobilise as were conscripts for the army.[19]

The question of Ottoman (and Egyptian) industrialisation in the nineteenth century is directly related to international crises, fluctuating commodity prices and an unstable political order – all of which drew the world into the First World War – but undoubtedly domestic resistance and lack of institutional stability plagued both Mahmud II and Mehmed Ali's reform agendas. In the 1820s, Mehmed Ali created his new army and successfully eliminated tax farming, but the net result was the creation of large landed estates and a form of plantation-style cotton farming which undoubtedly facilitated the intervention of foreign investment. His state-run factories, hastily assembled and often requiring forced labour, may have employed upwards of 30,000–40,000 people, and were deeply unpopular in agrarian settings. The 1838 Anglo-Ottoman Treaty removed the tariff protection his local industries needed. When combined with periodic fluctuations in world cotton prices, his monopoly on state commercial enterprises collapsed. His successors, Khedives Abbas (r. 1848–54), Said (r. 1854–63) and Ismail (r. 1863–79) struggled similarly. Ismail opened the Suez Canal in 1869, built by the French; the British took over the debt in the 1870s. Egypt owed £100 million sterling in international loans when, in 1876, Ismail was forced to accept a Public Debt Commission, just as Abdülhamid would in 1881. Foreign bureaucrats soon formed part of Ismail's government. Following the threat of a nationalist uprising, Egypt was effectively occupied by the British in 1882 and ruled indirectly by a British Consul until the Ottomans declared war in 1914.[20]

Selim III created or reorganised armament and gunpowder factories; his successors opened factories for uniforms and the like, but found themselves relying on foreign expertise and directors as well as financiers. Mahmud II's successors,

---

18   Coşkun Çakır, *Tanzimat Dönemi Osmanlı Maliye* [*Ottoman Finance in the Tanzimat Period*] (Istanbul, 2001), pp. 24–33, 55–76.

19   Donald Quataert, *Ottoman Manufacturing in the Age of the Industrial Revolution* (Cambridge, 2002), addresses the question of Ottoman nineteenth-century industrial and artisanal capacity.

20   Roger Owen, *The Middle East in the World Economy* (London, 1993), pp. 122–35.

Sultans Abdülaziz and Abdülmecid (r. 1861–76), addressed shortfalls by seeking foreign loans which began and continued through the Crimean War and moved the Ottoman economy, like that of Mehmed Ali's of Egypt, into the global market. They even experimented with paper money, which simply increased their reliance on the Ottoman Imperial Bank, which had to bail them out of the venture in 1862. In spite of its name, the Ottoman Imperial Bank was financed by British and French investors, even as it operated as the Ottoman state bank. The beneficiaries in Istanbul were largely non-Muslim families. The Ottomans defaulted on repayment of the interest on their loan in 1875–76, which stood then at £200 million. The result was the establishment in 1881 of the Public Debt Administration (PDA), an international agency which imposed European control over Ottoman finance and helped to restore some financial stability to the parts of the Ottoman economy under its control. It normally oversaw greater revenues than available to the sultan and his court. The PDA has often been likened to its successor, the International Monetary Fund.[21]

The late Ottomans proved incapable of safeguarding the traditional order or controlling their finances, and imposed a coercive political model on their subjects. Top-down reforms actually 'turned to the benefit of centripetal forces'.[22] While Mahmud II arguably thought in modern, secular terms, Abdülhamid II preferred to reinstate the status and influence of the religious classes. Installed on the throne by reform-minded administrators who constructed and promulgated a constitution in 1876, Abdülhamid quickly abrogated the document using the excuse of the Russo-Ottoman War of 1877–78, and his right to do so, which had been enshrined in the Gülhane constitutional document. Istanbul was then in the midst of the Great Eastern Crisis, as it is known, where an international commission was considering what to do with the Ottoman European territories which had been the scene of recent violent rebellions and repression by undisciplined Ottoman irregulars, called *bashibozuks*.

The international commission, ignoring the events unfolding in Istanbul, recommended the division of the Ottoman Balkans into three provinces: Eastern and Western Bulgaria and Bosnia-Herzegovina, with Western Bulgaria and Bosnia-Herzegovina acquiring semi-autonomous status and Eastern Bulgaria remaining as an Ottoman province. The Ottomans rejected the recommendations and went unprepared into a brief war with Russia, which proved to be an unmitigated disaster. In 1878, the Berlin Treaty awarded independence to Serbia, Romania and northern Bulgaria; Eastern Bulgaria (Rumelia) remained an Ottoman province.

This was the era of Gladstone's famous speech in parliament about the 'Turk' who should be ejected 'bag and baggage' from Europe: 'It is not a question of Mahometanism simply, but of Mahometanism compounded with the peculiar

---

21 Feroz Ahmad, *Turkey: The Quest for Identity* (Oxford, 2003), p. 193. Present-day Turks point with pride and bitterness to the fact that Republican Turkey acquired the Ottoman debt, and subsequently paid it off by the 1950s.

22 Dietrich Jung and Wolfango Piccoli, *Turkey at the Crossroads: Ottoman Legacies and a Greater Middle East* (London, 2001), p. 64.

character of a race … They were, from the black day when they first entered Europe, the one great anti-human specimen of humanity. Wherever they went, a broad line of blood marked the track behind them; and as far as their dominion reached, civilization disappeared from view.'[23] The Great Eastern Crisis altered the diplomatic relationships of the Ottomans. British public opinion essentially washed its hands of the Turkish barbarians as did British parliamentarians. The events of the period and the creation of the new Balkan states by the treaty of 1878 left the Ottomans with even less territory and fewer friends, except for the Germans, who offered both military and commercial expertise and financial assistance after the 1870s.

Ottoman Absolutism or Muslim Nationalism

Abdülhamid strove to reframe the empire as a modern, Muslim caliphate, at least partially in response to his bad press. Most historians have seen it as a defensive, mainly iconographic strategy in the face of the shrinking of territories, and the aggressive nationalism of the Balkans and the Caucasus. But, recently, the view concerning the worldwide challenge to British colonialism represented by Abdülhamid's pan-Islamism, which he himself may not have felt very deeply, is undergoing some revision.[24] Undoubtedly, he understood the value of iconography. Often painted as a rabid reactionary, Abdülhamid was, in fact, 'modern' in many senses of the word. He was engaged with presenting his empire in a favourable light, and was personally committed to what can legitimately be called a progressive agenda. Although he reinstated the old Ottoman model of political households in the palace, he understood the need for a stable, salaried bureaucracy, public schooling and literacy and the creation of a modern city. He remained deeply suspicious of the military, where most of the highly educated Muslim leadership was located, and he deliberately under-invested in military expenditures until the 1877–78 war required him to shift strategies.[25] His was the age of the telegraph and the railroad, and one of his final projects, the Hijaz railroad, was underwritten by Muslim subscription. His personal paranoia, however, drove a regime plagued by

---

23   Quoted in M. Şükrü Hanioğlu, *A Brief History of the Late Ottoman Empire* (Princeton, NJ, 2008), p. 111.

24   Engin Akarli, 'The Tangled Ends of an Empire: Ottoman Empire: Ottoman Encounters with the West and Problems of Westernization – an Overview', *Comparative Studies of South Asia, Africa and the Middle East* 26/3 (2006): pp. 353–66; Cemil Aydin, *The Politics of Anti-Westernism in Asia: Visions of World Order in Pan-Islamic and Pan-Asian Thought* (New York, 2007).

25   Selim Deringil, *The Well-Protected Domains: Ideology and Legitimation of Power in the Ottoman Empire, 1876–1909* (London, 1997); Butrus Abu-Manneh, *Studies on Islam and The Ottoman Empire in the Nineteenth Century, 1826–1876* (Istanbul, 2001); Virginia H. Aksan, 'The Ottoman Military and State Transformation in a Globalizing World', *Comparative Studies of South Asia, Africa and the Middle East* 27/2 (2007): pp. 259–72.

censorship and secret intelligence, more so even than the other dying empires of his neighbourhood.

Like his predecessor, Mahmud II, Abdülhamid II inflicted violence on his own populations without having real control over the instruments of that violence, such as the Kurdish Hamidiye militia, which he himself commissioned as new regiments, or the infamous semi-voluntary militias, the *bashibozuks* of the Balkans and Caucasus described above. Vastly understudied, because of the politically charged Armenian genocide debate, this period needs considerable dissection and recovery by Turkish and western historians alike as access to the archives of the period become more accessible.

Even though a time of great anxiety, as the limbs of the empire were torn asunder by the events described, the nineteenth century must have also been a vibrant, exciting time for emerging bourgeois sensibilities. It was the great age of nationalism and emergent literatures, connections with French internationalism and new forms of print. Ottoman subjects, largely non-Muslims, sent their families and children on the Ottoman equivalent of the grand tour to European cities. Many were educated abroad. Even Mahmud II ordered the sending of Muslim students to Europe for their studies: a handful went.[26] Regular embassies were established in major European cities; again, archival evidence of this is barely touched on in the historiographies. Ottoman historical, literary and periodical literature(s) emerged as parts of awakening national discourse(s), with profound implications for the survival of an Ottoman identity.

The reforms touched every aspect of Ottoman urban and rural life, be it dress, gender, families, censuses, conscription, municipal councils, new public schools, training academies for the military, provincial and land reforms (1864), taxes or the rule of law. What we once viewed as the complete Europeanisation of Ottoman society now looks much more like a singularly contested, embraced and lamented struggle about maintaining values understood as embedded in Muslim law and culture while recognising the need to improve the conditions of individual citizens. One of the most interesting of these has to do with the importation of legal systems, such as French and Italian civil and penal codes, and the systematic efforts to create a blended system of sharia/European law known as the *Mecelle*, a legal code never systematically imposed, but nonetheless still underlying much of the jurisprudence of the post-Ottoman states.[27]

Competing with the attempts to remake Ottoman diversity into universal citizenship was the bewildering variety of ethnic identities that coalesced into national narratives as the century unfolded. The creation of the Greek and Serbian nations are intertwined with the Eastern Question, interference of the European powers in what Sultan Mahmud II understood as a rebellion of his *reaya* (the 'flock'

---

26   The Turkish Republic continued the practice in the 1950s. Some of the first students of that era travelled on a converted US ship, decommissioned after the Second World War.

27   See, for example, the work of Ruth Miller, 'The Ottoman and Islamic Substratum of Turkey's Swiss Civil Code', *Journal of Islamic Studies* 11/3 (2000): pp. 335–61.

or 'peasants'). The Greek nation was imposed on the empire in 1831; the Serbian nation arose in the complex mix of Balkan and Russian competing views of how Eastern Europe should be organised following the expulsion of the Turk, and the Serbs began their march to independence in 1831, after several decades of revolt against Ottoman overlords. Typically, national sentiments began with the Orthodox Church where literacy largely lay until the mid-nineteenth century, but then were captured and often manipulated by Europeanised secular elites proposing separation from Ottoman rule, and constructing dictionaries and encyclopaedias of national languages and cultures, sometimes, as with the Albanians, for the first time. This was certainly true of Bulgaria, which in the eighteenth century acquired a separate patriarch with Ottoman approval, and then emerged in contest with Russia *and* the Ottomans in the nineteenth. Events were invariably complicated by Russian insistence that it had the right to protect its Orthodox brethren, one of the consequences of the 1774 Küçük Kaynarca treaty, and by the Muslim–non-Muslim ratio in the territories involved. The borders of the new Greek state, for example, enclosed only one-third of the Orthodox Greeks of the empire.

The national impulse, combined with European balance of power diplomacy, produced the 1878 Berlin Treaty, and would play out with further tragic consequences in the 1912–13 wars described below. Bosnia, Macedonia and Albania were far more diverse in terms of Muslim–Christian ratios, and, consequently, national sentiments arrived later. The Armenians, known as the loyal *millet*, were deeply entwined with Ottoman-Muslim identity and rule, and scattered in every corner of the empire, as merchants, agriculturalists, bankers, money-lenders and latterly state officials, serving on municipal councils and elsewhere. This was also the age of Zionism, and it should come as no surprise that representatives of political Zionism negotiated with the Ottomans for the right to settle in Palestine. The waves of refugee settlers began in the 1890s. The *Tanzimat* reforms empowered all such nationalist and religious groups who, tasting a bit of the freedom of equity, demanded much more of the government.

The lesser-known story of the nineteenth century is 'Muslim' nationalism. This evolved over the century from an attempt to create a non-religious Ottoman identity as a category of universal citizenship, to a Turkism, or pan-Turkism more restricted to the Muslim faith. Modern Turkish secular nationalism emerged only in the waning days of the empire under the aegis of the Committee of Union and Progress (see below). Similarly, Arab nationalism first arose as a call to an Arab brotherhood, Christian and Muslim, and an awakening as to the wealth of historical Arab civilisation. It is fair to say that the Arab nationalist project remains deeply contested and interrupted by the tragic events of post-Ottoman Arab societies.

Some historians estimate that, between the end of the Crimean War and 1918, perhaps as many as five million immigrants from Europe and the Caucasus, mostly Muslims, were forced to seek refuge in Anatolia. Work has just begun on the settlement policies of the late Ottoman government, which established a commission to take care of the Circassian and Tatar refugees pouring into the

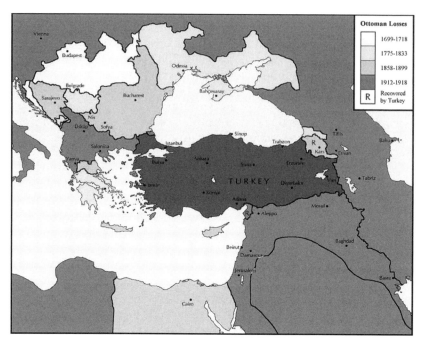

Map 6.1   Ottoman Losses. By Justin McCarthy. Used with permission from Middle East Studies Association

eastern provinces and into Romania and Bulgaria in the 1860s.[28] In Anatolia, such refugees encountered not just Armenians, but also Kurds, which resulted in a brutal disruption of settlement patterns, one of the explanations for later atrocities against the Armenians. A similar pattern of immigration occurred, in much smaller numbers, of Armenians into present-day Armenia and the Caucasus, especially in the 1830s and again in the 1860s. As with the Greek economic diaspora of a previous generation, Armenians living in Russia aspired to separation from the Ottomans. Nationalist sentiments turned into freedom societies such as the Hnchak and Dashnak Armenian Parties formed in 1887 and 1890 respectively. Demonstrations, and the occupation of the Ottoman Bank in Istanbul in 1896, precipitated harsh reprisals against innocent Armenian populations in the eastern territories and Istanbul alike.[29]

---

28   Justin McCarthy, *Death and Exile: The Ethnic Cleansing of Ottoman Muslims, 1821–1922* (Princeton, NJ, 1995), and his *The Ottoman Peoples and the End of Empire* (London, 2001). His statistics have been challenged by Armenian scholars. His core and reasonable observation was that the Muslim exile and exodus from Europe to Asia (west to east) remains almost untouched as a historical subject. James H. Mayer, 'Immigration, Return, and the Politics of Citizenship: Russian Muslims in the Ottoman Empire, 1860–1914', *International Journal of Middle East Studies* 39 (2007): pp. 15–32.

29   Edhem Eldem, *History of the Ottoman Bank* (Istanbul, 1999), pp. 233–9.

The events of 1894–96, generally referred to as the Armenian crisis, engendered disgust with Abdülhamid in European circles, and inspired further formation of revolutionary parties within the empire, notably in Macedonia, one of the most diverse provinces of the remaining Ottoman territories. Thessalonica, Macedonia's port city, was notable for its large numbers of Jews, more than 50 per cent of the population at the turn of the century. The next Ottoman crisis occurred around Macedonia, coveted by Greece, Bulgaria and Serbia alike, which now became the focus of a multitude of nationalist groups. In 1902, a series of guerrilla attacks were orchestrated by a Macedonian revolutionary group favouring union with Bulgaria; they were brutally suppressed by Ottoman forces.

By the eve of the First World War, Ottoman territories had effectively been reduced to present-day Thrace, Turkey and Mesopotamia (Map 6.1). Uprisings in Crete prompted the Ottoman war against Greece in Crete in 1897, which was won by the Turkish forces sent to put down the rebellion, but lost to British diplomacy in favour of the Greeks. Events there can be seen as the dividing line between state-sponsored Ottomanism and the spontaneous patriotism of the Turkish peasant army. It presaged the singular violence that would characterise the 1912–13 Balkan Wars. German observers and military advisors such as Colmar Freiherr von der Goltz predicted that the emerging moral energies of the Turkish 'volk', would spawn a Turco-Islamic culture.[30]

Turning Turk

It was in this context that Turkish nationalism first emerged on the peripheries. Military careerists such as Mustafa Kemal (later Atatürk, a native of Thessalonica), who had been trained in the secularised milieu of the prestigious Ottoman Military Academy, under the influence of the Prussian mission in Turkey since the 1870s, were instrumental in the creation of the revolutionary Committee of Union and Progress (hereafter the CUP, also called the Young Turks, or Unionists). The CUP began as a secret organisation among Ottoman officers in Thessalonica. The officers pressed for a restoration of the constitution, and the Third Army actually mutinied in Macedonia in 1908. On 23 July 1908, Abdülhamid reinstated the constitution, at least partially to forestall the challenge to his rule. Elections to a new chamber of deputies were held in 1908 (again in 1912 and 1914), and a bicameral parliament was convened by the sultan in December 1908, inaugurating what most historians now call the Second Constitutional Period. Most historians agree that this was a representative body, limited by gender and class, but embracing Ottoman diversity along ethnic and religious lines. The relatively independent body threatened the aims of both sultan and the CUP Central Committee core, which began to move to an authoritarian one-party rule. Initially an amorphous body of officers with

---

30   Kemal H. Karpat, *The Politicization of Islam: Reconstructing Identity, State, Faith, and Community in the Late Ottoman State* (New York, 2001), p. 24.

reformist intentions, the CUP was radicalised by Abdülhamid's countermeasures and censorship, widespread industrial unrest, and popular resistance to their turn to Turkism as national ideology.

The CUP ideologues found themselves in competition with the surviving Ottoman palace aristocracy, and their religious allies in the large Muslim intellectual class, whose loyalties were to the monarchy and the sharia, as well as to various divisive nationalist groups who clamoured for a larger voice in affairs. A counter-coup, probably engineered by the palace, and supported by disaffected military officers and Islamists, threatened CUP power in April 1909 (known in Turkish histories as the 31 March Incident). The CUP countered with a hastily mobilised Action Army, which defeated the mutinous soldiers on the streets of Istanbul, and resulted in the deposition and internal exile of Abdülhamid II, and the installation of his brother, Reşad, as Sultan Mehmed V. The retribution which followed was harsh, and inaugurated a more authoritarian period of CUP power. From 1909 to 1912, the CUP was primarily run by Enver (1881–1922), Cemal (1872–1922) and Talat (1874–1921) Pashas.

The ideological framework of revolutionary Turkism was supplied by sociologist Ziya Gökalp, who was heavily influenced by Durkheim, as were many of the new Turkish nationalist bourgeoisie. They argued that Ottoman society could be and ought to be Turkish, Muslim and modern: secular and scientific, but retaining its cultural roots in Islam.[31] These elites understood reform as enlightened social engineering by an oligarchy, but, of course, the need for state security and preservation of the vestigial Ottoman territories remained their top priority. Domestic reforms of the CUP secularised the legal system, improved the status of women, controlled elections and introduced 'economic nationalism', or 'state-created capitalist economy', which provided the later Kemalists with an organisational infrastructure on which to build the new Turkish Republic.[32] They cultivated a culture of corporate socialism which privileged Turkish Muslims over other nationalities as the European territories shrank.

In the face of much political opposition, and considerable effort to control the executive powers of the CUP, the triumvirate of Talat, Cemal and Enver assumed full powers in a 1912 coup, as Tripoli fell to the Italians and war threatened in the Balkans. It represented the effective end of the second constitutional experiment, although parliament continued to meet until 1918. The instrument of the CUP was the army, which it understood as the nation in arms. The Central Committee mobilised youths in paramilitary organisations and created a Special Organisation attached to the Ministry of War, responsible for military intelligence and counter-

---

31 M. Şükrü Hanioğlu, *Preparation for a Revolution: The Young Turks, 1902–1908* (Oxford, 2001) is monumental, tightly argued and heavily documented (one-third being notes and bibliography). For an influential earlier study, see Erik J. Zürcher, *The Unionist Factor: The Role of the Committee of Union and Progress in the Turkish National Movement* (Leiden, 1984). The debates over the nature of post-empire Turkey are well illustrated in Carter V. Findley, *Turkey, Islam, Nationalism and Modernity* (New Haven, 2011).

32 Jung and Piccoli, *Turkey,* p. 66.

insurgency. The CUP also tightly controlled the press, and used their publications as effective propaganda tools after 1913.[33]

Hence, the CUP was responsible for the disastrous defeats of the two Balkan Wars, 1912–13, and negotiating the secret alliance with Germany on the eve of world war. For the Ottomans, the First World War began in 1912. The Balkan declaration of war against the Ottomans in that year surprised Europe as much as the CUP. Montenegro, Greece, Serbia and Bulgaria, rivals since the 1878 Berlin Treaty, unexpectedly contrived an alliance against Istanbul. In spite of attempts by the Great Powers to intervene, the Balkans states declared war on the Ottomans in October 1912. Slow to mobilise, the Ottomans were beaten on all fronts. By December, Bulgarian troops, having taken the city of Edirne, were within 40 miles of Istanbul. The May 1913 Treaty of London, which halted the violence, heralded the end of the Ottomans in Europe. Ferocious fighting and much abuse of fleeing Muslim refugees characterised the short engagements. The erstwhile allies, however, began bickering about the division of the spoils, and while that was under way the CUP ordered the recapture of Edirne in July 1913, one indication of the Ottoman ability to recover and launch swift attacks. Hence, when the final treaties were signed, the Ottomans retained their foothold in Thrace, the only piece of good news to emerge from the two-year debacle, and still part of the Turkish Republic.

Efforts to acquire new European allies failed in 1913–14. Britain had long dismissed their former allies as a bad risk. Indeed, they could be said to be actively pursuing the protection of their territories in the Middle East in light of the inevitable collapse of the Ottoman Empire. Russia, Austria and France followed suit in the first half of 1914. As war loomed in the summer of 1914, Germany, previously uninterested, was persuaded to sign a treaty with the Ottoman government (2 August 1914). Enver Pasha is generally held responsible for pressing the secret negotiations with Germany to support reforms of both army and navy through military advisors, and to supply the Ottomans with arms. When war broke out in Europe in August 1914, the Ottomans, whose treaty with Germany did not require them to enter hostilities, declared armed neutrality and ordered empire-wide mobilisation, non-Muslim and Muslim.[34]

The Ottomans and the First World War

The Ottomans were eventually drawn into the war after a surprise attack on the Russian navy in the Black Sea (29 October 1914) by the German cruisers *Goeben* and *Breslau*. The war aims of the CUP may have been the recapture of lost territories

33 Hanioğlu, *Brief History*, p. 165; see also Ryan Gingeras, *Sorrowful Shores: Ethnicity and the End of the Ottoman Empire 1912–1923* (Oxford, 2009); Hasan Kayali, *Arabs and Young Turks: Ottomanism, Arabism, and Islamism in the Ottoman Empire 1908–1918* (Berkeley, CA, 1997).
34 Hanioğlu, *Brief History*, pp. 171–82.

in the Balkans and the consolidation over the remaining Mesopotamian (Arab) territories, as well as the incorporation of long autonomous regions such as the gulf, and the establishment of connections to the Muslim (largely Turkic) communities of the Caucasus, but Enver Pasha's dreams and the realities of an army recovering from the defeats of 1912–13 were two different things.

The Ottoman army of the First World War has long puzzled observers. The history of the Ottoman side of the Eastern (Asian front) is just beginning to receive the attention it has long deserved.[35] So too is the question of the dislocation of millions of people, not just the Armenians who were forced to leave their homes in eastern Anatolia, and march in untold misery and with accompanying atrocities, to Syria.[36]

In spite of the famine, raging fevers, poor equipment and underfed troops that characterised the state of the forces throughout the war, the Ottomans surpassed expectations. The first actual thrust was to cross the Sinai to Suez with 12,000–15,000 men, on rations of biscuits, dates and olives. Confrontations there with the British failed miserably. The major confrontations occurred in the Dardanelles at Gallipoli in 1915, and at Kut in Iraq in 1916 where, against all expectations, the Ottoman forces held up well. Initially underestimating Ottoman abilities to resist, the British reorganised their offensive lines, ordered reinforcements and gradually made their way deep into Syria. General Allenby's march into Jerusalem in early December 1917 was celebrated as the triumphal end of a crusade, and signalled the beginning of the end for the Ottoman troops. The government capitulated to the Allies in October 1918.

The social cost of the war was tremendous: 'Approximately 15% of the population, or one of two males beyond the civil service, was called to arms. By 1918, Ottoman casualties had reached the appalling figure of 725,000 (325,000 dead and 400,000 wounded) … More than a million deserters, constituting almost half the number of draftees, wreaked social havoc throughout the empire, especially in rural areas. Out of 2,608,000 men put in uniform, only 323,000 were still at their posts' in 1918. Most units existed on paper only.[37] Britain in the end was forced to deploy 2,550,000 men against the Ottoman army, and total allied casualties in the Middle Eastern arena are reckoned at 650,000. The Ottoman defence of Gallipoli, and subsequent withdrawal of the British, hastened the Bolshevik Revolution and

---

35 Mustafa Aksakal, *The Ottoman Road to War in 1914: The Ottoman Empire and the First World War* (Cambridge, 2008). An estimated 20 per cent of the civilian population, including the Armenians, perished in the wars in the region from 1912 until 1918, higher than any other participant in the First World War. The story of the wars has been ably told by Edward J. Erickson in several works: *Defeat in Detail: The Ottoman Army in the Balkans 1912–1913* (Westport, CT, 2003); *Ordered to Die: A History of the Ottoman Army in the First World War* (Westport, CT, 2000); see also Jonathan A. Grant, *Rulers, Guns and Money: The Global Arms Trade in the Age of Imperialism* (Harvard, MA, 2007).
36 For a review of some recent works, see Donald Quataert, 'The Massacres of Ottoman Armenians and the Writing of Ottoman History', *Journal of Interdisciplinary History* 37/2 (2006): pp. 249–59, and the discussion below.
37 Hanioğlu, *Brief History*, p. 181.

the collapse of Russia, which had deployed 702,000 troops in Anatolia and Iran, all of whom were withdrawn at the time of the Revolution.

As part of the Armistice Mudros in 1918, by which the Ottomans surrendered control of all garrisons outside Anatolia, the British occupied Istanbul (and the nominal government of the sultan) for the next five years. The last Ottoman parliament in 1920, decidedly anti-occupation and pro-nationalist, declared a National Pact, and called for the protection of minority rights, settlement of foreign debts (Public Debt Administration), independence, sovereignty and freedom of action, much to the outrage of the allies who were then devising the redistribution of the remaining Ottoman territories by the Treaty of Sèvres of 1920. The lasting impact of that treaty is notable even today in what historians call the 'Sèvres syndrome', the Turkish general paranoia about being carved up as once envisioned by the victorious allies.

Although the official histories exonerate Atatürk, founder of the Turkish Republic, of CUP excesses, he shared many of the ideas of the radical cells that began life in Thessalonica. He was also the popular hero of victory at Gallipoli, which catapulted him into the public arena. He spent most of the war, however, on the Syrian front, and not as part of the Central Committee. Ostensibly sent by the sultan after the armistice to the interior of Anatolia to disarm the remaining Ottoman forces, Atatürk succeeded in imposing the outlines of the contemporary republic on postwar Anatolia by rallying Muslims from all over Anatolia, and challenging both sultan and foreign occupiers. With his new popular Turkish army, he ultimately defeated the Greeks who, stimulated by the idea of reuniting Anatolia and Greece, and expecting allied backing, landed troops at Smyrna (Izmir). A brief and bloody civil war (known as the War of Independence in Turkey) ended when Atatürk's forces retook Izmir in 1922, forcing the withdrawal of the Greek army and masses of Ottoman Greek subjects. International negotiations ending in the 1923 treaty of Lausanne, where Ismet Inönü famously championed Turkish sovereignty and the right to self-determination, have been told ably elsewhere.[38]

The modern Turkish Republic was established in 1923. A 'Turk' was a citizen of the new Turkish Republic, regardless of ethno-religious identity. In reality, the notorious exchange of the Christian (1.5 million Turkish-speaking Greeks) populations of Anatolia for Muslims (600,000 Greek-speaking Turks) in Thrace, signed by Atatürk and Greek Prime Minister Venizelos, made certain that it stayed that way. One of Atatürk's most quoted refrains was: 'Yurtta sulh; cihanda sulh' ('Peace at home; peace in the world'), which signalled the new republic's intentions to stay within its borders. The Ottoman Empire was finished, literally and figuratively, as Atatürk proceeded to wipe most traces of it from the national narrative. All republican educational institutions embraced the Turkishness of the new nation, harked back to the Central Asian Turkish civilisations, and schooled their students to say 'Ne mutlu Türküm diyene', or 'How happy is he who can say "I am a Turk"'.

---

38 Especially well done in David Fromkin, *A Peace to End All Peace: Creating the Modern Middle East 1914–1922* (New York, 1989).

Ottoman Metanarratives

Students and scholars alike face a particularly interesting set of problems in approaching the study of an empire which straddles three continents and a vast array of cultures, Oriental and European. For one thing, the Ottoman house itself, while challenged continually by internal and external forces, was never actually toppled in its 600 years of existence. Secondly, in a Muslim civilisation legally, iconographically and culturally, none of the Ottoman sultans ever went on pilgrimage. Historians face further difficulties, not the least of which is the sacredness of much of the Middle Eastern space as the origin of western civilisation and monotheism in western imaginations. Equally important is the fact that post-Ottoman territories have comprised some 27 successor states since 1789.[39] Each of those states, in dozens of languages, has its own story to tell of the Ottoman experience, with predictable emphasis on the national triumph over the Turkish oppressor. The Turkish Republican version simply ignores the Ottoman past in favour of the story of the triumph of the secular nation-state, eliding the Armenian question. This wide diversity of views was typical of Ottoman historiography, which was singularly ill-developed until the 1980s, when historians began seriously to dismantle the teleological narrative(s) of westernisation and modernisation. Historians are now spending as much time writing about Ottoman difference with, as they are about Ottoman comparability to, other empires.[40]

Both popular and scholarly narratives have been produced in what appears to be an explosion of demand for an explanation of pre-modern Middle East history, driven in part by post-2001 events in the region and seemingly intractable conundrums such as the conflict between Israel and Palestine. For a long time, narratives of the Ottomans divided the 600 years into two empires: the 'classical' era of Süleyman the Magnificent (1520–66), extended to c. 1650 by most, and the era of *Tanzimat*, from 1839 to 1918 (or to 1923 if the narrative includes the emergence of the Turkish Republic). By and large, those who worked in the earlier period did not trespass into the nineteenth century. The reverse is also true, with the added complication that the Turkish revolutionary republican historiography tended to extend its shadow backwards to the eighteenth century. That is to say, the story of recovery and transformation was anachronistically applied to historical terrain not amenable to explanations based on the simple top-down transformative (westernised) model. Those who teach the region in North America normally find themselves covering much of the late empire, notably as an introductory appendage to myriad modern Middle East courses. The so-called Golden Age of the Ottomans is found most often in the middle of world history courses as part of the early modern or Mediterranean period.

The best illustration of the 'two' empires is the pair of Cambridge studies by Daniel Goffman *The Ottoman Empire and Early Modern Europe* and Donald Quataert

---

39   Hanioğlu, *Brief History*, p. 219 n. 4.
40   See Virginia Aksan, 'Locating the Ottomans Among Early Modern Empires', *Journal of Early Modern History* 3 (1999): pp. 104–134.

The Ottoman Empire 1700–1922. Goffman's history ends around 1600, while Quataert begins with 1700. Goffman challenges historians of the Renaissance by arguing strenuously for the enormous impact of the Ottomans on European consciousness.[41]

Donald Quataert's work is a useful survey of the economic and social history of the empire's last days which simply ignores the history of the disintegration described above. By contrast, Colin Imber's *The Ottoman Empire 1300–1650: The Structure of Power* presents the empire entirely in its own voice, and resists even the slightest inclination to draw comparative parallels or to go beyond the contemporary texts. Imber's work, although more readable, is very much in the tradition of the grand old man of Ottoman history, Halil İnalcık (especially his *Ottoman Empire*).[42]

The historiography of the modern era has been dominated by the twin subjects of national liberation and modernisation, focusing and concentrating on the passage from empire to successor states, the rise of Turkish nationalism, the despotism and brutality of Abdülhamid II, the Armenian question and the collapse of the empire in the First World War. Select examples of good late imperial (that is, Turkish) narratives include those of Douglas A. Howard, journalists Dietrich Jung and Wolfango Piccoli (who seek present-day Turkey's military oligarchy and over-bureaucratised state in Ottoman precedents) and Erik J. Zürcher (renowned for his studies of the Young Turks) whose political sketch of the late nineteenth century is good, but who is striking on the early nationalist period. Also good is the work of Şükrü Hanioğlu, the foremost Turkish scholar on the Young Turks and their Macedonian origins.[43]

Bernard Lewis' *Emergence of Modern Turkey* and Niyazi Berkes' *The Development of Secularism in Turkey* remain classics of a particularly recognisable type, obvious in the title of Berkes' work. That both are still in print reflects the state of the discussion around the national narrative which, in official Turkish historiography particularly, remains Turk-centric and claustrophobic. Justin McCarthy's *The Ottoman Turks: An Introductory History to 1923*, which continues the tradition in title and text, actually turns out to be a decent look at the Eurasian connections of the dynasty,

---

41   Goffman is among a growing body of scholars who are integrating the Ottomans into Braudelian Mediterranean history. Nicholas Doumanis reviews some of these works by Faroqhi, Goffman, Molly Greene, Masters and Quataert, in 'Durable Empire: State Virtuosity and Social Accommodation in the Ottoman Mediterranean', *Historical Journal* 49/3 (2006): pp. 953–66. Palmira Brummett expands on the Mediterranean as a fruitful research space in 'Imagining the Early Modern Ottoman Space: From World History to Piri Reis', in Virginia H. Aksan and Daniel Goffman (eds), *The Early Modern Ottomans: Remapping the Empire* (Cambridge, 2007), pp. 15–58, and in 'Visions of the Mediterranean: A Classification', *Journal of Medieval and Early Modern Studies* 37/1 (2007): pp. 9–55.

42   Colin Imber, *The Ottoman Empire, 1300-1650: The Structure of Power* 2nd ed. (Basingstoke, 2009); Halil İnalcık, *The Ottoman Empire: The Classical Age 1300–1600* (Westport, CT, 1973; London, 2002). See Leslie Peirce's 'Changing Perceptions of the Ottomans: The Early Centuries', *Mediterranean Historical Review* 19/1 (2004): pp. 7–8, where she makes much the same point about myopic studies of Ottoman uniqueness. The *MHR* issue is devoted to state-of-the-art reviews on the Middle East.

43   Douglas Howard, *The History of Turkey* (Westport, CT, 2001); Jung and Piccoli, *Turkey*; Erik J. Zürcher, *Turkey: A Modern History*, 3rd ed. (London, 2004); Hanioğlu, *Brief History*.

and a sympathetic look at social identity constructions of the nineteenth century as well as the human costs of the First World War and the republican period.[44] The Ottoman Arab and Balkan worlds are generally muted in the likes of Lewis, Berkes and McCarthy, but successive generations have moved into universal and thematic perspectives. Urban histories of all parts of the Ottoman realms use cityscapes to explore social interactions and the discourse on modernity, the economy and relations between religious communities. The *Tanzimat* itself has begun to serve as a *fin de siècle* moment.

Like Goffman and Quataert, James Gelvin's classroom text *The Modern Middle East*, with its post-colonial orientation, serves up a social history of lives in the Arab world. Jane Hathaway, whose expertise lies in Egypt, has recently published *The Arab Lands Under Ottoman Rule 1516–1800*.[45] Others have contributed scholarly texts on diverse regions of the empire: Jens Hanssen on Beirut; Beshara Doumani on Nablus; James Reilly on Hama and so forth. Long the domain of French and Arab scholars, urban social history continues to produce some of the best works for the period from 1650 to 1850.[46]

Consuming the Ottoman *longue durée* requires a strong stomach, partly because it *is* difficult to cover over 600 years of history, and there are minefields that await the unwary in ethno-religious sensitivities and national myths. Stanford Shaw's two-volume work *The History of Turkey* continues in print, as does Lord Kinross' popular *The Ottoman Centuries*. Most other comprehensive histories of the Ottomans are cartoons or fictionalised oriental tales, a particularly resilient way of portraying the Ottoman difference.[47] One happy exception is Caroline Finkel's *Osman's Dream:*

44 Bernard Lewis, *The Emergence of Modern Turkey* (Oxford, 1968); Niyazi Berkes, *The Development of Secularism in Turkey* (Montreal, 1964); Justin McCarthy, *The Ottoman Turks: An Introductory History to 1923* (Harlow, 1997).

45 James Gelvin, *The Modern Middle East: A History* (Oxford, 2005); Jane Hathaway with Karl Barbir, *The Arab Lands Under Ottoman Rule 1516–1800* (Harlow, 2007).

46 Jens Hanssen, *Fin de Siècle Beirut: The Making of an Ottoman Provincial Capital* (Oxford, 2005); Beshara Doumani, *Rediscovering Palestine: Merchants and Peasants in Jabal Nablus 1700–1900* (Berkeley, CA, 1995); James Reilly, *A Small Town in Syria: Ottoman Hama in the Eighteenth and Nineteenth Century* (Oxford, 2002); Merip Anastassiadou, *Salonique 1830–1912* (Leiden, 1997); André Raymond, *Cairo* (Cambridge, MA, 2000); Thomas Philipp, *Acre: The Rise and Fall of a Palestinian City 1730–1831* (New York, 2001); Abraham Marcus, *The Middle East on the Eve of Modernity: Aleppo in the Eighteenth Century* (New York, 1989); Bruce Masters, *The Origin of Western Economic Dominance in the Middle East: Mercantilism and the Islamic Economic in Aleppo 1600–1750* (New York, 1988); Abdul-Karim Rafeq, *The Province of Damascus 1723–1783* (Beirut, 1966); Linda Schatkowski-Schilcher, *Families in Politics: Damascene Families and Estates of the Eighteenth and Nineteenth Centuries* (Stuttgart, 1985), and James Grehan, *Everyday Life and Consumer Culture in Eighteenth-Century Damascus* (Seattle, WA, 2007).

47 Stanford Shaw, *History of the Ottoman Empire and Turkey* 2 vols. (Cambridge, MA, 1976-77); Lord Kinross, *The Ottoman Centuries: The Rise and Fall of the Turkish Empire* (New York, 1977). See Virginia Aksan 'The Ottoman Story Today', *Middle East Studies Association Bulletin* 25 (2001): pp. 35–42, which reviewed a number of the titles mentioned here; and, in the oriental tale category see, Jason Goodwin, *Lords of the Horizon* (New York, 2003)

The History of the Ottoman Empire.[48] The long-awaited four-volume *Cambridge History of Turkey*, mostly driven by the energy of Suraiya Faroqhi and Kate Fleet, began to appear in 2006.[49] Faroqhi's *Artisans of Empire* continues her prodigious publishing of more generalised social histories.[50] Daniel Goffman and Virginia Aksan's edited collection, *The Early Modern Ottomans*, broadens the chronological scope of the middle period of Ottoman history, challenging fellow historians in the title and body of the work to consider how and when the Ottomans can be said to have entered the modern age.

Debates Concerning Seventeenth-Century Crises

The three most repeated explanations for the Ottoman middle era, 1650–1800, are 'inexorable decline', or 'decentralisation', the latter intrinsically linked to the other two political and diplomatic metanarratives: 'westernisation' and its corollary, 'modernisation'. Decline theorists assert that the Ottomans lost control over their internal resources, over the ability to raise armies, as well as over taxation systems as early as 1600, and never recovered such control. The empire struggled on for 300 more years, motionless and unchanging. Hence, 'decline' has come in for considerable revision.[51] Ottomanist debates, prompted by those around the European global crisis of the seventeenth century, have focused on the incorporation of the Ottomans into the world economy, which initially meant challenging the theory of the Asiatic mode of production. Nonetheless, the debate has since given birth to myriad and robust studies on trade, agriculture, tax-farming and international economic systems, making the Ottomans a very real part of the world history canon.[52]

and Andrew Wheatcroft, *The Ottomans* (London, 1993). Leslie Peirce calls Wheatcroft quasi-scholarly and Goodwin breezy and anecdotal ('Changing Perceptions', p. 8).

48 Caroline Finkel, *Osman's Dream: The History of the Ottoman Empire* (New York, 2006). See Virginia Aksan's review on H-Turk of the Finkel work: 'The Long Ottoman Road' (www.h-net.org/reviews/showrev.php?id=13356); and Christine Woodhead's review article on a number of the titles mentioned here: 'Consolidation of the Ottoman Empire: New Works on Ottoman History, 1453–1839', *English Historical Review* 123/53 (2008): pp. 973–87.

49 Vol. 2, edited by Fleet and Faroqhi; vol. 3, edited by Faroqhi; and vol. 4, edited by Reşat Kasaba, were published in 2006–2009; vol. 1, edited by Kate Fleet, in 2010. A predecessor, still in print, Halil İnalcık and Donald Quataert's *Economic and Social History of the Ottoman Empire* (Cambridge, 2004) remains authoritative on the state of Ottoman economic history.

50 Suraiya Faroqhi, *Artisans of Empire: Crafts and Craftspeople Under the Ottomans* (Basingstoke, 2009); *Subjects of the Sultan: Culture and Daily Life in the Ottoman Empire* (Basingstoke, 2005); *The Ottoman Empire and the World Around It* (London, 2004).

51 See Douglas Howard, 'Genre and Myth in the Ottoman Advice for Kings Literature', in Aksan and Goffman (eds), *Early Modern Ottomans*, pp. 145–6.

52 Huri İslamoğlu-İnan (ed.), *The Ottoman Empire and the World-Economy* (Cambridge,

Westernisation or modernisation (the 'impact of the west'), the old way of representing Ottoman survival, has two schools of thought. One looks for the influence of secularism and constitutionalism on Ottoman institutions and intellectuals, the phenomenon of the phoenix rising from the ashes. The other is driven by assumptions of technological ineptitude, and the inability of native systems to adapt and regroup.[53] Kemal Karpat's *The Politicization of Islam* is a synthesis which reminds us that an internal Muslim discourse ran in the later Ottoman years as an alternative to the secularist version of the Ottoman future. Müge Göçek has mapped the bifurcation of the *Tanzimat* along the religious divide, in *Rise of the Bourgeoisie: Demise of Empire*.[54] Both books lead into more interesting questions than the widely prevalent 'Eastern Question' historiography, which maintains that the Ottomans survived because Europe allowed them to do so. There are, of course, just as many who suffer from neo-Ottoman nostalgia and pine for the 'tolerant' society of the Ottoman sixteenth and seventeenth centuries, or for the return of the caliphate, referring to Abdülhamid II as the last great caliph.

The early twenty-first-century debate about modernity and the arrival of western colonialism and imperialism in Middle Eastern societies promises a more nuanced examination of late Ottoman history. Abou El-Haj's influential *Formation of the Modern State: The Ottoman Empire Sixteenth to Eighteenth Centuries* sets out an agenda calling for a refocus on class, changing social order and fluidity rather than on state structures, Weberian bureaucracies and decline.[55] Ottoman dynamism, according to El-Haj, needed its own definition to explain the internal violence of the seventeenth century, and the upheavals among the elites around the sultan. Comparative studies, he argued, could avoid anachronistic assumptions about Ottoman social evolution (or lack of it) based on reading backwards from the nineteenth century.

The resistance to Ottoman sovereignty to which El-Haj alluded has received further consideration in Karen Barkey's *Bandits and Bureaucrats: The Ottoman Route to State Centralization*,[56] which offers a new model for the transitional period of the Ottoman state. Ottoman sultans and local grandees were recognised and rewarded

1987); Reşat Kasaba, *The Ottoman Empire and the World Economy: The Nineteenth Century* (Albany, NY, 1988); Donald Quataert, *Manufacturing in the Ottoman Empire and Turkey, 1500–1950* (Albany, NY, 1994).

53   Peter C. Perdue refers to that approach as the 'vocabulary of deficit' with which '[t]heorists examine non-European states to discover what essential ingredients [of the European success formula] they lacked'. 'Empire and Nation in Comparative Perspective: Frontier Administration in Eighteenth-Century China', *Journal of Early Modern History* 5/4 (2001): p. 282.

54   Bernard Lewis and Stanford Shaw remain the predominant representatives of such views: Karpat, *The Politicization of Islam*; Fatma Müge Göçek, *Rise of Bourgeoisie, Demise of Empire* (Oxford, 1996).

55   Rifa'at Ali Abou El-Haj, *Formation of the Modern State: The Ottoman Empire Sixteenth to Eighteenth Centuries* (Albany, 1991).

56   Karen Barkey, *Bandits and Bureaucrats: The Ottoman Route to State Centralization* (Ithaca, 1994).

for mobilising provincial reserve armies when needed, she argues, and dismissed or destroyed when no longer of use or when they had proved either too strong or too corruptible. The apparent tolerance of numerous sultans for blurred lines of legitimacy, and their perspicacity in constructing a model of inclusion and exclusion, bound Istanbul and provincial grandees in a cycle of punishment and amnesty.

Research on the question of 'belonging' to the Ottoman state, premised on access (guaranteed by a certificate) to some portion, however tiny, of the empire's wealth, has been strengthened by her paradigm, one of the few generated from within Ottoman historiography itself. There is massive documentary evidence of appeals by individuals and village collectives as well as provincial warlords and their armies to the sultan and his officials for lenience, amelioration and/or restoration of the contract between the 'state' and its 'subject'. This would appear to be at least one explanation for the continued acceptance of Ottoman rule.

Studies of these relationships, their households, their rivalries, their loyalty to Istanbul and success and failures as provincial warlords have increased dramatically. Volume 3 of the *Cambridge History of Turkey* devotes two chapters to the 'Semi-autonomous Forces in the Balkans and Anatolia', by Fikret Adanir and 'Semi-autonomous Forces in the Arab Provinces', by Bruce Masters. Adanir notes that the 'successful centralisation and monetarisation of the revenue mechanisms of the state, took place against the background of a reshuffling of the provincial administration', while Masters concludes that paradoxically, 'the rise of local elites and the devolution of economic resources [in the eighteenth century] made for widening the identity of the Arab *ayans* [notables] as *Ottomans*'.[57] Work such as this has liberated the seventeenth and eighteenth centuries from the shadow of nationalist narratives, themselves the subject of much revisionism since the collapse of the Soviet Union in 1989.

A handful of individuals have moved beyond the economic and political story to take up cultural questions of Ottoman modernity in the nineteenth century, some engaging with governmentality, others with state discipline, and still others with aesthetics, which is starting to bear fruit in new generations of students: works on education, architecture, city planning, gender, families have been added to the deep literatures on minorities, especially the Jews.[58] Most new students of the empire are surprised at how much of the late Ottoman record lies untouched in the libraries and archives of Istanbul.

---

57 Fikret Adanir, 'Semi-autonomous Forces in the Balkans and Anatolia', p. 167, and Bruce Masters, 'Semi-autonomous Forces in the Arab Provinces', p. 206, in Faroqhi, *Cambridge History of Turkey, vol. 3, Later Ottoman Empire 1603–1839*.

58 Cem Behar, *A Neighborhood in Ottoman Istanbul: Fruit Vendors and Civil Servants in the Kasap Ilyas Mahalle* (Albany, NY, 2003); Sibel Bozdoğan, *Modernism and Nation Building: Turkish Architectural Culture in the Early Republic* (Seattle, WA, 2001); Palmira Brummett, *Image and Revolution in the Ottoman Revolutionary Press, 1908–1911* (Albany, NY, 2000); Zeynep Çelik, *Displaying the Orient: Architecture of Istanbul at Nineteenth-Century World's Fairs* (Berkeley, CA, 1992); Benjamin Fortna, *Imperial Classroom: Islam, the State and Education in the Late Ottoman Empire* (Oxford, 2002); Timothy Mitchell, *Colonizing Egypt* (Berkeley, CA, 1988).

The Ottoman System and Its Critics

There are a number of ongoing debates about the Ottoman *longue durée*, which have evolved as more archives and chronicles are made available. The focus here will be on the debates around the question of slavery and relations with non-Muslims. Both discussions concern the question of Ottoman identities. What makes the Ottomans so fascinating, especially in the centuries before 1650, is precisely what makes them so difficult to study. The earliest eye-witnesses to the Ottomans wrote in Latin, Greek, Hungarian, Italian, various Slavic languages, Arabic, Persian and Turkish. The Ottomans emerged in a time of considerable social and political disorder and widespread antinomianism. The earliest official histories are rife with myths and fictive genealogies, written to celebrate and legitimate Ottoman rule. Of the few who have ventured into full translation of the official histories of the house, commissioned by Beyazid I and his successors, Colin Imber's *The Ottoman Empire 1300–1481* is most successful at evoking the period, as he has carefully reconstructed the Ottoman rise exclusively from surviving primary sources. Byzantine scholar Donald M. Nicol has rpublished a translation of an Italian work written in 1509 by Theodōros Spandounes, from a family of Greek refugees from conquered Istanbul after 1453. Along with Imber, *On the Origin of the Ottoman Emperors* broadens our understanding of the early centuries of the Ottoman conquest.[59] One of the persistent debates emerging from these cloudy beginnings has to do with relations between the Ottomans, their entourages and their non-Muslim (and non-Turkish Muslim) subjects). The debate is largely centred on two axes: the Ottomans as a slave state, and the role and fate of the *millet* (confessional) communities in larger Ottoman society.

Ottoman Janissaries were recruited from Christian boys, either war captives, or conscripts, often part of the capitulatory agreements made with conquered territories. Circumcised and raised as Muslims, they remained slaves of the sultan (*kul*), even though graduation into the ranks of Janissaries after an extended apprenticeship was accompanied by emancipation. Balkan historians, especially during the Soviet period, represented the Ottoman military slave system as the absolute death of pre-Ottoman Balkan society, inevitably the age of 'the Ottoman yoke'. The periodic round-up (*devşirme*) of the young boys and its catastrophic effects on Balkan villages is fundamental to all nationalist narratives of the Balkans, even though the field generally understands that some of these military slaves ended up as prominent leaders of the empire in the first two to three hundred years of the empire, and even on occasion endowed their homelands with charitable institutions. The round-ups were finished by the mid-seventeenth century, as sons of Janissaries, and other Muslim notables, clamoured for and received membership of the elite organisation. What then to make of these converted 'Ottomans' who were both loyal servants of the sultan, and often his severest critics?

---

59   Colin Imber, *The Ottoman Empire 1300–1481* (Istanbul, 1990); Theodōros Spandounes, *On the Origins of the Ottoman State*, trans. and ed. Donald MacGillivray Nicol (Cambridge, 2009).

Two books on slavery help to complicate the picture. Bernard Lewis' *Race and Slavery in the Middle East*, a slight work dedicated to pointing out that Muslims were capable of racism and slave practices, introduces the ambiguities of slaves in Muslim law. Emancipation was an exceptionally good deed in Muslim teachings, and children of concubines were considered free. More recently, Ehud Toledano and Hakan Erdem have placed Ottoman history in the context of the historiography of world slavery and its abolition in the nineteenth century (between the 1860s and the 1890s in the Ottoman realms).[60] The Janissary–sultan relationship, based on the original alienation of boys from their mothers, was couched always in Ottoman iconography as a father–son relationship, and early members of the corps could be relied on for unswerving loyalty to their master. The slave army became the moral compass of the empire, capable of seating and unseating sultans, and many of the rebellions attributed to them were based on real abuses: limiting of privileges, debasement of coinages and sending them on long and futile marches into Shi'ite territories particularly.[61]

Europe (Poland and Ukraine mostly, but the principalities, and the Habsburg territories as well) was also subject to enslavement in the periodic raids by the Muslim Tatar Khanate of the Crimea, either as an advance guard for Ottoman campaigns, or simply as part of their economy. The territories of the Khan became a client state of the Ottomans at the end of Mehmed II's reign. The Khan could command as many as 80,000 horsemen for campaigns, and was essential to the Ottoman military until 1783, when Catherine II unilaterally annexed the Crimea.[62] Thus, there was a continual stream of slaves to populate imperial and notable households, a system which continued well into the nineteenth century in the system of *evlatlik* (adopted or foster child). Circassians especially sold their children to city dwellers to be raised as servants in large households. Husrev Pasha (d. 1855), the towering figure behind the throne of Mahmud II, raised some 45 slaves in his personal household, most of whom became bureaucrats of the *Tanzimat*. His was the last of the great political households of the Ottoman imperial entourage.

Slavery existed elsewhere, of course. Work on the palace harem, or private quarters of the women and the sultan, most rife of all with stereotypes of Oriental fantasies, has undergone much revision, notably by Leslie Peirce (*The Imperial Harem*), who demonstrates the extent to which the harem represented a system of dynastic reproduction, where sultanic mothers and favourites were empowered with salaries and land grants, resulting in the construction of enormous charitable

---

60 Bernard Lewis, *Race and Slavery in the Middle East: A Historical Enquiry* (New York, 1990); Hakan Erdem, *Slavery in the Ottoman Empire and its Demise, 1800–1909* (New York, 1996); Ehud Toledano, *Slavery and Abolition in the Ottoman Empire* (Seattle, WA, 1998), and *As if Silent and Absent: Bonds of Enslavement in the Islamic Middle East* (New Haven, CT, 2007).

61 Virginia Aksan, 'War and Peace', in Faroqhi, *Cambridge History of Turkey*: vol. 3, pp. 81–117.

62 On Crimean Tatars, Brian Glyn Williams, *The Crimean Tatars: The Diaspora Experience and the Forging of the Nation* (Leiden, 2001).

projects such as the mosques of Istanbul.[63] The harem was populated with everything but Turks, mostly prized beauties from the Caucasus, and occasional European captives. Eunuchs arrived from Egypt in another form of slave system, black eunuchs serving the harem, while white eunuchs served the male equivalent of the harem quarters, where the male progeny of the reigning sultan resided in considerable seclusion from the mid-seventeenth century. The black eunuch was perhaps the most powerful member of the court, second only to the grand vizier, until the edge of the modern age in the eighteenth century.[64]

That prompts us to consider the question of Ottoman identity by investigating the self-representation of the imperial court which, after its arrival in Istanbul, never described itself as Turkish, a word which connoted an unsophisticated rustic until the end of the nineteenth century. An Ottoman was an educated Muslim, theoretically fluent in Arabic, Persian and Turkish, and cognisant of the religious sciences and law. Background was irrelevant as long as one was Muslim by birth or conversion. Converts were a ubiquitous part of the court. Much revisionism about the place of the convert (and the renegade and the minorities as well) in Ottoman circles is underway.[65] To be Ottoman, then, was first and foremost to be Muslim, and then to share in an imperial multi-lingual culture which included the ability to write poetry, one of the most frequently cited traits in the biographical dictionaries of Ottoman notables well into the nineteenth century. This was the Ottoman Muslim ruling house, and its elites were classified as the military class (*askeri*) as opposed to the ruled, or peasant class (*reaya*).

From Subject to Citizen: Ottoman Ethnographies

For most of the history of the empire, the *millets*, as the religious confessional groups were called, numbered three in Ottoman documents, as noted earlier. Such arrangements, largely ad hoc, were later extended to the Catholic (in the mid-eighteenth century) and Protestant (mid-nineteenth century) communities of the empire. How these so-called *millets* were construed, and to what extent the law represented the reality of even so limited an understanding of 'tolerance', has been a major source of historiographic debate. The impact of modernity on such non-differentiated identities raises a host of interesting questions. Historians disagree on

---

63 Leslie Peirce, *The Imperial Harem* (New York, 1993), Lucienne Thys-Şenocak, *Ottoman Women Builders: The Architectural Patronage of Hadice Turhan Sultan* (Aldershot, 2006).

64 Jane Hathway, *el Hajj Beshir Agha: Chief Eunuch of the Ottoman Imperial Harem* (Oxford, 2006).

65 Valensi, *The Birth of the Despot*; Daniel Goffman, 'Negotiating with the Renaissance State: The Ottoman Empire and the New Diplomacy', in Aksan and Goffman, *Early Modern Ottomans*, pp. 59–74; E. Nathalie Rothman, *Brokering Empire: Trans-Imperial Subjects Between Venice and Istanbul* (Ithaca, 2012).

whether *Tanzimat* legislation actually improved the lot of the non-Muslim subjects of the empire. Most agree that the economic and social condition of Muslims worsened, but disagree as to the impact on Christian or Jewish communities. As the *Tanzimat* bureaucrats turned to constitutionalism in the nineteenth century, they learned the new ethno-religious categories of emerging nationalism(s). Mahmud II always referred to his subjects as his *reaya* even when they rebelled, not as 'Serbians' or 'Greeks' as the great powers preferred. Learning to sort out the loyal Greeks from the rebellious meant acquiring new labels: loyal Greeks continued to be *Rum*, meaning of the Greek Orthodox *millet*, while the rebellious ones, subsequently the residents of the new Greek nation, became *Yunanli*, from 'Yunanistan', the Turkish word for Greece. From here it was but a short step to ethnographic categorisation of *aşiret*, for example, the ubiquitous and generic word for 'tribe' until the mid-nineteenth century, when Ottoman reforms and the arm of centralisation reached into Arab Bedouin communities in Syria and Iraq or Kurdish communities in eastern Anatolia and Iraq, some of whom developed a sense of tribal identity for the first time.[66]

Bruce Masters argues that Ottoman discrimination against *millet* populations was no different in the sixteenth or the nineteenth century, while Ussama Makdisi sees the development of sectarianism as a direct result of the 1856 recognition of the freedom of religion.[67] Others who examine the records of the sharia *kadi* (judge) court – the unique Ottoman institution which touched the lives of all subjects, Muslim or non-Muslim – see a preference among Christian women for divorce and inheritance adjudication in Muslim courts, while still others read racial and ethnic degradation (*Dhimmitude*) in the epistemology of court language around non-Muslim plaintiffs and defendants.[68] The grand paradox of the nineteenth century is that all central attempts to implement egalitarianism actually created further fissures in relations between the Muslim and non-Muslim communities. The impact of enumeration, the clarity of divisions around religious affiliation, the pressure to envision oneself as part of a new nation, great power intrigues, the economic opportunities of Christian communities to ally themselves with foreign consuls, the exclusion of non-Muslims of the 'nation under arms' all exposed a society that was probably beyond the moment when it could repair the cracks. The Armenian revolts and the Ottoman reaction to them which led to the tragic events of 1915 have to be seen as emerging from CUP paranoia about dissolution,

---

66 Eugene Rogan, *Frontiers of the State in the Late Ottoman Empire: Transjordan 1850–1921* (Cambridge, 1999); Reuven Aharoni, *The Pasha's Bedouin: Tribes and State in the Egypt of Mehemet Ali, 1801–1848* (London, 2007).

67 Bruce Masters, *Christians and Jews in the Ottoman Arab World: The Roots of Sectarianism* (Cambridge, 2001); Ussama Makdisi, *The Culture of Sectarianism: Community, History and Violence in Nineteenth Century Ottoman Lebanon* (Berkeley, CA, 2000).

68 Iris Agmon, *Family and Court: Legal Culture and Modernity in Late Ottoman Palestine* (Syracuse, NY, 2005); Avigdor Levy (ed.), *The Jews of the Ottoman Empire* (Princeton, NJ, 1984); Bat Ye'or, *The Dhimmi: Jews and Christians Under Islam* (Rutherford, NJ, 1985).

perceived decline of the Muslim bourgeoisie, the total collapse of the economy and a sense of betrayal of the most loyal of the *millets*.

Under international pressure, the debate about whether or not to recognise the Armenian genocide has been much broadened of late, as younger generations of Armenians and Turks outside Turkey talk to one another. Significant contributors to the debate include Ron Suny, Donald Bloxham, Müge Göçek and Taner Akçam.[69] Even in Turkey, where such debates are fraught with personal political consequences, the topic is on the table, as one more hurdle to becoming part of the extended European community. It has many in Turkey wondering about the virtue of joining the European Union, as they know perfectly well that the real issue has much more to do with the fact that the population is almost 100 per cent Muslim, simultaneously a testimony to the triumph of nation-state modernity and ethnic relocation as well as a badge of exclusion from Europe.

Future Research

The study of the Ottoman Empire has come of age in the twenty-first century. For a small field, it is in great demand in a post-9/11 world asking for historical explanations of present violence. The tension lies between the micro and the macro: the field still needs detailed and documented studies of the empire to a large degree, but Ottoman historians find themselves increasingly drawn into large thematic and comparative projects.[70] A quick glance at the Ottoman presence at the Annual Meeting of the Middle East Studies Association reveals a wide range of old and new approaches to many of the questions raised here. The definition and role of secularism in Turkey, studies of the Islamist parties, and religious identities such as the Alevis and Assyrians, stand side by side with panels on the Armenian and Kurdish questions. Biographies and subjecthood are emerging as a major subfield of Ottoman history, encompassing collective as well as individual experiences. New generations of young historians in Bulgaria and Greece are generating exciting work on the Ottoman experience of their populations, including urban settings and the trials and tribulations of migration and population exchanges. Colonialism, post-colonialism and gendered approaches to the east–west encounter

---

69   Taner Akçam, *From Empire to Republic: Turkish Nationalism and the Armenian Genocide* (London, 2004); Donald Bloxham, *The Great Game of Genocide: Imperialism, Nationalism, and the Destruction of the Ottoman Armenians* (Oxford, 2005); Fatma Müge Göçek, 'Turkish Historiography and the Unbearable Weight of 1915', in Richard G. Hovannisian (ed.), *The Armenian Genocide: Cultural and Ethical Legacies* (New Brunswick, NJ, 2007); Ronald Grigor Suny, Fatma Müge Göçek and Norman M. Naimark (eds), *A Question of Genocide: Armenians and Turks at the End of the Ottoman Empire* (Oxford, 2011).

70   This is changing. Facts on File published Gábor Ágoston and Bruce Masters' *Encyclopedia of the Ottoman Empire* (New York, 2008). *Historians of the Ottoman Empire* is an ongoing analytical online project of Harvard University and the University of Chicago, overseen by Hakan Karateke.

are evident in the renewed interest in the continuum from empire to nation state. Most impressive is the way that war and society, the impact of war and the First World War have become legitimate fields of endeavour. The experience of war, its remembrance and reconciliation and the distortion of state politics as a result of violence in the Middle East are all topics on the table in spite of the problem of accessibility to more recent documents in the Turkish archives. It is as if the young scholars are moving on, even as the intractability of contemporary Middle Eastern politics hinders attempts at transnational conversations. Most encouraging are the cross-imperial endeavours such as this one. The centrality of the Ottoman Empire to all the empires and seas of the pre-modern world – east, south, north and west – make it a natural fit for the research and concerns of historians regarding the populations and systems of pre-modern societies such as the Byzantines, Eurasian Mongol and Turkic civilisations, Safavid and Qajar Iran, Bourbon France, Austrian and Spanish Habsburgs, Russian Romanovs, Chinese Ming and Qing and Mughal and British India.

Mughal Empire

Michael H. Fisher

Through military victories, bureaucratic innovation, and cultural synthesis, the Mughal dynasty (1526–1858) built a vast, fabulously wealthy and ethnically diverse empire that eventually encompassed almost the entire Indian subcontinent and then, even after its decline, significantly shaped subsequent British colonial rule.[1] The dynasty's founder, Emperor Babur, conquered much of north India. His grandson, Emperor Akbar, and Akbar's three successors largely expanded their domain, despite repeated regional, as well as intra-dynastic, rebellions. At the peak in the late seventeenth century under Akbar's great-grandson, Emperor Aurangzeb Alamgir, the empire included over 1,250,000 square miles and some 100–200 million people. Even after its centralised control collapsed, the Mughal Empire continued for centuries as a powerful symbol and a precursor for British colonialism.

The Mughal Empire remained during its first two centuries an expansive military-fiscal state, with much of its energy going into revenue collection in order to support the constantly campaigning imperial armies, which included some 200,000 cavalry plus substantial artillery and massive infantry.[2] By establishing an elaborate administration centred on the emperor, with checks and balances among its hierarchically organised officeholders as well as extensive record-keeping, the empire enforced law and order and extracted huge land taxes and tariffs on trade. By custom, all high officers regularly came to the imperial court to renew their personal submission to the emperor as their symbolic patriarch.[3] Mughal emperors, their male and female relatives, and their courtiers composed and patronised works of history and literature, and commissioned paintings and other

---

1   Muzaffar Alam and Sanjay Subrahmanyam (eds), *Mughal State, 1526–1750* (Delhi, 1998); Irfan Habib, *Agrarian System of Mughal India, 1556–1707* (Delhi, 1999); Irfan Habib, *Atlas of the Mughal Empire* (Delhi, 1982); Shireen Moosvi, *People, Taxation, and Trade in Mughal India* (New York, 2008); John F. Richards, *Mughal Empire, The New Cambridge History of India*, part 1, vol. 5 (Cambridge, 1993); Douglas E. Streusand, *Formation of the Mughal Empire* (New York, 1989).

2   John Brewer, *The Sinews of Power: War, Money, and the English State, 1688–1783* (London, 1989).

3   Anooshahr Ali, 'The King Who Would Be Man: The Gender Roles of the Warrior King in Early Mughal History', *Journal of the Royal Asiatic Society* series 3, 18 (2008): pp. 327–40.

arts and crafts, palaces and monuments, that reflected and celebrated their power, ideologies and aesthetics.[4] The Empire's many battlefield victories, sophisticated imperial court culture and promising career opportunities with lavish economic rewards, all attracted the loyalties and service of elite Muslim immigrants, including courtiers, adventurers, literati and merchants especially from the central Asian and Iranian Safavid empires, Arabia and east Africa.[5] Many Indian converts to Islam, princes and scions of Hindu royal houses, and other regional notables also reached prominent positions serving Mughal emperors. Hereditary *zamindars* (landholders) largely accepted the authority of the Mughals and integrated with the imperial administration, collecting and passing on land revenues and also maintaining order in the countryside around them. In addition, vast numbers of Indian soldiers, administrators, merchant intermediaries and servants, as well as diverse immigrants from Asia, Africa and Europe, came to regard the Mughals as desirable employers.

Yet, weaknesses and limitations were inherent in the Mughal imperial system. Stability at the centre depended upon a strong emperor who could both hold together the constantly vying factions seeking his favour and constrain imperial princes seeking to displace him. Succession remained a constant source of instability. The Mughal dynasty did not recognise primogeniture. Thus, the many sons of the emperor, often with different mothers and factions of supporters, knew that only one of them could succeed while all others faced execution (although their followers might be forgiven if they adroitly accepted the new emperor's authority). In anticipation, princes strove to prove their worthiness for the throne, built their own constituencies and occasionally revolted against their father prior to his death.[6] The massive Mughal armies relied on impressive but expensive heavy cavalry, and did not innovate adequately when deployed in resource-poor regions or faced with guerilla tactics by locally based rebels. The imperial bureaucracy and ideology of rule worked effectively during periods of prosperity and expansion but attracted the support of diverse peoples only as long as it appeared invincible and the source of assured rewards. Further, the burgeoning Indian economy, which had empowered the Mughal state, reoriented towards the expanding northern European merchant corporations.

By the start of the eighteenth century, the Mughal imperial system was fragmenting. Over-expansion (especially in peninsular India), and resistance to

---

4   Catherine B. Asher, *Architecture of Mughal India: New Cambridge History of India*, part I, vol. 4 (Cambridge, 1992); Milo Cleveland Beach, *Mughal and Rajput Painting: New Cambridge History of India*, part I, vol. 3 (Cambridge, 1992); Ebba Koch, *Mughal Architecture: An Outline of Its History and Development (1526–1858)* (New York, 2002); Bonnie C. Wade, *Imaging Sound: An Ethnomusicological Study of Music, Art, and Culture in Mughal India* (Chicago, IL, 1998).

5   Richard C. Folz, *Mughal India and Central Asia* (Oxford, 2001); Naimur Rahman Farooqi, *Mughal-Ottoman Relations* (Delhi, 1989).

6   Munis D. Faruqui, 'The Forgotten Prince: Mirza Hakim and the Formation of the Mughal Empire', *Journal of the Economic and Social History of the Orient* 48/4 (2005): pp. 487–523.

institutional and cultural innovation and other unproductive imperial policies occasioned costly military defeats and overstrained both the empire's revenue base and its administrative capacity. These imperial crises lost the confidence of military officers and administrators, and alienated local notables and revenue payers. Regional rebellions increased in number, extent and success, while provincial governors and other officeholders began to exert their own de facto autonomy, although most continued to govern using the name of the emperor. Newly buoyant mercantile, banking, landholding, service-elite and artisan families found more attractive opportunities for themselves, including by dealing with the British and other European trading corporations as they expanded inland from their coastal enclaves.

The new opportunities that these European corporations represented for Indians included links to transoceanic trade networks and new markets, new commercial capital and more developed military, administrative, commercial, transportation and communications technologies. European recognition of the legal force of private property rights and contracts empowered and enriched some Indian landowning and commercial classes, often at the cost of the older service and landholding elites who had served the Mughals. Consequently, Europeans recruited Indians in growing numbers as financiers, business partners, revenue-paying landlords, officials and artisans, as well as soldiers, seamen, servants, labourers, and wives or mistresses.[7]

Over the eighteenth and early nineteenth centuries, a series of politically weak and militarily impotent Mughal emperors proved able to perpetuate only nominal authority, often as mere puppets in the hands of one or another warlord or regional ruler. In particular, the English East India Company asserted its power in innovative ways, militarily, politically and economically, across ever more of India during the century between 1757 and 1858, adopting, adapting and displacing the Mughal administrative, legal and economic systems as it went. Nonetheless, the Mughal dynasty remained in name sovereign over much of India until finally deposed by the British in 1858.

Down to the present, the Mughal Empire persists as a potent symbol, variously deployed by competing political interests. The British Raj (1858–1947) contrasted, for both European and Indian audiences, its own allegedly enlightened and modern rule with the supposedly archaic oriental despotism of the Mughal emperors. Modernising Indian bourgeois nationalist leaders, including those reflecting Marxist influences, have portrayed the Mughals as regressively feudal and, at best, only proto-capitalist, but nevertheless also as an Indian alternative to British colonialism.[8] Yet, the differences between what was practised in India and what was found in Japan, or European 'feudalism', has made it difficult to fit India into a Marxist teleology of modern capitalism.[9] Many secular Indians identify Emperor Akbar in particular as religiously eclectic and tolerant in sentiment and policies,

---

7   Ashin Das Gupta, *India and the Indian Ocean World: Trade and Politics* (Delhi, 2004).
8   Jawaharlal Nehru, *Discovery of India* (London, 1946).
9   Hermann Kulke (ed.), *State in India, 1000–1700* (Delhi, 1995).

and hence an admirable model for the post-1947 independent Indian republic.[10] However, some Hindu nationalists have denounced as threatening to *Hindutva* (the supposed 'Hinduness') of India the alleged 'sons of Babur', by whom these Hindu nationalists mean both the entire Mughal dynasty as alien Muslim invaders and also all 155 million Muslim citizens of today's Republic of India.[11] Conversely, some Muslim writers, especially those in Pakistan, condemn Akbar's putative betrayal of Islam and specially laud Emperor Aurangzeb as allegedly seeking to restore more virtuous Islamic policies.[12] Scholars debate how 'modern' the Mughal Empire was, and the process of transition – including the types of continuity versus change – to the British Raj. Hence, for nearly two centuries following its inception in 1526, the Mughal Empire conquered and ruled increasing amounts of India; over the three centuries since it lost substantial political power, around 1700, it has remained politically and culturally powerful but contested.

Origins: Emperors Babur and Humayun

Zahir al-Din Muhammad Babur (1483–1530), having spent much of his life seeking a kingdom to rule, invaded north India in 1526. From his youth, Babur – as one of the many descendants of two 'world conquerors', the Mongol Genghis Khan (1162–1227) and the Turkman Timur/Tamerlane (1336–1405) – contended for rule in central Asia and Afghanistan. In the dynastic tradition to which they belonged, sovereignty resided in the imperial clan collectively, so any one of its male members could aspire to the throne. Even after Babur's expulsion from his late father's city-state of Ferghana, which he had inherited at age eleven but ruled only briefly, Babur attracted a band of military adventurers seeking advancement under his leadership. After capturing Kabul in 1504, Babur launched raids into the nearby wealthy region of India's Punjab. In 1526, he led an army of some 12,000 Mughals, Turks and Uzbeks further into north India, defeating, among other enemies, the sultan then ruling in north India, Muhammad Ibrahim Lodi (r. 1517–26), an ethnic Afghan. Babur's creative mastery of cavalry tactics and firearms, including mobile field artillery, proved decisive. Subsequent military victories over various Muslim and Hindu regional rulers culminated in the establishment of his imperial authority in north India.

Neither Babur nor his Muslim, Hindu or other contemporaries regarded Indians as a nation. Rather, each of the many regions of the Indian subcontinent had its own history, mix of peoples and language or dialect; only rarely in history had any single ruler ever conquered even the majority of these regions. Nor was

---

10   Sri Ram Sharma, *Religious Policies of the Mughal Emperors* (London, 1940); Jadunath Sarkar, *India of Aurangzeb* (Calcutta, 1901).
11   Vinayak Damoda Savarkar, *Hindutva: Who is a Hindu?* 4th ed. (Poona, 1949).
12   Ishtiaq Husain Qureshi, *Ulema in Politics: A Study Relating to the Political Activities of the Ulema in the South-Asian Subcontinent from 1556 to 1947* (Karachi, 1972).

Babur the first Muslim ruler in India. India's western region of Sind had been under the rule of Muslims since 711. Over subsequent centuries, many Muslim families had immigrated from West Asia, Arabia and east Africa and settled in all regions of India, adding to the multiplicity of its peoples. From 1206 onward, five Muslim dynasties, variously from Afghanistan, Arabia or Central Asia, had ruled north and central India as Delhi Sultans. Their break-away governors and other Muslim families subsequently established five kingdoms in central India's Deccan plateau, based respectively at Ahmadnagar, Berar, Bidar, Bijapur and Golkonda. Further, the numerically largest number of Muslims in India were the descendants of Indians who had converted, often under the influence of Muslim Sufi mystics, especially in the Punjab and in India's eastern Bengal region. Thus, when Babur arrived, Islam and Muslims were already longstanding components of India's diverse polities and cultures.

Babur himself was pragmatic about Islam: he frequently used intoxicants but, on the eve of one decisive battle, vowed to Allah that he would give up his habit of drinking alcohol should he win. Further, he continued his Sunni Muslim clan's longstanding devotion to the orthodox Naqshbandi Sufi order by providing patronage for its diffusion in India. While many Muslims like Babur regarded Hindus as *kafir*s who followed a separate religion from themselves, they also recognised the diverse religious beliefs, *jati*s (castes), and ethnicities among peoples they called Hindustanis. Conversely, many people whom Babur would classify as Hindustani regarded him as a Turk, not part of a unified Muslim invasion.[13]

Even as Babur continued to conquer north India, he started to build his administration on foundations established by prior Muslim sultans. They themselves had drawn upon long-existing Indian systems of rule, to which they had added elements from the Islamic states of West and Central Asia. Persian became the language of imperial administration and high culture.[14] Despite the objections of particularly orthodox members of the Islamic *ulama*, who argued that Hindus had never been sent the Quran or a Prophet by Allah and therefore were not eligible to be 'people of the book', these sultans had largely recognised Hindus and followers of other indigenous Indian religions as *zimmi*s (protected non-Muslim subjects) – if they paid the *jizya* (graduated property tax). Babur continued this convention.

As Babur's humanistic autobiography, *Babur Nama*, recounts in his family's Turki language, he entered and ruled India as an outsider. He wondered at its – to him – exotic peoples, flora and fauna.[15] Babur prided himself on his skill in

---

13   David Gilmartin and Bruce B. Lawrence (eds), *Beyond Turk and Hindu: Rethinking Religious Identities in Islamicate South Asia* (Gainesville, FL, 2000).

14   Muzaffar Alam, *Languages of Political Islam: India, 1200–1800* (London, 2004).

15   Babur, *Baburnama*, trans. Annette Susannah Beveridge (London, 1921); Babur, *Baburnama: Memoirs of Babur, Prince and Emperor*, trans. Wheeler M. Thackston (New York, 2002); Stephen Frederic Dale, *Garden of the Eight Paradises: Babur and the Culture of Empire in Central Asia, Afghanistan, and India* (Leiden, 2004); Stephen Frederic Dale, 'Steppe Humanism: The Autobiographical Writings of Zahir al-Din Muhammad Babur, 1483–1530', *International Journal of Middle East Studies* 22 (1990): pp. 37–58.

constructing central-Asian-style water-filled pleasure gardens in his favourite sites, thus bringing comfort in north India's often hot and dry environment. Further, India's material wealth reconciled Babur to his life there. Thus, with relatively few followers of his own, Babur's constant campaigning drew much of north India's military manpower, administrative structures of rule and royal treasuries into his own service. However, at his death, only four years after his arrival in India, his imperial legacy remained fragile. He transferred the support of many of his followers to his eldest and favourite son, Humayun, but had yet to consolidate the Mughal Empire in India.

On his accession as emperor, Nasir al-Din Humayun (1508–1556) struggled to secure the loyalties of his father's followers and to mobilise sufficient resources to retain the throne. Following Timurid practice, he allotted provinces of his late father's realm to each of his four brothers. Having dynastic ambitions of their own, they eventually turned against him. Humayun's sister, Gulbadan Begum (1524–1603), described in rich detail the lives of their often contending imperial family in her book *Humayun Nama*.[16] She thereby revealed how the women of the imperial clan worked to advance the interests of their close kin and favourites, by arranging marriages and inheritances and by advising on policy, while Babur, Humanyun and their male relatives each struggled to expand his share of the family's conquered lands. Women in elite Mughal families often wielded considerable power. They provided political bonds between families, often proved influential in inheritance to the throne, formed key modes of communication and education (especially of younger children) and could at times exert a very visible influence over public policy. Imperial wives and princesses, including Nur Jahan and Jahanara Begum, proved vital in the politics of the imperial courts of their day. Norms of personal seclusion by respectable women, however, affected their public visibility at a time when personal charisma and a public presence often carried much weight.

Given the patrimonial basis of the Mughal Empire, dynamic personal leadership by the emperor and his continued military and revenue-collecting success proved decisive. Although Humayun won some military victories early in his reign, he also indulged himself in pleasures and intoxicants even more than his father had. During 1539–40, Humayun lost a desperately fought military campaign against the Sher Shah Suri (r. 1540–45), an ethnic Afghan who rose to power in eastern India. Consequently, after ten years of rule, Humayun had to flee; finding no secure haven in India, he eventually took shelter with the imperial Safavid court in Iran in 1544, at the cost of acknowledging the Shi'ite branch of Islam. His eldest and favourite son, Akbar, was born during this flight. With the military backing of Shah Tahmasp Safavid (1514–77), and after years of campaigning, Humayun was able to capture Kabul from his own half-brother, Mirza Kamran, in 1553. Only in 1555 was Humayun able to mobilise sufficient military and political support to reconquer north India from the contending heirs and governors of the fragmenting Suri state.

---

16   Begam Gulbadan, *History of Humayun*, trans. Annette Susannah Beveridge, 2 vols (London, 1902); Ruby Lal, *Domesticity and Power in the Early Mughal World* (Cambridge, 2005); Harbans Mukhia, *Mughals of India* (Malden, MA, 2004), pp. 113–55.

He did not live long to consolidate his reconquest, dying seven months later after falling down the steps of his imperial library.

Foundation of the Mughal Imperial System: Emperor Akbar

Jalal al-Din Muhammad Akbar (1542–1605) inherited his father's throne as a youth in 1556.[17] After five years living under the influence of regents, Akbar exerted his own personal power, conquering and reigning for nearly a half-century. His virtually unbroken string of military victories convinced his supporters, and many of his potential enemies, of his invincibility. Building on earlier administrative practices, particularly those of the Delhi Sultanate, Akbar and his high officials constructed a powerful Mughal imperial structure using what Max Weber would later term the 'patrimonial-bureaucratic ideal type'.[18] This advanced beyond the more traditional idea of the state as an extension of a patriarchal emperor's royal household to incorporate more 'rational bureaucratic' norms and a system of checks and balances among various appointed, rather than hereditary, officeholders. Simultaneously, as a charismatic ruler, Akbar actively created a sophisticated high-court culture and religious ideology that secured the loyal service of courtiers, administrators, military officers and subjects from a wide range of ethnicities and religions.

Akbar's decisive martial campaigns, often under his personal command, expanded his realm beyond north India to include Afghanistan, Bengal, Kashmir, Rajasthan, Sind and parts of the Deccan, among other regions. Those rulers who opposed Akbar were crushed militarily. Each conquest brought more seized treasuries, tributes to collect, and lands to tax, much of which went to further fund the ever-expanding Mughal military-fiscal state. Akbar took personal credit for a range of technological inventions, especially weapons.

Yet, the Mughal imperial centre could never establish its monopoly over the use of force of arms even within its borders. Much of Akbar's time and resources went into suppressing resistance from various Indian regional rulers and communities, his own generals and governors, and rival relatives, including his eldest son, Prince Salim (later Emperor Jahangir), who repeatedly rebelled against his long-lived father, only to be forgiven after each episode.

As Akbar's domain extended, his need for trustworthy officers and officials grew, as did his power to reward those loyal to him and punish those who opposed him. Broadening and deepening his military and administrative manpower base beyond those families and ethnicities who had long served his family, Akbar recruited rulers and noblemen of the formerly independent Indian kingdoms he conquered. Akbar and his close advisors organised, paid and bound these ever more numerous and diverse imperial officeholders to him through novel

---

17   Andre Wink, *Akbar* (Oxford, 2009).
18   Stephen P. Blake, 'The Patrimonial-Bureaucratic Empire of the Mughals', *Journal of Asian Studies* 39/1 (1979): pp. 77–94.

bureaucratic forms as well as court protocols and rituals. He and his high officers also hired soldiers from India's vast military labour pool and lower-level officials from families with traditions of service to other states.

Akbar's new model administration developed out of an earlier Mongol system of decimal military ranks and a similar, but more limited, practice used by Delhi Sultans of appanage – parcelling out to royal relatives or dependents military and administrative authority over regions or estates. Gradually, Akbar created a body of *mansabdars* (rank-holders) who combined administrative and military duties. Each held two *mansabs* (ranks) – one *zat* (personal) and one *suwar* (cavalry) – usually roughly equivalent in numerical value to each other, and ranging from ten up to several thousand (some 33 numerical values were actually used). Each official had personally to recruit, pay and command in the emperor's service the number of horsemen indicated by that rank. As of 1595, there were 1,823 *mansabdars* in total, with a collective obligation to provide some 141,000 cavalrymen in the emperor's service (in addition, there were considerable troops directly under the command of the emperor himself).[19]

Akbar assigned, promoted and demoted *mansabdars* at his will. *Mansab* ranks were not hereditary, so *mansabdars'* sons, known collectively as *khanazad* ([imperial] household born), had to work their way up the ranking. In practice, however, the sons of high *mansabdars* had accelerated careers. Further, favoured imperial princes and distinguished former enemies both started near the top. The personal property of each *mansabdar* was, in theory, inherited by the emperor and confiscated at his death, thereby continuing the dependence of each family of service elites on the emperor's benevolence.

Akbar proved successful in playing against each other the several rival, often ethnic-based, factions which divided his high *mansabdars*. In 1580, about 280 men held *mansabs* ranked 500 or above.[20] Sunni Muslim Turanis (central Asian Mughals, Turks and Uzbeks), long supporters of his dynasty, constituted about 35 per cent of these high *mansabdars*. Akbar counterbalanced these by recruiting more Shi'ite Muslim Iranians (who rose to 25 per cent). Continued Afghan resistance in India to Mughal rule kept members of this ethnicity largely out of imperial favour. However, some Arab and other Muslim immigrants did well. Among families long resident in India, a substantial proportion (about 18 per cent) were Indians whose ancestors had converted to Islam.

Many Hindu Rajput and other regionally ruling clans accepted Mughal sovereignty and service to the Empire; they constituted about 16 per cent of his *mansabdars*. Rising as *mansabdars* in the wider empire afforded them status, wealth

---

19   Shireen Moosvi, *Economy of the Mughal Empire, c. 1595: A Statistical Study* (Delhi, 1987), pp. 214–19.

20   M. Athar Ali, *Apparatus of Empire: Awards of Ranks, Offices, and Titles to the Mughal Nobility, 1574–1658* (Delhi, 1985), p. xx; Iqtidar Alam Khan, 'The Nobility under Akbar and the Development of His Religious Policy, 1560–1580', *Journal of the Royal Asiatic Society* 100/1 (1968): pp. 29–36.

and power greater than that of their locally based ancestors.[21] They served in regions far distant from their homelands, but often used their salaries and rewards to expand their natal estates.

Several of the highest Hindu Rajput royal houses married their daughters to Akbar or his successors, as part of the political and cultural process of formally recognising Mughal sovereignty. Since Rajputs practised hypergamy, the acceptance of the Mughal emperor as son-in-law meant acknowledgement of his social and political superiority. Providing a wife to the emperor elevated a family in status and influence, and also ensured their loyalty to the empire. Earlier Muslim rulers had also married Rajput and other Hindu women, but Akbar differed in permitting these wives to continue as Hindus rather than forcing them to convert to Islam. Consequently, many subsequent Mughal emperors had Hindu mothers. Further, these imperial wives, their male relatives and other Hindus adopted many of the Persianate customs that were developing in Akbar's court.

One continued tension for the Mughal emperors was between their military tradition of mobility in constant campaigns and a more stable reign where the emperor ruled from his capital city. Akbar and his successors until the end of the seventeenth century preferred mobility, often living in vast tent cities surrounded by their armies on the march. Yet, Akbar also built massive fortresses and city complexes across north India, including in Agra and Lahore. His most striking new city was Fatehpur Sikri, built in 1571 in the hills near the long-imperial city of Agra. Akbar designed and constructed Fatehpur around the shrine of Sufi mystic Salim Chishti (whose blessing had reportedly given Akbar his first son, Prince Salim), and yet modelled it on an imperial military encampment.[22] Owing to his need to resume campaigning in the empire's northwest and Fatehpur's perennial shortage of water, Akbar abandoned this city after fifteen years.

One vital innovation of Akbar's regime was to extend Mughal administrative control down to the level of villages. India was primarily an agricultural society, and the vast majority of its peoples lived in the countryside. Under the system existing prior to and throughout the Mughal period, *zamindars* (landholders) did not own lands, but rather their families held rights to various uses of it while other families held other rights to that same land. These rights could be inherited or sold. Thus, families of cultivators had the right to plant and harvest, local temples occasionally had the right to a fixed share of the crop, while the *zamindar* had the right to collect revenue, retaining a fixed proportion of it. Often, *zamindars* belonged to locally powerful lineages, holding perhaps several hundred villages collectively, and living as warrior-aristocrats, albeit local ones, with long traditions of armed resistance to tax collectors and the state. Akbar and his *mansabdars* began a process of 'political socialisation', converting these *zamindars* into disarmed quasi-officials who collected and passed on land taxes to the Mughal state and maintained local

---

21 Norman P. Ziegler, 'Rajput Loyalties during the Mughal Period', in John F. Richards (ed.), *Kingship and Authority in South Asia* (New York, 1998), pp. 242–84.

22 Michael Brand and Glenn D. Lowry (eds.), *Fatehpur-Sikri* (Bombay, 1987); Koch, *Mughal Architecture*.

order in the emperor's name.[23] Their sons often aspired to become *mansabdars*, or else soldiers in the victorious Mughal armies. Given the 1:100,000 ratio of *mansabdars* to population, the Mughal administration relied heavily on *zamindars* and other local elites.

From the 1580s, under Akbar's major new *zabt* (regulation) revenue system, Mughal officials periodically surveyed and assessed villages down to individual fields. Mughal administrators received cash payments of land revenue from the *zamindar* and provided written receipts. In provinces long under Mughal rule, about 90 per cent of the lands were *zabt*.[24] In more recently conquered or less fully controlled territories, none of the lands was to be *zabt*. Thus, the *zabt* system, in contrast to the practice of tribute-paying by semi-autonomous *zamindars* which had earlier prevailed, reflected the novel degree of centralised control exerted by Akbar and his successors down to the village level in core provinces.

This *zabt* system enabled Akbar to bureaucratise and retain power over the payment of his high officials. Each *mansabdar* received one or more *jagirs* (assignments of revenue from specific territories) of value sufficient to pay for his required corps of horsemen in addition to his personal household expenses. These revenue assignments were based on the assessed revenues of *zabt* land; under Akbar (but less so later in the empire), this assessed value largely matched the actual income which the *mansabdar* received. The assignments were rotated periodically and also conventionally allotted to the authority of another official rather than to the direct authority of the recipient. This worked to prevent officials from entrenching themselves in their *jagirs*, the major exception being that former rulers, most notably Rajputs, might have a *watan jagir* (homeland assignment) that recognised their pre-existing local roots.

The cash required to pay these land revenues invigorated regional economies. *Qasbas* (market towns) provided the locale where wholesale grain dealers purchased local crops for transport to cities or food-deficit regions. Large banking houses transferred considerable amounts of capital through *hundis* (bills of exchange) among the *qasbas* and cities of the empire.[25] Within *qasbas*, *zamindars*, merchants, moneylenders, artisans, entertainers and religious figures of various communities all interacted. Each *qasba* also had a *qazi* (judge), authorised by the Mughal central administration.

The judicial system of the Mughals applied the sharia (system of law based on the Quran and the sayings and acts of the Prophet Muhammad) of the Hanafi school of Sunni Islam, as interpreted by the emperor and his high officials. This was the basis both of criminal law for all and also of civil law for Muslims. Hindu and other religious communities under Mughal authority provided jurisprudent

---

23   Richards, *Mughal Empire*, p. 284.
24   Ibid., p. 189.
25   Karin Leonard, 'The "Great Firm" Theory of the Decline of the Mughal Empire', *Comparative Studies in Society and History* 21/1 (1979): pp. 151–67; Tapan Raychaudhuri and Irfan Habib (eds), *Cambridge Economic History of India*: vol. 1, *c. 1200–1750* (Cambridge, 1982).

advisors to assist Muslim *qazis*; many matters internal to these communities were settled by their own *panchayats* (village or *jati* councils conventionally of five male elders). Yet, the Mughals also chose to supervise some intra-community matters; they chose, for example, to determine the volition of a Hindu widow before she was permitted to demonstrate her fatal fidelity to her late husband as a *sati* (true wife). She had to appear personally before the emperor or his representative to seek permission, proving that the act of self-immolation which defined the *sati* was one of her own choice, rather than something into which she was being coerced by her late husband's or her natal family.

The Mughal state sought to extend its authority over all people within the territories it controlled, as subjects not citizens. The imperial state regarded forest-dwellers, nomads and pastoralists in particular as dangerously armed and difficult to tax or suppress, and thus largely unproductive.[26] Indeed, rebels and outlaws based in forests or on the margins of settled society continually threatened the Mughal order. Thus, while such marginal peoples actually provided vital resources to the economy, they often felt the brunt of Mughal military efforts to clear forests and settle itinerants, transforming them into more easily coerced, controlled and taxed agriculturalists.

Akbar and his close advisors designed his central and provincial administrations with sophisticated bureaucratic checks and balances, and made political information control one of the pillars of the imperial state. Although Akbar himself was illiterate (possibly due to dyslexia), his officials produced vast volumes of manuscript records and documents. Scribes recorded the every action of the emperor, from which the many extensive imperial histories were compiled. Various courtiers and scholars used the well-developed Persianate genre of *tarikh* (history) to record their representations and assessments of the salient events and peoples at the Mughal centre and throughout the empire.[27] Further, high officials and other rulers posted a *wakil* (representative) and an *akhbar nawis* (news reporter) to the imperial court, receiving detailed accounts and interpretive assessments of the emperor's inclinations and the constant factional politics of the court.

Within each province, separate officials held executive, revenue and judicial positions, and each reported independently to the Mughal centre. Extensive systems of news reporters wrote directly to the imperial court about the events and administrative successes and lapses of each Mughal official in that province. Regular networks of runners and other communications systems, including carrier pigeons, linked the imperial bureaucracy into an effective information order.[28]

---

26   Chetan Singh, 'Forests, Pastoralists and Agrarian Society in Mughal India', in David Arnold and Ramchandra Guha (eds.), *Nature, Culture, Imperialism* (Delhi, 1995), pp. 21–48.

27   Henry Miers Elliot, *History of India, as Told by Its Own Historians*, ed. John Dowson, 8 vols (London, 1867–77); Shahpurshah Hormasji Hodivala, *Studies in Indo-Muslim History* (Bombay, 1939).

28   C.A. Bayly, *Empire and Information: Intelligence Gathering and Social Communication in India, 1780–1870* (Cambridge, 1996), chap. 1. Scholars who rely on these central records tend to see the Empire from that perspective. Those scholars using regional records tend to see the more limited extent of the Mughal centre and persistence of local elites.

Thus, the Mughals imposed a relatively advanced administrative structure which nonetheless still depended on personal bonds of personal fealty between high officials and the emperor.

Akbar and his confidants synthesised and innovated powerful rituals and sartorial styles that bound his high *mansabdars* to his person, signifying their total submission to him and his paternalistic protection over them as symbolic dependents. Each high official periodically entered the imperial presence and offered his *nazr* (token of submission) to the emperor. In exchange, the emperor bestowed a *khil'at* (robe of honour) to this subordinate, nominally one or more pieces of clothing that had been worn by the emperor himself and therefore imbued with his substance. By thus symbolically clothing his subordinate, the emperor acted patriarchally towards him. This practice built upon central Asian traditions, but reached high levels of sophistication in elaborately graded qualities and quantities of the *khil'at*.[29]

Despite Akbar's many innovations, the openness of Mughals towards new ideas and peoples arriving from the lands and peoples of Europe was selective and limited. The Portuguese had been sailing around Africa directly to India since 1497, three decades prior to Babur's invasion. They established trading enclaves along India's western coast, annexing Goa in 1510 as the capital of their royal province in Asia. Portuguese emissaries, particularly Jesuits, ventured to Akbar's court, and remained there for extended periods, following their usual strategy for the conversion of a nation by starting with its ruler. Portuguese accounts detailed how Akbar occasionally donned Portuguese clothing, displayed reverence towards pictures of Christ and Mary, implied his intention to convert to Roman Catholicism, and encouraged at least one of his sons to do so. Emperor Akbar quizzed the Portuguese and other Europeans, comparing their descriptions and explanations about conditions in their competing homelands, playing Portuguese Jesuits off against English Protestants, for example. Around 1580, he dispatched an ambassador to King Philip II of Spain, although factional conflicts in the Mughal court meant the envoy never actually left India. Ultimately, however, Akbar frustrated Jesuit expectations for his own conversion.

Akbar's creative religious and political policies over his long reign reflect both his personal spiritual journey and his evolving imperial ideology.[30] Akbar's imperial ancestry, youthful elevation to rule, and the unstinting plaudits of his courtiers all testified to his unmatched status among men, with which he evidently concurred. He sought out intense spiritual relationships with the leading Sufi mystics of his day, particularly the Chisti order's Khwaja Muin al-Din and Shaikh Salim, as well as reputed holy men of diverse other traditions. Reorienting the imperial calendar around himself, Akbar invented a new solar-based revenue year. Akbar's court

---

29   Stewart Gordon (ed.), *Robes and Honor: The Medieval World of Investiture* (New York, 2001); Gordon (ed.), *Robes of Honour: Khil'at in Pre-colonial and Colonial India* (New York, 2003); Rosalind O'Hanlon, 'Manliness and Imperial Service in Mughal North India', *Journal of the Economic and Social History of the Orient* 42/1 (1999): pp. 47–93.
30   Khaliq Ahmad Nizami, *Akbar and Religion* (Delhi, 1989).

also created new forms of prostration and devotion to the Emperor. In Fatehpur, Akbar had leading figures from the many religions present in India stand debating below his feet, as he sat, questioning, provoking and arbitrating among them.

Thus, while Akbar relied on the support of the *ulema* (body of scholars [of the sharia and of Islamic sciences]), he refused subjection to their authority. Many Muslim religious figures had received or inherited *madad-i ma'ash* (tax-free land revenue grants) from earlier rulers. In 1578, Akbar ordered a thorough investigation of the legitimacy of these grants, confiscating many that were not documented. Akbar then lavishly redistributed such tax-free grants to members of the *ulema* who earned his respect and demonstrated loyalty to him. Further, in 1579, he required prominent *ulema* to sign a declaration recognising his authority as the *mujtahid* (arbiter of Islamic law) to decide what was legitimate in Islam whenever the *ulema* were not unanimous. Akbar reportedly modelled this on the concept of Papal infallibility which, though not yet Roman Catholic doctrine, was explained by Jesuits at Akbar's court.[31]

Many non-Muslims found Akbar worthy of devotion. He appeared daily before his subjects, bestowing *darshan* (auspicious appearance), customarily the term used when a Hindu deity reveals himself to devotees. Akbar abolished various special taxes on Hindus and other non-Muslims, most significantly *jizya*, and also awarded tax-free land grants to leaders and temples of Hindu and other religious traditions. He made *sulh kul* (absolute peace) a principle of his reign, meaning by this not the end to warfare but rather the peaceful coexistence and mutual respect among all his subjects.

Akbar's amanuensis, 'Abu al-Fazl (1551–1602), publicised the Emperor as the representative of God on earth and the 'perfect man' with the empire, even the entire world, as his bride.[32] This idea drew upon Sufi, Hindu, Zoroastrian and Christian ideas about the role of the monarch and his special relationship to the divine. Imperial service would be the main – perhaps the only – way for men to reach their highest virtue, with their own households as microcosms and themselves as perfect men within them.[33]

Akbar also made himself the centre of an imperial cult: *Din-i Ilahi* (Divine Religion). He and a core of his high officials devised rituals which implied his sacred status. They used the conventional Muslim expression *Allah-o Akbar* (Allah is Great) but implied its unconventional alternative meaning (Allah is Akbar). They wore images of Akbar on their turbans. Various esoteric rituals involving worship of fire and the sun also characterised this imperial cult, which bound high *mansabdars* in devotion to him. As the Hijri year 1,000 (1591/2 CE) approached, widespread Islamic millenarian movements expected the Mahdi to reveal himself and lead the faithful

31 'Abu al-Qadir Bada'uni, *Muntakhab al-Tawarikh*, trans. George S.A. Ranking, W.H. Lowe and Sir Wolsey Haig, 3 vols (Calcutta, 1925).

32 'Abu al-Fazl, *Akbar Nama*, trans. Henry Beveridge, 3 vols (Calcutta, 1902–1939); 'Abu al-Fazl, *A'in-i Akbari*, trans. Henry Blochmann and H.S. Jarrett, 3 vols (Calcutta, 1877).

33 Rosalind O'Hanlon, 'Kingdom, Household and Body: History, Gender and Imperial Service under Akbar', *Modern Asian Studies* 41/5 (2007): pp. 889–923.

to eternal salvation; some regarded Akbar as the prime candidate for this status. All this caused disquiet among orthodox Muslims, including Sheikh Ahmad Sirhindi (d. 1624) of the Naqshbandi Sufi order and *ulama* like Mulla Abd al-Qadir Bada'uni (b. 1540), who criticised Akbar and his initiates as heretics and also decried the apparent worship of the Emperor in defiance of the Quranic prohibition against worshipping any except Allah.[34] Indeed, Prince Salim gathered support from the critics of his father, rebelled in 1600, and arranged the assassination of 'Abu al-Fazl, only to be forgiven by Akbar, and succeed him as Emperor Jahangir.

The Institution of the Mughal Empire: Emperors Jahangir and Shah Jahan

Nur al-Din Jahangir (1569–1627) acceded in 1605 to a far more stable empire than had his father. Under Jahangir's direction (but rarely in his physical presence), the Mughal armies fought to extend virtually all imperial frontiers. His administration worked to extract revenues for these costly military campaigns and also the increasingly lavish imperial court, but Jahangir also drew deeply from the treasuries accumulated by his father. Jahangir was a renowned connoisseur of fine arts, both as political propaganda and also for art's own sake. As the imperial high culture grew ever richer and more sophisticated, the Mughals sought to impress the leaders of border regions and communities so that they would aspire to inclusion in it. At the same time, factions formed at the imperial centre that worked to gain power over the Emperor and his policies.

Throughout Jahangir's reign, imperial armies fought almost constantly to defend and expand the empire's frontiers in central Asia and India, as well as to suppress internal rebellions, including by his own family. Early in his reign, expensive military victories by Mughal armies, including in Rajasthan and the Himalayan foothills, reinforced the perception that the emperor could mobilise invincible force. Rather than opposing him, many regional rulers accepted service in the imperial administration or high military command, thus gaining transregional status.

Some regionally based communities, however, increased their resistance in the face of Mughal campaigns of coercion or cooption. Most prominently, Sikhism – begun by Guru Nanak (1469–1539) as a quietistic devotional movement in the Punjab – would prove a constant military and administrative problem for Jahangir and his successors. When the fifth Sikh Guru Arjun (1563–1606) supported Jahangir's repeatedly rebellious son, Mirza Khusrau (1588–1621), Jahangir had Arjun executed, making him a martyred rallying cry for Sikhs. In India's northeast, *mansabdar* Mirza Nathan fought frustrating campaigns; his *Baharistan-i Ghaybi* provides his extended account of the difficulties faced in attracting local rajas

---

34   Bada'uni, *Muntakhab al-Tawarikh.*

to assimilate into the empire and also in crushing local subalterns who resisted Mughal power.[35]

Jahangir's court rituals highlighted his glories. As his *Tuzuk-i Jahangiri* records, he personally redefined the official weights and measures and designed the largest imperial gold coin yet.[36] Personally favouring the Chishti Sufi order, Jahangir created a core of *shahids* (devotees) among his high *mansabdars*, who received imperial initiation, symbolised by a portrait of the emperor which they wore on their breast or turban. Books of etiquette, including Nur al-Din Qazi al-Khaqani's *Akhlaq-i Jahangiri*, instructed aspiring courtiers of the virtues and protocols of approaching and pleasing the imperial presence, which should far outweigh any monetary interests.[37] Personal influence over Jahangir brought great power.

An Iranian immigrant and widow, Nur Jahan (d. 1645), married Jahangir in 1611 and soon made herself the favourite among his twenty wives, thus entrenching herself, her family and their largely Iranian faction at the peak of the Mughal regime.[38] Having no children with Jahangir, she married her niece, famous as Mumtaz Mahal, to Jahangir's son Prince Khurram, and a daughter from her first marriage to another son, Prince Shahriyar (1604–1628). Especially from 1619, during the illness of Jahangir, Nur Jahan directed imperial affairs, including issuing coins in her own name, a mark of sovereignty. Yet, Prince Khurram frequently challenged both her and his own father, ultimately acceding as Emperor Shah Jahan on his father's death and sending Nur Jahan into retirement.

Shah Jahan (1592–1666) secured the throne in 1628 after executing his rival male relatives, and subduing opposition within the ranks of *mansabdars*. As a prince, his long and usually successful military campaigns had honed his skills and also demonstrated his worthiness for the throne. During his reign, he balanced martial prowess in the field with massive construction projects. India's economy gained from the import of new crops and specie via European trading corporations, but also acquired new weaknesses thereby.

At Shah Jahan's command, Mughal armies defeated various regional revolts. His forces also drove southward, seizing the Deccan sultanate of Ahmadnagar and winning victories over those of Bijapur and Golkonda. They also captured Kashmir and Assam plus Qandahar, Balkh, and other cities of central Asia, but could not retain them despite repeated and costly efforts to do so.

---

35 Mirza Nathan, *Baharistan-i-Ghaybi: A History of the Mughal Wars in Assam, Cooch Behar, Bengal, Bihar and Orissa*, trans. M.I. Borah, 2 vols (Gauhati, 1936); Gautam Bhadra, 'Two Frontier Uprisings in Mughal India', in Ranajit Guha (ed.), *Subaltern Studies II: Writings on South Asian History* (Delhi, 1983), pp. 43–59.

36 Jahangir, *Tuzuki-i Jahangiri*, trans. Alexander Rogers, ed. Henry Beveridge, 2 vols (London, 1909–1914); Corienne Lefèvre, 'Recovering a Missing Voice from Mughal India: The Imperial Discourse of Jahangir (r. 1605–1627)', *Journal of the Economic and Social History of the Orient* 50/4 (2007): pp. 452–89.

37 Mukhia, *Mughals*, pp. 72–111; Muhammad Baqir Najm Saini, *Advice on the Art of Governance, An Indo-Islamic Mirror for Princes: Mauizah-i Jahangiri of Muhammad Baqir Najm-i Saini*, trans. Sajida Sultana Alvi (Albany, NY, 1989).

38 Ellison Banks Findly, *Nur Jahan, Empress of Mughal India* (New York, 1993).

As celebrated in Shah Jahan's major regnal histories, including *Shah Jahan Nama* and *Padshah Nama*, in addition to exertions of martial prowess in the field, he created fixed displays of Mughal imperial power and wealth.[39] He constructed the fabled Peacock Throne which impressed all who saw or heard of it. To commemorate his favourite wife, Mumtaz Mahal, who died giving birth to her fourteenth child, he built the Taj Mahal in Agra as her tomb.[40] Near the site of earlier imperial cities of Delhi, he built his new capital, Shahjahanabad, with his Red Fort less as a military encampment in stone and more as a fortified pleasure garden evoking Paradise.[41] Thus, Shah Jahan sought to combine both the Mughal tradition of mobility in campaign and the model of an omnipotent monarch ruling from a stable capital.

Shah Jahan could afford these triumphs owing to a flourishing Indian economy. Owing to expanded territories and higher productivity, his empire's assessed revenue demand was double that of Akbar. American crops introduced by Europeans – including maize/corn, tobacco, tomatoes and chilli peppers – were widely adopted by Indian cultivators. In addition to cotton cloth, India also became a producer and exporter of silk, both raw and woven into cloth. Vast quantities of silver and gold, extracted from the Americas by Iberians and then paid to northern Europeans for their products, were subsequently imported into India by northern European trading companies to pay for spices, cloth, indigo, saltpetre and other goods.[42] Some silver entering India originated in Japan, brought by the Portuguese. Mughal mints converted the silver into imperial coins of standard weights and purity, and stamped in Persian with the emperor's name, titles and current regnal year. These both proclaimed the sovereignty of the emperor wherever they dispersed and also helped monetise the Indian economy. Coins in gold, silver and copper circulated widely, in addition to smaller and unofficial denominations like cowries (special seashells). This increased specie stimulated the Indian economy but also sparked inflation, which disrupted the Mughal system of *jagirs*; the purchasing power of *mansabdars* declined even as their numbers rose (in 1647 there were 60 per cent more *mansabdars* ranked at 500 or above than there had been under Akbar).[43] The numerical value of *mansabs* also inflated, with a growing gap between the nominal and the actual number of cavalrymen provided.

Shah Jahan favoured the eldest of his sons with Mumtaz Mahal, Prince Dara Shikoh (1614–59), raising him to an unprecedented *mansab* of 20,000 *zat* and 20,000 *sawar*.[44] While Shah Jahan supported an Islamic orthodoxy and the Naqshbandi

---

39   Inayat Khan, *Shah Jahan Nama*, trans. A.R. Fuller, eds W.E. Begley and Z.A. Desai (Delhi, 1990); Abdul Hamid Lahori, *King of the World: The Padshahnama*, ed. Milo Cleveland Beach and Ebba Koch, trans. Wheeler Thackston (London, 1997).

40   Ebba Koch, *Complete Taj Mahal: And the Riverfront Gardens of Agra* (London, 2006).

41   Stephen P. Blake, *Shahjahanabad: The Sovereign City in Mughal India, 1639–1739* (Cambridge, 1991).

42   The Dutch and English companies together imported into India an average of over 34 tons of silver and nearly half a ton of gold annually during the century 1660–1760. Richards, *Mughal Empire*, p. 198.

43   Athar Ali, *Apparatus*, p. xx; Richards, *Mughal Empire*, pp. 143–5.

44   Bikrama Jit Hasrat, *Dara Shikuh: Life and Works* (New Delhi, 1982).

Sufi order, Dara explored Hindu philosophies in order to reveal esoteric proofs of Islam. As Shah Jahan sickened, a premortem succession struggle erupted in 1657, which was won by his third son, Prince Aurangzeb, who executed Dara Shikoh and their brothers, and imprisoned Shah Jahan for eight years.

Extending the Empire to its Limits: Emperor Aurangzeb Alamgir

Aurangzeb (1618–1707) acceded as Emperor Alamgir in 1658.[45] He directed, and often personally led, costly military campaigns that extended the Mughal dominions to unprecedented extent, especially in peninsular India, overstraining the administration and army. Further, the Emperor shifted the ideology of his regime to Islamic piety, which resulted in the alienation of many officials, officers and subjects.[46] Thus, while he ruled more territories and peoples than his ancestors, his heirs experienced rapid fragmentation of the empire.

For his reign's first twenty years, Aurangzeb based himself largely in Shahjahanabad. From there, he attempted to extend his rule along the northern boundaries of the subcontinent, but with little gain. Thereafter, he shifted his throne to the seat of battle, particularly south to the Deccan, where he lived mainly in mobile military encampments during his last 30 years. There, Aurangzeb completed the conquest of the last two remaining Deccan sultanates: Bijapur and Golkonda. He also temporarily subdued the insurgent Maratha Hindu kingdom, based in western peninsular India. While his vast Mughal armies defeated virtually all enemies who confronted them in open battle, they proved less successful in suppressing guerilla and other localised resistance, while his court often failed in assimilating former enemies into Mughal imperial ideology. The expenses of these armies and efforts at co-optation also proved unsustainable by the Mughal military-fiscal state.

In his devotion to orthodox Islam, Aurangzeb downplayed his predecessors' claims to divinity. After ruling a decade, he ceased offering *darshan* to his subjects. His patronage of representative and performing arts generally declined, except for Islamic arts and sciences.[47] Thus, he ordered the cessation of the regnal history, *Alamagir Nama* (although unofficial histories continued).[48] Further, Aurangzeb commissioned the compilation of *fatwas* (written opinions) from leading Hanafi

---

45   Khafi Khan and Muhammad Hashim, *Khafi Khan's History of 'Alamgir*, trans. S. Moinul Haq (Karachi, 1975); Jadunath Sarkar, *History of Aurangzeb*, 5 vols (Calcutta, 1912–24).

46   M. Athar Ali, *Mughal Nobility under Aurangzeb* (Bombay, 1970).

47   Katherine Butler Brown, 'Did Aurangzeb Ban Music? Questions for the Historiography of His Reign', *Modern Asian Studies* 41/1 (2007): pp. 77–120.

48   For example, Muhammad Saqi Musta'idd Khan, *Maasir-i-`Alamgiri: A History of the Emperor Aurangzib-`Alamgir (reign 1658–1707 AD)*, trans. Sir Jadunath Sarkar (Calcutta, 1947).

Sunni Muslim *ulama* into the massive set of volumes *Fatawa-i Alamgiri*.[49] He appointed *muhtasibs* (censors) to scrutinise and Islamicise public behaviour in many *qasbas* and cities. Reinstating *jizya* (except for non-Muslims in his imperial service) in 1679, he also decreed – but did not fully enforce – a ban on new Hindu temples and Sikh gurdwaras. He ordered the ninth Sikh Guru Tegh Bahadur (r. 1664–75[?]) to be executed for resisting Aurangzeb's religious policies and, to flush out Sikhs from his service, ordered the shaving of beards, forbidden in Sikhism. Aurangzeb's sincere faith in the power of Islam thus became part of his various ideological and pragmatic efforts to strengthen and expand his empire.

In accord with Aurangzeb's policies to coopt former enemies, the ethnic distribution of his high *mansabdars* diverged from those of his predecessors. With the exception of a modest decline in Turanis, the proportions of various ethnicities had remained relatively stable from Akbar's time. Aurangzeb, however, enrolled 64 Deccani nobles (half at rank 5,000 *zat* or more), until they constituted 40 per cent of the highest *mansabdars*. While these men were Muslims, they were not *khanazad* and therefore alienated many of the old core of *mansabdars*. Even more discordant, another 96 newly enrolled *mansabdars* (34 ranked at 3,000 *zat* or more) were Maratha Hindus.[50] These men often knew none of the Persianate protocols and etiquette that characterised the elaborate imperial court culture. Established *mansabdars* resented their inability to defeat these Deccanis militarily and also denigrated these suddenly elevated new *mandabdars* as crudely uncivilised.

Most prominent among these imperfectly assimilated Maratha *mansabdars* was Shivaji (1627–1680).[51] Having risen by skill of arms and charismatic leadership of Maratha warriors, fighting first against the Bijapur Sultanate and then against Mughal armies, Shivaji not only evaded capture but even seized and looted the major Mughal port of Surat in 1664. Unable to crush Shivaji, Aurangzeb invested him with a *mansab* of 5,000 in 1666 and brought him to the imperial court at Agra. Feeling spurned and threatened, Shivaji escaped house arrest and fled back to his Maratha homeland. Then he plundered Surat again. To establish his own legitimate reign, he had himself crowned *Maharaja Chatrapati* (Emperor of the Four Quarters) in an elaborate Brahmanic ceremony in 1680. Aurangzeb's further efforts to defeat or assimilate Shivaji's heirs met only temporary success. They and other locally powerful enemies ultimately rejected Mughal authority.

By the late seventeenth century, the Mughal imperial system was breaking down. Inflated revenue assessments overtaxed peasants and also frustrated officials and soldiers whose pay was in arrears. The imperial fiscal and banking systems proved overstretched, and was disrupted by inflation. Local elites, upon whose collaboration

---

49   Richards, *Mughal Empire*, p. 164. This Arabic collection was compiled by Nizam Shaykh. For manuscripts and various translations, see D.N. Marshall, *Mughals in India: A Bibliographic Survey of Manuscripts* (London, 1985), pp. 377–8.

50   Athar Ali, *Apparatus*, pp. 26–30.

51   M.N. Pearson, 'Shivaji and the Decline of the Mughal Empire', *Journal of Asian Studies* 35/2 (1976): pp. 221–35; John F. Richards, 'The Imperial Crisis in the Deccan', *Journal of Asian Studies* 35/2 (1976): pp. 237–56.

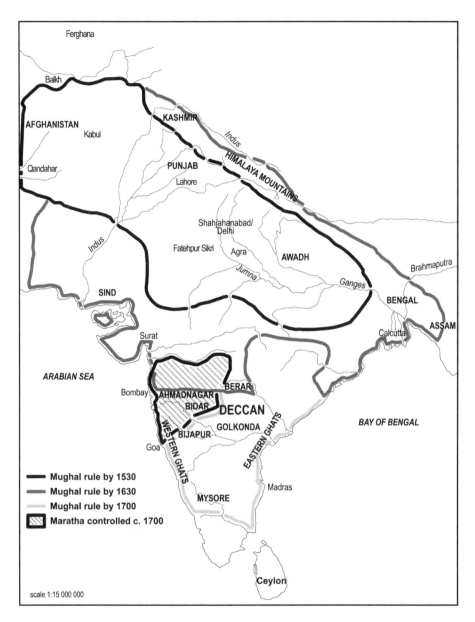

Map 7.1   The Mughal Empire

the Mughal administration depended, reasserted their local autonomy, attempting to retain their local control while also acquiring imperial powers through service to the emperor. Such affiliations depended upon expectation of future rewards from the Emperor, which in turn required the empire to expand and gain new resources. Yet, by strengthening these local bases of support, the empire became ever more

179

dependent upon them. Over time, merchant and popular conflicts and protests forced the empire into political bargains and accommodations that constricted its own policies and practices. The expansion and empowering of local supporters also diffused the personal bonds between the emperor and his officials. When Aurangzeb and his successors proved unable to provide victories or incomes, local power-holders sought alternatives.

Later Mughals of the Eighteenth and Early Nineteenth Centuries

When Aurangzeb died after a half-century of rule, his weak successors failed to restore the power of the imperial centre; fourteen largely ineffectual emperors reigned over the next 50 years.[52] One regional ruler or court faction after another seized power and used the Mughal emperor of the time as a figurehead. Many Mughal courtiers composed *Shahr Ashob* (City in Decline) literature, which bemoaned the Mughal decline.[53] Some Muslim scholars, including Shah Waliullah (1703–62), blamed the moral decay of Muslims, arguing that only a restoration of Islamic virtue would save the empire. Money and information flows bypassed the Mughal central administration. The revenue collection system largely broke down as entrepreneurs bid for tax collection rights and exploited their positions for immediate gain at the cost of long-term productivity. *Zamindars* resisted Mughal administrative demands and fought to restore their local autonomy. Further, the weakened empire could not fend off plundering incursions from Iran or central Asia. In 1739, Persian warlord Nadir Shah (r. 1736–47) invaded India, capturing and looting the Mughal court at Shahjahanabad. Invasions from Afghanistan followed, most notably eight by Ahmad Shah Abdali (r. 1747–73) between 1748 and 1767.

From the 1720s, imperial governors in several prime provinces – including Awadh, Bengal and Hyderabad – consolidated their personal power, effectively ruling as hereditary monarchs of successor states. Indeed, using provincial revenues, the most powerful of these provincial governors vied to control the person of the emperor and use him as a figurehead for their own aggrandisement.[54] Such was the power of the Mughal dynasty's symbolic authority, however, that these nominal provincial governors refrained from repudiating Mughal sovereignty, or from placing on the imperial throne someone from outside of the Mughal family.

---

52 Satish Chandra, *Parties and Politics at the Mughal Court, 1707–1740* (Delhi, 2002); William Irvine, *Later Mughals*, ed. Jadunath Sarkar, 2 vols (Calcutta, 1921–22).

53 Percival Spear, *Twilight of the Mughuls: Studies in Late Mughal Delhi* (Cambridge, 1951).

54 Muzaffar Alam, *Crisis of Empire in Mughal North India: Awadh and the Punjab, 1707–48* (Delhi, 1991); Munis D. Faruqui, 'At Empire's End: The Nizam, Hyderabad and Eighteenth-Century India', *Modern Asian Studies* 43/1 (2009): pp. 5–43; Satya Prakash Gupta, *Agrarian System of Eastern Rajasthan, c. 1650–c. 1750* (Delhi, 1986).

In other former imperial provinces, various regionally based peoples rejected Mughal control. Among the most powerful of these groups were Maratha warriors and their Brahmin officials. Various of Shivaji's generals, administrators and descendants established the loose Maratha confederacy which conquered much of west and central India over the eighteenth century. Other powerful regional kingdoms included the Sikhs in the Punjab, especially under Maharaja Ranjit Singh (1780–1839), and the Mysore kingdom, under Haider Ali (r. 1761–82) and his son Tipu Sultan (r. 1782–99).

The arrival and then economic, political and military expansion of northern Europeans would have profound but unanticipated effects on the declining Mughal Empire. In the early seventeenth century, various European powers chartered East India companies (joint-stock corporations), including the English (1600), the Dutch (1602) and the French (1664). At first, these companies struggled even for commercial access, having to petition the Mughal emperor for permission to trade in India. Based on their European concepts about international trade practices, and also their drive for profit, representatives of these corporations began to request special excise exemptions even as they started to reorient the Indian export economy. In particular, the English East India Company established outposts at Madras (now Chennai) in 1640, at Bombay (now Mumbai) in 1668, and at Calcutta (now Kolkata) in 1690, which employed, directly or indirectly, many of India's most skilled producers of fine cotton cloth and other luxury goods. From the mid-eighteenth century, these East India companies recruited armies of *sepoys* (Indian soldiers commanded by European officers) whose European-style discipline, uniform weapons and accoutrements, and reliable provisioning and pay enabled them to defeat the customarily larger but less efficiently equipped armies of Indian rulers.

Gradually, the English East India Company began to interfere in political affairs, making alliances and wars with various Indian rulers. English *sepoy* armies defeated those of the rival French and then, from 1757 with the battle of Plassey in Bengal, began piecemeal conquests of all the Mughal successor and regional kingdoms. In 1764, the English defeated the armies of Awadh, led nominally by Mughal Emperor Shah Alam II (r. 1759–1806). Yet, the Company respected Mughal sovereignty, restoring some of his territories and allowing his return to Shahjahanabad. In exchange, the Emperor appointed the East India Company as his official *Diwan* (chief fiscal officer) of the prosperous province of Bengal in 1765. That year, he also sent official envoys to London, submitting a *nazr* to King George III and requesting a British army to restore full Mughal power.[55] While the emperor thus demonstrated his awareness that he had a vital interest in learning about and influencing London politics, this came far too late for any realistic chance of success.

Nonetheless, the Mughal emperor continued to be a powerful symbol in north Indian politics. In 1803, the English East India Company captured the imperial capital, Shajahanabad, and again took Emperor Shah Alam II under its protection.

---

55   Michael H. Fisher, *Counterflows to Colonialism: Indian Travellers and Settlers in Britain, 1600–1857* (New Delhi, 2004), pp. 85–90.

Although the British continued to pay nominal *nazr* to him and his successors, they also confined them physically to that city. In 1831, Emperor Muhammad Akbar II (r. 1806–37), seeking fraternal ties with the British monarch (and a larger pension), sent to London another ambassador, Raja Rammohun Roy (1772–1833). Once again, this Mughal initiative came far too late to restore imperial power.

Indicative of the continuing symbolic significance of the Mughals to the peoples and polities of north India, Emperor Bahadur Shah II (r. 1837–58) returned to the centre of north Indian politics during the uprising of 1857–58, termed variously the 'First War for Indian Independence' and the 'Sepoy Mutiny'.[56] Many of the Indian *sepoys*, regional rulers and landholders who made up the bulk of the forces fighting the British regarded him as their restored emperor. In 1858, the victorious British ended the Mughal dynasty by summarily executing several of his sons, convicting this last Emperor of treason, and exiling him to Burma until his death in 1862.

The Mughals and the 'Riddle of the Modern'[57]

Rich historical evidence available from the Mughal Empire enables us to contribute to the decades-long, and hitherto unresolved, debates over the nature of 'modernity'. Indeed, as illustrated by this volume, scholars continue to use a variety of definitions of what constitutes 'modern imperial history'. One approach highlights chronology: the period from the mid-eighteenth century onward when most parts of the world began the connecting together, often – but not exclusively – through the expansion of European colonialism. The Mughal Empire during its final century proved significant in the transition in India to colonialism and also the transition in Britain to empire, although writers have taken a variety of positions about the degree and types of continuities versus changes that occurred.[58]

Another set of approaches seeks to find within the Mughal Empire itself elements generally considered 'modern', including literature revealing individuality, early forms of capitalism and an openness to the cultures and ideas of other peoples. Sanjay Subrahmanyam and Muzaffar Alam have studied the extensive body of Asian travel accounts about Mughal India, asserting thereby that Europeans cannot claim exclusive creation of the travel narrative genre.[59] Similarly, Stephen Dale has clearly found in Babur's autobiography, *Babur Nama*, a strikingly self-reflective

---

56   William Dalrymple, *Last Mughal: The Fall of a Dynasty: Delhi, 1857* (New York, 2007).
57   C.A. Bayly insightfully lays out the major scholarly debates over the nature of 'modernity' in his *The Birth of the Modern World* (Oxford, 2004), esp. pp. 9–12.
58   For scholarly articles debates about these transitions see: Seema Alavi (ed.), *Eighteenth Century in India* (Delhi, 2002) and P.J. Marshall (ed.), *The Eighteenth Century in Indian History: Evolution or Revolution?* (Delhi, 2003).
59   Muzaffar Alam and Sanjay Subrahmanyam, *Indo-Persian Travels in the Age of Discoveries, 1400–1800* (New York, 2007).

humanism.[60] Conventionally, both these literary forms reveal the emergence of modernity. Following a classical Marxist teleology, Irfan Habib has identified proto-capitalist features in the monetised Mughal economy and class conflicts within Mughal society from the sixteenth century onward.[61] Further, many scholars have seen in the policies and attitudes of some high Mughals – especially Emperor Akbar and Prince Dara Shikoh – an eclectic openness to diverse religious traditions or even a modern secularism. Extending this effort to see the Mughals as exhibiting ideological characteristics of modernity, William Dalrymple argues that, even in the final decades before its demise in 1858, the Mughal imperial court remained a site of cultural synthesis, where Indians and Europeans of diverse cultures and religions could interact creatively.[62]

These and other Mughal innovations constitute evidence of an autochthonous modernity or, at least, an early modernity. Indeed, Subrahmanyam argues for an 'Asian modernity', one independent of Europe. He seeks 'to delink the notion of "modernity" from a particular European trajectory (Greece, classical Rome, the Middle Ages, the Renaissance and thus "modernity"...), and to argue that it represents a more-or-less global shift, with many different sources and roots, and – inevitably – many different forms and meanings depending on which society we look at it from'. [63]

Despite these striking examples of 'modern' features within the Mughal Empire, however, many scholars concur that the Mughals did not produce during their three centuries of rule the linked array of developments comparable to the systemic modernity which emerged from Europe over this same time period. Instead, Mughal court culture retained an aristocratic and feudal orientation that derided commerce as crass. Artisans under Mughal rule made exquisite luxury goods and high-quality products like silk and cotton cloth, but the Mughals tended to see these commodities mainly as sources of tax revenue and their own adornment rather than as a means to empower the working or merchant classes.[64] Indeed, as Indian bourgeois nationalists like Jawaharlal Nehru argue, Mughal imperial policies suppressed the middle classes and also much productive investment of India's wealth, thus making India vulnerable to colonialism by Europe – where social, political and cultural revolutions of modernity were then occurring.[65]

Nor do most scholars find that the Mughals made much practical use of the orientations and technologies introduced by Europeans into their realm; they rarely changed their perspectives as a result of these new forms of knowledge. As Europeans began arriving at the Mughal court from the early sixteenth century,

---

60   Dale, 'Steppe Humanism'.
61   Irfan Habib, *Essays in Indian History: Toward a Marxist Perspective* (London, 2002).
62   Dalrymple, *Last Mughal*.
63   Sanjay Subrahmanyam, 'Connected Histories: Notes toward a Reconfiguration of Early Modern Eurasia', *Modern Asian Studies* 31/3 (July 1997): p. 737 (ellipsis in original); Sanjay Subrahmanyam, *Explorations in Connected History*, 2 vols (New York, 2005).
64   Richards, *Mughal Empire*, p. 285.
65   Nehru, *Discovery of India*.

they displayed their latest products and ideas in order to impress emperors and high officials.[66] As innovative as Emperor Akbar proved himself to be, he and his successors regarded these European printed books, globes, innovations in military hardware and software, and conceptions of the world's political geography as mere curiosities.

Printing presses with movable type had been available in the Portuguese enclaves of India from the sixteenth century. But the Mughals evidently made no effort to acquire or use them, nor did they value mass-produced books or the print-capitalism and public culture that these empowered in Europe. Instead, Mughal scribes generated many individual manuscript volumes which remained in elite libraries with little circulation.

Mughal emperors admired European-style globes. Many imperial paintings began to include depictions of them (as well as European-style cherubs). Yet, the Mughals used their images of globes as symbolic representations of the universal domain of the emperor, rather than as conveying knowledge of geography or for navigation.[67]

Despite the vast resources expended on Mughal armies, they did not systematically interest themselves in improvement in weaponry or tactics, including those being introduced from Europe.[68] The Mughal arsenals prized their artisan skills in casting ever larger and more impressive, if not more martially effective, cannon. Yet, associating the technical sciences of artillery aiming with Europe, the Mughals hired self-proclaimed (but often ignorant) Europeans as their expert artillerymen. Mughal infantrymen continued to use hand-made matchlocks, fired at will by individuals. While these matchlocks were often of impressive quality, they were slower, more expensive, individually variable and collectively carried less firepower than the flintlock musket volleyed by mechanically drilled infantry, as perfected by the professionalised armies of Europe from the seventeenth century. Indeed, these military innovations became the main foundation of the English East India Company *sepoy* armies that conquered India starting in the mid-eighteenth century.

Based on his close and extensive reading of Mughal texts, Simon Digby concludes that Mughals had very limited interest in knowledge produced by or about others:

> Although detailed information regarding Western Europe was available at the Mughal court and to other Indian princes from

---

66   Michael H. Fisher (ed.), *Visions of Mughal India: An Anthology of European Travel Writing* (London, 2007).

67   Sumathi Ramaswamy, 'Conceit of the Globe in Mughal Visual Practice', *Comparative Studies in Society and History* 49/4 (2007): pp. 751–82.

68   Jos Gommans, *Mughal Warfare: Indian Frontiers and Highroads to Empire, 1500–1700* (New York, 2002); Jos Gommans and Dirk H.A. Kolff (eds), *Warfare and Weaponry in South Asia, 1000–1800* (New York, 2001); Iqtidar Alam Khan, *Gunpowder and Firearms: Warfare in Medieval India* (Delhi, 2004).

> Europeans who could communicate in Persian or Turkish, Indo-Muslim sources of the seventeenth and early eighteenth centuries evince a profound ignorance of the geography of the world beyond the countries adjacent to India, and of Western European countries in particular … From the end of the sixteenth century there was some receptivity to European technical processes in contrast to the almost total failure to grasp the geographical knowledge of Europe which was simultaneously available.[69]

Thus, Europe as a place appeared to the Mughal dynasty (and indeed to most elite Indians until colonialism forced their attention onto Britain) as a distant curiosity, not a site for exploration.

Only from the late eighteenth century, after the Mughals were perforce dependent upon the English East India Company, did they send their own few envoys to Europe. Although working-class and other Indians had been travelling to Europe almost as long as Europeans had been sailing to India, these Indian travellers composed only oral accounts of what they discovered; the earliest written narratives by Indians who ventured to Europe date from the mid-eighteenth century.[70] Even then, these accounts mostly remained in manuscript, with limited readership.

In contrast, over the entire life of the Mughal Empire, Europeans developed ever more widespread commitments to the acquisition of Oriental knowledge and commodities, including published European explorers' accounts, texts and goods produced by Indians, and colonies there. Numerous European books about India had been printed and widely published for European readers from the seventeenth century onward – leading to what Edward Said has denoted 'Orientalism', with concomitant shifts in cultural power into European hands.[71] Hence, growing archives and books by Europeans about the Mughal Empire were affecting how India and its peoples were perceived and valued by the west, but there was no comparable literature about Europe for readers in India, even in the Mughal imperial court.

Some early Asian travel writers who went to Europe began to adopt perspectives that reflect the modern sensibilities of self-reflection and awareness of how others regarded them. As Mohamad Tavakoli-Targhi argues: 'Seeing oneself being seen, that is, the consciousness of oneself as at once spectator and spectacle, grounded all eighteenth- and nineteenth-century Orientals and Occidental *voy(ag)eurs'* narrative emplotment of alterity.'[72] Such self-awareness by these Asian authors

---

69   Simon Digby, 'An Eighteenth Century Narrative of a Journey from Bengal to England: Munshi Isma'il's New History', in Christopher Shackle (ed.), *Urdu and Muslim South Asia: Studies in Honour of Ralph Russell* (London, 1989), p. 49.

70   Gulfishan Khan, *Indian Muslim Perceptions of the West during the Eighteenth Century* (Karachi, 1998); Fisher, *Counterflows.*

71   Edward Said, *Orientalism. Western Conceptions of the Orient* (New York, 1978).

72   Mohamad Tavakoli-Targhi, *Refashioning Iran: Orientalism, Occidentalism, and Historiography* (New York, 2001), chap. 3.

measurably derives from their personal experiences of European cultures and was not characteristic of pre-colonial Asian authors.

Thus, the Mughal Empire became part of the process of development of modern European empires, even if it did not itself systematically produce or adopt modernity. The significant growth in India of many features of modernity – including print culture, capitalism, a uniform and drilled military, mechanised industry, widespread production and consumption of genres of literature such as the novel and autobiography, and the nation-state – were all subsequent to the fragmentation of the Mughal Empire and the onset of European colonialism. Nonetheless, the Mughal Empire, and the concomitant trade in goods and ideas between India and Europe, had considerable effects on the development of modernity in Europe and, through the imposition of colonialism that incorporated as well as distorted many Mughal concepts and institutions, in India.

European Empires

Philippa Levine

At the heart of European imperialism throughout its history lies massive population movement – among Europeans, those they enslaved and colonised, and those with whom they traded. Between the start of the sixteenth century and the early years of the nineteenth century, more than 2 million people left Europe bound for a variety of destinations, all of them colonial. In roughly the same period some 12 million Africans also left their homes, and they too, were headed for colonial destinations.[1] A good number of the Europeans left under duress as convicts or indentured labourers. Many more were spurred on by the prospect of a more affluent life.[2] In the case of the African migrants, choice was irrelevant; they left as slaves and those who survived the dangerous crossing arrived in the Atlantic to be sold in the market place. The English, Scots and Irish were the likeliest of Europeans to migrate, although Portuguese, Spanish, German and Dutch settlers were to be found in the Atlantic and in Africa by the middle of the seventeenth century. Over the course of that century, more than 700,000 people left England, of whom half went to the Americas. Between 1700 and 1760, only 23 per cent of trans-Atlantic migrants were not slaves, but most were under some form of indenture.[3]

While the nineteenth century saw a dip in slave migration as more and more nations abolished the trade, migration as a whole soared. By the 1750s, the Americas had perhaps 3.5 million settlers of European descent; they were far outnumbered in the region by slave migrants. Some 60 million left Europe between 1840 and 1940, bound mostly for current and former European colonies in the Americas,

---

1   H.L. Wesseling, *The European Colonial Empires, 1815–1919* (Harlow, 2004), p. 16. See also Julia Clancy-Smith, 'Marginality and Migration: Europe's Social Outcasts in Pre-Colonial Tunisia, c.1830–1881', in Eugene Rogan (ed.), *Outside In: On the Margins of the Modern Middle East* (London, 2002), pp. 149–82; Robin Cohen, *The Cambridge Survey of World Migration* (New York, 1995); Marc Donato, *L'Émigration des Maltais en Algérie au XIXème siècle* (Montpellier, 1985); David Eltis (ed.), *Coerced and Free Migration: Global Perspectives* (Stanford, CA, 2002).

2   Nicholas Canny, *Europeans on the Move: Studies on European Migration, 1500–1800* (Oxford, 1994).

3   David Eltis, *The Rise of African Slavery in the Americas* (Cambridge, 2000), p. 11.

Australasia and Africa.[4] There was also a huge flow of indentured labour from China, India and many of the Pacific Islands to Africa, Australia and colonies where slavery was no longer the principal source of manual labour. The laying of railway tracks, the cultivation and processing of sugarcane, and the mining of precious metals and jewels were in many places undertaken by indentured Indians and Chinese, a cheap and seemingly infinite source of docile labour.[5] As abolition spread in the nineteenth century, former slaves also often migrated in search of a better life or simply looking for work. In the late nineteenth century, the French established what they called *villages de liberté* in their African colonies for ex-slaves, although their location was predicated on ensuring a labour supply where it was most needed. By 1910 the system was abandoned, the residents having understood that their lives there were little better than they had been under slavery.[6]

Slaves and others born in the European colonies made their way to, or were brought without consent to, Europe, where some settled and many more passed through. Slave-owners brought slaves with them, students came for education, elites for leisure, activists to be heard. When the colonies began to break up in the years after the Second World War, much larger migrant populations entered France, Britain, Holland and other former colonial powers.[7]

While mass mobility is a critical variable within modern colonialism, it does not, of course, fully define it. Bouda Etemad sees the integration of what he calls 'full rule' with the 'dissemination of the home country's civilisation' as distinctive of modern empires, while John Darwin defines imperialism as 'the attempt to impose

---

4   Wesseling, *European Colonial Empires*, p. 17. See also C.A. Bayly, *The Birth of the Modern World, 1780–1914 Global Connections and Comparisons* (Malden, MA, 2004), p. 133; J.H. Elliott, *Empires of the Atlantic World: Britain and Spain in America, 1492–1830* (New Haven, CT, 2006), pp. xii, 52, 56; Lewis Gann, *White Settlers in Tropical Africa* (Baltimore, MD, 1962).

5   Madhavi Kale, *Fragments of Empire: Capital, Slavery, and Indian Indentured Labor Migration in the British Caribbean* (Philadelphia, PA, 1998); David Northrup, *Indentured Labor in the Age of Imperialism, 1834–1922* (Cambridge, 1995); Peter Richardson, 'The Recruiting of Chinese Indentured Labour for the South African Gold-Mines, 1903–1908', *Journal of African History* 18/1 (1977): pp. 85–108; Kay Saunders (ed.), *Indentured Labour in the British Empire, 1834–1920* (London, 1984).

6   Denise Bouche, *Les Villages de liberté en Afrique noire, 1887–1910* (Paris, 1968); Paul Lovejoy, *Transformations in Slavery: A History of Slavery in Africa* (Cambridge, 2000), p. 269.

7   Colin Brock, *The Caribbean in Europe: Aspects of the West Indian Experience in Britain, France, and the Netherlands* (London, 1986); Canny, *Europeans on the Move*; Brent Edwards, *The Practice of Diaspora: Literature, Translation, and the Rise of Black Internationalism* (Cambridge, MA, 2003); Gann, *White Settlers*; Alec Hargreaves, *Voices from the North African Immigrant Community in France: Immigration and Identity in Beur Fiction* (Providence, RI, 1991); David Killingray, *Africans in Britain* (London, 1994); Arthur Knoll and Lewis Gann, *Germans in the Tropics: Essays in German Colonial History* (New York, 1987); Neil MacMaster, *Colonial Migrants and Racism: Algerians in France, 1900–62* (Basingstoke, 1997); F.O. Shyllon, *Black People in Britain, 1555–1833* (London, 1977); Dominic Thomas, *Black France: Colonialism, Immigration, and Transnationalism* (Bloomington, IN, 2007).

one state's predominance of other societies by assimilating them to its political, cultural and economic system'.[8] In these readings, imperialism – as distinct from colonialism – is what Lenin famously called the 'highest stage of capitalism'. This is a useful distinction if empire is being read as a principally economic phenomenon, but distinguishing between colonialism and imperialism can also be helpful in understanding different political structures. While colonialism routinely involved forms of direct conquest and control (and often settlement in new lands), imperialism as a political system could function without formal colonies, as the existence of 'informal imperialism' suggests. The modern European empires utilised both forms, although colonialism was their dominant characteristic.[9] Armed conquest was the most likely means of creating a ruling polity and subordinate polities, but the distinction drawn by A.G. Hopkins between 'the exercise of state power in international relations' and imperialism adds a further refinement.[10] Antoinette Burton and Tony Ballantyne see empires as 'webs of trade, knowledge, migration, military power, and political intervention that allowed certain communities to assert influence and sovereignty over other groups'.[11] This latter designation usefully moves beyond political power as exclusively a state commodity. Still, modern empires have almost always ended with the creation of new nation states.[12] Whether we look to the independence movements of the late eighteenth and early nineteenth centuries which resulted in such new nations as the United States, Brazil, Haiti or Mexico, or to the much later era of twentieth-century anti-colonial nationalism which produced literally dozens of new nations across the globe, 'the experience of empire in the broadest sense was central to the creation and form of national states'.[13]

With the exception of Japan and the United States, modern imperial formations were European and forged out of changes on that continent from the eighteenth century.[14] Spain and Portugal had, of course, enjoyed large and extraordinarily profitable empires for two hundred and more years, but their star was waning by the middle of the eighteenth century and power was shifting, albeit unevenly, to

---

8   Bouda Etemad, *Possessing the World: Taking the Measurements of Colonisation from the Eighteenth to the Twentieth Century* (New York, 2007), p. 3. See also John Darwin, *After Tamerlane: The Global History of Empire since 1405* (London, 2007), p. 416.

9   Ania Loomba provides a concise discussion of these distinctions in chapter 1 of her *Colonialism/Postcolonialism* (London, 1998).

10   A.G. Hopkins, 'Comparing British and American Empires', *Journal of Global History* 2/3 (2007): p. 400. See also Susan Reynolds, 'Empires: A Problem of Comparative History', *Historical Research* 79/204 (2006): p. 152.

11   Tony Ballantyne and Antoinette Burton (eds), *Bodies in Contact: Rethinking Colonial Encounters in World History* (Durham, NC, 2005), p. 3.

12   Joseph Esherick, Hasan Kayali and Eric van Young, *Empire to Nation: Historical Perspectives on the Making of the Modern World* (Lanham, MD, 2006), p. 9.

13   Bayly, *Birth of the Modern World*, p. 2.

14   Japan and the United States became colonial powers at a much later date. See chapters in this volume by Ryūta Itagaki, Satoshi Mizutani and Hideaki Tobe on Japan and Mary Renda on North America.

the northern European nations. As many recent commentators have pointed out, there was nothing inevitable about the dominance of the modern west. Even at its height European colonialism was as precarious as it was profitable. From the first, European incursions into other continents met with resistance. The early years of European imperial expansion occurred at a time when many non-European empires – the Ottoman, the Safavid, the Moghul, the Qing – were still flourishing.[15] The slow disintegration of these rival empires offered Europeans an opportunity to exploit the fragmentation and instability that by the eighteenth century was widespread. By the mid-eighteenth century, imperial activity was overwhelmingly European.

This observation in no way invites an exceptionalist argument. There was nothing inevitable about Europe's rise and there were many moments at which its power was less than secure. And, like all empires, those of Europe came to an end. But, if not inevitable, it is nonetheless helpful to consider the particular contingencies that allowed a small group of European nations – often at odds with one another, and by no means cut from the same cultural cloth – to achieve so remarkable a dominance for the better part of two centuries.[16]

Many commentators have pointed to the maritime capabilities of the major European players as a pre-eminent factor in their dominance, allowing them to travel and trade across great distances, to transport fighters and settlers as well as goods to and fro.[17] Others emphasise European industrial technology as the major source of international power.[18] In reality these factors run together, for the growth of Europe's maritime and naval reach, and its interest and investment in industrial technology were equally indicative of the changes occurring in the eighteenth and expanding in the nineteenth century. Technology improved shipping. Shipping transported – whether as artillery, machinery or raw materials – technology. The application of technology was always uneven, but its presence was palpable by the end of the eighteenth century, if only as promise. Many of the goods that defined European industrialisation were dependent on colonial products; the processing of sugar in the West Indies, the hunger for textiles that facilitated particular forms of agricultural production at colonial sites, metal mining and more are simultaneously

---

15   Tonio Andrade, 'Beyond Guns, Germs, and Steel: European Expansion and Maritime Asia, 1400–1750', *Journal of Early Modern History* 14/1 (2010): pp. 165–86.

16   I would distance myself emphatically from the argument of Western superiority advanced in Niall Ferguson's *Civilization: The West and the Rest* (Harmondsworth, 2011).

17   Darwin, *After Tamerlane*, p. 96; Philip Curtin, *The World and the West: The European Challenge and the Overseas Response in the Age of Empire* (Cambridge, 2000).

18   Etemad, *Possessing the World*, p. 2. See also Michael Adas, *Machines as the Measure of Men: Science, Technology, and Ideologies of Western Dominance* (Ithaca, NY, 1989); Michael Adas, *Technology and European Overseas Enterprise: Diffusion, Adaptation and Adoption* (Aldershot, 1996); Jorge Cañizares-Esguerra, *Nature, Empire, and Nation: Explorations of the History of Science in the Iberian World* (Stanford, CA, 2006); Daniel Headrick, *The Tools of Empire: Technology and European Imperialism in the Nineteenth Century* (New York, 1981); Daniel Headrick, *The Tentacles of Progress: Technology Transfer in the Age of Imperialism, 1850–1940* (New York, 1988).

icons of industrialisation and of empire. They serve as a critical reminder that, in the European model, there is no stark separation between metropole and periphery.

Scholars have argued that the intellectual formations emerging in eighteenth-century Europe facilitated imperial expansion, although they have also recognised the dilemma of liberalism's associations with imperial rule.[19] Though the language of liberty flourished and often decried slavery, the institution of slavery disappeared only spottily and slowly.[20] After all, there was money to be made; there was always a struggle between profit and humanity. Attitudes to property ownership, finance and commerce, and labour practices in the colonising countries encouraged a commercially oriented imperialism. Over time, as we shall see, other and often more pious rhetoric emerged in connection with both imperial governance and expansion, but in the eighteenth century it was commercial and trade possibilities that drove European interest in empire.

The history of the European imperial world may be divided into four sequential phases: origin, expansion, maintenance and loss. This is neither an exact nor a strict sequence, for the histories of different national empires are uneven, and change was often a glacially slow business. The first three of these phases are the subject of this chapter; the fourth is the focus of another chapter in this collection, 'The Age of Imperial Crisis'.

Origins of the European Empires

Before the late eighteenth century, the focus of European imperialism was largely in the Atlantic, with smaller pockets of trade and influence in Asia and on the west and southern coasts of Africa. A tight connection bound the Atlantic and West Africa for the latter was where slave vessels boarded their human cargo, discharging those who survived the voyage in the Americas. The Treaty of Tordesillas (1494) had essentially recognised two spheres of European influence in the Atlantic, the Spanish and Portuguese. These two countries would dominate European imperialism for the next hundred and more years.[21]

These two powers emphasised different objectives. The Portuguese were more interested in a trading empire focused mostly on establishing fortresses and factories, while the Spanish leaned more towards settlement, frequently through conquest.[22] By the sixteenth century, the French, British and Dutch were starting

---

19   Uday Singh Mehta, *Liberalism and Empire: A Study in Nineteenth-Century British Liberal Thought* (Chicago, IL, 1999); Jennifer Pitts, *A Turn to Empire: The Rise of Imperial Liberalism in Britain and France* (Princeton, NJ, 2005). See also David Armitage, *Theories of Empire, 1450–1800* (Aldershot, 1998).

20   Bayly, *Birth of the Modern World*, p. 295.

21   James Lockhart, *Early Latin America: A History of Colonial Spanish America and Brazil* (Cambridge, 1983).

22   Elliott, *Empires of the Atlantic World*, p. 18; Wesseling, *European Colonial Empires*, p. 5. For

to compete seriously with the Spanish and Portuguese, and by the middle of the following century they, too, began to establish successful colonies.[23] By the 1640s, there were some 37,000 Britons on Barbados, which was rapidly becoming the most profitable of the new plantation colonies.[24] At the same time, the territory of Santo Domingo, which formed the western end of the large island of Hispaniola, began to move from Spanish to French control, and in the following decade Dutch settlement in South Africa grew rapidly.[25] By then, the French and British were a significant presence in North America.

The seventeenth century was the age of the European trading company. The Dutch created their East India and West Indies companies in 1602 and 1621 respectively. The French East India Company was formed in 1604 (re-established alongside a West India Company in 1664). The British boasted an enormous number of chartered companies, chief among them the East India Company (1600) and the Hudson's Bay Company (1670).[26] The Danish East India Company was founded in 1616, the Portuguese in 1628 and the Swedish in 1731. The Germans founded the Brandenburg African Company in 1682.

By this time Spain was an ailing imperial power, allowing the new European colonial powers to expand their interests in the region.[27] Britain, in particular, took advantage of Spain's weakness.[28] At first, however, it was the Dutch who looked likely to become the new leader in the field.[29] Dutch colonial influence and

---

the Spanish and Portuguese empires, see chapters in this volume by Andrien, and by Adas and Cagle.

23 J.H. Parry, *Europe and a Wider World, 1415–1715* (London, 1966).

24 Hilary Beckles, *White Servitude and Black Slavery in Barbados, 1627–1715* (Knoxville, TN, 1989); Hilary Beckles, *A History of Barbados: From Amerindian Settlement to Nation-State* (Cambridge, 1990); Richard Dunn, 'The Barbados Census of 1680: Profile of the Richest Colony in English America', *William and Mary Quarterly* 26/1, 3rd Series (1969): pp. 4–30.

25 François Blancpain, *La Colonie française de Saint-Domingue: de l'esclavage a l'indépendance* (Paris, 2004); James McClellan, *Colonialism and Science: Saint Domingue in the Old Regime* (Baltimore, MD, 1992); Richard Elphick and Hermann Giliomee (eds), *The Shaping of South African Society, 1652–1840* (Middletown, CT, 1989); Sidney Welch, *Portuguese and Dutch in South Africa, 1641–1806* (Cape Town, 1951).

26 Seema Alavi, *The Sepoys and the Company: Tradition and Transition in Northern India, 1770–1830* (Delhi, 1995); Robert Brenner, *Merchants and Revolution: Commercial Change, Political Conflict, and London's Overseas Traders, 1550–1653* (Princeton, NJ, 1993); Ann Carlos and Stephen Nicholas, 'Theory and History: Seventeenth-Century Joint-Stock Chartered Trading Companies', *Journal of Economic History* 56/4 (1996): pp. 916–24; K.N. Chaudhuri, *The English East India Company: The Study of an Early Joint-Stock Company, 1600–1640* (London, 1965); K.N. Chaudhuri, *The Trading World of Asia and the English East India Company, 1660–1760* (Cambridge, 1978); Philip Lawson, *The East India Company: A History* (London, 1993); Søren Mentz, *The English Gentleman Merchant at Work: Madras and the City of London 1660–1740* (Copenhagen, 2005).

27 Kenneth Andrien, *Crisis and Decline: The Viceroyalty of Peru in the Seventeenth Century* (Albuquerque, NM, 1985).

28 Elliott, *Empires of the Atlantic World*, p. 220 et seq.

29 Julia Adams, *The Familial State: Ruling Families and Merchant Capitalism in Early Modern*

possessions stretched from West and South Africa to the Caribbean. By the 1650s the Dutch were well entrenched along the South African coast, as well as in the Indonesian archipelago, and in Mauritius and Tasmania. This was a trading rather than a territorial empire. Backed by a robust Dutch economy and a skilled and efficient shipping fleet, Dutch colonial commerce prospered in the seventeenth century until the competing French and British forces attacked at both the economic and military level. While mercantilist laws, such as the English Navigation Acts of 1651 and 1660, and the French restrictive tariffs of the 1670s, cut into Dutch trade, both countries also warred against their wealthy neighbour. A series of Anglo-Dutch naval wars in the mid-seventeenth century, though inconclusive for both parties, were a costly undertaking. The French occupation of the Netherlands in the 1670s was likewise repulsed only at considerable expense.

After a brief period of alliance with the British, Dutch pre-eminence was eclipsed by the middle of the eighteenth century, and for a while rivalry between the French and British dominated imperial politics.[30] There were repeated clashes on colonial soil and in colonial seas between these two powers throughout the century. When France lost its North American territories after the Seven Years' War (1756–63),[31] Britain and Spain were once more the major European powers in the Atlantic, with Britain increasingly dominant.[32]

At the same time as war was reshaping the Atlantic region, Europeans were increasingly interested in the Indian subcontinent. The French and Portuguese had significant interests in India; the Portuguese had been there since 1498, with a viceroy in place from 1505. In the eighteenth century, however, the British emerged as a powerhouse in the region. The Battle of Plassey (1757) was the first land victory of the Europeans in Asia. With the defeat of the Bengali leader and his French allies, the British East India Company gained a significant economic and political foothold in eastern India. Over time it would become one of Britain's most significant imperial holdings, but in the eighteenth century British India was relatively small and the Caribbean remained the key arena of European colonialism.[33]

John Darwin has identified 'a huge extension of Europe's grip on the territorial resources of the world' between 1763 and the end of the eighteenth century.[34] The landscape of European colonialism was growing and non-European empires were increasingly under siege. The effect of these changes was felt not only at the political

Europe (Ithaca, NY, 2005).

30 Jacques Godechot, *France and the Atlantic Revolution of the Eighteenth Century, 1770–1799* (New York, 1965).

31 France regained some of Louisiana in 1800 but then sold it to the Americans in the Louisiana Purchase in 1803.

32 K.R. Andrews, Nicholas Canny and P.E.H. Hair (eds), *The Westward Enterprise: English Activities in Ireland, the Atlantic, and America, 1480–1650* (Liverpool, 1978).

33 Susan Dwyer Amussen, *Caribbean Exchanges: Slavery and the Transformation of English Society, 1640–1700* (Chapel Hill, NC, 2007); Robert Travers, *Ideology and Empire in Eighteenth Century India: The British in Bengal* (Cambridge, 2007).

34 Darwin, *After Tamerlane*, p. 174.

level, but in the daily lives of both those in the colonies and in Europe.[35] New goods and technologies traded back and forth between the colonies and Europe and also between colonies. Ever more voyages and ships increased the flow of goods. Communications improved and information as well as goods crossed oceans at faster speeds. Economies were quite literally internationalising, at the same time as, in Europe, they also began to industrialise.

Industrialisation, slow and piecemeal as it was in much of Europe, was part of a significant change in how labour was understood. The idea of free labour would have a massive impact on many societies. In the colonies, contract labour increasingly competed with slavery. In many colonial settings, manual labour and domestic service was shared between African slaves and poor European migrants under indenture, and indeed, in the earliest colonial eras, the distinction between them was blurred. Over the course of the eighteenth century, the boundaries between these groups were more sharply defined in legal and in racial terms most especially. European indentured labour began to taper off and more and more slaves were sold in the colonial marketplace, as well as consciously bred to produce new generations of enslaved workers.

The Atlantic slave trade was a racialised trade.[36] Within Africa, slavery was generally a result of military conquest; slaves were quite literally the spoils of war, put to work by their captors. Though slave trading was a practice of long standing in Africa, the scale and form of exchange in the Atlantic trade – one of the most characteristic elements of European imperialism – differed from the traditional trade, for slaves were bought and sold specifically as commercial objects.[37] Growing European demand increased slaving activities in Africa; more and more people were enslaved, not just through war but also via slave raids and kidnappings. In Africa, the enslaved were found in many occupations, but in the European colonies they were overwhelmingly tied to the plantation economies which provided the world with goods such as sugar, cotton and tobacco. They were also put to work alongside waged indigenous workers in the gold and silver mines of Brazil and Spanish America.[38] But it was sugar that was the key to the expansion of the Atlantic slave trade, and its production required a large labour force.[39] Recognition

---

35   Elizabeth Mancke and Carole Shammas (eds), *The Creation of the British Atlantic World* (Baltimore, MD, 2005).

36   Robin Blackburn, 'The Old World Background to European Colonial Slavery', *William and Mary Quarterly* 54/1, 3rd Series (1997): pp. 65–102.

37   For a discussion of other forms of slavery, see W.G. Clarence Smith, *Islam and the Abolition of Slavery* (Oxford, 2006).

38   P.J. Bakewell, *Silver Mining and Society in Colonial Mexico: Zacatecas, 1546–1700* (Cambridge, 1971).

39   Sidney Mintz, *Sweetness and Power: The Place of Sugar in Modern History* (New York, 1985). See too Stuart Schwartz, *Sugar Plantations in the Formation of Brazilian Society: Bahia, 1550–1835* (Cambridge, 1985) and Richard Sheridan, *Sugar and Slavery: An Economic History of the British West Indies* (Kingston, 2000).

of this spurred opponents to organise sugar boycotts as a way to help end New World slavery.[40]

In the sixteenth and seventeenth centuries, Spain and Portugal dominated the Atlantic slave trade. Spain profited the most among the European imperial powers, with its *asiento* system, by which a trader (or sovereign power) paid the Spanish crown for a monopoly on delivering slaves to Spanish-American colonies. Almost half a million slaves reached the Americas under the *asiento* system before its demise in 1750. The last of these agreements in 1713 was granted to Britain's South Sea Company. There was, of course, an unauthorised trade despite Spain's formal monopoly of the slave market. Spanish attempts to police the trade led in 1739 to a colonial war with Britain after Spanish coastguards, seeking illegal slave imports, raided a British merchant ship. The war dragged on indecisively for almost a decade, although not before there were costly battles in the Caribbean, in Florida and Georgia in North America and in Colombia (Cartagena) in South America. In the wake of the diplomatic resolution to the conflict, Britain paid Spain £100,000 to end the *asiento* and be permitted to trade without hindrance in Spanish America.

Slave populations in the Spanish colonies were relatively small in comparison with those in Portuguese Brazil and in the French and British colonies. The Dutch and Danish colonies in the Atlantic had by far the smallest slave populations, reflecting their smaller presence in the region. In the seventeenth century Brazil took 42 per cent and New Spain 22 per cent of slaves shipped to the western hemisphere.[41] In the eighteenth century, about 1.5 million slaves arrived in Brazil and the same number in the French West Indian colonies. Another 1.25 million were shipped to British colonies, but only about half a million to Spanish-America.[42] There were, moreover, many more free blacks in New Spain and Peru by the eighteenth century than in other European colonies.

Conditions for those unlucky enough to be or become enslaved were pitiful at the point of embarkation in Africa, during the voyage, and once they arrived at their destination. The insanitary conditions in the slave holds of ships were infamous even in the eighteenth century when laws and shipping regulations began to limit and regulate human cargo. Overcrowding, poor nutrition and disease aboard slave ships fed their high mortality rates. The practice of boarding slaves from different regions who did not share a common language was one of the ways in which ship captains and traders hoped to quell rebellion against the callous conditions of captivity. Nonetheless, concentrations of slaves from particular areas did grow up in the colonies, and helped to form distinctive new ethnic communities.[43]

---

40 The literature on slavery and abolition is vast and cannot be easily condensed here. Readers might refer to the chapters in this volume by Adas and Cagle, and by Troutt Powell for guidance on the literature.

41 Wesseling, *European Colonial Empires*, p. 93.

42 Herbert Klein, *The Atlantic Slave Trade* (Cambridge, 1999), p. 211.

43 Ira Berlin, *Many Thousands Gone: The First Two Centuries of Slavery in North America* (Cambridge, MA, 1998); Allan Kulikoff, *Tobacco and Slaves: The Development of Southern Cultures in the Chesapeake, 1680–1800* (Chapel Hill, NC, 1986).

Slavery was not the same experience in all locations. As in Africa where the enslaved worked in a wide variety of jobs, in New Spain it was not uncommon for slaves to oversee the work of indigenous manual labourers, a phenomenon that was unthinkable in British America. While Spain codified the conditions of slavery and manumission, English law recognised serfdom but not slavery, leaving slaves in many ways more vulnerable.

In the earlier years of colonial agriculture, white indentured labourers whose passages were paid by their employers in return for a set number of years of employment worked alongside slaves.[44] Many of the earliest French settlers in New France (eastern Canada) arrived under indenture, and in the Chesapeake region of English North America (Virginia and Maryland) indentured servants outnumbered slaves until late in the seventeenth century. North American settlement colonies attracted far more white indentured labourers than did their Caribbean counterparts; land was in greater supply and many of those under indenture hoped that, after serving a term or two, they would be able to acquire land and an ensuing economic independence.

In reality, indenture often lasted longer than many desired. Nonetheless, by the nineteenth century white indenture was rare and the abolition of slavery led to new forms of indenture across the colonial world emanating principally from South and East Asia. Just as the Atlantic slavery of European colonialism had produced a form of slavery centred on race, so would the needs of European colonialism produce an indenture organised around racial categories.

One signal effect, thus, of European colonialism in the Atlantic region with its vast movement of peoples from different parts of the world was to create newly diverse populations, and from that new forms of cultural expression, profound linguistic change and syncretic religions.[45] While the class divisions of the old world were by no means wholly abandoned, different (and not necessarily public) social and sexual mixing produced Creole populations and hybrid cultures whose effects still resonate today. These effects were not limited to the colonies but came 'home' to the heart of Europe. Masters brought their African slaves back to Europe with them. Sailors from Asia and Africa abandoned ships which docked at the trading ports of Europe, staying on in Liverpool and London, Marseilles and Nantes. There were between 4,000 and 5,000 slaves resident in France by 1770, enough to catalyse laws restricting their entry as well as their mobility within France.[46]

The position of women was a critical factor in how early colonial formations operated. Spanish conquistadores took noble Amerindian women as mistresses (and sometimes as wives), and elite Spanish woman as wives. Humbler women

---

44   Beckles, *White Servitude and Black Slavery*.
45   Catherine Hall, *Civilising Subjects: Metropole and Colony in the English Imagination, 1830–1867* (Chicago, IL, 2002); Derek Peterson and Darren Walhof (eds), *The Invention of Religion: Rethinking Belief in Politics and History* (New Brunswick, NJ, 2002).
46   Frederick Quinn, *The French Overseas Empire* (Westport, CT, 2000), p. 87. See also Sue Peabody, *'There Are No Slaves in France': The Political Culture of Race and Slavery in the Ancien Régime* (New York, 1996).

frequently formed temporary marriages with European men who also often had considerable access to slave women.[47] The often active discouragement in empires (such as the Dutch and British) to European female residence in the colonies made partnerships with indigenous women commonplace. Slave women were forced into sexual liaisons with other slaves as part of breeding programmes.

The effects of colonialism were apparent not just in these cultural, social and demographic ways, but also physically and ecologically.[48] The rise of the plantation economy profoundly altered agricultural production and with it the landscapes of the new colonies. Indigenous peoples in North and South America lost land, hunting grounds (and often the prey they hunted) and mobility as European property practices and new farming techniques marginalised them. The widespread assumption by the eighteenth century was that local populations would dwindle, unable to withstand the onslaught of modern civilisation. To many, this was the natural order of things, a logical and inevitable progression.[49] People fought back with energy, however: few colonies escaped resistance from those who European colonialism so rudely and rapidly displaced. Peasant insurgencies were widespread across the colonial world.[50]

Overall, disease was the largest factor in colonial mortality until well into the twentieth century. Europeans brought hitherto unknown diseases with them, and were themselves felled by other, frequently tropical, diseases they had never encountered before. The French attempt to settle in Guiana in the 1760s was dashed by disease. Less than 20 per cent of the settlers survived a year; the rest succumbed to malaria or yellow fever. In the other direction smallpox, for example, laid waste to indigenous communities in North America and in Australia, and, as migration between continents grew as a result of colonial trade and expansion, diseases spread further and further afield.[51] Waves of cholera, smallpox and other frequently fatal

47 Barbara Watson Andaya, 'From Temporary Wife to Prostitute: Sexuality and Economic Change in Early Modern Southeast Asia', *Journal of Women's History* 9/4 (1998): pp. 11–34.

48 William Beinart, *The Rise of Conservation in South Africa: Settlers, Livestock, and the Environment 1770–1950* (Oxford, 2003); William Cronon, *Changes in the Land: Indians, Colonists, and the Ecology of New England* (New York, 1983); Alfred Crosby, *Ecological Imperialism: The Biological Expansion of Europe, 900–1900* (Cambridge, 1986); Richard White, *The Middle Ground: Indians, Empires, and Republics in the Great Lakes Region, 1650–1815* (Cambridge, 1991).

49 Patrick Brantlinger, *Dark Vanishings: Discourse on the Extinction of Primitive Races, 1800–1930* (Ithaca, NY, 2003); Fiona Stafford, *The Last of the Race: The Growth of a Myth from Milton to Darwin* (Oxford, 1994).

50 Colonies were not alone in experiencing environmental change. The onset of industrial economies in Western Europe had a singular effect on the landscapes of many European nations as cities burgeoned, pollution intensified and railway tracks, mining works and canal cuttings appeared in what had hitherto been countryside. In Europe, though mortality rates among the urban poor were cause for concern and rural poverty grew, the scale of human destruction was generally far smaller than in the colonies.

51 Alfred Crosby, *The Columbian Exchange: Biological and Cultural Consequences of 1492* (Westport, CT, 1972); Philip Curtin, *Death by Migration: Europe's Encounter with the*

illnesses took their toll in the cities and villages of Europe as well, but, though their effects were everywhere monstrous, the worst hit populations were indubitably indigenous peoples in colonised environments. There a lack of immunity alongside the disruptive changes brought about by displacement, shifting economic mores, famine and warfare made diseases lethal for far longer periods and for larger segments of local populations. The slower rate of demographic recovery – in stark contrast to Europe which, by the mid-eighteenth century, was experiencing a population boom – seemed to endorse the widespread belief in the inevitable decline of 'primitive' peoples.

Disease was only one, if the major, factor in the high mortality rates in European colonies. Military conquest inevitably brought death in its wake, among both soldiers and the indigenous. European troops were far likelier to die from disease than in battle, certainly before the twentieth century. In the case of enslaved Africans, brutal labour practices and inadequate nutrition did little to improve overall health, although by the eighteenth century canny slave-owners understood slave health in economic terms and were often willing to protect their investments.[52]

These deep changes equally affected the contours and patterns of settler colonialism which, in the early years of European expansion, made up a very significant portion of the European imperial experience.[53] Prior to the nineteenth century, it was common for Europeans to establish or attempt colonies of settlement. Although the early Portuguese Empire focused largely on establishing trading enclaves in coastal Africa and Asia, by the 1540s their inroads into Brazil suggested that, like the Spanish, settlement was becoming the more typical Portuguese form of colonisation.[54] The Spanish and English most especially 'regarded the reconstitution of European civil society in an alien environment as the essential preliminary to

Tropical World in the Nineteenth Century (New York, 1989).

52   For the Caribbean, see Juanita De Barros, Steven Palmer and David Wright (eds), *Health and Medicine in the Circum-Caribbean, 1800–1968* (Hoboken, NJ, 2009); B.W. Higman, *Slave Populations of the British Caribbean, 1807–1834* (Baltimore, MD, 1984); Kenneth Kiple, *The Caribbean Slave: A Biological History* (New York, 1984); Richard Sheridan, *Doctors and Slaves: A Medical and Demographic History of Slavery in the British West Indies, 1680–1834* (Cambridge, 1985); Karol Weaver, *Medical Revolutionaries: The Enslaved Healers of Eighteenth-Century Saint Domingue* (Urbana, IL, 2006). For the nineteenth-century US, see Sharla Fett, *Working Cures: Healing, Health, and Power on Southern Slave Plantations* (Chapel Hill, NC, 2002); Todd Lee Savitt, *Medicine and Slavery: The Diseases and Health Care of Blacks in Antebellum Virginia* (Urbana, IL, 1978); Marie Jenkins Schwartz, *Birthing a Slave: Motherhood and Medicine in the Antebellum South* (Cambridge, MA, 2006); Steven Stowe, 'Obstetrics and the Work of Doctoring in the Mid-Nineteenth-Century American South', *Bulletin of the History of Medicine* 64/4 (1990): pp. 540–66.

53   James Belich, *Replenishing the Earth: The Settler Revolution and the Rise of the Anglo World, 1783–1939* (Oxford, 2009); Caroline Elkins and Susan Pedersen (eds), *Settler Colonialism in the Twentieth Century: Projects, Practices, Legacies* (New York, 2005); Daiva Stasiulis and Nira Yuval Davis (eds), *Unsettling Settler Societies: Articulations of Gender, Race, Ethnicity and Class* (London, 1995).

54   James Duffy, *Portugal in Africa* (Cambridge, MA, 1962).

their permanent occupation of the land'.[55] Needless to say, that process rarely went according to plan, but the goal of the earlier phases of colonial expansion generally revolved around settlement. The English had been active in this respect for some time, subduing Scotland and Wales, as well as the separate island of Ireland to their west. Indeed, the plantation was in use in Ireland before its translation to the Caribbean.[56] For the English, productive use of the land essentially settled the question of ownership, a position which would serve to displace indigenous inhabitants in many colonies.

For the most part, settlement colonies were located in the western hemisphere and, in the early years, largely in the Caribbean.[57] Serious attempt at settlement in North America came only in the seventeenth century. France's attempt in 1564 to establish a colony in what is now North Florida was a failure and its first success came in the early seventeenth century further north in Quebec. The first overseas French governor arrived there in 1665. By 1700, some 14,000 French settlers controlled 30,000 African slaves in the Caribbean. And, by the middle of the eighteenth century, some 3 to 4 million people of European descent were living in Spanish, French, British and Portuguese America.[58]

England's earliest attempts at American colonisation at Roanoke failed.[59] It was to the Chesapeake Bay area that by 1750 some quarter of a million Britons had migrated. Among them were some 50,000 convicts and many more indentured labourers. Large numbers of what the Americans early on called 'Scotch-Irish' (Protestant Scots who had settled in Ulster in the plantation years of the early seventeenth century) also arrived, along with Germans and Huguenots fleeing religious persecution in France. By the middle of the eighteenth century, 2 million Britons were living on the eastern shores of North America, compared with some 70,000 French settlers.[60]

The Spanish settlements in the Americas were considerably less diverse, since Spain permitted only Spaniards to settle there.[61] In the sixteenth century some half a million Spaniards settled in New Spain, but it was typically the British who saw the largest outflow of migrants to new settler colonies. Early British settlements differed from their Spanish and French counterparts not only in their commitment to religious liberty but in their less interventionist political strategies. Above all, their raison d'être was trade.

In the sixteenth century in particular, silver dominated trade and the Spanish Empire derived its wealth largely from silver. Until the nineteenth century the silver

55 Elliott, *Empires of the Atlantic World*, p. 36.

56 Nicholas Canny, *Kingdom and Colony: Ireland in the Atlantic World, 1560–1800* (Baltimore, MD, 1988).

57 Dutch settlement in South Africa from the seventeenth century and the piecemeal colonisation of the Australian continent from the 1780s were exceptions.

58 Darwin, *After Tamerlane*, p. 107.

59 Karen Ordahl Kupperman, *Roanoke: The Abandoned Colony* (Lanham, MD, 1991).

60 Quinn, *French Overseas Empire*, p. 67.

61 David Robinson, *Migration in Colonial Spanish America* (Cambridge, 1990).

specie standard, in which a fixed weight of the precious metal was the standard economic unit of account, governed international trade. The unsuccessful attempt in 1704 to unify the silver currency of the British colonies brought about the first tentative adoption of a Gold Standard in the British West Indies, though it would be 1821, in the wake of revolutions in Bolivia, Peru and Mexico, which seriously disrupted the supply of silver, before Britain formally adopted the Gold Standard.[62]

Spain's pre-eminence began to wane as economic competition from its European rivals grew in the seventeenth century. The emphasis on commerce and trade that characterised empires such as the Dutch and British afforded them increasing importance in the eighteenth century, as did their powerful naval presence. Britain's focus on trade was facilitated by an unusual fiscal system which kept interest on debt low and which pooled the risks taken by investors. Britain's credit-worthiness allowed it to invest in ships, goods and troops with which to maintain a vigorous overseas network and to manage more easily than its French rival the cost of wars. The Dutch adopted similar methods and indeed pioneered the joint-stock company as a means to minimise risk in expensive overseas voyages.

New and profitable products arose directly from colonial ventures and would strengthen the claims of the newer European colonial powers in the seventeenth century, especially the French and the British. In the 1620s, sugar and tobacco began to emerge as economic powerhouses: their export to eager consumers in Europe established these newer powers as fierce rivals to the Spanish and Portuguese. The British and the French were not alone in viewing the Atlantic as a source of revenue and profit: the Danish and the Dutch empires, albeit on a far smaller scale, claimed their share of the spoils, too.[63]

These trade-centred empires had looser governance structures than the tightly centralised Spanish model, which incorporated Spanish America into the metropolitan (Castilian) system. Both regarded their colonial practice as civilising, the Spaniards in their zeal to impose Catholicism and Spanish-style government on local populations, the trading empires through their belief that the development and encouragement of commerce helped civilise lesser peoples.

All of this came, though, at a cost. While profits could run high, the establishment of colonial control and trade was expensive. Outfitting and staffing ships and maintaining colonial outposts were costly and risky ventures, even with the innovative risk-sharing investment instruments pioneered in the sixteenth century. By the late eighteenth century these factors combined with a wave of new writings – from John Locke to Adam Smith – which redirected economic philosophy away from monopolies towards free trade. Britain in particular, needing to bring in raw materials for manufacture, began to champion free-trade policies designed to bring down import prices.

---

62 For discussions of currency history, see Barry Eichengreen and Marc Flandreau (eds), *The Gold Standard in Theory and History* (New York, 1985).

63 Denmark's most successful ventures were in Asia and those of the Netherlands in the East Indies.

It was principally to protect revenue that governments, in the early colonial period, committed resources to the colonies. Colonial funding and investment was generally private, although monarchs granted charters to companies in exchange for a cut of the profits. It was not merely ships and labour, goods and supplies, that were funded but also scientific research and exploration. Oceanic voyages frequently included not only a ship's surgeon to provide for the crew but frequently one or more naturalists, sometimes with government contracts though more often with private funding. Map-makers, botanists and anthropologists joined sea-faring expeditions, bringing back specimens and seeds, and cataloguing flora, fauna and people.[64] Their work was a crucial element of so-called Enlightenment practice, uncovering and discovering what Europeans widely regarded as the far-flung frontiers of the world. It was on such voyages, too, that countries often staked their colonial claims, although without subsequent occupation such claims were seldom successful.

Sometimes forgotten in the often celebratory story linking science and progress is that Europeans borrowed much from other mathematical, scientific and medical traditions even while they trumpeted the advance of western science.[65] The compass was a vital piece of maritime equipment that Europeans sailors took from Chinese and Arab sources. Early western treatments of sexually transmissible diseases, long the scourge of seafarers, were remarkably close to those already in use in medical systems in Asia. Such debts to non-western knowledge act as a useful reminder that, well into the eighteenth century, European empire-building had considerable competition from the Islamic empires and from sophisticated East Asian empires in China and Japan, often suspicious of or hostile to European interests. While Europeans were quick to take advantage of the weakening of their rivals, as was the case when the Safavid and Mogul empires ran into difficulties in the eighteenth century, they were by no means the pre-eminent economic, political or military forces of the day. It was only slowly that the balance of power shifted westward.

Moreover, in the eighteenth century wars between rival European powers sapped cash, energy and military power. Throughout the century European rivalries erupted over and over, and these theatres of war were frequently colonial, centred especially on the Atlantic. Perhaps the most bruising – and for the future of European colonialism, the most critical – of these encounters was the Seven Years' War, which pitted England and Prussia initially against France, Austria and Russia. Spain entered the war in 1762 against the British/Prussian alliance.

Although the war was fought mostly in North America, its broader reach suggests the extent to which this was centrally a colonial war. The British launched

---

64 Cañizares-Esguerra, *Nature, Empire, and Nation*; Richard Drayton, *Nature's Government: Science, Imperial Britain, and the 'Improvement' of the World* (New Haven, CT, 2000); Anne Godlewska, *Geography Unbound: French Geographic Science from Cassini to Humboldt* (Chicago, IL, 1999); Pamela Smith and Benjamin Schmidt (eds), *Making Knowledge in Early Modern Europe: Practices, Objects, and Texts, 1400–1800* (Chicago, IL, 2007).

65 Harold Cook, *Matters of Exchange: Commerce, Medicine, and Science in the Dutch Golden Age* (New Haven, CT, 2007).

attacks on French West Africa and the French Caribbean and invaded Spanish territories in Cuba and the Philippines. In the complicated peace treaty that ended hostilities, there was a great deal of colonial trading, in which European powers ceded colonised territory to one another, paying no attention to the desire of the indigenous inhabitants, a trend that would continue unabated. The Treaty of Paris, which ended the war, consolidated Britain's interests in North America; they gained almost all of what had been French territory as well as some Spanish territory. Though some Caribbean islands seized during the war were returned to France, Britain nonetheless made net gains in the region. But though 1763 saw the British dominant in the Atlantic, it was a dominance that would prove short-lived.

Within ten years, Britain's control of much of North America would be under attack. While the outcome of the Seven Years' War enriched Britain's territorial holdings, the cost of the war more than doubled Britain's national debt. Successive administrations in Britain sought to raise revenue through taxes and duties that American colonists resisted with considerable vigour. The amounts in question were not vast and the revenue was earmarked for local use, but the colonists' objections were less fiscal than political. During the 1760s and 1770s, first over sugar, then over stamp duties and finally over the import and export of tea, American rebels challenged the right of the British Parliament to impose such measures, arguing that only their local assemblies enjoyed the right of taxation. Initially there was little interest in rejecting all affiliation with Britain, but when Britain treated a 1774 ban on imports and exports championed by the Continental Congress as a rebellion, sending troops to Massachusetts in 1775, there was no going back. The American War of Independence gave rival European powers another opportunity to attack Britain; France offered help to the American rebels in 1778; Spain followed suit a year later. In all respects, then, this was a colonial war on all fronts: on the one hand, a protest against particular forms of colonial rule, and, on the other, an opportunistic theatre for intra-European colonial rivalry.[66] When Britain admitted defeat in 1783, the national debt had climbed even higher and the more southerly of the British American territories had been lost, leaving Britain with a much-reduced presence in what is now Canada.

The American Revolution was by no means the only bid for independence from colonial rule in this era. At the very end of the eighteenth century Britain faced a significant uprising in Ireland, one supported yet again by their French rivals. The upshot of this rebellion, which resulted in some 30,000 deaths, was the passing of the 1800 Act of Union which put Irish politicians in the British Parliament, dissolved the separate Irish Parliamentary body and set the stage for a long and bitter struggle between Irish nationalists and the English. The 1780s and 1790s proved just as tumultuous for the French and Spanish empires. Spain faced rebellions in Peru, Bolivia and New Granada in the early 1780s and, although they were quelled, dissatisfaction with the colonial state was growing rapidly, especially in South

---

66   There is a considerable literature on this topic. A good starting place would be Jack
      Greene (ed.), *The Reinterpretation of the American Revolution, 1763–1789* (New York,
      1968).

America.[67] In the early 1790s, it was the turn of France to experience serious colonial uprising, in this case the slave revolt that would culminate in the foundation of the independent state of Haiti.[68]

Saint-Domingue was the richest colony in the West Indies but had been wracked by slave rebellions and also by calls for independence among free whites and blacks who found French control onerous. In the 1790s a series of revolts among different populations culminated in massive slave rebellions across the country. By 1796 Toussaint l'Ouverture was governor and continued to press for autonomous rule until Napoleon re-captured the island, re-establishing slavery in 1802. The rebellions, however, did not evaporate, leading instead to a successful War of Independence, a substantial blow to the prowess of French colonialism.

At the start of the nineteenth century, then, France had lost most of its possessions in Canada and India, as well as its key Caribbean colony. Portugal and Spain's empires were on the verge of collapse. Yet these changes were by no means a prelude to European imperial decline. On the contrary, the nineteenth century would be a period of remarkable expansion with new imperial interests emerging as the contours of Europe itself changed. The growth of European nationalism fed the hunger for imperial conquest, and over time would also help sow the seeds of imperial collapse.

Expansion

As the nineteenth century began, the main colonial rivalries looked much as they had done for most of the previous century. The French, British, Spanish, Portuguese and Dutch continued to dominate European colonialism, especially in Asia, Africa and the Atlantic. Russian incursions eastward, and especially the annexation of the Crimea in 1783, had embroiled that empire in wars with the neighbouring Ottoman Empire, encounters which weakened the Ottomans. Increasing European influence in the Black Sea region had a long-term impact on European politics and colonialism, but it was the re-emergence of a French imperial threat under Napoleon which dominated the earliest years of the new century.

Napoleon's vision of a French empire spurred what is sometimes called his 'Eastern project', the military occupation of Egypt in 1798 and the unsuccessful attempt to move from there into Syria. The French presence met with hearty resistance and, driven out Egypt in 1802, Napoleon focused his attention on

---

67 These rebellions included the Peruvian uprising led by Túpac Amaru II (José Gabriel Condorcanqui) in 1780, the siege of La Paz in Bolivia in 1781 (led by Túpac Katari) and the Comuneros revolt in New Granada in the same year.

68 Laurent Dubois, *A Colony of Citizens: Revolution and Slave Emancipation in the French Caribbean, 1787–1804* (Chapel Hill, NC, 2004); Laurent Dubois, *Avengers of the New World: The Story of the Haitian Revolution* (Cambridge, MA, 2004); David Geggus, *The Impact of the Haitian Revolution in the Atlantic World* (Columbia, SC, 2002).

building an empire closer to home. Thomas Jefferson's controversial purchase of French territory in 1803 (the so-called Louisiana Purchase) helped Napoleon finance his colonising efforts in Europe, breaking up the Holy Roman Empire in 1806 and marching swiftly into many parts of Europe. His invasion of Portugal in 1807 and Spain in 1808 further destabilised these two imperial powers. Napoleon's eventual defeat and the accords made by the major European powers in 1815 led to a century of relative peace within Europe. There were far fewer intra-European wars than the eighteenth century had experienced, but a far greater degree of colonial expansion, even while Spain and Portugal lost the greater part of their empires. By the mid-1820s Spain's colonial possessions were reduced to Cuba and Puerto Rico in the Caribbean and the Philippines. Portugal retained a little more, although still a fraction of its former holdings: Goa in western India, Macao in the China Sea and, off the coast of West Africa, the Cape Verde Islands, San Tomé and Principe. Portugal also controlled East Timor and the central African territories between Angola and Mozambique.[69] Portugal's most significant defeat was the loss of Brazil in 1822.[70] By then, Spain had been ousted in Paraguay and Venezuela (1811), Argentina (then known as Rio de la Plata, 1816), Chile (1818) and Mexico and Peru (1821). Bolivia would declare its independence from Spain in 1825.

Thus, in the years before 1830, it was the British and Dutch who most energetically pursued colonial expansion, with France re-emerging on the scene in the 1830s. After the loss of the American colonies Britain began its 'swing to the east', concentrating on its Asian holdings as well as seeking lands for new penal colonies. These included most famously Britain's first incursion into the Australian landmass, the convict colony of New South Wales, established in 1788. Britain jockeyed with the Dutch for influence in Southeast Asia, outpacing the Dutch over time. By 1826 the British Straits Settlements comprised a number of key trading posts in the area, including Singapore, Penang and Malacca.[71] In Africa, Sierra Leone, founded initially in 1787 for rescued and freed slaves, was re-founded in 1808 after its initial failures, and Britain also established a coastal West African foothold in The Gambia as a base for its anti-slaving squadrons, following the abolition of the slave trade in 1806/1807.

The late eighteenth century had seen the penetration of the British into India, although in the early 1780s their success was by no means guaranteed.[72] The kingdom of Mysore in southern India, with the help of France, beat back the British

---

69   R.J. Hammond, *Portugal and Africa, 1815–1910: A Study in Uneconomic Imperialism* (Stanford, CA, 1966).

70   The independence of Brazil was a unique affair in that royalty remained at the head of the new nation. After Napoleon's invasion of Portugal in 1807, the royal family and its retinue left for Brazil, establishing it as the new capital of the Portuguese Empire. The Brazilian elite, fearful of revolutionary demands coming from Portugal in 1821 and 1822, asked Dom Pedro to become king of an independent Brazil whose constitution was markedly conservative, maintaining slavery and retaining Catholicism as the state religion.

71   For a useful summary of British–Dutch interactions in this period, see Nicholas Tarling, *The Cambridge History of Southeast Asia* (Cambridge, 1993), pp. 13–25.

72   C.A. Bayly, *Indian Society and the Making of the British Empire* (Cambridge, 1987).

incursion twice, finally succumbing in 1789. After the death of Tipu Sultan, Mysore's ruler, the British annexed much of the territory. Although early nineteenth-century British colonialism was focused heavily on India, this was not formally a government or a national venture but the undertaking of a private business, the East India Company, until 1858. The first half of the nineteenth century saw both considerable growth in the territories under their aegis, alongside an increasingly interventionist role for Company officials. The three presidencies of Bombay, Bengal and Madras operated increasingly as regional governments rather than trading offices. Parliament first instituted greater supervision of the Company's dealings in India in 1784, appointing a governor-general with jurisdiction throughout British India. In the 1820s and 1830s in particular, reforming zeal saw the passing of a series of laws addressing social and religious customs.[73]

The Dutch were simultaneously expanding their interest in Java. Following the bruising five-year Java War, they imposed the *kultuurstelsel* (cultivation system) from 1830, whereby the colonial government requisitioned both land and labour from the Javanese and imposed a monopoly on the sale and transportation of agricultural produce.[74] The policy was retained for some 40 years, enriching the Dutch Treasury and immiserating the local population. Famine ensued in the 1840s as a result of a downturn in rice production forced on Javanese farmers. In British India, similar monopolies enjoyed by the East India Company (in such products as tea, cotton and that most profitable of commodities, opium) were slowly whittled away in the first three decades of the century as free trade proponents got their way. Still, it was the 1830s before the company lost all of its monopolies; the free-trade system sometimes seen as the death of eighteenth-century mercantilism emerged only slowly and piecemeal.[75]

France reappeared on the imperial stage with the invasion of Algeria in the summer of 1830, just days before the fall of the Bourbon regime. Despite turmoil in France and organised resistance in Algeria, the French stayed on, developing a settlement colony which by 1840 had some 37,000 white settlers, growing to 250,000 by the early 1870s. In the late 1850s, the French invaded Indochina on grounds as flimsy as those which had justified the invasion of Algeria. Where in 1830 it was a dispute between a local ruler and the French consul that precipitated hostilities, in 1857 it was complaints from French Catholic missionaries that lit the fire. By 1860 it was clear that the resistance was determined, and the French withdrew from large parts of the country. They remained in Saigon, however, and from here cut Emperor Tu Duc's main rice supply, forcing concessions from him that allowed the establishment of a significant French presence in the region, including

---

73   Lata Mani, *Contentious Traditions: The Debate on Sati in Colonial India* (Berkeley, CA, 1998).
74   C. Fasseur, *The Politics of Colonial Exploitation: Java, the Dutch, and the Cultivation System* (Ithaca, NY, 1992).
75   Darwin, *After Tamerlane*, p. 185.

a protectorate in Cambodia (1863).[76] It was in these mid-century years, too, that France established a series of island footholds in the Pacific.[77]

By the time the French moved into Indochina and the Pacific, the second phase of European imperialism was in full swing. Some historians argue that the 1880s represent the high watermark of nineteenth-century imperialism, when the European powers divided the African continent amongst themselves. Yet, long before the 1880s, France, Britain and the Netherlands, in particular, were expanding busily; the significance of the last few decades of the nineteenth century lies principally in the development of new European colonial powers, notably Germany and Belgium and, to a lesser extent, Italy. Equally important in the nineteenth century is the decline of old empires. Alongside the losses of the Spanish and Portuguese, the mid-century saw the break-up of much of the Danish Empire. Denmark sold its Indian colonies to the East India Company in the 1830s and 1840s and ceded to Britain colonies it had acquired in the eighteenth century, its Gold Coast territory in 1849 and the Nicobar Islands in 1868.[78]

Britain's expansion was not limited to India or to possessions it acquired from other empires. Following expansion in India, Britain took a series of strategic colonies in the mid-century, designed either to expand important areas of trade or to provide naval, military or supply aid to the rest of the empire. Thus between the 1830s and the 1870s Britain's empire grew substantially, encompassing places as diverse as Aden (1839), New Zealand (1840), Hong Kong (1842), Natal (1843), Fiji (1874), Cyprus (1878) and more. Even before the 'Scramble for Africa', Britain had become a formidable colonial force.

This significant expansion was not without either its metropolitan critics or its colonised opponents. Some in Europe took a principled stand against colonialism (and certainly against the slaving which had so greatly enriched it), while others regarded it as an unnecessary expense. Those whose homelands were affected were not always inclined to accede, and revolts and rebellions were common throughout the period. It took a great deal of effort to establish French rule over Algeria, and Britain's acquisition of Hong Kong was the result of a maritime war with China over Britain's rights to bring opium into the region. In 1799 Sierra Leone had erupted over the refusal to allow black settlers freehold of the land; the revolt was suppressed by former runaway slaves from Jamaica. In 1857, the uprising of soldiers and their supporters that began in northern India and spread through large swaths of British-controlled India sufficiently alarmed the authorities in London and India that they imposed direct governmental rule in India, took away the East India Company's rights there and increased the presence of white soldiers on the subcontinent.[79]

---

76 Penny Edwards, *Cambodge: The Cultivation of a Nation, 1860–1945* (Honolulu, HI, 2007).
77 Matt Matsuda, *Empire of Love: Histories of France and the Pacific* (New York, 2005).
78 Denmark retained its Caribbean colonies until 1917, when it sold them to the United States.
79 There is a huge literature on what is now routinely known as the Sepoy Rebellion and used to be called the Indian Mutiny. A good starting point is Biswamoy Pati (ed.), *The*

Maintenance

Many intertwined factors drove this expansionist phase of European colonialism: a curious combination of greed, belief in European superiority, hunger for land in an increasingly urbanised world, and the shifting political landscape both within Europe itself and more globally. The massive and unprecedented attention to technology was amongst the critical elements which shaped nineteenth-century colonialism. New technologies affected military prowess, communications, extraction and manufacture, and the movement of goods as well as everyday lives. In almost all cases, perhaps the most important innovation was speed. News and people could travel faster, wars could be more quickly executed, buildings and goods could be speedily fashioned. The railway, just as in Europe, was often the most visible and potent symbol of this far-reaching revolution, although the building of rail lines in colonies occurred mostly in the late nineteenth century, later than in much of Europe. Capital-intensive technology – large-scale factories, railways and the like – were developed, if at all, far later in the colonies than in the home countries. Investment in colonial ventures was always regarded as risky, and as a result it was often delayed well beyond the moment when comparable developments emerged in Europe. But the steamship, the telegraph and increasingly efficient weaponry heralded, for the colonial world, the technological power harnessed by Europe. Science was as much the ally of empire as was its close cousin, technology. Improved mapping techniques, the growing use of statistics to survey countries and new medical understandings all helped further the spread of colonial authority and influence.[80] The reach of science and technology was slow and uneven, and often met with local resistance, yet, tentative as it sometimes was, science was critical for and representative of the incursions of Europe into other continents, and significantly expanded and eased the process of settlement.

1857 Rebellion (New Delhi, 2007).

80   On British colonialism, see David Arnold, *Colonizing the Body: State Medicine and Epidemic Disease in Nineteenth-Century India* (Berkeley, CA, 1993); David Arnold, *Science, Technology, and Medicine in Colonial India* (New York, 2000); Tony Ballantyne (ed.), *Science, Empire and the European Exploration of the Pacific* (Aldershot, 2004); Anna Crozier, *Practising Colonial Medicine: The Colonial Medical Service in British East Africa* (London, 2007); Matthew Edney, *Mapping an Empire: The Geographical Construction of British India, 1765–1843* (Chicago, IL, 1997); LaVerne Kuhnke, *Lives at Risk: Public Health in Nineteenth-Century Egypt* (Berkeley, CA, 1990); Lenore Manderson, *Sickness and the State: Health and Illness in Colonial Malaya, 1870–1940* (Cambridge, 1996); Megan Vaughan, *Curing Their Ills: Colonial Power and African Illness* (Cambridge, 1991). On French colonialism, see Florence Bretelle-Establet, 'Resistance and Receptivity: French Colonial Medicine in Southwest China, 1898–1930', *Modern China* 25/2 (1999): pp. 171–203; Nancy Rose Hunt, *A Colonial Lexicon of Birth: Ritual, Medicalization, and Mobility in the Congo* (Durham, NC, 1999); Eric Jennings, *Curing the Colonizers: Hydrotherapy, Climatology, and French Colonial Spas* (Durham, NC, 2006); P.M. Lorcin, 'Imperialism, Colonial Identity, and Race in Algeria, 1830–1870: The Role of the French Medical Corps', *Isis* 90/4 (1999): pp. 652–79.

While the eighteenth century had seen significant waves of emigration from Europe and colonialism was, at that time, virtually synonymous with migration and settlement, the flow of peoples from Europe increased greatly in the nineteenth century, creating new settlements, extending old ones and altering patterns of land-holding and of labour in the process. Germany's initial interest in building an empire was largely focused on settlement. In 1879 Friedrich Fabri's book *Bedarf Deutschland der Colonien? (Does Germany Need Colonies?)* promoted settlement as a solution to over-population, among other things.[81] The empire was already an arena in which those colonised within Britain – the Irish, the Scots and the Welsh – could move beyond the restrictions to which their marginal states often relegated them at home. Scottish migration to Jamaica accelerated rapidly after the 1707 Act of Union which had joined Scotland and England politically.[82] As the German Empire grew in the late nineteenth century, it, too, was an arena where those of lower status, including Jews, could find work.[83]

The same was so for those to whom settler life appealed. The chance to build a new social order or to acquire land was attractive to people of humble origin, and as transport options became both faster and cheaper so the constraints to emigration fell away. The growing phenomenon of settlement in South Africa and the Pacific often led to increased friction with prior inhabitants who invariably fared poorly as western-style cities emerged and new settlers claimed land. Even where formal treaties laid out indigenous rights (such as the 1840 Treaty of Waitangi in New Zealand), the new settlers invariably benefited most from these arrangements. Despite a treaty ceding western Algeria to Abd al Keder in 1837, the French kept up a war against him and his followers until he surrendered in 1847. Technically Algeria was a French *département* in the same way as any other region of France, and the Algerians were entitled to French citizenship (which very few wanted). But France ruled with an iron fist and rebellions, such as the Kabyle revolt of 1871, were frequent throughout the century. In 1887 the *Code de l'Indigénat* imposed different legal codes for Arabs and French, privileging the European settlers.[84]

---

81   Klaus Bade, *Friedrich Fabri und der Imperialismus in der Bismarckzeit: Beitrage zur Kolonial- und Uberseegeschichte* (Freiburg, 1975). For the debate over the motives of the German colonialism, see Wolfe Schmokel, *Dream of Empire: German Colonialism, 1919–1945* (New Haven, CT, 1964) and Woodruff Smith, *The German Colonial Empire* (Chapel Hill, NC, 1978) p. 28 et seq. See also W.O. Aydelotte, *Bismarck and British Colonial Policy: The Problem of South West Africa, 1883–1885* (Philadelphia, PA, 1937); Matthew Fitzpatrick, *Liberal Imperialism in Germany: Expansionism and Nationalism, 1848–1884* (Oxford, 2008); A.J.P. Taylor, *Germany's First Bid for Colonies, 1884–1885: A Move in Bismarck's European Policy* (London, 1938); Hans-Ulrich Wehler, 'Bismarck's Imperialism, 1862–1890', *Past and Present* 48/1 (1970): pp. 119–55.

82   Douglas Hamilton, *Scotland, the Caribbean, and the Atlantic World, 1750–1820* (Manchester, 2005); Angela McCarthy, *A Global Clan: Scottish Migrant Networks and Identity since the Eighteenth Century* (New York, 2006).

83   Smith, *German Colonial Empire*, pp. 134–6.

84   By 1914 the code was applied in most of French Africa and Indochina.

There was also involuntary settlement effected by the practice of transportation favoured by British and the French in the late eighteenth and early nineteenth century.[85] The French established a penal colony in Guiana in 1852 and at New Caledonia in the Pacific in 1853, shortly before the British ended transportation of British convicts to the Australian territories. Colonial as well as European convicts faced transportation, and France introduced transportation for political convicts in 1872. Transportation ended at New Caledonia in 1897 but the Devil's Island colony at Guiana existed until 1937.

While colonies intended as permanent settler outposts offered political freedoms to European settlers akin to those of their domestic counterparts, non-settler territories were ruled autocratically. The protectorate was a popular form of governance which allowed European interests maximum interference at minimum cost.[86] In essence it was a form of 'indirect rule' which kept in place a local authority under the thumb of the colonial power.[87] Direct rule, typified by what the British classified after 1815 as Crown Colonies, made no pretence of leaving extant indigenous authorities in place, though there was often a promise that local customs and beliefs would be honoured. Even as European polities moved in the direction of broader electorates and forms of democracy, these colonies were governed by small councils and cabinets, appointed rather than elected.

This distinction between settlements and dependencies (articulated by the French as *colonies de peuplement* and *colonies d'exploitation*) does not fully define the reach and complexity of European colonialism. Alongside variations on these themes (such as the penal colonies favoured by the French and the British and those places where the British installed 'residents' to advise local rulers, as in the Malay States after 1874), the palpable and widespread informal imperialism of the nineteenth and twentieth centuries enhanced colonial power at the expense of other areas of the world.[88] In former Spanish and Portuguese colonies in South

---

85   Clare Anderson, *Convicts in the Indian Ocean: Transportation from South Asia to Mauritius, 1815–53* (New York, 2000); A. Roger Ekirch, *Bound for America: The Transportation of British Convicts to the Colonies, 1718–1775* (Oxford, 1987); Stefan Petrow, 'Policing in a Penal Colony: Governor Arthur's Police System in Van Diemen's Land, 1826–1836', *Law and History Review* 18/2 (2000): pp. 351–95; A.G.L. Shaw, *Convicts and the Colonies: A Study of Penal Transportation from Great Britain and Ireland to Australia and Other Parts of the British Empire* (London, 1966); Stephen Toth, 'The Lords of Discipline: The Penal Colony Guards of New Caledonia and Guyana', *Crime, Histoire & Sociétés / Crime, History & Societies* 7/2 (2004): pp. 41–60.

86   Though this form of colonial rule is associated most closely with the late nineteenth century and early twentieth centuries, the French protectorate over Tahiti was an early example, established in 1842.

87   For a useful discussion of the differing styles of indirect rule adopted by the British and the French, see Michael Crowder, 'Indirect Rule: French and British Style', *Africa: Journal of the International African Institute* 34/3 (1964): pp. 197–205. In the British Empire, protectorates were not formally annexed.

88   Matthew Brown (ed.), *Informal Empire in Latin America; Culture, Commerce and Capital* (Oxford, 2008); H.S. Ferns, 'Britain's Informal Empire in Argentina, 1806–1914', *Past and*

and Central America, the British and later the Americans exercised an economic domination that made formal annexation unnecessary. The British acted similarly in the Persian Gulf, signing treaties that tied these states economically and politically to British interests.

Formal empire, in particular, also gave rise to a professionalisation of government service, although in France and Germany colonial postings lacked prestige and did not attract the best candidates.[89] In the British Empire, even after the introduction of competitive exams in the Civil Service in the 1850s, appointment was often secured through family connections rather than via concrete and measurable skills. The Dutch, Belgian and French established specialised training colleges for their colonial service. In Germany and in Britain universities began to offer courses in 'Oriental' languages and culture with an eye to training future officials. Yet, throughout the colonial era, there were seldom large numbers of European officers in the field. The Colonial Office was among the thinnest-staffed of British government departments. At the height of Britain's imperial influence, there were perhaps 6,000 British colonial officials in the colonies. French West Africa in 1912 had a mere 341 French nationals in formal colonial service, and in Java in 1890 there were some 300 Dutch civil servants.

These officials were uniformly male. Government service was not open to women and until well into the twentieth century colonial outposts were generally considered unsuitable, even dangerous, terrain for European women. In settler locations, male settlers outnumbered female settlers dramatically and ratios equalised only slowly in the twentieth century. In the 1860s, women comprised between 5 and 15 per cent of the white population of British Columbia, a proportion not atypical for early colonial settlement.[90] Settler populations routinely contained high numbers of young single men, as did colonial armies. Higher-ranking officials were often accompanied by wives and sometimes sisters, but only from the mid-nineteenth century was female emigration consciously encouraged. Though convict women arrived on the first transports from Britain to Australia, their numbers were small. Joy Damousi estimates that about 25,000 of the 160,000 convicts transported to Australia between 1788 and 1868 (when transportation ended) were women.[91] The French sent even fewer; of the more than 20,000 prisoners sent to New Caledonia in the nineteenth century, only around a thousand were women.[92]

Present 4/1 (1953): pp. 60–75; John Gallagher and Ronald Robinson, 'The Imperialism of Free Trade', *Economic History Review* 6/1, New Series (1953): pp. 1–15; David Mclean, *War, Diplomacy and Informal Empire: Britain, France and Latin America, 1836–1852* (London, 1995); Rory Miller, *Britain and Latin America in the Nineteenth and Twentieth Centuries* (London, 1993); M.D.D. Newitt, *Portugal in Africa: The Last Hundred Years* (London, 1981); D.C.M. Platt, *Latin America and British Trade, 1806–1914* (London, 1972).

89 Quinn, *French Overseas Empire*, p. 183; Smith, *German Colonial Empire*, pp. 134–6.

90 Adele Perry, *On the Edge of Empire: Gender, Race, and the Making of British Columbia, 1849–1871* (Toronto, 2001), p. 17.

91 Joy Damousi, *Depraved and Disorderly: Female Convicts, Sexuality and Gender in Colonial Australia* (Cambridge, 1997), p. 2.

92 Jane Lennon, 'Port Arthur, Norfolk Island, New Caledonia: Convict Prison Islands

By the 1850s societies encouraging female emigration to settler colonies were enjoying modest success, focusing on single women in 'feminine' occupations such as domestic service and school teaching, and invariably with the prospect of matrimony held out as the ultimate prize.[93] In British India, young single white women visiting their relatives were wryly known as the 'fishing fleet', their nets cast to attract husbands among the younger officials, military officers and businessmen working there. France acquired a society dedicated to sending women to the colonies only in the late 1890s, and it was short lived.[94] At the start of the twentieth century, Dutch women in Java numbered about 4,000.[95]

European men commonly sought companionship from local women, a tendency that could be, on the one hand, a source of tension and resentment, and, on the other hand, a profitable business. New forms of prostitution and concubinage grew in the wake of colonial expansion.[96] There was greater toleration of both intermarriage and cohabitation in the Spanish than in the early British Empire. Indeed, in 1514 the Spanish formally legitimised inter-ethnic marriage.[97] In the eighteenth century such arrangements went mostly unremarked, and were often seen as a useful strategy for infiltrating and understanding new cultures and languages. Non-western women, moreover, were widely regarded by Europeans as sexually freer than their white sisters, unencumbered by the restraints that governed the lives of white women. Their perceived hypersexuality became a justification not merely for the sexual convenience and 'needs' of male colonisers, but a key narrative of the 'civilising mission' which increasingly aimed to inculcate western standards on colonial populations.[98]

Britain and later Germany tended to have the most marked antipathy to interracial sexual relationships, passing laws early in the twentieth century to

in the Antipodes', in William Logan and Keir Reeves (eds), *Places of Pain and Shame: Dealing with 'Difficult Heritage'* (London, 2009), pp. 165–81.

93   Pamela Sharpe, *Women, Gender, and Labour Migration: Historical and Global Perspectives* (London, 2001). On British migrant women, see for example A. James Hammerton, *Emigrant Gentlewomen: Genteel Poverty and Female Emigration, 1830–1914* (London, 1979) and Rita Kranidis, *The Victorian Spinster and Colonial Emigration: Contested Subjects* (New York, 1999). There is yet to emerge a parallel history of female emigration in other European colonial settings.

94   Quinn, *French Overseas Empire*, p. 184.

95   Elsbeth Locher-Scholten, *Women and the Colonial State: Essays on Gender and Modernity in the Netherlands Indies, 1900–1942* (Amsterdam, 2000), p. 19.

96   Kenneth Ballhatchet, *Race, Sex, and Class Under the Raj: Imperial Attitudes and Policies and Their Critics, 1793–1905* (London, 1980); Durba Ghosh, *Sex and the Family in Colonial India: The Making of Empire* (Cambridge, 2006); Philippa Levine (ed.), *Gender and Empire* (Oxford, 2004).

97   Elliott, *Empires of the Atlantic World*, p. 81.

98   Jennifer Morgan, '"Some Could Suckle over Their Shoulder": Male Travelers, Female Bodies, and the Gendering of Racial Ideology, 1500–1770', *William and Mary Quarterly* 54/1, Third Series (1997): pp. 167–92; Felicity Nussbaum, *Torrid Zones: Maternity, Sexuality, and Empire in Eighteenth-Century English Narratives* (Baltimore, MD, 1995).

counter them.[99] A growing unease with interracial marriage in France from the 1870s led the French to encourage colonial officials to marry at home and go abroad with their wives.[100] Disapproval of interracial liaisons grew as the numbers of white women arriving in the colonies increased for, as Frances Gouda has put it, 'In virtually every colonial settler society, the social and sexual behaviour of women constituted a cornerstone of European domination.'[101] Gouda's observation is applicable not only to settler colonies but more broadly. The British government mandated a sex ratio so that ships carrying indentured South Asian labourers to their new workplaces included women, one of whose functions was to domesticate the men.[102] Penal colonies often emphasised family ties. French convicts with wives and children were entitled to financial help at the end of their sentences.[103] The wives of Indian convicts on the Andaman Islands were required to serve out the duration of their husbands' sentences. The softening effect of women was seen not just as a civilisational but as a political tool. Thus, in the early twentieth century, journalist Clara Brockmann urged German women to emigrate to South West Africa to help establish German domesticity. It was their wifely skills, she claimed, that would mark the new colony out as properly German. 'Without the presence of a *Hausfrau'*, she wrote, colonial farms would never be *heimisch*.[104] The act of colonial conquest was also often read in gendered terms. Subject populations were written off as effeminate, demasculinised by their very conquest, by their inability to fend off the more powerful colonisers.[105] Colonies were often represented as pliable and passive feminine entities requiring a firm paternal hand to guide their paths.

Nostalgia for what was seen as 'home' was a strong sentiment in settler societies, and many diaries and letters betray a longing for different climes and flora, or a distaste for the new environment. It was the task of European women to recreate,

---

99   Amirah Inglis, *The White Women's Protection Ordinance: Sexual Anxiety and Politics in Papua* (New York, 1975); Jock McCulloch, *Black Peril, White Virtue: Sexual Crime in Southern Rhodesia, 1902–1935* (Bloomington, IN, 2000); Lora Wildenthal, *German Women for Empire, 1884–1945* (Durham, NC, 2001).

100   Alice Conklin, *A Mission to Civilize: The Republican Idea of Empire in France and West Africa, 1895–1930* (Stanford, CA, 1997), pp. 20–21, 170; Emmanuelle Saada, 'Race and Sociological Reason in the Republic: Inquiries on the Métis in the French Empire (1908–37)', *International Sociology* 17/3 (2002): pp. 361–91; Owen White, *Children of the French Empire: Miscegenation and Colonial Society in French West Africa, 1895–1960* (Oxford, 1999).

101   Frances Gouda, *Dutch Culture Overseas: Colonial Practice in the Netherlands Indies, 1900–1942* (Amsterdam, 1995), p. 6.

102   B.V. Lal, 'Kunti's Cry: Indentured Women on Fiji Plantations', *Indian Economic & Social History Review* 22/1 (1985): pp. 55–71.

103   Stephen Toth, *Beyond Papillon: The French Overseas Penal Colonies, 1854–1952* (Lincoln, NE, 2006).

104   Nancy Ruth Reagin, *Sweeping the German Nation: Domesticity and National Identity in Germany, 1870–1945* (New York, 2007), p. 49.

105   Mrinalini Sinha, *Colonial Masculinity: The 'Manly Englishman' and the 'Effeminate Bengali' in the Late Nineteenth Century* (Manchester, 1995).

as Brockmann counselled, the trappings of European 'civilisation' in alien spaces.[106] Such attempts to recreate the familiar permeated not just the domestic world but the art and culture of colonialism too. Early Australian painting often depicted landscapes more reminiscent of England's countryside than of what painters actually saw. The radically different southern light was difficult for European-trained painters to capture at first. French nineteenth-century art frequently dwelt on colonial themes, from celebratory canvases of military campaigns to endless paintings of scantily clad women set against obviously colonial backgrounds. These latter images would also form a profitable segment of the picture postcard trade early in the twentieth century; exotically dressed and undressed women were a constant motif in this new industry fed in equal parts by travel and colonialism.[107]

In Europe the colonial exhibition became popular entertainment especially after Britain's Great Exhibition of 1851. Arts and crafts, technology and manufactured goods were celebrated as part of the bounty of colonialism, a tacit encouragement to European viewers not only to support but to invest in colonial ventures. Alongside the new manufactures so proudly displayed at these events, there were human exhibits too. The display of 'strange' colonials had been well established in Europe for some time. Native Americans had been displayed in London from the late sixteenth century.[108] Sara Baartman's display as the 'Venus Hottentot' in London and Paris in the 1810s is only the most celebrated of such exhibitions. Portraits of 'Esther the Hottentot' and 'Billy the Australian' flanked the entrance to the anthropology section of the Universal Exposition in Paris in 1889; the period from 1851 to the First World War was, in Peter Hoffenberg's words, one of 'exhibition mania'.[109] France saw a number of such exhibitions, culminating in the 1931 Colonial Exposition, which continued the nineteenth-century tradition of exhibiting people regarded in Europe as primitive.[110] The so-called Aztec twins went on display in London in 1853.[111] In Germany, the zookeeper Karl Hagenbeck put Pacific islanders and Laplanders on display in 1874.[112] Such exhibitions were

---

106 Perry, *On the Edge of Empire*.
107 Malek Alloula, *The Colonial Harem* (Minneapolis, MN, 1986); Christraud Geary and Virginia-Lee Webb, *Delivering Views: Distant Cultures in Early Postcards* (Washington, DC, 1998).
108 Richard Altick, *The Shows of London* (Cambridge, MA, 1978), p. 45.
109 Peter Hoffenberg, *An Empire on Display: English, Indian, and Australian Exhibitions from the Crystal Palace to the Great War* (Berkeley, CA, 2001), p. xiii.
110 Jean-Michel Bergougniou, Rémi Clignet and Philippe David, *'Villages noirs' et autres visiteurs africains et malgaches en France et en Europe: 1870–1940* (Paris, 2001); Laure Blévis et al., *1931: les étrangers au temps de l'Exposition coloniale* (Paris, 2008); Donna Jones, 'The Prison House of Modernism: Colonial Spaces and the Construction of the Primitive at the 1931 Paris Colonial Exposition', *Modernism/Modernity* 14/1 (2007): pp. 55–69.
111 Robert Aguirre, 'Exhibiting Degeneracy: The Aztec Children and the Ruins of Race', *Victorian Review* 29/2 (2003): pp. 40–63.
112 Eric Ames, 'From the Exotic to the Everyday: The Ethnographic Exhibition in Germany', in Vanessa Schwartz and Jeannene Przyblyski (eds), *The Nineteenth-Century Visual Culture Reader* (New York, 2004), pp. 313–27.

often dubbed ethnographic or ethnological, implying that they carried educational as well as entertainment value.[113]

Displays of this sort illuminate how race was fundamental to European understandings and justifications of imperial expansion.[114] The steady growth in importance of racial differentiation – measured scientifically and theologically, legislated, advertised and exhibited – began with the new form of slavery the Atlantic trade engendered but did not end with the slow move away from slave-trading and slave labour in the nineteenth century. On the contrary, imperial expansion became more and more closely associated with European dominion over peoples regarded as critically different – identified increasingly via skin colour, hair texture and physical characteristics – and as lesser. Nineteenth-century science purported to prove that such physical differences were matched by mental difference. David Killingray's claim that 'racial difference lay at the heart of the British empire' applies beyond Britain.[115]

Race was particularly provoking for missionaries who saw Christianity as a vital gift to colonial populations. Schooled on the one hand to regard all peoples as equal in the sight of God, and, on the other, to fear for the souls of the unconverted, missionaries were invariably unable to erase the importance of racial difference in their work. Protestant and Catholic empires alike invoked religion as a justification for their colonial activities. There were missionaries in the Canary Islands archipelago north of Morocco by the middle of the fourteenth century, and the Spanish and Portuguese established Catholic missions throughout their colonial domains. Protestant missions followed, the Dutch bringing their brand of Christianity to South Africa and Indonesia in the seventeenth century. Rome authorised and encouraged the Spanish and Portuguese efforts at conversion, working closely with both countries to strengthen the Christian presence. From the nineteenth century, the bulk of Catholic missionaries were French; 22 missionary orders were founded in France between 1816 and 1870.[116] In contrast to the East India Company, which kept missionaries out of British India until the nineteenth century, the Dutch East and West India Companies were required by their charters to promote the Dutch Reformed Church (the state church of the Netherlands) in their territories. Protestant missionary activity increased considerably in the late eighteenth century, reflecting both colonial expansion and the growing power of

---

113 Hagenbeck's Nubian display in 1878 was the catalyst for a petition organised by the Colonial Society to ban public exhibition of German colonial subjects on the grounds that their exhibition fostered a dangerous cross-ethnic identification: Ames, 'From the Exotic', p. 327, n. 52.

114 Pascal Blanchard, Gilles Boëtsch, Nanette Jacomijn Snoep and Lilian Thuram, *Exhibitions: L'invention du sauvage* (Paris, 2011).

115 David Killingray, '"A Good West Indian, a Good African, and, in Short, a Good Britisher": Black and British in a Colour-Conscious Empire, 1760–1950', *Journal of Imperial and Commonwealth History* 36/3 (2008): pp. 363–81. See too V.G. Kiernan, *The Lords of Human Kind: European Attitudes towards the Outside World in the Imperial Age* (Harmondsworth, 1972).

116 Quinn, *The French Overseas Empire*, pp. 121, 119.

Protestant evangelicalism. By the end of the nineteenth century some 10,000 British missionaries worked outside Britain, the vast majority in the empire.[117] Germany permitted Catholic missionaries in its empire after 1889. Missions in all the empires provided social infrastructure much as they did in Europe, furnishing the poor with access to educational and medical care alongside the equally serious business of saving souls. Religion certainly could and did act as a justification for empire, but it was not amongst its major ideological wellsprings. While religion could sanction empire, they were not mutually constitutive. Relatively few of those who left Britain for North America in the late seventeenth century did so for specifically religious reasons.[118] Religious freedom played a role, to be sure, but economic incentives were at least as critical a factor in the decision to relocate.

Catholicism grew deep roots in the Spanish and Portuguese empires, and shared its success with other forms of Christianity in Africa, the West Indies and elsewhere. Yet there was also considerable resistance in many areas to conversion, and missionaries frequently met with hostility, suspicion and resentment. Where they did make inroads, the versions of Christianity that proved most tenacious often combined the new religion with older forms of worship and ritual to the discomfort of many missionaries.

Nonetheless, religion was part of the rhetoric of the 'civilising mission' that so distinctively framed European colonialism. The association is a complex one, for the French version of this idea – the *mission civilisatrice* – emerged from the secular rationality of the French Revolution and was more concerned with culture. Elsewhere, where political secularism was less ingrained, the two merged more comfortably. Whether imbued with Christian principles or not, European colonists frequently and often self-righteously regarded their intervention as beneficent, raising the standards of more 'primitive' peoples to new heights through greater productivity, improved medical care, better education. Though the phrase is most associated with the later phases of colonialism, the civilising impulse had a long history. One goal of the plantation in seventeenth-century Ireland was to bring

---

117 For a discussion of British women missionaries, see Elizabeth Prevost, *The Communion of Women: Missions and Gender in Colonial Africa and the British Metropole* (Oxford, 2010). For broader missionary histories, see T.O. Beidelman, *Colonial Evangelism: A Socio-Historical Study of an East African Mission at the Grassroots* (Bloomington, IN, 1982); Jeffrey Cox, *Imperial Fault Lines: Christianity and Colonial Power in India, 1818–1940* (Stanford, CA, 2002); Elizabeth Elbourne, *Blood Ground: Colonialism, Missions, and the Contest for Christianity in the Cape Colony and Britain, 1799–1853* (Montreal, 2002); Richard Price, *Making Empire: Colonial Encounters and the Creation of Imperial Rule in Nineteenth-Century Africa* (Cambridge, 2008); Brian Stanley, *The Bible and the Flag: Protestant Missions and British Imperialism in the Nineteenth and Twentieth Centuries* (Nottingham, 1990); H. Henrietta Stockel, *Salvation Through Slavery: Chiricahua Apaches and Priests on the Spanish Colonial Frontier* (Albuquerque, NM, 2008); Susan Thorne, *Congregational Missions and the Making of an Imperial Culture in Nineteenth-century England* (Stanford, CA, 1999); Patrick Tuck, *French Catholic Missionaries and the Politics of Imperialism in Vietnam, 1857–1914: A Documentary Survey* (Liverpool, 1987).

118 Elliott, *Empires of the Atlantic World*, p. 54.

civilisation to the savage Irish. The plantation was, quite literally, a gardening metaphor: uprooting unproductive weeds in order to plant productive civility.

The relationship between the missionary impulse and the fact of imperialism was never simple. In the modern period missionaries were often critical of imperial policies, regarded by the authorities as trouble-makers. Missionaries had no hesitation in publicly denouncing policies they regarded as unethical, ranging from cruelty to workers to the toleration of prostitution. Harriet Colenso – daughter of the pro-African bishop of Natal, J.W. Colenso, who was removed from office for his outspoken views – robustly condemned European depradations in Africa in the late nineteenth century as 'the lust for power domineering or the lust for gold in dividends ... as though it [Africa] existed for our private advantage'.[119]

The military was often in the missionary firing line, in part because troops were the front line of conquest and in part because missionaries regarded military life as morally lax, with its toleration of non-marital sex and of the liberal use of alcohol. The hypermasculinity demanded of armies was largely incompatible with prevailing Christian precepts, and white colonial soldiers led peculiarly isolated lives. Yet the European soldier was out-numbered by indigenous troops in most colonial settings. Algeria was unusual in having been taken by an exclusively metropolitan army; it was far more common in the modern European empires for there to be a relatively small body of European troops and a far larger local army in colonial employ. Throughout Africa the French, Belgians, Germans, British and Portuguese recruited from amongst indigenous peoples they regarded as warlike, what the British called the 'martial races'. Not only were such troops cheaper to maintain but they were seen as inured to the hostile climates that took such a toll on European troops. The Germans maintained the smallest European forces in their empire, never numbering much more than 6,500, while the French and the British kept upwards of 60,000 white soldiers in Algeria and British India respectively from the late nineteenth century.

Native recruits, as they were known, were used widely. In the First World War, Britain and France used colonial regiments on the Western Front as well as in colonial theatres of war, and as a retaliatory move the French stationed black African soldiers in the demilitarised zone along the Rhine at the war's end, catalysing a firestorm of international protest against what was quickly dubbed the 'Black Horror on the Rhine'.[120]

---

119 Quoted in Jeff Guy, *The View Across the River: Harriette Colenso and the Zulu Struggle Against Imperialism* (Charlottesville, VA, 2002), p. 411.

120 See, for example, Jean-Yves Le Naour, *La Honte noire: L'Allemagne et les troupes coloniales françaises, 1914–1945* (Paris, 2004); Sally Marks, 'Black Watch on the Rhine: A Study in Propaganda, Prejudice and Prurience', *European History Quarterly* 13/3 (1983): pp. 297–334; Keith Nelson, 'The "Black Horror on the Rhine": Race as a Factor in Post-World War I Diplomacy', *Journal of Modern History* 42/4 (1970): pp. 606–627; Robert Reinders, 'Racialism on the Left: E.D. Morel and the "Black Horror on the Rhine"', *International Review of Social History* 13/1 (1968): pp. 1–28; Iris Wigger, *Die 'Schwarze Schmach am Rhein': Rassistische Diskriminierung zwischen Geschlecht, Klasse, Nation und Rasse* (Münster, 2006).

The French introduced conscription in French West Africa to provide troops for the 1914–18 war, though there was growing and increasingly organised resistance to it, starting in the Sudan in 1915 and spreading.[121] Britain recruited among its Indian subjects heavily, but never introduced conscription there, as it did in Britain in 1916.[122] The widespread use of indigenous troops, and their presence on European soil after 1915, raises interesting questions around colonial attitudes to assimilation and difference. The French policy of assimilation was an outgrowth of the 1848 revolution, and extended political rights to those in the French colonial possessions. The expectation was that Africans in French territories would transform themselves into culturally and linguistically French citizens.[123] By the end of the nineteenth century assimilation was being replaced by the idea of association, in which what were regarded as native institutions were retained and little effort was made to render the colonised French.

The French were not alone in weighing different methods of colonial rule. At a much earlier date, Thomas Macaulay's 'Minute on Education' – presented to the Governor-General of India, William Bentinck, in 1835 – famously envisaged 'a class of persons, Indian in blood and colour, but English in taste, in opinions, in morals, and intellect', who would act as 'interpreters between us, and the millions who we govern'.[124] His assimilationist perspective, to be achieved by education, held sway in British India until the rebellion of 1857, which many Britons saw as revealing the true barbarism of Indians who, henceforth, were regarded – and ruled – as dangerously different.

The Dutch switched policies at the start of the twentieth century when the new *Ethische Politiek* (Ethical Policy) articulated the responsibility of colonial governments, a sharp contrast to the *kultuurstelsel* which, from the 1830s to the 1870s, had transferred profits from the Dutch East Indies to the Netherlands. The Ethical Policy highlighted three major areas of responsibility: education, irrigation and transmigration (migration within the East Indies). Rather than emphasising cultural transformation, as did the 'civilising mission', this approach focused on

121 Conklin, *A Mission to Civilize*, pp. 142–8; Myron Echenberg, *Colonial Conscripts: The Tirailleurs Sénégalais in French West Africa, 1857–1960* (Portsmouth, NH, 1991); Richard Fogarty, *Race and War in France: Colonial Subjects in the French Army, 1914–1918* (Baltimore, MD, 2009); Adrian Muckle, 'Kanak Experiences of WWI: New Caledonia's Tirailleurs, Auxiliaries and "Rebels"', *History Compass* 6/5 (2008): pp. 1325–45; Melvin Page (ed.), *Africa and the First World War* (New York, 1987).

122 C.M. Andrew and A.S. Kanya-Forstner, 'France, Africa, and the First World War', *Journal of African History* 19/1 (1978): pp. 11–23; Shelby Cullom Davis, *Reservoirs of Men: History of the Black Troops of French West Africa* (Santa Barbara, CA, 1970); DeWitt C. Ellinwood and S.D. Pradhan (eds), *India and World War I* (Columbia, MO, 1978); Bill Gammage, *The Broken Years; Australian Soldiers in the Great War* (Canberra, 1974); Page, *Africa and the First World War*; Philippa Levine, 'Battle Colors: Race, Sex, and Colonial Soldiery in World War I', *Journal of Women's History* 9/4 (1998): pp. 104–130.

123 Raymond Betts, *Assimilation and Association in French Colonial Theory, 1890–1914* (Lincoln, NE, 2005), p. 8.

124 www.fordham.edu/halsall/mod/1833macaulay-india.asp, accessed 25 January 2012.

material improvement, although the budget available seldom allowed any radical alterations in the economic status quo.

These competing visions of colonial practice and motive reveal starkly the notion then in vogue that colonised peoples were radically different from Europeans. A good deal of nineteenth-century anthropology was devoted to sustaining that claim, both in its physical and intellectual manifestations. Justifications of black slavery had long been based on the idea that Africans were a race apart, whose enslavement violated neither humanistic nor Christian principles. The human sciences devoted considerable attention in the nineteenth century to investigating whether that held true across a broader canvas.

Attitudes such as these made it easy to dehumanise labour, and as many historians have pointed out European imperialism was built on the backs not just of slaves but of cheap colonised labour, whether locally derived or by indentured migrants. The abolition of slavery over the course of the nineteenth century was by no means uniform. Generally the trade and the institution were abolished separately, the former abandoned earlier. French abolition in 1794 was rescinded in 1802 and rekindled only in 1848, the same year in which Denmark abolished slavery (having abolished the slave trade in 1803, four years before the British). In the 1820s and 1830s slavery was abolished in most of Latin and South America as independence spread. Spain did not abolish slavery in its remaining colonies until late in the century, and it remained legal in Brazil until 1888.[125] Britain abolished slavery in the 1830s, but The Netherlands not until 1863, although the trade had been abolished there by 1820. Slavery nonetheless persisted in many areas under colonial control or influence, even after it was declared illegal.[126]

But even where the letter of the law was implemented, forms of coerced labour frequently replaced formal enslavement. The Belgian Congo was notorious in this respect in the early twentieth century, but the Belgian King, Leopold, was far from alone in his tactics. In German East Africa the penalty for non-payment of taxes was 'tribute labour', a form of forced labour which helped foment the Maji Maji rebellion in 1905. In West Africa, one consequence of the Herero uprising at much the same time was the compulsory labour implemented in the prisoner of war camps where the Germans interned Africans involved in the uprising. By the early twentieth century, labour extracted as a tax as well as labour requisitioning were commonplace in French West Africa.[127]

In Asia indenture dominated, a critical supply of manual labour as the European empires moved away from large-scale slave economies. British colonies provided a vast contingent of indentured labourers, principally from India. From the 1830s Indian indentured workers toiled on plantations in the Caribbean and Mauritius. Another wave of Indians moved to Fiji in the 1870s and another to East Africa

125 Robert Brent Toplin, *The Abolition of Slavery in Brazil* (New York, 1972).
126 Jan-Georg Deutsch, *Emancipation Without Abolition in German East Africa, c.1884–1914* (Oxford, 2006).
127 Catherine Ash, 'Forced Labor in Colonial West Africa', *History Compass* 4/3 (2006): pp. 402–406.

(largely for construction work) in the 1890s. The French recruited in India and Indochina, the Australians in the Pacific Islands to their north, and in China which provided workers, too, for German Samoa, for the gold and diamond mines in South Africa, and for construction work in the United States.

Despite the massive influx of indentured workers into the Caribbean after the 1830s, the West Indies declined in importance in the nineteenth century as beet sugar (which could be produced in Europe) competed with cane sugar and as new areas of sugar production such as north-eastern Australia emerged. An increasingly global economy overshadowed the Atlantic world which had dominated eighteenth-century European colonialism.[128] Asia, Africa, the Pacific and increasingly the Middle East became part of a massive interconnected world economy run largely by western bankers, manufacturers, shippers and merchants. Such a system depended on a good deal of collaboration. European colonists sought out, and sometimes set about creating, local elites with whom they could do business and on whom they could rely for support in political office, as economic partners and in maintaining social order. Educated elites were often mindful of the personal benefits that could accrue to them from colonialism. Rifles and ordnance were there when necessary, but it was often cheaper to persuade than to subdue.

The nineteenth century, then, saw a steady expansion of European colonialism. The colonial world in 1850 was a bigger and more widespread entity than it had been in 1750, and its centre of gravity shifted away from the Atlantic. In the last two decades of the nineteenth century there was a new and dramatic growth as the rival European colonies focused their energies and interests on the African continent. There had been European interest in Africa, of course, for centuries. It was the source of the slave trade and of precious luxury goods such as ivory. There had been small colonial settlements along the African coasts for centuries, but the 1880s witnessed a marked change in attitude as colonial powers moved into the African interior, funding explorations, commerce and trade on a hitherto unknown scale. This was also the moment at which the late-arriving European empires – Germany, Belgium and Italy – staked their claims.[129] The result was an upsurge in the long-simmering tensions between European rivals, and, more urgently, in severe hardships in many African populations. By 1914 only two African countries – Liberia and Ethiopia – remained uncolonised, though Italy briefly occupied portions of Ethiopia in the late 1930s.

This new phase of European colonialism began with the French occupation of Tunisia in 1881. Each new claim set off tensions between competing countries; their agreements with one another over how to divide territory ignored the wishes and needs of local peoples, and the resulting map of Africa frequently mingled

---

128 Elisabeth Wallace, *The British Caribbean from the Decline of Colonialism to the End of Federation* (Toronto, 1977).

129 W.O. Henderson, *The German Colonial Empire, 1884–1919* (London, 1993); Georges Nzongola-Ntalaja, *The Congo from Leopold to Kabila: A People's History* (London, 2002); Giorgio Rochat, *Il colonialismo italiano* (Turin, 1973).

populations previously hostile to one another or with nothing in common.[130] The most emblematic of such hubristic arrangements was the Berlin Conference, convened in 1884 by the German Chancellor, Otto Von Bismarck. While Europe generally profited from the deliberations of the Conference, it was King Leopold II of Belgium who won the greatest prize. The French and the British had been jostling over territory in the Congo, but the Conference awarded Leopold's Congo Society some 2 million square kilometres of Congo land. Leopold was the sole shareholder of the Society and despite lavish promises to work for the improvement of the 'natives' and to stem slavery, his Congo Free State was by the early twentieth century a byword for brutality and exploitation.[131] Leopold became fabulously rich before the Belgian state, responding to international outcry over his treatment of the indigenous population, annexed his territories in 1908. While it was in Africa that the bulk of new conquest and claim occurred in the closing decades of the century, the European colonial powers were also active elsewhere. The French presence in Indochina grew from the 1860s while in the Pacific, the Dutch, British and Portuguese jostled for territory. The Belgians had established a presence in the Sudan in 1894, trading concessions in China in 1902 and a protectorate over Ruanda-Urundi in 1916. Still, there were setbacks for European colonial powers. Between the 1870s and the 1890s, the Acehnese managed to hold off multiple Dutch attempts at conquest on their lands in northern Sumatra. Brute force at the end of the century finally brought the territory under colonial control. The Zulus famously held off the British in their territories until their defeat at the battle of Ulundi in 1879. The Ethiopians alone were successful in fully routing a colonial power, as they did the invading Italians in 1896. Riots and rebellions in the French colonial prisons in Indochina were constant.[132]

At the start of the twentieth century, the European empires controlled huge tracts of land on every continent. The Spanish and Portuguese empires were, of course, far smaller than they had been in the seventeenth and eighteenth centuries. The Dutch and Danish empires had shrunk too, but the French and British had grown significantly. More than 550 million people lived under some form of colonial European rule on the eve of the First World War. This was 'a global hierarchy of physical, economic and cultural power…an imperial world: of territorial empires … and of informal empires of trade, unequal treaties and extraterritorial privilege (for Europeans) – and garrisons and gunboats to enforce it – over most of the rest.'[133]

---

130 Raymond Betts, *The Scramble for Africa: Causes and Dimensions of Empire* (Lexington, MA, 1972); S.E. Crowe, *The Berlin West African Conference, 1884–1885* (Westport, CT, 1970); Stig Förster, Wolfgang Mommsen and Ronald Robinson (eds), *Bismarck, Europe, and Africa: The Berlin Africa Conference 1884–1885 and the Onset of Partition* (Oxford, 1988); Thomas Pakenham, *The Scramble for Africa, 1876–1912* (London, 1991).

131 Adam Hochschild, *King Leopold's Ghost: A Story of Greed, Terror, and Heroism in Colonial Africa* (Boston, MA, 1998); Nzongola-Ntalaja, *The Congo from Leopold to Kabila*.

132 Peter Zinoman, *The Colonial Bastille: A History of Imprisonment in Vietnam, 1862–1940* (Berkeley, CA, 2001), p. 5.

133 Darwin, *After Tamerlane*, pp. 298–9.

At the start of the twentieth century, then, European colonial power was substantial and widespread. Public perception may have seen it as unassailable but many in power were uncomfortably aware of the global tensions and the local rumblings that might yet topple this powerful phenomenon. As the last quarter of the twentieth century dawned, the age of formal European imperialism was certainly over: that is the topic of chapter 4, 'The Age of Imperial Crisis'.

Russian Empire, 1552–1917

Willard Sunderland

In 1838, Mikhail Pogodin had the following to say about the Russian Empire:

> Ten thousand versts in length, extending almost from the middle of
> Europe … to the faraway lands of America! And five thousand versts
> in width, running from Persia to the Polar Circle. What other state
> can compare to her in size? To half of her? How many states can even
> amount to a twentieth or fiftieth of her territory?[1]

Pogodin was a conservative historian and tutor to the tsarist family, so his
enthusiasm was to be expected. But even people who got on the wrong side of
the tsar could still feel the imperial mystique. In 1820 on his way to banishment
in the south for thinking too freely, the young poet Alexander Pushkin marvelled
at the Russian conquest of the Caucasus region ('the sultry frontier of Asia') and
imagined more glory to come. 'Perhaps', he wrote in his notebook, 'Napoleon's
chimerical plan for the conquest of India will come true for us.'[2]

And why not? Why not imagine the largest land empire in the world getting
even larger? The Russian Empire stood at the peak of its power in the first part of
the 1800s. The Russians had defeated Napoleon. In recent wars with the Turks they
had reached the outskirts of Constantinople. They ruled over a stunning array of
cultures – Finns, Poles, Armenians, Georgians, Turkic peoples, Siberian peoples,
Jews, to name just a few. They had become the greatest land power in Europe, the
counterpart to Britain's great empire of the sea.[3]

---

1   M.P. Pogodin, 'Pis'mo k gosudariu tsarevichu, velikomu kniaziu Aleksandru
    Nikolaevichu v 1838 godu', in *Istoriko-politicheskie pis'ma i zapiski vprodolzhenii Krymskoi
    Voiny 1853–1856* (Moscow, 1874), p. 2. A verst (Russian: versta) was the rough equivalent
    of a kilometre, or 0.6 miles.
2   Cited in T.J. Binyon, *Pushkin: A Biography* (New York, 2003), pp. 148–9.
3   For some thoughtful reflections on the contrasts between sea and land empires, see
    David Armitage, 'The Elephant and the Whale: Empires of Land and Sea', *Journal for
    Maritime Research* 9 (2007): pp. 23–36.

The second half of the nineteenth and early twentieth centuries would prove much rockier. Though Russia continued to grow by expanding into Central Asia and the Far East, the empire found itself forced to reform and modernise in order to compete with its European rivals. Political and social instability quickly followed. Military vulnerability at key moments made things worse, in particular the country's humiliating defeat in the war with Japan, which helped spark the great Revolution of 1905–1907.

The empire was far from doomed, however. Even amid its troubles, there were signs of progress and possibility. Yet by 1917 another war, the First World War, had grown so devastating that the problems became insurmountable. In February of that year, a spontaneous explosion of popular unrest in the imperial capital of Petrograd (formerly St Petersburg) overthrew the tsar. Then a few months later, in October, as the empire's agonies continued, the Bolsheviks, a radical socialist party, seized power and effectively terminated the imperial state. By 1922, after a ferocious civil war, the Bolsheviks would bury the old empire for good by inaugurating an entirely new type of state to replace it: the Union of Soviet Socialist Republics. The old Russian Empire, formally at least, was over.

Like most diverse and long-lasting states, the empire defies easy description. As we look into its history, we find, in fact, that it was often many different empires at once, defined by different habits of rule and cross-cultural life in different regions. We also see persistent contradictions. The tsars ruled in the name of Russian greatness, but Russians in the empire had no special privileges. (In fact, ordinary Russians had fewer privileges than many of the non-Russian peoples in the empire. They could be owned as serfs, for example, while many others could not.) The country's territory was huge but also hugely undergoverned. Meanwhile, the government was highly centralised yet had no single imperial policy. Finally, though many myths evolved to justify or explain the empire over its long history, they do not add up to a neatly coherent imperial idea. Was this an Orthodox empire claiming the legacy of Byzantium or an heir to the Mongol Empire of Genghis Khan? Was it a truly Russian empire or merely a multinational state ruled by a Russian tsar? Was the empire European, Asian or Eurasian?

We can sidestep these difficult questions for now by underscoring perhaps the most important point of all: regardless of how we might define the empire, its success as a political entity was remarkable. For well over 350 years, men and women who called themselves 'tsar' (a Russian derivation of Caesar) and later 'emperor' (*imperator*) ruled over the largest and most diverse territorial state in history. To understand how this came to pass, we need to look at how it expanded, what held it together and, ultimately, how it fell apart.

Expansion

The first Rus' princely states appeared in the ninth century, clustering around the centre of Kiev in what is now central Ukraine, but most historians situate the beginnings of the Russian Empire much later and farther to the north, in the year 1552 when the far younger principality of Moscow conquered the neighbouring Muslim Tatar state of Kazan on the Volga River. In truth, Moscow's expansion did not begin magically in this year – instead, it had been unfolding in fits and starts over the preceding two centuries as Muscovite princes gradually increased their power at the expense of the other Rus' principalities around them. But the conquest of Kazan is nonetheless important for it represents the first time that Moscow extended its power beyond its original neighbourhood. From this point on, the city became the kernel of a huge Russian state that would eventually grow in every direction across the Eurasian continent.

The expansion unfolded in stages. In the late sixteenth and seventeenth centuries, the Russians took over the rest of the Volga region, the Urals, Siberia and parts of Ukraine. In the early 1700s came the turn of what are today Estonia and Latvia; by the late eighteenth century, all of Lithuania, much of Poland, the entire northern shore of the Black Sea and the fringes of Alaska. Then over the course of the nineteenth century the expansion continued as the country incorporated (in rough chronological order) Finland, the southern Caucasus, the northern Caucasus, the Amur Region, Central Asia and, finally, Manchuria, where the tsarist government received a concession to build a railway in the early 1900s, and then proceeded to establish a de facto Russian colony on Chinese territory, replete with its own 'capital', the boomtown of Harbin, the so-called 'Paris of the East'.[4]

There were bumps in the road, of course, periodic defeats and retreats. Peter the Great, for example, wrested the southern port of Azov from the Crimeans and Ottomans in 1696 but found himself pressed to give it back shortly thereafter. Alexander II also famously 'let go' of Alaska by selling it to the United States in 1867, following in the footsteps of the Russian–American Company, which had sold off its outpost at Fort Ross in northern California some twenty years earlier. Yet even counting such cases of failed or reconsidered expansion, the state's growth was dramatic, rivalling the rise of any world empire in the modern period. Between 1500 and 1900, the empire's size expanded by more than eleven times, with its fastest rate of growth coming in the seventeenth century, the era of Siberian expansion, when it added on average some 51,000 square miles of territory every year.[5]

---

4   For a concise overview of Russian expansion in multiple directions, see Geoffrey Hosking, *Russia: People and Empire, 1552–1917* (Cambridge, MA, 1998), pp. 3–44.

5   See the graph provided in Rein Taagepera, 'An Overview of the Growth of the Russian Empire', in Michael Rywkin (ed.), *Russian Colonial Expansion to 1917* (London and New York, 1988), p. 5. The average annual growth rate for the seventeenth century that I provide here is based on my own crude calculations of the total territory of Siberia (5.1 million square miles) divided by 100 years. In fact, not all of what is considered Siberia was brought into the empire in the seventeenth century, as some of it was 'conquered' in the 1500s and some in the 1700s and 1800s, so this is only a very rough approximation. The overall expansion rate of the empire is based on an extrapolation from Taagepera's graph. The area of 51,000 square miles is roughly equivalent to the territory of modern Greece.

Not surprisingly, this long history of expansion has often been interpreted by Russia's neighbours and potential rivals as proof that the Russians are congenital expansionists who will stop at nothing to reach a warm-water port, or who simply lust to make their state bigger for bigness' sake. Some Russian thinkers of the nineteenth century encouraged these presumptions with their overheated visions of a universal empire of Russian Orthodoxy; excited Bolshevik calls for world revolution in the 1920s had a similar effect. In Russia today outspoken nationalists like the politician Vladimir Zhirinovsky still dream about Russian soldiers marching through the Middle East and 'washing their boots in the ... waters of the Indian Ocean'.[6]

In reality, however, Russian empire-building was far more complicated than this simple version suggests. Expansion into new lands was often a product of opportunity as much as ideology, and might be offensive or defensive in nature, or even both at the same time. Muscovy acquired immense amounts of territory in Siberia in the seventeenth century, for example, for the most part simply because there were no powerful rivals to stop it from doing so. At other times, by contrast, the Russians ended up absorbing territory because they feared that rivals might otherwise take it first. Such thinking helped to motivate the conquest of Central Asia in the mid to late nineteenth century, for example, which was partly about expanding Russian power in its own right but partly, too, about checking the British in Afghanistan and India. Lord Palmerston noted the curious passive-aggressive quality of Russian expansion at the time:

> The Russian government perpetually declares that Russia wants no increases of territory ... [b]ut while making these declarations in the most solemn manner, [it nonetheless] every year adds large tracts of territory ... not for the purpose of adding territory [as a goal in itself] but rather to occupy certain strategic points [so that] neighbouring states may be kept under control or threatened with invasion.[7]

In other words, Russian expansion as seen from the state's perspective was hardly absent-minded but neither was it single-mindedly aggressive. Instead both ambition and restraint flowed together, a contradictory mix that was influenced, at least in part, by the country's physical surroundings. Moscow began as a small princely seat in the twelfth century in the midst of an immense wooded plain crisscrossed with rivers. As its wealth and power grew, it faced few natural barriers to block its expansion, but, by the same token, it also had none to protect itself from its enemies. This combination of geographic openness and vulnerability had the effect

---

6   On Zhirinovsky's national-imperialist ideology and geopolitical visions, see Andreas Umland, 'Zhirinovsky's *Last Thrust to the South* and the Definition of Fascism', *Russian Politics and Law* 46/4 (2008): pp. 31–46.

7   Lord Palmerston in 1860 as quoted in John LeDonne, *The Russian Empire and the World, 1700–1917: The Geopolitics of Expansion and Containment* (New York, 1997), p. 368. I have slightly altered the text from the quotation as it appears in LeDonne's work.

of drawing the emerging Muscovite state outward towards ever more defensible frontiers. Even the Ural Mountains, the notional dividing line between Europe and Asia, are quite humble as mountains go (the range's highest peak is only about 6,000 feet). To the Russians approaching from the west, they never presented much of an obstacle to eastward expansion.

Instead, for centuries the more meaningful limits to territorial growth tended to be either political or ecological, or some combination of the two. Muscovite expansion to the west was much more difficult than to the east, for example, because on its western borders Muscovy faced the relatively well-organised military-fiscal states of early modern Europe, while in Asia its only formidable opponent was the new Qing Empire of China, which it ran up against – and was defeated by – in the environs of the Amur River in the late 1600s. By the same token, the Russians were unable for centuries to expand to the south because the immense grasslands north of the Black and Caspian seas were controlled by nomadic pastoralists whose fleet horsemen gave them a decisive military advantage over lumbering Muscovite armies. It was only in the second half of the eighteenth century that the Russians were able to break the power of the nomads and take over the region.[8]

As they pushed outwards, the Russians employed a wide range of methods. Of them, conquest was perhaps the most continuous inasmuch as we see it, albeit in varied forms, in almost every period of the empire's history. The conquest of Kazan was a textbook case. Laying siege to the town for six weeks with a massive army, the Muscovites ultimately overwhelmed the Kazanians and entered the town, plundering what they could. They then proceeded to transform it in their own image, as conquerors are wont to do, rebuilding the walled enclave of the kremlin in stone for themselves and forcing the town's defeated Muslims to relocate to a separate quarter while at the same time tearing down mosques and re-consecrating them as churches. To celebrate his victory, Tsar Ivan IV (the 'Terrible'), ordered a great cathedral to be built on Red Square in Moscow – the church we now know as St Basil's.[9] St Petersburg, which succeeded Moscow as the imperial capital in 1712, was itself a conquest city, built on land taken from the Swedes during the Great Northern War. The Caucasus was conquered by Russian armies, Central Asia as well.

---

8   On Russian expansion in the European steppe, see Michael Khodarkovsky, *Russia's Steppe Frontier: The Making of a Colonial Empire* (Bloomington and Indianapolis, IN, 2002); and my *Taming the Wild Field: Colonization and Empire on the Russian Steppe* (Ithaca, NY, 2004).

9   On the centrality of conquest and imperial expansion in the way that Russian monarchs represented their power, see Richard S. Wortman, *Scenarios of Power: Myth and Ceremony in Russian Monarchy* (Princeton, NJ, 1995), vol. 1; and also his 'Ceremony and Power in the Evolution of Russian Monarchy', in Catherine Evtukhov et al. (eds), *Kazan, Moscow, St Petersburg: Multiple Faces of the Russian Empire/Kazan', Moskva, Peterburg: Rossiiskaia imperiia vzgliadom raznykh uglov* (Moscow, 1997), pp. 23–5. On the building of St Basil's as a monument of conquest, see Isabel de Madariaga, *Ivan the Terrible: First Tsar of Russia* (New Haven, CT, 2005), p. 105. The word 'kremlin' in Russian means simply fort, or fortified town. The most famous kremlin is *the* Kremlin in Moscow, but many other towns had kremlins as well, including Kazan.

The Russians also acquired territory relatively peacefully. Some rulers, for example, petitioned the tsars to take them under their wing. This was the case with the kings of the Georgian kingdom of Kartli-Kakheti, who sought Russia's protection against the Ottomans in the late 1700s. The eastern part of what is today Ukraine entered the Russian domain under similar circumstances in the mid-1600s when the Cossack ruler Bohdan Khmelnytsky approached Moscow for a military alliance. In both cases, the leaders who initially sought Russian help undoubtedly expected something quite different than for their domains to disappear within the Russian state, but the tsars ultimately supported centralisation and both territories in time found themselves absorbed into the empire.

At other times, 'peaceful' expansion was assured through diplomacy. The partitions of Poland that ended up delivering roughly two-thirds of the territory of the former Polish-Lithuanian Commonwealth to Russia over a 30-year period in the late 1700s were the result of diplomatic agreements brokered with Prussia and Austria. The Russians also obtained some 360,000 square miles of territory in the Far East in the 1850s and 1860s through treaties with the Chinese.[10] The threat of military conquest, tacit or explicit, accompanied each of these expansions, though nominally at least, the gains were agreed to by other powers rather than forcibly imposed by the Russians themselves.

Many of the practices of conquest unfolded across vast spaces and long periods of time, which makes sense since the Russians, like all successful imperialists, were less interested in originality than in results. If a particular method worked, they simply used it again, sometimes repeatedly. The conquest of Siberia, for example, rather than the single dramatic battle often represented in national myth, unfolded instead as numerous smaller prosaic acts of domination repeated many times over. In the typical scenario, a band of Muscovite military men dispatched from a regional fort – Cossacks usually – would arrive at a settlement of native Siberians, pledging them protection as well as 'gifts' such as glass, cloth and metal bowls in return for furs, Siberia's soft 'gold' (vodka was also often included). They would then make the natives declare their loyalty to the great 'sovereign', usually in terms that the latter had no way of understanding but taking some of their people as hostages just in case in order to ensure their cooperation. This approach worked so well that the Russians continued to use it as they moved on from Siberia to the coasts of Alaska in the eighteenth century.[11]

---

10 L.R. Lewitter, 'The Partitions of Poland', in A. Goodwin (ed.), *The New Cambridge Modern History*: vol. 8, *The American and French Revolutions 1763–93* (Cambridge, 1965), pp. 333–59. For the surface area acquired from the Chinese in the Far East, see Robert H.G. Lee, *The Manchurian Frontier in Ch'ing History* (Cambridge, MA, 1970), p. 5.

11 James Forsyth, *A History of the Peoples of Siberia: Russia's North Asian Colony 1581–1990* (New York, 1992), pp. 28–47; Yuri Slezkine, *Arctic Mirrors: Russia and the Small Peoples of the North* (Ithaca, NY, 1994), pp. 11–45. On the continuities of Russian practices as they moved from Siberia to North America in the eighteenth century, see Gwenn A. Miller, *Kodiak Kreol: Communities of Empire in Early Russian America* (Ithaca, NY, 2010), pp. 11–27. In time, however, the Russian mode of rule and exploitation in their American possessions proved to be quite different from the situation in Siberia due in

Finally, perhaps the most important long-running form of empire-building, which the Russians rarely viewed as such, was peasant colonisation. And this, too, at least in part, was a function of geography. Just as the openness of the Russian plain invited state expansion, it also made it relatively easy for ordinary people to move. Russian peasants practised rudimentary agriculture. Surrounded by abundant land, when their fields began to give out, they often calculated – quite rightly, at least in the short run – that the easiest thing to do was to resettle to new lands somewhere else. By the late 1400s, migration of this sort had become so much the norm, in fact, that noble landlords found themselves constantly deprived of the labour they needed to work their lands. They predictably complained, and over time new laws gradually appeared to limit peasant mobility. By 1650, these restrictions evolved to the point of creating the most influential social institution of modern Russian history – serfdom, a full-fledged immobility 'regime' in which peasants became the property of their lords and any movement without their permission was illegal.[12]

Yet, even with the weight of this new 'unfreedom' pressing down on them, a good number of ordinary Russian folk moved anyway. Many simply fled their landlords to seek freedom on the frontier. We know this from the runaways' own stories but also from officials in the borderlands who would send reports back to the centre documenting the large numbers of roaming 'people' in their districts as well as the absent-minded souls who somehow always managed to forget their names and where they were from when they were picked up by state patrols. Other movement, by contrast, was actually encouraged by the government, which, though it needed to keep people in place, also required some of its subjects to relocate to the frontier in order to support its military defences.[13]

By the late eighteenth century, in part to pursue this longstanding goal and in part to address the new issue of rural 'overcrowding' in the centre of the country, the government began organising large-scale resettlements to the borderlands, mostly of peasants who resided on state lands and were therefore easier to move

part to geography but also to the nature of the hunting of the sea otter and the different dynamics of the fur trade in the region. For an argument that stresses the shift to a new method of rule in Alaska, see Ilya Vinkovetsky, *Russian America: An Overseas Colony of a Continental Empire, 1804-1867* (New York, 2011), esp. pp. 31-35.

12   The best recent treatment of the evolution of serfdom is David Moon's *The Russian Peasantry, 1600–1930: The World the Peasants Made* (London, 1999). The classic treatment in English is Jerome Blum, *Lord and Peasant in Russia: From the Ninth to the Nineteenth Century* (Princeton, NJ, 1961).

13   The late historian Richard Hellie argued that it was precisely the labour demands faced by 'middle servitors' on the frontier that gave rise to the establishment of serfdom. See his *Enserfment and Military Change in Muscovy* (Chicago, IL, 1971). On the southern defences as both a destination for runaways as well as a cordon to contain them, see Brian J. Boeck, 'Containment vs. Colonization: Muscovite Approaches to Settling the Steppe', in Nicholas B. Breyfogle, Abby Schrader and Willard Sunderland (eds), *Peopling the Russian Periphery: Borderland Colonization in Eurasian History* (New York, 2007), pp. 21–40.

than privately owned serfs. After the abolition of serfdom in the late nineteenth century, the migration flow increased. In all, some 15 million peasants resettled within the empire between 1700 and the First World War, with about 5 million moving in the two decades before 1917.[14]

The effects of this long history of colonisation were profound. In 1678, over two-thirds of Russian peasants lived in the traditional forest heartland of Muscovy; by the turn of the twentieth century, however, this figure had slipped to around 40 per cent, a reflection of the fact that large numbers of rural people had moved outward over the centuries, like the state itself.[15]

Some of these migrants literally pulled the train of expansion behind them, forcing the state to expand in order to catch up.[16] In other cases, the state conquered and the peasants followed. Yet, regardless of who moved first, once the colonists established themselves in significant numbers in the borderlands, their presence invariably changed the social and political balance. Settlers required state oversight and assistance. They had to be counted, their taxes collected. They also tended to encroach on or force out native communities, especially steppe nomads once the great shift to steppe settlement began in the late eighteenth century.

Borderland colonisation thus created the need for infrastructure and governance, which in turn reinforced state power. At the same time, the settlers' presence in the periphery, much like the basic fact of expansion itself, often stretched the state beyond what it could reasonably manage, overextending its limited resources and making it more fragile even as it was making it larger.

Patterns of Domination and Coexistence

The result of Russia's enormous expansion was thus a contradiction: a state that was vast in territory yet thin in terms of government pressed up against borders that were often ill-defined and hard to control, especially in the eastern and southern parts of the empire. Perhaps most importantly, the expansion transformed the country into a stunningly diverse domain. According to the imperial census of 1897, some 130 languages were spoken in the Russian state, while ethnic Russians known as Great 'Russians' in the parlance of the times, constituted less than half the population (45 per cent). Even adding up the large Eastern Slavic constituencies of the empire – the Great Russians, Ukrainians (Little 'Russians') and Belorussians (White Russians) – Orthodox Christians only amounted to about 70 per cent of

---

14   S.I. Bruk and V.M. Kabuzan, 'Migratsiia naseleniia v Rossii v xviii-nachale xx veka (chislennost', struktura, geografiia)', *Istoriia SSSR* 4 (1984): p. 59.

15   For these figures, see David Moon, 'Peasant Migration and the Settlement of Russia's Frontiers, 1550–1897', *Historical Journal* 40/4 (1997): p. 867, n. 4.

16   On this, see the remarks in Alfred J. Rieber, 'Persistent Factors in Russian Foreign Policy: An Interpretive Essay', in Hugh Ragsdale (ed.), *Imperial Russian Foreign Policy* (New York, 1993), p. 333.

the total. The remainder were Catholics, Protestants, Muslims, Buddhists, Jews, shamanists.[17] As Tsar Nicholas I noted to a foreign visitor in the 1830s, 'No country possesses a greater diversity of races, customs, religions, and ideas than Russia. Variety is the base, uniformity the surface, and unity only apparent.'[18]

Managing this diversity was a recurring challenge for Russia's rulers – we get a sense of this from the tsar's somewhat wistful remark about the lack of real unity in the country. Yet the empire nonetheless held together for centuries. How? What explains this impressive endurance? To answer this question, we need to look both at the realm of high state policy and at the patterns of cohabitation that defined the empire as a social world. And, to do this, it is helpful to divide Russia's history into two periods, the first from the 1550s to the mid-nineteenth century, when the empire and the sociopolitical system that defined it were largely stable and successful; and the second from the 1850s to the First World War, when the empire entered the age of nationalism and industrialisation and difficulties began to mount.

The first period, broadly speaking, was a good phase for the empire. During this long era, the state passed through major domestic and foreign crises, including the occupation of Moscow by foreign invaders on two occasions – by the Poles during the so-called Time of Troubles (*smuta*) of the early seventeenth century and by Napoleon's Grand Army in 1812. Yet overall the country grew in international standing to the point of emerging as one of the great powers of Europe and Asia by the mid-nineteenth century. Even as numerous other non-European states lost autonomy and influence or were simply destroyed by growing western might, Russia remained independent, in part by co-opting European practices, which it began to do with gathering intensity from the late seventeenth century.[19]

As a multinational order, the empire was also relatively successful. This is not because it was any more benevolent to its subjects than other empires. Russian policy could be fiercely intolerant, in particular in regards to non-Orthodox believers who were occasionally subject to forced conversions or saddled with restrictions. Steppe nomads, who were denounced as savage 'beasts' and regarded as deficient in terms of their way of life by the late eighteenth century, found themselves targeted for change through sedentarisation, while Jews, who entered the empire in large numbers as a result of the partitions of Poland, were prohibited by law from moving outside a special zone set up for them in the western part of the country – the so-called Pale of Settlement (*cherta osedlosti*). In addition to this soft form of imprisonment, they also faced discrimination in a range of other ways.

Yet along with such glaring examples of prejudice and intolerance, the empire was also characterised by toleration and accommodation. Prior to the late

---

17   On the imperial census, see David W. Darrow, 'Census as a Technology of Empire', *Ab Imperio* 4 (2002), pp. 145–76; and Juliette Cadiot, 'Le recensement de 1897: les limites du côntrole impérial et la représentation des nationalités', *Cahiers du monde russe* 45/3–4 (2004): pp. 441–64.

18   Marquis de Custine, *Letters from Russia* (New York, 1991), p. 82.

19   Marshall T. Poe argues that this is the singular accomplishment of early modern Russia. See his interesting essay, *The Russian Moment in World History* (Princeton, NJ, 2003).

nineteenth century, and even to a degree thereafter, the state's default position was something that might be called *laissez-faire* particularism. Each people had its own faith and customs and had entered the empire under its own circumstances. As a result, each had its own arrangement with the Russian state. Inevitably, this meant that some peoples fared better than others in the empire's hierarchy. But it also meant that almost every group ended up with a large degree of autonomy over its own affairs, including the most discriminated-against groups like the Jews, most of whom did not have to worry much about the state because they lived in largely self-governing communities. The traditional Russian Empire was premised on a simple rule: all of the peoples of the state owed their well-being to the tsar, and, in return for his benevolent concern, they each owed him something – taxes, recruits, service, obedience. Assuming these debts were taken care of they could count on being left largely alone.

The stability of the system was ensured by the Russians' greatest achievement of all in the area of empire maintenance – their success in creating and reproducing a multi-ethnic imperial elite. As a rule, when the state took over a new territory, rather than destroying or disbanding the people in charge, they were instead inducted into the imperial order. They kept their titles, or received comparable Russian ones. They retained their privileges and their lands. All they had to do in return, in most cases, was declare their loyalty to the tsar, which many of them were quite happy to do. After all, why not pledge allegiance to a crown that was wise enough to let you keep everything you had before they took over? The arrangement had obvious benefits for all parties concerned.

Over time, this *modus operandi* created a dazzling range of noble families: Tatar princes, Polish magnates, Ukrainian counts, Baltic German barons, Georgian *tavadis*. Many of these nobles gravitated towards Russia and willingly served the crown. Of these, a large number eventually converted to Orthodoxy. Their names became Russified. The richest noble family in the empire by the end of the monarchy, for example, was the Yusupovs, who were descended from a royal line of Nogay Tatars (Khan Yusuf) and whose later descendants, after a period of resistance, ultimately made their peace with the Russians and converted to Orthodoxy following the Kazan conquest.[20] With nobles like the Yusupovs as their servitors, the tsars were able to farm out the business of ruling the empire, leaving it largely in the hands of regional elites who, in turn, largely left things alone because they benefitted from the status quo. This arrangement favoured stability, and stability, overall, was good for the state.

Perhaps not surprisingly, one result of this system of multinational rule was the creation of a Russian empire that was not exactly Russian, or at least not entirely so. In fact, in part as a reflection of this curious situation, Russians in the

---

20 On the multi-ethnic complexity of the imperial nobility, see Dominic Lieven, *Russia's Rulers under the Old Regime* (New Haven, CT, 1989). At the end of the nineteenth century, Russian nobles accounted for only about 40 per cent of the country's hereditary nobles. The rest were non-noble families. See Andreas Kappeler, *The Russian Empire: A Multiethnic History* (Harlow, 2001), p. 299.

eighteenth century began to distinguish between two different terms for 'Russian': *russkii*, which described people and things related to Russian ethnicity or culture; and *rossiiskii*, which referred to the Russian state. The official title for the country after the period of Peter the Great, for example, was not *russkaia imperiia*, which would have suggested that the empire belonged to the Russian nation, but rather *rossiiskaia imperiia*, which made clear that the empire was made up of numerous peoples and was the state's, rather than the nation's, business.

In fact, it is hard to argue that the empire was especially favourable to ordinary Russians at all. Instead, much of the weight of the empire fell on their shoulders. Most of the army, for example, was made up of Russian peasant conscripts, while many non-Russians remained exempt from army service until the draft reforms of the 1870s. By the same token, and as noted earlier, Russian peasants could be owned as serfs, while many non-Russian peasants could not. Russians overall had lower rates of literacy and higher rates of infant mortality than numerous other ethnicities within the empire. Even data on average height, highly related to nutrition and diet, suggest that ordinary Russians were not eating much better than their non-Russian neighbours.[21]

For the majority of its history, imperial rule was thus not a matter of promoting the Russians as an imperial 'people' but rather of finding useful noble servitors for the tsar *regardless* of their ethnicity. Indeed, a non-Russian could even be tsar, as long as he or she was Orthodox. Catherine the Great, for example, began her life as a German princess named Sophie Auguste Friederike and only converted to Orthodoxy when she married the future Peter III and moved to St Petersburg. (This is also when she changed her name.) After overthrowing her husband in 1762, she ruled as an empress for over 30 years. Her German origins never amounted to a serious problem.[22]

By the early to mid-nineteenth century, however, this situation began to change. Influenced both by the rising appeal of national sentiment in Europe as well as by great events at home such as the victory over Napoleon in 1812, educated Russians began to adopt an increasingly national worldview. This did not mean that everything changed overnight. In fact, even as Russians grew increasingly impressed with their own national ways, the imperial system remained stubbornly multinational. Tsar Alexander I, for one, declared that he considered the Baltic German nobles his best 'servants'.[23] Officials in the borderlands also continued to identify with the idea of imperial paternalism rather than with a more explicitly pro-Russian form of rule. As the governor of the mixed Muslim–Christian region

---

21   Boris Mironov, *Blagosostoianie naseleniia i revoliutsii v imperskoi Rossii* (Moscow, 2010), pp. 391, 400, 405. Mironov's conclusions about relative average height are based on statistics for male army recruits in the 1906–1921 period.

22   On the role of foreignness in Catherine's life, see Hilde Hoogenboom, 'Catherine the Great', in Stephen M. Norris and Willard Sunderland (eds), *Russia's People of Empire: Life Stories from Eurasia, 1500–Present* (Bloomington, IN, 2012).

23   Cited in Baron Wilhelm von Wrangell, *Baron Wilhelm von Rossillon: Ein Lebensbild* (Dorpat, 1934), pp. 21–2.

of the Crimea wrote to his underlings in 1833, 'Our sovereign makes no distinction in his heart between the race and origins [*poroda i proiskhozhdeniia*] of his subjects. For him we are all as one – Russians and Tatars, his children, all of us living by the same laws … forming a single whole.'[24]

And yet a new national line was emerging, however inconsistently. By the 1820s, a term for designating seemingly backward non-Russian groups – *inorodtsy*, literally people of another 'birth', or 'aliens' – had entered official usage as a state-created social category, suggesting that elite Russians had begun to view their own people – the Russian *narod* – as a people apart. The government also enshrined nationality (*narodnost'*) as one of three principles behind a new formula for imperial rule that it unveiled in the 1830s: Autocracy, Orthodoxy, 'Nationality'. Of the three parts of the new triad, 'nationality' was the least familiar, and, as a result, its meanings tended to be the most variable, even in the state's own pronouncements.[25] But the very fact that the word was invoked at all was proof that things were shifting. For centuries, imperial rule had been premised on allegiance to the dynasty; now, it seemed, allegiance to the nation was to be important as well.

In practical political terms, however, the decisive move in this direction did not occur until a generation later, spurred on by two dramatic developments: the empire's defeat at the hands of the British, French and Ottomans in the Crimean War in 1856, and a massive secessionist revolt, followed by a brutal military crackdown, in Poland in 1863. The Crimean defeat – and especially the humiliating peace treaty that followed – pushed the government to enact sweeping reforms to modernise the country and restore its standing as a great power. Meanwhile the Polish Revolt precipitated the 'birth of Russification' – a bundle of new policies meant to shore up the integrity of the state by standardising administration and promoting, wherever practical, the presence of Russians and Russian culture.[26]

The adoption of this new course was proof that the empire had reached a portentous turning point. The full flowering of Russian nationalism was key to the change, as was a genuine fear of non-Russian separatism. (The Poles in this respect always figured as Exhibit Number One.) But changes in the ambitions and powers of government were equally important. The old Muscovite state had been too limited to intervene much in the social life of its peoples, nor did it especially aspire to do so. Achieving a reliable flow of tribute and taxes and defendable borders was good enough. The westernising reforms introduced by Peter the Great in the early

---

24 'O komandirovanii kady eskera Osmana Efendiia po gubernii dlia otobraniia ot Tatar vrednykh dlia nikh i obshchego spokoistva rukopisei', in *Derzhavnyi arkhiv v Avtonomnii Respublitsi Krym*, f. 26, op. 4, d. 456, l.2(b).

25 On this, see the interesting comments by Aleksei Miller, 'Priobretenie neobkhodimoe, no ne vpolne udobnoe: transfer poniatiia *natsiia* v Rossiiu (nachalo xviii–seredina xix v.)', in Martin Aust, Ricarda Vulpius and Aleksei Miller (eds), *Imperium inter pares: rol' transferov v istorii rossiiskoi imperii (1700–1917): sbornik statei* (Moscow, 2010), pp. 42–66, especially pp. 55–8.

26 The quoted phrase is drawn from Theodore Weeks, 'Nationalities Policy', in Dominic Lieven (ed.), *The Cambridge History of Russia*: vol. 2, *Imperial Russia, 1689–1917* (New York, 2006), p. 37.

eighteenth century introduced a much more assertive governing style, but even the early imperial state, for all of its pretensions, was a limited affair.

By comparison, the imperial order established by the last three tsars – Alexander II, Alexander III and Nicholas II – was much more interventionist. Indeed, even though all three tsars were conservative, the last two especially so, they were also modernisers who oversaw the country's transformation into a more dynamic and integrated imperial state. Russification, in effect, was the government's trusted road map to this destination, and it became all the more so after Alexander II was assassinated by radicals in 1881, and the state assumed what would become a lasting siege mentality.

Some aspects of the policy – the most notorious ones – were highly abusive. Non-Russian schools were closed and non-Russian communities saw much of their autonomy curtailed. Ukrainian intellectuals were told that their nation did not exist and publications in Ukrainian were banned. Chinese migrants in the Russian Far East came up against restrictive residential and hygiene laws, while others were deported. In Russian Poland and the Baltic provinces, new laws even clamped down on the privileges of the local nobilities, which was arguably the greatest departure of all from previous practices. 'It is tragic', wrote one German count from Estland (future Estonia) in 1890, 'but all that remains is exodus or death.'[27]

Yet other aspects of the Russification platform were more practical than punitive, the reflection of a desire to straighten out what were seen by the state as obsolete particularisms that had grown up over the years. Indeed, the goal of Russification for many of its supporters was less to turn the empire's subjects into Russians (though there were certainly Russian nationalists who dreamed of this outcome) than to reform diversity by making it more workable from the state's point of view. Some of this change was forced through by intolerant state initiatives. Much, however, was simply left to unfold more naturally, or at least less heavy-handedly, through the integration of imperial institutions (like the army) and the building of telegraph lines and railways, such as the Trans-Siberian Railroad, which not only carried goods, soldiers and colonists to new destinations, but also accelerated the standardisation of the state.[28]

At the same time, everything about Russification was complicated. Rather than just one variety, there were many – cultural Russification, administrative Russification, as well as different dimensions to the programme as it unfolded in the empire's various regions.[29] Thus we find curious contradictions, like the fact that, even though the government ardently curtailed the privileges of Germans and

---

27   Helene von Taube (ed.), *Graf Alexander Keyserling: Ein Lebensbild aus seinen Briefen und Tagebüchern* (Berlin, 1902), vol. 2, p. 599.

28   Weeks, 'Nationalities Policy', pp. 37–42. On the Trans-Siberian, see Steven G. Marks, *Road to Power: The Trans-Siberian Railroad and the Colonization of Asian Russia, 1850–1917* (Ithaca, NY, 1991).

29   On the variety of Russifications in the empire and an overview of scholarship on the question, see Aleksei Miller, *Imperiia Romanovykh i natsionalizm: esse po metodologii istoricheskogo issledovaniia* (Moscow, 2006), pp. 54–77.

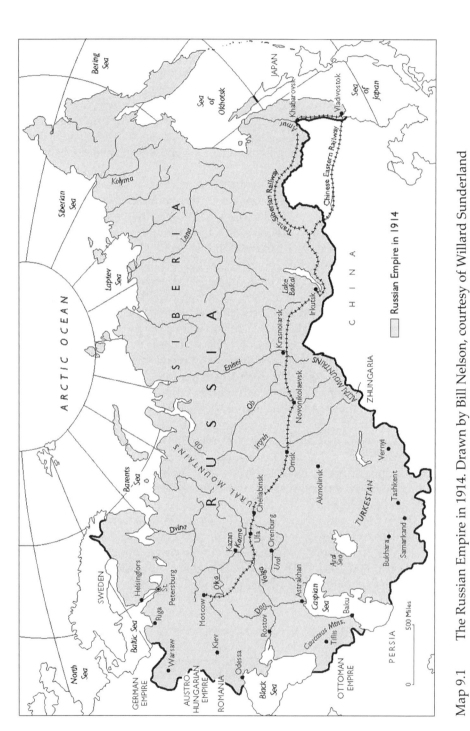

Map 9.1   The Russian Empire in 1914. Drawn by Bill Nelson, courtesy of Willard Sunderland

Poles, the two groups continued to make up close to 20 per cent of the imperial officer corps, while close to 40 per cent of all Russian diplomats serving abroad in the late nineteenth century were of German descent.[30] Even Jews, far and away the most discriminated group in the country, had opportunities to benefit from what one historian has called 'selective integration' within imperial society.[31] Russification in the administrative and economic realms was more straightforward and relatively easier to achieve, but in this arena, too, there were inconsistencies. The Finns, for example, had lost much of their autonomy by the end of the nineteenth century, but they retained their national currency – the Finnish *markka* – up to the fall of the empire, while Turkestan and the Caucasus, despite being slated to 'merge' with the Russian centre, remained de facto colonies, with their would-be colonial distinctiveness from Russia underscored and accentuated in government policy.[32]

In a sense, these contradictions are hardly surprising. Diversity was so central to the workings of the empire that it was simply impossible to standardise it with a single one-size-fits-all approach. Tsarist ministers, for all their shortsightedness, tended to recognise this fact and adapted their initiatives accordingly. At the same time, some of the contradictions of state policy also reflect the fact that the age of Russification coincided with a period of great 'acceleration' in which social and economic change was speeding up throughout the globe.[33] How could Russification hope to be consistent in a time of such flux and change? In retrospect, the government's great mistake was less that it attempted to modernise through Russification than the fact that it set about doing so without fully appreciating the volatility of modernisation itself (see Map 9.1).

30   P.A. Zaionchkovskii, *Samoderzhavie i russkaia armiia na rubezhe xix–xx stoletii, 1881–1903* (Moscow, 1973), p. 199; Mark von Hagen, 'Confronting Backwardness: Dilemmas of Soviet Officer Education in the Interwar Years, 1918–1941', in Elliott V. Converse III (ed.), *Forging the Sword: Selecting, Educating, and Training Cadets and Junior Officers in the Modern World* (Chicago, IL, 1998), pp. 86, 96, n. 15; Walter M. Pintner, 'The Nobility and the Officer Corps in the Nineteenth Century', in Eric Lohr and Marshall Poe (eds), *The Military and Society in Russia 1450–1917* (Leiden, 2002), pp. 250–51; and N.I. Ivanova, 'Nemtsy v ministerstvakh Rossii xix–nachala xx vekov', in *Nemtsy v Rossii* (St Petersburg, 2004), pp. 50–51.

31   Benjamin Nathans, *Beyond the Pale: The Jewish Encounter with Late Imperial Russia* (Berkeley, CA, 2002). For another work that emphasises the possibilities enjoyed by certain Jews in the empire in the late imperial era, see Jeffrey Veidlinger, *Jewish Public Culture in the Late Russian Empire* (Bloomington, IN, 2009).

32   On Finnish currency issues under the empire, see Ekaterina Pravilova, *Finansy imperii: dengi i vlast' v politike Rossii na natsional'nykh okrainakh, 1801–1917* (Moscow, 2006), pp. 353–66. For a discussion of the complicated question of tsarist colonies, see my 'The Ministry of Asiatic Russia: The Colonial Office That Never Was But Might Have Been', *Slavic Review* 69/1 (2010): pp. 120–50.

33   I borrow this term from C.A. Bayly. See his *The Birth of the Modern World, 1780–1914: Global Connections and Comparisons* (Oxford, 2004), pp. 451–87.

The End Game: Crisis, Possibility and Collapse

This volatility, however, was intense, and it showed itself in two massive revolutions that rocked the empire in the early twentieth century – those of 1905 and 1917. Indeed, it is helpful to think of these revolutions as the ultimate expression of the many complicated contradictions of Russian modernisation packed into a powder keg and then set off by a variety of fuses. The tsarist government survived the first of these great explosions by making enormous concessions but was undone by the second. By 1918, the imperial order itself had effectively ceased to exist.

Yet it is important to remember that this dynamic was not inevitable. Modernisation did not have to undo the empire. In fact, neither of the great revolutionary convulsions of the time was unambiguously anti-imperial.[34] That is, the revolutions of 1905 and 1917 were not in themselves revolts against the Russians or even against the idea of a shared multinational home, though feelings like this certainly existed and played a part in the general crisis of the period. Instead, just as the empire's complexity was ingrained in Russian life, it also became ingrained in the revolutions, making them hard to interpret in unambiguous terms.

For example, 1905 was an imperial revolution in that it raged as much, if not more, in the borderlands of the state than in the centre, but much of the unrest on the periphery was shaped by local and regional factors, which makes the revolution difficult to read overall as a rebuke of the imperial order. Some non-Russians took advantage of the general tumult to clamour against the restrictions of Russification and demand greater autonomy. Others vented their frustration against the national communities around them. In the process, class and national antagonisms intersected and overlapped in complicated ways. Thus Estonian peasants and workers ransacked the manors of Baltic German landlords led, in some cases, by Russian radicals; an Armenian–Tatar 'War' broke out in places like Baku in the South Caucasus while anti-Jewish pogroms erupted across what is today Moldova and southern Ukraine. We see some of the complexity of the moment in Irkutsk in Eastern Siberia where Buryat students rallied to slogans like 'Everyone for our people!' and 'Everyone for the Buryats!' but the placards they carried were in Russian rather than their own language.[35]

The government responded to the surge of unrest in 1905 in mixed ways, which in turn produced a mixed situation for the peoples of the empire in the last years of the regime. On the one hand, the revolution resulted in clear gains for national and non-Orthodox communities: some of the most reviled Russification laws were rescinded; A new law on religious toleration was adopted; and the new parliament, or Duma, created by the October Manifesto, quickly emerged as a forum for debating nationality issues and a venue for new 'types' of non-Russians

---

34 Jane Burbank also stresses this point. See her 'The Rights of Difference: Law and Citizenship in the Russian Empire,' in Ann Laura Stoler, Carole McGranahan, and Peter C. Perdue (eds.), *Imperial Formations* (Santa Fe, NM, 2007), p. 77.

35 On the 'Buryat revival' in 1905, see the comments in M. Bogdanov, 'Buriatskoe "vozrozhdenie"', *Sibirskie voprosy*: 3 (1907): pp. 38–9.

to participate in imperial politics.[36] Yet the government also used massive violence to repress anti-state activity in the borderlands, including executing thousands of people in hastily convoked field 'trials' in the Baltic and other areas in 1905–1907; then, as the new quasi-constitutional order took shape in the aftermath of the revolution, it consistently blocked real reform on national issues coming out of the Duma.[37]

Taking all this into account, is it right to see the Russian Empire as a going 'concern' on the eve of the Great War?[38] Probably not. Considering the country's many social and political tensions, this seems like an overly rosy description. But the state was at least muddling through in regards to its nationality 'question'. The most important effect of 1905 was the politicisation of nationality on a mass scale. The basic challenge facing the tsarist leadership after 1905 was thus to control this new political factor in order to avoid another great revolution, and, in the few years it had between 1905 and 1914, at least, it was able to do this. It curtailed the electoral law to help fashion a conservative consensus on nationality politics in the Duma, and it continued to make the trade-offs it had long negotiated with the non-Russian nobility, while building new alliances among new non-Russian business elites in the borderlands. Perhaps most importantly, it managed to keep the disruptive influences of Russian nationalism in check, though less by design than because of its own divisions on the question. On the one hand, extremely conservative figures, like Tsar Nicholas himself, embraced the xenophobia and anti-Semitism of the new Russian politics and supported the work of Russian chauvinist organisations. Yet other government leaders, like Premier Petr Stolypin, though highly conservative and pro-Russian in their own right, rightly saw the danger this sort of majority chauvinism posed to the imperial system and acted to mitigate its effects.

Thus as the country approached the eve of the First World War a shaky arrangement was holding on the national 'question', and we can see similar *modi vivendi* holding together on other questions as well. Perhaps if the war had been short and limited, the various arrangements might have held together longer, but instead the conflict ground on for over three years and, as its costs compounded, the possibilities for political compromise eroded away. The scale of the event was a key determinant. In just the first five months of the war (August–December 1914), the empire lost a quarter of a million men. This was over three times the mortality rate it had suffered in the entire course of the war with Japan a decade earlier. For a time, the economy kept up with the voracious demands and dislocations of

---

36 On the significance of the new parliament for national politics in the empire, see the useful overview in Rustem Tsiunchuk, 'Peoples, Regions, and Electoral Politics: The State Dumas and the Constitution of New National Elites', in Jane Burbank, Mark von Hagen and Anatolyi Remnev (eds), *Russian Empire: Space, People, Power, 1700–1930* (Bloomington, IN, 2007), pp. 366–97.

37 Peter Holquist, 'Violent Russia, Deadly Marxism? Russia in the Epoch of Violence, 1905–1921', *Kritika: Explorations in Russian and Eurasian History* 4/3 (2003): pp. 632–3; and Kappeler, *Russian Empire*, 328–48.

38 I borrow this characterisation from Aviel Roshwald. See his *Ethnic Nationalism and the Fall of Empires: Central Europe, Russia, and the Middle East, 1914–1924* (New York, 2001), p. 33.

the war, but food and industrial supply ultimately began to falter, as did support for the conflict, among elites and in the army and broader Russian society. One peasant conscript remembered a left-leaning junior officer telling him in the fall of 1914 that the great slaughter around them was nothing but a miserable battle over capital, with ordinary folk serving as cannon fodder for the bourgeoisie:

> As someone with no understanding of politics or of the revolutionary movement, I found [the officer's] words hard to follow, but I nonetheless knew instinctively that they were true. Indeed, who has the right to send millions of peasants and workers to their deaths … to fight over the made-up claim that one nation should rule over another?[39]

This kind of thinking, multiplied many times over in the army and more broadly in Russian society, eventually undermined the legitimacy of the war and of the tsarist system itself.

The war also profoundly altered the state's relations with its national constituencies – markedly for the worse in most cases. Though the conflict began with statements of non-Russian loyalty, over time, just as Russians lost their enthusiasm for the war, non-Russians did as well, and, as they did, nationality became a touchstone for resistance. Some groups found themselves effectively removed from the empire altogether, such as the Poles whose Russian-ruled lands ended up under German occupation as early as 1915. But the war even changed relations with non-Russian groups well behind the front. The most obvious example of this was the great Steppe Revolt of 1916, which erupted when the government announced its plan to impose a special labour levy on Kazakh nomads to help with the war effort. The uprising took the lives of thousands of Russian settlers on the steppe and perhaps tens of thousands of Kazakhs. The state eventually regained control but only after repressing the nomads with brutal severity.[40]

The war, in effect, brought out all the difficult contradictions of the empire as a nationalising multinational state. On the one hand, the war intensified some of the darker sides of Russian nationalism. Along the front lines in places like the Baltic and western Ukraine, whole populations were designated as 'unreliable' and deported en masse, Russian Germans and Jews in particular. Foreigners and non-Russians became increasingly suspect. 'Spymania' became a national obsession.[41] Yet, at the same time, the tsarist army never ceased to be a multinational fighting force, with

---

39   D. Os'kin, *Zapiski soldata* (Moscow, 1929), p. 61.

40   On the 1916 revolt and the colonial context in Russian Central Asia, see Daniel Brower, *Turkestan and the Fate of the Russian Empire* (London, 2003), pp. 1–25, 152–75. For a creative examination of Russian-Kazakh relations and mutual perceptions during the revolt, see Jörn Happel, *Nomadische Lebenswelten und zarische Politik: der Aufstand in Zentralasien 1916* (Stuttgart, 2010).

41   On these issues, see Eric Lohr, *Nationalizing the Russian Empire: The Campaign Against Enemy Aliens During World War I* (Cambridge, MA, 2003); and William C. Fuller, *The Foe Within: Fantasies of Treason and the End of the Russian Empire* (Ithaca, NY, 2006).

ranks made up of soldiers and officers from a wide range of the empire's peoples. Thus even as Russian generals denounced Jews for what they saw as a lack of patriotism and made excuses for anti-Jewish pogroms committed by their troops, some half a million Jewish soldiers fought for Russia during the war. Similarly, the empire's Cossack forces, widely touted as 'true sons of the Russian nation' in popular texts and imagery, nonetheless included Buddhist Buryats and Muslim Bashkirs.[42]

Indeed, for all that the war intensified the power of nationalism in imperial life, it is hard to say that nationalism itself destroyed the empire. Instead, the real culprit in this respect was the revolutionary upheaval of 1917, which was driven, in part, by the unresolved national tensions of the imperial system but by many other factors besides. Three long years of war simply exhausted the country, laying bare all of its problems. The monarchy, for example, lost the last trimmings of its legitimacy not just with revolutionaries, who already despised it, but with wider groups as well. The fragile accommodations made between government and society prior to the war eroded and then cracked apart. The economy crumbled. The war, in effect, produced a massive crisis that eventually became a crisis of authority, with 1917 marking the crucial tipping point, the decisive moment when the old order slipped and crashed, and the country turned in new directions.

The year, in fact, produced two revolutions. The first, in February, deposed the tsar, replacing the autocracy with the rule of a so-called Provisional Government made up of liberal and moderate representatives from the old Duma. Then in the autumn, after months of tension and failed compromise and against the backdrop of continuing war, the Bolsheviks, the most radical socialist and anti-imperialist party in the Russian spectrum, staged a military coup and overthrew the Provisional Government in turn. In the process, the empire died not once but twice. The February Revolution ended the monarchy, the traditional fulcrum of the imperial system. The Bolshevik takeover, led by Vladimir Lenin and Leon Trotsky, followed up by destroying the system itself.

The Imperial Postmortem

Perhaps the most important point to make about the end of the Russian Empire, however, is that it unfolded quite differently from the other imperial deaths that came about as a result of the First World War. The Ottoman and Habsburg empires, like Russia, were also overwhelmed and ultimately undone by the war, but they unravelled completely and were replaced by a patchwork of independent states and mandates. The Russian Empire, by contrast, was largely resuscitated after the Bolshevik Revolution in the new form of the USSR, which then went on to survive for another 70 years until its collapse in 1991.

---

42   Zvi Y. Gitelman, *A Century of Ambivalence: The Jews of Russia and the Soviet Union, 1881 to the Present* (Bloomington, IN, 2001), p. 55; and Stephen M. Norris, *A War of Images: Russian Popular Prints, Wartime Culture, and National Identity* (DeKalb, IL, 2006), pp. 140–41.

Indeed, one of the great ironies of the October Revolution is that, even though its leaders were sworn enemies of international imperialism, they nonetheless shared much in common with their opponents because they, too, were imperial people. Having been shaped by the ways of tsarist state and society, they saw an obvious logic to combining peoples and territories in large conglomerations. Their goal was simply to destroy what they saw as the conjoined twins of capitalist and imperialist exploitation. A society made up of multiple peoples, by contrast, they saw as a good thing. In fact, they saw this kind of society as essential, the very way of the future. The diverse society of tomorrow just had to be a modern multinational *socialist* society led by the Communist Party rather than a backward, capitalist, autocratic one ruled over by the tsars.

The USSR and the Russian Empire were organised on radically different principles, of course, so it is simplifying too much to suggest that the one somehow lived on in the other. And yet the deeper structures and many of the habits of cohabitation that characterised Russia's imperial state and society did indeed carry over across the revolutionary divide, and, to a degree, we still see them in Russia today. The Soviet Union is gone and (almost certainly) never coming back), but three-quarters of its territory (and roughly half of its former population) are still gathered together in one state.[43] What better proof could there be of the complicated longevity of Russian empire-building?

---

[43] Rein Taagepera, 'Expansion and Contraction Patterns of Large Polities: Context for Russia', *International Studies Quarterly* 44 (1997): p. 491.

North American Empire

Mary A. Renda

Richard Olney and the Long History of North American Empire

In 1895, US Secretary of State Richard Olney asserted a bold claim for his nation. The United States was, he declared, 'practically sovereign' over all the Americas.[1] Olney spoke in response to an invitation from Venezuela to bring his nation's diplomatic weight to bear in a long-standing dispute over the rich Orinoco River Delta and the western boundary of British Guiana. Elaborating upon President James Monroe's 1823 doctrine that the Americas were henceforth to be considered closed to future European colonisation, in one breath Olney affirmed considerations of right, justice and national self-determination as integral to Monroe's message and to the continuing disposition of the United States towards Latin America. In another breath, he more famously confronted the British Foreign Minister, Lord Salisbury, and the empire he represented, with the stark reality of American power. The United States' 'fiat is law upon the subjects to which it confines its interposition', he insisted, 'not simply by reason of its high character as a civilised state, nor because wisdom and justice and equity are the invariable characteristics of the dealings of the United States', but also 'because its infinite resources and isolated position render it master of the situation and practically invulnerable as against any or all other powers'.[2] The naked terms of this assertion of US might vis-à-vis Europe, and of mastery over the western hemisphere, proclaimed the ascendance of the United States on the world stage.

Richard Olney's 1895 interpretation of the Monroe Doctrine speaks both to the long history of North American imperialism and to the particularity of US power in

---

1   Richard Olney to Thomas F. Bayard, 20 July 1895, in *Papers Relating to the Foreign Relations of the United States 1895*, vol. 1 (Washington, DC, 1896), p. 558. See also Mary A. Renda, 'Practical Sovereignty: The Caribbean Region and the Rise of US Empire', in Thomas H. Holloway (ed.), *A Companion to Latin American History* (Malden, MA, 2008). Thanks to Elena Cohen for research assistance on this chapter.

2   Olney, *Papers Relating to the Foreign Relations of the United States*, p. 588.

the late nineteenth century. His attention to matters of right, justice and democracy as essential to expansive claims for the nation followed a long tradition of imperial imaginings, traceable at least to Thomas Jefferson's vision of the United States as an 'empire for liberty'. At the same time, his insistence that his nation was at last 'practically invulnerable' was attributable, in his view, to its success at marshalling the 'infinite resources' of the North American continent. The achievement of US international power was, he implied, rooted in the historical process of continental exploration, conquest, settlement and 'improvement' through which the American people had established their sovereignty over – and extracted enormous wealth from – vast expanses of North America. Olney reinforced the point three years later: 'This country was once the pioneer, and is now the millionaire', he wrote in 1898 on the eve of war with Spain. 'It behooves it to recognize the changed conditions, … to realize its great place among the powers of the earth [and] … to accept the commanding position belonging to it.'[3]

While Olney saw the emergence of US power as a unique national process, his emphasis on continental conquest points to an even longer and wider history of North American empire. Patterns of settlement, struggles over land and sovereignty and new forms of racism took shape in distinct ways in different parts of North America during the colonial era, and these colonial patterns and precedents continued to have a shaping force on the continent's new nations. What began centuries earlier, with the claims of European powers to great swaths of land that they could neither rule nor control, culminated in the appearance of novel imperial formations. Indian peoples reorganised themselves to maintain their sovereignty, sometimes establishing their own imperial reach over significant land masses, while the United States, Mexico and Canada each in their own ways pushed beyond previously established political borders or areas of effective control to claim lands, resources and labour.[4] After the 1783 Treaty of Paris, the as-yet incomplete process of establishing dominion over vast portions of the continent held by native peoples thus passed from the European empires to the new nations of North America.

These changes prefigured yet another set of imperial transitions in the late nineteenth and twentieth centuries, when industrial development helped to entrench state power in these three North American nations, and when the project of anointing populations as capable or incapable of self-rule provided the ideological basis for further US military action and economic interventions across national borders and beyond the continent. The imperative to delineate who was and who was not fit for citizenship, who was and was not owed civil rights and respect, gained force in the United States in the context of massive labour immigration to serve the needs of an industrialising economy, and in time would be extended to overseas populations as US capital sought wider fields of involvement. In the twentieth century, the United States, along with the European imperial powers,

---

3   Quoted in Walter LaFeber, *The New Empire: An Interpretation of American Expansion, 1860–1898* (Ithaca, NY, 1998), p. 257.

4   With the horse as an especially effective instrument of economic and military power. See Pekka Hämäläinen, *The Comanche Empire* (New Haven, CT, 2008).

guarded the entrances to national self-determination in the international arena, a development with significant consequences for the evolving nature of US power and all manifestations of North American empire.

This chapter will thus suggest, in line with arguments in the literature of empire discussed below, that the process of defining and shaping nations in and beyond North America was the work of modern empire. It made possible the appropriation of land, the assertion of rule over the original inhabitants of that land, and the spread of capitalist economic organisation to extract wealth from both. In these ways, the persistence of empire shaped all three internationally recognised North American nations, even as the United States became the dominant American imperial presence and, eventually, the seat of a singular global empire.

Precisely because the dominant form of North American empire has been based in a conceit of popular sovereignty, its history has entailed successive renunciations of empire. This entwining of imperial assertion and renunciation, the embrace of empire and its erasure, the conceit of its rejection, characterises the modern imperial forms that emerged out of North American struggles over land and livelihood, and out of the international relations and transnational connections shaping those struggles.[5] The tension between self-mastery and mastery over others, between sovereignty as self-determination and sovereignty as rule, came to define the dominant pattern of imperial enterprises mounted by North Americans in the national and international contexts of the nineteenth and twentieth centuries and beyond.

Three Phases of North American Empire

1. Republics and Dominions, 1783–1867

In the new United States, the fixing of borders and the assertion of federal rule over vast expanses of land claimed, inhabited and often controlled by native peoples, as well as the exclusion of those peoples from the polity, proceeded hand-in-hand with a new conceit of sovereignty.[6] In the logic of liberal republicanism, sovereignty connoted not imperial rule but individual and collective freedom of action and

---

5   On the international and transnational contexts of US history, see Thomas Bender, *A Nation among Nations: America's Place in World History* (New York, 2006) and Ian Tyrrell, *Transnational Nation: United States History in Global Perspective since 1789* (New York, 2007).

6   Beth Saler, 'An Empire for Liberty, A State for Empire: The US National State before and after the Revolution of 1800', in James P. Horn, Peter S. Onuf and Jan Lewis (eds), *The Revolution of 1800: Democracy, Race, and the New Republic* (Charlottesville, VA, 2002), pp. 360–82. See also Anders Stephanson, 'A Most Interesting Empire', in Lloyd C. Gardner and Marilyn B. Young (eds), *The New American Empire: A Twenty-First Century Teach-In on US Foreign Policy* (New York, 2005), pp. 253–75.

popular governance, not mastery over others but self-mastery as the basis for self-determination. Yet citizens of the new nation could also understand themselves to be, in the words of George Washington, 'lords and proprietors of a vast continent'.[7] In Mexico and Canada, liberalism also framed the emergence of national polities and shaped the projects of rule that would perpetuate colonial domination of the indigenous peoples of North America.

For the United States, the process of asserting national rule over Native American lands was uneven and conflicted, both because it met with a wide variety of Indian initiatives and responses and because it was driven by diverse and contending agendas within the new nation. Those who fashioned the institutions of governance and set policy for the newly created government sought to shape the nation according to their particular visions for the republic: Jefferson and Madison saw the vastness of the continent as a resource that could provide the foundation for a virtuous republic of yeoman farmers, whereas Federalists tended to envision a national domain developed through trade, and encompassing some Indian peoples who would remain subordinate to, and protected by, the federal government.[8] States with claims to land beyond the crest of the Appalachians sought the advantages of sale or settlement. Slave owners saw lands awaiting tobacco or cotton cultivation, while those making legislative arguments for and against slavery gleaned the prospect of augmented political weight within the union. Missionaries hoped to reap souls; military men, honours and their rewards; traders, markets and goods. Land companies and speculators set their sights on easy money, and tended to prevail in the attempt. Surveyors mapped metes and bounds, creating the documents that brought native lands within the grasp of legalism for profit and settlement.[9] Individual white men and women saw room to settle their families, make their fortunes and claim their American freedoms and identities. In all, by 1820, nearly two million Euro-Americans made their way west, past the mountains, where they were confronted by an Indian population seeking 'to maintain land and sovereignty', in some areas driven to unwelcome accommodation with newcomers, in some still exercising considerable power on their own terms.[10]

The exclusion of Native Americans from the polity, the process of turning them into outsiders in their own lands, was simultaneously contradictory and integral to the establishment of a republican body politic in the United States. As Philip Deloria has shown, identification with (and imitation of) Indians formed a crucial basis on which Americans differentiated themselves from the British to claim their

---

7   Cited in Saler, 'An Empire for Liberty, A State for Empire', pp. 360–361.

8   Peter S. Onuf, *Jefferson's Empire: The Language of American Nationhood* (Charlottesville, VA, 2000).

9   Robert D. Mitchell and Paul A. Groves, *North America: The Historical Geography of a Changing Continent* (Totowa, NJ, 1987), p. 155.

10   Ibid., p. 165. Quotation from Philip J. Deloria, *Playing Indian* (New Haven, CT, 1998), p. 37.

independence and to fashion themselves as republican citizens.[11] Perceptions of Indian savagery, as well as black slavery, provided the mirror that reflected back to white Americans their own self-possession and civilised self-mastery. Even where whites were able to imagine a future more open to Indian participation, inclusion most often rested on the promise of Native American conformity and cultural erasure. Thus, Thomas Jefferson's vision of an 'empire for liberty' encompassed a plan for the assimilation of Indians, in which Indian men would own property and 'take the labor of the earth from the women'. In this way, he told the Mohican leader Hendrick Aupaumut, among others, 'You will … form one people with us and we shall all be Americans. You will mix with us by marriage. Your blood will run in our veins, and will spread with us over this great land.'[12] Jefferson's insistence on the necessary 'sameness' of the nation thus made room for incorporation, but only through erasure.[13]

From the establishment in 1783 of the Mississippi River as the western boundary of the nation to the acquisition of California and half the territory claimed by Mexico at the end of the Mexican War (1846–48), the addition of new territories and the spread of Anglo-Americans over the land went forward in conjunction with the social, economic and cultural knitting together of the nation, a process that repeatedly affirmed the primacy of private property, relied on considerable violence and reproduced forms of racial hierarchy and subordination, threaded with gendered and sexual meanings and imperatives, at each stage of national development.[14] The Louisiana Purchase, secured for the US in 1803 as a result of Haiti's revolutionary triumph, doubled the nation's landmass, providing vast new areas for the expansion and entrenchment of the institution of slavery. In parts of the south, the subsequent effect of this expansion and entrenchment combined

---

11 Deloria, *Playing Indian*. Dreams of liberty may indeed have been cultivated in part by perceptions of Indian freedom and by the model of representative governance found in the Iroquois example, a much debated point. See Donald A. Grinde, Jr and Bruce E. Johansen, *Exemplar of Liberty: Native America and the Evolution of Democracy* (Los Angeles, CA, 1991).

12 Thomas Jefferson, 'Address to Captain Hendrick, the Delawares, Mohicans, and Munries' (21 December 1808), in Albert Ellery Bergh (ed.), *The Writings of Thomas Jefferson*, vol. 16 (Washington, DC, 1907), p. 452.

13 Saler, 'An Empire for Liberty, A State for Empire', p. 374.

14 Amy Kaplan, *The Anarchy of Empire in the Making of US Culture* (Cambridge, MA, 2002); Shelley Streeby, *American Sensations: Class, Empire, and the Production of Popular Culture* (Berkeley, CA, 2002); Reginald Horsman, *Race and Manifest Destiny: The Origins of American Racial Anglo-Saxonism* (Cambridge, MA, 1981); Thomas R. Hietala, *Manifest Design: Anxious Aggrandizement in Late Jacksonian America* (Ithaca, NY, 1985); Lori Merish, *Sentimental Materialism: Gender, Commodity Culture, and Nineteenth-Century American Literature* (Durham, NC, 2000); Patricia Nelson Limerick, *The Legacy of Conquest: The Unbroken Past of the American West* (New York, 1987), pp. 55–77; Gretchen Murphy, *Hemispheric Imaginings: The Monroe Doctrine and Narratives of US Empire* (Durham, NC, 2005). On the social and economic integration of North American hinterlands, see, for example, William Cronon, *Nature's Metropolis: Chicago and the Great West* (New York, 1991).

with class pressures to produce a more thorough link between race and property, including the reinforcement of whiteness as a form of property.[15] In 1834, Congress designated a portion of the Louisiana Purchase 'Indian Territory', to which indigenous peoples of the southeast, recently recast as 'domestic dependent nations', were forcibly removed.[16] The acquisition of Florida in 1819; the Transcontinental Treaty, which garnered for the US a corridor to the Pacific that same year; and the settlement of disputes with Britain over the northern boundary of the nation, which claimed Oregon Territory for the United States in 1846, further expanded the realm of settlement and conflict with Indians including the Comanche Empire, the Sioux who dominated the Great Plains and the nations of the northwest.[17] The mid-century discovery of gold in California accelerated and reshaped a process already deemed the 'manifest destiny' of the nation.[18]

Canadians and British North American subjects in what would later become Canada moved towards their own form of imperial nationhood between 1763 and 1867, driven by some of the same cultural and economic logics, but propelled too by important political and geographical differences. This process did not wait for the British North America Act of 1867 which, uniting Ontario, Quebec and the Maritime Provinces in a quasi-independent confederation, established the Dominion of Canada. It began sooner, in experimental rearrangements of colonial sovereignty and in the forging of assimilationist frameworks for cultivating industrious, property-owning subjects, fit for liberal self-government.[19]

In the wake of the Seven Years' War and prior to the American Revolution, British authorities adopted a number of relatively accommodating policies towards both the conquered French Canadians and their own indigenous allies, policies they would abandon as circumstances changed. When the American Revolution brought

---

15 Lacy K. Ford, Jr, 'Making the "White Man's Country" White: Race, Slavery, and State-Building in the Jacksonian South', *Journal of the Early Republic* 19/4 (1999): pp. 736–7; Cheryl Harris, 'Whiteness as Property', *Harvard Law Review* 106 (1993): pp. 1709–1791.

16 Cherokee Nation v. Georgia 30 US 1 (1831). See also Theda Perdue and Michael D. Green, *The Cherokee Nation and the Trail of Tears* (New York, 2007).

17 William Earl Weeks, *John Quincy Adams and American Global Empire* (Lexington, KY, 1992); Richard H. Immerman, *Empire for Liberty: A History of American Imperialism from Benjamin Franklin to Paul Wolfowitz* (Princeton, NJ, 2010), pp. 60–97. For an introduction to Indian resistance, including the important roles played by Neolin, Tenskwatawa and Tecumseh, see R. Douglas Hurt, *The Indian Frontier, 1763–1846* (Albuquerque, NM, 2002). For literature that rejects the model of resistance, see Hämäläinen, *Comanche Empire*, especially pp. 365–6, n. 3.

18 On the concept of 'manifest destiny', see Anders Stephanson, *Manifest Destiny: American Expansion and the Empire of Right* (New York, 1995); Linda S. Hudson, *Mistress of Manifest Destiny: A Biography of Jane McManus Storm Cazneau, 1807–1878* (Austin, TX, 2001), pp. 46–8, 205–210. Hudson shows that the phrase, commonly attributed to John L. O'Sullivan, was authored by Storm, a.k.a., Cora Montgomery.

19 John S. Milloy, 'The Early Indian Acts: Developmental Strategy and Constitutional Change', in J.R. Miller (ed.), *Sweet Promises: A Reader on Indian-White Relations in Canada* (Toronto, 1991), pp. 145–54.

Loyalist settlers to the northern shores of the eastern Great Lakes, policy veered towards concessions to the growing British population with the establishment of Upper Canada (Ontario) in 1791, a new English-speaking province carved out of lands formerly claimed by Quebec. The First Nations of North America still had strong claims, however, given their role in the defence of Canada during both the American Revolution and the War of 1812. With increasing British settlement, Indian peoples faced growing hostility as well as severe cutbacks in the gifts and annuities provided by the British.[20] As settlers claimed more land Canada began to establish Indian reserves, initially within existing areas of native residence rather than at a distance.

As in the United States and Canada, empire took shape in Mexico in the forms of liberal nationhood as Mexican Liberals such as Benito Juárez and Miguel Lerdo de Tejada crafted a programme for their nation's modernisation that sought to remake the Mexican people, and to render them fit for rational, republican self-government and economic advancement. The programme sought to rationalise landowning, transform agriculture, restrict the power of the Catholic Church, knit the nation together with railroads and canals, redress the persistence of indigenous 'myth' and 'superstition', and eliminate continuing opposition from independent Indians in the now-truncated north. Coming to power in 1854, the Liberals decried peonage and the ill-treatment of Indian labourers as part of the failure of the nation to establish a rational approach to the cultivation of its fertile land.[21] But in seeking to garner all 'unused lands' for a properly organised agricultural programme, Liberals also took aim at Indian communities themselves and at forms of protection previously extended to them by the federal government and the church. They called for individual land ownership, an end to 'indolence' in the existing population, colonisation of supposedly 'virgin lands' by immigrants, education and concessions to foreign capital.[22] A central goal was to bring Indians into the nation as industrious and prosperous citizens. The results were uneven at best. In some locales indigenous villagers were able to manage the process, limit its effects, and even in some cases amass wealth. But many Indians were forced further into debt servitude as wealth came to be concentrated in the hands of the very few, whether Mexicans or *Norteamericanos* – that is, US citizens.[23]

---

20   R. David Edmunds, 'Native Americans and the United States, Canada, and Mexico', in Philip J. Deloria and Neal Salisbury (eds), *A Companion to American Indian History* (Malden, MA, 2002), pp. 397–421; Roger L. Nichols, *Indians in the United States and Canada* (Lincoln, NE, 1998).

21   Luis González y González, 'Liberals and the Land', in Gilbert M. Joseph and Timothy J. Henderson (eds), *The Mexico Reader: History, Culture, Politics* (Durham, NC, 2002), p. 240.

22   Dreams of colonisation through immigration went unfulfilled.

23   González y González, 'Liberals and the Land', p. 247; John Mason Hart, *Revolutionary Mexico: The Coming and Process of the Mexican Revolution* (Berkeley, CA, 1987), pp. 37–8, 358–61; Raymond B. Craib, 'Standard Plots and Rural Resistance', in Gilbert M. Joseph and Timothy J. Henderson (eds), *The Mexico Reader: History, Culture, Politics* (Durham, NC, 2002), pp. 252–62; Karen D. Caplan, 'Indigenous Citizenship: Liberalism, Political

In the early nation-building phases of North American empire, the sovereign self was effectively joined to the ideal of dominion over a given expanse of territory to birth modern democratic republicanism and the North American liberal nation-state. Empire, a project of rule over native peoples and their lands, was joined to nationhood, a project of collective self-fashioning and sovereign self-assertion. At the same time, with labouring populations tuned to the strains of economic need and opportunity, financiers, engineers and industrial entrepreneurs set their minds to exploiting the continent's natural resources. By the 1870s, all three recognised North American nations, unlike the indigenous nations (and empires) that persisted in their midst, had centralised governments operating in conjunction with capital to pursue economic development and to produce wealth, both public and private. Thus, while the growing power of the industrialising North would generate assaults on Mexican sovereignty in the century to come, the form of Mexican society itself had already in some respects reproduced North American empire within the nation, preparing the ground for the growing power of 'El Norte'. In the decades that followed, Mexican oligarchs in Yucatan grew rich on forced Yaqui labor and contracts for hemp destined to become bailing twine on the Great Plains of Canada and the United States while a rapidly expanding US expatriate community in the north increasingly took title to Mexican land and resources.[24]

2. Imperial Embrace, 1860–1917

In all three countries, the consolidation of the liberal nation-state in the 1860s and 1870s went hand-in-hand with wage labour, the appropriation and redistribution of 'federal' lands at the expense of indigenous and African-heritage people, greater efficiency in transportation and communication and new negotiations of race and citizenship, often through the cultural mechanisms of gender and sexuality.[25] Yet, despite similarities in state forms and nation-building projects, widening inequalities and national differences increasingly defined the contours of modern North American empire between 1860 and 1917.

In the United States, the outlines of a new capitalist empire took shape in a series of political, economic and social changes, including the growth of the federal government during the Civil War; the triumph of waged and other intermediate forms of labour over slavery, and of corporate rule over widely shared notions of commonweal; the deployment of the US Army against workers within the United States, notably but not solely in the Great Uprising of 1877; the amassing

---

Participation, and Ethnic Identity in Post-Independence Oaxaca and Yucatán', in Andrew B. Fisher and Matthew D. O'Hara (eds), *Imperial Subjects: Race and Identity in Colonial Latin America* (Durham, NC, 2009), pp. 225–47.

24 Sterling Evans, *Bound in Twine: The History and Ecology of the Henequen-Wheat Complex for Mexico and the American and Canadian Plains, 1880–1950* (College Station, TX, 2007).

25 Ann Laura Stoler, *Haunted by Empire: Geographies of Intimacy in North American History* (Durham, NC, 2006).

of individual fortunes in connection with mining, agriculture and railroad construction; and the establishment of powerful financial houses to underwrite such enterprises.[26] Washington privatised federal lands and resources through such measures as the Homestead Act and the National Mineral Act, expanded the nation's borders through the acquisition of Alaska in 1867, and deployed the Army to eradicate Native American opposition to colonisation as well as to restore the confederate states to the Union. While relying on missionaries and reformers to make proper citizen-workers of immigrants and freed people, the federal government abdicated its responsibility towards its citizens by acquiescing to both lynching and the institutionalisation of deepening racial hatreds in segregation and disfranchisement.[27] At the same time, overseas imperial pursuits included missionary efforts to inculcate industrious New England values in Hawaiian plantation workers and experiments with direct investment in railroads, mining, agricultural production and manufacturing in Latin America and the Pacific.[28] The cultivation of an ideology of Anglo-Saxon racial superiority through science, sideshows and world's fairs, and the use of the US military to guarantee a friendly field for the operation of capital beyond US borders, gave form and substance to an evolving empire that could now begin to vie with the overseas empires of Europe.[29]

Meanwhile, between the 1860s and the early twentieth century, Mexico came increasingly under the weight of US economic dominance, while Canada incrementally shed its status as a colony. Mexican leaders invited US capital to develop mining, agriculture, an oil industry and railroads, and to provide arms as necessary to control labour uprisings and to address persistent indigenous resistance to the Liberal programme of national development.[30] By the first decade of the twentieth century, US investments accounted for half of all foreign investment in Mexico and fully one-quarter of all US foreign investments.[31] The Mexican Revolution, which broke out at the end of that decade in the northern

26   Eric Foner, *Reconstruction: America's Unfinished Revolution, 1863–1877* (New York, 1989); Thomas O'Brien, *The Revolutionary Mission: American Enterprise in Latin America, 1900–1945* (Cambridge, 1996), pp. 13–43.

27   Matthew Frye Jacobson, *Barbarian Virtues: The United States Encounters Foreign Peoples at Home and Abroad, 1876–1917* (New York, 2000); Derek Chang, *Citizens of a Christian Nation: Evangelical Missions and the Problem of Race in the Nineteenth Century* (Philadelphia, PA, 2010).

28   Jon Kamakawiwo'ole Osorio, *Dismembering Lāhui: A History of the Hawaiian Nation to 1887* (Honolulu, HI, 2002). Earlier private imperial adventures included filibustering expeditions in the 1850s, notably those of William Walker. See for example Michel Gobat, *Confronting the American Dream: Nicaragua under U.S. Imperial Rule* (Durham, NC, 2005).

29   Emily S. Rosenberg, *Spreading the American Dream: American Economic and Cultural Expansion, 1890–1945* (New York, 1982).

30   Greg Grandin, *Empire's Workshop: Latin America, The United States, and the Rise of the New Imperialism* (New York, 2006), p. 29; Hart, *Revolutionary Mexico*, pp. 74–186.

31   Hart, *Revolutionary Mexico*, p. 177; Grandin, *Empire's Workshop*, p. 17. See also O'Brien, *Revolutionary Mission*, pp. 253–4.

state of Sonora, proved a formidable challenge to the US Empire and ultimately contributed to key shifts in US policy, as Washington confronted the reality of Latin American nationalism. In Canada, dominion status came in 1867, followed closely by new laws governing the First Nations, specifically designed to break up hereditary chiefship, impose elections as part of tribal governance itself, unilaterally impose Canadian citizenship and dismantle the reserves. With these moves, the economic assault of an expanding Euro-American and Canadian economy was compounded by expectations for participation in the liberal state and renunciation of collective land use and communal life. By the early twentieth century, Canadians would take their place in British imperial conferences as partners collaborating with other white colonies to influence policy for the West Indies and India.[32]

In the years that followed the 'Venezuela Crisis' of 1895, the United States' embrace of imperialism materialised in myriad policy initiatives and military ventures. United States American men threw themselves into the conflict with Spain in the Caribbean and the Pacific, and the nation emerged with its first overseas colonies, including Puerto Rico, Guam and the Philippines, as well as Hawaii, which was claimed by a separate colonial process.[33] Although legislators had vowed, as a condition for the declaration of war on Spain, not to take Cuba as a colony, the decades that followed US victory saw the tightening of political and economic control in the Caribbean through a series of innovations – including formal protectorates, customs receiverships, client constabularies, military occupations and counter-insurgency warfare – that would set the stage for the extension of US 'informal' empire beyond the hemisphere.[34] The strategy of fomenting and abetting

---

32   Jennifer Henderson, *Settler Feminism and Race Making in Canada* (Toronto, ON, 2003), pp. 22–5.

33   Kristin Hoganson, *Fighting for American Manhood: How Gender Politics Provoked the Spanish-American and Philippine-American Wars* (New Haven, CT, 1998). On Puerto Rico, see Fernando Picó, *1898: la guerra despúes de la guerra* (Rio Piedras, 1987); Eileen J. Suárez Findlay, *Imposing Decency: The Politics of Sexuality and Race in Puerto Rico, 1870–1920* (Durham, NC, 1999); Christina Duffy Burnett and Burke Marshall (eds), *Foreign in a Domestic Sense: Puerto Rico, American Expansion, and the Constitution* (Durham, NC, 2001); Laura Briggs, *Reproducing Empire: Race, Sex, Science, and US Imperialism in Puerto Rico* (Berkeley, CA, 2002). On Guam, see Stephanson, 'A Most Interesting Empire', p. 262; Arnold H. Leibowitz, *Defining Status: A Comprehensive Analysis of United States Territorial Relations* (Dordrecht, 1989). On Hawaii, see Sally Engle Merry, *Colonizing Hawai'i: The Cultural Power of Law* (Princeton, NJ, 2000); Noenoe K. Silva, *Aloha Betrayed: Native Hawaiian Resistance to American Colonialism* (Durham, NC, 2004); Eric T. Love, 'White is the Color of Empire: The Annexation of Hawaii in 1898', in James T. Campbell, Matthew Pratt Guterl and Robert G. Lee (eds), *Race, Nation and Empire in American History* (Chapel Hill, NC, 2007), pp. 75–102. On the Philippines, see Vicente Rafael, *White Love and Other Events in Filipino History* (Durham, NC, 2000); Julian Go and Anne L. Foster (eds), *The American Colonial State in the Philippines: Global Perspectives* (Durham, NC, 2003); Paul A. Kramer, *The Blood of Government: Race, Empire, the United States, and the Philippines* (Chapel Hill, NC, 2006). See also Alison Schneider, *Suffragists in an Imperial Age: US Expansion and the Woman Question, 1870–1929* (Oxford, 2008).

34   The Teller Amendment, which foreswore the annexation of Cuba as a goal for the War

local insurgencies served the material interests of US investors and entrepreneurs and the strategic goals of the state, which made possible, among other things, a cross-isthmian canal project in the new nation of Panama, formerly a region of the less accommodating Colombian nation.[35] Henceforth, the opening of that crucial route to the Pacific would reinforce perceptions of the need to maintain US dominance in the Caribbean region, contributing to the justification for repeated and extended military occupations in Cuba, Haiti, the Dominican Republic, Nicaragua and Mexico. All this seemed to answer late nineteenth-century calls for masculine, Anglo-Saxon imperialist assertiveness made by such influential leaders as Alfred Thayer Mahan, Josiah Strong and Theodore Roosevelt.[36]

Yet such straightforward, relatively un-camouflaged assertions of US power characterised a moment that would soon pass. While Mahan's new navy was being readied to command the Caribbean and the Pacific, Latin Americans voiced their opposition to the growing power of what Cuban nationalist José Marti called 'the savage and brutal North'.[37] News of US atrocities in the war to suppress Filipino independence between 1899 and 1903 opened northern ears to such accusations, inciting fears in the United States of a degenerating American manhood, contaminated by contact with a supposedly savage people.[38] The debacle of war in the Philippines marked for many the contradiction that was now evident between bald assertions of US sovereign status over far-flung lands and official pretensions to the protection and maintenance of popular sovereignty. Led by Mexico, opposition to US imperialism in Latin America and the Caribbean mounted.[39] Moreover,

of 1898, was largely a reflex of widespread fear of the incorporation of 'darker peoples' into the nation. Eric T.L. Love, *Race over Empire: Racism and US Imperialism, 1865–1900* (Chapel Hill, NC, 2004). For a summary of US policy and action in the Caribbean region during this period, including Theodore Roosevelt's important 'corollary' to the Monroe Doctrine, see Renda, 'Practical Sovereignty'.

35   This is not to deny the significance of pre-existing political opposition to local rulers, such as in Panama. Alfredo Castillero Calvo, *El café en Panamá: una historia social y económica: siglos XVIII–XX* (Panama, 1985); Julie Greene, *The Canal Builders: Making America's Empire at the Panama Canal* (New York, 2010).

36   Gail Bederman, *Manliness and Civilization: A Cultural History of Gender and Race in the United States, 1880–1917* (Chicago, IL, 1995); Rosenberg, *Spreading the American Dream*, pp. 44–5.

37   José Marti, Letter to Manuel Mercado, 18 May 1895, in Robert H. Holden and Eric Zolov (eds), *Latin America and the United States: A Documentary History* (Oxford, 2000), p. 63. Other signal protests against US domination in this period included the Calvo Clause and the Drago Doctrine.

38   Hoganson, *Fighting for American Manhood*, pp. 133–55.

39   Wilson ordered the occupation of Veracruz in 1914 in an attempt to staunch the radicalism of Mexico's revolution. See Thomas O'Brien, *Making the Americas: The United States and Latin America from the Age of Revolutions to the Era of Globalization* (Albuquerque, NM, 2007), p. 37. On Latin American opposition in the twentieth and twenty-first centuries, see Alan McPherson, *Yankee No! Anti-Americanism in US-Latin American Relations* (Cambridge, MA, 2003); Fred Rosen (ed.), *Empire and Dissent: The United States and Latin America* (Durham, NC, 2008).

limitations on US trade and investment arising from European colonial competition contributed to an official anti-imperialist stance. In response to circumstances in China in 1899, US Secretary of State John Hay's first 'Open Door Note' proclaimed the United States' opposition to closed-sphere imperialism in favour of the liberal values of free trade and freedom of the seas.[40]

3. Internationalism as Empire, 1918–2001

The First World War provided the occasion, and Woodrow Wilson the leadership, to forge a new open-door approach to empire for the twentieth century, one that was to be anti-colonial, internationalist, nominally based on universalist principles and friendly to the supremacy of capital. The keystone of this new approach was world leadership for the United States based on its putative defence of democracy and national sovereignty. Wilson's Fourteen Points, spelled out in an address to the US Congress in January 1918, articulated his vision of a world without imperial boundaries, a world in which all nations would, eventually, enjoy the ideal of national 'self-determination' and benefit from a lively commerce in ideas and civilised values as well as material goods.

Wilson's desire to supersede the existing European imperial system was nurtured by a larger progressive effort 'to end all wars' and to refine government structures in the service of human welfare, but this partially liberatory project had more complex roots and goals.[41] The growing strength of radical internationalism, its role in Mexico, its triumph in Russia and its spread through immigration, as well as Lenin's role as spokesperson for a growing anti-capitalist revolution, forced Wilson to lead with the emancipatory elements of his liberal vision. At the same time, his belief that peace would come through a common framework modelled on US economic development conveniently accommodated the advance of US capital and political leadership. His concept of national sovereignty, rooted in exclusivist notions of an Anglo-Saxon genius for liberty that distinguished a racially superior class of world leaders, suggested the need to tutor less developed nations in the arts of democracy.[42] Wilson's programme thus presented the economic imperative of open trade alongside the political and geographical project of constituting

---

40 On the Open Door, see Rosenberg, *Spreading the American Dream*; Jacobson, *Barbarian Virtues*; and LaFeber, *The New Empire*. On economic opportunity in China, see Eileen P. Scully, 'Taking the Low Road to Sino-American Relations: "Open Door" Expansionists and the Two China Markets', in *Journal of American History* 82/1 (1995): pp. 62–83. See also Eileen P. Scully, *Bargaining with the State from Afar: American Citizenship in Treaty Port China, 1844–1942* (New York, 2001).

41 Thomas J. Knock, *To End All Wars: Woodrow Wilson and the Quest for a New World Order* (Princeton, NJ, 1992).

42 Mary A. Renda, *Taking Haiti: Military Occupation and the Culture of US Imperialism, 1915–1940* (Chapel Hill, NC, 2001), pp. 91–115; Rosenberg, *Spreading the American Dream*, pp. 63–75.

bounded nations closed to foreign territorial acquisition, properly governed by states committed to liberal principles and open to capitalist markets.

Political opposition led by Senator Henry Cabot Lodge routed Wilson's plan for US membership in the League of Nations, the substance of his fourteenth point, but his programme of liberal internationalism provided the blueprint for a distinctly modern US empire. Economic circumstances at war's end made possible the partial materialisation of Wilson's vision. With European economies devastated, the United States' status as the world's 'millionaire' facilitated a turn from military action to financial administration, significantly extending the reach of US influence.[43] Under Herbert Hoover's leadership, the Department of Commerce supplanted the Department of State as the critical bureaucratic hub where US international relations were recast, fostering corporate expansion in oil, rubber, communications and more. In this new framework, nominal and sometimes substantive support for national self-determination became a necessary corollary to US international power, while an increasing turn towards covert operations and the suppression of dissent, both honed in the circum-Caribbean occupations and interventions of the 1920s, masked the persistence of naked power in the United States' liberal approach to empire-building.[44] More immediately, these changes facilitated the renunciation of the Monroe Doctrine that Latin American protests and broader political circumstances now required. The new internationalism seemed to harmonise the discordant strains of US policy and rhetoric, even as military occupations, administrative protectorates, client militarism, economic dictation – and indeed, US colonies – persisted.

This new iteration of US empire continued to take shape in the troubled global contexts of the 1930s. In 1933, Franklin Roosevelt's Good Neighbor policy announced a retreat from outright dictation to Latin American client states. The new policy created a kind of deniability, making it possible to emphasise the United States' distance from regional dictators when necessary, while maintaining financial oversight in some cases and reaping the benefits of 'stability' for US corporate ventures. It also relieved the nation of a financial burden at a time of deepening economic depression. In 1934, Roosevelt experimented with new international economic structures through the establishment of the Export-Import Bank, designed to strengthen the global economy in significant measure by promoting the international profile of key US industries such as oil, electricity and automobile production. Having forged an accommodation during the recession between capital and labour in the name of a higher standard of living through increased productivity, Roosevelt then enlisted both in opposition to the Axis powers.[45] Thus, notwithstanding widespread 'isolationist' sentiment during the

---

43 The phrase is from Olney, *Papers Relating to the Foreign Relations of the United States*; Emily S. Rosenberg, *Financial Missionaries to the World: The Politics and Culture of Dollar Diplomacy, 1900–1930* (Cambridge, MA, 1999).

44 Renda, 'Practical Sovereignty'; Ellen Meiksins Wood, *Empire of Capital* (London, 2003).

45 O'Brien, *Making the Americas*, p. 155. These moves also masked the impact of powerful US companies abroad: see Paul J. Dosal, *Doing Business with the Dictators: A Political*

1930s, Roosevelt pressed forward with a liberal, reform-minded, internationalist programme for US global leadership.

While Washington retooled the political and economic machinery of its international relations and pledged the nation to fair dealing with Latin America in the interwar years, other facets of North American empire, involving what some have called 'internal colonialism', revealed the contradictions embedded in US and Canadian promises of sovereignty.[46] Whether facing social and political exclusion or forced inclusion on unacceptable terms, those targeted by white racism in its various forms often perceived the links between domestic oppression and imperialism and pressed their claims for independence and respect in part by calling on transnational connections that bridged those differences. Thus, in the interwar years, African Americans claimed sovereignty over their own lives increasingly through transnational organising and international radicalism.[47] In the early 1920s some Native American and First Nation peoples in Canada and the United States considered the new League of Nations a possible forum for the redress of grievances. In the case of the Iroquois Six Nations resident on land claimed by Canada, incursions on the reserve and interference with self-government, linked with the passage of new legislation designed to integrate Indian peoples more fully into the Canadian nation and to dislodge them from collective ownership of their land, led one leader, Deskaheh (born Levi General), to make an application for membership for his nation in the League of Nations. While his plea, 'The Redman's Appeal for Justice', failed, he got support from a half-dozen governments, including those of Panama, Ireland and Japan, and proclaimed to members of his and other First Nations and to the world the rightful sovereignty they had never forfeited.[48]

During these years, the contradictions of US paternalism toward Filipinos, still under formal colonial rule, engendered racial violence in the US west. Encouraged by the need for agricultural labour, and seeking relief from economic recession, single Filipino men came to the western United States in increasing numbers during the 1920s, only to run headlong into 'the ideology of white entitlement to the resources of the West' – and to the bodies of white women. When anti-Filipino whites attempted to circumvent the legal requirements of the empire with explicit racial restrictions to limit the movement that Filipinos enjoyed as US nationals, their alternative was to throw their support behind formal independence for the

History of United Fruit in Guatemala, 1899–1944 (Wilmington, DE, 1993).

46 For an excellent discussion of the term, see Linda Gordon, 'Internal Colonialism and Gender', in Ann Laura Stoler (ed.), *Haunted by Empire: Geographies of Intimacy in North American History* (Durham, NC, 2006), pp. 427–51.

47 Kaplan, *Anarchy of Empire*, pp. 171–212; Penny M. Von Eschen, *Race Against Empire: Black Americans and Anticolonialism, 1937–1957* (Ithaca, NY, 1997); Michelle Ann Stephens, *Black Empire: The Masculine Global Imaginary of Caribbean Intellectuals in the United States, 1914–1962* (Durham, NC, 2005); and Glenda Gilmore, *Defying Dixie: The Radical Roots of Civil Rights, 1919–1950* (New York, 2008).

48 Ronald Niezen, 'Recognizing Indigenism: Canadian Unity and the International Movement of Indigenous Peoples', *Comparative Studies in Society and History* 42 (2000): pp. 119–48; Nichols, *Indians in the United States and Canada*, pp. 268–70.

Philippines, resulting, ironically, in the Tydings–McDuffie Bill of 1934, and in the redoubled desire of Filipino migrants, in particular, for national independence from a hostile United States.[49]

The Second World War created an unprecedented opening for those fighting for racial justice, civil rights and national sovereignty within US contexts by rendering racism politically anathema as a justification for empire. The internment of Japanese Americans, the conduct of the war against Japan, racial segregation in the military, race riots targeting African Americans and Mexican Americans and continuing discrimination attested to the persistence of US racism. Yet the Allies' defeat of enemies who had waged war in the name of racial supremacy, the revelation of Nazi genocide and, not least, the existence of a worldwide anti-colonial movement with eyes and ears attuned to the inconsistencies of US claims to leadership in the name of universal principle, made it politically unfeasible for proponents of US global power to continue to use explicitly racist criteria to mark out who was and was not capable of self-rule.[50]

In other ways, too, the Second World War fundamentally changed the terrain on which peoples of colour struggled and on which modern US empire operated. In August 1941, several months before Pearl Harbor and the US declaration of war, Roosevelt succeeded in getting Churchill to agree, if not without some bristling and a caveat, to an 'Atlantic Charter' stating the broad outlines of his vision for a postwar world of open markets and equal access to economic wealth for all nations.[51] While Roosevelt could not prevent the British and the Soviets from brokering a postwar division of territorial influence for each, the devastation of war broke the back of western Europe's empires and created openings for anti-colonial nationalism. It also consolidated US economic production and military power, positioning the nation to claim its place as 'leader of the free world' after the war's end. Not least of the developments that solidified this outcome was the advent of atomic weaponry and its deployment on Hiroshima and Nagasaki in August of 1945. But mass mobilisation of the population and the economy, and other advances in wartime technology, laid the foundation for postwar prosperity and global leadership.[52] By 1944, the United States had also fostered the creation of an international institutional framework to ensure postwar open markets, economies strong enough to withstand the appeal of socialism, and a measure of international governance based on national sovereignty. The World Bank and the International Monetary Fund, created in 1944, would provide the economic framework, while the new United Nations would be the political face of internationalism. Roosevelt

49   Mae Ngai, *Impossible Subjects: Illegal Aliens and the Making of Modern America* (Princeton, NJ, 2004), pp. 96–126; quote, p. 109.

50   Von Eschen, *Race Against Empire*; Howard Winant, *The World is a Ghetto: Race and Democracy since World War II* (New York, 2001).

51   Walter LaFeber, *American Age: United States Foreign Policy at Home and Abroad since 1750* (New York, 1989), pp. 380–381.

52   Michael Adas, *Dominance by Design: Technological Imperatives and America's Civilizing Mission* (Cambridge, MA, 2006).

gained a further advantage just after the 1945 Yalta conference by negotiating postwar access to Saudi Arabian oil in exchange for military protection from the United States.[53] Throughout the war, Roosevelt attempted to limit US commitments that might strengthen British colonialism and, particularly after 1943, he worked to draw Stalin into partnership under the banner of an open-market internationalism.[54]

After the war, the US empire-building programme continued with unprecedented force.[55] Despite Roosevelt's efforts, the United States' wartime alliance with the Soviet Union devolved into Cold War opposition, with Stalin consolidating Soviet control over Eastern Europe (albeit within boundaries agreed upon at Yalta) and refusing to accept US aid contingent upon open markets as the framework for postwar reconstruction. Military force had, between 1918 and 1920, been an element of US opposition to Bolshevism, but prior to the Second World War the United States defended itself against Communism primarily by strengthening the appeal of capitalism and deflecting Soviet criticisms of US imperialism with anti-subversion campaigns and suppression of dissent.[56] In 1947, the withdrawal of British aid to those fighting socialist contenders in Greece alongside Soviet pressure in Turkey prompted President Harry Truman to draw a line of military containment against the Soviets to establish the principle of US military aid in contests for freedom around the globe. Truman's failure to contain communism in Asia was highlighted by the triumph of the Chinese Communists in 1949, and Republicans seized the opportunity to push to further strengthen US defences. By 1950, the Soviet Union had its own atomic bomb, Communist China had entered into a pact with Moscow and Chinese forces loomed at the border of Korea. That year, an influential architect of US policy stated outright that the United States must now establish itself as a 'world-dominating force'.[57] Notwithstanding the advent of a series of regional treaties and treaty organisations designed to institutionalise cooperative military defence, US military spending rose to new heights in the ensuing three years of war in Korea.[58]

Linked inextricably with the military dimension of postwar US power were the economic and the ideological. The Marshall Plan put in place a common economic framework, which Charles Maier has dubbed 'the empire of production'.[59] It incorporated economic growth based on the prevailing American business

---

53   Michael T. Klare, *Blood and Oil: The Dangers and Consequences of America's Growing Petroleum Dependency* (New York, 2004), p. 33; David Harvey, *The New Imperialism* (Oxford, 2003), p. 53.

54   LaFeber, *American Age*, pp. 392–429.

55   Neil Smith, *American Empire: Roosevelt's Geographer and the Prelude to Globalization* (Berkeley, CA, 2003), p. 373.

56   On the 1918–1920 intervention, see David Fogelsong, *America's Secret War Against Bolshevism: US Intervention in the Russian Civil War, 1917–1920* (Chapel Hill, NC, 1995).

57   James Burnham, quoted in Stephanson, 'A Most Interesting Empire', p. 267.

58   The first of these was the Rio Pact of 1947, followed in 1949 by NATO. See Grandin, *Empire's Workshop*, p. 40; LaFeber, *American Age*, pp. 463–9.

59   Charles Maier, *Among Empires: American Ascendancy and Its Predecessors* (Cambridge, MA, 2006).

model, welfare states, wages high enough to keep workers away from the lure of Communism and vigilance with regard to radical threats to the system.[60] The scale of aid – $13 billion over five years – was sufficient to bring Western Europe into play as a market for US goods on an entirely new level, a crucial element for growing productivity and steady economic health for the new imperial centre, where, at war's end, fully half the world's goods were produced.[61] This 'market empire' strengthened by the Marshall Plan was neither completely new to the postwar moment nor solely the product of actions taken by the US state, but the infusion of aid and influence produced a new legitimacy for US consumer society even as Europe's leaders chafed against the curtailment of national sovereignty that resulted from the shaping force of consumerism.[62] The hegemonic impact of modernity played a crucial role in this process, as marketing successfully sold the American way of doing things as the 'natural, modern, and good way'.[63]

The defence against Communism took a different form in many parts of what came to be known as the Third World. There, modernisation theory enhanced earlier paternalist logic for bringing the so-called 'undeveloped' and 'developing' nations into the international capitalist system under the influence of the United States. The perceived need for US guidance in Latin America, Africa and Asia, no longer explicitly cast as racial inferiority, was now attributed to the weight of tradition and ignorance that needed to be purged to make possible a nation's advancement, assisted by enlightened scientific expertise.[64] In 1949, Truman announced his 'Point Four' aid programme, highlighting the importance of 'industrial progress', 'scientific advances' and 'technical knowledge' as the means to address problems he attributed to the 'primitive and stagnant' economic life of poor countries. Philanthropic foundations also contributed, while keeping to narrow ideological frameworks that precluded, at least at first, attention to structural inequalities in land ownership and taxation.[65] Meanwhile, US dollars and expertise sought to reform intimate lives thought to exacerbate poverty and

---

60   Ibid. See also Melvyn P. Leffler, 'The Cold War: What Do "We Now Know"?' *American Historical Review* 104/2 (1999): pp. 501–524.

61   LaFeber, *American Age*, pp. 434, 455.

62   Victoria de Grazia, *Irresistible Empire: America's Advance through Twentieth-Century Europe* (Cambridge, MA, 2005). On the prewar US presence in Europe, see also Frank Costigliola, *Awkward Dominion: American Political, Economic, and Cultural Relations with Europe, 1919–1933* (Ithaca, NY, 1984); Rosenberg, *Financial Missionaries*. On the Marshall Plan, see also Geir Lundestad, 'Empire by Invitation', *Diplomatic History* 23 (1999): pp. 189–217.

63   De Grazia, *Irresistible Empire*, p. 8. The United States devised cultural diplomacy to address European and worldwide resistance through directed, state-sponsored efforts at cultural imperialism: see Reinhold Wagnleitner, *The Coca-colonization of Europe: The Cultural Mission of the United States in Austria after the Second World War* (Chapel Hill, NC, 1994); Penny M. Von Eschen, *Satchmo Blows Up the World: Jazz Ambassadors Play the Cold War* (Cambridge, MA, 2004).

64   O'Brien, *Making the Americas*, pp. 179–207.

65   Ibid., 191.

further threaten the First World through overpopulation. This approach to Third World development, according to Laura Briggs, was pioneered before the war in Puerto Rico, a US colonial setting, and later applied in neo-colonial contexts in part based on studies carried out there.[66] Meanwhile, popular culture and philanthropy produced images of Asian and African children in need of parental guidance and adoption into upstanding middle-class American homes.[67] America's was to be a 'benevolent supremacy' that could guide, protect and discipline.[68]

Third World peoples had their own ideas about the nature of development that would best suit their societies, and found in the United Nations Commission for Latin America, led by Argentine economist Raúl Prebisch, an institutional base for cultivating a more nationalist approach. By the 1950s, Argentina, Chile and Uruguay were beginning to have some success strengthening their economies on this model. But whereas welfare states were part of the European bargain, and were at first tolerated in Latin America as well, managed economies that sought to nationalise private enterprises in the Third World were interpreted as extensions of the Soviet system and called for firm opposition. An increase in economic aid to Latin America, designed to direct economic development along capitalist lines, came in 1961. Casting socialism as a form of 'tyranny', President John F. Kennedy announced his 'Alliance for Progress' with a call to 'awaken ... the American revolution until it guides the struggles of people everywhere – not with an imperialism of force or fear but the rule of courage and freedom and hope for the future of man'.[69]

Force, however, was a frequent visitor and, for some, an ever-present reality in the Third World neighbourhoods of the 'Free World'. There the United States pursued its aims through economic coercion, military intervention, political subversion, support for compliant dictators and campaigns of terror.[70] National Security Council Memorandum No. 68 made it possible for the United States to curtail the sovereignty of countless nations, whenever their political processes and economic planning ran athwart US Cold War aims, such as when they pursued nationalist economic development on their own terms. Interventions followed

---

66   Briggs, *Reproducing Empire*, pp. 108, 140.
67   Christina Klein, *Cold War Orientalism: Asia in the Middlebrow Imagination* (Berkeley, CA, 2003).
68   Melani McAlister, *Epic Encounters: Culture, Media, and US Interests in the Middle East since 1945*, updated edition, with a post-9/11 chapter (Berkeley, CA, 2005), p. 47.
69   John F. Kennedy, Address by President Kennedy at a White House Reception for Latin American Diplomats and Members of Congress (13 March 1961), *Department of State Bulletin* 44/1136 (3 April 1961): pp. 471–4; Stephen G. Rabe, *The Most Dangerous Area in the World: John F. Kennedy Confronts Communist Revolution in Latin America* (Chapel Hill, NC, 1999).
70   On the relation of Third World dictators to US empire, see Eric Paul Roorda, *The Dictator Next Door: The Good Neighbor Policy and the Trujillo Regime in the Dominican Republic, 1930–1945* (Durham, NC, 1998); David Schmitz, *Thank God They're on Our Side* (Chapel Hill, NC, 1999); Gobat, *Confronting the American Dream*.

across the globe, from Iran to Guatemala, the Congo, Chile and beyond.[71] In addition to influencing elections and managing *coups d'état*, Washington disciplined those who opposed US dictates by training lethal security agencies and, as had been the case in some earlier military interventions, by overseeing torture operations that terrorised oppositional populations.[72] Founded in Panama in the mid-1940s and later relocated to the United States, the US Army's School of the Americas acquainted Latin American military officers with US American ways and aims.[73] Training manuals from the 1960s and later provide detailed evidence of training in methods of torture that had been systematically and scientifically developed for such purposes.[74]

A mixed posture towards non-Soviet empires emerged as US global aims and strategic needs evolved in the postwar period. European and Asian colonialisms were allowed to go forward when they served the interests of US empire. The military occupations of Germany and Japan served to rehabilitate these defeated powers, preparing them to function within the system of international capitalism and to host US military bases essential to the defence against Communism.[75] In a sense, the United States also 'occupied' Trinidad from 1941 to 1947, when it established military bases there, an arrangement with Britain that would play a significant and complex role in Trinidad's transition to an independent nation.[76] When the Chinese invaded and occupied Tibet in 1949, Washington chose not to engage, and

---

71   Grandin, *Empire's Workshop*, p. 49; O'Brien, *Making the Americas*, 220–27; Stephen Schlesinger and Stephen Kinzer, *Bitter Fruit: The Story of the American Coup in Guatemala* (Cambridge, MA, 1999); Walter LaFeber, *Inevitable Revolutions: The United States in Central America* (New York, 1993); J. Patrice McSherry, *Predatory States: Operation Condor and Covert War in Latin America* (New York, 2005); Adam Hochschild, *King Leopold's Ghost: A Story of Greed, Terror, and Heroism in Colonial Africa* (New York, 1998). History Commons maintains a well-documented website detailing some interventions that are not yet treated thoroughly in the historical literature. See www.historycommons.org/ project.jsp?project=us_interventions_project.

72   Grandin, *Empire's Workshop*, p. 49; Alfred W. McCoy, *A Question of Torture: CIA Interrogation, from the Cold War to the War on Terror* (New York, 2006).

73   McCoy, *A Question of Torture*.

74   Darius Rejali, *Torture and Democracy* (Princeton, NJ, 2007).

75   On Japan, see Mire Koikari, *Pedagogy of Democracy: Feminism and the Cold War in the US Occupation of Japan* (Philadelphia, PA, 2008); John W. Dower, *Embracing Defeat: Japan in the Wake of World War II* (New York, 1999). On Germany, see, Carolyn Woods Eisenberg, *Drawing the Line: The American Decision to Divide Germany, 1945–1949* (Cambridge, 1996); Jessica C.E. Gienow-Hecht, *Transmission Impossible: American Journalism as Cultural Diplomacy in Postwar Germany 1945–1955* (Baton Rouge, LA, 1999); Uta Poiger, *Jazz, Rock, and Rebels: Cold War Politics and American Culture in a Divided Germany* (Berkeley, CA, 2000); Maria Höhn, *GIs and Frauleins: The German-American Encounter in 1950s West Germany* (Chapel Hill, NC, 2002).

76   Harvey R. Neptune, *Caliban and the Yankees: Trinidad and the United States Occupation* (Chapel Hill, NC, 2007). On the rise of US empire in the British West Indies, see also Gerald Horne, *Cold War in a Hot Zone: The United States Confronts Labor and Independence Struggles in the British West Indies* (Philadelphia, PA, 2007).

in the Suez Crisis of 1956 the United States opposed British intervention in Egypt, winning credit and trust in the Middle East. As the United States established its own military bases in the region, that response shifted dramatically.[77] Elsewhere, the Pentagon eyed British holdings. In the mid-1960s, Mauritius seemed to be ideal for an Indian Ocean air base to serve US military needs in Southeast Asia. Washington called for three islands, the largest of which was Diego Garcia, to be set aside by the British from the rest of Mauritius, which would be granted independence in 1968. US claims to protect national sovereignty ran up against the inconvenient reality of a population of about 2,000 Chagossians, as the islanders are known. The US arranged a deal with the British to acquire the islands – without the consent of the Chagossians, who were deported from their homeland to make room for the base.[78] These processes all contributed to the United States' success in ringing the world with its navy, air force, army and marine corps bases, numbering over 700 in recent years.[79]

Like earlier iterations of US empire, the postwar project of building, shaping and re-directing other nations to produce cooperative military and economic partners had its domestic corollary in attempts to build, shape and re-direct the nation at home. The social organisation of race, gender, sexuality and class had the potential to bolster or undermine national interests defined in terms of capitalist markets and corporate profits. Thus US Cold War ideology, premised on a profound sensitivity to the danger of threats both external and internal, worked its way into the capillaries of the nation through hyper-differentiated, class-specific norms of gender and sexuality.[80] One expert in the growing field of sex research voiced Cold War fears when he warned in 1955 that homosexuality was linked to a dangerous long-term trend marked by 'the ascendancy of women' and 'the destruction of masculine males' that could 'foreshadow for Western civilization a decline and fall such as that of the Roman Empire'.[81] Structures of gender and sexuality were intimately linked with other axes of social power as middle-class suburban norms became the dominant manifestation of a national ideology of class.

---

77   Rashid Khalidi, *Resurrecting Empire: Western Footprints and America's Perilous Path in the Middle East* (London, 2004).

78   John Pilger, 'The Secret Files That Reveal How A Nation Was Deported', Z-Net (22 October 2004), www.zcommunications.org/the-secret-files-that-reveal-how-a-nation-was-deported-by-john-pilger. Accessed 4 August 2010. See also Marjorie Miller, 'Britain Illegally Expelled Chagos Islanders for US Base, Court Rules', *Los Angeles Times* (4 November 2000).

79   Chalmers Johnson, *The Sorrows of Empire: Militarism, Secrecy, and the End of the Republic* (New York, 2004), p. 154.

80   K.A. Cuordileone, *Manhood and American Political Culture in the Cold War* (New York, 2005); Margot Canaday, *The Straight State: Sexuality and Citizenship in Twentieth Century America* (Princeton, NJ, 2009).

81   George Henry, *All the Sexes* (1955), quoted in Donna Penn, 'The Meanings of Lesbianism in Postwar America', in Barbara Melosh (ed.), *Gender and American History* (London, 1993), p. 114.

These intertwined imperatives of gender, sexuality and class played out in particular ways in the Civil Rights movement of the 1960s, in the lives of peoples of colour and in the racial subjectivity of white US Americans. The Second World War produced an opening for advances in African-American civil rights, but only on condition that the movement shed its radical critiques of capitalism and discipline its ranks with respect to sexuality and properly gendered comportment.[82] Japanese-American citizens' experiences with military service and education derived from personal goals and patriotism, but these were also the means to liberation from wartime imprisonment in the internment camps of the west. War brides who arrived from Japan, and later Korea, and Chinese women who were admitted to the country after decades of exclusion, saw paths forward within and as part of the nation, on the condition that they accept the terms of assimilation.[83] In 1965, people of Asian heritage would be exalted as a 'model minority', their successes attributed to a culture of hard work, deployed as a tool for disciplining and excluding others.[84]

Exclusion was particularly pointed for Native Americans who had, only two decades earlier, gained legal recognition for their status as 'tribes' with rights to live by their own collective self-determination while having their status as citizens of the United States preserved and guarded. In the new Cold War context, the emphasis on cultural traditions that had animated John Collier's Indian New Deal (1934) ran headlong into the imperatives of modernisation theory, with its denigration of traditionalism and its charge that primitive peoples failed to exploit the natural resources and economic opportunities in their lands. The result was an about-face in federal policy to a programme of 'termination', by which tribes lost their status and individuals were expected to assimilate to the dominant culture.[85]

War in Vietnam broke open the conceits of sovereignty on many levels. In 1945, Ho Chi Minh declared the independence of Vietnam in language borrowed directly from the American declaration of 1776, but, like the Haitian revolutionary leader Jean-Jacques Dessalines in 1804, failed in his appeal to the United States for recognition of his nation's post-colonial independence.[86] After the Vietnamese

---

82 Brenda Gayle Plummer, *Rising Wind: Black American and US Foreign Affairs, 1935–1960* (Chapel Hill, NC, 1996); Ruth Feldstein, *Motherhood in Black and White: Race and Sex in American Liberalism, 1930–1965* (Ithaca, NY, 2000).

83 Ji-Yeon Yu, *Beyond the Shadow of Camptown: Korean Military Brides in America* (New York, 2002); Xiaolan Bao, 'When Women Arrived: The Transformation of New York's Chinatown', in Joanne Meyerowitz (ed.), *Not June Cleaver: Women and Gender in Postwar America, 1945–1960* (Philadelphia, PA, 1994); Ngai, *Impossible Subjects*; Roger Daniels, *Guarding the Golden Door: American Immigration Policy and Immigrants since 1882* (New York, 2004).

84 Thanks to Francie Chew for pointing this out.

85 On termination and the Cold War, see Paul C. Rosier, *Serving Their Country: American Indian Politics and Patriotism in the Twentieth Century* (Cambridge, MA, 2009), pp. 109–201.

86 Mark Bradley, *Imagining Vietnam and American: The Making of Postcolonial Vietnam, 1919–1950* (Chapel Hill, NC, 2000). See, also, Lloyd C. Gardner, *Approaching Vietnam: From World War II to Dienbienphu* (New York, 1988); and Marilyn B. Young, *The Vietnam Wars, 1945–1990* (New York, 1991).

defeat of the French at Dien Bien Phu in 1954, the United States, despite its nominal commitment to popular sovereignty, refused to recognise the Geneva Accords, under which the Vietnamese would set their own political course as a unified country, opting instead for a lethal and ill-conceived nation-building project below the seventeenth parallel. As US military engagement deepened, those with knowledge of Vietnamese culture and history warned that the war might be unwinnable, but decision-makers allowed themselves to be guided instead by their belief in the technical supremacy of the American war machine and by abstract statistical modelling based on data skewed by racial assumptions.[87] Such 'arrogant miscalculations' were manifestations of racism flying under the flag of neutrality and objectivity.[88] While US leaders posited abstract scientific approaches to planning and policy as the very antithesis of Soviet-style ideological politics, their own ideological shortsightedness turned out to be encoded in their uses of science and technology. With the political imperatives of the post-war racial moment, policy-makers could render the Vietnamese people neither as mere instruments of American will nor as child-like people racially unprepared for self-government. Nation-building seemed instead to posit the readiness of the Vietnamese for US-style democracy, but it proceeded on the logic that American leadership, objective modelling and overwhelming military technology would bring it about, regardless of South Vietnamese opposition to the project.

This refusal to consider the human consequences of policy did not abate after the debacle of Vietnam. Though outright racism was discredited after the Second World War, neither the success of technocratic administration and weapons technology as a means to accomplish genocide, nor their subsequent failure in Vietnam to subdue anti-capitalist opposition turned US policy-makers away from their allure. In the coming decades, *laissez-faire* economics appeared to be a technical panacea for debt crises in the Third World and for financial crises in the United States. As the International Monetary Fund imposed structural adjustment programmes on poor nations as a condition for aid, the costs in human suffering registered nowhere in its ledgers. Moreover, the distanced abstractions of techno-war continued to restrict the imagination of national security planners, the ethical scope of bomber pilots' vision and the moral compass of a civilian population presented with such supposed wonders as the 'surgical strike'.[89]

While failure in Vietnam did not dismantle US militarism, it did break open the long-term denial of US empire and strengthen opposition to it. During the war, a younger generation of US Americans broke ranks with 'the establishment', and dissent reached the higher echelons of Washington's policy-making elite. In the decades that followed, activists built international solidarity movements focused,

---

87   Adas, *Dominance by Design*, pp. 281–302.
88   The phrase is from ibid., p. 281.
89   Michael S. Sherry, *The Rise of American Air Power: The Creation of Armageddon* (New Haven, CT, 1987). See also Carol Cohn, 'Wars, Wimps, and Women: Talking Gender and Thinking War', in Miriam Cooke and Angela Woollacott (eds), *Gendering War Talk* (Princeton, NJ, 1993).

for example, on El Salvador, Nicaragua and South Africa, and circumvented the policies of their government in a sanctuary movement that welcomed refugees and asylum-seekers fleeing regimes of terror supported by the United States. These forces within the United States added their mite to a global movement against imperialism.

After the fall of Saigon, defeat fell heavy on the United States. For many it seemed not merely a military defeat but one of principle and confidence, and it arrived just as the United States faced the need for adjustment in the form of its empire.[90] Competition from Europe and Japan in the area of manufacturing, rising oil prices (a gambit to which Washington was a party, designed to trouble the nation's competitors), fiscal crisis resulting in part from the costs of the Vietnam War, stagflation and the recent exposure of the Watergate scandal troubled the nation.[91] For people whose daily life depended on automobiles, who believed in the exceptional power of their nation and whose patriotism was rooted in a deep sense of moral righteousness, this was a challenging time. In the coming decades, key industries starting with textiles and steel became more mobile. As the empire of production rusted and rotted in the cities and the heartland of a once cocky and prosperous America, racism and xenophobia surged. Immigrants arriving to staff the emerging service economy became scapegoats. African Americans took the fall for the security fears of whites, in wars on crime, drugs and welfare that cast black people as predators on an innocent white society.

The United States' subsequent attempts to establish itself as 'practically sovereign' over a rapidly changing world called for the further extension of both military force and aggressive financial policies in the late twentieth and early twenty-first centuries. In Central America, movements towards socialism and economic democracy gained strength in the 1970s in large measure in response to the legacies of heavy-handed US military intervention and strangling economic dominance, maintained in alliance with local elites.[92] Bloody 'counter-insurgency warfare' defeated these efforts to a significant degree in the 1980s, and undermined democratic struggles elsewhere in the years to come, notably in Haiti, where CIA involvement culminated in the removal of President Jean-Bertrand Aristide in 2004 to make way for a more compliant technocratic leader. Meanwhile, the Iran–Contra scandal of 1986 linked conservative engagement in Central America to the Middle East, where the Iranian Revolution of 1979 that ousted the Shah had alarmed Washington on multiple levels. Since the Second World War, the United States had relied heavily on Iran, along with Saudi Arabia and Israel, as its steady surrogates and allies in the region. By the late 1960s, US companies controlled nearly 60 per cent of Middle Eastern oil.[93] Faced with the threat to its control over that oil, President Jimmy Carter ruled that the United States would use its military force to maintain open routes for the extraction of oil from the region by significantly increasing

---

90   Harvey, *The New Imperialism*, pp. 60–63.
91   Ibid., pp. 62–4.
92   LaFeber, *Inevitable Revolutions*.
93   Harvey, *The New Imperialism*, p. 20.

the US military presence. Under three subsequent administrations, Washington fuelled the war between Iraq and Iran, patrolled no-fly zones in Iraq, and pressed aerial bombing campaigns against that nation.[94] But financial tools were also critical to late twentieth-century empire, and Bill Clinton's neo-liberal economic reforms of the 1990s, then associated with the term globalisation, deepened and extended subordination to the demands of North American power in a newly post-Soviet environment, even as economic rivals gained strength around the world.

After the aerial attacks on New York on 11 September 2001, the wars in Afghanistan and Iraq, the Bush doctrine of pre-emptive intervention, the tightening of domestic control through the Homeland Security Act, the unlawful detention of suspected terrorists at Guantanamo Naval Base, the uses of torture and its justification as a legal and acceptable tool committed the United States to an ever balder imperial stance. These changes seemed to many to constitute a sharp departure from all precedent in the United States' conduct of its international policy and in its prosecution of war and empire. In another light, however, these twenty-first-century developments were the newest manifestations of a long-standing, continuously adaptable imperial project, based, as earlier iterations had been, in the conceit that the power of the United States stood for democratic self-determination and freedom, the calculation of national interests and opportunities to pursue them.

Approaching North American Empire: The Historiography

The first decade of the twenty-first century saw an explosion of scholarship on US empire that both built on scholarly developments long in the making and responded to the ratcheting up of imperial stakes after 9/11 under President George W. Bush. Especially relevant scholarly work dates back to the 1960s, when materialist analysis of US imperialism, fed by longer-standing Marxist theoretical traditions, emerged in the context of the war in Vietnam. By the 1990s new departures in the study of empire opened the field considerably, and the richness and the challenge of this historiography lie in its sheer diversity. American colonial history, once largely preoccupied with the British colonies of the eastern seaboard, has expanded by turns in relation to transatlantic contexts, Native American histories, multiple geographical orientations and circumstances precedent to the emergence of Mexico and Canada as well as the United States.[95] The 'new western history'

---

94   Thus, the Gulf War of President George H.W. Bush was not an isolated response to the Iraqi invasion of Kuwait, but part of a longer strategy for control in the Middle East.

95   Peter Linebaugh and Marcus Rediker, *The Many Headed Hydra: Sailors, Slaves, Commoners, and the Hidden History of the Revolutionary Atlantic* (Boston, MA, 2000); Richard White, *The Middle Ground: Indians, Empires, and Republics in the Great Lakes Regions, 1650–1815* (New York, 1991); Ned Blackhawk, *Violence over the Land: Indians and Empires in the Early American West* (Cambridge, MA, 2006).

has foregrounded the problem of borders and borderlands, giving prominence to questions about migration and ethnicity.[96] Both Asian-American and Chicano histories have grown in connection with the new western history, contributing enormously to our understanding of the tensions that shaped exclusive assertions of people-hood and national belonging.[97] Overlapping with these fields, and in many respects leading the way towards new interpretations of empire in North America, Native American history has both forced and enabled cognate fields to take account of diverse indigenous perspectives and experiences and to consider the imprint of Native American leadership, institutions and cultures on the non-indigenous.[98]

Different approaches to the history of North American empires, and particularly US empire, have come from diplomatic and military history.[99] Here, treatments of empire – whether focused on continental expansion, the taking of colonies, the high imperialism of the late nineteenth century or what many diplomatic historians prefer to call 'informal empire' – build on deep familiarity with a particular state archive and an understanding of the to and fro of negotiation at the inter-state level.[100] Work focused on particular leaders – either individually or grouped in

96   Limerick, *Legacy of Conquest*; William Cronon, Howard Lamar and Jay Gitlin (eds), *Under an Open Sky: Rethinking America's Western Past* (New York, 1992); Robert V. Hine and John Mack Faragher, *The American West: A New Interpretive History* (New Haven, CT, 2000); Susan Lee Johnson, *Roaring Camp: The Social World of the California Gold Rush* (New York, 2000); Dorothy B. Fujita-Rony, *American Workers, Colonial Power: Philippine Seattle and the Transpacific West, 1919–1941* (Berkeley, CA, 2003). See also Donald Worster, *Rivers of Empire: Water, Aridity, and the Growth of the American West* (New York, 1985).

97   Sucheng Chan, *Asian Americans: An Interpretive History* (New York, 1993); George Sanchez, *Becoming Mexican American: Ethnicity, Culture, and Identity in Chicano Los Angeles, 1900–1945* (Oxford, 1993).

98   Peter C. Mancall and James H. Merrell (eds), *American Encounters: Natives and Newcomers from European Contact to Indian Removal, 1500–1850*, 2nd ed. (New York, 2007); Philip J. Deloria and Neal Salisbury (eds), *A Companion to Native American History* (Malden, MA, 2002); Daniel K. Richter, *Facing East from Indian Country: A Native History of Early America* (Cambridge, MA, 2001); Brian DeLay, *War of a Thousand Deserts: Indian Raids and the US-Mexican War* (New Haven, CT, 2008).

99   On military dimensions, see Allan R. Millett, *Semper Fidelis: The History of the United States Marine Corps* (New York, 1980); Brian McAlister Linn, *Guardians of Empire: The US Army in the Pacific, 1902–1940* (Chapel Hill, NC, 1997); Hans Schmidt, *Maverick Marine: General Smedley D. Butler and Contradictions of American Military History* (Lexington, KY, 1987); Renda, *Taking Haiti*.

100 An essential resource is the journal *Diplomatic History*, published by the Society for Historians of American Foreign Relations. For an overview of this vast literature, including the concept of 'informal empire', see Frank Ninkovich, 'The United States and Imperialism', in Robert D. Schulzinger (ed.), *A Companion to American Foreign Relations* (Malden, MA, 2006), pp. 79–102. See also Bruce Cumings, *Dominion from Sea to Sea: Pacific Ascendancy and American Power* (New Haven, CT, 2009); Michael H. Hunt, *The American Ascendancy: How the United States Gained and Wielded Global Dominance* (Chapel Hill, NC, 2007); Michael J. Hogan (ed.), *America in the World: The Historiography of American*

ways that illustrate important patterns of imperial thought, action and engagement – shed light on major policy questions and sometimes broader trends in empire-building.[101] Within diplomatic history, authors associated with the Wisconsin School (or the Open-Door School), founded by William Appleman Williams with *The Tragedy of American Diplomacy* (1959), emphasise the economic dimensions of empire.[102]

Latin American critiques of US power have also had an important impact. Raúl Prebisch, writing in the 1950s, emphasised structural inequalities between nations in his writings on dependency theory.[103] He argued that Latin American and other nations on the 'periphery' of the capitalist world economy suffered 'strangulation from abroad'.[104] In the mid-1960s the Brazilian and Chilean sociologists Fernando Henrique Cardoso (later president of Brazil) and Enzo Faletto articulated dependency theory for an even wider audience.[105] Eduardo Galeano, the Uruguayan novelist, penned a scathing critique in 1971 of European and North American domination, *Open Veins of Latin America*, which, like Ariel Dorfman and Armand Mattelart's critique of US cultural imperialism in Latin America, *How to Read Donald Duck: Imperialist Ideology in the Disney Comic*, was initially kept from US audiences.[106] By the mid-1980s, Dorfman and Mattelart, in particular, reached an enthusiastic audience in the US academy.[107]

Leading figures in African American history laid the foundations for an understanding of the connections between race and empire.[108] Important works

---

Foreign Relations since 1941 (Cambridge, 1995). A work that treats the emergence of formal and informal empire together, from the legal field, is Bartholomew H. Sparrow, *The Insular Cases and the Emergence of American Empire* (Lawrence, KS, 2006).

101 Fred Anderson and Andrew Cayton, *The Dominion of War: Empire and Liberty in North America, 1500–2000* (New York, 2005); Immerman, *Empire for Liberty*; Thomas J. McCormick and Walter LaFeber, *Behind the Throne: Servants of Power to Imperial Presidents, 1898–1968* (Madison, WI, 1993).

102 William Appleman Williams, *The Tragedy of American Diplomacy* (New York, 1959) and *Empire as a Way of Life: An Essay on the Causes and Character of America's Present Predicament along with a Few Thoughts about an Alternative* (New York, 1980); Lloyd C. Gardner (ed.), *Redefining the Past: Essays in Diplomatic History in Honor of William Appleman Williams* (Corvallis, OR, 1986).

103 Raúl Prebisch, *The Economic Development of Latin America and Its Principal Problems* (Lake Success, NY, 1950).

104 Antonio H. Obaid, Review of Raúl Prebisch, *Hacia una dinámica del desararollo para Latinoamerica* (1963), *Hispanic American Historical Review* 44/3 (1964): p. 400.

105 Fernando Henrique Cardoso and Enzo Faletto, *Dependency and Development in Latin America* (Berkeley, CA, 1979).

106 Eduardo Galeano, *Open Veins of Latin America* (New York, 1973); Ariel Dorfman and Armand Mattelart, *How to Read Donald Duck: Imperialist Ideology in the Disney Comic* (New York, 1975).

107 See also Holden and Zolov, *Latin America and the United States*, pp. 267, 272.

108 W.E.B. Du Bois, 'The African Roots of War' (1915), in Herbert Aptheker (ed.), *Writings by W.E.B. DuBois in Periodicals Edited by Others* (Millwood, NY, 1982); Rayford W. Logan, *The Betrayal of the Negro: From Rutherford B. Hayes to Woodrow Wilson* (New York, 1965);

on the continental dimensions of race appeared in the 1980s, including Reginald Horsman's account of the novel, historically specific formulations of Anglo-Saxon racism that attended US continental expansion.[109] Historians have begun to bring the history of slavery into conversation with other aspects of empire-building and national expansion, illustrating the role of expansion in tightening the slave system.[110] The significance of racism in US overseas ventures has received extensive attention, including work focused on the contributions of racism to imperialist ideology.[111] Yet racism contributed crucially to opposition to imperialism as well as to its support.[112] Recently, historians have turned to the ways imperial ventures created laboratories for the reformulation of distinct forms of racism and how different forms collided with one another in different imperial contexts.[113] African-American experiences of overseas empire were the focus of Willard Gatewood's 1975 collection of letters written home by soldiers fighting in Cuba and the Philippines.[114] In recent decades, a number of important works have turned attention to African-American opposition to empire in its various stages.[115] Historical scholarship has addressed whites who opposed US imperialism and its inherent racism as well as the role of imperialism in permitting eastern and southern European immigrants a place in the US nation, and polity, as whites.[116] The role of gender in the advent

and Willard B. Gatewood Jr, *Black Americans and the White Man's Burden, 1898–1903* (Urbana, IL, 1975).

109 Horsman, *Race and Manifest Destiny*; Hietala, *Manifest Design*. See also Michael Rogin, *Fathers and Children: Andrew Jackson and the Subjugation of the American Indian* (New York, 1975); Richard Slotkin, *Regeneration Through Violence: The Mythology of the American Frontier, 1600–1860* (Norman, OK, 1973); Richard Drinnon, *Facing West: The Metaphysics of Indian-Hating and Empire-Building* (Minneapolis, MN, 1980).

110 Adam Rothman, *Slave Country: American Expansion and the Origins of the Deep South* (Cambridge, MA, 2005); Walter Johnson, *River of Dark Dreams: Slavery, Capitalism, and Imperialism in the Mississippi Valley* (Cambridge, MA, forthcoming).

111 Michael H. Hunt, *Ideology and US Foreign Policy* (New Haven, CT, 1987); Robert Rydell, *All the World's A Fair: Visions of Empire at American International Expositions, 1876–1916* (Chicago, IL, 1984).

112 Love, *Race over Empire*; Robert Beisner, *Twelve Against Empire: The Anti-Imperialists, 1898–1900* (New York, 1968).

113 Kramer, *Blood of Government*; and 'Making Concessions: Race and Empire Revisited at the Philippine Exposition in St Louis, 1901–1905', *Radical History Review* 73 (1999): pp. 74–114; Warwick Anderson, *Colonial Pathologies: American Tropical Medicine, Race, and Hygiene in the Philippines* (Durham, NC, 2006).

114 Willard B. Gatewood, Jr, *'Smoked Yankees' and the Struggle for Empire: Letters from Negro Soldiers, 1898–1902* (Urbana, IL, 1971).

115 Hazel V. Carby, '"On the Threshold of Woman's Era": Lynching, Empire, and Sexuality in Black Feminist Theory', *Critical Inquiry* 12 (1985): pp. 262–77; Von Eschen, *Race against Empire*; Nikhil Pal Singh, *Black is a Country: Race and the Unfinished Struggle for Democracy* (Cambridge, MA, 2004).

116 Robert David Johnson, *The Peace Progressives and American Foreign Relations* (Cambridge, MA, 1995) and *Ernest Gruening and the American Dissenting Tradition* (Cambridge, MA, 1988); Renda, *Taking Haiti*, pp. 266–75; On the last point, see Matthew Jacobson, *Special*

of North American racism and the racism of white women have been important elements in feminist historical scholarship.[117]

Recently, new emphases in the international and transnational history of the United States have grown out of women's history. Studies of white US prostitutes, missionaries and wives have illuminated women's varied roles in relation to empire-building.[118] The experiences of women and men faced with the impositions of US power, and at times the openings provided by it, have illuminated the workings of North American empire at home and abroad.[119] The emergence of gender as a focus of historical scholarship beyond the history of women has also yielded important work on men and manhood in US imperial history.[120]

Cultural histories of US empire have emphasised connections across different phases of the nation's history to track the cultivation and emergence of the

---

Sorrows: The Diasporic Imagination of Irish, Polish, and Jewish Immigrants in the United States (Berkeley, CA, 2002), pp. 177–216 and *Whiteness of a Different Color: European Immigrants and the Alchemy of Race* (Cambridge, MA, 1998).

117 Jennifer L. Morgan, *Laboring Women: Reproduction and Gender in New World Slavery* (Philadelphia, PA, 2004); Louise Newman, *White Women's Rights: The Racial Origins of Feminism in the United States* (New York, 1999); Laura Wexler, *Tender Violence: Domestic Visions in an Age of US Imperialism* (Chapel Hill, NC, 2000).

118 On prostitutes, see for example Scully, 'Taking the Low Road'. On wives, see Linda Gordon, *The Great Arizona Orphan Abduction* (Cambridge, MA, 1999); Rafael, *White Love*. On missionaries, see Barbara Reeves-Ellington, Connie Shemo and Kathryn Kish Sklar (eds), *Competing Kingdoms: Women, Mission, Nation, and Empire* (Durham, NC, 2010); Karen K. Seat, *Providence Has Freed Our Hands: Women's Missions and the American Encounter with Japan* (Syracuse, NY, 2008); Peggy Pascoe, *Relations of Rescue: The Search for Female Moral Authority in the American West, 1874–1939* (Oxford, 1990); Patricia R. Hill, *The World Their Household: The American Woman's Foreign Mission Movement and Cultural Transformation, 1870–1920* (Ann Arbor, MI, 1985); Jane Hunter, *The Gospel of Gentility: American Women Missionaries in Turn-of-the-century China* (New Haven, CT, 1984).

119 Lara Putnam, *The Company They Kept: Migrants and the Politics of Gender in Caribbean Costa Rica, 1870–1960* (Chapel Hill, NC, 2002); Catherine Ceniza Choy, *Empire of Care: Nursing and Migration in Filipino American History* (Durham, NC, 2003); Findlay, *Imposing Decency*; Gordon, *The Great Arizona Orphan Abduction*; Nancy Shoemaker (ed.), *Negotiators of Change: Historical Perspectives on Native American Women* (New York, 1995); Ramona Ford, 'Native American Women: Changing Statuses, Changing Interpretations', in Elizabeth Jameson and Susan Armitage (eds), *Writing the Range: Race, Class, and Culture in the Women's West* (Norman, OK, 1997); Devon Mihesuah, *Cultivating the Rosebuds: The Education of Women at the Cherokee Female Seminary, 1851–1909* (Urbana, IL, 1998); Deena Gonzalez, *Refusing the Favor: The Spanish-Mexican Women of Santa Fe, 1820–1880* (Oxford, 1999); Vicki L. Ruiz, *Out of the Shadows: Mexican Women in Twentieth-Century America* (Oxford, 1999).

120 Amy Greenberg, *Manifest Manhood and the Antebellum American Empire* (Cambridge, 2005); Robert D. Dean, *Imperial Brotherhood: Gender and the Making of Cold War Foreign Policy* (Amherst, MA, 2001); Renda, *Taking Haiti*; Christian G. Appy (ed.), *Cold War Constructions: The Political Culture of United States Imperialism, 1945–1966* (Amherst, MA, 2000); Roorda, *Dictator Next Door*; Hoganson, *Fighting for American Manhood*; Bederman, *Manliness and Civilization*.

imperial within the frame of the national; across geopolitical borders to reveal the international and transnational dimensions of historical developments once imagined to have been merely domestic; and across disciplinary lines that once separated the study of policymaking and military history from the study of culture, gender, sexuality, myriad forms of intimacy and identity and the daily lives and experiences of immigrants and workers.[121] Particularly important are works that emphasise the complexity of intercultural connections or 'the close encounters of empire' and the perspectives of those outside the United States. Those who have worked in multiple national archives have looked to develop bi-national or multiregional frames to examine particular areas of US overseas ventures.[122]

The varied phases in the history of North American empire reveal a search for mastery – institutional, systemic, individual, subjective, cultural. But this mastery was neither all that was sought nor fully what was obtained. More was sought in the sense that myriad actors and intentions determined the shape of each new phase of empire; and more resulted, among other things, because even where hegemonic forms of empire emerged as dominant, those targeted for subordination took what was produced and put it to their own uses. While these rejoinders, like that of the Iroquois leader, Deskaheh, often did not prevail or succeed in bringing about a widely altered immediate reality, they did establish alternative interpretations and alternative paths, often shifting the terms or altering the shape of subsequent imperial domination and always revealing varied, subaltern perspectives on the realities of North American empire.

---

121 Especially notable in the evolution of this work are Amy Kaplan and Donald E. Pease (eds), *Cultures of United States Imperialism* (Durham, NC, 1993) and Edward Said, *Culture and Imperialism* (New York, 1993).

122 Gilbert M. Joseph, et al. (eds), *Close Encounters of Empire* (Durham, NC, 1998); Findlay, *Imposing Decency*; Roorda, *The Dictator Next Door*; Gobat, *Confronting the American Dream*; Kramer, *The Blood of Government*; Louis Perez, *On Becoming Cuban: Identity, Nationality, and Culture* (Chapel Hill, NC, 1999); Daniela Spenser, *The Impossible Triangle: Mexico, Soviet Russia, and the United States in the 1920s* (Durham, NC, 1999); Steve Striffler and Mark Moberg (eds), *Banana Wars: Power, Production, and History in the Americas* (Durham, NC, 2003); Silva, *Aloha Betrayed*.

Japanese Empire

Ryūta Itagaki, Satoshi Mizutani and Hideaki Tobe[1]

In a collective project such as this volume, where different modern imperial formations are discussed side by side, it is tempting to see our chapter on the Japanese Empire as an unassuming addition to what may be called 'comparative imperial studies'.[2] Just as in the British and French empires, Japanese 'modernisation' was used to justify the ways in which acquired territories and conquered peoples were transformed and mobilised ultimately for the benefits of the imperial metropole. Modern Japan emerged as a geopolitical 'centre' whose relationship to the 'peripheries' was one of hierarchical order and insurmountable inequality. Unlike its European counterparts, however, Japanese imperialism involved domination over peoples who appeared infinitely familiar to – rather than different from – the colonising nation in terms of both race and culture. Of particular importance was the fact that much of the East Asian region that fell under the sway of Japanese imperialism had already been culturally unified in its common use of Chinese characters as a medium of writing and intellectual discourse.[3] In such a context, the asymmetrical relationship across national borders was legitimised not just by the notion of *jinshu* ('race' in European racial theory),[4] but even more importantly

---

1   All three authors are members of DOSC (Doshisha Studies in Colonialism), a research group based at Doshisha University, Kyoto, Japan. We thank all other members of DOSC and Professor Sebastian Conrad of Freie Universität Berlin for their suggestions and comments on an early version of this chapter. We also thank the Japan Society for the Promotion of Science and the Institute for the Study of Humanities and Social Sciences (Doshisha University) for funding the whole research of DOSC, one of the direct results of which is this chapter .

2   All direct quotations from Japanese or Korean texts will appear in their translated form only. The titles of these non-English texts will appear in translation in the main text whilst appearing in their original forms (romanised) in the footnotes.

3   For example, this had a tremendous effect on the language and educational policies in Taiwan under Japanese rule. See Chen Peifeng, *Dōka' no Dōshōimu: Nihontouchika Taiwan no Kokugokyōikushi Saikou* (Tokyo, 2001).

4   For a cogent discussion as to how Japanese intellectuals approached the European notion of racial difference, see Tessa Morris-Suzuki, 'Debating Racial Science in Wartime Japan', *Osiris*, 2nd Series, 13 (1998): pp. 354–75.

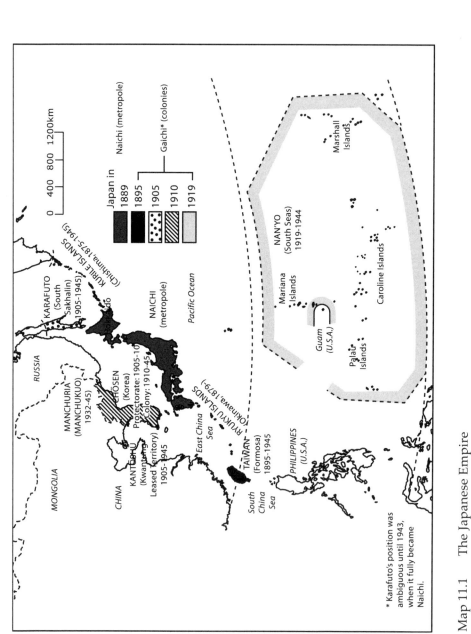

Map 11.1   The Japanese Empire

by that of *minzoku* ('ethnos') used to denote people, folk, group and nation, as well as race.[5] One of the merits of using *minzoku* was that it allowed the colonising Japanese to emphasise a putative solidarity among the 'Asian race' without apparently contradicting the rigidly hierarchised differences within it.

It would be possible – and might have been necessary under other circumstances – to continue enumerating the 'characteristics' of the Japanese Empire by comparing them with those of the 'model' empires of Britain and France. Our present chapter, however, will *not* be such a 'comparative study' of Japanese imperialism. Up to a certain point, comparison can certainly be useful, but it can also be as misleading and self-disabling. In a thought-provoking essay, Ann Stoler and Carole McGranahan have argued that all empires, even the supposedly pioneering British and French ones, claimed to be historically unique and exceptional, if in different ways and with different degrees of emphasis. This is because the creation and continuation of an empire often involved uncertainties and ambiguities, necessitating a *politics of comparison* in which the empire simultaneously emulated *and* criticised other empires.[6]

Although the comparative historiography of colonial empires is of great relevance to scholars of the Japanese Empire, who have been tempted to characterise it through comparison, there are dangers to this approach. Takeshi Komagome has recently warned that, if we are not careful, we could easily end up comparing Japanese to European colonialism without giving due attention to the ideological ways in which comparison was historically mobilised by the agents of colonialism themselves. Preoccupied with the knowledge that Japanese imperialism was both a late comer and 'non-European', comparative historiography tends to proceed by setting up 'universal' standards of colonial rule – largely based on the modern British or French experience – and turns these into evaluative criteria for historical judgement. Japanese imperialism is assessed, and its 'characteristics' carved out, with reference to these standards.[7] The imposition of such standards has led one historian to argue that the Japanese Empire was nothing but an 'anomaly of modern history', being 'the only non-Western imperium of recent times'.[8] It is doubtful if such comparative wisdom can help us to go beyond the complex politics of comparison that had actually been played by Imperial Japan itself.

Academic discourses on imperialism have thus been an integral part of the history of the politics of comparison, and this may well still obtain in our own

5   On *minzoku*, see, for example, Kevin M. Doak, 'What is a Nation and Who Belongs? National Narratives and the Ethnic Imagination in Twentieth Century Japan', *American Historical Review* 102 (1997): pp. 283–309; Richard Siddle, *Race, Resistance and the Ainu of Japan* (Oxford, 1996), pp. 6–25.

6   Ann Laura Stoler and Carole McGranahan, 'Introduction: Refiguring Imperial Terrains', in Ann Laura Stoler, Carole McGranahan and Peter C. Perdue (eds), *Imperial Formations* (Santa Fe, NM, 2007), pp. 3–42.

7   Takeshi Komagome, '"Teikoku no hazama" kara kangaeru', *Nen'pō Nihon Gendaishi* 10 (2005): pp. 1–21.

8   Mark R. Peattie, 'Introduction', in Ramon Hawley Myers, Mark R. Peattie and Qingqi Chen (eds), *The Japanese Colonial Empire, 1895–1945* (Princeton, NJ, 1984), p. 6.

post-imperial age. Indeed, how Japanese academia has responded to Anglophone post-colonial studies is itself an interesting question of comparison with distinctive political implications. For instance, the critique of Eurocentrism – perhaps the single most important practice of post-colonial theory – can never be a straightforward business in East Asia, not least because many ideologues of Japanese imperialism were themselves explicitly anti-western. In fact, some philosophers in Imperial Japan might be seen as having already been in some sense 'postmodern' in their eloquent exhortation to 'overcome modernity'.[9] Post-colonial theory can enrich the historiography of Japanese colonialism in a number of ways, but its introduction cannot be a simple matter of 'application', or 'modified use'. As Leo T.S. Ching has argued, blind acceptance of theoretical assumptions developed in Euro-American academia might have unwittingly involved us in – but not absolved us from – the politics of comparison.[10]

For example, in his preface to the Japanese translation of his own *Post-colonialism: A Very Short Introduction* (2003), Robert Young – one of the most renowned post-colonial theorists writing today – recommends the reader to rethink the Japanese Empire in light of its contributions to the anti-western cause of non-European nations since the late nineteenth century. Stressing the landmark nature of Japan's victory in the Russo-Japanese War (1905), Young points out how the rise of Japan as a modern imperial power was an inspiration for many Asians and Africans suffering under the yoke of European imperialism and racism. He even argues, in much the same way as those advocating the 'theory of colonial modernisation' (discussed below), that the rapid economic advancement of some Asian countries has been thanks to Japanese colonialism, which went to great lengths in industrialising conquered societies.[11] We do not doubt Young's great contribution to the development of post-colonial theory since the early 1990s, but, in the East Asian context, nothing is more questionable than endorsing Japan's anti-western cause in the way he does here. 'Anti-west' may have unproblematically meant anti-colonial in most cases, but not always so in the case of the Japanese Empire. Young's view overlooks how the rhetoric of anti-Eurocentrism was itself an indispensable ingredient of the politics of comparison that justified Japan's colonial domination. Because of this, a prominent post-colonial scholar ironically ends up expressing a view which is little different from the neo-colonialist perspective.

---

9   There are a number of works on the famous 'Kyoto School of Philosophy'. See, for example, Harry Harootunian, *Overcome by Modernity: History, Culture, and Community in Interwar Japan* (Princeton, NJ, 2000).

10 Leo T.S. Ching, *Becoming 'Japanese': Colonial Taiwan and the Politics of Identity Formation* (Berkeley, CA, 2001), pp. 30–1. For a similar argument, see Tani E. Barlow, 'Introduction: On "Colonial Modernity"', in Barlow (ed.), *Formations of Colonial Modernity in East Asia* (Durham, NC, 1997), p. 6.

11 Robert Young, 'Nihongoban eno jobun', in Robert Young, *Issatsu de wakaru: Post-colonialism*, trans. Tetsuya Motohashi (Tokyo, 2005) [Japanese translation of R. Young, *Post-colonialism: A Very Short Introduction* (2003)], pp. i–ix. The English original of this preface can be found at www.robertjcyoung.com/VSIJapanPreface.pdf (accessed on 29 December 2010).

Thus, while introducing the topic to an English-speaking readership, our aim here is *not* to illuminate Japanese imperial history in light of Anglophone (post-) colonial studies. Rather, this chapter is a survey of a preliminary nature, focusing less on the *history* than on the *historiography* of the Japanese Empire since the end of the Second World War. The complex trajectories of how this empire has been studied by historians are little known.[12] A history of historiographies, we hope, will turn out to be an important first step towards a new paradigm of historical research under which no modern empire – including that of Japan – would figure as either exceptional or standard.[13] Of particular importance is why the question of modernity has long been part of the historiographical discourse in Japan, Korea and elsewhere in East and Southeast Asia. One of the most hotly debated themes in today's (post-)colonial studies is the question of 'colonial modernity', and this is certainly true of the recent historiography of Japanese colonialism. We will pay great attention to this debate by focusing on the historiography of colonial Korea. But before addressing this point, the chapter will first trace the preceding developments in historiography, showing how the changing historical circumstances in East Asia – from decolonisation through the Cold War (and its end) to the rise of South Korea as one of the 'NIEs' (newly industrialising economies) – have served to delimit the modes and areas of historical research on the Japanese Empire.

Categories and Boundaries of Rule

Before embarking on a discussion of historiography, it is helpful to offer a few details on the Japanese colonial empire and its basic geopolitical structures. What did 'colonies' historically mean under Japanese rule? How were they conceptualised under the political and legal systems of the Japanese empire-state? Which territories, both within and beyond the Japanese Isles, fell into the specific category of colonies? As far as the official taxonomy goes, 1889 – the year the Imperial Constitution of Japan was enforced – marked a decisive moment. Those territories that were found within Japan's national borders before then were to be recognised later as belonging to the mainland. By definition, these territories were not colonies but instead combined to form a 'metropole' (*naichi*). On the other hand, all territories which were acquired thereafter were to be regarded as colonies. The inhabitants

---

12 However, there have appeared several review-articles of importance. See, for example, Asobu Yanagisawa and Makio Okabe, 'Kaisetsu: Teikokushugi to shokuminchi', in Yanagisawa and Okabe (eds), *Tenbō Nihonrekishi 20: Teikokushugi to Shokuminchi* (Tokyo, 2001), pp. 1–12; Makio Okabe, 'Teikokushugiron to shokuminchikenkyu', in Nihonshokuminchikenkyūkai (ed.), *Nihonshokuminchikenkyu no Genjō to Kadai* (Tokyo, 2008), pp. 20–54; Hideaki Tobe, 'Post-colonialism to teikokushikenkyū', in Nihonshokuminchikenkyūkai (ed.), *Nihonshokuminchikenkyu no Genjō to Kadai*, pp. 56–88.
13 On the need for such a holistic paradigm for research, see Stoler and McGranahan, 'Introduction'.

there were defined as the 'colonial subjects' of the empire, and were not treated equally with *naichi-jin* (people of the mainland). Following this classificatory order, Japan's colonies included Taiwan (acquired in 1895), Karafuto [Sakhalin] (1905), Korea (first made a protectorate in 1905, and later annexed as a colony in 1910), the Kwantung Leased Territory (1905) and the Nan'yō, or the equatorial Pacific Islands (conquered in 1914 and made a mandatory territory in 1922).

However, the Japanese approach to the category 'colony' was never straightforward. Since the earliest years of the Japanese colonial empire, there was a reluctance to use the term *shokuminchi* (colony). The issue was highlighted, for instance, during the parliamentary debates at the beginning of the twentieth century as to whether or not the Governor-General of Taiwan should be allowed to keep his power to issue law-like decrees independently of Tokyo, the seat of imperial government. What is noteworthy is that, though the law was eventually renewed for the third time in March 1905, many of the politicians attending the parliamentary session had expressed anxieties over the outward image of Taiwan as a colony. To be sure, Taiwan was nothing but a colony in practice, but the use of the term *shokuminchi* was 'appalling' for these politicians.[14] In the ears of many Japanese, *shokuminchi* sounded too strong a term, evoking the colonialism of white European nations. According to Shirō Kiyomiya, a Japanese scholar of constitutional law, by the 1930s *shokuminchi* was no longer the preferred term, and the term *gaichi* (outer land) had started to be used instead. In his 1944 book on the legal status of Japanese colonies, Kiyomiya argued that 'the word [*shokuminchi*] turned out to be unsuitable for correctly denoting the fundamental objective of our empire's rule of new territories'. This was because 'it easily sounded associated with such unusual ideas as imperialist exploitation, just as it did when expressed in its original form (colony in English, German and French)'.[15] Clearly, this change in nomenclature had been motivated by an imperial politics of comparison, claiming a uniqueness for Japanese imperialism – among 'modern' empires – on account of its being 'non-European'. Such comparison must be seen as problematic not least because it was meant to disguise the nature of Japanese colonialism, which in actuality was every bit as exploitative, violent and 'racist' as the colonialisms of European nations.

The system of racial classification used in the Japanese Empire also threatens to cover up what may be called modern Japan's 'internal colonialism'. The Ainu of the Ezō district (in the northeastern periphery of the archipelago) were not ethnically 'Japanese': they were an indigenous people of a largely uncultivated land, having hitherto been integrated only loosely in the mainland polity under

---

14   Yūzō Yamamoto, *Nihon Shokuminchi Keizaishikenkyū* (Nagoya, 1992), pp. 9–10. One of the most influential studies on this law has been Meitetsu Haruyama's article, 'Kindai nihon no shokuminchitōchi to Hara Takashi' published in 1980. The article has recently been reprinted in Meitetsu Haruyama, *Kindainihon to Taiwan* (Tokyo, 2008), pp. 155–221.

15   Shirō Kiyomiya, *Gaichihō Jyosetsu* (Tokyo, 1944). pp. 1–2. On the latest discussion of the legal order of the metropole and colonies under Japanese imperialism, see Toyomi Asano, *Teikokunihon no Shokuminchihōsei* (Nagoya, 2008).

the 'pre-modern' status order. The emerging Meiji state (established in 1868) was quick to claim the Ainu lands as a 'national' territory of the Japanese, naming the area Hokkaido in 1869 and sending settlers there from the mainland. Similarly, in 1879 Japan asserted that the Ryūkyū Islands (in the western Pacific Ocean at the eastern limit of the East China Sea) fell within the bounds of the new nation-state and would be called Okinawa, with the Ryūkyū Kingdom losing its 450-year independence. Today, few would deny that the integration of the Ainu and Ryūkyū peoples represents a modern form of colonialism. These peoples have been not so much *governed* as *ruled* by foreign intruders having scant regard for the former's irreducible historical particularities. It is with good reason, therefore, that a number of radical intellectuals have resisted the official distinction between *naichi* and *gaichi,* and choose to see the history of Hokkaido and Okinawa as a field for critical reflections on Japanese colonialism.[16]

The official categorisation of the politico-legal orders of Imperial Japan also obfuscates the ambivalent position occupied by Manchukuo, or the State of Manchuria (*Manshūkoku*), which lasted from 1932 to 1945. Officially, Manchukuo was not a colony but an independent nation-state. That it was merely a puppet state, existing to serve Japanese interests, has long been recognised. It is therefore crucial to go beyond its official designation as a sovereign state and read traces of imperial rule into the Manchurian experience. This does not mean that the ambivalent political status of Manchukuo should be resolved so that this form of state could be regarded as just one among other colonial states within the Japanese Empire. In a number of respects, Manchukuo was distinct from both the metropole and its formal colonies overseas. As Hiroshi Yamamoto reminds us, one of its distinguishing features was its position between the metropole and colonies, allowing it to serve as a kind of transnational hub through which both people and knowledge circulated within complex intra-imperial relations.[17] Also, for some historians, such as Prasenjit Duara, the kind of imperial rule represented by the Japanese management of Manchukuo can be seen as a new form of imperialism – imperialism without colonies – thus contributing to the ongoing effort to refresh (post-)colonial studies in English-speaking academia and beyond.[18]

Another crucial issue regarding the categories and boundaries of the Japanese empire-state is how to approach the sociocultural mechanisms of inclusion and exclusion. It has been conventionally assumed that Japanese colonialism was assimilationist in a way not dissimilar to the French model, in large part because *dōka*

---

16   See for example, David L. Howell, *Geographies of Identity in Nineteenth-Century Japan* (Berkeley, CA, 2005), pp. 110–96; Richard Siddle, *Race, Resistance and the Ainu of Japan* (Oxford, 1996); Glenn D. Hook and Richard Siddle (eds.), *Japan and Okinawa: Structure and Subjectivity* (London, 2003).

17   Hiroshi Yamamoto, 'Manshū', in Nihonshokuminchikenkyūkai, *Nihonshokuminchikenkyu*, p. 238.

18   Prasenjit Duara, 'The Imperialism of 'Free Nations': Japan, Manchukuo and the History of the Present', in Stoler, McGranahan and Perdue, *Imperial Formations*, pp. 211–39.

(assimilation) underpinned the official imperial ideology, supported by the Pan-Asianist creed of solidarity among Asians in their common cause against western imperialism. *Dōka*, however, was deeply contradictory, rhetorically hoisted to mask – rather than counteract – the intrinsic impulse of a multi-ethnic empire-state to differentiate and hierarchically order its diverse populations.[19] The imperial effort to 'Japanise' colonised subjects was never truly inclusionary in the first place. In 1918, there emerged a legal concept of *chi'iki* (region) that supposedly left no room for arbitrary interpretation. According to this framework, those overseas regions (now called Taiwan, Korea and so forth) were designated as 'different regions'. And it was in part by the Law of Family Register that the exclusionary nature of such a legal order was to be reinforced: whoever was born into a non-Japanese family could never become 'Japanese' even when he or she migrated to and became domiciled in *naichi*. Even during the last years of the war, when the Empire needed to Japanise its colonised subjects for military mobilisation, racial exclusion never ceased to be the imperial norm.[20] The Koreans in these years were even forced to discard their Korean names and adopt Japanese ones. But, even then, they never became formally *naichi-jin* because they had been 'registered' as Korean under the aforementioned law.[21]

The 'Theory of Imperialism'

Much of colonial studies before and during the Second World War was complicit with the notion of colonialism as a civilising mission. Colonialism was defined as an act of benevolence by the already civilised Japanese to bring the uncivilised 'rest' of Asia along the progressive path of history. Such a view of Japanese imperial rule survived into the postwar era, if not so openly, among state officials as well as conservative politicians and intellectuals. For example, a confidential report by the Japanese Ministry of Finance (dated 20 June 1946) insisted that the Japanese rule of Korea was not as exploitative, aggressive or authoritarian as had been claimed by critics at the end of the war. According to the report, 'there was sufficient ground to refute such criticism', since 'ideally, the Japanese government of Korea did not intend itself to be a form of so-called colonial rule'.[22] It was partly as a reaction against such trends that the human and social sciences in postwar Japan made a

19   Takeshi Komagome, *Shokuminchiteikokunihon no Bunkatōgō* (Tokyo, 1996), pp. 10–24.
20   See Setsuko Miyata, *Chōsenminshū to 'Kōminka' Seisaku* (Tokyo, 1985).
21   See, Yŏngdal Kim, 'Sōshikaimei no seido', in Yŏngdal Kim, Setsuko Miyata and T'aeho Yang (eds), *Sōshikaimei* (Tokyo, 1992), pp. 41–75.
22   Ōkurashōkanrikyoku (ed.), *Nihonjin no Kaigaikatsudo ni kansuru Rekishitekichōsa 11* (1950), pp. 1–2. The Japanese government was so quick in preparing itself against possible criticisms partly because of its fear to be forced to make formal reparations to former colonised nations. For the current debates on Japan's 'colonial responsibility', see, for example, Ryūta Itagaki, 'Datsu-reisen to shokuminchishihaisekinin no tsuikyū', in Puja Kim and Toshio Nakano (eds), *Rekishi to Sekinin* (Tokyo, 2008), pp. 260–84.

new start, and, in this, historians were to play a crucial role. Radical academics were compelled to ask why Japan's aggressive war in Asia and the Pacific – the so-called 'Fifteen Years' War' (1930–45) – occurred in the way it did, causing great suffering to millions of people in the colonies and China. The self-assigned role of postwar historiography would be to explore the possibilities for a 'new Japanese nation', whilst interrogating the sources of 'backwardness' – fascism and militarism in particular – that had plagued the old regime.

Marxism appealed to a section of Japanese historians, allowing them to view historical phenomena in terms of progress and development. The unit of analysis for their historiography was almost invariably the nation state, such that a 'national people' (*kokumin*) became the subject-agent of history. These trends were to determine how postwar Japanese historiography sought to reconstruct the modern history of East Asia. The goal of this historiography was to describe and explain the imperialist expansion of Japan and the inevitability of its collapse as manifestations of the Marxist law of history. Not surprisingly, the forms of anti-colonial nationalism whose emergence Japanese historians enthusiastically welcomed were those socialist-oriented movements of the 'Third World'. In this historiography, the idea of progress was paramount, with the overthrow of capitalist imperialism through the creation of a socialist state defined as the final stage of history. It was this Marxist reading of imperialism as a vehicle for capitalist expansion on a transnational scale – much influenced by Lenin – that heavily informed colonial studies in the first two decades after the war.

Whilst unmistakably radical, this historiography inevitably had its ethnocentric, or 'Orientalist', aspect, as post-colonial scholars have pointed out. China, for instance, was often cited as an example of Asiatic stagnation, partly because of its supposedly pre-modern social structure and partly because of its semi-colonisation.[23] Much the same was said about Korea, with the influence of Tokuzō Fukuda – an economic historian much influenced by the German Lujo Brentano – particularly important. It is not certain to what extent Fukuda's writings (published from the beginning of the century) directly influenced later historians, but they were certainly pivotal in laying down the ethnocentric framework within which the latter were to work. Thus, between the 1920s and 1945, historians readily compared Japan and Korea, arguing that the former experienced a universal historical development while the latter did not. Such a view was founded on an argument that Japanese society at its pre-capitalist stage had a secure feudal base, one comparable to that of pre-capitalist European societies. Japanese society, unlike Korean society, was thus able to move smoothly into the capitalist stage of historical development because of its mature feudal structure. Marxist historiography inherited this ethnocentric historiography: in fact, it was mainly through the spread of academic Marxism in

---

23   On this point, see Sebastian Conrad, 'What Time is Japan? Problems of Comparative (Intercultural) Historiography', *History and Theory* 38 (1999): pp. 75–81; Stefan Tanaka, *Japan's Orient: Rendering Pasts into History* (Berkeley, CA, 1993).

Japan from the 1920s onwards that the view of early modern Japan as properly feudal established itself in *Sengorekishigaku* (postwar Japanese historiography).[24]

Despite these problems, postwar historiography was significant in creating a vision of modern East Asian history as one of domination and resistance, with a clear-cut demarcation between the imperialiser and imperialised. In the 1960s, the so-called 'theory of imperialism' (*teikokushugi ron*) became influential. The origins of this theory can be traced back to the 1950s, when several historical studies of importance on China, Manchuria, South-East Asia as well as Korea, appeared. It was by building on these works that the 1960s and the early 1970s witnessed a growth of empirical studies broadly framed under the rubric of this theory. One of the clearest articulations of this theory appeared in the work of Kyōji Asada, who argued that the subject-agent of radical historical transformation would be those 'national' peoples in Asia who formed racial collectivities in the course of their united struggle against Japanese imperialism.[25]

This theory of imperialism was not without its limits. Because it prioritised economics, the theory tended to overlook the heterogeneous ways in which imperial penetration affected the formations of the colonised societies at political and sociocultural levels. Theorists of imperialism ended up proposing a rather one-dimensional view of colonial rule as an ideological justification for crude economic exploitation. The task of exploring anti-colonial resistance was simply left to those historians – usually from former colonised countries such as the two Koreas – who wrote on anti-imperialist agency from the vantage point of nationalist struggle.

This nationalist historiography tended to focus exclusively on those forms of resistance that were driven by a historical consciousness towards independent sovereignty. Such consciousness was seen as necessary for the ultimate goal of national self-determination, while forming the embryo of the development of a modern state – whether liberal or socialist – in the subsequent post-colonial era. Collaboration between nationalist and Marxist historiographies, however, did not always work harmoniously, nor did it manage to cover a sufficiently comprehensive range of areas and themes. Nationalist historiography was too constrained by its own teleological bias, downgrading the significance of any other forms of struggle, including religion-inspired popular movements. And the theory of imperialism generally failed to question the colonial situation. Its primary focus was fixed on the expansion of Japanese capitalism to Manchuria, and, through it, across mainland China as a whole: the formal colonies could thus easily be treated as of secondary importance.

---

24 Hiroshi Miyajima, 'Nihon ni okeru "kokushi" no seiritsu to kankokushi ninshiki – hōkenseiron wo chūshin ni', in Hiroshi Miyajima and Young-Deok Kim (eds), *Kindaikōryūshi to Sōgoninshiki I* (Tokyo, 2001), pp. 329–63; Hiroshi Miyajima, 'Nihonshi chōsenshi kenkyu ni okeru 'hōkensei'ron – 1910–45 nen', in Hiroshi Miyajima and Young-Deok Kim (eds), *Kindaikōryūshi to Sōgoninshiki II* (Tokyo, 2005), pp. 283–312.
25 Ryūichi Tanaka, *Manshūkoku to Nihon no Teikokushihai* (Tokyo, 2007), p. 4.

Diversification of Colonial Studies

It was primarily in the late 1970s that colonial studies grew substantially in terms of both volume and methodological pluralism. While studies on Korea and Manchuria continued to be conducted, historians also started to work seriously on colonial Taiwan for the first time in four decades.[26] The aforementioned theory of imperialism remained influential, but it was evident that a new generation of historians found its economism too outmoded. This framework appeared to be something to overcome rather than modified through internal critique.[27] It was partly because of this that the decade from the mid-1970s witnessed an immense diversification of colonial studies. Empirical studies focused on manifold aspects of imperialism, including such themes as settler colonialism and development, as well as older themes related to capitalism. This involved interdisciplinary collaborations with other research fields as diverse as fascism studies, migration studies and the history of social thought.[28]

Towards the end of the 1980s a series of events would fundamentally influence the direction of research in the following decade and, to a great extent, even today. First of all, the rise of the so-called newly industrialising economies (NIEs) was crucial because they included South Korea and Taiwan – countries whose modern history had been irreversibly marked by Japan's colonial rule. In the face of the rapid economic growth of these countries, historians were urged to ask how and to what extent Asian societies were historically transformed by Japanese colonialism, and whether or not such a transformation had a positive effect on their economic development in the post-colonial period. Have these formerly colonised societies economically 'succeeded' *because of* or *despite* Japanese rule? Secondly, the spectacular collapse of the socialist regimes in the Soviet Union and Eastern Europe rendered historical materialism irrelevant in the eyes of many historians of Japanese colonialism. Marxism would have to be fundamentally transformed if it was to remain at all relevant. It was during this period that the works of Edward Said and Benedict Anderson were translated into Japanese and widely read, serving to direct colonial studies further away from older theories of imperialism towards a multiplicity of new approaches, including post-colonial theory and the theory of nationalism.[29]

It was not necessarily the case, however, that what is called post-colonialism in English-speaking academia set up its stronghold in Japan's historical profession overnight. As far as historiography is concerned, the introduction of Anglophone post-colonialism has remained slow and rather superficial. For one thing, the way in which decolonisation proceeded in East Asia had long created a collective amnesia among the Japanese about their imperialist past. Unlike its British or French counterparts, the Japanese colonial empire suddenly disintegrated with the

---

26   Yanagisawa and Okabe, 'Kaisetsu', pp. 3–4.
27   Okabe, 'Teikokushugiron', p. 28.
28   Yanagisawa and Okabe, 'Kaisetsu', pp. 5–7.
29   Ibid., p. 8.

end of the Second World War. The loss of colonies concurred with the defeat in the war. It was topics relating to war that dominated the nation's collective memory of the recent past: colonialism tended to be recollected, if at all, only in relation to these topics. The emerging Cold War also helped Japan to evade the issue of its colonial responsibility and further indulge in the aforementioned amnesia. Thus while there emerged a public discussion on war and fascism, colonialism tended to pass into oblivion, much to the fury of the Korean and Chinese communities remaining in Japan across generations. Moreover, unlike in states of the former European empires, Japan has not accepted immigrants from ex-colonies in any large numbers. Such an anti-immigration policy not only served the postwar emergence of the myth of a homogeneous nation, but also prevented the memory of the Japanese colonial empire from being inscribed in the public consciousness of the nation.

Having said this, since the 1990s historical circles in Japan have been well aware that no historiography of modern Japan is legitimate without a central consideration of its overseas colonies. The publication of *Modern Japan and Its Colonies* (1992–93) reflected this new awareness.[30] This eight-volume series, published by Iwanami Press – arguably the most prestigious of all academic publishers in Japan – contains 89 articles on a wide range of themes. Many of the articles were prepared in the midst of the collapse of the Cold War regime, and represented both old and new historiographical perspectives. The 1990s also saw the publication of a number of influential monographs. Ichiro Tomiyama's *Modern Japan and the 'Okinawans'* (1990) has been acknowledged as a sophisticated study of the deprived lives of Okinawans. It discusses not only their subjugation on their own islands but also how they were exploited by Japanese capitalism when many of them migrated as industrial workers to urban areas in the mainland, especially Osaka. What makes this study distinctive is its sharp focus on how the two categories 'Okinawan' and 'Japanese' related to one another as these migrants were integrated into the host society as labourers.[31] Takeshi Komagome's *The Cultural Integration of the Japanese Colonial Empire* (1996) has been another influential study. Using the concept of cultural integration, it showed how the Japanese colonial empire ruled different *minzoku* groups through education and other sociocultural means. Imperial integration, however, was a deeply contradictory project. As Komagome convincingly argues, it was inevitably at odds with the exclusionary nature of Japan's nationalism, which was based on an ideology of blood purity.[32] Eiji Oguma's 800-page monograph *The Boundaries of the Japanese* (1998) is another widely known study, examining the historical construction of Japaneseness by focusing on its boundaries drawn in and around Japan's (internal) colonies – namely, Okinawa, Hokkaido, Taiwan and Korea.[33]

---

30 Shinobu Ōe, et al. (eds), *Iwanamikōza: Kindainihon to Shokuminchi*, vols 1–8 (Tokyo, 1992–93).
31 Ichiro Tomiyama, *Kindainihonshakai to 'Okinawajin'* (Tokyo, 1990).
32 Komagome, *Shokuminchiteikokunihon no Bunkatōgō*.
33 Eiji Oguma, *<Nihonjin> no Kyōkai* (Tokyo, 1998).

As these works reflect in detail, colonial studies since this period has been more concerned with *empire* than *imperialism*, and, as such, has been framed within 'empire studies', rather than the theory of imperialism. During the last decade, empire studies has marshalled a variety of approaches and perspectives, and it would be neither possible nor practical to try to enumerate all of them here.[34] Komagome nonetheless claims that this new approach typically examines how metropole and colonies intersected with one another in ways that affected their internal structures at many levels; it does not analyse the metropole and the colonies separately but attempts to explain how both developed within a relationship of mutual influence. Particularly important in this context is the question of how colonial events and experiences helped shape the contours of social formations in the metropolitan context, a dimension that has long escaped critical examination. Furthermore, empire studies overcomes the narrow economism that has plagued the theory of imperialism, opening up new research fields for political and cultural history. Such work also argues that certain categories of historical analysis, such as 'nation' and 'culture', can no longer be taken as self-evident: these units of analysis should themselves be investigated in ways that contextualise them in the imperialist production and hierarchical ordering of different identities.[35]

From the end of the 1990s to the present, this diversification has continued to reshape Japanese colonial studies. If anything, it appears to have gained further momentum, partly thanks to the increasing currency of the concept of 'colonial modernity'. This new concept – with postmodern and poststructuralist theories as its backbones – has become so influential that it is highly likely that it will find itself at the centre of historiographical debates in the years to come. Thus, in what follows, we focus attention on the historiography of Japanese colonial modernity. As a case study, we will take up recent historical research on colonial Korea.

The Idea of Colonial Modernity: The Case of Korea under Japanese Rule

In the years after 1945, historians such as Kentarō Yamabe, working on modern Korea, played a significant role in the spread of the theory of imperialism. Their work, however, was soon found problematic by other historians, particularly for its blind emphasis on the transnational spread of capitalism as the prime determinant of Korean history. The theory of imperialism seemed to imply, rather disturbingly, that the path to modern civilisation was opened up for Koreans only when capitalism arrived in Korea via Japanese colonialism: the Koreans were not

---

34   Many of its fruits have been available in an eight-volume series published by Iwanami Press, Aiko Kurasawa, et al. (eds), *Iwanamikōza: Ajia-Taiheiyōsensō*, vols 1–8 (Tokyo, 2005–2006).

35   Takeshi Komagome, '"Teikokushi" kenkyū no shatei', *Nihonshikenkyu*, 452 (2000), p. 224.

recognised as agents of their own history.[36] In fact, by the 1940s, Korean Marxist historians had already come to hold the view that Korean society had sown the seeds of its own modern historical development before it was exposed to western and Japanese influences. Such a perspective – which became dominant after the war in the North[37] – was inseparable from the perceived need to overcome the colonialist historiography of modern Korea, which regarded the country as backward compared not just with the west but also with Japan (see above). Inspired by this trend in Korea, the Japanese historian Hideki Kajimura proposed an influential 'theory of autonomous development' (naizaiteki hatten ron). This theory in many ways diametrically opposed the theory of imperialism, which was still haunted by the ghost of Fukuda's imperialist historiography. According to Kajimura, the potentials for capitalist development – regarded as a universal mode of historical development preceding socialism – were evident within Korean society.[38]

Kajimura's theory of autonomous development was widely disseminated and further refined. Into the 1980s, however, it found itself under attack by those who saw it as too constrained by its belief in the western model of modernisation as the universal measure of historical transformation. In the eyes of its critics, the theory seemed to contradict itself when it praised the self-modernisation of the Koreans whilst at the same time condemning that of the Japanese: how in such a view could modern development ever be appreciated as a universal model?[39] But the declining influence of Kajimura's radical historiography was not purely theoretical: it had a lot to do with a series of historical events in and outside the Korean peninsula. In the 1970s, the economic stagnation of North Korea gradually became evident while, in stark contrast, South Korea went through an economic miracle. This served to make forms of historical materialism (including Kajimura's) look increasingly out of touch with the realities of the present.

The economic development of South Korea has had a far-reaching impact on academic discussions of the historiography of modern Korea. Above all, it led to the emergence of the so-called 'theory of colonial modernisation', some variants of which have explicit links with the neo-conservative politics of the New Right in South Korea. It is not the case, however, that radical historiography has disappeared. The 1980s was also pivotal for South Korea in terms of political democratisation. The new political climate – coming after a long period of military dictatorship – enabled a new generation of historians to pursue a history from below: a non-elitist historiography (even influenced by Marxism) with a new interest in such research fields as popular movements.

---

36   Takashi Mitsui, 'Chōsen', in Nihonshokuminchikenkyūkai, Nihonshokuminchikenkyu, pp. 95–6. Mitsui's work concisely reviews the history of colonial studies within the field of Korean Studies in Japan and in the Koreas.
37   In the South, where Marxism was suppressed, historians tended to pursue rather conservative lines of inquiry.
38   Hideki Kajimura, Chōsen ni okeru Shihonshugi no Keisei to Tenkai (Tokyo, 1977).
39   Masahito Namiki, 'Sengonihon ni okeru Chōsenkindaishikenkyū no gendankai', Rekishihyōron, 482 (1990): pp. 21–6.

From 'Modernisation' to 'Modernity'

In the field of modern Korean history, a new historiography based on the theory of colonial modernity (*shokuminchi kindaisei ron*) emerged in the late 1990s and has grown ever more influential, provoking discussions and debates that are worth close examination. There have been several multi-authored books representing the views of this historiography, most notably, *The Modern Subject and Colonial Disciplinary Power* (1997),[40] *Colonial Modernity in Korea* (1999)[41] and *The Perspective of Colonial Modernity – Korea and Japan* (2004),[42] published in Korea, the US and Japan respectively.[43] The publication of Kyŏngdal Chŏ's recent polemic, provocatively entitled 'A Critique of the Theory of Colonial Modernity' (2008), shows the extent to which the theory of modernity has become part of the everyday talk among scholars working in the field of (post-)colonial studies.[44] Gi-Wook Shin, Michael Robinson, Hae-dong Yun, Masahito Namiki and Takenori Matsumoto are among its most vocal advocates. They do not necessarily hold the same opinions on all matters concerned: their perspectives differ in terms of kinds and areas of research and points of emphasis. However, they agree on most of the basic historiographical assumptions, allowing us to see them as loosely constituting a collective. It is to this theory and the debates circulating around it, that the rest of this chapter is devoted, but, first, it is necessary to discuss the theory of colonial modernisation (*shokuminchi kindaika ron*).

By the 1980s, the rapid economic growth of South Korea rendered the hitherto dominant theory of autonomous development obsolete. Against this historical background, Byŏngjik An, a South Korean economic historian, reversed his former position and argued that the post-independence growth of the South Korean economy had its basis in the process of modernisation initiated by the colonising Japanese. Contrary to the autonomous development thesis, he identified the colonial industrialisation of the early twentieth century as one of the main conditions for the economic catch-up of postwar South Korea.[45] An was not alone in holding this idea of the colonial origins of Korean modernisation. The early

---

40   Jingyun Kim and Gŭnsik Chŏng (eds), *Kŭndaejuch'e wa Singminji Kyuyul Kwŏlryŏk* (Seoul, 1997).

41   Gi-Wook Shin and Michael Robinson (eds), *Colonial Modernity in Korea* (Cambridge, MA, 1999).

42   Hiroshi Miyajima, Sŏngsi Lee, Hae-dong Yun and Ji-hyŏn Im (eds), *Shokuminchikindai no Shiza* (Tokyo, 2004). The Korean version of this volume is Sŏngsi Lee and Ji-hyŏn Im (eds), *Kuksa ŭi Sinhwa rul Nŏmŏsŏ* (Seoul, 2004).

43   One should remember, though, that not all contributors to these volumes, including Ryūta Itagaki and Myŏnhwoe Do, are unequivocally supportive of the notion of colonial modernity.

44   Kyŏngdal Chŏ, 'Shokuminchikindaiseiron hihan', in his *Shokuminchikichōsen no Chishikijin to Minshū* (Tokyo, 2008), pp. 9–32.

45   His first article written from this perspective was published in 1989, and a further refined version of the argument appeared in Byŏngjik An, 'Hanguk kŭnhyŏndaesa yŏngu ŭi saeroun p'aerŏdaim', *Ch'angjak gwa Bip'yŏng* 98 (1997): pp. 39–58.

1990s saw the publication of two historical studies – both by US scholars – which pointed to an inseparable link between Japanese colonialism and the development of Korean capitalist enterprises, namely Dennis L. McNamara's *The Colonial Origins of Korean Enterprise, 1910–1945* (1990) and Carter Eckert's *Offspring of Empire: The Koch'ang Kims and the Colonial Origins of Korean Capitalism 1876–1945* (1991).[46] In any case, An's view came to be perceived as representative of the theory of colonial modernisation, soon finding itself hotly debated by critics and historians. In 1997, the South-Korean journal *Creation and Criticism* organised and published a debate session where An's view was criticised by other participants. One of the clearest articulations of the counter-argument can be found in Suyŏl Hŏ, *Development without Development* (2005), which argues that colonialism never modernised Korea for Koreans themselves: if anything, it served to hold back the country while the benefits of industrialisation were stolen by the Japanese.[47]

What is characteristic of the controversy over the theory of colonial modernisation is that both proponents and critics tend to confine the debate to the narrowly economic dimension of the colonial modern. Both arguments focus their attention on the extent to which Japanese colonialism socioeconomically developed or underdeveloped Korea in quantitative, statistical terms. In contrast, the emerging theory of colonial modernity has concerned itself much more with the non-economic dimensions of colonial rule. This historiography refuses to take for granted the supposedly emancipatory nature of modernisation; rather, it calls the very *idea* of modernisation into question.

Rethinking Resistance and the Political

Another important feature of the theory of colonial modernity is its critique of conventional nationalist historiography. While acknowledging 'the important contribution that nationalist historiography has made in effectively refuting colonialist interpretations of Korean history',[48] theorists of colonial modernity have criticised nationalist historiography for its perceived moralistic reductionism and thematic narrowness. Nationalism has served as an important vehicle for the political struggle against foreign domination; nationalist historiography, however, has become too dominant, while its value-laden approach to colonial history has prevented scholars from contemplating *resistance* in any flexible way. This approach identifies 'national heroes' whilst trying to hunt down 'pro-Japanese traitors'. Ordinary Koreans are either pushed to the background as irrelevant and

---

46   Dennis L. McNamara, *The Colonial Origins of Korean Enterprise, 1910–1945* (Cambridge, 1990); Carter Eckert, *Offspring of Empire: The Koch'ang Kims and the Colonial Origins of Korean Capitalism 1876–1945* (Seattle, WA, 1991).
47   Suyŏl Hŏ, *Kaebal Omnŭn Kaebal* (Seoul, 2005).
48   Gi-Wook Shin and Michael Robinson, 'Introduction: Rethinking Colonial Korea', in Shin and Robinson, *Colonial Modernity in Korea*, p. 7.

marginal or, worse still, morally suspect for not apparently resisting – and thus ending up indirectly collaborating with – the colonising Japanese.[49] '[B]etween those who fought colonialism and everyone else who collaborated', as Gi-Wook Shin and Michael Robinson lament, 'there are no shades of gray'.[50]

Such 'shades of gray' are precisely what interest historians of colonial modernity, for they encourage historians to go beyond the dichotomous thinking of nationalist historiography, and to take a more flexible view of resistance. Efforts to change the terms of power *from within the empire* – demands for universal franchise or for a dominion status, for example – would no longer be dismissed or made secondary to the heroic anti-colonial challenge staged abroad by 'freedom fighters' in exile. Certain forms of resistance were possible precisely because the colonised engaged with the colonisers, whether one terms such engagement collaborationist or not.[51] On the part of the Japanese, colonial rule was considered possible only by achieving a degree of cultural hegemony among the colonial subjects, and such a hegemonic project would be inconceivable without the extensive employment of Koreans as intermediaries, internalising and then trying to transmit the normative and practical values of modernity introduced by the colonisers.

Both the Japanese who administered colonial rule and the Koreans who opposed it engaged in modernity, albeit for different ends. In this sense, as Andre Schmid has argued, colonialism and anti-colonialism were ambiguously complicit with one another in their common investment in colonial modernity.[52] Thus, while nationalist historiography would 'posit a disjunction between colonialism and modernity', the new historiography would see the two as inseparable.[53] Accordingly, analysis of the political should take the impact of modernity into account, and not confine its attention to *ethnos*-based nationalism: the field of inquiry should be widened to include the various forms of negotiation within what may be aptly called the colonial public sphere – local government, reformist movements in the countryside as well as in cities and feminist and labour movements whose

---

49 Kyu Hyun Kim, 'Reflections on the Problems of Colonial Modernity and "Collaboration" in Modern Korean History', *Journal of International and Area Studies* 11 (2004): p. 95; Kyu Hyun Kim, 'War and the Colonial Legacy in Recent South Korean Scholarship', *International Institute for Asian Studies Newsletter* 38 (2005): p. 6; Masahito Namiki, 'Shokuminchikōkyōsei to Chōsenshakai – shokuminchikōhanki wo chūshin ni', in Choong-Seok Park and Hiroshi Watanabe (eds), *'Bunmei', 'Kaika', 'Heiwa': Nihon to Kankoku* (Tokyo, 2006), pp. 221–46; Hae-dong Yun, 'Shokuminchininshiki no "gray zone"', *Gendaishisō*, 30/6 (2002): pp. 132–47; Hae-dong Yun, *Singminji ŭi Hwoesaekjidae* (Seoul, 2003). For a detailed discussion on the postwar politics over 'collaboration' in South Korea, see Koen De Ceuster, 'The Nation Exorcised: The Historiography of Collaboration in South Korea', *Korean Studies* 25 (2002): pp. 207–242.

50 Shin and Robinson, 'Introduction', p. 7.

51 Yun, 'Shokuminchininshiki no "gray zone"', p. 136; Yun, *Singminji ŭi Hwoesaekjidae*, p. 31.

52 Andre Schmid, *Korea between Empires, 1895–1919* (New York, 2002), pp. 266–7.

53 Shin and Robinson, 'Introduction', p. 5.

elements of resistance should be granted a historical significance of their own, and not dismissed as insufficiently 'nationalist' or 'anti-Japanese'.[54]

Haedong Yun argues that even the March First Movement – the first and last nationwide insurrection against Japanese rule – can be seen as a culmination not of an *ethno*-national consciousness but of colonial modernity. According to Yun, the ordinary people in the countryside had already been made 'modern', for instance, through a new concept of time adopted for more effective agricultural production. Korean farmers had already come to understand the world in more rational, quantitative terms. It was here that the Movement came in: it facilitated rationality's explosive spread by *nationalising* it through a nationwide struggle against Japanese rule.[55] The Movement marked the birth of a mass society, whose members had already begun to internalise modernity and move away from their pre-modern customs and traditions. Albeit still in a rough and incomplete way, ordinary Koreans had rapidly internalised values of modernity, and thus become individuals on and through whom modern disciplinary power could operate. It was on this basis of modern social transformation that nationalist elites and intellectuals could manipulate the political aspirations of the people for their own ends.

The post-nationalist approach to the political adopted by theorists of colonial modernity has been criticised on several counts. The Korean-Japanese historian Kyŏngdal Chō, for example, has argued that peasants in the Movement had their own pre-modern logic of political action. Their nationalism had nothing to do with a modern yearning for their own nation-state but was of a primordial or archaic kind. For their part, the nationalist leaders – with their internalised standards of modernity – despised the peasants for their perceived ignorance and uncontrollability, and did not even try to make modern subjects out of them.[56] Myŏnggyu Pak has criticised the new approach for a different reason. Reviewing Gi-wook Shin's work, Pak argues that their characteristic reliance on postmodern theory has allowed theorists of colonial modernity to focus exclusively on *colonial discourse*. This has not always served to widen the scope of historical inquiry as they have proclaimed, but has ironically narrowed it by confining historians' attention to the linguistic and representational features of colonialism. Shin's seemingly radical analysis of the political has not gone beyond describing the meanings of a given discourse in fragmented, isolated ways. Almost no interest has been taken in how each of such discourses was related to concrete political practices under specific historical circumstances.[57]

---

54 Yun, 'Shokuminchininshiki no "gray zone"', pp. 137–9; Yun, *Singminji ŭi Hwoesaekjidae*, pp. 34–8.

55 Hae-dong Yun, 'Shokuminchikindai to taishūshakai no tōjō', in Miyajima, Lee, Yun and Im, *Shokuminchikindai no Shiza*, p. 50; Yun Hae-dong, 'Singminji knead wa daejungsahwoe ŭi tŭngjang', in Miyajima, Lee, Yun and Im, *Kuksa ŭi Sinhwa rul Nŏmŏsŏ*, p. 236.

56 Chō, *Shokuminchikichōsen*, pp. 26–7.

57 Myŏnggyu Pak, 'Singminji yŏksa-sahoehag ŭi sigonggangsŏng e taehayŏ', in Sŏk Hyŏnho and Yu Sŏkch'un (eds), *Hyŏndae Hanguk-sahoe Sŏngkyŏk-nonjaeng* (Seoul, 2001), p. 44.

Colonial Hegemony and Discipline

From the perspective of the new historiography, older explanations of Japanese colonial power are insufficient because they have reduced the sheer complexities of colonial social interactions into a dichotomous model of political repression versus rebellion, or of economic exploitation and passive dispossession. By explaining away Japanese colonial power as an 'Asian' form of coercive violence and naked exploitation, they have masked rather than unpacked the minute structures of domination–subordination relations. Thus Chulwoo Lee argues that to dismiss Japanese colonialism as 'non-western' is to remain haunted by an old-fashioned understanding of modernity. Such a view allows for an unhelpful notion of Japanese colonialism as too 'deviant' and 'abnormal' to be framed as one among the several alternative forms of hegemonic project emerging on a global scale in the early twentieth century.[58] A new historiography based on the concept of colonial modernity would have to go beyond such self-constricting models towards one with a renewed understanding of modern domination. For Gi-Wook Shin and Michael Robinson, it is none other than the 'Foucauldian notion of discourse and the Gramscian conception of hegemony' that help us to understand such domination.[59]

Through appropriating such post-Marxist and post-structuralist perspectives on the nature of power, the theory of colonial modernity has called for a comprehensive re-examination of the role of intermediary classes. Whether as subordinate bureaucrats, school teachers, doctors or social reformers, the emerging classes of Korean intermediaries set about 'civilising and enlightening' the masses. Their historical significance became crucial in the period following the 1919 uprising, when the Governor-General's office embarked on the so-called Cultural Rule in place of the former Military Rule.

For the authors of *The Modern Subject and Colonial Disciplinary Power*, to examine the operations of colonial disciplinary power as observed in schools, factories, the family and hospitals, and in social-reformist measures, has been an indispensable *political* practice.[60] The authors identified the origins of today's social contradictions in the colonial period. In other words, the hegemonic power of colonial modernity was such that its imprints have been found in post-colonial South Korean society. But at this point one might wonder: what occurred in the countryside where the majority of the Koreans lived in this period? Was not modern disciplinary power able to operate only through specific types of institutions located predominantly in the urban areas? Theorists of colonial modernity do recognise that there was a characteristic unevenness in the way in which modern institutions were distributed. They also try to show, however, that the disparity between the modernising urban centres and the under-modernised peripheries in the countryside did not prevent modernity from extending the spheres of its hegemonic influence into the latter.

---

58   Chulwoo Lee, 'Modernity, Legality, and Power in Korea Under Japanese Rule', in Shin and Robinson, *Colonial Modernity in Korea*, p. 22.

59   Shin and Robinson, 'Introduction', p. 7.

60   Kim and Chŏng (eds), *Kŭndaejuch'e wa Singminji Kyuyul Kwŏlryŏk.*

One crucial example of such hegemonic projects in the countryside was an agrarian reform movement called the Rural Revitalisation Campaign (1932–40). Through this reform, the colonial state sought to extend its control over village communities by using young Korean villagers as intermediary agents. Launched by the colonial government to alleviate the economic distress of Korean villages, the reform was a deeply ideological project with the covert aim of deflecting class conflicts whilst facilitating a penetration of state control deep into the quotidian lives of agrarian society. The former model of colonial control, heavily dependent upon the traditional authority of Korean landowners, was to be replaced by a new model based on modern disciplinary power inscribed in the inner subjectivity of each village member. For Go-Wook Shin and Do-Hyun Han, such shift signalled a growing interest in the domination of consciousness: 'Although the Japanese never abandoned coercion and repression as means of colonial control, they also attempted to exercise ideological/hegemonic domination.'[61]

A similar argument has been made by Takenori Matsumoto in his study of sanitation policy in the Campaign. Matsumoto focuses on how some Korean intermediary groups – including local civil servants, private reformers and some young villagers – became involved in what was essentially a colonialist initiative. They took reform as an opportunity to teach the values of modern public health to the uneducated masses in the countryside. For their part, the common people in the village would gradually integrate the norms of modern sanitation which used to be foreign to them. In actuality, farmers had only limited experiences of modern medicine and sanitation, but through the guidance of these intermediary groups they had come to possess at least some knowledge of them. This helped the formation of a discursive basis upon which the village farmers willingly embraced, rather than simply being coerced into, the modern values of sanitation. The colonial state would now be able to create a modern space with minimum costs, further extending areas in which they could intervene.[62]

For Kyŏngdal Chō, however, such a model of historical explanation is hardly acceptable. Chō criticises Matsumoto for assuming a docile readiness on the part of ordinary villagers to accept modern ideas. Chō argues that the very notion of colonial modernity is deeply flawed because its effort at cultural hegemonisation stumbled in the face of an impenetrable world of ordinary villagers deeply influenced by religious and folkloric world-views inherited from the early modern age. In *The History of Korean Popular Movements* (2002), he argues that non-elite Koreans, who were largely illiterate (illiteracy ran at 77.7 per cent in 1930), were not merely unable to absorb, but were defiantly indifferent to the lofty ideals of civilisation and enlightenment preached by the literati, let alone the colonising Japanese. The self-modernising elites did not so much try to understand the non-elites as simply regard them as a target for civilisation. In the meanwhile, the

---

61   Gi-Wook Shin and Do-HyunHan, 'Colonial Corporatism: The Rural Revitalization Campaign, 1932–1940', in Shin and Robinson, *Colonial Modernity in Korea*, p. 71.

62   Takenori Matsumoto, *Chōsen'nōson no <Shokuminchikindai> keiken* (Tokyo, 2005), pp. 49–94.

common people themselves remained uninfluenced by the secularised ideals of order and progress disseminated by the elites, living instead in a world of their own which was based on an early-modern sense of 'community'.[63]

The Emergence of Hybrid Identities

The notion of multiple and hybrid identities has strongly informed the development of the theory of colonial modernity. The historical construction of gender identities has been discussed most widely, and particularly noteworthy is the recent growth of interest taken in the so-called 'new women' – that is, Korean women who aspired to embrace modernity during the period of Japanese rule.[64] The formation of this new identity has been theorised hand-in-hand with the emerging notion of colonial modernity. One of the most sharply articulated examples is found in Kyeong-Hee Choi's work collected in *Colonial Modernity in Korea*, where she reads a paradoxical impact of colonial modernity into Wansô Pak's novel 'Mother's Stake 1' (1980), a story about a Korean mother who desires to raise her daughter as a 'modern' girl freed from the shackles and prejudices of the patriarchal system of traditional Korean society.[65] According to Choi, the problem for the emerging new women in Korea was that modernity came from their foreign oppressors, the Japanese. The more they desired to be liberated from the patriarchal order of their own society, the more they found themselves under the hegemony of Japanese colonialism. The point of Choi's analysis of the novel is to think through this paradoxical attitude of Korean women towards modernity, foregrounding a hybrid mode of identity which was neither colonial nor national. Choi argues that the grand narrative of nationalist historiography is inadequate not just because of its male-centredness but because of its problematic tendency to suppress what Homi Bhabha calls 'the anxious, split truths and double destinies of those who are minoritised and marginalized'.[66]

Burgeoning research on the new woman has shed light on the historical formations of gendered identities in colonial Korea. Japanese colonialism did in some ways contribute to the inclusion of Korean women into the sphere of

---

63   Kyŏngdal Chō, *Chōsen'minshū'undō no Tenkai* (Tokyo, 2002), pp. 239–41.

64   For one of the most recent discussions of this subject in English, see Theodore Jun Yoo, *The Politics of Gender in Colonial Korea: Education, Labor, and Health, 1910–1945* (Berkeley, CA, 2008), pp. 58–94.

65   Kyeong Hee Choi, 'Neither Colonial Nor National: The Making of the "New Woman" in Pak Wansŏ's "Mother's Stake I"', in Shin and Robinson, *Colonial Modernity in Korea*, pp. 221–47; for a critical review of Choi's essay, see Ha Jŏng-il, 'Haebang Jŏnhusa ŭi Jaeinsik ŭi minjok gwa minjokjuŭi: Cho Gwanja wa Kim Ch'ŏl ŭl Chungsim uro', in *Ch'ang-jak gwa Bip'yŏng* 135 (2007): pp. 350–51.

66   The expressions are taken from Homi K. Bhabha, 'Anxious Nations, Nervous States', in Joan Copjec (ed.), *Supposing the Subject* (London, 1994), p. 216, quoted in Choi, 'Neither Colonial Nor National', p. 222.

modernity; however, protagonists tend to be rather vague about the actual degree of such inclusion – particularly in quantitative terms – making them vulnerable to counter-arguments. For example, exactly *which sections* and *how many* of the female population came from family backgrounds economically secure enough to allow them to pursue a career or way of life that made them modern women? And all this, at a time when the majority of colonised Koreans, men as well as women, were severely disadvantaged compared to the resident Japanese in terms of formal school education?[67] Here Puja Kim's detailed historical research, which draws on numerous statistical data, is highly suggestive. It demonstrates that the deprivation of educational opportunities was gendered, Korean women being more deprived than Korean men. But this was not all: there was also an unmistakable class gap *among Korean women themselves*, leaving a mere handful in a privileged position to practise new womanhood.[68] Furthermore, Sujin Kim has shown that even those more fortunate Korean women who did receive education in colonial Seoul often found it difficult to make their way into the clerical and service sectors of the economy. Japanese women dominated the modern sector of occupations available to educated women.[69]

Kim's research suggest that discriminations based on *minzoku* and class remained fundamental to the formation of gender identities under colonial rule. The increasingly fashionable focus on hybrid identities may produce stimulating reflections on modernity, but it does not always help us to deal with the discriminatory practices of colonialism. As Myŏnhwoe Do has pointed out, to focus merely on the hybrid, multiple nature of identity formations does not explain why and how only *certain* modes of identity, particularly those based on *minzoku* and class, became more relevant under particular historical circumstances.[70] In understanding such hybrid identities as new womanhood, it is almost as important to acknowledge the socioeconomic restrictions that were imposed on them: the hybridity of the groups in question should be carefully measured vis-à-vis the structured hierarchies of colonial society, which often left their position simply *marginalised*, rather than *ambivalent* or *in-between*.

Retreat of the Colonial

The idea of colonial modernity is pervasive in recent work on Japanese imperialism. Albeit in different degrees and kinds, *all* colonial subjects – regardless of their class,

---

67 Sŏngch'ŏl Oh, *Singminji Ch'odŭng Kyoyug ŭi Hyŏngsŏng* (Seoul, 2000).

68 Puja Kim, *Shokuminchikichōsen no Kyōiku to Gender* (Kanagawa, 2005).

69 Sujin Kim, '1930 nyŏndae Kyŏngsŏng ŭi Yŏhaksaeng gwa "Chigŏp Buin" ŭl t'onghae bon sinyŏsŏng ŭi kasisŏng gwa chubyŏnsŏng', in Jeuk Kon and Gŭnsik Chŏng (eds), *Sinminji ŭi Ilsang: Chibae wa Kyunyŏl* (Seoul, 2006), pp. 489–524.

70 Myŏnhwoe Do, 'Singminjuŭi ga nurak doen "singminji kŭndaesŏng"', *Yŏksa Munje Yŏngu* 7 (2001), pp. 268–9.

status or gender – are supposed to have come under the hegemonic influence of Japanese rule. By focusing on the analysis of the modern, the theory of colonial modernity has extended the sphere of the colonial, thematising areas that had been completely ignored by conventional historiographies, whether colonialist or nationalist. For some scholars, however, this has caused a retreat of the colonial within historiography. Reviewing *Colonial Modernity in Korea*, for example, Myŏnhwoe Do expressed discomfort that the authors give too little weight to colonialism: he argues that the book's explorations of modernity have been at the expense of the significance of colonialism, the effects of which have been downplayed.[71] Myŏnggyu Pak makes the same point, complaining that 'the colonial gets reduced into just another word for colonial modernity, as the former is treated merely as one particular aspect of the latter'. Theorists of colonial modernity have been trapped in 'a confusion caused by failing to see the colonial as a structure connected with specific times and places'.[72]

Indeed, it is as though the question 'What is modernity?' has become more important than 'What is colonialism?' Or perhaps it would be more correct to say that the colonial context has been given by the theory of colonial modernity a privileged position from which to deconstruct modernity. The idea of colonial modernity is necessary, argues Soon-Won Park, precisely because it can show that, when engaged by Koreans, modernity could be altered into something beyond the intentions of the colonising Japanese.[73] The ambiguous inclusion of the colonised Korean into the sphere of modernity must be recognised by historians for its very ambiguity: it would destabilise the dichotomous distinction between the Japanese and the Koreans, between the coloniser and the colonised. It is at this juncture that Takenori Matsumoto describes Korean civil servants as exemplifying a characteristically ambivalent mode of identity which is not dissimilar to 'colonial mimicry', famously formulated by post-colonial theorist Homi K. Bhabha.[74] The sort of colonial ambivalence as formulated by such postmodern theorists as Bhabha presupposes the inclusion of the colonised into the sphere of a transplanted modernity, via their representation under categories of colonial discourse.[75] As we have seen, such an inclusionary model of colonial modernity has been severely criticised by Kyŏngdal Chō. For Chō, the very use of modernity as an analytic category is outrightly harmful to the paradigmatic construction of his own historiography for and about the people.

On the surface, the two perspectives above are diametrically opposed to one another. But is this really the case? Following Su Hŏ's lead, a suggestive comparison may be made here with the case of the Subaltern Studies group (hereafter SS).

---

71   Ibid., pp. 263–5.
72   Pak, 'Singminji yŏksa-sahoehag', pp. 51–2.
73   Soon-Won Park, 'Colonial Industrial Growth and the Emergence of the Korean Working Class', in Shin and Robinson, *Colonial Modernity in Korea*, pp. 131, 159.
74   Matsumoto, *Chōsen'nōson*, p. 128.
75   Satoshi Mizutani, 'Hybridity and History: A Critical Reflection on Homi K. Bhabha's "Post-Historical" Thought', *Zinbun* 41 (2008): p. 16.

Hŏ points out, first of all, that the kind of *minshū* historiography represented by Chō is rather similar to the SS in its early stage with Ranajit Guha as its theoretical leader.[76] As Kyŏngdal Chō himself has made clear in a recent essay, his historiography has affinities with the SS during its 'history from below' phase, when the primary focus was on the 'autonomous' nature of Indian popular uprisings under British rule.[77] Since his first monograph, *Heretical Popular Uprisings* (1998), Chō's own work has been couched in the view that in Korea, from the nineteenth century onwards, popular insurgencies were anchored in an 'autonomous nature' of the common people's world.[78] After recognising such convergence, the subsequent step of Hŏ's argument is that *minshū* historiography not only resembles the initial phase of the SS but also shares the latter's theoretical inconsistencies.

Hŏ reminds us that the SS's early emphasis on autonomy was criticised from within by those who took a 'deconstructive' approach, as opposed to the 'constructivist' one, to the question of subaltern history. While the former approach still relies on history as a means to represent the authentic voice of the subaltern,[79] the latter questions the very idea of historical representation, calling instead upon an unrepresentable otherness of the subaltern.[80] From the perspective of the latter, the former has not freed itself from an 'essentialist' view of history: if the subalterns were completely autonomous from the modern world, how can a historian ever represent their subjectivity – supposedly incommensurable to the modern mind – using the linguistic and conceptual conventions of modern historiography? Hŏ's point is that *minshū* historiography is surely admirable for its emphasis on historical agency, but at the same time is potentially vulnerable to the kind of critique directed at the early SS. In the case of the SS, many of its most prominent members, including Guha himself, have moved with relative ease from their initial 'constructivist' approach to a 'deconstructive' one.[81] It remains to be seen how *minshū* historiography will respond to such possible criticism from the 'deconstructionist' position. At present, Hŏ argues that 'the same historiography has not thoroughly endeavoured to overcome the difficulties involved in such process of representation (even though it does take note of the difficulties themselves). Consequently, its representation of the common people does not seem very convincing.'[82]

---

76   Su Hŏ, 'Saeroun singminji yŏngu ŭi hyŏnjuso: "Singminji kŭndae" wa "minjungsa" rŭl chungsim ŭro', *Yŏksa munje yŏngu* 16 (2006): p. 24.
77   Chō, *Shokuminchikichōsen*, pp. 23–4.
78   Kyŏngdal Chō, *Itan no Minshūhanran* (Tokyo, 1998).
79   See Ranajit Guha, *Elementary Aspects of Peasant Insurgency in Colonial India* (Durham, NC, 1999) as the most representative of this approach.
80   One of the most famous works based on this approach is Dipesh Chakrabarty, *Provincializing Europe: Post-colonial Thought and Historical Difference* (Princeton, NJ, 2000).
81   Guha's recent book is on historiography. See Ranajit Guha, *History at the Limit of World-History* (New York, 2002). For an account of this paradigm shift, see Gyan Prakash, 'Post-colonial Criticism and Indian Historiography', *Social Text* 31/32 (1992): p. 9.
82   Hŏ, 'Saeroun singminji', p. 24.

This problem of representation notwithstanding, *minshū* historiography offers a useful corrective against exaggerating the significance of colonial modernity as a hegemonic power. First of all, its idea of the archaic nature of political action among ordinary Koreans may be extended to include the world of the educated classes, exploring their possibly 'non-modern' behaviours: even when and where Korean intermediaries were assimilated into the sphere of 'colonial modernity', their aspirations and logics of action should not always have matched the intentions of the imperial rulers. Second, it calls into question the very idea of the inclusion of colonised elites. In the paradigm of colonial modernity, their experience of colonialism appears more about inclusion than about exclusion, compared to that of the classes below them. Yet such a picture does not pay sufficient attention to the extent to which Imperial Japan did *not* intend to assimilate the Koreans as much as it actually did. As Takeshi Komagome forcefully argues, in Korea (as well as in Taiwan), the Governor-General's government had the power to decide what kinds of modernity were to be promoted, whilst simultaneously leaving other kinds unavailable to the colonised.[83] Even the elite classes could easily remain excluded from the realm of modernity simply because they were not Japanese but Korean.

In this context, one crucial problem of the idea of colonial modernity is its disproportionate interest in the 'metaphysical' aspect of modernity to the relative neglect of the social: it has tended to lead its supporters and critics alike to reduce the metropole into an abstract, anonymous force of modern historical transformation. Thus, in discussing Gi-wook Shin's work, Myŏnggyu Pak has shrewdly pointed out that while Ann Stoler and Frederick Cooper have argued for treating metropolitan and colonial social formations under a single analytic framework,[84] 'most of Gi-wook Shin's work has dealt with the colony as a standalone entity with its [imperial] centre having disappeared from view'; 'No traces of the imperial metropole can be discerned in such a colony as is engaged by him.'[85] The asymmetrical relationship between the metropole and the colony, or between the Japanese and the Koreans, should be examined on concrete social levels as well as on discursive ones: it should not be conceived of merely as a hegemonic relationship between the giver and the recipient of modern ideas and institutions.

In the Japanese Empire, the Koreans were ruled under a legal system different from the one for *naichi-jin*. The Imperial Diet's 'Law for the Election of the Members of the House of Representatives' was not extended to Korea. Nor were any independent legislative bodies established there. Even more importantly for our discussion here, Korean civil servants were placed in a *structurally* subordinated position within the imperial bureaucratic regime. Those Koreans who worked as intermediary agents of imperial rule also found themselves stuck in a structure of organised exclusion and exploitation. They were certainly more privileged than

---

83 Komagome, *Shokuminchiteikokunihon*, p. 371.
84 See Frederick Cooper and Ann Laura Stoler (eds), *Tensions of Empire: Colonial Cultures in a Bourgeois World* (Berkeley, CA, 1997), pp. 238–62.
85 Pak, 'Singminji yŏksa-sahoehag', pp. 42–3.

ordinary Koreans, but their colonial experience turned out to be as much marked by colonial racism as by their equivocal relationship to modernity.

To illustrate this point, the historian Makiko Okamoto's recent work on the colonial civil services in Korea and Taiwan is highly suggestive. In her thoroughly researched historical study, *The Political History of Colonial Bureaucrats* (2008), Okamoto demonstrates that the recruitment and promotion systems involving Japanese and Korean civil servants had been doubly hierarchised. On the one hand, the Japanese servants working in colonial Korea had a lower prestige than those selected for service in the imperial metropole. On the other hand, these same Japanese enjoyed a higher status and greater economic benefits than their Korean colleagues. Japanese civil servants were given special benefits and allowances, the official explanation for which was that they deserved special treatment for serving in a foreign milieu. All such privileges were denied to native Koreans, making their terms of employment unattractive in comparison. Such a gap, it should be noted, corresponded to the insurmountable barriers of *minzoku* that had been erected between ruler and ruled despite the Pan-Asianist ideology of assimilation. Okamoto's meticulous historical research clearly shows that Korean civil servants were sharply aware of the discriminatory dimension frustrating their career prospects.[86]

The awareness of material inequalities, as shown in the case of Korean civil servants, should be recognised as *historical*, and as such would not be adequately framed by the paradigm of colonial modernity with its post-historicist prioritisation of cultural hybridity. It was *not* that awareness came into being because the intermediary Koreans in question were under the hegemonic influence of the 'mimicable' Japanese, but rather their consciousness became politically charged precisely because they realised they had been excluded and materially exploited. Their colonial experience cannot simply be explained either by their supposed proximity to modernity or by their putative separation from the world of the common people.

Also problematic is a tendency among some theorists of colonial modernity to stress modernity disproportionally, making it seem as if all colonial phenomena had their origins in the advent and spread of modernity in Korea. According to such a historical perspective, the social order of the pre-colonial era crumbled away rapidly, freeing the colonised people from early modern customs and conventions. Such a view does not give sufficient consideration as to how, under colonialism, newness and oldness interacted in complex and shifting ways. Neither does it do justice to the fact that the actors of history were not confined to the usual three – the colonisers, the intermediaries and the subaltern classes. In Sangju (a region in the southeast of the peninsula), for example, Korean society came to exhibit the formations of a multi-layered social structure, where colonial power defined – and operated through – the internal tensions between older and modern values, between traditional and emerging new elites. The value system of the early modern order did not simply disappear even in the 1920s and 1930s. Within the administrative

---

86 Makiko Okamoto, *Shokuminchikanryō no Seijishi* (Tokyo, 2008), pp. 659–734.

unit called *ŭp*, the elites of Sangju continued to exert a degree of social influence over the population, utilising or even extending clan-based networks surviving from the early modern period. In terms of civilisation and enlightenment, they commanded the respect of the people because of their mastery of classical Chinese. Despite the gradual spread of modern 'new schools' under Japanese rule, these elites managed to establish old-style ones, catering to the needs of those children whose parents could not afford to send them to the new schools. This does not mean that the ways of the early modern survived into the colonial period in their purely original form. However, such a development can be taken to imply that modernity did not infiltrate into the colonised society as readily as the notion of colonial modernity seems to imply. There certainly were those 'new' Korean elites who identified more with the modern than the early modern culture, but they found themselves in conflict with these other elites, whose influence over the people in the district could be far-reaching.[87]

If colonialism was so fundamental to the formation of new social structures, it was not simply because it transplanted modernity but because it deeply affected the complex and even contradictory ways in which Korean society shifted from its early modern to its modern phase of historical formation. Colonial power had manifold facets – physical violence, political coercion and economic exploitation as well as cultural-hegemonic work – and all these had to operate in and through the multi-layered structures of a society in transition. This multifarious nature of the colonising process would not be adequately captured by any generalised ideas of colonial modernity. The relationship between the colonial and the modern should remain a matter of cautious historical investigation. No doubt the theory of colonial modernity has done much to open up new areas of inquiry. Yet it will also be necessary for future studies of the Japanese Empire to rethink these new areas in ways that put colonialism in question more squarely.

---

87   On these points, see Ryūta Itagaki, *Chōsenkindai no Rekishiminzokushi* (Tokyo, 2008).

PART III
Themes

Governance

Jon E. Wilson

Governance is hard to write about. Colonial writing about it was perfunctory and formulaic. Texts about colonial governance were produced in such vast quantities they are almost impossible for the historian to handle successfully; historians find narratives about conquest or academic accounts of the non-European world far more interesting to read. As a consequence, the history of governance often gets submerged under more exciting stories about either elite politics or – more recently – narratives about the academic knowledge produced in Europe about the non-European world. In either case, there is a danger of reducing the complex and uncertain practices of colonial administration to the history of the rather more stable categories, concepts and stereotypes that metropolitan Europeans used to describe the non-European world.

Colonial discourses centred in Europe seem to have had only a marginal relationship to the practice of colonial governance itself. The languages articulated in Oxford or Leiden Universities, or in the council rooms of London or Paris, cannot be straightforwardly used to explain the practice of imperial rule in the dispersed scenes of colonial governance. Administrators rarely possessed a very clear set of concepts to understand what they were doing in the first place, regardless of the source of those ideas. In fact, throughout the colonised world, colonial officials experienced a pervasive form of anxiety about both the purpose of colonial rule, and the sources of knowledge used to guide its conduct. That anxiety was caused by the gap between what colonial officials actually did and what they thought they were supposed to be doing. It is this central component within the world of colonial governance – which played an important role in the rise, character and fall of European empires throughout the non-European world – that this chapter traces.

More than anything else, imperial governance was boring for those doing it. Battles, violent uprisings, thrilling trials, heroic missionary expeditions and daring acts of espionage were of course central to imperial propaganda published in Europe. But they occupied a very small part of the time which most European imperial officials – or their much larger number of African, Asian or Caribbean employees – devoted to the task of actually governing empire. The actions which had the greatest impact on the non-European populations ruled by European imperial regimes were small in scale and dull for those who carried them out. These are the actions that Jeffrey Auerbach describes as 'the banality of empire'.[1] Tasks such as the delineation of a landed estate's boundary, the collection of land or property taxes, the adjudication of a property dispute, or the licensing and regulation of this or that species of local trade often had the implicit threat of devastating violence behind them. Frequently they were possible only because a colonial state had established itself through acts of conquest, war and treachery. But these tasks were neither violent nor exciting in themselves, and so often tended to be overlooked. The seventeenth-century Spanish jurist and colonial governor Geronimo de Uztáriz complained that 'historians [were] more inclined to speak of battles, sieges, revolutions and other strange events, than to transmit to the public measures in favour of commerce and other policies of government'.[2] More than a century and half and a world later, the *Calcutta Review* noted 'the frightful boredom, loneliness, absence of amusement' of the life of the British administrator in India. The judge Courtney Smith wrote that 'terrible sameness pervades our life, time wears on heavily and all my wishes and thoughts tend to an abandonment of this service'.[3] Incrementally, though, the acts in which the readers of the *Calcutta Review* engaged dramatically transformed the behaviour of the populations they ruled.

This chapter emphasises the differences rather than similarities between forms of colonial governance, stressing in particular the rupture between early modern and modern forms of empire. If it has a single argument, the chapter suggests that imperial governance was intrinsically crisis-prone. And if that crisis-prone character had a single origin, it lay with the gap which existed between the banal actions that colonial governors performed in specific colonial contexts, and the exciting narratives and often rather extraordinary ambitions that imperial officers and politicians used to explain what they were doing in large parts of the non-European world.

But what is 'governance'? Since the last decade of the twentieth century, the word has become increasingly popular within both academic and broader public writing, and has a variety of meanings. At its most basic level 'governance' consists in the act of trying to get someone else to do what the governing institution or individual wants them to do. Governance involves small-scale acts which cajole, coerce or persuade people to do things which the governing power claims are in their best interests: refraining from charging their tenants or customers too much, paying their taxes on time, improving the kind of crops they cultivate, celebrating religious festivals in an orderly way, and so on.

Governance is different from the exercise of sovereignty. Firstly, governance can be carried out by institutions that don't have sovereign power (missionaries,

---

1   Jeffrey Auerbach, 'Imperial Boredom', *Common Knowledge* 11/2 (2005): pp. 283–305.
2   Geronimo de Uztáriz, *Theory and Practice of Commerce and Maritime Affairs* (London, 1751), vol. 1, p. 186, quoted by Gabriel Paquette, *Enlightenment, Governance and Reform in Spain and its Empire, 1759–1808* (Basingstoke, 2008), p. 152.
3   Anon., 'India in English Literature', *Calcutta Review* 65 (1859): p. 46; Courtney Smith to his father, 30 April 1831, Mss. Eur. C247, Oriental and India Office Collections, British Library, London.

or private corporations), and sovereigns can exist without governing. The idea of governance presupposes the operation of power through complex systems and networks; it assumes that power is far more complex than the ability of a legitimate sovereign to command.[4] Secondly, governance presupposes that the welfare of individual subjects is the main object of rule. But 'welfare' is understood in terms defined by whoever governs. Local acts of governance are, therefore, often accompanied by efforts to delegitimise the knowledge-systems and forms of local understanding with which the subjects of colonial rule previously understood their lives. Governance presumes intention, that peoples are driven by rational motives that the ruler then tries to shape. The institutions of governance rest, however, on the assumption that the governor knows what is best for those being ruled.[5] Institutions articulating this language of welfare often treat their subjects as if they were concerned with nothing other than their own material self-interest. The process of governance tries to make the complex ethical and political personalities of the non-European peoples it rules into easily classifiable and governable, economic and sometimes cultural subjects. In doing so, colonial governors imagine their subjects to be purely economic rather than political and ethical beings. Colonial administration often denies the people it rules the ability to articulate their own political views with any authority. Inevitably, though, imperial policies and practices are appropriated and resisted by subjects whose political intentions cannot be suppressed, making resistance an ever-present part of the logic of colonial governance.

The kind of governance with which this chapter is primarily concerned emerged as a consequence of the processes and practices of imperial rule during the late eighteenth and early nineteenth centuries. It was preceded by a phase of imperial politics in which both European and Asian 'empires' were conceived more as a disparate series of largely self-governing polities clustered under a single monarch, rather than as a single machinery for governing a population dispersed across the globe. As this chapter will suggest, the collapse of composite empires in Europe and the Americas, the Middle East and Asia at the end of the eighteenth century led to the emergence of new forms of governance across the territories which came under European rule.

The following pages offer an account of three phases in the history of modern European colonial governance. Firstly, the chapter shows how, from the sixteenth to late eighteenth century, imperial states relied on alliances with local or creole power structures within heteroglot polities that might be described as trans-Oceanic composite polities, states which simply extended the structure of Europe's

---

4   For a critical account of this notion of governance, see Mark Bevir, 'The Construction of Governance', in Mark Bevir and Frank Trentmann (eds), *Governance, Consumers and Citizens: Agency and Resistance in Contemporary Politics* (Basingstoke, 2007), pp. 25–48.

5   Michel Foucault, 'Governmentality', in Graham Burchell *et al.* (eds), *The Foucault Effect: Studies in Governmentality* (London, 1991), pp. 87–104. See also Michel Foucault, *Security, Territory, Population: Lectures at the Collège de France, 1977–1978*, ed. Michel Sellenart (Basingstoke, 2009).

empires on an inter-continental scale. Such a flexible system of rule did not survive the shock of worldwide war and fiscal crises that occurred in the last third of the eighteenth and first decade of the nineteenth century; as importantly, its loose configuration did not provide metropolitan authorities with a clear and justifiable sense of how overseas empire was being ruled.

Secondly, then, we consider the attempt by authoritarian military colonial states to rule using reconstructed versions of local systems of knowledge. The militaristic attempt to rule through 'native' knowledge collapsed under its own internal contradictions. This resulted in a wave of non-European resistance that swept Europe's empires during the middle decades of the nineteenth century. Thirdly, empire in the mid-nineteenth century led to the creation of a 'rule of experts' in which technically sophisticated forms of European knowledge were wielded by colonial bureaucrats, now divided between different departments and knowledge-regimes. This 'rule of experts' incorporated areas of the colonised world into a global, imperial economy and society far more emphatically than previous modes of governance had done. But, as we will see, in order to cut costs it abandoned equally large areas of the colonial hinterland to rule by under-resourced and therefore weak indigenous rulers. These areas contained tensions which exploded into often violent conflict during the mid-twentieth century, tensions which continued in post-colonial societies until at least the 1970s.

Empire as Composite Monarchy

In 1975 H.G. Koenigsberger coined the term 'composite state' to describe the regimes of early modern Europe. For Koenigsberger a composite state was a state with 'more than one country under the sovereignty of one ruler'.[6] Before the French revolution, Europe was dominated by polyglot empires that bound together different peoples, languages, religions and constitutional forms under a single monarch. These empires united kingdoms through wars of conquest and dynastic marriage contracts, but the emperor rarely attempted to assimilate the different parts of the empire under a single style of rule. Imperial rule consisted of the art of recognising the intentions of often powerful subjects who had a clear political agenda of their own. Governance remained in the hands of local elites and continued to be conducted through local customs for the most part; 'These kingdoms', as the seventeenth-century Spanish jurist Juan de Solózano Pereira put it, 'must be ruled and governed as if the king who holds them all together were king only of each one of them.'[7] Spain was the classic example of such a composite monarchy. The European kingdoms of Aragon, Naples, Sicily, Sardinia, Portugal

---

6   H.G. Koenigsberger, *Politicians and Virtuosi: Essays in Early Modern History* (London, 1986), pp. 12–13.

7   Quoted in J.H. Elliott, 'A Europe of Composite Monarchies', *Past and Present* 137 (1992): p. 53.

and the southern provinces of the Netherlands were united by their formal subjugation to the Castilian crown, but retained their local assemblies and courts of nobles. Imperial governance relied on negotiation between a tiny group of royal officials and regional notables. Despite the rhetoric of absolutism, France was no less disparate; the assemblies and estates of regions such as Brittany, Languedoc and Burgundy remained powerful until the revolution in 1789. Even Britain was no exception: Scotland and England were separate kingdoms, with a separate Scottish parliament until 1707 and a separate church and legal system into the present day.

In the sixteenth and seventeenth centuries, Spain and Portugal expanded their extended monarchies across the Atlantic; in doing so they established new viceroyalties and captaincies that had a complex but largely autonomous relationship with the Spanish or Portuguese Crown. The early Dutch and English empires expanded as chartered companies and corporate bodies governed newly colonised territories, or tried to establish monopolistic commercial relations with parts of the non-European world. In each case, forms of governance that developed in Europe were being expanded across the Americas in particular to form transoceanic empires. In each case, although authority was formally vested in the European capital, governing power was actually diffused amongst notables and local elites across widely dispersed provinces.

As in Europe, rule over these transcontinental European composite monarchies was a complex process of negotiation between the centre and local elites. Order was enforced and welfare functions performed almost entirely by local, often creole elites. The greater distance and absence of regular traffic between the 'metropole' and 'colony' allowed constitutional assumptions and political cultures to develop more autonomously from those which emerged in European states. Distance allowed the gap to widen between what colonial rulers actually did and what metropolitan elites thought they should be doing.

Metropolitan and provincial political cultures came into conflict with one another, particularly at moments of financial crisis. The greatest point of tension occurred as the monarch demanded greater contributions to the treasury to fund empire-wide war. Often a ruler was able to manage opposition from one part of the empire by relying on the countervailing support of another, but general crises could occur where the complex set of centre–periphery negotiations that bound the empire together collapsed entirely. The Spanish king pressured his provinces to pay more revenue to the centre in the 1640s. The result was a revolt of the Catalan *cortes* (parliament) and the creation of an alliance of local nobilities across the Spanish Empire that led to the independence of Portugal from the Spanish Crown, contributed to the final defeats of the Spanish Habsburg forces in the Thirty Years' War, and nearly provoked a French invasion.[8]

The British Atlantic empire that collapsed with the War of American Independence was, as Jack Greene notes, 'a consensual empire composed of a loose association of essentially self-governing polities in which authority and

---

8   Koenigsberger, *Politicians and Virtuosi*, p. 14.

effective power were distributed between the center and the peripheries'.[9] Like the Spanish and Portuguese empires, this was a global polity founded above all on the permanent movement of people, whether African slaves, or free (although often indentured) British and German settlers. Settlers travelled with their language, religion and a loose cluster of political ideas, but they did not bring laws or concrete forms of political legitimacy with them. As Greene notes, 'the earliest settlers did not so much bring *authority* with them across the ocean as the license to create their own authorities'.[10] This dispersal of authority allowed the creation of local cultures of governance. As Daniel Hulsebosch notes, 'the common law was inseparable from the institutions that applied, practiced, and taught the common law'. Where there were different institutions – as in British America, or, indeed British-ruled India – there were different laws.[11]

Just as in the seventeenth-century Spanish Empire, the conflicts which marked British North American politics from the mid-1750s were driven by tensions between local and metropolitan political and legal cultures at moments of fiscal crisis. Once peace returned after the defeat of France in the Seven Years' War, British parliamentarians once again demanded resources from Americans – people who the British believed had been 'nourished up by [their] Indulgence' and 'protected by our arms' – to contribute to empire-wide defence.[12] The result was the Stamp Act of 1765, a piece of legislation which violated the culture of republican self-government that had emerged in the thirteen colonies, and led to a weakening of Britain's imperial connections across the Atlantic.

Britain's growing eighteenth-century presence in South Asia was dominated by a similar set of dynamics and contradictions. The gap between metropolitan and local political cultures widened at a moment when imperial finances were under pressure. South Asia had its creole political cultures. The three fortified towns of Madras, Bombay and Calcutta were governed through forms of English legal procedure that had evolved to meet local conditions. Also founded in the late seventeenth century, Pondicherry and Chandernagore, the largest French settlements, were ruled in a similar fashion, with local variants of French institutions supporting a resident Indian merchant class.[13] Yet, as British political power extended into the hinterland through conquest and the cession of territory following war with France and rival Asian powers, the East India Company began to collect revenue and establish an administrative infrastructure beyond walled

9   Jack P. Greene, 'The American Revolution', *American Historical Review* 105/1 (2000): pp. 93–102; Greene (ed.), *Negotiated Authorities: Essays in Colonial, Political and Constitutional History* (Charlottesville, VA and London, 1994).
10 Jack P. Greene, '"By Their Laws Shall Ye Know Them": Law and Identity in Colonial British America', *Journal of Interdisciplinary History* 13/2 (2002): pp. 247–60.
11 Daniel J. Hulsebosch, 'The Ancient Constitution and the Expanding Empire: Sir Edward Coke's British Jurisprudence', *Law and History Review* 21/3 (2003): pp. 439–82.
12 Fred Anderson, *The Crucible of War: The Seven Years' War and the Fate of Empire in British North America, 1754–1766* (New York, 2000).
13 K. Mukund, 'New Social Elites and the Early Colonial State: Construction of Identity and Patronage in Madras', *Economic and Political Weekly* 38/27 (5 July 2003): pp. 2857–64.

port towns, and the creole presence became less important. If the expansion of territory was largely rooted in military force, the East India Company nonetheless acted as a characteristically European composite sovereign by negotiating with the local power structures it conquered. In the eastern Indian province of Bengal, for example, Warren Hastings' insistence in 1772 that disputes between Indians were to be decided by Hindu and Muslim law was an attempt to retain the voice of Indian legal practitioners within the growing colonial state. As Robert Travers notes, 'at this early stage of colonial state-building, the embodied authority of *pandits* and *maulvis* [Indian legal officers] as interpreters of Hindu and Muslim law was more important to the working of the Company's courts than translated codes'.[14] Further, P.J. Marshall suggests that the British consolidated their authority in India by doing what they had failed to do in the thirteen American colonies – incorporating local or creole power structures into their polity in a way that eventually allowed the collection of revenue and establishment of institutions sufficient to sustain the state.[15]

Yet, in Britain's growing Asian empire, this process of negotiation did not last long. As the fiscal centre of the British Empire swung eastwards, and pressure on Asian allies and interlocutors increased, the attempt to govern distant subjects through a transcontinental form of composite state began to break down. The kinds of ad hoc Anglo–Indian relationships which governors such as Robert Clive and Warren Hastings built failed to produce either a regular and substantial profit for the East India Company, or a set of political justifications able to convince the British public that Britain's empire in India had a solid moral foundation. The financial failure of the East India Company during the 1770s led to a sustained moral critique in the 1780s, and to the reconstruction of the practical and ideological basis of British rule in the 1790s.[16] That moral critique was a consequence of the acute contradictions between imperial ideologies designed for domestic consumption, which emphasised both the virtue and profitability of empire, and the local reality of *ad hoc* negotiation with non-European polities and the continuous threat of financial disaster.

The cost of long periods of global warfare in the second half of the eighteenth and first fifteen years of the nineteenth centuries played a powerful role in reshaping patterns of governance both within and outside the structures of European-ruled empires. The loose, negotiated relationship between centre and periphery that characterised early modern composite monarchies was incapable of bearing the fiscal strain of global warfare. The extraordinary period of revolution and war the world experienced between 1780 and 1815 witnessed the creation of states which made far greater claims to govern and tax local populations than their predecessors. It also saw the emergence of a new moral justification for the exercise

---

14   Robert Travers, *Ideology and Empire in Eighteenth-Century India: The British in Bengal* (Cambridge, 2007), p. 124.

15   P.J. Marshall, *The Making and Unmaking of Empires: Britain, India and America, c.1750–1783* (Oxford, 2005).

16   Travers, *Ideology and Empire*; Jon E. Wilson, *The Domination of Strangers: Modern Governance in Eastern India, 1780–1835* (Basingstoke, 2008), chap. 2 passim.

of state power, both in Europe and beyond. In 1790, the revolutionary government of France issued paper currency based on the value of confiscated church lands in order to prevent the bankruptcy of the French state. Three years later, the English East India Company's government of the one-time Mughal province of Bengal declared that the value of land possessed by Indian landholders would underpin its own solvency.[17] As in France, a mechanism for directly taxing wealthy property-holding sections of the population replaced a tax-farming system premised on the existence of local intermediaries who had a substantial degree of autonomy over how they taxed and governed the areas under their power.[18] The exercise of state power was justified in the name of the welfare and improvement of the population – although, in India, the new British concern with the welfare of the population emerged alongside a highly pejorative language used to describe the *populus* being ruled.

Despotic Reconstructions of Indigenous Law

In Europe's overseas empires during the first half of the nineteenth century the practice of imperial governance was dominated by the attempt to find, understand and tax sources of local revenue which were able to sustain the growing imperial state financially. The politics of tax was, of course, crucial to the transformation in governance which occurred in post-1789 Europe itself, as the Revolutionary and Napoleonic state and its adversaries found more efficient ways to raise revenue and troops to fight a two-decade-long war. Things were different outside Europe though, as regimes struggling to raise revenue quickly found they were faced with a breakdown in their ability not merely to tax but effectively to understand the societies they ruled. Already imbued with negative stereotypes about non-European peoples, expanding colonial regimes tried to raise revenue from populations which were regarded as potentially both incomprehensible and ungovernable by European officials. Fiscal crises quickly turned into what C.A. Bayly calls 'information panics' and more general crises of colonial knowledge.[19]

The states constructed by Britain, France and the Netherlands – the major colonial powers of the period in the first half of the nineteenth century – to govern colonial subjects in Africa and Asia had two characteristics in common. First of all, they were predominantly military regimes. Ruled as often as not by soldiers, their primary purpose was to raise revenue to pay for large standing armies even

---

17   Wilson, *Domination of Strangers*, chap. 2 and Ranajit Guha, *A Rule of Property for Bengal: An Essay on the Idea of Permanent Settlement* (Paris, 1963).

18   For a comparison with Britain where the land tax was also locally administered, see Colin Brooks, 'Public Finance and Political Stability: The Administration of the Land Tax, 1688–1720', *Historical Journal* 17/2 (1974): pp. 281–300.

19   C.A. Bayly, *Empire and Information: Intelligence Gathering and Social Communication in India, 1780–1870* (Cambridge, 1996).

where they were administered by civilians. From the appointment of Charles, Earl Cornwallis, as Governor-General of Bengal in 1786 until the 1850s, military personnel dominated the highest ranks of British governance in India. Arthur Wellesley, Duke of Wellington, nineteenth-century Europe's most famous general, began his career in India and spent some time governing newly conquered Indian territory. His style of militaristic authoritarianism dominated British Indian politics for a generation, as friends or sons of friends were appointed to the post of Governor-General. A cadre of soldier-bureaucrats who came of age in his brother Richard Wellesley's Indian administration between 1798 and 1805 dominated the East India Company's civil service from the 1810s through the 1830s. This group, which included Thomas Munro, Mountstuart Elphinstone and John Malcolm, was marked by its linguistic skills, apparent local knowledge, paternalistic style of rule and belief in the primacy of the sword over other instruments of persuasion. Even the most 'liberal' Governor-General of the period, Lord Bentinck, was a soldier, concerned primarily to maintain stability and cost-effectiveness within what Douglas Peers describes as a 'garrison state'.[20] Soldiers, often soldiers with experience in India, occupied the highest positions of British imperial authority elsewhere. The province of Canada was ruled continuously by soldiers from 1805 to 1835. New South Wales' first non-military Governor (the first four in post after 1788 were sailors not soldiers) was the Bombay-born conservative politician Lord Lisgar, appointed only in 1861.

After the conquest of 1830, colonial rule in Algeria was even more explicitly proconsular and militaristic. Occupied areas of French-ruled Algeria came under the *régime de sabre* ruled by a military Governor-General responsible to the French minister of war. Like British imperialism in India, French rule in North Africa created a class of soldier-bureaucrats; as in India, these officers were primarily concerned to create a stable, taxable society by settling an otherwise mobile population. In contrast to the situation in India – and as was commonly the case in European-settled agricultural colonies such as Canada, Australia or New Zealand – these French officers encouraged white colonisation as the most viable means to create social order. And although it was more common for the Governors-General of the Dutch East Indies to be colonial civil servants than their counterparts in British India, many senior officials of the Dutch colonial state were nonetheless military men.

Early nineteenth-century colonial governance was dominated by military personnel in part because European colonial states were on a constant war footing. But conquest was about more than geopolitics. Territories were annexed because they offered a potential supply of revenue or a location for European colonisation as well as the chance to neutralise a potential military foe. As often as not 'expansion' occurred as European states used their global credit networks to monopolise the military labour market. Prince Dipanagara's resistance to Dutch imperialism in Java in the 1820s petered out as he found it more and more difficult to recruit

---

20   Douglas M. Peers, *Between Mars and Mammon: Colonial Armies and the Garrison State in India, 1819–1835* (London, 1995).

insurgents to his army.[21] Despite their belief that they had won because of superior military technology and tactics, Arthur Wellesley's and Lord Lake's defeat of the Maratha polity was rooted in the British ability to monopolise the Indian military labour market, and thus disturb western Indian states' ability to retain the loyalty of their followers.[22]

The extension of European power created violent frontier regions, as soldiers unable to find employment in indigenous states and unable to join European forces maintained themselves through plunder and warlordism. In Afghanistan, northeastern India, the uplands of Southeast Asia and southern Algeria, for example, highland and desert regions became lawless zones, where those fleeing European imperialism found refuge amidst 'tribal' polities that refused to assimilate themselves to the pattern of ordered governance that existed on the plains. The new kind of stateless politics that emerged in these places was treated by Europeans as a sign of what life was like before the colonial intrusion, and yet another justification for imperial rule.[23] The instability and wildness of these regions meant they attracted the disproportionate attention of paranoid colonial states, often providing the spark that ignited large-scale military conflagrations.

If the first aspect of Europe's expanding early nineteenth-century colonial states was their dominance by military logic and personnel, their second most important characteristic was the extent to which they were primarily concerned to establish settled social orders, and used – or attempted to use – indigenous laws and customs to create such stability. Colonial cities such as Batavia, Algiers or Calcutta were dominated by highly mobile forms of imperial capital, providing spaces for the creation of hybrid, Euro-indigenous elites at home both in European and indigenous languages and culture. Many of these urban elites dominated later nationalist movements. Between the cities and the distant, troublesome and often upland frontiers lay the bulk of the colonised population. This increasingly settled population inhabited territory ruled by a relatively small number of European colonial administrators who insisted that their property, economic activity and family life should be rigidly fixed by 'indigenous' rules peculiar to that place. Colonial states, and later nationalist elites, vastly under-estimated the extent to which prior Asian and African social and economic relations in this zone relied on the movement of people.[24] It was here, in the attempt to rule supposedly settled agrarian societies by despotic imperial regimes, that the colonial language of welfare and improvement found its first target. But the gap between the realities of everyday colonial practice and the ideologies of order and improvement which

---

21 Peter B.R. Carey, *Babad Dipanagara: An Account of the Outbreak of the Java War, 1825–30* (Kuala Lumpur, 1981).

22 Randolph G.S. Cooper, *The Anglo-Maratha Campaigns and the Contest for India* (Cambridge, 2003).

23 James C. Scott, *The Art of Not Being Governed: An Anarchist History of Upland Southeast Asia* (New Haven, CT, 2009).

24 Arjun Appadurai, 'Putting Hierarchy in its Place', *Cultural Anthropology* 3/1 (1988): pp. 33–49.

administrators used to justify their conduct created the conditions for waves of colonial rebellion in the mid-nineteenth century.

The attempt to create order through the governance of supposedly immobile colonial spaces generated expertise amongst European colonial officials about 'native' culture. In doing so, it produced a complex and fraught relationship between European officers and their non-European interlocutors and informants. The law was one institution in which this territorially rooted colonial knowledge was constructed; it was also an important site of engagement and miscommunication between ruler and ruled. During the late eighteenth and early nineteenth centuries, colonial legal practice tended to remove the direct agency of local juridical decision-makers who had been incorporated into early modern composite empires, replacing them with colonial judges who governed with European transcriptions and translations of 'native' texts. The first half of the nineteenth century saw a vast expansion in books that guided European rulers through Asian and African cultures. These works relied heavily on an engagement with indigenous intellectuals, but were also intended to stifle 'native' voices from directly influencing the process of colonial decision-making, exalting supposedly 'native' knowledge at the same time as they restricted the agency of Africans, Asians or Australasians. Colonial texts offered a simplistic, one might almost say parodied, version of the complex political practices that had governed pre-colonial societies; in doing so, they often transformed indigenous societies in ways that administrators did not intend. Often 'native' law consolidated the power of those local elites who most readily conformed to European stereotypes, and were able to articulate most effectively their interests to the colonial regime. In India, for example, the British codification of Hindu and Muslim law dramatically restricted the power of Indian women to possess property in the name of 'native' custom and religious law.[25]

Other institutions within the networks of imperial governance played an important role in the governance of the supposedly settled colonial spaces in early nineteenth-century Europe's absolutist military overseas empires. Medical corps, often attached to conquering armies, were significant in British India and French North Africa. Military surgeons were an important source of practical colonial knowledge, offering generalised and often highly racialised accounts of the conditions of colonised subjects in Algeria and elsewhere.[26] Missionaries often had a tense relationship with imperial authorities, but were a source of expertise about the languages and ways of life of subject populations.[27] In New Zealand, missionaries produced the misleading translation of the Treaty of Waitangi with which sections of the Maori population exchanged sovereignty over their polity for protection of their land rights.[28] Here, missionaries and colonial governors

25   Wilson, *Domination of Strangers*, chaps 3 and 4.

26   Patricia M.E. Lorcin, 'Imperialism, Colonial Identity and Race in Algeria, 1830–1870: The Role of the French Medical Corps', *Isis* 90/4 (1999): pp. 652–79.

27   Andrew Porter, *Religion versus Empire? British Protestant Missionaries and Overseas Expansion, 1700–1914* (Manchester, 2004).

28   Mark Hickford, 'Making Territorial Rights of the Natives: Britain and New Zealand,

collaborated in their attempt to ensure Maori social stability and colonial order threatened by the growing process of white settlement; initially, Maori land rights were championed not in order to increase indigenous prosperity, but to block the rise of unruly settler populations. Despite their common participation in the colonial project of establishing order, though, the missionaries' presence was framed principally around a desire to transform the religious practices of indigenous society; on occasion this led to clashes with colonial governments.

Officers of the French army's Bureaux Arabes performed a similar role in Algeria, attempting to preserve Arab and Kabyle property against colonisers from north of the Mediterranean.[29] In each place, the settlement of a 'native' population with secure land rights and protection from the encroachment of European settlers were seen as the best way to ensure the stability of the colonial regime, and to prevent the pressure on military expenditure which an anti-colonial or anti-settler rebellion would cause. The failure of these attempts in both New Zealand and Algeria was shown by the persistence of anti-colonial resistance in Algeria and the onset of the New Zealand Wars in the late 1840s.[30]

The governmental regimes that ruled Europe's overseas empires during the first two-thirds of the nineteenth century presumed that non-European populations could be denied political power and governed despotically so long as their 'native' social existence was settled and protected. The assumption was made that settled indigenous legal and cultural systems needed only to be correctly interpreted and upheld by European administrators for colonial empires to be secure. But these presuppositions existed alongside European hostility to non-European religious and cultural practice, and brought with them a complex series of tensions and anxieties. European missionaries as well as military and civil officers, keen to uphold local property rights, frequently articulated their desire (albeit a desire they rarely believed could quickly be put into practice) to convert Asians, Africans and Australasians into Christians. Such a hostile attitude to non-European society, the poor linguistic abilities of European officers and the itinerant character of colonial careers made it very difficult for the colonial regime to engage practically with the subjects it ruled. Despite claims to represent indigenous social order, the forms of practical knowledge used by the colonial revenue collector, judge or administrator in everyday official life was in fact a thin and abstract projection of the imperial mind onto the complexity of indigenous society. The structure of colonial power was increasingly centralised as it attempted to concentrate knowledge about indigenous society into a limited number of texts that colonial officials could control. Officials were aware of the fragile basis of their connection to local society,

---

1830–1847', DPhil dissertation, Oxford University, 1999; Paul McHugh, *The Maori Magna Carta*: *New Zealand Law and the Treaty of Waitangi (Oxford, 1991).*

29   Kenneth P. Perkins, 'Pressure and Persuasion in the Policies of the French Military in Colonial North Africa', *Military Affairs* 40/2 (1976): pp. 74–8.

30   Julia Clancy-Smith, *Rebel and Saint: Muslim Notables, Populist Protest, Colonial Encounters (Algeria and Tunisia, 1800–1904)* (Berkeley, CA, 1994); James Belich, *The New Zealand Wars and the Victorian Interpretation of Racial Conflict* (Auckland, 1986).

and relied heavily on the projection and occasional actual use of military force to retain order.

Thus the practice of early nineteenth-century governance within Europe's colonial territories themselves was never sure of its political or intellectual footing, continually oscillating between the cautious attempt to govern with existing custom, and the authoritarian assertion of imperial command. In Europe, particularly after the criticisms of the late eighteenth century, politicians committed to empire needed to justify fragile and sprawling colonial institutions with a rather more certain set of languages. Thus, politicians and intellectuals in Europe articulated a language of moral purpose that often projected rather more ambitious intentions onto the colonial enterprise than those held by colonial administrators themselves. Officials 'on the spot' believed that their purpose was to ensure the military and fiscal stability of the colonial regime, maintain social order, uphold property rights and so allow the 'improvement' of local society to occur. Critics challenged the limited nature of these intentions, arguing that empire should conduct a broader process of moral reformation, sometimes including conversion to Christianity, but always more frequently assimilating local populations to what had begun to be defined as 'European civilisation'. Yet until the twentieth century this more ambitious sense of imperial mission was the preserve of missionaries, metropolitan radicals and a small and ultimately marginal set of officers sent to Africa or Asia with grand ideas about transformation who frequently returned home with a sense of failure. Thomas Macaulay is a good example of such a figure; Macaulay went to India in 1834 to write a new system of criminal law and to introduce the benefits of a supposedly more 'advanced' civilisation to the subcontinent. He returned home four years later having failed to have his code enacted, with a newfound sympathy for the soldier-administrators who founded the British Empire in the east, and the project of establishing well-regulated states without engaging in the dangerous scenario of dramatically transforming local society.

Delocalised Logic of Expert Knowledge

The mid-nineteenth century witnessed a wave of anti-colonial rebellion across the colonised world. This spate of revolt occurred as contradictions inherent within the logic of colonial governance intersected with the cycles of an increasingly interconnected global economy. Worldwide economic depression in the 1830s and early 1840s led colonial regimes to intensify the extraction of resources from the hinterland of their colonies or from formally annexed territory they were previously able to exploit without directly ruling.[31] As Ronald Robinson and John Gallagher famously noted, '[b]etween 1840 and 1851 Great Britain occupied or annexed New

---

31 C.A. Bayly, *Rulers, Townsmen and Bazaars: North Indian Society in the Age of British Expansion* (New Delhi 1983); Sanjay Sharma, *Famine, Philanthropy and the Colonial State* (Delhi, 2001).

Zealand, the Gold Coast, Labuan, Natal, the Punjab, Sind and Hong Kong'. With further damage to the East India Company's financial position inflicted by a second international depression, Awadh was annexed in 1856.[32] The depression also drove the emigration of Europeans to Europe's colonial empires, which benefited the metropolis but placed additional pressure on colonial regimes.

With the deteriorating fiscal position of colonial regimes as a backdrop, anti-colonial rebellion was sparked by the intrusion of European settlers, or the paranoid, punitive violence of colonial regimes whose attempt to govern with indigenous law was breaking down. So, for example, the New Zealand Wars, which escalated from the mid-1840s until the early 1870s, occurred because settlers attempted to seize Maori land which the imperial state had promised to protect. As the scope of institutions which represented the white population expanded, the state was increasingly forced to side with settlers.[33] Similarly, conflict in Algeria was fuelled by the encroachment of *colons* upon territory the colonial regime had initially demarcated as Arab. Both the Indian Rebellion of 1857–58 and the Morant Bay revolt in Jamaica in 1865 occurred when local populations were angered by panicky colonial attempts to punish minor instances of disobedience with what locals perceived as excessive violence.[34] Ideas about the radically transformative intentions of colonial states seeped from metropolitan political argument, or from more radical fringes of the colonial network such as pockets of missionary or settler activity into the circuits of informal non-European communication. Rumours imputed the *ad hoc* coercive acts of the colonial regime with a radical and systematic desire to undermine the norms and structures of Indian, North African or post-emancipation Caribbean society. In doing so, they justified concerted campaigns of resistance against European states throughout the colonised world which often erupted with unanticipated force. As C.A. Bayly argues, local spies and indigenous information-gatherers had been replaced with more abstract, often statistical forms of knowledge that Europeans could collect without extensive reliance on 'native' agency.[35] The result was that colonial regimes were increasingly oblivious to growing rumours of rebellion.

This era of mid-Victorian imperial disorder pulled the practice of colonial governance in two contradictory directions. On the one hand, the period saw a redoubling of colonial efforts to penetrate indigenous society with the supposedly universal norms of western science, governance and law. It was only after the Indian Rebellion that a revised version of Macaulay's penal code was made law in 1860. The following three decades saw the rationalisation of colonial jurisprudence in India with the enactment of codes to govern the law of evidence and contract, for example. Codes modelled on Macaulay's penal law were introduced in Sudan

---

32 John Gallagher and Ronald Robinson, 'The Imperialism of Free Trade', *Economic History Review* 6/1, New Series (1953): p. 2.

33 Belich, *New Zealand Wars*.

34 Clare Anderson, *The Indian Uprising of 1857–8: Prisons, Prisoners and Rebellion* (London, 2007), pp. 55–94.

35 Bayly, *Empire and Information*, pp. 338–64.

in 1899, and in northern Nigeria in 1959.[36] The early twentieth century also saw the expansion of the European scientific and medical establishments in India and elsewhere, and the introduction of a range of science-based practices from agronomy to psychiatry, whereas in the mid-nineteenth century administrators had conceded the need to work with indigenous legal, medical and scientific systems, if only because they thought the best survival for European knowledges might be their grafting onto local roots. By the early twentieth century, these hybridities had been replaced by the aim of subjugating what were regarded as inferior non-European systems of knowledge to the supposedly universal norms of European science (see chapter in this volume by Sivasundaram).

The last years of the nineteenth and first half of the twentieth century saw the intensification of attempts to control African, Asian and Caribbean populations. These efforts saw the beginning of attempts to govern not merely commerce and social relations but the bodies of ordinary colonial subjects. In rapidly growing cities such as Bombay and Hong Kong, for example, what David Arnold calls a 'new interventionism' witnessed the segregation and incarceration of patients deemed at risk of contagious diseases such as cholera and plague, and the detention of women suspected of carrying sexually transmitted diseases. These efforts often mirrored the approach taken to manage and police the poor in European domestic environments, yet, within the zones in which it had an effect, colonial interference was more interventionist than domestic governance. So, for example, the confinement under colonial regulation of female sex workers suspected of carrying contagious diseases occurred before domestic initiatives.[37]

In the early twentieth century, disciplines such as colonial town planning, agricultural science, psychiatry, forestry and statistics offered rival ways of measuring and in many cases intervening in the daily lives of local populations that exceeded the degree of intervention possible at 'home'. This was, for example, the period of intensive cadastral mapping in many colonial environments. A detailed map defining land rights began to be produced by Egypt's British rulers in 1898; no such map had been produced for most of the United Kingdom by the end of the twentieth century. Within this new 'rule of experts' (as Timothy Mitchell puts it) colonial territories were defined as being occupied by populations whose conduct could be mapped and calculated in an increasingly abstract and scientific statistical form.[38] The use of these disembodied and delocalised systems of expertise made the stereotyped but locally oriented knowledge systems which had underpinned mid-nineteenth century colonial rule less and less legitimate. Governance

36 Alan Gledhill, *The Penal Codes of Sudan and Northern Nigeria* (London and Lagos, 1963); H.F. Morris, 'How Nigeria got its Penal Code', *Journal of African Law* 14/3 (1970): pp. 137–54.

37 David Arnold, *Colonizing the Body: State Medicine and Epidemic Disease in Nineteenth-Century India* (Berkeley, CA, 1993); Philippa Levine, *Prostitution, Race and Politics: Policing Venereal Disease in the British Empire* (New York, 2003); John Marriott, *The Other Empire: Metropolis, India and Progress in the Colonial Imagination* (Manchester, 2003).

38 Timothy Mitchell, *Rule of Experts: Egypt, Techno-Politics, Modernity* (Berkeley, CA, 2002).

seemed possible from greater distances. Detailed mapping made possible aerial anti-insurgency bombing campaigns, for example. They also allowed dramatic alterations in political boundaries at the stroke of a pen. Mapping and statistics allowed the lawyer and Oxford fellow Sir Cyril Radcliffe to determine the boundary between independent India and Pakistan with no previous knowledge of the Indian subcontinent. It also enabled the colonial state in post-war Tanganyika to spend millions marking out territory, removing local farmers and planting peanuts in wholly unsuitable soil. The groundnut scheme saw not a single nut harvested.[39]

There were, however, at least two ambiguities that cut across the reach of colonial governance in the early twentieth century. With limited budgets, anxieties about the limits on their power and affective affiliations thousands of miles away, colonial officials only cared for the late colonial project of 'modernising' non-European society in a half-hearted fashion. Institutions whose purpose was ostensibly to radically transform colonial societies were capable of extraordinary inertia and stasis. Despite its importance in consolidating racial difference and colonial power structures, the intensification of governance in the last years of the nineteenth and first part of the twentieth century was only possible with the substantial involvement of local elites. African, Asian and Caribbean interlocutors of colonial states often saw fruitful combinations between modern science and non-European knowledge systems. And, as importantly, many doubted how far the imperial character of colonial governance was able to transform the non-European world.[40] Eventually, within new post-colonial structures of sovereignty, the techniques and institutions of late colonial governance were redirected away from imperial purposes to buttress the process of post-colonial state formation in many parts of the non-European world. For example, early in his career the Bengali statistician Prashanta Chadra Mahalanobis worked on the physical measurements of different racial groups, allying new statistical techniques to the colonial (and deeply racist) science of anthropometry. A close friend of Rabindranath Tagore, Mahalanobis was nonetheless central to the creation of a university at Santiniketan, the aim of which was to regenerate indigenous culture. He went on to play a powerful role in one of the post-colonial Indian state's most important instruments of social transformation, the Planning Commission, the body responsible for allocating state resources in post-colonial India.

The careers of scientist-administrators such as Mahalanobis demonstrate that the delocalised logic of governmental expertise allowed colonial governing practices to be untethered from their supposedly European moorings for very different purposes and consequences. Yet the anxieties of colonial administrators about indigenous opposition acted to limit the intensification of modern forms of governance in many places. Fear of rebellion led European administrators to try to root the practice of colonial rule in local power structures. Colonial power and knowledge sometimes acted in a paradoxical way to limit their own reach,

---

39   Alan Wood, *The Groundnut Affair* (London, 1950).

40   See, for example, Gyan Prakash, *Another Reason: Science and the Imagination of Modern India* (Princeton, NJ, 1999).

establishing forms of 'indirect rule' where European administrators defined large areas of territory as falling under the rule of supposedly authentic African or Asian sovereignties. Indirect rule was underpinned by fiscal imperatives, being significantly cheaper and less risky than direct governance.[41] Sometimes the search for non-European 'partners' or 'collaborators' in governing empire was driven by the anti-democratic sensibilities of colonial administrators, who saw colonial territories as an opportunity to protect the kind of aristocratic social structure they believed was being too rapidly undermined back home. By the early twentieth century, however, authoritarian polities were more frequently supported in Africa and Asia by men and women who were democrats back 'home'. Here, indirect rule relied on a strong sense of the difference and inferiority of non-European peoples. Colonial difference was buttressed by colonial forms of racial and cultural knowledge that used 'science' to justify claims about the unsuitability of democracy for Asia or particularly African personality.[42]

To a certain degree, indirect rule involved a return to the composite state that had characterised Europe's early modern overseas empires. Rhetorically at least, authority was shared by European states and non-European elites. Yet there were important differences from the early modern model. For the most part, symbolism mattered far more than actual governmental power. Indirect rule strongly emphasised the symbolic aspects of sovereignty, being an attempt to enshrine the status of indigenous rulers in complex forms of rituals. Formal political arrangements varied. In large Indian 'princely states' such as Hyderabad, and Jammu and Kashmir, rulers governed independently in all areas but defence. On the other hand, small African chieftaincies were easily over-awed and out-gunned by powerful British residents.[43] In all cases, however, indirect rule presupposed that imperial sovereignty possessed an 'absolute authority' to appoint and dismiss local rulers. As Peter K. Tibenderana points out, '[a]s the British conceived it, indirect rule was a system of colonial administration through which the traditional chiefs were regarded as an integral part of the machinery of government' not as a wholly separate form of authority.

In the middle third of the twentieth century, colonial authority fractured under growing financial pressure and the rising resistance of its non-European subjects. The post-colonial states which emerged after European personnel and sovereignty retreated from the colonial world inherited governmental structures wracked by the tensions and contradictions this chapter has examined. Most importantly

---

41 Olufemi Vaughan, 'Chieftaincy Politics and Communal Politics in Western Nigeria, 1893–1951', *Journal of Africa History* 44 (2003): pp. 283–302.

42 David Cannadine, *Ornamentalism: How the British Saw their Empire* (London, 2002); Homi K. Bhabha, 'The Other Question: Difference, Discrimination and the Question of Colonialism', in Francis Barker *et al.* (eds), *Literature, Politics and Theory: Papers from the Essex Conference 1976–1984* (London, 1986), pp. 148–72; Mahmood Mamdani, *Citizen and Subject: Contemporary Africa and the Legacy of Late Colonialism* (Princeton, NJ, 1996), pp. 148–72.

43 Bernard S. Cohn, 'Representing Authority in Victorian India', in Eric J. Hobsbawm and Terence Ranger (eds), *The Invention of Tradition* (Cambridge, 1983), pp. 165–210.

perhaps, they inherited but radically transformed the colonial state's mission to modernise the non-European world. Nationalist politicians argued that, unless African, Asian and Caribbean people governed their own societies, modernisation would be impossible. Nationalist states replaced the languid and often ambivalent approach of colonial officials to social change with a fervent commitment to reform, a commitment that often led to the rapid growth in size and power of the state after independence.

Yet post-colonial states frequently employed expanded but unreformed colonial bureaucracies to achieve their nationalist reforming ambitions. Nationalist movements had also often relied strongly on seemingly non-modern or 'traditional' forms of identity and community to mobilise resistance to colonial rule, and these could not be abandoned at independence. Forms of group belonging such as caste and tribe which, under colonial rule, marked African and Asian politics as different from their European counterparts have remained important markers of identity and political mobilisation, even though they have been transformed by the expansion of the modern post-colonial state, by capitalism and by global forms of communication. Changes in the way citizens of post-colonial states produce, socialise, trade and communicate with one another since independence have meant that any attempt to argue that post-colonial politics or governance has been straightforwardly determined by the structures of colonial rule is bound to fail. But the fact that new ways of living occur within institutions that were not significantly transformed means that the complex tensions and crises of governance this chapter has examined are not wholly irrelevant to understand the post-colonial world.

Perhaps the most important difference between the worlds of colonial and post-colonial governance is the different degree of commitment its practitioners, at least within the highest levels of government, felt towards the populations they ruled. Colonial administrators were occasionally passionate about particular reforming projects, often liable to moments of incandescent anger when the colonial world wasn't as pliable under their efforts to order and transform as they expected. But for the most part the mood of imperial governance was listless boredom and not passionate determination. From the early nineteenth century, the lives of colonial officers in India, Africa and the Caribbean was based around a small, parochial community of Europeans who shared a sense of disengagement from non-European society. Colonial officers rarely intended to settle in the African, Asian and Caribbean societies they ruled. The fact that Britons could imagine colonies of settlement such as Australia, New Zealand and Canada as a permanent home contributed to the very different dynamics of governance there. In the non-white empire, though, a posting to a colonial territory was imagined as a relatively short sojourn marked by hard work and a lack of comfort, to be followed by years of bucolic retirement to a country seat or a re-immersion into European political life after the much-longed-for return 'home'. The most important thing about a colonial career was the fact that it would come to an end. The transitory character of individual Europeans' relationships with the colonies they governed made serious commitment to the project of imperial governance rare. Empire was, of course, based on the collection of information about those who were being ruled; colonial governors needed to respond constantly to the demands of the governed. But sustained efforts to engage intellectually with non-white populations on an equal basis were always few and far between.

It was this lack of commitment that made the practice of colonial governance seem extremely dull. In their efforts both to justify empire and to make it liveable for themselves, colonial administrators often seem to have forgotten the everyday history of the power relations between rulers and ruled that constituted the practice of imperial governance. Instead they, like many historians, assumed that the history of empires could be explained by more exciting narratives about the clash of imperial ideologies or the controversies about empire in metropolitan politics. This chapter has suggested instead that it is to the seemingly tedious history of colonial governance in colonial territories that one needs to look to explain both the rise and fall of empires, and the impact of imperial regimes on the non-European world. Precisely because it has so often been forgotten, the everyday practice of colonial governance was important.

Finance

Søren Mentz

When Akbar the Great died in 1605 the value of the treasuries in Mughal India was approximately 56 million ducats. At the time of Philip II's death, only a few years earlier in 1598, the debt of the Spanish Empire was some 85 million ducats. The difference between east and west is not only striking but also highly relevant in the study of world empires, for despite rising national deficits several European states expanded in the period from 1500 to 1850, a growth made possible by fiscal innovations and changing financial policies.

The wealth of the Mughal Empire derived primarily from agricultural taxation raised through an elaborate fiscal system introduced in the late sixteenth century. According to M.N. Pearson, direct taxation of agriculture covered all imperial expenses:

> The revenue needs of the empire, vast though they were, could be met from massive amounts of land revenue collected by a rather articulated and efficient chain of government officials. What could be easier than to tax a peasant population numbering many tens of millions, who by definition had to stay put and so could easily be taxed?[1]

As such, the central Mughal government was disinclined to change the fiscal practice of the empire. China reveals similar characteristics. The Ming (1368–1644) and Qing (1644–1912) dynasties were not compelled to make radical changes to the fiscal system, since emperors could raise enough money through existing means of taxation. Labour was abundant, and so an increasing population secured economic growth and gave the imperial government no incentive for innovation. In other words, large populations became a deterrent to technological innovation in the agricultural and industrial sectors, creating what Mark Elvin has labelled a 'high-level equilibrium trap'.[2]

---

1   M.N. Pearson, 'Merchants and States,' in J.D. Tracy (ed.), *The Political Economy of Merchant Empires: State Power and World Trade 1350–1750* (Cambridge, 1991), p. 52.
2   M. Elvin, *The Pattern of the Chinese Past* (Stanford, CA, 1973).

European rulers, by contrast, controlled smaller territories than Asian emperors. As revenue from agriculture alone could not meet the rising demand for capital, fiscal alternatives were explored. Governments established ties with the commercial sector as a means of taxing the financial resources of trade. In return, members of the merchant elite gained political influence. In eighteenth-century Britain, for example, the expanding number of wealthy financiers and merchants in London, whose widespread commercial networks represented in miniature the geography of the British Empire, demonstrated how innovation and enterprise at home led to achievement and success abroad.[3] Furthermore, the landed aristocracy who ruled the country established a political partnership with large-scale merchants thereby creating a vital source of national stability.[4]

As the century progressed commercial revenues and excise duties became a major source of state income. Great Britain managed to raise the necessary capital to fight France in the long century from 1688 to 1815 by transforming itself into a 'fiscal-military' state capable of administering an overseas empire.[5] Commercial capital was also invested in government bonds as new mechanisms for the management of short-term debt and long-term borrowing were created. As such, the most original fiscal device introduced in Europe was the national debt, and not the steady influx of American silver which the power of Philip II had come to depend upon during the second half of the sixteenth century.[6]

European states thus created the economic structures of world empires by directing their attention to sectors largely ignored by their imperial predecessors in Mughal India and imperial China. India and China did experience growing commercialisation during the seventeenth and eighteenth centuries, but, although this process stimulated the economy of the provinces, it did not affect the imperial centre.

This chapter will explore the financial activities of imperial governments and their relationships with local power structures and merchant elites. Empires were not just centres of power. They were also sources of authority whose effectiveness depended upon the degree of legitimacy that regimes were able to exert over civil society. Rulers had to accommodate the interest of various social groups if, for example, the level of taxation was to be raised without causing unrest or rebellion. As such, the relationship between governments and subjects is highly relevant to the study of imperial finance.

---

3   H.V. Bowen, *Elites, Enterprise and the Making of the British Overseas Empire, 1688–1775* (London, 1996), p. 4.
4   L. Colley, *Britons, Forging the Nation 1707–1837* (London, 1994), p. 61.
5   J. Brewer, *The Sinews of Power: War, Money and the English State, 1688–1783* (London, 1989).
6   P.G.M. Dickson, *The Financial Revolution: A Study in the Development of Public Credit, 1688–1756* (London, 1967); N. Steensgaard, 'The Seventeenth-Century Crisis and the Unity of the Eurasian History', *Modern Asian Studies* 24/4 (1990): pp. 683–97; J.H. Parry, *The Spanish Seaborne Empire* (New York, 1966, reprinted 1990), p. 246.

Small-Scale Empire: The Case of Denmark–Norway 1500–1800

The study of small scale imperial finance using the example of Denmark–Norway offers an excellent introduction to the fiscal options available to imperial powers. As we have seen, small states had fewer resources than larger empires, and so the Danish government was forced to intervene in agriculture, trade and manufacture to meet rising military costs during the seventeenth and eighteenth centuries. Geographically, the Danish kingdom was a vast conglomerate including Norway, the southern provinces of present-day Sweden, Iceland, Greenland, the Faroe Islands and the duchies of Schleswig and Holstein in North Germany. In size, it was surpassed only by the Habsburg Empire of Charles V; in structure, it resembled that of a traditional maritime-cum-imperial power.[7] However, it was sparsely populated with between 1.5 and 2 million people living in the realm.

Denmark was an agrarian economy; revenue from agriculture was its most important source of income. Prior to 1660 half of the cultivated land belonged to the king, who was expected to run the state on this income. Approximately 60,000 rixdollars, the standard Danish currency, were collected on his behalf in 1559, and though the sum was raised to 134,000 rixdollars in 1602 by increasing the export of cattle to north Europe, the amount only covered half the state's expenditure in peacetime. Hindered by the fact that part of the revenue was paid in kind, the state was forced to reorganise the revenue system as a whole in order to meet rising costs. The leading members of the Danish aristocracy, however, opposed reform because they controlled a good deal of the land, and enjoyed exemption from taxes. The ensuing struggle between king and nobility ended in 1660 when an absolute monarchy was introduced after a devastating war with Sweden. A process of centralisation began, and Denmark was gradually transformed into a military-fiscal state. Large parts of the crown estate were sold off, and tax reforms were introduced. The process was completed in 1688 when an assessment of the entire country laid down how much tax each administrative unit in the kingdom had to pay to the state coffers. The Great Assessment raised the national income from agriculture to almost 890,000 rixdollars per annum. The exemption of manor houses from taxation established a new understanding between monarchy and the old nobility, as a result of which the aristocracy became loyal servants to the absolute monarch. The tax burden was laid upon the peasants, whose standard of living accordingly fell. According to British ambassador Robert Molesworth, who published an account of Denmark in 1694, 'the weight of [taxes, etc.] is so great, that the Natives have reason rather to wish for, than defend their Country from an Invader; because they have little or no Property to lose'.[8] Although he may have exaggerated the desperation of the peasantry, Molesworth reveals how far impoverishment was the price of centralisation.

---

7   D. Cannadine (ed.), *Empire, the Sea and Global History: Britain's Maritime World, c.1760–c.1840* (London, 2007), p. 3.

8   R. Molesworth, *An Account of Denmark as it Was in the Year 1692* (London, 1694), p. 120.

Christian IV (1577–1648), who ascended to the Danish throne in 1596, aimed to expand central authority at home and increase the state revenues by transforming Denmark into a leading commercial nation. The Sound Dues paid by all merchants entering or leaving the Baltic Sea were an important source of income for the Crown. As the Baltic trade expanded, the Danish king exploited his control over the Sound in order to tax merchant vessels. Although Denmark grew rich from the Sound Dues, the country acquired an unenviable reputation as a parasitical power, alienating the leading commercial nations in Europe.

The commercial sector had great potential, however, and the export of Norwegian timber in particular provided the state with considerable revenue. The king's commercial endeavours were intended to 'bring honour to us [the king] and, God willing, no harm to the merchants', and he developed one of the first mercantilist programmes in Europe.[9] The Danish East India Company was founded in 1616. Christian IV held 12.5 per cent of the shares and, because it was difficult to attract foreign investment, he pressed Danish nobles and merchants into buying the rest of them. The company was regarded as a state enterprise, headed by the king, and an unsafe investment for merchants. The capital of the company could not sustain a regular trade. A mere eighteen ships sailed for Tranquebar, the Danish factory on the east coast of India, between 1618 and 1639 – and of these only seven returned. Denmark's overseas trade was therefore disappointing and Christian IV's personal losses were huge. In 1624 alone, he poured an additional 300,000 rixdollars into the Danish East India Company without receiving returns on the investment.

Mercantilist policies were still relatively new in Europe, and if Christian IV demonstrated a degree of naivety, it was because there was little experience upon which he could draw. Although many of his projects failed, mercantilist policy would be successfully adopted by future governments. During the Nine Years War (1688–97), when the greater part of Europe was engaged in war, Denmark–Norway remained neutral and secured commercial and maritime advantages. According to annual ship inventories prepared by custom house officials, the duties of Bergen, the largest port town in Norway, more than doubled while other Norwegian customs districts rose even more. No figures exist for Copenhagen, but the tonnage of the capital undoubtedly increased considerably more than that of any other shipping port of the realm.[10]

The government had an interest in protecting and regulating Danish trade. The expansion of commercial activity resulted in rising customs duties, which increased the annual income of the state. This success was the result of closer cooperation between merchants and central government. The German merchant Heinrich Schimmelmann (1724–82) was brought to Copenhagen in 1762 to help to improve the national economy. He served as finance minister and headed the leading merchant house of Copenhagen, which was involved in the slave trade and sugar

---

9   P.D. Lockhart, *Denmark 1513–1660: The Rise and Decline of a Renaissance Monarchy* (Oxford, 2007), p. 134.

10   D. Jørgensen, *Danmark-Norge mellom stormakterne 1688–1697* (Oslo, 1976), English summary, p. 323.

production on the Danish possessions in the Virgin Islands. He was also a major shareholder in the Danish East India Company.[11] This cooperation was especially successful in the last decades of the eighteenth century, when Danish involvement in overseas trade expanded as a result of the country's neutrality in the European wars. Vessels registered in Denmark and equipped with Danish documents transported goods belonging to French merchants in order to break the British maritime blockade of the Continent. The Danes claimed that neutral shipping could trade with any nation, but it was a dangerous policy especially when supported by a state in need of customs revenue, and resulted in a national disaster.[12] The British attacked Copenhagen twice in the first decade of the nineteenth century and took the Danish navy as war booty in 1807. Denmark lost its commercial potential and thus the ability to finance a potent small-scale imperial state.

Agrarian Empires

Mughal India was a vast agrarian empire with a population of over 100 million and a standard of living comparable to Europe. The revenue raised by the emperor Akbar (1542–1605) in 1595–96 was 99 million rupees, and, although the greatest part of the budget was devoted to supporting a massive military establishment, an annual surplus of 4 or 5 million rupees was often generated.[13] Owing to this ability historians such as Irfan Habib and J.F. Richards regard the Mughal state during the seventeenth and the first decades of the eighteenth century as an instrument of political and fiscal centralisation.[14]

Buoyed by conquest and plunder, Akbar created an administration capable of steady expansion, adding new provinces to the empire. As the Mughals penetrated local structures of power, *zamindars* were gradually reshaped into a quasi-official service class, and a new revenue system, *zabt*, was introduced.[15] The great advantage from an imperial point of view was that the *zabt* system enabled the administration to predict with great certainty its future revenue from agriculture. Mughal officials collected data on average yields and harvest by cultivator and village for the previous ten years, and local market prices for all crops were collected. These data enabled Mughal officials to calculate a standard assessment for each *pargana* and

---

11   C. Degn, *Die Schimmelmanns im atlantischen Dreieckshandel* (Neumünster, 1974).

12   Studies in eighteenth-century commercial policies of the Danish state have been done by O. Feldbæk: 'Dutch Batavia Trade via Copenhagen 1795–1807: A Study in Colonial Trade and Neutrality', *Scandinavian Economic History Review* 21 (1973): pp. 43–75; 'Eighteenth Century Danish Neutrality: Its Diplomacy, Economies and Law', *Scandinavian Journal of History* 8 (1983): pp. 3–21.

13   S. Moosvi, *The Economy of the Mughal Empire c. 1595: A Statistical Study* (Delhi, 1987), p. 195.

14   I. Habib, *Agrarian System of Mughal India, 1556–1707* (Delhi, 1999); J.F. Richards, *Mughal Empire*: vol. 5, *The New Cambridge History of India* (Cambridge, 1993).

15   Richards, *Mughal Empire*, p. 83.

for each individual crop.[16] Tapan Raychaudhuri claims that this elaborate fiscal system enabled the Mughals to extract from a third to a half of the profits from agricultural output.[17]

Raising taxes on such a scale year after year demanded an efficient revenue system and a centralised, bureaucratic state. The emperor commanded the services of a body of warrior-aristocrats who served as provincial governors and filled high administrative positions throughout the empire. These imperial administrators, *mansabdars*, were given a rank and a number of soldiers to maintain, and received either a cash payment from the imperial treasury or were granted *jagirs*. A *jagir*-holder possessed the fiscal rights of an imperial territory and raised taxes from the countryside. In 1595, some 1,800 men held *mansabs* and commanded above 140,000 soldiers, mostly heavy cavalry with their own horses and equipment. By the early eighteenth century, military expenses consumed 82 per cent of the total annual budget.[18]

According to J.F. Richards, the crucial moment in Mughal history was the 1680s, when the emperor Aurangzeb (1618–1707) led his army southwards and conquered the Deccan states of Golconda and Bijapur. Although initially successful, the Mughals never managed to incorporate the new territories in the empire and bring stability to the south. Aurangzeb spent most of his time with the army trying to repel the rising power of the Marathas, using large sums of money on military campaigns. With Aurangzeb thus occupied, imperial expansion in rural Indian society ceased and the central administration began to collapse as local *zamindars* and peasants resisted the demands of the weakened centralised state.[19]

Sanjay Subrahmanyam and Muzaffar Alam have contested these arguments, claiming that Mughal India never was a centralised state, and that at least one-third of the revenue was collected by means other than the *zabt*-system.[20] Such views support C.A. Bayly's research. He has described the Mughal Empire as a loose regime where *zamindars*, Hindu rajas and other groups of regional magnates controlled resources and authority in the villages. The local gentry prospered in Mughal service but began to separate themselves from the imperial centre, fight off demands for taxes, and assert their status as warrior kings in their own right.[21] The flow of taxes from the provinces dried up during the first half of the eighteenth century while provinces such as Bengal, Awadh and the Deccan slipped out of the control of Delhi and established independent states.

---

16 I. Habib, 'Agrarian Relations and Land Revenue', in I. Habib and T. Raychaudhuri (eds), *The Cambridge Economic History of India*, vol. 1 (Cambridge, 1982), p. 237.
17 T. Raychaudhuri, 'The State and the Economy' in T. Raychudhuri and I. Habib (eds), *The Cambridge Economic History of India*, vol. 1 (Cambridge, 1982), p. 173.
18 Richards, *Mughal Empire*, p. 63.
19 Ibid., p. 296.
20 M. Alam and S. Subrahmanyam, 'Introduction', *The Mughal State 1526–1750* (Oxford, 1998), p. 15.
21 C.A. Bayly, *Indian Society and the Making of the British Empire* (Cambridge, 1987), p. 13.

This regional perspective is similar to that taken by historians of the Ottoman Empire in recognition of the astonishing diversity of territories that it encompassed. Extending from Basra to the Balkans, a variety of regional fiscal and power structures grew in the Ottoman Empire, based as much on compromise as on force. Many areas – Egypt, Yemen, Baghdad and Basra – were more monetised and adopted fiscal systems based on the institutions of older elites rather than of the Ottoman state.[22]

In China, the Ming (1368–1644) and Qing (1644–1912) governments chose to make agriculture the foundation of its resource base, thereby basing fiscal security on the economic prosperity of peasants. Social and political stability thus rested on agricultural production. The Chinese economy had light agricultural taxation; although there were numerous surtaxes, the general level of taxation was a modest 10 per cent.[23] The tax revenue which reached the central government was low in comparison to the actual tax burden of the peasants as local authorities took their share of the money before sending it to the central government. But the amount that reached the imperial treasury was sufficient to pay the costs of a government which maintained only a thin veneer of administration.[24] The revenue increase experienced during the first Qing emperors was an effect of population growth. As the number of Chinese increased threefold, the area under cultivation expanded, almost doubling between 1650 and 1800.[25] However, the empire failed to take advantage of the growth of the economy, for the tax system did not provide the government with extra funds; revenue remained in the provinces and strengthened local power structures.

Commercial Empires

From the late sixteenth century, the Dutch Republic became the economic miracle of Western Europe. Trade was the dynamic sector and Dutch merchants dominated the Baltic trade, bringing naval stores and grain to the growing cities of the region. The Dutch pursued their imperial ambitions beyond Europe, and created a seaborne empire in Asia with Java at the centre. From the city of Batavia (Jakarta), the Dutch controlled the international spice trade through most of the seventeenth century.[26]

---

22 B. McGowan, *Economic Life in Ottoman Europe: Taxation, Trade and the Struggle for Land, 1600–1800* (Cambridge, 1981). For an advocate of the Ottoman Empire as a centralised state, see H. İnalcık, *The Ottoman Empire: The Classical Age 1300–1600* (Westport, CT, 1973; London, 2002).

23 R. Bin Wong, 'Relationship between the Political Economies of Maritime and Agrarian China, 1750–1850', in W. Gungwu and N. Chin-keong (eds), *Maritime China in Transition 1750–1850* (Wiesbaden, 2004), p. 21.

24 J.A.G. Roberts, *The Complete History of China* (London, 2006), p. 181.

25 S. Adshead, *China in World History* (London, 1995), p. 253.

26 H. Furber, *Rival Empires of Trade in the Orient 1600–1800* (Minnesota, 1976), p. 52.

Though the Danish monarch Christian IV referred to the Netherlands as the 'peddler-nation', he studied Dutch methods of commerce in an attempt to emulate them. Dutch success was based on the favourable environment provided for merchant groups by the republic. The state generals intervened, for example, in Scandinavian power struggles several times in order to secure a free passage in the Baltic by curtailing the powers of Denmark or Sweden. As Josiah Child (1630–99), director of the British East India Company, observed in the 1660s, 'The prodigious increase of the Netherlands in their domestic and foreign trade, riches and multitude of shipping, is the envy of the present and may be the wonder of future generations'.[27]

Holland was the leading province in the Dutch Republic and paid almost 60 per cent of the cost of government. Amsterdam alone raised half of this amount but also possessed the bulk of the commerce, shipping and industry, which provided tax revenue in the form of customs and excise duties. Holland was 'the cement that held the state together' while the rest of the Dutch revenue system was decentralised.[28] Each of the seven provinces in the Republic raised revenue by means of a separate tax system. In the predominantly rural provinces it was impossible to administer excises as efficiently as in the urban context, and so it made more sense to collect a higher proportion of taxation from traditional direct taxes on land and houses.[29] By the late eighteenth century the Dutch Republic was covered by an abundance of taxes, duties and levies. The lack of centralisation and fiscal unity posed a major problem for the Netherlands, and attention turned to the establishment of a national system that would merge the debts of the various provinces into a single national debt helping to reduce interest rates and enable the republic to meet its rising expenses.

During the eighteenth century the Netherlands was superseded by Britain as Europe's leading commercial nation. Britain had challenged Dutch commercial supremacy by creating commercial protection. The Navigation Act of 1651 (renewed 1665–66 and again 1672–74) ensured that goods imported to Britain arrived directly from the producer and were carried on British ships rather than passing through the hands of the Dutch.[30] The laws created an area of free trade between the British Isles and their colonies in the Atlantic Ocean which was protected from foreign competition and provided a basis for economic growth; the subsequent expansion of the colonial economy contributed to the commercial development of the mother country. Colonial trade led to an expansion of British manufacture in response to overseas demands. Seventy eight per cent of North American imports before 1775 came from Britain, covering a range of products such as textiles, household goods and metal wares.

---

27   J. Child, *A New Discourse of Trade* (London, 1694).
28   I. Wallerstein, *The Modern World-System*: vol. 2, *Mercantilism and the Consolidation of the European World-Economy, 1600–1750* (San Diego, CA, 1980), p. 62.
29   J. Israel, *The Dutch Republic: Its Rise, Greatness, and Fall 1477–1806* (Oxford, 1995), p. 291.
30   A. McFarlane, *The British in the Americas 1480–1815* (London, 1994) p. 99.

Huw Bowen has argued that although the foundations of the Atlantic trading system were laid by individual merchants, the British Atlantic empire and maritime strength were developed with the needs of the state in mind.[31] Merchant ships registered in England rose from 340,000 tons in 1686 to 2,477,000 tons by 1815. The tonnage of ships (the aggregate weight of goods carried in the cargo spaces of all vessels) cleared through British ports for the Caribbean, North America and Asia rose in the same period from 82,000 tons to 467,000. The Navigation Acts thus contributed to the rise of the British 'commercial revolution'.[32]

With the foundation of the English East India Company in 1600, a regular commerce with Asia was established and large quantities of Indian textiles were imported to London. From the eighteenth century, English merchants also began to visit Canton annually to buy tea. In contrast to the open trade of the Atlantic, Asian commerce was regulated by a chartered company that monopolised importation. From a fiscal point of view it was easier to tax the activities of one company instead of many merchants, and each time the charter was to be renewed the state could extract money from the directors in order to preserve the privileged trade.[33]

Earnings from customs also became an important source of state income. There was a steep rise in the level of duties paid as overseas trade was exploited for revenue purposes, and many new commodities were caught in the customs net. Still more striking was the growth of excise. Between 1670 and 1780 customs duties accounted for 25–30 per cent of total tax income whereas the level of excise in the same period rose from 23 per cent of total tax income to 56 per cent in 1780 (Table 13.1). This growth in government income was considerably greater than that enjoyed by other European states. As Dickson and Sperling have shown, Britain trebled its revenue between 1697 and 1714, compared with a 50 per cent increase in Holland and a fall in France.[34]

Imports of colonial goods were much greater than could be consumed by the domestic market, and so products such as tobacco, rice and coffee were re-exported by British merchants to northern Europe, thereby augmenting custom revenue. The favourable balance of trade in re-exports was used to transfer money to the European continent and finance military activities without draining the domestic

---

31 Bowen, *Elites, Enterprise and the Making of the British Overseas Empire*, p. 32; see also D. Hancock, *Citizens of the World: London Merchants and the Integration of the British Atlantic Community, 1735–1785* (Cambridge, 1995).

32 P. O'Brien, 'Inseparable Connections: Trade, Economy, Fiscal State and the Expansion of Empire, 1688–1815', in P.J. Marshall (ed.), *The Oxford History of the British Empire: The Eighteenth Century* (Oxford, 1998), p. 54.

33 N. Steensgaard, 'The Growth and Composition of the Long-distance Trade of England and the Dutch Republic before 1750', in J.D. Tracy (ed.), *The Rise of Merchant Empires: Long-distance Trade in the Early Modern World 1350–1750* (Cambridge, 1990), pp. 123–31.

34 P.G.M. Dickson and J. Sperling, 'War Finance 1689–1715', in J.S. Bromley (ed.), *New Cambridge Modern History*, vol. 6, (London, 1971), p. 313.

Table 13.1 Levels of tax income (£ million), Great Britain, 1670–1780

Year	Excises and stamps	Customs	Direct tax	Total tax income
1670	0.3	0.4	0.6	1.3
1690	0.9	0.7	1.4	3.0
1720	2.8	1.7	1.6	6.1
1750	3.5	1.4	2.0	6.9
1780	6.6	2.6	2.6	11.8

Sources: G. Holmes, *The Making of a Great Power: Late Stuart and Early Georgian Britain 1660–1720* (London, 1993), p. 268; for the tax income 1665–1720, see p. 433. For the period 1720–80, see G. Holmes and D. Szechi, *The Age of Oligarchy: Pre-Industrial Britain 1722–1783* (London, 1993), p. 369.

economy for cash.[35] Furthermore, the income financed the imports of useful raw materials such as iron, hemp and tar that helped to keep the merchant fleet and the British navy at sea.

Great Britain managed the burden of rising military commitments during the eighteenth century by radically increasing taxation. In the 1690s land tax provided 42 per cent of all tax revenue.[36] After 1714, indirect taxes, most notably customs and excise, became important sources of state income. Foreign trade served to increase the wealth of the nation, and British foreign policy favoured trade. The contribution that colonial trades were making to the British economy and to British public finances was universally recognised, and the eighteenth century witnessed a vigorous growth of a British empire built on transcontinental trade.[37] However, when parts of India were annexed as a British colony during the second half of the eighteenth century, the function of the East India Company was transformed from a merchant trading company to a tax collector remitting surplus revenue from land to Britain. By 1793, £500,000 per annum was going into the exchequer in London from Bengal. Indian revenue also financed British trade with China, and established Britain as a huge continental military power with a standing army of 220,000 soldiers. India was recognised as the most important possession. 'We cannot now', wrote a pamphleteer in 1773, 'relinquish those possessions without endangering our future freedom and independency as a nation'.[38]

35　D.W. Jones, *War and Economy in the Age of William III and Marlborough* (London, 1988), p. 78.
36　Brewer, *The Sinews of Power*, p. 95.
37　O'Brien, 'Inseparable Connections', p. 53; P.J. Marshall, 'Empire and British Identity: The Maritime Dimension', in D. Cannadine (ed.), *Empire, The Sea and Global History: Britain's Maritime World, c. 1763–c. 1840* (London, 2007), p. 48; J. Black, *Trade, Empire and British Foreign Policy, 1689–1815* (London, 2007), p. 13.
38　Quoted in Marshall, 'Empire and British Identity', p. 54; see also P. Lawson, *The East India Company: A History* (London, 1993), p. 131; H.V. Bowen, *Revenue and Reform: The Indian Problem in British Politics 1757–1773* (Cambridge, 1991), pp. 151–69.

Agrarian Empires and Trade

As we have already seen, the general approach to trade and commerce was somewhat different in agrarian Asia. Although the Chinese Qing dynasty kept an eye on the country's commercial activity during the eighteenth century, the state did not rely significantly on commercial revenues, and had little fiscal incentive to promote trade.[39] Close ties between merchants and the state never existed. Chinese merchants had to struggle against the orthodox Confucian view that they were at the bottom of the sociopolitical scale, and that they should not be allowed to use commercial wealth to acquire political power either directly through official appointments or indirectly through higher status.[40]

Not all Asian rulers were indifferent to the world of commerce. Shah Abbas (1587–1624), the ruler of Safavid Iran (Persia), has been called 'the largest capitalist in the kingdom'.[41] His commercial policies involved bringing thousands of Armenians to the newly established capital of Isfahan in 1606.[42] Under the patronage of the Shah, Armenians were granted trading privileges and soon controlled the lucrative export trade in Persian silk. Abbas's successor, Shah Safi (1629–42), consolidated the Armenian hold on internal trade in Iran by encouraging entrepreneurs to set up shops in the bazaars, create networks of contacts throughout the country, and develop international markets, promoting in particular Iran's foreign trade in raw silk.[43] Through such policies the Safavid dynasty was not only attempting to secure the state a higher income, but also to consolidate power, for example, by suppressing the commercial operations of the Tajiks, a group of political opponents.[44] Sanjay Subrahmanyam has argued that the Tajiks left the Safavid territories and moved to countries such as India and Thailand, where they gained political influence and were appointed to high posts within the state administration. Thus, the sort of 'state mercantilism' espoused in Iran by Shah Abbas was brought to other places in Asia

39 Wong, 'Relationships between the Political Economies of Maritime and Agrarian China', pp. 22, 27.
40 W. Gungwu, 'Merchants Without Empire: The Hokkien Sojourning Communities', in J.D. Tracy (ed.), *The Rise of Merchant Empires: Long-distance Trade in the Early Modern World 1350–1750* (Cambridge, 1990), p. 400. For studies that may provide a more nuanced picture of Chinese merchants, see J.K. Chin, 'The Hokkien Merchants in the South China Sea: 1500–1800', and R. Ptak, 'The Ryukyu Network in the Fifteenth and Early Sixteenth Centuries', in Om Prakash (ed.), *Trading World of the Indian Ocean 1500–1800* (Delhi, 2012), pp. 433-62 and 463-82 respectively.
41 Alam and Subrahmanyam, 'Introduction', p. 8.
42 S. Mentz, 'The Commercial Culture of the Armenian Merchant: Diaspora and Social Behaviour', *Itinerario* 1 (2004): pp. 20–21.
43 P. Jackson (ed.), *The Timurid and Safavid Periods*: vol. 6, *The Cambridge History of Iran* (Cambridge, 1986), p. 457.
44 S. Subrahmanyam, 'Persians, Pilgrims and Portuguese: The Travails of Masulipatnam Shipping in the Western Indian Ocean, 1590–1665', *Modern Asian Studies* 22/3 (1988): pp. 503–530.

by these 'portfolio capitalists'.[45] By combining political activity with long-distance trade their activities resembled European mercantile capitalism. However, their numbers were too few to make a profound difference in the Asian trading world.

In Mughal India merchants generally received little support from the state, and operated in a free trade zone, for the authorities and the merchants lived in demarcated worlds in which contact was negligible. Customs duties were minimal, around 5 per cent of the value of the goods. The separation of trade and state administration had its consequences. Without an active and protective state it was impossible for commercial capitalism to emerge in India. The commercial sector in India was a closed system in which merchants had no opportunity to invest in real estate or government bonds. The Indian merchant could only reinvest his capital in commercial transactions, and this led to an uncontrolled growth in the course of which a personal fortune neither ensured the merchant an improved social position nor reduced his risk of bankruptcy by spreading his investment activities. Commercial firms were thus vulnerable to changing political conditions and fluctuations of the market.[46]

Trade and commercial taxes may not have represented a great source of revenue for the emperor in Delhi, but, for the *zamindars* and provincial governors, taxes on trading activities were an important income supplement. India's export boom during the seventeenth century created increasing affluence in the provinces which benefited from economic growth. This increasing commercialisation strengthened regional authorities, merchants and financiers, and promoted provincial wealth and social power which could not easily be controlled from Delhi.[47] Alliances between the governors of provinces, *zamindars* and local financiers created the basis for new power structures, and former provinces in the heartland of the Mughal Empire initiated a process of secession that led to the setting up of such independent states as Bengal, Awadh and Hyderabad. Over the course of the eighteenth century these regions ceased to be provinces in the Mughal Empire and became successor states, autonomous and independent of the empire.[48]

---

45 S. Subrahmanyam, 'Iranians Abroad: Intra-Asian Elite Migration and Early Modern State Formation', in S. Subrahmanyam (ed.), *Merchant Networks in the Early Modern World* (London, 1996), p. 72; C.A. Bayly and S. Subrahmanyam, 'Portfolio Capitalists and the Political Economy of Early Modern India', *Indian Economic and Social History Review* 25/4 (1988): pp. 401–425.

46 K.N. Chaudhuri, *Trade and Civilisation in the Indian Ocean: An Economic History from the Rise of Islam to 1750* (Cambridge, 1985), pp. 212–14.

47 Bayly, *Indian Society*, p. 10.

48 M. Alam, *Crisis of Empire in Mughal North India: Awadh and the Punjab 1707–1748* (Delhi, 1991).

Creating the National Debt: The Financial Revolution

The success of Britain and its rise to great power status was a consequence in part of a highly efficient financial system. By the early eighteenth century London had become an international trading entrepôt with a dynamic service sector and a prosperous merchant community.[49]

Trade was a risky business. A sensible merchant would secure himself by spreading his capital around different types of investments. As such, commercial ventures to different destinations were mixed with financial transactions. Lending money on interest, or investment in real estate, represented alternatives, and although the profit rates were lower than on trade ventures they were more secure forms of investment. The merchant financier and East India Company director Sir John Banks, for example, withdrew almost entirely from commercial activity during the 1670s, after which 48 per cent of his capital was invested in real estate and 39 per cent in government bonds and mortgages. He kept 4 per cent in cash and invested only 9 per cent in trade.[50]

Contemporary observers were concerned about the volume of capital being channelled away from commerce and invested in financial transactions, claiming that it threatened to ruin the country. Their fears were unfounded; the British commercial and service sector continued to expand. In C.H. Lee's view, 'the key essentials of a financial market, dealing in securities by specialists, legal recognition of transfers, a banking system, and sufficient wealth available for investment, were all conditions fulfilled in London by the late seventeenth century'.[51] The City of London played an important role in overseas activities, financing planters in the Caribbean, settlers in Chesapeake and private merchants in India.[52]

The commercial and financial sector contributed to the consolidation of Britain's political and economic status after the War of Spanish Succession in 1714. Military actions had to be financed and the state's acute lack of capital brought drastic changes to the financial sector, the most notable of which was the creation of the National Debt. The National Debt had been introduced in 1692–93 when the government raised a loan of £1 million by offering the investors annuities, and secured the payments of interest on future tax revenues.[53] According to Patrick O'Brien, long-term borrowing provided the state with the means to mobilise the forces of the Crown speedily by avoiding the burden of sharp and immediate rises in taxation.[54] The National Debt increased from £2 million in 1680 to £14 million in

---

49   O'Brien, 'Inseparable Connections', pp. 60–61.

50   D.C. Coleman, *Sir John Banks, Baronet and Businessman: A Study of Business, Politics and Society in Later Stuart England* (Oxford, 1963), p. 56.

51   C.H. Lee, *The British Economy since 1700: A Macroeconomic Perspective* (Cambridge, 1986), p. 60.

52   S. Mentz, *The English Gentleman Merchant at Work: Madras and the City of London 1660–1740*, (Copenhagen, 2005); Hancock, *Citizens of the World*; Bowen, *Elites, Enterprise and the Making of the British Overseas Empire*.

53   Holmes, *The Making of a Great Power*, p. 270.

54   O'Brien, 'Inseparable Connections', p. 66.

1700, but this was nothing compared with the £133 million the British state owed its creditors in 1763 or the £700 million in 1815.[55] It was the ability of the state to tap the wealth of the merchant elite that secured the outcome of the Anglo-French warfare in the period from 1689 to 1815; Britain could always finance another army while France collapsed under the burden of military expenses. Economic development did suffer occasional setbacks, like that of the South Sea Bubble in the 1720s. The South Sea Company had lent almost £12 million to the state by converting government bonds into Company shares. When the public discovered how the shares were without real value, panic broke out and all share holders tried to sell at the same time. Many small-scale investors lost their savings and it took time before the confidence to the British government and the financial system was restored.

Central to the financial revolution was the Bank of England. Created in 1694 the Bank serviced the financial needs of the government, receiving deposits, making loans and handling the national debt; J.H. Clapham has characterised the Bank as a money-raising machine which received privileges in exchange for providing the state with loans.[56] From the second half of the eighteenth century, the East India Company also provided the government with loans. The Company began to issue short-term bonds in order to raise capital, and these bonds became popular investments for the British middle class. The East India Company was becoming a public domain rather than a private organisation, and politicians gave 'cast-iron guarantees' that the Company's position in East would remain unchanged.[57] The government would not experience another financial crisis akin to the South Sea Bubble.

National Debts and Asian Empires

When Aurangzeb commenced his large-scale campaign against the Deccan sultanates of Golconda and Bijapur, he had no need to borrow money for the war. Unlike European leaders, the emperor was able to draw upon accumulated reserves in the provincial treasuries.[58] When Aurangzeb died in 1707 the Mughals controlled most of the Indian subcontinent. But the imperial finances were drained and without money the power of the central government diminished. The Mughal Empire was collapsing by the time of emperor Farrukhsiyar's death in 1719.

Although we know little of the influence of public loans in Mughal India, there are no indications of either a financial sector or a banking system which provided the state with loans. Yet Indian merchant bankers played an important role in the Mughal Empire during the seventeenth century. Karen Leonard has argued that

---

55 H. Roseveare, *The Financial Revolution 1660–1760* (London, 1991), pp. 3, 52; Dickson, *The Financial Revolution*.

56 J. Clapham, *The Bank of England, 1694–1797* (London, 1945), chap. 1.

57 Lawson, *The East India Company*, p. 76.

58 Richards, *Mughal Empire*, p. 185.

indigenous banking firms performed services for the Mughal state, organising trade in agricultural products and using credit notes (*hundis*) to move money from one part of the country to another.[59] But merchant wealth was not tapped as in Europe, and no political partnership was established which could have provided the Mughal state with liquidity in times of trouble.

When central authority collapsed, Hindu trader-bankers and Muslim revenue farmers assisted regional power structures in creating independent states. However, the alliance was seldom successful and successor states struggled with poor finances. During the Anglo-French wars of the 1740s, the Nawab of Arcot, Muhammad Ali (1717–95), secured his rule in the Carnatic with help from the British army. The Nawab is one example of an independent ruler who failed to create a financial system that could cope with the rising debts of his state. To finance his warfare Mohammed Ali borrowed money from several Indian merchants, such as Bukkanji Kasi Das – a Gujarati with agents at all the principal towns – at exhorbitant rates of interest. The lending rate in 1759 was 1.5 per cent per month plus the commission on the *hundi*, which could be another 1.5 per cent per month. In addition, Indian merchants wanted adequate security in jewels or gold. These high rates of interest forced the Nawab to borrow capital from the British. In 1766 his debts to the East India Company stood at 1,365,104 pagodas (£546,041) and he owed an even greater sum to private British merchants. The private loans had also been borrowed at excessive rates of interest ranging from 20 to 36 per cent.[60] Despite his financial deficits, Muhammad Ali was considered one of the richest princes in South India, but the situation became more critical year by year as large proportions of the land's revenue were going into the payment of interest on the debts. In 1773 the Nawab's private secretary, George Paterson, described the desperate economic situation in the following manner:

> When the necessities of the state made great payments necessary, the Nawab had nothing, and was obliged to raise money at an exorbitant interest from money lenders of every denomination, ruining his finances, bringing him into disgrace with the public. Thereafter his payments were precarious and uncertain.[61]

The Nawab of Arcot and other rulers of Indian successor states did not create a national debt equivalent to the British. Without money or credit their states could not withstand British pressure and fell under the influence of the East India Company.

---

59   K. Leonard, 'The "Great Firm" Theory of the Decline of the Mughal Empire', *Comparative Studies in Society and History* 21/2 (1979): p. 399.

60   S. Arasaratnam, *Maritime Commerce and English Power (Southeast India 1750–1800)* (Delhi, 1996), p. 14.

61   George Paterson's diary 1773, quotation from J.D. Gurley, 'The Debts of the Nawab of Arcot, 1763–1776', DPhil dissertation, Oxford University, 1968, p. 226.

Public and Private Domains

Government finance in Asia and in Europe followed different paths from the late seventeenth century onwards. As we have seen, Mughal India concentrated on raising revenue from the agricultural sector without involving the commercial and financial sectors to any considerable degree in state affairs. Rising production and monetisation of the rural economy put more resources at the disposal of the local gentry.[62] The regions prospered under the loose regime of the Mughals and used their wealth to separate themselves from Delhi. According to J.F. Richards, the failure of the central government to intervene in rural society increased 'the confidence and the resources of the zamindars', and encouraged 'conflict with more prominent gentry and trading groups'.[63] Even in imperial China the capacity of the Qing emperor to mobilise the bureaucracy to influence local affairs remained significantly circumscribed.[64]

In Britain a close alliance between the landed aristocracy and the commercial and financial elite dictated the general pattern of economic development and overseas expansion in the eighteenth and nineteenth centuries, creating what Cain and Hopkins have dubbed 'the gentleman capitalist'.[65] Leading members of the gentlemanly elite were drawn from across Britain into a tight-knit political and business community centred on London, the financial and political capital of the Empire. They benefited from metropolitan involvement in a wide variety of overseas activities and enterprises: 'Bankers, politicians, military officers, landowners and merchants contributed capital and skills to the development of the empire and, in return, drew benefit in the form of employment, opportunity, prestige and profit.'[66]

British subjects generally accepted rising taxation, even by the 1780s, when the rate was two and a half times that in France.[67] But rising tax levels could have serious consequences. When the British government tried to make the North American colonies contribute financially to the rising military expenses by introducing the Stamp Act in 1765 and the Coercive Acts in 1774 political animosity was created which led eventually to American independence.

In his *Inquiry into the Nature and Causes of the Wealth of Nations* (1776), Adam Smith reflects over the progress of societies and argues that nations must go through four stages of development, each of which will shape the mode of production and political institutions. The final stage is characterised by the division of labour and free trade between nations, effectively superseding mercantilism. The advantages

---

62   Bayly, *Indian Society*, pp. 3–4.
63   Richards, *Mughal Empire*, p. 296.
64   C.M. Isett, *State, Peasant and Merchant in Qing Manchuria, 1644–1862* (Stanford, CA, 2007), p. 10.
65   P.J. Cain and A.G. Hopkins, *British Imperialism: Innovation and Expansion 1688–1914* (London, 1993).
66   Bowen, *Elites, Enterprise and the Making of the British Overseas Empire*, p. 48.
67   P. Mathias and P. O'Brien, 'Taxation in England and France, 1715–1810: A Comparison of the Social and Economic Incidence of Taxes Collected for the Central Governments', *Journal of European Economic History* 5 (1976): pp. 601–650.

of free trade were seen soon after the creation of the United States of America when the former colony resumed trade with Britain. In 1781–85 US trade with Britain was worth £1.8 million; ten years later its value had trebled to £7.4 million.[68] A new phase of imperial finance had begun.

The Craze for Markets: Financing the Nineteenth-Century Empire

With the repeal of the Corn Laws in 1846 Britain opened its markets to all the nations of the world. The Prime Minister Robert Peel (1788–1850) believed that free trade would promote civilisation and peace, a vision he shared with many intellectuals of the early Victorian age.[69] The repeal was seen as a victory for middle-class ideas, and together with the reforms of the 1830s the middle class were attached to the constitution and had, in the words of Lord Grey, become 'the real and efficient mass of public opinion … without whom the power of the gentry is nothing'.[70]

For most of the nineteenth century, Britain was an industrial nation whose interest lay in trade. Satellite economies were established all over the world and regions such as Central and South America became part of an informal empire subjugated to British economic interests. These activities increased the government's income from customs and excise duties (Table 13.2). Britain's policy-makers were aware of the need to provide industries, especially cotton goods, with overseas markets and to deal with problems of foreign competition. Free trade would generate additional revenues, allowing the tax burden to be eased and the national debt to be reduced. The City of London and the British service sector gained from this policy, and 'by the mid-Victorian period, free trade and overseas investment were propelling the City towards the leadership of a global economy instead of merely a colonial one'.[71] By 1850 invisible earnings began to assume importance in the balance of payments as overseas investments, marine insurances and other services secured the British state a sizable income.

India became the most important possession in the British Empire but it took time before the British state actually gained from the take-over of provinces such as Bengal, Awadh, Sind and the Punjab. British India was administered by the East India Company until the Indian Mutiny in 1857, when civil authority was transferred to the Crown. The company was a private organisation, and the abolition in 1813 of the company's monopoly of trade with India allowed private

68   McFarlane, *The British in the Americas*, p. 286.
69   A. Howe, 'Free Trade and Global Order: The Rise and Fall of a Victorian Vision', in D. Bell (ed.), *Victorian Visions of Global Order: Empire and International Relations in Nineteenth-Century Political Thought* (Cambridge, 2007), p. 26.
70   T.W. Heyck, *The Peoples of the British Isles: A New History from 1688 to 1870* (Belmont, CA, 1992), p. 307.
71   Cain and Hopkins, *British Imperialism*, p. 84.

Table 13.2   Levels of tax income (£ million), Great Britain, 1800–1850

Year	Customs	Excise	Land tax
1801–1805	8.2	15.6	5.4
1826–30	19.4	21.3	5.2
1846–50	22.1	14.7	4.5

Source: Compiled from E.J. Evans, *The Forging of the Modern State: Early Industrial Britain 1783–1870* (London, 1983), p. 389.

merchants to make their way into new markets. Agency houses invested private capital in various types of commercial ventures, exploiting the political power of the company, and, while the private merchants gained fortunes, the East India Company was faced with rising deficits due to military expenditure, a bill that British taxpayers at home unwillingly helped to cover.[72]

When these problems gradually eased after 1857, India contributed to the imperial finances in different ways. Land tax was the largest source of state revenue followed by the sale of opium, which was a government monopoly. The British introduced individual ownership of land with fixed money rents. If landowners were unable to meet the regular revenue demand of the government and fell into debt, they were forced to sell or had their land confiscated. The pattern of rural life was breaking up as old feudal masters were displaced by new ones. The British Empire did also profit by selling products to the Indians. In 1850 nearly one-fifth of Britain's exported cotton goods went to India, and the economic development of the colony was directed towards the production of foodstuffs and raw materials in exchange for clothing and other manufactured goods.[73]

As the century progressed, European powers like Germany and France industrialised, as did the United States of America. Britain's global interests were threatened and the craze for markets and colonies intensified. Although free trade characterised the nineteenth century, the traditional agrarian empire also revived. Russia was the fastest-expanding country owing to her growing interest in central Asia. The repopulation of the Crimea in the late eighteenth century was an attempt to exploit the economic potential of the territory. Foreign immigrants were encouraged to settle in Russia in order to make the underpopulated areas more productive. German farmers cultivated the land, while Greeks, Armenians and Jews exploited commercial connections with their places of origin and established trade routes to Russia. The port city of Odessa prospered especially,

72   Furber, *Rival Empires of Trade*, pp. 290–92; S. Mentz, 'European Private Trade in the Indian Ocean 1500–1800', in Om Prakash (ed.), *Trading World of the Indian Ocean 1500–1800*, pp. 483-518; Cain and Hopkins, *British Imperialism*, p. 323.

73   B. Porter, *The Lion's Share: A Short History of British Imperialism 1850–1995* (London, 1996), pp. 42–3.

receiving an average of 300 ships a year.[74] During the nineteenth century Russian territorial expansion was directed towards Central Asia, a region where the only European opponent was the British presence in India. With these areas secured, the population of the Romanov empire rose from 36 million in 1800 to 60 million by 1850, creating a huge increase in taxpayers and representing a protected market for Russian industrial products.[75]

While an agrarian revenue system was the fundamental platform for any empire, the commercial and financial sectors represented alternatives with enormous potential. In Asia where land was plentiful, rising expenditure was met by increasing agricultural revenue, while European states used indirect taxation and long-term borrowing as ways of raising capital. Growing commercialisation in the years after 1600 favoured the approach taken by European statesmen, although it was not a straightforward success. Philip II of Spain, for example, could not control the national debt, although he commanded a vast empire with great economic potential. He resorted to bankruptcy several times to escape from his enormous indebtedness to international bankers. However, in Britain the financial revolution provided cash in periods of war by postponing the payment to the future. As the state managed to reduce interest rates, government bonds did not lead to bankruptcy but was considered a secure investment for the general public. It was an option that few Asian rulers had. They could command large armies, but only as long as the treasuries were full.

The Danish historian Niels Steensgaard has called the comparative study of taxation 'a specialty with few friends',[76] perhaps for obvious reasons – it is a laborious task to follow the money – but it is rewarding, and the results will reveal why some empires prospered while others collapsed. Future research must give the centralised fiscal system more attention by focusing on the relationship between the imperial core and various regions, and by using a comparative approach to create a better understanding of the vital role fiscal mechanisms played in world empires.

---

74   J. Pallot and D. Shaw, *Landscape and Settlement in Romanov Russia* (Oxford, 1990), p. 83.

75   P. Longworth, *Russia's Empires: Their Rise and Fall: From Prehistory to Putin* (London, 2005), p. 208.

76   Steensgaard, 'The Seventeenth-Century Crisis', p. 683.

Consumption

Erika Rappaport

Since the early 1990s, historians, anthropologists and literary critics have expanded our understanding of the motives for empire-building, and the nature and consequences of the colonial encounter. They have urged us to look at imperialism as something which happens both in the metropole and in the colonies, and to regard colonialism as a form of exchange between the colonised and coloniser. These shifts have significantly altered the study of imperial economies and cultures. Where once commodities were regarded as quantifiable evidence of the value of colonies, they are now studied in their own right as carriers of meaning, sites of contestation and lenses through which we can see the making and unmaking of imperial, sub- and trans-imperial relationships. This new approach to commodities has been premised upon a dynamic understanding of the consumer and consumerism as critical to the history of imperialism.

Those who debated the economics of formal and informal empires typically measured consumers but did not analyse their role in process of colonisation. Studies of imperial political economy presented consumers as shadowy figures reacting to activities that happened elsewhere. They could be either beneficiaries or victims but seldom directed the show. In the last few years, however, we have begun to delineate the historical conditions which enabled consumers to play a role in local, national, imperial and post-imperial economies and cultures. Initially this approach focused on western industrialised settings and essentially showed how Euro-American consumers were complicit in the imperial project. Scholars soon moved beyond the west, however, to illuminate how consumer practices and material cultures were a central aspect of the colonial encounter. Some have focused on how consumer-based identities also contributed to organised anti-colonial struggles. Others have employed the metaphor of the commodity chain to show how non-European consumers shaped the history of global economies before, during and after European colonisation. By looking at consumers in Europe, the Americas, Africa, and South and East Asia, this research has scrutinised and rewritten Eurocentric assumptions about the birth and consequences of the global economy. It has recast our understanding of the motives and justifications for colonisation, the players involved in the colonial process, and the ways in which colonisation was experienced and resisted. Most of this work maintains the linkages between economics and empire but questions the distinction between formal/informal/irresistible empires, and the shift between an empire of free trade to one of formal conquest in the late nineteenth century.

European Consumerism as Imperialism

Much recent work has emphasised how consumerism was a driving force behind early modern and modern forms of globalisation and contributed to the establishment of Europe's overseas empires. European consumers' taste for tropical commodities fed expansion into Asia, Africa and elsewhere, at least from the sixteenth century.[1] As luxury items increasingly gave way to mass-consumed commodities such as foodstuffs, drugs and cotton textiles, average men and women became implicated in the imperial project. As they shopped for and consumed foods and fashions, men and women far removed from colonial spaces were enacting a mundane but central role of colonial acquisition. This scholarship shifts our gaze from producer to consumer and reveals how empire operates in metropolitan spaces as well as in formal and informal colonial settings.

In the nineteenth and twentieth centuries, advertisements, museums and exhibitions relied upon and promoted similar Orientalist discourses that acknowledged Europe's colonial history yet sugar-coated this story. Popular culture taught Europeans that their daily comforts and pleasures derived from faraway lands, but, as Joanna de Groot has written, this culture also rendered the most exploitive aspects of imperial power relations invisible.[2] Lipton tea advertisements,

---

1   There are numerous works that develop this point. One of the best examples is Marcy Norton, *Sacred Gifts, Profane Pleasures: A History of Tobacco and Chocolate in the Atlantic World* (Ithaca and London: Cornell University Press, 2008). Also see John Brewer and Roy Porter (eds), *Consumption and the World of Goods* (London, 1993); Maxine Berg, *Luxury and Pleasure in Eighteenth Century England* (New York, 2005); Peter N. Stearns, *Consumerism in World History: The Global Transformation of Desire* (London, 2001); Elizabeth Kowaleski-Wallace, *Consuming Subjects: Women, Shopping and Business in the Eighteenth Century* (New York, 1997); and D. Woodruff Smith, *Consumption and the Making of Respectability, 1600–1800* (New York, 2002).

2   Joanna de Groot, 'Metropolitan Desires and Colonial Connections: Reflections on Consumption and Empire', in Catherine Hall and Sonya O. Rose (eds), *At Home with the Empire: Metropolitan Culture and the Imperial World* (Cambridge, 2006), p. 170. There is a very large body of work on British imperial popular culture. See, for example, John MacKenzie, *Propaganda and Empire: The Manipulation of British Public Opinion, 1880–1960* (Manchester, 1984); MacKenzie (ed.), *Imperialism and Popular Culture* (Manchester, 1987); Anne McClintock, *Imperial Leather: Race, Gender and Sexuality in the Colonial Contest* (New York, 1995); Thomas Richards, *Commodity Culture in Victorian England: Advertising and Spectacle, 1851–1914* (Stanford, CA, 1990); Peter H. Hoffenberg, *An Empire on Display: English, Indian and Australian Exhibitions from the Crystal Palace to the Great War* (Berkeley, CA, 2001).

for example, frequently illustrated how the crop was grown and manufactured on plantations in Ceylon, but did not reveal the more exploitative aspects of plantation labour systems.[3] These advertisements conveyed notions of racial and cultural superiority, and literally made colonialism palatable. This imperial propaganda could also be effective in countries with relatively small 'formal' empires, such as the nineteenth-century United States. Kristin Hoganson, for example, has shown how American consumer culture was layered with imperial ideologies even before it entered its most expansive and 'imperialistic' phase. By acknowledging informal and cultural forms of imperialism, work such as Hoganson's has placed middle-class female shoppers in the role of coloniser.[4]

The consumer-imperialist may have become an even more ubiquitous figure in the early twentieth century when governments as well as quasi-political agencies such as Britain's Empire Marketing Board began to argue that consumers were imperial citizens who had a patriotic duty to buy empire goods. In Britain and France, for example, interwar displays of colonial produce and peoples were often conscious state efforts to win populations over to the imperial project. The Colonial Exhibition held in Paris in 1931, for example, contained tens of thousands of square metres of display space explaining to French citizens how and why colonies aided their ailing economy.[5] Politicians and their allies recognised that colonies were not always profitable but they used the promise of future riches as a justification for empire.[6] Even if the markets and cheap raw materials hoped for from colonial exploitation were not always realised, advertisements and exhibitions sold the idea of empire as a desirable commodity.

As valuable as this new consumer-oriented approach has been it has, in many respects, replicated past understandings of empires as serving European bodily needs and desires. Most Victorian politicians and businessmen would no doubt have agreed with this materialist conception of colonialism. A typical mid-nineteenth-century English tea advertisement, for example, informed consumers that 'Every land under the Sun is ransacked to provide the good things in life for Englishmen and Englishwomen and there is no other country in which the women have such

3   Anandi Ramamurthy, *Imperial Persuaders: Images of Africa and Asia in British Advertising* (Manchester, 2003). Piya Chatterjee makes a similar point in *A Time for Tea: Women, Labor and Post/Colonial Politics on an Indian Plantation* (Durham, NC, 2001).
4   Kristin L. Hoganson, *Consumers' Imperium: The Global Production of American Domesticity, 1865–1920* (Chapel Hill, NC, 2007).
5   Patricia Morton, *Hybrid Modernities: Architecture and Representation at the 1931 Colonial Exhibition, Paris* (Cambridge, MA, 2000). Also see Thomas G. August, *The Selling of Empire: British and French Imperialist Propaganda, 1890–1940* (Westport, CT, 1985); Steven Constantine, '"Bringing the Empire Alive": The Empire Marketing Board and Imperial Propaganda, 1926–33', in John MacKenzie (ed.), *Imperialism and Popular Culture* (Manchester, 1986), pp. 192–231.
6   On the French colonial lobby and its promotion of Empire trade, see, for example, Robert Aldrich, *Greater France: A History of French Overseas Expansion* (London, 1996) and D.K. Fieldhouse, *Economics and Empire, 1830–1914* (London, 1973), especially pp. 22–6.

chances of making a pleasant and happy home.'[7] The advertisement recognised and even celebrated the fact that metropolitan domesticity was derived from the pillage of much of the rest of the world. In this Victorian advertisement, and in much recent historical work, the image of the consumer has been reduced to that of receptacle of new things and/or a spectator of a commodified entertaining empire. This scholarship has acknowledged the consumer's centrality to imperial political economies but has maintained an essentially passive and feminised construct of the consumer.

Another problem which critics have been quick to point out is that it is not clear what type of knowledge consumers actually gleaned from visiting an exhibition, drinking a cup of tea or purchasing a Kashmiri shawl.[8] Did commercialised forms of imperialism lead to greater political support for empire or even sell more goods? Did consumers engage in patriotic purchasing when an inexpensive non-imperial commodity was available? What role did merchants and retailers play in this story? Did they always agree that selling empire was a good or profitable thing?[9] What about 'imperial' goods that travelled from the colonies but which were not heavily advertised or even acknowledged as bearing colonial origins?[10] Finally, what were the conditions which enabled consumers to move beyond being passive recipients of imperialistic propaganda? I have argued elsewhere that consumer knowledge often became important at moments of crisis or scarcity, when legal or state structures changed, or when public issues such as food scares raised awareness about the healthiness or morality of globally traded goods.[11] It is fairly clear now that imperial traces saturated metropolitan consumer culture and that consumers were participants in the colonial endeavour. However, we have not yet fully

---

7   Advertisement, c. 1865. Tetley Group Archive, Acc# 4364/01/002, London Metropolitan Archive.

8   See my discussion of this point in 'Imperial Possessions, Cultural Histories, and the Material Turn', *Victorian Studies* 50/2 (Winter 2008): pp. 289–96.

9   For an example of when merchants resisted the promotion of empire, see Erika Rappaport, 'Art, Commerce or Empire? The Rebuilding of Regent Street, 1880–1927', *History Workshop Journal* 53 (2002): pp. 95–118.

10   For a discussion of these sorts of commodities, see the series of papers presented as part of the 'Commodities of Empire' research project run by Sandip Hazareesingh, Jean Stubbs and Jonathon Curry-Machado based at London Metropolitan University. See, for example, Ayodeji Olukoju, 'The United Kingdom and the Political Economy of the Global-Oil Producing Nuts and Seeds during the 1930s', *Commodities of Empire Working Paper*, 5 (London, 2008).

11   Erika Rappaport, 'Packaging China: Foreign Articles and Dangerous Tastes in the Mid-Victorian Tea Party', in Frank Trentmann (ed.), *The Making of the Consumer: Knowledge, Power and Identity in the Modern World* (London, 2006), pp. 125–46. Also see, Frank Trentmann, 'Knowing Consumers – Histories, Identities, Practices: An Introduction', in the same volume, pp. 1–29; Susan Freidberg, *French Beans and Food Scares: Culture and Commerce in an Anxious Age* (Oxford, 2004) and Lowell J. Satre, *Chocolate on Trial: Slavery, Politics and the Ethics of Business* (Athens, OH, 2005).

considered the significance of these developments either on an individual level or in broader economic, social or political terms.

Some of these issues have been addressed by research that has explored European consumer practices in the colonies. These studies have posited a highly politicised consumer-subject who consciously and subconsciously used European foods, fashions and architectural styles to erect and maintain racial, class and gender boundaries in the empire. Things from home, for example, often became crucial tools in the forging of social networks among white colonists and thereby contributed to the maintenance of European authority.[12] Personal acts of clothing took on especially powerful notions of cultural superiority when performed in a colonial setting.[13] At times the desire for metropolitan commodities proved difficult and could lead to dramatic instances of domestic violence and family disharmony.[14] Consumerism in the empire could thus undermine as well as cement the bonds of white colonial society. Despite these problems, however, colonial settlers used the acquisition and display of goods to maintain boundaries, and colonise subject peoples.

Consumer Politics and the Colonial Encounter

Consumer goods and their uses were, however, not merely a source of power to the coloniser. In colonial settings the purchase, display and rejection of consumer goods were crucial ways in which colonialism was experienced, reworked and, on occasion, rejected. Ironically, though consumers could and did use goods to protest against colonialism this did not necessarily imply a rejection of consumerism or global capitalism *per se*. Indeed, much scholarship has shown how important non-western consumers were to the growth of the modern global economy. All of this work has assumed a relatively dynamic relationship between buyers and sellers and thereby developed a more nuanced view of how consumers incorporate and redefine commodities to create new hybrid colonial cultures.

Much of the new work on consumerism in colonial settings has focused on the late eighteenth and early nineteenth century, a period which witnessed the growth in what historians have labelled consumer society, but also on theorising about the nature of the consumer and consumerism. Political economists, moralists, scientists and others argued about who should consume goods, and what, how and where objects should be purchased and displayed. The intensification of cottage industries, growth of global trade in cheap rather than luxury items, and

---

12   Alan Lester, *Imperial Networks: Creating Identities in Nineteenth-Century South Africa and Britain* (London, 2001), especially pp. 74–7.

13   Nicola J. Thomas, 'Embodying Imperial Spectacle: Dressing Lady Curzon, Vicereine of India, 1899–1905', *Cultural Geographies* 14/3 (2007): pp. 369–400.

14   Erika Rappaport, 'The Bombay Debt: Letter Writing, Domestic Economies and Family Conflict in Colonial India', *Gender and History* 16/2 (2004): pp. 233–60.

expansion of state power based on the taxation of colonial commodities raised questions about the legitimacy of consumption and imperialism. Eighteenth- and early nineteenth-century imperial economic policy was one arena in which the value of the consumer and primary commodities first emerged. A fully theorised consumer-citizen is a more recent development and something that we are just beginning to understand.[15] However, in the American colonies, in Great Britain and in China we find a new politically potent consumer emerging at the end of the eighteenth century as various parties debated slavery, free trade and taxation policy. The debates transformed commodities such as tea, sugar, cotton and opium into symbols of foreign oppression and/or national and individual liberty. Clare Midgley has shown how in 1790s Britain, for example, abolitionists launched a campaign to abstain from using slave-produced sugar and related commodities. This effort particularly incorporated women into the political process, but Midgley carefully points out that the emphasis was placed on abstaining from using and eating, not from buying *per se*. The consumer being called upon to exert pressure on Parliament and planters was defined more as a user of goods than a modern-day shopper.[16] Nevertheless, this movement asked consumers to contemplate the nature of the labour that produced their comforts and to recognise that everyday choices influenced workers across the Atlantic. This consumer-oriented politics privileged free labour and free trade while encouraging the growth of new forms of imperialism in South Asia and elsewhere.

This politicisation of slave-produced goods occurred in North America, but anti-colonial politics also elevated the significance of Americans' consumer choices. Timothy Breen has revealed how the economic slump following the Seven Years' War, coupled with an increased debt burden in the North American colonies, shifted colonial self-perceptions and politicised British imports. Consumer boycotts and organised protests such as the Boston Tea Party were the product and generator of a new view of the consumer. Even a working-class consumer could be virtuous if he or she abstained from purchasing imported goods. Indeed, Breen emphasises that after the passage of the Tea Act in May 1773 the ideological shift from non-

---

15 See Frank Trentmann, 'The Modern Genealogy of the Consumer: Meanings, Identities and Political Synapses', in Trentmann (ed.), *Consuming Cultures, Global Perspectives: Historical Trajectories, Transnational Exchanges* (Oxford, 2006) pp. 19–69 and Trentmann, *Free Trade Nation: Commerce, Consumption and Civil Society in Modern Britain* (Oxford, 2008). Most work on the role of consumers in formal politics has looked at the late nineteenth and early twentieth centuries and focused on European and American settings. See, for example, Susan Strasser, Charles McGovern and Matthias Judt (eds), *Getting and Spending: European and American Consumer Societies in the Twentieth Century* (Cambridge, 1998) and Matthew Hilton, *Consumerism in Twentieth-Century Britain: The Search for a Historical Movement* (Cambridge, 2003). There has also been a recent interest in Asian consumer politics. See, for example, Sheldon and Patricia L. Maclachan (eds), *The Ambivalent Consumer: Questioning Consumption in East Asia and the West* (Ithaca, NY, 2006), and Patricia L. Maclachan, *Consumer Politics in Postwar Japan* (Ithaca, NY, 2002).

16 Clare Midgley, *Women Against Slavery: The British Campaigns, 1780–1870* (London, 1995).

importation to non-consumption forced the issue of individual responsibility and everyday choices.[17]

Consumerism and resistance to colonial state authority were interdependent in late-colonial America. Yet what were the long-term consequences for this nation founded in part on a narrative of anti-colonial, democratic consumerism? Was there any connection between the revolutionary and progressive eras, when consumerism came to be articulated as one of the founding pillars of American national identity and the modern face of imperialism?[18] Scholars such as Victoria de Grazia have begun to trace how specific institutions and commodities aided the overseas expansion of American consumer culture, establishing what she argues was a new form of imperialism based on markets for goods and ideas that proved irresistible to many Europeans in the late nineteenth and twentieth century.[19] More work on the globalising tendencies of early nineteenth-century American business would help us to see the transition between an era when consumerism signified anti-imperial politics and a time when it became the visible face of a newly powerful informal empire.[20]

Anti-colonial consumer politics also emerged in nineteenth-century China, but there they left a legacy of state control rather than a celebratory culture of individual acquisitiveness. At virtually the same time that North Americans were rejecting British imports, the Chinese imperial government sought to limit the consumption of what had come to be seen as an especially nefarious 'British-identified' commodity, opium. As in the American colonies, resistance to imports became central to state policy, led to armed conflict and cast the consumer as an important figure in a nationalist struggle against imperialism. Opium was originally a luxury item important to diplomacy between early modern China and other areas of Asia, and a facet of an indigenous sex-recreation industry. However, the expansion of opium consumption in the early nineteenth century shifted understandings of the

---

17   Timothy Breen, *The Marketplace of Revolution: How Consumer Politics Shaped American Independence* (Oxford, 2004), p. 298.

18   There is now a huge literature on the making of American consumer cultures. See, especially, Lizabeth Cohen, *A Consumers' Republic: The Politics of Mass Consumption in Postwar America* (New York, 2003); Charles F. McGovern, *Sold American: Consumption and Citizenship, 1890–1945* (Chapel Hill, NC, 2006); William Leach, *Land of Desire: Merchants, Power, and the Rise of a New American Culture* (New York, 1993); T. Jackson Lears, *Fables of Abundance: A Cultural History of Advertising in America* (New York, 1994).

19   There is also vast scholarship on Americanisation, of which one of the most helpful works is Victoria de Grazia, *Irresistible Empire: America's Advance through Twentieth-Century Europe* (Cambridge, MA, 2005).

20   An example is David Hancock's study of how American boycotts of Madeira during the Revolutionary War encouraged British firms to seek new markets in India, Southeast Asia and China. The search for consumers thus migrated eastward as armed conflict shut off one lucrative market. See David Hancock, '"An Undiscovered Ocean of Commerce Laid Open": India, Wine and the Emerging Atlantic Economy, 1703–1813', in H.V. Bowen, Margarette Lincoln and Nigel Rigby (eds), *The Worlds of the East India Company* (Suffolk, 2002), pp. 163–8.

drug, and it increasingly came to be seen as a product which degenerated those who used it.[21] The British shared this view of opium, seeing it as a pernicious influence undermining Victorian society, although that did not stop them from peddling it in the South China Seas.[22] In nineteenth-century Great Britain and China opium consumers were cast as weak links providing an avenue to foreign invasion.

Despite these similarities with England, British propaganda branded Qing attempts to maintain closed-door policies as proof that China was backward, uncivilised and anti-commercial. This European interpretation has been challenged in recent years by scholars who have charted a flourishing indigenous consumer culture dating at least to the years of the Ming dynasty (1368–1644). According to Craig Clunas, wealthy Ming homes were filled with art, furniture and other objects similar to those which adorned European households.[23] Kenneth Pomeranz has further suggested that both luxury and mass consumption were features of the Qing era and that the consumption of silver was an important aspect of this consumer world, with obvious repercussions for those labouring in the mines of Spanish America. Pomeranz forcefully notes that 'China's silver demand' was 'every bit as much an active force in creating the global economy as was the west's demand for porcelain, tea, and so on'.[24] Chinese consumer culture thus emerged as a parallel development to that in Europe rather than a western creation, a revisionist interpretation that necessarily alters our understanding of the 'rise of the west'.

Though scholars have appreciated the distinct growth of early modern Chinese consumerism, by the late nineteenth century the forced 'opening' of China and its reduction to semi-colonial status altered its consumer culture. China's inability to set up tariffs to keep out foreign goods, and the growing influence of western goods and styles in Shanghai and treaty-port cities, meant that here too imports came to signify subject status. Karl Gerth has shown how Chinese consumer culture was 'nationalised' in the early twentieth century in response to the continued onslaught of western and Japanese things. In a way not unlike Revolutionary America and quite similar to twentieth-century Britain and France, Chinese business leaders and their allies enfranchised consumers as they asked them to abstain from buying and

---

21 Zheng Yangwen, *The Social Life of Opium* (Cambridge, 2005). See also Carl A. Trocki, *Opium, Empire and Political Economy: A Study of the Asian Opium Trade, 1750–1950* (London, 1999) and Timothy Brook and Bob Tadashi Wakabayashi (eds), *Opium Regimes: China, Britain, and Japan, 1839–1952* (Berkeley, CA, 2000).

22 Barry Milligan, *Pleasures and Pains: Opium and the Orient in Nineteenth Century British Culture* (London, 1995). Consumers of other substances defined as drugs also came to be seen as foreign or at least allowing for foreign invasion. See, for example, James H. Mills, *Cannabis Britannica: Empire, Trade, and Prohibition* (Oxford, 2003).

23 Craig Clunas, *Superfluous Things: Material Culture and Social Status in Early Modern China* (Cambridge, 1991).

24 Kenneth Pomeranz, *The Great Divergence: China, Europe, and the Making of the Modern World Economy* (Princeton, NJ, 2000), p. 161. For a broad examination of early modern Asian consumption, see K.N. Chaudhuri, *Asia before Europe: Economy and Civilization of the Indian Ocean from the Rise of Islam to 1750* (Cambridge, 1990).

using foreign things, which were now specifically assigned imperialist meanings.[25] In the 1920s and 1930s especially, consumerism was yoked to nationalist rather than individual aspirations for autonomy and independence. This nationalist turn was not unique to China, however. The inter-war period saw the growth of international agencies regulating the flow of commodities but it also witnessed the counter-development of nations aspiring to economic self-sufficiency. Both tendencies elevated the collective power of consumers to act on the political stage.

Whether in the 1760s or the 1930s, colonial boycotts theorised consumers as active subjects. Individual choices took on new meanings when harnessed to social movements that sought to overturn labour systems, challenge political arrangements or support local rather than foreign businesses. In some respects these boycotts could be viewed as early forms of anti-globalisation struggles, but they were not anti-materialist or consumerist as such. Indeed, they nearly always promoted certain forms of consumer activity as morally legitimate. The presence of a boycott movement also did not necessarily imply the existence of a consumer-based subjectivity. In some cases, such as in Nationalist era China, businessmen and politicians were the leading forces behind the consumer movement. Nevertheless, under certain conditions colonial and semi-colonial polities set the stage for particularly powerful consumer movements, and perhaps identities.

Work on colonial boycotts has highlighted how consumer collectivity can undermine colonial hegemony. Other scholarship has examined how religious, cultural and racial difference framed the colonial encounter as an arena for contests over goods. Missionaries especially constructed legitimate/illegitimate forms of consumption as they denigrated indigenous material culture. John and Jean Comaroff's influential study of colonialism in nineteenth-century Southern Africa illuminated how English Christian missionaries tried to inculcate new attitudes towards markets and money, labour and consumerism as part of their effort to create new African Christian subjectivities. Missionaries viewed certain forms of consumption and particular items as bearing especially sacred significance, and, though they certainly were not mere lackeys for British business interests, Victorian missionaries did fantasise about the vast 'dark continent' attired in 'Manchester goods'.[26] In fact, wherever they saw these goods present, the British believed that they had encountered people who were at least semi-civilised. Commenting on the trade in 'India-rubber, ebony and wax for Manchester, Birmingham and Sheffield goods' among the hill tribes of Upper Assam, one Victorian writer smugly wrote that '[t]he red borderlands of savagery are now the proudest conquests of progress'.[27] The mere presence of British goods proved both the benefits of conquest, and the introduction of a new culture of consumption. Consumption then was an integral

25   Karl Gerth, *China Made: Consumer Culture and the Creation of the Nation* (Cambridge, MA, 2003).

26   John L. and Jean Comaroff, *Of Revelation and Revolution: The Dialectics of Modernity on a South African Frontier*, vol. 2 (Chicago, IL, 1997), especially chaps 4 and 5.

27   E.M. Clerke, 'Assam and the Indian Tea Trade', *Asiatic Quarterly Review* 5 (1888): pp. 381–3.

aspect of the colonial conquest but it was not something directly imposed upon subject peoples. Europeans and Africans together generated 'an economy at once material and moral, social and symbolic, stylistic and sensuous'.[28]

Africans incorporated imports into their cultures and economies in a variety of unexpected ways. Though writing about a much later period, Timothy Burke's analysis of soap consumption in Zimbabwe beautifully illuminates this point. Burke shows how Africans reworked European conceptions of the body, cleanliness and the toiletries that were promoted by missionaries and their allies as well as by European businesses. At times this reinterpretation maddened European businessmen who were frustrated by the 'inappropriate' ways that their products were being used even though these practices led to greater sales. Conquest was revisited in daily practices such as eating, washing and clothing oneself as hybrid colonial consumer cultures remained arenas of contestation long after colonial regimes were officially stabilised.[29]

Work on African fashion systems has also underscored how colonial and post-colonial consumer cultures have been implicated in and resisted colonisation, and created new identities and sources of conflict within colonised societies. Jean Allman's *Fashioning Africa: Power and the Politics of Dress* reiterates the need to throw out Eurocentric paradigms which have cast modernity as something either happening in Europe or brought by Europeans. In addition to exploring indigenous notions of dress and the body, the authors in this collection delineate one of the Comaroffs' central points that 'Western dress ... opened up a host of imaginative possibilities for Africans', but could also create new points of contention.[30] Margaret Jean Hay's essay emphasised this latter point when she described how the gradual adoption of western clothing in Kenya between the turn of the century and the 1940s paralleled the broader colonial struggles at stake. During the early 1900s, European colonial officials and missionaries were dismayed by the persistence of western Kenyan modes of dress and undress yet they were equally wary about the wholesale adoption of 'European' styles, which implied a kind of racial mimicry.[31] Instead, they sought to impose a 'coastal mode of dress', which approximated styles worn in Zanzibar and along the Swahili coast. Assuming that clothing should be a fairly transparent representation of difference and hierarchy, British settlers encouraged chiefs to reject knock-off European styles and dress in robes which were 'appropriately ceremonial'. Early Anglican missionaries felt that their parishioners should wear clothing to be sure, but believed that European modes

---

28   Comaroff, *Of Revelation and Revolution*, p. 220.

29   Timothy Burke, *Lifebuoy Men, Lux Women: Commodification, Consumption, and Cleanliness in Modern Zimbabwe* (Durham, NC, 1996).

30   Jean Allman (ed.), *Fashioning Africa: Power and the Politics of Dress* (Bloomington, IN, 2004), p. 7.

31   For a comparative discussion, see Bernard S. Cohn, 'Cloth, Clothes, and Colonialism: India in the Nineteenth Century', in *Colonialism and its Forms of Knowledge: The British in India* (Princeton, NJ, 1996), pp. 106–162; and Emma Tarlo, *Clothing Matters: Dress and Identity in India* (Chicago, IL, 1996).

of dress failed to reflect the 'African character' of the church. The British instead sought to clothe Kenyans in 'ideal forms of African clothing' derived from that worn by Swahili or Somali domestic servants in Mombasa and Nairobi.[32] Conflicts over clothing thus erupted between the coloniser and colonised, but Hay also shows how clothing struggles revealed divisions between Christians and non-Christians, elders and young men, fathers and daughters, as well as husbands and wives. Objects and their circulation thereby created new fault lines along axes of age, gender and religion, as well as class and race.

Colonial Consumers and the Making of the Global Economy

Though European conquest gradually transformed the material worlds of Africans, the adoption of western things was not always a byproduct of formal conquest.[33] At times, as Jeremy Prestholdt has argued, consumerism may have delayed the 'need' for formal colonisation and yet still contributed to the growth of global capitalism. His work is part of body of scholarship which has returned to the issue of consumer demand as a driving force behind global capitalism; but, as much work on China has suggested, non-European consumers are now seen as equally critical actors in this story. In a strikingly original book on the history of consumer desires in nineteenth-century East Africa, Prestholdt has shown how the consumption of western things in a pre-colonial setting shaped the development of industries across the globe. He specifically looks at East Africa *before* colonialism to argue that African demand was crucial to the emergence of the global economy long before European governments fully acknowledged the centrality of African markets. The East African coast had been a thriving hub of global economic activity for thousands of years, but in the nineteenth century this region became more deeply embedded in interoceanic commercial circuits that connected it more directly with Europe, America and India. Those who wished to sell their wares in places like Zanzibar had to appeal to consumer tastes which, as elsewhere, seemed difficult to predict. At a time when communications were relatively slow and knowledge about consumer demand was limited at best, whole cargoes of manufactured goods would sometimes have to be returned. In the 1840s, American, English, French, German and Indian merchants responded by acknowledging that they needed to send samples ahead to Zanzibar lest whole cargoes of cloth, guns or

---

32   Margaret Jean Hay, 'Changes in Clothing and Struggles over Identity in Colonial Western Kenya', in Jean Allman (ed.), *Fashioning Africa: Power and the Politics of Dress* (Bloomington, IN, 2004), pp. 67–83.

33   Indeed, recent scholarship on Africa has examined how 'western-style' consumer culture can be used by states to forge to new 'postcolonial' identities. See, for example, Bianca Murillo, 'Ideal Homes and the Gender Politics of Consumerism in Postcolonial Ghana, 1960–1970', *Gender and History* 21/3 (2009): pp. 560–75.

the wrong gauge brass wire be shipped home unsold.[34] Zanzibari consumers had sophisticated tastes. In the 1850s, for example, these consumers demonstrated a dramatic preference for chintz produced in France and Germany rather than England. They also seemed to reject imitations. One Hamburg firm evidently tried to import a knock-off of a blue turban cloth made in Muscat (Oman), but found to their dismay that, even though it was cheaper, consumers disliked its overly bright colours which they interpreted as signifying poor quality. Middlemen, such as caravan leaders, often found it necessary to remake the consumer goods they had in their possession, reconfiguring cloth to suit the tastes of young Maasai men, and restringing beads in lengths that consumers would find more acceptable.[35]

Such examples chart the access points for consumer intervention in the economy. Indeed, employing a commodity-chain approach, Prestholdt also shows how Zanzibari tastes influenced macro-level economic development in places such as the northeastern United States and southern India. East Africa was an important market for New England manufactured goods in the early nineteenth century, and Salem's economy in particular was increasingly dependent on Zanzibar, where New England merchants sold not only cotton cloth, but also furniture, shoes and glassware. A typical early nineteenth-century ship's manifest reveals a highly varied trade, including 'cloth, brass wire, specie, gun powder, loaf sugar, muscats, and flour'. Others included hundreds of boxes of soap, rocking chairs, lustre plates, gold watches, bread, ice and even ham.[36] By the 1840s, the expansion of African demand for cotton cloth beyond the elite classes stretched the capacity of the Lowell cotton mills and led to rapid inflation. During the Civil War the trade between America and East Africa collapsed; Bombay firms took advantage of this and began to flood East African markets with unbleached cotton cloth produced in English mills. By the later years of the century, East African consumer demand provided an important stimulus for the industrialisation of Bombay's textile industry and thereby inadvertently contributed to the decline of Indian craft industries, and the exploitation of Indian labourers.

Prestholdt's work challenges the conventional understanding that formal colonisation was driven by a search for markets. In Zanzibar, at least, African desires for European things grew from a dialogue between eighteenth- and early nineteenth-century global trading relationships and local cultural conditions, including notions of selfhood. This conclusion does, however, resurrect the question of whether or not these trading relationships were in some degree colonial in nature – that is, more controlled by Europeans than Prestholdt has suggested. If so, the commercialisation of East Africa might still be regarded as a product of what Robinson and Gallagher long ago labelled the imperialism of free trade.[37] Furthermore, though Prestholdt

---

34 Jeremy Prestholdt, *Domesticating the World: African Consumerism and the Geneologies of Globalization* (Berkeley, CA, 2008), p. 65.

35 Ibid., pp. 67–8.

36 Ibid., p. 74.

37 John Gallagher and Ronald Robinson, 'The Imperialism of Free Trade', *Economic History Review*, 6/1, New Series (1953): pp. 1–15. Also compare Prestholdt's conclusions

clearly reveals how African consumers influenced the nineteenth-century global economy, how did this situation change after the transition to formal empire at the end of the century? Did East African consumers have the same economic agency after European states solidified their control in the region?

A number of works have in fact suggested that in formal and semi-formal colonial settings consumers can and did alter global economic relationships and modes of production. Michelle Maskiell has shown how a global trade in expensive Kashmiri shawls between the late eighteenth and late nineteenth centuries was not, as art historians have posited, initially fed or directed by European demand. Shawl design and long-distance trade were influenced by the political and religious practices of the Iranian and Mughal court cultures between the sixteenth and nineteenth centuries. Rather than being subsumed into western-controlled trade, a thriving intra-Asian overland trade continued well into the nineteenth century, and was as important to the changes in production as was growing Euro-American demand.[38] Together, elite Asian, American and European demand determined the global trade in Kashmiri shawls.

Recent work on Latin American consumption has similarly questioned a western-focused narrative. Steven Topik's study of *domestic* markets prior to the onset of a fully globalised coffee economy dramatically rewrites the history of this commodity and of globalisation.[39] Heretofore scholars have assumed that Europeans brought coffee from the Middle East to Europe and then transferred it to Latin America and other growing regions primarily as an export commodity destined for European markets. Latin Americans (and other non-western labourers) have been studied primarily as producers of this global good, while scholars have also noted the place of coffee in Northern–Southern American foreign-policy conflicts. Topik argues instead that, although Europeans originally brought coffee to the Americas in the 1720s, coffee consumption grew first in the Caribbean and then was slowly transferred to Mexico, Brazil and other regions of the Americas. Unlike Europe and North America, coffee consumption was not spread solely by a male-dominated café culture. In places like Veracruz, women purchased coffee in the marketplace and drank it at home. Peasants were known to grow and consume

---

with Robinson and Gallagher's interpretation of the region in *Africa and the Victorians: The Official Mind of Imperialism* (London, 1961), pp. 41–52. Basically, Robinson and Gallagher and Prestholdt differ on how much the British were already in control of the region prior to formal colonisation.

38 Michelle Maskiell, 'Consuming Kashmir: Shawls and Empires, 1500–2000', *Journal of World History* 13/1 (2002): pp. 27–65.

39 Steven Topik, Consuming Coffee in Central America, 1850–1930', *Diálogos: Revista Electrónica de Historia* 9 (2008): http://historia.fcs.ucr.ac.cr/dialogos.htm. See also William Gervase Clarence-Smith and Steven Topik (eds), *The Global Coffee Economy in Africa, Asia and Latin America, 1500–1989* (Cambridge, 2003). Work on Middle Eastern consumer cultures during and after the Ottoman and European colonial eras has been an important contribution. See, for example, Donald Quataert (ed.), *Consumption Studies and the History of the Ottoman Empire, 1550–1922* (New York, 2000) and Relli Shechter (ed.), *Transitions in Domestic Consumption and Family Life in the Modern Middle East* (New York, 2003).

their own coffee, and indeed in this region even coffee produced for export was grown on smallholdings until the twentieth century.[40] In other contexts, such as in late-colonial Tamilnadu in Southern India, coffee consumption was very much a product of colonialism, as was tea drinking throughout the subcontinent.[41]

Sven Beckert's study of the global cotton trade during and after the American Civil War posits a similarly complex story of the global economy but one which maintains a dramatic shift in the late nineteenth century. He argues that the war contributed to a massive restructuring in global cotton commodity chains, freeing labour in the American south but leading to the intensification of imperialism in Asia and Africa. New bureaucratic regimes of politicians and industrialists from 'cotton-consuming' countries began to scour the globe for new supplies of raw cotton and new sources of cheap and reliable labour. As early as the summer of 1862, the combination of the northern blockade and the southern policy of banning all exports led to a near collapse of the global cotton economy.[42] Beckert highlights the role of the American war in the shift from informal to formal forms of imperialism in the later part of the century. He does not focus on the role of consumers as such, but his approach raises the question of whether or not consumers may have had a greater influence on global economies in the early nineteenth century before the merchant-driven cotton economy gave way to greater state control. With the growth of colonial state bureaucracies a more balanced multi-directional relationship between consumers and producers may have broken down.

However, locally oriented consumer–merchant relationships still existed in the colonial period and played an important role in the growth of global consumer cultures. Richard Roberts' study of cotton and colonialism in the French Soudan, for example, suggests that West African consumers and producers together restrained the economic impact of the French colonial state. Beginning in the post-Napoleonic period, the French government encouraged cotton production as a means to aid their home economies and secure the economic viability of their colonial possessions. Nevertheless, the French were unable to reorient cotton production in their West African colonies towards metropolitan ends. An indigenous cotton trade, based on a handcraft industry which served local, regional and long-distance markets, had existed prior to the arrival of the French. This economy was transformed but not obliterated as West Africa increasingly served the demands of world markets. Local growers were able to resist colonial encroachments and continue to sell to African producers, who paid them a better price for their raw

---

40   Topik, 'Consuming Coffee in Central America', p. 13.

41   A.R. Venkatachalapathy, '"In those Days there was no Coffee": Coffee Drinking and Middle-Class Culture in Colonial Tamilnadu', *Indian Economic and Social History Review* 39/2 (2002): pp. 301–316.

42   Sven Beckert, 'Emancipation and Empire: Reconstructing the Worldwide Web of Cotton Production in the Age of the American Civil War', *American Historical Review* 109/5 (2004): pp. 1405–1419. Other studies of the global cotton trade posit a similar scenario. See, for example, D.A. Farnie, *The English Cotton Industry in the World Market, 1815–1896* (Oxford, 1979). Farnie emphasises the significance of English cotton goods produced for export; particularly central to his story is the Indian market, which peaked at mid-century.

cotton. These producers relied upon handcraft rather than industrialised methods in part because their wares were particularly appealing to consumers across West Africa. Roberts reveals a resilient, flexible local economy, which did not crumble with the arrival of the French colonial state. These dynamics changed during and after the First World War, but Roberts suggests this should not cause us to overlook the early and continued importance of African markets in the nineteenth-century global cotton economy.[43]

Work on South Asia has similarly highlighted the existence of multiple economies during and after colonisation, suggesting a space both for local merchants and consumers to influence macro-level economic developments. Claude Markovits, for example, has traced how diasporic communities of Indian traders remained central to the trade with the rest of Asia, Africa and especially with the world explored by Jeremy Prestholdt. A vast trade between India and East Africa, centred in Zanzibar until the 1890s, was largely in the hands of Gujarati capitalists. Although these merchants did not figure very prominently in British colonial discourse, they were increasingly prominent in global trade especially but not exclusively within the territories of the British Empire.[44] This trade fed European demand for 'oriental' goods and Asian demands for 'western goods', promoting consumer desires in Europe and Asia throughout the nineteenth and early twentieth century.

European desires for exotica did ignite the desire for colonies. At home and in the colonies, European consumerism also enacted the unequal power relations that defined colonialism. However, these desires were not natural or inherent and, as Markowitz and others have shown, they might have been ignited by Asian and other non-European merchants who sought European markets for their goods. At the same time, non-European consumer desires were also a significant factor shaping the expanding global economy. At times such demand enabled resistance to colonial occupation but it could also lead to formal conquest. It could secure continued reliance on handcraft production but also encouraged the shift towards industrialised highly exploitive forms of production.

Scholarship on global consumer cultures has ultimately questioned the utility of empires as a framework for analysis since commodities, consumers and merchants rarely respected imperial or national borders. However, as we turn to metaphors such as the commodity chain to understand the history of global capitalism, it is

---

43   Richard L. Roberts, *Two Worlds of Cotton: Colonialism and the Regional Economy in the French Soudan, 1800–1946* (Stanford, CA, 1996). The role of consumers and local conditions can become more visible when one examines commodities that were not especially 'global' in their origins. See, for example, Brenda Chalfin, *Shea Butter Republic: State Power, Global Markets, and the Making of an Indigenous Commodity* (New York, 2004). It is also perhaps easier to see the power of demand for goods that are important to elite consumer practices. See, for example, Carlos Marichal, 'Mexican Cochineal and European Demand for American Dyes, 1550–1850', in Steven Topik, Carlos Marichal and Sephyr Frank (eds), *From Silver to Cocaine: Latin American Commodity Chains and the Building of the World Economy, 1500–2000* (Durham, NC, 2007).

44   Claude Markovits, *The Global World of Indian Merchants, 1750–1947: Traders of Sind from Bukhara to Panama* (Cambridge, 2000).

nevertheless still important to ask how and where imperialism and consumerism intersected in the past.[45] In doing so, we can highlight embedded nineteenth-century assumptions lurking in contemporary social and economic theories. For good or ill, marginalised individuals did not just labour in the global economy. Their consumer desires participated in the complex processes that made and unmade empires.

---

45 For a history of the term 'commodity chain', see the introduction to Jennifer Bain (ed.), *Frontiers of Commodity Chain Research* (Stanford, CA, 2009), pp. 1–34.

Soldiery

Richard Smith

Three primary tasks were demanded of imperial armies: acquiring territory, protecting colonies from incursions by rival powers and policing to subdue or preempt indigenous dissent. Characteristically, these imperatives necessitated the pressed or voluntary enlistment of subject peoples as soldiers, militia, police, auxiliaries, military labourers and provisioners to replenish the ranks and sustain imperial campaigns which otherwise would have soon exhausted the resources of the metropolitan power. The enlistment of colonial subjects thus provides significant insights into the dynamics of imperial government and struggles over identity and status – in particular, the inherent tensions and ambiguities of imperial rule which in many cases led to its ultimate demise. Therefore this chapter focuses principally on military service by the colonised, rather than recruits from the coloniser nations.[1]

Military life is a developing but still under-researched area of imperial scholarship. Research on the British and French empires predominates, much of it focused around the experience of colonial soldiery in the two world wars. This study surveys the wider literature beyond this narrow perspective to address three central themes to provide both comparative insight and possible direction for future research. The first two of these strands – the role of slavery within military

---

1   Examples in the latter category include Martin Bossenbroek, 'The Living Tools of Empire: The Recruitment of European Soldiers for the Dutch Colonial Army, 1814–1909', *Journal of Imperial and Commonwealth History* 23/1 (1995): pp. 25–53; Roger Norman Buckley, *The British Army in the West Indies: Society and the Military in the Revolutionary Age* (Gainesville, FL, 1998); Keith Jeffrey, *The British Army and the Crisis of Empire, 1918–22* (Manchester, 1984); A.S. Kanya-Forstner, 'The French Marines and the Conquest of the Western Sudan, 1880–1899', in Jaap de Moor and H.L. Wesseling (eds), *Imperialism and War: Essays on Colonial Wars in Asia and Africa* (Leiden, 1989); Brian McAllister Linn, *Guardians of Empire: The US Army and the Pacific, 1902–1940* (Chapel Hill, NC, 1997); Stewart Lone, *Japan's First Modern War: Army and Society in the Conflict with China, 1894–95* (London, 1994); Martin Thomas, 'Order Before Reform: The Spread of French Military Operations in Algeria, 1954–1958', in David Killingray and David Omissi (eds), *Guardians of Empire: The Armed Forces of the Colonial Powers c. 1700–1964* (Manchester, 1999).

labour regimes and the emergence of martial race theories – seek to define the military industrial complex of modernity and racial divisions of labour within empire. The final section explores the impact of imperial military recruitment on another key formation of modernity – the emergence of independent nation states as imperial power declined.

Military Service and Slavery

At first sight, soldier and slave may seem irreconcilable categories. The increasing association of military service and citizenship, evident in discourses of the European social and national revolutions from the late eighteenth century, underlined idealized distinctions between slave and soldier. The decision, in any epoch, to arm slaves and thereby provide the opportunity for potential rebellion might seem an act of extreme folly. In practical terms, however, the use of slaves as soldiers provided an immediate solution to manpower shortages in colonial armies and drew on many historical precedents. In the empires of antiquity, the deployment of slave soldiers was routine. Livy recorded that during the Second Punic War (218–201 BCE), the Roman army complemented its volunteer legions with 8,000 slaves who were rewarded with manumission and enfranchisement to circumvent the prohibition on slave arms-bearing. There is also evidence of the deployment of slaves by both sides in the Peloponnesian War (431–404 BCE).[2]

From the premodern era the most extensive use of military slaves occurred in the Islamic caliphates. Between 632 and 750 CE, Arabian armies of the Rashidun and Umayyad dynasties conquered Syria, Egypt, North Africa, Iran, Iraq, much of the Caucasus and Iberia. Widespread military slavery in the caliphates developed from the increasing use of non-Arab troops and convert prisoners-of-war – the *malawi* – during territorial expansion. By the reign of Abu Ishaq al-Mutasim (833–42), the exemplar enslaved military caste – the *mamluks* – drawn from the non-Muslim Turkic and Caucasian periphery, carried strategic weight in the caliphate forces. The *mamluks* developed to become ruling dynasties, most notably in Egypt (1250–1517). Their origins and deployment, however, anticipated many of the tactical and political considerations to exercise imperial military minds in the modern era. The *mamluks'* initial lowly status, difference and enforced isolation from local populations were thought to ensure discipline and loyalty. They were also held to possess innate martial capability; Turkic peoples especially were portrayed as exceptional horsemen and archers, capable of decisive mobility and offensive spirit. This identity was effectively sustained over a millennium, as

---

2   Peter Hunt, 'Arming Slaves and Helots in Classical Greece', in Christopher Leslie Brown and Philip D. Morgan (eds), *Arming Slaves: From Classical Times to the Modern Age* (New Haven, CT, 2006), pp. 15–17; Christopher Leslie Brown, 'Arming Slaves in Comparative Perspective', in Brown and Morgan (eds), *Arming Slaves*, p. 331; Orlando Patterson, *Slavery and Social Death* (Cambridge, MA, 1982), p. 288.

evident in the favoured presence of the *mamluks* in Napoleon's Imperial Guard, the only non-French soldiers to which this honour was extended.[3] *Ghilman*,[4] slaves drafted as soldiers or employed as bodyguards, provided the basis for the *mamluk* armies. But the enlistment of enslaved youths permeated the Islamic world beyond the caliphates, accounting for the presence of military slaves in the Delhi Sultanate during the fourteenth century and, to a lesser extent, the Mughal Empire.[5] And prior to the *devshirme* (forced levy of Christian youths), which sustained the *yeniceri* (janissary guards) in the Ottoman Empire from the late fourteenth to late seventeenth centuries, *ghilman* had provided many recruits.[6]

This historic link between slavery, military service and citizenship was evident from the earliest days of the European empires, although jurisprudence regarded the slave and the soldier as mutually exclusive stations.[7] The industrial scale of slavery which supported the plantation system in the Americas provided a potential source of coerced military labour. Even before the development of plantation societies, European conquest was partially dependent upon slave soldiers imported from Africa or snatched from among indigenous populations. The Portuguese army, which ousted the Dutch from Brazil in 1649, included many slaves and counted among its officers Henrique Dias, a former bondsman.[8] Military slavery in the colonies was often regarded as a temporary solution to an emergency such as an incursion by another European power or indigenous unrest. In 1555, for example, the Spanish impressed both local Indians and black slaves to defend Havana from French pirates. Slaves defended other Spanish possessions including Puerto Rico, Cartagena and Santo Domingo during the remainder of the sixteenth century.[9]

From the early decades of conquest, European colonisers were outnumbered by their slaves, producing a constant tension between short-term pragmatism and long-term political interests whenever slaves were recruited as soldiers. Manumission,

3   Matthew S. Gordon, *The Breaking of a Thousand Swords: A History of the Turkish Military of Samarra, AH 200–275/815–889 CE* (Albany, NY, 2001); Reuven Amitai, 'The Mamluk Institution, or One Thousand Years of Military Slavery in the Islamic World', in Brown and Morgan (eds), *Arming Slaves*; Patterson, *Slavery*, pp. 310–11. For further reading on the emergence of *mamluk* military and political power see James Waterson, *The Knights of Islam: The Wars of the Mamluks* (London, 2007); Michael Winter and Amalia Levanoni (eds), *Mamluks in Egyptian and Syrian Politics and Society* (Leiden, 2003); Thomas Philipp and Ulrich Haarmann (eds), *The Mamluks in Egyptian Politics and Society* (Cambridge, 2007).
4   Singular *ghulam*, Arabic for youth or boy.
5   Peter Jackson, *The Delhi Sultanate: A Political and Military History* (Cambridge, 2003).
6   B. Lewis *et al.* (eds), *Encyclopaedia of Islam* (Leiden, 1965), vol. 2, pp. 211–13, 1084–9; Godfrey Goodwin, *The Janissaries* (London, 1994), pp. 29–53.
7   Hendrik Kraay, 'Arming Slaves in Brazil from the Seventeenth to the Nineteenth Century', in Brown and Morgan (eds), *Arming Slaves*, pp. 146–7.
8   Charles R. Boxer, *The Golden Age of Brazil: Growing Pains of a Colonial Society, 1695–1750* (Manchester, 1995), p. 142.
9   The most comprehensive survey of slave soldiers in this region is Peter M. Voelz, *Slave and Soldier: The Military Impact of Blacks in the Colonial Americas* (New York, 1993).

along with a share in booty, provided the means to demobilise, disperse and appease slaves serving under arms, who might otherwise prove troublesome. Although dependent upon the apparatus of plantation slavery, military service provided a significant route out of chattel servitude. Slaves released after some form of military duty accounted for much of the free non-white population in the Americas from the sixteenth century, and the more conservative elements of this layer of colonial society in turn provided a bulwark against slave insurgency and post-emancipation insurrection.[10]

While military service offered the slave prospects for manumission, a more certain route to freedom was escape. *Grand marronage* – the establishment of communities by runaway slaves – was a feature of most settler societies in the New World. In many cases, these maroon communities provided a significant threat to European control, most notably contributing to the overthrow of colonial rule in Saint-Domingue (modern Haiti).The seventeenth-century black state of Palmares in Brazil provides another notable example.[11] Of perhaps greatest renown are the maroons of Jamaica, where *marronage* can be traced to the 1650s, when Juan de Bolas led liberated Africans against the Spanish occupation. De Bolas assisted the British takeover of the island in 1655, but on condition that his people would remain unmolested once the Spanish were expelled. Maroon communities formed by slaves deserting the sugar plantations kept the British at bay for much of the eighteenth century. The treaty concluding the First Maroon War (1739–40) granted permanent land settlement for the maroons, but also stipulated that future runaways must be returned to the plantations. The British also deployed maroons to quell slave unrest and to pursue escaped slaves. This highlighted the ambiguous accommodations such semi-militarised communities could be forced to make in the face of increasing imperial might. The Second Maroon War of 1796 culminated in a more humiliating treaty which ordered the dispersal of some maroons to Nova Scotia and Sierra Leone. However, the relationship with imperial authority endured to the extent that the maroons collectively volunteered for service in the British army at the outbreak of the First World War.

The British West Indies provided the recruiting ground for the most systematic scheme to recruit military slaves in the modern imperial experience. Faced with appalling losses from disease and poor provisioning, and the need to defend British territories following the outbreak of war with republican France in 1793, the British army established a scheme to conscript slaves. During the American Revolutionary War (1775–83), the British had formed the Carolina Corps from American slaves and free black loyalists. After 1796, the British procured slaves directly from the

---

10 See for example, Matthew Restall, 'Black Conquistadors: Armed Africans in Early Spanish America', *The Americas* 57/2 (2000): pp. 171–205; Seth Meisel, '"Fruits of Freedom": Slaves and Citizens in Early Republican Argentina', in Jane G. Landers and Barry M. Robinson (eds), *Slaves, Subjects, and Subversives: Blacks in Colonial Latin America* (Albuquerque, NM, 2006).

11 R.K. Kent, 'Palmares: An African State in Brazil', in Richard Price (ed.), *Maroon Societies: Rebel Slave Communities in the Americas* (Baltimore, MD, 1979).

transatlantic trade as plantation owners were often reluctant to sell their prized human possessions. Until the abolition of the slave trade in 1807, twelve regiments of black troops, the West India Regiments (WIR), were raised in this manner, supplemented by slaves captured from the French or handed over by royalist deserters. Some 13,400 slaves were purchased for military service, accounting for around 7 per cent of slave exports to the British West Indies during the twelve years before abolition. Post-abolition, many Africans freed by British navy patrols were used to replenish the ranks of the WIR, a practice which continued until 1844.[12]

During the Haitian revolutionary struggle (1791–1804), diverse modes of slave soldier recruitment developed owing to shifting internal alliances and successive invasions by foreign states. These included plantation guards and irregular forces raised by political factions, slave insurgents formed into regular army troops, and corps of both insurgents and slaves established by the British and Spanish armies of intervention.[13] Slave insurgency broke out in the North province of Saint-Domingue when the struggle for political power between the *gens de couleur libres* (free black and coloured population) and the whites did not result in emancipation. Some slaves remained loyal to their masters and were often armed to defend plantations from insurgent attacks, continuing to defend their plantations even after the planters had fled as a means to lay claim to the soil on which they had laboured. From September 1791, the *gens de couleur* began to raise bands of slave auxiliaries and maroons, known as the Swiss, who were initially manumitted as a reward. However, tensions emerged in a subsequent alliance between the *gens de couleur* and some whites around universal emancipation, and the Swiss were subsequently deported to the Mosquito coast by the western provincial assembly.[14]

The radical whites of Port au Prince enlisted slaves into the Company of Africans to pursue their struggle against the *gens de couleur*, and white royalists recruited a manumitted slave, Jean Kina, to lead black auxiliaries in attacks on slave insurgents. The European powers attempting to gain a foothold in Saint-Domingue also exploited the ample supply of military labour comprising slave insurgents. Spain formed a pragmatic alliance with the black general Toussaint l'Ouverture, although he would later lead the forces which expelled both the Spanish and British. French republicans recruited many former slaves into the National Guard in Saint-Domingue, manumitting many on the grounds that they had previously taken up arms in defence of their masters' property. The British formed black *chasseur* regiments to make good the catastrophic losses of white troops who had succumbed to disease. In August 1793, emancipation was announced by Sonthonax, the republican France's representative in Saint-Domingue. Henceforth

---

12   Brian Dyde, *The Empty Sleeve: The Story of the West India Regiments of the British Army* (St Johns, Antigua, 1997), pp. 29–32, 136; Roger Norman Buckley, *Slaves in Red Coats: The British West India Regiments, 1795–1815* (New Haven, CT, 1979).

13   David Patrick Geggus, 'The Arming of Slaves in the Haitian Revolution', in Brown and Morgan (eds), *Arming Slaves*.

14   David Patrick Geggus, *Haitian Revolutionary Studies* (Bloomington, IN, 2002), pp. 99–115.

all black men were recruited as free men to an army which ultimately secured the independent republic of Haiti inaugurated on 1 January 1804.[15]

Haiti provides the pre-eminent example of a revolutionary slave insurrection in modern European empires. But, throughout the Americas, armed slaves were deployed in struggles between white colonisers and imperial powers until the abolition of slavery in Cuba (1886) and Brazil (1888).[16] Beyond the Americas, schemes for the recruitment of slave troops were also considered. At the time of the Indian Rebellion (1857) the Portuguese governor of Goa considered the possibility of importing Mozambiquan slave soldiers as a bulwark against local unrest.[17]

From the earliest European incursions into Senegambia in the seventeenth century, Africans had been engaged to supplement battalions of European soldiers who suffered high attrition rates due to disease and existing ill-health. The French demand for African troops increased steadily from the 1820s, to supply not only West African garrisons but also those further afield, such as Madagascar, French Guiana and later Morocco. France's increasing reliance on its African colonies as a 'reservoir of men' was dependent upon slavery practices which provided around 75 per cent of recruits to the *tirailleurs sénégalais*, recruited from all French West African territories, not Senegal alone. The *rachat* system of recruitment provided for bounty payments to masters whose slaves were indentured into service for between twelve and fourteen years. At first the indentured men served as military labourers, a status regarded with some disdain in West African societies. As French ambitions grew, however, a corps was formed in 1857 and they were thereafter indentured as *tirailleurs sénégalais*.

After France permanently abolished slavery in 1848, *rachat* became a source of some embarrassment, and attempts were made to reduce the colonial army's dependency on the system. Proponents of African recruitment endeavoured to bolster voluntary enlistment by insisting on the *tirailleurs'* infantry status, producing attractive uniforms and reducing the demeaning tasks expected of them. Nevertheless, the direct purchase of slaves was still used to fill the ranks on occasion. Although *rachat* was phased out between 1882 and 1895, other slavery-related practices remained. These included the payment of bonuses to slave masters who released their slaves into military service, the conscription of prisoners-of-war in the West African campaigns, and the imposition of military labour on local peasant communities. In some cases, peasants performing military labours were forcibly transferred to the infantry. Dependency on such methods increased as the consolidation and defence of territory demanded greater numbers of troops than had the initial conquest. The mass deployment of *sénégalais* in the French Moroccan campaigns of 1912–13 resulted in further pressure on the West African recruitment

---

15 Geggus, 'Arming of Slaves'.

16 See for example, Hendrik Kraay, 'Slavery, Citizenship and Military Service in Brazil's Mobilization for the Paraguayan War', *Slavery and Abolition* 18/3 (1997): pp. 228–56; Seth Meisel, 'Fruits of Freedom'.

17 Timothy Walker, 'Slaves or Soldiers?', in Indrani Chatterjee and Richard M. Eaton (eds), *Slavery and South Asian History* (Bloomington, IN, 2006).

system. This culminated in the introduction of formal conscription, paving the way for the mass mobilisation of around 200,000 Africans by France in the First World War.[18]

Military Labour Regimes and Martial Race Theories

All the European combatant nations deployed forced or conscripted labour in vast numbers during the First World War. Egypt, South Africa, China, Fiji and India were among the chief sources of military labour deployed on the Western Front and in Italy, Mesopotamia and the Middle East. France in turn drew on its Far Eastern possessions and China. In the East African theatre, the British enlisted up to 1 million Africans from fifteen countries as camp followers, labourers and members of the Carrier Corps (*kariakor*). Particularly significant was the military's adoption of the labour recruitment structures developed for other imperial projects such as railway- and road-building. The Native Followers Ordnance of 1915 entrenched this relationship by permitting district commissioners to place limitless quotas on local chiefs to produce military labour. A casualty rate of 14.6 per cent among those contracted for longer terms of service, and the subsequent dislocation and diminishment of populations resulting from this vast demand for military labour, shows that large-scale human tragedy was not confined to the Western Front.[19]

Labour regimes and recruitment patterns highlighted another key feature of imperial military policy – the separation of subject peoples into martial and non-martial races. Labourers and other auxiliaries were regarded as an inferior element in the military hierarchy, despite their indispensable contribution to military operations. From foraging, rearing livestock and forming baggage trains to building railways and roads, digging trenches, and manning docks and supply depots, military labour sustained armies in the field throughout the era of modern empire. However, deployment to labour companies often served as an individual or collective punishment, or as a humiliating reminder of a soldier's place in the hierarchy of empire. British soldiers who showed insufficient combative spirit during the opening days of the Battle of the Somme were disarmed and demoted

---

18   Myron Echenberg, *Colonial Conscripts: The Tirailleurs Sénégalais in French West Africa, 1857–1960* (Portsmouth, NH, 1991); Richard S. Fogarty, *Race and War in France: Colonial Subjects in the French Army, 1914–1918* (Baltimore, MD, 2008); Gregory Mann, *Native Sons: West African Veterans and France in the Twentieth Century* (Durham, NC, 2006); Joseph Lunn, '"Les Races Guerrières": Racial Preconceptions in the French Military about West African Soldiers during the First World War', *Journal of Contemporary History* 34/4 (1999): pp. 517–36.

19   Geoffrey Hodges, *Kariakor: The Carrier Corps: The Story of the Military Labour Forces in the Conquest of German East Africa, 1914 to 1918* (Nairobi, 1999), pp. 34–5; Anthony Clayton and Donald C. Savage, *Government and Labour in Kenya, 1895–1963* (London, 1999), pp. 81–107. For a recent overview see Edward Paice, *Tip and Run: The Untold Tragedy of the Great War in Africa* (London, 2007).

to the labour battalions as an example to others.[20] The denial of arms-bearing underlined low civic status and racial subordination, emphasising exclusion from the civil rights, duties and rewards associated with the emergence of citizen armies during and after the French revolution.[21] The regulation of arms-bearing established a military discourse which underpinned wider imperial gendered and racialised categories. Black men and white women were variously represented as physically weaker, irrational and intellectually inferior to preserve the white male domain of the front line. During the First World War, the British Army opposed the use of women and black troops on the Western Front, arguing in the same breath that both lacked the necessary 'strength, coolness and courage'.[22]

The arbitrary demarcation between military labour and armed service institutionalised social and racial inequalities with far-reaching consequences. This was vividly demonstrated by the fate of the Ottoman Army's Armenian labour battalions during the First World War. Modernisation, or, more accurately, Europeanisation of the army was one of the key priorities of the Young Turk Revolution (1908–1918). In 1909, conscription for national service was extended to the non-Muslim population of the Ottoman Empire, partly as a way of achieving a degree of unity among its ethnically diverse subjects.[23] Previously, the recruitment of non-Muslims had been limited to the janissary corps until its annihilation in the Auspicious Event of 1826.[24] Non-Muslim conscripts tended to be drafted into labour units, rather than infantry and cavalry regiments, as military leaders were fearful they might prove unreliable should conflict erupt with the Ottoman Empire's Christian rivals. The neighbouring Russian imperial army shared similar concerns about the potential for religious turbulence in its ranks. After Catherine the Great annexed the Crimea in 1783, the loyalty of Russia's Muslim Tartar subjects was routinely called into question, despite their protestations of loyalty during crises such as the Crimean War. Imperial officials were ever fearful of the potential for divisions along ethno-religious lines to become more overt or even decisive. Such anxieties were not assuaged by the Tartars' awesome fighting reputation, and Russian policy wavered between assimilation and semi-autonomy. It was resolved that subject peoples, particularly those with martial traditions such as the Tartars and Don Cossacks, should provide military service to the tsars in native units under their own leaders, but they were also simultaneously encouraged to regard themselves as subjects of greater Russia.[25]

---

20 Anthony Babington, *Shell Shock: A History of the Changing Attitudes to War Neurosis* (London, 1997), pp. 78–80.
21 George L. Mosse, *Fallen Soldiers: Reshaping the Memory of the World Wars* (Oxford, 1990).
22 Richard Smith, *Jamaican Volunteers in the First World War: Race, Masculinity and the Development of National Consciousness* (Manchester, 2004), p. 79.
23 Erik Jan Zürcher, 'The Ottoman Conscription System, 1840–1914', *International Review of Social History* 43 (1998): pp. 437–49. On the Europeanisation of Asian armies, see David B. Ralston, *Importing the European Army: The Introduction of European Military Techniques and Institutions into the Extra-European World, 1600–1914* (Chicago, 1990).
24 Goodwin, *Janissaries*, pp. 214–28.
25 Kelly O'Neill, 'Between Subversion and Submission: The Integration of the Crimean

The Ottoman army's avowedly segregationist policy became further entrenched during the First World War. Armenian Christians constituted around 75 per cent of the labour battalions, a proportion which increased from February 1915. Those serving elsewhere were transferred to labour companies by a high command fearful of mass desertions to the Russians in the wake of the defeat at Sarıkamış. The Armenians were henceforth deprived of the means to defend themselves, both within the army and in the Ottoman Empire at large. When attacks on the Armenian community accelerated in April 1915, Armenian labour conscripts were primary targets, even though the ensuing slaughter deprived the Ottoman army of vital infrastructure.[26] The Turkish army was disproportionately dependent upon its labour battalions as transport systems, especially railways, were underdeveloped in the Ottoman Empire. In general, despite the shortage of manpower faced by imperial armies throughout the First World War, racial ideology ensured the confinement of many potential soldiers to labour units. On the Western Front, where sensitivities surrounding the deployment of black troops against white opponents were most evident, the British West Indies Regiment provides the most widely cited example of an imperial unit confined to non-combatant duties. However, black South Africans, Maoris and Chinese were treated similarly by the British.[27]

As we have seen in the case of *mamluk* and Tartar recruitment, the belief that certain 'races' had innate martial capability was a phenomenon of longstanding. From the mid-nineteenth century, however, as the armies of the European empires were subject to increasing bureaucratisation, conscription and scientific organisation, systematic beliefs around martial prowess became more evident. In the British imperial context, the Indian Rebellion of 1857 was pivotal in determining recruitment on racial lines. Non-whites were increasingly caricatured as unreliable and potentially traitorous, as well as falling short of British ideals of heroism, military elan and steadfastness. In the metropolitan army, the recruitment of black

---

Khanate into the Russian Empire, 1783–1853', PhD dissertation, Harvard University, 2006; Robert F. Baumann, 'Subject Nationalities in the Military Service of Imperial Russia: The Case of the Bashkirs', *Slavic Review* 46/3–4 (1987): pp. 489–502; Mark von Hagen, 'The Limits of Reform: The Multiethnic Imperial Army Confronts Nationalism, 1874–1917', in David Schimmelpennick van der Oye and Bruce Menning (eds), *Reforming the Tsar's Army: Military Innovation in Imperial Russia from Peter the Great to the Revolution* (Cambridge and Washington, DC, 2004), pp. 34–55.

26   Erik Jan Zürcher, 'Ottoman Labour Battalions in World War I', in Hans-Lukas Kieser and Dominik J. Schaller (eds), *Der Völkermord an den Armeniern und die Shoah: The Armenian Genocide and the Shoah* (Zürich, 2002), pp. 187–96. For further background, see Edward J. Erickson, *Ordered to Die: A History of the Ottoman Army in the First World War* (Westport, CT, 2000).

27   Santanu Das, *Race, Empire and First World War Writing* (Cambridge, 2011) provides an excellent overview of the diverse sources from which military labour was recruited. See also Glenford Howe, *Race, War and Nationalism: A Social History of West Indians in the First World War* (Kingston, 2002); Brian Willan, 'The South African Native Labour Contingent, 1916–18', *Journal of African History* 10 (1978): pp. 61–86; Michael Summerskill, *China on the Western Front: Britain's Chinese Work Force in the First World War* (London, 1982).

and Asian soldiers was heavily controlled, and those who did enlist were barred from attaining commissioned officer status.[28] Anxieties around the recruitment of subject peoples into imperial armies were not limited to the overseas empires. The Austro-Hungarian army, for example, had experienced wholesale desertions among its Italian troops during the Lombardy campaigns of 1848.[29] In India, the imperial forces required a steady stream of recruits to contain potential internal unrest and discourage perceived Russian ambition on the subcontinent. Pre-existing attitudes around race and military capability were increasingly codified in order to determine the most reliable local recruiting grounds.

The recruitment practices of the Mughal Empire (1526–1707) provided the basis for some of the ethnic and caste categories – particularly Pashtuns and Rajputs respectively –upon which martial race theory came to rest. However, the Mughals ultimately eschewed ethnicity and caste in favour of patronage, household affiliation and other social networks necessary to ensure loyalty and military effectiveness in a semi-nomadic empire. The Mughal emperors depended upon two highly differentiated sources – the jamadars and zamindars – for military labour. The jamadars were landless, mounted nomadic war bands who offered their services to those who could command the highest price. Jamadars remained semi-independent even in military service, recruiting their own followers and retainers from among their tribal hinterlands in Central Asia, Iran and Afghanistan. The zamindars were settled members of the Indian gentry with relatively circumscribed spheres of influence from which they recruited small numbers of cavalry, relying on local artisans and peasants as the main source of their armed bands.[30]

Western interpretations of past military traditions were particularly significant in the case for the Sikhs and the Gurkhas. Both groups provided formidable opposition to British expansion in the Anglo-Nepalese War (1814–16) and the Anglo-Sikh Wars (1845–49), before emerging as pivotal elements of the Indian Army through the remainder of the imperial era.[31] They also formed part of the exoticised spectacle in which imperial racial ideology was rendered and extended to other martial groups such as the Highland Scots and the West India regiments. These groups continue to retain symbolic and strategic significance, in post-colonial Britain *and* the subcontinent. Despite composing only 2 per cent

---

28   David Killingray 'All the King's Men: Blacks in the British Army in the First World War, 1914–1918', in Rainer Lotz and Ian Pegg (eds), *Under the Imperial Carpet: Essays in Black History, 1780–1950* (Crawley, 1986), p. 168.

29   Gunther Rothenberg, *The Army of Francis Joseph* (West Lafayette, IN, 1998), pp. 25–6.

30   Jos Gommans, *Mughal Warfare: Indian Frontiers and Highroads to Empire, 1500–1700* (New York, 2002), pp. 68–9. Gommans' *The Rise of the Indo-Afghan Empire, c.1710–1780* (Leiden, 1995), provides much information throughout on military developments in the subcontinent during the decline of Mughal power.

31   Lionel Caplan, *Warrior Gentleman: 'Gurkhas' in the Western Imagination* (Oxford, 1995); Amandeep Singh Madra and Parmjit Singh, *Warrior Saints: Three Centuries of The Sikh Military Tradition* (London, 1999); David Omissi, *The Sepoy and the Raj: The Indian Army, 1860–1940* (London, 1994), pp. 10–32; Heather Streets, *Martial Races: The Military, Race and Masculinity in British Imperial Culture, 1857–1914* (Manchester, 2004), pp. 62–9.

of the Indian population, Sikhs made up around 8 per cent of the Indian army at the beginning of the twenty-first century.[32]

Martial race theory presented significant advantages to imperial rule in India, as was most notably evident in the recruitment strategies outlined by Lord Roberts and Sir George MacMunn in the late nineteenth and early twentieth centuries.[33] The martial races were seen as separate from subject populations as a whole, who were generally regarded as irredeemably inferior. Martial distinctiveness circumscribed the potential number of recruits, fulfilling the wish of military policy-makers to ensure that the number of colonial subjects receiving military training was kept as low as practicable. Martial races were deployed within their indigenous region to suppress dissent among groups regarded as less loyal, or they could be transported across continents to serve as 'reliable aliens'.[34]

After 1857, the British military establishment insisted that northern Indians made the best soldiers and that the peoples of the south lacked courage and manliness, even though the southern regiments had tended to prove more reliable during the Rebellion. The favouring of the northern, generally lighter-skinned 'Aryan' peoples was centred around the notion of a common Euro-Indian culture. The prevalence of endogamous marriage in the north was believed to ensure racial purity by the British, who regarded exogamy as enfeebling and feminising. The northern hills, from which Gurkha and Pathan recruits were drawn, for example, were held to be invigorating in contrast to the tropical southern climates, perceived as enervating and dissipating of manliness.[35] Again, this emphasised the profoundly gendered character of imperial military discourses, which served to legitimize hierarchical concepts of race, pitting the manly, energetic, resourceful and brave white warrior/ frontiersman against the effeminate, cowardly, ineffectual and devious imperial subject. These imperial imaginings served to bolster white masculinity not only in the face of crises such as the Indian Mutiny, but also in relation to gender anxieties

---

32   Omar Khalidi, 'Ethnic Group Recruitment in the Indian Army: The Contrasting Cases of Sikhs, Muslims, Gurkhas and Others', *Pacific Affairs* 74/4 (2002): pp. 529–52.

33   Brian Robson (ed.), *Roberts in India: The Military Papers of Field Marshal Lord Roberts, 1876–1893* (Stroud, 1993); George Fletcher MacMunn, *The Armies of India* (London, 1911); MacMunn, *The Martial Races of India* (London, 1933).

34   David Killingray, 'Guarding the Extending Frontier: Policing the Gold Coast, 1865–1913', in David M. Anderson and David Killingray (eds), *Policing the Empire: Government, Authority and Control, 1830–1940* (Manchester, 1991), p. 116. By contrast, the Japanese imperial authorities in Taiwan, Kantō and Korea during the 1920s and 1930s increasingly adopted a strategy of self-policing for subject peoples. Locally raised police and, in the case of the Chinese colonies, the indigenous community-based *baojia* (*pao-chia*) system of policing were preferred over an overt military policing presence (Ching-chih Chen, 'Policy and Community Control Systems in the Empire', in Ramon H. Myers and Mark R. Peattie (eds), *The Japanese Colonial Empire, 1895–1945* (Princeton, NJ, 1984).

35   Omissi, *Sepoy and the Raj*, pp. 12–24; Douglas M. Peers, 'Martial Races and South Asian Military Culture in the Victorian Indian Army', in Daniel Marston and Chandar Sundaram (eds), *A Military History of Modern India* (New York, 2006).

closer to home as mid-Victorian society grappled with debates around womanly virtue and the place of women in the public sphere.[36]

British recruitment policy in Africa from the 1880s was also informed by martial race ideology, often put into practice by army officers with previous Indian experience. Among them was Lord Lugard who administered the amalgamation of the Nigerian colonies (1912) and promoted the policy of indirect rule in Britain's African colonies during the 1920s.[37] Lugard had served in the Afghan and Burma campaigns during the 1870s and 1880s and formed the West African Frontier Force in 1897. As both soldier and administrator, he advocated the maintenance of order through the deployment of non-local occupying forces and the disruption of ethnic affinity to ensure that groups with military service traditions did not challenge imperial authority. One of the most damaging legacies of martial race policy, particularly in West Africa, was post-independence ethnic strife. The disproportionate representation of martial races in newly formed national armies seriously undermined faith in the military as an independent institution.[38] In British imperial Africa, men from remote, impoverished regions were often recruited in the belief they could survive on irregular food supplies and had natural scouting skills. As on the Indian subcontinent, peoples who had resisted colonial rule, such as the Nandi of Kenya or Asante of the Gold Coast (Ghana), were also favoured.[39] It was held that martial effectiveness could only be fully realised under white tutelage and leadership. Paradoxically, however, martial race prowess was regarded as an inherent quality, rather than latent potential that could be realised through training and discipline. According to Viscount Wolseley, leader of the Asante Campaign (1873–74) and commander-in-chief of the British Army from 1895 to 1901, the African soldier's 'want of intelligence' was compensated by his 'intuitive knowledge of wild animals'. This presented him 'an immense advantage over the ordinary town-bred soldier' by providing for 'the easy acquisition of a soldier's duties'.[40] Wolseley's assessment highlighted how martial characteristics imagined in the subject races could be appropriated to inject fresh vigour into the imperial military which, toward the close of the nineteenth century, was regarded as beset by the alleged debilitating effects of city life and domesticity. Representations of the martial 'other' were particularly potent at the contested frontiers of empire and during imperial crises.[41]

---

36   Streets, *Martial Races*, pp. 42–3.

37   Daniel Tetteh Osabu-Kle, *Compatible Cultural Democracy: The Key to Development in Africa* (Peterborough, 2000), pp. 44–8.

38   J. 'Bayo Adekson, 'Ethnicity and Army Recruitment in Colonial Plural Societies', *Ethnic and Racial Studies* 2/2 (1979): pp. 152–3. Timothy H. Parsons, '"Wakamba Warriors Are Soldiers of the Queen": The Evolution of the Kamba as a Martial Race, 1890–1970', *Ethnohistory* 46/4 (1999): p. 671.

39   Timothy H. Parsons, *The African Rank and File: Social Implications of Colonial Military Service in the King's African Rifles, 1902–1964* (Oxford, 1999), p. 54.

40   Viscount Wolseley, 'The Negro as a Soldier', *Fortnightly Review* 44/264 (1888): pp. 689–90.

41   Robert H. MacDonald, *Sons of the Empire: The Frontier and the Boy Scout Movement, 1890–1918* (Toronto, ON, 1993).

Imperial recruitment tended to be inconsistent and pragmatic, underlining the ambiguous and ill-defined characteristics held to constitute a martial race. The Gurkhas, for example, rather than constituting an ethnic group, can be regarded as an element of Nepalese society favoured by army recruiters.[42] Peoples classified as soldierly might subsequently be regarded as otherwise if they contested the terms of military service, became disenchanted with military life or showed signs of discontent. Reliability, loyalty and discipline were favoured by colonial recruiters over apparent innate valour, fearlessness and fighting skill. Whereas Muslim soldiers were regarded as the most martial and reliable in India, African Muslims came to be regarded as distinctly undependable, particularly after Sudanese troops mutinied in 1897. Politically disorganised and disparate pagan groups, who might otherwise be considered as less civilised and socially advanced, could be preferred over the Hausa and Fulani of north and northeastern Nigeria, who shared Islamic beliefs.[43]

Education or business acumen was regarded as a sign that a previously warlike tribe had become 'too soft'. In the British Empire particularly, this reflected the broader suspicion with which learning was regarded in the military's anti-intellectual milieu. During the Second World War, when African candidates were finally accepted as candidates for commissions, education was largely disregarded in the selection process. Attitudes to military prowess were also influenced by patterns of European settlement. In West Africa, coast dwellers had been regarded as more civilised and capable of military duty, but, as Europeans advanced into the hinterland, inland areas became the preferred recruiting ground.[44] The presence of a larger white settler population could result in resistance to the recruitment and advancement of indigenous soldiers.[45] Resentment towards indigenous troops increased in the aftermath of the two world wars, partly due to fears that veterans would prove politically volatile. Equally important, however, was the policy of Africanisation of the officer corps developed by metropolitan governments. Settler colonies were characterised by greater social stratification among the white population, potentially leading to competition and insecurity in the distribution of senior positions. Africanisation was therefore often delayed in settler colonies, and resistance to the process may have partly accounted for the particular bitterness of independence struggles in colonies such as Malaya, Kenya, Algeria and Congo.

France's anxieties about its demographic deficit with Germany produced a major shift in policy towards the deployment of African soldiers on European soil. In 1910, the military strategist General Charles Mangan argued that sufficient men of a martial disposition could be found in France's African territories to provide a 'reservoir of men' in a future European conflict. However, France continued to follow the general tenor of European thought in its racial attitudes towards African recruits. In a similar vein to Viscount Wolseley, Mangan suggested 'warrior

---

42   Caplan, *Warrior Gentleman*, pp. 10–12.
43   Anthony H.M. Kirk-Greene, '"Damnosa Hereditas": Ethnic Ranking and the Martial Races Imperative in Africa', *Ethnic and Racial Studies* 3/4 (1980): pp. 400–401.
44   Adekson, 'Ethnicity': pp. 154–7; Kirk-Greene, 'Damnosa Hereditas': pp. 395–6, 406–407.
45   Adekson, 'Ethnicity': p.162.

instincts ... remain extremely powerful in primitive races', and argued that Africans possessed innate abilities to cope with harsh climates and the capacity to carry heavy loads. A less-developed nervous system, the patriarchal nature of African society and a habitual familiarity with war endowed the African martial races with the ideal attributes to make disciplined and efficient soldiers.[46] The most martial of Africans were credited with the potential to reinvigorate 'French fury', 'their cold-blooded and fatalistic temperament [would] render them terrible in the attack', particularly in 'delivering the final shock'.[47] Critics of Mangan argued that blacks were not sufficiently intelligent to meet the demands of modern warfare. They also opposed the deployment of Africans on logistical and climatic grounds, and urged military policy-makers to consider the social impact of black soldiers on French soil. Such hostility was overridden, however, by more pragmatic attitudes during the First World War as French losses mounted and unrest became evident in the army. Large sections of the French army mutinied after the Second Battle of the Aisne in May 1917, and the widespread use of African troops met with little resistance.[48]

Caricatures of martial fitness were not limited to black and Asian imperial subjects. The unequal contest between Britain and its Celtic periphery, for example, provided the conditions for a pool of military labour which generated associations of martial prowess, regarding the Scots in particular, and the Welsh and Irish to a lesser extent.[49] The latter, while regarded ambiguously within the British military establishment, provided a source of military labour for many states in mainland Europe.[50] By the end of the nineteenth century, the British Empire increasingly looked to its dominions for images of reinvigorating masculinity. After the First World War, the 'digger' soldiers of Australia and New Zealand provided the most enduring renditions of martial efficiency, and were a prominent feature of emerging national identity, mirrored also in postwar Canadian and white South African culture. Another significant example is the emergence of postwar Unionist and Loyalist identities in the north of Ireland.[51]

---

46   Lunn, 'Les Races Guerrières', p. 521. For French attitudes towards the military capability of imperial subjects in Indo-China, see Sarah Womack, 'Ethnicity and Martial Races: The *Garde Indigène* of Cambodia in the 1880s and 1890s', in Karl Hack and Tobias Rettig (eds), *Colonial Armies in South East Asia* (London, 2006).

47   Lunn, 'Les Races Guerrières', p. 525.

48   Ibid. For German policy on the recruitment of Africans, see Erick J. Mann, *Mikono ya damu: 'Hands of Blood': African Mercenaries and the Politics of Conflict in German East Africa, 1888–1904* (New York, 2002).

49   Steve Murdoch and Andrew Mackillop (eds), *Fighting for Identity: Scottish Military Experience c. 1550–1900* (Leiden, 2002); Edward M. Spiers, *The Scottish Soldier and Empire, 1854–1902* (Edinburgh, 2006).

50   Moisés Enrique Rodríguez, 'The Spanish Habsburgs and their Irish Soldiers (1587–1700)' *Irish Migration Studies in Latin America* 5/2 (2007): pp. 125–30; Harman Murtagh, 'Irish Soldiers Abroad, 1600–1800', in Thomas Bartlett and Keith Jeffery (eds), *A Military History of Ireland* (Cambridge, 1996).

51   Christopher Pugsley, *The Anzac Experience: New Zealand, Australia and Empire in the First World War* (Auckland, 2004); Graham Seal, *Inventing Anzac: The Digger and National*

Imperial Military Service and New National Identities

The two world wars consolidated links between citizenship and military service, rationalised and institutionalised the commemoration of the war dead, enshrined the self-determination of nations as an universal ideal and undermined the claim of white imperial nations to possess innate supremacy over their non-white subjects. These factors tended to steer imperial subjects engaged in military labour to the forefront of self-determination struggles, either as active participants or emblems of nationhood. However, as the examples which follow highlight, pursuing the rewards of military service, such as nationhood and citizenship, were deeply gendered undertakings. While the deeds of 'great men' were privileged in narratives of nation and empire, the lure of immortality was also held out to ordinary male citizens and subjects in return for imperial military service.

Military volunteers were linked with the identity and interests of the nation, rather than simply acting as servants of the state. Soldiering had traditionally been regarded as a dishonourable occupation recruiting mercenaries, the rural and urban poor, and criminals. But the figure of the citizen-volunteer to emerge from the French Revolution could be an educated and respectable idealist, who fought and died defending not only national integrity but national ideals. As was evident in the raising of the Polish Legions during the Napoleonic era, military service on the part of another power could be a strategy to build support for a national homeland. This tactic was further developed in the formation of the Czech Legions during the First World War. Habsburg Czechs, often former prisoners of war who had served in the Austro-Hungarian forces, volunteered for service in the Russian and French armies in pursuit of self-determination.[52] The volunteer ideal was reinforced by the Romantic tradition, exemplified by the participation of Lord Byron in the Greek War of Independence. Byron, like the war poet Rupert Brooke nearly a hundred years later, died of disease, rather than battle wounds. But both were immortalised as fallen heroes within the national canon welding the masculine self-sacrifice of the volunteer to nationhood and righteous causes.[53] By contrast, conscripts, who increasingly dominated the ranks of modern armies in wartime, were often regarded in lower standing. Whereas volunteering was a public gesture of active masculinity and commitment,'[t]he conscript was the passive subject of a bureaucratic hand'.[54]

Mythology (St Lucia, QLD, 2004); Alistair Thomson, *Anzac Memories: Living with the Legend* (Melbourne, 1994); Jonathan F. Vance, *Death So Noble: Memory, Meaning, and the First World War* (Vancouver, BC, 1997); Jeremy Krikkler, *White Rising: The 1922 Insurrection and Racial Killing in South Africa* (Manchester, 2005); Brian Graham and Peter Shirlow,'The Battle of the Somme in Ulster Memory and Identity', *Political Geography* 21 (2002): pp. 881–904.

52 Edwin P. Hoyt, *The Army Without a Country* (New York, 1967).

53 Mosse, *Fallen Soldiers*, pp. 15–32.

54 Ilana R. Bet-El, 'Men and Soldiers: British Conscripts, Concepts of Masculinity and the Great War', in Billie Melman (ed.), *Borderlines: Genders and Identities in War and Peace, 1870–1930* (London, 1998), p. 76.

Martial narratives linking male sacrifice to citizenship, and national interests and ideals were not unique to European societies. As Mimi Sheller has shown, in Haiti martial roles and narratives arose from preoccupations with the defence of the newly independent state and to ensure the 'elevation of the black man out of the depths of slavery into his rightful place as father, leader, and protector of his people'.[55] The Haitian revolution drew on the African-oriented warrior figures of Boukman and Makandal as well as the tradition of the male arms-bearing citizen from the American and French Revolutions. However, the privileging of male arms-bearers contributed to the emergence of an authoritarian regime dominated by military elites thereby undermining the radical promise of the Haitian Revolution.[56]

We have already noted the importance of voluntary military service in the assertion of demands for self-determination among European national groups such as the Poles and Czechs. In the founding myths of the Australian nation, military service in the First World War figures large, serving to produce symbolic male procreative power. Whereas women might be called upon to sacrifice their sons in war 'their collective death would bring forth immortal life, the birth of a nation .... Men's deeds ... were rendered simultaneously sacred and seminal'.[57] For some Australians, veteran status carried significant prestige and the promise of employment, housing, land and welfare benefits. Australian participation in the Gallipoli landings of 1915 was pivotal, even though the campaign had ended in ignominious defeat. But it was not the outcome that was significant so much as that 'southern manhood was put to a supreme test and did not fail. [Australia] had leapt from the cradle of her nationhood into the front rank of the bravest of the brave.'[58]

After the First World War, national movements in the European colonies tended to articulate demands and aspirations through established meanings of military service. Although many imperial subjects who participated in the world wars were conscripted, pressed or even enslaved, those who enlisted freely were often inspired by such depictions of the citizen volunteer and hoped wartime sacrifice would confer higher social and economic status to themselves, their communities and their nation. And, as Laura Tabili has argued, black and Asian servicemen manipulated British claims to fairness and justice in support of demands for non-discriminatory treatment in the metropole.[59] A particularly illuminating case in the post-imperial context is the campaign of South Moluccans for Dutch citizenship. As the favoured martial race of Dutch imperialism in Indonesia, the Moluccans

---

55   Mimi Sheller, 'Sword-Bearing Citizens: Militarism and Manhood in Nineteenth-Century Haiti', *Plantation Societies in the Americas* 4/2–3 (1997): p. 241.
56   Ibid., pp. 234, 242.
57   Marilyn Lake, 'Mission Impossible: How Men Gave Birth to the Australian Nation – Nationalism, Gender and Other Seminal Acts', *Gender and History* 43 (1992): pp. 305–322.
58   Ibid., p. 307. Imperial military service and the formation of independent national identities is also discussed in Smith, *Jamaican Volunteers* and Kevin Blackburn, 'Colonial Armies as Postcolonial History: Commemoration and Memory of the Malay Regiment in Modern Singapore and Malaysia' in Hack and Rettig, *Colonial Armies*.
59   Laura Tabili, *'We Ask For British Justice': Workers and Racial Difference in Late Imperial Britain* (Ithaca, NY, 1994).

were subject to increasing marginalisation after independence in 1949. Following an unsuccessful attempt to establish an autonomous Moluccan state, former soldiers were resettled in the Netherlands where it was not until the late 1970s that many were awarded citizenship.[60]

Within the growing movements for national independence, and in contrast to the experience of soldiers from the white dominions of Australia, New Zealand, Canada and South Africa, the exclusion of black and Asian ex-servicemen from both the material and symbolic rewards of military manhood, and the *non-commemoration* of male sacrifice became central themes within nationalist narratives. Black and Asian masculine and racial self-confidence grew as the myth of European invincibility was eroded from the late nineteenth century onwards. This was evident in the increasing failure of potential recruits to meet the minimum standards of army fitness evident during the South African War (1899–1902), a theme which recurred after 1914. The mental toll of modern warfare, epitomised by the prevalence of psychiatric casualties in the First World War, also undermined white claims of rationality and self-control. Of more direct impact was the routing of European armies at Adwa, Ethiopia (1896), in the Russo-Japanese War (1904–1905) and at Singapore (1942).[61] Imperial military service had a considerable impact on the processes and pace of national independence. But as Rudolf von Albertini reminds us in his early comparative work on decolonisation, we must not underestimate other key forces at work such as economic and social changes within the colonial powers themselves.[62]

This chapter has traced the development of military labour systems among colonised populations. Some key historical and spatial continuities, particularly in the enlistment of slaves and martial tradition have been highlighted. Perhaps the most widespread characteristic was the tendency of pragmatism to override other considerations, particularly those of race, in order to ensure an adequate supply of military labour. Strict codes of race and status were upheld, or re-ordered, when alternative sources of military labour were available. The adoption of a comparative approach therefore reaffirms the importance of identifying specific historical conditions and contingencies in the emergence of imperial military labour systems. Colonial politics, the size of settler communities, availability of slaves, disease and imperial rivalries were among the factors accounting for differing recruitment practices. Equally important was the role of the colonised themselves, not least in sharing the rhetoric of military service, which was ultimately mobilised in support of national independence.

---

60   Jaap de Moor, 'The Recruitment of Indonesian Soldiers for the Dutch Colonial Army, c. 1700–1950', in Killingray and Omissi (eds), *Guardians of Empire*.

61   See, for example, Frank Furedi, 'The Demobilized African Soldier and the Blow to White Prestige', in Killingray and Omissi (eds), *Guardians of Empire*; James K. Matthews, 'World War I and the Rise of African Nationalism: Nigerian Veterans as Catalysts of Change', *Journal of Modern African Studies* 20/3 (1982): pp. 493–502.

62   Rudolf von Albertini, 'The Impact of Two World Wars on the Decline of Colonialism', *Journal of Contemporary History* 4/1 (1969): pp. 17–35.

Circulation and Migration

Michael Mann

Connecting Past and Present

The migration of Indian 'coolies' (*kuli*)[1] has been at the top of the economic, social and lately also labour agenda of South Asian historians since the last decade of the twentieth century. Scholars from around the world have contributed to the emerging field of mobility and migration with special reference to the 'indentured labourer', as the Indian *kuli* was judicially termed.[2] Some books on Indian migration had appeared on the academic market in the 1970s and early 1980s and yet were hardly noticed.[3] Two reasons may be responsible for this. First, as an academic subject migration remained restricted to the trans-Atlantic world until the fall of the Berlin Wall in 1989 and the end of the Cold War in 1992. Second, the Indian government's politics of economic liberalisation introduced by Rajiv Gandhi at the end of the 1980s encouraged Indian migration overseas with a consequent increase in remittances sent back home. These remittances became an important factor in the country's economic and fiscal system amounting up to 3 per cent of annual GDP at the end of the twentieth century. The same is true for other South Asian countries, particularly Pakistan, Bangladesh and Sri Lanka.[4]

---

1   It may be noted here that the term *kuli* originates most probably from the Tamil word 'kuli' designating a hired or wage labourer. It also indicates that the colonial system of indentured labour was developed in the Tamilnad region of southern India: Henry Yule and A.C. Burnell, *Hobson-Jobson: A Glossary of Colloquial Anglo-Indian Words and Phrases, and of Kindred Terms, Etymological, Historical and Discursive* (London 1889), new edn by William Crooke (London, 1903), reprint (London, 1989), 'cooly', pp. 249–50.

2   Marina Carter, *Servants, Sirdars and Settlers: Indians in Mauritius 1834–1874* (Oxford, 1995); Crispin Bates (ed.), *Community, Empire and Migration: South Asians in Diaspora* (Basingstoke, 2001).

3   Hugh Tinker, *A New System of Slavery: The Export of Indian Labour Overseas, 1830–1920* (Bombay, 1974), and Tinker, *Separate and Unequal: India and the Indians in the British Commonwealth, 1920–1950* (London, 1976); Kay Saunders (ed.), *Indentured Labour in the British Empire, 1834–1920* (London, 1984).

4   International Monetary Fund, Balance of Payments Statistics, calculated by Samuel M. Maimbo *et al.* (eds), *Migrant Labor Remittances in South Asia* (Washington, DC, 2005),

Migrant Indians living overseas were valorised by the Hindu-nationalistic government from the 1990s until 2004. Not only did 'guest workers' – the post-colonial term for the *kuli* – in the states around the Persian Gulf (and Indian academics in the US) become part of that constructed 'diaspora', but also residents of British India who had emigrated as *kulis* to the islands of the Caribbean and to Canada, to South Africa, Mauritius, Malaya and Fiji more than a century previously, were now regarded as part of a global Indian diaspora. And in the 'Age of Globalisation', stressing some sort of 'Indianness' could create the feeling of a global Indian community sharing common cultural values ranging from Bollywood movies to Masala cuisine rather than a common belief or religion. Seen from an historical point of view, however, it seems inappropriate, even misleading, to characterise the contemporary global presence of Indians as a 'global Indian diaspora', for that phrase serves political and ideological rather than historical and sociological ends. Other South Asian governments, significantly, do not view their citizens living abroad as members of a global diaspora.[5]

From an historical perspective, migration from South Asia was part of a global phenomenon which gained momentum from the middle of the nineteenth century, and reflected the incorporation of an Indian labour force into international markets. From 1846 to 1940, migration from South Asia and southern China amounted to about 52 million, European transatlantic migration was 58 million, and migrants from northeastern Asia and Russian Siberia were 51 million, indicating that migration was not merely trans-Atlantic but truly global.[6] However, problems remain in grasping the dynamics of these global diasporas. It is not clear, for example, why migrants from South Asia are counted alongside migrants from southern China simply because they belonged to the same system of temporal labour contracts operating in the Indic, Atlantic and Pacific Oceans. And Africa is almost excluded or, owing to an assumed lack of sources, neglected.

More than 32 million South Asian migrants left the Indian subcontinent over this period. Of these about 14 million went to Burma, roughly 8 million migrated to Ceylon and probably up to 3 million to the islands of the Caribbean. Most likely the same number migrated to Mauritius and eastern Africa, and approximately 2 million people from South Asia went as indentured labourers to Malaya. Additionally, up to 2 million traders, merchants and lawyers migrated temporarily or permanently to all the colonies of the British Empire.[7] However,

---

p. ix and p. 13. In Sri Lanka, for example, the rate ranged from 6.8 to 7.9 per cent of the GDP between 1999 and 2003.

5   Steven Vertovec, *The Hindu Diaspora: Comparative Patterns* (London, 2000) and Judith M. Brown, *Global South Asians: Introducing the Modern Diaspora* (Oxford, 2006).

6   Adam McKeown, 'Global Migration, 1846–1940', *Journal of World History* 15/2 (2004): pp. 155–89, esp. pp. 156–8.

7   Kingsley Davis, *The Population of India and Pakistan* (Princeton, NJ, 1951), Table 35: 'Estimated Total Migration to and from India, 1834 to 1937', p. 99; K.S. Sandhu, *Indians in Malaya* (Cambridge, MA, 1969), pp. 373–80; Ian van den Driesen, *The Long Walk: Indian Plantation Labour in Sri Lanka in the Nineteenth Century* (New Delhi, 1997); Marina Carter, *Voices from Indenture: Experiences of Indian Migrants in the British Empire*

since statistics refer only to official numbers, migration numbers are incomplete. 'Informal migration' organised by private recruitment agencies or individuals, as well as massive numbers of single migrants, remain obscured and therefore unquantifiable. The statistics are also misleading with respect to the mode of counting, since they indicate only the embarkation of individuals and give no information on subsequent re-migrations. Out of the calculated 32 million migrants, at least 25 million re-migrated because labour contracts were limited to five years and included return shipping, suggesting some 6 million *kulis* actually did emigrate.[8]

In some countries, particularly on the islands of the Indian Ocean and the Caribbean, Indian migration resulted in considerable demographic shifts. During the century from 1840 to 1940 many countries received permanently settling indentured labourers from South Asia: Ceylon 2,321,000, Malaya 1,911,000, Mauritius 455,000, Natal (South Africa) 153,000, Reúnion 75,000 and eastern Africa 39,500. Additionally, Indian *kulis* permanently settled in the Caribbean and the Pacific: 239,000 in British Guiana, 150,000 in Trinidad, 39,000 in Jamaica, 79,000 in the French Caribbean, 35,000 in Dutch Guiana and 61,000 in Fiji.[9] The impact of this migration is sharply brought in to relief if we consider these numbers in proportion to the indigenous population: in Mauritius immigrants from South Asian constituted about 60 per cent of the overall population by the fourth decade of the twentieth century, in Trinidad roughly 30 per cent, in Jamaica about 34 per cent, in British Guiana 42 per cent, in Ceylon 23 per cent, and in Fiji 44 per cent.[10] Most migrants, however, received an 'Indian identity' when disembarking, and it was only after 1920 that official British papers identified people from British India as Indian nationals.

Seen against this background it seems reasonable that almost all research on South Asian migration has been concerned with the culture, integration and economic progress of emigrants. The seminal study of Marina Carter on *Servants, Sirdars and Settlers: Indians in Mauritius, 1834–1873*, and her most innovative book, *Voices from Indenture: Experiences of Indian Migrants in the British Empire*, are successful attempts to chart the movement of and give voice to the subaltern. Many studies deal with the history and culture of the Indians as industrious and therefore important settlers abroad, thereby contributing to the emerging field of mobility and migration with special reference to the 'indentured labourer'. Crispin Bates, *Community, Empire and Migration: South Asians in Diaspora*, K.O. Laurence,

(Leicester, 1996), pp. 22–3; Claude Markovits, 'Indian Merchant Networks Outside India in the Nineteenth and Twentieth Century', *Modern Asian Studies* 33 (1999): pp. 883–911, esp. p. 895.

8   Davis, *The Population of India and Pakistan*, Table 35: 'Estimated Total Migration to and from India, 1834 to 1937', p. 99.

9   Sugata Bose, *A Hundred Horizons: The Indian Ocean in the Age of Global Empire* (Cambridge, MA, 2006), pp. 76–7.

10   Carter, *Voices from Indenture*, pp. 22–3; Joseph E. Schwartzberg (ed.), *A Historical Atlas of South Asia* (Chicago, IL, 1978), 2nd imp., with additional material (New York, 1992), p. 115, Map B.

A Question of Labour: Indentured Immigration into Trinidad and British Guiana, 1875–1917, and the special edition of the *Internationales Asienforum* on the cultural history of South Asian migrants in historical as well as contemporary perspective indicate a growing general interest into a hitherto rather neglected world region, although trans-Atlantic migration from the eighteenth to the twentieth centuries still accounts for the majority of publications and academic research.[11] Various other themes such as the forging of the Sikh community in Canada or the reshaping of Muslim communities in Mauritius, the social and cultural history of miner-*kulis* and merchant-settlers in South Africa also feature in migration studies.[12]

Substance for such intense and forward-thinking research is provided by a unique archive. Bureaucratic registrations, records of medical inspections and shipping lists contribute to a comprehensive collection of individual names, places of origin, destination and duration of employment. Probably no other group of migrant people, apart from the European Jews whose registration, migration and extermination were enforced by an efficient German administration between 1933 and 1945, has been so meticulously registered and recorded as the Indian *kuli*.

Historical Setting

Migration of people to the cities and countries along Indian Ocean took place from the twelfth century onwards. Merchants, traders, seamen and travellers from South Asia and other regions bordering the Indian Ocean, particularly East Africa, Arabia and the Persian Gulf on the western side and Sumatra and Malaya on the eastern side, developed and created an inter-continental and translocal arena which has been depicted and described as the civilisation of the India Ocean.[13] This transoceanic region came into existence through tight-knit networks which reached, at least from the eighteenth century onwards, the southern parts of Africa via the Mascarenes, East Africa and the Arabian Peninsula, South Asia and the western fringe of what is known as Southeast Asia, sometimes also including mainland and insular Southeast Asia. During the heyday of European and British

---

11   Carter, *Servants, Sirdars and Settlers*; Carter, *Voices from Indenture*; K.O. Laurence, *A Question of Labour: Indentured Immigration into Trinidad and British Guiana, 1875–1917* (Kingston, 1994). See, also, the excellent collection of articles in the special volume of *Internationales Asienforum* 33 (2002) and Bates (ed.), *Community, Empire and Migration*.

12   For the Sikh community of Canada see amongst many publications, Radhika Seshan and Sushma J. Varma (eds), *Fractured Identities: The Indian Diaspora in Canada* (Jaipur, 2003). For *kulis* in South Africa, see, for example, Vishnu Padayachee and Robert Morrell, 'Indian Merchants and Dukawallahs in the Natal Economy, c. 1875–1914', *Journal of Southern African Studies* 17 (1991): pp. 71–102.

13   Kirti N. Chaudhury, *Asia before Europe: Economy and Civilisation of the Indian Ocean from the Rise of Islam to 1750* (Cambridge, 1990). See also Ravi A. Palat, *From World-Empire to World-Economy: Southeastern India and the Emergence of the Indian Ocean World-Economy (1350–1650)* (Ann Arbor, MI, 1988).

imperialism in the Indian Ocean, the Indian Subcontinent and its itinerant people became an important element of the global British Empire, the British Raj serving as model for administration and as an indispensable centre of human resources between 1860 and 1920.[14] The demography of the British Empire was thus shaped less by central administrative decisions and bureaucrats on the spot than by the willingness of people from British India to become members of the emerging empire's labour market.

In the nineteenth century the Indian merchant diaspora ranging from Sofala and Hormuz to Melaka and Johore was superseded by the mass migration of indentured labourers. The number of temporary indentured labourers was unprecedented in scale and dimension, yet not entirely new in its direction and organisation. Human trafficking between the eastern African and western Indian coasts had existed at least since the fifteenth century. Likewise, temporary migration and circulation of traders, merchants, monks and labourers to and from Sri Lanka took place from the tenth century. Here, for example, migration was organised by a well-established South Indian *kangany* recruitment agency and financed by the Chettiyar merchant community.[15] Recruiting *kulis* in the nineteenth century, therefore, followed established local and regional migration and recruitment patterns, particularly in the case of migrants from Tamilnad to Ceylon. This model dominated the recruitment of indentured labourers from South India to Burma, Ceylon and Malaya, setting into motion up to 25 million people in the western Indian Ocean.[16] After the abolition of the slave trade and slavery in the British Empire in 1807 and 1834, ex-slaves did not wish to work as wage labourers on the sugar and cotton plantations of their former masters. Slaves, therefore, had to be replaced by a new labour force. To solve the labour problem which threatened to affect the sugar industry on the Caribbean and the Mascarene islands of the western Indian Ocean, plantation owners started to look for substitute labourers. Until 1842, representatives of the plantocratic regimes – including the British government of Mauritius and that of several islands in the Caribbean, the British Indian government and the Imperial government in London – elaborated a sequence of laws according to which recruitment, transport and shipment of the *kuli* as well as his or her temporary employment as a wage labourer was organised. Supplementary legislation during the second half of the nineteenth

14 Thomas Metcalf, *Imperial Connections: India and the Indian Ocean Arena, 1860–1920* (Berkeley, CA, 2007).
15 Frank Heidemann, *Kanganies in Sri Lanka and Malaysia: Tamil Recruiter-cum-Foreman as a Sociological Category in the Nineteenth and Twentieth Century* (Munich, 1992); Hans-Dieter Evers, 'Chettiar Moneylenders in Southeast Asia', in Denis Lombard and Jean Aubin (eds), *Asian Merchants and Businessmen in the Indian Ocean and the China Sea* (Delhi, 2000), pp. 197–221; Michael Adas, 'Immigrant Asians and the Economic Impact of European Imperialism: The Role of the Indian Chettiar in British Burma', *Journal of Asian Studies* 33 (1974): pp. 385–401.
16 Eric Meyer, 'Labour Circulation between Sri Lanka and South India in Historical Perspective', in Claude Markovits, Jaques Pouchepadass and Sanjay Subrahmanyam (eds), *Society in Circulation: Mobile People and Itinerant Cultures in South Asia, 1750–1950* (Delhi, 2003), pp. 55–88.

century regulated sanitary and health conditions in the Indian depots and on board the ships with, however, rather minimal results. Official recruitment operated until 1917 when leading representatives of the Indian National Congress successfully agitated against any prolongation of the labour regime.[17]

Among the migrating *kulis* we find, as one would expect, many landless poor people, but also small and middling landowners, petty artisans, and former soldiers disbanded after the rebellion against colonial rule in 1857–58, as well as Brahmans originating mostly from southern India. The Indian migrant population was, like all such populations, far from homogeneous; social bindings and alliances which shaped group identities formed around familial, local and regional traditions including language, habits, custom, beliefs and rituals, rather than along lines of 'class or caste'.[18]

Approximately 80 per cent of migrants returned to South Asia, re-settling in the valleys and villages from where they were recruited. So far, however, the history of the returning *kuli* as part of a circulatory regime of family members and village inhabitants multifariously moving between their places of origin and the plantation, thereby also creating and moving goods and money, new ideas and new habits, has been neglected by academic research, reflecting the dominant colonial discourse of that history.[19] Since contemporary urban Indian as well as British colonial elites regarded 'coolies' with an adivasi (tribal) or dalit ('out-caste') background as savages who, driven through the streets and concentrated in the depots of Calcutta and Madras, were the scum of an imagined Indian society, they were and still are regarded as unworthy representatives of an imagined 'Indian nation' as well as an 'Indian national history'. In this respect only the fate of the exploited and exhausted Indian labourer, on the one hand, and the industrious and improving settler, on the other, seems to have been an adequate subject of historical research.

This is not to diminish the role of 'Indian communities' living abroad in Trinidad, Mauritius, Natal or Fiji. On the contrary, research in these areas has been innovative because it not only deals with the formation of communities or identities

---

17 Amarjit Kaur, 'Indian Labour, Labour Standard, and Worker's Health in Burma and Malaya, 1900–1940', *Modern Asian Studies* 40/2 (2006): pp. 425–75; Tinker, *A New System of Slavery*, pp. 116–19, and, on the background of indentured labour abolition, pp. 134–67.
18 Carter, *Voices from Indenture*, pp. 42–4; Ravindra K. Jain, *Indian Communities Abroad: Themes and Literature* (Delhi, 1993), pp. 23–7. See also the impressive but almost forgotten early study of Morton Klass, *East Indians in Trinidad: A Study of Cultural Persistence* (New York, 1961).
19 Contributions to *dalit* and *adivasi* recruitment do not tackle the position of the returnees other than in their role as recruiters. See Prabhu P. Mohapatra, 'Coolies and Colliers: A Study of the Agrarian Context of Labour Migration from Chota Nagpur, 1880–1920', *Studies in History* 1/2 (1985): pp. 247–303; and Crispin Bates and Marina Carter, 'Tribal and Indentured Migrants in Colonial India: Modes of Recruitment and Forms of Incorporation', in Peter Robb (ed.), *Dalit Movements and the Meanings of Labour in India* (Delhi, 1996), pp. 159–85.

but tries to reconstruct the 'agency' of indentured labourers abroad.[20] It also tries archaeologically to elaborate a distinct consciousness among South Asian migrants and settlers, lately dubbed 'Coolitude'. Analogous to 'Negritude' – the African cultural movement of the 1960s – Coolitude aims to build and strengthen the self-consciousness of former Indian indentured labourers as present-day citizens and settlers far from their ancestral homes and families. Descendants of the ex-*kulis* appear to accept a hybrid history as a constitutive part of their local societies and cultures.[21]

The settlement of *kulis* was on the recruitment agenda of neither the British Indian nor the local colonial governments. Planters, however, were keen to establish a durable but flexible labour regime consisting of indentured labourers during their first period of contract. Second-term *kulis* were more expensive, but settling Indians were welcomed either as small, stable and reliable labour force on the plantations or, as in most cases, as petty traders in villages and towns, and as garden cultivators in the countryside supplying planters and the local population with fruit and vegetables. This mix of labour fitted the plantation owners' desire to control rapidly growing numbers of labourers on their plantations according to economic necessities. For the same reasons planters welcomed, after some reluctance, an increasing number of female labourers as sexual partners or wives for the male labour force regarding the founding of families as helpful for stabilising the plantation/plantocratic regime.[22]

Although Indian settlements abroad were not on the agenda of the British Indian colonial state, East Africa was an exception. As mentioned above, merchants from western Indian regions like Kathiawar, Kachh and Gujarat had for centuries established trading posts and merchant communities along the coast and, since the middle of the nineteenth century, also in the hinterland of eastern Africa. This was particularly so in the coastal strip opposite the island of Zanzibar after the region officially became a British colony. More Indians than ever before migrated to British East Africa. In 1895–96 almost 7,000 Indians migrated - double that of the previous year. More indentured Indians came to East Africa when British authorities decided to develop the country's agrarian economy by means of a railway line from the coast of the Arabian Sea to Lake Victoria. From 1896 to 1902, roughly 31,000 railway builders temporarily migrated.[23] Most of them returned after their

20   See, for example, Marina Carter (ed.), *Across the Kalapani: The Bihari Presence in Mauritius* (Port Louis, 1999).
21   Marina Carter and Khal Torabully (eds), *Coolitude: An Anthology of the Indian Labour Diaspora* (London, 2002), pp. 143–214.
22   Joe Beall, 'Women under Indenture in Colonial Natal, 1860–1911', in Colin Clarke, Ceri Peach and Steven Vertovec (eds), *South Asians Overseas: Migration and Ethnicity* (Cambridge, 1990), pp. 57–74; Pieter C. Emmer, 'The Meek Hindu: The Recruitment of Indian Indentured Labourers for Service Overseas, 1870–1916', in Emmer (ed.), *Colonialism and Migration: Indentured Labour Before and After Slavery* (Dordrecht, 1983), pp. 187–207, esp. p. 198; Brij Lal (ed.), *Plantation Workers: Resistance and Accommodation* (Honolulu, HI, 1993).
23   Metcalf, *Imperial Connections*, pp. 171, 200.

contracts expired; some 7,000 however remained in the country, settling in towns and villages along the railway line and living, like many Indian immigrants, as *dukawallas* (petty shopkeepers).[24]

Though constantly increasing numbers of Indian indentured labourers and immigrants may indicate a similar demographic and/or economic pressure in South Asia, just the opposite happened. At the turn of the nineteenth century the 'Scramble for Africa' turned into a scramble for *kulis* in the British Indian province of Punjab in the Northwest, as well as in adjacent regions. This was because the number of policemen, soldiers and labourers in East Africa and other colonies of the British Empire in the Indian Ocean arena remained chronically deficit. The main recruitment areas for the indentured labourers had been Chota Nagpur in present Indian Union states of Chattisgarh, Jharkhand and parts of West Bengal, as well as the Tondaimandala region in present-day southern Tamil Nadu. Recruitment was organised along established indigenous local patterns and infrastructure. During the second half of the nineteenth century professional recruitment agencies run by South Asians extended the 'catchment area' up country, including the United Provinces of Agra and Oudh and finally reaching the Punjab. At the end of the nineteenth century labourers were also recruited in western India, however mainly for internal migration to the industrial centres of Bombay and Ahmedabad.

Kuli recruitment in India turned into a highly competitive private and public undertaking despite the fact that recruitment in the Indian countryside was welcomed by neither British revenue collectors nor Indian landowners, since a decreasing agricultural labour force could not provide for increasing agricultural outputs and, to put it in financial and fiscal terms, thus provide for rents and revenues. As the revenue system of British India was still based on its agricultural productivity, the diminishing supply of agricultural labourers threatened to undermine the colonial state's fiscal base.[25]

In the 1860s, British administrators in East Africa suggested for the first time the idea of establishing British East Africa as a settlement colony for Indian peasants. Local colonial administrators imagined Indian rural settlers in the hinterland of the country as civilising missionaries teaching black Africans the basics of agriculture to improve cash crops; that is, the plantation economy. As a contemporary Briton put it, East Africa was to become 'America for the Hindus', the promised land where they could settle as free farmers. The idea, however, was rejected by British settlers in East Africa who feared, among many other things, racial tensions. Yet the plan was revived at the end of the First World War when the former German East Africa was to be turned into a settlement colony for Indian soldiers and for others willing to colonise and develop the country. British colonial authorities saw the opening of East Africa for Indian colonisation as compensation for military services during the

---

24   Robert G. Gregory, *South Asians in East Africa: An Economic and Social History, 1890–1980* (Boulder, CO, 1993), pp. 10–15. Similarly for Natal, South Africa, Vishnu Padayachee and Robert Morrell, 'Indian Merchants and Dukawallahs in the Natal Economy, c. 1875–1914', *Journal of Southern African Studies* 17 (1991): pp. 71–102.

25   Carter, *Voices from Indenture*, pp. 38–9, 45; Metcalf, *Imperial Connections*, pp. 166–87.

Great War. Additionally, it was believed that this kind of sub-colonialism would put British India on a similar footing to South Africa and Australia, because this semi-independent British settler colony now acted as a mandatory power within the League of Nations administering former German colonies. This proposition also came to nought.[26]

During the interwar period there were two notable developments in patterns of long-term migration. First, it has barely been recognised that despite the fact that the migration of South Asian indentured labourers had begun a hundred years previously, and despite global economic depression and the dramatic collapse of prices for agricultural as well as natural resources, the number of migrants from India peaked shortly before the outbreak of the Second World War. This is remarkable given that the indentured labour system had been officially abolished in 1917, and in 1922–23 was finally superseded by new imperial immigration rules. Obviously unofficial migration was able to provide an immense reserve of Indian labourers desperately needed in the eastern Indian Ocean to develop the rubber plantation economy. In particular, the *kangany* recruiter mentioned above helped to prolong and intensify the privately organised and in some respect self-sustaining or, rather, multiplying indentured labour supply to Malaya.[27] It was during the 1930s that the idea of guest workers (as they would come to be known after the Second World War) emerged. When the British in 1920 acquired the mandate over Iraq, they tried to develop its oil industry as well as that in the neighbouring Arabian Emirates. British and American oil companies were willing to invest capital, but the countries lacked labourers. Pressed by British imperial interests and British Indian experience, the governments of the Emirates along the Trucial Coast agreed to implement contracts allowing American and British companies to employ Indian labourers. Yet these contracts could not disguise a close similarity to those previously applied to indentured labourers in strictly regulating recruitment, transport, working hours and repatriation. By 1950 more than 15,000 guest workers from South Asia worked temporarily in the states along the southern coast of the Persian Gulf.[28]

Continuities and Change

The end of the Second World War launched the end of worldwide colonialism. The first colony gaining independence was British India in 1947, to be followed by Ceylon in 1948. Yet, whereas the independence of Ceylon was smooth and peaceful –

---

26   Metcalf, *Imperial Connections*, pp. 142–52 passim.
27   Davis, *The Population of India and Pakistan*, Table 35: 'Estimated Total Migration to and from India, 1834 to 1937', p. 99; Kaur, 'Indian Labour, Labour Standard, and Worker's Health', p. 430.
28   L.J. Secombe and R.I. Lawless, 'Foreign Worker Dependence in the Gulf, and the International Oil Companies, 1910–1950', *International Migration Review* 20/3 (1986): pp. 548–74.

which is why the event was hardly noticed – independence of British India with the partitioning of the subcontinent caused profound human tragedies. Partition along religious lines created two nation states, India and Pakistan, and induced the exodus of Hindus and Sikhs from Pakistan to India and of Muslims the other way round. Approximately 12 million people migrated, of whom about 1 million were killed. Even today this massive 'demographic exchange' is visible in many cities of Pakistan and India. In Lahore, the capital of the former Sikh rajadom, no Sikhs can be found nowadays. In Karachi, the then major port city of Pakistan, many Muslim refugees from northern India were resettled and, within a decade, became a class of its own, the *muhajirs* (literally translated: migrants). At the same time, the Mughal residence Shahjahanabad, otherwise known as Old Delhi, where Muslim and Hindu populations were more or less at par during the previous centuries, emigration of almost all Muslims caused a massive change not only in the demographic composition but in the economic activities of the city.[29]

Atrocities which went along with partition, expulsion and flight were hardly describable, yet literati of both countries tried hard to comprehend the incomprehensible.[30] Apart from that, Partition as such seemed anachronistic in the moves towards constitutional reform and national self-determination of both the successor states of British India. Problems of separation and integration dominated the interior politics of both states. Soon, the numbers of mass migration became widely known but the history of that emigration, which fundamentally changed the human (besides the political) face of the subcontinent within a decade, was not written for another half-century. Only in the new millennium did historians from Pakistan and some from India, but more from the Anglo-American academia, begin to investigate this period of dramatic transition and fundamental change. For the first time after partition the consequences of this caesura are becoming slowly and fragmentarily visible.[31] Consequently, future research will have to elaborate on the history of partition and migration as part of a subcontinental and therefore transnational history.

The history of partition and migration is very much comparable to the events occurring in Europe after the collapse of the Nazi-German Empire. Millions of German, Polish and Russian people were driven away from their homelands after

---

29   Sarah Ansari, *Life after Partition: Migration, Community and Strife in Sindh, 1947–62* (Karachi, 2005); Ravinder Kaur, 'Planning Urban Chaos: State and Refugees in Post-Partition Delhi', in Evelin Hust and Michael Mann (eds), *Urbanization and Governance in India* (Delhi, 2005), pp. 229–50.

30   Kushwant Sing, *Train to Pakistan* (New Delhi, 1988); Ravikant and Tarun K. Saint (eds), *Translating Partition: Stories by Attia Hosain et al* (New Delhi, 2001); Sukashi Kamra, *Bearing Witness: Partition, Independence, End of the Raj* (Calgary, 2002; New Delhi, 2003); Naiz Zaman, *A Divided Legacy: The Partition in Selected Novels of India, Pakistan and Bangladesh* (Dhaka, 1999); Prasada Rao and V. Pala, *India–Pakistan: Partition Perspectives in Indo-English Novels* (New Delhi, 2004).

31   Ian Talbot, *Divided Cities: Partition and its Aftermath in Lahore and Amritsar, 1947–1957* (Karachi, 2006); Ian Talbot and Shinder Thandi (eds), *People on the Move: Panjab Colonial and Post-Colonial Migration* (Karachi, 2004).

the re-drawing of borders in central and eastern Europe. Some 14 million Germans were evicted from eastern Europe, and nearly 3 million Polish people 'repatriated' from Ukraine to the new parts of western Poland. Additionally, almost 1.5 million Jews left Europe, the Middle East and Africa for the newly founded state of Israel, whereas in East and Central Asia approximately 3 million Japanese settlers on the Asian mainland were 'repatriated'. Some 2 million Chinese people from Taiwan and perhaps 5 to 6 million Tibetans migrated to India after 1950.[32] Estimates vary greatly and are often exaggerated, but at least 30 million people were re-settled in Europe and Asia within a decade after the end of the Second World War.

Apart from internal migration on the Indian subcontinent, external migration steadily increased. The circulation of guest workers accelerated after the oil crises of the 1970s; the crisis for the oil-consuming states of the west turned into an economic boom for oil-producing states around the Persian Gulf. Large investment in infrastructure and construction demanded an additional labour force easily provided by people from South Asian states. According to estimates for the year 1990, about 2 million guest workers from India, 1.5 million from Pakistan, 200,000 from Bangladesh and 70,000 from Sri Lanka had stayed, so far, temporarily as guest workers in the Gulf States. Labour contracts were generally for one year, only exceptionally up to five years. Once the contracts expired, guest workers had to return to the country of their origin, but could re-engage after the lapse of a year. Despite strict immigration laws, a small number of the guest workers were able to stay in Gulf States, legally, if their employees were able to receive exceptions from the law, or illegally, clandestinely protected by their employers, who were in dire need of labourers.[33]

Migrating to the Gulf promised social uplift and economic improvement. Traditionally, rural migrants invested their remittances in land and agricultural implements. Yet much money was also spent on the improvement of houses, often turning mud and thatch into brick and tile constructions. In the 1980s and 1990s, money was (and still is) also spent on better nutrition, medical and health care, and, last but not least, education. In this context it is interesting to note that particular circulants, that is, migrant workers, from the Pakhtun area of Pakistan situated along the Afghan border invest much of the remittances in the education of their offspring, including daughters. And it is also interesting that female migrants from Sri Lankan villages working as housemaids in the Gulf adapted the veil as part of a modern dressing habit, indicating that it was appropriate for women to cover their face in public. This does not indicate a puristic or even fundamentalist attitude let alone consciousness, but expresses the Muslim women's desire to dress appropriately. Both examples, however, do in any case indicate that in many rural

---

32   Partha S. Ghosh, *Migrants and Refugees from South Asia: Political and Security Dimensions* (Shillong, 2001), pp. 1–27; R.P. Chari, *Missing Boundaries: Refugees, Migrants, Stateless and Internally Displaced Persons in South Asia* (New Delhi, 2003).

33   Hasan N. Gardezi, 'Asian Workers in the Gulf States of the Middle East', *Journal of Contemporary Asia* 21 (1991): pp. 179–94, esp. pp. 189–90; Jonathan S. Addleton, *Undermining the Centre: The Gulf Migration and Pakistan* (Karachi, 1992), pp. 63–74, 82–3.

families and village societies sometimes substantial changes took and still take place, and that mobility and migration are essential for transforming and, at the same time, modernising South Asian societies.[34]

British Empire and the Commonwealth of Nations

Structures established during the time of the British Empire, particularly in the first half of the twentieth century, provided the ways and means by which migration of people from independent South Asian countries was organised in the post-colonial era. This is not to maintain that such migration structures prolonged colonial rule setting the frame for a neocolonialism of the former imperial power, but rather that the effect of such structures remained powerful, affecting the decision-making processes of willing migrants to particular countries which were, most likely, former colonies of the British Empire. Another post-colonial effect was the secondary migration of second- or third-generation Indian indentured labourers to Great Britain, be that from eastern Africa or from the Caribbean. For that reason it is important not to terminate the history of migration at the end of the British Empire but to look at the long-term effect of colonial labour politics.

The migration of people from South Asia was not restricted to indentured labourers and *dukawalas* accompanied by traders and lawyers to plantation colonies or for railway constructions in the colonies of the British Empire. In the twentieth century, Indians migrated to all the colonies of the British Empire, including white settler colonies such as Canada. Sikh migration from the Punjab into Canada is the most prominent example among the many histories of South Asian migratory groups and has attracted detailed research. Sikh migration to Canada began early in the twentieth century. As early as 1908 the Canadian government implemented anti-immigration laws to prevent Asian immigration. At that time, some 5,000 Indians lived in Canada, mainly in and around British Columbia's capital, Vancouver. Since only relatives were allowed to immigrate after 1908, many Sikhs put their wives and brothers on the immigration lists. This explains why in the middle of the 1930s some 95 per cent of all Indian immigrants were Sikhs. Most of them originated from a few villages in the Punjab, often reproducing in Canada almost identical Punjabi social and familial structures.[35] As in other parts of the world, immigration laws became less restrictive over time in Canada because of the growing postwar labour shortage in industrial and semi-industrial countries. In

---

34   Pong-Sul Ahn (ed.), *Migrant Workers and Human Rights: Out-Migration from South Asia* (New Delhi, 2004); Katy Gardner and Filipo Osella, 'Migration, Modernity and Social Transformation in South Asia: An Overview', *Contributions to Indian Sociology* 37/1–2 (2003): pp. v–xxviii; Godfrey Gunatilleke (ed.), *The Impact of Labour Migration on Households: A Comparative Study in Seven Asian Countries* (Tokyo, 1992).

35   Acharna B. Verma, *The Making of Little Punjab in Canada: Patterns of Immigration* (New Delhi, 2002), pp. 182–97.

1991 immigrants from all South Asian countries to Canada had risen to more than 220,000 people, nearly half of them Sikhs. The high percentage of Sikhs among the South Asian migrants can be explained by the early twentieth-century migration patterns inducing chain-migration based on a continuous flow of information.[36]

Immigrants from South Asia, and in particular the Indian Union, do not constitute a single homogeneous society within a 'host society'. Immigrants from Tamilnad, for example, differ considerably in familial structures, social behaviour and cultural customs when compared with Sikh immigrants from the Punjab.[37] There is also a big difference between immigration from before the Second World War and post-Partition immigration after 1967. Only then did the Sikhs from the Punjab develop a distinct diasporic community consciousness, for they were now seen to constitute a people evicted from their ancestral homeland, and to represent true Sikh values.[38] It was the Sikh community of Canada which strongly supported the Sikh demand of an independent state 'Khalistan' during the Indian Union's turbulent 1970s and 1980s, in particular when troops of the Indian Union stormed the Golden Temple in Amritsar, and when Hindu riots against Sikh property and life were launched after Prime Minister Indira Gandhi was assassinated by a Sikh bodyguard in 1984.[39]

The effects of global migration may also be traced in Great Britain, the core of a vanishing empire and emerging commonwealth, which may be regarded as early evidence of what is presently called globalisation. Increasing wages and prices in the textile sector in postwar industrial nations put recently decolonised nations like India and Pakistan in a favourable position as they could produce textiles cheaply. Owing to this immense competitive advantage, western nations insisted on a globally regulated market realised by the 'Multifibre Arrangement' in 1974. The 'arrangement' organised imports from 'Third World' producers to industrialised countries. Here, however, producers looked for countries not affected by this international arrangement, among them the young state of Bangladesh, which had separated from Pakistan in 1971. Within the decade 1976–85, the number of textile factories in Bangladesh increased from about 500 to 700, most of them situated in and around Dhaka and Chittagong. During the same period the textile market of Great Britain collapsed, putting a third of the mainly female labourers out of work. Many among them were immigrants from former British Bengal and East Pakistan.[40]

Before the restrictive 'Commonwealth Immigration Bills' of 1962 and 1968, investors from Great Britain regarded 'Oriental women' as willing, humble, yet diligent labourers, which is why agencies recruited women from districts of

---

36   Gurcharn S. Basran and B. Singh Bolaria, *The Sikhs in Canada: Migration, Race, Class and Gender* (New Delhi, 2003), pp. 96–7, 104–107, 164–7, 198–203.

37   Varma and Seshan (eds), *Fractured Identity.*

38   Bhagat Singh, *Canadian Sikhs Through a Century (1897–1997)* (Delhi, 2001), pp. 317–51.

39   For an up-to-date version of a visionary Sikh nation, see www.khalistan.net.

40   Naila Kabeer, *Bangladeshi Women Workers and Labour Market Decisions: The Power to Choose* (New Delhi, 2001).

eastern Bengal like Sylhet and Chittagong. Judicial restrictions, however, did not prohibit the immigration of relatives. The same 'empire effect' which characterised Sikh migration to Canada determined Bengali and Bangladeshi immigration to London's East End. Soon men started to open small restaurants and shops whilst their women worked as textile workers, many of them as freelance homeworkers. In 1981 some 29,000 officially registered female textile workers were supplemented by an estimated labour force of 40,000 unofficial homeworkers.[41] Despite the Commonwealth immigration laws, immigration of people from South Asia into Great Britain was not interrupted. On the contrary, between 1961 and 1991 the number of immigrants from South Asia increased from 100,000 to more than 1.4 million people. Most immigrants came from a few districts in the Punjab, from Gujarat and Bangladesh.

Additionally, secondary migration of Indians from East Africa caused a dramatic increase in Britain's immigration numbers in the 1970s. The first group of such migrants came to Britain after Idi Amin forced Indians to leave Uganda in 1972; approximately 300,000 Indians left eastern Africa. Almost at the same time Indian secondary immigration from the Caribbean islands caused some confusion among the British population. Most British regarded the Caribbean as the home of black Africans, not Indians. Indians having directly migrated and settled in Great Britain, however, viewed Indian immigrants from Trinidad, Jamaica and British Guyana as curious contemporaries differing much in language, habits and customs from their South Asian 'compatriots'. As descendants from former indentured labourers, Caribbean Indians had adapted some specifics of the local Caribbean creole culture but, in general, they remained a distinct society of various groups trying to protect their cultural heritage. Yet because they preserved their cultures and customs, secondary immigrants seemed different and curious. The politics of identity and ethnicity during the 1950s and 1960s redefined Indian communities in the Caribbean. Many of its members received better education, which enabled some 50,000 to 60,000 Caribbean people of South Asian origin to emigrate to Great Britain.[42]

Enabling and establishing migration within the British Empire, supported by an imperial administration and institutions in London as well as various colonial institutions and administrations, induced a sophisticated system of recruitment, collection, concentration, transport and distribution: in short, a new infrastructure. This reorganised the labour market of the British Empire and helped physically to maintain it until the Second World War. Yet migration is not only about infrastructure (though this is an important aspect, which has only lately been placed on the historical research agenda). It is also about the transformation and modernisation of people and societies within and without such an empire. Much has already been said on the plantation colonies; much, however, will have to be

---

41 Ibid., pp. 193–201.
42 Steven Vertovec, 'Caught in an Ethnic Quandary: Indo-Caribbean Hindus in London', in Roger Ballard (ed.), *Desh Pardesh: The South Asian Presence in Britain* (London 1994), pp. 272–90.

said on the returnees to, and re-settlers in, South Asia, in particular with respect to the modernising aspects of migration and mobility. Research on the social and economic as well as cultural history of returning indentured labourers will be the most interesting aspect of future academic scrutiny and certainly the most profitable, as it may help to explain the effects of 'slow modernisation' in some regions as well as the prolonged so-called 'backwardness' of people in some other regions of South Asia.[43] In any case it has become clear that running the British Empire consisted of more than imperial decisions and bureaucratic measures. To some extent it depended upon the willingness of Indian labourers to migrate and to shape the routes of migration not only according to the empire's needs but to meet their own ends. Exploring the kuli's agency could be a rather profitable field for subaltern studies.

Structures of the British Empire, including infrastructures, were still very much at work after decolonisation, and still are. Established patterns of migration, settlement, employment, legislation regulating emigration and immigration seem to determine decisions to regulate and to direct global migration. This process has to be seen in a wider context, that of new empires emerging whilst old ones try to hold on to their fading influence let alone power. The US and the EU, as well as the Republic of China and the Indian Union, may serve as contemporary examples of preserving and forging empires of global dimension. Whether or not to regulate immigration into and emigration from these empires is highly debated by politicians, sociologists and demographers. Migration and the way immigration is judiciously dealt with, and the way immigrants as well as returnees are socially integrated will prove the ability of all contemporary empires to modernise their societies. That question, however, was never on the mind of the British Empire's politicians, who simply aimed at the control of its labour market, yet did not develop any particular interest in modernising South Asia's societies.

---

43   Michael Mann, 'Migration – Re-migration – Circulation: South Asian Kulis in the Indian Ocean and Beyond, 1840-1940', in Donna R. Gabaccia and Dirk Hoerder (eds), *Connecting Seas and Connected Ocean Rims. Indian, Atlantic and Pacific Oceans and China Seas Migrations from the 1830s to the 1930s* (Leyden and Boston, MA, 2011), pp. 108–33.

Crime

Lauren Benton

As key elements in the constitution and consolidation of empires, crime and criminal law promoted practices of exclusion and inclusion. The simple act of trying and convicting someone of a crime implied an act of inclusion by affirming the legitimacy of a claim to jurisdiction. This authority could not be taken for granted in empire but required the support of wider arguments about the scope of imperial authority and the status of colonial subjects. At the same time, the trial, sentencing and punishment of criminals created groups of political and legal outsiders. The tensions between inclusion and exclusion produced complex and fluid imperial legal orders. The expansion of the colonial state's criminal jurisdiction developed alongside measures generating spatial and temporal variations in the treatment of crime and criminals. Acts of legal experimentation included the proliferation of penal colonies, declarations of martial law and campaigns to suppress piracy and banditry. Imperial bureaucracies enacted measures that created legally differentiated zones within empires and multiplied status distinctions among imperial subjects while also working to establish more systematic and nearly complete control over crime and criminal justice.

This chapter explores such tensions within empires between 1500 and 1900. It focuses on three interconnected phenomena. The first involved representations and uses of imperial spaces as destinations for shipments of convicted criminals. This surprisingly widespread policy, which we will examine mainly in European empires, simultaneously produced a proliferation of colonial penal colonies and fostered a cultural association between empire and criminality. A second, related aspect of empire was the representation of imperial peripheries as conducive to crime, especially acts disruptive of the exercise of sovereign authority. Piracy and treason featured in accounts of European empires as crimes encouraged by distance from metropolitan centres and facilitated by decentralised and layered systems of rule. Third, criminal prosecutions in empires were at the heart of a vibrant jurisdictional politics. Struggles over definitions of crime often served as focal points for larger conflicts, in particular tense negotiations and recurring violence surrounding the incorporation of culturally different peoples within imperial legal orders. These three trends reveal the ways in which crime and criminality operated at the intersection of the consolidation of empires and processes of imperial fragmentation.

Banishment and Exile

Banishment was a widely occurring feature of imperial law, one with some surprising similarities across legal systems. Exile served in most empires as a punishment for common criminals and political subversives. Transported convicts faced uncertainty about their legal status after they arrived at designated places of banishment, although it was clear that prisoners of high and low status were generally subjected to different treatment.

Exile was not a purely European imperial phenomenon. It was a well-established punishment in the Qing Empire between 1758 and 1820, for example, particularly for elites accused of sedition. Banishment in China formed part of a colonising project to incorporate the northwestern frontier regions that had recently been brought into the empire. The end of the northwestern campaigns in 1759 prompted the movement of thousands of people as exiles into the 'new territories' of Xinjiang. While banished elite exiles retained the hope of returning, more numerous common criminals were sentenced to perpetual exile as an alternative to execution. In a society privileging family ties, banishment was an especially painful and socially debilitating punishment.[1]

Islamic law also recognised banishment. The Quran mentions it, and classical jurisprudence from the ninth to the thirteenth century discussed it mainly as a punishment for banditry and illicit sex. Banishment was almost exclusively a punishment for males, though it could be applied to women, who would have been accompanied by male relatives in exile. In the Ottoman criminal code, it figured as a sentence mainly for people perceived to be a danger to the religious or social order, such as gypsies, lepers, irreligious people or arsonists. We know that banishment was preserved in the criminal codes created in the mid-nineteenth century, but the codes tell us little about the full range of uses of exile since local communities were empowered to impose the penalty on undesirables. Egypt banished criminals to the Sudan in the 1860s, and there are doubtless other, little-studied examples of transporting political and common criminals.[2]

In Europe, exile and banishment entered early modern practice mainly though not exclusively through Roman law, which prescribed sentences ranging from expulsion from a city or province (in perpetuity or for a fixed term) to deportation to a fixed location with forfeiture of rights of citizenship and property. Banishment in Rome could be applied to anyone, but it was used mainly for elites and often imposed as a reaction to political crimes or other acts against the public order. In some periods of Roman history, the threat of exile became a weapon against people merely suspected of being capable of fomenting disorder, such as gypsies, astrologers or Jews.[3]

---

1   J. Waley-Cohen, *Exile in Mid-Qing China: Banishment to Xinjiang, 1758–1820* (New Haven, CT, 1991).

2   R. Peters, *Crime and Punishment in Islamic Law: Theory and Practice from the Sixteenth to the Twenty-First Century* (Cambridge, 2005).

3   R.G. Caldwell, 'Exile as an Institution', *Political Science Quarterly* 58/2 (1943): pp. 239–62;

Not surprisingly, given the wide influence of Roman law across European legal orders, Atlantic European powers adopted banishment to serve imperial ventures from an early period. From the fifteenth century, Portuguese expeditions relied on convicts as scouts and employed them as forced colonists.[4] Soon after Columbus' first voyage, the Spanish monarchs weighed the wisdom of dispatching convicts to help settle Hispaniola.[5] New France became another site of colonisation by criminals on expeditions led by La Roque, Cartier and de la Roche; the last abandoned 60 convicts on tiny Sable Island in the North Atlantic, and a later French expedition found only twelve survivors.[6] The English talked of using convicts as forced colonists when planning Martin Frobisher's second voyage across the North Atlantic in 1577. By the early seventeenth century, the English crown sought ways to establish transportation as an act of mercy in criminal cases while also identifying particular destinations for transported criminals in the North Atlantic and East and West Indies.[7] Officials in Virginia called for the importation of convicts in the early seventeenth century, and contingents of criminals were shipped to Tangier to work on the construction of its massive sea barrier. In addition to these experiments, Portugal, Spain and France relied on the use of criminals as forced labourers on galleys, a practice that lasted until the mid-eighteenth century.

Despite substantive differences in law, the structure of bureaucracies and the timing and goals of imperial expansion, early convict transportation practices shared some key features across empires. First, distinctions were commonly made between criminals of high and low status. For example, Spanish and Portuguese convicts from the nobility were often shipped to garrisons in North Africa, while low-status offenders were condemned to the galleys, sometimes in perpetuity. Second, convict transportation figured everywhere as a punishment for both political acts and common crimes. Offences defined very differently at law were thus linked, as they were in France, where the status of legal non-person was attached to political prisoners, leading to their exile and preparing the way for a larger wave of transported criminals.[8] Third, as in Roman law, convicts transported from European polities arrived in their designated places of banishment to find

M.V. Braginton, 'Exile Under the Roman Emperors', *Classical Journal* 39/7 (1944): pp. 391–407; O.F. Robinson, *The Criminal Law of Ancient Rome* (Baltimore, MD, 1995).

4   See, for example, 'Letter of Pedro Vaz de Caminha to King Manuel', pp. 3–32 in W.B. Greenlee (ed.) *The Voyage of Pedro Álvares Cabral to Brazil and India from Contemporary Documents and Narratives* (London, 1938); see also M.D.D. Newitt, *A History of Portuguese Overseas Expansion, 1400–1668* (London and New York, 2005).

5   Archivo General de Indias, Seville, Patronato, 295, N.35; Archivo Histórico Nacional, Madrid, Diversos Colecciones, 41, N. 22.

6   Jacques-Guy Petit, 'La Colonizzazione Penale del Sistema Penitenziario Francese', in M. Da Passano (ed.), *Le Colonie Penali nell'Europa dell'Ottocento* (Rome, 2004), pp. 37–65.

7   G. Morgan and P. Rushton, *Eighteenth-Century Criminal Transportation: The Formation of the Criminal Atlantic* (New York, 2004).

8   M. Spieler, *Empire and Underworld: Captivity in French Guiana* (Cambridge, MA, 2012); and see also E. Rothschild, 'A Horrible Tragedy in the French Atlantic', *Past and Present* 192 (2006): pp. 67–108.

their legal status largely undefined. For example, the courts of British Atlantic colonies made no meaningful distinctions between transported criminals and indentured servants until well into the eighteenth century.[9]

These broadly similar conditions developed alongside practices that varied by empire. In Britain, the numbers of transported criminals declined during the first part of the eighteenth century as they were instead pressed into service as soldiers and sailors. The 1718 Transportation Act altered the legal framework for transportation, converting it into a sentence that courts could impose directly rather than merely substitute in acts of mercy for other punishments. Servile bondage was being institutionalised as an element of criminal law, though the legal status and rights of transported convicts still remained unspecified.[10] The vast majority of convicts transported from Britain in the eighteenth century were sent to just two Atlantic colonies, Virginia and Maryland.

In Iberian empires, exile continued to be a routine punishment in the courts, but with different results: the formation of a truly imperial system for Portugal and a more decentralised, ad hoc practice of banishment in the Spanish Empire. Portugal used convicts (*degredados*) as forced colonists from the fifteenth century and moved more quickly than other European powers towards a system in which convicts were moved from one colonial site to another.[11] Courts in Spain and in the Spanish colonies routinely sentenced criminals to *destierro* (exile), both for fixed and indefinite periods, and in response to a wide range of crimes including acts of sedition. But until the late eighteenth century, and with the notable exception of the practice of sentencing men to forced labour on the galleys, penal transportation was not applied systematically as an imperial policy in the Spanish Empire.[12]

In the late eighteenth century the transportation of convicts surged across European empires and became more closely aligned with imperial goals. Part of the impetus for this trend lay in changes in the criminal law in Europe, in particular in widespread measures to criminalise vagrancy. Another stimulus was the intensification of global inter-imperial rivalries. New patterns of long-distance maritime trade created increased incentives for establishing far-flung bases and defending sea approaches to distant spheres of influence, trends connected to the widespread militarisation of empires. Interest in founding penal settlements in strategically located sites formed part of this broader process of global competition.

We see the pairing of penal transportation and militarisation clearly in the Spanish Empire, where anxieties about the rise of British global power in the wake of the Seven Years War stimulated plans for the construction by forced labour of

---

9   A. Atkinson, 'The Free-born Englishman Transported: Convict Rights as a Measure of Eighteenth-Century Empire', *Past and Present* 44 (1994): pp. 88–115.

10 See ibid.; B. Kercher, 'Perish or Prosper: The Law and Convict Transportation in the British Empire, 1700–1850', *Law and History Review* 21/3 (2003): pp. 527–54; and J.M. Beattie, *Crime and the Courts in England, 1660–1800* (Oxford, 1986).

11 T.J. Coates, *Convicts and Orphans: Forced and State-Sponsored Colonizers in the Portuguese Empire, 1550–1755* (Stanford, CA, 2001).

12 R. Pike, *Penal Servitude in Early Modern Spain* (Madison, WI, 1983).

new fortifications in colonial garrisons (*presidios*). Spanish officials began massing criminals, many of them soldiers accused of desertion, in a few Spanish ports for transportation to colonial sites. While some convicts, especially those of elite status, continued to be sent to the garrisons of North Africa, criminals were now also shipped to work on colonial fortifications in San Juan, Havana and the Philippines, places that had been attacked and held by the English during the Seven Years War. An existing practice of moving men from one colony to another after they had been convicted of crimes in colonial courts – from New Spain to the Philippines, for example – was now also expanded. Colonial convicts joined men sent from Spain as forced labourers in *presidios*, and on other public works in imperial sites.[13]

As with Spain, geopolitical considerations influenced British convict transportation. The American Revolution disrupted the shipment of convicts to North American colonies, leading British authorities to place convicts on disabled ships, or hulks, in the Thames River while casting around for alternative sites of exile. It was not only the build-up of the convict population in the hulks that made the search for a new site so pressing. British officials considered convict transportation as a means of supplying forced colonists for strategically located points in empire. Botany Bay, selected after officials considered and rejected alternatives such as Nova Scotia, Florida, the Falkland Islands and the island of Lemain in the Gambia River, supported British designs in the Pacific, where a French presence and even the arrival of American whalers were considered potential threats to British hegemony. As one historian has put it, 'transportation was the mode but not the motive of Britain's colonisation of Australia'.[14] France also moved to utilise convict transportation in support of imperial designs. The exile of political prisoners before and during the French Revolution led to the more systematic exile of forced colonisers to French Guiana, and later also to New Caledonia. Convicts poised for transportation were parked in the *bagnes*, sites of imprisonment under naval administration in France.[15]

The expansion of convict transportation as an imperial system was accompanied by a shift towards tightening restraints on convicts in places of exile. In the Spanish Empire, the trend created an administrative novelty, the placement of civilian convicts under military authority. Soldiers, mainly deserters, and civilian convicts laboured together in *presidios*, where civilians now found themselves without avenues for appeal. This legal limbo had precedence only in the treatment of galley slaves; it was otherwise anomalous in an empire in which subjects everywhere had traditionally enjoyed the prerogative of petitioning the king for mercy, and for relief from corrupt

---

13 Ibid.; E.M.S.C. Segurado, '"Vagos, Ociosos y Malentretenidos": The Deportation of Mexicans to the Philippines in the Eighteenth Century', unpublished paper delivered at the American Historical Association Annual Meeting, Atlanta, GA, 5 January 2007.

14 A. Frost, *Botany Bay Mirages: Illusions of Australia's Convict Beginnings* (Carlton, VC, 1994), p. 40; Emma Christopher, *A Merciless Place: The Fate of Britain's Convicts after the American Revolution* (Oxford and New York, 2011).

15 Spieler, *Empire and Underworld*.

local commanders.[16] One of the few records of a convict protesting this anomalous status is a petition written by Bernardino de Valcárel, a lawyer transported to the *presidio* at San Juan in 1791. Valcárel complained, probably to no avail, that he had been 'punished without a hearing … [and] made a criminal without having any charges filed'. He noted that there were no established procedures in the *presidio* to consider grievances or to challenge arbitrary punishments.[17]

The rising influence of military law in empire can also be observed in the British Empire. The penal colony of New South Wales was under martial law only between 1792 and 1795, and again briefly after the rebellion against Governor Bligh in 1808.[18] But the influence of military law extended further. Governors at New South Wales initially enjoyed broad civilian and military authority and could unilaterally assign convicts to private masters, award pardons and decide civil cases on appeal. The chief judge of the colony held the military title of Judge Advocate until 1809.[19] The more striking uses of martial law occurred in the secondary penal colonies such as Van Diemen's Land and Norfolk Island where civilian institutions were slower to develop. Within two years of its settlement in 1788, martial law was declared at Norfolk Island to allow the island commander to order severe punishments for convicts or settlers stealing from the dwindling stores. After 1800, the colony endured the command of a series of military officers who imposed a harsh disciplinary regime with few checks on their actions. Especially during the period between 1827 and 1840, when the settlement took on the characteristics of a brutal prison camp, Norfolk Island acquired a reputation as a site outside the regular system of law and legal administration.[20]

Transportation to colonial penal colonies decreased in the first decades of the nineteenth century, but neither the phenomenon nor the legal questions it raised disappeared from colonial practice. Britain created a penal colony in the Andaman Islands for criminals and political prisoners transported from India in the second half of the nineteenth century.[21] In the Spanish Empire and in the South American republics, men who favoured independence from Spain or opposed new republican governments were sent to island penal colonies such as Más-a-Tierra, one of the Juan Fernández Islands off the coast of Chile, and to the Isla de Pinos off Cuba, which José Martí made the subject of an anti-Spanish tract in 1871.[22]

---

16 See A. Cañeque, *The King's Living Image: The Culture and Politics of Viceregal Power in Colonial Mexico* (New York, 2004); S. Serulnikov, *Subverting Colonial Authority: Challenges to Spanish Rule in Eighteenth-Century Southern Andes* (Durham, NC, 2003).
17 Archivo General de Simancas, SGU,7136,9.
18 B. Kercher, *Debt, Seduction, and Other Disasters: The Birth of Civil Law in Convict New South Wales* (Sydney, 1996); B. Kercher, 'Resistance to Law under Autocracy', *Modern Law Review* 60/6 (1997): pp. 779–97.
19 See Kercher, 'Perish or Prosper'.
20 For a detailed look at martial law on Norfolk Island, see Lauren Benton, *A Search for Sovereignty: Law and Geography in European Empires, 1400–1900* (Cambridge, 2010), chap. 4.
21 A. Vaidik, *Imperial Andamans: A Spatial History of an Island Colony* (Basingstoke, 2010).
22 J. Martí and C. Manzoni, *El Presidio Político en Cuba: Último Diario y Otros Textos* (Buenos Aires, 1995).

Rumblings about the dangers of such experiments began early in the nineteenth century and continued as long as the penal colonies were in use. This critical commentary was connected to a wider discourse about martial law in empire and, more broadly still, about the viability of imperial constitutions under conditions in which parts of empire were held to be legally anomalous and some subjects were deemed to hold different, and inferior, sets of rights. The most striking example of debates about such issues occurred in London in the wake of the court martial and hanging of a moderate opposition leader in Jamaica, George Gordon, who was indicted for taking part in the 1865 Morant Bay revolt. In order to take advantage of the state of emergency, officials moved the trial from one part of the island to another, where martial law had been declared. Though not directly connected to the question of criminal transportation, the controversy sparked by this event centred on familiar questions about the legitimacy of defining certain spaces in empire as legally exceptional.[23] In particular, worried metropolitan observers speculated that compromising imperial subjects' rights might lead to attacks on the rights of citizens at home.

The Criminal Empire

Increased reliance on martial law in parts of European empires in the late eighteenth and nineteenth centuries encouraged an association of empires with political danger and crimes against the state. Such associations also built upon a much longer history. Treason cases had flourished in imperial settings from an early date. European agents jockeyed for political position and future patronage by accusing rivals in fledgling colonies of treason. Indigenous leaders were also at times punished for treason – dramatic reminders that they had become vassals of distant sovereigns. Piracy, a crime related to treason and sedition, meanwhile became increasingly linked to maritime violence in waters far from Europe. Spectacular punishments of pirates, as occurred in the British campaign against piracy in the 1720s, advertised the legal reach of imperial institutions and warned subjects against the risks of detaching themselves from imperial sponsorship. Publicising such crimes against order simultaneously created cultural connections between empire and criminality and worked to extend the reach of imperial law.

Examples of treason cases in early European empires are surprisingly varied. Spaniards accused other Spaniards and Indians of treason, playing on the crown's anxieties about the usurpation of royal authority and the skimming of royal profits on the other side of the Atlantic. Pizarro was executed for treason after rising against crown authority in Peru, and many less celebrated cases crowd the historical record, such as Álvar Núñez Cabeza de Vaca's execution of an Indian leader for

---

23   N. Hussain, *The Jurisprudence of Emergency: Colonialism and the Rule of Law* (Ann Arbor, MI, 2003); R.W. Kostal, *A Jurisprudence of Power: Victorian Empire and the Rule of Law* (Oxford, 2005).

treason, followed a short time later by his own arrest by rivals for treasonous acts supposedly committed on an expedition inland near Asunción. Such cases were by no means peculiar to the Spanish Empire. In 1609, Samuel de Champlain engineered the trial and execution of a locksmith in the newly founded outpost of Quebec for plotting to hand the small fort over to Spaniards. Placing the traitor's head on a post was probably intended to shore up Champlain's authority among his own troops as much as to warn other Europeans and Indians of his resolve. In Jamestown, John Smith arrived in chains, having been charged with plotting a mutiny on the voyage, and he was later accused again by rivals of disloyalty, particularly in his relations with Indians. Sir Walter Raleigh was embroiled in a transatlantic politics of treason; convicted of trumped-up charges of plotting to overthrow the monarch, he was confined to the Tower of London in 1603 and then freed in 1616 to undertake a second voyage to Guiana to find gold. When he failed and, in the process, stirred up tensions with Spain, his earlier treason conviction was used to justify his execution.[24]

These diverse examples share a number of interesting characteristics. First, imperial agents invoked treason in situations of acute political tension, a condition common in places remote from centres of power. The result was to nurture an association between distant parts of empire and criminality, particularly the perceived danger of the usurpation of crown authority. Second, this association itself became at times a weapon within a wider politics of empire. Raleigh's game attempt to reverse his conviction for treason by travelling to Guiana played upon the idea that distant territories posed political dangers – temptations that he would claim to have resisted and that rivals would portray as the source of fresh offences against the crown. Third, these representations of distant imperial places as politically treacherous did not require them to be rendered as spheres outside the law. On the contrary, European sojourners carried legal rituals with them, and insisted upon them in jockeying for royal patronage and approval. Spaniards routinely called for notaries to record depositions and declarations for future use in metropolitan courts. Although Spaniards have been singled out as especially legalistic (and litigious), other Europeans also avidly performed legal rituals in distant outposts and participated in a transatlantic discourse about the duties and rights of subjecthood and the risks of disloyalty.[25]

Responses to piracy showed another way in which the extension of imperial criminal jurisdiction was paired with increasing anxiety over criminality in

---

24   For an analysis of these cases, see Benton, *A Search for Sovereignty*, chap. 2.

25   On Spanish litigiousness, see R.L. Kagan, *Lawsuits and Litigants in Castile, 1500–1700* (Chapel Hill, NC, 1981). On discourses about the rights of Englishmen in the colonies, see D.J. Hulsebosch, *Constituting Empire: New York and the Transformation of Constitutionalism in the Atlantic World, 1664–1830* (Chapel Hill, NC, 2005). Indigenous peoples quickly learned the language of subjecthood in making legal appeals, as shown in J. Pulsipher, *Subjects unto the Same King: Indians, English, and the Contest for Authority in Colonial New England* (Philadelphia, PA, 2005) and B. Owensby, *Empire of Law and Indian Justice in Colonial Mexico* (Stanford, CA, 2008).

empires. It is important to note that the popular image of the pirate as a stateless agent clashes with the historical record in most times and places. Pirates and privateers were close cousins, and mariners shifted from one category to the other in periods of war or peace, and depending upon whom they chose as the victims of sea raids. Mariners knew how to play upon these ambiguities and to profit from shifting diplomatic winds. They constructed alternative stories, backed by paper trails, about having authorisation for sea raiding. Establishing ties to legitimate sponsors offered avenues for securing prizes and sometimes an escape from the gallows. Efforts of mariners to position themselves legally paralleled attempts by imperial powers to extend legal controls over maritime violence. During the first several centuries of European maritime empire, piracy cases were tried mainly in metropolitan courts. As the volume of trade and interest in controlling it grew, Atlantic European powers made legal adjustments, beginning especially in the last decades of the seventeenth century, to permit the trial of pirates and adjudication of prize cases in colonial courts.[26]

Paradoxically, policy shifts that enhanced the authority of colonial legal forums provided a crucial tool in the 'campaign' against piracy while also burnishing pirates' reputation for lawlessness. As British officials in particular sought to inhibit sea raiding in an effort to protect trade, including the growing slave trade, in the early eighteenth century, they aggressively pursued mariners who refused the king's pardon. It was these scattered bands that resembled the 'stateless' pirates of popular culture. Public executions of pirates, together with an emerging genre of pirate literature in Europe (with its detailed reports of pirate trials and lurid accounts of pirate hangings), encouraged the image of pirates as criminal outcasts. The story of good men corrupted by bad men made better copy than a narrative about the expansion of imperial legal institutions and the redefinition of occasional servants of the crown as outlaws.

Reports about acts of treason and piracy no doubt comprised an important strand within a broader European discourse about 'lawlessness' and criminality in empire.[27] But this labelling of extra-European zones as lawless did not make them so. Imperial subjects, including pirates, carried legal authority with them and reproduced claims about their loyalty and subjecthood in the face of criminal accusations. Their actions often worked to extend the reach of imperial law.

Jurisdictional Politics and Crime

Polities with widely different legal traditions in the early modern world shared a structure of legal pluralism; both empires and the societies with which they

---

26 L. Benton, 'Legal Spaces of Empire: Piracy and the Origins of Ocean Regionalism', *Comparative Studies in Society and History* 47/4 (2005): pp. 700–724.

27 E. Gould, 'Zones of Law, Zones of Violence: The Legal Geography of the British Atlantic, circa 1772', *William and Mary Quarterly* 60/3 (2003): pp. 471–510.

came into contact housed multiple legal authorities. Even well into the nineteenth century, imperial officials continued to recognise the semi-autonomy, or quasi-sovereignty, of subpolities within empires and to award them some degree of local control over law. One result of these multicentric and layered legal structures was that jurisdictional tensions pervaded imperial legal orders. Sometimes in quick succession, officials proposed ways to define with precision and to hold stable the relation of different jurisdictions, then made adjustments or abandoned the plans altogether in response to jurisdictional jockeying by legal actors.[28]

Definitions of crime played a central role in these jurisdictional disputes. Expanding criminal jurisdiction was not an obvious and easy imperial policy for elites and officials to embrace. It involved significant costs of staffing courts and sending out legal personnel, and it prompted challenges to criminal jurisdiction by indigenous inhabitants, including elites whose legal authority was partly supplanted by imperial officials. For colonisers, claiming criminal jurisdiction was politically and culturally momentous because it implied recognising potential criminals as imperial subjects, a status that created not only the possibility of punishment but also the obligation to admit testimony, recognise property rights and extend other legal protections. Indigenous and non-elite actors perceived this connection and, even in situations in which they appeared nearly powerless, adopted legal strategies in response to criminal cases that raised questions about the jurisdiction of the courts, and, by extension, the legitimacy of imperial rule. This section discusses variants of these patterns and presents examples of the strains created in the expansion of imperial criminal jurisdiction.

At early stages of conquest or imperial encounters, culturally different groups often faced each other in settings where no one group held a monopoly on violence. Imperial histories in such sites feature cases in which groups had to adjust to the criminal legal procedures of others in punishing crimes along frontiers of settlement. For example, in the Pays d'en Haut region written about by Richard White as a 'middle ground' of encounter between French and Indians in North America, settlers learned to exact payment from Indian communities for violent acts by their members rather than insist on the perpetrators' punishment as criminals.[29] In the early decades of the Cape Colony, Dutch officials handed Khoi criminals over to their chiefs for punishment and sometimes held Khoi or their cattle as hostages until their communities made restitution for crimes against property.[30] Such practices should not be read as signalling mutual understanding, or an abandonment of claims to jurisdiction. Sometimes both colonial officials and local leaders insisted that accused criminals should be turned over to them, or at least punished according to their own standards and procedures.

---

28   L. Benton, *Law and Colonial Cultures: Legal Regimes in World History, 1400–1900* (Cambridge, 2002).

29   R. White, *The Middle Ground: Indians, Empires, and Republics in the Great Lakes Region, 1650–1815* (Cambridge, 1991).

30   R. Ross, *Beyond the Pale: Essays on the History of Colonial South Africa* (Hanover, NH, 1993), pp. 170–77.

Where power shifted to the hands of colonisers, they were able to redefine criminal acts and increasingly assert jurisdiction over locals. Still, colonised societies held tightly to their own visions of criminality, categorising the actions of colonisers accordingly. Consider the example of New South Wales where, as settlers extended sheep grazing and farming into lands where Aborigines had controlled access to resources, acts of frontier violence escalated. The colonial courts initially heard few cases involving Aborigines, then increasingly began to bring them in as criminal defendants, claiming jurisdiction over violence and property crimes by Aborigines against whites but continuing to rule that acts by Aborigines against Aboriginal victims were not under the purview of the courts. Many cases fit uneasily within these guidelines. In some cases brought against Aborigines for stealing sheep or cattle, for example, not guilty verdicts were rendered after testimony or arguments that Aborigines had 'little knowledge of the rights of property'.[31] Even more challenging for the courts were cases in which Aborigines were accused of acts of violence that were probably punitive reactions to perceived infractions or violence committed by settlers.[32]

In New South Wales and in other colonies, the appearance of indigenous people in colonisers' courts also required judgements about whether their testimony should be accepted. Non-Christian testimony was generally not admitted in European colonial courts on the grounds that pagans could not swear to tell the truth since they had no fear of divine retribution for breaking oaths. Slaves could also not testify in court. But these rules were not hard and fast. When non-Christian subjects or slaves were the only witnesses to crimes or conspiracies, courts found ways to enter their testimony, often through statements by Christian, free witnesses. In some cases, and probably in more instances than we can see in the historical record, people managed to influence the outcome of court cases even though they had no legal standing as witnesses or subjects.[33]

In some imperial settings, jurisdictional jockeying took place not along frontiers but at points of intersection between multiple legal systems. In late-eighteenth-century India, British officials constructed a plural legal order in which courts

---

31   Quote is from *R. v. Dundomah and others*, Supreme Court of New South Wales, 1840 reported in *Sydney Herald*, 10 November 1840, *Decisions of the Superior Courts of New South Wales, 1788–1899*, published by the Division of Law, Macquarie University, www. law.mq.edu.au/scnsw/cases1840–41/RvDundomah,1840.htm. See also *R. v. Boatman or Jackass and Bulleyes*. For a detailed discussion of crime and the jurisdictional problems along the frontier, see L. Ford, *Settler Sovereignty: Jurisdiction and Indigenous People in America and Australia, 1788–1836* (Cambridge, MA, 2010).

32   On the punitive actions of Aborigines, see I. Clendinnen, *Dancing with Strangers: Europeans and Australians at First Contact* (Cambridge, 2005); and Benton, *Law and Colonial Cultures*, chap. 5.

33   For example, *R. v. Fitzpatrick and Colville*, Supreme Court of New South Wales, 1824 reported in *Sydney Gazette*, 24 June 1824, *Decisions of the Superior Courts of New South Wales, 1788–1899*, Division of Law, Macquarie University,   http://www.law.mq.edu. au/research/colonial_case_law/nsw/cases/case_index/1824/supreme_court/r_v_ fitzpatrick_and_colville/

administering Hindu and Muslim law operated alongside forums applying English law to English subjects and East India Company employees. Initially, imperial officials envisioned a plural legal order that would leave criminal jurisdiction in most cases to courts applying Muslim law. Increasingly, though, control of crime came to be identified as one of the main competencies and obligations of the Raj. Rural banditry was singled out as a threat to imperial order from as early as the late eighteenth century, but after the 1857 revolt the campaign against it developed a legal dimension that included new efforts of 'policing mobile populations' and legislation, most notably the Criminal Tribes Act of 1871, establishing ways for designating whole communities as 'criminal tribes' outside the law.[34] Tensions over administering the criminal law erupted at multiple points during the middle decades of the nineteenth century. These conflicts included a series of controversial, high-profile cases involving Indian princely states, which retained criminal jurisdiction inside their borders as a property of 'quasi-sovereignty'. For example, British officials moved to depose the leader of the princely state of Baroda in 1875 after he was accused of plotting to murder a key British official. Here and in other cases, the British elaborated and promoted a rationale for substituting acts of political control and repression for criminal prosecutions, which they were still prevented by jurisdictional rules from pursuing.[35]

In conflicts over definitions of crime, criminal procedure and jurisdiction, imperial subjects and officials perceived the stakes to be very high. Protecting legal prerogatives, including and especially authority over crime, symbolised broader capacities and served as a shorthand for sovereignty. Indigenous groups perceived this connection in seeking to retain local control over crime. So did colonial settlers, who often operated semi-independently from imperial officials and advanced territorial control by asserting first authority over settler-on-settler crime, then claiming jurisdiction over indigenous violence against settlers and finally asserting purview over acts committed by anyone, indigenous or settler, within particular territories.[36] This process of expanding criminal jurisdiction was never smooth. Nor were settlers the only parties who advocated the trend. In the nineteenth century in particular, precisely because criminal jurisdiction was symbolically linked to sovereignty, indigenous subjects insisted on the prosecution of Europeans for crimes against locals and complained about unequal treatment of defendants depending on ethnicity and race.[37] As with the creation and management of penal

---

34   R. Singha, 'Settle, Mobilize, Verify: Identification Practices in Colonial India', *Studies in History* 16/2 (2000): pp. 151–98; Mark Brown, 'Colonial History and Theories of the Present: Some Reflections upon Penal History and Theory', in B. Godfrey and G. Dunstall (eds), *Crime and Empire 1840–1940: Criminal Justice in Local and Global Context* (Cullompton, 2005), pp. 76–91.

35   L. Benton, 'From International Law to Imperial Constitutions: The Problem of Quasi-Sovereignty, 1870–1900', *Law and History Review* 26/3 (2008): pp. 595–620. The British also extended rule by asserting jurisdiction over the violence of whites. See E. Kolsky, *Colonial Justice in British India: White Violence and the Rule of Law* (Cambridge, 2010).

36   Ford, *Settler Sovereignty*.

37   Martin Wiener, *An Empire on Trial: Race, Murder, and Justice under British Rule, 1870–1935*

colonies, an expanding criminal jurisdiction was associated with periodic extra-legal interventions. Perceived political threats blended with imagined dangers of rampant criminality. Much like 'national security' in the late twentieth and early twenty-first centuries, crime and its control motivated the expansion of imperial legal institutions while creating circumstances in which politics clearly trumped law.

Neither imperial systems of banishment nor the expanding apparatus for the control and adjudication of crime in empires should be understood as constructing imperial peripheries as places of 'lawlessness'. To be sure, a rhetoric about lawlessness flourished, and it was associated in turn with an older discourse about colonisers as the bearers of civility and colonised peoples as culturally backward. But there was more to the cultural construction of the 'criminal empire' than its contrast to Europe as a zone of law and civility.[38] Acts of exclusion were also acts of inclusion in the imperial legal order.

Early European experiments with banishment and criminal transportation left the legal status of convicts in empire open-ended. This legal indeterminacy shifted in the late eighteenth century, when the global militarisation of European empires and the proliferation of forms of coerced labour gave rise to harsh disciplinary regimes in penal 'work camps'. Convict transportation was related to a broader criminalisation of vagrancy and regimes of harsher penalties for property crimes in Europe, while new penal colonies created zones in which transported convicts were more explicitly stripped of political and legal rights. These acts of exclusion were integral parts of the imperial order. Observers compared the legal status of convicts to that of slaves precisely because they recognised that transportation represented one of many arrangements in which subjects were placed under the semi-autonomous and potentially arbitrary punishment regimes of delegated legal authorities. Even declarations of martial law fitted within the vision of a multi-layered imperial sovereignty in which local authorities supposedly protected the whole of the imperial order by exercising tighter control at the local level. Transportation and forced labour excluded criminals at the same time that imperial sovereignty incorporated them into a coherent imagination of empire as a hierarchy in which part-sovereignties nested under overarching imperial authority.

Jurisdictional disputes over crime had much the same effect. As maritime raids became less of a boon to expanding European empires without large established navies and more of a danger to growing trade, popular conceptions of the sea as a space of lawlessness gained currency. These ideas coexisted with institutional changes designed to bring both trade and maritime crime under the purview of imperial courts. Jurisdictional tensions over indigenous peoples and the acts they committed meanwhile generated familiar legal patterns across empires. Initial

---

(Cambridge, 2008), especially chaps 6 and 7.

38   This formulation figures prominently in Carl Schmitt's analysis of how the 'bracketing' of violence outside Europe enabled the region to fashion itself as the centre of an international legal community. For a critique of this seductive idea, see L. Benton, 'Empires of Exception: History, Law, and the Problem of Imperial Sovereignty', *Quaderni di Relazioni Internazionali* 6 (2008): pp. 54–67.

compromises over punishment between European settlers and indigenous groups faltered, and colonial courts haltingly pursued the criminalisation of a range of acts by indigenous people – not just violence against colonial settlers but also the defence of resources and the seizure of property. Imperial agents and indigenous inhabitants negotiated and sparred over definitions of crime and appropriate punishments, with ruptures and larger-scale violence often following perceived injustices on both sides as occurred on the edges of the Cape Colony and with settler–Aboriginal relations in New South Wales.

The designation of new groups of criminal outsiders paradoxically reinforced imperial law and extended its reach. Historians should resist the temptation to follow historical actors in characterising the peripheries of empire (which were after all often central to imperial spheres of influence) as places of criminality. Even in penal colonies and on pirate ships, or in times of the suspension of law and imposition of martial law in response to perceived crises of order, crime and its control produced new legalities. Late imperial legal orders claimed expanding authority over criminal law while also prompting new conflicts over jurisdiction, stimulating debates about the limits of law, and multiplying legally differentiated imperial zones.

Slavery

Eve M. Troutt Powell

Slaves as Tourist Sites

The slave trade had been made illegal in Egypt for over a decade when, in 1885, the Baedeker brothers published an updated version of their handbook to Lower Egypt and Sudan. In apparent answer to the interest of British and other European tourists, the guidebook introduces slavery in the following way:

> The slave-trade is now very rapidly approaching complete extinction in Egypt, not so much owing to the penalties imposed (which the rapacious officials take every opportunity of enforcing), as from changes in the mode of living, and the growing preference of the wealthy for paid servants. Down to 1870 the trade was still carried on but since then it has been at a standstill.[1]

Though the slave trade was waning, slaves lived in the present tense in the Cairo of 1885, indexed in Baedeker under the entry for 'Negroes'. The guidebook asserts that the government had, since 1878, kept a complete register of domestic slaves, and that 'special officials are appointed to watch over their interests'.[2] This is all true, but these details omit any description of the forces that enabled 'special officials' to watch over the interest of domestic slaves in Egypt. Perhaps the tourist readers of the guidebook knew that in 1876 Egypt's ruler, the Khedive Isma'il, unable to pay back loans to British and French banks, was forced to declare the country bankrupt. Maybe these visitors to Egypt were aware that the Khedive had submitted the treasury to the financial supervision of a new administrative institution, the Public Debt Administration, run by a team of British and French officials and led by Evelyn Baring, a member of the powerful banking company.[3] Maybe these tourists, already interested in Egyptian affairs, had read newspaper accounts of the Khedive's abdication in favour of his son, or of the 1881 rebellion

---

1   K. Baedeker, *Handbook for Lower Egypt* (Leipzig, 1885), p. 51.
2   Ibid., p. 52.
3   Roger Owen, *Lord Cromer: Victorian Imperialist, Edwardian Proconsul* (New York, 2005), p. 35.

led by army officers against the increasing British and French control of Egypt's political infrastructure. Whether they were aware of these details, surely they knew that, three years before the Baedekers reissued their guidebook, British forces had attacked the rebelling forces, and had occupied Egypt in the autumn of 1882. Evelyn Baring, now Lord Cromer, in effect ran the Egyptian government as proconsul. And one service his administration provided was the establishment of manumission bureaux across Egypt, where slaves could turn if they sought their freedom. British officials freed hundreds of slaves in this way, and the Baedeker guidebook gives credence to the effectiveness of these bureaux.[4]

The slaves presented by Baedeker were all older, settled into patterns of dependence upon the families for whom they worked. Most, the guidebook says, refused to seek the emancipation the government offered because they would then have had to provide for themselves. Eunuchs, those expensive slaves who served in only the most elite of households, are described as the most obsolete, and they 'very seldom avail themselves of this opportunity of regaining their liberty, as their emancipation would necessarily terminate the life of ease and luxury in which they delight'.[5] It is as if all of these slaves, who were 'treated more like members of the family than like servants', could not see a future for themselves other than in their continued participation in traditional labour networks so economically ineffective as to no longer serve a purpose.

Baedeker repeats the equation of 'negro' with 'slave'. While it was true that the majority of slaves in Egypt in 1885 were Sudanese, Baedeker's guide never mentions the networks or trade in Circassians, another ethnic group who, as slaves or as slave-owners, figured prominently in the upper echelons of Ottoman and Egyptian society. And although most of the slaves in Egypt were women, whether of Sudanese, Circassian or Ethiopian descent, Baedeker's guide barely mentions female slaves. With its short entries about the peoples of the Nile Valley, the Baedeker guide does not provide much biographical information, certainly not about slaves or their owners. But it does unveil for us a fascinating scene, giving us a sense of which Europeans were interested in knowing more about the slaves, and why, and what the slaves do or do not know about themselves:

> Ethnographers, linguists or other scientific men who desire to see specimens of as many different races as possible should obtain an introduction to an Arabian merchant in the Gameliyeh, who will conduct them to merchants from every part of the interior and of the African coast, each attended by his staff of negro servants. The latter, however, especially if long resident in Egypt, cannot give trustworthy information about their country and their origin. Some of them have forgotten their mother tongue and even the name of their native country.[6]

---

4   Diane Robinson-Dunn, *The Harem, Slavery and British Imperial Culture* (Manchester, 2006), pp. 13–14.
5   Baedeker, *Handbook*, p. 51.
6   Ibid., p. 52.

It is a jarring idea that would-be anthropologists and linguists would turn to illicit slave markets as a source for conducting research into the cultures, origins and languages of black slaves in Egypt. Baedeker's promise – that the Arabian merchant can lead inquisitive foreign eyes to a view of 'specimens of as many different races as possible' – invites photographers as well. Not only is it important, the guide implies, to study these races, but it is crucial to see and observe them. And because any such viewing could only take place while the illegal trade was being conducted, there is a frisson of the illicit that hangs over such a meeting. Because of the slave trade's illegality, no Egyptian wealthy enough to own slaves would have allowed a curious European 'ethnographer' into his or her home to inspect the slaves, just as they would never have permitted a male foreigner to meet the women of the household. Male Europeans were forbidden these views of the intimate; hence Baedeker's advice that ethnographers, linguists and other scientific men make their surreptitious way to Gamaliyeh to find African slaves demonstrates how enticing such observations had become, at this point in the history between Egypt and Europe.

And even if those slaves could be found, the guidebook told its readers, they would be a disappointment. Nineteenth-century 'scientific men' on tour would only be disillusioned by their informants' lack of knowledge of their own origins and languages. These were slaves who knew only Egypt, condemned by a gentle yet forced assimilation into Egyptian culture to permanent alienation from their own cultural, linguistic and familial past. The guidebook said of these slaves that 'the latter, however, especially if long resident in Egypt, cannot give trustworthy information about their country and their origin'.[7] In Baedeker's account, these enslaved men had lost their authenticity as Africans on their path to coping with their roles and lives in Egyptian society. The intimacy of slaves' connections to the families in which they worked, and by whom they had been purchased, mostly unseen by interested European observers, was pathologised. The fact that these slaves had to assimilate into these societies and often did so successfully was dismissed. The slaves' catastrophic loss of their own social identity and their subsequent adaptation to a new culture denied the European ethnographer the sought-after evidence.

This chapter will explore how mostly British officials and 'men of science' who were interested in the slaves of the Ottoman Empire in general, and Egypt and Sudan in particular, created and disseminated their own images of Sudanese slaves. Following the desire of the Baedekers' specialists, who hoped to remedy what seemed to them the slaves' tragic loss of identity, this chapter will investigate photographs taken by men in the field, most of them military officers, of the slaves they encountered in Sudan, the source of most of Egypt's slave trade. I have begun my chapter in Cairo, with the ethnographers' search for slaves, but I will move now with the soldiers and photographers of the British Empire to Sudan. In 1899, the Egyptian army, led by General Herbert Kitchener and other British officers, defeated the forces of the Islamic movement known as the Mahdiyya, and

---

7   Ibid.

began to set up government in Khartoum.[8] The new governors of Sudan relied heavily on photographers for visual information about the Sudanese landscape and its inhabitants; among these, its slaves and its slave-owners. Many of these photographers were soldiers. At times, their mission included the regularisation of the abolition of the slave trade which had provided slaves for generations to Egypt and other parts of the Ottoman Empire. I will explore what these pictures tell us about, and why it was so important, at certain times, to point a camera at an enslaved person who had, it was believed, been emptied of their past. And, finally, I will follow how these photographs can be attempts, sometimes futile, to locate the pictured slaves' origins, and how photographs could be used to 'capture' the voices of the slaves themselves.

Taking the Camera to the Source: Photographing Slaves in Sudan

By the end of the nineteenth century, political circumstances gave British experts a panoptic view of slaves and the slave trade in Egypt and Sudan. In 1882, British forces occupied Egypt and dominated the government's administration. From London, the powerful British and Foreign Anti-Slavery Society lobbied many of these officials, demanding that they do more to enforce anti-slave trade laws established in Egypt in 1877. Manumission bureaux, monitored by the British occupying government, were set up in different parts of Egypt, as official sites where slaves could seek liberation, and documentation of their manumission.[9] The records of the Foreign Office from the 1880s are filled with complaints against Egyptian slave-buyers. In 1892, bowing to pressure from the Anti-Slavery Society, Lord Cromer established the Cairo Home for Freed Slave Women, a home that welcomed mostly Sudanese and Ethiopian slave women and girls and trained them to work like English domestic servants.[10] And while British administrators in Egypt were mindful of Circassian slavery, they considered themselves less empowered to take on what they saw as a much deeper and entrenched system of slavery that involved the entire Ottoman Empire.[11] Drawing in part from Great Britain's involvement in the trans-Atlantic slave trade, and from reports of anti-slavery officials and missionaries in central and East Africa, those officials mobilising to suppress the slave trade in Egypt 'often regarded black slaves as subject to greater exploitation and oppression than the others'.[12] As Diane

---

8   Richard L. Hill, *A Biographical Dictionary of the Anglo-Egyptian Sudan* (Oxford, 1951), p. 204.
9   Eve M. Troutt Powell, *A Different Shade of Colonialism: Egypt, Great Britain and the Mastery of the Sudan* (Berkeley, CA, 2003), pp. 138–40.
10   Robinson-Dunn, *The Harem*, p. 86.
11   Ehud R. Toledano, *Slavery and Abolition in the Ottoman Middle East* (Seattle, WA, 1998), p. 33.
12   Robinson-Dunn, *The Harem*, p. 18.

Robinson-Dunn asserts, 'Black slaves moreover came closest to a contemporary English idea of how a slave looked, an idea which had already become a part of British imperial culture through representations made by anti-slavery workers during the early part of the century.'[13]

And how did a slave look? A slave looked African and a slave was naked. Such images came from Britain's own involvement in the African slave trade, and from the drawings of European explorers and missionaries in Africa. The Khedive Isma'il had begun the practice of employing British officials to stop the slave trade at its biggest source, Sudan, in the late 1860s, when he hired Sir Samuel Baker to arrest and bring to justice the largest of the Sudanese *jallaba* (slave-traders). Baker thus joined a growing number of anti-slavery Britons whose letters, articles, sketches and photographs of slaves fuelled the growth and the financial support of the abolition movement in England. The images of slaves disseminated by the abolition movement became, for most Europeans in the late nineteenth century, the only ways in which slaves were seen. As Jan Pieterse described this visualisation:

> The abolition movement had an enormous cultural effect. If images from slavery from the pro-slavery point of view were scarce, the image production of abolitionism was abundant. Almost all the images of slavery with which we are familiar are in fact abolitionist images. The typical iconography of abolitionism displays the movement's Christian pathos: the recurring image is the blacks kneeling with hands folded and eyes cast upward.[14]

One of the most important producers of these images was David Livingstone, and his sketches became emblems for the message of the Anti-Slavery Society. Drawn in the diaries he wrote in the 1850s and 1860s, these sketches showed the downtrodden figures of recently enslaved people in Central Africa. One powerful sketch (Figure 18.1) drew an act of terrible violence: slave raiders in the process of murdering slaves too weak to continue on the caravan. By just looking at the drawing, there is no way to know where these slaves come from, while other details, such as the caps on the heads of the slave traders, indicate a distinctive, vaguely non-African identity. The act of violence extends to the upper left part of the picture, where, if you squint, you can see a tiny child being led along the slave caravan.

An act of murder like the one depicted here could never have been photographed. There could never have been a western witness with heavy and large camera apparatus given access to such a crime. Yet this sketch was believable. The accusatory nature of the picture – its capture of the murderers *in flagrante* – speaks to a nineteenth-century reliance on this kind of imagery as factual. Livingstone hired an artist as well as his photographer brother for this expedition. As James Ryan puts it, 'although their equipment was different and the resulting images held

---

13   Ibid., p. 18.
14   Jan Nederveen Pieterse, *White on Black: Images of Africa and Blacks in Western Popular Culture* (New Haven, CT, 1998), p. 58.

Figure 18.1 Sketch by David Livingstone of recently enslaved people in Central
Africa

different currencies of veracity, the roles of expeditionary artist and photographer
were closely associated'. In many ways, this drawing can be seen as 'the artist's
attempt to stamp his pictures with the authority of a photograph'.[15] Its careful detail,
drawn perhaps from memory, perhaps from the accounts of slaves, bears solemn
testimony to the suffering of slaves, and to the cruelty and violence, as imagined by
abolitionists like Livingstone, of the slave-raiders who came from Muslim tribes.
In the late 1850s, the sketches of Livingstone's artist, Thomas Baines, dominated
the imagery of Africa envisioned by members of the Royal Geographic Society, but
increasingly they also responded to images projected by what was then cumbersome
photographic equipment. Livingstone's brother, Charles, accompanied him on
the 1858–64 Zambezi Expedition as 'official photographer and cartographer'.[16]
The practice of photography, as Ryan has written, 'was shaped clearly in accordance

15   James R. Ryan, *Picturing Empire: Photography and the Visualization of the British Empire*
      (Chicago, IL, 1997), p. 35.
16   I have not yet found evidence that Charles Livingstone photographed slaves. By the
      1870s, however, photographs of David Livingstone's porters, Chuma and Susi, were
      taken and published in England. For more on the visual presence of Susi and Chuma,
      see Claire Pettit, *Dr Livingstone, I Presume? Missionaries, Journalists, Explorers and Empire*
      (Cambridge, 2007), pp. 156–68.

with the aims of the expedition and, despite the bulky apparatus necessary, was embraced as a powerful new means of recording permanently the landscapes, inhabitants, flora and fauna of the area to be explored'.[17]

Slaves in Central Africa thus offered pliable examples of the landscape. They were examples of ethnic types, whose faces and bodies revealed 'characteristics of the race', at a time when exploration and photography were important instruments in the ongoing discourse of 'race' and 'types'. In this discourse, professionals like Livingstone concerned themselves with how to systematise a classification of humans. Livingstone made this clear to his photographer brother when he instructed Charles to 'secure characteristic specimens of the different tribes ... for the purposes of Ethnology'.[18] As Ryan points out, 'the language and imagery of "race" occupied a central place within Victorian culture, where it was used variously as a measure of bodily difference and as a description of national identity'.[19] Racial 'types' were laid bare for theorists of physiognomy, phrenology and the sciences of ethnology and anthropology. The characteristics of a face in Sudan or Australia were read as universal signs of the character of that person's race.

Wherever Africans were sent, either free or as slaves, this practice of visualisation followed them. Livingstone's contemporaries in other countries used other forms of picture-taking to classify Africans. One of the most dramatic examples of the photographic seizure of slaves occurred in the southern United States, to be later displayed in the Peabody Museum of Harvard University. In the 1850s, Louis Agassiz, the famous Swiss naturalist then teaching at Harvard, commissioned a series of daguerreotypes of Gullah slaves living and working in Columbia, South Carolina. The point of the commission was to investigate the racial difference between Africans and Europeans. Much has been written about these photographs, but here I will discuss only a few of them, as a point of reference for how slaves were viewed through camera lenses. I have chosen these two because they represent an older slave and his daughter, so there is a relationship between the subjects that the captions narrate, but that relationship is not in itself clear from the daguerreotypes. Figure 18.2 shows Renty, an older man. He is thin, he is stark, and if he does wear clothing it has been pulled down to reveal the physiognomy of his torso. Renty's torso and facial characteristics gave Agassiz what he thought was information about Congolese Africans' bodies and character. One can also see, although not recorded in the captions, the effects of hard agricultural labour on this older man's muscled body.

Next follows Renty's daughter, Delia. It is clear that her blouse has been pulled down to reveal her chest and musculature (Figures 18.3 and 18.4). These three pictures are only a part of a series of daguerreotypes that displayed seven slaves, born in Africa or the children of African parents, who lived and worked on a South Carolina plantation. Maybe Brian Wallis' description equates to your reaction:

---

17 Ryan, *Picturing Empire*, p. 32.
18 Ibid., p. 146.
19 Ibid., pp. 146–7.

If it is a shock to see full frontal nudity in early American photography, it is even more surprising to see it without the trappings of shame or sexual fantasy. Here, the seated women calmly reveal their breast, and the standing men are naked. But their attitudes are detached, unemotional, and workmanlike. In what seems to be a deliberate refusal to engage with the camera or its operator, they stare into the lens, their faces like masks, eyes glazed, jaws clenched.[20]

The starkness of Renty and Delia's mutual nakedness heightens the isolation into which each daguerreotype puts this father and his daughter. Certainly they were made to sit, or stand, for the camera for many minutes; the long exposure time required by photographic equipment at in the 1850s made being the subject of such a photo very uncomfortable.[21] But there is greater and unspoken sadness in the exposure of their bodies, and in our knowledge that the old man could not protect his daughter, nor she protect her ageing parent, from the eyes that explored both of their bodies.

Agassiz commissioned these daguerreotypes for two reasons: 'to analyze the physical differences between European whites and African blacks', and to use them as 'evidence to prove his theory of "separate creation", the idea that the

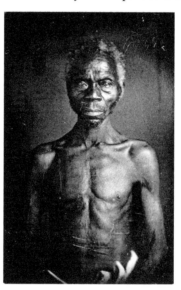

Figure 18.2   Louis Agassiz's daguerreotype of Renty, 1850. Courtesy of the Peabody Museum of Archaeology and Ethnology, Harvard University [35-5-10/53037 (D1)]

---

20   Brian Wallis, 'Black Bodies, White Science: Louis Agassiz's Slave Daguerreotypes', *American Art* 9/2 (1995): p. 40. All the Agassiz images here come from this article.

21   Sarah Graham-Brown, *Images of Women: The Portrayal of Women in Photography of the Middle East, 1860–1950* (New York, 1988), p. 36.

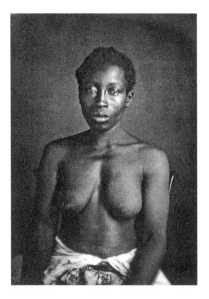

Figure 18.3   Louis Agassiz's daguerreotype of Renty's daughter, Delia (front view) 1850. Courtesy of the Peabody Museum of Archaeology and Ethnology, Harvard University [35-5-10/53040 (D4)]

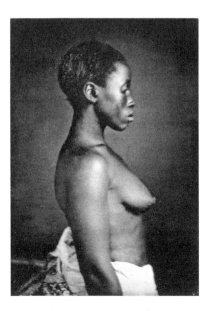

Figure 18.4   Louis Agassiz's daguerreotype of Renty's daughter, Delia (side view) 1850. Courtesy of the Peabody Museum of Archaeology and Ethnology, Harvard University [35-5-10/53039 (D3)]

various races of mankind were in fact separate species'.[22] Agassiz had come to South Carolina to tour plantations, and picked several slaves to be photographed. They were selected either because they had been born in Africa, giving Agassiz the chance to examine 'Ebo, Foulah, Gullah, Guinea, Coromontee, Mandrigo and Congo Negroes' or were only one generation removed from Africa. As Brian Wallis discovered, their names were as carefully recorded as their African origins and 'the current ownership of the slaves'.[23]

In a way, this careful depiction of the slaves' origins tells us, viewing these pictures over 160 years after they were taken, several things. We see how the slaves were related, we learn their origins (although we do not learn how that was conveyed and by whom), and we witness how much continual control over their bodies their owner had, repeated in the brief but commanding hold that the photographer caught in his lens. We witness just how overly exposed Delia and Renty were. Their nudity excludes them completely from mainstream American society. There were other daguerreotypes and photographs taken of slaves in the 1850s, 1860s and 1870s, in which slaves were clothed and their images hung in frames on walls or on mantlepieces.[24] But the Agassiz daguerreotypes could not be framed and exhibited in homes; as Mandy Reid has written, such nudity 'was not suitable material for the albums of the Anglo families the slaves served'.[25] They were cast out, as she writes, 'from the familial realm for they were neither individuals whose relationships by blood and marriage were recognised by society nor were they members of the Anglo family of humankind, as Agassiz's espousal of polygenesis makes clear'.[26] These were meant for scientific, not domestic, consumption.

I would like now to turn to photographs of Sudanese slaves to explore the relationships between the photographer and the enslaved. Several decades after Agassiz commissioned those daguerreotypes, abolitionists could rely on more sophisticated and portable technology to capture the reality of enslavement in the Nile Valley and East Africa. In 1880, shortly before the British occupied Egypt, the camera was developed.[27] More portable than the equipment needed for daguerreotypes, with no need for heavy glass plates, the camera quickly became an important military instrument as well. By 1899, the British had achieved a much deeper and wider control of Sudan following the re-conquest in 1899 from the Mahdiyya. Now, these officials could take their search for slaves and the slave trade directly to areas of Sudan that the Mahdiyya had blocked from them. Now they could search for the origins of slaves, continuing the quest of those 'learned' men who, in Baedeker's 1885 guidebook, seek the slaves' real pasts. And for years, as the photographic collection

---

22   Ibid., p. 40.
23   Ibid., p. 45.
24   Laura Wexler, *Tender Violence: Domestic Visions in an Age of US Imperialism* (Chapel Hill, NC, 2000), pp. 70–71.
25   Mandy Reid, 'Selling Shadows and Substance: Photographing Race in the United States, 1850–1870s' *Early Popular Visual Culture* 4 (2006): p. 290.
26   Ibid., p. 290.
27   Ariella Azoulay, *The Civil Contract of Photography* (New York, 2008), p. 91.

of the Sudan Archive reveals, learned (and not-so-learned) British officials in charge of different regions of Sudan took pictures of slaves around them.

The rest of the photographs of slaves used in this chapter were all taken between 1900 and 1920. The slave trade had long been outlawed, in both Egypt and Sudan, but for many reasons the British had found the outright abolition of slavery too complicated and provocative to enforce in Sudan. These pictures of slaves bear witness to the continuation of slavery, but I am less clear if they do so in the spirit of protest or in the quest for documentation. The first two are photographs of slave women, taken by an unknown photographer. The caption for Figure 18.5 in the archive reads: 'young slave woman washing clothes by the bank of the Nile, probably Khartoum Province (1900–20)'.[28] She has no name, and could be washing in any year within a two-decade period: neither her scanty clothes nor the scenery around her offers any more identification. Those familiar with the different styles of hair braiding among different tribes may be able to identify which tribe she came from, but then she might have braided her hair in whatever style was easiest, or considered appropriate by her owner. To me, she looks as if she has been interrupted, but little registers across her face.

The next photograph, taken in 1908, also shows a slave woman (Figure 18.6). The famous administrator and early anthropologist H.A. MacMichael, may have taken this photograph – it is in his collection. As you can see from the caption scribbled at the bottom the photograph identifies this woman as a 'Kababish slave woman at 'Id el Merach job'.[29] This unnamed Kababish woman was carrying water from wells in a part of Kordofan, paying no attention to the camera at all. There is little that distinguishes her, except her movement and how busy she is. It is one of the only pictures I have found of a slave in motion.

Like the enslaved woman Delia, from South Carolina, these women are half-naked, breasts bared. Do their eyes or clenched jaws give the same hint of being controlled that the Agassiz daguerreotypes do? I wonder if Brian Willis' words apply to these Sudanese slaves? 'The emphasis on the body occurs at the expense of speech; the subject is already positioned, known, owned, represented, spoken for, or constructed as silent; in short, it is ignored.'[30] Or is that a luxury – are these women too busy to even take the camera and the photographer seriously? I also wonder under what circumstances the pictures were taken, whether or not these women worked on or near a military centre where British officers felt in control, or whether or not their owners were nearby. Who was in authority? The captions offer so little that they have become victims of what T. Jack Thompson calls 'the anonymous African syndrome'.[31]

---

28 From the collection of K.D.D. Henderson, Sudan Archive, Durham (SAD), 540/1/116.
29 H.A. MacMichael Collection, SAD, 587/1/193.
30 Wallis, 'Black Bodies, White Science', p. 54.
31 T. Jack Thompson, 'Capturing the Image: African Missionary Photography as Enslavement and Liberation', Day Associates Lecture, 29 June 2007, Yale University Divinity School, New Haven, CT.

Figure 18.5   Photograph of 'young slave woman washing clothes by the bank of the Nile, probably Khartoum Province (1900–20)'. From the collection of K.D.D. Henderson, Sudan Archive, Durham (SAD, 540/1/116). Reproduced by permission of Durham University Library

Figure 18.6   Photograph of a 'Kababish slave woman at "Id el Merach job"' (1908) from the H.A. MacMichael Collection (SAD, 587/1/193). Reproduced by permission of Durham University Library

What may well link the photographed circumstances of the South Carolina slaves to the Sudanese slaves is that they were not asked if their pictures could be taken. This question of consent, or even being paid to consent to be photographed, began when the distribution of photographs became cheap and popular, in the nineteenth century. In the middle of the century, as Ariella Azoulay has written, 'access was provided to images of people, objects and places that in the absence of photography would have remained outside the modern citizen's visual field'.[32] This ease of access caused people looking at these photographs to forget that the photograph was 'the result of an encounter with another, and with an other, and, as such, does not have one obvious, constant owner'. Azoulay continues,

> It is an encounter that always and inescapably involves a measure of violence, even when the situation is one of full and explicit consent between the participant parties. The violence is inherent in the instrumentalization of the photographed person in order to produce an image of him, within which context the photographed person can have as much of a vested interest as the photographer.[33]

Azoulay's work specifically raises questions about how Palestinians, caught on camera in moments of catastrophe with Israeli authorities, exercise a right to citizenship by the display of the violence committed against them. Her work is pertinent, too, to the photography of the enslaved Sudanese whose very presence as slaves bears historical witness to an act of violence – their kidnapping. But Azoulay is also fortunate in the sense that she knows the context of the photographs she writes about. The last two photographs bear no such information. These two women cope with their enslavement and what violence may have been meted to them, but they work. No pain, no scar tissue can be seen. Neither as a viewer nor as a historian do I have any idea for whom these pictures were taken, or why. The relationships implied in the act of taking the picture are removed.

Jane Hogan and M.W. Daly also explored the question of political context in photographs of servants and subordinates and the relationships they represent, specifically within the photographic collections of the Sudan Archive, where the photographs of slaves reproduced here are located. There is less violence here than in Azoulay's interpretation and a different sense of who the officers were and for whom the photographs were meant when they write:

> so a photograph that appears to one observer to depict an event may to another illustrate a person, or a place, or the weather. A district officer's photograph of a Sudanese servant may have been intended to put a face to the name in letters home, or as proof of a supposed racial characteristic, or to illustrate the flowering shrub in the background, and may have been posed or 'candid', deliberately taken

32   Azoulay, *The Civil Contract*, p. 98.
33   Ibid., p. 99.

when the servant was filthy from cleaning a stone, or dazzling in his Friday jallabiyya.[34]

So what can we learn from these photographs of naked Sudanese slave women working? Were these photographs sent home to England to show what daily life was like in a particular village, and how different such life was from village life back home? The women are busy, less engaged by having to submit to the camera than the American slaves, Renty or Delia. The institution of slavery represented by these women who are identified as slaves appears everyday, calm, bustling and normal. What we may also observe is a lack of any of the emotive power evoked by the sketches that David Livingstone commissioned, or even by the daguerreotypes of Louis Agassiz. Here the photographer's construction of the picture reveals an acceptance of the slave women's status; perhaps the picture was taken to show how the process of washing laundry in Sudan compared to washing in Great Britain.

British rhetoric about slavery, so strong in the late nineteenth century, did little to abolish slavery in Sudan once the British took over the administration of the country. Part of this was due to 'some senior British officials' perception of Sudanese slavery, which was framed by western intellectual and historical experience. They feared that sudden abolition would lead to vagrancy and prostitution.'[35] And in the first decades of the Anglo-Egyptian Condominium, the British government of Sudan worked very closely with former Mahdist rebels and tribal leaders, many of whom were slave owners themselves. One official, H.C. Jackson, summed up the Armageddon that sudden abolition would create:

> Liberation would have resulted in the abandonment of most of the cultivation along the river-banks, the loss of many of the flocks and herds of the nomad Arabs and the consequent deaths of thousands of innocent individuals who, through no fault of their own, had been brought up under a social system that was repugnant to Western ideas, but accepted as an indispensable condition of their everyday lives. More than this, to have freed all the slaves would have meant letting loose upon society thousands of men and women with no sense of social responsibility, who would have been a menace to public security and morals.[36]

As Ahmad Sikainga sees it, this kind of attitude caused the British to deny 'the existence of slavery', to turn a blind eye. But it was not blind eyes that put the slaves in focus and took the pictures. For whatever reason, the photographer took the time to take these photographs.

---

34   M.W. Daly and Jane R. Hogan, *Images of Empire: Photographic Sources for the British in Sudan* (Leiden, 2005), p. 71.

35   Ahmad Alawad Sikainga, *Slaves Into Workers: Emancipation and Labor in Colonial Sudan* (Austin, TX, 1996), p. 37.

36   Ibid., p. 38.

Enslaved children seemed to have provoked more outrage than working older slave women. The next group of photographs offers what I consider to be a clearer statement of purpose about slavery. These were all taken in 1916, and though the photographer is unnamed, many of the people in the photographs are identified. They are from R.V. Savile's collection in the Sudan Archive. Savile was the governor of Dar Fur Province from May 1917 until his resignation in November 1923. Before beginning his service as governor, he fought for the British-led Sudan Government's conquest of Dar Fur (which was completed during the First World War). While on this mission, he encountered many slaves.

Here are these pictures in succession. The archive's caption for Figure 18.7 reads: 'two officers with a kidnapped slave child recovered from the Gura'an, during the Dar Fur campaign'.[37] Dar Fur was the last and most independent province of Sudan to be conquered by the British, and the conquest in 1916 over the forces of its leader, Sultan Ali Dinar, was hard fought. This may have given British participants a greater feeling of indignation about and protectiveness towards the slaves they liberated, particularly when they were as small as this little boy. I hope you can see how the officer on the left is turning the child's face towards the camera, while holding one of his small hands. The other smiling officer holds the child's other hand. It is a photograph that captures a moment in a unique relationship, filled with pity, outrage and European adult domination.

In the next photograph, the relationship changes (Figure 18.8). The little boy in the front is the same little boy pictured with the two officers, but now he is photographed from below, perhaps by one of those same soldiers, now indulging him.[38] The little boy is eating something and looks almost as relaxed as his friend, who smiles, perhaps at the photographer. They sit companionably together, and look comfortable on the camel. These two photos tell a story, of the children's connectedness, of the soldiers' tenderness toward them, and of the liberating power the officers carry, by being able to stage such pictures. Even more, liberation has soothed these small, perhaps parentless, children, and has put smiles on their faces.

The next photograph (Figure 18.9) shows a starker version of the drama of enslavement. The full caption for the photo reads: 'Group of kidnapped children recovered from the Gura'an, during the Dar Fur campaign.'[39] From the positioning of the children, I read a greater neediness, and a harsher indignation directed at what kidnapping and enslavement did to them. Without the officers standing next to them, or directly under the camel on which they had been indulgently placed, this larger group of children seems unsure of where to look, even of what to do with their arms. The viewer can feel the photographer's anger at the Gura'an here.

The last picture of this collection is also the most complicated, and not only because it offers the most information (Figure 18.10). From the documentation I have found, I believe the photographer is R.V. Savile. Savile took this photograph in Kordofan, in 1910. The two officers seated and listening to one of the Sudanese

---

37 From the R.V. Savile collection (1916), SAD, 675/4/22.
38 Ibid., SAD, 675/4/23.
39 Ibid., SAD, 675/4/22.

Figure 18.7   Photograph of 'two officers with a kidnapped slave child recovered from the Gura'an, during the Dar Fur campaign' 1916. From R.V. Savile's collection in the Sudan Archive (SAD, 675/4/22). Reproduced by permission of Durham University Library

Figure 18.8   Photograph of two freed slave children sitting on a camel. From the R.V. Savile collection (1916) in the Sudan Archive (SAD, 675/4/23). Reproduced by permission of Durham University Library

Figure 18.9   Photograph of a 'group of kidnapped children recovered from the Gura'an, during the Dar Fur campaign' 1916. From R.V. Savile's collection in the Sudan Archive (SAD, 675/4/22). Reproduced by permission of Durham University Library

men were A.L. Hadow and R.B. Black. The description for the photo, one of the most detailed I found, mentions that they were talking to 'Murgan, an Arabic and English-speaking Nuba man who was sold into slavery as a child before joining a travelling company and visiting various European cities'.[40] If you look closely, you can see it is Murgan, sitting naked in front, motioning with his right arm as he perhaps describes his journeys. But we have more than this photograph and this description. Savile kept a diary of his travels through Kordofan, and here is what he wrote of this encounter:

> After breakfast spent most of the morning interviewing various meks [local chiefs] etc. while the Camel Corps watered their camels. Hadow went exploring up the hill and met the mek Toto and with him a stark naked savage who knew Arabic. He talked to this man and showed him his glasses. When the man had looked at them he returned them with the words 'thank you' in English. Hadow got a good deal of his story out of him and brought him down with the mek to see me. The man's name was Murgan and he had had a very varied existence. He had been kidnapped as a boy by a Hamrawi and sold to a slave trader who had sold him in Alexandria. Later he had joined some sort of a travelling company, representing an African village, and had gone to

---

40   Ibid., SAD, A12/51.

London, Portsmouth, Cardiff and various other English towns and eventually went to Paris. He had remained 6 years in this company, chiefly in England, and had then returned to Alexandria, where he was enlisted in the XIV Sudanese in which he served 8 years.[41]

And that is all he wrote. But even though he changed the subject so abruptly, he considered Murgan's story compelling enough to write it down, and to photograph the man (first called 'savage') in the act of telling as well.

As I read it, Murgan announced himself to these officers by expressing an interest in the glasses that belonged to one of them, and then speaking to them in English. That sparked their attention, as did his ability to converse in Arabic. He is even shown telling his story actively. What is learned of Murgan's past and his identity is that he was Nuba, and that he had been enslaved several times; what is less clear is his status at the time of this encounter. On leaving the XIVth Sudanese regiment, had he been enslaved again? Was he the *mek*'s slave?

Murgan's trajectory through slavery, in Egypt, in Sudan and in Europe, was also visual. He described the remarkable experience of having spent years in Europe, most of them in England, touring as a part of a travelling company where he was a re-enactor of Nubian cultural practices in a recreated African village. I do

Figure 18.10 Photograph of two British officers talking to 'Murgan, an Arabic and English-speaking Nuba man who was sold into slavery as a child before joining a travelling company and visiting various European cities'. From R.V. Savile's collection in the Sudan Archive (SAD, A12/51). Reproduced by permission of Durham University Library

41   Journal of R.V. Savile, 10 February 1910, SAD, 427/7/16 (v).

not know if he did this as a slave or as a free man, but his body and his presence were used to provide a visual authenticity to the exhibition of African life (seen far outside of Africa). But his photograph with the officers ended up in an archive in the north of England, perhaps not too far from one of the towns where he played at being an African. And his photograph, unlike any other photograph of a slave that I have seen, shows him talking, commanding the attention of not only the officers who lean toward him to listen intently, but also of the *mek*, his social superior and perhaps his master.

Much of the literature about imperialism and photography explores the power of the Europeans' gaze, here instrumentalised in the form of a camera. James Ryan writes about the harshness of this gaze as a means of European photographers conveying, to their viewers back home and to the natives in the colony, their 'cultural superiority': 'Optical devices in general, from looking-glasses to cameras, were influential within the European encounter with Africa at least in part because of the significance of metaphors of light, sight and vision with western Christian conceptions of self.'[42] And I think that Delia and Renty's faces embody at least the fear, if not the suspicion, with which the African sitters for photographs looked at the camera: 'those sitters whom photographers did manage to capture had neither knowledge nor control over the uses and meanings of their likenesses'.[43] And yet, there is Murgan, looking comfortable in front of the camera and at ease telling his story in front of the British officers. As in the other photographs of slaves, Murgan is naked, yet not alone. He sits with officers, not only in front of the one behind the lens. It is not only his experience with enslavement that inspired the taking of the picture, but his telling the story of how he got there. As many questions as his story raises, I think we can appreciate that part of Murgan's ease in front of the camera was as a result of his travelling across Europe as a professional African villager in the exhibits of African, Aboriginal, Asian and Middle Eastern cultures displayed in the international exhibitions of the late nineteenth and early twentieth centuries. He was not responsible for taking the photograph but he commands the camera, shown in the act of telling his story. If the camera captured anything, it caught a moment in which this man, a slave, told the story of his own enslavement.

The international exhibitions in which the Nubian Murgan participated brought home to Europeans a chance to see living Africans engaged in supposedly realistic re-enactments of their cultures and lives at home. Much has been written about these native villages, designed to educate French, British and other audiences about peoples on conquered continents and to display the span and power of each European empire.[44] In fact, the timing of the addition of these native villages to the exhibitions, beginning with the Nubian exhibition in the Paris Exposition of

---

42   Ryan, *Picturing Empire*, p. 143.

43   Ibid.

44   For broader discussions of imperialism and the international exhibition, see Timothy Mitchell, *Colonizing Egypt* (Berkeley, CA, 1998) and Paul Greenhalgh, *Ephemeral Vistas: The Expositions Universelles, Great Exhibitions and World's Fairs, 1851–1939* (New York, 1988), particularly chap. 4, 'Human Showcases'.

1889, coincided with the advances made in camera technology that enabled British officials and military officers to more easily and quickly take photographs of Nubians back in Sudan.

Many of these Nubians and other Africans were profoundly affected by their experience overseas. As Paul Greenhalgh has written:

> The presence of thousands of people at international exhibitions as exhibits had dramatic cultural and social spin-offs. This was particularly the case with those contained within imperial displays. Many of the Senegalese, Somalis and Dahomeyans who toured the world became westernized in some degree, could conceivably have married into local populations and most certainly affected their own people if and when they returned home.[45]

And if they were not as profoundly affected as Greenhalgh hoped, they were usually, at least paid, and thus, as Fatimah Tobing Rony and Debra Willis consider, complicit in the display. Willis, quoting Rony, writes of Senegalese performers in exhibitions that

> Blacks negotiated representations of themselves in performance and role-playing for money. Many performers at world's fairs were paid for their work, just as indigenous peoples sometimes received compensation for allowing themselves to be photographed by anthropologists and tourists. While it was common for exhibited people to be paid for the duration of their residencies, it is unknown whether any of the subjects discussed here were additionally compensated for being photographed. Although first person accounts do now survive, their complicity cannot be discounted.[46]

I read, in that last paragraph, a wish on the authors' part for these black performers to have asserted more than their rights to compensation for time and labour, but also for them, performing in their fake villages or posing stiffly in their photographs, to have somehow pushed through stereotypical imagery-making and created a new image of themselves. So little is known about how these performers or people in the photographs that we have much to learn about the circumstances of their participation. In Murgan's case, what were his choices? What of the slave who was returned from an exhibit back into slavery? We have glimpsed Murgan in his revelatory moment of seizing the stage, but much of Savile's information about him implies he was still a slave. If it is encouraging to think that many Africans and other imperial subjects were learning first how to cooperate and profit from their involvement with European public display by 1910 when Murgan was discovered

---

45   Greenhalgh, *Ephemeral Vistas*, p. 109.
46   Deborah Willis and Carla Williams, 'The Black Female Body in Photographs from World's Fairs and Expositions', *exposure* 33/1 and 2 (2000): p. 9.

by R.V. Savile, it also makes sense that liberation from these images came about in a different form, when Africans began to take their own pictures of themselves, costumed as they saw fit.[47]

In this chapter I have for the most part discussed photographs taken by British officers in the Sudan government. I have discussed the images, but remain unsure of the motivations of these photographers – they left few captions and no footnotes detailing why they chose to document slaves visually. From what I can gather, these photographers were not commissioned by abolitionist societies, nor were they owners taking pictures of their own slaves. On some occasions, like the drama of finding kidnapped children, or hearing a slave speak of London in English, circumstances were striking enough to inspire photographing the historical moment. Perhaps a landscape, urban or rural, that still included so many slaves, needed to be recorded – how many pictures of poor children in slums in Cairo or Mumbai have made their way into the albums or computers of contemporary tourists? And no relationships were commemorated here, unlike the posed slave and master couples photographed in Khartoum right before the Mahdiyya in 1884 by Louis Vossion.[48] I have also not gone further here into the photographic and literary work of Catholic and Protestant missionary societies, all active in Sudan by the end of the nineteenth century and for whom photographing slaves and former slaves charted the progress of Christian conversion. For those Sudanese still enslaved or recently liberated in the early decades of the twentieth century, it was in the publications and pictures of the missions that slaves were documented as they turned into free people. Increasingly, freed Sudanese slaves were encouraged to write or dictate the narratives of their enslavement, and their transformation from non-monotheistic belief to members of the Christian faithful. Photographs were very important to this process. As T. Jack Thompson has stated: 'though largely constrained by the demands and the ideas of the missionary photographer, Africans still found it possible to make themselves known, to begin to come to terms with the new world with which they had to deal – a world filled with new ideas, customs and technologies, of which the camera was merely one small part'.[49] Perhaps from reading their narratives as well, we can learn more about their predecessors, those slaves who were photographed anonymously years before.

---

47 Reid, 'Selling Shadows', pp. 10–14. Reid shows how Sojourner Truth composed herself for the camera, carefully dressed, and countering the enforced nudity that Renty and Delia had to endure decades before.
48 http://gallica.bnf.fr/ark:/12148/btv1b7702294z. These photographs were commissioned by Prince Bonaparte, and published under the title 'Types du Soudan'. I am including them in a longer chapter about the photographs of Sudanese slaves in my *Tell this is my Memory: Stories of Enslavement from Egypt, Sudan and the Ottoman Empire* (Stanford, CA, 2012).
49 Thompson, 'Capturing the Image', p. 21.

Race

Damon Salesa

The relationships between modern empires and racial discourses were multiple,
deep, persistent and synergetic. Just as race provided key, central and pervasive
modalities for modern empires, modern empires catalysed and energised
developing concepts of race. These concepts of race, barely evident in the European
experience of the sixteenth century, had by the nineteenth century become
pervasive, moving from the provinces of intellectuals, or colonial populations,
to the very centres of European, American – even global – politics. By the close
of the nineteenth century, race had become an organising principle of colonial
and imperial statecraft, and racial discourses had proven to be critical grounds
upon which new fields of knowledge were constituted. Racialised knowledge and
practice had become an ordinary condition of the administration of empires and
colonies, and governed important dimensions of life in empires, whether one was
ruling or ruled. At their most intense, racial discourses proved so pervasive and
powerful that they made race itself seem a self-evident and 'natural' condition of
the world: race could explain the past and outline the future, and through race
much of the present might be experienced, directed and understood.

But these histories of race and empire were far from singular or straightforward.
'Perhaps it is wrong to speak of [race] at all as "a concept"', W.E.B. Du Bois once
noted, 'rather than as a group of contradictory forces, facts, and tendencies.'[1]
Looking at a period in which empires supposedly ruled most of the world, this
insight is salutary. What is needed are ways to study race and empire that can
encompass, yet not flatten, these 'contradictory forces, facts, and tendencies'.
The multiple, complicated, histories of race and empire will not produce a single
straightforward, synthetic narrative, but require the recognition and entertaining of
diversities, contradictions and intricacies, in order to reconstruct accurate histories
of their interconnected genealogies, developments and distribution.

Framing this chapter is the argument that racial discourses were distinctively,
perhaps uniquely, 'modern'. This did not mean, of course, that stark inequalities
between groups of people – a setting apart due to appearance or skin colour, or

---

1   W.E.B. Du Bois, *Dusk of Dawn: an Essay Toward an Autobiography of a Race Concept* (New
     Brunswick, NJ, 2002), p. 133.

of strangers or foreigners, or 'others' more generally – were uniquely modern practices. Social and political distinctions seem to have been made within all polities or societies – including all empires – and these were often modal for many kinds of hierarchies and inequalities. Whether in the sumptuary laws of the Aztec Empire, or in the use of gender, political status and other abstract qualities and characteristics in Ancient Greece, most states and empires possessed a variety of 'ordering devices'.[2] Many of these distinctions seem analogous to race, in that they shape and produce inequality and hierarchies; but they were not homologous. Even when these distinctions drew upon or were indexed to perceived physical differences, they cannot all be usefully reduced to concepts of race. Race concepts, by constrast, had particular contents, or at least common strands; these included particular understandings that all people existed in *races*; that there was a relationship between physical type and character or capacity; that the group acted upon the individual; that these races could be ordered in hierarchies; and that there was a 'knowledge-based politics', as Tvetzan Todorov has put it, compellingly, 'the need to embark on a political course that brings the world into harmony' with these racialised conceptions.[3] This knowledge-based politics illustrated how race was irreducible to a sequence or collection of concepts. Instead, race comprised *discourses* which brought empire and race into such intense engagement. The discursive character of race meant that it established its own topics, and produced the objects of its knowledge. Consequently, racial discourses governed 'the way that a topic [could] be meaningfully talked about and reasoned about'.[4]

Racial discourses were articulated with social and political practices and institutions of particular kinds: state formations and practices, epistemological, discursive and political conditions that can be usefully understood as 'modern'.[5] Many of these elements were distinctively European in origin, but many others were not. To be sure, empires that stood more or less apart from certain European genealogies nonetheless came to share, appropriate or reinvent racial discourses – but this was usually contemporary with a raft of other changes. Japan's empire, for instance, drew from and was modelled on European empires, but traditional Japanese ideas about their own national and cultural superiority were recast in racial modes at the same time as the Japanese state was dramatically remade as an empire.[6] Similarly, Chinese scholars of race emerged contemporaneously with new forms of statecraft, and through which they intensified their encounters

---

2   Inga Clendinnen, *Aztecs: An Interpretation* (Cambridge, 1991), p. 69.

3   Tzvetan Todorov, *On Human Diversity: Nationalism, Racism and Exoticism in French Thought*, trans. Catherine Porter (Cambridge, 1993), pp. 91–4.

4   Stuart Hall, 'The Work of Representation', in Stuart Hall (ed.), *Representation: Cultural Representations and Signifying Practices* (Milton Keynes, 1997), p. 44.

5   C.A. Bayly, *The Birth of the Modern World, 1780–1914. Global Connections and Comparisons* (Oxford, 2004), pp. 9–12; David Theo Goldberg, *The Racial State* (Malden, MA, 2002).

6   John Dower, *War Without Mercy: Race and Power in the Pacific War* (New York, 1986); Louise Young, *Japan's Total Empire: Manchuria and the Culture of Wartime Imperialism* (Berkeley, CA, 1999).

with non-Chinese racial discourses.[7] Not just these racial and imperial forms, but these kinds of exchanges characterised modern empires. Most of the empires that coexisted from the late eighteenth through to the mid-twentieth centuries were not just contemporaneous, but kindred – and racial discourse was a characteristic of this kinship.[8] Racial discourses were able to circulate not just within, but across, empires, and were not the property of, nor quarantined within, any particular historical or national variant of empire. Indeed, a defining feature of 'modern' empires was that they were racial.

Deep, even unchanging, differences and inequalities between races appeared to be the order of the world, and empires and colonialism appeared to align with this 'natural' state. Rather than being challenged by new knowledges, this 'natural' condition was rearticulated, refined and reified by science, scholarship and 'common sense'. As Stuart Hall notes, race could translate 'historically-specific structures into the timeless language of nature; decomposing classes into individuals and recomposing those disaggregated individuals into the reconstructed unities, the great coherences, of new ideological "subjects"'.[9] Race was a formation that could make an overwhelming kaleidoscope of different peoples, languages and societies intelligible, and narrow or fix differences in ways that could be repeated or sorted, and circulated. *'Working together*, race and nature legitimate particular forms of political representation, reproduce social hierarchies, and authorise violent exclusions – often transforming contingent relations into eternal necessities.'[10] The peculiar optical or visual qualities of race – that it putatively could be seen and was self-evident – furthered this appeal to the natural: 'the virtual realities of race'.[11] Race, like gender, was made natural, integral to the natural order – and the two articulated and reinscribed one another.

Genealogies of Race

The intellectual genealogies of race remain contested, but one of the points of agreement amongst historians of race has been that the later eighteenth century was a forge of modern racial discourses. This was visible in the changing power of the

7 Frank Dikötter, *The Discourse of Race in Modern China* (Stanford, CA, 1992).
8 For serious attempts to establish longer genealogies of race largely outside a European genealogy: Bernard Lewis, *Race and Slavery in the Middle East: An Historical Inquiry* (New York, 1992); Peter Robb (ed.), *The Concept of Race in South Asia* (New Delhi, 1997).
9 Stuart Hall, 'Race, Articulation and Societies Structured in Dominance', in UNESCO, *Sociological Theories: Race and Colonialism* (Paris, 1980), p. 342.
10 Donald S. Moore, Anand Pandian and Jake Kosek, 'Introduction: The Cultural Politics of Race and Nature: Terrains of Power and Practice', in Moore, Pandian and Kosek (eds), *Race, Nature, and the Politics of Difference* (Durham, NC, 2003), p. 3.
11 Paul Gilroy, *Against Race: Imagining Political Culture Beyond the Color Line* (Cambridge, MA, 2000), p. 11.

scala naturae, the 'Great Chain of Being'.[12] In his famous work of that name, Arthur Lovejoy emphasised many of the continuities this understanding of the world shared with Plato and Aristotle. Works in the vein of the Great Chain observed gradations and continuities in nature that spanned from the highest forms of life (people) to the lower and inanimate. 'How many gradations may be traced between a stupid Huron, or a Hottentot, and a profound philosopher?' inquired William Smellie in 1790.

> Here the distance is immense; but Nature has occupied the whole by almost infinite shades of discrimination. ... Man, in his lowest condition, is evidently linked, both in the form of his body and the capacity of his mind, to the large and small orang-outangs. These again, by another slight gradation, are connected to the apes.[13]

This envisioned a world that was hierarchical, ordered and stable, but also one that was continuous and in series. Yet it appeared able to incorporate or explain important new 'facts' or knowledge – from orang-utans to Native Americans – that had become pressing as the domains of empire and exploration expanded.

But the European political, social, religious and moral orders with which the Great Chain had proven so compatible were themselves facing multiple challenges. These wider changes were entwined with shifts in thinking about human differences: in gender, class or social status and race. Understandings of race retained some key continuities: 'climate' remained a central preoccupation, for instance; the Bible retained a privileged, if complicated, position; 'white' races were still placed at the apex of humanity.[14] But the changes were unmistakable. One telling and increasingly important move was evident in 'stadial' theory, which recast the Great Chain to give it a temporal dimension. Stadial theory understood that societies developed through a sequence of stages, usually four: hunting, herding, agriculture and then commerce. Particularly contrasted with the Great Chain, it was more dynamic. A handful of Western European societies were placed in a singular position at the terminal stage, while other races were interpreted as earlier, more primitive or savage, stages of development: anachronisms in a modern world. Catalysed by the later work of Baron Montesquieu, there was soon an impressive chorus of stadial theorists including luminaries such as Anne-Robert Jacques Turgot, François Quesnay, Claude Adrien Helvétius, Dugald Steward, Alexander Dalrymple, the Marquis de Condorcet and Lord Kames (Henry Home).[15] But none put the matter quite as dramatically, or influentially, as three scholars

---

12   Arthur O. Lovejoy, *The Great Chain of Being: A Study of the History of an Idea* (Cambridge, 1936).
13   William Smellie, *The Philosophy of Natural History* (Edinburgh, 1790), vol. 2, p. 431.
14   Clarence Glacken, *Traces on the Rhodian Shore: Nature and Culture in Western Thought from Ancient Times to the End of the Eighteenth Century* (Berkeley, CA, 1967).
15   The most important survey remains Ronald L. Meek, *Social Science and the Ignoble Savage* (Cambridge, 1976).

integral to the Scottish Enlightenment: John Millar, William Robertson and Adam Smith. Stadial theory furnished what were to be lasting and powerful readings of racial difference: that certain races were in some way not modern even as they existed in the present; that there was a preferred, singular path of development; and that certain races – typically deemed to be 'hunters', such as the aborigines of Australia, the races of Patagonia, and the 'Hottentots' of southern Africa – were considered the most savage, and to have limited claims on law, property and even the lands upon which they lived. Stadial history, though current in the salons of Paris, Berlin, London, Edinburgh and Glasgow, was a manufacture that relied on a complex of encounters, many of which were in some way imperial. Quesnay was a noted sinophile, known as the 'Confucius of Europe', for instance; William Robertson's *opus magnum* was his eight volume *History of America*; Alexander Dalrymple was the key geographer directly behind the expeditions of James Cook.[16]

Clearly, a powerful impetus for innovation amongst metropolitan intellectuals before, during and after the Enlightenment were the engagements with foreign societies and places occasioned by empires. This was particularly evident with regard to race, as Enlightenment modes of rationality, liberalism, secularisation and science converged on 'man's' relationship with nature, knowledge and God. Most historical accounts of the leading intellectual figures of the Enlightenment have depicted race as marginal to, or absent in, their work, although for most of these figures race was at least at the margins, and not uncommonly at the centre. The Comte de Buffon, Carl von Linné, Immanuel Kant, David Hume, Johann Gottfried von Herder, Georges Cuvier and Georg Wilhelm Hegel each addressed race directly and substantially.[17] For some, such as Kant, the study of anthropology and geography – two sciences explicitly concerned with human variety, territorial expansion and exploration – were clearly central to his intellectual agenda. And for all the many specific differences between European thinkers, there was surprisingly broad agreement on the differences between people, and on the superiority of white people. 'Humanity exists in its greatest perfection in the white race', Kant asserted. 'The yellow Indians have a smaller amount of talent. The Negroes are lower, and the lowest are a part of the American peoples.'[18] Some have even argued, for instance, that is was Kant who 'invented' race.[19]

The spaces of empire catalysed changes within Europe in remarkable ways, particularly, though not only, from the mid-1700s. On occasion the conditions of empire provided impetus in ways that were still, in some sense, separate from

---

16   E. Fox-Genovese, *The Origins of Physiocracy: Economic Revolution and Social Order in Eighteenth-century France* (Ithaca, NY, 1976), p. 74.

17   See Emmanuel Chukwudi Eze (ed.), *Race in the Enlightenment: A Reader* (Cambridge, 1997).

18   Quoted in Katherine M. Faull, *Anthropology and the German Enlightenment: Perspectives on Humanity* (Lewisburg, PA, 1995), p. 218; see also Susan Shell, 'Kant's Concept of a Human Race', in Sara Eigen and Mark Larrimor (eds), *The German Invention of Race* (New York, 2006), pp. 55–72.

19   Robert Bernasconi, 'Who Invented the Concept of Race? Kant's Role in the Enlightenment Construction of Race', in Bernasconi (ed.), *Race* (Oxford, 2001), p. 11.

empire and European expansion: a good example of this was the famous debate over the state of 'natural man', where Denis Diderot addressed Jean-Jacques Rousseau following the publication of Louis Antoine, Comte de Bougainville's account of visiting Tahiti (Diderot's work was published as an *Supplément au voyage de Bougainville*).[20] Here Bougainville's voyage provided the occasion for a largely familiar exchange. More importantly, though, empire was a powerful catalyst for *new* developments and innovations, ones that specifically addressed, drew from, or were set in contexts of empire (or European expansion). Few things captured Enlightenment sensibilities and projects as powerfully as the voyages of Captain James Cook. Cook was perhaps the greatest icon of Enlightenment knowledge, humanity and curiosity; his fellow explorers, most notably Joseph Banks and Johann Forster, exercised profound influence on men of learning from Berlin to London, and many others associated with the journeys, from naturalist Daniel Solander to artist William Hodges, made smaller but important impressions.[21] Furthermore, certain elements in the Enlightenment(s) – for, as J.G.A. Pocock argues, one can accurately pluralise 'enlightenment into a number of movements in both harmony and conflict with each other' – can be usefully regarded as local responses to wider developments, from the global reordering of empire after the Seven Years' War (1756–63), to the new conditions of empire and political revolution, perhaps even of 'globality', that this may have signalled.[22] Moreover, the encounter of Europe with its new territories, new people and the new more generally, repeatedly introduced moments, things, people and material that traditions and conventions struggled to accommodate or explain. Whether it was the platypus confounding Enlightenment taxonomies, or the 'discovery' of Polynesians that required Johann Friedrich Blumenbach to add another race to his taxonomy of human kinds, empire was present, and articulate, at the Enlightenment(s).

Throughout learned circles in Europe and beyond, the decades before and after 1800 created new possibilities for racial discourse, not just intellectually, but through new cultural formations, institutions and sociabilities. Most obvious was the consolidation of 'science', and the crafting of new disciplines within it. The word biology, for instance, was first used in French (by Jean-Baptiste Lamarck) and in English right at the beginning of the nineteenth century; this can serve as a marker for many new medical and scientific formations all emerging with a particular investment in human variety. By the early decades of the nineteenth century, whether in learned societies in Europe or its colonies, there were few serious alternatives to talking about human diversity in terms of race, and a host of spaces had been established where working on, and in, race was a central

---

20 Denis Diderot, *Supplément au voyage de Bougainville, ou dialogue entre A et B* ([Paris], 1772).

21 Bernard Smith, *European Vision and the South Pacific, 1769–1850: A Study in the History of Ideas* (Oxford, 1960).

22 J.G.A. Pocock, *Barbarism and Religion* (Cambridge, 1999), vol. 1, p. 7. On the central role of difference to key Enlightenment sociabilities – especially 'civility' – see Dena Goodman, 'Difference: an Enlightenment Concept', in Keith Baker and Peter Reill (eds), *What's Left of Enlightenment: A Postmodern Question* (Stanford, CA, 2001), pp. 129–47.

activity. As Nancy Stepan has put it, before this scientific reorientation there was 'an emphasis on the fundamental physical and moral homogeneity of man, despite superficial differences, [whereas afterward there was] an emphasis on the essential heterogeneity of mankind, despite superficial similarities'.[23] This reorientation was entwined with a new emphasis on the perceived differences between male and female – one that understood these 'sex' differences not only as predictably hierarchical, but also as analogous to the differences between races.[24] This coupling of gendered and racial differences often stemmed from the same, or overlapping, techniques of knowledge. Moreover, the collapsing or entangling of gender and racial differences worked to integrate and shore up both, and shared analogies and metaphors of difference proved critical in directing subsequent thinking and activity.[25]

This new preoccupation with difference can be charted through a discursive shift – in English, French and German – in what 'race' signified. Beforehand 'race' had seemed a fairly elastic and sweeping concept, represented by a word that had stood in for 'lineage' or even 'nation'. Increasingly it was recast into a concept more proximate to 'type'.[26] This was bound up with increasing interest in the extent of these typical differences, and the very nature of these types. By the turn of the nineteenth century these developments seemed to break with older ways. A marker of this was the tentative advancing of questions that were to prove durable and pressing, an incitement to a new intensity of discourses. Were different races actually different species? Could different races procreate together? Should they? What climates suited which races? Were some races destined to disappear? Did different races have different intellectual, cognitive, and physical capacities? Each of these questions was entangled with, and bore directly upon, practical, political and social dimensions of life and government, in metropole and colony alike.

23   Nancy Stepan, *The Idea of Race in Science: Great Britain, 1800–1960* (Hamden, 1982), p. 4.

24   Lacqueur and Schiebinger have presented this as a shift from a 'one-sex' to a 'two-sex' model: Thomas Laqueur, *Making Sex: Body and Gender from the Greeks to Freud* (Cambridge, 1990); Londa Schiebinger, *Nature's Body: Gender in the Making of Modern Science* (Boston, MA, 1989). Though compare Karen Harvey, *Reading Sex in the Eighteenth Century: Bodies and Gender in English Erotic Fiction* (Cambridge, 2005); Michael Stolberg, 'A Woman Down to Her Bones: The Anatomy of Sexual Difference in the Sixteenth and Early Seventeenth Centuries', *Isis* 94 (2003): pp. 274–99.

25   Nancy Leys Stepan, 'Race and Gender: The Role of Analogy in Science', *Isis* 77 (1986): pp. 261–77.

26   Michael Banton, *Racial Theories*, 2nd edn (Cambridge, 1998), pp. 44–80; Stepan, *The Idea of Race in Science*, pp. 93–103.

Racial Politics and Empire

'*Like all politics*', Zygmunt Bauman has argued, race '*needs organization, managers and experts*'.[27] The distribution of the organisations, managers and experts enmeshed by racial discourses was a marker of just how complicated, uneven and widespread the terrains of racial discourses were becoming. Few of the 'modern' discourses that integrated empires and colonies did not have recognisable, distinctive, racial modalities. This did not mean that all expertise on race was directly instrumental; many disciplines and realms of racial study were ethereal, or esoteric, or simply strange or otherwise marginal (titles such as 'On Some of the Racial Aspects of Music').[28] But whether or not a specific racial expertise seemed directly instrumental to identifiable personal, social or state activities, they were elements of larger regimes of racial discourse. It was telling, for instance, that the French Empire could energetically avoid the use of explicitly racial terms by state practitioners yet, as Emmanuelle Saada has observed of Indochina, the 'legal statuses of "citizen" and "subject" are almost exactly superimposed on the social categories of French and indigène, defined in terms of place of birth and racial identity'.[29] The habitat for racial concepts, debates and arguments was not framed by discrete realms whether they were science or scholarship or bureaucracy, but traversed more diverse and expansive terrains of politics and society.

A powerful, sweeping illustration of the integral connections between modern imperial statecraft and racial discourses is in the junctures that produced the formal ending of slavery. These are also instructive, because despite the remarkable variety of intellectual and political traditions among empires, there was an eerie comity over slavery in the New World. There was also a striking comity in the rolling back of slavery, and centuries of slavery ended in just a few decades – between the abolition of slavery in the British Empire (1832–36) and that in the Brazilian/Portuguese Empire (1888).

New World slavery also marked the ancestral relationships between ancient and modern empires. There were critical continuities between ancient and 'modern' slavery – both real and asserted – and ancient slavery proved especially important in buttressing and legitimating the continuation of slavery. This became acutely important as shifts in politics, faith and public sentiment made slavery increasingly disreputable. A proximate remaking of Christianity helped loosen the biblical precedents and support for slavery.[30] No less important had been the sanction of antiquity, where Aristotle, Plato and Augustine, amongst others, cast slavery as integral to a moral, disciplined world. The idea of the 'natural slave', which for

---

27 Zygmunt Bauman, *Modernity and the Holocaust* (Ithaca, NY, 1989), p. 74. Italics in the original.

28 Joseph Kaines, 'On Some of the Racial Aspects of Music', *Journal of the Anthropological Institute of Great Britain and Ireland* 1 (1872): pp. xxviii–xxxvi.

29 Emmanuelle Saada, 'Empire of Law: Dignity, Prestige, and Domination in the "Colonial Situation"', *French Politics, Culture and Society* 20/2 (2002): p. 111.

30 David Brion Davis, *The Problem of Slavery in Western Culture* (Ithaca, NY, 1966).

centuries was powerful coin in many slave realms, was encapsulated by – and referred back to – Aristotle: 'the lower sort are by nature slaves, and it is better for them as for all inferiors that they should be under the rule of a master'.[31] But the similarities between ancient and modern, whether in Brazil, the Caribbean or North America, had real limits: in crucial ways the Atlantic slavery of the modern era was of its own kind: 'racial slavery', as Winthrop Jordan called it.[32]

The end of racial slavery – as with other near contemporary declarations of putative universality, equality or freedom – worked to make racial discourses more, rather than less, important. Without the extraordinary power of slave laws and other institutions overtly to intervene and govern inequalities amongst populations, colonial states turned to comparatively more refined yet powerful workings of racial discourse, statecraft and rhetoric.[33] Likewise, other contemporary schemes of liberal modernisation, formal equality among races or understandings of universal progress and civilisation – from the Declaration of Independence and US Constitution through the *Déclaration des droits de l'homme et du citoyen* to the 1830s reforms in the British empire – continued to mobilise racial modalities, particularly in articulation with gender. Writing of the largest of all the formal colonies, British India, Partha Chatterjee observed that the difference that 'united the ruling bloc and separated it from those over whom it ruled', was marked by race. Rather than receding into the background as the colonial state modernised and a political language of universalism was broadly espoused, 'the more the logic of a modern regime of power pushed the processes of government in the direction of a rationalisation of administration and the normalisation of the objects of its rule, the more insistently did the issue of race come up to emphasise the specifically colonial character of British dominance'.[34] In India, as elsewhere, new standards of presumptive universalism and equality increasingly turned on the routinised ability to apportion and administer unequally. These were particularly marked in post-slavery societies, but were evident in most colonial situations from the mid-nineteenth century onward.

Evidently, not all peoples and societies were to be admitted to the equalities and universalisms that modern empires increasingly proclaimed. Many people failed to meet what Uday Mehta has described as an 'anthropological minimum' – a 'thicker set of social credentials that constitute the real bases of political inclusion'.[35] This 'anthropological minimum' was largely crafted through race and

---

31   Aristotle, *The Politics of Aristotle*, trans. Benjamin Jowett, (Oxford, 1885), p. 8.

32   Winthrop Jordan, *White Over Black: American Attitudes Toward the Negro* (Chapel Hill, NC, 1968), pp. 91–101.

33   Frederick Cooper, Thomas C. Holt and Rebecca J. Scott, *Beyond Slavery: Explorations of Race, Labor and Citizenship in Postemancipation Societies* (Chapel Hill, NC, 2000).

34   Partha Chatterjee, *The Nation and Its Fragments: Colonial and Postcolonial Histories* (Princeton, NJ, 1993), p. 19.

35   Uday Mehta, 'Liberal Strategies of Exclusion', in Ann Stoler and Frederick Cooper (eds), *Tensions of Empire: Colonial Cultures in a Bourgeois World* (Berkeley, CA, 1997), p. 61. An important, different, view holds romanticism rather (or more) than liberalism/universalism as key in the intensifying of racial discourse: see, for instance, Kenan

gender, but also factored in age, literacy and property-holding. Each of these had a critical importance in modulating which peoples could be ruled and in what ways, in metropolitan and colonial spaces. (Age, literacy and property could also be deployed as proxies for race and gender – especially when women or non-white races were held as 'juvenile'.) The diverse endings of racial slavery, 'the problem of freedom' as Thomas Holt has phrased it, repeatedly demonstrated the intense intersections between race, labour, citizenship and political rights.[36] Elsewhere, in places like North America, New Zealand, Hawaii, Argentina or Australia, where settlers were dislodging indigenous peoples, land frequently replaced or augmented the element of labour. The profound connections between race, gender, political rights and subjecthood or citizenship were palpable and ordinary.

Racial Discourses and New Techniques of Empires

As well as being collections of territories, material and people, modern empires were collections of knowledge. Racial discourses were never simply arcane or esoteric diversions – although they were often that – but modalities through which this knowledge could be produced, organised and mobilised. Empires were extraordinarily complicated assemblages, and race furnished some capacity to engage and govern them. Empires were not often efficient, and were frequently contradictory, but for considerable periods of time over large territories they managed. Philippa Levine has noted the 'contradictory impetus [that] combined a clear dismissal of colonial populations as multitudinous and unindividual, and yet insisted on minutely refining racial categories. Characteristically it showed a disregard for divisions other than those meaningful to colonial power.'[37] Chief amongst these 'meaningful divisions' was race; and one of the chief reasons it was meaningful was that it proved compatible with new forms of statecraft, working across many registers in what Adam Smith once called 'the science of a statesman or legislator'.[38]

Smith might have added more humble participants in this new articulation of the state. There were many officials and soldiers, doctors and teachers, settlers and missionaries, and myriad other kinds of racial and imperial 'practitioners'. The new science of the state was theirs too, and in the various domains of empire race remained amongst the most powerful and meaningful languages in their

Malik, *The Meaning of Race: Race, History, and Culture in Western Society* (Houndmills, 1996).

36   Thomas C. Holt, *The Problem of Freedom: Race, Labor, and Politics in Jamaica and Britain 1832–1938* (Baltimore, MD, 1992).

37   Philippa Levine, *Prostitution, Race and Politics: Policing Venereal Disease in the British Empire* (New York, 2003), p. 202.

38   Adam Smith, *An Inquiry into the Nature and Causes of the Wealth of Nations* (London, 1776), vol. 2, p. 217.

lives, working and private. The synergies between emerging imperial and colonial statecraft and racial discourses paralleled the synergies that seemed to exist in very different scales. In one scale, for instance, empires dealt with the unimaginably large, the geopolitical, international laws and treaties; yet, in others, they delved into matters less large, even the most intimate details of colonised subjects, repeatedly seeking to govern carnal relations and the constitution of households and families.

Recent studies of empire have unveiled the ways in which racial discourses worked in the most intimate of domains. Informed by work pioneered by feminist and postcolonial historians, the home, family and personal lives of those in empires have shifted from being seen as relatively unimportant to being considered central to an analysis of imperial and colonial enterprises.[39] Racial discourses were indispensable to these intimate registers, and were bound up with the careful discriminations of gender and class or status. These connections were regularly apparent in the most obvious interventions of state governance into intimate relations – the regulation and instituting of marriage. This remained, for most of the lives of modern empires, a profoundly unequal relationship, where women commonly ceded their property and many of their rights, often also their citizenship or public legal identity. But attempts to govern the carnal were hardly restricted to marriage laws. Most strikingly, mixed-race children, often outside of legal marriage, dramatised the coordinated, unequal, workings of race and gender: at stake were often questions not just of legal but of social paternity, as well as those of property and succession, entitlements to rights, privileges and standing.[40] Most dramatically, children born of enslaved mothers, with free fathers, were usually born as slaves. In many other ways besides, the intimate was tied to the public and expansive through racial discourses.

Racial discourses were articulated in a variety of intimate registers. There were new disciplines of colonial medicine and public health – particularly those informed by the highly studied fields of tropical or racial 'hygiene', widespread attempts to regulate venereal disease and 'prostitution', the governing of domestic labour, colonial education, new disciplines of sport and athletics, and urban planning and architecture. These intimate registers made clear that discourses of race, and empires, were always gendered. The hierarchies of race and gender could not be separated: as one expert put it in 1847, 'the uterus is to the Race what

---

39   See, for example. Ann Stoler, *Carnal Knowledge and Imperial Power: Race and the Intimate in Colonial Rule* (Berkeley, CA, 2002); Catherine Hall, *White, Male and Middle Class: Explorations in Feminism and History* (Cambridge, 1992); Levine, *Prostitution, Race and Politics*; Adele Perry, *On the Edge of Empire: Gender, Race and the Making of British Columbia, 1849–1871* (Toronto, ON, 2001); Durba Ghosh, *Sex and the Family in Colonial India: The Making of Empire* (Cambridge, 2006).

40   See, for example, Damon Salesa, *Racial Crossings: Victorian Britain, Colonial New Zealand and the Problem of the Races* (Oxford, 2011); Ann Stoler, *Race and the Education of Desire: Foucault's* History of Sexuality *and the Colonial Order of Things* (Durham, NC, 1995); Owen White, *Children of the French Empire: Miscegenation and Colonial Society in French West Africa, 1895–1960* (Oxford, 1999).

the heart is to the individual'.[41] This was evident in all kinds of racial formations, such as eugenics, which specifically addressed reproduction, children and family, and these developments had numerous precedents, including the equally popular racialised discourse of phrenology. But while these intimate domains were 'dense transfer points' for state, imperial and colonial power, they were also zones for engagement that localised discourses and made them amenable to resistance.[42] Women, men and families did not lie prostrate before empires and their agents; they were usually unruly, and frequently hostile or resistant. A turn to the intimate regularly shows that racial discourses were in many ways effective, though in other ways less so, were always uneven, and were never perfect. Indeed, the intimate often most strongly marked both the power and the limits of both racial discourses and colonial statecraft.

Pulling at one strand of racial discourse tightens multiple, often unexpected, parts of the complicated web of empires. For historians there is no more prescient and powerful example of this than recognising that race worked on, and in, the archives. Racial discourses produced archival principles, governing the way that archives were generated, how they were stored and the ways in which they were retrieved. The archives of empire, in their multiple forms and locations, were not simply innocent records of activity, compiled for later use; rather they were, as Nicholas Dirks succinctly put it, archives *for* rule, not just *of* rule.[43] Accordingly, archival organisation was racially conditioned. Whether it was in court records, land titles, certificates, entitlements, taxation, virtually every kind of population statistic, conjugal and parental rights, or access to and participation in the market, institutions, schools, hospital or the franchise, the marking of race in these archives is indelible. Of course, the specifications of archives varied tremendously, but the utility and ubiquity of race was usually apparent.

The significance of race in modern statecraft was not restricted to imperial contexts. Racial discourses commonly, and powerfully, worked on metropolitan populations. In Britain, France, Spain, the German-speaking regions, the growing Russian Empire and Italy, as well as in other existing or establishing empires, there were new racial ways of casting and describing these 'domestic' diversities. Britain, for example, was acutely conscious of its multiplicity of peoples, not just because of its obvious 'Celtic Fringe' – in Scotland, Wales, Ireland and Cornwall (a massive proportion of its population) – but because it was generally held that the English themselves were a mixed people, formed of a union between Angles, Saxons, Normans, Danes and Teutons, in proportions that shifted between accounts.[44]

---

41   W. Tyler Smith, 'Lectures on Parturition, and the Principles and Practice of Obstetrics', *The Lancet* 50, no. 1264 (20 November 1847): p. 544.

42   Stoler, *Race and the Education of Desire*.

43   Nicholas Dirks, *Castes of Mind: Colonialism and the Making of Modern India* (Princeton, NJ, 2001), p. 107.

44   David Eastwood and Laurence Brockliss (eds), *A Union of Multiple Identities: The British Isles, c.1750–c.1850* (Manchester, 1997); Robert J.C. Young, *Colonial Desire: Hybridity in Theory, Culture and Race* (London, 1995).

In Britain, as elsewhere, these domestic peoples and regions were recast as primitive and backward, vestiges of a past that had anachronistically persisted. The French cast similar kinds of linguistic, regional, 'cultural' difference in racial discourses, as the Spanish did of the south, and Russians of the eastern frontier.[45] Likewise, it was widely supposed that there was a distinct southern race in Italy and Sicily, which Cesare Lombroso famously thought was disposed to 'great criminality'.[46] All of these were powerful varieties of 'racialised nationalisms' that would become widely evident throughout Europe.[47]

As in the case of overseas empires and racial discourses, these domestic representations were articulated with state practices to remake or govern areas and peoples. The project at hand was, in a key sense, the nation itself, and the ability to make the metropolitan state functional, effective and seemingly natural. The means by which this was advanced were localised and myriad: from land 'reform' to public education, through taxation policy, to banking and the judiciary, emigration policies, imprisonment and a galaxy of other different practices.[48] The correspondence between these activities and those that were often undertaken in the farther reaches of empire has not escaped historians. These processes of 'self-colonisation' or 'internal colonialism' were not just analogous to processes conducted in more distant regions, but contemporaneous, and usually genealogically related.[49] But differences were also apparent, particularly regarding strategies of inclusivity: commonly, though far from usually, these domestic races could be included in the widening of the suffrage, incorporated with ruling races, whether by invitation or compulsion – though a number of constituencies persisted who were commonly cast as defying progress.[50]

The racial experts who charted all of these developments were a diverse crowd. In the late eighteenth and early nineteenth centuries these experts were usually amateurs, often themselves officials or missionaries, already working 'in' empire. Explorers, missionaries and travellers all brought libraries with them, and all kinds of circuits for this knowledge were available from the early decades of the nineteenth century. Empires often read, in a sense, each other's mail, tracking innovations and developments overseas or in neighbouring colonies. Those in charge of colonies travelled with libraries and had transnational, transimperial

---

45   On the Russian case, see the forum in *Slavic Review* 61/1 (2002): pp. 1–65.

46   Cesare Lombroso, *Crime: Its Causes and Remedies*, trans. Henry P. Horton (Boston, MA, 1912), p. 25.

47   See, for example, Bruce Baum, *The Rise and Fall of the Caucasian Race* (New York, 2006), pp. 118–61.

48   See, for example, Eugen Weber, *Peasants into Frenchmen: The Modernization of Rural France, 1870–1914* (Stanford, CA, 1976); Saskia Sassen, *Guests and Aliens* (New York, 1999), pp. 69–73; James Lehning, *Peasant and French: Cultural Contact in Rural France During the Nineteenth Century* (Cambridge, 1995).

49   Weber, *Peasants Into Frenchmen*; Michael Hechter, *Internal Colonialism: the Celtic Fringe in British National Development*, 2nd edn (New Brunswick, NJ, 1999).

50   John Marriott, *The Other Empire: Metropolis, India and Progress in the Colonial Imagination* (Manchester, 2003).

networks of correspondence and patronage.[51] Science was a particularly powerful medium for building transnational networks, as were religious organisations. By the early twentieth century developments in transportation and communications meant that further steps could be taken, and religious, scientific and political conferences brought together constituencies that held high stakes in racial discourses. International Congresses of Eugenics were held in 1912, 1921 and 1932, for example; a pivotal 'World Missionary Conference' was held in Edinburgh in 1910, and Universal Races Congresses were held intermittently from 1911 until 1939. These constituted 'publics' that were implicated in racial discourses, and which not only integrated specific empires, but made individual racial problems modular, commensurate and transferable.

The instrumental effects of some of these larger, more broadly circulating racial discourses is striking. The ability to make discourses of transracial brotherhood and Christian grace compatible – in conjunction with shifts in the market and the metropolitan polity – helped to produce the abolition of the British slave trade. Almost universally held ideas about the decline and imminent extinction of dozens of colonised races – common through the entire nineteenth century – had a pivotal effect on imperial and colonial policy in North America, Oceania and Africa. Similarly, discourses about the orient facilitated the establishment of predatory and autocratic colonial regimes. Readings of native effeminacy proved pivotal in some locations, as did racialised understandings of religion in others. A swath of other recognisable formations of racial discourse, such as eugenics, population control, 'tribalism' and 'the lazy native' – the list could truly go on – were also deeply implicated in direct colonial action. Entire administrative techniques, focus and apparatus grew out of these racial discourses, including new schemes of 'protection', 'civilisation', public works, urban planning, forced schooling or 'adoption', hygiene and 'pacification'.

The expert discourses of race continued to be altered by a succession of new technical capacities. Amongst the most important were those that trafficked in the perceived gravitas and exactitude of science. These techniques made race even more visible, sortable and useful for statecraft and policy. The actual innovations were dramatically different, but each significant development seemed to offer new ways of measuring, classifying, interpreting and working on, or through, race. These technical capacities tended to operate at different scales, sometimes targeting racialised populations, other times individual racialised bodies, or even particular physical features.

The most important of new techniques in racial discourse, and one that marks the trajectory of modern empire and race, was the remarkable rise of statistics. Though statistics now seem such a natural part of everything from medicine to statecraft, the production of statistics was relatively recent, contemporary with

---

51   Tony Ballantyne, *Orientalism and Race: Aryanism in the British Empire* (Houndmills, 2002); Dominic Lieven, *Empire: The Russian Empire and its Rivals* (New Haven, CT, 2000); Bayly, *The Birth of the Modern*; Alan Lester, *Imperial Networks: Creating Identities in Nineteenth-Century South Africa and Britain* (London, 2001).

the rise not only of modern nation-states, but of modern empires. As historians from Benedict Anderson to Zoë Laidlaw have argued, statistics were particularly important – and pioneered – in imperial and colonial contexts.[52] Not only was the empire 'new', and thus more amenable to the impositions of new tasks and duties for officials (though they often remained reluctant or unable to collect even the most rudimentary statistics), statistics – along with, for instance, cartographic representations – were one of the few ways of representing the massive, diverse, far-flung entities that were empires. In particular, the development of colonial censuses was acutely important. Colonial censuses were not simply enumerating individuals, but calculating and defining racial and subject populations, and delineating domains of rule. Almost all imperial or colonial censuses not only tallied according to locality, but constituted categories of rule such as 'sex', age (adult or minor), as well as 'race': which varied from set schemes of 'castas' as in Latin America or algorithms of religion, origin and language, to the more generalised 'native'. In other situations, particularly in colonies of settlement, the census was a tabulation of subjects and citizens. Statistics, however, were far more complicated than they appeared. On the one hand they appeared administratively efficient, uniformly reducing practice to columns and volumes. On the other hand, statistics stemmed from and masked practices that were always far less perfect and powerful than they seemed. In many, perhaps most, places the inability to administer even the most rudimentary census indexed the continuing strength of local resistance or independence, and the comparative weakness of the colonial state. This was magnified when the statistics were more targeted and precise, and thus opened onto the kinds of slipperiness and complexity that statistics were partly engineered as a response to.

Few things rivalled the massive, unprecedented scale of the colonial, even the imperial, census; but in smaller scales racial technicians were no less laborious. At the scale of the body there were innumerable, changing, racial measurements – the measurement of various parts of the anatomy, compounded statistical tools like facial angles and intelligence measures, the use of calibrated photography, the enumeration of birth rates and illness – which went from accidental and amateur to become serious science and knowledge-making. These kinds of metrics seemed peculiarly susceptible to fashion. It was common for multiple methods and terminologies to be in the field, and to rise and fall from prominence quickly. But certain preoccupations proved enduring. The racial features that were almost fetishes to race experts were the width and breadth of the head, 'cranial capacity', the supposed breadth of the nose, the 'facial angle', lips, and the texture and colour of hair. At this scale it was also apparent that these racial discourses produced not only new data, but new ways of actually encountering people, places and discourses. Certain measurements could only be made artefactually, on skeletons; others required visits to the field, and new ways of 'seeing' people. But whether

---

52   Zoë Laidlaw, *Colonial Connections, 1815–1840: Patronage, the Information Revolution and Colonial Government* (Manchester, 2005); Benedict Anderson, *Imagined Communities: Reflections on the Origin and Spread of Nationalism* (London, 1991).

the item to be measured was a disembodied skeleton – a skull, in another revealing consistency, was usually the most prized – or a living 'native' or 'negro', the element most evident in these and later measurements was the element of power or control required to make them. Again some races, whom many desired to measure, were simply too unruly or difficult, too powerful or independent even to count in censuses, let alone to get close enough to apply the measuring scheme of your chosen expert. Thus, at both the largest and the most intimate of scales, the experts of race seemed to require, in some guise, the power of empire.

The most important forms of these investigations and studies were in the forms of, or under the aegis of what was become known as, science. It was not, however, pseudo-science – as some who want to disown a badly behaved predecessor have claimed – though it may well have been, as Nancy Stepan points out, bad science.[53] Science was an emerging powerhouse in metropolitan and imperial statecraft, and was thoroughly entwined with the practices of empire. These forms of race recognition, measurement and new technologies were often raised on faulty assumptions, or not consistent with their own methodological claims. They were commonly reliant on bad, or no evidence, and were frequently not reproducible, often defective, and surprisingly often fraudulent. But the naturalness of race made many of their findings, however they were produced, expected. This meant that these faults – and there were some who ventured to find them – were largely immaterial; what mattered was the authority and relevance the work conveyed. Moreover, the controversies over the minutiae or esotericisms of racial discourse served to make less visible the larger consensus, and the fields of power in which they were articulated.

One of the common threads that ran through much of the knowledge making about race – scientific, statistical, medical, sociological, anthropological and so on – was that it converted knowledge that was analogue into digital forms. Race could inhere in disembodied, numerical forms, could be represented in charts and diagrams, could appear in formulas and footnotes. If the census was this process on a large scale, it was only one example, and one scale. John Carson has described how Paul Broca, a leading French scientist, called for 'individual observations', 'collected through simple, uniform procedures, sheltered from the imagination, and repeated *on a large number of individuals chosen by chance*'. These observations were conditioned by instruments, 'uniform and mechanical procedures, that permit the results of each observation to be expressed in numbers'.[54] The intensity and laboriousness of measurement was soon enough legion, with the density of numbers producing the proof of scientific method, and allied to a wider process of statisticalisation, digitisation and standardisation. Broca's student, Paul Topinard, consequently measured 44 skulls nearly 4,500 times. By such means individuals were disembodied even as their bodies were measured, and races were made as subjects even as they were unmade as people.

---

53   Stepan, *The Idea of Race in Science*, p. xvi.
54   John Carson, *The Measure of Merit: Talents, Intelligence, and Inequality in the French and American Republics, 1750–1940* (Princeton, NJ, 2007), p. 100.

This conversion from analogue to digital altered the technical status of race, and meant that – particularly as the nineteenth century progressed – one could work with the facts of race, or in racial modalities, and yet be at a remove, often several removes, from the experiences, cognitive and sorting acts that produced them. For one thing this allowed a consistency in racial data and theories – even when, as was often the case, such consistencies did not provide accurate indices, and elided moments of resistance, unevenness and incompleteness. In these ways the digitisation of race mirrored and contributed to larger efforts to stabilise imperial and colonial archives, to consolidate, organise and shore up imperial and colonial rule. A simple census, a map of territory, an assignation of a tribe or race to a particular territory: each of these was an achievement as well as a foreshadowing or aspiration of empire, and tracked as well as enabled very real material and practical achievements. Consequently race, as a metric, a shorthand, a sorting code or an archival principle, was constitutive, central and foundational in changing, often innovative, modes. Racial discourse proved a compelling currency of empire, integrating and making commensurate disparate and contradictory elements.

In each of these ways racial discourses had epistemological consequences, governing not just policy or statements, but perceptions and experiences. Races were 'natural', as we have seen, and ordered experience, observation, understanding and comment, as well as actions and policy. But these developments were always imperfect, often vulnerable to dissonance or discrepancy. As racial discourses were epistemological, they were not simple hypotheses: certain kinds of claims or knowledge that was demonstrably incongruent or contradictory to individual experiences and observations about race hardly led to a collapse, and rarely even to adjustments, in many racial discourses. Discrepant experiences and observations could themselves be delegitimated or disavowed, categorised as inauthentic or non-authoritative, even by the people who themselves experienced them.[55] The thousands of offspring produced by individuals of different races that some experts asserted could never procreate, repeatedly proved an insufficient rebuttal. Similarly, it was surprisingly common for individuals to arrive and depart from the spaces of empire – and to still understand themselves to never have seen or accessed 'real', 'pure' or authentic experiences – that is, experiences consistent with their expectations and prior knowledge.

Remaking Racial Discourses, Remaking Empires

The Second World War was a turning point not only in the fortunes of empires, globally, but in the parameters of their public conduct: a new regime of discourse, typified by the United Nations Charter, sounded a new international public decorum concerning race. (Though the Soviet Union had proclaimed racial

---

55   Edward Said, *Orientalism: Western Conceptions of the Orient* (New York, 1978).

equality considerably earlier, and declared itself a 'raceless society'.[56]) The atrocities perpetrated during the Second World War – death camps, attempted genocides, mass bombings of civilians, deployment of nuclear weapons – were not only of a scale unprecedented in human history, killing millions, but had been clearly conditioned by race – 'by the propagation ... through ignorance and prejudice, of the doctrine of the inequality of men and races', the preamble to the UNESCO Constitution stated.[57] The most horrific example of this, the attempted extermination of European Jews, was to prove a lasting motivation for anti-racism. It was clear that, after the war, even if empires wanted and were able to continue business as usual – and one could point to the events in Indochina or Kenya or the Suez or any number of other locations where this appeared to be the case – empires had to work through new discourses and confront dramatically changed circumstances. Both sides of the Cold War, led by the US and the Soviet Union, scrambled to claim the mantle of anti-imperialism and racial equality, even if neither ultimately did so in a manner that was very convincing. For the US, particularly, the continued racialisation of domestic citizenship and rights proved to be an ongoing Achilles heel in international contexts.[58] A third grouping, that of the Non-Aligned Movement, or the Third World, made a more compelling claim, but was ultimately largely unsuccessful; many of the postcolonies themselves struggled with the problems of races under new postcolonial regimes, often violently so.

Racial discourses had sustained inequalities from slavery into freedom, and in parallel ways worked to formulate continuities from formal empire and colonialism into 'decolonisation'. Decolonisation was, and is, a partial project, in both senses of that word; only partially completed, and completed in a way that was partial to metropolitan powers and interests. Despite the formal declaration of racial equality, and the official declarations that the differences amongst people were not to matter, there was no question that decolonisation did not erase or expunge the valence of race. The coarsest measure of this was the continued supremacy of certain (particularly 'white') races that had been conditioned and enabled by racial discourse as both an end and a modality of rule. The 'end' of empires did produce, in many respects, a limiting and remaking of earlier racial privileges, but the elements that continued were equally apparent. The durability of race, and its

---

56   See both the 1918 Constitution of the Russian Soviet Federated Socialist Republic, (especially chap. 5, article 22) and the 1924 Soviet Constitution; Meredith Roman, 'Racism in a "Raceless" Society: Racial Violence at the Stalingrad Giant of Socialist Industry and Images of Soviet Racial Equality, August 1930', *International Labor and Working-Class History* 71 (2007): pp. 185–203.

57   George L. Mosse, *Toward the Final Solution: A History of European Racism* (New York, 1980); Robert Proctor, *Racial Hygiene: Medicine Under the Nazis* (Cambridge, 1988); Dower, *War Without Mercy*; Ronald Takaki, *Hiroshima: Why America Dropped the Atomic Bomb* (Boston, MA, 1995).

58   Penny Von Eschen, *Race Against Empire: Black Americans and Anticolonialism, 1937–1957* (Ithaca, NY, 1997); Nikhil Pal Singh, 'Culture/Wars: Recoding Empire in an Age of Democracy', *American Quarterly* 50/3 (1998): pp. 471–522.

ability to remain an organising power, and a living set of discourses, quite clearly exceeded the formal ending of the age of empires.

Racial discourses continued to hold together diverse, often contradictory constituencies. Similarly, a kaleidoscope of postwar projects – including anti-racism, and anti-imperialism, nationalism, civil rights and human rights movements, as well as decolonisation itself – found utility or validity for racial discourses. The enduring, almost visceral power of race – as a 'virtual reality', as 'natural' – meant that it also remained obvious and in practice. But, even as decolonisation was 'invented', racial differences found new deployment in familiar hands, used to craft powerful internal discriminations within metropolitan and post-imperial states. Race could specifically attach to bodies and populations as they moved across state lines in former imperial realms, as empires contracted into nation-states. As Jamaicans and South Asians moved to Britain; as Turks moved to Germany; as Algerians and West Africans moved to France; as Hmong, Vietnamese, Chamorros and Filipina/os moved to the US; as Congolese moved to Belgium; as Niuginians moved to Australia, or Samoans to New Zealand, race modulated new relationships with the state and society.[59] Racial discourse could be renovated and energised in new ways, increasingly to manage not only external frontiers, but interior ones. 'Race riots' were to be found broadly, in Jakarta and Detroit, Marseilles and Oldham. Racial discourses were intense and palpable at the end of the twentieth century: whether in Eastern Europe and the Balkans, Rwanda or South Africa, if not always in familiar ways.

After the war there had been explicit legal, organisational and political attempts to outlaw or in some way regulate discourses of race. These occurred within the frames of national states, in postcolonial constitutions, in the United Nations, even FIFA – but unfolded over decades, and often with impressively little or limited impact. Even at the upper echelons of diplomacy, as Frank Furedi has observed, for many years 'race was a central category in international relations'.[60] The decrease in explicitly racial discourses in some places coexisted with their heightening elsewhere, as well as the rise of many kinds of proxy languages – which were often agile and changing, frequently fastening onto new terms, even tracking into new domains. A variety of historians have shown in compelling ways that racial discourses remained powerfully relevant in putatively non-racial and non-imperial projects such as 'development', 'modernisation', 'international philanthropy', transnational adoption, foreign intervention, aid distribution and scientific

---

59   Rita Chin, *The Guest Worker Question in Postwar Germany* (Cambridge, 2007), pp. 148–55; Damon Salesa, 'New Zealand's Pacific', in G. Byrnes (ed.), *The New Oxford History of New Zealand* (Oxford, 2009), pp. 149–72; Catherine Ceniza Choy, *Empire of Care: Nursing and Migration in Filipino American History* (Durham, NC, 2003); Todd Shepard, *The Invention of Decolonization: The Algerian War and the Remaking of France* (Ithaca, NY, 2006).

60   Frank Furedi, *Silent War: Imperialism and the Changing Perception of Race* (London, 1998), p. 1.

experimentation (such as medical trials). It is evident that racial discourses chart one of many 'visible connections between the colonial and the global'.[61]

Relatively quickly in the postwar period the kind of scholarly practice that had distilled, and made natural, racial inequality had fallen widely into disrepute. The eugenic and racialist research of the 1930s had no simple counterpart in the 1960s and 1970s. But it was not difficult to find influential proponents of racial discourse that seemed remarkably familiar and consistent with the centuries of racial discourse. The idea of polygenesis – that some races were so different as to be different species, with different origins – had long been seen as the starkest enunciation of racial inequality. It had been denounced by its critics as discredited when it was first advanced in the 1700s, and had been supposedly refuted by everything from the Bible, evolution and mixed-race children to modern genetics. The critical voices were strident: one insisted that 'all human races are of one species and one family'; another, that 'All human beings belong to a single species and are descended from a common stock'. But no less remarkable than the volume of the critics was that these two statements, though only a few words different, were written 150 years apart. The first was the last sentence of James Cowles Prichard's *Natural History of Man* (1845), while the second was the first sentence of the first article of the United Nations' 'Declaration on Race and Racial Prejudice' (1978).[62] Just as empires decolonised, but never went away, racial discourses continued to haunt long after they had been repeatedly, and demonstratively, entombed.

---

61   Tony Ballantyne and Antoinette Burton (eds), *Bodies in Contact: Rethinking Colonial Encounters in World History* (Durham, NC, 2005), p. 13. See also Frederick Cooper, *Colonialism in Question: Theory, Knowledge, History* (Berkeley, CA, 2005).

62   James Cowles Prichard, *The Natural History of Man*, 2nd edn (London, 1845), p. 546; 'Declaration on Race and Racial Prejudice', 27 November 1978.

Gender

Elsbeth Locher-Scholten

> In language, character, practice and effects, imperialism was never gender-neutral.

This statement is a near-cliché, even if many historians of colonialism remain reluctant to take gender to heart. As a result of women's and gender studies, postcolonial and subaltern writing, and 'new' social history, creative research questions concerning the functioning of gender and prescribing roles for women and men have sharpened our understanding of empire.

Reading imperialism through gender is a relatively new field, dating largely from the 1980s.[1] While women, both colonial and colonised, are marginal or non-existent in the traditional archives and therefore easily overlooked, researchers have been creative in finding sources which throw light on women in the empire.[2] Such studies have shifted in focus: from an emphasis on the victimisation of colonised women to an interest in their agency; from blaming western women for the fall of empires to recognising them as supporters of empire or critical-colonial actors;[3] from separating gender issues in metropole and periphery to interactions, contacts and contests between both. In line with the history of colonialism in general, this broad subject has evolved from the 'West to the Rest', and recently to their multiple relations that are now generally studied 'in a single analytic field'.[4]

---

1   For a discussion of the (lack of) attention to women in the connected field of world history see Tony Ballantyne and Antoinette Burton, 'Introduction: Bodies, Empires, and World Histories', in Ballantyne and Burton (eds), *Bodies in Contact: Rethinking Colonial Encounters in World History* (Durham, NC, 2005), pp. 1–15.

2   Antoinette Burton, *Dwelling in the Archive: Women, Writing, House, Home and History in Late Colonial India* (New York, 2003).

3   Claudia Knapman, *White Women in Fiji, 1835–1935: The Ruins of Empire?* (Sydney, 1986); Beverley Gartrell, 'Colonial Wives: Villains or Victims?', in H. Callan and S. Ardener (eds), *The Incorporated Wife* (London, 1984), pp. 165–86, esp. p. 165; Nupur Chaudhuri and Margaret Strobel (eds), *Western Women and Imperialism: Complicity and Resistance* (Bloomington, IN, 1992).

4   Ann Laura Stoler and Frederick Cooper, 'Between Metropole and Colony: Rethinking a Research Agenda', in Cooper and Stoler (eds), *Tensions of Empires: Colonial Cultures in*

Until the middle of the 1990s, gender studies focused primarily on female roles and actual behaviour; then issues of masculinity appeared on the scene. Empires had always flourished on and by a gendered rhetoric in which men played a dominant role. In popular imagery, for instance, men explored and penetrated virgin countries and constructed male-oriented communities of heroic pioneers, opening up new land for rubber, tobacco or other crops and industries. Colonial projects asked for and created new constructions of manliness. Colonial masculinity was defined in opposition to 'effeminate' colonised peoples, whether Bengali or Javanese, though a few allegedly martial races always remained exempted, such as the Moluccan soldiers in the Dutch colonial army, and the Ghurka among British troops.[5]

Hence, gender is now defined as 'actual relations between men and women, the assignment of roles and the definition of the attributes of each sex, the feminine and the masculine',[6] or more succinctly as 'a set of social and symbolic relations'.[7] Despite this broad understanding of gender I will focus here on women since they remain the neglected part of humankind, and I will only incidentally discuss masculinity. My leading questions will centre on how imperialism itself was gendered and how it affected women, gender relations and gender conceptions of coloniser and colonised. Since gender, as one of the markers of difference, always appears in tandem with ethnicity (or race), class, and even age and religion, racial difference will also serve as one of my organising principles.[8]

The examples will be drawn mainly from the Indonesian archipelago, since truly comparative colonial histories of gender are difficult to realise, or achieve at most 'a parallel play'.[9] There was no uniform colonial experience for women in European empires, a situation complicated further when the US, Russian, Ottoman and other empires are taken into account.[10] Moreover, while there is an impressive amount of high-quality work on gender in the British Empire, work on other

---

     a Bourgeois World (Berkeley, CA, 1997), pp. 1–55.

5   Mrinalini Sinha, *Colonial Masculinity: The 'Manly Englishman' and the 'Effeminate Bengali' in the Late Nineteenth Century* (Manchester and New York, 1995).

6   Peter N. Stearns, *Gender in World History* (London and New York, 2000), p. 11.

7   Nancy Rose Hunt, Tessie P. Liu and Jean Quataert (eds), *Gendered Colonialisms in African History* (Oxford, 1997), p. 4.

8   Anne McClintock, *Imperial Leather: Race, Gender and Sexuality in the Colonial Contest* (New York, 1995). The relationship between different social markers has been defined as 'intersectionality'. For a recent appraisal, see Kathy Davis, 'Intersectionality as Buzzword: A Sociology of Science Perspective on what Makes a Feminist Theory Successful', *Feminist Theory* 9 (2008): pp. 67–85.

9   Ann Laura Stoler, *Carnal Knowledge and Imperial Power: Race and the Intimate in Colonial Rule* (Berkeley, CA, 2002), p. 209; Julia Clancy-Smith, 'The Intimate, the Familial, and the Local in Transnational Histories of Gender', *Journal of Women's History* 18/2 (2006): pp. 174–83, esp. p. 177.

10   Cheryl Johnson-Odim and Margaret Strobel, 'Introduction: Conceptualizing the History of Women in Africa, Asia, Latin America and the Caribbean, and the Middle East and North Africa', in Barbara N. Ramusack and Sharon Sievers (eds), *Women in Asia: Restoring Women to History* (Bloomington, IN, 1999), p. xlvii.

empires lags behind in this respect.[11] My focus on the Indonesian example offers both an examination of one of the lesser-known empires and a good opportunity to flesh out the general issues around 'women, gender and empire' that emerge from the international historiography.[12]

Gender and Rhetoric in Early Modern Southeast Asia

As other chapters in this volume have shown, trade laid the foundation of the European empires in Asia.[13] Chartered by the States-General of the Dutch republic, the United East India Company (VOC; 1602–1796) exerted sovereign rights over trade and contracts, war and peace. In the many islands of the Indonesian archipelago – such as Java, Sumatra and the Moluccas – the new traders entered societies in which economic circumstances had provided women with a rather favourable position.[14] The economic and religious importance of agriculture and the ritual meaning of weaving had given them status. The cultivation of rice and other food products was largely a female responsibility, and their local activities in the market were valued. Maternal descent was important, and inheritance practices routinely included daughters. Among the matrilineal Minangkabau population on Sumatra, where descent was reckoned primarily through the female line, men were expected to migrate in search of land and it was women who inherited land. The birth of a daughter was celebrated because her marriage might lift the debts from the family through the bride price, and bring the physical labour of her husband to the family.[15]

Political power was in the hands of elite family networks, in which women also played a pivotal role, although their direct political power was limited. Tony Day has argued that the concept of the precolonial 'states' in Southeast Asia should be replaced by a focus on familial networks, since the latter more fully includes women.[16] Javanese history, for instance, was above all family history. In general,

---

11   In monographs and in edited volumes, for instance, Clare Midgley (ed.), *Gender and Imperialism* (Manchester, 1998); Philippa Levine (ed.), *Gender and Empire* (Oxford, 2004).

12   For a historiographical survey of gender in African colonial history, see for instance, Nancy Rose Hunt, 'Introduction', in Hunt, Liu and Quataert (eds), *Gendered Colonialisms in African History*, pp. 1–15.

13   With its focus on Java and the Moluccas in the archipelago and its myriad of forts and factories (trade posts) elsewhere in Asia, the VOC developed as a dominant player in the trade relations of the region at large. In the seventeenth and eighteenth centuries, the VOC extended its political power in Java and the coastal areas of the other islands.

14   Barbara Watson Andaya, *The Flaming Womb: Repositioning Women in Early Modern Southeast Asia* (Honolulu, HI, 2006).

15   There is scant historiography on indigenous women in the early modern period. Andaya, *Flaming Womb*, pp. 7, 110–12, 116.

16   Tony Day, 'Ties that Unbind: Families and States in Premodern Southeast Asia', *Journal of Asian Studies* 55 (1996): pp. 384–409.

women held strong positions at the Central Javanese courts where they served in the military bodyguard of the sultan, heavily armoured and as capable of shooting as the best male snipers. Here, women were also responsible for money transactions and capital investment.[17] Different Malay regions, including Islamic Aceh in North Sumatra, had female sultans at times.[18] But even where women did not enjoy this supreme position, they linked families, possessing direct access to centres of authority in their roles as wives and mothers. Similar to their position in medieval and early modern Europe, they acted as 'women behind the throne' and as mothers of possible rulers-to-be. Thus they could be part of the repeating succession struggles which accompanied Islamic polygamy and added to the characteristic contests of the precolonial indigenous state in the region.[19] The sultans of Central Java could have four official and numerous unofficial wives (up to 25 or 30, later 50), which resulted in many offspring (up to 50 or 80) and much potential disharmony.

In societies in which families were valued as the foundational unit of a rural economy, women held strong positions that were reflected in cultural rhetoric. Gender ideals in the Javanese folk culture of *wayang* (shadow play), for instance, praised vigorous women as courageous, energetic and determined. In mythology, strong female goddesses provided the Central Javanese rulers with power, and princesses with a 'flaming womb' expressed authoritative sexuality.

A more male-oriented rhetoric of the family prevailed in political culture. This rhetoric was a common political tool in the hands of the indigenous elite. In southeast Sumatra, for instance, *raja* (princes) expressed diplomatic endeavours for peace by their wish 'to live as brothers'. Even the new coloniser might be included in

---

17 Peter Carey and Vincent Houben, 'Spirited Srikandhis and Sly Sumbradas: The Social, Political and Economic Role of Women at the Central Javanese Courts in the Eighteenth and Early Nineteenth Centuries', in Elsbeth Locher-Scholten and Anke Niehof (eds), *Indonesian Women in Focus: Past and Present Notions* (Leiden, 1992), pp. 13–17; 29. The official marriages of a sultan were limited to three, while the fourth place was left open for temporary marriages to the many co-wives mothering his children. These rich marriage networks connected courts and countryside: Nancy Florida, *Writing the Past, Inscribing the Future: History as Prophecy in Colonial Java* (Durham, NC, 1995), pp. 102–103, 280. For examples of strength see the wrathful behaviour of one queen with her weapons, chasing her husband over the palace wall; John Pemberton, *On the Subject of 'Java'* (Ithaca, NY, 1994), pp. 40–41.

18 Cheah Boon Kheng, 'Power Behind the Throne: The Role of Queens and Court Ladies in Malay History', *Journal of the Malaysian Branch of the Royal Asiatic Society* 66 (1993): pp. 1–21; Leonard Andaya, '"A Very Good-Natured but Awe-Inspiring Government": The Reign of a Successful Queen in Seventeenth-Century Aceh', in Elsbeth Locher-Scholten and Peter Rietbergen (eds), *Hof en handel: Aziatische vorsten en de VOC 1620–1720, opgedragen aan Jurriën van Goor* (Leiden, 2004), pp. 59–84. For pre- and early colonial elite families in South Asia, see Indrani Chatterjee (ed.), *Unfamiliar Relations: Family and History in South Asia* (New Brunswick, NJ, 2004).

19 Michael Adas, 'From Avoidance to Confrontation: Peasant Protest in Precolonial and Colonial Southeast Asia', *Comparative Studies in Society and History* 32 (1981): pp. 217–47.

this rhetoric, legitimating his presence. South Sumatra rulers sometimes addressed the highest Dutch official, the governor-general, as a 'father'.[20] According to a Javanese legend, the marriage between a princess 'with a flaming womb' and the 'upstart lord of Jakarta' ended in her pitiful exile, because the fire from her genitals prevented its consummation. Abroad she married a Dutch prince, reigning in Spain. Their son, Mur Jankung (Han Pieterszoon Coen, founder of Batavia in 1619), revenged his mother and took Jakarta. Hence, Dutch victories could be justified in Javanese gender terms, the colonisers being a kind of 'relative' or family member, returning unexpectedly.[21]

Effects of Early Colonialism

What did indigenous women from the diverse multitude of kingdoms and ethnic groups, from different regions and classes, notice of the new regional trade partner from distant Europe? With a few exceptions, they never met any of the hundreds of VOC representatives, who remained white dots in a colourful tropical surrounding.[22]

Changes came in a more indirect way. New long-distance trade patterns, new cash crops such as indigo and pepper in demand by the VOC, and rising numbers of wage labourers, as well as the growth of a slave market, expanded the economic possibilities more for men than for women. There were a few exceptions: members of the female guard of the Sultan van Jogjakarta (Central Java), for example, profited from the private trade in gold and precious stones as well as from their ties to a market near the palace. Yet, in general, the gap between a 'male' and a 'female' economy gradually widened. In eighteenth-century Java, the VOC preferred to trade with men, as they considered women – wrongly – to have little access to capital. Women were also often reluctant to deal with European men whom they despised for their disdain and sometimes outright outrageous behaviour towards Javanese women. New urban centres like Batavia were an ugly demonstration of a growing female poverty, while prostitution, legally prohibited, went hand-in-hand with a growing slave market and an expanding male migration.[23]

---

20   Barbara Watson Andaya, *To Live as Brothers: Southeast Sumatra in the Seventeenth and Eighteenth Centuries* (Honolulu, HI, 1993).

21   On sources, see Andaya, *Flaming Womb*, chap. 2; on the flaming womb, see p. 58; and Carey and Houben, 'Spirited Srikandhis and Sly Sumbradas', pp. 13–17, 29.

22   This could be a mutual experience, or as a Dutch traveller in Southeast Borneo (now Kalimantan) from the early eighteenth century remarked: 'as to their women, I never saw any of them, and so can give no account of them'. Quoted in Andaya, *Flaming Womb*, p. 64.

23   Slave owners could thereby enhance their income, while manumitted female ex-slaves often did not have resources other than the sex trade. Andaya, *Flaming Womb*, pp. 118–23, 125, 130–33, 137, 230–31. For insults by VOC men to women, see Andaya, *To Live as Brothers*, pp. 171, 193, 215.

Gender relations were also affected by the coming of male-dominated world religions, either before (Islam) or during early empire formation (Christianity). Islamic traders had reached the Indonesian archipelago by the end of the fourteenth century. In Java, Islam adapted itself to extant Buddhism and Hinduism and developed a Javanese religious practice, including offerings and fertility rituals.[24] The veiling and the strict seclusion of the Middle East were not found here. Although women lost some ground, their ritual power remained intact in the fertility rituals of rice cultivation. Where Islam expanded in reaction to the 'kafir' Dutch trade company VOC, it stimulated polygamy and the exclusion from public life of elite women.[25] The VOC itself was not interested in proselytising outside its own Protestant company circle; it was more concerned about its Roman Catholic rivals, such as Portugal, than about Islam.

Intimate Relations and their Offspring during the *Ancien* Régime

In all empires a new group of subjects emerged, the children of male colonisers and colonised women, the hybrid mestizo in-betweens. They could be found in all social classes of colonial societies. Indigenous women were victims and agents in these sexual 'contact zones'.[26]

Empires differed in their appreciation of mestizos, varying from a more or less easy acceptance (the Portuguese and Spanish empires) to a strong uneasiness among the British in India. By the late eighteenth century, British distrust of 'corrupting' Indian vices discouraged interracial relations and promoted prostitution as a device to keep the 'white race' 'pure'. By 1835 the East India Company had prohibited marriages between its senior officials and Indian women. One of the consequences was that most of the cross-racial connections in British India were kept secret or at the least did not end up in an official marriage. In the late-colonial state with its legal divisions of the population according to race this would result in counting Anglo-Indians among the native population group.[27]

The situation in the Dutch East Indies was markedly different. Here relations between the indigenous peoples and European newcomers were always hybrid

---

24 This Javanese version of Islam got the name *abangan* in the nineteenth century, contrasting with the more strict *santri* group: M.C. Ricklefs, *Polarizing Javanese Society: Islamic and Other Visions (c.1830–1930)* (Leiden, 2007).

25 See for instance Gerrit Knaap, 'Pants, Skirts and Pulpits: Women and Gender in Seventeenth-Century Amboina', in Barbara Watson Andaya (ed.), *Other Pasts: Women, Gender and History in Early Modern Southeast Asia* (Honolulu, HI, 2000), pp. 147–73.

26 For contact zones, Mary Louise Pratt, *Imperial Eyes: Travel Writing and Transculturation* (London, 1992).

27 Philippa Levine, 'Sexuality, Gender and Empire', in Levine (ed.), *Gender and Empire*, p. 138; Durba Ghosh, *Sex and the Family in Colonial India: The Making of Empire* (Cambridge, 2006), pp. 8–10.

and fluid. The VOC favoured pragmatism.[28] The pursuit of profits required stable marriages; therefore, the VOC permitted formalised interracial relations between Dutch men and local women, on the condition that these women entered the Protestant religion officially and spoke and understood some basic Dutch. The Protestant religion and 'Dutchness' (as well as high social status and one's relation to the VOC) became far stronger social markers than race. Cohabitation was not allowed; sexual relations between non-Christian women and Dutch men were even punishable to death. The reality, of course, differed from the law. The fact that regulations fixing these rules were repeatedly invoked illustrates that they were not followed rigidly.[29]

Mestizo women occupied a highly favourable position among the elite in Batavia, the centre of the VOC trade empire in Asia. Indigenous women, whether originally slave or free, gained European status and the inheritance rights of Dutch women by marriage to a VOC servant, and they and their daughters could become important family assets. Young, strong and better adapted to the climate than their woollen-clad husbands, these (Eur)asian women often survived them and inherited fortunes that made them attractive marriage partners to other male members of the elite, as Jean Gelman Taylor has argued.[30] While the sons of these mixed-race marriages were sent to Holland for education, daughters remained in the colony and cemented families and fortunes through their marriages. These women created an Indies mestizo culture of clothing, language, and habits such as betel chewing.[31] Although Taylor's thesis has been criticised recently, as other social marriage and migration patterns can be discerned as well,[32] there is no doubt that a Eurasian culture of female origin was part and parcel of VOC colonialism.

The agency and power of at least one of these mestizo elite women, the seventeenth-century Cornelia van Nijenroode, is known. Daughter of a VOC official and a Japanese woman (the VOC imperium ran from East Asia to the Near East, including sexual relations among its highly mobile personnel), she married into the highest VOC circles of Batavia. In 1672, her husband died leaving her in her forties as a widow with a legendary fortune. She soon consented to a second marriage

---

28 This policy was developed after some failed experiments with shiploads of virgin orphans as brides-to-be from the Dutch Republic. Once in the Indies, these women failed to live up to the expected marital moral standards.

29 Eric Jones, 'Courts and Courtship: An Examination of Legal Practice in Dutch Asia', *Leidschrift* 21/2 (2006): pp. 31–50.

30 Jean Gelman Taylor, *The Social World of Batavia* (Madison, WI, 1983).

31 As in India, VOC officials (but outside Batavia) could now have harem-like family structures. This tendency was reinforced when at the end of the eighteenth century wars with the English and the French made contact and travel by Dutch women more difficult. Ulbe Bosma and Remco Raben, *Being 'Dutch' in the Indies: A History of Creolisation and Empire, 1500-1920* (Athens, OH, 2008), p. 70.; Ghosh, *Sex and the Family*.

32 Other marriage patterns than those between VOC families did exist as well, for instance with women from Europe, or from elsewhere in Asia, while among the Batavia elite the ideal of marrying as white as possible remained intact. Bosma and Raben, *Being 'Dutch' in the Indies*, pp. 67–70.

with the (penniless) VOC lawyer Joan Bitter, who had just arrived in Batavia. Conflict and violence were her lot, as Bitter tried to take control of her money, which according to contemporary laws was still hers. Their divorce resulted in a twenty-year legal struggle. Cornelia did not give in to the greedy demands of her husband Bitter, and took recourse to all legal weapons she could muster, amongst others different religious, legal and political authorities. She fully lived up to her surname: untamable. Her death (or disappearance from the sources) in 1691 put an end to the conflict. Her case is one of the few examples of a forceful mestizo woman's voice of the *ancien régime*.[33]

During the brief period in the Napoleonic era when the British took over from the Dutch in the archipelago (under Thomas Stamford Raffles, 1811–16), the conspicuous wealth and behaviour of the Eurasian VOC ladies put to shame British men and women concerned with racial purity and distance. Lady Olivia M. Raffles and others were horrified by what they saw as rude Batavian mores. Yet subsequently in the nineteenth century five Dutch governor-generals, representing the King of the Netherlands in the archipelago, would marry locally born Eurasian women.[34] Only at the end of the century did Social Darwinist theories and a greater influx of white women from the Netherlands relegate Eurasian family patterns to the rural estates in the interior of Java and to specific parts of the archipelago (such as Central Java, Ambon and North Celebes/Sulawesi) where the majority of the European population group were Eurasian.

State Colonialism: The Nineteenth Century

In the nineteenth century, European governments discarded the older trade organisations that had laid the foundation of the expanding territorial empires. After the bankruptcy of the VOC, the Napoleonic period and the British interregnum, the Dutch state assumed colonial authority in the archipelago. The new state imperialism on Java directly affected the courts of Central Java, where women were crucial. After the bloody Java War (1825–30), fought between the Dutch troops and the Javanese-Islamic followers of Prince Dipo Negoro, the local courts became politically impotent. The Dutch also infringed on the functions of Javanese women. The female military units were withdrawn.[35] While the financial role of women remained largely intact, sexuality was one of the few remaining idioms of male Javanese power and potency. It was elaborated in the nineteenth century, stressing Javanese male fantasies of control of women, as Nancy Florida has convincingly argued. In this Javanese gender idiom, racial and gender positions

---

33 Leonard Blussé, *Bitter Bonds: A Colonial Divorce Drama of the Seventeenth Century* (Princeton, NJ, 2002).
34 L.P. van Putten, *Ideaal en werkelijkheid: Gouverneurs-generaal van Nederlands-Indië* (Rotterdam, 2003).
35 Carey and Houben, 'Spirited Srikandhis and Sly Sumbradas', pp. 13–17, 29.

were even reversed: European wives were critically described as being hardly able to suppress their lust for a sexually attractive king and their desire to be part of his harem.[36]

Little is known of the changing role of women and gender perceptions in the rural areas of Java and other islands in the nineteenth century. The effects on indigenous women of the so-called Cultivation System, the production of export crops that was required by the colonial state between 1830 and 1870 (and even longer in practice), have not been researched. The system involved households instead of individuals, hence both female and male labour patterns must have been affected, for, as a traditional Javanese saying has it, in agriculture the ideal couple of man and wife acted as 'a pair of oxen before the plough'.[37]

The Twentieth Century: Political Background

Like all historiography about gender and empires, that of the Dutch Empire in the twentieth century has much more to offer than that of the nineteenth century. Dutch imperialism swept through the archipelago at the end of the nineteenth century, putting an end to the independence of indigenous princes and sultans. However, the Dutch expanded 'in depth' instead of enlarging their territory. The government remained within the already internationally recognised borders of the archipelago. Around 1900 colonial state formation received a strong impetus with the so-called Ethical Policy, a new policy designed by the Dutch to develop the colony and its population on a European model under Dutch guidance.[38] Like Kipling's 'White Man's Burden' symbolising the new colonial plight of the British, and the *mission civilisatrice* of the French, the Ethical Policy was a vehicle of modernity. It influenced education, technology, medicine and health, culture and politics as well as the new nationalism.

Indonesian nationalism emerged in the first decade of the twentieth century initially as a regional movement among the western-educated lower nobility. The economic crises and nationalist uprisings of the 1920s brought the semi-progressive policies of Ethical Policy to a standstill in the 1920s, and by the 1930s there was outright repression of nationalism and the imposition of a far more authoritarian law–and–order regime. The Japanese occupation of 1942–45 erased the Dutch presence in Indonesia physically (by internment) as well as culturally. The

---

36 Nancy Florida, 'Sex Wars: Writing Gender Relations in Nineteenth-Century Java', in Laurie J. Sears (ed.), *Fantasizing the Feminine in Indonesia* (Durham, NC, 1996), pp. 207–224.

37 There is a remarkable gap in gender studies concerning indigenous women in the nineteenth century between the Dutch and the British Empire. *Sati* (widow burning) did not occur in the Dutch colony; concomitant moral issues about women and domesticity did not draw colonial attention in that century.

38 Elsbeth Locher-Scholten, *Sumatran Sultanate and Colonial State: Jambi and the Rise of Dutch Imperialism 1839–1907* (Ithaca, NY, 2003).

proclamation of the Indonesian Republic by the nationalist leaders Sukarno and Mohamad Hatta two days after the capitulation by Japan (15 and 17 August 1945) resulted in a lengthy struggle for independence by means of war and diplomacy. In December 1949 the Dutch Empire ended officially through the transfer of sovereignty.

Indonesian Feminism and Gender Ideals

Although male-dominated nationalism frequently put gender equality on hold while the nationalist ideal was pursued, feminism among the colonised very often went hand-in-hand with the rise of nationalism, while both were stimulated by new education facilities of the colonial state.[39] Indonesian feminism was no exception. In line with the earlier court tradition of strong women, the Javanese noblewoman Raden Ajeng Kartini (1879–1904) was one of the first women to express a national Javanese consciousness. Inspired by her Dutch elementary schooling and her longing for further education, she championed the teaching of Javanese girls and the development of Javanese crafts. She strongly opposed polygamy in her letters to one of her Dutch intellectual 'godmothers', the wife of a civil servant. Her explanations of Javanese culture, values and norms were (and are) a contribution to a renewed Javanese self-respect. Her letters were published after her death in 1911 and brought her long-lasting fame, both among the Dutch and among Indonesians. Moderate and well-voiced as she was, she became the darling of progressive Dutchmen who considered her the civilised emblem of the advantages of colonial modernity. Indonesian nationalism made her into an early national heroine. As a feminist, however, she remained within the confines of her class and Javanese culture. At the wishes of her father – and fearing magic tricks (*guna-guna*) from an unknown suitor, as complete publication of her letters has shown – she did not long reject polygamy: she married an older polygamous *regent* (Javanese prince) and died in childbirth, 24 years old.[40]

Kartini was one of the few among the Indonesian millions who could speak and write in Dutch. Even if the Dutch language was considered the gateway to the west, the Indies government was slower than other colonial governments in introducing a full-fledged education system from kindergarten to universities, in which women occupied a second place. The government preferred quality of education to quantity of pupils; it was always in need of teachers; it was apprehensive of the costs and afraid to create a white-collar proletariat. Hence, it did not answer the general longing for western education among the Indonesian elite.[41] While the early decades of the twentieth century saw a great spurt in the number of women

---

39 Kumari Jayawardena, *Feminism and Nationalism in the Third World* (London, 1986).
40 Joost Coté (ed. and trans.), *Letters from Kartini, an Indonesian Feminist, 1900–1904* (Clayton, VC, 1992).
41 Susan Blackburn, *Women and the State in Modern Indonesia* (Cambridge, 2004), p. 4.

in elementary village schools from 3,000 in 1909 to 37,000 in 1919, girls' education remained of secondary importance. In 1939 around 2 million Indonesian children attended one of the many elementary schools of the complicated colonial education system, of which 620,000 were girls (31 per cent of all pupils). The number of women with a Dutch university degree remained limited to a handful of daughters of the Javanese elite. Together with female teachers, the latter were to become the leaders of the so-called 'secular' women's movement in the 1920s and 1930s.[42]

The women's movement in Indonesia would always be divided into a 'secular' wing of nominal Muslims, and the women's branches of the large Muslim organisations, whether political or social. While the secular women's movement counted its members by the thousands, the Muslim women's movement counted them by a figure that was ten or even a hundred times more than this. In the late 1920s both movements joined in an association of Indonesian women which strove for political representation and the right to vote.[43]

In the 1920s and 1930s, education and political debates stimulated female members of the 'secular' Indonesian elite to formulate their gender perceptions of the so-called 'new woman', a modern ideal with a specific Indonesian touch in which modernity and Javanese Islam went hand-in-hand. Secular feminism did not do away with Islam but recognised its moderate forms as part of an Indonesian identity. Being a mother (*ibu*) in Indonesia had always implied responsibility for the family and the social community at large. Motherhood evolved as a woman's highest calling, a vision which fused harmoniously with Islamic domesticity but aimed at a nuclear family and in this way differed from the earlier diffuse pattern of polygamic family relations with its many mothers.[44] Fusing western notions of domesticity with Islamic ideals of the family, motherhood became an emblem for health and modernity, providing women with a means to act in the public sphere also.[45]

This femininity was expressed in direct relation to the imagined Indonesian nation. In the 1930s, a 'companionate feminism', underlining harmony in the home and cooperation with men in the outside world, became an even more dominant theme in the gender rhetoric of Indonesian women's organisations. Female authors identified their true nature as equal to men, yet at the same time feminine and harmonious; they saw themselves as a help and inspiration to their husbands. They championed emancipation but rejected the western pursuit of individual well-being. In accordance with Javanese cultural values of refinement (*halus*) as proper female behaviour and in line with national solidarity, the values of these women fit

42   *Volkstelling 1930/Census 1930. Overzicht voor Nederlandsch-Indië* (Batavia, 1936), Tables 18–19. For India, see, for instance, Meena Bhargava and Kalyani Dutta, *Women, Education and Politics: The Women's Movement and Delhi's Indraprastha College* (New Delhi, 2005).

43   Saskia Wieringa, *The Politicization of Gender Relations in Indonesia: The Indonesian Women's Movement and Gerwani until the New Order State* (Amsterdam, 1995), pp. 77–85.

44   Blackburn, *Women and the State*, pp. 138–42.

45   Partha Chatterjee, *The Nation and its Fragments: Colonial and Postcolonial Histories* (Princeton, NJ, 1993).

neatly with those of the nationalist leader Sukarno who saw women as helpmates to the cause of independence instead of pursuing their own interests.[46]

As a voluntary act of self-sacrifice, these women preferred Indonesian unity to the woman's cause. For instance, in massive protests in the late 1930s against a proposed marriage law that opted for voluntary monogamy, secular elite women preferred unity with their sisters in Islamic organisations who defended polygamy, rather than voicing their personal preference for monogamy.[47] Indonesian feminism thus followed Kartini's example, sacrificing personal ideals to the Indonesian culture and community at large. In the uneasy marriage between these two projects of modernity – feminism and nationalism – Indonesian women opted for nationalism and 'tradition'. This choice would continue to affect gender perceptions during the Revolution and after empire.[48]

Clean of Body and Soul: Health

In the twentieth century, empires dealt with health and sexual matters – marriage, cohabitation and prostitution – according to western norms of cleanliness of character and body.[49] Medicine in the Dutch Empire was western and largely dealt with men. Nursing had begun as a male activity in the health service of the colonial army, and in nineteenth-century vaccination campaigns that in indigenous opinion put the 'Dutch stamp' – that is, the small-pox inoculation scars – on their bodies. Medicine remained largely in male hands even after the development of a state-run colonial health service in the 1910s. Because there were so few nurses (male or female) in the colony, Indonesian nurses were tasked with curing more than caring at the bedside; more than in the western world they were involved in medical treatment and in vaccinating. Feminisation of the nursing profession started in the Christian missions, which introduced 'nursing by vocation', requiring character and motivation alongside technical education. Indonesian women entered the nursing profession in significant numbers only when the nursing diploma opened the possibility of training as a midwife in the 1920s and 1930s, a traditionally respected profession in indigenous circles. At last, and by a different route from that in the west, hospital nursing became identified with the female sphere.[50]

---

46 Colin Brown, 'Sukarno on the Role of Women in the Nationalist Movement', *Review of Indonesian and Malayan Affairs* 15 (1981): pp. 68–92.

47 Elsbeth Locher-Scholten, 'Morals, Harmony and National Identity: "Companionate Feminism" in Colonial Indonesia in the 1930s', *Journal of Women's History* 14/4 (2003): pp. 38–58. On the construction of masculinity and femininity among British and Hindu nationalism in British India, see Sikata Bannerjee, *Make Me a Man! Masculinity, Hinduism and Nationalism in India* (Albany, NY 2005).

48 Saskia Wieringa, *Sexual Politics in Indonesia* (Basingstoke, 2002), pp. 52–96.

49 McClintock, *Imperial Leather*.

50 Rosalia Sciortino, 'The Multifariousness of Nursing in the Netherlands Indies', in Peter Boomgaard, Rosalia Sciortino and Ines Smyth (eds), *Health Care in Java: Past and*

Marriage

All western colonial empires were centrally concerned with the issue of marriage control. All projected their own ideals – of a happy, heterosexual, voluntary union, headed by a male breadwinner – onto their colonial subjects. In indigenous societies where marriage was considered the only proper status – especially for women – two approaches to marriage collided: the more individualised couple-based western arrangement and the indigenous community-oriented reading of marriage. In the latter, marriage served a community interest, bonding families in economic and political networks.

The marriage issue was invariably a thorny one for foreign rulers. The fact that Hinduism required marital obedience until death and Islam permitted polygamy complicated the subject further. However, unlike its British counterpart, the colonial government in the Indies took little legal action regarding marriage. As Hinduism was restricted to the isle of Bali, which kept its self-governance until the early twentieth century, there were no acts governing *sati* or widow remarriage. Only the marriages of Christian Indonesians were regulated by law, including a minimum age (in 1933 15 for women and 18 for men), free partner choice and monogamy. The custom of child marriage, a sensitive 'private institution' and therefore difficult to control by the colonial state, was left to the campaigning activities of Indonesian women's organisations.[51]

Yet Islamic marital customs posed problems for western rulers. European colonisers considered women's marital position as well as education as a yardstick of progress and modernity, and implicitly as the foundation stone to rights of citizenship and political identity.[52] Seclusion, veiling and polygamy were considered counterproductive to female progress. In the Netherlands Indies, where veiling and seclusion never took the strict form of the Maghreb and the Middle East, polygamy was the critical issue, the more so as it was the secular women's movement which put the topic on the agenda. Marriage customs and regulations interfered directly with notions of gender, ethnicity/race and religion. While marriages of white men and local women might be frowned upon or even be illegal, in all European empires mixed marriages between local men and white women were widely rejected. These relations remained an exception but their number grew slightly in the 1930s, when the male Indonesian elite reached a

---

Present (Leiden, 1996), pp. 23–50. On midwives see also Liesbeth Hesselink, *Genezers op de koloniale markt: Inheemse dokters en vroedvrouwen in Nederlands Oost-Indië, 1850–1915* (Amsterdam, 2009).

51   Sita van Bemmelen 'The Marriage of Minahasa Women in the Period 1861–1933: Views and Changes', in Locher-Scholten and Niehof, *Indonesian Women in Focus*, pp. 181–204; Blackburn, *Women and the State*, pp. 111–27.

52   Alice L. Conklin, 'Redefining 'Frenchness': Citizenship, Race, Regeneration and Imperial Motherhood in France and West Africa, 1914–1940', in Julia Clancy-Smith and Frances Gouda (eds), *Domesticating the Empire: Race, Gender, and Family Life in French and Dutch Colonialism*, (Charlottesville, VA: 1998), pp. 65–83.

higher education level and its members became more attractive marriage partners to European women.

Marriage also caused administrative and 'moral' problems. In the Indies, an 1898 law had ruled that a wife was classified by her husband's population group upon marriage – these groups being 'Europeans' (including Indo-Europeans), 'Foreign Orientals' (Chinese and Arabs) and 'Natives' (Indonesians). Hence, European women married to 'Natives' or Indonesians would become 'Natives' and could be subjected to polygamy. To counter this possibility, in 1937 the colonial government proposed the already mentioned law on voluntary monogamous civil marriage for Indonesians. Islamic groups considered this an attack on polygamy and on their religion as well as an unwanted meddling of the government with a private institution. Massive protests forced the withdrawal of the proposal and no action was taken within the Dutch Empire. Eventually, the Dutch effort to reform marriage in the colony failed dramatically.[53]

Cohabitation

Other aspects of the regulation of sexual relations concerned the indigenous housekeeper or concubine (*nyai*), the prostitute (including women forced into prostitution) and the homosexual. Attitudes towards concubinage across the European empires were mixed. In French Algeria, concubinage between the coloniser and a Berber or Muslim woman was unusual.[54] In French Cambodia it was an approved practice; in British India it was frowned upon; while in the Dutch Empire it was a common feature of society.[55] Until the 1890s 50 per cent of European men in the Dutch Empire lived with a concubine. Concubinage was common among young plantation personnel from Europe. Until 1922 Europeans arriving in the plantation world of Sumatra were not allowed to marry until after some six years, during which time a female coolie from China or Java usually served their domestic and sexual needs and, as a 'walking dictionary', might teach them the language. These women were not expected to become pregnant, and if they did they either had to leave or the child, legally recognised by the father, was taken from them. The *nyai* thus had no rights and had to remain invisible.[56]

Large-scale concubinage was widespread in the Indies army.[57] Soldiers were not allowed to marry, but could have an indigenous or mestizo *nyai* in the

---

53   Locher-Scholten, *Women and the Colonial State*, pp. 187–218.
54   Julia Clancy-Smith, 'Islam, Gender and Identities in the Making of French Algeria, 1830–1962', in Clancy-Smith and Gouda (eds), *Domesticating the Empire*, pp. 154–74.
55   Penny Edwards, 'Womanizing Indochina: Fiction, Nation and Cohabitation in Colonial Cambodia, 1890–1930', in Clancy-Smith and Gouda (eds), *Domesticating the Empire*, pp. 108–130.
56   Reggie Baay, *De njai: Het concubinaat in Nederlands-Indië* (Amsterdam, 2008).
57   Baay, *De njai*; Petra Groen, 'Zedelijkheid en martialiteit: Het kazerneconcubinaat in

barracks. Coming from poor areas, these women found some economic security in this exchange. The Royal Netherlands-Indies Army (KNIL) was the only army that allowed women to live in its compounds. Until the interwar years of the twentieth century, colonial authorities regarded such relations as a stimulus to military morale, a counter-measure to homosexuality and venereal diseases (since they reasoned that these soldiers did not visit infected prostitutes), and as a basis for 'domesticity' among soldiers belonging to the rough and alcohol-prone lowest echelons of colonial society. These women offered another advantage: if the garrison was attacked, they could be fierce fighters themselves.

Stories of power differences and (gruesome) violence towards concubines in and outside the army are more numerous than the few reports of tender love. In European public opinion and colonial literature, the *nyai* were the female 'other', feared as unreliable, jealous and poisonous or praised as pliable, sweet and feminine.[58] Indonesian nationalism had other opinions about these women: their position was an insult to Indonesian culture. However, as nationalists were unable to end the practice, they urged colonial authorities to protect the *nyai* by law.[59] In the twentieth century, European morality gradually won out. Concubinage in the barracks was abolished in 1919 and in the army in the late 1920s. Just before the Second World War, marrying 'the mother of one's children' became a common practice.[60]

Prostitution

The decline of concubinage went hand-in-hand with an increase in prostitution. Prostitution was another 'evil' that fell under the spell of civilising imperialism. Its regulation was dictated by concerns of morality and health, and reflected colonial opinions on the free sexuality of colonised women, considered as one of the dangers of uncivilised people in general. In most colonies, whether French, British or Dutch, indigenous women were often identified as likely prostitutes.[61] Prostitution had existed before and after the arrival of the Dutch, but increased dramatically in the nineteenth century as a direct effect of the imperial economy.[62] The expanding

---

Nederlands-Indië rond 1890', in Marieke Bloembergen and Remco Raben (eds), *Het koloniale beschavingsoffensief: Wegen naar het nieuwe Indië, 1890–1950* (Leiden, 2009), pp. 25–52.

58 Present-day prostitution tourism has a long colonial tradition: Edwards, 'Womanizing Indochina'.

59 Locher-Scholten, *Women and the Colonial State*, p. 200.

60 Baay, *De njai*.

61 Clancy-Smith, 'Islam, Gender and Identities', p. 158; Philippa Levine, *Prostitution, Race and Politics: Policing Venereal Disease in the British Empire* (New York, 2003); Liesbeth Hesselink, 'Prostitution: A Necessary Evil. Particularly in the Colonies: Views on Prostitution in the Netherlands East Indies', in Locher-Scholten and Niehof (eds), *Women in Focus*, pp. 204–224.

62 So-called *ronggèng* (dancing girls) were professional prostitutes, possibly a remnant of

plantation system, the improvement of transport facilities and the growth of harbours and cities resulted in a circular labour migration by single men with cash to spend on sex.

All colonial empires tried in vain to control prostitution. Both in the British and the Dutch Empire regulations issued between 1850 and 1875 required medical examination of prostitutes, which were highly unsuccessful. Under pressure from fierce opposition to state-regulated prostitution in the metropole and the Indies, these medical examinations were ended and the use of prostitutes forbidden by law in Java in 1911. Stimulated by the anti-prostitution campaigns of Muslim nationalists, regional and local councils introduced new regulations in 1920. Yet, in the 1930s, prostitution and venereal disease (VD) tended to increase rather than diminish. In colonial cities where there were large numbers of single men, prostitution and VD were always higher than in cities in Europe.[63] Women of all population groups (Indonesian, Chinese and European) were involved in the business, both on a regular and on a temporary basis. The colonial structure prescribed the hierarchies within the sex trade; while (Indo-)European and Chinese women only serviced their own ethnic group, Indonesians were there for all. And while Europeans tended to accept prostitution by Indonesian women more easily than they would have done in the metropole, they considered that European prostitution undermined white prestige, one of the main 'sins' during imperialism.[64]

Homosexuality

Lesbian studies is a new field of scholarly interest, yet little explored as far as empire is concerned, owing to the archival invisibility of same-sex practices.[65] Javanese sources from around 1800, however, are quite frank about homosexual and lesbian relations at the central-Javanese courts, and about the interchangeability of sex

---

temple prostitution.

63   As many government and private reports of the nineteenth and first half of the twentieth centuries in the Indies acknowledged. John Ingleson, 'Prostitution in Colonial Java', in David P. Chandler and M.C. Ricklefs (eds), *Nineteenth and Twentieth Century Indonesia: Essays in Honour of Professor J.D. Legge* (Clayton, VC, 1986), pp. 123–40, esp. p. 132.

64   Ingleson, 'Prostitution in Colonial Java'. Army prostitution had a long history in the European empires. During the Second World War the Japanese Empire continued the tradition of improving military morale by (forced) prostitution of so-called comfort women, a form of organised rape or sex slavery in which 200,000 victims were misled, deported or stolen from their homes. Yoshimi Yoshiaki, *Comfort Women: Sexual Slavery in the Japanese Military during World War II* (New York, 2000); Margaret Stetz and Bonnie B.C. Oh (eds), *Legacies of the Comfort Women of World War II* (Amonk, NY, 2001).

65   Research on this topic is only just beginning. Saskia E. Wieringa, Evelyn Blackwood and Abha Bhaiya (eds), *Women's Sexualities and Masculinities in Globalizing Asia* (New York, 2007); Pete Sigal (ed.), *Infamous Desire: Male Homosexuality in Colonial Latin America* (Chicago, IL, 2003); Robert Aldrich, *Colonialism and Homosexuality* (London, 2003).

roles and clothing.[66] Even if the colonial state had proclaimed its own laws of moral purity, these were applied only once – in 1938 – in a large-scale persecution of male homosexuals, involving hundreds of high-ranking Europeans. This 'scandal' – an attempt to clean the colony of 'sinful practices' – broke out at the instigation of a Christian political party who mentioned the involvement of one of the highest civil servants. It concerned only men, for in the Dutch (and the British) Empire female same-sex practices wholly escaped attention.[67] This controversy should be situated within the general nervousness at the breaking of the world order at the end of the 1930s.

White Women's Colonial Tasks and Civilising Offensives

All empires were concerned with racial boundaries, western morality and sexual mores.[68] White women entering the colonised world in larger numbers around 1900 were often considered – and considered themselves – the custodians of moral, social and racial boundaries, maintaining 'white prestige'.[69] Nineteenth-century notions of white ethnic superiority as well as a new social 'maternalism' became dominant. Closely connected to other axes of inequality such as class and gender, whiteness now was the explicit norm for mapping the hierarchies and identity politics of empire.[70]

Around 1900 the colony served the formation of national identity among white men and women in the Netherlands. At the large-scale exhibition on female labour in The Hague in 1898, for instance, Dutch elite women – organisers and visitors alike – envisioned white women taking care of native women and their crafts.[71] Combining feminine beauty and masculine power, the young Queen Wilhelmina (r. 1898–1948) toured the exhibition, yet she never visited one part of her colonial realm. And, unlike the ceremony full of invented traditions of her British relative of 1877, she was never crowned as empress. Yet, it was in her name that the Ethical

66 Carey and Houben 'Spirited Srikandhis and Sly Sumbradas', pp. 17–19.
67 Levine, 'Sexuality, Gender and Empire', p. 152. It remains to be seen whether the described prevalence of a same-sex pattern in Asia and Southeast Asia of female masculinity (butch; tomboy) and femme has its roots in history. Sticking to the dominant gender ideology of male–female difference or masculine and feminine, the femme claims sexual normalcy while the masculine woman (or tomboy) takes to the appreciated male characteristics and is classified as a man (see Wieringa, Blackwood and Bhaiya, *Women's Sexualities*).
68 Ann Laura Stoler, *Carnal Knowledge and Imperial Power: Race and the Intimate in Colonial Rule* (Berkeley, CA, 2002,).
69 Ibid.
70 Ibid.
71 Maria Grever and Berteke Waaldijk, *Transforming the Public Sphere: The Dutch National Exhibition of Women's Labor in 1898* (Durham, NC, 2004).

Policy of 'uplifting the Native' and modernising colonial society was officially launched in 1901.

In the Ethical Policy, women played their role and played it well. White women took their task of 'making empire respectable' to heart.[72] Older Eurasian patterns of cooking and clothing were replaced by European food, Parisian fashion and home-made summer dresses. Europe became the dominant north of the cultural compass, white women the markers of domestic modernity. Fears of 'going native' hovered above daily life.

Sexual relations with indigenous women were now ideally limited to lower-class European soldiers and were socially frowned upon. Eurasian women taught their daughters 'to marry as white as possible'. As mentioned above, Dutch sexual purity was even at stake in state efforts to regulate marriage by law. Yet, in contrast to the British Empire in New Guinea and Africa, laws and regulations in the Indies never manifested fears of a 'black peril', of colonised men menacing white women sexually.[73]

Married white women tended to become what Beverley Gartrell first called 'incorporated wives' more easily in the colonies than in the metropole.[74] European women in the Indies also took the ethical task to elevate the 'native' seriously. A Dutch student on a three-month private course in the 1920s in The Hague, which prepared Dutch women for their future colonial domicile, learnt, as she stated, 'that she also has a national task, that is, to create bonds of appreciation and devotion between the people of the Netherlands and the people of Insulinde [the Indonesian archipelago]'.[75] Most white women put this task of elevating and bonding to work in their own households among their servants who were, after all, the only colonised people they met on a regular basis.[76]

However, these activities also reached outside the archipelago. It was women who made the colony familiar to their relatives at home. The Dutch tradition of weekly letters served as the 'umbilical cord' between colony and periphery; women kept the colonial connection and spread the word about race and class, about the ease, the luxury or the penuries of daily colonial life. From the 1930s on these letters were often accompanied by either photographs or even home movies.[77]

---

72   Stoler, *Carnal Knowledge*.

73   Jock McCulloch, *Black Peril, White Virtue: Sexual Crime in Southern Rhodesia, 1902–1935* (Bloomington, IN, 2000).

74   Incorporated wives can be defined as women whose status and agency were identified by their husbands' position in society. See Callan and Ardener (eds), *The Incorporated Wife*. See also Mary Procida, *Married to the Empire: Gender, Politics and Imperialisms in India, 1883–1947* (Manchester, 2002).

75   Locher-Scholten, *Women and the Colonial State*, p. 98.

76   See the more than 700 interviews (nearly 3,000 hours) of the Foundation for the Oral History of Indonesia/SMGI at the Royal Institute of Linguistics and Anthropology/ KITLV, Leiden, composed between 1997 and 2001. Fridus Steijlen (ed.), *Memories of 'The East': Abstracts of the Dutch Interviews about the Netherlands East Indies, Indonesia and New Guinea (1930–1962) in the Oral History Collection* (Leiden, 2002).

77   Eveline Buchheim, 'Geschreven levens: Brieven van Nederlandse vrouwen in Indië

The Cult of Domesticity

The cult of domesticity, developed in nineteenth-century Europe and the United States, was exported to the colonies and transmitted to colonial and indigenous middle classes alike.[78] Strongly developed in the Netherlands, it also set the agenda in the Dutch Empire. As a result, the proportion of working women remained low in comparison with men, White women entering the labour market were few; only 15 per cent of the European labour force was female compared with 24 per cent in the Netherlands. In the 1930s women in the Netherlands could pursue a university education designed to train them as colonial civil servants, but they were not allowed to enter the service itself, as it was only open to men. White women found work in teaching and nursing, in offices and in domestic service.[79] In the first half of the twentieth century there were no female scholars in the Netherlands working on (parts of) the empire as there were in the United Kingdom.[80] Colonial society was conservative and parochial, and in the 1930s the European population group numbered no more than 240,000 (0.4 per cent of the total population) but lived in a region that reached from Ireland to the Urals.

The cult of domesticity reinforced a colonial rhetoric of the family, rooted in Christianity and cherished in all empires. Colonial subjects were included in this rhetoric as children to be educated by benevolent and paternalistic western guardians. Colonial unity between metropole and periphery might be expressed in the metaphor of a (happy) marriage (east and west belonging to each other as a man and a woman), and in the maternal relationship between a *mère patrie* (mother country) and a childlike colony. In England the Empire Family became a new trope, combining metropole and colony in one.[81] On a smaller scale in the Indies itself, this rhetoric included the indispensable indigenous domestic servants, while 'othering' them at the same time. Here, the rhetoric of the family merged happily with existing indigenous political rhetoric, mentioned earlier. It gendered

1919–1940', MA thesis, University of Amsterdam, 1999. Fridus Steijlen and Erik Willems (eds), *Met ons alles goed: Brieven en films uit Nederlands-Indie van de familie Kuyck* (with DVD; Zutphen, 2008).

78 Judith Walsh, *Domesticity in Colonial India: What Women Learned When Men Gave Them Advice* (Lanham: 2004); Swapna M. Banerjee, *Men, Women and Domestics: Articulating Middle Class Identity in Colonial Bengal* (Oxford, 2004).

79 Locher-Scholten, *Women and the Colonial State*, pp. 123–4. The number of nurses was limited: in 1930 a little more than two hundred nurses with a European degree (headnurses) worked among the 60 million inhabitants. Sciortino, 'Multifariousness of Nursing', p. 39.

80 Barbara Bush, 'Gender and Empire: The Twentieth Century', in Levine (ed.), *Gender and Empire*', pp. 88–9, 103–104; Catherine Hall, 'Of Gender and Empire': Reflections on the Nineteenth Century', in Levine (ed.), *Gender and Empire*, pp. 46–76.

81 Frances Gouda and Julia Clancy-Smith, 'Introduction', in Clancy-Smith and Gouda (eds), *Domesticating the Empire*, p. 7; Bush, 'Gender and Empire', p. 79; Elizabeth Buettner, *Empire Families: Britons and Late Imperial India* (Oxford, 2004).

the colonial project and brought family, women and structures of rule under one linguistic roof.[82]

Dutch domesticity in the colony was stimulated by the presence of white children cared for by indigenous servants. In the interwar years, fears that children would 'go native' grew stronger; white mothers tended to take education away from the indigenous *baboe* (nursemaid) or to appoint white nannies. Unlike the custom in British India, children of colonial families in the Netherlands East Indies were rarely sent to the Netherlands for education. The Netherlands did not have a tradition of boarding schools, while a colonial school system following the Netherlands system developed in the larger colonial cities as of the early twentieth century. Hence, while in British India, as Mary Procida has argued, white women developed a companionate behaviour, focusing on their husbands and their masculine pastimes in reaction to the temporary absence of their children, such attitudes were rare in the Indies.[83]

Political Influence

White women's political influence remained scant. In British India, women of all racial groups won a limited right to vote – for provincial legislatures and restricted by property and literacy – in the 1920s, almost at the same time as in the United Kingdom itself. France did not recognise female voting rights until after the Second World War, either in the metropole or in its colonies. While in the Netherlands Dutch women won the vote in 1918, it would be another seventeen years before a woman was nominated in the Indies proto-parliament, the People's Council. Women of all population groups in the Indies got active voting rights for city councils only in 1941, two weeks before the Japanese attack on Pearl Harbor, when the loyalty of all subjects was in the highest demand. The privilege was limited to elite women who, like male voters, were literate and paid taxes, a mere 2 per cent of Indonesian women. Of the intersecting categories of gender, race and class, class remained the decisive category of exclusion. The outbreak of the Second World War in the Pacific meant that women did not exert their voting rights in the colonial period, but had to wait until the first Indonesian elections of 1955.[84]

In the struggle for the vote in the Indies, Dutch women who belonged to right-wing political parties were the most active champions, convinced of the value of empire and of their Dutch-national rights to defend colonial interests. Efforts to

---

82   It was a rhetoric that nationalists could use ironically as well. Frances Gouda, 'Good Mothers, Medeas, or Jezebels: Feminine Imagery in Colonial and Anticolonial Rhetoric in the Dutch East Indies, 1900–1942', in Clancy-Smith and Gouda (eds), *Domesticating the Empire*, pp. 236–55.

83   Buchheim, 'Geschreven levens'; Buettner, *Empire Families*; Hall, 'Of Gender and Empire', pp. 73–4; Procida, *Married to the Empire*.

84   Locher-Scholten, *Women and the Colonial State*, pp. 151–86.

join forces in this respect with the Indonesian women's movement failed, owing to their claims of superior European experiences. Dutch feminism in the Indies remained embedded in Dutch colonialism and nationalism. Like their British white sisters Dutch women demanded citizenship as the maternal saviours of the empire. Dutch women, too, corroborated their cause with arguments of 'social motherhood' and 'maternal or familial feminism' as educators of the younger generation, and domesticity at large.[85]

The self-appointed colonial task of white women ended in 1942 with the coming of the Japanese to the archipelago. The occupation saw the internment of Europeans, separating white women and children from prisoners of war and male civilians. Only those European women and children who could prove their descent from an Indonesian ancestor were allowed to live outside the camps, leading a life that was hardly less difficult than those interned. After the war, this internment resulted in new perceptions by white men who now admired women who had managed to survive as 'strong heroines'.[86] Yet despite their necessarily independent behaviour during the war, most women returned remarkably easily to their original role as 'incorporated wives'. They did not claim the leading positions they had had in the women's internment camps. After the years of war and diplomacy (1945–49) of the Indonesian Revolution, their physical presence and influence disappeared from the colony. Repatriated to the Netherlands, women (and men) had to find their way in new surroundings, which often led to loss of status and of servants, to social destitution and hard work on a lower level than in the Indies.[87] In independent Indonesia, Indonesian women had to struggle to find their way in politics and administration. Endowed with voting rights and legal equality, they did not see their services to the revolution easily remunerated.[88]

Until now little has been written on the topic of gender and the end of empire; studies on gender and post-colonial memory are more numerous.[89] Both in the colonies and in the metropoles these memories tend to fit a national or nationalist context. In the former colony, memories of the successful revolution have obliterated memories of Dutch colonialism.[90] Moreover, identification with the new

85 Antoinette Burton, *Burden of History: British Feminists, Indian Women, and Imperial Culture, 1865–1915* (Chapel Hill, NC, 1994); Barbara Southard, 'Colonial Politics and Women's Rights: Woman Suffrage Campaigns in Bengal, British India in the 1920s', *Modern Asian Studies* 27 (1993): pp. 397–439.

86 Esther Captain, *'Achter het kawat was Nederland': Indische oorlogservaringen en – herinneringen 1942–1995* (Kampen, 2002).

87 Eveline Buchheim, 'Passie en missie: Huwelijken van Europeanen in Nederlands-Indie/ Indonesië 1920–1958', PhD dissertation, Amsterdam University, 2009.

88 Wieringa, *Sexual Politics*.

89 On gender rhetoric of the period see Frances Gouda, 'Gender and Hypermasculinity as Post-Colonial Modernity during Indonesia's Struggle for Independence, 1945–49', in Antoinette Burton (ed.), *Gender, Sexuality and Colonial Modernities* (New York, 1999), pp. 161–74.

90 William H. Frederick, 'Reflections in a Moving Stream: Indonesian Memories of the War and the Japanese', in Remco Raben (ed.), *Representing the Japanese Occupation of*

nation has inhibited the full deployment of feminist demands, and has determined gender perceptions. In opposition to a more or less despised materialist western womanhood, formerly colonised women have tried to adapt these demands to their indigenous culture and religion. Outright rejection of western ends has been slight to non-existent in Indonesia.[91]

In the west, colonial remembrances remain strongly gendered. European women were and are active agents in the memory industry, stimulating vernacular memorising against the backdrop of the dominant post-colonial narratives and reproducing some of the 'colonial complicities of Western women' of the colonial past.[92] Around 1970, Indies women in the Netherlands were among the first to organise commemorations of the Japanese internment.[93] Influential female authors like Maria Dermout, Hella S. Haasse and Beb Vuyk, Aya Zikken and Marion Bloem[94] have voiced their images of the Indies of the past. Embedded in individual national discourses of historical re-imagination, these memories reflect nostalgia for a lost paradise in a myriad of ways. These memories should be analysed within the context of national histories of empire, as Sara de Mul has recently argued.[95] Yet, these memories may also productively be compared transnationally. In a globalised world, the development of a memory culture, whether of the Second World War or of empire, transcends national borders and reflects similar patterns internationally. There is work to do. The subject of imperialism and gender has not only a past but, without question, also a fruitful future.

    Indonesia (Zwolle, Amsterdam, 1999), pp. 16–35.

91   Wieringa, *Sexual Politics*.

92   Sarah P.J. de Mul, '"Yesterday does not go by": The Return to the Colonial Past in Women's Travel Writing and the Contingencies of Dutch and British Cultures of Remembrance', PhD dissertation, Amsterdam University, 2007, p. 269; Alison Blunt, *Domicile and Diaspora: Anglo-Indian Women and the Spatial Politics of Home* (Oxford, 2005).

93   Elsbeth Locher-Scholten, 'From Urn to Monument: Dutch Memories of World War II in the Pacific, 1945–1995', in Andrea L. Smith (ed.), *Europe's Invisible Migrants* (Amsterdam, 2003), pp. 115–20.

94   De Mul, 'Yesterday does not go by'.

95   Ibid.

Ideology

Ben Silverstein and Patrick Wolfe

For Karl Marx and Friedrich Engels, luminaries of the critique of ideology, ideologies were ideas imposed by a dominant social group on society as a whole. 'The ideas of the ruling class are in every epoch the ruling ideas, i.e. the class which is the ruling *material* force of society, is at the same time its ruling *intellectual* force.'[1] This formulation should not be taken as narrowly as the intellectualist terminology might suggest. As we read on, the 'ideas' that Marx and Engels had in mind emerge as more than formal propositions. They were cultural outlooks or world-views that comprehensively sustained the dominance of one social group over others:

> Insofar, therefore, as they [the ruling class] rule as a class and determine the extent and compass of an epoch, it is self-evident that they do this in its whole range, hence among other things rule also as thinkers, as producers of ideas, and regulate the production and distribution of the ideas of their age: thus their ideas are the ruling ideas of the epoch.[2]

This is not a one-way process. When subordinate groups contest the dominance of a ruling group, they mobilise countervailing ideas to do so. A clash of ideologies ensues. 'For instance, in an age and in a country [Marx and Engels clearly meant France] where royal power, aristocracy, and bourgeoisie are contending for mastery and where, therefore, mastery is shared, the doctrine of the separation of powers proves to be the dominant idea and is expressed as an "eternal law".'[3] As the phrase 'eternal law' suggests, a key feature of ideologies is that they represent a ruling group's dominance as given in nature rather than as historical, the result of human activity.

For Marx and Engels, the ideologies of primary concern were class ideologies – in particular, the ideology sustaining the dominance of the capitalist ruling class – but their understanding of ideology is of more general application, characterising sectional hegemonies such as patriarchy, white supremacism, and religious or

---

1   Karl Marx and Frederick Engels, *The German Ideology* (New York, 1970), p. 64.
2   Ibid., pp. 64–5.
3   Ibid., p. 65.

other cultural forms of domination, all of which have been mobilised in the service of imperialism. This generality stems from ideology's anchorage in representations of nature. Attributing a group's suzerainty to natural processes is a particularly powerful mode of legitimation since it renders the situation seemingly eternal and unchangeable. Just as, for Marx and Engels, bourgeois ideology ascribed capitalist social relations to the eternal propensities of *homo economicus*, so, for instance, does patriarchy appeal to putatively natural endowments, typically ranging from greater physical strength to a superior capacity for reason, whereby men are destined to hold sway over women.

When European powers began to assert their domination over the world outside Europe, domestic ideologies proved themselves readily adaptable to the global setting. In a Catholic context, religious difference provided enduring grounds for the denigration of others, principally Jews within and Muslims without. To a significant extent, Europe became Europe – as opposed to the heterogeneity encompassed under the rubric of western or Latin Christendom – through the 'reconquest' of Muslim Iberia (*alAndalus*), a procedure that was completed a few months before Columbus set off on the voyage (partly financed by funds expropriated from banished Muslims and Jews) that was to take him to the 'New' World.[4] In the Americas, Christian discourses on Jews and Muslims became adaptable to a range of novel alterities, peoples who were not only heathen but whose relationship to Adam was at best uncertain. For Francisco de Vitoria, writing on the cusp of modernity, though the natives of the Indies lacked access to the gospel, they participated in a universal rationality whereby all people created by God could discern the order in His creation. This universal competence obliged Indians and Europeans alike to adhere to the Law of Nations (*jus gentium*), a responsibility that the inhabitants of the New World, with their alleged cannibalism and related depravities, were conspicuously failing to discharge. Though natural law was there for all to divine, some could divine it better than others. From the outset, therefore, universalism indicted colonial difference: on the one hand, natives were equivalent to Europeans in being possessed of reason while, on the other, the uses to which they put that universal human endowment were at odds with the *jus gentium*. Thus the Indians required Spanish intervention, an occurrence rendered likely by the fact that the Spanish were entitled to enforce their right to travel, trade and proselytise in the Indians' country.[5]

As Spanish and Portuguese imperialism confronted the global ascendancy of Protestant Holland and England, the language of European hegemony became increasingly bourgeois and secular. In colonial practice, the Law of Nations

---

4   See, for example, A. Hamdani, 'An Islamic Background to the Voyages of Discovery', in S.K. Jayyusi (ed.), *The Legacy of Muslim Spain* (Leyden, 1992), pp. 273–304; C. Verlinden, *The Beginnings of Modern Colonization* (Ithaca, NY, 1970).

5   Ernest Nys (ed.), *De Indis et De Iure Belli Relectiones being parts of Relectiones Theologicae XII by Franciscus de Victoria* (Washington, DC, 1917), p. 157. See also Robert A. Williams, Jr., *The American Indian in Western Legal Thought: The Discourses of Conquest* (Oxford, 1991), pp. 96–118.

concerned relations between colonial powers rather than between Europeans and natives.[6] To understand the full presumption of, say, the English claim to New York, it is not enough to see it as a denial of Iroquois sovereignty, since the competing sovereignties that the English were principally concerned to deny were not Iroquois but Dutch, French and Swedish. In the secularised doctrine of discovery, the axiomatic discrepancy between natives and Europeans found expression in the utilitarian distinction between dominion, which inhered in European sovereigns, and occupancy, a use-right assigned to natives that was subject to extinguishment at the will of European sovereigns. The total dispensation that this doctrine assigned to European sovereigns in the colonies predated – and, accordingly, furnishes a possible model for – the development of monarchical absolutism in Europe. (This possibility remains available for research.) Though arguably continuing older justifications for taking the land of subjugated peoples, in particular the Roman *vacuum domicilium* and the medieval Norman Yoke, the distinctive configuration of efficiency, utility, rationality and individual enterprise that suffused bourgeois-liberal discourse hallmarked an altogether new concept of property that would have transformative implications abroad as well as at home.

It is a commonplace that capitalism required colonial expansion for its development. Colonies both produced and consumed, furnishing labour and raw materials for capitalist production and markets for its finished products. In the process, both periphery and metropole were transformed. The development of this global network of unequal relationships, whereby the 'west' and the 'rest' historically co-produced each other, was both ideological and material. In Frantz Fanon's incisive inversion, 'Europe is literally the creation of the Third World'.[7] Exported into the colonies, the bourgeois-liberal critique of hereditary landed privilege became a critique of wasteful native occupancy, making nobles of its savages. At its core, this versatile ideology enshrined a concept of efficiency: settled agriculture rendered land capable of sustaining a higher population than it could have supported if left in its natural state, whether as an aristocratic hunting estate in Europe or as unenclosed territory 'roamed by nomads' in the colonies. John Locke's formulation would become canonical:

> [H]e who appropriates land to himself by his labour, does not lessen but increase the common stock of mankind. For the provisions serving to the support of humane life, produced by one acre of inclosed and cultivated land, are (to speak much within compass) ten times more, than those, which are yeilded [sic] by an acre of Land, of an equal richnesse, lyeing wast in common.[8]

---

6   See, for example, L.C. Green, 'Claims to Territory in Colonial America', in Green and Olive P. Dickason (eds), *The Law of Nations and the New World* (Alberta, 1989), pp. 125–6.

7   Frantz Fanon, *The Wretched of the Earth* (New York, 2004), p. 81.

8   John Locke, *Two Treatises of Government* (Cambridge, 1964), vol. 2, chap. 5 ('Of Property'), para. 37.

Exported to the New World, this formula provided grounds for dispossession. 'All the world', as Locke famously put it, had once been America, a primordial condition that was above all distinguished by the failure to cultivate.[9] Two centuries later, in an antipodean portion of the southern ocean that had been unknown to Locke, the same resilient principle – conventionally glossed as the doctrine of *terra nullius* – would provide that, in failing to cultivate, to irrigate and to fence, Australian Aborigines had failed to attain a level of historical development that was consonant with property ownership. The land did not belong to them. It was there for the taking.[10]

But early colonial ideology did not restrict itself to free-market principles. As many scholars have noted, a symbolic universe left over from preceding eras of European culture furnished a rich demonology that was readily displaced outward onto the native realm. In addition to the blood libel and other outrages attributed to Jews and Muslims, European folklore was replete with witches, wild men, anthropophages, werewolves and the like, most of whom duly became reborn in the colonial world, providing a warrant for colonial violence.[11] As Charles Zika has demonstrated, for instance, the iconography of witchcraft in early modern Germany included a set of coded representations, in particular the cannibal barbecue, common to coeval representations of the natives of the New World.[12] Indeed, such was the opportunism of colonial ideology that practically minded commercial adventurers could be capable of believing in fairy tales so long as they took place outside Europe.

As selected into colonial discourse, however, the timeless figures of European folklore acquired historical specificity. They were put to particular ideological uses under particular historical circumstances. The cannibal, for instance, is a figure of the frontier, of the violent interlude when European domination had yet to be consolidated. Hence the hapless European in the giant cooking-pot was stereotypically a missionary, harbinger and emblem of the colonial advance guard. Whether in age-of-exploration Fiji (the 'Cannibal Islands'), scrambled-for Africa, Maori-War New Zealand or frontier Australia, natives who remained capable of military resistance to European intrusion became invested with the reproach of cannibalism. At its simplest, the consumption of human flesh was such a depraved activity that it marked its practitioners out as deserving of extirpation. It also violated the rigorous differentiation of self and other, of coloniser and colonised, that imperial ideology required, which was confounded by the pre-cultural universality of shared flesh. Moreover, given its resonance with Christianity's

---

9   Ibid., vol. 2, chap. 5, para. 49. The immediate referent was the use of money ('for no such thing as *Money* was anywhere known' – i.e., when all the world was America).

10   Alan Frost, 'New South Wales as *Terra Nullius*: The British Denial of Aboriginal Land Rights', in S. Janson and S. Macintyre (eds), *Through White Eyes* (Sydney, 1990), pp. 65–76.

11   See, for example, Roger Barta, *Wild Men in the Looking Glass: The Mythic Origins of European Otherness* (Ann Arbor, MI, 1994) and Rudolf Wittkower's classic 'Marvels of the East: A Study in the History of Monsters', *Journal of the Warburg and Courtauld Institutes* 5 (1942): pp. 159–97.

12   Charles Zika, 'Cannibalism and Witchcraft in Early Modern Europe: Reading the Visual Images', *History Workshop Journal* 44 (1997): pp. 77–105.

central rite, cannibalism had a particular purchase on European sensitivity, lending piquance to Shakespeare's anagrammatic Caliban, which would be corroborated in its association with missionaries. Thus cannibals in the colonial world were much more than simple reincarnations of the generic anthropophages of European mythology. Indeed, they even owe their name to colonialism. When Columbus first landed in the Americas, he immediately inaugurated one of imperialism's characteristic techniques of domination, that of divide and rule, distinguishing between the good natives, Tainos and Arawaks, who welcomed and cooperated (some would say collaborated) with him, and the hostile Caribs, after whom the Caribbean was named. The Caribs were to lend their name to more than a sea. The friendly natives feared them as eaters of human flesh, a propensity that led Columbus to link the Caribs to Herodotus' anthropophages ($\alpha\nu\theta\rho\omega\pi\sigma\varsigma$ – human; $\phi\alpha\gamma\epsilon\iota\nu$ – to eat).[13] By way of Spanish and Romance, 'carib' became 'canib', a specifically colonial invention manufactured from historically European materials.

Thus we should not see imperial ideology as inertly channelling eternal European themes. As Edward Said recognised in dating orientalism from the eighteenth century,[14] the rise of Islamophobia in contemporary western societies is not simply a reactivation of the ideology of the Crusades, seen as imperviously waiting in the wings of history. Indeed, the very idea that certain themes have an abiding potency that transcends the historical process is itself an ideological (not to say fundamentalist) construct, since it renders that potency immutable. Winthrop Jordan made this mistake when he attributed Europeans' negative attitude to Africans to a deeply sedimented cultural opposition between the timeless archetypes light/white, which was positively valued, and dark/black, which was correspondingly denigrated.[15] Accounting for racism in this way not only makes it hard to resist, it also dilutes the historical specificity of the particular ideologies that accompanied institutional practices such as chattel slavery in the United States. Semantically, the quality of blackness may provide a superficial link between Othello and scientific racism's negro, but the two shared little else.

The Moor's primary ideological characteristic was a religious lack, the state of being non-Christian, rather than a set of essential deficits attaching to the colour of his skin. As is apparent from Islamophobia in the modern world, racism does not require the biogenetic vocabulary that was historically associated with, say, slavery in the United States or anti-semitism in Nazi Germany. Indeed, discrimination does not require race. Exclusionary ideologies can employ a range of registers, whether biological (heredity, blood, genes) or cultural (religion, civilisation, mind), typically in combination, to compatible ends. The point is the exclusion rather than the idiom through which it is expressed. In turning to one of imperialism's master-ideologies, that of race, then, it is important to dispense with the idea, still apparent in some

---

13 Peter Hulme, 'Columbus and the Cannibals', in his *Colonial Encounters: Europe and the Native Caribbean, 1492–1797* (London, 1986), pp. 13–43.
14 Edward W. Said, *Orientalism: Western Conceptions of the Orient* (New York, 1979).
15 Winthrop Jordan, *White Over Black: American Attitudes Toward the Negro* (Chapel Hill, NC, 1968).

anti-racist scholarship, that racial ideology operates on a naturally present set of attributes that are already given outside history. Racial identities are constructed in and through the very process of their exclusion. The process, exclusion, is prior. It produces the ontology. To illustrate this point, we can remain with the settler-colonisation of America.

Imperial Ideologies of Race

The regimes of race that were respectively imposed on enslaved people and natives in the course of constructing the empire state were revealingly antithetical. As exported into Euroamerican colonial ideology, Lockean discourse became racially coded. The premise that private property accrued from the mixture of labour and land acquired a supplement: blacks provided the former and Indians the latter – the application of enslaved black people's labour to expropriated Indian land produced the white man's property, a primitive accumulation if ever there was one. It followed that, where black people were valuable commodities, Indians, with their counter-claim to land, only obstructed the expansion of settler society. This disparity between blacks and Indians produced a corresponding antithesis in the ways in which the two groups were racialised. Black people's value as labour was registered in a racial calculus whereby no amount of miscegenation would affect a person's status as a slave, and, in the wake of emancipation, as a black person – a regime that culminated in the so-called 'one-drop rule', whereby any amount of black ancestry, regardless of physical appearance, makes a person black.[16] The founding logic of this calculus is brutally obvious – it maximised the reproduction of slaves. In the case of Indians, by contrast (as in the case of Indigenous people in Australia), rather than being endlessly resistant to admixture, non-white blood became highly unstable. White blood had the cuckoo-like effect of breeding nativeness out – an assimilationist extension of frontier homicide that was diametrically opposed to the one-drop rule that applied to the formerly enslaved. Thus there is nothing stable or essential about being black, since black people in Australia were targeted for biocultural elimination in a manner antithetical to the racial targeting of black people in the United States.[17] Whether classified red or black, Indigenous people in both countries have been racialised in almost indistinguishable ways.[18] Accordingly,

16 F. James Davis, *Who Is Black? One Nation's Definition* (University Park, PA, 1991); Pauli Murray, *States' Laws on Race and Color* (Athens, GA, 1997 [1950]).
17 National Inquiry into the Separation of Aboriginal and Torres Strait Islander Children from their Families, *Bringing Them Home: Report of the National Inquiry into the Separation of Aboriginal and Torres Strait Islander Children and their Families* (Canberra, 1997); Anna Haebich, *Broken Circles: Fragmenting Indigenous Families 1800–2000* (Freemantle, WA, 2000). For a cogent comparative study, see Katherine Ellinghaus, 'Biological Absorption and Genocide: A Comparison of Indigenous Assimilation Policies in the United States and Australia', *Genocide Studies and Prevention* 4/1 (2009): pp. 59–79.
18 Patrick Wolfe, 'Land, Labor, and Difference: Elementary Structures of Race', *American*

we should not see exclusion simply negatively, as withholding or as banishment. Rather, outcast (in this case, racial) categories are positively constituted through being excluded. To say that social categories are excluded in different ways is, therefore, to say that excluded categories are constituted differently.

Race's multifaceted versatility was sufficient to accommodate imperialism's complexity. For every articulation – relations of slavery, of indenture, of dispossession, of compradorship, (inter)mediation, mercantile exchange – a corresponding racial category could spring into discourse. Accordingly, just as, for Durkheim, religion was society speaking,[19] so, we might say, race is imperialism speaking, in idioms whose diversity reflects the variety of unequal relationships into which Europeans have coopted conquered populations.

Viewed only in practice, however, as orchestrating imperialism's local hierarchies of difference, race might seem to constitute an ideology without an idea. Running through and discursively binding together all the local racialisations was the taxonomic inheritance of Enlightenment natural science, the 'analytic of finitude' which, as Michel Foucault pointed out, finally rendered humanity of a piece with surrounding nature.[20] There is general agreement that the modern concept of race became recognisably consolidated in the late eighteenth century.[21] We may cite 1795, the year in which, in the third edition of his *De generis humanae varietate*, Johann Friedrich Blumenbach first linked five distinct races of man to five human skull types as viewed from (where else?) above, the *norma verticalis*. But a precise moment of origin is not so important as the fact that racial science brought together the two principal strands of Enlightenment discourse – namely, liberal politics and taxonomic natural philosophy (which was yet to be called science). Liberalism was born of exclusion, the beneficiaries of its ostensibly universal entitlements being distinctly particular.[22] To this we might add that the taxonomies of eighteenth-century science were quintessentially hierarchical. To incorporate different categories of humanity into these taxonomies was, therefore, to imbue the hierarchical ranking of human groups with the objective imprimatur of natural science. This is ideology in the strictest definitional sense that we noted at the outset, the assimilation of human power relations to nature.

Enlightenment racial science provided an organising grammar of imperial control. In late-eighteenth-century thought, the stages of human social development came to be seen not only hierarchically (neither the ancient Greeks nor the Hebrews doubted that urban society was superior to nomadism) but cumulatively as well.

Historical Review 106 (2001): pp. 865–905; cf. Ellinghaus, 'Biological Absorption and Genocide'.

19   Emile Durkheim, *The Elementary Forms of Religious Life* (Oxford, 2001).

20   '[M]an appears in his ambiguous position as an object of knowledge and as a subject that knows', Michel Foucault, *The Order of Things: An Archaeology of the Human Sciences* (London, 1974), p. 312.

21   See, for example, Ian Hannaford, *Race: The History of an Idea in the West* (Baltimore, MD, 1996); Kenan Malik, *The Meaning of Race: Race, History and Culture in Western Society* (Houndsmills, 1996).

22   Uday Mehta, 'Liberal Strategies of Exclusion', *Politics and Society* 18 (1990): pp. 427–54.

For Adam Smith, John Millar and other scions of the Scottish Enlightenment, it was not just that settled agriculturalists were superior to nomadic pastoralists. Rather, settled agriculturalists had once been pastoralists themselves, but had passed through this stage and improved upon it, subsequently progressing still further to the commercial city.[23] Thus developed the fateful imperialist formula that 'their' (colonial) present was 'our' (European) past. This view collapsed time and space: to leave Europe was to travel back in time, whether to the moribund avatar of European feudalism that was held to obtain in India or to the old stone age that was seen to persist in Australia. With a plenitude reminiscent of the Great Chain of Being, unilinear evolutionism had a niche for everyone.[24]

Politically, Enlightenment thought confronted a contradiction: globally, the bourgeois class that was counterposing the liberal-democratic rights of man to aristocratic privilege was simultaneously subjecting certain subordinate categories of humanity, notably enslaved Africans, to particular forms of treatment that were at odds with universalist political rhetoric. As a taxonomy, race resolved this embarrassment, categorically separating the bearers of the rights of man from other species within the heterogeneity making up *genus* (or was it?) *homo*. Contradictory as it was, this perspective did not pass unchallenged. There were always those – emancipationists, abolitionists, the Exeter Hall group – who sought to hold imperialism to account on its own, generally lofty, terms. Such opposition was not always as philanthropic as it claimed. It could, for instance, stem from an interest in investments in the East – as opposed to the West – Indies.[25] Nonetheless, significant opposition was voiced. In addition to domestic dissent, we should emphasise the less-compromised protests of the colonised themselves, whether voiced in the genteel phraseology of incipient colonial nationalism or in the more explicit terminology of slave, native or sepoy insurgency, already dubbed 'terrorism' by the early twentieth century.[26] Again, therefore, we should not view imperial ideology as a one-way process. As well as its failure to capture non-European systems of meaning and sources of resistance, it generated its own opposition and incubated its own contradictions, in many cases with ultimately emancipatory consequences – though the settler-colonised are, on the whole, still waiting.

Marx observed that, in producing an urban proletariat to staff its factories, the industrial bourgeoisie had managed to create a standing army in its midst.[27]

---

23   Ronald L. Meek, *Social Science and the Ignoble Savage* (Cambridge, 1976).

24   Arthur O. Lovejoy, *The Great Chain of Being: A Study of the History of an Idea* (Cambridge, MA, 1936).

25   Catherine Hall, *Civilising Subjects: Metropole and Colony in the English Imagination, 1830–1867* (Chicago, IL, 2002).

26   John C. Ker, *Political Trouble in India* (Delhi, 1917).

27   'But not only has the bourgeoisie forged the weapons that bring death to itself; it has also called into existence the men who are to wield these weapons – the modern working class – the proletarians ... Masses of labourers crowded into the factory are organised like soldiers.' Karl Marx and Friedrich Engels, *The Communist Manifesto* (Harmondsworth, 2002), chap. 1 ('Bourgeois and Proletarians').

Less specifically, Foucault asserted that power generates its own opposition.[28] As Hobson and, following him, Lenin would point out, industrial capitalism relied on imperialism for its expansion.[29] The European proletariat were not the only docile bodies that industrialisation required. In settler colonies, factory discipline had long been prefigured, albeit unfreely, in plantation slavery's coercive regimes.[30] Towards the end of the eighteenth century, however, the industrial revolution began to inaugurate a profound shift in European capitalism's management of its colonial trade (for a key date, we might choose 1793, two years prior to Blumenbach's cranial hierarchy, when Cornwallis unveiled his Permanent Settlement of Bengal). Compared with the close control of production and consumption that industrialists would come to require, the mercantile relationships that had centred about coastal entrepôts had been relatively unintrusive. Like the intercultural middle ground about the Great Lakes that Richard White has magisterially narrated, with its assorted boundary-straddlers, *coureurs du bois*, mixed marriages, *métis* and related hybridities, mercantilism had produced dependency but not – at least, not on a general scale – directed exploitation.[31] The indigenous goods exchanged on the colonial market had not been produced under European control. Native dependency had not extended to the wholesale directedness that would characterise labour on the plantations and in the mines, railways, timber-mills and fisheries of industrial capitalism's expansive global network. Industrialisation required that both supply and demand, production and consumption, be strictly regulated. This requirement caused colonial modernity's disciplinary regimes to penetrate Native societies ever more intrusively – scrutinising, prescribing and controlling down to levels of life more intimate than those that mercantilism had sought to incorporate. These more intrusive regimes of control generated novel forms of anti-colonial resistance.

They also sought to form novel colonial subjectivities, a project that has recently conduced to post-colonial analyses in which imperial ideology has acquired a psychosomatic comprehensiveness that exceeds an ideational critique of historical consciousness. Understood, in Foucauldian terms, as positivity, imperial ideology provided very particular descriptions of otherness that simultaneously incorporated their subjects into the global frame of empire.

In concert with our charting of imperialism's global career – of macrophenomena such as the shift from mercantilism to industrialisation; imperial rivalries and the consolidation of the nation-state; the global shrinkage brought about by steam, railway and the telegraph; settler population growth and the explosion of European migration; the nineteenth-century revolution in techniques of warfare; the ascendancy of the US and the decline of the Ottomans – we need to inscribe the

---

28   Michel Foucault, *The History of Sexuality: An Introduction* (London, 1978), pp. 95–6.
29   J.A. Hobson, *Imperialism: A Study* (London, 1902); V.I. Lenin, *Imperialism, the Highest Stage of Capitalism* (Peking, 1964 [1916]).
30   For discussion and references, see Robin Blackburn, *The Making of New World Slavery: From the Baroque to the Modern, 1492–1800* (London, 1997), pp. 332–3.
31   Richard White, *The Middle Ground: Indians, Empires, and Republics in the Great Lakes Region, 1650–1815* (Cambridge, 1991).

local ideologies of difference that were shaped in colonial encounters, in the clash of cultures and economies, in ambivalent contexts of fragmentary universalism and haunting insecurity.[32] These ideologies were anchored in asymmetrical relationships that not only set out classes of rulers and ruled but were also sites of contest over the manner of rule: the form of a colonised population was inextricably bound up in the form of its colonial state. To map this heterogeneity requires deeply specific studies of colonial agendas and cultures that were ubiquitously riven with conflict and fluidity. This is nowhere more apparent than in the heterogeneous local elaborations of imperialism's master category of race, the bedrock operator of white supremacism that Partha Chatterjee has termed (with questionable singularity) the 'rule of colonial difference'.[33]

Introducing a collection of works on race, Henry Louis Gates, Jr, cites the case of Phillis Wheatley. In 1772, eighteen of Boston's most notable colonists undertook an oral examination of Wheatley, then an eighteen-year-old slave who claimed to have written a short book of poems. The group's interrogation was intended to ascertain whether she had, in fact, done so by herself. The 'Attestation' the group produced, which formed the preface to her book, enabled the publication of her work. The signatories acknowledged that 'Numbers would be ready to suspect they were not really the Writings of Phillis.'[34] But it was in fact possible for an African to write poetry, to produce art. Africans, it could now be argued, could learn to possess reason, write, and become fully human, no longer destined to be enslaved forever. Race, within this early emancipationist discourse, was not an ultimate barrier to progress.

The liberal idea that people of non-white (or non-Anglo-Saxon) races could become civilised – through education, conversion, work, wealth or, in the Jamaican case, 'apprenticeship' – expressed an imperial optimism that prevailed well into the nineteenth century.[35] This was not an uncontested optimism. In the United States, for every northern emancipationist, there was a seigneurial southerner who insisted on his human property's irretrievable debasement. When it came to natives, moreover, even liberal northerners could endorse Indian Removal, a policy that refused any possibility of assimilation or improvement.[36] So far as subject races – which is to say, those scheduled for exploitation rather than elimination – were concerned, however, liberal ideology in the first half of the nineteenth century presupposed

---

32   Nicholas Thomas, *Colonialism's Culture: Anthropology, Travel and Government* (Cambridge, 1994), p. 15.

33   Partha Chatterjee, *The Nation and Its Fragments: Colonial and Postcolonial Histories* (Princeton, NJ, 1993).

34   Phillis Wheatley, Preface to *Poems on Various Subjects, Religious and Moral* (London, 1773), cited in Henry Louis Gates, Jr, 'Writing "Race" and the Difference It Makes', in Henry Louis Gates, Jr (ed.), *'Race,' Writing and Difference* (Chicago, IL, 1986), pp. 7–8.

35   See Uday Mehta, *Liberalism and Empire: A Study in Nineteenth-Century British Liberal Thought* (Chicago, IL, 1999).

36   Richard B. Latner, *The Presidency of Andrew Jackson: White House Politics 1829–1837* (Athens, GA, 1979), pp. 97–8. See also Laurence M. Hauptman, *Tribes and Tribulations: Misconceptions about American Indians and their Histories* (Albuquerque, NM, 1995), p. 39.

a benign mutability on the part of the colonised. A major victory for the civilising mission was the 1829 British abolition of the practice of *sati*, which required Indian widows to burn alive on the funeral pyres of their husbands. Exemplifying the colonial warrant that Gayatri Chakravorty Spivak famously characterised as 'white men rescuing brown women from brown men', the controversial abolition performed a white masculinity that would intervene in the colonies for the benefit and progress of subject peoples, here embodied in the feminised victim of tradition.[37] This pointed not only to 'the genius of the race' for colonising and governing, but also to a vision of subject races as improvable, if only they could be liberated from the tyranny of custom. Thus the use of Wheatley's writing to evidence her capacity for reason and civilisation would find an echo, half a century later and in a very different theatre of empire, in the native education policies of Lord Macaulay. Macaulay's 1835 'Minute on Indian Education' overturned the sanskritised policies of Orientalists such as William Jones and Warren Hastings. In their stead, he prescribed an anglicised education for an emergent Indian middle class, immortalising the aim of British liberalism in India:

> We must at present do our best to form a class who may be interpreters between us and the millions whom we govern [–] a class of persons Indian in blood and colour, but English in tastes, in opinions, in morals and in intellect.[38]

Race was something to be worked around: Indians could attain a mimetic Englishness, though the recalcitrance of blood and colour was emphatic. In Homi Bhabha's celebrated phrase, the anglicised Indian would always confront the visible barrier that his Englishness was 'almost the same, but not quite'.[39] While, for colonisers, this resemblance could approach unsettlingly close to the real thing, its 'not-quiteness', an achievement of the work of race, imposed an absolute limit on the educated Indian's access to a universal ambience that was indelibly coded white.

The second half of the nineteenth century saw a progressive abandonment of British liberal optimism in favour of a hardened racial supremacism, prefigured in Thomas Carlyle's 1853 pamphlet, *Occasional Discourse on the Nigger Question*, that

37   Gayatri Chakravorty Spivak, 'Can the Subaltern Speak?', in Cary Nelson and Lawrence Grossberg (eds), *Marxism and the Interpretation of Culture* (Urbana, IL, 1988), pp. 271–313. See also Lata Mani, *Contentious Traditions: The Debate on Sati in Colonial India* (Berkeley, CA, 1998). Cf. Patrick Wolfe, 'Can the Muslim Speak? An Indebted Critique', *History and Theory* 41 (2002): pp. 367–80.

38   'Minute Recorded in the General Department by Thomas Babington Macaulay, law member of the governor-general's council, dated 2 February 1835', in Lynn Zastoupil and Martin Moir (eds), *The Great Indian Education Debate: Documents Relating to the Orientalist-Anglicist Controversy, 1781–1843* (Richmond, Surrey, 1999), p. 171. For a history of colonial pedagogy in India, see Sanjay Seth, *Subject Lessons: The Western Education of Colonial India* (Durham, NC, 2007).

39   Homi K. Bhabha, 'Of Mimicry and Man', in *The Location of Culture* (London, 1994), pp. 121–31.

took hold in response to the widespread local resistance provoking the expansion of empire. This shift reflected a series of imperial crises, each of which could be attributed to a failure of the civilising mission. The Indian 'Mutiny' of 1857–58, the New Zealand Land Wars of the 1860s, the US Civil War of 1861–65, the Morant Bay Rebellion of 1865, the continuing violence and instability of the South African and Queensland frontiers, combined with Fenianism in Ireland and such worrying developments as the catastrophic colonial death rates being recorded throughout the Pacific, prompted a reformulation of the nature of racial difference and the ends of colonialism.[40] The ideology of universal progress in which all could participate, albeit in different time frames, gave way to a more selective programme that would prepare different colonial subjects for different visions of progress. Not only was there a shift in imperial ideologies; ideology produced the empire differently.

Controlling Ideologies

In a reversal of agency, anti-colonial resistance was represented not as a response to oppression but as a failure of command, command itself being seen to rest on knowledge. Thus imperialism came to be viewed as vulnerable to failures of knowledge. The most common English explanation for the Indian Mutiny was that an offence had been caused to native religious sentiment, the entire conflagration being reduced to the single spark of a cavalry regiment rising up in support of colleagues who had been punished for refusing to use cartridges coated in a mixture of pork and beef fat, offensive to Hindu and Muslim sepoys alike. The lesson, therefore, was one of attending to the precariousness of a colonial regime that rested on inadequate knowledge. Without a better and more penetrating understanding of native manners and customs, colonial rule would continue to produce populations whose instability would undermine the steady march of progress.[41] In similar fashion, the Morant Bay Rebellion of 1865, an imperial scandal that followed on the heels of the Mutiny, was presented as an issue of both racial governance and the ends of colonisation. Following a small riot over a disputed fine, Governor Edward Eyre, citing fear of a wider uprising, declared martial law and sent in the troops, killing hundreds and destroying over a thousand homes.

---

40 Bernard Porter, *The Lion's Share: A Short History of British Imperialism*, 4th edn (Harlow, 2004), pp. 49–67; Chris Youé, 'Mamdani's History', *Canadian Journal of African Studies* 34/2 (2000): pp. 397–408; Thomas C. Holt, *The Problem of Freedom: Race, Labor and Politics in Jamaica and Britain 1832–1938* (Baltimore, MD, 1992); James Belich, *The New Zealand Wars and the Victorian Interpretation of Racial Conflict* (Auckland, 1986); David Routledge, *Matanitu: The Struggle for Power in Early Fiji* (Suva, 1985).

41 The gendered English satire of the educated Bengali *babu*, whose effeminacy came to stand for the degeneracy of educated Indians as a whole, is an important example. See Seth, *Subject Lessons*, pp. 47–78; Mrinalini Sinha, *Colonial Masculinity: The 'Manly Englishman' and the 'Effeminate Bengali' in the Late Nineteenth Century* (Manchester and New York, 1995).

He was recalled to England, where his actions prompted furious public debate as to whether the use of force against black subjects was inevitable or whether some form of improvement could be achieved.[42]

Along with the need to reform native subjectivities, controversies such as these were also narrated in the imperial imagination as necessitating a reconstruction of white masculinity. The Mutiny figured incessantly as a story of Indian men doing unspeakable things to white women, the colonial spectre of interracial sexual assault constituting a general outrage against British womanhood and providing the opportunity for a powerful yet protective manhood.[43] Fascination with such violence was also central to re-tellings of the Morant Bay Rebellion, as debate in the metropole revolved around different notions of masculinity.[44] If white men were to re-assert their power to protect white women, let alone brown or black ones, they would need to re-establish their commanding knowledge of other societies.[45] The fragmentation of racial difference that constructed colonial subjects as incessantly tribal, or as members of unchanging castes, was thus also a project of white masculine reconstruction, consolidating a relational position of total and universal knowledge. White men were situated above and panoptically looking down on all others, casting a penetrating scientific gaze into racial differences and enumerating further subdivided populations.

In British India, 'Hindus' (almost everyone other than Muslims) came to be comprehended in terms of caste divisions (*varna* rather than *jati*) derived from brahmanical scripture. Two post-1857 projects, the census and the *Imperial Gazetteer of India*, solidified caste as the central organising principle of Indian society.[46] A colonial invention, caste was inscribed in this form at the intersection of race and occupation, a joinder which, in the case of 'criminal castes and tribes', could constitute an irredeemable state of exception. William Hunter, creator of the *Gazetteer*, wrote that:

> [W]hile caste has thus its foundations deep in the distinctions of race, its superstructure is regulated by another system of division, based on the occupations of the people. The early classification of the people

42 Catherine Hall, *White, Male and Middle Class: Explorations in Feminism and History* (New York, 1992), pp. 280–83; Julie Evans, *Edward Eyre, Race and Colonial Governance* (Dunedin, 2005), pp. 133–49.

43 Catherine Hall, 'Of Gender and Empire: Reflections on the Nineteenth Century', in Philippa Levine (ed.), *Gender and Empire* (Oxford, 2004), p. 72; Angela Woollacott, *Gender and Empire* (Basingstoke, 2006), p. 7.

44 Hall, *White, Male and Middle Class*, pp. 255–95; Hall, *Civilising Subjects*.

45 Trinh T. Minh-Ha, *Woman, Native, Other: Writing Postcoloniality and Feminism* (Bloomington, IN, 1989), pp. 48–9. Cf. Sara Mills, *Discourses of Difference: An Analysis of Women's Travel Writing and Colonialism* (London, 1991).

46 Nicholas B. Dirks, *Castes of Mind: Colonialism and the Making of Modern India* (Princeton, NJ, 2001). On the census, see Bernard Cohn, 'The Census, Social Structure and Objectification in South Asia', in Cohn, *An Anthropologist among the Historians and Other Essays* (Oxford, 1987), pp. 224–54.

may be expressed either ethnically as 'twice-born' Aryans, and 'once-born' non-Aryans; or socially, as priests, warriors, husbandman, and serfs. On these two principles of classification, according to race and employment, still further modified by geographical position, has been built up the ethnical and social organization of Indian caste.[47]

A colonial mytho-history, in which Aryan invaders from the northwest mixed to varying extents with indigenous races, provided a colour-coded schedule of castes, significantly dominated by European criteria, at the same time as it mapped an evolutionary hierarchy onto the caste system's distinctive division of labour.[48] In liberal discourse, caste provided the antithesis par excellence to bourgeois society's allegedly achieved distinctions. Caste stood for the dead hand of tradition – for birth rather than merit, for status rather than contract – in a manner that refurbished the domestic critique of aristocratic privilege for colonial export. Standing in for Europe's feudal past, Hindu society was counterposed to a versatile ideological formation that was simultaneously dispossessing natives at opposite ends of the earth, whether as *terra nullius* in Australia or as Manifest Destiny in the United States. As in the case of race, therefore, so in the diverse ontologies of caste or tribe, the issue is not the classificatory details but the colonising function of classification itself.

In Britain's sub-Saharan African colonies, the totalising unit of colonial knowledge was the tribe. Every African everywhere came to be understood as submerged in the tribe, ruled by a chief and inertly subject to the rigidities of customary law. This preoccupation with order and stability amidst rapid change, valuing 'tradition' even as precolonial social forms were radically transformed, was, of course, multiply contradictory. The colonial transformation notwithstanding, tribes figured as changeless, eternal and primordial.[49] The 'Hamitic hypothesis' – whereby, much like the Aryan invasions of India, a lighter-skinned racial group was said to have invaded from the north – differentiated racialised populations throughout Africa. Some tribes – monolithically, predictably, each to their place – were born to work, some were born lazy. Some, more ominously, were born warriors.[50] Race here became spatial rather than temporal. Thus South African Prime Minister B.J. Vorster could still claim, in 1973, that: 'If I were to wake up one morning and find myself a black man, the only major difference would be geographical.'[51]

---

47 William Wilson Hunter, *The Indian Empire: Its Peoples, History, and Products* (London, 1886), p. 192, cited in John Marriott, *The Other Empire: Metropolis, India and Progress in the Colonial Imagination* (Manchester, 2003), p. 210.
48 Marriott, *The Other Empire*, pp. 212–13.
49 For the colonial construction of the tribe, see Leroy Vail (ed.), *The Creation of Tribalism in Southern Africa* (London, 1989), and Mahmood Mamdani, *Citizen and Subject: Contemporary Africa and the Legacy of Late Colonialism* (Princeton, NJ, 1996).
50 Edith R. Sanders, 'The Hamitic Hypothesis: Its Origin and Functions in Time Perspective', *Journal of African History* 10/4 (1969): pp. 521–32. Cf. Cheikh Anta Diop, *Civilization or Barbarism: An Authentic Anthropology* (Chicago, IL, 1991).
51 Cited in David Theo Goldberg, *Racist Culture: Philosophy and the Politics of Meaning* (Oxford, 1993), p. 185.

From the late nineteenth century onward, a focus on race in such colonies illuminates the workings of exclusion. As such, it tells us much about the basic order of colonial difference and about the whiteness constructed in colonial and 'post'colonial societies. As Mahmood Mamdani argues, however, it has less to tell us about the ideological formation of the colonial state.[52] For this, we need to attend to the divisive ideologies of incorporation whereby colonial subjects came to be conceived, below the level of race, as caste-bound or tribal. These theories of societies intersected with and constituted ideologies of colonial government. Thus the shift towards understanding subject populations as fragmentary coincided with, and conduced to, a change in colonial governmentality, whether to indirect rule, as in the British Empire, or to *association*, as in the French.[53]

Many historians link the transition to such forms of government as reflective of a conservative opposition to progress, as a desire to preserve native societies in an antiquarian state. While there may have been a step away from the more extravagant claims of the civilising mission, the ideal of material improvement – a key component of Victorian progress and the French Third Republic's *mission civilatrice* – was never abandoned. Thus, in Frederick Lugard's classic account of the work of colonial administration, *The Dual Mandate in British Tropical Africa*, the duality referred both to trusteeship of the advancement of subject races and to the development of colonial resources for the benefit of all mankind. Such advancement and development could be encouraged by disciplining the productive power of native labour:

> The Bantus, and most other negroes, are physically fine specimens of the human race. Powerfully built, they are capable of great feats of strength and endurance. Individuals will carry a load of 100 lbs. on their heads from morning till night, up hills and through swamps, with but brief intervals for rest.[54]

Tribalised within the overall category of race ('The Bantus, and most other negroes'), ethnographic divisions of labour could be mobilised in the interests of progress, providing a basis for both development and a re-thought civilising mission.

These units of colonial control rested on a discursive paradox that Karuna Mantena describes as a 'holistic vision of native society as both functionally intact and vulnerable to imminent dissolution'.[55] This perception of vulnerability, which

---

52 Mahmood Mamdani, 'Historicizing Power and Responses to Power: Indirect Rule and Its Reform', *Social Research* 66/3 (1999), p. 864.

53 On indirect rule, see Frederick Lugard, *The Dual Mandate in British Tropical Africa* (Edinburgh, 1922) and William Malcolm Hailey, *An African Survey: A Study of Problems Arising in Africa South of the Sahara* (London, 1938). On association, see Raymond F. Betts, *Assimilation and Association in French Colonial Theory, 1890–1914* (Lincoln, NE, 2005).

54 Lugard, *The Dual Mandate*, p. 68.

55 Karuna Mantena, 'Henry Maine and the Theoretical Origins of Indirect Rule', in Andrew Lewis and Michael Lobban (eds), *Law and History* (Oxford, 2003), p. 184.

she traces to the work of Henry Maine, suggested a form of colonial rule that diverged from the civilising mission. Rather, a technique of governmentality that worked to harness the forces within native societies became normalised. Maine, in this way, prefigures the development of functionalist anthropology in the 1920s, with its now obvious affinities with the developing colonial ideologies of government.[56]

The ethnographic ideologies of caste and tribe were inherently fragmentary, suppressing potential solidarities that were an unwelcome byproduct of the rule of colonial difference. Moreover, as noted, their rise was contemporaneous with a shift in the form of colonial exploitation. By the late nineteenth century, the reconfiguration of colonial economies in the interest of metropolitan capital, combined with domestic pressure to assuage the growing discontent of the metropolitan working class, intensified the exploitation of colonial labour. In post-slavery empires, organisational hierarchies such as the specialist caste or the authoritarian tribe furnished divisions of labour that could be recruited both to maximise the efficiency of colonial societies' productive forces and to obstruct the development of anti-colonial solidarities.[57]

This is not to say that European colonisers produced these objects of knowledge out of nothing, without reference to the lives or experiences of colonised people. Placing caste and religion at the centre of Indian society reflected the perspective of conservative Brahmins, while the African tribe was informed by the desire of many African men to exercise control over land, labour and women.[58] In such cases, the crucial question was which sections of native society could exercise influence over European understandings of traditional custom. Colonial ideologies were sites of interaction and struggle. Important affinities were established between European and Native elites, which provided both ideological and material means of cooptation into the universalised hierarchies of colonial discourse.[59]

The immense work that went into making caste and tribal identities real was also an enterprise that incorporated colonial elites. The invention of tradition was less an imposition than the outcome of a weighted dialogue that interpellated colonial subjects.[60] The effects of this interpellation were diagnosed by Frantz Fanon in his

---

56 See, for example, Talal Asad (ed.), *Anthropology and the Colonial Encounter* (London, 1973).

57 Terence Ranger, 'Race and Tribe in Southern Africa: European Ideas and African Acceptance', in Robert Ross (ed.), *Racism and Colonialism: Essays on Ideology and Social Structure* (The Hague, 1982), pp. 121–42.

58 Dirks, *Castes of Mind*; Susan Bayly, *Caste, Society and Politics in India from the Eighteenth Century to the Modern Age* (Cambridge, 1999); Terence Ranger, 'The Invention of Tradition Revisited: The Case of Colonial Africa', in Terence Ranger and Olufemi Vaughan (eds), *Legitimacy and the State in Twentieth-Century Africa: Essays in Honour of A.H.M. Kirk-Greene* (Basingstoke, 1993) pp. 62–111; Martin Chanock, *Law, Custom and Social Order: The Colonial Experience in Malawi and Zambia* (Cambridge, 1985).

59 Bruce Berman and John Lonsdale, *Unhappy Valley: Conflict in Kenya and Africa*, vol. 1 (London, 1992), p. 79.

60 See Shula Marks, *The Ambiguities of Dependence in South Africa: Class, Nationalism and the State in Twentieth-Century Natal* (Baltimore, MD, 1986).

Black Skins, White Masks. The alienation of the black man, he wrote, is the outcome of both economic exploitation which produces his inferiority and 'the internalization – or, better, the epidermalization – of this inferiority'.[61] Ideology and psychology converged in whiteness or, most destructively, in the lack of it: an interiority of inferiority, the skin within. 'I discovered', Fanon wrote, 'my blackness, my ethnic characteristics; and I was battered down by tom-toms, cannibalism, intellectual deficiency, fetishism, racial defects, slave-ships, and above all else, above all: "Sho' good eatin' "'.[62] This visceral production of inequality could only be resisted, he argued, by a redemptive violence.[63]

Settler Colonialism and Ideology

But redemptive violence organised around blackness hardly presents a viable option for Aboriginal parents in Australia, whose resistance to assimilation has included tactics such as blackening their children's skin with charcoal and grease in the hope of preventing them from being officially kidnapped as 'half-castes'. As we have stated, in addition to the macrohistorical shifts at the centre of empire, we need to inscribe the heterogeneity among local ideologies of difference. Where functionalist anthropology assisted in the exploitation of some natives, it assisted in the disappearance of others. Projected onto the survivors of settler genocide, the image of a timeless, harmoniously functioning native tradition effaced the immiseration of structural functionalism's empirical informants, whose ethnographic testimony was often enough elicited in police lock-ups or on island leprosariums. Scholarly acquiescence in nation-state boundaries, the current vogue for transnationalism notwithstanding, has depoliticised the domestic management of settler-colonised natives, converting invasion into a welfare issue.

Indigenous people's colonisers never went home. National independence only deepened the settlers' stranglehold on their lives. To tell someone from India or Kenya that they are still colonised would be to insult that person's mentality. To say the same thing to an Indigenous person from Australia, Palestine, Tibet, Aotearoa/New Zealand, Hawai'i or the United States is to acknowledge that person's continuing history. This is not to understate the limitations of formal decolonisation or the continuing inequities of neocolonialism and globalisation in the 'post'colonial third world. It is simply to state the specifically territorial character of settler colonialism. A society premised on the exploitation of colonised labour requires the continuing reproduction of its human providers. By contrast, a society premised on the expropriation of native people's land requires that those who provided it should not be allowed back. Across the post-conquest generations, what settler colonialism reproduces is not human potential but human elimination,

---

61   Frantz Fanon, *Black Skin, White Masks* (London, 1970), p. 10.
62   Ibid., p. 79.
63   Fanon, *The Wretched of the Earth*, pp. 1–52.

whether this is achieved biologically (extermination), territorially (removal) or demographically (assimilation). Assimilation policies continue elimination into the post-frontier history of the settler nation-state, demographically eroding the native constituency. Accordingly, the native case obliges us to adjust the critique of democracy – levelled by Marxism, feminism and post-colonialism alike[64] – that liberal universalism relies on practical exclusions, since democracy's intolerance of difference has operated through inclusion as much as through exclusion. Some differences are absorbed rather than excluded. Bhabha's 'sly civility' hardly disrupts a situation in which 'not quite' was more than white enough for an assimilation programme that was not in the least confounded to see its own image reflected, albeit caricatured, in the native mirror.[65] There is no unified discourse of race and (*pace* Chatterjee) no single rule of colonial difference.

    Different places, different races – or, to put it more generally, different imperial populations, different ideologies. The ideologies that differentiated, and thereby divided, colonised subjects from each other varied in tune with the respective histories of these peoples' incorporation into global relations of inequality. The ideologies of the 'dying Aborigine' and the 'vanishing Indian' alike reflected their human counterparts' unwanted persistence on the land that settlers were stealing from them. As they vanished, Indians would be replaced by imported labour: Africans, valued only for their bodies, whose homelands had yet to become objects of colonial desire. Correspondingly, enslaved people's fitness for labour found ideological encapsulation as a natural sense of rhythm. Across the globe, in Britain's principal franchise colony and at a level below that of race, the lettered ones incorporated as intermediaries and administrators would duly become the shifty, feminised Bengali *babus*, while those most conspicuously recruited to fight for their conquerors became the manly Sikhs, to whom strategic concessions were appropriate. Race operates as a trace of history, one of many finely calibrated rules of imperial difference that together made up the one ideological difference that ultimately mattered, that of whiteness.

---

64   See, for example, Karl Marx, 'On the Jewish Question', in *Early Political Writings* (Cambridge, 1994); Carole Pateman, *The Sexual Contract* (Cambridge, 1988); Mehta, 'Liberal Strategies of Exclusion'. See also Charles W. Mills, *The Racial Contract* (Ithaca, NY, 1997).
65   Bhabha, *The Location of Culture*, pp. 89, 93–101.

ASHGATE
RESEARCH
COMPANION

Religion

Derek R. Peterson[1]

Between 2002 and the time of writing in 2012 eight books were published with the word 'invention' and the name of a religion in the title.[2] This academic fashion is not confined to the study of religion. Since the publication of Hobsbawm and Ranger's pioneering book *The Invention of Tradition* in 1983, the Cambridge University Library has catalogued no less than 223 books with titles beginning with 'The invention of'.[3] Carried along on this tide, scholars have revealed that purportedly timeless religions are in fact creations and re-creations of self-interested entrepreneurs. By introducing us to the agents who standardised doctrines, choreographed rituals, and conjured up deities, the 'invention' school has distanced the study of religion from metaphysics, and opened up an important new field of inquiry for secular historians.

Too often, though, scholars interested in the 'invention of religion' do not leave the library. They presume that religion is primarily a scholarly construct, created and sustained by the protocols of the modern university.[4] In her 2005 book

1   I wish to acknowledge the support of the Leverhulme Trust, whose Philip Leverhulme Prize gave me time to pursue research for this article. Michael Dodson and Chandra Mallampalli offered valuable criticism of earlier drafts.
2   See, among others, Brian Pennington, *Was Hinduism Invented?: Britons, Indians, and the Construction of Religion in Colonial Bengal* (New York, 2005); James R. Lewis and Olav Hammer (eds), *The Invention of Sacred Tradition* (Cambridge, 2007); Derek R. Peterson and Darren Walhof (eds), *The Invention of Religion: Rethinking Belief in Politics and History* (New Brunswick, NJ, 2002); Craig Phillips, *The Invention of Religion: Reason, Identity, and the Colonialist Imagination* (Basingstoke, 2003); and Tomoko Masuzawa, *The Invention of World Religions: Or, How European Universalism was Preserved in the Language of Pluralism* (Chicago, IL, 2005).
3   See Derek R. Peterson, 'Culture and Chronology in African History', *Historical Journal* 50 (2007): pp. 483–97.
4   The scholarship I have in mind here includes Russell McCutcheon's *Manufacturing Religion* (New York, 1997); McCutcheon, *The Discipline of Religion: Structure, Meaning, Rhetoric* (London, 2003); Jonathon Z. Smith, *Relating Religion: Essays in the Study of Religion* (Chicago, IL, 2004); and Richard King, *Orientalism and Religion: Post-colonial Theory, India, and 'the Mystic East'* (London, 1999).

The Invention of World Religions, for example, Tomoko Masuzawa argues that the conceptualisation of 'world religions' was 'initially developed in the European academy'. Masuzawa explores the genesis of comparative theology in European universities in the nineteenth century, traces the sudden rise of 'Buddhism' as a textual construct, and spends a chapter with F. Max Müller, the scholar most often credited as the founder of comparative religion. She spares a few words in her preface to acknowledge that 'the stubborn factivity of [world religions] today' is 'obviously not of the European academy's making'. But she argues that a more 'holistic view' compassing the world outside the university could only emerge as an 'after-effect', an 'image conjured up by some efficacious assembling of so many particular, historically and regionally specific, comparative studies'.[5] Like many contemporary critics of the scholarly practice of religious studies, Masuzawa walls herself into the library, and narrows her focus to study the cadre of European intellectuals who 'invented' Buddhism, Hinduism and other religions.

But there was a much wider cast of characters involved in the making of world religions. Even as Max Müller furiously worked to edit and publish his *magnum opus*, nationalists in India, Africa and Japan were actively configuring their intellectual traditions and ritual practices as religions. For colonised people, being religious – possessing a defined religious system as cultural property – was a powerful means of exercising political agency. In this chapter I explore how Indians, Africans, Japanese and other people valorised their history, invented religions, and relativised European Christians' claims to superior cultural attainment. The invention of religion, in other words, was a means by which colonial subjects could exercise agency on a terrain defined by European imperialism. And for nationalist entrepreneurs, inventing religion was also a potent instrument of internal political organisation. By elevating a God over the human landscape, culture-builders could invite their people to overlook their differences and align themselves. In clarifying and elaborating on Hinduism, Shinto or African religion, nationalists established a certain pattern of behaviour as invariant, created a unitary language, and configured imagined communities.

The invention of religion was a drill sergeant mustering people into formation as national subjects, as Indians, Japanese or Gikuyus. In this regimented landscape, where religious identities overlap with political geography, movement was heresy. For nationalists were also nativists: they sought to fix people in place as indigenes, as believers in a religion that had been assigned to them by virtue of their position within a particular political community. Converts undermined this population-building exercise by setting themselves in motion. Here, therefore, I also examine two conversion movements: the 1956 conversion of Bhimrao Ambedkar, which drew hundreds of thousands of 'untouchables' into Buddhism; and the 'East African Revival', a Christian conversion movement that spread from Rwanda into Kenya, Tanzania and Uganda during the 1940s and 1950s. In their conversion, Indian Buddhists and East African revivalists put distance between themselves and the national communities that claimed them as constituents. Converts were

---

5   Masuzawa, *Invention of World Religions*, pp. xiv–xv.

dissenters: they were pursuing the possibilities of cosmopolitanism, and refusing to comport themselves as patriots.

The Invention of Religion?

For missionaries, nationalists and other cultural entrepreneurs, God was a useful character. In India and in eastern Africa, Christian missionaries needed conversation partners. They did ethnography, wrote dictionaries, and composed treatises on comparative religion as a means of identifying the essential beliefs that Hindus, Africans and other peoples held. In so doing they created the basis for comparative conversations about God. Nationalists were likewise devoted to a singular deity. Searching for grounds on which to answer missionaries' claims, nationalists in colonised societies valorised their own institutions and proclaimed that they, too, possessed a religion to be proud of. But their monotheism was not simply a reply to missionaries' arrogance. In identifying their people's essential religion, nationalists also sought to unify disparate patterns of political thought and practice. 'God' allowed nation-builders to identify a mainstream in their people's history, and to label dissent as both traitorous and unorthodox.

Language Work and the Definition of Hinduism

Hinduism was more than an invention of India's colonial history: it has a long history, defined in part by the rhetorical opposition between 'native' Indian practices and Islam. The earliest recorded reference to 'Hindus' as a demographic group comes from circa 990 CE, when the poet al-Biruni composed a general account of Indian religion, history and customs. By the early 1300s, the expansion of Islamic dynasties into Andhra Pradesh had evidently created a sharper sense of political and religious identity among India's people: an inscription from 1352 entitles the Muslim ruler 'Sultan among Hindu kings'.[6] In the early fifteenth century, the poet Vidyapati contrasted the religious customs of Hindus and Muslims: 'one calls the faithful to prayer. The other recites the Vedas', he wrote. 'One butchers animals by bleeding. The other cuts [off their heads].'

But it was Christian missionaries who first composed a systematic theology for the Hindu religion.[7] In their search for vernacular phraseology with which to preach the Gospel, missionaries helped to consolidate 'Hinduism' as an ordered, doctrinal religious system. In 1613, for example, the Italian missionary Roberto Nobili composed a study of Brahminical thought, traditional Indian sciences and

---

6   These examples are derived from David Lorenzen, 'Who Invented Hinduism?' *Comparative Studies in Society and History* 41/4 (1999): pp. 630–59.

7   Argued most effectively in Geoffrey Oddie, *Imagined Hinduism: British Protestant Missionary Constructions of Hinduism, 1793–1900* (Thousand Oaks, CA, 2006).

sartorial customs. He settled on 'brahman' as 'the most general name for God'.[8] Other missionary linguists similarly sifted through Sanskrit for analogues to Christian nomenclature. Heinrich Roth composed the first Sanskrit grammar in the seventeenth century; the Pondicherry missionary J. Pons wrote a Sanskrit grammar in Latin in the early eighteenth century. In these and in other venues, missionaries identified parallels between Sanskrit words and Christian concepts, allowing them to think of Hinduism as a religious system, with scriptures, rituals and an omniscient deity. The Jesuit J. Bouchet compared the authors of the Vedas with Moses, the law-giver of Christian (and Jewish) history.[9] By these means Hinduism was inducted into a pre-determined historical trajectory: just as Judaism had given way to the 'new covenant' of Christianity, so too would Hindus eventually recognise Christ from within their own religious system. So embracing was this teleology that missionaries felt themselves authorised to compose new Vedas. In the 1770s Jesuits published a Veda as a device to Christianise Hindu readers.[10] Missionaries actively sought to shape Hinduism, in order to induct Hindus into a trajectory leading towards Christianity.

Perhaps the most creative missionary thinker about Hinduism and language was James Robert Ballantyne, superintendent of the government-run Benares College during the mid-nineteenth century. Ballantyne encouraged the study of Sanskrit in Benares, presenting western learning 'less as a contradiction of what is false in [their own] systems, than as a legitimate development of that which is true'.[11] He created word lists representing the nomenclature of European science with Sanskrit terms. Hydrogen, for example, he rendered as *jalakara*, the 'maker of water'; while chlorine was *harita*, 'greenish coloured'.[12] Ballantyne sought to show that India's pre-existing language could be the starting point for a programme of learning about the west. In his 1859 tract 'Christianity contrasted with Hindu philosophy', Ballantyne listed a series of controversial subjects – the chief end of man, for example – and for each he laid out Christian and Hindu dogmas, and explained how Christian views surpassed Hinduism. The missionary J.N. Farquar took this 'fulfilment theology' to its logical conclusion. The Vedanta, he argued in 1913, was a 'presentiment to Christian truth'. 'It is our belief that the living Christ will sanctify and make complete the religious thought of India', wrote Farquar. 'For centuries … her saints have been longing for him, and her thinkers … have been thinking his thoughts.'[13]

---

8   Wilhelm Halbfass, *India and Europe: An Essay in Understanding* (Albany, NY, 1988), p. 40.

9   Halbfass, *India and Europe*, pp. 45–6.

10 See Ludo Rocher (ed.), *Ezourvedam: A French Veda of the Eighteenth Century* (Philadelphia, PA, 1984).

11 Michael Dodson, *Orientalism, Empire, and National Culture: India, 1770–1880* (Basingstoke, 2007), pp. 101–102.

12 Ibid., p. 136.

13 J.N. Farquar, *The Crown of Hinduism* (London, 1913). Quoted in Halbfass, *India and Europe*, pp. 51–2.

Ballantyne, Farquar and other missionaries were working to enlist Indians into a conversation about comparative religion. But missionaries were not the only ones composing Hindu doctrine. Indian intellectuals and activists worked in parallel with missionary translators. They likewise sought to make Hinduism look like a religion, the better to contrast missionary ideas with Hindu concepts.[14] Born in 1772, Rammohan Roy was an accomplished scholar who in the late 1810s helped Baptist missionaries to translate the New Testament into Bengali.[15] The first of his English language writings, published in 1816, was an abridgement of the Vedas.[16] In this and in other texts, Roy challenged the *adhikara*, the rules confining the study of Hindu sacred scriptures to high-caste men. He was opening out Hindu texts, and convoking a new audience, an egalitarian readership that would engage directly with the divine.

Monotheism was a critical aspect of this agenda. One of the earliest appearances of the word 'Hinduism' in the English language came in 1817, when Roy published a tract arguing that the Upanisads manifested a pure monotheism. The 'doctrines of the unity of God are real Hinduism', he wrote.[17] In his translations and in his other writings, Roy challenged high-caste men's hold over Hinduism. In the same breath, he worked to free Hindu religion of the idols and rituals that marked the popular practice of religion. Roy used monotheism to summon a new, egalitarian Hindu community into being. He aimed to draw Indians together, not as practitioners of idiosyncratic and heterodox rituals, nor still as members of hidebound castes, but as one people under God.[18]

Roy was challenged by high-caste Hindus, who argued that his feckless egalitarianism undermined India's social order.[19] But his effort to clarify and standardise disparate Hindu religious practices shaped Indians' thinking about their religion. Roy's confidence in the unity and integrity of Hindu religion can be seen, for example, in Swami Vivekanada's address at the 1893 World Parliament of Religions:

> Sect after sect have arisen in India ... but like the waters of the seashore in a tremendous earthquake, [the religion of the Vedas] receded only for a while, only to return in an all absorbing flood ... and when the

---

14   Argued most forcefully in Pennington, *Was Hinduism Invented?*
15   Torkel Brekke, 'Mission Impossible? Baptism and the Politics of Bible Translation in Early Protestant Missions in Bengal', *History of Religion* 45 (2006): pp. 213–33.
16   Halbfass, *India and Europe*, pp. 204–6.
17   Lorenzen, 'Who Invented Hinduism?', pp. 631–2; see also Brian Hatcher, 'Remembering Rommohan: An Essay on the Re-emergence of Modern Hinduism', *History of Religions* 46 (2006): pp. 50–80. Geoffrey Oddie identifies an older occurrence of 'Hindoo-ism' in a 1787 letter authored by Charles Grant, a prominent East India Company merchant and an evangelical (*Imagined Hinduism*, p. 71).
18   For Roy's liberal project, see C.A. Bayly, 'Rammohan Roy and the Advent of Constitutional Liberalism in India, 1800–30', *Modern Intellectual History* 4 (2007): pp. 25–41.
19   Halbfass, *India and Europe*, p. 210.

tumult of the rush was over, they have been all sucked in, absorbed and assimilated.[20]

Vivekanada was positioning Indians alongside Christians, Muslims and other peoples as believers in a world religion, and simultaneously defining India as necessarily and organically Hindu. In their effort to draw Indians together as practitioners of a singular religion, Hindu nationalists made heterodoxy look deviant.

This definitional work was more than a theological undertaking. In their efforts to choreograph Indians' religious lives, Rammohan Roy and other reformers were also engaged in a gendered project. The makers of modern Hinduism were also husbands and fathers, and in their religious work they also sought to control deviant wives and daughters. In 1905, the moralist Sannulal Gupta published *Strisubodhini*, a domestic manual aimed primarily at women living in the north Indian city of Lucknow.[21] He adopted the voice of an elder married sister, instructing her younger sister on proper behaviour. A wife 'should be of service to her husband with her body, soul and choice', he wrote. 'However bad a husband is … she should always love him and be ready to serve him.'[22] As he sought to tame independent wives, Gupta also sought to reform the idiosyncratic religious practices in which women engaged. His book inveighed against the practice of worshipping at the tombs of Muslim saints, arguing that such actions showed disrespect for Hindu religion. He condemned the practice of keeping feasts and other 'false rituals'. And he mocked women who believed in the miracles of soothsayers, arguing that their successes were based on simple chemical reactions. Lucknow's women, he argued, had better worship God in their own homes, to avoid entangling themselves in 'webs of deceit of spirits, demons, and possession'.[23] For Hindu thinkers, the definition of religious orthodoxy and the reinforcement of patriarchy were joint projects.

Hindu reformers and Christian evangelists worked from different angles, but they together sought to fashion, address and mobilise a singular Hindu community. Missionaries clarified words' meanings, drawing parallels between Christian theology and Sanskrit vocabulary. By this linguistic work they sought to lead Indians into a conversation about comparative religion. Hindu nationalists likewise did ethnographic and linguistic work. Seeking to define cultural property that was uniquely their own, they emphasised the monotheistic aspects of their own tradition, creating a religion that could be set alongside Christianity and Islam. And as they elevated God to a novel position, reformers also drew India's people together, not as believers in soothsayers, nor as cloistered brahmins, nor still as troublesome women, but as one nation under God. The definition of Hinduism was an aspect of the making of the Indian public sphere.

---

20   Quoted in Masuzawa, *The Invention of World Religions*, p. 264.
21   S. Gupta, *Strisubodhini* (Lucknow, 1954 [23rd edition]).
22   Quoted in Sanjay Joshi, *Fractured Modernity: The Making of a Middle Class in Colonial North India* (New Delhi, 2001), pp. 63–4.
23   Joshi, *Fractured Modernity*, pp. 117–18.

Directing Ritual in Meiji Japan

Like Hinduism, Shinto was defined spatially, as the religion of a particular nation. And like Rammohan Roy and Sannulal Gupta, Japan's nationalists found in religious reform a means to consolidate disparate patterns of practice and to clarify their people's identity. For Japan's people did not, all at once, present themselves as co-sharers of a religious tradition. The worship of *kami*, Japan's local tutelary deities, had since the first millennium been interwoven with Buddhist rituals and institutions.[24] Buddhist images were enshrined in *kami* institutions, alongside gods of a more local provenance. Shrines were built in a deliberately ambiguous fashion, allowing Buddhists and followers of the *kami* to worship together. For practitioners, Buddhism and Shinto were not separable religious systems. The word *shûkyô*, 'religion', was introduced into Japanese language in the 1860s to denote the religious freedoms that resident foreigners were, by treaty, to enjoy.[25] The word had not previously meant 'religion' in the generic sense: in the Buddhist lexicon it had meant 'sectarian teachings'.

In the 1850s and 1860s, however, Japanese polity-builders began to sort out their cultural property. With Russian and American ships encroaching on Japanese waters, intellectuals associated with the Kokugaku school insisted that, in order to restore its political integrity, Japan had to recover its ancient culture. Kokugaku men invested the worship of the *kami* with a political theology, arguing that these deities were in fact the makers of the natural world and upholders of a foreordained political order, headed by the emperor.[26] In 1868, nativist intellectuals helped to topple the Tokugawa shogunate and establish a new imperial regime. That same year, the new Meiji government ruled that worship of the *kami* should be separated from that of the buddhas. Under the reform programme shrine sites were cleared of Buddhist elements, and Buddhist priests were obliged to practice Shinto exclusively.[27] In 1871 the government instituted a programme of registration by which every subject at birth became a parishioner of a local shrine.[28] Japan's new government was imposing a demographic order on its people, creating a constituency anchored to a particular place, and orienting subjects' loyalties toward the emperor.

---

24 Kuroda Toshio, 'Shinto in the History of Japanese Religion', *Journal of Japanese Studies* 7 (1981): pp. 1–21; Ian Reader and George Tanabe, *Practically Religious: Worldly Benefits and the Common Religion of Japan* (Honolulu, HI, 1998), pp. 147–55; Sarah Thal, *Rearranging the Landscape of the Gods: The Politics of a Pilgrimage Site in Japan, 1573–1912* (Chicago, IL, 2005), chaps 5 and 6.

25 Sarah Thal, 'A Religion that was not a Religion: The Creation of Modern Shinto in Nineteenth-Century Japan', in Peterson and Walhof (eds), *The Invention of Religion*, pp. 100–114.

26 Helen Hardacre, 'Creating State Shinto: The Great Promulgation Campaign and the New Religions', *Journal of Japanese Studies* 12/1 (1986): pp. 29–63.

27 See Thal, *Rearranging the Landscape of the Gods*, chap. 6.

28 Helen Hardacre, *Shinto and the State, 1868–1988* (Princeton, NJ, 1989), pp. 28–9.

As shrines were made instruments of government oversight, so was Shinto ritual directed towards the empire's political centre. During the early years of the Meiji dynasty, government reformed tax collection and established a national military draft. Opposition was widespread, and the 1870s and early 1880s were marked by riots, protests and the assassination of public figures. In the context of social tumult, Shinto priests and politicians found in ritual a means of anchoring Japan's disparate people to the new order. Insisting that the 'way of the *kami*' arose spontaneously from nature, they contrasted Shinto ritual with the 'beliefs' that set people at odds. 'Shrines are sites at which the *kami* of Heaven and Earth, the spirits of imperial loyalists, and the righteous heroes of patriotism are enshrined and worshipped', wrote one Shinto thinker, and 'Churches ... are the places where people celebrate the spirits of each individual faith'.[29] Japan's intellectuals were contrasting the decorum and civility of Shinto rituals with the divisive, contentious character of other religions. In 1882, the government ruled that priests should not preach at the shrines at which they worked. Preaching and instruction in doctrine were to be conducted at a distance from the shrine precincts. Shinto was being rendered as ritual in which the Japanese, regardless of their religious or doctrinal convictions, could participate.

It was this account of Shinto – as a natural pattern of participatory ritual – that the architects of the Meiji state used to corral the diverse inhabitants of Japan. Nation-builders actively suppressed religious movements that challenged the centralised system of state Shinto. The Omotokyo movement, for example, was founded in 1892 when Deguchi Nao was possessed by the spirit of Konjin. She and her followers preached of a coming era in which the emperor would be overthrown and a utopian social order established.[30] In 1921 and again in 1935 government police destroyed the group's headquarters, arresting hundreds of its followers. Omotokyo was declared an 'evil religion', its followers unpatriotic antagonists of civil order. The Holiness Church of Japan was likewise disbanded in the 1930s. Its members anticipated a judgement day determined by God.[31] These and other groups were dissidents because they would not abide by the ordered practice of ritual in imperial Japan. Their religious vision, oriented towards an alternate future, led them to behave in ways that upset the pattern of conduct that government upheld. Where older practices of religion had oriented worshippers in a variety of directions – towards Buddha, towards local deities – Shinto invited its worshippers to fix their loyalties on the emperor. And where older religious practices had been heterodox and dynamic, the architects of modern Shinto imposed a template to guide ritual behaviour. Shinto helped Japanese nationalists to orient their would-be constituents' loyalties, and identified heterodox patterns of ritual as traitorous.

---

29   Quoted in Thal, 'A Religion that was not a Religion', p. 106.
30   Emily Groszos Ooms, *Women and Millenarian Protest in Meiji Japan: Deguchi Nao and Omotokyo* (Ithaca, NY, 1993).
31   Hardacre, *Shinto and the State*, p. 127.

Remaking Religion in Central Kenya

Africa's traditional religions never earned a place in Max Müller's list of world religions.[32] But in Africa, as in India and Japan, God proved to be politically useful, both for Christian evangelists and for African political organisers. In defining and elaborating on the doctrines of traditional religion, cultural entrepreneurs elevated a deity over the social world, and invited disparate people to see themselves as children of one father. The linguistic and theological work that missionaries and African entrepreneurs did, in other words, helped to define political communities as a fraternity.

Central Kenya was one forum where an African traditional religion was constituted. Pioneering immigrants came from all over eastern Africa to settle in the highland forests of central Kenya in the late seventeenth century.[33] The pioneers called themselves Gikuyu, after a fig tree that grows in well-watered soil. As a society of forest clearers, Gikuyu thought about human civilisation spatially. Dying men and women were taken from their homes and left in the forest by their relatives fearful that death would extend its reach to the living. Ancestors (*ngoma*) were unpredictable, sometimes causing sickness or dementia among relatives who ignored them. Unpredictable *ngoma* needed to be controlled if human society was to prosper. When faced with an inexplicable disease in their family, or worried over the failure of crops, elders slaughtered a fattened ram at a fig tree located on land possessed by their clan.[34] They poured the fat at the base of the tree and ate some of its roasted meat. These ritual actions were *kūhaka magongona* – to 'put side by side', or 'to separate'.[35] The work of *kūhaka magongona* was the religious dimension of elders' larger duty to wall human society off from the wilderness.

Some problems needed wider solutions. When plague killed people indiscriminately, elders from several clans banded together to –*haka magongona* for 'God'.[36] About a transcendent God this practically minded people was necessarily imprecise. Elders in different regions invoked different names when making territorial *magongona*: some used *Githuku*; others used *Maagũ*.[37] The name most widely used was *Ngaĩ*. Etymologically, *Ngaĩ* was a foreign term, adopted from Maasai pastoralists. *Ngaĩ* had little resonance for Gikuyu people: it belonged to the class of nouns associated with inanimate objects. 'Sacrifices' to *Ngaĩ* were infrequent, offered only during times of calamity. Prayers asked *Ngaĩ* for protection

---

32 But see John Mbiti, *African Religions and Philosophy* (New York, 1969); and Mbiti, *Introduction to African Religion* (Portsmouth, 1975).

33 K.R. Dundas, 'Notes on the Origin and History of the Kikuyu and Dorobo Tribes', *Man* 8 (1908): pp. 136–9.

34 L.S.B. Leakey, *The Southern Kikuyu Before 1903* (London, 1977), 1107–1109; Jomo Kenyatta, *Facing Mount Kenya* (London, 1938), chap. 10.

35 T. Benson, *Kikuyu–English Dictionary* (Oxford, 1964), p. 138.

36 Leakey, *Southern Kikuyu*, pp. 202–203.

37 A.R. Barlow, 'Notes on *Githuku* and *Maagũ*', Edinburgh University Library Archives (Scotland) (hereafter EUL) Gen. 1785/1.

against drought, famine or plague. Nowhere does the evidence record prayers that dwell on the abstract qualities of *Ngaī*.

It is impossible to know what Gikuyu actually thought about *Ngaī* in the nineteenth century. *Ngaī* was a label, not a deity: it helped elders get a grip on the unknown. The relationship between Gikuyu people and *Ngaī* was not ritualistic worship between created and Creator. Gikuyu householders boxed *Ngaī* out, as part of their larger work of cordoning human society off from the unknowable forest. The absence of abstract theological discourse about *Ngaī* highlights the material, pragmatic nature of Gikuyu religious practice.

Protestant missionaries arrived in central Kenya in the late nineteenth century. Their evangelistic practice worked by inducting *Ngaī*, and *magongona*, into a natural religion. By translating situational Gikuyu practices into the atemporal categories of comparative religion, missionaries sought to create a world of rituals and propositions, a world to be converted through sermons about God. They sought to identify similarities between Gikuyu and Christian religion, to make Christianity look like a natural extension of the old beliefs. They bridged the two religions by creating matching lists of words. One Presbyterian missionary made the following list:

absolve from sin	*ehereria*
belief	*wītikio*
divination	*ūgo, ūragūri*
evil	*ūūru, waganu*
govern	*atha*
king	*mwathani, mūthamaki*[38]

Arrayed in columns, lists like these linked theological concepts to Gikuyu words. At the core of this project was the equation between the Christian God and *Ngaī*. For if *Ngaī* could be made into a law-giving, otherworldly and absolutely powerful 'God', then missionaries could make comparisons between Gikuyu and Christian ways of dealing with the divine. A key text in missionaries' theology of *Ngaī* was 'The Choice Between Gikuyu and Christian Religion', a Gikuyu-language catechism. The catechism opened by developing a character for *Ngaī* in Gikuyu religion:

1. The thinking about *Ngaī*
   a. The Gikuyu believe with no doubt that there is *Ngaī*. …
   e. Also they think that *Ngaī* is the origin of life, of birth, of all in earth. He is the one who gives children, livestock and food. …
   g. They also believe *Ngaī* stays in heaven because they at times say 'Ngaī wa Igūrū' [*Ngaī* of above]. …

---

38   A.C. Madan, An Outline Dictionary (London, 1905). The quoted copy is in the Presbyterian Church of East Africa Archives (Nairobi, Kenya) (here*after PCEA), I/Z/4.*

l. Also Gikuyu believe that *Ngaĩ* is the King because it is stated that 'Nĩwe Ngaĩ wa Gikuyu' [He is the *Ngaĩ* of the Gikuyu], and their *kĩrĩra* [here 'laws'] were given by Ngaĩ.[39]

The catechism plucked *Ngaĩ* out of the world of human interaction and located it firmly in heaven, establishing a totalitarian economy between God and humanity. The author's strategy for establishing this hierarchy was linguistic. By reinterpreting elders' aphorisms and redefining Gikuyu words, the catechism created a systematic theology for *Ngaĩ*. Point g above, for example, linked the vernacular phrase *Ngaĩ wa Igũrũ* with the religious concept 'heaven'. *Igũrũ* was the direction 'up'. In elders' parlance, the phrase *Ngaĩ wa Igũrũ* ('God of above') contrasted *Ngaĩ* with the ancestors, who were said to dwell 'underground' on specific plots of land. The catechism took this name for the unknown and made it into a heavenly realm, pinning *Ngaĩ* down in a cloudy Christian otherworld.

With *Ngaĩ* seated in heaven, ruling over its subjects as an omnipotent king, missionary linguists could make comparisons between Christian and Gikuyu systems of belief. Here Protestants found useful parallels in the Old Testament. Like the Jewish temple sacrifices described in the Old Testament, *magongona*, argued missionaries in their catechism, foreshadowed the Christian practice of Communion.

> Sacrificing for God under a fig tree can be equated to some of the Israelites' practices … The lamb that was used for magongona under a fig tree was to be unblemished. The same was done by the Israelites … Also some meat was left for Ngaĩ in the altar and the rest was divided amongst the elders. This is comparable with Holy Communion among Christians.

Gikuyu religion was thereby incorporated into a predetermined historical trajectory: just as Christianity had superseded Judaism, so too would Gikuyu religion give place to the Gospel. This teleology made comparative religion easy. In 1922, missionary tutors had Gikuyu divinity students write essays showing 'where Kikuyu religion is defective in its worship [*magongona*] as compared with Christianity'.[40]

This reduction of a fluid social world into a hierarchy of truth was more than a mistake. Gikuyu knew human civilisation to be a kinetic bargain with a threatening wilderness. Missionaries sought to standardise Gikuyu social praxis with atemporal religious nomenclature. *Magongona* in missionary discourse were formulaic rituals, not socially creative actions. Elders were priests playing out a ritual script, not inventive experimentalists. And *Ngaĩ* was the author of creation, not a name that separated humanity from the unknown. By inducting *Ngaĩ*, *magongona* and other words into the lexicon of modern religion, missionaries worked to standardise Gikuyu thought and practice, the better to compare it with the tenets of their

39   A.R. Barlow, 'Guthura Uhoro wa Gikuyu na wa Ukristiano', n.d., Tumutumu Church Archives, Karatina (Kenya), 'Notes for catechists' file.
40   Junior Preacher exam, 3 June 1922, PCEA II/C/41.

own faith. Gikuyu 'traditional religion' was an evangelistic strategy, a means by which missionaries inducted their hearers into comparative conversations about belief systems.

But it was not only missionaries who made Gikuyu religion. Educated in Protestant schools, early Gikuyu converts took missionaries' vocabulary and built a culture out of it. They used missionaries' vocabulary to weld central Kenya's disparate people together. Converts found useful phraseology in the 1924 Protestant reading primer, whose first sentence read: '*Ngaĩ* gave the Gikuyu a good country that lacks neither food nor water or forests. It's therefore good for the Gikuyu to be praising *Ngaĩ*, for he has been very generous to them'.[41] Central Kenya's early nationalists found this a rousing recruiting speech. Writing in the Kikuyu Central Association's newspaper *Mwigwithania* in 1929, one editorialist personified the missionaries' origin story: he referred to 'our ancestor, Kikuyu', to whom God, from his seat on Mount Kenya, had once given the land from Kabete to Meru.[42] Another writer noted that 'there is a name for the father of a man, but what is the name of a man's mother? Know that a man's mother's name is Muumbi'.[43] As the father and mother of all Gikuyu people, Gikuyu and Muumbi turned disparate clans into a homogeneous people with a common parentage. The genesis story shrouded the Gikuyu people's diverse origins, and helped cultural entrepreneurs to call their constituents to filial obedience.

Missionaries' standardised conception of religion papered over Gikuyu people's differences, and gave nation-builders the rhetorical and intellectual leverage with which to draw disparate people together. Writing in 1931, an unnamed editorialist reminded readers that 'the land we have was given to us by our father, *Ngaĩ*'.[44] 'WAKE UP! WAKE UP', he wrote in capital letters, as if to awaken the Gikuyu body politic by force of words, 'and take care of the country together.' Nothing about their labour history invited Gikuyu readers to think about 'the land' as a gift given by God to an identifiable people. Pioneers had wrenched their farms from the forbidding forest by dint of hard work. In 1902, anthropologists could report that 'in all directions spreads one huge garden, every square inch of it ... [with] carefully marked boundaries'.[45] Gikuyu political divisions were physically marked out on the landscape. The nation-builders of the 1930s asked their constituents to overlook the boundaries that divided them, to think of their property as a national territory given to them by God. Their surveying work allowed activists to cast themselves as defenders of a fatherland, and (therefore) as spokesmen for a people. As early as 1926, Kikuyu Central Association organisers were complaining that government officials and missionaries were snatching 'Kikuyu land' from its

---

41   Marion Stevenson, *Karirikania* (Nyeri, 1924).

42   Ng'ondu wa Kabuitu, 'Preserving Kikuyu Characteristics', *Mwigwithania* 2/2 (July–August 1929); Kenya National Archives (hereafter KNA), DC Machakos 10B/13/1.

43   H.M. Gichuiri, 'A Parable', *Mwigwithania* 1/7 (November 1928).

44   Kikuyu Central Association (Karura), *Mwigwithania* 4 (September 1931).

45   Quoted in Arthur Barlow, 'Kikuyu Land Tenure and Inheritance', *Journal of the East African and Uganda Natural History Society* 45–46 (1933): pp. 56–66.

rightful owners.[46] By lumping householders' estates together, intellectuals were also clearing the ground on which to constitute a Gikuyu polity.

In central Kenya as in colonial India, the codification and standardisation of changeable social practice was at the heart of the Christian missionaries' project. Like the Jesuit Nobili, like the Sanskrit linguist Ballantyne, missionaries in central Kenya composed word lists, did ethnography, and illuminated parallels between Christianity and the old religion. They sought to consolidate Gikuyu religious life, to make *Ngaī* look like God, in order to create the grounds on which to do comparative religion. Gikuyu 'traditional religion' was in part an evangelistic strategy, a means by which missionaries mustered up a community of talking partners.

Whether or not they became Christians, Gikuyu found missionaries' vocabulary useful. Just as missionaries papered over local differences in their analysis of Gikuyu religion, so did central Kenya's nation-builders seek to paper over their people's parochial political culture. Just as missionaries elevated God to a singular place in the cosmos, so did Gikuyu find their heavenly father to be a helpful parent. Like Rammohan Roy, Gikuyu monotheists sought to level out their people's differences, to bring them into a singular relationship with God. And, like the architects of Shinto religion, Gikuyu monotheists sought to shape their people's behaviour and orient their loyalties. It is not a mistake that the politician Jomo Kenyatta titled his 1938 treatise on Gikuyu social life *Facing Mount Kenya*.[47] Mount Kenya was, by Kenyatta's time, firmly established as the seat of *Ngaī*. In central Kenya as in Japan and India, God summoned disparate people to face the same direction, to identify themselves as co-sharers of an identity, and a future.

Conversion and Dissent in India and Eastern Africa

In a world in which religion defines majoritarian cultures and cements political identities, conversion is an act of dissent. Where missionaries and nationalists in Japan, India and Kenya sought to anchor to a particular religious tradition, converts were on the move, both physically and as subjects. Where nation builders established certain forms of ritual behaviour as normative, converts upset the social rules that undergirded political communities. And where nation builders assigned people to particular demographic and religious categories by virtue of their birth, converts would not stay in place. They passed from one life to another, and in so doing they challenged the prescriptions that nationalists made for them.

---

46   H. Mundia *et al.* to District Commissioner Nyeri, 10 July 1926, KNA PC Central 8/5/2. See Derek R. Peterson, '"Be Like Firm Soldiers to Develop the Country": Political Imagination and the Geography of Gikuyuland', *International Journal of African Historical Studies* 37 (2004): pp. 71–101.

47   Kenyatta, *Facing Mount Kenya*.

Ambedkar, Buddhism and Political Agency in India

Born in 1891 to a Mahar untouchable family in Mhow, in the Central Provinces, Bhimrao Ambedkar was one of the most highly educated Indians of his generation. He took a PhD in anthropology from Columbia University in New York, and completed a DSc from the University of London. His doctoral work at Columbia concerned the historic origins of India's caste system. After his return to India, Ambedkar was nominated to the Legislative Council as one of two representatives of the depressed classes. He was named Jawaharlal Nehru's first Law Minister in 1947, and was largely responsible for drafting the Republic of India's first constitution.[48] On 14 October 1956, a day historically associated with the Emperor Ashoka's conversion to Buddhism, Bhimrao Ambedkar publicly pledged to observe the Five Precepts and to avoid the practices of Hinduism. Ambedkar was joined in his conversion by some 380,000 people, most of them untouchables, who watched as he made his pledge and to whom he, in turn, administered the vows. In all some 500,000 people converted to Buddhism over a 36-hour period following Ambedkar's conversion.[49]

The convert Ambedkar was not only engaged in a private act of religious piety. While post-colonial India's politics were avowedly secular, even Jawaharlal Nehru, the architect of modern India's bureaucracy, discovered India's essential identity in what he called the 'ancient wisdom' of the Vedas.[50] In a polity that had been defined as organically and naturally Hindu, Ambedkar's conversion was a means of distancing himself and his followers from the nationalists' hold. In their conversion, untouchables refused to play out the religious and political role that India's nation-builders had assigned them.

Ambedkar was Mahatma Gandhi's contemporary, and a comparison of their political thought illuminates the distance that Ambedkar put between himself and the mainstream of Indian nationalism. Gandhi idealised the caste system as a force for good in India's society. The *varna* system clarified Indians' social and economic roles, he thought, diminishing the prospect of class warfare and helping to preserve traditional skills. 'The law of varna teaches us that we have each one of us to earn our bread by following the ancestral calling', he wrote. 'It defines not our rights but our duties … there is no calling too low and none too high. All are good, lawful and absolutely equal in status'.[51] For Ambedkar, by contrast, the rural society that Gandhi valorised was a 'chamber of horrors'. 'The iron law of caste', he wrote in

---

48   Dhanajay Keer, *Dr Ambedkar: Life and Mission* (Bombay, 1971).
49   Described in Christopher Queen, 'Ambedkar, Modernity and the Hermeneutics of Buddhist Liberation', in A.K. Narain and D.C. Ahir (eds), *Dr Ambedkar, Buddhism, and Social Change* (Delhi, 1994), pp. 99–122.
50   In his *Discovery of India* (New Delhi, 1946), Jawaharlal Nehru argued that India needed to break with 'all the dust and dirt of the ages that have covered her up and hidden her inner beauty and significance. We have to cut away these excrescences and remember afresh the core of that ancient wisdom.' Quoted in Joshi, *Fractured Modernity*, pp. 127–8.
51   Quoted in Nicholas Dirks, *Castes of Mind: Colonialism and the Making of Modern India* (Princeton, NJ, 2001), pp. 267–8.

1945, 'the heartless law of Karma and the senseless law of status by birth are to untouchables veritable instruments of torture which Hindusm has forged.'[52] Where Gandhi sought to reform the abuses of the caste system, Ambedkar argued that caste was essential to the definition of Hinduism. 'Hindus observe caste not because they are inhumane or wrong headed', wrote Ambedkar in his *The Annihilation of Caste*. 'They observe caste because they are deeply religious'.[53]

Ambedkar's diagnosis of Hinduism – as a religion that necessarily upheld social inequity and disadvantaged untouchables – made him see conversion as a means by which untouchables could take their future in their own hands. At a 1935 gathering in Yeola, he famously told some 10,000 leaders of India's depressed classes to consider their religious identity as a matter of choice, not a fact of destiny:

> If you want to gain self-respect, change your religion. If you want to create a cooperating society, change your religion. If you want power, change your religion. If you want equality, change your religion. If you want independence, change your religion.[54]

For Ambedkar, though, conversion was not a straightforward transfer of allegiance from one religion to another. For twenty years after his announcement at Yeola, Ambedkar conducted research about world religions. He sent out a stream of emissaries to attend and report back on religious conferences, and carried on correspondence with thinkers from a variety of traditions. The former Nizam of Hyderabad offered him 50 million rupees for the wholesale delivery of India's untouchables to Islam. The Methodist Episcopal bishop of Bombay assured Ambedkar that untouchables would be welcome to convert to Christianity.[55] Ambedkar meditated in newspaper editorials and other venues about the benefits and disadvantages that each religious tradition offered untouchables. By the late 1940s, he had settled on Buddhism as the most politically enabling religion for India's untouchables.[56] For Ambedkar, Buddhism was validated by historical precedent: it was an Indian religion that had, in ancient times, been overtaken by the tyranny of the Brahmins.

Ambedkar spent much of his adult life researching and planning his conversion. He lived at a crossroads, not in a homeland. Indian nation-builders from Rammohan Roy through to Ghandi sought to anchor Indians to a particular religion. They codified Hindu rituals and beliefs, sorted orthodoxy from deviance,

---

52 Bhimrao Ambedkar, *What Congress and Gandhi Have Done to the Untouchables* (Bombay, 1945), p. 277. Quoted in A.K. Narain, 'Dr Ambedkar, Buddhism and Social Change: A Reappraisal', in Narain and Ahir (eds), *Dr Ambedkar, Buddhism, and Social Change*, p. 85.
53 Bhimrao Ambedkar, *The Annihilation of Caste* (Jalandar, 1936), p. 111. Quoted in Timothy Fitzgerald, *The Ideology of Religious Studies* (New York, 2000), p. 124.
54 Quoted in Keer, *Dr Ambedkar*, p. 255.
55 Queen, 'Ambedkar, Modernity and the Hermeneutics of Buddhist Liberation'.
56 Gauri Viswanathan, *Outside the Fold: Conversion, Modernity, and Belief* (Princeton, NJ, 1998), pp. 231–2.

and marshalled up an Indian community defined by its obedience to a unitary God. Ghandi scorned Ambedkar: 'Religion is not like a house or a cloak, which can be changed at will', he wrote. 'It is a more integral part of one's self than one's own body'.[57] But Ambedkar would not be subjected to Ghand's culture-building project. He would not be fixed in place. Converts were experimenting with novel religious postures, following paths that led in divergent directions. Their mobility challenged the demographic project in which Hindu culture-builders were engaged, and opened up novel avenues of political agency.

Revivalism and Patriotism in Central Kenya

The East African Revival was a Christian conversion movement that began in southern Uganda and northern Rwanda in the early 1930s and spread through Kenya, Tanzania and Burundi during the 1940s and 1950s. Its converts – many of them women – thought it was their religious duty to confess their most intimate sins in public. In the Ankole region of Uganda, where Revival evangelists were preaching in 1936, converts were known for their never-ending sermons.[58] In Bukoba, on Tanganyika's Lake Victoria's shore, revivalist preaching was so offensive that church leaders banned them from talking in church.[59] By 1944, even sympathetic observers were complaining about Gikuyu converts' 'tendency ... towards competitive confessing, sometimes of sins which are better not mentioned in front of large mixed audiences'.[60]

In central Kenya as in colonial India, religious conversion was an act of political dissent. The women and men of the East African Revival were not untouchables, challenging civic disabilities. Neither did their leaders publish learned theological treatises, or write essays criticising the political order of their time. But like the hundreds of thousands of untouchables who converted in 1956, East Africa's converts were on the move. In their testimonies of conversion, revivalists put distance between themselves and the political communities that claimed them as constituents. Gikuyu nationalists sought to summon people up as members of a particular community, to shape their manners, loyalties and identities in conformity with a template. Revivalists would not play the role they had been assigned. As converts, they unsettled the constituency that Gikuyu nation-builders sought to construct.

Gikuyu people made themselves converts through narrative. To be converted, revivalists gave 'testimonies' that illuminated the distance they had travelled

---

57   Quoted in ibid., p. 231.
58   E. Maari, 'The Balokole Movement in Nyabushozi Country of Ankole', in A. Byaruhanga-Akiiki (ed.), *Occasional Research Papers*, vol. 22 (Kampala, 1974).
59   John Iliffe, *A Modern History of Tanganyika* (Cambridge, 1979), p. 365.
60   Rev. O. Wigram, July 1944, Church Missionary Society Archive, University of Birmingham, annual letters.

between the old life and the new.[61] They mapped their passage by drawing lines through the whole spectrum of human social activity, distinguishing right conduct from iniquity. Early converts recalled the shock with which they saw, for the first time, that previously uncontroversial actions made them sinful. Bedan Ireri was lying in bed after an intimate encounter with a young man when he 'saw a big light, and a cloud. Then the Voice spoke to me and said, "You commit fornication", and I said Yes. "You are a liar". … "You are a thief".'[62] The next morning, Ireri repented of his sins in prayer with other revivalists. Walter Mwangi Rurie was eating at table when he heard a voice tell him, 'Walter, you are full of sins – very many sins'. He lost his appetite, went to his room, and pleaded forgiveness from God.[63] Converts were prompted to see themselves in a new light. They sorted through their relationships and their remembered actions, classifying otherwise unremarkable actions – a night spent drinking beer, a disagreement with a spouse – as sinful.

Their forensic work generated evidence that converts could use in plotting their passage to a new life. With the proof spread out before them, converts could make public confession of their misdeeds. Eunice Kagio was saved after she realised that her life had become a 'stinking thing' to God. In her testimony, she described how Jesus' blood had washed her clean from sin.[64] In their testimonies revivalists distinguished themselves from the dark lives they had formerly led. By this classificatory work they set themselves on a new path, and took up a new position in the social world. In 1945, Bedan Ireri had a vision that lasted some two weeks: each evening, he saw himself on a pilgrimage towards heaven. The vision, he remarked, was 'like television'.[65] Revivalist preachers often illustrated their sermons using posters of life's travellers on two ways, one to destruction and the other to the Eternal City.[66] Converts were in motion, travelling from one life to another.

Gikuyu patriots were appalled at revivalists' incendiary talk. In their view, revivalists' testimonies undermined public order. More than etiquette was at stake here. The pioneers who had cleared the forest around Mount Kenya had exercised a stern discipline over their kin: they knew that 'home affairs must not go into the

61 Published testimonies include Joe Church, *Quest for the Highest* (Exeter, 1981); Dorothy Smoker, *Ambushed by Love: God's Triumph in Kenya's Terror* (Fort Washington, PA, 1994); Edith Wiseman, *Kikuyu Martyrs* (London, 1958); and Joe Church, *Awake Uganda!* (Kampala, 1957). See also Derek Peterson, *Creative Writing: Translation, Bookkeeping and the Work of Imagination in Colonial Kenya* (Portsmouth, 2004), chap. 7.
62 Interview with Bedan Ireri, 26 May 1988, Jocelyn Murray papers, London Mennonite Centre.
63 Smoker, *Ambushed*, p. 195.
64 Ibid., p. 263.
65 Interview with Bedan Ireri, 26 May 1988, Jocelyn Murray papers, London Mennonite Centre.
66 Irvine, Chogoria Annual Report, 1949, PCEA II/BA/10.

open', in the words of one proverb.[67] Soft words made homes cool and prosperous.[68] Public argument between husbands and wives, by contrast, destroyed families' hard-won reputation. Revivalists' testimonies made their most intimate affairs subject to public examination. Where straight-backed pioneers earned honour by their discipline and hard work, converts talked endlessly about their sins. In a 1948 pamphlet, the newspaperman Henry Muoria instructed his readers 'don't spend time praying at home without doing anything, only crying on account of your sins'. Instead, Gikuyu people ought to pray for the 'strength to work', and for 'good thoughts so that they undertake good actions'.[69] Hard-working patriots like Muoria scorned gossiping converts for their moral and physical lassitude. At some point in the 1940s, Gikuyu people began using the verb -goco, the root of the revivalists' oft-repeated phrase *Mwathani arogocwo* ('Praise the Lord'), to mean 'disturbing chatter causing disorder or discord'.[70] Revivalists' loose tongues made many people doubt their morals. There were rumours that travelling evangelists had sexual access to women converts.[71] In the view of many conservatives, revivalists were derelict in their conjugal and political duties. One editorialist described in 1949 how at a Revival convention thousands of people had happily sung about their salvation. Reminding his readers that the British had stolen their lands, the editorialist argued that 'anybody who says that he is joyful when many of our people are oppressed slaves and left in landless poverty is deceiving himself'.[72] Revivalists absconded on their duty to their homeland.

Henry Muoria and other Gikuyu political organisers were terrified by the Revival because they were, even while the Revival took form, actively working to draw central Kenya's disparate people together as compatriots. In earlier decades activists had used missionaries' vocabulary and language primers as vehicles of political mobilisation. In the late 1940s, Gikuyu activists were again sorting through their history and summoning partisans to duty. In a 1947 editorial Henry Muoria opened up the missionaries' 1924 primer (above) and reminded his readers that 'Mr Gikuyu gave us all the land from Meru to Ngong'. But European colonists had 'cunningly robbed us of most of our land and left us with very little'.[73] Muoria called on his readers to defend their homeland. 'The present battle is the brain battle', he wrote.[74] With pen in hand, Muoria was summoning up a Gikuyu community

---

67   G. Barra, *1000 Kikuyu proverbs* (Nairobi, 1994 [1939]), no. 20.

68   Barlow, 'Kikuyu Linguistics', EUL Gen. 1786/6.

69   Henry Muoria, *Writing for Kenya: The Life and Works of Henry Muoria*, ed. Wangari Muoria-Sal, B.F. Frederiksen, John Lonsdale and Derek R. Peterson (Leiden, 2009), p. 147.

70   Barlow, notes on –*goco*, EUL Gen 1785/1.

71   'Papers on –Isms' file: 'Report on Ruanda Activities', 10 August 1950, Africa Inland Mission Archives (Nairobi).

72   Josiah Magu in *Mumenyereri*, 12 September 1949, Anglican Church of Kenya Archives, North Highlands Rural Deanery file.

73   *Mumenyereri*, 6 October 1947. Quoted in Director of intelligence and security to Chief Native Commissioner, 21 October 1947, KNA MAA 8/106.

74   *Mumenyereri*, 24 November 1947. Quoted in Director of intelligence and security to Chief Native Commissioner, 28 November 1947, KNA MAA 8/106.

that shared a history, a founding myth, a homeland and a stern social discipline. The project of historical reconstruction and the work of political mobilisation went hand-in-hand.

The guerrillas of central Kenya's 'Mau Mau' movement carried this patriotic project forward. Mau Mau was, in one of its aspects, a nationalist war against British colonialism. It was also a conservative struggle against indiscipline, against the social irresponsibility that revivalists seemed to promote. Men of the Kikuyu Central Association began administering oaths against the Revival in 1948. Oath-takers promised not to reveal secrets to outsiders.[75] Female oath-takers were obliged to obey their husbands. In 1952 the Kenyan government, alarmed at the growth of the movement they called Mau Mau, declared a State of Emergency and brought in the British army. Thousands of Gikuyu men and women went into central Kenya's forests to join guerilla gangs. Mau Mau's organisers sought to transform these scattered, disunited gangs into a patriotic army through bureaucracy. Mau Mau agents in Nairobi printed off identity cards, with 'Kenya Land Freedom Army' inscribed on them.[76] The cards identified Mau Mau's partisans, and shaped their actions. Each guerilla camp was to keep ten record books, including a register, a hymn book, a history book, and a list of friends and enemies.[77] Mau Mau's leaders wanted memorial halls constructed after Kenya's independence to house the registers. The books immortalised fighters' deeds, and endowed them with a heritage: Mau Mau's leaders promised fighters that, when they died, their descendants would 'take your share of the land and enjoy the freedom you died for'.[78] By ensuring that readers of the future would learn of their heroic deeds, record books shaped partisans' actions in their contemporary world. The practice of record-keeping invited wavering people to comport themselves as activists, single-mindedly fighting for their country.

Revivalists were Mau Mau's chief dissenters. They would not conform their biographies, and their loyalties, to the directions Mau Mau organisers gave. Revivalists refused to bear arms during the war, either for Mau Mau or for the British. And in their endless talk about their private lives, converts undermined the discipline that Mau Mau promoted. Mau Mau's 'oath of unity' promised that those who revealed secrets would have their tongues pierced with a red-hot iron, their eyes plucked out, and their hands cut off.[79] Mau Mau organisers used violence to silence revivalists who talked too much. Converts who kept silent were generally left to live in peace. One revivalist explained that 'Mau Mau hated being talked

---

75 Robert MacPherson, 'East African Revival', *Kikuyu News* 193 (September 1950); Mau Mau confession forms, 1955, PCEA II/G/4.

76 Gucu G. Gikoyo, *We Fought for Freedom* (Nairobi, 1979), p. 22.

77 Donald Barnett and Karari Njama, *Mau Mau from Within: An Analysis of Kenya's Peasant Revolt* (New York, 1966), pp. 246–7.

78 Maina wa Kinyatti, *Kimathi's Letters* (Nairobi, 1986), p. 26.

79 Pittway, letter to prayer partners, 23 January 1954, Anglican Church of Kenya Archives.

about. ... If you were talking about them too much, then they would fight you. If you kept silent, they wouldn't touch you.'[80]

Mau Mau partisans' war against talkative revivalists highlights the regimentation that Gikuyu polity-builders imposed on their would-be constituents. Mau Mau's organisers claimed for themselves the power to author other people's destiny. They sought to enclose disparate people within an all-encompassing Gikuyu homeland, unify them as children of a single family, and mobilise them as activists of a cause. Revivalists were on a different path. As converts, they were obliged to narrate their passage from one life to another. By their testimonies they contrasted darkness with light, sin with new life, and the past with the future. Their narratives made their conversion real and visible, in their eyes and in others. Converts could not march in lockstep with the constituency that Gikuyu politicians sought to create. Where political organisers sought to fix people in place as natives of a homeland, converts were on a journey towards another home. Where political organisers fixed people's identities in record books, converts were authoring their own destiny. Where political organisers sought to reform constituents' morals and curb their tongues, converts kept talking. And where political organisers assigned partisans a role to play, converts were actors in a different drama. East Africa's revivalists were not, like Ambedkar, converting to a minority religion. Their conversion did not challenge a majoritarian religion's hold over public space. But, like Ambedkar, revivalists authored their own biographies. Their life stories set them on a path leading to a different homeland.

In India, Japan and eastern Africa, the 'invention of religion' was a chapter in the social history of patriotism. 'Religion' was a tendentious translation project, carried off by missionaries eager to start conversations about God, and by nationalists working to unify their people. Political organisers sought to anchor people in place as natives of a fatherland. As they standardised national languages, did historical research, disciplined refractory women and imagined communities, nativists also elevated a God to stand over the parochial terrain.[81] They thereby invited disparate, divided people to regard themselves as a brotherhood bound together by a shared heritage. But not everyone would lift their eyes and follow political organisers' directions. Converts acted as dissidents on this religio-political landscape: they engaged in forensic and investigatory work, set themselves in motion, crossed boundaries and took up a novel place in the political world. In their pilgrimages they opened up a path of political agency.

The scholarship on the 'invention of religion' has walled itself into an intellectual dead end. Writing from within the university library, advocates of the 'invention' school have shown that purportedly timeless religions are in fact creations of human intellectual history. What this deconstructive project lacks is a forward momentum, a vision for how politics might differently work. Africans, Indians and Japanese today inhabit a world that has already been mapped, where human populations

---

80 Interview: Timothy Gathu Njoroge, Kangema, Nyeri, 29 June 1994.
81 Benedict Anderson, *Imagined Communities: Reflections on the Origin and Spread of Nationalism* (London, 1991).

have already been assigned roles to play. On a terrain where religious and political identities overlap, converts pioneered a home-grown form of deconstruction. They were setting themselves in motion, and refusing to acknowledge the claims that nationalists made on their bodies or their beliefs. Their religious practice lets us see conversion as cultural criticism, and allows us to imagine a wider itinerary for post-imperial history.

Culture

Lara Kriegel

When asked in February 1899 by an American reporter about the nascent work of US empire-building in Cuba and the Philippines, British imperialist, Rhodesia governor, and diamond magnate Cecil Rhodes declared, 'You are taking to it like mother's milk'. Rhodes endorsed the American imperial project 'with the greatest delight' whilst on board the steamship *Hapsburg*, which was crossing the Mediterranean on its way to Egypt, where he was to work on the Cape to Cairo Railway and Telegraph. Impressed by the progress of the new imperial nation, Rhodes predicted that, within a century, the United States would certainly rule the entire western hemisphere, with the exception of Canada. He railed against critics of US imperialism, whom he dismissed as 'selfish', and claimed, 'It is the duty of civilized nations to take charge of the barbarians and give them a white man's government. The United States is one of the great powers, and cannot escape this duty.' And so, as a representative of the leading imperial nation, Rhodes spoke for mother Britain as he urged the fledgling United States on its newfound imperial path.[1]

Rhodes' words were just one expression of a broader enthusiasm for empire – and especially for the civilising mission of imperialism – evident in the Anglo-American world and beyond in 1899. It was a high moment for imperial expression, for, in the same month that Rhodes praised American colonial aspirations, Rudyard Kipling published his famous poem 'The White Man's Burden', in both *The Times* and *McClure's Magazine*. Like Rhodes' statement aboard the steamer *Hapsburg*, the poem had a tutelary and parental spirit. It was meant to laud the new imperial nation that had embarked on the rigorous course of uplifting inferior races, while warning it of the many treacheries of the imperial endeavour. The poem gave Kipling newfound acclaim as it prompted several derivatives, both endorsements and parodies, which attested to the heady and varied nature of imperial discourse at the *fin de siècle*.[2] At that time, American historian Frank Ninkovich notes, the world witnessed the 'unprecedented diffusion of both power and culture' under the aegis

---

1   'Mr Rhodes on Expansion', *New York Times*, 3 March 1899, p. 1.
2   See David Gilmour, *The Long Recessional: The Imperial Life of Rudyard Kipling* (New York, 2002), pp. 126–32.

of the civilising mission, the mantle taken up by the British and the Americans, and, in a distinctly republican tenor, by the French, too.[3] To be sure, the civilising mission has a long history as the cultural logic of empire, but it coalesced in the era between 1870 and First World War as the governing logic of east–west and north–south global relations. Within this framework, imperial nations employed ideas of racial and national superiority as they engaged in exercises of domination and control that promised improvement – both moral and material – on the part of the west in the east and on behalf of the north in the south.

In his particular iteration of civilising mission discourse, Rhodes suggested that the mission was a duty, the inevitable result of western modern enterprise and Anglo-Saxon racial superiority. He also indicated that there was something inevitable and *natural* about the will to power on the part of Anglo-Saxon nations. The United States, after all, had taken to the imperial project like an infant taking to mother's milk. The simile rests, of course, on a distortion of the process of breastfeeding, just as it hinges on a myth about the imperial project that cultural historians and cultural critics have done much to disabuse. The publication of Edward Said's *Orientalism* in 1978 sparked a body of scholarship known often as the new imperial history that has sought to show that the colonial order of the modern era was not natural but, rather, constructed. *Orientalism* was the most 'iconic text' in this body of literature 'which linked culture with colonialism'.[4] In one distillation of this scholarship, historian Catherine Hall has argued that 'the task of ruling the unruly' across the globe required 'particular frames of mind and fields of vision as well as technologies of power'.[5] The civilising mission that Rhodes, Kipling and others championed is one such frame of mind – and one that was buttressed by particular hierarchies of gender and race, not to mention by institutions of high and popular culture. While Rhodes may have understood it as the natural outcome of Anglo-Saxon superiority, a generation of new imperial historians has identified the civilising mission as a cultural and ideological imperative. It was just one component of an imperial consciousness that was made legible and material through governmental and civic 'institutions of colonialism'.[6]

As it has sought to identify and understand the application of knowledge, discipline and pleasure to the task of colonial rule, the new imperial history has built on the work of Said and post-colonial critics. In the process, it has placed culture and its institutions front and centre in its analysis of colonialism. It has been

3 Frank Ninkovich, *The United States and Imperialism* (Oxford, 2001), p. 10.
4 Catherine Hall, 'Culture and Identity in Imperial Britain', in Sarah Stockwell (ed.) *The British Empire: Themes and Perspectives* (Oxford, 2008), p. 199.
5 Catherine Hall, 'William Knibb and the Black British Subject', in Martin Daunton and Rick Halperin (eds), *Empire and Others: British Encounters with Indigenous Peoples* (Philadelphia, PA, 1999), pp. 300–324, esp. p. 303. See also Catherine Hall, *Civilising Subjects: Metropole and Colony in the English Imagination, 1830–1867* (Chicago, IL, 2002).
6 Annie Coombes, *Reinventing Africa: Museums, Material Culture, and Popular Imagination in Late Victorian and Edwardian England* (New Haven, CT, 1994), p. 5; Alice Conklin, *A Mission to Civilize: The Republican Idea of Empire in France and West Africa, 1895–1930* (Stanford, CA, 1997), p. 3.

aided by Said's contravention of the understanding of culture as a superstructural or epiphenomenal effect, a residue, perhaps, of political and economic processes of domination.[7] Practitioners of the new imperial history have insisted that 'cultural practice' is 'inseparable from the political and economic dimensions of imperialism'.[8] A generation of historians has shown that 'culture may be understood' as 'the processes of signification through which people – consciously and unconsciously, intentionally and unintentionally – structure both social relationships and the material world'.[9] This understanding of culture has allowed imperial historians to take seriously notions like the civilising mission, which had long been written off as the racist cavils of men like Rhodes, the opportunistic rationalisation of military forces, the cynical promotion of ambitious governments or the false consciousness of the working classes. Ultimately, the civilising mission was not 'window dressing' for empire.[10] Nor was it a 'moral fig leaf', obscuring brute power, racial arrogance and material greed.[11] It was not a veneer, nor either an obvious good or a racist ploy. To treat the civilising mission as such hinders us from getting at the 'whole constellation of meanings, images, ideas and values that helped to shape and direct' empires in the nineteenth and twentieth centuries, for it provided a powerful and persuasive organising logic for imperial ventures and imperial critique throughout the modern era.[12]

As they have probed the workings of empire in the modern age, cultural historians have identified race and gender as central organising devices that have underwritten the notion of civilisation and enabled the ideal of the civilising mission to flourish.[13] At the heart of the civilising mission in its Anglo-American variant was the conviction that the world was divided into barbaric and elevated races. If, at the beginning of the nineteenth century, race was largely a moral category, connected to stages of development and to habits of labour, by the century's end it had assumed a biological guise, measurable through eugenic means. *Fin-de-siècle* proclamations about the inevitable triumph of the United States and European powers evident in the writings of Rhodes and Kipling, among others, reflected the intensification of racial thinking around the civilising mission over the course of the nineteenth century. The words of Rhodes and Kipling also remind us that

7   Edward Said, *Culture and Imperialism* (New York, 1993); Edward Said, *Orientalism: Western Conceptions of the Orient* (New York, 1978); Saloni Mathur, *India By Design: Colonial History and Cultural Display* (Berkeley, CA, 2007), p. 7.
8   John M. MacKenzie, 'Empire and Metropolitan Cultures', in Andrew Porter (ed.), *Oxford History of the British Empire*: vol. 3, *The Nineteenth Century* (Oxford, 1999): pp. 270–94, esp. pp. 272–3.
9   Mary A. Renda, *Taking Haiti: Military Occupation and the Culture of US Imperialism* (Chapel Hill, NC, 2001): p. 24.
10   Conklin, *A Mission to Civilize*, p. 2.
11   Ninkovich, *The United States and Imperialism*, p. 90.
12   Renda, *Taking Haiti*, p. 15.
13   See, especially, Gail Bederman, *Manliness and Civilization: A Cultural History of Gender and Race in the United States, 1880–1917* (Chicago, IL, 1995), chap. 1.

gender performed critical ideological work in the maintenance of imperialism.[14] At the core of the civilising mission ideal resided a manly colonialist who would identify vocation, fulfil destiny and find meaning in an expanding empire. This notion of Anglo-Saxon masculinity developed alongside changing understandings of African, Asian and Hispanic masculinity that coalesced during the nineteenth and twentieth centuries. So, too, were the trope and the ideal of femininity central to the civilising mission of empire. Exploiting their power in his proclamations aboard the *Hapsburg*, Rhodes had suggested the maternal qualities of imperialism as he offered the vision of a nurturing Britain leading an infant United States on its way. The broader maternal capacities of empire were not lost on imperial women themselves, who jockeyed – in their various capacities as missionaries' wives, social reformers and political figures – to become 'necessary partners' in empire. Like their male counterparts, they had recourse to the white woman's burden as they made claims for their special capacity to uplift their darker-skinned, and, resultantly, less fortunate, sisters around the globe.[15] Examining these dynamics around race and gender brings to light the fact that the civilising mission, like the broader imperial project itself, relied upon a dynamic and complex intellectual and cultural apparatus that had a series of invented binaries at its heart. To probe these is to take up the call to unmask the workings of imperial power that has been made by many historians, and especially those inspired by feminist theory.[16]

The new imperial history has also sought to interrogate yet another binary – that of colony and metropole. By discussing imperialism under the framework of exchange and encounter, historians have placed metropole and colony in the same field of analysis.[17] Taking the lead from the work of Said and others, historians have argued that empire and colony had a 'symbiotic' relationship.[18] Building on this line of argument, still others have held that empire actually 'permeated', 'saturated', 'steeped' or 'suffused' the home front and its cultural contours, especially in the urban centres of Europe.[19] A subset of this literature has taken a visual and material

---

14   On the relationship between the two, see Gilmour, *The Long Recessional*, p. 137.
15   Lora Wildenthal, *German Women for Empire, 1884–1945* (Durham, NC, 2001), p. 130; Antoinette Burton, *Burdens of History: British Feminists, Indian Women, and Imperial Culture, 1865–1915* (Chapel Hill, NC, 1994).
16   See, for example, Joan Scott, *Gender and the Politics of History* (New York, rev. edn, 1999); Mrinalini Sinha, *Colonial Masculinity: The 'Manly Englishman' and the 'Effeminate Bengali' in the Late Nineteenth Century* (Manchester and New York, 1995); Philippa Levine, *Prostitution, Race, and Politics: Policing Venereal Disease in the British Empire* (New York, 2003).
17   Ibid. See also Antoinette Burton, *At the Heart of the Empire: Indians and the Colonial Encounter in Later Victorian England* (Berkeley, CA, 1998); Hall, *Civilising Subjects*; Catherine Hall and Sonya O. Rose (eds), *At Home with the Empire: Metropolitan Cultures in an Imperial World* (Cambridge, 2006); MacKenzie, 'Empire and Metropolitan Cultures', pp. 270–71.
18   Conklin, *A Mission to Civilize*, p. 5.
19   Stephen Howe, 'Empire and Ideology', in Sarah Stockwell (ed.), *The British Empire: Themes and Perspectives* (Oxford, 2008), p. 161.

turn, as it has concentrated on the ubiquity of artefacts, advertisements and exhibitions that, together, translated the civilising mission into spectacular form in the service of developing a consensual, cross-class public that endorsed the imperial enterprise.[20] These lines of inquiry have led to the formulation of a new orthodoxy that has held that 'colony and metropole are terms which can be understood only in relation to each other' – and, ultimately, that 'without colonialism, there would have been no Europe'.[21] At one time, this new orthodoxy met a strong challenge from Bernard Porter, who vigorously questioned the degree to which empire played a necessary and pervasive role in the formation of Britain's domestic culture.[22] Ostensibly an argument about empire, this now largely concluded discussion was itself a refraction of a larger debate about evidence, causation and culture.[23]

Sidestepping this debate to examine the workings of the civilising mission, this chapter endorses the consensus that 'cultural expressions of Empire were undoubtedly highly pervasive' and influential during the long nineteenth and early twentieth centuries, whether in the British or the American case.[24] It engages the theme of the civilising mission as a way of appreciating the contributions of the cultural history of empire, of rectifying the shortcomings of the new imperial history and of forging new directions for cultural analyses of empire. Many new imperial histories took their inspirations from literary and cultural studies, and the field 'has continued to be marked by its origin'.[25] Therefore, historians have examined empire through language and representation. As they have sought to bring material and social heft to these analyses, historians have embraced the notion that imperial discourse is 'a set of practices' and processes that are tied to institutions and 'technologies of power'.[26] The civilising mission in its changing guises has provided an effective site for such analysis – and revisiting this theme allows us to move beyond the discursive and the textual, connecting the 'amorphous stuff of culture' to such enterprises as engineering, diplomacy and military practice.[27] As it evolved through the nineteenth and twentieth centuries, the Anglo-American civilising mission encompassed not only representations, but also social relations; it concerned itself not just with the software of empire, but also with the hardware of empire; and, finally, it was preoccupied not simply with imagination, but additionally with infrastructure. Guns, medicines, canals

---

20 Coombes, *Reinventing Africa*, p. 3; MacKenzie, 'Empire and Metropolitan Cultures', esp. p. 291.

21 Hall, *Civilising Subjects*, pp. 12, 15; Conklin, *A Mission to Civilize*; Howe, 'Empire and Ideology', p. 161.

22 Howe, 'Empire and Ideology', p. 161; Bernard Porter, *The Absent-Minded Imperialists: Empire, Society, and Culture in Britain* (Oxford, 2004).

23 See Hall, 'Culture and Identity in Imperial Britain', p. 200.

24 MacKenzie, 'Empire and Metropolitan Cultures', p. 291.

25 Howe, 'Empire and Ideology', p. 164.

26 Hall, 'Culture and Identity in Imperial Britain', pp. 202–203.

27 Kristin Hoganson, *Fighting for American Manhood: How Gender Politics Provoked the Spanish-American and Philippine-American Wars* (New Haven, CT, 1998), p. 3; Howe, 'Empire and Ideology', p. 159; Hall, 'Culture and Identity', p. 200.

and harbours were not just feats of technology or engineering; rather, they were regarded in the west as the 'great work of civilization'.[28] Ultimately, to consider the history of the civilising mission is to address imperial culture in its fullest dimensions. Indeed, steamers like the *Hapsburg*, on which Cecil Rhodes sailed to work on the Cape to Cairo Canal and Railway, provided the very stage for the articulation of civilising mission discourse.

Rhodes' speech aboard the *Hapsburg* suggests still another important direction for revising the cultural history of empire. Even in their most dynamic forms, cultural histories of empire have often taken the form of national stories. Yet, as Rhodes' words remind us, the civilising mission was part of an international, even transnational discussion of global domination. His pronouncements highlight the existence of connected histories of national development whose chronicling requires a distinctly 'transnational thinking'.[29] As a contribution towards this effort, this chapter reprises the national histories of the civilising mission discourse as it developed in the Anglo-American context, where the civilising mission was steeped in Christianity, morality and race thinking. In the conclusion, this chapter gestures towards transnational possibilities for writing future histories of the civilising mission.[30]

Ultimately, by considering the civilising mission, we can assess past histories and future possibilities for understanding for the cultural logic of empire. The cultural history of empire has been written as a history of interchange, with metropole and colony both figuring as laboratories for addressing imperial dreams and realities.[31] Moreover, imperial historians have shown the cultural encounter to be, by nature, 'complex, ambiguous, and unstable', uneven and dialogical rather than unidirectional.[32] Like culture itself, the civilising mission was dynamic, evolving throughout its career to address shifting colonial and metropolitan realities. It was a dominating script of colonialism that proved difficult, even impossible, to govern, much like modern empires themselves. In the end, like Anglo-American imperialism itself, the career of the civilising mission was a story of disappointment, refashioning, reversal and rebirth. It required constant reworking and it invited manifold responses throughout its rich career in the modern era.

---

28 Ninkovich, *The United States and Imperialism*, p. 106.
29 Hall, *Civilising Subjects*, pp. 7, 9.
30 Renda, *Taking Haiti*, p. 25.
31 Conklin, *A Mission to Civilize*, p. 3.
32 T.C. McCaskie, 'Cultural Encounters: Britain and Africa in the Nineteenth Century', in Andrew Porter (ed.), *Oxford History of the British Empire*: vol. 3, *The Nineteenth Century* (Oxford, 1999), esp. p. 663.

Great Britain and the Emergence of the Civilising Mission

The civilising mission had a long, dynamic career within British imperial history. From the later eighteenth to the mid-twentieth century, notions of civilisation were tied in variable ways to race and gender.[33] They helped to organise a changing 'grammar of difference' and superiority that was central to the operation, maintenance and promotion of Britain's empire.[34] Nineteenth-century imperialists of all stripes heralded the global spread of 'civilisation': an intellectual, material, scientific and cultural quality embodied in the ideas, commodities, bodily practices, technologies, social formations and institutions of urban, industrial society.[35] The civilising mission would congeal in a visible fashion in the metropole through the forms of commodity capitalism and world's fairs at the moment of the high imperialism of the later nineteenth century, but the notion dates back to the later eighteenth century. At that moment of transition between the first and second British empires, the imperatives of commerce, civilisation and Christianity combined to inform an imperial mission that bound diverse locations in an imperial whole, all the while helping to forge a sense of Britishness within the metropole. As a discourse and a project, the civilising mission would allow a range of historical actors and cultural interlocutors to take their places as part of the imperial enterprise.

At its inception in the later eighteenth century, many embraced the civilising mission as an expressly secular, humanitarian project. It eventually grew into a religious, moral endeavour. In the early nineteenth century, an array of imperial actors – religious and secular, male and female – rallied around the mission, as they sought to forge an improving, moral civilisation through myriad reforming efforts across the globe. These ameliorative projects never proceeded without division; nor did they lack for detractors. But it was India's Sepoy Rebellion of 1857 and Jamaica's Governor Eyre controversy of 1865 that bred decisive and widespread doubt and disillusionment with the promises of reform.[36] As the century wore on, the civilising mission assumed an increasingly racialised form in the face of the Scramble for Africa, as Rhodes' *Hapsburg* sentiments suggest. This shift was underwritten by a hardening of Social Darwinist and eugenic thinking, by an accumulation of ethnographic and geographical knowledge, and by a range of pictorial, journalistic and material representations.[37] These alterations in the civilising mission provide a window onto the 'shifting tone of empire' in the nineteenth century, when conceptions of domination became increasingly bellicose

---

33   Catherine Hall, 'Of Gender and Empire: Reflections on the Nineteenth Century', in
     Philippa Levine (ed.), *Gender and Empire* (Oxford, 2004), p. 49.
34   Hall, 'Culture and Identity in Imperial Britain', p. 205; Hall, *Civilising Subjects*, p. 17;
     Howe, 'Empire and Ideology', p. 166.
35   Mackenzie, 'Empire and Metropolitan Cultures', pp. 270-71; Hall, *Civilising Subjects*;
     Levine, *Prostitution, Race, and Politics*, p. 61.
36   See, for example, John Marriott, *The Other Empire: Metropolis, India, and Progress in the
     Colonial Imagination* (Manchester, 2003), pp. 130, 133, 143, 155, 166, 222, 229.
37   See Porter, Introduction, p. 24.

and popular.[38] By century's end, the civilising mission would be reborn in an aggressive, racialised popular imperialism that was exemplified by the Scramble for Africa and in the Anglo-Boer War. It would also be ready for export to the United States of America.

Many historians have pointed to James Mill's *History of British India* as a *locus classicus* for articulating the civilising mission in its early nineteenth-century liberal guise. In Mill's rendition, civilisation was tied explicitly to gender order and especially to the status of women. Writing of the gender order in the east and west, Mill observed, 'Among rude people, the women are generally degraded; among civilized people they are exalted'.[39] In the minds of Mill and his contemporaries, civilising meant setting gender relations on their proper course or aligning them with the middle-class domestic ideal. From the 1780s onward, the crusade to abolish *sati*, or widow-burning, provided an effective avenue to rectify the high-caste Hindu woman's status as the 'degraded victim of her barbaric society' and so to engage in the civilising mission.[40] The campaign to abolish *sati*, which culminated in the 1829 legal prohibition, provides a particularly effective window onto the cultural dynamics of the production of imperial reforming consciousness. Orientalist scholars assiduously sought to sediment *sati* as a Brahmanic scriptural practice in the later eighteenth and nineteenth centuries, evangelical preachers brought it to the consciousness of metropolitan and provincial audiences, visual images kindled broader sympathy for *sati*'s victims, and Parliamentary testimony honed in on alleged Hindu depravity.[41] In this 'process of symbolic cultural constitution' which linked metropole and colony, the high-caste Hindu woman came to the fore. Perceived as the victim of barbarism and superstition, she became the living proof of Indian depravity, writ large. In turn, *sati* became a 'potent symbol of what was wrong with India'. And it became imperative that the high-caste Hindu woman, the victim of *sati*, 'be saved by the civilising power of the colonial state'. The practice was so abominable – so 'undermining to British notions of civilisation' – in the British reforming mind as to lead to a departure from practices of religious toleration that had technically marked the rule of subject peoples in India.[42]

This early intervention in the gender politics of India had long-lasting effects in enabling women to become cultural and political agents of imperial reform. As Mrinalini Sinha, Antoinette Burton and others have noted, the 'degraded 'Hindoo woman' held enduring freight in the nineteenth century, whether in debates over child marriage, the *zenana* or the age of consent. As this figure 'traveled across the circuits of empire', a range of women entered the political sphere as advocates who fought for civilisation, and ultimately, sought the vote on behalf of their subaltern

---

38 MacKenzie, 'Empire and Metropolitan Cultures', p. 272.
39 James Mill, *The History of British India* (1808, London, 1858), p. 309.
40 Hall, 'Of Gender and Empire, p. 51.
41 Lata Mani, *Contentious Traditions: The Debate on Sati in Colonial India* (Berkeley, CA, 1998), pp. 2, 15.
42 Hall, 'Of Gender and Empire', pp. 53–5, esp. p. 53.

sisters.[43] Well into the twentieth century, the Englishwoman's 'quest for inclusion in the imperial state was predicated' on the cultural construction of the Indian woman in the public sphere, and especially in the feminist press, as a helpless victim – a 'less civilised female other'. Along with the women of Central Africa, Turkey, Egypt, Tibet and China, she awaited redress by metropolitan reform on the part of such women as Mary Carpenter, Millicent Garret Fawcett and Eleanor Rathbone, all of whom participated in the imperial civilising mission. Such a notion was especially potent in the global campaign to repeal the Contagious Diseases Acts, wherein Josephine Butler and other crusaders sought to rise to the level of 'imperial purifiers' as they married the civilising mission to a medico-moral discourse.[44] White women would continue in this role as the moral and physical cleansers of empire well into the twentieth century, when they taught hygienic and domestic practices to African women as part of an effort to produce 'clean and proper-looking African bodies'.[45]

If the civilising mission facilitated the elevation of women the world over, it also allowed for the uplift of the African male and his family, and the cleansing of the British Caribbean, through the process of emancipation – first, by the abolition of the slave trade in 1807, and later by the ending of slavery itself in 1834. Like the banning of *sati*, the anti-slavery campaign has a history dating back to the eighteenth century, when abolitionists drew up schemes for free labour in Africa that would allow for the rise of civility, while transforming slaves into subjects.[46] Abolition took an evangelical turn in the later eighteenth century. Christopher Leslie Brown has argued that early advocates of anti-slavery may have been accidental abolitionists, concerned more with the promulgation of religion than with the end of bondage, invested more in morality than in labour.[47] However, evangelical Christianity became increasingly central to the cause of emancipation, and to a variegated civilising mission discourse, as missionaries proclaimed from the pulpit the evils of slavery to a provincial public comprising the middle classes, lower middle classes and artisans.[48] One exemplar of this missionary caste was William Knibb, a representative of the Baptist Missionary Society, who imagined emancipation in Jamaica as a 'great experiment' in forming 'new colonial subjects' who were the 'subjects of a new cultural order and a new gender order' that would be forged to mirror British middle-class domesticity. For Knibb and his colleagues, emancipation and evangelicalism were, together, the vehicles for civilising Jamaican

---

43 Ibid., pp. 58, 54–5; Clare Midgley (ed.), 'Gender and Imperialism: Mapping the Connections', in Midgley, (ed.) *Gender and Empire* (Manchester, 1998), pp. 1–21; Sinha, *Colonial Masculinity*.

44 Burton, *Burdens of History*, pp. 7–9, 17, 94, 105, 152.

45 Timothy Burke, *Lifebuoy Men, Lux Women: Commodification, Consumption, and Cleanliness in Modern Zimbabwe* (Durham, NC, 1996), pp. 52, 84, 125; Anne McClintock, *Imperial Leather: Race, Gender and Sexuality in the Colonial Contest* (New York, 1995).

46 Christopher Leslie Brown, *Moral Capital: Foundations of British Abolitionism* (Chapel Hill, NC, 2006), pp. 226–30.

47 Brown, *Moral Capital*.

48 Patricia Grimshaw, 'Faith, Missionary Life, and the Family', in Levine, *Gender and Empire*, p. 264.

slaves. In Knibb's mind, emancipation would facilitate the creation of 'new Christian subjects, babes in Christ washed clean, capable of transformation into labouring men and domesticated women'. For men such as Knibb, emancipation truly had a 'double meaning', like the civilising mission more generally.[49] It promised to cleanse not only the slave, but the slaveholder as well. Under the regime of slavery, Knibb noted, it was not only Africans, but white men, too, who became 'savages, uncultivated and uncivilized'. Although emancipation became a reality in 1834, the long process of apprenticeship proved to be a disappointment. Attempts to remake the emancipated black subject as free, docile and Christian did not meet the hopes of their progenitors. William Knibb's civilising dream of a 'family of man' characterised by a 'harmonious racially mixed society' died with him in 1845, and new, racialised stereotypes came to the fore in the 1850s.[50]

Like the campaign to end *sati*, the crusade for emancipation had an afterlife across the empire that enabled the spread of the civilising mission. The particularly Christian civilising discourse to which it gave rise facilitated the entry of women into the missionary cause. In the mid-nineteenth century, mission work became a feminised enterprise, with wives as the 'helpmeets' of their men and as useful agents of civilisation.[51] This was the case not only in the Caribbean, but across the empire. Christianity gave women a special place within the civilising mission, allowing them to make claims of 'redemptive authority'.[52] This sort of opening would pave the way for women's sustained intervention in the empire later in the century when motherhood became a dominant trope. Aiding this strategy was a growing preoccupation with the improvement of childhood, which, as Fiona Paisley has noted, became a central project and metaphor for promoting 'the reinvigoration of the imperial and colonial nation'. Middle-class white women seized on the rhetorical and pragmatic opportunities that this turn afforded. They deemed themselves especially well suited to take up the role of social mothering at home and abroad, aiming to 'bring civilisation' both to urban slums and to 'childlike lesser races'.[53] The campaign for abolition also gave rise to new heroes who were lauded in British newspapers and popular literature as exemplars of the civilising mission. One of the best examples is David Livingstone, who continued the 'Christian fight' against slavery in Africa in the tradition of earlier luminaries like William Wilberforce and contemporary leaders including General Gordon.[54]

These reverberations and continuities notwithstanding, the tenor and thrust of the civilising mission – and of British imperialism more generally – shifted after

49   Hall, *Civilising Subjects*, p. 21.
50   Hall, 'William Knibb and the Black British Subject', pp. 305, 313–14, 320–21.
51   Hall, 'Of Gender and Empire', p. 60; Grimshaw, 'Faith, Missionary Life, and the Family', p. 265; Susan Thorne, *Congregational Missions and the Making of an Imperial Culture in Nineteenth-Century England* (StanfordStanford, CA, 1999).
52   Burton, *Burdens of History*, pp. 42–5.
53   Fiona Paisley, 'Childhood and Race: Growing Up in the Empire', in Levine, *Gender and Empire*, pp. 241–2.
54   McCaskie, 'Cultural Encounters', p. 674; MacKenzie, 'Empire and Metropolitan Cultures', p. 275.

mid-century as social openness gave way to cultural containment and as liberal reform ceded to bureaucratic rule. Together, emancipation, the Sepoy Revolt and the Governor Eyre controversy – all publicised in the press at home – exposed the limits of the civilising mission in its liberal and Protestant variant. These perceived limitations effected changes in the mode of government and the culture of daily life in the colonies in palpably material ways. Not only did the Mutiny mark the demise of the East India Company, the Revolt also gave rise to new habits of dress, eating and childrearing that sought to weave a 'web of Britishness' around the vulnerable British body.[55] These changes were evident in the built environment and cultural geography of India under the Raj, as embodied in its Hill Stations and clubs.[56]

Even more than the changes in India and the Caribbean, however, it was the turn to African colonisation that epitomised the shifts in the civilising mission and in the cultural logic of imperial rule as the century drew to a close. As T.C. McCaskie notes, the encounter with Africa was longstanding, developing throughout the nineteenth century as engagement with the continent shifted from trade with the West African Coast to interior exploration and occupation. During the later part of the century, imperial acceleration gave rise to an increasingly assiduous desire to 'civilise' Africa, 'not simply by the putatively humane enterprises of missionary enterprise and free trade, but also by exposing its peoples to all of the many ordering technologies and secular disciplines of modern bourgeois life'.[57] Hardened notions of biological race and national destiny underwrote these enterprises. The later nineteenth century saw 'an increasing racial awareness being added to early Victorian paternalism', as experiments like the foundation of Freetown, Sierra Leone, designed to create a self-sustaining community of free labour, gave way to punitive invasions and exploitative investment in the interior of Africa.[58] Oftentimes, this racial thinking was anything but benevolent, drawing as it did upon base versions of Social Darwinism, eugenics and jingoistic Anglo-Saxon superiority as exemplified in the words and writings of Cecil Rhodes. Technological innovation, too, in the form of communications, weaponry and medicine augmented the 'capacity for cultural transmission' in the latter decades of the nineteenth century. During the Scramble for Africa, the civilising mission became a markedly racist and particularly technocratic enterprise. Ultimately, McCaskie writes, during the later nineteenth century, 'African cultures succumbed to the onslaught of a Britain (and Europe)

---

55   E.W. Collingham, *Imperial Bodies: The Physical Experience of the Raj, c.1800–1947* (Cambridge, 2001), pp. 7, 92, 112, as cited in Hall, 'Of Gender and Empire', p. 72.

56   Dane Kennedy, *The Magic Mountains: Hill Stations and the British Raj* (Berkeley, CA, 1996); Mary Procida, *Married to the Empire: Gender, Politics and Imperialism in India* (Manchester, 2002); Mrinalini Sinha, 'Britishness, Clubability and the Imperial Public Sphere: The Genealogy of an Imperial Institution in Colonial India', *Journal of British Studies* 40 (2001): pp. 481–529; Elizabeth Buettner, *Empire Families: Britons and Late Imperial India* (Oxford, 2004).

57   McCaskie, 'Cultural Encounters', p. 675.

58   Ibid., pp. 685–6.

now organized, translated and mobilized through the ever accelerating pace of modernity'.[59]

In Britain, commodity culture popularised the notion of racial superiority on which the civilising mission hinged at the *fin de siècle*. The advertisements for Pears Soap that promised to whitewash the Dark Continent in the name of civilisation are only the best-known exemplars of commodity culture's service to the civilising mission. Thanks to corporations like Pears Soap, the dirty, savage and often naked African body became a 'pervasive part of colonial sentiment and white subjectivity'. Western commodification promised cleanliness and civilisation, as it linked goods and market expansion to civilised society.[60] Legitimated by ethnography and anthropology, visual culture, too, underwrote this racial and geographical hierarchy. As Philippa Levine has shown, the undress of the ethnographic photograph helped to drive home understandings of Africans as savage or infantile.[61] Finally, exhibitions and world's fairs such as the Stanley and African Exhibition of 1890, held in London, used spectacular practice to make Africa available for consumption under the guise of the scientific primitive. Through its displays of weapons and arts, the organisers cast the natives of the continent as primitive and heathen, yet susceptible to uplift.[62] Even more strikingly, its human showcases of live Africans snatched from the continent and placed on display crudely employed the spectacle of race to highlight the difference between 'British enterprise' and 'African primitivism'. Given their power and popularity, it proved difficult to govern the outcomes of these mass spectacles, and especially the living displays. It was possible, Felix Driver has noted, for exhibits to 'depart from the scripts', for the popular exhibitions 'promised an exchange of sorts, between observers and observed, colonizers and colonized'.[63] This was certainly the case at another late-nineteenth-century show, the Colonial and Indian Exhibition of 1886. One visitor, T.N. Mukharji, noted that the former prisoners who constituted the living displays at the Exhibition went against the grain of the display's intent of juxtaposing primitivism and progress. He reported that the living subjects at the show were remarkably dignified in their bearing. They stood in stark and striking contrast to the teeming poor of greater London. Ultimately, Mukharji's metropolitan sojourn prompted him to question the status of London as the 'very fountain-head of modern civilization'.[64] With such an allegation, Mukharji cast doubt on the certainty of the imperial hierarchies that the Colonial and Indian Exhibition, like so many others, sought to enshrine. Such allegations would fuel a nascent nationalist

59   Ibid., p. 688.
60   Burke, *Lifebuoy Men, Lux Women*, pp. 17–24, esp. p. 23.
61   Philippa Levine, 'States of Undress: Nakedness and the Colonial Imagination', *Victorian Studies* 50/2 (2008): pp. 189–219; see also James Ryan, *Picturing Empire: Photography and the Visualization of the British Empire* (Chicago, IL, 1997).
62   Coombes, *Reinventing Africa*, p. 81.
63   Felix Driver, *Geography Militant: Cultures of Exploration and Empire* (Oxford, 2001), pp. 148–9.
64   Mathur, *India By Design*, p. 68; Antoinette Burton, 'Making A Spectacle of Empire: Indian Travelers in Fin de Siècle London', *History Workshop Journal* 42 (1996): pp. 126–46.

movement in India and, later, inform anti-colonial discourse. This is just once instance of the ways in which these living villages and the reflections they yielded led to a broader questioning of the very hierarchies of metropole and colony as well as civilised and uncivilised that underwrote the late nineteenth-century imperial mission.[65]

A very different spectacle of technology was on display in the Anglo-Boer War and in First World War. Like the ethnographic shows in the metropole, these cataclysmic events gave way to pressing questions about western superiority and the civilising mission. Michael Adas and Daniel Headrick have both illustrated the pivotal role played by science and technology in 'creating the reality of Europe's power overseas and the myth of its superior civilization'.[66] Technology and the virtues that it suggested, including reason and masculinity, were the properties of Europe, whereas primitivism, fatalism and femininity were the tendencies of Asians and Africans. To be sure, there were those who questioned this formulation before the Great War. But it was the calamitous effects of First World War which gave rise to an expressly anti-colonial critique. During the Great War, colonial troops witnessed the destructive ends of technology not only in Africa, Asia and the Arab world, but also in the very heart of Europe. These experiences allowed critics of empire to attack the technological promises of the civilising mission as 'unmatched hubris'.[67] Among these ranks we can count not only western intellectuals, but also colonial critics including Tagore, Ghose and, of course, Mahatma Gandhi, whose *Hind Swaraj* famously mounted a critique of the civilising mission by undoing the supposed alignment of moral improvement and industrial progress. Turning accepted hierarchies on their heads, Gandhi declared, 'Civilization is not an incurable disease, but it should never be forgotten that the English are at present afflicted by it'.[68]

The United States and the Adoption of the Civilising Mission

Ten years earlier, on the eve of the American century, British imperialist Cecil Rhodes had encouraged the United States, a nation relatively new to the modern imperial project, to take up the Anglo-Saxon civilising mission. In the decade

---

65 Burton, *At the Heart of the Empire*, p. 71.
66 Conklin, *A Mission to Civilize*, p. 70; see also Michael Adas, *Machines as the Measure of Men: Science, Technology, and Ideologies of Western Dominance* (Ithaca, NY, 1989); Daniel J. Headrick, *The Tools of Empire: Technology and European Imperialism in the Nineteenth Century* (New York, 1981).
67 Michael Adas, 'Contested Hegemony: The Great War and the Afro-Asian Assault on the Civilizing Mission Ideology', *Journal of World History* 15/1 (2004): pp. 31–63, esp. p. 41.
68 M.K. Gandhi, *Hind Swaraj* (1909), as excerpted in Homer A. Jack (ed.), *The Gandhi Reader: A Sourcebook of his Life and Writings* (New York, 1994), p. 107.

leading up to First World War, American enthusiasts for empire gladly endorsed its rhetorical mantle and racial imperative as they sought to enter into a dense and complex imperial field that had been dominated by European states for centuries.[69] It was, of course, the US conquest of the Philippines that inspired Rudyard Kipling's poem 'The White Man's Burden', which characterised the civilising mission as a particular combination of 'racial destiny and humanitarian martyrdom'.[70] A cultural commodity in its own right, the poem has become the best-known symbol of the Anglo-Saxon civilising mission at the turn of the century. At that time, the United States gravitated to the imperial project. To be sure, there were many enthusiasts, but not everyone took immediately to the endeavour like an infant to 'mother's milk'. And in the end the mission proved, for many charged with its deliverance, to be far from natural.

Arguably the American west was one of the first imperial locales in the nineteenth century, as enthusiasm for Manifest Destiny suggested. As the frontier closed and this first 'expansive moment' came to an end, Americans looked to Hawaii and eventually to Cuba and Puerto Rico to find a rightful home for their civilising mission.[71] In these islands as in the Philippines, they would seek to supplant the dishonourable, dysfunctional Spanish Empire of old. It was not just the closure of the frontier, but industrial unrest, economic depression, agricultural crisis and immigration that kindled imperial sentiment. Gail Bederman and other scholars have tied these troubles to a broader cultural ferment that had at its centre a national crisis of masculinity. Threatened by demographic and industrial shifts, American men embraced a notion of civilisation that had taken hold in the nineteenth century when the nation became 'obsessed' with the connections between 'manhood and racial dominance'.[72] They sought to develop an 'advanced manliness' whose expression was found in strenuousness, 'intelligence, altruism, and morality'.[73] According to its advocates, this form of manliness was at once quintessentially American, but also wholly cosmopolitan. In the spirit of Rhodes, it advocated the creation of a global civilisation based on Anglo-Saxon race superiority as it yoked 'male dominance and white supremacy to a Darwinist version of Protestant millennialism'.[74]

Manly civilisation provided a logic for the Spanish-American War, as Kristin Hoganson has shown. Reluctant interventionists, Americans rose to defend Cuba against Spanish soldiers, who were portrayed in American culture alternately as effeminate, weak and aristocratic, or as 'savage rapists who lacked the moral

---

69   Paul Kramer, *The Blood of Government*, *The Blood of Government: Race, Empire, the United States, and the Philippines* (Chapel Hill, NC, 2006), p. 11.
70   Ibid., p. 120.
71   Allison L. Sneider, *Suffragists in an Imperial Age: US Expansion and the Woman Question, 1870–1929* (New York, 2008), p. 5.
72   Bederman, *Manliness and Civilization*, p. 4. See also Ninkovich, *The United States and Imperialism*, pp. 35, 41.
73   Bederman, *Manliness and Civilization*, p. 185.
74   Kramer, *The Blood of Government*, p. 46.

sensibilities and self restraint of civilized men'.[75] This endeavour of rescuing manly Cubans from debased or decrepit Spaniards offered a variety of repair work for war enthusiasts, much like that prescribed by William Knibb of the Baptist Missionary Society, who had advocated slave emancipation on the nearby island of Jamaica nearly 70 years before. Ultimately, the struggle in Cuba promised to rescue American manhood from a form of excessive, effete culture associated with urbanisation, commodity capitalism and modernity, and so to set civilisation on its proper course.[76] As in the British case, the deployment of the rhetoric of manliness and civilisation had longstanding effects. One outcome was to produce lines of political inclusion and exclusion. Honour and brotherhood were, in the minds of the advocates of intervention, decidedly male characteristics. Subsequently, in the years after the war, men often pointed to military service and heroism as indicators of future political promise and governmental discernment as they sought to enter the American body politic. In the face of this shoring up of the boundaries of political practice as distinctly male, it should not surprise us that many who opposed intervention in Cuba – not incidentally, in the name of civilisation – were women. However, as the war became a *fait accompli*, women with political ambitions sought to forge a place for themselves in the US Empire, much like their British sisters had done. Notably, they recast the feminine propensity for national housekeeping, important to the maintenance of both changing nation and nascent empire, as a particular variety of military prowess. And, as they adopted the mantle of empire, black and white suffragists alike added 'political rights for women to the list of markers symbolizing the achievement of "civilisation" on a global stage'.[77]

Its appeal notwithstanding, the discourse of 'chivalry' that was deployed in the case of Cuba tended to find its undoing in a self-aggrandising war.[78] In the process, the promises of manly civilisation were 'quickly put to the test'. This was evident during the occupation, which sought to counter centuries of decline under Spain by whitewashing Cuba with improved schools, public works and cleanliness regimes. As in the British case, such a literal and figurative whitewashing endeavoured to inculcate 'social discipline and civilised status'. Yet, like 'political godliness', 'American-imposed cleanliness' proved to be an empty promise for the Cubans. The occupation did not bring enlightened and refined rule to the island. Instead, America's punitive discipline replaced Spain's antiquated barbarism. Violations of the new civic code were punished, for example, through public whippings.[79]

Once reluctant imperialists, the new American converts would bring their hopes for civilisation to the Philippines. More than any other, this imperial venture has become emblematic of the American civilising mission, its promises and its ironies. Despite the high hopes of Roosevelt and his advocates for a 'civilised

---

75   Hoganson, *Fighting for American Manhood*, p. 11.
76   Ibid., p. 139.
77   Sneider, *Suffragists in an Imperial Age*, p. 136.
78   Hoganson, *Fighting for American Manhood*, p. 133.
79   Thomas F. O'Brien, *Making the Americas: The United States and Latin America from the Age of Revolutions to the Era of Globalization* (Albuquerque, NM, 2007), p. 99.

war' that would elevate American manhood, the enterprise in the Pacific was, in truth, a 'squalid little war' that held out little possibility for manly rehabilitation. Stories of wartime atrocities and fears of cultural meltdown abounded in the public sphere.[80] Rather than an 'uplifting and ennobling experience', the fighting 'made a mockery of arguments that imperialism would be a school for building character and manufacturing manhood'.[81] Instead of offering an edifying experience, the dehumanising and bloody war held out the threat of racial degeneration in the sensual tropics. Moreover, the occupation and the resulting failure to develop the islands laid bare the 'vast gap between imperialist promise and performance'. It failed to effect the cultural transformation that the civilising mission had promised for the native population, which was to benefit from missionary activity, commodity capitalism and expanded education, especially in technical and industrial fields, not to mention in the bodily tutelage of grooming and dining. Nor did the 'Engineer's Imperialism' of improving roads, railroads and harbours bring the transformation that civic works purportedly augured.[82] American capitalists who looked to the Philippines to profit were to be disappointed; there was no El Dorado to be found in the islands.[83] Ultimately, the civilising mission was undone, historians have argued, by a number of factors. It was thwarted by the unforeseen challenges of tropical environs; it was also complicated by the legacy of Spanish colonialism. Notably, Spanish colonialism had fostered an indigenous elite class, whose existence complicated any simple efforts at uplift. The simple precepts of the civilising mission broke down in the face of the indigenous elite: 'rather than civilizing savages it appeared that the United States was savaging exemplars of civilization'.[84]

The civilising mission in the Philippines took centre stage in American culture at the 1904 St Louis World's Fair, which, Paul Kramer argues, 'emerged out of colonial institutions and dynamics'. One of its highlights was a Philippine display, which intended to 'convey hegemonic messages about race, capitalism, and US national superiority', all the while showcasing the imperial mission in the Philippines as a story of a movement from 'pathos to progress'.[85] The organisers sought to show the islands as a distinctively 'modern zone of production and consumption', with exhibits on agriculture and forestry. At the same time, they aimed to cast the relationship between the Philippines and the United States as a largely tutelary one, exemplified by the Model Schoolhouse at the centre of the exhibit. Through such strategies, they would endorse the possibilities of the civilising mission and the fruits that had already been garnered in less than five years of US occupation of the islands. In creating the display, the organisers sought the support of Filipino elites.

---

80   Kramer, *Blood of Government*, pp. 90, 146–9; Bederman, *Manliness and Civilization*.
81   Ninkovich, *The United Staes and Imperialism*, pp. 52–3.
82   Michael Adas, *Dominance by Design: Technological Imperatives and America's Civilizing Mission* (Cambridge, MA, 2006), chap. 3.
83   Ninkovich, *The United States and Imperialism*, pp. 67, 234.
84   Hoganson, *Fighting for American Manhood*, p. 185.
85   Kramer, *The Blood of Government*, pp. 230–32.

The native elites proved to be reluctant partners, for they feared that the display would not show Filipinos as cultured, but rather as savage. Their fears were well founded. Ultimately, the racialised notion of primitivism that was embedded in the narrative of the civilising mission turned out to overwhelm promises of uplift. During the Exhibition, the living displays of non-Christian tribes situated in a putatively 'natural' environment occupied the front page in the American press and in the American mind. In particular, the unclad Igorots, who allegedly ate dogs, became the most magnetic representatives of the Philippines. In the end, it was the naked native, aligned with ethnography, on the one hand, and with blackface minstrelsy, on the other, who represented the Philippines at the Fair. Despite concerted efforts to offer an alternate message, the primitive undertones of civilising mission discourse proved all too powerful, and the grammar of the spectacle all too rigid. The native elites had been wise in their recalcitrance. As Paul Kramer explains, fairgoers were drawn to the Igorots not simply out of salacious interest or because of prior prejudices. Instead, it was because they were hungry for the exhibitionary narrative of 'evolutionary progress toward civilization'. As the Filipino elite had feared, it turned out that 'progress was difficult to make into spectacle'.[86]

In the western hemisphere, the civilising mission retained its currency well into the twentieth century, as the US occupation of Haiti under the aegis of 'interventionist paternalism' shows. According to Mary Renda, cultural politics were integral to – and, indeed, inseparable from – the military, political and economic project of the occupation. In turn, the occupation precipitated a 'rich and varied cultural engagement' with Haiti in the United States, as performance art, radio shows, fiction and visual culture made clear.[87] Such productions employed a paternalism based on notions of racial and social superiority, and in the process sought to make the occupation a desirable and necessary enterprise, especially for the troops who were subject to cultural conscription. Myriad 'cultural tools' were geared to enabling marines, themselves often men from the civilian working poor, to engage in the 'Darwinian encounter between civilized man and primitive savage' – including the White City, the Rough Riders, Tarzan and Buffalo Bill's Wild West. At the same time, marines were encouraged to see themselves as would-be father figures of the Haitian people.[88] However, as in the prior cases, the neat hierarchies that propelled the civilising mission collapsed, even when it came to a land that many associated with cannibalism and voodoo. This breakdown is evident in Eugene O'Neill's The Emperor Jones, which featured the story of a land grab by a black convict who became governor of a West Indian Island. Similarly, James Weldon Johnson rejected the opposition between 'civilised self and primitive

86 Kramer, The Blood of Government, p. 269.
87 Renda, Taking Haiti, pp. 11, 18, 20. On Puerto Rico, see Laura Briggs, Reproducing Empire: Race, Sex, Science, and US Imperialism in Puerto Rico (Berkeley, CA, 2002). On Trinidad, see Harvey Neptune, Caliban and the Yankees: Trinidad and the United States Occupation (Chapel Hill, NC, 2007).
88 Renda, Taking Haiti, p. 16.

other'. He portrayed Haitians as civilised while he turned his critical gaze to the evident savagery of the slums of London and New York. Furthermore, if cultural production proved difficult to govern, the lived experience of marines on the ground turned out to be even more unpredictable.[89] Often, these marines came to question the logic of interventionist paternalism and the hierarchies of the civilising mission as they spent time in Haiti. While on the island, they often found that they grew sympathetic to practices deemed beyond the pale of civilisation, including voodoo. Whether in colony or metropole, the script of the civilising mission showed itself to be unruly and unmanageable.

The Recurrence, Resilience and Reprisal of the Civilising Mission

In her analysis of the American occupation of Haiti, Mary Renda argued that the operation of culture was integral to the workings of colonialism, its unpredictability notwithstanding. More specifically, she showed that a 'whole constellation of meanings, images, ideas and values helped to shape and direct' the relationship of the United States with former European colonial possessions, if not in wholly governable ways.[90] The discussion herein has aimed to substantiate and to broaden this assertion by investigating the Anglo-American career of the civilising mission in the modern age. At the turn of this century, this enterprise was a largely collaborative one, with shared notions of race, language and democratic heritage binding Great Britain and the United States. As if to ratify this understanding, Cecil Rhodes had declared aboard the steamer *Hapsburg* that England and the United States stood together in 1899.[91]

When he endorsed the American imperial project, Rhodes attested to the portability of the civilising mission within the Anglo-American context. While Rhodes understood the civilising mission as a particularly Anglo-American ideal, the writings of other scholars attest to its broader currency and flexibility as an overarching cultural logic for modern imperialism. It certainly extended to Greater France, where the *mission civilisatrice* took on a distinctly republican inflection. In her archaeology of the *mission civilisatrice*, Alice Conklin charted the career of 'a particularly French concept', which was invented in the eighteenth century and carried especial freight under the empire of the Third Republic, following 1870, when the French expanded their power across the globe from Africa to Indochina. It shared with the British and American variants a belief in the superiority of western culture. And, like the Anglo-Saxon strain, the *mission civilisatrice* was buttressed by the bureaucratic, scientific and industrial institutions of the west.[92]

---

89   Ibid., pp. 187, 195.
90   Ibid., pp. 18, 15.
91   'Mr Rhodes on Expansion', p. 1.
92   Conklin, *A Mission to Civilize*, p. 1.

It structured itself along the binary of civilisation and barbarism, which had racial and geographic distinctions. And, as the *mission civilisatrice* matured, it embraced an increasingly technocratic vision, centred on health, hygiene, knowledge and reason. For all that the Gallic *mission civilisatrice* shared with its Anglo-Saxon correlate, it also had a particularly French slant in its secular tendencies, its Enlightenment heritage, its reliance on expert knowledge, its scepticism about aristocracy and its elevation of the 'universal principles of 1789'.[93] These tendencies would prove a challenge in several areas, including educational policy, where the French sought to forge an adapted form of education which addressed local particularities, while holding fast to the universalism of France's revolutionary heritage. In the end, these negotiations tended to break down on the ground, where lack of funds and a shortage of teachers combined to make the civilising mission a failure.[94] Its limits notwithstanding, the French *mission civilisatrice* proved to be notably fungible, as J.P. Daughton has demonstrated. The French mission was especially capacious, able to accommodate the work and words of the Jesuit missionaries, priests and nuns who had provided the foundations of empire in such disparate locales as Indochina, Tahiti and Madagascar.[95] In the interwar era, Gary Wilder has shown, the mission became especially technocratic under the aegis of colonial humanism. And, in an ironic reversal, black intellectuals pointed to the potentials of humanism as race uplift, as they embraced a cosmopolitan vision of *négritude*.[96]

In the interwar era, the civilising mission ceased to be the purview of the liberal democracies of the west. Under Stalin, the Soviet Union embraced 'state sponsored evolutionism' – and such technologies of rule as the census, map and museum long associated with liberal governmentality – as it sought to forge a nation out of its internal empire.[97] And, in a related move, Russian reformers, both men and women, crusaded against the pervasiveness of the veil in the Muslim provinces. In the process, they situated the Muslim women of central Asia in a subject position akin to that occupied by the Hindu woman of the Indian subcontinent – the epitome of backwardness, abjectness and tribalism.[98] If the civilising mission was portable to the Stalinist left, it proved to be equally adaptable to the Fascist right. Given his endorsement of Greco-Roman heritage it should be no surprise that even Mussolini cleaved to the civilising mission as he sought to civilise the 'savages' of Ethiopia in the name of fascist glory.[99]

---

93   Ibid., p. 75.

94   Ibid., pp. 137–9.

95   J.P. Daughton, *An Empire Divided: Religion, Republicanism, and the Making of French Colonialism, 1880–1914* (Oxford, 2008).

96   Gary Wilder, *The French Imperial Nation-State: Negritude and Colonial Humanism between the World Wars* (Chicago, IL, 2005).

97   Francine Hirsch, *Empire of Nations: Ethnographic Knowledge and the Making of the Soviet Union* (Ithaca, NY, 2005).

98   Douglas Northrop, *Veiled Empire: Gender and Power in Stalinist Central Asia* (Ithaca, NY, 2004).

99   A.J. Barker, *The Civilizing Mission: A History of the Italo-Ethiopian War of 1935–36* (New York, 1968), pp. 231, 288, 309; see also Neptune, *Caliban and the Yankees*, pp. 4, 38.

The enduring career of the civilising mission at the end of Europe's imperial age attests to the flexibility and tenacity of the notion. In the twentieth century, as multinational organisations and NGOs took up the role of mediating between the first and third worlds, they too adopted a version of the civilising mission, a postcolonial humanism concerned primarily with education, development, health and human rights.[100] Finally, at the beginning of the twenty-first century, the notion experienced a curious rebirth in the wake of the 9/11 attacks. In many ways, it was a 'predictable revival', with the wars in Afghanistan and Iraq predicated, among other things, upon reductive binaries that pitted democracy against despotism and Judeo-Christian tradition against Islam.[101] To be sure, modes of cultural communication had accelerated and expanded in ways that nineteenth-century bearers of the civilising mission could hardly have imagined. But there are important continuities all the same. As in the nineteenth century, the liberation of women from backwardness became a central issue in a transformed public sphere. Additionally, the technology of destruction became, once again, a mode of enforcement and a focus of debate, particularly when it came to matters of access, truth and proper use. Given the particular Anglo-American career of the civilising mission, it should be no surprise that the world leader who rose to support President George Bush was Britain's Prime Minister Tony Blair. Only this time there was a reversal of Rhodes' formulation, with Britain as the junior partner in this mother-and-child reunion. And, in this reprisal, the civilising mission took on a distinctly retaliatory reasoning and tone for a post-imperial age. But, once again, the civilising mission has proven its resilience, in a most strange and mournful way. It remains flexible and fungible in its application, while also being improbable and perhaps even impossible in its execution. Were Cecil Rhodes to look upon the current state of affairs, he might declare, as he was purported to have done on his deathbed, 'So little done, so much to do'.[102]

---

100 Mrinalini Sinha, *Specters of Mother India: The Global Restructuring of an Empire* (Durham, NC, 2006), p. 74; James Vernon, *Hunger: A Modern History* (Cambridge, 2007).

101 Adas, *Dominance by Design*, p. 206.

102 Thomas Elkins Fuller, *The Rt Honourable Cecil John Rhodes: A Monograph and a Reminiscence* (London, 1910), p. 263.

Art

Natasha Eaton

> *Empire follows art and not vice versa as English men suppose.*
> – William Blake, 'Annotations to Sir Joshua Reynolds'
> 'Discourses' (1808)

This chapter takes seriously Blake's annotation that art articulates, even directs empires. According to Nicholas Thomas, 'colonialism has always been a cultural process; its discoveries and processes are imagined and energized through signs, metaphors and narratives; even what would seem its purest moments of profit and violence have been mediated and enframed by structures of meaning'.[1] Despite the emphasis on colonial ideology, race and Orientalism, the fraught and complex relations between art and empire have been until very recently a relatively marginal concern (at best an annotation) for both historical studies and art history.[2] Yet artists, artworks and cultural institutions generated, endorsed, criticised and resisted imperial projects: as such, they highlighted the problematic agency and genealogy of both colonialism and the category of art.

My chapter examines the ways in which scholars have addressed the question of art, or, more broadly, visual culture across empires. Firstly, it explores the involvement of the visual in what Martin Jay has termed 'scopic regimes of

---

1   Nicholas Thomas, *Colonialism's Culture: Anthropology, Travel and Government* (Oxford, 1994), p. 4.
2   This new interest in art and empire is demonstrated by the appearance of a number of essays which deal very broadly with the subject. See the essay by Jeffrey Auerbach, 'Art and Empire', in Robin Winks (ed.), *Oxford History of The British Empire*, vol. 5 (Oxford, 1999), pp. 571–83, and, more recently, Douglas Fordham, 'New Directions in British Art History of the Eighteenth Century', *Literary Compass* 5 (2008): pp. 906-917; Romita Ray and Angela Rosenthal, 'Britain and the World Beyond, c.1600–c.1900', in David Bindman (ed.), *History of British Art*, vol. 2 (London, 2008), pp. 86-115; Christopher Pinney, 'The Material and Visual Culture of British India, in Douglas M. Peers and Nandini Gooptu (eds), *India and the British Empire: Oxford Companion to the British Empire* (Oxford, forthcoming, 2012).

modernity'.[3] Following Foucault and Said, visibility has been cast as the central means for controlling, rendering docile, even for constructing bodies and the governmental measure of population – a mode of thought which has been used by scholars of empire in relation to Orientalist painting, photography and practices of collecting. Secondly, I consider the limits of this approach in terms of the uncanny, disorienting experience of art in empire. Since the early 1990s the so-called 'New Art History' has aimed at making imperialism far more central to the study of western European (especially French and British) visual culture: this desire for imperial hegemony may have produced several valuable works but it is also polemical both in its unquestioned emphasis on European colonialism, and in a certain unwillingness to engage with other empires, or to disrupt the metropole–colony dichotomy. As an attempt to think past this blind spot, the third part of this chapter turns to recent anthropological approaches towards the agency of art objects in relation to imperialism. A focus on the circulation and the context-making potential of artworks has the potential to break free from a conventional historiography which treats images as either merely illustrative or as semantically equivalent to textual sources. The concluding section of this chapter teases out a few of the strands of contemporary artistic practice in relation to post-coloniality – the problematic of identity politics, the new world order of what can be dubbed 'contemporary empire'.[4]

Visibility: Representation

The first generation of scholars to engage critically with the matter of the agency of art in empire has taken up Said's concern with institutionalised knowledge and his suggestion that the Orient acts as a filter through which to view and then control empire. Although Said wrote relatively little on art, his examination of 'racial, ideological and imperialist stereotypes', and the European production of a 'complex Orient suitable for study in the academy, for display in the museum, for theoretical illustration in anthropological, biological, linguistic, racial and historical theses about mankind' is intensely visual.[5] Following Foucault, power/knowledge is predicated on visibility.

Linda Nochlin's essay 'The Imaginary Orient' transplanted Said's key ideas, perhaps most obviously in her reading of Gérôme's *Snake Charmer* (1889), which appeared on the cover of the first edition of *Orientalism*.[6] She reads this painting through its aura of mystery – the beguiling rear view of the boy holding a snake

---

3   Martin Jay, 'The Scopic Regimes of Modernity', in Hal Foster (ed.), *Vision and Visuality* (Seattle, WA, 1988), pp. 3–23.
4   Giorgio Agamben, *Homo Sacer: Sovereign Power and Bare Life* (Stanford, CA, 1998).
5   Edward Said, *Orientalism: Western Conceptions of the Orient* (New York, 1978), pp. 16–17.
6   Linda Nochlin, 'The Imaginary Orient', in *The Politics of Vision: Essays on Nineteenth-century Art and Society* (London, 1983).

– inferring an erotic, sexually charged occultism which operated as a standard trope for the Orient. At the same time this mystery is represented by a radical realism which Said had also defined as a principal feature of western texts on the east. According to Nochlin, Gérôme achieves this 'effect of the real' through his painstaking, almost 'ethnographic' attention to detail – the snake's wrinkles, the seated men's dress, the richly patterned carpet and the intricacies of the tiles. Keen to provide a play between presence and absence (put forward in Foucault's reading of Velasquez's *Las Meninas* 1656, in *Les mots et les choses*), Nochlin points to the lack of any sign of modernisation or colonisation.[7] She argues that this representation of oriental cultures occurred at the very moment that Europe was destroying them. The same colonial societies that were engaged in wiping out local customs also wanted to preserve them at the level of *representation* in the form of postcards, academic oil paintings, simulated streets and villages at worlds' fairs, and ethnographic photographs, and as the subject of museum displays. Nochlin's argument has been challenged by several scholars intent on showing the limits of colonial power in a range of imperial contexts. John MacKenzie, Mary Roberts and Roger Benjamin have shown how the Orient could also be seen as a radical, new and positive source of artistic inspiration.[8] Benjamin in particular highlights the intricate relationships between painters, exhibitions and collectors and the pathways of post-colonial legacies. After all, one of the early twenty-first century's biggest markets for Orientalist painting is generated by collectors in North Africa, Turkey, the Middle East, Saudi Arabia and the Gulf states.

Said's concern with the production of a 'complex Orient' has inspired several important publications preoccupied with the colonial dimensions of what cultural theorist Tony Bennett has termed the 'exhibitionary complex'.[9] Rigorous in his use of Foucault's concern with scopic regimes of power where vision can render subjects docile, Bennett's exhibitionary complex consists of an archipelago of cultural institutions and practices whose agenda was to instruct and to make self-aware the heterogeneous public which emerged during nineteenth-century British imperial expansion. Aside from his discussion of the first world's fair held at Crystal Palace in 1851, however, Bennett has relatively little to say about empire in relation to the exhibitionary complex.[10] Nevertheless, his provocative hypothesis has been adapted by Timothy Mitchell in his celebrated book *Colonizing*

---

7   Michel Foucault, *Les Mots et les choses* (Paris, 1971); Nochlin, *The Politics of Vision*, pp. 35–59.

8   John MacKenzie, *Orientalism: History, Theory and the Arts* (Manchester, 1995); Mary Roberts, *Intimate Outsiders: The Harem in Ottoman and Orientalist Art and Literature* (Durham, NC, 2005); Roger Benjamin, *Orientalist Aesthetics: Art, Colonialism and French Northern Africa, 1880–1930* (Berkeley, CA, 2003); Benjamin, 'Postcolonial Taste: Non-western Markets for Orientalist Art', in Benjamin (ed.) *Orientalism: From Delacroix to Klee* (Sydney, 1997), pp. 32–40.

9   Tony Bennett, *The Birth of the Museum: History, Theory, Politics* (London, 1995).

10 Tony Bennett has subsequently written a 'follow-up' to *Birth of the Museum* which considers non-western museums, *Pasts Beyond Memory: Evolution, Museums, Colonialism* (London, 2004).

Egypt.[11] Like Nochlin, Mitchell focuses on colonial perspectivism – that is, the imperial quest for a privileged and distant point of view, a 'position from which ... one could see and not be seen'.[12] In an analysis of nineteenth-century Parisian *expositions universelles* which draws on Heidegger's essay 'The Age of the World Picture', Mitchell highlights the modern European penchant for transforming the world into representation.[13] His central point is that Orientalism is not just a general problem of how one culture portrays another, nor is it merely an aspect of colonial domination: Orientalism is central to the methods of order and truth constituting European modernity. Modernity is thus driven by the paradoxical desire to render the world as an object of representation and to lose oneself in this object world – to experience it directly. The simulated Egyptian streets at the 1889 Paris World's Fair relied on imperial investment in the certainty of representation – namely, on a deliberate difference in time and displacement in space that separated the representation from the real thing. Two parallel pairs of distinction were maintained – between the visitor and the exhibit, and between the exhibit and what it represented.[14]

There are pressure points where distinctions collapse, where the intensities of affect disrupt the work of representation. Nineteenth-century western European travellers to North Africa expressed dissatisfaction at not being able to frame a view necessary to maintaining a comforting, aesthetic distance from their surroundings. But many others, including the artist John Frederick Lewis, assumed oriental dress, learnt Arabic, or in the case of painter Mary Walker worked with royal Ottoman women in an attempt to embed themselves in Ottoman and Palestinian culture.[15] Lewis' detailed interiors and 'picturesque' alleys, and the wide-angle genres of the panorama and the diorama, offered what Oliver Grau has termed the aesthetic of immersion, which sought to instil the observer within the picture.[16] As a 'space of presence' this aesthetic allied tourism and colonisation with the aim of trapping the viewer in the real. The scopic structure of the panorama transformed the format of Bentham's panopticon (so central to Bennett's explanation of the exhibitionary complex) by reworking the relationship between the central, all-seeing surveillance tower designed to observe potentially all prison inmates to focus instead on the projected sovereignty of viewers intent on surveying the painted vista. This experience of surveying the 360-degree painted panorama from an elevated central platform placed the observers in a position of virtual authority. Such an experience of virtual reality sealed off the observer – hermetically – from everything extraneous to the view. Were it 'not hermetic, there would be no feeling of presence or virtuality'.[17]

---

11 Timothy Mitchell, *Colonizing Egypt* (Berkeley, CA, 1987).

12 Mitchell, *Colonizing Egypt*, p. 24. See also C. Hirschkind's critique, 'Egypt at the Exhibition: Reflections on the Optics of Colonialism', *Critique of Anthropology* 11/3 (1991): pp. 279–98.

13 Martin Heidegger, 'The Age of the World Picture', in *The Question Concerning Technology and Other Essays* (New York, 1977).

14 Mitchell, *Colonizing Egypt*.

15 For Mary Walker, who spent 30 years in Constantinople, see Roberts, *Intimate Outsiders*.

16 Oliver Grau, *From Illusion to Immersion* (Cambridge, MA, 2003).

17 Ibid., p. 111.

Scholarly monographs on Orientalist paintings, panoramas, world's fairs, and museums and monuments (for instance the South Kensington Museum, the Imperial Institute) have generated a lucrative 'culture industry' in academic publishing.[18] Three studies in particular have taken on Mitchell's insistence on the centrality of empire to 'Cartesian perspectivism'. Annie Coombes explores how colonialists invented competing ideas of Africa through processes of collecting in the period 1880–1930. Her detailed and extensive research focuses on the conflicts as much the complicity amongst missionaries, colonial officials and curators in their scramble for African artefacts.[19]

Arindam Dutta and Saloni Mathur concentrate on globalising pathways in relation to nineteenth-century India, world's fairs and cultural policy.[20] Both Mathur and Dutta attempt to reconceptualise the British imperial regime of vision and indeed what might be the 'shape' of empire. Taking her lead from Said's *Culture and Imperialism*, Mathur insists that empire be viewed as a single analytical field where colony and metropole must be read contrapuntally in, through and against one another.[21] Her approach foregrounds transcultural flows of things and people in the hope that their extreme crossings can be read as symptomatic of the anxieties of empire – a method which draws on anthropologist Arjun Appadurai's discussion of circulation and transformation of commodities.[22] In a study of the most ambitious project to emerge from the Great Exhibition of 1851 – the Department of Science and Arts (DSA) – Dutta constructs alternative multilateral flows. Whilst at first glance the preservative, localising and decentralising DSA apparatus in colonial India might appear to be an extension of metropolitan reform, Dutta argues that liberal practice does not play out there in the same way. Victorian imperialism is binocular: one eye sees to clarify and classify, the other is blind and reliant on *ad hoc* tactics.

Both Dutta and Mathur set out to challenge our understanding of the imperial metropolis. Given their interest in migration and translation it comes perhaps as no surprise that the conventional view of late nineteenth-century London as a burgeoning centre of finance and politics celebrated in literature on the Crystal Palace, the Grand Durbar Hall of the new Foreign Office, the Imperial Institute and the extensive development of a cultural complex at South Kensington is undermined.[23] Mathur breaks the city up into a series of spaces for reversed

18 For the continuing popularity of Orientalist painting, see *The Lure of the East* exhibition, Tate Britain, summer 2008.

19 Annie E. Coombes, *Reinventing Africa: Museums, Material Culture, and Popular Imagination in Late Victorian and Edwardian England* (New Haven, CT, 1994).

20 Arindam Dutta, *The Bureaucracy of Beauty: Design in the Age of Global Reproducibility* (London, 2006); Saloni Mathur, *India by Design: Colonial History and Cultural Display* (Berkeley, CA, 2007).

21 Edward Said, *Culture and Imperialism* (New York, 1993), p. xi.

22 Arjun Appadurai, 'Introduction', in *The Social Life of Things: Commodities in Cultural Perspective* (Cambridge, 1996).

23 For imperial architecture in Victorian London, see G. Alex Bremner, *The Gothic Revival and Empire: Religious Architecture and High Anglican Culture in Britain and the British*

colonisation. An Indian Village in Liberty's, demonstrations in Battersea Park, the Colonial and Indian Exhibition at the South Kensington Museum and the East End, only properly function through the presence of non-Europeans. London was simply a floating signifier of undefined urban agglomeration, twice the size of Paris, controlling 75 per cent of the flow of global capital by 1900; Dutta contends that the city had less connection with its surroundings than with India. In effect, London was oracular, an entity without a body, inhabiting the future of others without being able to announce its own presence.[24]

Dutta argues for the centrality of beauty to the economic enterprise of empire. He stresses that the DSA saw itself as nothing less than the full-blooded enterprise of economic stratification through aesthetic means, an issue also taken up by Lara Kriegel and Abigail McGowan in their explorations of craft and colonial museums.[25] The DSA dominated design in Britain and India from its inception in 1857 to the 1920s, commanding 180 design schools in Britain and many others in India. It was also responsible for hosting all the world exhibitions in London.[26] At its heart was a liberal agenda, informed by John Stuart Mill's perception of industrial depredation and the need to reform public institutions to benefit workers. In tying the aesthetic to the logistic of the commodity, the DSA melded the German idealist philosophy of Kant with an English history of workshop-based pedagogy.

Mathur and Dutta demonstrate how Asiatic production for display in exhibitions and museums was located not in the timeless village ideal put forward by colonial officials but in Indian prisons. The apparatus of the jail was not a replacement for artisanal work in any conventional sense but rather acted as the mechanism for introducing uncontracted and unpaid labour. The DSA encouraged the establishment of 'Jail and Bazaar Factories' throughout India, effectively jettisoning craft from its idealised space in ancient customs to become a reformative

---

Colonial World, 1840–1870 (forthcoming).

24 For imperial London, see Jonathan Schneer, *London 1900* (New Haven, CT, 1999); Lynda Nead, *Victorian Babylon: People, Streets and Images in Nineteenth-Century London* (New Haven, CT, 2000); M.H. Port, *Imperial London: Civil Government Building in London, 1850–1915* (New Haven, CT, 1995); John Marriott, *The Other Empire: Metropolis, India and Progress in the Colonial Imagination* (Manchester, 2003).

25 Lara Kriegel, *Grand Designs: Labor, Empire and the Museum in Victorian Culture* (Durham, NC, 2007); Abigail McGowan, *Crafting the Nation in Colonial India* (New York, 2009).

26 See Carol Breckenridge, 'The Aesthetics and Politics of Collecting: India at the World's Fairs', *Comparative Studies in Society and History* 31/2 (1989): pp. 195–216; Mark Crinson, *Empire Building: Orientalism and Victorian Architecture* (London, 1995); Peter H. Hoffenberg, *An Empire on Display: English, Indian, and Australian Exhibitions from the Crystal Palace to the Great War* (Berkeley, CA, 2001); Jeffrey Auerbach, *The Great Exhibition: A Nation on Display* (New Haven, CT, 1999); Jeffrey Auerbach and Peter Hoffenberg, *Britain, the Empire, and the World at the Great Exhibition of 1851* (Farnham, 2008); Paul Young, *Globalization and the Great Exhibition: The Victorian New World Order* (Basingstoke, 2009); Louise Purbrick (ed.), *The Great Exhibition of 1851: New Interdisciplinary Essays* (Manchester, 2001); Tim Barringer, *Men at Work: Art and Labor in Victorian Britain* (New Haven, CT, 2005).

industry, a process which had parallel practices in Britain and the United States. But given the celebrated status of Indian products in Britain, these jail-made commodities were frequently advertised as rare, luxury products with no hint of their means of production.[27] This involved far more than the growing argument among reform groups about the rehabilitative aspect of 'proper' labour. Dutta and Swaminathan show how from the 1860s prison productions, carpets in particular, became a critical space for the DSA's experimentation with systems of design.[28] In her exploration of prisoners exhibited at the 1886 Colonial and Indian Exhibition in London, Mathur suggests that the public understood craft to be located in the timeless Indian village characterised by caste-based industry. No one seemed to know or care that many of these men, women and children were in fact inmates of Agra gaol forced to learn the necessary skills to please metropolitan expo-goers.[29] Although it was not common practice to put prisoners on display in this way, by the 1880s colonial officials were writing extensively about the technologies and processes of such crafts whilst increasingly devising exhibitions featuring villagers performing labour.[30]

Art History and the Imperial Turn

Aside from the fine work of Mathur, Coombes and Dutta, very few art-historical studies have taken seriously Mitchell's claim that there is in these High Imperial cultural practices (1870s–1920s) something uncanny, subliminal or even radically disorienting. Against the grain, cultural commentators from outside the discipline have attempted to articulate these unsettling practices through a focus on mimicry and mimesis in the colonial encounter. This space between mimicry and mimesis can act as a valuable means for thinking about more unexpected visual practices. The 'uncanny of cultural difference', the slippage involved in replicating cultural practices outside of Europe and the resultant mimicry-menace are explored by Homi Bhabha in a series of seminal essays published collectively in 1994 as *The Location of Culture*.[31] Taking up theories of the gaze and engaging with scopic regimes of modernity, Bhabha argues that there is an intensely visual aspect to colonialism.[32] He sees a connection between mimicry and camouflage; not a

27 McGowan, *Crafting the Nation*, chaps 2 and 3.
28 Dutta, *Bureaucracy of Beauty*; P. Swaminathan, 'Prison as Factory: A Study of Jail Manufactures in the Madras Presidency', *Studies in History* 11/1 (1995): pp. 77–100. The carpets made by Indian prisoners have been the subject of an exhibition, *Jail Birds: An Exhibition of Indian Carpets* (Mall Galleries, London, 1987).
29 Saloni Mathur, 'Living Ethnological Exhibits: The Case of 1886', *Cultural Anthropology* 15/4 (2000): pp. 492–524.
30 See McGowan, *Crafting the Nation*, chap. 3.
31 Homi K. Bhabha, *The Location of Culture* (London, 1994).
32 This is made explicit in Bhabha's essay 'The Other Question: Homi Bhabha Reconsiders the Stereotype and Colonial Discourse', *Screen* 24/6 (1983): pp. 18–36.

harmonisation or repression of difference but a form of resemblance that differs from and defends presence by displaying it in part metonymically.[33] Hence the acts of Indian *subaltern* imitation subvert that which is being represented (colonialism) and in consequence the question of power begins to vacillate. Not everyone would agree: what about the complicity argument? Anthropologist Michael Taussig stages imperial anthropology as a privileged site for mimetic encounter.[34] He revives the idea of mimetic aptitude as an anthropological constant, suggesting that the ability to mime – and mime well – is precisely the capacity to Other. He works out the practices of 'sentient knowing' – that is, mimetic acts by which the copy acquires power over the original. Through a subtle reading of colonial copies of metropolitan originals – for instance, Cuna needlework which includes western motifs of gramophones – he arrives at the notion of 'mimetic excess' – mimesis turned on itself, leading to mimetic self-awareness. Mimesis is articulated as a 'space between, a space permeated by the colonial tension of mimesis and alterity, in which it is far from easy to say who is the imitator and who is the imitated, which is copy and which is original'.[35]

Surprisingly, Bhabha's and Taussig's questions of cultural hybridity, mimicry and mimesis firmly anchored to a series of localised and historicised encounters in India and South America have been glossed over by the majority of art historians who tend either to overdetermine or downplay the agency of imperialism in artistic projects.[36] Colonialism is either absent or all pervading in the *kunstwollen* of artistic production and consumption. The 'Imperial Turn' in the western academy has meant that in recent years imperialism has begun to move from the margins to occupy the centre, especially in current investigations of British and North American art.[37] Following the impact of gender studies, 'race' and 'empire' have become liberal buzzwords for highlighting the activities of both major and minor European artists in relation to imperialism. At least in the field of eighteenth- and nineteenth-century British art, empire is now taking the place of the more overtly Marxist agenda of the 1970s and 1980s focused on class and ideology.

One important scholarly innovation has been the shift from a study of nationalism and the 'Englishness of English art' to a focus on British visual culture as resolutely imperial not only in the colonies but also back home.[38] This interest in

---

33   Homi K. Bhabha, 'Of Mimicry and Man', in *Location of Culture*, pp. 44–58.
34   Michael Taussig, *Mimesis and Alterity: A Particular History of the Senses* (New York, 1993).
35   Ibid., p. 45.
36   Important exceptions are Stephen F. Eisenman, *Gaugin's Skirt* (London, 1997); Roberts, *Intimate Outsiders*; Christopher Pinney, *Camera Indica: The Social Life of Indian Photographs* (Chicago, IL, 1997).
37   'The central premise of the essays collected here is that the concept of empire belongs at the centre rather than in the margins of the history of British art … This book aims to reinsert empire as a fundamental category for the analysis of British art', Geoff Quilley, Tim Barringer and Douglas Fordham (eds), *Art and the British Empire* (Manchester, 2006), p. 3.
38   The thesis for the Englishness of English art was put forward in Nikolaus Pevsner's *The Englishness of English Art* (New York, 1956).

the imperial dimension of British art was put forward by Bernard Smith in his *Place, Taste and Tradition* (1945), where he noted that Winckelmann wrote up the results of his explorations in the ruins of Pompeii and Herculaneum in the same year that General Wolfe captured Quebec and Clive consolidated the gains of the Battle of Plassey in Bengal. Smith suggested that the relationship between the commercial policy that led to imperialist expansion and the archaeological investigations that led to Classicism still needs to be examined in depth.[39] With the passing of the Rococo in the 1760s, which Smith described as the last original art style, European art modelled itself on cultural others, in the form of the past, the exotic or the imperial. From the 1760s, the taste for the Rococo and the exotic would be usurped by overtly imperialist themes.[40] For instance, the redecoration of London's leading pleasure ground, Vauxhall Gardens' Grand Pavilion, centred on four enormous history paintings of recent British victories in the Seven Years' War (1756–63), whilst monumental tombs commemorating imperial heroes began to appear in Westminster Abbey precisely at the time it was being reinvented as a national pantheon.[41] Through its ambitious reconstruction of its London headquarters, its commissioning of extremely expensive marble busts and statues of its servants, and its encouragement for artists to work in India, the English East India Company constituted one of the few 'public' patrons of art in eighteenth-century Britain. At this time too, Sir Joshua Reynolds, the first President of the Royal Academy, lectured on the importance of creating a British school of art for the new imperial nation.[42]

This new emphasis on the relationship between art and empire has also been instrumental in excavating forgotten artists such as William Hodges and Agostino Brunias, whose painterly experiments with landscape, whiteness and ethnography in India, the Pacific and the West Indies have justifiably become 'hot topics'.[43] Hodges trained with the leading Welsh, Rome-trained landscape painter Richard Wilson,

---

39 Bernard Smith, *Place, Taste and Tradition: A Study of Australian Art since 1788* (London, 1945), p. 16.

40 For detailed exploration of this shift to the imperial, see Douglas Fordham, *Allegiance and Autonomy: British Art and the Seven Years' War* (Philadelphia, PA, 2010).

41 David Solkin, *Painting for Money: The Visual Arts and the Public Sphere in Eighteenth-Century England* (New Haven, CT, 1993); Miles Ogborn, *Spaces of Modernity: London's Geographies, 1680–1780* (New York, 1998); Joan Coutu, *Persuasion and Propaganda: Monuments and Eighteenth-Century British Empire* (Montreal, 2007).

42 Sir Joshua Reynolds, 'Discourse Seven', in Robert Wark (ed.), *Discourses on Art* (New Haven, CT, 1981), pp. 115–42. Reynolds' views would be attacked by William Blake: see David Erdman, *Blake: Prophet Against Empire* (London, 1978).

43 Geoff Quilley and John Bonehill (eds), *William Hodges 1744–1797: The Art of Exploration* (London, 2004); Kay Dian Kriz, *Slavery, Sugar and Refinement: Representing the British West Indies, 1700–1840* (London, 2008); Geoff Quilley and Kay Dian Kriz (eds), *An Economy of Colour: Visual Culture and the Atlantic World, 1660–1830* (Manchester, 2003); Angela Rosenthal and A. Lugo-Ortiz (eds), *Invisible Subjects? Slave Portraiture in the Circum-Atlantic World, 1630–1890* (Cambridge, forthcoming); P. Hamilton and R.J. Blyth (eds), *Representing Slavery: Art, Artefacts and Archives in the Collections of the National Maritime Museum, Greenwich* (Farnham, 2007).

before embarking on Cook's second voyage to the Pacific. He would join a cohort of artists and scientists, most notably Sydney Parkinson, John Webber, Sir Joseph Banks, and Georg and J.R. Forster, who travelled with Cook in the period 1768–82. None of the three principal painters, Parkinson, Webber or Hodges, was trained in life drawing of the human body, which is perhaps suggestive of the voyage's focus on trade, natural history, astronomy and cartography at the expense of portraiture, history painting and ethnography. All three artists would produce hundreds of stunning images which went far beyond their initial brief to record flora, fauna and coastal profiles.[44] Parkinson focused on Maori tattooing, Hodges produced ambitious seascape oil sketches and red chalk portraits, and Webber drew scenes of 'ethnographic' encounters between Cook and a number of indigenous peoples.[45] Bernard Smith's seminal research on the art of Cook's voyages argues that a real tension emerges between 'on the spot' eye-witness sketching and its translation into the neo-classical style favoured by London engravers.[46] Nicholas Thomas, likewise, demonstrates the difficulties faced by printmakers in their attempts at visually explaining the exotic objects collected during the voyages.[47]

Cohn, Pinney and Eaton have argued that portraits as gifts at Indian courts held a highly contentious status.[48] Although several Indian rulers presented their likenesses as gifts to colonial officials, they were possibly coerced into doing so by the East India Company, which frequently forced them into patronising European artists. Art, then, contributed to the enormous debts and war reparations that rulers like Asaf ud-daula, sovereign of the state of Awadh, owed to the British. One consequence was the Company's forced annexation of rulers' land in lieu of the repayment of such debts, thus increasing the grass-roots work of colonisation. Full-face, full-length oil-painted likenesses could hardly be more different from the watercolour and gold leaf Indian miniatures favoured by these rulers. Pinney suggests that photography enjoyed greater success, partly due to the prominence

---

44   R. Joppien and B. Smith, *The Art of Cook's Voyages*, 4 vols (London, 1985).
45   See Harriet Guest, 'Curiously Marked: Tattooing, Masculinity and Nationality in Eighteenth-Century British Perceptions of the South Pacific', in John Barrell (ed.), *Painting and the Politics of Culture* (Cambridge, 1992), pp. 101–134; Guest, 'The Great Distinction: Figures of the Exotic in the Work of William Hodges', *Oxford Art Journal* 12/2 (1989) pp. 36–58.
46   Bernard Smith, *European Vision and the South Pacific, 1769–1850: A Study in the History of Ideas* (London, 1960); Smith, *Imagining the Pacific* (New Haven, CT, 1992).
47   Nicholas Thomas, *Entangled Objects: Exchange, Material Culture and Colonialism in the Pacific* (Cambridge, MA, 1991). Also concerned with collecting in the Pacific is T.C. Mitchell (ed.), *The British Museum Yearbook*, vol. 3 (London, 1979); Nicholas Thomas, *Possessions: Indigenous Art/Colonial Culture* (London, 1999); Nicholas Thomas and Diane Losche (eds), *Double Vision: Art Histories and Colonial Histories in the Pacific* (London, 1999).
48   See Bernard Cohn's classic essay 'Representing Authority in Victorian India' in Eric J. Hobsbawm and Terence Ranger (eds), *The Invention of Tradition* (Cambridge, 1983), pp. 165–210; Natasha Eaton, 'Between Mimesis and Alterity: Art, Gift and Diplomacy in Colonial India', *Comparative Studies in Society and History* 46/4 (2004): pp. 816–44; Christopher Pinney, *The Coming of Photography in India* (London, 2008).

of certain vernacular practitioners, most notably Lala Deen Dayal and Sayyid Ali Khan, who experimented with a number of fantastical poses and dresses for their subjects (for instance seating them in mock-up planes) which enabled them to play with the demands of western physiognomy and its serious and moral link to the revelation of character. Likeness becomes something magical and the projection of character a game of role-playing. Pinney argues that such images indicate very different ideas of personhood and photographic practice which he dubs a 'chamber of dreams'.[49] He suggests that, instead, copying the modern and colonial idea of the individual who was bound to perform certain roles (the hunter, the statesman, and so on), Indians devised imaginative new forms of self-representation, which privileged the idea of the 'dividuated' personality. This dividuation was projected into these ludic and fantastic photographic portraits.

Aside from this interest in portraiture, landscape was the principal genre favoured by British imperial artists and it has deservedly become a veritable 'culture industry' in art history. Somewhat misleadingly, scholars have tended to homogenise the aesthetic experience of places as far apart as the West Indies and Australia under the aegis of the Imperial Picturesque.[50] However, the shock of the new frequently forced painters to forge radical solutions when confronted with strange landscapes which defied the conventions of ruins and overgrown glades associated with the Picturesque aesthetic in Britain.[51] Dixon and Carter have argued that, in Australia, the Picturesque occupied a specific stage in the colonial civilising process; it emerged alongside a second generation of settlers intent on creating landscaped country parks reminiscent of aristocratic estates in Britain.[52] However, there was also the possibility of the bad prospect and the melancholy pastoral. Most poignantly, John Glover's views of Aboriginal dancing in Tasmania represent a joyful population which had in fact already been decimated; in his work the dancers signify as spectral presences in the colonial landscape.[53]

49 Pinney, *The Coming of Photography*, pp. 14–34; Pinney, *Camera Indica*; see also Julie F. Codell (ed.), *Photography and the Imperial Durbars of British India* (London, 2010).
50 This is certainly the case with an older generation of scholars. See, for instance, Mildred Archer, 'Balthasar Solvyns and the Picturesque', *The Connoisseur* (1969): pp. 12–18. For the Imperial Picturesque in India, see G.H.R. Tillotson, *The Artificial Landscape* (Aldershot, 1999). Jeffrey Auerbach seeks to challenge the category of the Picturesque in his essay 'The Picturesque and the Homogenisation of Empire', *British Art Journal* 5/1 (2004): pp. 47–54; Glenn Cooper (ed.), *Landscape and Empire, 1770–2000* (Aldershot, 2005).
51 For the Picturesque aesthetic in Britain, see Malcolm Andrews, *The Search for the Picturesque* (New Haven, CT, 1981); Peter Garside and Stephen Copley (eds), *The Politics of the Picturesque* (London, 1994); Kim Michasiw, 'Nine Revisionist Theories of the Picturesque', *Representations* 38 (1992): pp. 76–100.
52 R. Dixon, *The Course of Empire: Neoclassical Culture in New South Wales, 1788–1860* (Melbourne, 1986); Paul Carter, *The Road to Botany Bay: An Essay in Spatial History* (London, 1987). See also T. Hughes-d'Aeth, 'Pretty as a Picture: Australia and the Imperial Picturesque', *Journal of Australian Studies* 53 (1997): pp. 99–107.
53 For the ghost-like appearance of indigenous figures in the Australian/Tasmanian landscape, see Ian MacLean, *White Aborigines: Identity Politics in Australian Art*

The minor artist Benjamin Duterreau celebrated in paint the infamous protector of Aborigines, George Augustus Robinson, known as 'The Conciliator' (responsible for the deportation and confinement of indigenous peoples) with the last surviving Tasmanian, Trucanini. Fearing riots after her death in 1876, the colonial authorities buried her in secret in the chapel of Hobart gaol. Two years later her body was exhumed; the flesh was sloughed from her bones, which were boiled and nailed in a case for keeping apples before being put in a glass case in Hobart Museum, where they remained on display until 1947.

The power and violence of a range of prints, satires and paintings in the formation of a modern biopolitical regime in Britain and the colonies have been closely studied. Kay Dian Kriz's examination of artistic practice in the British West Indies – notably, the development of a creole landscape and crudely racialised visual jokes – as well as Stephanie Pratt's research on the representation of indigenous peoples of North America are fine examples. So too are Leonard Bell's work on the Maori and David Bindman's investigation of physiognomy and racism.[54] Bindman has been instrumental in reviving Hugh Honour's hugely ambitious 'encyclopaedic' project, *The Image of the Black in Western Art*, whilst also giving empire due space in his recent edited volume *History of British Art*.[55] Marcus Wood and David Dabydeen have produced highly emotive accounts of the role of Africans in Hogarth's work and in the pornographic and alienating representation of torture and racial atrocity in the slave-trading world between France, Britain, western Africa, North America and the Caribbean which Paul Gilroy has named as the 'Black Atlantic'.[56] In this line of thinking, race becomes an organising grammar for the production, reception and circulation of invidious images.

In the later nineteenth century, the belief that race could be fixed by being visualised and that it was intimately linked with emergent theories of evolutionism and eugenics came to play a standardising role in science, art theory and photography. In the painting of race, Jordanna Bailkin has argued that a desire to standardise the representation of different skin tones became a preoccupation for art instructors as never before.[57] This concern with 'objectivity' in relation to

---

(Cambridge, 1998); David Hansen, *John Glover and the Colonial Picturesque* (Hobart, 2003); T. Bonyhady, *Images In Opposition: Australian Landscape Painting, 1801–1890* (Oxford, 1985); A. Cerwonka, *Native to the Nation: Disciplining Landscapes and Bodies in Australia* (Minneapolis, 2004).

54   Kriz, *Slavery*; David Bindman, *Ape to Apollo: Aesthetics and the Idea of Race in the Eighteenth Century* (London, 2002); Stephanie Pratt, *American Indians in British Art, 1700–1840* (London, 2006); Leonard Bell, *Colonial Constructs: European Images of Maori, 1840–1914* (London, 1991).

55   David Bindman, *History of British Art, 1600–1870*, vol. 2 (London, 2008).

56   Marcus Wood, *Blind Memory: Visual Representations of Slavery in England and America* (Manchester, 2000); David Dabydeen, *Hogarth's Blacks: Images of Blacks in Eighteenth Century English Art* (Kingston-upon-Thames, 1987); Paul Gilroy, *The Black Atlantic: Modernity and Double Consciousness* (London, 1993). Still relevant is Stephen J. Gould's classic *The Mismeasure of Man* (New York, 1981).

57   Jordanna Bailkin, 'Indian Yellow: Making and Breaking the Imperial Palette', *Journal*

race also set the benchmark for the governmental use of photography. French policeman Alphonse Bertillon and British scientist Francis Galton, as Allan Sekula and Carlo Ginzburg have shown, used the police filing cabinet and an objectified measurement of the body in combination with the mug shot or composite photograph as key methods for archiving and reproducing race.[58] Race became intimately linked with the emergent discipline of criminology, one of whose effects was to demonise certain ethnic groups in India under the Criminal Tribes Act of 1870 The first three editions of the 'handbook' for colonial anthropology, *Notes and Queries*, placed heavy emphasis on the body as the cultural and racial site of difference, where anthropometry and photography took centre stage.[59] These projects were frequently met with opposition, as Edgar Thurston, superintendent of the Madras Museum, recorded in relation to his anthropometric investigations in southern India: 'The Paniyan women of the Wynaad when I appeared in their midst ran away believing that I was going to have the finest specimens among them stuffed for the museum. Oh that this were possible!'[60] As anthropologists George Stocking, Henrika Kuklick and James Urry have noted, this near obsession with recording biological difference at the level of the visual would form the basis of early experimental psychology.[61] Following the advice of Francis Galton, the anthropologists Arthur C. Haddon, W.H.R. Rivers and Charles Seligman carried out experiments in relation to the aesthetic sensibility, vision and artistic inclinations of the recently missionised peoples of the Torres Strait.[62] Although they concluded that there seemed to be no abstract terms for colour – indicative of an impoverished intellect and lack of aesthetic appreciation of nature – they concluded that there was little difference in the development of the senses, in particular vision, between so-called 'primitive' people and modern Europeans; indeed, they found greater

---

of *Material Culture* 10/2 (2005): pp. 197–214. See also Mary Cowling, *The Artist as Anthropologist* (Cambridge, 1989).

58   Allan Sekula, 'The Body and the Archive', in R. Bolton (ed.), *The Contest of Meaning: Critical Histories of Photography* (Cambridge, MA, 1992), pp. 343–89; Carlo Ginzburg, 'Family Resemblances and Family Trees: Two Cognitive Metaphors', *Critical Inquiry* 30/3 (2004): pp. 537–56.

59   Elizabeth Edwards (ed.), *Anthropology and Photography* (London, 1992); James Ryan, *Picturing Empire: Photography and the Visualization of the British Empire* (Chicago, IL, 1997).

60   Edgar Thurston, 'Anthropology in Madras', Educational Department, August 1, 1896, Nos. 454, 455 (app. F), India Office Records, British Library, London. Thurston also noted in appendix E of the same file that 'the measurement appliances sometimes frighten the subjects, especially the goniometer for determining the facial angle which is mistaken for an instrument of torture'.

61   George W. Stocking Jr, *Victorian Anthropology* (New York, 1987); Henrika Kuklick, *The Savage Within: The Social History of British Anthropology, 1885–1945* (Cambridge, 1991); James Urry, *Before Social Anthropology: Essays on the History of British Anthropology* (Reading, 1993). See also Peter Pels and Oscar Salmink (eds), *Colonial Subjects: Essays on the Practical History of Anthropology* (Ann Arbor, MI, 1999).

62   A.C. Haddon (ed.), *Cambridge Expedition to the Torres Straits*, 6 vols (Cambridge, 1901–1935); A. Herle and S. Rouse (eds), *Cambridge and the Torres Straits* (Cambridge, 1998).

visual acuity among the 'primitives'. Their findings clearly disputed ideas of racial inferiority and laid the basis for a diffusionist view of culture based on more unpredictable events than the linear progress advocated by Darwin and Galton.[63]

From maritime painting to picturing slavery and photographing race, empire is now seen by scholars to capture the 'spirit of the age' of eighteenth- and nineteenth-century visual culture. The editors of a recent collection of essays entitled *Art and Empire* sum up this approach: 'despite the silence of many scholars and curators, empire remains an unspoken presence, stalking the museums' picture stores and haunting the footnotes of journals and monographs'.[64] But there is the danger of making empire all pervasive; as anthropologist Nicholas Dirks warned several years ago of this delusional margin, 'calling for the study of the aesthetics of colonialism' is often little more than a 'chic version of Raj nostalgia'.[65] There are two striking problems with this proliferation of imperial art studies – the space and extent of empire and the tactics for resisting its epistemology. If you look for it, empire seems to be omnipresent in much French or British art. In reaction against this 'imperial gestalt', historian Bernard Porter questions whether Britain was in fact an imperial society at all.[66] Using a range of visual sources he argues that, before the 1870s, very few Britons thought of themselves as imperial. Only political and economic crises forced the British government to devise a propaganda machine which invested heavily in monuments, institutions and art works such as Watts' *Physical Energy*.[67] Although Porter's point is valid, his rather basic quantitative evidence (the number of art objects which he sees as directly dealing with empire) is extremely problematic. His approach ignores the more subtle and unsettling presence of empire which could assume numerous complicated manifestations.

Whilst the emphasis on the 'hegemony' of empire has led to some valuable work on colonial representation in the British Empire, much of this scholarship is still far from heeding Dipesh Chakrabarty's call to 'provincialize Europe'.[68] Chakrabarty exposes the ways in which '"Europe" has remained the sovereign, theoretical subject of all histories'.[69] In his terms the *margin* – that is, the 'third world' – is radically different from its vague and problematic status in art history, which is largely preoccupied with European visual culture outside of Europe. In contrast to both these positions, post-colonial cultural critical Rustom Bharucha suggests that not only must Europe be pushed to the margins – that is, provincialised through

---

63   Elazar Barkan, *The Retreat of Scientific Racism* (Cambridge, 1991); G. Richards, *Race, Racism and Psychology* (London, 1997); Diana Donald and Jane Munro (eds), *Endless Forms: Charles Darwin, Natural History and the Visual Arts* (Cambridge, 2009); Shearer West (ed.), *The Victorians and Race* (London, 1996).

64   Quilley, Barringer and Fordham (eds), *Art and the British Empire*, p. 4.

65   Nicholas B. Dirks, 'Introduction', *Colonialism and Culture* (Ann Arbor, MI, 1992), p. 3.

66   Bernard Porter, *The Absent-minded Imperialists: Empire, Society and Culture in Britain* (Oxford, 2004).

67   Ibid., pp. 88–109.

68   Dipesh Chakrabarty, *Provincializing Europe: Postcolonial Thought and Historical Difference* (Princeton, NJ, 2000).

69   Ibid., p. 27.

the dismantling of its claims to epistemic, even ontological hegemony – but that Europe's deeply 'parochial' view of the world must be fully exposed.[70] However, there are a select number of studies which privilege the nuanced analyses of exchange and demonstrate this marginality – Bernard Smith, Nicholas Thomas and Stephen Eisenmann on colonial encounters in the Pacific, and Tapati Guha-Thakurta's and Partha Mitter's exemplary studies of Indian artists' struggle against colonial rule.[71] Guha-Thakurta and Mitter outline the formation of a collective of Japanese and Bengali artists and writers keen to stress an alternative 'Pan-Asian' aesthetic to the Victorian colonial salon art. Through their use of Japanese wash and compositions inspired by sixteenth-century Mughal miniatures and Sanskrit treatises (*silpa sastras*), Abanindranath Tagore and Nandalal Bose fashioned an aesthetic which dismantled the hegemony of western art. The resultant nationalist art provides an alternative to Orientalism and a space for experimenting with a pan-Asianist agenda. Both Tagore and Bose carried out extensive archaeological investigations in India's Buddhist cave complexes; they worked closely with Japanese artists and they wrote extensively on the importance of meditation and colour. Bose's murals at Rabindranath Tagore's university campus at Sanitiniketan are a wonderful example of this cerebral and reactionary aesthetic approach. His use of wash, fresco and earth colours seeks to reject the legacies of colonial art in favour of a synthetic aesthetic which alludes to Rabindranath's poetry and plays as well as to ancient Sanskrit epics. Murals served Bose as a political tool: he worked closely with Gandhi at the annual Congress exhibitions held at Lucknow and Haripurs in the late 1930s, where he designed the exhibition complexes. Murals brought art to the people; Bose's artistic references were meant to 'update' village art and to show how art could be a political device in the fostering of nationalism.

Despite post-colonial critic Peter Hallward's call for academic recognition of the importance of *other ontologies*, rigorous studies of how European artists and collectors negotiated with, or emulated, the cultural practices of other empires – the Mughals, Ottomans, Incas, Safavids, the Ching dynasty – are still few and far between.[72] For the most part, the disciplinary 'Orientalist' division between western and non-western art continues to inform the ways in which art historians approach cultural encounters – with one important exception. A methodology focused on networks, nomads and rhizomes in social sciences and philosophy (Latour, Deleuze and Guattari) is beginning to shape the study of art and empires.[73] This

---

70   See Rustom Bharucha's critique of *Provincializing Europe*, 'Infiltrating Europe: Outside the Borders of Postmodern Cool', in Iftikhar Dadi and Salar Hussan (eds), *Unpacking Europe: Towards a Critical Reading* (Rotterdam, 2002), pp. 216–31.

71   Smith, *European Vision and the South Pacific*; Thomas, *Entangled Objects*; Eisenman, *Gauguin's Skirt*; Tapati Guha-Thakurta, *The Making of a New Indian Art* (Cambridge, 1992); Partha Mitter, *Art and Nationalism* (Oxford, 1994).

72   Peter Hallward, *Absolutely Postcolonial: Writing between the Singular and the Specific* (Manchester, 2001).

73   Bruno Latour, *Pandora's Hope: Essays on the Reality of Social Sciences* (London, 1998); Gilles Deleuze and Félix Guattari, *A Thousand Plateaus: Capitalism and Schizophrenia* (London, 2002).

emphasis on unexpected interconnectedness has the potential to create excellent work on the southern Atlantic (including cultural exchange between the Congo and Georgia); the taste for Chinoiserie in sixteenth-century Mexico, the negotiation of alterity in Safavid Iran through the lens of Indian and Chinese art, and the strategic deployment of Turkish architecture by the rulers of Poland.[74] In all these cases, circulation, translation and hybridity indicate the many forms of power available to images across empires, and the capacity of art to exist beyond western bounds.

Post-Colonial Legacies

The question of the 'Other' has been a long-term project for artist/writer/activist Rasheed Araeen. After migrating to Britain in the 1960s from Pakistan, he soon found that fellow artists and curators expected him to produce nothing but 'traditional' Asian art. In reaction, he devised a disruptive agenda which turned a self-critical eye on the museological process of Othering. His exhibition, *The Other Story* (1990, Hayward Gallery, London), located African and Asian artists within and against ideas of art constructed by the west. He asked and continues to question why western art institutions still close their eyes to the importance of post-colonial artists. In his view, the British institutional solution has been to adopt a cultural theory that would connect these artists' works to their supposedly original cultures in Africa and India and then to evaluate their significance in relation to their own traditions, while providing a space alongside western artists for the circulation of their works. Thus while western art can be posited as serving a universal need, non-western artists remain tied to a culture outside the western tradition.

According to art historian Jorella Andrews, artists of colour in Britain are now 'losing labels and liking it'.[75] Many artists have rejected the collective identity politics of the 1980s as reductive and disabling. An emphasis on globalisation and new media has shifted the agenda of contemporary art. Critic and curator Okwui Enwezor warns that attempts to classify today's artistic practice risk reiteration of the hegemony of an increasingly virtual but nonetheless powerful model of 'Europe'. His agenda for the major international art forum *Documenta 11* in 2002 aimed at forging an alternative curatorial strategy to the increasingly predictable biennale circuit which promotes a select number of internationally recognised artists 'thoroughly disciplined and domesticated within the scheme of Empire'.[76]

---

74   Cécile Fromont, 'Christian Icons: Kongo Symbols', PhD dissertation, Harvard University, 2008; David Roxburgh, *Prefacing the Image: Art History in Sixteenth-Century Iran* (Leiden, 2001); Naby Avcioglu, 'A Palace of One's Own: Stanislas I's Kiosks and the Idea of Self-representation', *Art Bulletin* 85 (2003): pp. 662–84; Dana Leibsohn, *Script and Glyph: Prehistory, Colonial Bookmaking and Historia Toleteca-chichimoca* (Cambridge, MA, 2009).

75   Jorella Andrews, 'Losing Labels and Liking It', in Heather Maitland (ed.), *Navigating Difference: Cultural Diversity and Audience Development* (London, 2004), pp. 141–7.

76   Okwui Enwezor, 'Preface', *Documenta 11* (Kassel, 2002), p. 3.

By using the term 'Empire' here he follows Negri's and Hardt's identification of a new world order determined by the forces of globalisation and the ascendancy of America as the replacement of modern European colonial powers.[77] Instead, Okwui Enwezor argues that a different set of regulatory and resistance models has to be found to counterbalance empire's attempt at totalisation. According to Enwezor, Negri and Hardt, 'empire' refers to the promulgation of a global order which is producing a new form of sovereignty characterised by a single power (the US) that is imperial rather than imperialist in its aim to absorb countries into an international network, but whose racialising ideologies are, as Etienne Balibar suggests, perhaps no less rigid than their colonial predecessors.[78]

These racialising ideologies, the aesthetic of immersion, the power of objects and the emphasis on transit underpinning Hazoumé's *La Bouche du Roi* can act as a useful endnote to my discussion of art and empire. The deck of empty gin bottles, combs and other trading objects which the artist refers to as fetishes, indicate the multiple, often precarious lives of objects in empire. The petrol cans standing in for the bodies of Africans sold into slavery also demonstrate the affective power of objects which the artist has collected from the situation of 'economic bondage' in Benin. The slave ship is only part of an installation which features a post-colonial panorama of the downriver trading port from whence the slaves would have been sent to north America or the Caribbean. With its huge scale and low lighting (perhaps reminiscent of the dimly lit displays of imperial museums) there is something profoundly disturbing about *La Bouche du Roi* which serves to undermine the imperialist agenda of the exhibitionary complex, the display of colonised bodies at world's fairs and the harsh labour in the service of empire. It performs as a timely reminder not only that the investigation of visual culture and imperialism involves the linkage of visibility and power, but that imperial legacies and the contemporary presence of empire entail something far more unsettling, even disorienting, which can highlight practices of resistance and bring into being new forms of post-colonial becoming.

---

77   Michael Hardt and Antonio Negri, *Empire* (London, 2000).
78   Ibid.; Etienne Balibar, 'Racism and Nationalism', in Balibar and I. Wallerstein, *Race, Nation, Class: Ambiguous Identities* (London, 1991), pp. 37–67.

Science, Medicine and Technology

Sujit Sivasundaram

In the introductory essay to his 1893 Romanes Lecture, Thomas Henry Huxley noted: 'the colony is a composite unit introduced into the old state of nature; and thenceforth, a competitor in the struggle for existence, to conquer or to be vanquished'.[1] This utilisation of evolution as an analogy for the imperial process should not come as a surprise, for Huxley was amongst the chief popularisers of Darwinian ideas. He is credited with establishing the modern idea of the professional scientist as a secular prophet. This 'devil's disciple' and 'high priest of evolution', as one historian has described Huxley, saw colonialism as providing further proof of the efficacy of evolution.[2] If the colonists were 'slothful, stupid and careless', then their colonies would be overtaken by the 'old state of nature'. Using the example of a shipload of 'English colonists' landing in Tasmania he noted: '[t]he native savage will destroy the immigrant civilized man; of the English animals and plants some will be extirpated by their indigenous rivals, others will pass into the feral state and themselves become components of nature'. To ensure that this did not occur, Huxley spelt out the importance of protection against extreme heat and cold in the form of housing and clothing; he advocated drainage and irrigation works which would deter the effects of excessive rain and drought; roads, bridges, canals and ships that would overcome natural barriers to transport; 'mechanical engines [which] would supplement the natural strength of men and their draught animals', and hygiene which would deter the onset of disease. 'With every step of this progress of civilization, the colonists would become more and more independent of the state of nature; more and more their lives would be conditioned by a state of art.' Colonialism would thus be subject to natural processes. But colonial power would be forged as it overcame and transformed nature, and, even at its highpoint, empire would be susceptible to defeat by evolution. But

---

1   All citations from the lecture are from 'Prolegomena' and 'Evolution and Ethics', in Alan P. Barr (ed.), *The Major Prose of Thomas Henry Huxley* (Athens, GA, 1997), pp. 292–4.
2   Adrian Desmond, *Huxley: The Devil's Disciple*, 2 vols (London, 1994); Desmond, *Huxley: From Devil's Disciple to Evolution's High Priest* (London, 1998).

by this point of the nineteenth century, the last of the Tasmanian aboriginals was deemed dead.[3]

The literature on the relationship between imperialism and science, technology and medicine is a vibrant one. Yet Huxley's lecture demonstrates some of the difficulties in theorising the precise relationship. At the surface of contact between these ideologies, each took on new forms and reinvented itself. Empires drew on technical information and technological prowess; indeed, modern imperialism as a process was redefined and refracted through the vocabulary of expert knowledge. Symmetrically, the vocation of the scientist and a series of new scientific disciplines emerged out of imperialism in such a way that science as an activity and a way of thought was itself radically reshaped by the imperial age. The sciences were therefore imperial, in as much as modern empires were scientific enterprises.

The assemblage of ideas that make up science, technology, medicine and empire were fundamentally interwoven; yet this does not mean that the entanglement of these ideas didn't involve contradictions. As illustrated by Huxley's lecture, science, technology and medicine represented tangible modes of imperial work as well as forms of imperial speech and imagination, linked to the creation of mentalities and identities. Science, technology and medicine marked a sense of progress while exposing some of the problems that might cause imperial collapse, such as degeneration or the spread of disease. They also provided solutions by specifying how it would be possible to create global empires immune from natural processes. The sciences were therefore symptoms of both imperial anxiety and optimism, and their application was marked by failure as much as success, as was true for imperialism also.

Another contradiction is evident in Huxley's explanation of the scientific method: for Huxley, it was that which set the civilised apart from the savage, and yet science's methodology was defended as universal, palpably contradicting this critical nineteenth-century distinction. In pointing to science's universalism, Huxley famously described the disciplinary method as 'methodised savagery'; scientists followed the intellectual work of any 'savage', who read animal tracks and worked out the causes of such tracks.[4] It was this universalism which, in the end, saw nationalist movements in colonial territories, adopting, responding and recasting their own histories of science in the phase of imperial collapse.

The range of contradictions in usage, rhetoric, symbolism and philosophy generated by the imperial sciences makes a singular thesis or model about their

---

3   See James Paradis, '*Evolution and Ethics* in Victorian Context', in James Paradis and George C. Williams (eds), *Evolution and Ethics: T.H. Huxley's Evolution and Ethics, With New Essays on Its Victorian and Sociobiological Context* (Princeton, NJ, 1989), pp. 52–5. For the metaphorical entanglement between evolutionary language and colonialism, see David Amigoni, *Colonies, Cults and Evolution: Literature, Science and Culture in Nineteenth-Century Writing* (Cambridge, 2007).

4   Cited and discussed in James G. Paradis, *T.H. Huxley: Man's Place in Nature* (Lincoln, NE, 1978), p. 34.

entanglement impossible. I propose three arguments that have emerged from the literature: a *thesis of power*, a *thesis of limits* and a *thesis of globalisation and modernity*.[5]

The *thesis of power* is connected to the traditional statement of knowledge being equal to power. Yet I argue that speaking of science *and* empire is a simplification, for the power that was generated out of the meeting of these entangled ideologies was more fundamental than one of cause and effect. Separating them into science *and* empire reduces the multiple levels at which they were united. The *thesis of limits*, which I present next, is a revisionist position which urges that power had boundaries. Knowledge cannot be cast into monolithic blocks, separated merely by the placement of its creators on either side of the power differential between colonisers and colonised. The imperial sciences may be fragmented into rival and competing discourses of knowledge, in as much as indigenous knowledge had different forms, but should not be reified. In contact zones, different traditions of science came face to face, and there was an intense exchange of ideas, alongside moments of resistance. The *thesis of globalisation and modernity* takes these questions forward to the era of anti-colonialism and nationalism, and delves into debates about mimicry and derivation. Why did political movements in disparate parts of the world utilise science, technology and medicine for ideological resistance? I urge that nationalist science was derived from colonial ideas, but not wholly so, and that globalisation and modernity are better concepts for thinking through these ideas than is a linear explanation of causation that links colonisers and colonised. Both the *thesis of limits* and the *thesis of globalisation and modernity* point to the importance of thinking beyond empires to global processes in making sense of the status of science, technology and medicine on the world stage.

The French Empire and the Thesis of Power

It has now become a commonplace amongst historians to see science, technology and medicine as languages of command. The literature on the French Empire exemplifies the basic claims of this position very well, and this section will use this literature to illustrate the *thesis of power*. It is vital to stress that the French were not exceptional in combining science and empire in this manner, and much of what follows might have been supported by examples from the better-known story of the British Empire instead. However, the French imperial regime of science was distinctive in several ways: for instance, with respect to early professionalisation and to the heavy involvement of the state in the institutions of science.[6]

---

5   Since this chapter was first written, I have edited a forum of essays in *Isis* which bear out the need for new global histories of science. See, Sujit Sivasundaram (ed.),. 'Global histories of science', *Isis* 101 (2010): pp. 95-158.

6   For a survey, see Michael Osborne, 'Science and the French Empire', *Isis* 96 (2005): pp. 80–87.

The early and formative involvement of *savants* in the imperial project is illustrated by Napoleon's use of 150 intellectuals when he invaded Egypt in 1798.[7] These scholars represented a range of disciplines from natural history and engineering to medicine. Soon after their arrival this group set up the Institute of Egypt. It might seem incongruous to think of *savants* delivering papers in Egypt, given the precarious political context there while the British held the French army to ransom, yet papers continued to be delivered at the Institute of Egypt until March 1801, six months before the French capitulation to the British.

Why did Napoleon engage *savants* in such a sensitive mission, which was intended to strike at an artery of British colonialism and threaten access to India? Napoleon saw his *savants* as akin to soldiers, to be deployed as the shock troops of his empire. While in Egypt the *savants* paid attention to problems that affected the French presence overseas: for instance, they attempted to discover the ancient canal that linked the Gulf of Suez to the Nile. Elsewhere, too, science and militarism came together in French expansionism: in 1794–95, a commission for science travelled with France's army; and in Amsterdam it confiscated the Stadholder's natural historical collection, bringing it back to Paris. The collections of the Musée d'Histoire naturelle were substantially expanded by acquisitions from other conquered lands.[8] Napoleonic science was, then, a militarised form of knowledge, placed at the core of imperial rivalry. It maintained, albeit in a new mould, the Old Regime combination of science and colonialism seen in the plantation complex of Saint Domingue in the Caribbean.[9]

It was to the Musée d'Histoire naturelle, which had been nationalised after the Revolution, that Geoffroy Saint-Hilaire brought back his mummified ibis specimens from the expedition to Egypt. On returning to Paris, Saint-Hilaire was party to one of the best-known controversies of nineteenth-century science, with his former friend and new rival, Georges Cuvier.[10] The controversy erupted in public debate in 1830 before the Académie des sciences in Paris. In simple terms this can be interpreted as a contest about scientific methodology, between the broad view of natural philosophical theorising represented by Saint-Hilaire and a more specialist and institutional knowledge embodied in Cuvier. For Cuvier, fieldwork such as that undertaken by St Hilaire was for a lesser category of naturalist. Therefore overseas colonialism was critical to this debate, and it minted the hierarchies already evident

---

7   This paragraph relies on Charles C. Gillispie, 'The Scientific Importance of Napoleon's Egyptian Campaign', *Scientific American* 271/3 (1994): pp. 78–85 and Gillispie, 'Scientific Aspects of the French Egyptian Expedition, 1798–1801', *Proceedings of the American Philosophical Society* 33 (1989): pp. 447–74. See also Fernand Beucour, Yves Laissus and Chantal Orgogozo, *The Discovery of Egypt* (Paris, 1990).

8   Richard W. Burkhardt, 'The Leopard in the Garden: Life in Close Quarters at the Muséum d'Histoire Naturelle', *Isis* 98/4 (2007): p. 684.

9   See James E. McClellan, *Colonialism and Science: Saint Domingue in the Old Regime* (Baltimore, MD, 1992).

10 This paragraph relies on Toby Appel, *The Cuvier-Geoffroy Debate: French Biology in the Decades before Darwin* (New York, 1987) and Dorinda Outram, *Georges Cuvier: Vocation, Science and Authority in Post-revolutionary France* (Manchester, 1984).

in the period prior to the Revolution, between travellers in colonial lands – namely, field naturalists – and theorists in metropolitan centres, called cabinet naturalists.[11] Those in Europe came to rely in material terms on the findings, specimens and assistance of those in colonial territories, and yet saw themselves as superior in having the right to pronounce final judgement. The Napoleonic Empire made possible the methods advocated by Cuvier – that is, the examination of specimens from across the breadth of nature. The most famous corpse to be examined at the Musée d'Histoire naturelle, by Cuvier himself, was that of the Khoisan woman, Sara Baartman, the so-called 'Hottentot Venus', who had first arrived in Paris, after her display in London, as a typification of the sexualised savage.[12]

The study of nature represented by the new disciplines of the early nineteenth century had a material bearing on the running of the French Empire, and its lived experience. As Michael Osborne writes: 'Kew Gardens and the Paris Muséum National d'Histoire Naturelle were hubs in the wheels of international scientific exchange and colonial agriculture.'[13] *Agronomie* was first a French word, and by the late eighteenth century had become connected with experiments to increase the return on the land.[14] It was the French context that also gave rise to the term 'acclimatisation', in connection with a project to introduce merino sheep into France. This is not to suggest that acclimatisation was exclusively a French concern, but that the French side of the story is a useful site for my purposes.[15] Debates about acclimatisation were also connected to theories of race: the monogenists, who advocated the unity of humankind and a single creation, were especially enthusiastic about acclimatisation because it held out the possibility of adaptability as an explanation of current human difference. By 1860, the French Société zoologique d'acclimatation, had 2,600 members and a garden in Paris where it displayed flora, fauna and peoples from abroad, and stimulated interest in imperial territories. Away from the centre in Algeria, ambitious experiments in acclimatisation were conducted with yak and llama, bamboo and quinine, and with an attempt to start up a silk industry.

Beyond the natural sciences, the physical sciences were themselves moulded by the imperial age. Though the British case has received more attention, telegraphy was a key technology for French colonialism as well. In the aftermath of the revolution, the Chappe brothers assumed a central role in devising a working optical telegraph which would allow the French government to convey messages

---

11   For the earlier history of French natural history, see Emma Spary, *Utopia's Garden: French Natural History from Old Regime to Revolution* (Chicago, IL, 2000).

12   Sadiah Qureshi, 'Displaying Sara Baartman, The 'Hottentot Venus', *History of Science* 42 (2004): pp. 233–57.

13   Michael Osborne, 'Acclimatizing the World: A History of the Paradigmatic Colonial Science', *Osiris* 15 (2000): p.136. For a more extended treatment of the science of acclimatisation, see Osborne, *Nature, the Exotic and the Science of French Colonialism* (Bloomington, IN, 1994).

14   Simon Schaffer, 'Enlightenment Brought Down to Earth', *History of Science* 41 (2003): pp. 257–68.

15   Osborne, 'Acclimatizing', p. 137.

with speed and to receive messages of victory from newly conquered territories.[16] The building of telegraph lines was embraced with enthusiasm in the nineteenth century, sustaining a system that stretched over 4,000 kilometres, linking 500 stations in France with territories as far afield as Egypt and Indochina.[17] The technological needs of empire drove research in physical sciences: the empire can be seen as a vast space, or a laboratory, where experiments were conducted in order to test theories. The French created a grid of observatories, weather stations and surveying sites linked to their army, navy and consular agencies. This was a network of surveillance: the collection, passage and decoding of information all relied on the utilisation of the physical sciences of astronomy, geophysics, hydrography, cartography and physics.

As the century proceeded, the colonial arena provided an important road to career advancement for French scientists hoping to return to more senior postings in France. The growing bureaucratisation of the French Empire thus reformulated the earlier hierarchy between metropolitan theorists and field workers in the periphery. The increasing number of colonial research institutes, colonial universities and, in 1912, an Association of Colonial Scientists, was critical to the internationalisation of science within a colonial framework of metropolitan hegemony. Colonial scientists, proclaimed Edouard de Martonne, head of the geographical service of French West Africa, in 1930, 'are the agents of the propagation of French culture, just as colonists and functionaries are the agents of social and economic expansion'.[18]

These words by Martonne typify the discursive elements of the entanglement of science with empire, which have attracted attention in the light of Edward Said's argument that the French expedition to Egypt set in motion an Orientalist view of Egypt, culminating in the territories' submission to European imperialism.[19] However, the forms of representation and imagination which were foundational to science were imperialist in more complex ways than the simple creation of an Orientalised other.

A study of the Prussian Alexander von Humboldt, who was resident in Paris from 1804 to 1827 upon returning from South America, makes this point well. While von Humboldt was not French, he typified 'German science' and its Romantic view of nature in Paris, and was popular amongst the city's *savants*, who worked with him on his 30 volumes of information which were published in French after his return from his travels.[20] Humboldt was a universal theorist who straddled

---

16   Ben Marsden and Crosbie Smith, *Engineering Empires: A Cultural History of Technology in Nineteenth-Century Britain* (New York, 2005), chap. 5.
17   See Daniel Headrick, *The Tentacles of Progress: Technology Transfer in the Age of Imperialism, 1850–1914* (New York, 1988), pp. 122–4.
18   Cited in Lewis Pyenson, *Civilizing Mission: Exact Sciences and French Overseas Expansion, 1830–1940* (Baltimore, MD, 1993), p. 334.
19   Edward Said, *Orientalism: Western Conceptions of the Orient* (New York, 1978), p. 87ff.
20   Michael Dettlebach's work on Humboldt is excellent. See, for instance, 'Romanticism and Resistance: Humboldt and German "Natural Philosophy" in Napoleonic France', *Boston Studies in the Philosophy of Science* 241 (2007): pp. 247–58, and 'The Stimulations of Travel: Humboldt's Physiological Construction of the Tropics', in Felix Driver and

disciplines from astronomy to geology, and carried a mass of instruments in order to collect the impression of the tropics on his own body. Yet scientific travel was also a linguistic enterprise: region, nation, state, kingdom, province, outpost, colonist and even tramp, appear as terms to describe the geographical distribution of animals and plants in the biogeographical tradition initiated by Humboldt and taken on board by many others.[21] Scientific forms of representation and language did not only 'other', they neutralised and naturalised a multiplicity of political and social categories of imperialism.

One historical context which saw the articulation of multiple colonial classifications was the display of peoples. In early twentieth-century France, it was possible to view a typical 'native' village; the people on display were given materials with which to build their traditional dwellings and asked to perform religious rituals.[22] The 1931 Paris *Exposition International Coloniale* included temples, pagodas and mosques, alongside a large botanical garden built on site. Such exhibitions, like their counterparts elsewhere in Europe and the United States, ranked societies in a developmental hierarchy with the imperial nation at the pinnacle in an attempt to create both universal knowledge and imperial legitimacy.

The exhibitions were also closely connected to the consolidation of anthropology, 'the science of man'.[23] The Musée d'Ethnographie was formed after the 1878 *Exposition Universelle* and inherited many artefacts from that exhibition. The new Musée d'Homme was founded in 1938, out of the earlier museum, by the socialist anthropologists Paul Rivet and Marcel Maussin, in an attempt to create a progressive anthropology which could convince Europeans of the full humanity of the peoples of the French Empire. Despite the reorganised museum's socialist leanings, a colonial subsidy was critical to its operation, as were collecting expeditions in French colonies. The changing history of these museums denotes the shifting methods of anthropology, away from an earlier evolutionary perspective where cultures could be ranked in stadial fashion, to an allegedly non-racialised functionalist brand where cultures could be studied on their own terms.

Influential discussions of the entanglement of science with empire have emerged from the study of French colonial medicine and psychiatry. French medicine sought to assimilate colonial peoples into French culture, citizenship and religion. The professionalisation of medicine made it possible for the individual to be an object of scrutiny open to the gaze of the doctor, in this period invariably

---

Luciana Martins (eds), *Tropical Visions in an Age of Empire* (Chicago, IL, 2005), pp. 43–58.

21   Janet Browne, 'Biogeography and Empire', in N. Jardine, J.A. Secord and E.C. Spary (eds), *Cultures of Natural History* (Cambridge, 1996), pp. 305–321. See also Londa Schiebinger, *Plants and Empire: Colonial Bioprospecting in the Atlantic World* (Cambridge, MA, 2004), chap. 5.

22   Paul Greenhalgh, *Ephemeral Vistas: The Exposition Universelles, Great Exhibitions and World's Fairs, 1851–1939* (Manchester, 1988), p. 83ff.

23   Alice L. Conklin, 'Civil Society, Science, and Empire in Late Republican France: The Foundation of Paris's Museum of Man', *Osiris* 17 (2002): pp. 255–90. See also Fredrick Barth et al., *One Discipline Four Ways: British, German, French and American Anthropology* (Chicago, IL, 2005).

a white male.[24] Colonial psychiatric practice became an arena in which to theorise race and psychopathology, and in particular to essentialise the Islamic mind in a North African context.[25]

The post-colonial history of medicine and psychiatry draws in particular on the work of several theorists who emerge out of or engage with the French context. First there are the writings of Frantz Fanon which drew from his experience working as a psychiatrist in French Algeria before joining the National Liberation Front. Fanon saw his patients as victims of the alienation imposed by colonialism and necessitating violent liberation.[26] Second there is Michel Foucault's critique of medical discourse as essential to the philosophising of the finitude of humanity, and the emergence of the clinic as a space where the medical gaze of surveillance can create and control the individual and the social order.[27] Third there is the work of Bruno Latour, who presented a theorisation of the impact of the French chemist Louis Pasteur, in what has become known as 'actor-network theory'.[28] Louis Pasteur successfully proposed that disease had to be understood at the level of the micro-organism. Since micro-organisms were invisible to the naked eye and required professional equipment to be seen, such work allowed experts to entrench their position. Pasteur institutes for medical and sanitary research quickly spread across the empire: Saigon (1891), Tunis (1893), Algiers (1894), Nha Trang (1895), Tangiers (1914), Hanoi (1922), and Tananarive in Madagascar (1927).[29] Pasteurisation also enabled the rise of the laboratory as a site of theatrical control, for micro-organisms could be reproduced which were equivalent to those in the field, allowing the technician to manipulate these at will. The discovery of the bacillus for bubonic plague, which threatened French Indochina, is one example: within months of arriving in Hong Kong a team of French scientists were able to publish a complete description of the bacillus in the *Annales* of the Pasteur Institute, and later developed a serum and a vaccine. Following Latour, the power of science to act at a distance lies through these channels of institutionalisation, which allow

---

24 For historiographical surveys, see Warwick Anderson, 'Where is the Postcolonial History of Medicine?' *Bulletin of the History of Medicine* 72 (1998): pp. 552–80, and Shula Marks, 'What Is Colonial about Colonial Medicine? And What Has Happened to Imperialism and Health?', *Social History of Medicine* 10 (1997): pp. 205–219. For the emergence of colonial subjectivities, see Megan Vaughan, *Curing their Ills: Colonial Power and African Illness* (Cambridge, 1991).

25 Richard Keller, *Colonial Madness: Psychiatry in French North Africa* (Chicago, IL, 2007).

26 For commentary on Fanon and psychiatry, see Sloan Mahone and Megan Vaughan (eds), *Psychiatry and Empire* (Basingstoke, 2007), particularly the introduction. See also Keller, *Colonial Madness*.

27 See Michel Foucault, *The Birth of the Clinic: An Archaeology of Medical Perception* (Bristol, 1973).

28 Bruno Latour, *The Pasteurization of France* (Cambridge, MA, 1988).

29 Anne Marcovich, 'French Colonial Medicine and Colonial Rule: Algeria and Indochina', in Roy Macleod and Milton Lewis (eds), *Disease, Medicine and Empire: Perspectives on Western Medicine and the Experience of European Expansion* (London, 1988), pp. 103–118.

the reproduction and manipulation of natural phenomena within the controlled conditions of laboratories spread across the world.

Putting the theoretical writings of Fanon, Foucault and Latour together with those of Said, it is possible to look back at the literature on the French Empire in order to summarise the *thesis of power*. There was a powerful entanglement of ideologies around empire, science, technology and medicine which might be seen as a discourse which worked structurally, determining and shifting the delineation of disciplinary boundaries, and making an engagement with imperial territories and information essential to the task of being a scientist. Yet the fusion of the sciences with imperialism was also about methodology: in a search for laws, collections and classifications, the scientific method was redefined through empire, in as much as imperialism could become a neutral project through scientific claims to universality. Languages of civilisation, rationality and othering, in addition to ideas of race, arose simultaneously from empires and sciences. The practical workings of science saw the emergence of centres of collection such as museums, learned societies and universities reliant on data sent from distant lands. Precise instructions to travellers, and attention to the development of technology, allowed science to emerge as a trusted international language centred in imperial capitals. Yet the science of empire was not merely produced or consumed by an elite; a public science of exhibitions, for instance, existed in tension with expert renditions.

The British Empire and the Thesis of Limits

Recent work in the history of science has challenged the explanatory value of a framework focused exclusively on European power in uniting science with empire. There is increasing attention to the contingencies, failures and limits of imperial science. This is less an attempt to question the effects of power than one to understand its boundaries and to trace how the colonised responded to science. The literature on science in the British Empire has recently showcased what I call the *thesis of limits*, which is a revisionist position of this kind.

British imperial science encountered scientific knowledge in existing empires which had already turned to science and technology, such as the late Qing Empire of the nineteenth century. Documenting the passage of natural history specimens sent from Canton to Britain before the Opium War (1839–42), Fa-ti Fan argues that there was 'mingling, interaction, accommodation, hybridisation and confluence as well as conflicts' between British and Chinese knowledge about nature.[30] At Canton, sea-captains visited nursery gardens and shipped plants back to Britain. Gentlemanly naturalists corresponded with their counterparts in Britain. Gardeners working for the Royal Horticultural Society of London collected specimens in Canton. All these groups were dependent upon Chinese traders for their wares. Most of the specimens sent to the Zoological Society of London arrived from markets

---

30   Fa-ti Fan, *British Naturalists in Qing China* (Cambridge, MA, 2004), p. 3.

in Canton rather than from journeys into the interior, to which westerners were largely forbidden access since the Qing Empire closely guarded trade. Even when, in the late nineteenth century, more access became possible, British naturalists relied heavily on local informants, and British research on natural history became entangled with Sinological work on Chinese texts about plants, herbs and animals.

In the late Mughal Empire and its Hindu successor states of the eighteenth and nineteenth centuries, British men of science found indigenous rulers who relied on runners, astrologers, physicians, spies and wandering holy men.[31] Precolonial rulers in India determined the time for war, agricultural activity and politics through observation of the stars, which gave astronomers high status at courts. British officers attempted to engage with Indian astronomy through patronage of *pandits* or indigenous scholars, and by the collection of Sanskrit manuscripts. Over time the British asserted the superiority of their own astronomy and attempted to convert Indians to Copernican thought. Yet the rise of British astronomy did not serve as the death knell of astronomical knowledge based on ancient Hindu texts; in the world of print, a popular genre was that which mixed Puranic cosmology with Hindu mythology and astronomy. Colonial knowledge did not, thus, enjoy unbounded or simple power.

These examples from the late Qing and Mughal empires suggest that scientific and natural knowledge was utilised to bolster rule in non-European imperial formations, and then adopted by the British. Yet even where there were no formalised structures of imperialism prior to their arrival, the British relied on extant traditions of scientific knowledge. Captain Cook's three epic late eighteenth-century voyages inaugurated a new empire of science, yet they were characterised by complex practices of exchange in language, natural historical specimens and nautical information. Recent scholarship intriguingly argues that some sections of Cook's first voyage can be reinterpreted as the voyage of Tupaia, the Tahitian priest and navigator who Cook took on board. Tupaia joined the voyage voluntarily but was treated as an exotic creature: he directed the sailing from Tahiti to Huahine and Raiatea.[32] For the naturalist Joseph Banks, who was on board, Tupaia's value was 'his experience in the navigation of these people and knowledge of the Islands in these seas; he has told us the names of above 70, the most of which he has himself been at'.[33] Cook's use of Tupaia was not anomalous; other Pacific navigators were

---

31 C.A. Bayly, *Empire and Information: Intelligence Gathering and Social Communication in India, 1780–1870* (Cambridge, 1996), chap. 7 in particular. See also Michael Dodson, *Orientalism, Empire and National Culture, 1770–1880* (Basingstoke, 2007), and Sujit Sivasundaram, '"A Christian Benares": Science, Orientalism and the Serampore Mission of Bengal', *Indian Economic and Social History Review* 44 (2007): pp. 111–45.

32 For work that picks up this claim, see Anne Salmond, *The Trial of the Cannibal Dog: The Remarkable Story of Captain Cook's Encounters in the South Seas* (New Haven, CT, 2003); and David Turnbull, 'Cook and Tupaia:A Tale of Cartographic Méconnaissance?' in Margarette Lincoln (ed.), *Science and Exploration in the Pacific: European Voyages to the Southern Oceans in the Eighteenth Century*, (London, 1998), pp. 117–32.

33 J.C. Beaglehole (ed.), *The Endeavour Journal of Sir Joseph Banks, 1768–1771* (Sydney, 1962), vol. 1, entry for 12 July 1769, pp. 312–13.

taken captive by Europeans for use in similar ways. Tupaia's story shows how British exploration arose in part out of indigenous traditions of travel.

European reliance on local knowledge was critical, too, at the Cape Colony. Botanical explorations by Europeans in southern Africa relied on indigenous peoples who alerted travellers to the uses of plants, and whether they were edible or poisonous.[34] A similar account emerges in the Caribbean slave plantation.[35]

This symmetry in the cultural encounter suggests that we need a more robust framework than that suggested by 'indigenous knowledge' to recover the agency of the colonised. 'Indigenous knowledge' arose as the oppositional term to 'scientific knowledge', implying a lesser knowledge. Given the racial and colonial agenda which surrounded historic uses of the category of 'indigenous knowledge', contemporary writers must be careful not to adopt these same hierarchies in their classification and recovery of knowledge.[36] One way out of this conundrum is to replace 'indigenous knowledge', a concept which brings to mind an abstract conceptualisation of knowledge, with a view of knowledge as a body of work. Following the work of Pierre Bourdieu, historians of science have begun to stress the need to see science as practice, meaning a skill that is learnt and which is embodied by individuals in society.[37] For these writers, science is no longer theory, but is about the workings of the body, and contexts of production. Scholarship that leads to a more fragmented account of knowledge will pay attention to the making of knowledge, rather than seeing it as already fully formed. This includes a new strand of writing that comes out of South Asian historiography, which stresses movement and circulation as key to the emergence of scientific ideas.[38]

Yet deconstructing science into a set of practices that circulate should not mean that we ignore resistance. In the Pacific, missionary naturalists sought to inculcate a reverent appreciation for nature on the part of islanders. Islanders, however, frequently reinterpreted this message of natural theological adoration. One reportedly planted a nail and hoped that it would grow.[39] Apocryphal or

---

34   Elizabeth Green Musselman, 'Plant Knowledge at the Cape: A Study in African and European Collaboration', *International Journal of African Historical Studies* 36 (2003): pp. 367–92.

35   See Susan Scott Parish, 'Diasporic African Sources of Enlightenment Knowledge', in James Delbourgo and Nicholas Dew (eds), *Science and Empire in the Atlantic World* (New York and London, 2008), pp. 281–310. For slave knowledge and the limits of the colonial network, see Londa Schiebinger, *Plants and Empire: Colonial Bioprospecting in the Atlantic World* (Cambridge, MA, 2004).

36   See Helen Tilley, 'Global Histories, Vernacular Science and African Genealogies; or is the History of Science Ready for the World?', *Isis* 101 (2010): pp.110–19.

37   David Wade Chambers and Richard Gillespie, 'Locality in the History of Science: Colonial Science, Technoscience, and Indigenous Knowledge', *Osiris* 15 (2000): pp. 221–40.

38   Kapil Raj, *Relocating Science: Circulation and the Construction of Knowledge in South Asia and Europe: Seventeenth to Nineteenth Centuries* (Delhi, 2006); and David Arnold, *The Tropics and the Travelling Gaze: India, Landscape and Science, 1800–1856* (Seattle, WA, 2006).

39   Sujit Sivasundaram, *Nature and the Godly Empire: Science and Evangelical Mission in the Pacific, 1795–1850* (Cambridge, 2005), p. 161.

not, this account gestures towards the registers of adaptation open to islanders in responding to western science. This individualised response might usefully be compared with the response generated by the carefully stage-managed high points of late Victorian science, the solar eclipse expeditions. Sponsored by the Royal Astronomical Society, the Royal Society and the British Association for the Advancement of Science, these expeditions transported delicate instruments such as telescopes, spectroscopes and cameras to the colonies, with a team of observers to await the magical moment of the solar eclipse. Yet the meanings the inhabitants of colonial territories ascribed to eclipses came into conflict, sometimes forcefully, with those represented by western science. British commentators noted what they termed the superstition and fear of the indigenous people. In 1830 in Africa, local people were reported to have run away in terror from an eclipse. In India, Brahmin ceremonies occurred side by side with expedition science. In 1882, a crowd of Egyptians threatened to invade the camp of the astronomers, and had to be controlled by the army and police.[40]

The history of colonial medicine has also served up varied instances of resistance to western methods. In early twentieth-century Uganda, patients understood pills as charms, and contextualised diagnosis within their own religious systems. They insisted on being provided with particular remedies and dismissed the instructions of doctors. Some Africans also believed that Europeans were seeking their blood to cure white diseases, or that their blood was drunk by the doctor. Medicine became entangled with long-held traditions of vampires and bloodsucking.[41]

Yet a simple dichotomy of colonised and colonising inadequately represents the reception of western medicine in the colonies: in east and central Africa, for example, colonial male elders and administrators came together to form a discourse around sexually transmitted disease in order to exercise control over black women.[42] Interventionist British responses to plague epidemics in late nineteenth- and early twentieth-century India generated neither popular resistance nor elite collaboration; instead they sat side by side.[43] Perhaps the most common local response to plague measures was flight, given the rigours of quarantine and containment.

Debates surrounding vaccination and variolation in India are perhaps the best-known episode of resistance to British colonial medicine.[44] British accounts

---

40 Alex Soojung-Kim Pang, *Empire and the Sun: Victorian Solar Eclipse Expeditions* (Stanford, CA, 2002), pp. 77–81.

41 Luise White, *Speaking with Vampires: Rumor and History in Colonial Africa* (Berkeley, CA, 2000), chap. 3.

42 Vaughan, *Curing their Ills*, chap. 6.

43 Rajnarayan Chandavarkar, 'Plague, Panic and Epidemic Politics in India, 1896–1914', in Terence Ranger and Paul Slack (eds), *Epidemics and Ideas: Essays on the Historical Perception of Pestilence* (Cambridge, 1992), pp. 203–240.

44 See David Arnold, *Science, Technology and Medicine in Colonial India* (New York, 2000), pp. 71–5 and Arnold, *Colonizing the Body: State Medicine and Epidemic Disease in Nineteenth-Century India* (Berkeley, CA, 1993), chap. 3. See also Sanjoy Bhattacharya, Mark Harrison and Michael Worboys, *Fractured States: Smallpox, Public Health and Vaccination Policy in British India, 1800–1947* (New Delhi, 2005).

of variolation, or inoculation with live smallpox matter, were initially positive but turned negative around 1800, with the introduction of a regime of colonial vaccination. Inhabitants of the subcontinent resisted vaccination for a range of reasons: they saw it a polluting practice involving the transfer of fluids; they objected to it as an ungodly way of dealing with the goddess Sitala, who was equated with smallpox; and they also saw it as an infringement of gender, because it involved female contact with unknown men, rather than known *tikadars*, the hereditary group that dispensed variolation. Yet even this narrative of conflict has recently been recast, to indicate something other than a simple meeting of rational western science with the religious Indian customs of the body; for Indians were utilised within the vaccinating regime, and vaccination became part and parcel of middle-class urban Indian life by the end of the nineteenth century.[45]

Recent work on the British Empire has further developed the boundedness of imperial science, evident from a focus on resistance, by stressing not just the achievements of colonial science but its repeated failures. This is particularly evident in the realm of engineering and technology. Britons sought to apply their techniques in new environments, with different weather, soil and access to raw materials; in such contexts roads, bridges, irrigation schemes and experiments often simply did not work. In colonial Sri Lanka, soon after the 1815 victory over the last remaining indigenous kingdom in the interior, the British attempted to build a grand military road to the interior. They soon discovered that their road would be washed away in monsoonal conditions.[46] Later in the century, the monsoon was often a setback to railway construction in India, as was the terrain. Laying a track up the precipitous ghats was a severe challenge; the extreme topography meant that the line took seven years and required 38 tunnels, 81 bridges and 14 viaducts.[47]

Daniel Headrick's work sketches three phases of technological history: the penetration phase, connected to steamers and quinine; the conquest phase, linked to rapid-firing rifles and machine guns; and the consolidation phase, which brought steam lines, telegraphs and railroads.[48] This schema ignores how failure and struggle invariably marked the history of technology and empire. Indeed, Headrick's own later work on the telegraph bears this out. In India 'insects, storms, monkeys, elephants, and humans conspired to pull down the wires'.[49]

The *thesis of limits* is a revisionist position which allows for a more symmetrical understanding of the entanglement of the sciences and imperialism, by acknowledging the agency of the colonised. The non-European world was never a space devoid of science, medicine and technology, awaiting the liberation of the European Enlightenment. What is distinctive about modern imperialism is

---

45   See Bhattacharya, *Fractured States.*

46   Sujit Sivasundaram, 'Tales of the Land: British Geography and Kandyan Resistance in Sri Lanka, c. 1803–1850', *Modern Asian Studies* 41 (2007): pp. 925–61.

47   Headrick, *Tentacles of Progress,* p. 69.

48   Daniel Headrick, *The Tools of Empire: Technology and European Imperialism in the Nineteenth Century* (New York, 1981), p. 12.

49   Headrick, *Tentacles of Progress,* p .121.

the intensity with which knowledge traditions were circulated, displaced and changed, because of the spread of new imperial technologies. As new traditions were moved across the world by empires, they were met by resistance in many forms. The programme of applying science in empire also involved dramatic failures in the application of knowledge – for knowledge was being transferred to new situations with greater speed and less time for adaptation. In seeking to apply science, technology and medicine, the British sought to consolidate power, but sometimes discovered that they did not have a monopoly on this combination of interests.

The Decolonising World and the Thesis of Globalisation and Modernity

In the twentieth-century as anti-colonialism, nationalism and decolonisation came in succession, there were new contestations to the limits of imperial science. The sciences became part of a global discourse tied to new nationalist movements and economic critiques of colonialism. The history of nationalist science must be placed in relation to the work of creole and indigenous intellectual elites in a prior age. This long perspective on nationalist uses of science has been a key point of the most critical question in the literature on this area: was nationalist science derived from the colonial regime? Yet I argue nationalist science must also be set in the context of globalisation and transnational modernity.

By the early twentieth century, the Dutch had introduced new technologies in colonial Indonesia, ranging from railways to trams, and from the telephone to the radio.[50] Technology generated dramatic change and was adopted practically, socially and metaphorically as a cornerstone of anti-colonialism. Take, for instance, the 1930s nationalist journal *Sopir*, whose title translates as 'Chauffeur'. At the head of each article was an illustration of a driver behind the wheel of a car. The journal encouraged solidarity between drivers, and fed into a trade union of drivers. It was among office clerks, railway workers, radio repairmen and laboratory assistants that nationalism took root. While the Dutch attempted to utilise these newly introduced technologies to enforce segregation of coloniser and colonised and to legitimise rule, Indonesian nationalists saw technology as a site to articulate freedom from colonial rule. Railway strikes were one expression of this: in 1923 rails and sleepers were torn off, and a strike took as its battle cry 'tracks crushing'.[51]

In the Spanish and Portuguese empires, meanwhile, nationalists used western science to frame their own identity. The universal monarch so defining of the early modern era was tied to an imperial command over nature and the seas. The demise of this political philosophy allowed creole elites in these empires to

---

50   This paragraph is derived from Rudolf Mrázek, *Engineers of Happy Land: Technology and Nationalism in a Colony* (Princeton, NJ, 2002), p. xvi.
51   Ibid., p.16.

monopolise scientific activity.[52] With the advent of nationalist stirrings, the creole cultural traditions based on the work of Alexander Humboldt gave rise to a genre of landscape painting that sought to define the modern nation as neither European nor indigenous but *mestizaje* and urban-centred, so as to critique colonial visions of Mexico as a wilderness.[53] Critically for the argument here, Jorge Cañizares-Esguerra sees this nationalism not as simply derivative – not an embarrassing mimicry of Europe – but as the evolution of a lengthy South American natural historical tradition.

Other scholars have added further layers to this argument: for instance, natural history museums in Brazil and Argentina in the late nineteenth century were instrumental in forging a distinctive and nationalist palaeontology which claimed South America as the birth place of humans. The museums filled in blank spaces on maps through their collections of archaeological and physical remains.[54] Here was the new nation on display. In the Caribbean states of Colombia, Venezuela, Puerto Rico and Cuba, the traditions of creole science continued into a post-colonial era: governments sought to subjugate and domesticate wild landscapes by national inventories of plants, to eradicate yellow fever and malaria, to build railroads and overcome natural barriers, and to exploit natural commodities.[55] The continuity from creole science to national science makes neat differentiations of empires and nations too simple. These nationalist uses of the sciences are indicative of globalisation. By the twentieth century, intellectuals and politicians were living in an age where ideas shifted context with great speed, but also in an age with many rival scientific schools. In this global age, the pre-colonial, the colonial and post-colonial came to be seen as equally plausible places from which to forge a nationalist agenda, as the displacements of modernity allowed multiple posturing.

Such an argument is especially useful in making sense of the processes through which Japanese and Chinese reformers, patriots and nationalists adopted the discourses of science, medicine and technology. The traditional story of the late Qing Empire is told around the narrative of how the Chinese came increasingly to feel technologically and scientifically inadequate. This account, however, holds too strongly to a dichotomy of tradition and modernity, playing up the differences between China and the west.[56] In reality, Japan played a substantial role in the late reforms of the Qing Empire.[57] Over ten thousand Chinese studied in Japan between

---

52 Juan Pimentel, 'The Iberian Vision: Science and Empire in the Framework of a Universal Monarchy, 1500–1800', *Osiris* 15 (2001): pp. 17–30.

53 Jorge Cañizares-Esguerra, *Nature, Empire, and Nation: Explorations of the History of Science in the Iberian World* (Stanford, CA, 2006).

54 Maria Margaret Lopes and Irina Podgorny, 'The Shaping of Latin American Museums of Natural History, 1850–1990', *Osiris* 15 (2000): pp. 108–118.

55 Stuart McCook, *States of Nature: Science, Agriculture, and Environment in the Spanish Caribbean, 1760–1940* (Austin, TX, 2002).

56 Fa-ti Fan, 'Redrawing the Map: Science in Twentieth-Century China', *Isis* 98 (2007): pp. 524–38. See also the other essays in this Focus section in *Isis* on China in the twentieth century.

57 The following is a summary of Benjamin A. Elman, *On Their Own Terms: Science in*

1902 and 1907, where they encountered new and western sciences. The Japanese Meiji scholars adopted some of their science from Chinese sources. The mutual influence of Japan and China draws a more complex picture of transnational intellectual linkages in science, rather like the Latin American story.

In the late Qing Empire, reformers claimed Chinese origins for much western science and questioned the successes of western medicine. When the Guomindang sought to abolish traditional Chinese medicine in the late 1920s, Chinese doctors called a national convention supported by strikes at pharmacies and surgeries across the nation. Yet, in the Republican period in the early twentieth century, Chinese scientists travelled to the United States and Europe while universities in China employed both Chinese and foreign scientists, expanding scientific contacts and collaborations between China and other parts of the world. The Society for the Preservation of National Learning, founded in Shanghai in 1905, sought to translate the work of western intellectuals such as Spencer, Darwin, Huxley and J.S. Mill into Chinese.[58] Yet at the same time there was the competing claim that China required a restoration of pre-Qing learning: 'Put differently, in order to digest western learning, China must have a strong Chinese stomach.'[59] The classics, Confucian thought, natural history and evolutionary theory were all present here in a complicated mix which resisted a categorization of science being imported from outside or generated from within China. Chinese national science therefore drew on the west whilst laying claim to its past. Arguably, even with the advent of the Chinese Communist Party and its purge of intellectuals, an interest in tying the old and the new in order to support power carried through: take for example the Chinese Communist Party's active promotion of Chinese traditional medicine.[60]

If there is a regional history which has seen wide debate of the idea of nationalist discourses of science and technology as derivative from colonialism, it is in the rich work on twentieth-century India. Gyan Prakash has argued: 'Nationalism arose by laying its claim on revived traditions, by appropriating classical texts and traditions of science as the heritage of the nation'.[61] Prakash does not deny that nationalists turned to precolonial traditions of India, or that their renditions of science were a mixture of indigenous and western, but his point is that this reverence for reason was derived from colonialism's own fascination for science. His account starts with how British colonists created the state of India through their surveys, histories and censuses, and through the technologies of roads, railways and canals that welded far-flung provinces together. The colonists staged

---

China, 1550–1900 (Cambridge, MA, 2005), chap. 11. See, also, James R. Bartholomew, *The Formation of Science in Japan: Building a Research Tradition* (New Haven, CT, 1989).

58   Fa-ti Fan, 'Nature and Nation in Chinese Political Thought: the National Essence Circle in Early Twentieth-Century China ', in Lorraine Daston and Fernando Vidal (eds), *The Moral Authority of Nature* (Chicago, 2004), pp. 409-37.

59   Fan, 'Nature and Nation', p. 416.

60   Kim Taylor, *Chinese Medicine in Early Communist China, 1945–1963: A Medicine of Revolution* (London and New York, 2005).

61   Gyan Prakash, *Another Reason: Science and the Imagination of Modern India* (Princeton, NJ, 1999), pp. 6–7.

the magic of science in colonial exhibitions and museums in India in order to show the superiority of colonial rationalities, and the inability of the colonised to respond to reason without recourse to what the British termed superstition. It was this context which laid the groundwork for the nationalist elites' turn to science. Early leaders of the Indian National Congress, such as Madan Mohan Malaviya or Romesh Chunder Dutt, saw British colonialism as generative of poverty in India. Indian economic historians in the nationalist era charged the British with turning India into a base for agriculture in order to finance Britain's industrial revolution, thereby critiquing the impact of colonial technology. This primed a nationalist cry for the need to renovate India's technology and science, and eventually fed into the centralised socialism exemplified by Jawaharlal Nehru, India's first Prime Minister, who believed the scientific method would answer India's problems. But Nehru himself embraced western science, again pointing to the impossibility of wholly disentangling western and subcontinental traditions.

A new strand of work on India seeks to connect political thought and history of science, and to move beyond the position advocated by Prakash. Shruti Kapila has studied the uses of Herbert Spencer's evolutionary ideas by Indian nationalists looking to critique liberalism.[62] Sunil Amrith's work on the politics of hunger and the welfare state shows how Gandhi employed ideas of nutritional science in his religious and ethical beliefs.[63] Nationalists sought to create solidarity with the hungry through a critique of colonialism, and made welfare a priority for the newly independent nation. The turn to the transformations of scientific political thought and to the practices of internationalising science point to the tiredness of the debate about the connection between the imperial order of science and the decolonising one. Scholars have concluded that the earlier debate cannot be solved by recourse to a simple story of mimicry, or indeed a linear narrative of the history of national science. This was a global age of knowledge, where ideas travelled in multiple directions together with migrating students and scientists, and where the local, the national, the regional and the transnational were registers open to the same idea, sometimes at different times.

The recent literature on modern colonial science is making it inevitable that there will be a reworking of the European history of science, with its marking points of the Scientific Revolution, the Enlightenment and Industrialisation. Yet at the same time the term 'colonial science' is itself being opened up in radically new ways; its lineaments are being questioned. Science was not separable from empire, and so talk of how imperialism allowed the diffusion of science from colonial centres to the peripheries, or how science was either a cause or an effect of empire, is misguided.[64]

62 Shruti Kapila, 'Self, Spencer and Swaraj: Nationalist Thought and Critiques of Liberalism, 1890–1920', *Modern Intellectual History* 4 (2007): pp. 109–127.

63 Sunil S. Amrith, 'Food and Welfare in India, c. 1900–1950', *Comparative Studies in Society and History* 50 (2008): p. 1019.

64 I have made no reference thus far, on purpose, to the model that dictated the terms

In outlining my *thesis of power*, I pointed to the powerful symbiosis of sciences with empires, making these ideas a site where each could reinvent itself in complicated ways. Such reinventions stretched from the structural format of science, technology and medicine, including careers and disciplines, to the methods adopted by the sciences. Scientific correspondence between theorists and field workers was an imperial network, and metropolitan institutions set themselves up as interpreters of the data that flowed from the field. Imperial science separated the elite theorist from the amateur collector.

Yet this hierarchical reckoning had its limits. Science, technology and medicine were also made in 'contact zones' between cultures, which allowed new ideas to emerge through the processes of circulation made possible by imperialism. To understand the workings of science in imperialism, it is important to think beyond a simply dichotomy of coloniser and colonised. It is also vital to adopt terminology that encompasses a range of traditions of knowledge, without a bias towards European practices of science. A recourse to embodiment and skill might make such a widened project viable. Attending to the hybrid and already changing traditions of science which came into contact with empires, and to the limits of the applicability of such sciences, characterises a *thesis of limits*.

Moving chronologically forward, the field has seen vibrant debate about the nationalising of science in the age of imperial decline. Was this a derivative discourse? I have argued, from my *thesis of globalisation and modernity* that although nationalising elites adopted European scientific traditions to make themselves modern, this observation cannot tell the full story. There were legacies from the precolonial as well as the creole and early colonial periods. Nationalist science did not represent a radical break in the meetings of different traditions of science, merely a new rendition for a time of imperial collapse. The globalisation of nationalism allowed anti-colonial ideas of science to circulate. At the same time, tradition and modernity were interlinked in the twentieth century around discourses of science. In particular this thesis gestures to the fact that a focus on empires clouds a wider global history of science.

From our standpoint, an understanding of science, technology and medicine on the modern imperial stage provides a context for the rise of the information age and its technologies of colonialism, and the still pervasive occurrence of brain drain, underdevelopment and intellectual property theft from indigenous peoples. Just as much as science, technology and medicine were utilised to form the nation-state out of empires, they are now part of the contestation and fragmentation of the system of nation-states, in a new age of the colonial politics of knowledge.

---

of the field for too long: George Basalla, 'The Spread of Western Science', *Science* 156 (1967): pp. 611–22. A more recent model has been provided by Roy MacLeod, 'On Visiting the "Moving Metropolis": Reflections on the Architecture of Imperial Science', *Historical Records of Australian Science* 5 (1982): pp. 1–16.

Environment[1]

Richard Grove and Vinita Damodaran

Environmental history has been described variously as the interdisciplinary study of the relations among culture, technology and nature through time,[2] and as the story of the life and death, not of human individuals, but of societies and species in terms of their relationship with the world around them.[3] Some environmental historians argue from a materialist/structuralist perspective while others argue from a much more cultural perspective. There are thus divergent opinions over the extent to which nature influences human affairs, some taking the position of limited environmental determinism, others insisting that culture determines all. Worster straddles both worlds by asserting that the cultural history of nature is as significant as the ecological history of culture.[4] Disagreements exist on whether the natural world constitutes any kind of order or pattern that we can know and, if it does, whether that order can be comprehended by means of science. There is also debate on what is natural and what is not, whether indigenous people managed the whole environment or only some part of it, how much was wilderness and how much of this wilderness was mythical.

---

1   A version of this essay appeared in R. Grove and V. Damodaran, 'Imperialism, Intellectual Networks and Environmental Change: Origins and Evolution of Global Environmental History, 1676–2000', *Economic and Political Weekly* 41/42 (2006): pp. 4345–54, 4497–5006. A version of a section has also appeared in Vinita Damodaran, 'Environment and Empire: A Major Theme in World Environmental History', in Mary Harris and Csaba Levai (eds), *Europe and its Empires* (Pisa, 2008), pp. 129–39.

2   D. Worster, *Nature's Economy: A History of Ecological Ideas* (Oxford, 1985).

3   Mark Elvin, *The Retreat of the Elephants: The Environmental History of China* (New Haven, CT, 2004); Richard Grove, *Green Imperialism: Colonial Expansion, Tropical Island Edens and the Origins of Environmentalism* (Cambridge, 1995). For the history of environmental history, see John McNeill, 'Observations on the Nature and Culture of Environmental History', *History and Theory* 42 (2003): pp. 5–43.

4   For works that examine the cultural history of nature, see Paul Carter, *The Lie of the Land* (London, 1996); Simon Schama, *Landscape and Memory* (New York, 1996); D. Cosgrove and S. Daniel, *The Iconography of the Landscape: Essays on the Symbolic Representation, Design and Use of Past Environment* (Cambridge, 1989).

Environmental history, then, seeks to address the absence of nature in the study of history by developing new perspectives. Several studies have achieved wide resonance: Carolyn Merchant, *The Death of Nature* (1980), Alfred Crosby, *Ecological Imperialism* (1986), Donald Worster, *Rivers of Empire* (1985), William Cronon, *Nature's Metropolis* (1991), Richard Grove, *Green Imperialism* (1995) and John McNeill, *Something New Under the Sun* (2000).[5] Some of these are works of synthesis while others present new approaches which are large scale and comparative in scope, with relevance for the environmental history of empire.[6] Grove's idea of the 'unnatural' history of the empire, for example, has taken root in studies of empire. This idea argues that the development of an environmental sensibility can be traced to the encounter of seventeenth- and eighteenth-century western Europeans (especially naturalists, medical officers and administrators) with the startlingly unfamiliar environments of the tropics, and to the attendant environmental damage. In arguing that global environmental history is not new – it was already being written by the mid-nineteenth century – this theory challenged the deep misconception that the integration of narratives of human history into ecological contexts began in the 1990s.[7]

From the mid-nineteenth century on, environmental history developed primarily in the form of 'historical geography', which was partly displaced in the mid-twentieth century by a more consciously global environmental history.[8] This was also a period in which European decolonisation began in earnest, and in which writings about the possibility of global nuclear catastrophe and pesticide pollution (particularly by Rachel Carson in the United States and Kenneth Mellanby in Britain)[9] helped to stimulate the early green shoots of a worldwide populist environmental movement which bloomed in the early 1970s.

---

5   Carolyn Merchant, *The Death of Nature: Women, Ecology and the Scientific Revolution* (San Francisco, CA, 1982); Alfred Crosby, *Ecological Imperialism: The Biological Expansion of Europe, 900–1900* (Cambridge, 1986); D. Worster, *Rivers of Empire: Water, Aridity and the Growth of the American West* (New York, 1985); William Cronon, *Nature's Metropolis: Chicago and the Great West* (New York, 1991); John McNeill, *Something New Under the Sun: An Environmental History of the Twentieth-Century World* (New York, 2000). See also Sverker Sorlin and Paul Warde, 'The Problem of the Problem of Environmental History: A Re-reading of the Field', *Environmental History* 12/1 (2007): pp. 107–130, and Caroline Ford, 'Nature's Fortunes: New Directions in the Writing of European Environmental History', *Journal of Modern History* 79 (2007): pp. 112–33.
6   Sorlin and Warde, 'The Problem of the Problem', p. 5.
7   See, for example, Richard C. Foltz, 'Does Nature Have Historical Agency? World History, Environmental History, and How Historians Can Help Save the Planet', *History Teacher* 37 (2003): pp. 9–28.
8   William L. Thomas (ed.), *Man's Role in Changing the Face of the Earth* (Chicago, IL, 1956).
9   Rachel Carson, *The Sea Around Us* (New York, 1951); Carson, *Silent Spring* (New York, 1962); G.J. Marco, *Silent Spring Revisited* (New York, 1987); Kenneth Mellanby, *Pesticides and Pollution* (London, 1967).

Environmentalism, Desiccationism and Environmental History

It is no accident that the earliest writers to comment specifically on rapid environmental change in the context of empires were scientists involved in ecological issues. The early environmental critique of the European and American empires depended upon an historical perception of rapid rates of ecological change.[10] As early as the mid-seventeenth century, intellectuals and natural philosophers living in the colonies – Richard Norwood and William Sayle in Bermuda,[11] Thomas Tryon in Barbados[12] and Edmond Halley and Isaac Pyke on St Helena[13] – were aware of the high rates of soil erosion and deforestation in the colonial tropics, and of the urgent need for conservationist intervention to protect forests and threatened species. On St Helena and Bermuda this early conservationism led in 1715 to the gazetting of the first colonial forest reserves and forest protection laws.

On French colonial Mauritius (Isle de France), Pierre Poivre and Philibert Commerson framed pioneering forest conservation legislation designed specifically to prevent rainfall decline in the 1760s.[14] In India, William Roxburgh, Edward Balfour, Alexander Gibson and Hugh Cleghorn (all Scottish medical scientists) wrote alarmist narratives relating deforestation to the danger of climate change.[15] Their distinctively modern environmentalist views owed a great deal to the precocious commentaries of Alexander von Humboldt in his *Personal Narrative*.[16] East India Company scientists in the eighteenth century were also aware of French attempts to prevent deforestation and rainfall change in Mauritius.[17] William Roxburgh, together with Alexander Beatson on St Helena, observed the incidence of global drought events which we know today were globally linked or teleconnected.[18] The rise of imperial networks of information thus enabled the emergence of a new global environmental awareness as well as the first accurate accounts of global change.

---

10   Grove, *Green Imperialism*.
11   J.H. Lefroy, *Memorials of the Discovery and Early Settlement of the Bermudas or Somers Islands, 1515–1685: Compiled from the Colonial Records and other Original Sources* (London, 1877–79).
12   Thomas Tryon, *Friendly Advice to the Gentlemen-planters of the East and West Indies: In Three Parts by Philotheos Physiologus* (London, 1684).
13   Grove, *Green Imperialism*, p. 114.
14   Ibid., pp. 168–264.
15   Ibid., pp. 380–473.
16   A. von Humboldt, *Personal Narrative of Travels to the Equinoctial Regions of the New Continent, 1799–1804* (London, 1819).
17   Edward Balfour, Papers and Correspondence, V/27/560/107, Oriental and India Office Collections, British Library, London.
18   R. Grove, 'Revolutionary Weather: The Climatic and Economic Crisis of 1788–1795 and the Discovery of El Nino', in T. Sherratt (ed.), *A Change in the Weather: Climate and Culture in Australia* (Canberra, 2005), pp. 128–40. Teleconnections refers to links among climate anomalies over large distances.

The writings of Balfour and Cleghorn in the late 1840s illustrated the extent of the permeation of a global environmental consciousness.[19] In similar fashion, Baron Ferdinand Von Mueller in Australia, George Perkins Marsh and Franklin Benjamin Hough in the United States and John Croumbie Brown in South Africa all displayed formidable knowledge of global environmental change, which they used to warn of the dangers of future environmental profligacy and global ruin.[20] Most of these men published their most important texts during the 1860s, a period which we might appropriately name the 'first environmental decade'.

It was in the colonial periphery that what we now term 'environmentalism' first made itself felt. Colonial proponents were often in a position to make use of historical evidence for environmental change in government records and thus became *de facto* environmental historians. Victorian texts such as Paul Strzelecki, *Physical Description of New South Wales* (1845), Berthold von Ribbentrop, *Forestry in the British Empire* (1899), J.C. Brown, *Hydrology of South Africa* (1875), Hugh Cleghorn, *The Forests and Gardens of South India* (1861) and George Marsh, *Man and Nature* (1864) were not only vital to the onset of environmentalism, they were also meticulously documented works in environmental history.[21] One preoccupation, which owed much of its strength to notions circulating from the eighteenth century linking climate, civilisational degeneration and racial types, stands out: the growing interest in the human impact on climate change, a fear that human activity, especially deforestation, might lead to global desiccation.[22] This fear grew steadily in the wake of colonial expansion and fed into post-colonial fears about desertification articulated in the late twentieth century by international bodies and global NGOs. It also critically affected the early direction of environmental history.

After the 1860s, and even more after the great Indian famines of 1876 and 1899–1902, the connections between the human and the natural world stimulated the idea that human history and environmental change might be linked. Historians played surprisingly little part in this process; instead they inherited a fully fledged thesis developed, in the main, by historical geographers whose ideas were then picked up and developed by *annaliste* historians such as Fernand Braudel and W.G. Hoskins. Meanwhile, mainstream desiccationist thinking developed among foresters, geographers and natural scientists working mainly in the colonial tropics

---

19 See, for example, H.F. Cleghorn, *The Forests and Gardens of South India* (Edinburgh, 1861).

20 See, for example, Ferdinand von Mueller, *Australian Vegetation, Considered especially in its Bearing on the Occupation of Territory* (Melbourne, 1867); George Marsh, *The Earth as Modified by Human Action* (London, 1874); and Franklin Hough, *On the Activity of Governments in the Preservation of Forests* (Salem, MA, 1873).

21 Paul Strzelecki, *Physical Description of New South Wales* (London, 1845); Berthold von Ribbentrop, *Forestry in the British Empire* (London, 1899); J.C. Brown, *The Hydrology of South Africa* (London, 1875); George Marsh, *Man and Nature, or, Physical Geography as Modified by Human Action* (London, 1864).

22 See, for example, the work of G.-L. Leclerc, Comte de Buffon, *Histoire naturelle: générale et particulière* (Paris, 1749–1804).

of Britain and France, and to some extent in the USSR and the American west as well as the new Pacific and Caribbean empire of the United States.

In the mid-nineteenth century, the British explorer David Livingstone linked lake shoreline features in the Kalahari to past rainfall episodes and subsequent desiccation.[23] In southern Africa, John Croumbie Brown suggested that human agency may have been involved in the deterioration of local conditions.[24] The discovery towards the end of the nineteenth century of moraines (heaps of rocks which glaciers push up in front of them) on Mount Kenya and Kilimanjaro (in Tanzania), far below the tongues of present glaciers, made it plain that the climate of Africa had been cooler in the past. In West Africa, J.D. Falconer described extensive fields of linear dunes, covered in vegetation and supporting a large population, stretching well into northern Nigeria, far to the south of the current limits of the Sahara.[25] About the same time, Jean Tilho found evidence of a great lake having existed in the Bodele depression in Chad between Tibesti and Lake Chad.[26]

The years around 1900 thus saw a renewed interest in essentially millennial theories of global desiccation closely related to convictions about the 'inevitable' extinction of both indigenous peoples and large tropical mammals such as the African elephant. These theories were reinforced by climatic events. By the end of the nineteenth century it was evident that the short-term vicissitudes of the African climate were of considerable economic importance. In East Africa the level of Lake Victoria rose suddenly in 1878 after unusually heavy rains. A few months later there was abundant rain over the Blue Nile's catchment in Ethiopia, followed by the disastrous Nile floods in Egypt. Severe droughts affected southern Africa in 1862, and again between 1881 and 1885. In 1911, Alexander Knox pointed to what he saw as a decline in rainfall in nineteenth-century Senegal.[27]

At the same time, American geographers started to investigate post-glacial desiccation in central Asia and China. Dry water courses and lakes as well as abandoned settlements in central Asia suggested that deteriorating environmental conditions had spurred successive nomadic invasions during periods of increased aridity. An early exemplar of this theory was Ellsworth Huntington, a geographer and environmental determinist. His book *The Pulse of Asia* (1907) set an agenda for both desiccationism and environmental determinism.[28]

A small group of geographers, increasingly influenced by their professional contacts with a globally distributed set of colonial scientists and geographers, began to think in terms of global relations between environmental change, imperial

---

23   David and Charles Livingstone, *Narrative of an Expedition to the Zambesi and its Tributaries: And of the Discovery of the Lakes Shirwa and Nyassa, 1858–1864* (New York, 1866).

24   J.C. Brown, *The Hydrology of South Africa* (London, 1875).

25   J.D. Falconer, *On Horseback through Nigeria; or, Life and Travel in the Central Sudan* (London, 1911).

26   J. Tilho, *Documents scientifiques de la Mission Tilho, 1906–1909* (Paris, 1910–1911).

27   Alexander Knox, *The Climate of the Continent of Africa* (Cambridge, 1911), p. 158.

28   Ellsworth Huntington, *The Pulse of Asia: A Journey in Central Asia Illustrating the Geographic Basis of History* (Boston, MA, 1907).

power and societal change. The scene was set by Halford Mackinder's *Britain and the British Seas*, a highly selective historical interpretation of nature, geography and super-power political economy, which appeared a year after H.B. George's innovative *The Relations of Geography and History*.[29] After the First World War, a flurry of publications linking climate and history appeared, starting with the works of C.E.P. Brooks.[30] As a colonial scientist, Brooks used his field observations from places as far apart as the Falkland Islands and Uganda, to draw conclusions about changes in the world climate. This body of work from the interwar years reflected a connection between the environmental decline of ancient empires and contemporary fears about imperial disturbances, thereby encouraging the emergence of anti-colonial nationalisms.

Similarly, some of the political and existential anxieties immediately prior to the First World War had been created by such doom-laden books as William Macdonald's widely read *Conquest of the Desert* (1913).[31] After the war a generalised revulsion at the enormity of the wartime slaughter was reflected in a strengthened awareness of the potential for human destruction on a world scale. This prompted major retrospective views on comparable narratives of mass human disruptions of life and environment. A flurry of colonial publications and commissions on the connections between drought and human activity appeared in the early 1920s. It was in semi-arid South Africa that the gospel of desiccation found its most pronounced and didactic interwar expression. The highly alarmist 1922 report of the South African Drought Commission revealed for the first time the beginnings of a North American influence on British colonial soil.[32] Two of the Afrikaner members of the commission had worked in the US as refugees after the South African War (1899–1902). One of the first South Africans to write systematic historical studies of pastures, T.D. Hall, studied agriculture in Illinois between 1910 and 1913. His work was followed by other worrying studies, most notably, J.C. Smuts' 1926 *Holism and Evolution*, a work heavily influenced by the ecological theories of the British ecologist Arthur Tansley, who made connections among climate, ecology and 'climax' individuals and communities.[33]

---

29   H.J. Mackinder, *Britain and the British Seas* (London, 1902); H.B. George, *The Relations of Geography and History* (Oxford, 1901); George, *A Historical Geography of the British Empire* (London, 1904).

30   C.E.P. Brooks, *The Evolution of Climate* (London, 1922), Brooks, *Climate through the Ages* (London, 1926); Brooks, *Climate and Weather of the Falkland Islands and South Georgia* (London, 1920); Brooks, *Variations in the Levels of Central African Lakes, Victoria and Albert* (London, 1923).

31   William Macdonald, *The Conquest of the Desert* (London, 1913).

32   'Interim Report of the South African Drought Investigation Committee' (Capetown, 1922).

33   A.G. Tansley, English botanist and pioneer in the field of ecology. He was founding editor of the journal *New Phytologist* in 1902. Climax refers to a biological community of plants and animals which through a process of ecological succession has reached a stable state.

In Africa the concerns of the 1920s now began to embrace colonial territories that had not featured at all in the environmental literature of the prewar years, but which were now the subject of considerable colonial interest and infrastructural investment. Anglo-Egyptian Sudan attracted some of the first literature on desert-spreading or desertification. A pioneer in this area was E.W. Bovill, and his ideas were in turn taken up by G.T. Renner, who painted Africa as a potentially famine-ridden continent.[34]

The emergence of a period of environmental anxiety in North America, catalysed by the prolonged 'dustbowl' droughts in the southern United States in the early 1930s, supplemented existing colonial panic over desert-spreading.[35] Soil erosion had been a prominent issue in India from 1890, and huge investments to control it were made – for example, in the Etawah region of the United Provinces of northern India. These efforts, like similar measures in West and South Africa, long predated American 'dustbowl' alarmism. In 1934, E.P. Stebbing, a prominent Indian forester, visited West Africa.[36] His short visit, made during the dry season, provoked him to write a feverish warning on the dangers of desert-spreading. While Stebbing's somewhat hysterical warnings were downplayed by local scientists who had much greater experience of the causes, rates and seasonality of local desertification and erosion, his terminology was taken up with alacrity by governing circles in Paris and London, and led directly to the founding of the Anglo-French Boundary Forest Commission in 1934.[37] He was not alone in his concerns. In 1931, Keith Hancock (later a prominent historian of the British Empire and Commonwealth) published a virulent attack on profligate deforestation and land-clearing by settlers.[38] His work was followed in 1938 by that of Francis Ratcliffe who, fresh from his investigations of the causes of soil erosion in South Australia and Queensland, published a savage indictment of the impact of extensive outback agriculture.[39]

Global Environmental Thinking from the 1930s

By the 1930s, therefore, there was an innovative convergence of analytical and descriptive writings by geographers, anthropologists, archaeologists and ecologists, many of them taking a global and increasingly anxious and prescriptive view of human–environment interactions. The Australian archaeologist Vere

---

34 E. Bovill, 'The Encroachment of the Sahara on the Sudan', *Journal of the Royal African Society* 20 (1921): pp. 23–45; G.T. Renner, 'A Famine Zone in Africa: The Sudan', *Geographical Review* 16 (1926): pp. 583–96.

35 Donald Worster, *Dust Bowl: The Southern Plains in the 1930s* (New York, 1979).

36 E.P. Stebbing, *The Forests of India* (Edinburgh, 1922).

37 E.P. Stebbing, *The Creeping Desert in the Sudan and Elsewhere in Africa: 15 to 13 Degrees Latitude* (Khartoum, 1953).

38 W.K. Hancock, *Australia* (New York, 1931).

39 Francis Ratcliffe, *Flying Fox and Drifting Sand: The Adventures of a Biologist in Australia* (New York, 1938).

Gordon Childe placed his theories of pre-historic development on a world scale.[40] Daryll Forde's *Habitat, Economy and Society*, published in 1934, drew on a highly structured and global approach to history and human societies. He incorporated case studies from Malaya, the Kalahari, Siberia, the Arctic, West Africa and the Pacific, many of them the work of a new breed of anthropologists and geographers in colonial employ.[41]

Colonial environmental agendas were again decisive in defining the form of global environmental geography, history and anthropology in the 1930s. Perhaps the most interesting of those who adopted this approach was L. Dudley Stamp, an oil geologist in Burma before he became the first professor of geography at Rangoon University. Like Jan Smuts, Stamp was an adherent of Arthur Tansley and interested in the evolution and climatic history of the Burma landscape.[42] Stamp's surveys in both Burma and Britain (where he developed the official land utilisation survey between 1930 and 1940) were preoccupied with evolutionary changes in the succession of vegetation types over time.[43] For many years Stamp's approach influenced the philosophy and methods of postwar colonial natural resource survey in other colonies.[44] This was an important development since the globalisation of soil and land-use survey methods encouraged efficient use of land long after decolonisation.

After the Second World War, environmental accounts often became confessionals or apologias for imperial environmental misdeeds, particularly under a British Labour government fated to impose far more interventionist imperial 'development' policies than any previous prewar Conservative government had dared. Colonial expertise, not least from Australia, played a major role in the new postwar debates about the global environment, especially in the tropics. Australian geologist Frank Debenham, a member of Scott's *Terra Nova* expedition, typified this new generation. In 1946 he and Laurens van der Post undertook a series of reports on the natural resource potential of Bechuanaland and Nyasaland for the Colonial Office and the Commonwealth Development Corporation.[45] Such work often took

---

40 Vere Gordon Childe's *Dawn of European Civilization* (London, 1925), echoing the title of J.L. Myres' 1911 work, *The Dawn of History*, was soon followed by *New Light on the Most Ancient East* (London, 1933) and *Man Makes Himself* (London, 1936).

41 Daryll Forde, *Habitat, Economy and Society* (London, 1934).

42 See, for example, L.D. Stamp, 'Notes on the Vegetation of Burma', *Geographical Journal* 43 (1924): pp. 231–3; Stamp, 'Burma: A Survey of a Monsoon Country', *Geographical Review* 20 (1930): pp. 86–109; Stamp, 'The Irrawady River', *Geographical Journal* 95 (1940): pp. 329–56; Stamp, 'The Aerial Survey of the Irrawady Delta Forests', *Journal of Ecology* 15 (1924): pp. 262–76.

43 The first land-utilisation survey was carried out by amateurs, including school children. The second land-utilisation survey was carried out after the Second World War and was still largely official.

44 At the Gold Coast Robert Wills carried on a decade-long study of agriculture and its evolution in the Gold Coast, adopting the methods of both Stamp and Henry Darby, author of *The Domesday Geography of Eastern England* (Cambridge, 1952).

45 F. Debenham, *Kalahari Sands* (London, 1953); Debenham, *Nyasaland: The Land of the*

place within an emergent development ideology, and sometimes under contract to the young United Nations agencies, where ex-colonial natural resource specialists easily found employment.

Africanists, Classicists and Global Environmental History

In the 1960s and 1970s a new range of environmental accounts appeared. Another pioneer of environmental history, Clarence Glacken, explored the role of humans as environmental agents on a global scale that moved beyond European thought and encompassed imperial thinking about nature from the Akkadian to the European maritime empires. Glacken's *Traces on the Rhodian Shore* (1967) inspired a group of studies taking themes directly from different periods of global environmentalism.[46] Donald Hughes pursued the proto-environmentalism and the alleged ecologically caused demise of Classical Greece and Rome. Keith Thomas, a historian of early modern England, published *Man and the Natural World* (1984), a work which filled in gaps left by Glacken in his treatment of English environmental ideas.[47] Thomas argued that between 1500 and 1800 a fundamental change in people's perception of nature had occurred as a result of the move from a premodern, precapitalist magical world to a modern, capitalist one.

After Glacken we see both a range of worldwide environmental treatises being produced and an ambitious series of major regional environmental histories of a kind that had not previously been attempted. Perhaps perversely this pattern was initiated by Africanist and South Americanist archaeologists in regions where documentary data were very scarce, above all in Sub-Saharan Africa and the Amazon.[48] From an initial interest in the climatological and quaternary geological history of Africa, A.T. Grove and A.S. Goudie branched out to develop a wider interest in the regional environmental history of Africa, the Mediterranean and southern Europe, and (in the case of Goudie) to survey human impacts globally.[49] Polly Hill, particularly in her 1963 book on migrant cocoa farmers in southern

Lake (London, 1955); J.D.F. Jones, *Teller of Many Tales: The Lives of Laurens Van Der Post* (London, 2001).

46 Clarence Glacken, *Traces on the Rhodian Shore: Nature and Culture in Western Thought from Ancient Times to the End of the Eighteenth Century* (Berkeley, CA, 1967).

47 Donald Hughes, *Pan's Travail: Environmental Problems of the Ancient Greeks and Romans* (Baltimore, MD, 1996); K. Thomas, *Man and the Natural World* (Oxford, 1984). Like Glacken, Thomas felt compelled to halt his essay at 1800 leaving a lacuna in environmental history for the nineteenth century.

48 Thurstan Shaw (ed.), *Discovering Nigeria's Past* (Ibadan, 1975); Betty J. Meggers, *Amazonia: Man and Culture in a Counterfeit Paradise* (Chicago, IL, 1971).

49 A.S. Goudie, *The Human Impact* (Oxford, 1984); A. T. Grove, *Land Use and Soil Conservation on the Jos Plateau* (Zaria, 1952).

Ghana, linked anthropology to detailed environmental history, overturning a welter of mistaken theories about West African plantation agriculture.[50]

An even broader approach, pioneered by Claudio Vita-Finzi's 1969 *The Mediterranean Valleys*,[51] cleared the path for two major works on the environmental history of the Mediterranean. The first was *The Mountains of the Mediterranean World* by John McNeill, the junior scion of a remarkable father-and-son duo of world environmental historians. The elder McNeill similarly extended his reach to write a series of world histories with an increasingly ecological bias starting with *The Origins of Civilization* in 1968, and moving on to interpret the global history of epidemics in *Plagues and Peoples* in 1976.[52] The McNeills jointly wrote *The Human Web* (2003), which implicitly argued that environmental history could not be understood properly outside the context of the progressive globalisation of the history of ideas. In this, it built on and extended ideas first developed by Janet Abu-Lughod in *Before European Hegemony*, which had underscored the importance of global processes in this early period.[53]

Millennial and Socioecological Environmental History

What some have considered to be the 'closing' of the globalised world by communication and the internet became the occasion for a series of retrospectives on the contribution of European and Chinese imperialisms to the transformation of the world environment. The increasing scholarly interest taken by Americans seems to have paralleled the rapid growth in the United States' imperial interests and ambitions after 1945, despite the quite separate introspective nature of environmental history in the United States itself. It may well have been this awareness of new superpower status, as well as the Cold War itself, that encouraged Paul Colinvaux and Jared Diamond, both tropical ecologists, to attempt socioecological explanations of world history, respectively in the *Fates of Nations* (1980) and in *Guns, Germs and Steel* (1997).[54] These best-selling books used concepts such as Colinvaux's 'the learned niche' and Diamond's less profound

---

50   Polly Hill, *Migrant Cocoa Farmers of Southern Ghana* (Cambridge, 1963); and see her *Development Economics on Trial: The Anthropological Case for a Prosecution* (Cambridge, 1984).

51   Claudio Vita-Finzi, *The Mediterranean Valleys: Geological Changes in Historical Times* (Cambridge, 1969).

52   W. McNeill, *The Origins of Civilization* (New York, 1968); McNeill, *Plagues and Peoples* (New York, 1976).

53   J.R. McNeill, *The Mountains of the Mediterranean World: An Environmental History* (Cambridge, 2003); J.R. McNeill and William H. McNeill, *The Human Web: A Bird's Eye View of World History* (New York, 2003); Janet Abu-Lughod, *Before European Hegemony: The World System AD 1250–1350* (New York, 1991).

54   Paul Colinvaux, *The Fates of Nations: A Biological Theory of History* (New York, 1980); Jared Diamond, *Guns, Germs and Steel: The Fates of Human Societies* (New York, 1997).

'differences in environmental real estate' to explain the differential economic trajectories of Europeans versus African or aboriginal societies. Neither of these authors attached primacy to the coalescence of networks of ideas in the context of globalisation to explain technological differentiation, as the McNeills did so much more satisfactorily in 2003. Differences in intellectual training clearly counted in this instance.

Asianists and Global Environmental History

In contrast to the global views of the socioecologists, a refreshing and less culturally triumphalist view of the environmental impact of apparently 'successful' expansionist imperial societies has been taken by a distinctive group of historians of China, beginning with Lester Bilsky in 1980.[55] Drawing mainly on the translated works of Mencius, Hsuntze and Chan-kuo Ts'e, Bilsky pointed to the prolific evidence for local social collapse and famine-caused wars in the first millennium. Much more detailed evidence was published in the ensuing twenty years for what Elvin called 'three thousand years of unsustainable growth'.[56] Peter Perdue and Robert Marks, like Elvin, drew attention to the massive ecological transformation wrought by the westward expansion of successive Chinese empires, findings which helped to place European colonial expansion in perspective and re-emphasised its comparable ecological impact.[57]

A comparable shift towards an ecological questioning of conventional agrarian history developed among historians of South Asia in the early 1980s. Richard Tucker and John Richards were convinced that ecological changes accompanying economic transition in the seventeenth to nineteenth centuries, while clearly large-scale, had never been properly quantified. Almost immediately they realised that their questioning could not be confined to South Asia but required answers within a wider global economic history, particularly with the advent of an era in which the connections between deforestation, carbon dioxide production and global warming were becoming major popular anxieties in what Teresa Brennan was calling the 'Age of Paranoia'.[58] They set out to review the global history of deforestation, especially in the tropics.[59]

---

55   Lester Bilsky (ed.), *Historical Ecology: Essays on Ecology and Social Change* (Port Washington, NY, 1980).

56   Mark Elvin, 'Three Thousand Years of Unsustainable Growth: China's Environment from Archaic Times to the Present', *East Asian History* 6 (1993): pp. 7–46.

57   Robert B. Marks, *Tigers, Rice, Silk and Silt: Environment and Economy in Late Imperial South China* (New York, 1997); Peter Perdue, *Exhausting the Earth: State and Peasant in Hunan, 1500–1850* (Cambridge, MA, 1987).

58   Teresa Brennan, *Globalisation and its Terrors* (London, 2003).

59   Richard P. Tucker and John F. Richards (eds), *Global Deforestation in the Nineteenth Century World Economy* (Durham, NC, 1983); Tucker and Richards, *World Deforestation in the Twentieth Century* (Durham, NC, 1988).

Tucker and Richards had come to global environmental history as part of a realisation that the ecological impacts of empire, especially as forerunners of 'modern' globalisation, had been startlingly neglected. In making the quick and logical intellectual leap from South Asia to world history, Richards and Tucker had ironically left the environmental history of South Asia itself largely untouched with the exception of some very limited essays, regional studies and essay collections.[60] This lacuna has been addressed more recently by developments in South Asian environmental history. In particular, the work of K. Sivaramakrishnan, Mahesh Rangarajan, Ravi Rajan, Rohan D'Souza and Vasant Saberwal, among others, attempt regional and local environmental histories of India.[61] These works have made their presence felt in mainstream South Asian history writing and, in terms of an institutional advance, South Asian environmental history is becoming well entrenched.

Imperial Historians, Historians of Science and Global Environmental History

The difficulty in writing a history of globalising colonial empires in terms of an expanding resource frontier lies in the need to produce snapshots of different parts of that frontier worldwide, focusing on a smorgasbord of commodities and periods. In Richards' work, this permitted an effective broadbrush picture of material change and resource consumption in the early modern period, but he did not set out to explain the reasons, methods and motivation of the ecological transformation in terms of the history of science, history of ideas or imperial organisation. Some of these ways of understanding the 'empires of nature', to use Mackenzie's term, were already well developed.[62] In particular, Roy Macleod, Deepak Kumar and Satpal Sangwan had, in their early excursions into the 'science of the Raj', started to unravel the complex matrix of British imperial science in India, finding it necessary to overturn Louis Pyenson's and George Basalla's portrayals of colonial science

---

60   R. Guha and M. Gadgil, *This Fissured Earth: Towards an Ecological History of India* (Delhi, 1992). For a review of other work in the field see introduction to R. Grove, V. Damodaran and S. Sangwan (eds), *Nature and the Orient: The Environmental History of South and Southeast Asia* (Oxford, 1998). See also R. D'Souza, 'Nature, Conservation and Environmental History: A Review of Some Recent Environmental Writings on South Asia', *Conservation and Society* 1/2 (2003): pp. 117–32.

61   K. Sivaramakrishnan, *Modern Forests, State Making and Environmental Change in Eastern India* (Delhi, 1999); Vasant Saberwal, *Pastoral Politics: Shepherds, Bureaucrats, and Conservation in the Western Himalaya* (Delhi, 1999); Mahesh Rangarajan, *Fencing the Forest* (Delhi, 1999); Rohan D'Souza, *The Drowned and the Dammed: Colonial Capitalism and Flood Control in Eastern India* (Delhi, 2006); Ravi Rajan, *Modernising Nature, Forestry and Imperial Eco-development* (Oxford, 2008).

62   Deepak Kumar, *Science and the Raj, 1857–1905* (Oxford, 1995).

as the handmaiden of metropolitan science.[63] John MacKenzie and Richard Grove found rich veins to excavate in the history of imperial conservationism, some of them intersecting histories of hunting and natural history collecting.[64]

Henry Hobhouse and Alfred Crosby focused on the effects of the introduction of crops and diseases by Europeans to the settler colonies and the West Indies.[65] Their work ignored the longer pre-European histories of plant transfer and disease in Old World Africa, Asia and Oceania. Lucille Brockway, in her pathbreaking *Science and Colonial Expansion*, explored the role of the Royal Botanic Gardens at Kew in promoting imperial botanic gardens and exchanges.[66] Then Ray Desmond, using expertise gathered as an archivist at the India Office library in London, published *The European Discovery of the Indian Flora* in 1992. Both he and Richard Drayton developed this theme in further closely related books on the history of Kew Gardens and the impact of explorer-curators such as Joseph Hooker on imperial 'improvement' schemes.[67] Donal McCracken usefully supplemented these works in a global guide to the history of colonial botanic gardens.[68]

All these scholars had been foreshadowed to some extent by Ian Burkhill's 1965 treatise on *Chapters in the History of Indian Botany*.[69] Burkill afforded remarkable insights into the significance of environmental thinking in British India. He pointed, for example, to the highly precocious advent of ecological thinking in botanical science before 1857, particularly by John Edgeworth and Ellerton Stocks, surgeon-botanists employed by the East India Company, who were important in the early development, structuring and methods of the Bombay Presidency's Forest Department.[70]

A more global ecological perspective in the imperial context underscored Peder Anker's *Imperial Ecology* (2001).[71] Anker argued that the structures of what appeared to be a globally referential 'science' were at least in part composed of a medley of

63   George Basalla, *The Evolution of Technology* (Cambridge, 1999); Louis Pyenson, *Cultural Imperialism and the Exact Sciences: German Expansion Overseas, 1900–1930* (New York, 1985).
64   John MacKenzie, *The Empire of Nature: Hunting, Conservation and British Imperialism* (Manchester, 1988); Grove, *Green Imperialism*.
65   Henry Hobhouse, *Seeds of Change: Five Plants that Transformed the World* (London, 1985); Crosby, *Ecological Imperialism*; Crosby, *The Columbian Exchange: Biological and Cultural Consequences of 1492* (Westport, CT, 1972).
66   Lucille Brockway, *Science and Colonial Expansion* (New York, 1979).
67   Ray Desmond, *The European Discovery of the Indian Flora* (Oxford 1992); Desmond, *The History of the Royal Botanic Gardens, Kew* (Cumbria, 1997); Richard Drayton, *Nature's Government: Science, Imperial Britain, and the 'Improvement' of the World* (New Haven, CT, 2000).
68   Donal McCracken, *Gardens of Empire: Botanical Institutions of the Victorian British Empire* (Leicester, 1997).
69   I. Burkill, *Chapters in the History of Indian Botany* (Calcutta, 1965).
70   Grove, *Green Imperialism*, p. 457.
71   Peder Anker, *Imperial Ecology: Environmental Order in the British Empire, 1895–1945* (Cambridge, MA, 2001).

holistic notions of the kind pursued by Jan Smuts, laced with notions of Freudian psychology in the work of Arthur Tansley, but above all based on military, racial and social nationalism. He showed too that Smuts, Tansley and Charles Elton, an animal zoologist associated with modern population and community ecology (who, along with Frederic Clements, led the new global and imperial ecology), had made early connections among climate, ecology and 'climax' individuals and communities (p. 572).[72] Deep and discriminatory fears about extreme climatic events, racial difference and identity run right through the histories of empires and formulations of global environmental and climate change.

An accumulation of knowledge about the chronology of extreme climate events and a more limited understanding of their dynamics might have been expected to reduce these fears by offering the prospect of a more predictable world. Indeed, global climate histories are now the most rapidly developing aspect of global environmental history and, as we have seen, they have always formed a vital aspect of the field. However, global climate history and its practitioners, upon whom global climate modellers are entirely dependent, has in the first decade of the twenty-first century offered, in its presentation of global warming trends, a prospect almost as grim as that of the spread of modern epidemics of auto-immune disease, an aspect of global environmental history which we have touched on but little here.

We end with noting the global possibilities of environmental history. The strengths are that it looks beyond the old geographical boundaries that have long governed approaches to history. It has the capacity to be world history in a uniquely dynamic and comprehensive way as diseases, plants and animals move or are moved from one continent to another, or as climatic shifts affect regions of the world far distant from each other. In a sense, imperial history has always had this advantage as empires could only be studied on a global scale. Global environmental history, then, like all other global history, 'means transcending national boundaries or local concerns in order to grasp the linkages that today bind all peoples and all eco-systems together and to understand how that happened and what the consequences have been'.[73] As Kate Showers has noted, global environmental history does not preclude local, regional or national environmental histories; rather, it simply asks that the richness of local examination be linked to the broader intellectual evolution of ideas about environments, environmental function and environmental change.[74] It is in this global context that environmental histories of empire have their greatest relevance.

---

72 A climax community, or climatic climax community, is a biological community of plants and animals which, through the process of ecological succession – the development of vegetation in an area over time – has reached a steady state. This equilibrium occurs because the climax community is composed of species best adapted to average conditions in that area.

73 Donald Worster quoted in Gabriella Corona (ed.), 'Forum: What is Global Environmental History?', *Global Environment* 2 (2008): p. 233.

74 Kate Showers, 'Themes in Environmental History, Method and Fieldwork', unpublished paper delivered at History and Sustainability Conference, Cambridge, 10 January 2009.

Modernity

John Marriott

I choose to think of colonial modernity as the condition created by the process of modernisation attendant on western global expansion. Through European colonisation in particular, attempts were made to inscribe imperial subjects within the space of modernity.[1] Such a project experienced varying degrees of success, for, although universalising in intent, it lacked coherence and met significant resistance from subjects opposed to western influence. In its global reach, however, colonial modernity forged complex relationships which transcended discrete and elemental units such as nation states or civilisations, and in so doing shaped the contemporary world.[2] The notion of colonial modernity therefore touches on a range of vital questions about the origins of modernity, the nature of colonial rule, and the relationship between colonies and the imperial metropolis, all of which this chapter hopes to address. To begin, let us investigate modernity itself, and consider whether it operates in the plural or singular.

Plural versus Singular

Implicit in this rough-hewn definition is a sense that colonial modernity was driven by western imperatives. At first sight such a claim may seem uncontentious, for much of the considerable historiography on modernity has been concerned to chart the course of western modernity or the so-called Enlightenment Project. Thus, for example, Marshall Berman's influential *All That is Solid Melts into Air* includes among the defining features of modernisation the industrialisation of production, rapid and often cataclysmic urban growth, increasingly powerful nation states, immense demographic upheavals and great discoveries in the physical sciences,

1 Achille Mbembe, 'On the Power of the False', trans. Judith Inggs, *Public Culture* 14 (2002): p. 634.
2 Tani E. Barlow, 'Introduction: On "Colonial Modernity"', in Barlow (ed.), *Formations of Colonial Modernity in East Asia* (Durham, NC, 1997).

all of which are seen as part of a western experience.[3] And yet the claim does not meet with unambiguous approval; on the contrary, many thoughtful scholars have in recent years contended that to equate modernity with the west simply replicates the familiar exercise of power, and that we should more usefully talk of *modernities* – that is, modernities which were forged relatively independently of, and perhaps in opposition to, the west. *Alternative Modernities*, edited by Dilip Gaonkar, is fairly representative of this current of thought. Among the contributors is the philosopher Charles Taylor, who sets out to distinguish between cultural and acultural theories of modernity.[4] Cultural theory stresses the transformations seen in the modern west which create a culture with its own distinct understandings of the individual, nature, good, and so forth. Acultural theory, on the other hand, focuses on transformations brought about by processes including industrialisation, demographic change and urbanisation which are seen to be culturally neutral in their impact. According to Taylor, acultural theories have dominated the intellectual agenda, resulting in an impoverished and distorted view of both the west and the cultures it encounters:

> The belief that modernity comes from a single, universally applicable operation imposes a falsely uniform pattern on the multiple encounters of non-Western cultures with the exigencies of science, technology, and industrialization. As long as we are bemused by the enlightenment package, we will believe that all cultures have to undergo a range of cultural changes, drawn from our own experience – for example, secularization or the growth of atomistic forms of self-identification … The march of modernity will end up making all cultures look the same. This means, of course, that we expect they will end up looking Western.[5]

A cultural theory of modernity which recognises its historical specificity offers different prospects. If we view the transition of modernity as marking the rise of a new culture such as the conversion of the Roman Empire to Christianity, or parts of India to Islam then the starting point will continue to exert an influence on the resultant culture. Thus modernity which was impelled by the Enlightenment – and with which it can be seen as coterminous – has shaped different civilisations with divergent starting points to create a range of variant modernities. Instead of a singular, all-encompassing modernity, Taylor concludes, we should think in terms of 'alternative modernities' as evidenced by, say, Japanese modernity, Indian modernity and multiple Islamic modernities.

---

3   Marshall Berman, *All that is Solid Melts into Air: The Experience of Modernity* (London, 1983). The same arguments apply to David Harvey's important *The Condition of Postmodernity: An Enquiry into the Origins of Cultural Change* (Oxford, 1989).
4   Dilip Gaonkar (ed.), *Alternative Modernities* (Durham, NC, 2001).
5   Charles Taylor, 'Two Theories of Modernity', in Gaonkar (ed.), *Alternative Modernities*, pp. 180–81.

This theme is taken up by other contributors to the volume who are intent to demonstrate how indentured labourers, members of the African diaspora, Bengali elites and the Russian imperial bourgeoisie, amongst others, mobilised their cultural resources in creatively adapting to the forces of modernity. These alternative modernities, states Gaonkar in his introduction to the collection, produce surprising combinations: *'everywhere, at every national/cultural site, modernity is not one but many'.*[6]

Some scholars have taken the argument further by claiming that non-western cultures displayed 'modern' characteristics predating western modernisation. Rationalisation, bureaucratic structures, scientific methodology, double-entry bookkeeping and capitalist practices are among the features identified in Indian, Chinese and Arabic societies, suggesting that these cultures were on the high road to modernisation before western expansion.[7] It might be tempting under such circumstances to argue that particular cultures eventually took their own, distinct path to the modern world, but most studies conclude that, even when modern features are seen to have existed in particular cultures, they were forced to engage with, and hence were modified by, western modernisation.

The most powerful body of literature within this paradigm is that produced by members of the Subaltern Studies collective. Working broadly within political science and cultural theory, Partha Chatterjee, Dipesh Chakrabarty, Gyan Prakash and others have described what they consider to be the distinctive forms of an Indian modernity.[8] In a lecture entitled 'Our Modernity', Chatterjee lays out the arguments. There exist multiple modernities, the forms of which depend upon specific historical circumstances. If there is a universal modernity it is one that teaches us to employ reason to identify our own modernities. Thus Indian modernity can be understood only as a legacy of a colonised past. Struggles have taken place to create a space where Indians can assert their independence from the debilitating structures of western universalism, but there remains a lack of belief in the ability to reject the modernities of others and forge their own distinct forms.[9]

There is something inherently attractive in these arguments confronting as they do perspectives built around a putative western triumphalism. Indeed, much recent work on China, Africa and the Mediterranean world rests comfortably

6   Dilip Gaonkar, 'On Alternative Modernities', in Gaonkar (ed.), *Alternative Modernities*, p. 23.
7   For a good review, see Jack Goody, *The East in the West* (Cambridge, 1996).
8   Partha Chatterjee, *Nationalist Thought and the Colonial World: A Derivative Discourse* (London, 1993) and *The Nation and its Fragments: Colonial and Postcolonial Histories* (Princeton, NJ, 1993); Dipesh Chakrabarty, *Provincializing Europe: Postcolonial Thought and Historical Difference* (Princeton, NJ, 2000); Gyan Prakash, 'Writing Post-Orientalist Histories of the Third World: Perspectives from Indian Historiography', and 'Can the Subaltern Ride? A Reply to O'Hanlon and Washbrook', in Vinayak Chaturvedi (ed.), *Mapping Subaltern Studies and the Postcolonial* (London, 2000), pp. 163–90 and 220–38.
9   Partha Chatterjee, 'Our Modernity', in *The Present History of West Bengal* (Delhi, 1997), pp. 193–210.

within their contours.[10] However, such work suffers from a number of potentially life-threatening weaknesses derived from an undue reliance upon a current in postmodern thought that eschews grand narratives:

1. If plural modernities can be identified across time and space with distinct origins and structures, then the concept of modernity loses its analytical power.[11] It makes no more sense to talk of alternative modernities than to propose alternative capitalisms.

2. The notion of plural modernities exhibits an uncomfortable relativism. Modernity comes to be defined in such a way that it embraces a seemingly endless variety of cultural pursuits identified by interested scholars. This can produce surprises when, for example, the ancient practices of witchcraft in Cameroon and bardic rituals in Rajasthan are incorporated into the modern canon.[12] Under such circumstances it can logically be argued that nothing need necessarily be left out. To secure the integrity of 'modernity' against the incursion of relativism it is therefore necessary to work on a definition – grounded in historical experience – with which the variety of conditions seen to be modern can be evaluated.

3. Implicit in the notion of an alternative modernity is the question: alternative to what? The answer is inevitably western modernity, and so a duality is constructed between cultural traits seen as paradigmatically western, and others viewed almost exclusively in relation to the west. Thus Chinese, Indian and Islamic modernities all come to be understood in terms of the extent to which they depart from the condition of the west.

4. Colonial experience is too frequently neglected. Thus, for example, while the *Alternative Modernities* collection draws together case studies from specific instances of the colonial experience, the question of the relationship between colonialism and modernity is understated; indeed, colonial modernity is not mentioned. Given the critical role of colonialism in the promotion of modernity this is a worrying silence.

There is another, more promising approach which I believe has the potential to overcome these problems. It is a return to the idea that modernisation and modernity are best understood respectively as a process and a condition kick started, promoted

---

10   Lisa Rofel, *Other Modernities: Gendered Yearnings in China after Socialism* (Berkeley, CA, 1999); Carol A. Breckenridge (ed.), *Consuming Modernity: Public Culture in a South Asian World* (Minneapolis, MN, 1995); Jan-Georg Deutsch, Peter Probst and Heike Schmidt (eds), *African Modernities: Entangled Meanings in Current Debate* (Portsmouth, 2002); Chatterjee, *The Nation and its Fragments*; Leila Fawaz and C.A. Bayly (eds), *Modernity and Culture: From the Mediterranean to the Indian Ocean* (New York, 2002).

11   Frederick Cooper, *Colonialism in Question: Theory, Knowledge, History* (Berkeley, CA, 2005), p. 114.

12   Peter Geschiere, *The Modernity of Witchcraft: Politics and the Occult in Postcolonial Africa* (Charlottesville, VA, 1997); Jeffrey Snodgrass, *Casting Kings: Bard and Indian Modernity* (New York, 2006).

and sustained by western globalisation. The identity between modernity and the west is made possible, indeed necessary, by the recognition that only the west could lay claim to universality because only it had power which reached across the global stage. The contrast here with putative alternative modernities is evident. Even if we could accept the existence of an Islamic or Chinese modernity, neither could be seen as universalising. This reading of western modernity as authoritative, powerful and singular, however, does not replicate outdated perspectives on the ascent of the west, or elevate 'messy histories into a consistent project'.[13] Since the success of western modernisation depended upon its exportation to the non-western world, modernity was a product not of the west but of the interaction between the west and the rest.[14] The dialogical nature of modernity thus challenges the notion of alternative modernities as variations of a western model; from the outset, the non-western world was constitutive of western modernity.

In foregrounding historical interaction, this approach also draws attention to the vital role that colonial modernity can play in opening up perspectives on capitalist modernisation. Marx famously locates the beginnings of industrial capitalism not in the textile factories of England but in the colonial system. It was the flow of plunder from the colonies into England, and the establishment of a world market, which enabled financiers and entrepreneurs to lubricate the process of accumulation. As he put it, employing characteristically graphic terms:

> The discovery of gold and silver in America, the extirpation, enslavement, and entombment in the mines of the aboriginal population, the beginning of the conquest and looting of the East Indies, the turning of Africa into a warren for hunting black skins, signalised the rosy dawn of capitalist production. These idyllic proceedings are the chief momenta of primitive accumulation. On their heels treads the commercial war of the European nations, with the globe for a theatre.[15]

More recent studies have suggested that the origins of capitalist production and labour are to be found in the production of sugar rather than cotton. It was in the plantations of the Caribbean that distinctly capitalist methods of labour discipline, division and organisation were first developed in the seventeenth century.[16] Simultaneously, we witnessed the emergence of the first international proletariat on board the ships used to transport human and material goods across the trading networks of empire. The ship was a prototype of the factory for on its decks and in its cabins moved large numbers of waged workers involved in complex and

---

13   Cooper, *Colonialism in Question*, p. 117.
14   This point is well made by Timothy Mitchell, 'The Stage of Modernity', in Mitchell (ed.), *Questions of Modernity* (Minneapolis, MN, 2000), p. 2, upon whose arguments I have here relied.
15   Karl Marx, *Capital* (New York, 2007), vol. 1, p. 823.
16   Sidney Mintz, *Sweetness and Power: The Place of Sugar in Modern History* (New York, 1985).

synchronised tasks under harsh disciplinary regimes. This was the workforce that kept alive a radical Atlantic tradition after the political tumults of the Civil War in seventeenth-century England had receded.[17]

Thought of in this way, colonial modernity problematises many conventional narratives of capitalist development, colonial intervention and the relationship between the west and the rest. I will have cause to return to this question later using the experience of slavery, but first I wish to provide some preliminary notes on a specific but formative episode in the history of colonial modernity – namely, British intervention in India. India provided the British as a colonial power with great opportunity but also a host of problems around governance and administration with which they were unfamiliar, and for which they were unprepared. And even though lessons were learnt that were later applied to other colonial contexts, the particularity of India should not be underestimated.

India as a British Colony

John Darwin has recently reminded us of the distinction between the formal and informal modes of control which constituted the 'globe-spanning juggernaut' of the British Empire.[18] But this overused distinction barely captures the multiplicity of economic and political relationships between Britain and its territories. Within the formal empire were a variety of dominions and dependencies, each having distinct connections with Britain. The informal empire of influence rather than direct rule was also diverse. Argentina, for example, while possessing political sovereignty had an economy determined largely by British enterprises. In Egypt after 1882, on the other hand, the British claimed to act in an advisory capacity to the government but in fact asserted a degree of control as complete as in parts of the formal empire. The picture that emerges is not one of an integrated empire built on despotic metropolitan power and shaped by a unified vision, but of a patchwork of seemingly inchoate connections forged by pragmatism, even ad hocery, the precise nature of which was determined by the unfolding of individual relationships over time.

The early phases of British intervention in India have yet to be explained satisfactorily: debates continue on how British ascendancy was linked to the decline of the Mughal Empire, and the remarkable transformation of the East India Company from a trading to an imperial power in the second half of the eighteenth century.[19] In India the British encountered a civilisation about which

---

17 Peter Linebaugh and Marcus Rediker, *The Many-Headed Hydra: The Hidden History of the Revolutionary Atlantic* (London, 2000).
18 John Darwin, 'Britain's Empires', in Sarah Stockwell (ed.), *The British Empire: Themes and Perspectives* (Oxford, 2008), pp. 1–20.
19 P.J. Marshall (ed.), *The Eighteenth Century in Indian History: Evolution or Revolution?* (Delhi, 2003); Seema Alavi (ed.), *The Eighteenth Century in India* (Delhi, 2002); Eric Stokes, *The Peasant and the Raj: Studies in Agrarian Society and Peasant Rebellion in Colonial*

they knew little. Seventeenth-century travellers had published accounts of the wealth and splendour of the Mughal court, and the strange customs of the indigenous population, but these publications went out of fashion as a result of which knowledge of India among the eighteenth-century British probably receded even further.[20] This ignorance, combined with the Company's avowed reluctance to interfere unduly in the customs, rituals and laws of the country, hardly produced conditions which were propitious for colonisation.

And yet colonisation did follow. It was heralded by the defeat inflicted by Robert Clive on the young nawab Siraj-ud-daulla at the Battle of Plassey in 1757, less through military prowess than the traitorous act of Siraj's general Mir Jaffar who had been bribed to withdraw his forces. More important was the Battle of Buxar in 1764, when Clive overcame the last organised resistance to Company authority in Bengal. Within a year *diwani* rights passed into the hands of the Company, authorising it to collect and administer land revenues which were used not only to enrich its servants but to purchase the goods of Bengal and so create revenue to finance colonial annexation of neighbouring territories.[21] Such an ambitious and profitable venture could no longer be ignored by the British state, particularly when the Company's profligacy was linked to corruption at all levels. At stake was the future of the British presence in India, and so, following periods when the Company faced financial ruin, the 1773 Regulating Act and 1784 India Act were introduced as a means of providing a degree of parliamentary authority over its operations – the first faltering steps on a path leading to supersession of the Company in 1858. Government representatives were appointed to the Council of the Presidency of Bengal, one of whom, Philip Francis, entered into a bitter series of disputes with the Governor-General Warren Hastings which exposed deep antagonisms between London and Calcutta on how British India should be governed.

This is all familiar to historians of modern India. The events reveal just how fragmented and diffuse the exercise of power was among the government Board of Control, and East India Company Board of Directors in London, and the Governor-General in India. Ideological differences between the state and the Company, and the impossibility of monitoring routine administration on the ground, rendered impractical the exercise of a coherent colonial policy. This was complicated further by the existence of indigenous structures and cultures which predated the British and which, despite a certain weakening attendant on the dissolution of the Mughal order, could be neither ignored nor overridden in pursuit of imperial ambitions. Given the ignorance of Company servants about Indian culture and the stated reluctance to create potential dissent by undue interference in indigenous customs,

India (Cambridge, 1978).

20 John Marriott, *The Other Empire: India, Metropolis and Progress in the Colonial Imagination* (Manchester, 2003).

21 Sugata Bose and Ayesha Jalal, *Modern South Asia: History, Culture, Political Economy* (Delhi, 1999), p. 60. This remains one of the most thoughtful and accessible general histories of India.

the first decades of British rule were therefore characterised by an ongoing dialogue between colonial administrations and an institutional system created largely by Mughal and Hindu elites. The work of Eric Stokes before his untimely death in 1978 explored this interaction. His classic *The English Utilitarians and India* detailed the emergence of utilitarian thought and its impact on colonial policy in India. If his approach tended to overstate the ability of the British to modify pre-colonial systems, the series of studies which followed paid due regard to the processes of interaction and adaptation, so challenging the oversimplifications of both imperialist perspectives which stressed the dominance of the British, and nationalist accounts which focused on the vacuum created by the decline of Mughal authority.[22] Thus the homologies or congruencies between trajectories of previously independent historical processes help explain the course of British ascendancy, and the survival of indigenous structures in the colonial regime well into the nineteenth century.[23]

The process of interaction stalled reform to a greater extent than has generally been supposed. Initially, the Company under Hastings attempted to use extant systems to collect and administer land revenue; only when these came to be seen as corrupt and inefficient was indirect rule abandoned, intermediaries eliminated, and direct responsibility placed in the hands of an official bureaucracy using British models. These and other attempts at anglicisation introduced by Lord Cornwallis from the 1780s were, however, strictly limited:

> On grounds of both policy and expediency the East India Company continued to act in many respects as an Indian ruler, striking its coinage with the image of the puppet emperor at Delhi, maintaining the use of Persian in official correspondence and in the law courts, administering Hindu and Muslim law, repressing Christian missionary activity and upholding the religious institutions of the country.[24]

Other studies appeared from what has been loosely labelled the Cambridge School, which explored in finer detail the structural foundations of British rule. Christopher Bayly's *Rulers, Townsmen and Bazaars* provides a textured analysis of a powerful class of north Indian merchants, landholders and moneylenders who mediated between the state and agrarian society in the eighteenth century. They were created by, or inherited, the apparatus of the Mughal state, and through collaboration with the British provided an appropriate infrastructure for Company trade and ultimately for colonialism: 'conditions in Indian society', writes Bayly, 'determined the emergence and form of British India'.[25] David Washbrook is also

---

22 Eric Stokes, *The English Utilitarians and India* (Oxford, 1959); Stokes, *The Peasant and the Raj*.

23 Burton Stein, 'Eighteenth-Century India: Another View', in Marshall (ed.), *The Eighteenth Century in Indian History*, p. 65.

24 Eric Stokes, 'The First Century of British Colonial Rule', *Past and Present* 58 (1973), reprinted in *The Peasant and the Raj*, p. 28.

25 C.A. Bayly, *Rulers, Townsmen and Bazaars: North Indian Society in the Age of British*

intent on revealing how the British appropriated indigenous networks of commerce and finance. Focusing on south India, he demonstrates that Indian financiers of the eighteenth century provided the capital with which the Company and its servants conducted their businesses, thereby helping to establish the context for capitalist imperialism.[26]

This early experience of British rule in India suggests that the introduction of 'modern' governance was neither coherent nor uncontested. The British could not readily draw upon historical precedent to exercise authority over a land and people of which they were profoundly ignorant. Deep fissures opened up on how this task should be undertaken, fissures that could not be closed while the Company continued to exercise authority, nor while communications between London and Calcutta were interminably slow. This lack of authority, combined with a reticence in some influential circles to interfere unduly in indigenous customs and beliefs, forced the British into a dialogue with Indian elites on the nature and course of governance. In the light of these considerations, I wish to pause and consider in more detail one of the most decisive measures imposed by the British at the time – namely, the Permanent Settlement of 1793.

The Permanent Settlement

Ranajit Guha's seminal study *A Rule of Property for Bengal* has carefully traced the intellectual history of the settlement.[27] Although the settlement was formally imposed by 1793 Regulation I, deliberations on the vital issue of the administration of land revenue had begun at least twenty years earlier.[28] With the acquisition of the rights to administer land and collect revenue in 1765, land became the Company's principal source of income. The moment, however, was not propitious. The Bengal famine of 1770 which wiped out up to a third of the population had unsettled the minds of influential senior Company administrators, and the Company itself was experiencing financial difficulties and was under pressure from the British parliament to put its affairs in order. From this crisis emerge a determination to

---

    Expansion, 1770–1870 (Cambridge, 1983), p. 2.

26   David Washbrook, *The Emergence of Provincial Politics: The Madras Presidency, 1870–1920* (Cambridge, 1976); Washbrook, 'Progress and Problems: South Asian Economic and Social History, c. 1720–1860', *Modern Asian Studies* 22 (1988): pp. 57–96; Washbrook, 'South Asia, the World System and World Capitalism', in Sugata Bose (ed.), *South Asia and World Capitalism* (Delhi, 1990), pp. 40–84.

27   Ranajit Guha, *A Rule of Property for Bengal: An Essay on the Idea of Permanent Settlement* (Paris, 1963). See also P.J. Marshall, 'Parliament and Property Rights in the Late Eighteenth-Century British Empire', in John Brewer and Susan Staves (eds), *Early Modern Conceptions of Property* (London, 1996), pp. 530–44.

28   For facsimile reproductions of the Act and influential contributions to the debate, see John Marriott and Bhaskar Mukhopadhyay (eds) *Britain in India, 1765–1905*, 6 vols (London, 2006), vol. 2, *Land Revenue and Trade*.

provide a measure of stability and security, and the state's representative, Philip Francis, applied himself to the task. When he arrived in Calcutta in 1774 Francis found Bengal in a state of decay; blaming the Company's administration he worked feverishly on a plan of fundamental reform, at the heart of which lay the matter of land revenue. The plan of 1776 drew upon French physiocratic thought – in particular its insistence on the critical importance of private property as a source of wealth and stability – to propose that *zemindars* – that is, indigenous landholders – be granted permanent proprietary rights over land as a means of securing regular and permanent revenue for the Company. Some have viewed the plan as a fundamental challenge to ancient Indian property rights which did not recognise private ownership, but Francis thought differently. In arguing for *zemindars*, he declared, he was attempting to restore the hereditary rights that had been sustained under the Mughals only to be subverted by British rule. Without such rights, *zemindars* would not be encouraged to improve the productivity of their lands through investment in irrigation, scientific management, cultivation of waste land and the marketing of crops.

Details of the plan were scrutinised by senior Company servants, among them John Shore, who had expert knowledge of the administration of land revenue from his experience as a collector. At first Shore approved of the main outline of Francis' plan. In a memorial of 1782 he pronounced that *zemindars* were the most appropriate people to manage the land revenues of their districts and that their assessment should be moderate. By 1789, however, at a time when Cornwallis was ready to implement the Permanent Settlement based largely on the recommendations of Francis, Shore launched a devastating attack on the policy. The events of the French Revolution had persuaded him of the essential worth of the English constitution and the fallibility of ill-considered reform. Underpinning his critique was a decisive shift in his views of *zemindars*, whom he now saw as worthless, corrupt and inefficient – not the sort of people to be granted permanent rights over property when the Company had little experience of administration. And yet simultaneously he claimed no objection to the general principles of the plan, 'but the application of them must be directed by circumstances of time and situation'.[29] He was opposed to any grand categories forged by thought alone. The true test of all measures must be experience; without this, he decided, any settlement should not be permanent but restricted to ten years.

Ultimately, however, the decision had to be taken by Cornwallis who, with characteristic single-mindedness, resolved to implement a plan based largely on the arguments of Francis. It was a vote of confidence in the *zemindars*, not as they had traditionally functioned in Indian society as landholders but as improving landlords. They were divested of feudal, pre-modern privileges including the power to collect transit duties and adjudicate in civil cases, and it was hoped that through education and the gift of private property for life, they would be

---

29   John Shore, Minute of 21 December 1789, cited in Guha, *Rule of Property in Bengal*, p. 204.

persuaded to invest their capital in the land, and thereby be transformed into capitalist entrepreneurs modelled on the progressive English gentleman farmer.[30]

Based on the experience of Bengal, and embedded in a Burkean emphasis on the importance of continuity to the maintenance of societal cohesion, the Permanent Settlement met with insurmountable difficulties when as part of the expansion of British rule it encountered other provinces with very different traditions of property rights. The first challenge came from the Ceded and Conquered Provinces annexed during the military campaigns of Wellesley early in the nineteenth century. Regulation X of 1807 was introduced to secure permanent settlement; within a year it faced resistance from colonial authorities, who reported that they had considerable practical difficulties in revenue collection and advised that the scheme be postponed. More influential in the long term were the objections of Thomas Munro, the Principal Collector of Madras, who argued that the assessment and collection should be more closely directed to the *ryots* (small peasant landholders), particularly since Permanent Settlement had led to their impoverishment at the hands of *zemindars*. Due regard also needed to be paid to fluctuating outputs caused by conditions beyond the control of *ryots*. The *ryotwar* settlement Munro proposed as an alternative was later introduced in Madras when he became Governor of that Presidency.

Many of the features of the experience of reform in the administration of land were evident in other spheres of colonial intervention. Religion, culture, education, jurisprudence, science and economics were all subject to colonial intervention, almost always with limited success and unanticipated results. Considerable discrepancies existed between the formal statement of policies and their implementation, and one should not be read from the other.[31] Thirty years after the Permanent Settlement the colonial state entered its grand phase of reform, but for all the vigour and determination of William Bentinck little progress was made in promoting education among the Indian masses, in altering the customs of widow remarriage, child marriage or bonded labour, or in eliminating disease and famine.[32] Missionaries were continually frustrated by the small numbers of Indians who converted to Christianity. Part of the reason was that the colonial state had neither the financial means nor the communications networks it needed to reach the mass of the Indian population; even after 1860 when the Company had been superseded, planned reform by the British state accelerated, but ignorance of Indian culture remained a considerable barrier. And here we are not talking exclusively of the masses; significant sections of the indigenous intellectual and cultural elite were never entirely won over to the modernising impulses of British rule. Apart from small groups such as the brilliant cohort of scholars around the Young Bengal movement, the vast majority of the Brahmin elite – even the reformers among them – clung tenaciously onto the precepts of ancient Hindu teaching.

---

30   Ibid., pp. 182–5.

31   This point is made well by Stokes, 'First Century of British Rule', p. 30.

32   The banning of *sati* in 1829 is generally thought of as Bentinck's crowning achievement as a reformer, but even here Indians never strictly adhered to the law.

This brief survey of the foundational phase of British rule reveals something of the nature of colonial modernity. Intervention was informed by an imperative of modernisation. At the heart of the Permanent Settlement was a vision of improvement in agricultural productivity using the figure of the English gentleman farmer. The connections with agrarian patriotism as it gathered pace during the 1780s were unmistakable. British landowners were encouraged to build and repair roads, bridges and canals, and adopt scientific farming practices not only to increase the productivity of the land but also to promote a moral community of great landholders, yeoman farmers and professionals.[33] It was hardly coincidental that the scheme was implemented in the same year as the Pitt administration set up the Board of Agriculture to champion agrarian patriotism as an article of faith. Plans to rationalise Indian jurisprudence, clean up the streets of Calcutta, provide preventive medical care through mass vaccination against smallpox, make available western thought through education (albeit to a small elite), eliminate immoral cultural practices, and save Indian souls from perdition by rescuing them from pagan practices were among 'progressive' measures designed to bring Indians into the modern world, thereby rendering them more amenable to British rule.

Despite the racial violence and tyranny of this rule at ground level, British intervention lacked a coherent and unified philosophy derived from a confident intellectual tradition. Previous experience of colonial rule proved of limited value in the alien environment that was India, and so policy emerged awkwardly from the uneasy tensions which existed among orientalists, evangelicals, utilitarians and military despots. The apparatus of rule was deeply riven by competing interests and the practical difficulties of implementation. Only in the second half of the nineteenth century when the colonial state took control and more effective means of telegraphic communication were available was it possible to rule with a degree of coherence and consistency. Even then the activities of the school of free-trade radicals committed to the idea of an informal empire, and of colonial reformers advocating a middle-class empire stripped of patronage and privilege, remind us of the continued presence in the imperial heartland of powerful critiques of British rule in India.[34]

In India the British encountered a people inhabiting cultures which they neither understood nor cared for. In one of those pleasantly ironic historical episodes, this ignorance was dispelled briefly when a group of committed scholars including Warren Hastings and William Jones brought to the attention of an amazed Europe a body of Sanskrit texts displaying remarkable intellectual and literary achievements.[35] The effect, writes Raymond Schwab, was equal to that created

---

33 C.A. Bayly, *Imperial Meridian:The British Empire and the World, 1780–1830* (Harlow, 1989), pp. 80–81.

34 Bernard Semmel, *The Rise of Free Trade Imperialism: Classical Political Economy, the Empire of Free Trade Imperialism, 1750–1850* (Cambridge, 1970).

35 William Jones travelled to India to take up a post as a judge at the Supreme Court in Calcutta. He is best remembered, however, for his astonishing ability as a linguist with which, for example, he demonstrated that Indian and European languages had a

by the arrival of Greek manuscripts after the fall of Constantinople in the late fifteenth century.[36] The promise offered by this oriental renaissance, however, was sequestered by censorious commentators of the early nineteenth century. British evangelicals and historians, fronted by James Mills' *History of British India* (1817), concluded that, while India had possessed an advanced ancient civilisation, its progress had since stalled under the weight of religious orthodoxy, and it had entered into a protracted period of stagnation and decline culminating in a state of material, moral and intellectual poverty.

In the meantime, the Company, guided by an unadulterated empiricism, embarked on an energetic campaign to gather information about India and its peoples. Ambitious topographical surveys were undertaken, the land was mapped, Hinduism investigated, indigenous languages learnt, and ethnographic studies carried out which were to lay the foundations of anthropology. Much of the information gathered was recognised to be unreliable, as if India was beyond knowledge. This combined with a seeming determination to avoid undue interference with indigenous customs encouraged policy makers to enter into a dialogue with extant systems and beliefs. So long as it was thought practicable, traditions of indigenous administration and Indian officials were used by the Company to prioritise reform in areas such as land revenue and jurisprudence. Furthermore, missionary activity, which was held responsible for the most flagrant violations of indigenous culture, was banned; only with the renewal of the Company's charter in 1813 were missionaries allowed to work in India, and even then with limited licence.[37]

Metropolis and Colony

These considerations raise important questions about the nature of the relationship between the imperial metropolis and the colonies. Perspectives which argued for an all powerful metropolis have been replaced by an emphasis on reciprocity – that is, influence flowing in both directions. More persuasive for me is Bernard Cohn's notion of a unitary field of knowledge.[38] From the later eighteenth century, India and Britain were brought together in a shared epistemological terrain evidenced by the investigative modalities used to know them. Homologies therefore appeared

---

common source.

36   Raymond Schwab, *The Oriental Renaissance* (New York, 1984), p. 11. Written nearly sixty years ago, this wonderful account has not been surpassed, but see also Ronald Inden, *Imagining India* (Bloomington, IN, 2000).

37   Periodic renewal of the Company charter was one way in which parliament was able to exercise a degree of control; 1813 was of particular significance not only in allowing missionaries to operate, but also in marking the end of the Company's monopoly trading privileges to the East.

38   Bernard S. Cohn, *Colonialism and its Forms of Knowledge: The British in India* (Princeton, NJ, 1996).

between the metropolis and India as objects of inquiry. The British may have exercised hegemony but the experience of colonial rule in India facilitated the expression of indigenous forms of knowledge. The articulating principle of this common knowledge was progress, for this was the moment when the idea of progress captivated some of the most influential sections of bourgeois thought in Europe, so wedding colonialism to modernity.[39]

How, therefore, was this unitary field constituted? How did the experience of colonial rule in India help to determine the course of modernity in Britain? These questions have never commanded the serious attention they deserve. Stokes begins his study of utilitarianism by considering India's role in transforming English mentality. India exerted little influence, he argues, on 'fashioning the distinctive qualities of English civilization'. In the later years of the nineteenth century anxieties surfaced that the exercise of despotic colonial power ran counter to Liberal opinion and had fatally weakened the cause of liberty in Britain.[40] But precedents had been established in the early decades of British rule when India acted as a laboratory in which movements that helped to define an ascendant middle class were tested. Here battles were fought over evangelicalism, utilitarianism and free trade waged by the most prominent liberal protagonists including James and John Stuart Mill, Jeremy Bentham and Thomas Babington Macaulay. Bernard Cohn argues similarly that the Indian Civil Service, which with the Military Service composed the two great bureaucracies of the East India Company, provided the model for the domestic British Civil Service. And it was on Indian soil that the investigative methods, including the historiographic, survey and enumerative were developed, thereby laying the foundations for the disciplines of ethnology, cartography and tropical medicine.[41]

Although these arguments have been developed from the experience of British India, I believe they have a wider application. China was never colonised totally by the British or the Japanese but in many respects we can detect the same complex dialogical processes during the formative stages of its modern thought.[42] China was first introduced to western science and technology in the books brought by Jesuit missionaries at the close of the Ming dynasty. Rather than attempting to convert the Chinese to western thought, however, missionaries encouraged collaboration with Confucianism by encouraging the Chinese to interpret the books in their own way and using their own language. With the ascent of the west, many Chinese scholars proposed the wholesale adoption of western science including mathematics, optics and cartography as a means of self-improvement. Colleges of natural sciences were established in the late nineteenth century, and science subjects introduced

---

39 These ideas are developed much more fully in Marriott, *The Other Empire*.

40 Stokes, *English Utilitarians*, p. xi.

41 Cohn, *Colonialism and its Forms of Knowledge*, p. 4.

42 Wang Hui, 'The Fate of "Mr Science" in China: The Concept of Science and its Application in Modern Chinese Thought', in Barlow (ed.), *Formations of Colonial Modernity in East Asia*, pp. 21–81. Barlow rather unhelpfully describes China's experience as one of semi-colonialism.

into the curricula of many Chinese schools. In response to the criticism that these developments risked abandoning Chinese scientific methodology, influential arguments were voiced that western science actually had its origins in Chinese teaching, and that there was thus a profound congruity between the two, applicable to both the east and the west. Chinese thinkers interpreted the works of Comte, Huxley, Spencer, Darwin and others against a backdrop of traditional Chinese epistemology. Thus, while Baconian positivism was thought to have advanced science by promoting rational scientific methodology, ultimately science itself both illustrated, and provided a means of understanding, organic connections between the universe, the world, society and human behaviour – matters which had figured prominently in eastern traditions of intellectual inquiry.

Using examples from a later period, Lydia Liu has similarly mapped the ways in which western discourses on individualism were deployed by Chinese intellectuals in the process of nation-building during the first decades of the twentieth century.[43] Through translations of western liberal and nationalist theories by Japanese scholars, individualism was introduced into China at the turn of the century and promised much to help resolve dilemmas over modern nationhood and selfhood. Drawing upon a post-Enlightenment European thought exemplified by the writings of Rousseau, Hegel, Ibsen and others, Chinese intellectuals sought to reclaim an authentic individualism as a challenge to the rampant materialism of contemporary Chinese society. Later the New Youth movement extended the critique by charging Confucianism with sacrificing individual well-being to the interests of ritual and an outdated social morality. The noble ideals of individualism embodied by the French Revolution, it was argued, would provide autonomy and self-development to subjects, sons and wives who inhabited a slave mentality based on ritualised dependency. 'The free development of the individuals for the Common Welfare' expressed an ambition which could be achieved only through the truth of western science and humanism rather than inferior indigenous intellectual traditions such as Buddhism and Confucianism. Older ideals of nationalism and social collectivism, however, were never abandoned, particularly when more critical perspectives appeared claiming that western individualism was a bourgeois ideology formed out of the rise of the free market, capitalism and the Enlightenment. With the establishment of the People's Republic in 1949 the Chinese state appropriated this leftist critique of individualism, translating it into a negative western trait as a means of reconstituting power relations between the east and the west, and between the state and the indigenous intelligentsia.

These tantalising glimpses of how western thought was negotiated by Asian subjects, however, have rarely provoked the work necessary to reveal how the colonial experience reached back into the metropolis to shape domestic policy. Some fine studies have recently appeared on aspects of colonial policy which demonstrate the pervasive but contested nature of British rule, and yet evidence of how India shaped the thinking of domestic policy-makers, or how China influenced

---

43   Lydia H. Liu, 'Translingual Practice: The Discourse of Individualism between China and the West', in Barlow (ed.), *Formations of Colonial Modernity in East Asia*, pp. 83–112.

modern science are not adequately explored, perhaps because such conscious influences are not easily traced, or because of a reluctance to recognise the colonial dimensions of modernity.[44] One area which has promised to shed light on this question is evangelicalism, which has attracted much recent scholarship. According to Stokes, evangelicalism gained much of its early momentum from intervention in India.[45] Charles Grant and John Shore, for example, were both senior members of the East India Company, members of the Clapham Sect and tireless promoters of Indian missions despite the Company's hostility to missionary endeavour. William Wilberforce himself at times laid greater stress on the salvation of Indian souls than on the abolition of slavery. From these circles generations of civil servants were dispatched; committed to doing good works and with earnestness of purpose they laid the foundations of the service ideal underpinning neo-Platonist forms of colonial rule later in the century. India, however, was not the only site of missionary activity; at the same time as early evangelical intervention in the subcontinent, China figured largely in the Protestant imagination as one of its biggest challenges, but from the late eighteenth century, when the Baptist Missionary Society, the London Mission Society and Church Mission Society were founded, India became the main focus.[46]

Given that missionary intervention in India and China predated the massive phase of missionary work in London by some 40 years, it is tempting to see the episode as a useful case study of how the colonial experience reached back into the heartland. The practice of intensive house-to-house visits adopted among the London poor as the best means of effecting a moral regeneration of society was almost certainly modelled on evangelical work in India. And many missionaries who had worked in India drew upon their experiences to compare the two sites. To give just one example, on his return to England, Joseph Mullens, Foreign Secretary of the LMS, published *London and Calcutta* in which he stated that, though the slums of London are violent and vice-ridden, those of heathenism found in Calcutta reach the 'very horrors of immorality'.[47] And yet such evidence has not been used to illuminate the dialogic nature of evangelicalism in the context of empire. We have fine studies of English evangelicalism which see it as an exclusively domestic product, and of overseas missions which, while recognising the nexus

44 Among the best of many studies are Mark Harrison, *Public Health in British India: Anglo-Indian Preventive Medicine, 1859–1914* (Cambridge, 1994); Matthew Edney, *Mapping an Empire: The Geographical Construction of British India, 1765–1843* (Chicago, IL, 1997); Radhika Singha, *A Despotism of Law: Crime and Justice in Early Colonial India* (Delhi, 1998); Peter Robb, *Ancient Rights and Future Comforts: Bihar, the Bengal Tenancy Act of 1885, and British Rule in India* (Richmond, 1997); Jon Wilson, *The Domination of Strangers: Modern Governance in Eastern India, 1780–1835* (Basingstoke, 2008).
45 Stokes, *English Utilitarians*, p. xii.
46 Susan Thorne, *Congregational Missions and the Making of an Imperial Culture in Nineteenth-Century England* (Stanfordo, CA, 1999); Andrew Porter, *Religion Versus Empire? British Protestant Missionaries and Overseas Expansion, 1700–1914* (Manchester, 2004).
47 Joseph Mullens, *London and Calcutta, Compared in their Heathenism, their Privileges and their Prospects* (London, 1869), p. 53, quoted in Marriott, *The Other Empire*, p. 122.

with London, consider the lines of influence acting in one direction only.[48] Thus the most comprehensive of recent studies advocating an integrated approach to missions and empire, starts well by challenging a certain orthodoxy justifying localised, internal studies of missionary work on the grounds that what took place in Africa, China and India had more to do with conditions found there than with traditions of metropolitan thought.[49] Instead, Andrew Porter argues that while indigenous responses and resistance to missions may have 'shaped a process of cultural exchange which often bore little relation to broader imbalances of material power between colonisers and colonised', evangelicalism as a practical philosophy was developed by an interaction between metropolis and empire, and to ignore either results in a distorted picture.[50] And yet again, how that interaction refracted back on metropolitan thought and practices, or indeed on missionary activity at other sites, remains largely unexplored in the literature.

This last point, made more broadly to encompass colonialism as a whole, is an important one. If India was the first great laboratory of British colonial rule, what lessons were learnt and applied as the empire encroached on other countries? How did the extensive network of doctors, engineers, administrators, teachers, missionaries, soldiers and other agents facilitate the transmission of what was considered best practice from one colony to another? It is evident that despite shifts which occurred in ideologies underpinning the colonial state of the nineteenth century, the Indian army and civil service provided models used later by the British in Africa, that the administration of public works in India was copied elsewhere, and that the extension of education and medical provision was based on the Indian experience.[51] The precise flow of knowledge and personnel, however, has rarely been explored beyond the confines of individual biographies.

The Modernity of Atlantic Slavery

I wish to finish by returning to the question of the extent to which the experience of Atlantic slavery was constitutive of colonial modernity. Here the most commanding arguments have been developed by Paul Gilroy in *The Black Atlantic*.[52] His premise is that debates over modernity have failed adequately to take account of the ways in which ideas about nationality, ethnicity and authenticity have shaped

---

48   Boyd Hilton, *The Age of Atonement: The Influence of Evangelicalism on Social and Economic Thought, 1785–1865* (Oxford, 1988); D.M. Lewis, *Lighten their Darkness: The Evangelical Mission to Working-Class London, 1828–67* (New York, 1986); Thorne, *Congregational Missions*; Porter, *Religion Versus Empire?*

49   Porter, *Religion Versus Empire?*, p. 4.

50   Ibid., p. 322.

51   Andrew Thompson, 'Empire and the British State', in Stockwell (ed.), *The British Empire*, pp. 39–61.

52   Paul Gilroy, *The Black Atlantic: Modernity and Double Consciousness* (London, 1993).

the transformations of the post-Enlightenment world. European colonisers, the Africans they enslaved, and the Indians they subjugated were not isolated from one another, but tied into processes of cultural negotiation and hybridisation from which emerged ethnic identities and political strategies, and dynamic senses of the west as a cultural community. Recognition of the intimate historical relationship between slavery and modernity, he contends, thus forces on to the agenda a number of critical issues which together promise to transcend unproductive debates between a Eurocentric rationalism 'which banishes the slave experience from its account of modernity', and an occidental anti-humanism which 'locates the origins of modernity's current crisis in the shortcomings of the Enlightenment project'.[53] Among the issues raised by this recognition are:

1. The seductive idea of history as progress, including schema built around teleological notions of a stages theory of societal development.[54]
2. Those narratives and periodisations attendant on the dialectic of the Enlightenment which foregrounded the inexorable moves toward rationalisation, secularisation, liberalisation and democratisation.
3. The experience of racial brutality and terror, resulting in what Orlando Patterson has described as the social death of the enslaved.[55]

Many of the advances that have come to be accepted as integral to modernity, contingent as they were on the power of the dominant racial grouping to define them as such, were in fact partial and incomplete. Given this, it is necessary to reconstruct the history of modernity from the slaves' point of view, not simply as a means of including them in a more complete picture, but in order to look afresh at the putative coherence and integrity of the Enlightenment project. Gilroy proceeds to reveal how black artistic, literary and musical expression, while conscious of the promise of the modern world, mounted a critique from both within and without, thereby forcing a reassessment of foundational concepts including power, freedom, identity and citizenship. This was not an alternative modernity but a distinctive *counterculture* of modernity which 'defiantly reconstructs its own critical, intellectual, and moral genealogy in a partially hidden public sphere of its own'.[56] Thus in the writings of Richard Wright, Frederick Douglass, W.E.B. Du Bois and Martin Delany, and in the music of a host of artists from the Fisk Jubilee Singers to contemporary hip-hop, are to be found dialogues voicing profound anxieties about modernity's contradictions.

The memory of slavery embedded in its descendants refused the separation of culture and politics to pose a new set of questions about the bases for ethics and aesthetics different from those immanent within western modernity. To understand

53 Ibid., pp. 53–4.
54 For this, see the magisterial David Brion Davis, *Slavery and Human Progress* (New York, 1986).
55 Orlando Patterson, *Slavery and Social Death* (Cambridge, MA, 1982).
56 Gilroy, *Black Atlantic*, pp. 37–8.

the consequence and contemporary relevance of this task requires diligent scrutiny of the complex interaction of African and European bodies of philosophical and cultural inquiry to create a concept of modernity which can contribute, for example, to 'an analysis of how the particular varieties of radicalism articulated through the revolts of enslaved people made selective use of the ideologies of the western Age of Revolution and then flowed into social movements of an anti-colonial and decidedly anti-capitalist type'.[57] More tellingly, perhaps, a scepticism towards Enlightenment narratives demands the dismantling of the biological hierarchies of scientific racism – one of their more durable and pernicious products – and their replacement with more complex understandings of cultural differences in the contemporary world.

It seems to me that if for slavery we read colonialism, and for slave we read colonised subject, Gilroy's arguments lose none of their relevance or potency, for they have purchase in other contexts. Used appropriately, they can illuminate the emergence of counter-modernities in colonial and post-colonial formations around the world, from the millenarian inspired nationalisms in Africa to the Chinese Community Party's take on individualism.

Modernity was framed by the Enlightenment and came through the ascendancy of the west to claim universality. The moment of its formation was inscribed by the experience of slavery and colonialism from which emerged the need to examine notions such as the individual, citizenship, nationality, race, governance, liberty and sexuality which have remained at the very core of modernity and its contradictions. This universality could never act with an overpowering authority. Colonial formations were replete with internal tensions and conflicts, and colonial rule operated out of ignorance rather than knowledge, and was subject to forms of resistance – countercultures of modernity – forcing colonial powers to enter into dialogues with indigenous systems and cultures. This epistemological terrain bringing together metropolis and colony was therefore one of hegemonic struggle, and, because of this, colonial modernity was uneven and incomplete.

The concept of colonial modernity is of value in forcing us to address the colonial experience when thinking of modernity. If, on the other hand, that experience is recognised from the start to be constitutive of modernity and our discussions necessarily address this formative experience as a matter of routine, then the term colonial modernity will hopefully become tautological and obsolete.

---

57   Ibid., p. 44.

Aftermath

Christopher J. Lee

On 24 October 1945, the United Nations (UN) came into being, thus completing a series of diplomatic meetings during the Second World War that sought to establish a peaceful world order for the postwar period. Seeking to restore the principles of the failed League of Nations (1920–46) within a new institutional body, the UN launched a representative assembly, a security council, an international court of justice and other organs to resolve future international tensions by peaceful, diplomatic means. At the centre of this undertaking was the primacy of the nation-state. The intellectual and moral foundations of the new body originated with US President Woodrow Wilson's Fourteen Points delivered in 1918, and the 1941 Atlantic Charter drafted by British Prime Minister Winston Churchill and US President Franklin D. Roosevelt. In keeping with these beginnings, the UN validated a world order based on self-determination and sovereign nation-states, not empires.[1] Although British, French and Portuguese empires would remain intact, if in declining form, until the last decades of the twentieth century, imperialism as a stated political practice would be viewed as increasingly illegitimate, a stance solidified by the active inclusion of post-colonial countries as UN members. Yet the advent of the Cold War and its bipolar structure of world power compromised the dimensions and possibilities of post-colonial autonomy. Political independence appeared to be in name only, with the structural legacies of modern imperialism continuing to inform political and economic realms at local and global levels. The diverse cultural impact of western imperialism – through religion, gender, sexuality, racial difference, consumer taste, language and aesthetic forms of literature, architecture, music and other arts – looked just as irreversible.

This chapter is concerned with this complex aftermath. As a research topic, the predicaments of the post-colonial era have garnered wide attention since the aforementioned wave of decolonisation during the latter half of the twentieth century. However, the expression 'aftermath of empire' raises immediate questions of time and place. Which empire, and during what period? Furthermore, it risks

---

1   Erez Manela, *The Wilsonian Moment: Self-Determination and the International Origins of Anticolonial Nationalism* (Oxford, 2007); Elizabeth Borgwardt, *A New Deal for the World: America's Vision for Human Rights* (Cambridge, MA, 2005).

demarcating epochal change for political, economic and cultural shifts that are defined as much by continuity as by departure from the past. To this end, Frederick Cooper has recently contended that empire-states, rather than nation-states, have been central to world history. Only recently has the nation-state model fully emerged as a normative political form, despite views that stress its establishment by the 1648 Peace of Westphalia that ended the Thirty Years' War in Europe.[2] Such observations on the recurrence and durability of imperialism as a political routine dovetail with contemporary work on globalisation and state power that has suggested the renewed relevance of empire-like formations.[3] In sum, efforts to achieve global political reach and influence, whether formally or informally, are unlikely to disappear.[4] Yet the expression 'aftermath of empire' holds resonance and meaning for individuals, communities and countries that experienced imperialism and embraced efforts, often at great cost, to end it. Decolonisation signals a moment of fundamental political change, however limited, with attendant shifts in economy, law, culture and other social realms. It indicates a perspective and consciousness different from that found under imperialism.

This chapter therefore outlines three inter-related areas through which the aftermath of imperialism can be understood: political rights and representation, economic integration and structural inequality, and cultural knowledge. These themes do not represent issues solely 'beyond' empire as such, nor does this chapter pretend to offer a comprehensive account of each. But these topics do locate areas of interconnection and contestation that have defined the boundaries and content of imperial and post-imperial orders. Indeed, the broad argument put forward by this chapter is that the aftermath of imperialism is best understood as a set of mutually constituted outcomes – between 'colonisers' and the 'colonised', metropoles and colonies, and other related variations – that underscore the multiple origins and diverse factors that shaped imperialism and its ends. This approach to understanding the legacies of empire and the birth of new patterns of history further points to a general need for interdisciplinary dialogue between sociocultural history, diplomatic history and political economy, in addition to

---

2   Frederick Cooper, *Colonialism in Question: Theory, Knowledge, History* (Berkeley, CA, 2005), chap. 6. For related engagements, see Antoinette Burton (ed.), *After the Imperial Turn: Thinking With and Through the Nation* (Durham, NC, 2003); Gary Wilder, *The French Imperial Nation-State: Negritude and Colonial Humanism Between the Two World Wars* (Chicago, IL, 2005).

3   Michael Hardt and Antonio Negri, *Empire* (London, 2000); Niall Ferguson, *Empire: The Rise and Demise of the British World Order and the Lessons for Global Power* (New York, 2003); Noam Chomsky, *Hegemony or Survival: America's Quest for Global Dominance* (Boston, MA, 2003); Chalmers Johnson, *The Sorrows of Empire: Militarism, Secrecy, and the End of the Republic* (New York, 2004); Rashid Khalidi, *Resurrecting Empire: Western Footprints and America's Perilous Path in the Middle East* (London, 2004). For an overview, see Frederick Cooper, 'Empire Multiplied', *Comparative Studies in Society and History* 46 (2004): pp. 247–72.

4   On 'formal' and 'informal' imperialism, see Ronald Robinson and John Gallagher with Alice Denny, *Africa and the Victorians: The Official Mind of Imperialism* (New York, 1961).

the commonly referenced insights of post-colonial theory. A multifaceted set of techniques serves to highlight the idea of imperialism as generative of power – that its end does not necessarily entail a decline of political power as such but more often its relocation, with results that complicate received periodisations of 'colonial' and 'post-colonial'. In sum, a consistent need exists to integrate the experiential complexity and contradictions of imperial history and its repercussions with the broadly conceived claims of anti-colonial political rhetoric and post-colonial theory alike.

Anti-Colonialism and Decolonisation: The Global Circulation of Rights and Representation

Decolonisation poses fundamental challenges for the historian. From an empirical standpoint, it represents a contingent moment of political independence *and* the culmination of a process with deep roots, often originating with the act of initial colonisation itself. It is an experience that is at once uniquely individual – to people, communities, and nation-states alike – and in retrospect seemingly universal. This ubiquity paradoxically contributes to its relative disregard for uniform frames of analysis or time. With the American Revolution (1776–83) and the Haitian Revolution (1791–1804) subverting the imperial presence of Great Britain and France in North America and the Caribbean, decolonisation in the western hemisphere preceded that of Africa and Asia by almost two centuries. Indeed, the early modern political independence of states in North and South America antedated the formal colonisation of Africa, in ways that influenced this continental shift in imperial direction during the nineteenth century. Asia similarly experienced imperialism within a different time frame. Initial western intrusion concurred with imperial endeavours in the Americas during the fifteenth century and finished with Great Britain's late handover of Hong Kong to China in 1997 and Portugal's separate transfer of Macao to China in 1999. Our generic method of periodisation through the terms 'pre-colonial', 'colonial' and 'post-colonial' consequently faces the challenge of synchronicity when applied on a global scale. Furthermore, informal 'anti-colonial imperialism' and sub-imperialist endeavour by ex-colonies such as the United States represent developments that usefully de-centre Europe, but also introduce new complications for interpreting the precursors and aftermaths of imperialism in world history.[5]

---

5   On modern decolonization and its variability, see, for example, Prosser Gifford and Wm Roger Louis (eds), *The Transfer of Power in Africa: Decolonization, 1940–1960* (New Haven, CT, 1982); Gifford and Louis (eds), *Decolonization and African Independence: The Transfers of Power, 1960–1980* (New Haven, CT, 1988); John Darwin, *The End of the British Empire: The Historical Debate* (Oxford, 1991); M.E. Chamberlain, *Decolonization: The Fall of the European Empires* (Oxford, 1999); John Springhall, *Decolonization Since 1945: The Collapse of European Overseas Empires* (New York, 2001); James D. Le Sueur (ed.), *The Decolonization Reader* (New York, 2003); Prasenjit Duara (ed.), *Decolonization: Perspectives*

The political process of decolonisation, which is central to understanding post-imperial history, is consequently poised between local conditions and global trends. It is not an expression easily transferred between geographic or temporal contexts with a universal meaning intact. Like the nation-state with which it is intrinsically connected, decolonisation lends itself to wide use as a baseline for transitional political independence and autonomy, as well as historical narratives of economic development and modernisation. However, as with these teleologies, decolonisation requires scrutiny. Recent work has pointed to the qualitative differences between settler and non-settler colonies in directing political outcomes, but broader geopolitical contexts – the Cold War, for example – must likewise be seen as crucial factors in shaping decolonisation and at times prolonging its denouement, as late twentieth-century conflicts in Southeast Asia and southern Africa have demonstrated.[6] At a conceptual level, the term 'post-colonial', to which decolonisation is also intrinsically tied, poses equal risks of essentialisation, through interpretive claims that have sought to read and inscribe a common set of experiences across the former colonial world. The universality of condition imparted by such terminology demands critical vigilance.[7] Overall, the categories and frameworks associated with imperialism and its aftermaths present an ongoing predicament between a need for comparative analysis and attention to situated case studies that refine broader patterns of event and meaning across space and time. Rather than signalling a linear transfer of power that can be transposed on a number of different situations, decolonisation constitutes a complex and frequently unstable intersection of competing views and claims over colonial pasts, transitional presents and inchoate futures. Once these dimensions and their ambiguities are acknowledged, a more meaningful sense of imperial aftermaths can be achieved.[8]

---

from Now and Then (New York, 2004); Ronald Hyam, *Britain's Declining Empire: The Road to Decolonisation, 1918–1968* (Cambridge, 2006). On 'anti-colonial imperialism' as applied to the United States, see William Appleman Williams, *The Tragedy of American Diplomacy* (New York, 1959).

6   Caroline Elkins and Susan Pedersen (eds), *Settler Colonialism in the Twentieth Century: Projects, Practices, Legacies* (New York, 2005); Odd Arne Westad, *The Global Cold War: Third World Interventions and the Making of Our Times* (Cambridge, 2006).

7   For critiques of the term 'post-colonial', see Ella Shohat, 'Notes on the Postcolonial', *Social Text* 31/32 (1992): pp. 99–113; Anne McClintock, 'The Angel of Progress: Pitfalls of the Term "Postcolonialism"', *Social Text* 31/32 (1992): pp. 84–98; Arif Dirlik, *The Postcolonial Aura: Third World Criticism in the Age of Global Capitalism* (Boulder, CO, 1997); David Scott, *Refashioning Futures: Criticism After Postcoloniality* (Princeton, NJ, 1999). For an overview of post-colonial thought, see Robert J.C. Young, *Postcolonialism: An Historical Introduction* (Oxford, 2001).

8   For recent examples that address this complexity, see Matthew Connelly, *A Diplomatic Revolution: Algeria's Fight for Independence and the Origins of the Post-Cold War Era* (Oxford, 2002); Todd Shepard, *The Invention of Decolonization: The Algerian War and the Remaking of France* (Ithaca, NY, 2006); David Luis-Brown, *Waves of Decolonization: Discourses of Race and Hemispheric Citizenship in Cuba, Mexico, and the United States* (Durham, NC, 2008).

Take, for example, the case of Haiti, among the earliest examples of modern post-colonial nationhood and one of the most dramatic given its birth in the crucible of plantation slavery. Saint-Domingue, as Haiti was then known, had become a key producer of sugar during the eighteenth century. Although class and racial tensions escalated over time, the French Revolution (1789–99) and its Declaration of the Rights of Man and of the Citizen (1789) provided a political rationale and catalyst for rebellion, demonstrating not only the quick and powerful effects that revolutionary ideas could have, but how they were reconfigured and applied to local political situations. In his acclaimed work *The Black Jacobins* (1938), C.L.R. James argues that to understand the Haitian and French Revolutions it is necessary to understand the imperial context in which they coexisted. Each made similar claims to an imagined political future, if from different vantage points.[9] Recognition of the ways in which ideas circulated between metropoles and colonies – and the role that activists and intellectuals such as Toussaint l'Ouverture, the leader of Haiti's slave rebellion, and James have had in embracing and interpreting these ideas – has since become an accepted feature of political histories of imperialism.[10] Indeed, twentieth-century activist-intellectuals such as Aimé Césaire, Frantz Fanon and Albert Memmi further pointed to the tensions of purported 'civilising missions' by western imperial powers that in practice conflicted with 'native' policies which discriminated on the basis of race and culture. Such contradictions informed and often destabilised political binaries of native/settler and citizen/subject that attempted to limit the possibilities of political change and equality, and ultimately served to spur anti-colonial movements and their designs for self-determination.[11]

The global proliferation of ideas about political rights and citizenship has therefore been a key feature of the aftermath of imperialism – informing anti-colonial and post-colonial politics alike – but their reception, use and influence have been dependent upon time and place. The early independence of Haiti, for example, did not avert later French colonialism in Africa, Asia and the Middle East. Principles like self-determination depended upon local leaders and receptive popular audiences. Nor were such ideas necessarily confined to the geographic

---

9   C.L.R. James, *The Black Jacobins: Toussaint L'Ouverture and the San Domingo Revolution* (New York, 1989). See also Laurent Dubois, *Avengers of the New World: The Story of the Haitian Revolution* (Cambridge, MA, 2004); Dubois, *A Colony of Citizens: Revolution and Slave Emancipation in the French Caribbean, 1787–1804* (Chapel Hill, NC, 2004); Sibylle Fischer, *Modernity Disavowed: Haiti and the Cultures of Slavery in the Age of Revolution* (Durham, NC, 2004); Jeremy D. Popkin, *Facing Racial Revolution: Eyewitness Accounts of the Haitian Insurrection* (Chicago, IL, 2007).

10 See especially Frederick Cooper and Ann Laura Stoler (eds), *Tensions of Empire: Colonial Cultures in a Bourgeois World* (Berkeley, CA, 1997); Kathleen Wilson (ed.), *A New Imperial History: Culture, Identity, and Modernity in Britain and the Empire, 1660–1840* (Cambridge, 2004).

11 Aimé Césaire, *Discourse on Colonialism* (New York, 2000); Frantz Fanon, *The Wretched of the Earth* (New York, 2004); Albert Memmi, *The Colonizer and the Colonized* (Boston, MA, 1967). See also Alice L. Conklin, *A Mission to Civilize: The Republican Idea of Empire in France and West Africa, 1895–1930* (Stanford, CA, 1997).

boundaries of empire. Modern anti-colonial struggles intersected with civil-rights movements seeking political reform and representation, producing transregional political phenomena such as Pan-Africanism. They also overlapped with other types of internationalism, especially socialism, as illustrated by the 1927 League Against Imperialism meeting sponsored by the Communist International, which sought to conjoin the revolutionary interests of anti-colonial movements with those of the Comintern. International meetings of this kind, centred on identifying shared notions of political and economic rights, continued into the post-colonial period with the 1955 Asian-African Conference held in Bandung, Indonesia as well as the Tricontinental Conference held in Havana, Cuba in 1966. Both asserted the importance of 'Third World' solidarity during the Cold War. Indeed, transnational organisations like the Non-Aligned Movement (NAM) and the Cairo-based Afro-Asian Peoples' Solidarity Organization (AAPSO) which came out of these events sought to continue their political momentum by addressing issues of intercontinental concern that ranged from women's rights to the surreptitious manner in which the Cold War policies of the US and Soviet Union reproduced power imbalances reminiscent of imperialism, compromising the political autonomy of many post-colonial nation-states. The political ideas that founded independence struggles therefore continued to be protected and refashioned according to changing circumstances, extending legacies of activism rooted in the experience of imperialism.[12]

Parallel to the global transmission of a discourse of rights has been the ascendance of the nation-state as a political form. Indeed, the most palpable end result of imperialism has been the establishment of new states. A proliferation of sovereign countries has occurred since the end of the Second World War up to the recent break-up of the Soviet Union, but a deeper trajectory of this phenomenon can be located in the western hemisphere during the eighteenth and nineteenth centuries.[13] Noting this, Benedict Anderson has contended that the origins of the nation-state partly rest in colonial Latin America, not exclusively Europe.[14] The topic of nationalism has consequently attracted widespread attention with some, like Anderson, arguing for its populist, imagined characteristics and others, like Partha Chatterjee, emphasising its derivative, applied nature to contexts outside Europe.[15]

---

12   Westad, *The Global Cold War*.

13   On the USSR as an empire, see Ronald Grigor Suny and Terry Martin (eds), *A State of Nations: Empire and Nation-Making in the Age of Lenin and Stalin* (Oxford, 2001); Francine Hirsch, *Empire of Nations: Ethnographic Knowledge and the Making of the Soviet Union* (Ithaca, NY, 2005); Vladislav M. Zubok, *A Failed Empire: The Soviet Union in the Cold War from Stalin to Gorbachev* (Chapel Hill, NC, 2007).

14   Benedict Anderson, *Imagined Communities: Reflections on the Origin and Spread of Nationalism* (London, 1991). See also Sara Castro-Klarén and John Charles Chasteen (eds), *Beyond Imagined Communities: Reading and Writing the Nation in Nineteenth-Century Latin America* (Baltimore, MD, 2003).

15   Partha Chatterjee, *Nationalist Thought and the Colonial World: A Derivative Discourse* (London, 1993). See also Geoff Eley (ed.), *Becoming National: A Reader* (New York 1996); John D. Kelly and Martha Kaplan, *Represented Communities: Fiji and World Decolonization*

Both approaches have attempted to explain the positive and negative effects of nationalism. Beyond its celebrated attributes of popular agency and power, for example, nationalism has often been racially exclusive as observed in former colonies such as South Africa, Brazil, Australia and the United States.[16] Ethnic identities that were reinforced by colonial policies have periodically been a source of post-colonial division and tension, as seen in episodic communal violence in India and the tragic case of the 1994 Rwandan genocide.[17] Beside these ideological legacies, structural features of imperialism have also proved tenacious. Colonial bureaucracies have frequently resulted in post-colonial 'gatekeeper' states that are highly centralised and offer limited opportunities for popular participation.[18] Combining these elements, a central paradox of many post-colonial countries has been not only a failure to achieve the political principles that informed anti-colonial struggles – a 'historic failure of the nation to come to its own' as once cited by Ranajit Guha – but the reproduction of autocratic state institutions and power, with their attendant social disparities as predicted by Frantz Fanon.[19] Such continuities between the colonial and post-colonial periods are located not only in the political realm. To understand their full impact, the question of economic autonomy must also be considered.

Independence and Dependence: Structural Inequality in the World Economy

Contemporary media images from Africa, Asia and Latin America are often suffused with themes of poverty, disease, weak infrastructure and the rudimentary aspects of rural life. Accompanying these representations have been policy-oriented keywords such as 'development' and 'modernisation' which, as supported by institutions like the World Bank and the International Monetary Fund (IMF), encompass a discourse that has reinforced western perspectives that 'modernity' has not yet been achieved by 'least developed countries' (LDCs). These views speak to a general problem – that post-colonial sovereignty did not translate into

---

(Chicago, IL, 2001).

16   George M. Fredrickson, *White Supremacy: A Comparative Study in American and South African History* (New York, 1981); Anthony Marx, *Making Race and Nation: A Comparison of South Africa, the United States, and Brazil* (Cambridge, 1998).

17   Gyanendra Pandey, *Routine Violence: Nations, Fragments, Histories* (Stanford, CA, 2005); Mahmood Mamdani, *When Victims Become Killers: Colonialism, Nativism, and the Genocide in Rwanda* (Princeton, NJ, 2001).

18   On the term 'gatekeeper' state, see Frederick Cooper, *Africa Since 1940: The Past of the Present* (Cambridge, 2002). For similar engagements, see Jean-François Bayart, *The State in Africa: The Politics of the Belly* (London, 1993); Achille Mbembe, *On the Postcolony* (Berkeley, CA 2001).

19   Ranajit Guha, 'On Some Aspects of the Historiography of Colonial India', in Guha (ed.), *Subaltern Studies I: Writings on South Asian History and Society* (New Delhi, 1982), p. 7; Fanon, *The Wretched of the Earth*, chap. 3.

economic independence. Haiti again provides a vivid example of this dilemma, having achieved self-rule over two hundred years ago but ranking among the poorest countries in the world today. The post-colonial writings of such twentieth-century political leaders as Kwame Nkrumah and Julius Nyerere further speak to this predicament.[20] Indeed, the adoption of socialism by many anti-colonial nationalist movements during the last century was a strategic recognition that self-determination required not only political change but economic control and self-sufficiency. However, as observed with the political quandaries of many post-colonial countries, the economic transition from colonial to post-colonial status was often thin on autonomy and thick with ongoing entanglements. What is important to emphasise, then, is the historically-constructed nature of such material inequalities and their social effects. Poverty, malnutrition and environmental crises such as famine are not intrinsic to certain places. They have a history.[21]

Early twentieth-century critics such as J.A. Hobson, Rosa Luxemburg and Vladimir Lenin were among the first to argue that imperialism at its root was economically driven. Drawing upon Marxist theory, Luxemburg and Lenin outlined how capitalist interests based in industrialised European nation-states sought resources and new markets through the establishment of overseas colonies. In Lenin's words, imperialism comprised 'the highest stage of capitalism'. Based on his experience as a journalist, Hobson witnessed this kind of economic acquisition first-hand during the South African War (1899–1902), when Great Britain sought to take over the gold- and diamond-rich territories governed by the Afrikaner Orange Free State and the South African Republic. During the 1970s and 1980s, world-systems analysis outlined by Immanuel Wallerstein, Andre Gunder Frank and others built upon these earlier theories to propose a sweeping interpretation of global history based on the rise of a capitalist world economy since the fifteenth century. Imperialism played a crucial role in its foundation and subsequent expansion. At its heart, this research model has attempted to explain both the integration of different parts of the world into a global economy and the imbalances of wealth that have resulted. The 'world system' is consequently defined by a 'core' – consisting of countries such as the United States and those in Western Europe where financial capital has been centred – and a 'periphery' – where 'underdeveloped' countries lacking a comparable industrial base exist. The core has drawn resources from the periphery and in turn has sold manufactured goods to these peripheral areas, an interaction that has left little material gain for the latter. Beyond the academic incentive of synthesising disparate fields of area-studies knowledge, this ambitious paradigm equally sought to address the basic question, then palpable during the

---

20   Kwame Nkrumah, *Neo-Colonialism: The Last Stage of Imperialism* (New York, 1965); Nkrumah, *Consciencism: Philosophy and the Ideology for Decolonization* (New York, 1970); Julius K. Nyerere, *Ujamaa: Essays on Socialism* (Oxford, 1968).

21   Amartya Sen, *Poverty and Famines: An Essay on Entitlement and Deprivation* (Oxford, 1981); Mike Davis, *Late Victorian Holocausts: El Niño Famines and the Making of the Third World* (London, 2001).

1970s, as to why post-colonial countries in Africa, Asia and Latin America did not take off economically after the end of imperialism.[22]

This question was even more pressing to post-colonial leaders and intellectuals. In his Lenin-inspired polemic *Neo-Colonialism: The Last Stage of Imperialism* (1965), Kwame Nkrumah – the first president of Ghana which, in 1957, was the first country to gain independence in Sub-Saharan Africa – contended that imperial influence had not ended, but that a neo-colonial order had taken hold whereby western countries sought to maintain the economic inequalities created by colonialism.[23] In parallel, Walter Rodney, a historian and activist from Guyana, argued that an ineluctable legacy of European imperialism was the 'underdevelopment' of former colonial areas, thus echoing concurrent ideas in world-systems analysis. In his influential study *How Europe Underdeveloped Africa* (1972), Rodney proposed that weak economic growth in post-colonial Africa was due to long-term imperial policies of resource extraction combined with low investment in infrastructure.[24] Given the risk of continued economic dependence, some leaders actively sought to establish indigenous forms of economic expansion. President Julius Nyerere of Tanzania (1964–85), for example, attempted a form of African socialism through his *ujamaa* (family-hood) programme during the late 1960s and 1970s. Inspired by Chinese collective agriculture as well as what he viewed as community-based African cultural values, *ujamaa* intended to spur economic growth and social egalitarianism through a national 'villagisation' plan. It eventually failed in the face of weak economic demand and unpopularity – a reflection of a top-down approach that misunderstood local agricultural knowledge in addition to dislocating people against their will.[25] Nevertheless, given the context of the Cold War, other countries in Africa, Latin America, the Middle East and Asia embraced socialism as a means of achieving economic autonomy, often with financial backing from the Soviet Union. If nonalignment remained elusive in the political realm, it was likewise in the economic sphere. Soviet and Chinese support provided a distinct alternative and break from connections with the west that had been established through imperialism.

Yet western states and institutions have remained a powerful influence, especially since the denouement of the Cold War. Established shortly after the end of the Second World War to help reconstruct Europe, the World Bank and IMF have since become key lenders to 'developing' countries on the so-called periphery. Efforts have been made by post-colonial nation-states to limit their financial sway through proposals such as the 1974 New International Economic Order, which sought to

---

22 For world-systems theory, see Andre Gunder Frank, *World Accumulation, 1492–1789* (New York, 1978); Giovanni Arrighi, *Chaos and Governance in the Modern World System* (Minneapolis, MN, 1999); Immanuel Wallerstein, *World-Systems Analysis: An Introduction* (Durham, NC, 2004). An important critique is Frederick Cooper *et al.* (eds), *Confronting Historical Paradigms: Peasants, Labor, and the Capitalist World System in Africa and Latin America* (Madison, WI, 1993).

23 Nkrumah, *Neo-Colonialism*.

24 Walter Rodney, *How Europe Underdeveloped Africa* (Washington DC, 1972).

25 James C. Scott, *Seeing Like a State: How Certain Schemes to Improve the Human Condition Have Failed* (New Haven, CT, 1998), chap. 7.

revise their policies in favour of Third World countries. Producer cartels like the Organization of the Petroleum Exporting Countries (OPEC), established in 1960, have similarly aspired to coordinate the economic strengths of countries outside the west. The creation of trade blocs such as the Southern African Development Community, the Andean Community of Nations and the South Asian Free Trade Area has correspondingly aimed to generate regional growth and limit external dependence. Nevertheless, financial support and investment from Euro-American sources has continued. International aid through non-governmental organisations like the Rockefeller, Ford, and, more recently, Gates Foundations has had a positive impact, funding disease prevention programmes in Sub-Saharan Africa and 'green revolutions' in Mexico and India. But general efforts at 'development' have also garnered criticism for placing national economies within ill-fitted teleologies of 'modernisation' that ignore local social dynamics. These modes of intervention and the application of western criteria for measuring growth have reproduced forms of power and inequality, not simply in a material sense but in terms of knowledge and perspective. Indeed, the contemporary discourse of development has deep roots extending back to the imperial period, when figures like David Livingstone advocated 'Christianity, commerce and civilisation' as part of Europe's imperial project. In sum, post-colonial economies remain a site of contestation involving questions of sovereignty, cultural norms and the meanings of present growth and future wealth. Fiscal inequities between the global 'north' and 'south' continue to be one of imperialism's more enduring legacies. But, as the case of Livingstone additionally demonstrates, so is western culture, the topic of the next section.[26]

Toward a New Humanism: Post-Colonialism and the Transformation of Knowledge

The geographic expansion of European power since the fifteenth century resulted in an unprecedented level of cultural contact and social mobility, as Michael Adas and Hugh Cagle note elsewhere in this volume. These twin processes led to an extraordinary growth of information and the redefinition of humanity itself. Indeed, the field of post-colonial studies as conventionally understood has been primarily about this legacy of knowledge production and cultural discourse, rather than contemporary political or economic analysis. Scholars like Edward Said, Gayatri Spivak and Robert J.C. Young helped to set these parameters by drawing from their backgrounds in literature and critical thought to propose that the western

---

26   James Ferguson, *The Anti-Politics Machine: 'Development', Depoliticization, and Bureaucratic Power in Lesotho* (Cambridge, 1990); James Ferguson, *Expectations of Modernity: Myths and Meanings of Urban Life on the Zambian Copperbelt* (Berkeley, CA, 1999); Arturo Escobar, *Encountering Development: The Making and Unmaking of the Third World* (Princeton, NJ, 1995); Akhil Gupta, *Postcolonial Developments: Agriculture in the Making of Modern India* (Durham, NC, 1998).

canon across the humanities was part of a power/knowledge structure mobilised and reinforced by the experience of overseas imperialism. Western knowledge – including scientific and political thought as well as languages, religious ideas and aesthetic forms – became an intrinsic component of imperial projects, enabling technological efficiency but also a set of rationales for justifying foreign rule.[27] Building upon long-held notions of geographic and religious difference, European civilisation was viewed by colonial agents as the pinnacle of the human intellect and its imposition perceived as benevolent and even inevitable. The 'civilising mission' captured this sensibility, with the establishment of Christian missions, secular schools and other institutions giving form to this diverse cultural endeavour. Yet it is equally important to emphasise the more quotidian ways in which European practices and perspectives spread, confirming cultural differences while also converting colonial subjects into 'Black Englishmen', Portuguese *assimilados* and other categories signalling western acculturated status.[28] In his influential study *Orientalism* (1978), Edward Said outlines the role that personal travelogues, memoirs and scientific expeditions had in the service of empire, however seemingly disconnected on the surface, through the construction of difference at micro- and macro-discursive levels.[29] Meanwhile, other scholars have since demonstrated how fashion, sports and parallel forms of consumption and leisure transcended cultural divides to redefine racial, class and gender identities in novel ways.[30]

This intrinsic tension of perceived difference and its transgression has underscored the importance of social discourse and the analytic uses of a cultural framework to surpass domination-resistance binaries of 'coloniser' and 'colonised'. Indeed, the critical project of post-colonial studies has been marked by a broad turn from identifying interpretive structures of difference to locating forms of cultural engagement and similitude. Homi K. Bhabha's *The Location of Culture* (1994) exemplifies this shift with its focus on hybridity as a condition of colonialism, while other scholars like Said have extended this argument to underscore that European metropolitan cultures have been fundamentally shaped by imperialism.[31] In short, the western canon is not as 'western' as once imagined. This line of critique has therefore not been about resistance to the imposition of European custom as such,

---

27 On technology, see Michael Adas, *Machines as the Measure of Men: Science, Technology, and Ideologies of Western Dominance* (Ithaca, NY, 1990).

28 For different studies of this issue, see, *inter alia*, G. Wesley Johnson, *The Emergence of Black Politics in Senegal: The Struggle for Power in the Four Communes, 1900–1920* (Stanford, CA, 1971); Leo Spitzer, *The Creoles of Sierra Leone: Responses to Colonialism, 1870–1945* (Madison, WI, 1974); Mrinalini Sinha, *Colonial Masculinity: The 'Manly Englishman' and the 'Effeminate Bengali' in the Late Nineteenth Century* (Manchester and New York, 1995); Jeanne Marie Penvenne, *African Workers and Colonial Racism: Mozambican Strategies and Struggles in Lourenço Marques, 1877–1962* (Portsmouth, NH, 1995).

29 Edward W. Said, *Orientalism: Western Conceptions of the Orient* (New York, 1978).

30 See, for example, Anne McClintock, *Imperial Leather: Race, Gender, and Sexuality in the Colonial Contest* (New York, 1995).

31 Homi K. Bhabha, *The Location of Culture* (London, 1994); Edward W. Said, *Culture and Imperialism* (New York, 1993).

but exploring interactions created through empires that have resulted in complex webs of influence and social change.[32] Once associated strictly with industrialised Euro-American life, modernity itself has been redefined as the outcome of this global interplay. Scholars such as Paul Gilroy and Walter Mignolo, for example, have sought to position 'counter-modernities' and 'alternative modernities' within existing frameworks of empire and global capital as a means of capturing subaltern forms of agency and knowledge in the making of modern life.[33] Discrete cultural and geographic distinctions between 'the West' and 'the Rest' have experienced a subsequent pressure to dissolve, with ideas of multiculturalism and cosmopolitanism proposed to take their place. Yet there is still a consensus that the intellectual legacies of imperialism are difficult to escape. Dipesh Chakrabarty has charted this predicament in *Provincializing Europe* (2001), noting that western knowledge can neither be wholly rejected nor uncritically embraced.[34] Archival limitations, the Eurocentric epistemology of academic method, and the sociopolitical realities of many post-colonial countries have ensured a situation of continued critical engagement.

In sum, the intellectual aftermath of imperialism has involved the dismantling of Eurocentric discourses of knowledge and power that created biased hierarchies of intellectual and aesthetic value tilted towards the west. If imperialism resulted in an increase in knowledge about different societies and cultures, it did so in a way that valorised European civilisation. A key task since then has been to decentre this intellectual regime with the purpose of outlining a new and more inclusive humanism respectful of global diversity. Beyond the work of post-colonial studies, the United Nations Educational, Scientific and Cultural Organization (UNESCO), founded in 1945, has exemplified this agenda through conferences, publishing ventures and historical and natural heritage projects. During the Cold War, universities around the world embraced area studies as a means of funding and organising research on countries and regions beyond Europe and the United States, typically with a continental focus in mind. 'Third World' writers and intellectuals similarly sought to 'decolonise the mind', in Kenyan novelist Ngũgĩ wa Thiong'o's memorable phrase, by reviving the practice of local languages and aesthetic forms.[35] Such efforts have been both political and intellectual, connected to post-colonial nation-building as well as broader geopolitical contexts, namely

---

32   Paul Rabinow, *French Modern: Norms and Forms of the Social Environment* (Cambridge, MA, 1989); Nicholas B. Dirks (ed.), *Colonialism and Culture* (Ann Arbor, MI, 1992); Said, *Culture and Imperialism*; Cooper and Stoler (eds), *Tensions of Empire*; Wilson (ed.), *A New Imperial History*.

33   Paul Gilroy, *The Black Atlantic: Modernity and Double Consciousness* (London, 1993); Walter D. Mignolo, *Local Histories/Global Designs: Essays on the Coloniality of Power, Subaltern Knowledges, and Border Thinking* (Princeton, NJ, 2000); Dilip Gaonkar (ed.), *Alternative Modernities* (Durham, NC, 2001). See also John Marriott's chapter in this volume.

34   Dipesh Chakrabarty, *Provincializing Europe: Postcolonial Thought and Historical Difference* (Princeton, NJ, 2001).

35   Ngũgĩ wa Thiong'o, *Decolonising the Mind: The Politics of Language in African Literature* (London, 1986).

the dynamics of the Cold War. In the present, the politics of knowledge continues to be important as contemporary globalisation has continued to produce and shape new 'communities of fate' beyond the nation-state – the emergence of transnational religious identities, indigenous peoples movements and ethnically based diasporas being several key examples. What can be surmised overall is that the historical forces of cultural contact and exchange unleashed by imperialism will continue into the future, posing ongoing questions of power and identity amidst trends of cultural interaction and critique in order that greater, more inclusive senses of the human experience are achieved.

Returning to the opening discussion of this chapter, to speak of the 'aftermath of empire' is to risk essentialisation in the same fashion that 'empire' as a political unit or 'imperialism' as a process hazard a totalising view of historical experience. Yet this epochal terminology still enables an intellectual space for locating patterns of similarity and difference across geographic space and historical time, in addition to recognising the fundamental importance of political independence to those who endured and struggled against foreign rule. Approached from a different vantage point, too often the historical connections between Africa, Asia, Latin America and the Middle East have been occluded by the geographic compartmentalisation of area studies since the 1960s. Though comparative and diasporic histories have pushed these boundaries in useful ways, regional and continental knowledge has typically been centred either by historical change emanating from Europe or by the dynamics of local communities making their own history, if not always under conditions of their choosing. The backdrop to both approaches has been the experience of imperialism. Not only did forms of western intervention serve as defining moments in many locales – inaugurating modernity itself, as some scholars have asserted – but they have left durable legacies as to how such events and processes would be interpreted after their denouement. Scholars poised between such legacies and the possibilities of their critique have undertaken a range of theoretical and empirical efforts to interrogate the views and contradictions of the colonial archive and, more generally, the uncritical reproduction of imperial knowledge. However, a task that remains, beyond recovering a space of agency and history situated against the power of the west, is to examine more fully the interrelationships between these regions that are often out of conversation with one another, thus achieving a more diverse and holistic sense of what the afterlives of imperialism are.[36]

---

36   On the introduction of 'modernity', see, *inter alia*, Bhabha, *The Location of Culture*; Mignolo, *Local Histories/Global Designs*; Chakrabarty, *Provincializing Europe*. On interrogating archival knowledge, see essays by Ranajit Guha and Gayatri Spivak in Guha and Spivak (eds), *Selected Subaltern Studies* (New York, 1988); Ann Laura Stoler, *Along the Archival Grain: Epistemic Anxieties and Colonial Common Sense* (Princeton, NJ, 2009). On area studies knowledge, see Arif Dirlik, Vinay Bahl and Peter Gran (eds), *History After the Three Worlds: Post-Eurocentric Historiographies* (Lanham, MD, 2000); David Szanton (ed.), *The Politics of Knowledge: Area Studies and the Disciplines* (Berkeley, CA, 2004).

Equally important is the challenge of addressing the relocations of political, economic, and cultural power. Decolonisation did not signal the end of these forms of power, but rather their regeneration in different places and guises. Independence and nation-state sovereignty reflected the expression of local political will, but post-colonial economic and security arrangements like the Southeast Asia Treaty Organization (1954) and the Baghdad Pact (1955), which sought to reinforce western strategic interests against communist influence, defined a new global Cold War structure of power that echoed earlier imperial ambitions. Continuity as well as change must therefore be understood as shaping the contours of post-coloniality. This observation, moreover, speaks to a contemporary need to explore how critical knowledge about past imperialism can be mobilised to address current political dilemmas. David Scott and Arif Dirlik, for example, have underscored the growing disjuncture between the politics of post-colonial criticism as originally conceived and the political predicaments of the present, such as continuing poverty, global class inequality and environmental exploitation in 'the majority world'.[37] In a fashion evocative of Frantz Fanon, Frederick Cooper has similarly pointed to empirical gaps in recent critical work that has assigned blame for post-colonial impasses on past colonial projects. In his view, this approach obscures the importance of the late colonial and early post-colonial periods in shaping the present – what Fanon would cite as the failure of nationalist leaders to bring about decisive, revolutionary change supportive of popular will.[38] In sum, questions have arisen as to whether the continued interrogation of a receding imperial past is still politically valid. The events and processes of the post-colonial period have continued apace, demanding a renewal of focus on the evolving relationships between sovereignty, political economy and cultural life that were once defined by imperial formations, but increasingly extend beyond their immediate legacies.

This type of attention towards the present is equally attuned to the potential for imperialism's re-emergence. Recent scholarship has explored the calculated and surreptitious ways in which one-time colonies have ascended to superpower status, the United States being a case in point.[39] Such research has offered insight into the contemporary context of American military intervention in the Middle East and Central Asia, but this *longue durée* view of political transformation has also highlighted a general phenomenon of the reproduction and relocation of state power that is imperial-like in practice. The growing regional authority and sway of such countries as China and South Africa – to offer two other examples – if not composed of active territorial acquisition as such nevertheless mirror earlier patterns of political and economic influence. In parallel, rhetoric over 'humanitarian intervention' and other questions of international law and human

---

37   Dirlik, *The Postcolonial Aura*; Scott, *Refashioning Futures*.

38   Cooper, *Colonialism in Question*, chap. 1; Fanon, *The Wretched of the Earth*.

39   Among many titles, see Greg Grandin, *Empire's Workshop: Latin America, the United States, and the Rise of the New Imperialism* (New York, 2006); Michael Adas, *Dominance by Design: Technological Imperatives and America's Civilizing Mission* (Cambridge, MA, 2006); George C. Herring, *From Colony to Superpower: US Foreign Relations Since 1776* (Oxford, 2008).

rights have raised perplexing questions over culture, agency and the appropriate sovereign authority to adjudicate such matters. The effectiveness of the UN and the International Court of Justice in achieving international security and equity apply here. Multinational companies such as ExxonMobil and Halliburton – distant descendants of such global precursors as the Dutch East India Company (1602) and the British South Africa Company (1889) – moreover point to the persistence of transnational financial interests that continue to intervene and shape national and regional economies.

To discuss the 'aftermath' of empire is therefore not only to query time and place, but to draw attention to the dormant and active characteristics of imperialism. Indeed, it is to raise the possibilities of its renewal, redefinition and evolution as a political form. At stake is not necessarily identifying its formal presence, but considering why global situations of poverty, violence and other abuses of political power exist, and whether such predicaments are owing to the unfair reach and impact of a select group of countries. These ongoing tasks can, of course, create a dispiriting sense of difference between the failures of the present and the vibrant post-colonial futures once envisioned during moments of decolonisation. But opportunities are provided in this set of tensions as well. Thinking through 'aftermaths' provides a point of renewal, for reconsidering the specific conditions and local causes for political change, in addition to the more broadly experienced historical themes, as described here, that have attended such shifts. 'Appeals to the past are among the commonest strategies in interpretations of the present', Edward Said has written. 'What animates such appeals is not only disagreement about what happened in the past and what the past was, but uncertainty about whether the past is really past, over and concluded, or whether it continues, albeit in different forms, perhaps.'[40] Given the persistent challenge of interpreting contemporary politics and their future outcomes, recourse to history is not only useful, but urgently necessary.

---

40   Said, *Culture and Imperialism*, p. 3.

Bibliography

Aarsse, Robert, 'Le Saminisme ou le refus non-violent de révoltés', in Pierre Brocheux and Robert Aarsse (eds), *Histoire de l'Asie du Sud-Est: revoltes, reformes, revolutions* (Lille, 1981), pp. 17–29.

Abernethy, David B., *The Dynamics of Global Dominance: European Overseas Empires, 1415–1980* (New Haven, CT, 2000).

Abeyasinghe, Tikiri, *Portuguese Rule in Ceylon* (Colombo, 1964).

Abu-Lughod, Janet L., *Before European Hegemony: The World System AD 1250–1350* (New York, 1991).

Abu-Manneh, Butrus, *Studies on Islam and the Ottoman Empire in the Nineteenth Century, 1826–1876* (Istanbul, 2001).

Abugideiri, Hibba, *Gender and the Making of Modern Medicine in Colonial Egypt* (Farnham, 2010).

Adams, Julia, *The Familial State: Ruling Families and Merchant Capitalism in Early Modern Europe* (Ithaca, NY, 2005).

Adanir, Fikret, *The Ottomans and the Balkans: A Discussion of Historiography* (Leiden, 2002).

— 'Semi-autonomous Forces in the Balkans and Anatolia', in Suraiya N. Faroqhi (ed.), *Cambridge History of Turkey*: vol. 3, *The Later Ottoman Empire 1603–1839* (Cambridge, 2006), pp. 157–85.

Adas, Michael, 'Immigrant Asians and the Economic Impact of European Imperialism: The Role of the Indian Chettiar in British Burma', *Journal of Asian Studies* 33 (1974): pp. 385–401.

— 'From Avoidance to Confrontation: Peasant Protest in Precolonial and Colonial Southeast Asia', *Comparative Studies in Society and History* 32 (1981): pp. 217–47.

— *Machines as the Measure of Men: Science, Technology, and Ideologies of Western Dominance* (Ithaca, NY, 1989).

— *Technology and European Overseas Enterprise: Diffusion, Adaption and Adoption* (Aldershot, 1996).

— 'Contested Hegemony: The Great War and the Afro-Asian Assault on the Civilizing Mission Ideology', *Journal of World History* 15/1 (2004): pp. 31–63.

— *Dominance by Design: Technological Imperatives and America's Civilizing Mission* (Cambridge, MA, 2006).

Addleton, Jonathan S., *Undermining the Centre: The Gulf Migration and Pakistan* (Karachi, 1992).

Adekson, J., 'Bayo, 'Ethnicity and Army Recruitment in Colonial Plural Societies', *Ethnic and Racial Studies* 2/2 (1979): pp. 151–65.

Adshead, Samuel, *China in World History* (London, 1995).

Agamben, Giorgio, *Homo Sacer: Sovereign Power and Bare Life* (Stanford, CA, 1998).

Ageron, Charles-Robert, *Histoire de l'Algérie contemporaine, 1830–1970* (Paris, 1970).

Agmon, Iris, *Family and Court: Legal Culture and Modernity in Late Ottoman Palestine* (Syracuse, NY, 2005).

Ágoston, Gábor and Bruce Masters, *Encyclopedia of the Ottoman Empire* (New York, 2008).

Aguirre, Robert, 'Exhibiting Degeneracy: The Aztec Children and the Ruins of Race', *Victorian Review* 29/2 (2003): pp. 40–63.

Aharoni, Reuven, *The Pasha's Bedouin: Tribes and State in the Egypt of Mehemet Ali, 1801–1848* (London, 2007).

Ahmad, Feroz, *Turkey: The Quest for Identity* (Oxford, 2003).

Ahn, Pong-Sul (ed.), *Migrant Workers and Human Rights: Out-Migration from South Asia* (New Delhi, 2004).Akarli, Engin, 'The Tangled Ends of an Empire: Ottoman Empire: Ottoman Encounters with the West and Problems of Westernization – an Overview', *Comparative Studies of South Asia, Africa and the Middle East* 26/3 (2006): pp. 353–66.

Akçam, Taner, *From Empire to Republic: Turkish Nationalism and the Armenian Genocide* (London, 2004).

Aksakal, Mustafa, *The Ottoman Road to War in 1914: The Ottoman Empire and the First World War* (Cambridge, 2008).

Aksan, Virginia, 'Locating the Ottomans among Early Modern Empires', *Journal of Early Modern History* 3 (1999): pp. 104–134.

— 'The Ottoman Story Today', *Middle East Studies Association Bulletin* 25 (2001): pp. 35–42.

— 'War and Peace', in Suraya N. Faroqhi (ed.), *Cambridge History of Turkey*: vol. 3, *The Later Ottoman Empire 1603–1839* (Cambridge, 2006), pp. 81–117.

— 'The Ottoman Military and State Transformation in a Globalizing World', *Comparative Studies of South Asia, Africa and the Middle East* 27/2 (2007): pp. 259–72.

— *Ottoman Wars 1700–1873: An Empire Besieged* (Harlow, 2007).

— and Daniel Goffman (eds), *The Early Modern Ottomans: Remapping the Empire* (Cambridge, 2007).

al-Fazl, Abu, *A'in-i Akbari*, trans. Henry Blochmann and H.S. Jarrett, 3 vols (Calcutta, 1877).

— *Akbar Nama*, trans. Henry Beveridge, 3 vols (Calcutta, 1902–1939).

Alam, Muzaffar, *Crisis of Empire in Mughal North India: Awadh and the Punjab, 1707–48* (Delhi, 1991).

— *Languages of Political Islam: India, 1200–1800* (London, 2004).

— and Sanjay Subrahmanyam (eds), *Mughal State, 1526–1750* (Delhi, 1998).

— and Sanjay Subrahmanyam, *Indo-Persian Travels in the Age of Discoveries, 1400–1800* (New York, 2007).

Alam, S.M. Shamsul, *Rethinking the Mau Mau in Colonial Kenya* (New York, 2007).

Alavi, Seema, *The Sepoys and the Company: Tradition and Transition in Northern India, 1770–1830* (Delhi, 1995).
— (ed.), *The Eighteenth Century in India* (Delhi, 2002).
Albertini, Rudolf von, 'The Impact of Two World Wars on the Decline of Colonialism', *Journal of Contemporary History* 4/1 (1969): pp. 17–35.
Alden, Dauril, *The Making of an Enterprise: The Society of Jesus in Portugal, Its Empire, and Beyond, 1540–1750* (Stanford, CA, 1996).
Aldrich, Robert, *Greater France: A History of French Overseas Expansion* (London, 1996).
— *The Last Colonies* (Cambridge, 1998).
— *Colonialism and Homosexuality* (London, 2003).
Ali, Anooshahr, 'The King Who Would Be Man: The Gender Roles of the Warrior King in Early Mughal History', *Journal of the Royal Asiatic Society* series 3, 18 (2008): pp. 327–40.
Ali, M. Athar, *Mughal Nobility under Aurangzeb* (Bombay, 1970).
— *Apparatus of Empire: Awards of Ranks, Offices, and Titles to the Mughal Nobility, 1574–1658* (Delhi, 1985).
Allman, Jean (ed.), *Fashioning Africa: Power and the Politics of Dress* (Bloomington, IN, 2004).
Alloula, Malek, *The Colonial Harem* (Minneapolis, MN, 1986).
Altick, Richard, *The Shows of London* (Cambridge, MA, 1978).
Altman, Ida, *Emigrants and Society: Extremadura and America in the Sixteenth Century* (Berkeley and Los Angeles, CA, 1989).
— *Transatlantic Ties in the Spanish Empire: Brihuega, Spain, and Puebla Mexico, 1560–1620* (Stanford, CA, 2000).
Ambedkar, Bhimrao, *The Annihilation of Caste* (Jalandar, 1936).
— *What Congress and Gandhi Have Done to Intouchables* (Bombay, 1945).
Ames, Eric, 'From the Exotic to the Everyday: The Ethnographic Exhibition in Germany', in Vanessa Schwartz and Jeannene Przyblyski (eds), *The Nineteenth-Century Visual Culture Reader* (New York, 2004), pp. 313–27.
Amigoni, David, *Colonies, Cults and Evolution: Literature, Science and Culture in Nineteenth-Century Writing* (Cambridge, 2007).
Amitai, Reuven, 'The Mamluk Institution, or One Thousand Years of Military Slavery in the Islamic World', in Christopher L. Brown and Philip D. Morgan (eds), *Arming Slaves: From Classical Times to the Modern Age* (New Haven, CT, 2006), pp. 40–78.
Amrith, Sunil S., 'Food and Welfare in India, c. 1900–1950', *Comparative Studies in Society and History* 50 (2008): pp. 1010–1035.
Amussen, Susan Dwyer, *Caribbean Exchanges: Slavery and the Transformation of English Society, 1640–1700* (Chapel Hill, NC, 2007).
An, Byŏngjik, 'Hanguk kŭnhyŏndaesa yŏngu ŭi saeroun p'aerŏdaim', *Ch'angjak gwa Bip'yŏng* 98 (1997): pp. 39–58.
Anastassiadou, Merip, *Salonique 1830–1912* (Leiden, 1997).
Andaya, Barbara Watson, *To Live as Brothers: Southeast Sumatra in the Seventeenth and Eighteenth Centuries* (Honolulu, HI, 1993).

— 'From Temporary Wife to Prostitute: Sexuality and Economic Change in Early Modern Southeast Asia', *Journal of Women's History* 9/4 (1998): pp. 11–34.

— *The Flaming Womb: Repositioning Women in Early Modern Southeast Asia* (Honolulu, HI, 2006).

Andaya, Leonard, '"A Very Good-Natured but Awe-Inspiring Government": The Reign of a Successful Queen in Seventeenth-Century Aceh', in Elsbeth Locher-Scholten and Peter Rietbergen (eds), *Hof en handel: Aziatische vorsten en de VOC 1620–1720, opgedragen aan Jurriën van Goor* (Leiden, 2004), pp. 59–84.

Anderson, Benedict, *Imagined Communities: Reflections on the Origin and Spread of Nationalism* (London, 1991).

Anderson, Clare, *Convicts in the Indian Ocean: Transportation from South Asia to Mauritius, 1815–53* (New York, 2000).

— *The Indian Uprising of 1857–8: Prisons, Prisoners and Rebellion* (London, 2007).

Anderson, David, *Histories of the Hanged: The Dirty War in Kenya and the End of Empire* (New York, 2005).

Anderson, Fred, *The Crucible of War: The Seven Years' War and the Fate of Empire in British North America, 1754–1766* (New York, 2000).

— and Andrew Cayton, *The Dominion of War: Empire and Liberty in North America, 1500–2000* (New York, 2005).

Anderson, John, *The Struggle for the School: The Interaction of Missionary, Colonial Government and Nationalist Enterprise in the Development of Formal Education in Kenya* (London, 1970).

Anderson, Warwick, 'Where is the Postcolonial History of Medicine?' *Bulletin of the History of Medicine* 72 (1998): pp. 552–80.

— *Colonial Pathologies: American Tropical Medicine, Race, and Hygiene in the Philippines* (Durham, NC, 2006).

Andrade, Tonio, 'Beyond Guns, Germs, and Steel: European Expansion and Maritime Asia, 1400–1750', *Journal of Early Modern History* 14/1 (2010): pp. 165–86.

Andrew, C.M. and A.S. Kanya-Forstner, 'France, Africa, and the First World War', *Journal of African History* 19/1 (1978): pp. 11–23.

Andrews, Charles McLean, *The Colonial Period in American History* (New Haven, CT, 1934).

Andrews, Jorella, 'Losing Labels and Liking It', in Heather Maitland (ed.), *Navigating Difference: Cultural Diversity and Audience Development* (London, 2004), pp. 141–7.

Andrews, K.R., Nicholas Canny and P.E.H. Hair (eds), *The Westward Enterprise: English Activities in Ireland, the Atlantic, and America, 1480–1650* (Liverpool, 1978).

Andrews, Malcolm, *The Search for the Picturesque* (New Haven, CT, 1981).

Andrien, Kenneth J., *The Kingdom of Quito, 1690–1830: The State and Regional Development* (Cambridge, 1985).

— *Crisis and Decline: The Viceroyalty of Peru in the Seventeenth Century* (Albuquerque, NM, 1985).

Anker, Peder, *Imperial Ecology: Environmental Order in the British Empire, 1895–1945* (Cambridge, MA, 2001).

Anon, 'India in English Literature', *Calcutta Review* 65 (1859).

Ansari, Sarah, *Life after Partition: Migration, Community and Strife in Sindh, 1947–62* (Karachi, 2005).

Appadurai, Arjun, 'Putting Hierarchy in its Place', *Cultural Anthropology* 3/1 (1988): pp. 33–49.

— *The Social Life of Things: Commodities in Cultural Perspective* (Cambridge, 1996).

Appel, Toby, *The Cuvier-Geoffroy Debate: French Biology in the Decades before Darwin* (New York, 1987).

Appy, Christian G. (ed.), *Cold War Constructions: The Political Culture of United States Imperialism, 1945–1966* (Amherst, MA, 2000).

Arasaratnam, Sinnappah, *Dutch Power in Ceylon, 1658–87* (Amsterdam, 1958).

— *Maritime Commerce and English Power (Southeast India 1750–1800)* (Delhi, 1996).

Archer, Mildred, 'Balthasar Solvyns and the Picturesque', *The Connoisseur* (1969): pp. 12–18.

Aristotle, *The Politics of Aristotle*, trans. Benjamin Jowett (Oxford, 1885).

Armitage, David, *Theories of Empire, 1450–1800* (Aldershot, 1998).

--- 'The Elephant and the Whale: Empires of Land and Sea', *Journal for Maritime Research* 9 (2007): pp. 23–36.

— and Michael J. Braddick (eds), *The British Atlantic World, 1500–1800* (London, 2002).

Arnold, David, *Colonizing the Body: State Medicine and Epidemic Disease in Nineteenth-Century India* (Berkeley, CA, 1993).

— *Science, Technology, and Medicine in Colonial India* (New York, 2000).

— *The Tropics and the Travelling Gaze: India, Landscape and Science, 1800–1856* (Seattle, WA, 2006).

Arrighi, Giovanni, *Chaos and Governance in the Modern World System* (Minneapolis, MN, 1999).

Arroyo, Anthony M. Stevens, 'The Inter-Atlantic Paradigm: The Failure of Spanish Medieval Colonization of the Canary and Caribbean Islands', *Comparative Studies in Society and History* 35/3 (1993): pp. 515–43.

Asad, Talal (ed.), *Anthropology and the Colonial Encounter* (London, 1973).

Asano, Toomey, *Teikokunihon no Shokuminchihōsei* (Nagoya, 2008).

Ascherson, Neal, *The King Incorporated: Leopold II in the Age of Trusts* (London, 1963).

Ash, Catherine, 'Forced Labor in Colonial West Africa', *History Compass* 4/3 (2006): pp. 402–406.

Asher, Catherine B., *Architecture of Mughal India*: vol. 4, *New Cambridge History of India*, part 1 (Cambridge, 1992).

Atkinson, Alan, 'The Free-born Englishman Transported: Convict Rights as a Measure of Eighteenth-Century Empire', *Past and Present* 44 (1994): pp. 88–115.

Atwell, William S., 'Volcanism and Short-Term Climatic Change in East Asian and World History, c. 1200–1699', *Journal of World History* 12/1 (2001): pp. 29–98.

Atwill, David G., *The Chinese Sultanate: Islam, Ethnicity, and the Panthay Rebellion in Southwest China, 1856–1873* (Stanford, CA, 2005).

Auerbach, Jeffrey, *The Great Exhibition: A Nation on Display* (New Haven, CT, 1999).

— 'Art and Empire', in Robin Winks (ed.), *Oxford History of The British Empire*, vol. 5 (Oxford, 1999), pp. 571–83.

— 'The Picturesque and the Homogenisation of Empire', *British Art Journal* 5/1 (2004): pp. 47–54.

— 'Imperial Boredom', *Common Knowledge* 11/2 (2005): pp. 283–305.

— and Peter Hoffenberg, *Britain, the Empire, and the World at the Great Exhibition of 1851* (Farnham, 2008).

August, Thomas G., *The Selling of Empire: British and French Imperialist Propaganda, 1890–1940* (Westport, CT, 1985).

Aust, Martin, 'Writing the Empire: Russia and the Soviet Union in Twentieth-Century Historiography', *European Review of History* 10/2 (2003): pp. 375–91.

Avcioglu, Naby, 'A Palace of One's Own: Stanislas I's Kiosks and the Idea of Self-representation', *Art Bulletin* 85 (2003): pp. 662–84.

Avellaneda, José Ignacio, *The Conquerors of the New Kingdom of Granada* (Albuquerque, NM, 1996).

Ayao, Hoshi, *The Ming Tribute Grain System* (Ann Arbor, MI, 1969).

Aydelotte, W.O., *Bismarck and British Colonial Policy: The Problem of South West Africa, 1883–1885* (Philadelphia, PA, 1937).

Aydin, Cemil, *The Politics of Anti-Westernism in Asia: Visions of World Order in Pan-Islamic and Pan-Asian Thought* (New York, 2007).

Axtell, James, *The Invasion Within: The Contest of Cultures in Colonial North America* (Oxford, 1985).

Azoulay, Ariella, *The Civil Contract of Photography* (New York, 2008).

Baay, Reggie, *De njai: Het concubinaat in Nederlands-Indië* (Amsterdam, 2008).

Babington, Anthony, *Shell Shock: A History of the Changing Attitudes to War Neurosis* (London, 1997).

Babur, *Baburnama*, trans. Annette Susannah Beveridge (London, 1921).

— *Baburnama: Memoirs of Babur, Prince and Emperor*, trans. Wheeler M. Thackston (New York, 2002).

Bada'uni, 'Abu al-Qadir, *Muntakhab al-Tawarikh*, trans. George S.A. Ranking, W.H. Lowe and Sir Wolsey Haig, 3 vols (Calcutta, 1925).

Bade, Klaus, *Friedrich Fabri und der Imperialismus in der Bismarckzeit: Beitrage zur Kolonial- und Uberseegeschichte* (Freiburg, 1975).

Baedeker, K., *Handbook for Lower Egypt* (Leipzig, 1885).

Bailkin, Jordanna, 'Indian Yellow: Making and Breaking the Imperial Palette', *Journal of Material Culture* 10/2 (2005): pp. 197–214.

Bain, Jennifer (ed.), 'Introduction', in *Frontiers of Commodity Chain Research* (Stanford, CA, 2009), pp. 1–34.

Bakewell, P.J., *Silver Mining and Society in Colonial Mexico: Zacatecas, 1546–1700* (Cambridge, 1971).

Balibar, Etienne, 'Racism and Nationalism', in Balibar and I. Wallerstein, *Race, Nation, Class: Ambiguous Identities* (London, 1991), pp. 37–67.

Ballantyne, Tony, *Orientalism and Race: Aryanism in the British Empire* (Houndmills, 2002).

— (ed.), *Science, Empire and the European Exploration of the Pacific* (Aldershot, 2004).

— and Antoinette Burton (eds), *Bodies in Contact: Rethinking Colonial Encounters in World History* (Durham, NC, 2005).

Ballhatchet, Kenneth, *Race, Sex, and Class Under the Raj: Imperial Attitudes and Policies and Their Critics, 1793–1905* (London, 1980).

Bannerjee, Sikata, *Make Me a Man! Masculinity, Hinduism and Nationalism in India* (Albany, NY 2005).

Banerjee, Swapna M., *Men, Women and Domestics: Articulating Middle Class Identity in Colonial Bengal* (Oxford, 2004).

Banks, Kenneth, *Chasing Empire Across the Sea: Communications and the State in the French Atlantic, 1713–1763* (Montreal, QC, 2002).

Banton, Michael, *Racial Theories*, 2nd edn (Cambridge, 1998).

Bao, Xiaolan, 'When Women Arrived: The Transformation of New York's Chinatown', in Joanne Meyerowitz (ed.), *Not June Cleaver: Women and Gender in Postwar America, 1945–1960* (Philadelphia, PA, 1994), pp. 19–36.

Barkan, Elazar, *The Retreat of Scientific Racism* (Cambridge, 1991).

Barker, A.J., *The Civilizing Mission: A History of the Italo-Ethiopian War of 1935–36* (New York, 1968).

Barkey, Karen, *Bandits and Bureaucrats: The Ottoman Route to State Centralization* (Ithaca, NY, 1994).

— *Empire of Difference: The Ottomans in Comparative Perspective* (Cambridge, 2008).

Barlow, Arthur, 'Kikuyu Land Tenure and Inheritance', *Journal of the East African and Uganda Natural History Society* 45–6 (1933): pp. 56–66.

Barlow, Tani. E., 'Introduction: On "Colonial Modernity"', in Barlow (ed.), *Formations of Colonial Modernity in East Asia* (Durham, NC, 1997).

— (ed.), *Formations of Colonial Modernity in East Asia* (Durham, NC, 1997)

Barnett, Donald and Karari Njama, *Mau Mau from Within: An Analysis of Kenya's Peasant Revolt* (New York, 1966).

Barr, Alan P. (ed.), *The Major Prose of Thomas Henry Huxley* (Athens, GA, 1997).

Barringer, Tim, *Men at Work: Art and Labour in Victorian Britain* (New Haven, CT, 2005).

Barta, Roger, *Wild Men in the Looking Glass: The Mythic Origins of European Otherness* (Ann Arbor, MI, 1994).

Barth, Fredrick, *et al.*, *One Discipline Four Ways: British, German, French and American Anthropology* (Chicago, IL, 2005).

Bartholomew, James R., *The Formation of Science in Japan: Building a Research Tradition* (New Haven, CT, 1989).

Bartlett, Beatrice S., *Monarchs and Ministers: The Grand Council in Mid-Ch'ing China, 1723–1820* (Berkeley, CA, 1991).

Basalla, George, 'The Spread of Western Science', *Science* 156 (1967): pp. 611–22.

— *The Evolution of Technology* (Cambridge, 1999).

Bashford, Alison, *Imperial Hygiene: A Critical History of Colonialism, Nationalism and Public Health* (Basingstoke, 2004).

Basran, Gurcharn S. and B. Singh Bolaria, *The Sikhs in Canada: Migration, Race, Class and Gender* (New Delhi, 2003).

Bates, Crispin (ed.), *Community, Empire and Migration: South Asians in Diaspora* (Basingstoke, 2001).

— and Marina Carter, 'Tribal and Indentured Migrants in Colonial India: Modes of Recruitment and Forms of Incorporation', in Peter Robb (ed.), *Dalit Movements and the Meanings of Labour in India* (Delhi, 1996), pp. 159–85.

Baum, Bruce, *The Rise and Fall of the Caucasian Race* (New York, 2006).

Bauman, Zygmunt, *Modernity and the Holocaust* (Ithaca, NY, 1989).

Baumann, Robert F., 'Subject Nationalities in the Military Service of Imperial Russia: The Case of the Bashkirs', *Slavic Review* 46/3–4 (1987): pp. 489–502.

Bayart, Jean-François, *The State in Africa: The Politics of the Belly* (London, 1993).

Bayly, C.A., *Rulers, Townsmen and Bazaars: North Indian Society in the Age of British Expansion* (New Delhi 1983).

— *Indian Society and the Making of the British Empire* (Cambridge, 1987).

— *Imperial Meridian: The British Empire and the World, 1780–1830* (Harlow, 1989).

— *Empire and Information: Intelligence Gathering and Social Communication in India, 1780–1870* (Cambridge, 1996).

— *The Birth of the Modern World, 1780–1914: Global Connections and Comparisons* (Oxford, 2004).

— 'Rammohan Roy and the Advent of Constitutional Liberalism in India, 1800–30', *Modern Intellectual History* 4 (2007): pp. 25–41.

— and Tim Harper, *Forgotten Armies: The Fall of British Asia, 1941–1945* (Cambridge, MA, 2005).

— and S. Subrahmanyam, 'Portfolio Capitalists and the Political Economy of Early Modern India', *Indian Economic and Social History Review* 25/4 (1988): pp. 401–425.

Bayly, Susan, *Caste, Society and Politics in India from the Eighteenth Century to the Modern Age* (Cambridge, 1999).

Beach, Milo Cleveland, *Mughal and Rajput Painting*: vol. 3, *New Cambridge History of India*, part 1 (Cambridge, 1992).

Beaglehole, J.C. (ed.), *The Endeavour Journal of Sir Joseph Banks, 1768–1771* (Sydney, 1962).

Beall, Joe, 'Women under Indenture in Colonial Natal, 1860–1911', in Colin Clarke, Ceri Peach and Steven Vertovec (eds), *South Asians Overseas: Migration and Ethnicity* (Cambridge, 1990), pp. 57–74.

Beattie, J.M., *Crime and the Courts in England, 1660–1800* (Oxford, 1986).

Beckert, Sven, 'Emancipation and Empire: Reconstructing the Worldwide Web of Cotton Production in the Age of the American Civil War', *American Historical Review* 109/5 (2004): pp. 1405–1419.

Beckles, Hilary McD., *White Servitude and Black Slavery in Barbados, 1627–1715* (Knoxville, TN, 1989).

— *A History of Barbados: From Amerindian Settlement to Nation-State* (Cambridge, 1990).

Bederman, Gail, *Manliness and Civilization: A Cultural History of Gender and Race in the United States, 1880–1917* (Chicago, IL, 1995).

Behar, Cem, *A Neighborhood in Ottoman Istanbul: Fruit Vendors and Civil Servants in the Kasap Ilyas Mahalle* (Albany, NY, 2003).

Beidelman, T.O., *Colonial Evangelism: A Socio-Historical Study of an East African Mission at the Grassroots* (Bloomington, IN, 1982).

Beinart, William, *The Rise of Conservation in South Africa: Settlers, Livestock, and the Environment 1770–1950* (Oxford, 2003).

Beisner, Robert, *Twelve Against Empire: The Anti-Imperialists, 1898–1900* (New York, 1968).

Belich, James, *The New Zealand Wars and the Victorian Interpretation of Racial Conflict* (Auckland, 1986).

— *Replenishing the Earth: The Settler Revolution and the Rise of the Anglo World, 1783–1939* (Oxford, 2009).

Bell, David, 'The Unbearable Lightness of Being French: Law, Republicanism and National Identity at the End of the Old Regime', *American Historical Review* 106/4 (2001): pp. 1215–35.

Bell, Leonard, *Colonial Constructs: European Images of Maori, 1840–1914* (London, 1991).

Bemmelen, Sita van, 'The Marriage of Minahasa Women in the Period 1861–1933: Views and Changes', in Elsbeth Locher-Scholten and Anke Niehof (eds), *Indonesian Women in Focus: Past and Present Notions* (Leiden, 1992), pp. 181–204.

Bender, Thomas, *A Nation among Nations: America's Place in World History* (New York, 2006).

Benjamin, Roger, 'Postcolonial Taste: Non-western Markets for Orientalist Art', in R. Benjamin (ed.), *Orientalism: From Delacroix to Klee* (Sydney, 1997), pp. 32–40.

— *Orientalist Aesthetics: Art, Colonialism and French Northern Africa, 1880–1930* (Berkeley, CA, 2003).

Benjamin, Thomas, *The Atlantic World: Europeans, Africans, Indians and their Shared History, 1400–1900* (Cambridge, 2009).

Bennett, Tony, *The Birth of the Museum: History, Theory, Politics* (London, 1995).

— *Pasts Beyond Memory: Evolution, Museums, Colonialism* (London, 2004).

Benson, T., *Kikuyu–English Dictionary* (Oxford, 1964).

Benton, Lauren, *Law and Colonial Cultures: Legal Regimes in World History, 1400–1900* (Cambridge, 2002).

— 'Legal Spaces of Empire: Piracy and the Origins of Ocean Regionalism', *Comparative Studies in Society and History* 47/4 (2005): pp. 700–724.

— 'From International Law to Imperial Constitutions: The Problem of Quasi-Sovereignty, 1870–1900', *Law and History Review* 26/3 (2008): pp. 595–620.

— 'Empires of Exception: History, Law, and the Problem of Imperial Sovereignty', *Quaderni di Relazioni Internazionali* 6 (2008): pp. 54–67.

— *A Search for Sovereignty: Law and Geography in European Empires, 1400–1900* (Cambridge, 2010).

Berg, Maxine, *Luxury and Pleasure in Eighteenth Century England* (New York, 2005).

Bergougniou, Jean-Michel, Rémi Clignet and Philippe David, *'Villages noirs' et autres visiteurs africains et malgaches en France et en Europe: 1870–1940* (Paris, 2001).

Berkes, Niyazi, *The Development of Secularism in Turkey* (Montreal, 1964).

Berlin, Ira, *Many Thousands Gone: The First Two Centuries of Slavery in North America* (Cambridge, MA, 1998).

Berman, Bruce and John Lonsdale, *Unhappy Valley: Conflict in Kenya and Africa*, vol. 1 (London, 1992).

Berman, Marshall, *All that is Solid Melts into Air: The Experience of Modernity* (London, 1983).

Bernasconi, Robert, 'Who Invented the Concept of Race? Kant's Role in the Enlightenment Construction of Race', in Bernasconi (ed.), *Race* (Oxford, 2001), pp. 11–36.

Bet-El, Ilana R., 'Men and Soldiers: British Conscripts, Concepts of Masculinity and the Great War', in Billie Melman (ed.), *Borderlines: Genders and Identities in War and Peace, 1870–1930* (London, 1998), pp. 73–94.

Bethencourt, Francisco and Diogo Ramada Curto, *Portuguese Oceanic Expansion, 1400–1800* (Cambridge, 2007).

Betts, Raymond, *The Scramble for Africa: Causes and Dimensions of Empire* (Lexington, MA, 1972).

— *Assimilation and Association in French Colonial Theory, 1890–1914* (Lincoln, NE, 2005).

Beucour, Fernand, Yves Laissus and Chantal Orgogozo, *The Discovery of Egypt* (Paris, 1990).

Bevir, Mark, 'The Construction of Governance', in Mark Bevir and Frank Trentmann (eds), *Governance, Consumers and Citizens: Agency and Resistance in Contemporary Politics* (Basingstoke, 2007), pp. 25–48.

Bhabha, Homi K., 'The Other Question: Homi Bhabha Reconsiders the Stereotype and Colonial Discourse', *Screen* 24/6 (1983): pp. 18–36.

— 'The Other Question: Difference, Discrimination and the Question of Colonialism', in Francis Barker *et al.* (eds), *Literature, Politics and Theory: Papers from the Essex Conference 1976–1984* (London, 1986), pp. 148–72.

— *The Location of Culture* (London, 1994).

— 'Anxious Nations, Nervous States', in Joan Copjec (ed.), *Supposing the Subject* (London, 1994), pp. 201–217.

Bhadra, Gautam, 'Two Frontier Uprisings in Mughal India', in Ranajit Guha (ed.), *Subaltern Studies II: Writings on South Asian History* (Delhi, 1983), pp. 43–59.

Bhargava, Meena and Kalyani Dutta, *Women, Education and Politics: The Women's Movement and Delhi's Indraprastha College* (New Delhi, 2005).

Bharucha, Rustom, 'Infiltrating Europe: Outside the Borders of Postmodern Cool', in Iftikhar Dadi and Salar Hussan (eds), *Unpacking Europe: Towards a Critical Reading* (Rotterdam, 2002), pp. 216–31.

Bhattacharya, Sanjoy, Mark Harrison and Michael Worboys, *Fractured States: Smallpox, Public Health and Vaccination Policy in British India, 1800–1947* (New Delhi, 2005).

Bilsky, Lester (ed.), *Historical Ecology: Essays on Ecology and Social Change* (Port Washington, NY, 1980).

Bindman, David, *Ape to Apollo: Aesthetics and the Idea of Race in the Eighteenth Century* (London, 2002).

— *History of British Art, 1600–1870*, vol. 2 (London, 2008).

Binyon, T.J., *Pushkin: A Biography* (New York, 2003).

Black, Jeremy, *Trade, Empire and British Foreign Policy, 1689–1815* (London, 2007).

Blackburn, Carole, *Harvest of Souls: The Jesuit Missions and Colonization in North America, 1632–1650* (Montreal, AC and Kingston, ON, 2000).

Blackburn, Kevin, 'Colonial Armies as Postcolonial History: Commemoration and Memory of the Malay Regiment in Modern Singapore and Malaysia', in Karl Hack and Tobias Rettig (eds), *Colonial Armies in Southeast Asia* (London, 2006), pp. 302–327.

Blackburn, Robin, 'The Old World Background to European Colonial Slavery', *William and Mary Quarterly* 54/1, 3rd Series (1997): pp. 65–102.

— *The Making of New World Slavery: From the Baroque to the Modern, 1492–1800* (London, 1997).

Blackburn, Susan, *Women and the State in Modern Indonesia* (Cambridge, 2004).

Blackhawk, Ned, *Violence over the Land: Indians and Empires in the Early American West* (Cambridge, MA, 2006).

Blake, Stephen P., 'The Patrimonial-Bureaucratic Empire of the Mughals', *Journal of Asian Studies* 39/1 (1979): pp. 77–94.

— *Shahjahanabad: The Sovereign City in Mughal India, 1639–1739* (Cambridge, 1991).

Blancpain, François, *La Colonie française de Saint-Domingue: de l'esclavage a l'indépendance* (Paris, 2004).

Blanks, David (ed.), *Images of the Other: Europe and the Muslim World Before 1700* (Cairo, 1997).

Blaufarb, Rafe, 'The Western Question: The Geopolitics of Latin American Independence', *American Historical Review* 112/3 (2007): pp. 742–63.

Blévis, Laure *et al.*, *1931: les étrangers au temps de l'Exposition coloniale* (Paris, 2008).

Bloxham, Donald, *The Great Game of Genocide: Imperialism, Nationalism, and the Destruction of the Ottoman Armenians* (Oxford, 2005).

Blum, Jerome, *Lord and Peasant in Russia: From the Ninth to the Nineteenth Century* (Princeton, NJ, 1961).

Blunt, Alison, *Domicile and Diaspora: Anglo-Indian Women and the Spatial Politics of Home* (Oxford, 2005).

Blussé, Leonard, *Bitter Bonds: A Colonial Divorce Drama of the Seventeenth Century* (Princeton, NJ, 2002).

Boahen, A. Adu, *Africa Under Colonial Domination, 1880–1935* (Berkeley, CA, 1990).

Boeck, Brian J., 'Containment vs. Colonization: Muscovite Approaches to Settling the Steppe', in Nicholas B. Breyfogle, Abby Schrader and Willard Sunderland (eds), *Peopling the Russian Periphery: Borderland Colonization in Eurasian History* (New York, 2007), pp. 21–40.

Bogdanov, M., 'Buriatskoe "vozrozhdenie"', *Sibirskie voprosy* (1907).

Bonyhady, T., *Images In Opposition: Australian Landscape Painting, 1801–1890* (Oxford, 1985).

Borah, Woodrow and Sherburne Cook, *The Aboriginal Population of Mexico on the Eve of the Spanish Conquest* (Berkeley, CA, 1963).

Borgwardt, Elizabeth, *A New Deal for the World: America's Vision for Human Rights* (Cambridge, MA, 2005).

Bose, Sugata, *A Hundred Horizons: The Indian Ocean in the Age of Global Empire* (Cambridge, MA, 2006).

— and Ayesha Jalal, *Modern South Asia: History, Culture, Political Economy* (Delhi, 1999).

Bosma, Ulbe and Remco Raben, *Being 'Dutch' in the Indies: A History of Creolisation and Empire, 1500–1920* (Athens, OH, 2008).

Bossenbroek, Martin, 'The Living Tools of Empire: The Recruitment of European Soldiers for the Dutch Colonial Army, 1814–1909', *Journal of Imperial and Commonwealth History* 23/1 (1995): pp. 25–53.

Bossenga, Gail, *The Politics of Privilege: Old Regime and Revolution in Lille* (Cambridge, 1991).

Bouche, Denise, *Les Villages de liberté en Afrique noire, 1887–1910* (Paris, 1968).

Boucher, Philip, 'The "Frontier Era" of the French Caribbean, 1620s–1690s', in Christine Daniels and Michael V. Kennedy (eds), *Negotiated Empires: Centers and Peripheries in the Americas, 1500–1820* (New York, 2002), pp. 207–234.

Bourne, Edward Gaylord, *Spain in America, 1450–1580* (New York, 1904).

Bovill, E. William, 'The Encroachment of the Sahara on the Sudan', *Journal of the Royal African Society* 20 (1921): pp. 23–45.

Bowen, H.V., *Revenue and Reform: The Indian Problem in British Politics 1757–1773* (Cambridge, 1991).

— *Elites, Enterprise and the Making of the British Overseas Empire, 1688–1775* (London, 1996).

Boxer, C.R., *Salvador de Sá and the Struggle for Brazil and Angola, 1602–1688* (London, 1952).

— *The Dutch in Brazil, 1624–1654* (Oxford, 1957).

— *Four Centuries of Portuguese Expansion, 1415–1825: A Succinct Survey* (Johannesburg, 1965).

— *The Dutch Seaborne Empire, 1600–1800* (London, 1973).

— *The Church Militant and Iberian Expansion, 1440–1770* (Baltimore, MD and London, 1978).

— *The Golden Age of Brazil: Growing Pains of a Colonial Society, 1695–1750* (Manchester, 1995).

Boyajian, James C., *Portuguese Trade in Asia under the Habsburgs, 1580–1640* (Baltimore, MD, 1993).

Boyd-Bowman, Peter, *Índice geobiográfico de cuarenta mil pobladores españoles de América en el siglo XVI*, 2 vols (Bogotá, 1964).

Bozdoğan, Sibel, *Modernism and Nation Building: Turkish Architectural Culture in the Early Republic* (Seattle, WA, 2001).

Brading, D.A., *The First America: The Spanish Monarchy, Creole Patriots, and the Liberal State, 1492–1867* (Cambridge, 1991).

Bradley, Mark, *Imagining Vietnam and American: The Making of Postcolonial Vietnam, 1919–1950* (Chapel Hill, NC, 2000).

Braginton, M.V., 'Exile Under the Roman Emperors', *Classical Journal* 39/7 (1944): pp. 391–407.

Branch, Daniel, *Defeating Mau Mau, Creating Kenya: Counterinsurgency, Civil War, and Decolonization* (Cambridge, 2009).

Brand, Michael and Glenn D. Lowry (eds), *Fatehpur-Sikri* (Bombay, 1987).

Brantlinger, Patrick, *Dark Vanishings: Discourse on the Extinction of Primitive Races, 1800–1930* (Ithaca, NY, 2003).

Braudel, Fernand, *The Mediterranean and the Mediterranean World in the Age of Philip II*, vol. 1 (London, 1972).
— *Civilization and Capitalism, 15th–18th Century*: vol. 3, *The Perspective of the World*, trans. Sian Reynolds (New York, 1984).
Breckenridge, Carol A., 'The Aesthetics and Politics of Collecting: India at the World's Fairs', *Comparative Studies in Society and History* 31/2 (1989): pp. 195–216.
— (ed.), *Consuming Modernity: Public Culture in a South Asian World* (Minneapolis, MN, 1995).
Breen, Timothy, *The Marketplace of Revolution: How Consumer Politics Shaped American Independence* (Oxford, 2004).
Brekke, Torkel, 'Mission Impossible? Baptism and the Politics of Bible Translation in Early Protestant Missions in Bengal', *History of Religion* 45 (2006): pp. 213–33.
Bremner, G. Alex, *The Gothic Revival and Empire: Religious Architecture and High Anglican Culture in Britain and the British Colonial World, 1840–1870* (forthcoming).
Brennan, Teresa, *Globalisation and its Terrors* (London, 2003).
Brenner, Robert, *Merchants and Revolution: Commercial Change, Political Conflict, and London's Overseas Traders, 1550–1653* (Princeton, NJ, 1993).
Bretelle-Establet, Florence, 'Resistance and Receptivity: French Colonial Medicine in Southwest China, 1898–1930', *Modern China* 25/2 (1999): pp. 171–203.
Brewer, John, *The Sinews of Power: War, Money, and the English State, 1688–1783* (London, 1989).
— and Roy Porter (eds), *Consumption and the World of Goods* (London, 1993).
Briggs, Laura, *Reproducing Empire: Race, Sex, Science, and US Imperialism in Puerto Rico* (Berkeley, CA, 2002).
Brock, Colin, *The Caribbean in Europe: Aspects of the West Indian Experience in Britain, France, and the Netherlands* (London, 1986).
Brockway, Lucille, *Science and Colonial Expansion* (New York, 1979).
Brokaw, Cynthia Joanne, *Commerce in Culture: The Sibao Book Trade in the Qing and Republican Periods* (Cambridge, MA, 2007).
Brook, Timothy, *Praying for Power: Buddhism and the Formation of Gentry Society in Late-Ming China* (Cambridge, MA, 1993).
— *The Confusions of Pleasure: Commerce and Culture in Ming China* (Berkeley, CA, 1998).
— and Bob Tadashi Wakabayashi (eds), *Opium Regimes: China, Britain, and Japan, 1839–1952* (Berkeley, CA, 2000).
Brooks, C.E.P., *Climate and Weather of the Falkland Islands and South Georgia* (London, 1920).
— *The Evolution of Climate* (London, 1922).
— *Variations in the Levels of Central African Lakes, Victoria and Albert* (London, 1923).
— *Climate through the Ages* (London, 1926).
Brooks, Colin, 'Public Finance and Political Stability: The Administration of the Land Tax, 1688–1720', *Historical Journal* 17/2 (1974): pp. 281–300.
Brooks, George, *Eurafricans in Western Africa: Commerce, Social Status, Gender, and Religious Observance from the Sixteenth to the Eighteenth Century* (Athens, OH, 2003).
Brower, Daniel, *Turkestan and the Fate of the Russian Empire* (London, 2003).

Brown, Christopher Leslie, *Moral Capital: Foundations of British Abolitionism* (Chapel Hill, NC, 2006).
— 'Arming Slaves in Comparative Perspective', in Christopher Leslie Brown and Philip D. Morgan (eds), *Arming Slaves: From Classical Times to the Modern Age* (New Haven, CT, 2006), pp. 330–53.
— and Philip D. Morgan (eds), *Arming Slaves: From Classical Times to the Modern Age* (New Haven, CT, 2006).
Brown, Colin, 'Sukarno on the Role of Women in the Nationalist Movement', *Review of Indonesian and Malayan Affairs* 15 (1981): pp. 68–92.
Brown, J.C., *The Hydrology of South Africa* (London, 1875).
Brown, Judith M., *Global South Asians: Introducing the Modern Diaspora* (Oxford, 2006).
Brown, Katherine Butler, 'Did Aurangzeb Ban Music? Questions for the Historiography of His Reign', *Modern Asian Studies* 41/1 (2007): pp. 77–120.
Brown, Mark, 'Colonial History and Theories of the Present: Some Reflections upon Penal History and Theory', in B. Godfrey and G. Dunstall (eds), *Crime and Empire 1840–1940: Criminal Justice in Local and Global Context* (Cullompton, 2005), pp. 76–91.
Brown, Matthew (ed.), *Informal Empire in Latin America: Culture, Commerce and Capital* (Oxford, 2008).
Browne, Janet, 'Biogeography and Empire', in N. Jardine, J.A. Secord and E.C. Spary (eds), *Cultures of Natural History* (Cambridge, 1996), pp. 305–321.
Bruk, S.I. and V.M. Kabuzan, 'Migratsiia naseleniia v Rossii v xviii-nachale xx veka (chislennost', struktura, geografiia)', *Istoriia SSSR* 4 (1984): pp. 41–59.
Brummett, Palmira, *Image and Revolution in the Ottoman Revolutionary Press, 1908–1911* (Albany, NY, 2000).
— 'Imagining the Early Modern Ottoman Space: From World History to Piri Reis', in Virginia H. Aksan and Daniel Goffman (eds), *The Early Modern Ottomans: Remapping the Empire* (Cambridge, 2007), pp. 15–58.
— 'Visions of the Mediterranean: A Classification', *Journal of Medieval and Early Modern Studies* 37/1 (2007): pp. 9–55.
Bryant, Joseph M., 'The West and the Rest Revisited: Debating Capitalist Origins, European Colonialism, and the Advent of Modernity', *Canadian Journal of Sociology/Cahiers canadiens de sociologie* 31/4 (2006): pp. 403–444.
Buchheim, Eveline, 'Geschreven levens: Brieven van Nederlandse vrouwen in Indië 1919–1940', MA dissertation, University of Amsterdam, 1999.
— 'Passie en missie: Huwelijken van Europeanen in Nederlands-Indie/Indonesië 1920–1958', PhD dissertation, Amsterdam University, 2009.
Buckley, Roger Norman, *Slaves in Red Coats: The British West India Regiments, 1795–1815* (New Haven, CT, 1979).
— *The British Army in the West Indies: Society and the Military in the Revolutionary Age* (Gainesville, FL, 1998).
Buettner, Elizabeth, *Empire Families: Britons and Late Imperial India* (Oxford, 2004).
Bulag, Uradyn Erden, *The Mongols at China's Edge: History and the Politics of National Unity* (Lanham, MD, 2002).

Burbank, Jane, 'The Rights of Difference: Law and Citizenship in the Russian Empire', in Ann Laura Stoler, Carole McGranahan, and Peter C. Perdue (eds), *Imperial Formations* (Santa Fe, NM, 2007), pp. 77-111.

— and Frederick Cooper, *Empires in World History: Power and the Politics of Difference* (Princeton, NJ, 2010).

Burke, Timothy, *Lifebuoy Men, Lux Women: Commodification, Consumption, and Cleanliness in Modern Zimbabwe* (Durham, NC, 1996).

Burkhardt, Richard W., 'The Leopard in the Garden: Life in Close Quarters at the Muséum d'Histoire Naturelle', *Isis* 98/4 (2007): pp. 675–94.

Burkholder, Mark A. and D.S. Chandler, *From Impotence to Authority: The Spanish Crown and the American Audiencias, 1687–1808* (Columbia, MO, 1977).

Burkill, Isaac Henry, *Chapters in the History of Indian Botany* (Calcutta, 1965).

Burnard, Trevor, 'The British Atlantic', in Jack P. Greene and Philip D. Morgan (eds), *Atlantic History: A Critical Appraisal* (Oxford, 2009), pp. 111–36.

Burnett, Christina Duffy and Burke Marshall (eds), *Foreign in a Domestic Sense: Puerto Rico, American Expansion, and the Constitution* (Durham, NC, 2001).

Burton, Antoinette, *Burdens of History: British Feminists, Indian Women, and Imperial Culture, 1865–1915* (Chapel Hill, NC, 1994).

— 'Making A Spectacle of Empire: Indian Travelers in Fin de Siècle London', *History Workshop Journal* 42 (1996): pp. 126–46.

— *At the Heart of the Empire: Indians and the Colonial Encounter in Later Victorian England* (Berkeley, CA, 1998).

— *Dwelling in the Archive: Women, Writing, House, Home and History in Late Colonial India* (New York, 2003).

— (ed.), *After the Imperial Turn: Thinking With and Through the Nation* (Durham, NC, 2003).

Bush, Barbara, 'Britain's Conscience on Africa: White Women, Race and Imperial Politics in Inter-war Britain', in Clare Midgley (ed.), *Gender and Imperialism* (Manchester, 1998), pp. 200–223.

— 'Gender and Empire: The Twentieth Century', in Philippa Levine (ed.), *Gender and Empire* (Oxford, 2004), pp. 77–111.

Cadiot, Juliette, 'Le recensement de 1897: les limites du côntrole imperial et la representation des nationalités', *Cahiers du monde russe* 45/3–4 (2004): pp. 441–64.

Cain, P.J., *Hobson and Imperialism: Radicalism, New Liberalism, and Finance 1887–1938* (Oxford, 2002).

— and A.G. Hopkins, *British Imperialism: Innovation and Expansion 1688–1914* (London, 1993).

Çakır, Coşkun, *Tanzimat Dönemi Osmanlı Maliye [Ottoman Finance in the Tanzimat Period]* (Istanbul, 2001).

Caldwell, R.G., 'Exile as an Institution', *Political Science Quarterly* 58/2 (1943): pp. 239–62.

Callan, Hilary and Shirley Ardener, *The Incorporated Wife* (London, 1984).

Calvo, Alfredo Castillero, *El café en Panamá: una historia social y económica: siglos XVIII–XX* (Panama, 1985).

Canaday, Margot, *The Straight State: Sexuality and Citizenship in Twentieth Century America* (Princeton, NJ, 2009).

Cañeque, A., *The King's Living Image: The Culture and Politics of Viceregal Power in Colonial Mexico* (New York, 2004).

Cañizares-Esguerra, Jorge, *Nature, Empire, and Nation: Explorations of the History of Science in the Iberian World* (Stanford, CA, 2006).

— 'Entangled Histories: Borderland Historiographies in New Clothes', *American Historical Review* 112/3 (2007): pp. 787–99.

— 'The Core and Peripheries of Our National Narratives: A Response from IH-35', *American Historical Review* 112/5 (2007): pp. 1423–33.

Cannadine, David, *Ornamentalism: How the British Saw their Empire* (London, 2002).

— (ed.), *Empire, the Sea and Global History: Britain's Maritime World, c.1760–c.1840* (London, 2007).

Canny, Nicholas, *Kingdom and Colony: Ireland in the Atlantic World, 1560–1800* (Baltimore, MD, 1988).

— *Europeans on the Move: Studies on European Migration, 1500–1800* (Oxford, 1994).

— *Making Ireland British, 1580–1650* (Oxford, 2001).

Cao, Xueqin, *The Story of the Stone* (New York, 1973).

Caplan, Karen D., 'Indigenous Citizenship: Liberalism, Political Participation, and Ethnic Identity in Post-Independence Oaxaca and Yucatán', in Andrew B. Fisher and Matthew D. O'Hara (eds), *Imperial Subjects: Race and Identity in Colonial Latin America* (Durham, NC, 2009), pp. 225–47.

Caplan, Lionel, *Warrior Gentleman: 'Gurkhas' in the Western Imagination* (Oxford, 1995).

Captain, Esther, *'Achter het kawat was Nederland': Indische oorlogservaringen en – herinneringen 1942–1995* (Kampen, 2002).

Carby, Hazel V., '"On the Threshold of Woman's Era": Lynching, Empire, and Sexuality in Black Feminist Theory', *Critical Inquiry* 12 (1985): pp. 262–77.

Cardoso, Fernando Henrique and Enzo Faletto, *Dependency and Development in Latin America* (Berkeley, CA, 1979).

Carey, Peter B.R., *Babad Dipanagara: An Account of the Outbreak of the Java War, 1825–30* (Kuala Lumpur, 1981).

Carey, Peter and Vincent Houben, 'Spirited Srikandhis and Sly Sumbradas: The Social, Political and Economic Role of Women at the Central Javanese Courts in the Eighteenth and Early Nineteenth Centuries', in Elsbeth Locher-Scholten and Anke Niehof (eds), *Indonesian Women in Focus: Past and Present Notions* (Leiden, 1992), pp. 12–42.

Carlos, Ann and Stephen Nicholas, 'Theory and History: Seventeenth-Century Joint-Stock Chartered Trading Companies', *Journal of Economic History* 56/4 (1996): pp. 916–24.

Carney, Judith and Richard Nicholas Rosomoff, *In the Shadow of Slavery: Africa's Botanical Legacy in the Atlantic World* (Berkeley, CA, 2009)

Carson, John, *The Measure of Merit: Talents, Intelligence, and Inequality in the French and American Republics, 1750–1940* (Princeton, NJ, 2007).

Carson, Rachel, *The Sea Around Us* (New York, 1951).

— *Silent Spring* (New York, 1962).

Carter, Marina, *Servants, Sirdars and Settlers: Indians in Mauritius 1834–1874* (Oxford, 1995).

— *Voices from Indenture: Experiences of Indian Migrants in the British Empire* (Leicester, 1996).

— (ed.), *Across the Kalapani: The Bihari Presence in Mauritius* (Port Louis, 1999).

— and Khal Torabully (eds), *Coolitude: An Anthology of the Indian Labour Diaspora* (London, 2002).

Carter, Paul, *The Road to Botany Bay: An Essay in Spatial History* (London, 1987).

— *The Lie of the Land* (London, 1996).

Castro-Klarén, Sara and John Charles Chasteen (eds), *Beyond Imagined Communities: Reading and Writing the Nation in Nineteenth-Century Latin America* (Baltimore, MD, 2003).

Çelik, Zeynep, *Displaying the Orient: Architecture of Istanbul at Nineteenth-Century World's Fairs* (Berkeley, CA, 1992).

Cell, Gillian T., *English Enterprise in Newfoundland, 1577–1660* (Toronto, ON, 1969).

Cerwonka, A., *Native to the Nation: Disciplining Landscapes and Bodies in Australia* (Minneapolis, MN, 2004).

Césaire, Aimé, *Discourse on Colonialism* (New York, 2000).

Chadya, Joyce M., 'Mother Politics: Anti-colonial Nationalism and the Woman Question in Africa', *Journal of Women's History* 15/3 (2003): pp. 153–7.

Chafer, Tony, *The End of Empire in French West Africa: France's Successful Decolonization?* (Oxford, 2002).

Chakrabarty, Dipesh, *Provincializing Europe: Postcolonial Thought and Historical Difference* (Princeton, NJ, 2000).

Chakravarti, Uma, 'Whatever Happened to the Vedic Dasi? Orientalism, Nationalism, and a Script for the Past', in Kumkum Sangari and Sudesh Vaid (eds), *Recasting Women: Essays in Indian Colonial History* (New Delhi, 1989), pp. 27–87.

Chakravarty, Suhash, *Afghanistan and the Great Game* (Delhi, 2002).

Chalfin, Brenda, *Shea Butter Republic: State Power, Global Markets, and the Making of an Indigenous Commodity* (New York, 2004).

Chamberlain, M.E., *Decolonization: The Fall of the European Empires* (Oxford, 1999).

Chambers, David Wade and Richard Gillespie, 'Locality in the History of Science: Colonial Science, Technoscience, and Indigenous Knowledge', *Osiris* 15 (2000): pp. 221–40.

Chan, Sucheng, *Asian Americans: An Interpretive History* (New York, 1993).

Chandavarkar, Rajnarayan, 'Plague, Panic and Epidemic Politics in India, 1896–1914', in Terence Ranger and Paul Slack (eds), *Epidemics and Ideas: Essays on the Historical Perception of Pestilence* (Cambridge, 1992), pp. 203–240.

Chandra, Satish, *Parties and Politics at the Mughal Court, 1707–1740* (Delhi, 2002).

Chang, Derek, *Citizens of a Christian Nation: Evangelical Missions and the Problem of Race in the Nineteenth Century* (Philadelphia, PA, 2010).

Chang, Hsin-Pao, *Commissioner Lin and the Opium War* (Cambridge, MA, 1964).

Chang, Michael, *A Court on Horseback: Imperial Touring and the Construction of Qing Rule, 1680–1785* (Cambridge, MA, 2007).

Chanock, Martin, *Law, Custom and Social Order: The Colonial Experience in Malawi and Zambia* (Cambridge, 1985).

Chari, R.P., *Missing Boundaries: Refugees, Migrants, Stateless and Internally Displaced Persons in South Asia* (New Delhi, 2003).

Chatterjee, Indrani (ed.), *Unfamiliar Relations: Family and History in South Asia* (New Brunswick, NJ, 2004).

Chatterjee, Partha, *The Nation and Its Fragments: Colonial and Postcolonial Histories* (Princeton, NJ, 1993).

— *Nationalist Thought and the Colonial World: A Derivative Discourse* (London, 1993).

— 'Our Modernity', in *The Present History of West Bengal* (Delhi, 1997), pp. 193–210.

Chatterjee, Piya, *A Time for Tea: Women, Labor and Post/Colonial Politics on an Indian Plantation* (Durham, NC, 2001).

Chaturvedi, Vinayak (ed.), *Mapping Subaltern Studies and the Postcolonial* (London, 2000).

Chaudhuri, K.N., *The English East India Company: The Study of an Early Joint-Stock Company, 1600–1640* (London, 1965).

— *The Trading World of Asia and the English East India Company, 1660–1760* (Cambridge, 1978).

— *Trade and Civilisation in the Indian Ocean: An Economic History from the Rise of Islam to 1750* (Cambridge, 1985)

— *Asia before Europe: Economy and Civilisation of the Indian Ocean from the Rise of Islam to 1750* (Cambridge, 1990).

Chauduri, Nupur and Margaret Strobel (eds), *Western Women and Imperialism: Complicity and Resistance* (Bloomington, IN, 1992).

Chaunu, Huguette and Pierre Chaunu, *Seville et l'Atlantique, 1504–1650*, 8 vols (Paris, 1955–59).

Chaunu, Pierre, *Les Philippines et le Pacifique des Ibériques (XVIe, XVIIe, XVIIIe siècles): introduction méthodologique et indices d'activité* (Paris, 1960).

— *L'Expansion Européenne du XIIIe au XVe siècle* (Paris, 1969).

Chen, Ching-chih, 'Policy and Community Control Systems in the Empire', in Ramon H. Myers and Mark R. Peattie (eds), *The Japanese Colonial Empire, 1895–1945* (Princeton, NJ, 1984), pp. 213–39.

Child, Josiah, *A New Discourse of Trade* (London, 1694).

Childe, Vere Gordon, *Dawn of European Civilization* (London, 1925).

— *New Light on the Most Ancient East* (London, 1933).

— *Man Makes Himself* (London, 1936).

Chin, J.K., 'The Hokkien Merchants in the South China Sea: 1500–1800', in Om Prakash (ed.), *Trading World of the Indian Ocean 1500–1800* (Delhi, 2012), pp. 433-62.

Chin, Rita, *The Guest Worker Question in Postwar Germany* (Cambridge, 2007).

Ching, Leo T.S., *Becoming 'Japanese': Colonial Taiwan and the Politics of Identity Formation* (Berkeley, CA, 2001).

Chō, Kyŏngdal, *Itan no Minshūhanran* (Tokyo, 1998).

— *Chōsen'minshū'undō no Tenkai* (Tokyo, 2002).

— 'Shokuminchikindaiseiron hihan', in *Shokuminchikichōsen no Chishikijin to Minshū* (Tokyo, 2008).

Choi, Kyeong Hee, 'Neither Colonial Nor National: The Making of the "New Woman" in Pak Wansŏ's "Mother's Stake I"', in Gi-Wook Shin and Michael Robinson (eds), *Colonial Modernity in Korea* (Cambridge, MA, 1999), pp. 221–47.

Chomsky, Noam, *Hegemony or Survival: America's Quest for Global Dominance* (Boston, MA, 2003).

Choy, Catherine Ceniza, *Empire of Care: Nursing and Migration in Filipino American History* (Durham, NC, 2003).

Christopher, Emma, *A Merciless Place: The Fate of Britain's Convicts after the American Revolution* (Oxford and New York, 2011).

Church, Joe, *Awake Uganda!* (Kampala, 1957).

— *Quest for the Highest* (Exeter, 1981).

Cipolla, Carlo, *Guns, Sails, and Empires: Technological Innovation and the Early Phases of European Expansion 1400–1700* (New York, 1965).

Clancy-Smith, Julia, *Rebel and Saint: Muslim Notables, Populist Protest, Colonial Encounters (Algeria and Tunisia, 1800–1904)* (Berkeley, CA, 1994).

— 'Islam, Gender and Identities in the Making of French Algeria, 1830–1962', in Julia Clancy-Smith and Frances Gouda (eds), *Domesticating the Empire: Race, Gender, and Family Life in French and Dutch Colonialism*, (Charlottesville, VA, 1998), pp. 154–74.

— 'Marginality and Migration: Europe's Social Outcasts in Pre-Colonial Tunisia, c.1830–1881', in Eugene Rogan (ed.), *Outside In: On the Margins of the Modern Middle East* (London, 2002), pp. 149–82.

— 'The Intimate, the Familial, and the Local in Transnational Histories of Gender', *Journal of Women's History* 18/2 (2006): pp. 174–83.

Clapham, J., *The Bank of England, 1694–1797* (London, 1945).

Clarence-Smith, William Gervase and Steven Topik (eds), *The Global Coffee Economy in Africa, Asia and Latin America, 1500–1989* (Cambridge, 2003).

Clay, Christopher, *Gold for the Sultan* (London, 2000).

Clayton, Anthony and Donald C. Savage, *Government and Labour in Kenya, 1895–1963* (London, 1999).

Cleghorn, H.F., *The Forests and Gardens of South India* (Edinburgh, 1861).

Clendinnen, Inga, *Aztecs: An Interpretation* (Cambridge, 1991).

— *Dancing with Strangers: Europeans and Australians at First Contact* (Cambridge, 2005).

Clerke, E.M., 'Assam and the Indian Tea Trade', *Asiatic Quarterly Review* 5 (1888): pp. 381–3.

Cline, Catherine, *E.D. Morel, 1873–1924: The Strategies of Protest* (Belfast, 1980).

Clunas, Craig, *Superfluous Things: Material Culture and Social Status in Early Modern China* (Cambridge, 1991).

Coates, T.J., *Convicts and Orphans: Forced and State-Sponsored Colonizers in the Portuguese Empire, 1550–1755* (Stanford, CA, 2001).

Codell, Julie F. (ed.), *Photography and the Imperial Durbars of British India* (London, 2010).

Cohen, Lizabeth, *A Consumers' Republic: The Politics of Mass Consumption in Postwar America* (New York, 2003).

Cohen, Paul A., *Discovering History in China: American Historical Writing on the Recent Chinese Past* (New York, 1984).

— *History in Three Keys: The Boxers as Event, Experience, and Myth* (New York, 1997).

Cohen, Robin, *The Cambridge Survey of World Migration* (New York, 1995).

Cohn, Bernard S., 'Representing Authority in Victorian India', in Eric J. Hobsbawm and Terence Ranger (eds), *The Invention of Tradition* (Cambridge, 1983), pp. 165–210.

— 'The Census, Social Structure and Objectification in South Asia', in Bernard S. Cohn, *An Anthropologist among the Historians and Other Essays* (Oxford, 1987), pp. 224–54.

— *Colonialism and its Forms of Knowledge: The British in India* (Princeton, NJ, 1996).

Cohn, Carol, 'Wars, Wimps, and Women: Talking Gender and Thinking War', in Miriam Cooke and Angela Woollacott (eds), *Gendering War Talk* (Princeton, NJ, 1993), pp. 227–46.

Cole, Juan, *Napoleon's Egypt: Invading the Middle East* (London, 2007).

Coleman, D.C., *Sir John Banks, Baronet and Businessman: A Study of Business, Politics and Society in Later Stuart England* (Oxford, 1963).

Colinvaux, Paul, *The Fates of Nations: A Biological Theory of History* (New York, 1980).

Collett, Nigel, *The Butcher of Amritsar: Brigadier-General Reginald Dyer* (London, 2005).

Colley, Linda, *Britons, Forging the Nation 1707–1837* (London, 1994).

Collingham, E.W., *Imperial Bodies: The Physical Experience of the Raj, c.1800–1947* (Cambridge, 2001).

Comaroff, John L. and Jean, *Of Revelation and Revolution: The Dialectics of Modernity on a South African Frontier*, vol. 2 (Chicago, IL, 1997).

Conekin, Becky, Frank Mort and Chris Waters (eds), *Moments of Modernity: Reconstructing Britain 1945–1964* (London, 1999).

Conklin, Alice L., *A Mission to Civilize: The Republican Idea of Empire in France and West Africa, 1895–1930* (Stanford, CA, 1997).

— 'Redefining "Frenchness": Citizenship, Race, Regeneration and Imperial Motherhood in France and West Africa, 1914–1940', in Julia Clancy-Smith and Frances Gouda (eds), *Domesticating the Empire: Race, Gender, and Family Life in French and Dutch Colonialism* (Charlottesville, VA: 1998), pp. 65–83.

— 'Civil Society, Science, and Empire in Late Republican France: The Foundation of Paris's Museum of Man', *Osiris* 17 (2002): pp. 255–90.

Connelly, Matthew, *A Diplomatic Revolution: Algeria's Fight for Independence and the Origins of the Post-Cold War Era* (Oxford, 2002).

Conrad, Sebastian, 'What Time is Japan? Problems of Comparative (Intercultural) Historiography', *History and Theory* 38 (1999): pp. 75–81.

Constantine, Stephen, *The Making of British Colonial Development Policy, 1914–1940* (London, 1984).

— '"Bringing the Empire Alive": The Empire Marketing Board and Imperial Propaganda, 1926–33', in John MacKenzie (ed.), *Imperialism and Popular Culture* (Manchester, 1986), pp. 192–231.

Cook, Harold, *Matters of Exchange: Commerce, Medicine, and Science in the Dutch Golden Age* (New Haven, CT, 2007).

Cook, Noble David, *Born to Die: Disease and New World Conquest, 1492–1650* (Cambridge, 1998).

— 'Sickness, Starvation, and Death in Early Hispaniola', *Journal of Interdisciplinary History* 32/3 (2002): pp. 349–86.

Coombes, Annie E., *Reinventing Africa: Museums, Material Culture, and Popular Imagination in Late Victorian and Edwardian England* (New Haven, CT, 1994).

Cooper, Frederick, *Decolonization and African Society: The Labor Question in French and British Africa* (Cambridge, 1996).

— *Africa Since 1940: The Past of the Present* (Cambridge, 2002).

— 'Empire Multiplied', *Comparative Studies in Society and History* 46 (2004): pp. 247–72.

— *Colonialism in Question: Theory, Knowledge, History* (Berkeley, CA, 2005).

— and Ann Laura Stoler (eds), *Tensions of Empire: Colonial Cultures in a Bourgeois World* (Berkeley, CA, 1997)

—, Thomas C. Holt and Rebecca J. Scott, *Beyond Slavery: Explorations of Race, Labor and Citizenship in Postemancipation Societies* (Chapel Hill, NC, 2000).

— et al. (eds), *Confronting Historical Paradigms: Peasants, Labor, and the Capitalist World System in Africa and Latin America* (Madison, WI, 1993).

Cooper, Glenn (ed.), *Landscape and Empire, 1770–2000* (Aldershot, 2005).

Cooper, Randolph G.S., *The Anglo-Maratha Campaigns and the Contest for India* (Cambridge, 2003).

Cope, R. Douglas, *The Limits of Racial Domination: Plebeian Society in Colonial Mexico City, 1660–1720* (Madison, WI, 1994).

Corona, Gabriella (ed.), 'Forum: What is Global Environmental History', *Global Environment* 2 (2008).

Cosgrove, D. and S. Daniel, *The Iconography of the Landscape: Essays on the Symbolic Representation, Design and Use of Past Environment* (Cambridge, 1989).

Costa, Emilia Viotti da, *The Brazilian Empire: Myths and Histories*, 2nd edn (Chapel Hill, NC, 2000).

Costigliola, Frank, *Awkward Dominion: American Political, Economic, and Cultural Relations with Europe, 1919–1933* (Ithaca, NY, 1984).

Coté, Joost (ed. and trans.), *Letters from Kartini, an Indonesian Feminist, 1900–1904* (Clayton, VC, 1992).

Coutu, Joan, *Persuasion and Propaganda: Monuments and Eighteenth-Century British Empire* (Montreal, QC, 2007).

Cowling, Mary, *The Artist as Anthropologist* (Cambridge, 1989).

Cox, Jeffrey, *Imperial Fault Lines: Christianity and Colonial Power in India, 1818–1940* (Stanford, CA, 2002).

Craib, Raymond B., 'Standard Plots and Rural Resistance', in Gilbert Michael Joseph and Timothy J. Henderson (eds), *The Mexico Reader, History, Culture, Politics* (Durham, NC, 2002), pp. 252–62.

Crinson, Mark, *Empire Building: Orientalism and Victorian Architecture* (London, 1995).

Cronon, William, *Changes in the Land: Indians, Colonists, and the Ecology of New England* (New York, 1983).

— *Nature's Metropolis: Chicago and the Great West* (New York, 1991).

—, George Miles and Jay Gitlin (eds), *Under an Open Sky: Rethinking America's Western Past* (New York, 1992).

Crosby, Alfred, *The Columbian Exchange: Biological and Cultural Consequences of 1492* (Westport, CT, 1972).

— *Ecological Imperialism: The Biological Expansion of Europe, 900–1900* (Cambridge, 1986).

Crossley, Pamela Kyle, *A Translucent Mirror: History and Identity in Qing Imperial Ideology* (Berkeley, CA, 1999).

—, Helen F. Siu and Donald S. Sutton (eds), *Empire at the Margins: Culture, Ethnicity, and Frontier in Early Modern China* (Berkeley, CA, 2006).

Crowder, Michael, 'Indirect Rule: French and British Style', *Africa: Journal of the International African Institute* 34/3 (1964): pp. 197–205.

Crowe, S.E., *The Berlin West African Conference, 1884–1885* (Westport, CT, 1970).

Crozier, Anna, *Practising Colonial Medicine: The Colonial Medical Service in British East Africa* (London, 2007).

Cumings, Bruce, *Dominion from Sea to Sea: Pacific Ascendancy and American Power* (New Haven, CT, 2009).

Cuordileone, K.A., *Manhood and American Political Culture in the Cold War* (New York, 2005).

Curtin, Philip D., *The Atlantic Slave Trade: A Census* (Madison, WI, 1969).

— *Cross-Cultural Trade in World History* (New York, 1984).

— *Death by Migration: Europe's Encounter with the Tropical World in the Nineteenth Century* (New York, 1989).

— *The World and the West: The European Challenge and the Overseas Response in the Age of Empire* (Cambridge, 2000).

Custine, Marquis de, *Letters from Russia* (New York, 1991).

Dabydeen, David, *Hogarth's Blacks: Images of Blacks in Eighteenth Century English Art* (Kingston-upon-Thames, 1987).

Dale, Stephen Frederic, 'Steppe Humanism: The Autobiographical Writings of Zahir al-Din Muhammad Babur, 1483–1530', *International Journal of Middle East Studies* 22 (1990): pp. 37–58.

— *Garden of the Eight Paradises: Babur and the Culture of Empire in Central Asia, Afghanistan, and India* (Leiden, 2004).

Dalrymple, William, *Last Mughal: The Fall of a Dynasty: Delhi, 1857* (New York, 2007).

Daly, M.W. and Jane R. Hogan, *Images of Empire: Photographic Sources for the British in Sudan* (Leiden, 2005).

Damodaran, Vinita, 'Environment and Empire: A Major Theme in World Environmental History', in Mary Harris and Csaba Levai (eds), *Europe and its Empires* (Pisa, 2008), pp. 129–39.

Damousi, Joy, *Depraved and Disorderly: Female Convicts, Sexuality and Gender in Colonial Australia* (Cambridge, 1997).

Daniels, Roger, *Guarding the Golden Door: American Immigration Policy and Immigrants since 1882* (New York, 2004).

Darby, Henry, *The Domesday Geography of Eastern England* (Cambridge, 1952).

Darling, Linda, 'Public Finances: The Role of the Ottoman Centre', in Suraiya N. Faroqhi (ed.), *Cambridge History of Turkey*: vol. 3, *The Later Ottoman Empire 1603–1839* (Cambridge, 2006), pp. 118–31.

Darrow, David W., 'Census as a Technology of Empire', *Ab Imperio* 4 (2002): pp. 145–76.

Darwin, John, *Britain, Egypt, and the Middle East: Imperial Policy in the Aftermath of War, 1918–1922* (Basingstoke, 1981).

— *The End of the British Empire: The Historical Debate* (Oxford, 1991).

— *After Tamerlane: The Rise and Fall of Global Empires, 1400–2000* (Harmondsworth, 2008).

— 'Britain's Empires', in Sarah Stockwell (ed.), *The British Empire: Themes and Perspectives* (Oxford, 2008), pp. 1–20.

— *The Empire Project: The Rise and Fall of the British World-system, 1830-1970* (Cambridge, 2009).

Das, Anirban and Ritu Sen Chaudhuri, 'The Desired "One": Thinking the Woman in the Nation', *History Compass* 5 (2007): pp. 1483–99.

Das, Santanu, *Race, Empire and First World War Writing* (Cambridge, 2011).

Das Gupta, Ashin, *India and the Indian Ocean World: Trade and Politics* (Delhi, 2004).

Daughton, J.P., *An Empire Divided: Religion, Republicanism, and the Making of French Colonialism, 1880–1914* (Oxford, 2008).

Davis, David Brion, *The Problem of Slavery in Western Culture* (Ithaca, NY, 1966).

— *Slavery and Human Progress* (New York, 1986).

Davis, F. James, *Who Is Black? One Nation's Definition* (University Park, PA, 1991).

Davis, Kathy, 'Intersectionality as Buzzword: A Sociology of Science Perspective on what Makes a Feminist Theory Successful', *Feminist Theory* 9 (2008): pp. 67–85.

Davis, Kingsley, *The Population of India and Pakistan* (Princeton, NJ, 1951).

Davis, Mary, *Sylvia Pankhurst: A Life in Radical Politics* (Sterling, VA, 1999).

Davis, Mike, *Late Victorian Holocausts: El Niño Famines and the Making of the Third World* (New York, 2001).

Davis, Shelby Cullom, *Reservoirs of Men: History of the Black Troops of French West Africa* (Santa Barbara, CA, 1970).

Day, Tony, 'Ties that Unbind: Families and States in Premodern Southeast Asia', *Journal of Asian Studies* 55 (1996): pp. 384–409.

Dean, Robert D., *Imperial Brotherhood: Gender and the Making of Cold War Foreign Policy* (Amherst, MA, 2001).

De Barros, Juanita, Steven Palmer and David Wright (eds), *Health and Medicine in the Circum-Caribbean, 1800–1968* (Hoboken, NJ, 2009).

De Bary, William Theodore (ed.), *Self and Society in Ming Thought* (New York, 1970).

Debenham, F., *Kalahari Sands* (London, 1953).

— *Nyasaland: The Land of the Lake* (London, 1955).

Decisions of the Superior Courts of New South Wales, 1788–1899, Published by the Division of Law, Macquarie University, www.law.mq.edu.au/scnsw/cases1840–41/RvDundomah,1840.htm.

De Ceuster, Koen, 'The Nation Exorcised: The Historiography of Collaboration in South Korea', *Korean Studies* 25 (2002): pp. 207–242.

Degn, C., *Die Schimmelmanns im atlantischen Dreieckshandel* (Neumünster, 1974).

de Groot, Joanna, 'Metropolitan Desires and Colonial Connections: Reflections on Consumption and Empire', in Catherine Hall and Sonya O. Rose (eds), *At Home with the Empire: Metropolitan Culture and the Imperial World* (Cambridge, 2006), pp. 166–90.

DeLay, Brian, *War of a Thousand Deserts: Indian Raids and the US-Mexican War* (New Haven, CT, 2008).

Deleuze, Gilles and Félix Guattari, *A Thousand Plateaus: Capitalism and Schizophrenia* (London, 2002).

Deloria, Philip J., *Playing Indian* (New Haven, CT, 1998).

— and Neal Salisbury (eds), *A Companion to Native American History* (Malden, MA, 2002).

de Madariaga, Isabel, *Ivan the Terrible: First Tsar of Russia* (New Haven, CT, 2005).

de Moor, Jaap, 'The Recruitment of Indonesian Soldiers for the Dutch Colonial Army, c. 1700–1950', in David Killingray and David Omissi (eds), *Guardians of Empire: The Armed Forces of the Colonial Powers c. 1700–1964* (Manchester, 1999), pp. 53–69.

de Mul, Sarah P.J., '"Yesterday does not go by": The Return to the Colonial Past in Women's Travel Writing and the Contingencies of Dutch and British Cultures of Remembrance', PhD dissertation, Amsterdam University, 2007.

Deringil, Selim, *The Well-Protected Domains: Ideology and Legitimation of Power in the Ottoman Empire, 1876–1909* (London, 1997).

Derrick, Jonathan, *Africa's 'Agitators': Militant Anti-Colonialism in Africa and the West, 1918–1939* (New York, 2008).

Desmond, Adrian, *Huxley: The Devil's Disciple*, 2 vols (London, 1994).

— *Huxley: From Devil's Disciple to Evolution's High Priest* (London, 1998).

Desmond, Ray, *The European Discovery of the Indian Flora* (Oxford 1992).

— *The History of the Royal Botanic Gardens, Kew* (Cumbria, 1997).

Dettlebach, Michael, 'The Stimulations of Travel: Humboldt's Physiological Construction of the Tropics', in Felix Driver and Luciana Martins (eds), *Tropical Visions in an Age of Empire* (Chicago, IL, 2005), pp. 43–58.

— 'Romanticism and Resistance: Humboldt and German "Natural Philosophy" in Napoleonic France', *Boston Studies in the Philosophy of Science* 241 (2007): pp. 247–58.

Deutsch, Jan-Georg, *Emancipation Without Abolition in German East Africa, c.1884–1914* (Oxford, 2006).

—, Peter Probst and Heike Schmidt (eds), *African Modernities: Entangled Meanings in Current Debate* (Portsmouth, 2002).

de Uztáriz, Geronimo, *Theory and Practice of Commerce and Maritime Affairs* (London, 1751.

de Vries, Jan, 'The Dutch Atlantic Economies', in Peter Coclanis (ed.), *The Atlantic Economy During the Seventeenth and Eighteenth Centuries: Organization, Operation, Practice and Personnel* (Columbia, SC, 2005), pp. 1–29.

Diamond, Jared, *Guns, Germs and Steel: The Fates of Human Societies* (New York, 1997).

Dickson, P.G.M., *The Financial Revolution: A Study in the Development of Public Credit, 1688–1756* (London, 1967).

— and J. Sperling, 'War Finance 1689–1715', in J.S. Bromley (ed.), *New Cambridge Modern History*, vol. 6 (London, 1971), pp. 284–314.

Diderot, Denis, *Supplément au voyage de Bougainville, ou dialogue entre A et B* ([Paris], 1772).

Digby, Simon, 'An Eighteenth Century Narrative of a Journey from Bengal to England: Munshi Isma'il's New History', in Christopher Shackle (ed.), *Urdu and Muslim South Asia: Studies in Honour of Ralph Russell* (London, 1989), pp. 49–65.

Dikötter, Frank, *The Discourse of Race in Modern China* (Stanford, CA, 1992).

Diop, Cheikh Anta, *Civilization or Barbarism: An Authentic Anthropology* (Chicago, IL, 1991).

Dirks, Nicholas B., *Colonialism and Culture* (Ann Arbor, MI, 1992).

— *Castes of Mind: Colonialism and the Making of Modern India* (Princeton, NJ, 2001).

Dirlik, Arif, *The Postcolonial Aura: Third World Criticism in the Age of Global Capitalism* (Boulder, CO, 1997).

— Vinay Bahl and Peter Gran (eds), *History After the Three Worlds: Post-Eurocentric Historiographies* (Lanham, MD, 2000).

Dixon, R., *The Course of Empire: Neoclassical Culture in New South Wales, 1788–1860* (Melbourne, 1986).

Do, Myŏnhwoe, 'Singminjuŭi ga nurak doen "singminji kŭndaesŏng"', *Yŏksa Munje Yŏngu* 7 (2001).

Doak, Kevin M., 'What is a Nation and Who Belongs? National Narratives and the Ethnic Imagination in Twentieth-Century Japan', *American Historical Review* 102 (1997): pp. 283–309.

Dodson, Michael, *Orientalism, Empire, and National Culture: India, 1770–1880* (Basingstoke, 2007).

Donald, Diana and Jane Munro (eds), *Endless Forms: Charles Darwin, Natural History and the Visual Arts* (Cambridge, 2009).

Donato, Marc, *L'Émigration des Maltais en Algérie au XIXème siècle* (Montpellier, 1985).

Dorfman, Ariel and Armand Mattelart, *How to Read Donald Duck: Imperialist Ideology in the Disney Comic* (New York, 1975).

Dosal, Paul J., *Doing Business with the Dictators: A Political History of United Fruit in Guatemala, 1899–1944* (Wilmington, DE, 1993).

Doumani, Beshara, *Rediscovering Palestine: Merchants and Peasants in Jabal Nablus 1700–1900* (Berkeley, CA, 1995).

Doumanis, Nicholas, 'Durable Empire: State Virtuosity and Social Accommodation in the Ottoman Mediterranean', *Historical Journal* 49/3 (2006): pp. 953–66.

Dower, John W., *War Without Mercy: Race and Power in the Pacific War* (New York, 1986).

— *Embracing Defeat: Japan in the Wake of World War II* (New York, 1999).

Drayton, Richard, *Nature's Government: Science, Imperial Britain, and the 'Improvement' of the World* (New Haven, CT, 2000).

Dreyer, Edward, *Zheng He: China and the Oceans in the Early Ming Dynasty, 1405–1433* (New York, 2007).

Driesen, Ian van den, *The Long Walk: Indian Plantation Labour in Sri Lanka in the Nineteenth Century* (New Delhi, 1997).

Drinnon, Richard, *Facing West: The Metaphysics of the of Indian-Hating and Empire-Building* (Minneapolis, MN, 1980).

Driver, Felix, *Geography Militant: Cultures of Exploration and Empire* (Oxford, 2001).

D'Souza, Rohan, 'Nature, Conservation and Environmental History: A Review of Some Recent Environmental Writings on South Asia', *Conservation and Society* 1/2 (2003): pp. 117–32.

— *The Drowned and the Dammed: Colonial Capitalism and Flood Control in Eastern India* (Delhi, 2006).

Duara, Prasenjit, *Rescuing History from the Nation: Questioning Narratives of Modern China* (Chicago, IL, 1995).

— (ed.), *Decolonization: Perspectives from Now and Then* (New York, 2004).

— 'The Imperialism of "Free Nations": Japan, Manchukuo, and the History of the Present', in Ann L. Stoler, Carole McGranahan and Peter C. Perdue (eds), *Imperial Formations* (New York, 2007), pp. 211–39.

Du Bois, W.E.B., 'The African Roots of War' (1915), in Herbert Aptheker (ed.), *Writings by W.E.B. DuBois in Periodicals Edited by Others* (Millwood, NY, 1982).

— *Dusk of Dawn: An Essay Toward an Autobiography of a Race Concept* (New Brunswick, NJ, 2002).

Dubois, Laurent, *A Colony of Citizens: Revolution and Slave Emancipation in the French Caribbean, 1787–1804* (Chapel Hill, NC, 2004).

— *Avengers of the New World: The Story of the Haitian Revolution* (Cambridge, MA, 2004).

Duffy, James, *Portugal in Africa* (Cambridge, MA, 1962).

Dumett, Raymond E. (ed.), *Gentlemanly Capitalism and British Imperialism: The New Debate on Empire* (London, 1999).

Duncan, T. Bentley, *Atlantic Islands: Madeira, the Azores, and the Cape Verdes in Seventeenth Century Commerce and Navigation* (Chicago, IL, 1972).Dundas, K.R., 'Notes on the Origin and History of the Kikuyu and Dorobo Tribes', *Man* 8 (1908): pp. 136–9.

Dunn, Richard, 'The Barbados Census of 1680: Profile of the Richest Colony in English America', *William and Mary Quarterly* 26/1, 3rd Series (1969): pp. 4–30.

Durkheim, Emile, *The Elementary Forms of Religious Life* (Oxford, 2001).

Dutta, Arindam, *The Bureaucracy of Beauty: Design in the Age of Global Reproducibility* (London, 2006).

Duval, Eugène-Jean, *La Révolte des sagaies: Madagascar 1947* (Paris, 2002).

Dyde, Brian, *The Empty Sleeve: The Story of the West India Regiments of the British Army* (St Johns, Antigua, 1997).

Dyke, Paul A. van, *The Canton Trade: Life and Enterprise on the China Coast, 1700–1845* (Hong Kong, 2005).

Eastwood, David and Laurence Brockliss (eds), *A Union of Multiple Identities: The British Isles, c.1750–c.1850* (Manchester, 1997).

Eaton, Natasha, 'Between Mimesis and Alterity: Art, Gift and Diplomacy in Colonial India', *Comparative Studies in Society and History* 46/4 (2004): pp. 816–44.

Eccles, W.J., *France in America* (New York, 1972).

Echenberg, Myron, *Colonial Conscripts: The Tirailleurs Sénégalais in French West Africa, 1857–1960* (Portsmouth, NH, 1991).

Eckert, Carter, *Offspring of Empire: The Koch'ang Kims and the Colonial Origins of Korean Capitalism 1876–1945* (Seattle, WA, 1991).

Edgerton-Tarpley, Kathryn, *Tears from Iron: Cultural Responses to Famine in Nineteenth-Century China* (Berkeley, CA, 2008).

Edmunds, R. David, 'Native Americans and the United States, Canada, and Mexico', in Philip J. Deloria and Neal Salisbury (eds), *A Companion to American Indian History* (Malden, MA, 2002), pp. 397–421.

Edney, Matthew, *Mapping an Empire: The Geographical Construction of British India, 1765–1843* (Chicago, IL, 1997).

Edwards, Brent, *The Practice of Diaspora: Literature, Translation, and the Rise of Black Internationalism* (Cambridge, MA, 2003).

Edwards, Elizabeth (ed.), *Anthropology and Photography* (London, 1992).

Edwards, Penny, 'Womanizing Indochina: Fiction, Nation and Cohabitation in Colonial Cambodia, 1890–1930', in Julia Clancy-Smith and Frances Gouda (eds), *Domesticating the Empire: Race, Gender, and Family Life in French and Dutch Colonialism* (Charlottesville, VA, 1998), pp. 108–130.

— *Cambodge: The Cultivation of a Nation, 1860–1945* (Honolulu, HI, 2007).

Ehret, Christopher, 'Sudanic Civilizations', in Michael Adas (ed.), *Agricultural and Pastoral Societies in Classical History* (Philadelphia, PA, 2001), pp. 224–74.

Eichengreen, Barry and Marc Flandreau (eds), *The Gold Standard in Theory and History* (New York, 1985).

Eisenberg, Carolyn Woods, *Drawing the Line: The American Decision to Divide Germany, 1945–1949* (Cambridge, 1996).

Eisenman, Stephen F., *Gauguin's Skirt* (London, 1997).

Ekirch, A. Roger, *Bound for America: The Transportation of British Convicts to the Colonies, 1718–1775* (Oxford, 1987).

El-Haj, Rifa'at Ali Abou, *Formation of the State: The Ottoman Empire Sixteenth to Eighteenth Centuries* (Albany, NY, 1991).

Elbourne, Elizabeth, *Blood Ground: Colonialism, Missions, and the Contest for Christianity in the Cape Colony and Britain, 1799–1853* (Montreal, QC, 2002).

Eldem, Edhem, *History of the Ottoman Bank* (Istanbul, 1999).

— 'Capitulations and Western Trade', in Suraiya N. Faroqhi (ed.), *Cambridge History of Turkey*: vol. 3, *The Later Ottoman Empire 1603–1839* (Cambridge, 2006), pp. 283–335.

Eley, Geoff (ed.), *Becoming National: A Reader* (New York 1996).

Elkins, Caroline, *Imperial Reckoning: The Untold Story of Britain's Gulag in Kenya* (New York, 2005).

— and Susan Pedersen (eds), *Settler Colonialism in the Twentieth Century: Projects, Practices, Legacies* (New York, 2005).

Ellinghaus, Katherine, 'Biological Absorption and Genocide: A Comparison of Indigenous Assimilation Policies in the United States and Australia', *Genocide Studies and Prevention* 4/1 (2009): pp. 59–79.

Ellinwood, DeWitt C. and S.D. Pradhan (eds), *India and World War I* (Columbia, MO, 1978).

Elliot, Henry Miers, *History of India, as Told by Its Own Historians*, ed. John Dowson, 8 vols (London, 1867–77).

Elliott, J.H., *The Revolt of the Catalans: A Study in the Decline of Spain, 1580–1640* (Cambridge, 1963).

— 'A Europe of Composite Monarchies', *Past and Present* 137 (1992): pp. 48–71.

— *Empires of the Atlantic World: Britain and Spain in America, 1492–1830* (New Haven, CT, 2006).

Elliott, Mark C., *The Manchu Way: The Eight Banners and Ethnic Identity in Late Imperial China* (Stanford, CA, 2001).

Elman, Benjamin, *From Philosophy to Philology: Intellectual and Social Aspects of Change in Late Imperial China* (Cambridge, MA, 1984).

— *On Their Own Terms: Science in China, 1550–1900* (Cambridge, MA, 2005).

Elphick, Richard and Hermann Giliomee (eds), *The Shaping of South African Society, 1652–1840* (Middletown, CT, 1989).

Eltis, David, *The Rise of African Slavery in the Americas* (Cambridge, 2000).

— (ed.), *Coerced and Free Migration: Global Perspectives* (Stanford, CA, 2002).

Elvin, Mark, *The Pattern of the Chinese Past* (Stanford, CA, 1973).

— 'Three Thousand Years of Unsustainable Growth: China's Environment from Archaic Times to the Present', *East Asian History* 6 (1993): pp. 7–46.

— *The Retreat of the Elephants: The Environmental History of China* (New Haven, CT, 2004).

Emmer, Pieter C., 'The Meek Hindu: The Recruitment of Indian Indentured Labourers for Service Overseas, 1870–1916', in Pieter C. Emmer (ed.), *Colonialism and Migration: Indentured Labour Before and After Slavery* (Dordrecht, 1983), pp. 187–207.

Enwezor, Okwui, 'Preface', *Documenta 11* (Kassel, 2002).

Erdem, Hakan, *Slavery in the Ottoman Empire and its Demise, 1800–1909* (New York, 1996).

Erdman, David, *Blake: Prophet Against Empire* (London, 1978).

Erickson, Edward J., *Ordered to Die: A History of the Ottoman Army in the First World War* (Westport, CT, 2000).

— *Defeat in Detail: The Ottoman Army in the Balkans 1912–1913* (Westport, CT, 2003).

Erimtan, Can, *The Origins of the Tulip Age and its Development in Modern Turkey* (London, 2008).

Eschen, Penny M. von, *Race Against Empire: Black Americans and Anticolonialism, 1937–1957* (Ithaca, NY, 1997).

— *Satchmo Blows Up the World: Jazz Ambassadors Play the Cold War* (Cambridge, MA, 2004).

Escobar, Arturo, *Encountering Development: The Making and Unmaking of the Third World* (Princeton, NJ, 1995).

Esherick, Joseph W., *Reform and Revolution in China: The 1911 Revolution in Hunan and Hubei* (Berkeley, CA, 1976).

— *The Origins of the Boxer Uprising* (Berkeley, CA, 1987).

— Hasan Kayali and Eric van Young, *Empire to Nation: Historical Perspectives on the Making of the Modern World* (Lanham, MD, 2006).

Etemad, Bouda, *Possessing the World: Taking the Measurements of Colonisation from the Eighteenth to the Twentieth Century* (New York, 2007).

Evans, E.J., *The Forging of the Modern State: Early Industrial Britain 1783–1870* (London, 1983).

Evans, Julie, *Edward Eyre, Race and Colonial Governance* (Dunedin, 2005).

Evans, Martin, *The Memory of Resistance: French Opposition to the Algerian War (1954–1962)* (Oxford, 1997).

Evans, Sterling, *Bound in Twine: The History and Ecology of the Henequen-Wheat Complex for Mexico and the American and Canadian Plains* (College Station, TX, 2007).

Evers, Hans-Dieter, 'Chettiar Moneylenders in Southeast Asia', in Denis Lombard and Jean Aubin (eds), *Asian Merchants and Businessmen in the Indian Ocean and the China Sea* (Delhi, 2000), pp. 197–221.

Eze, Emmanuel Chukwudi (ed.), *Race in the Enlightenment: A Reader* (Cambridge, 1997).

Fahmy, Khaled, *Mehmed Ali: From Ottoman Governor to Ruler of Egypt* (Oxford, 2009).

Fairbank, John K. (ed.), *The Cambridge History of China*: vol. 10, *Late Ch'ing, 1800–1911*, part 1 (Cambridge, 1978).

— and Kwang-Chih Liu (eds), *The Cambridge History of China*: vol. 11, *Late Ch'ing, 1800–1911*, part 2 (Cambridge, 1980).

Falconer, J.D., *On Horseback through Nigeria; or, Life and Travel in the Central Sudan* (London, 1911).

Fan, Fa-ti, *British Naturalists in Qing China* (Cambridge, MA, 2004).

— 'Nature and Nation in Chinese Political Thought: the National Essence Circle in Early Twentieth-Century China ', in Lorraine Daston and Fernando Vidal (eds), *The Moral Authority of Nature* (Chicago, 2004), pp. 409-37.

— 'Redrawing the Map: Science in Twentieth-Century China', *Isis* 98 (2007): pp. 524–38.

Fanon, Frantz, *Black Skin, White Masks* (London, 1970).

— *The Wretched of the Earth* (New York, 2004).

Farid, Hilmar and Razif, '*Batjaan liar* in the Dutch East Indies: A Colonial Antipode', *Postcolonial Studies* 11/3 (2008): pp. 277–92.

Farnie, D.A., *The English Cotton Industry in the World Market, 1815–1896* (Oxford, 1979).

Farooqi, Naimur Rahman, *Mughal-Ottoman Relations* (Delhi, 1989).

Faroqhi, Suraiya, *The Ottoman Empire and the World Around It* (London, 2004).

— *Subjects of the Sultan: Culture and Daily Life in the Ottoman Empire* (London, 2005).

— (ed.), *The Cambridge History of Turkey: The Later Ottoman Empire, 1603–1839* (Cambridge, 2006).

— *Artisans of Empire: Crafts and Craftspeople Under the Ottomans* (Basingstoke, 2009).

Farquar, J.N., *The Crown of Hinduism* (London, 1913).

Faruqui, Munis D., 'The Forgotten Prince: Mirza Hakim and the Formation of the Mughal Empire', *Journal of the Economic and Social History of the Orient* 48/4 (2005): pp. 487–523.

— 'At Empire's End: The Nizam, Hyderabad and Eighteenth-Century India', *Modern Asian Studies* 43/1 (2009): pp. 5–43.

Fasseur, C., *The Politics of Colonial Exploitation: Java, the Dutch, and the Cultivation System* (Ithaca, NY, 1992).

Faull, Katherine M., *Anthropology and the German Enlightenment: Perspectives on Humanity* (Lewisburg, PA, 1995).

Fawaz, Leila and C.A. Bayly (eds), *Modernity and Culture: From the Mediterranean to the Indian Ocean* (New York, 2002).

Fay, Peter Ward, *The Forgotten Army: India's Armed Struggle for Independence, 1942–1945* (Ann Arbor, MI, 1993).

Feldbæk, O., 'Dutch Batavia Trade via Copenhagen 1795–1807: A Study in Colonial Trade and Neutrality', *Scandinavian Economic History Review* 21 (1973): pp. 43–75.

— 'Eighteenth Century Danish Neutrality: Its Diplomacy, Economies and Law', *Scandinavian Journal of History* 8 (1983): pp. 3–21.

Feldstein, Ruth, *Motherhood in Black and White: Race and Sex in American Liberalism, 1930–1965* (Ithaca, NY, 2000).

Ferguson, James, *The Anti-Politics Machine: 'Development', Depoliticization, and Bureaucratic Power in Lesotho* (Cambridge, 1990).

— *Expectations of Modernity: Myths and Meanings of Urban Life on the Zambian Copperbelt* (Berkeley, CA, 1999).

Ferguson, Niall, *Empire: The Rise and Demise of the British World Order and the Lessons for Global Power* (New York, 2003).

— *Civilization: The West and the Rest* (Harmondsworth, 2011).

Fernández-Armesto, Felipe, *Before Columbus: Exploration and Colonization from the Mediterranean to the Atlantic, 1229–1492* (Philadelphia, PA, 1987).

Ferns, H.S., 'Britain's Informal Empire in Argentina, 1806–1914', *Past and Present* 4/1 (1953): pp. 60–75.

Ferro, Marco, *Colonization: A Global History* (London, 1997).

Fett, Sharla, *Working Cures: Healing, Health, and Power on Southern Slave Plantations* (Chapel Hill, NC, 2002).

Fieldhouse, D.K., *Economics and Empire, 1830–1914* (London, 1973).

— *Western Imperialism in the Middle East 1914–1958* (Oxford, 2006).

Findlay, Eileen J. Suárez, *Imposing Decency: The Politics of Sexuality and Race in Puerto Rico, 1870–1920* (Durham, NC, 1999).

Findley, Carter V., *Turkey, Islam, Nationalism and Modernity* (New Haven, CT, 2011).

Findly, Ellison Banks, *Nur Jahan, Empress of Mughal India* (New York, 1993).

Finkel, Caroline, *Osman's Dream: The History of the Ottoman Empire* (New York, 2006).

Finnane, Antonia, *Speaking of Yangzhou: A Chinese City, 1550–1850* (Cambridge, MA, 2004).

Fischer, Sibylle, *Modernity Disavowed: Haiti and the Cultures of Slavery in the Age of Revolution* (Durham, NC, 2004).

Fisher, Michael H., *Counterflows to Colonialism: Indian Travellers and Settlers in Britain, 1600–1857* (New Delhi, 2004).

— (ed.), *Visions of Mughal India: An Anthology of European Travel Writing* (London, 2007).

Fitzgerald, Timothy, *The Ideology of Religious Studies* (New York, 2000).

Fitzpatrick, Matthew, *Liberal Imperialism in Germany: Expansionism and Nationalism, 1848–1884* (Oxford, 2008).

Florida, Nancy, *Writing the Past, Inscribing the Future: History as Prophecy in Colonial Java* (Durham, NC, 1995).

— 'Sex Wars: Writing Gender Relations in Nineteenth-Century Java', in Laurie J. Sears (ed.), *Fantasizing the Feminine in Indonesia* (Durham, NC, 1996), pp. 207–224.

Fogarty, Richard S., *Race and War in France: Colonial Subjects in the French Army, 1914–1918* (Baltimore, MD, 2008).

Fogelsong, David, *America's Secret War against Bolshevism: US Intervention in the Russian Civil War, 1917–1920* (Chapel Hill, NC, 1995).

Foltz, Richard C., *Mughal India and Central Asia* (Oxford, 2001).

— 'Does Nature Have Historical Agency? World History, Environmental History, and How Historians Can Help Save the Planet', *History Teacher* 37 (2003): pp. 9–28.

Foner, Eric, *Reconstruction: America's Unfinished Revolution, 1863–1877* (New York, 1989).

Ford, Caroline, 'Nature's Fortunes: New Directions in the Writing of European Environmental History', *Journal of Modern History* 79 (2007): pp. 112–33.

Ford, Jr, Lacy K., 'Making the "White Man's Country" White: Race, Slavery, and State-Building in the Jacksonian South', *Journal of the Early Republic* 19/4 (1999): pp. 713–37.

Ford, Lisa, *Settler Sovereignty: Jurisdiction and Indigenous People in America and Australia, 1788–1836* (Cambridge, MA, 2010).

Ford, Ramona, 'Native American Women: Changing Statuses, Changing Interpretations', in Elizabeth Jameson and Susan Armitage (eds), *Writing the Range: Race, Class, and Culture in the Women's West* (Norman, OK, 1997), pp. 42–68.

Forde, Daryll, *Habitat, Economy and Society* (London, 1934).

Fordham, Douglas, 'New Directions in British Art History of the Eighteenth Century', *Literary Compass* 5 (2008): pp. 906–917.

— *Allegiance and Autonomy: British Art and the Seven Years' War* (Philadelphia, PA, 2010).

Förster, Stig, Wolfgang Mommsen and Ronald Robinson (eds), *Bismarck, Europe, and Africa: The Berlin Africa Conference 1884–1885 and the Onset of Partition* (Oxford, 1988).

Forsyth, James, *A History of the Peoples of Siberia: Russia's North Asian Colony 1581–1990* (New York, 1992).

Fortna, Benjamin, *Imperial Classroom: Islam, the State and Education in the Late Ottoman Empire* (Oxford, 2002).

Foucault, Michel, *Les Mots et les choses* (Paris, 1971).

— *The Birth of the Clinic: An Archaeology of Medical Perception* (Bristol, 1973).

— *The Order of Things: An Archaeology of the Human Sciences* (London, 1974).

— *The History of Sexuality: An Introduction* (London, 1978).

— 'Governmentality', in Graham Burchell *et al.* (eds), *The Foucault Effect: Studies in Governmentality* (London, 1991), pp. 87–104.

— *Security, Territory, Population: Lectures at the Collège de France, 1977–1978*, ed. Michel Sellenart (Basingstoke, 2009).

Foust, Clifford M., *Muscovite and Mandarin: Russia's Trade with China and its Setting, 1727–1805* (Chapel Hill, NC, 1969).

Fox-Genovese, Elizabeth, *The Origins of Physiocracy: Economic Revolution and Social Order in Eighteenth-century France* (Ithaca, NY, 1976).

Frank, Andre Gunder, *World Accumulation, 1492–1789* (New York, 1978).

— *ReOrient: The Silver Age in Asia and the World Economy* (Berkeley, CA, 1998).

Frederick, William H., 'Reflections in a Moving Stream: Indonesian Memories of the War and the Japanese', in Remco Raben (ed.), *Representing the Japanese Occupation of Indonesia* (Zwolle, Amsterdam, 1999), pp. 16–35.

Fredrickson, George M., *White Supremacy: A Comparative Study in American and South African History* (New York, 1981).

Freidberg, Susan, *French Beans and Food Scares: Culture and Commerce in an Anxious Age* (Oxford, 2004).

Fromkin, David, *A Peace to End All Peace: Creating the Modern Middle East 1914–1922* (New York, 1989).

Fromont, Cécile, 'Christian Icons: Kongo Symbols', PhD dissertation, Harvard University, 2008.

Frost, Alan, 'New South Wales as *Terra Nullius*: The British Denial of Aboriginal Land Rights', in S. Janson and S. Macintyre (eds), *Through White Eyes* (Sydney, 1990), pp. 65–76.

— *Botany Bay Mirages: Illusions of Australia's Convict Beginnings* (Carlton, VIC, 1994).

Fujita-Rony, Dorothy B., *American Workers, Colonial Power: Philippine Seattle and the Transpacific West, 1919–1941* (Berkeley, CA, 2003).

Fuller, Mia, *Moderns Abroad: Architecture, Cities and Italian Imperialism* (London, 2007).

Fuller, Thomas Elkins, *The Rt Honourable Cecil John Rhodes: A Monograph and a Reminiscence* (London, 1910).

Fuller, W.C., *Strategy and Power in Russia, 1600–1914* (New York, 1992).

— *The Foe Within: Fantasies of Treason and the End of the Russian Empire* (Ithaca, NY, 2006).

Furber, H., *Rival Empires of Trade in the Orient 1600–1800* (Minnesota, 1976).

Furedi, Frank, *Silent War: Imperialism and the Changing Perception of Race* (London, 1998).

— 'The Demobilized African Soldier and the Blow to White Prestige', in David Killingray and David Omissi (eds), *Guardians of Empire: The Armed Forces of the Colonial Powers c. 1700–1964* (Manchester, 1999), pp. 179–98.

Galeano, Eduardo, *Open Veins of Latin America* (New York, 1973).

Gallagher, John and Ronald Robinson, 'The Imperialism of Free Trade', *Economic History Review* 6/1, New Series (1953): pp. 1–15.

Games, Alison, 'Atlantic History: Definitions, Challenges, and Opportunities', *American Historical Review* 113/3 (2006): pp. 741–56.

— *The Web of Empire: English Cosmopolitans in an Age of Expansion, 1560–1660* (Cambridge, MA, 2008).

Gammage, Bill, *The Broken Years: Australian Soldiers in the Great War* (Canberra, 1974).

Gann, Lewis, *White Settlers in Tropical Africa* (Baltimore, MD, 1962).

Gaonkar, Dilip (ed.), *Alternative Modernities* (Durham, NC, 2001).

Gardezi, Hasan N., 'Asian Workers in the Gulf States of the Middle East', *Journal of Contemporary Asia* 21 (1991): pp. 179–94.

Gardner, Katy and Filipo Osella, 'Migration, Modernity and Social Transformation in South Asia: An Overview', *Contributions to Indian Sociology* 37/1–2 (2003): pp. v–xxviii.

Gardner, Lloyd C. (ed.), *Redefining the Past: Essays in Diplomatic History in Honor of William Appleman Williams* (Corvallis, OR, 1986).

— *Approaching Vietnam: From World War II to Dienbienphu* (New York, 1988).

Garfield, Robert, *A History of São Tomé Island, 1470–1655: The Key to Guinea* (San Francisco, CA, 1992).

Garside, Peter and Stephen Copley (eds), *The Politics of the Picturesque* (London, 1994).

Gartrell, Beverley, 'Colonial Wives: Villains or Victims?', in Hilary Callan and Shirley Ardener (eds), *The Incorporated Wife* (London, 1984), pp. 165–86.

Gaspar, David Barry and David Patrick Geggus (eds), *A Turbulent Time: The French Revolution and the Greater Caribbean* (Bloomington, IN, 1997).

Gates, Jr, Henry Louis, 'Writing "Race" and the Difference It Makes', in Henry Louis Gates, Jr (ed.), *'Race,' Writing and Difference* (Chicago, IL, 1986).

Gatewood, Jr, Willard B., *'Smoked Yankees' and the Struggle for Empire: Letters from Negro Soldiers, 1898–1902* (Urbana, IL, 1971).

— *Black Americans and the White Man's Burden, 1898–1903* (Urbana, IL, 1975).

Geary, Christraud and Virginia-Lee Webb, *Delivering Views: Distant Cultures in Early Postcards* (Washington, DC, 1998).

Geggus, David, *The Impact of the Haitian Revolution in the Atlantic World* (Columbia, SC, 2002).

— *Haitian Revolutionary Studies* (Bloomington, IN, 2002).

— 'The Arming of Slaves in the Haitian Revolution', in Christopher Leslie Brown and Philip D. Morgan (eds), *Arming Slaves: From Classical Times to the Modern Age* (New Haven, CT, 2006), pp. 209–232.

Geiger, Susan, *TANU Women: Gender and Culture in the Making of Tanganyikan Nationalism, 1955–1965* (Portsmouth, NH, 1997).

Gelvin, James, *The Modern Middle East: A History* (Oxford, 2005).

George, H.B., *The Relations of Geography and History* (Oxford, 1901).

— *A Historical Geography of the British Empire* (London, 1904).

Gerth, Karl, *China Made: Consumer Culture and the Creation of the Nation* (Cambridge, MA, 2003).

Geschiere, Peter, *The Modernity of Witchcraft: Politics and the Occult in Postcolonial Africa* (Charlottsville, VA, 1997).

Ghosh, Durba, *Sex and the Family in Colonial India: The Making of Empire* (Cambridge, 2006).

Ghosh, Partha S., *Migrants and Refugees from South Asia: Political and Security Dimensions* (Shillong, 2001).

Gibson, Charles, *The Aztecs under Spanish Rule* (Stanford, CA, 1964).

— *Spain in America* (New York, 1966).

Gichuiri, H.M., 'A Parable', *Mwigwithania* 1/7 (November 1928): n.p.

Gienow-Hecht, Jessica C.E., *Transmission Impossible: American Journalism as Cultural Diplomacy in Postwar Germany 1945–1955* (Baton Rouge, LA, 1999).
Gifford, Prosser and Wm Roger Louis (eds), *The Transfer of Power in Africa: Decolonization, 1940–1960* (New Haven, CT, 1982).
— and Wm Roger Louis (eds), *Decolonization and African Independence: The Transfers of Power, 1960–1980* (New Haven, CT, 1988).
Gikoyo, Gucu G., *We Fought for Freedom* (Nairobi, 1979).
Gillispie, Charles C., 'Scientific Aspects of the French Egyptian Expedition, 1798–1801', *Proceedings of the American Philosophical Society* 33 (1989): pp. 447–74.
— 'The Scientific Importance of Napoleon's Egyptian Campaign', *Scientific American* 271/3 (1994): pp. 78–85.
Gilmartin, David and Bruce B. Lawrence (eds), *Beyond Turk and Hindu: Rethinking Religious Identities in Islamicate South Asia* (Gainesville, FL, 2000).
Gilmore, Glenda, *Defying Dixie: The Radical Roots of Civil Rights, 1919–1950* (New York, 2008).
Gilmour, David, *The Long Recessional: The Imperial Life of Rudyard Kipling* (New York, 2002).
Gilroy, Paul, *The Black Atlantic: Modernity and Double Consciousness* (London, 1993).
— *Against Race: Imagining Political Culture Beyond the Color Line* (Cambridge, MA, 2000).
Gimple, Jean, *The Medieval Machine* (New York, 1983).
Gingeras, Ryan, *Sorrowful Shores: Ethnicity and the End of the Ottoman Empire 1912–1923* (Oxford, 2009).
Ginio, Ruth, *French Colonialism Unmasked: The Vichy Years in French West Africa* (Lincoln, NE, 2006).
Ginzburg, Carlo, 'Family Resemblances and Family Trees: Two Cognitive Metaphors', *Critical Inquiry* 30/3 (2004): pp. 537–56.
Gitelman, Zvi Y., *A Century of Ambivalence: The Jews of Russia and the Soviet Union, 1881 to the Present* (Bloomington, IN, 2001).
Glacken, Clarence, *Traces on the Rhodian Shore: Nature and Culture in Western Thought from Ancient Times to the End of the Eighteenth Century* (Berkeley, CA, 1967).
Gledhill, Alan, *The Penal Codes of Sudan and Northern Nigeria* (London and Lagos, 1963).
Go, Julian and Anne L. Foster (eds), *The American Colonial State in the Philippines: Global Perspectives* (Durham, NC, 2003).
Gobat, Michel, *Confronting the American Dream: Nicaragua under US Imperial Rule* (Durham, NC, 2005).
Göçek, Fatma Müge, *Rise of Bourgeoisie, Demise of Empire* (Oxford, 1996).
— *Social Constructions of Nationalism in the Middle East* (Albany, NY, 2002).
— 'Turkish Historiography and the Unbearable Weight of 1915', in Richard G. Hovannisian (ed.), *The Armenian Genocide: Cultural and Ethical Legacies* (New Brunswick, NJ, 2007), pp. 336–68.
Godechot, Jacques, *France and the Atlantic Revolution of the Eighteenth Century, 1770–1799* (New York, 1965).

Godlewska, Anne, *Geography Unbound: French Geographic Science from Cassini to Humboldt* (Chicago, IL, 1999).

Goffman, Daniel, 'Negotiating with the Renaissance State: The Ottoman Empire and the New Diplomacy', in Virginia H. Aksan and Daniel Goffman (eds), *The Early Modern Ottomans: Remapping the Empire* (Cambridge, 2007), pp. 59–74.

Goldberg, David Theo, *Racist Culture: Philosophy and the Politics of Meaning* (Oxford, 1993).

— *The Racial State* (Malden, MA, 2002).

Gommans, Jos, *The Rise of the Indo-Afghan Empire, c.1710–1780* (Leiden, 1995).

— *Mughal Warfare: Indian Frontiers and Highroads to Empire, 1500–1700* (New York, 2002).

— and Dirk H.A. Kolff (eds), *Warfare and Weaponry in South Asia, 1000–1800* (New York, 2001).

Gonzalez, Deena, *Refusing the Favor: The Spanish-Mexican Women of Santa Fe, 1820–1880* (Oxford, 1999).

González y González, Luis, 'Liberals and the Land', in Gilbert M. Joseph and Timothy J. Henderson (eds), *The Mexico Reader: History, Culture, Politics* (Durham, NC, 2002), pp. 239–51.

Goodfriend, Joyce (ed.), *Revisiting New Netherland: Perspectives on Early Dutch America* (Leiden, 2005).

Goodman, Dena, 'Difference: An Enlightenment Concept', in Keith Baker and Peter H. Reill (eds), *What's Left of Enlightenment: A Postmodern Question* (Stanford, CA, 2001), pp. 129–47.

Goodman, Jordan, *The Devil and Mr Casement: One Man's Battle for Human Rights in South America's Heart of Darkness* (New York, 2010).

Goodwin, Godfrey, *The Janissaries* (London, 1994).

Goodwin, Jason, *Lords of the Horizon* (New York, 2003).

Goody, Jack, *The East in the West* (Cambridge, 1996).

Gordon, David, *The Passing of French Algeria* (London, 1966).

Gordon, Linda, *The Great Arizona Orphan Abduction* (Cambridge, MA, 1999).

— 'Internal Colonialism and Gender', in Ann L. Stoler (ed.), *Haunted by Empire: Geographies of Intimacy in North American History* (Durham, NC, 2006), pp. 427–51.

Gordon, Matthew S., *The Breaking of a Thousand Swords: A History of the Turkish Military of Samarra, AH 200–275/815–889 CE* (Albany, NY, 2001).

Gordon, Stewart (ed.), *Robes and Honor: The Medieval World of Investiture* (New York, 2001).

— (ed.), *Robes of Honour: Khil'at in Pre-colonial and Colonial India* (New York, 2003).

Gorst, Anthony, *The Suez Crisis* (London, 1997).

Gouda, Frances, 'The Gendered Rhetoric of Colonialism and Anti-Colonialism in Twentieth-Century Indonesia', *Indonesia* 55 (1993): pp. 1–22.

— *Dutch Culture Overseas: Colonial Practice in the Netherlands Indies, 1900–1942* (Amsterdam, 1995).

— 'Good Mothers, Medeas, or Jezebels: Feminine Imagery in Colonial and Anticolonial Rhetoric in the Dutch East Indies, 1900–1942', in Julia Clancy-Smith and Frances Gouda (eds), *Domesticating the Empire: Race, Gender, and Family Life in French and Dutch Colonialism* (Charlottesville, VA, 1998), pp. 236–55.

— 'Gender and Hypermasculinity as Post-Colonial Modernity during Indonesia's Struggle for Independence, 1945–49', in Antoinette Burton (ed.), *Gender, Sexuality and Colonial Modernities* (New York, 1999), pp. 161–74.

— and Julia Clancy-Smith (eds), *Domesticating the Empire: Race, Gender, and Family Life in French and Dutch Colonialism* (Charlottesville, VA, 1998).

Goudie, A.S., *The Human Impact* (Oxford, 1984).

— 'Entangled Worlds: The English-Speaking Atlantic as a Spanish Periphery', *American Historical Review* 112/3 (2007): pp. 764–86.

— 'Entangled Atlantic Histories: A Response from the Anglo-American Periphery', *American Historical Review* 112/5 (2007): pp. 1415–22.

Gould, Eliga H., 'Zones of Law, Zones of Violence: The Legal Geography of the British Atlantic, circa 1772', *William and Mary Quarterly* 60/3 (2003): pp. 471–510.

Gould, Stephen J., *The Mismeasure of Man* (New York, 1981).

Graham, Brian and Peter Shirlow, 'The Battle of the Somme in Ulster Memory and Identity', *Political Geography* 21 (2002): pp. 881–904.

Graham-Brown, Sarah, *Images of Women: The Portrayal of Women in Photography of the Middle East, 1860–1950* (New York, 1988).

Grandin, Greg, *Empire's Workshop: Latin America, The United States, and the Rise of the New Imperialism* (New York, 2006).

Grant, Jonathan A., *Rulers, Guns and Money: The Global Arms Trade in the Age of Imperialism* (Harvard, MA, 2007).

Grau, Oliver, *From Illusion to Immersion* (Cambridge, MA, 2003).

Grazia, Victoria de, *Irresistible Empire: America's Advance through Twentieth-Century Europe* (Cambridge, MA, 2005).

Green, L.C., 'Claims to Territory in Colonial America', in L.C. Green and Olive P. Dickason (eds), *The Law of Nations and the New World* (Alberta, 1989), pp. 1–140.

Greenberg, Amy, *Manifest Manhood and the Antebellum American Empire* (Cambridge, 2005).

Greenberg, Michael, *British Trade and the Opening of China* (Cambridge, 1951).

Greenlee, W.B. (ed.), *The Voyage of Pedro Álvares Cabral to Brazil and India from Contemporary Documents and Narratives* (London, 1938).

Greene, Jack P. (ed.), *The Reinterpretation of the American Revolution, 1763–1789* (New York, 1968).

— *Pursuits of Happiness: The Social Development of Early Modern British Colonies and the Formation of American Culture* (Chapel Hill, NC, 1988).

— 'Negotiated Authorities: The Problem of Governance in the Extended Polities of the Early Modern Atlantic World', in Jack P. Greene (ed.), *Negotiated Authorities: Essays in Colonial Political and Constitutional History* (Charlottesville, VA and London, 1994).

— 'The American Revolution', *American Historical Review* 105/1 (2000): pp. 93–102.

— '"By Their Laws Shall Ye Know Them": Law and Identity in Colonial British America', *Journal of Interdisciplinary History* 13/2 (2002): pp. 247–60.

— and Philip D. Morgan (eds), *Atlantic History: A Critical Appraisal* (New York, 2008).

Greene, Julie, *The Canal Builders: Making America's Empire at the Panama Canal* (New York, 2010).

Greenhalgh, Paul, *Ephemeral Vistas: The Expositions Universelles, Great Exhibitions and World's Fairs, 1851–1939* (New York, 1988).

Greer, Allan, *Mohawk Saint: Catherine Tekakwitha and the Jesuits* (Oxford, 2005).

Gregory, Robert G., *South Asians in East Africa: An Economic and Social History, 1890–1980* (Boulder, CO, 1993).

Grehan, James, *Everyday Life and Consumer Culture in Eighteenth-Century Damascus* (Seattle, WA, 2007).

Grever, Maria and Berteke Waaldijk, *Transforming the Public Sphere: The Dutch National Exhibition of Women's Labor in 1898* (Durham, NC, 2004).

Grimshaw, Patricia, 'Faith, Missionary Life, and the Family', in Philippa Levine (ed.), *Gender and Empire* (Oxford, 2004), pp. 260–80.

Grinde, Jr, Donald A. and Bruce E. Johansen, *Exemplar of Liberty: Native America and the Evolution of Democracy* (Los Angeles, CA, 1991).

Groen, Petra, 'Zedelijkheid en martialiteit: Het kazerneconcubinaat in Nederlands-Indië rond 1890', in Marieke Bloembergen and Remco Raben (eds), *Het koloniale beschavingsoffensief: Wegen naar het nieuwe Indië, 1890–1950* (Leiden, 2009), pp. 25–52.

Grove, A. T., *Land Use and Soil Conservation on the Jos Plateau* (Zaria, 1952).

Grove, Richard, *Green Imperialism: Colonial Expansion, Tropical Island Edens and the Origins of Environmentalism* (Cambridge, 1995).

— 'Revolutionary Weather: The Climatic and Economic Crisis of 1788–1795 and the Discovery of El Nino', in T. Sherratt (ed.), *A Change in the Weather: Climate and Culture in Australia* (Canberra, 2005), pp. 128–40.

— and V. Damodaran, 'Imperialism, Intellectual Networks and Environmental Change: Origins and Evolution of Global Environmental History, 1676–2000', *Economic and Political Weekly* 41/42 (2006): pp. 4345–54, 4497–5006.

—, V. Damodaran and S. Sangwan (eds), *Nature and the Orient: The Environmental History of South and Southeast Asia* (Oxford, 1998).

Guest, Harriet, 'The Great Distinction: Figures of the Exotic in the Work of William Hodges', *Oxford Art Journal* 12/2 (1989): pp. 36–58.

— 'Curiously Marked: Tattooing, Masculinity and Nationality in Eighteenth-Century British Perceptions of the South Pacific', in John Barrell (ed.), *Painting and the Politics of Culture* (Cambridge, 1992), pp. 101–134.

Guha, Ranajit, *A Rule of Property for Bengal: An Essay on the Idea of Permanent Settlement* (Paris, 1963).

— 'On Some Aspects of the Historiography of Colonial India', in Guha (ed.), *Subaltern Studies I: Writings on South Asian History and Society* (New Delhi, 1982), pp. 1–8.

— *Elementary Aspects of Peasant Insurgency in Colonial India* (Durham, NC, 1999).

— *History at the Limit of World-History* (New York, 2002).

— and M. Gadgil, *This Fissured Earth: Towards an Ecological History of India* (Delhi, 1992).

— and Gayatri Spivak (eds), *Selected Subaltern Studies* (New York, 1988).

Guha-Thakurta, Tapati, *The Making of a New Indian Art* (Cambridge, 1992).

Guitard, Odette, *Bandoung et le réveil des peuples colonisés* (Paris, 1976).

Gulbadan, Begam, *History of Humayun*, trans. Annette Susannah Beveridge, 2 vols (London, 1902).

Gunatilleke, Godfrey (ed.), *The Impact of Labour Migration on Households: A Comparative Study in Seven Asian Countries* (Tokyo, 1992).

Gungwu, W., 'Merchants Without Empire: The Hokkien Sojourning Communities', in James D. Tracy (ed.), *The Rise of Merchant Empires: Long-distance Trade in the Early Modern World, 1350–1750* (Cambridge, 1990), pp. 400–422.

Gupta, Akhil, *Postcolonial Developments: Agriculture in the Making of Modern India* (Durham, NC, 1998).

Gupta, S., *Strisubodhini* (Lucknow, 1954 [23rd edn]).

Gupta, Satya Prakash, *Agrarian System of Eastern Rajasthan, c. 1650–c. 1750* (Delhi, 1986).

Gurley, J.D., 'The Debts of the Nawab of Arcot, 1763–1776', DPhil dissertation, Oxford University, 1968.

Guy, Donna J. and Thomas E. Sheridan (eds), *Contested Ground: Comparative Frontiers on the Northern and Southern Edges of the Spanish Empire* (Tucson, AZ, 1998).

Guy, Jeff, *The View Across the River: Harriette Colenso and the Zulu Struggle Against Imperialism* (Charlottesville, VA, 2002).

Guy, R. Kent, *The Emperor's Four Treasuries: Scholars and the State in the Late Ch'ien-Lung Era* (Cambridge, MA, 1987).

Habib, Irfan, *Atlas of the Mughal Empire* (Delhi, 1982).

— 'Agrarian Relations and Land Revenue', in I. Habib and T. Raychaudhuri (eds), *The Cambridge Economic History of India*, vol. 1 (Cambridge, 1982), pp. 235–48.

— *Agrarian System of Mughal India, 1556–1707* (Delhi, 1999).

— *Essays in Indian History: Toward a Marxist Perspective* (London, 2002).

Haddon, A.C. (ed.), *Cambridge Expedition to the Torres Straits*, 6 vols (Cambridge, 1901–1935).

Haebich, Anna, *Broken Circles: Fragmenting Indigenous Families 1800–2000* (Freemantle, WA, 2000).

Hagen, Mark von, 'Confronting Backwardness: Dilemmas of Soviet Officer Education in the Interwar Years, 1918–1941', in Elliott V. Converse III (ed.), *Forging the Sword: Selecting, Educating, and Training Cadets and Junior Officers in the Modern World* (Chicago, IL, 1998), pp. 82–98.

— 'The Limits of Reform: The Multiethnic Imperial Army Confronts Nationalism, 1874–1917', in David Schimmelpennick van der Oye and Bruce W. Menning (eds), *Reforming the Tsar's Army: Military Innovation in Imperial Russia from Peter the Great to the Revolution* (Cambridge and Washington, DC, 2004), pp. 34–55.

Hailey, William Malcolm, *An African Survey: A Study of Problems Arising in Africa South of the Sahara* (London, 1938).

Halbfass, Wilhelm, *India and Europe: An Essay in Understanding* (Albany, NY, 1988).

Haliczer, Stephen, *Inquisition and Society in the Kingdom of Valencia* (Berkeley, CA, 1990).

Hall, Catherine, *White, Male and Middle Class: Explorations in Feminism and History* (Cambridge, 1992).

— 'William Knibb and the Black British Subject', in Martin Daunton and Rick Halperin (eds), *Empire and Others: British Encounters with Indigenous Peoples* (Philadelphia, PA, 1999), pp. 303–324.

— *Civilising Subjects: Metropole and Colony in the English Imagination, 1830–1867* (Chicago, IL, 2002).

— 'Of Gender and Empire: Reflections on the Nineteenth Century', in Philippa Levine (ed.), *Gender and Empire* (Oxford, 2004), pp. 46–76.

— 'Culture and Identity in Imperial Britain', in Sarah Stockwell (ed.) *The British Empire: Themes and Perspectives* (Oxford, 2008), pp. 199–217.

— and Sonya O. Rose (eds), *At Home with the Empire: Metropolitan Cultures in an Imperial World* (Cambridge, 2006).

Hall, Gwendolyn Midlo, *Slavery and African Ethnicities in the Americas: Restoring the Links* (Chapel Hill, NC, 2005).

Hall, Stuart, 'Race, Articulation and Societies Structured in Dominance', in UNESCO, *Sociological Theories: Race and Colonialism* (Paris, 1980), pp. 305–345.

— 'The Work of Representation', in Stuart Hall (ed.), *Representation: Cultural Representations and Signifying Practices* (Milton Keynes, 1997), pp. 13–74.

Hallward, Peter, *Absolutely Postcolonial: Writing between the Singular and the Specific* (Manchester, 2001).

Hämäläinen, Pekka, *The Comanche Empire* (New Haven, CT, 2008).

Hamdani, A., 'An Islamic Background to the Voyages of Discovery', in S.K. Jayyusi (ed.), *The Legacy of Muslim Spain* (Leyden, 1992), pp. 273–304.

Hamilton, Douglas, *Scotland, the Caribbean, and the Atlantic World, 1750–1820* (Manchester, 2005).

Hamilton, P. and R.J. Blyth (eds), *Representing Slavery: Art, Artefacts and Archives in the Collections of the National Maritime Museum, Greenwich* (Farnham, 2007).

Hammer, Ellen, *The Struggle for Indochina* (Stanford, CA, 1954).

Hammerton, James, *Emigrant Gentlewomen: Genteel Poverty and Female Emigration, 1830–1914* (London, 1979).

Hammond, R.J., *Portugal and Africa, 1815–1910: A Study in Uneconomic Imperialism* (Stanford, CA, 1966).

Hancock, David, *Citizens of the World: London Merchants and the Integration of the British Atlantic Community, 1735–1785* (Cambridge, 1995).

— '"An Undiscovered Ocean of Commerce Laid Open": India, Wine and the Emerging Atlantic Economy, 1703–1813', in H.V. Bowen, Margarette Lincoln and Nigel Rigby (eds), *The Worlds of the East India Company* (Suffolk, 2002), pp. 153–68.

Hancock, W.K., *Australia* (New York, 1931).

Hanioğlu, M. Şükrü, *Preparation for a Revolution: The Young Turks, 1902–1908* (Oxford, 2001).

— *A Brief History of the Late Ottoman Empire* (Princeton, NJ, 2008).

Hannaford, Ian, *Race: The History of an Idea in the West* (Baltimore, MD, 1996).

Hansen, David, *John Glover and the Colonial Picturesque* (Hobart, 2003).

Hanssen, Jens, *Fin de Siècle Beirut: The Making of an Ottoman Provincial Capital* (Oxford, 2005).

Happel, Jörn, *Nomadische Lebenswelten und zarische Politik: der Aufstand in Zentralasien 1916* (Stuttgart, 2010).

Harbi, Mohammed and Benjamin Stora, *La Guerre d'Algérie* (Cheltenham, 2005).

Hardacre, Helen, 'Creating State Shinto: The Great Promulgation Campaign and the New Religions', *Journal of Japanese Studies* 12/1 (1986): pp. 29–63.

—. *Shinto and the State, 1868–1988* (Princeton, NJ, 1989).

Hardt, Michael and Antonio Negri, *Empire* (London, 2000).

Hargreaves, Alec, *Voices from the North African Immigrant Community in France: Immigration and Identity in Beur Fiction* (Providence, RI, 1991).

Haring, C.H., *The Spanish Empire in America* (New York, 1947).

Harootunian, Harry, *Overcome by Modernity: History, Culture, and Community in Interwar Japan* (Princeton, NJ, 2000).

Harris, Cheryl, 'Whiteness as Property', *Harvard Law Review* 106 (1993): pp. 1709–1791.

Harrison, Mark, *Public Health in British India: Anglo-Indian Preventive Medicine, 1859–1914* (Cambridge, 1994).

Hart, John Mason, *Revolutionary Mexico: The Coming and Process of the Mexican Revolution* (Berkeley, CA, 1987).

Haruyama, Meitetsu, 'Kindai'nihon no shokuminchi'tōchi to Hara Takashi', in Meitetsu Haruyama, *Kindainihon to Taiwan* (Tokyo, 2008), pp. 155–221.

Harvey, David, *The Condition of Postmodernity: An Enquiry into the Origins of Cultural Change* (Oxford, 1989).

— *The New Imperialism* (Oxford, 2003).

Harvey, Karen, *Reading Sex in the Eighteenth Century: Bodies and Gender in English Erotic Fiction* (Cambridge, 2005).

Hasrat, Bikrama Jit, *Dara Shikuh: Life and Works* (New Delhi, 1982).

Hatcher, Brian, 'Remembering Rommohan: An Essay on the Re-emergence of Modern Hinduism', *History of Religions* 46 (2006): pp. 50–80.

Hatfield, April Lee, *Atlantic Virginia: Intercolonial Relations in the Seventeenth Century* (Philadelphia, PA, 2007).

Hathway, Jane, *el Hajj Beshir Agha: Chief Eunuch of the Ottoman Imperial Harem* (Oxford, 2006).

— with Karl Barbir, *The Arab Lands Under Ottoman Rule 1516–1800* (Harlow, 2007).

Hauptman, Laurence M., *Tribes and Tribulations: Misconceptions about American Indians and their Histories* (Albuquerque, NM, 1995).

Havard, Gilles and Cécil Vidal, *Histoire de l'Amerique française* (Paris, 2003).

Havinden, Michael, *Colonialism and Development: Britain and its Tropical Colonies, 1850–1960* (London, 1993).

Hay, Margaret Jean, 'Changes in Clothing and Struggles over Identity in Colonial Western Kenya', in Jean M. Allman (ed.), *Fashioning Africa: Power and the Politics of Dress* (Bloomington, IN, 2004), pp. 67–83.

Headrick, Daniel, *The Tools of Empire: Technology and European Imperialism in the Nineteenth Century* (New York, 1981).

— *The Tentacles of Progress: Technology Transfer in the Age of Imperialism, 1850–1940* (New York, 1988).

Headrick, Rita, 'African Soldiers in World War II', *Armed Forces and Society* 4/3 (1978): pp. 501–526.

Healy, Michael S., 'Colour, Climate, and Combat: The Caribbean Regiment in the Second World War', *International History Review* 22/1 (2000): pp. 65–85.

Hechter, Michael, *Internal Colonialism: The Celtic Fringe in British National Development*, 2nd edn (New Brunswick, NJ, 1999).

Heidegger, Martin, *The Question Concerning Technology and Other Essays* (New York, 1977).

Heidemann, Frank, *Kanganies in Sri Lanka and Malaysia: Tamil Recruiter-cum-Foreman as a Sociological Category in the Nineteenth and Twentieth Century* (Munich, 1992).

Hellie, Richard, *Enserfment and Military Change in Muscovy* (Chicago, IL, 1971).

Heming, John, *Red Gold: The Conquest of the Brazilian Indians, 1500–1760* (Cambridge, MA, 1978).

Henderson, Jennifer, *Settler Feminism and Race Making in Canada* (Toronto, ON, 2003).

Henderson, W.O., *The German Colonial Empire, 1884–1919* (London, 1993).

Herle, Anita and S. Rouse (eds), *Cambridge and the Torres Straits* (Cambridge, 1998).

Herring, George C., *From Colony to Superpower: US Foreign Relations Since 1776* (Oxford, 2008).

Hesselink, Liesbeth, 'Prostitution: A Necessary Evil. Particularly in the Colonies: Views on Prostitution in the Netherlands East Indies', in Elsbeth Locher-Scholten and Anke Niehof (eds), *Indonesian Women in Focus: Past and Present Notions* (Leiden, 1992), pp. 204–224.

— *Genezers op de koloniale markt: Inheemse dokters en vroedvrouwen in Nederlands Oost-Indië, 1850–1915* (Amsterdam, 2009).

Hevia, James L., *English Lessons: The Pedagogy of Imperialism in Nineteenth-Century China* (Durham, NC, 2003).

Heyck, T.W., *The Peoples of the British Isles: A New History from 1688 to 1870* (Belmont, CA, 1992).

Heywood, Linda M. and John K. Thornton, *Central Africans, Atlantic Creoles, and the Foundation of the Americas, 1585–1660* (New York, 2007).

Hickford, Mark, 'Making Territorial Rights of the Natives: Britain and New Zealand, 1830–1847', DPhil dissertation, Oxford University, 1999.

Hietala, Thomas R., *Manifest Design: Anxious Aggrandizement in Late Jacksonian America* (Ithaca, NY, 1985).

Higman, B.W., *Slave Populations of the British Caribbean, 1807–1834* (Baltimore, MD, 1984).

Hill, Patricia R. *The World Their Household: The American Woman's Foreign Mission Movement and Cultural Transformation, 1870–1920* (Ann Arbor, MI, 1985).

Hill, Polly, *Migrant Cocoa Farmers of Southern Ghana* (Cambridge, 1963).

— *Development Economics on Trial: The Anthropological Case for a Prosecution* (Cambridge, 1984).

Hill, Richard L., *A Biographical Dictionary of the Anglo-Egyptian Sudan* (Oxford, 1951).

Hilton, Anne, *The Kingdom of Kongo* (Oxford, 1985).

Hilton, Boyd, *The Age of Atonement: The Influence of Evangelicalism on Social and Economic Thought, 1785–1865* (Oxford, 1988).

Hilton, Matthew, *Consumerism in Twentieth-Century Britain: The Search for a Historical Movement* (Cambridge, 2003).

Hine, Robert V. and John Mack Faragher, *The American West: A New Interpretive History* (New Haven, CT, 2000).

Hirsch, Francine, *Empire of Nations: Ethnographic Knowledge and the Making of the Soviet Union* (Ithaca, NY, 2005).

Hirschkind, C., 'Egypt at the Exhibition: Reflections on the Optics of Colonialism', *Critique of Anthropology* 11/3 (1991): pp. 279–98.

Hŏ, Suyŏl, *Kaebal Omnŭn Kaebal* (Seoul, 2005).

— 'Saeroun singminji yŏngu ŭi hyŏnjuso: "Singminji kŭndae" wa "minjungsa" rŭl chungsim ŭro', *Yŏksa munje yŏngu* 16 (2006): pp. 9–32.

Hobhouse, Henry, *Seeds of Change: Five Plants that Transformed the World* (London, 1985).

Hobson, J.A., *Imperialism: A Study* (London, 1902).

Hochschild, Adam, *King Leopold's Ghost: A Story of Greed, Terror, and Heroism in Colonial Africa* (Boston, MA, 1998).

Hodgen, Margaret, *Early Anthropology in the Sixteenth and Seventeenth Centuries* (Philadelphia, PA, 1964).

Hodges, Geoffrey, *Kariakor: The Carrier Corps: The Story of the Military Labour Forces in the Conquest of German East Africa, 1914 to 1918* (Nairobi, 1999).

Hodges, Tony and Malyn Newitt, *São Tomé and Príncipe: From Plantation Colony to Microstate* (Boulder, CO, 1988).

Hodivala, Shahpurshah Hormasji, *Studies in Indo-Muslim History* (Bombay, 1939).

Hoffenberg, Peter H., *An Empire on Display: English, Indian, and Australian Exhibitions from the Crystal Palace to the Great War* (Berkeley, CA, 2001).

Hogan, Michael J. (ed.), *America in the World: The Historiography of American Foreign Relations since 1941* (Cambridge, 1995).

Hoganson, Kristin L., *Fighting for American Manhood: How Gender Politics Provoked the Spanish-American and Philippine-American* Wars (New Haven, CT, 1998).

— *Consumers' Imperium: The Global Production of American Domesticity, 1865–1920* (Chapel Hill, NC, 2007).

Höhn, Maria, *GIs and Frauleins: The German-American Encounter in 1950s West Germany* (Chapel Hill, NC, 2002).

Holland, Heidi, *The Struggle: A History of the African National Congress* (London, 1989).

Hollis, Christopher, *Italy in Africa* (London, 1941).

Holmes, G., *The Making of a Great Power: Late Stuart and Early Georgian Britain 1660–1720* (London, 1993).

— and D. Szechi, *The Age of Oligarchy:Pre-Industrial Britain 1722–1783* (London, 1993).

Holquist, Peter, 'Violent Russia, Deadly Marxism? Russia in the Epoch of Violence, 1905–1921', *Kritika: Explorations in Russian and Eurasian History* 4/3 (2003): pp. 632–3.

Holt, Thomas C., *The Problem of Freedom: Race, Labor, and Politics in Jamaica and Britain 1832–1938* (Baltimore, MD, 1992).

Hoogenboom, Hilde, 'Catherine the Great', in Stephen M. Norris and Willard Sunderland (eds), *Russia's People of Empire: Life Stories from Eurasia, 1500–Present* (forthcoming, Bloomington, IN, 2012).

Hook, Glenn D. and Richard Siddle (eds), *Japan and Okinawa: Structure and Subjectivity* (London, 2003).

Hopkins, A.G., 'Comparing British and American Empires', *Journal of Global History* 2/3 (2007): pp. 395–404.

Horne, Alistair, *A Savage War of Peace: Algeria 1954–1962* (London, 1977).

Horne, Gerald, *Cold War in a Hot Zone: The United States Confronts Labor and Independence Struggles in the British West Indies* (Philadelphia, PA, 2007).

Horowitz, Richard S., 'International Law and State Transformation in China, Siam, and the Ottoman Empire in the Nineteenth Century', *Journal of World History* 15/4 (2004): pp. 445–86.

Horsman, Reginald, *Race and Manifest Destiny: The Origins of American Racial Anglo-Saxons* (Cambridge, MA, 1981).

Hosking, Geoffrey, *Russia: People and Empire, 1552–1917* (Cambridge, MA, 1998).

Hough, Franklin, *On the Activity of Governments in the Preservation of Forests* (Salem, MA, 1873).

Howard, Douglas, *The History of Turkey* (Westport, CT, 2001).

— 'Genre and Myth in the Ottoman Advice for Kings Literature', in Virginia H. Aksan and Daniel Goffman (eds), *The Early Modern Ottomans: Remapping the Empire* (Cambridge, 2007), pp. 137–67.

Howe, Anthony, 'Free Trade and Global Order: The Rise and Fall of a Victorian Vision', in Duncan Bell (ed.), *Victorian Visions of Global Order: Empire and International Relations in Nineteenth-Century Political Thought* (Cambridge, 2007), pp. 26–46.

Howe, Glenford, *Race, War and Nationalism: A Social History of West Indians in the First World War* (Kingston, 2002).

Howe, Stephen, *Anticolonialism in British Politics: The Left and the End of Empire, 1918–1964* (Oxford, 1993).

— 'Empire and Ideology', in Sarah Stockwell (ed.), *The British Empire: Themes and Perspectives* (Oxford, 2008), pp. 157–76.

Howell, David L., *Geographies of Identity in Nineteenth-Century Japan* (Berkeley, CA, 2005), pp. 110–96.

Hoyt, Edwin P., *The Army Without a Country* (New York, 1967).

Hsu, Immanuel C.Y., 'The Great Policy Debate in China 1874: Maritime Defense vs. Frontier Defense', *Harvard Journal of Asiatic Studies* 25 (1964–65): pp. 212–28.

Huang, Ray, *Taxation and Governmental Finance in Sixteenth Century Ming China* (Cambridge, 1974).

— *1587: A Year of No Significance* (New Haven, CT, 1981).

Hucker, Charles O., *The Traditional Chinese State in Ming Times (1368–1644)* (Tucson, AZ, 1961).

Hudson, Linda S., *Mistress of Manifest Destiny: A Biography of Jane McManus Storm Cazneau, 1807–1878* (Austin, TX, 2001).

Hughes, Donald, *Pan's Travail: Environmental Problems of the Ancient Greeks and Romans* (Baltimore, MD, 1996).

Hughes-d'Aeth, T., 'Pretty as a Picture: Australia and the Imperial Picturesque', *Journal of Australian Studies* 53 (1997): pp. 99–107.

Hui, Wang, 'The Fate of "Mr Science" in China: The Concept of Science and its Application in Modern Chinese Thought', in Tani S. Barlow (ed.), *Formations of Colonial Modernity in East Asia* (Durham, NC, 1997), pp. 21–81.

Hulme, Peter, *Colonial Encounters: Europe and the Native Caribbean, 1492–1797* (London, 1986).

Hulsebosch, Daniel J., 'The Ancient Constitution and the Expanding Empire: Sir Edward Coke's British Jurisprudence', *Law and History Review* 21/3 (2003): pp. 439–82.

— *Constituting Empire: New York and the Transformation of Constitutionalism in the Atlantic World, 1664–1830* (Chapel Hill, NC, 2005).

Humboldt, A. von, *Personal Narrative of Travels to the Equinoctial Regions of the New Continent, 1799–1804* (London, 1819).

Hunt, Michael H., *Ideology and US Foreign Policy* (New Haven, CT, 1987).

— *The American Ascendancy: How the United States Gained and Wielded Global Dominance* (Chapel Hill, NC, 2007).

Hunt, Nancy Rose, 'Domesticity and Colonialism in Belgian Africa: Usumbura's *Foyer Social*, 1946–1960', *Signs* 15/3 (1990): pp. 447–74.

— *A Colonial Lexicon of Birth: Ritual, Medicalization, and Mobility in the Congo* (Durham, NC, 1999).

—, Tessie P. Liu and Jean Quataert (eds), *Gendered Colonialisms in African History* (Oxford, 1997).

Hunt, Peter, 'Arming Slaves and Helots in Classical Greece', in Christopher Leslie Brown and Philip D. Morgan (eds), *Arming Slaves: From Classical Times to the Modern Age* (New Haven, CT, 2006), pp. 14–39.

Hunter, Jane, *The Gospel of Gentility: American Women Missionaries in Turn-of-the-century China* (New Haven, CT, 1984).

Hunter, William Wilson, *The Indian Empire: Its Peoples, History, and Products* (London, 1886).

Huntington, Ellsworth, *The Pulse of Asia: A Journey in Central Asia Illustrating the Geographic Basis of History* (Boston, MA, 1907).

Hurt, R. Douglas, *The Indian Frontier, 1763–1846* (Albuquerque, NM, 2002).

Hussain, N., *The Jurisprudence of Emergency: Colonialism and the Rule of Law* (Ann Arbor, MI, 2003).

Hyam, Ronald, *Britain's Declining Empire: The Road to Decolonisation, 1918–1968* (Cambridge, 2006).

Iliffe, John, *A Modern History of Tanganyika* (Cambridge, 1979).

Imber, Colin, *The Ottoman Empire 1300–1481* (Istanbul, 1990).

— *The Ottoman Empire, 1300-1650: The Structure of Power*, 2nd ed. (Basingstoke, 2009).

Immerman, Richard H., *Empire for Liberty: A History of American Imperialism from Benjamin Franklin to Paul Wolfowitz* (Princeton, NJ, 2010).

İnalcık, Halil, *The Ottoman Empire: The Classical Age 1300–1600* (Westport, CT, 1973; London, 2002).
— and Donald Quataert *Economic and Social History of the Ottoman Empire* (Cambridge, 2004).
Inden, Ronald, *Imagining India* (Bloomington, IN, 2000).
Ingleson, John, 'Prostitution in Colonial Java', in David P. Chandler and M.C. Ricklefs (eds), *Nineteenth and Twentieth Century Indonesia: Essays in Honour of Professor J.D. Legge* (Clayton, VC, 1986), pp. 123–40.
Inglis, Amirah, *The White Women's Protection Ordinance: Sexual Anxiety and Politics in Papua* (New York, 1975).
Innis, Harold, *The Fur Trade in Canada* (Toronto, 1956).
'Interim Report of the South African Drought Investigation Committee' (Capetown, 1922).
Irvine, William, *Later Mughals*, ed. Jadunath Sarkar, 2 vols (Calcutta, 1921–22).
Isett, C.M., *State, Peasant and Merchant in Qing Manchuria, 1644–1862* (Stanford, CA, 2007).
İslamoğlu-İnan, Huri (ed.), *The Ottoman Empire and the World-Economy* (Cambridge, 1987).
Israel, Adrienne M., 'Measuring the War Experience: Ghanaian Soldiers in World War II', *Journal of Modern African Studies* 25/1 (1987): pp. 159–68.
Israel, J., *The Dutch Republic: Its Rise, Greatness, and Fall 1477–1806* (Oxford, 1995).
Itagaki, Ryūta, *Chōsenkindai no Rekishiminzokushi* (Tokyo, 2008).
— 'Datsu-reisen to shokuminchishihaisekinin no tsuikyū', in Puja Kim and Toshio Nakano (eds), *Rekishi to Sekinin* (Tokyo, 2008), pp. 260–84.
Ivanova, N.I., 'Nemtsy v ministerstvakh Rossii xix–nachala xx vekov', in *Nemtsy v Rossii* (St Petersburg, 2004).
Jack, Homer A. (ed.), *The Gandhi Reader: A Sourcebook of his Life and Writings* (New York, 1994).
Jackson, Peter, *The Timurid and Safavid Periods*: vol. 6, *The Cambridge History of Iran* (Cambridge, 1986).
— *The Delhi Sultanate: A Political and Military History* (Cambridge, 2003).
Jacobs, Jaap, *New Netherland: A Dutch Colony in Seventeenth-Century America* (Leiden, 2005).
Jacobson, Matthew Frye, *Whiteness of a Different Color: European Immigrants and the Alchemy of Race* (Cambridge, MA, 1998).
— *Barbarian Virtues: The United States Encounters Foreign Peoples at Home and Abroad, 1876–1917* (New York, 2000).
— *Special Sorrows: The Diasporic Imagination of Irish, Polish, and Jewish Immigrants in the United States* (Berkeley, CA, 2002).
Jahangir, *Tuzuki-i Jahangiri*, trans. Alexander Rogers, ed. Henry Beveridge, 2 vols (London, 1909–1914).
Jain, Ravindra K., *Indian Communities Abroad: Themes and Literature* (Delhi, 1993).
James, C.L.R., *The Black Jacobins: Toussaint L'Ouverture and the San Domingo Revolution* (New York, 1989).

Jay, Martin, 'The Scopic Regimes of Modernity', in Hal Foster (ed.), *Vision and Visuality* (Seattle, WA, 1988), pp. 3–23.

Jayawardena, Kumari, *Feminism and Nationalism in the Third World* (New Delhi, 1986).

— *The White Woman's Other Burden: Western Women and South Asia During British Colonial Rule* (New York, 1995).

Jefferson, Thomas, 'Address to Captain Hendrick, the Delawares, Mohicans, and Munries' (21 December 1808), in Albert Ellery Bergh (ed.), *The Writings of Thomas Jefferson*, vol. 16 (Washington, DC, 1907).

Jeffrey, Keith, *The British Army and the Crisis of Empire, 1918–22* (Manchester, 1984).

Jenks, Robert Darrah, *Insurgency and Social Disorder in Guizhou: The 'Miao' Rebellion, 1854–1873* (Honolulu, HI, 1994).

Jennings, Eric, *Curing the Colonizers: Hydrotherapy, Climatology, and French Colonial Spas* (Durham, NC, 2006).

Johnson, Chalmers, *The Sorrows of Empire: Militarism, Secrecy, and the End of the Republic* (New York, 2004).

Johnson, G. Wesley, *The Emergence of Black Politics in Senegal: The Struggle for Power in the Four Communes, 1900–1920* (Stanford, CA, 1971).

Johnson, Robert David, *Ernest Gruening and the American Dissenting Tradition* (Cambridge, MA, 1988).

— *The Peace Progressives and American Foreign Relations* (Cambridge, MA, 1995).

Johnson, Susan Lee, *Roaring Camp: The Social World of the California Gold Rush* (New York, 2000).

Johnson, Walter, *River of Dark Dreams: Slavery, Capitalism, and Imperialism in the Mississippi Valley* (Cambridge, MA, forthcoming).

Johnson-Odim, Cheryl and Margaret Strobel, 'Introduction: Conceptualizing the History of Women in Africa, Asia, Latin America and the Caribbean, and the Middle East and North Africa', in Barbara N. Ramusack and Sharon Sievers (eds), *Women in Asia: Restoring Women to History* (Bloomington, IN, 1999), pp. xvii–li.

Jones, Donna, 'The Prison House of Modernism: Colonial Spaces and the Construction of the Primitive at the 1931 Paris Colonial Exposition', *Modernism/ Modernity* 14/1 (2007): pp. 55–69.

Jones, D.W., *War and Economy in the Age of William III and Marlborough* (London, 1988).

Jones, Eric, 'Courts and Courtship: An Examination of Legal Practice in Dutch Asia', *Leidschrift* 21/2 (2006): pp. 31–50.

Jones, E.L., *The European Miracle: Environments, Economies and Geopolitics in the History of Europe and Asia* (Cambridge, 1981).

Jones, J.D.F., *Teller of Many Tales: The Lives of Laurens Van Der Post* (London, 2001).

Jŏng-il, Ha, 'Haebang Jŏnhusa ŭi Jaeinsik ŭi minjok gwa minjokjuŭi: Cho Gwanja wa Kim Ch'ŏl ŭl Chungsim uro', *Ch'ang-jak gwa Bip'yŏng* 135 (2007).

Joppien, R. and B. Smith, *The Art of Cook's Voyages*, 4 vols (London, 1985).

Jordan, Winthrop, *White Over Black: American Attitudes Toward the Negro* (Chapel Hill, NC, 1968), pp. 91–101.

Jørgensen, D., *Danmark-Norge mellom stormakterne 1688–1697* (Oslo, 1976).

Joseph, Gilbert M. *et al.* (eds), *Close Encounters of Empire* (Durham, NC, 1998).

Joseph, Gilbert M. and Timothy J. Henderson (eds), *The Mexico Reader: History, Culture, Politics* (Durham, NC, 2002).

Joshi, Sanjay, *Fractured Modernity: The Making of a Middle Class in Colonial North India* (New Delhi, 2001).

Julien, Charles-André, *L'Histoire de l'Algérie contemporaine*, vol. 1 (Paris, 1964).

Jung, Dietrich and Wolfango Piccoli, *Turkey at the Crossroads: Ottoman Legacies and a Greater Middle East* (London, 2001).

Kabeer, Naila, *Bangladeshi Women Workers and Labour Market Decisions: The Power to Choose* (New Delhi, 2001).

Kabuitu, Ng'ondu wa, 'Preserving Kikuyu Characteristics', *Mwigwithania* 2/2 (July–August 1929): n.p.

Kagan, R.L., *Lawsuits and Litigants in Castile, 1500–1700* (Chapel Hill, NC, 1981).

Kagarlitsky, Boris, *Empire of the Periphery: Russia and the World System* (London, 2007).

Kahin, George, *Nationalism and Revolution in Indonesia* (Ithaca, NY, 2003).

Kaines, Joseph, 'On Some of the Racial Aspects of Music', *Journal of the Anthropological Institute of Great Britain and Ireland* 1 (1872): pp. xxviii–xxxvi.

Kajimura, Hideki, *Chōsen ni okeru Shihonshugi no Keisei to Tenkai* (Tokyo, 1977).

Kale, Madhavi, *Fragments of Empire: Capital, Slavery, and Indian Indentured Labor Migration in the British Caribbean* (Philadelphia, PA, 1998).

Kamen, Henry, *Inquisition and Society in Spain: Sixteenth and Seventeenth Centuries* (London, 1985).

— *Empire: How Spain Became a World Power, 1492–1763* (New York, 2003).

Kamra, Sukashi, *Bearing Witness: Partition, Independence, End of the Raj* (Calgary, 2002; New Delhi, 2003).

Kanya-Forstner, A.S., 'The French Marines and the Conquest of the Western Sudan, 1880–1899', in Jaap de Moor and H.L. Wesseling (eds), *Imperialism and War: Essays on Colonial Wars in Asia and Africa* (Leiden, 1989), pp. 121–45.

Kapila, Shruti, 'Self, Spencer and Swaraj: Nationalist Thought and Critiques of Liberalism, 1890–1920', *Modern Intellectual History* 4 (2007): pp. 109–127.

Kaplan, Amy, *The Anarchy of Empire in the Making of US Culture* (Cambridge, MA, 2002).

— and Donald E. Pease (eds), *Cultures of United States Imperialism* (Durham, NC, 1993).

Kappeler, Andreas, *The Russian Empire: A Multiethnic History* (Harlow, 2001).

Karpat, Kemal H., *The Politicization of Islam: Reconstructing Identity, State, Faith, and Community in the Late Ottoman State* (New York, 2001).

Kasaba, Reşat, *The Ottoman Empire and the World Economy: The Nineteenth Century* (Albany, NY, 1988).

— *A Moveable Empire: Ottoman Nomads, Migrants and Refugees* (Seattle, WA, 2009).

Katz, Friedrich, *Ancient American Civilizations* (New York, 1972).

Kaur, Amarjit, 'Indian Labour, Labour Standard, and Worker's Health in Burma and Malaya, 1900–1940', *Modern Asian Studies* 40/2 (2006): pp. 425–75.

Kaur, Ravinder, 'Planning Urban Chaos: State and Refugees in Post-Partition Delhi', in Evelin Hust and Michael Mann (eds), *Urbanization and Governance in India* (Delhi, 2005), pp. 229–50.

Kayali, Hasan, *Arabs and Young Turks: Ottomanism, Arabism, and Islamism in the Ottoman Empire, 1908–1918* (Berkeley, CA, 1997).

Keer, Dhanajay, *Dr Ambedkar: Life and Mission* (Bombay, 1971).

Keller, Richard, *Colonial Madness: Psychiatry in French North Africa* (Chicago, IL, 2007).

Kelly, John D. and Martha Kaplan, *Represented Communities: Fiji and World Decolonization* (Chicago, IL, 2001).

Kennedy, Dane, *The Magic Mountains: Hill Stations and the British Raj* (Berkeley, CA, 1996).

Kennedy, John F., Address at a White House Reception for Latin American Diplomats and Members of Congress (13 March 1961), *Department of State Bulletin* 44/1136 (3 April 1961).

Kent, R.K., 'Palmares: An African State in Brazil', in Richard Price (ed.), *Maroon Societies: Rebel Slave Communities in the Americas* (Baltimore, MD, 1979), pp. 170–90.

Kenyatta, Jomo, *Facing Mount Kenya* (London, 1938).

Ker, John C., *Political Trouble in India* (Delhi, 1917).

Kercher, B., *Debt, Seduction, and Other Disasters: The Birth of Civil Law in Convict New South Wales* (Sydney, 1996).

— 'Resistance to Law under Autocracy', *Modern Law Review* 60/6 (1997): pp. 779–97.

— 'Perish or Prosper: The Law and Convict Transportation in the British Empire, 1700–1850', *Law and History Review* 21/3 (2003): pp. 527–54.

Kerslake, R.T., *Time and the Hour: Nigeria, East Africa and the Second World War* (London, 1997).

Khalidi, Omar, 'Ethnic Group Recruitment in the Indian Army: The Contrasting Cases of Sikhs, Muslims, Gurkhas and Others', *Pacific Affairs* 74/4 (2002): pp. 529–52.

Khalidi, Rashid, *Resurrecting Empire: Western Footprints and America's Perilous Path in the Middle East* (London, 2004).

Khan, Gulfishan, *Indian Muslim Perceptions of the West during the Eighteenth Century* (Karachi, 1998).

Khan, Inayat, *Shah Jahan Nama*, trans. A.R. Fuller; W.E. Begley and Z.A. Desai (eds) (Delhi, 1990).

Khan, Iqtidar Alam, 'The Nobility under Akbar and the Development of His Religious Policy, 1560–1580', *Journal of the Royal Asiatic Society* (1968): pp. 29–36.

— *Gunpowder and Firearms: Warfare in Medieval India* (Delhi, 2004).

Khan, Khafi and Muhammad Hashim, *Khafi Khan's History of 'Alamgir*, trans. S. Moinul Haq (Karachi, 1975).

Khan, Muhammad Saqi Musta'idd, *Maasir-i-`Alamgiri: A History of the Emperor Aurangzib-'Alamgir (reign 1658–1707 AD)*, trans. Sir Jadunath Sarkar (Calcutta, 1947).

Kheng, Cheah Boon, 'Power Behind the Throne: The Role of Queens and Court Ladies in Malay History', *Journal of the Malaysian Branch of the Royal Asiatic Society* 66 (1993): pp. 1–21.

Khodarkovsky, Michael, *Russia's Steppe Frontier: The Making of a Colonial Empire* (Bloomington, IN, 2002).

Kiernan, Ben, *Blood and Soil: A World History of Genocide and Extermination from Sparta to Darfur* (New Haven, CT, 2007).

Kiernan, V.G., *The Lords of Human Kind: European Attitudes towards the Outside World in the Imperial Age* (Harmondsworth, 1972).

Killingray, David, 'The Maintenance of Law and Order in British Colonial Africa', *African Affairs* 85/340 (1986): pp. 411–37.

— 'All the King's Men: Blacks in the British Army in the First World War, 1914–1918', in Rainer Lotz and Ian Pegg (eds), *Under the Imperial Carpet: Essays in Black History, 1780–1950* (Crawley, 1986), pp. 164–81.

— 'Guarding the Extending Frontier: Policing the Gold Coast, 1865–1913', in David M. Anderson and David Killingray (eds), *Policing the Empire: Government, Authority and Control, 1830–1940* (Manchester, 1991), pp. 106–125.

— *Africans in Britain* (London, 1994).

— '"A Good West Indian, a Good African, and, in Short, a Good Britisher": Black and British in a Colour-Conscious Empire, 1760–1950', *Journal of Imperial and Commonwealth History* 36/3 (2008): pp. 363–81.

Kim, Hodong, *Holy War in China: The Muslim Rebellion and State in Chinese Central Asia, 1864–1877* (Stanford, CA, 2004).

Kim, Jingyun and Gŭnsik Chŏng (eds), *Kŭndaejuch'e wa Singminji Kyuyul Kwŏlryŏk* (Seoul, 1997).

Kim, Kyu Hyun, 'Reflections on the Problems of Colonial Modernity and "Collaboration" in Modern Korean History', *Journal of International and Area Studies* 11 (2004): pp. 95–111.

— 'War and the Colonial Legacy in Recent South Korean Scholarship', *International Institute for Asian Studies Newsletter* 38 (2005): p. 6.

Kim, Puja, *Shokuminchikichōsen no Kyōiku to Gender* (Kanagawa, 2005).

Kim, Sujin, '1930 nyŏndae Kyŏngsŏng ŭi Yŏhaksaeng gwa "Chigŏp Buin" ŭl t'onghae bon sinyŏsŏng ŭi kasisŏng gwa chubyŏnsŏng', in Jeuk Kon and Gŭnsik Chŏng (eds), *Sinminji ŭi Ilsang: Chibae wa Kyunyŏl* (Seoul, 2006), pp. 489–524.

Kim, Yŏngdal, 'Sōshikaimei no seido', in Yŏngdal Kim, Setsuko Miyata and T'aeho Yang (eds), *Sōshikaimei* (Tokyo, 1992), pp. 41–75.

Kimble, Judy and Elaine Unterhalter, '"We Opened the Road for You, You Must Go Forward": ANC Women's Struggles, 1912–1982', *Feminist Review* 12 (1982): pp. 11–35.

King, Richard, *Orientalism and Religion: Post-colonial Theory, India, and 'the Mystic East'* (London, 1999).

Kinross, Lord, *The Ottoman Centuries: The Rise and Fall of the Turkish Empire* (New York, 1977).

Kinyatti, Maina wa, *Kimathi's Letters* (Nairobi, 1986).

Kiple, Kenneth F., *The Caribbean Slave: A Biological History* (New York, 1984).

Kirk-Greene, Anthony H.M., '"Damnosa Hereditas": Ethnic Ranking and the Martial Races Imperative in Africa', *Ethnic and Racial Studies* 3/4 (1980): pp. 393–414.

Kiyomiya, Shirō, *Gaichihō Jyosetsu* (Tokyo, 1944).

Klare, Michael, *Blood and Oil: The Dangers and Consequences of America's Growing Petroleum Dependency* (New York, 2004).

Klass, Morton, *East Indians in Trinidad: A Study of Cultural Persistence* (New York, 1961).

Klein, Christina, *Cold War Orientalism: Asia in the Middlebrow Imagination* (Berkeley, CA, 2003).

Klein, Herbert, *The Atlantic Slave Trade* (Cambridge, 1999).

— and Ben Vinson III, *African Slavery in the Caribbean and Latin America* (New York, 2007).

Klooster, Wim, 'The Dutch Atlantic, 1600–1800: Expansion Without Empire', *Itinerario* 23 (1999): pp. 48–69.

— 'Other Netherlands Beyond the Sea: Dutch America between Metropolitan Control and Divergence, 1600–1795', in Christine Daniels and Michael V. Kennedy (eds), *Negotiated Empires: Centers and Peripheries in the Americas, 1500–1820* (New York, 2002), pp. 171–5.

Knaap, Gerrit, 'Pants, Skirts and Pulpits: Women and Gender in Seventeenth-Century Amboina', in Barbara Watson Andaya (ed.), *Other Pasts: Women, Gender and History in Early Modern Southeast Asia* (Honolulu, HI, 2000), pp. 147–73.

Knapman, Claudia, *White Women in Fiji, 1835–1935: The Ruins of Empire?* (Sydney, 1986).

Knight, Franklin W., *The Caribbean: The Genesis of a Fragmented Nationalism*, 2nd edn (New York, 1990).

Knock, Thomas J., *To End All Wars: Woodrow Wilson and the Quest for a New World Order* (Princeton, NJ, 1992).

Knoll, Arthur and Lewis Gann, *Germans in the Tropics: Essays in German Colonial History* (New York, 1987).

Knox, Alexander, *The Climate of the Continent of Africa* (Cambridge, 1911).

Koch, Ebba, *Mughal Architecture: An Outline of Its History and Development (1526–1858)* (New York, 2002).

— *Complete Taj Mahal: And the Riverfront Gardens of Agra* (London, 2006).

Koenigsberger, H.G., *Politicians and Virtuosi: Essays in Early Modern History* (London, 1986).

Koikari, Mire, *Pedagogy of Democracy: Feminism and the Cold War in the US Occupation of Japan* (Philadelphia, PA, 2008).

Kolsky, E., *Colonial Justice in British India: White Violence and the Rule of Law* (Cambridge, 2010).

Komagome, Takeshi, *Shokuminchiteikokunihon no Bunkatōgō* (Tokyo, 1996).

— '"Teikokushi" kenkyū no shatei', *Nihonshikenkyu*, 452 (2000).

— '"Teikoku no hazama" kara kangaeru', *Nen'pō Nihon Gendaishi* 10 (2005): pp. 1–21.

Kostal, R.W., *A Jurisprudence of Power: Victorian Empire and the Rule of Law* (Oxford, 2005).

Kovalenko, I., 'Bandung: Past and Present', *Far Eastern Affairs* 3 (1980): pp. 17–28.

Kowaleski-Wallace, Elizabeth, *Consuming Subjects: Women, Shopping and Business in the Eighteenth Century* (New York, 1997).

Kraay, Hendrik, 'Slavery, Citizenship and Military Service in Brazil's Mobilization for the Paraguayan War', *Slavery and Abolition* 18/3 (1997): pp. 228–56.

— 'Arming Slaves in Brazil from the Seventeenth to the Nineteenth Century', in Christopher Leslie Brown and Philip D. Morgan (eds), *Arming Slaves: From Classical Times to the Modern Age* (New Haven, CT, 2006), pp. 146–79.

Kramer, Paul A., 'Making Concessions: Race and Empire Revisited at the Philippine Exposition in St Louis, 1901–1905', *Radical History Review* 73 (1999): pp. 74–114.

— *The Blood of Government: Race, Empire, the United States, and the Philippines* (Chapel Hill, NC, 2006).

Kranidis, Rita, *The Victorian Spinster and Colonial Emigration: Contested Subjects* (New York, 1999).

Kriegel, Lara, *Grand Designs: Labor, Empire and the Museum in Victorian Culture* (Durham, NC, 2007).

Krikkler, Jeremy, *White Rising: The 1922 Insurrection and Racial Killing in South Africa* (Manchester, 2005).

Kriz, Kay Dian, *Slavery, Sugar and Refinement: Representing the British West Indies, 1700–1840* (London, 2008).

Kuhn, Philip A., *Rebellion and Its Enemies in Late Imperial China: Militarization and Social Structure* (Cambridge, MA, 1970).

— 'The Taiping Rebellion', in John K. Fairbank (ed.), *The Cambridge History of China*: vol. 10, *Late Ch'ing, 1800–1911*, part 1 (Cambridge, 1978), pp. 264–317.

— *Soulstealers: The Chinese Sorcery Scare of 1768* (Cambridge, MA, 1990).

Kuhnke, LaVerne, *Lives at Risk: Public Health in Nineteenth-Century Egypt* (Berkeley, CA, 1990).

Kuklick, Henrika, *The Savage Within: The Social History of British Anthropology, 1885–1945* (Cambridge, 1991).

Kulikoff, Allan, *Tobacco and Slaves: The Development of Southern Cultures in the Chesapeake, 1680–1800* (Chapel Hill, NC, 1986).

Kulke, Hermann (ed.), *State in India, 1000–1700* (Delhi, 1995).

Kumar, Deepak, *Science and the Raj, 1857–1905* (Oxford, 1995).

Kupperman, Karen Ordahl, *Settling with the Indians: The Meeting of English and Indian Cultures in America, 1580–1640* (Totowa, NJ, 1980).

— *Roanoke: The Abandoned Colony* (Lanham, MD, 1991).

Kurasawa, Aiko *et al.* (eds), *Iwanamikōza: Ajia-Taiheiyōsensō*, vols 1–8 (Tokyo, 2005–2006).

LaFeber, Walter, *American Age: United States Foreign Policy at Home and Abroad since 1750* (New York, 1989).

— *Inevitable Revolutions: The United States in Central America* (New York, 1993).

— *The New Empire: An Interpretation of American Expansion, 1860–1898* (Ithaca, NY, 1998).

Lahori, Abdul Hamid, *King of the World: The Padshahnama*, ed. Milo Cleveland Beach and Ebba Koch, trans. Wheeler Thackston (London, 1997).

Laidlaw, Zoë, *Colonial Connections, 1815–45: Patronage, the Information Revolution and Colonial Government* (Manchester, 2005).

Lake, Marilyn, 'Mission Impossible: How Men Gave Birth to the Australian Nation –Nationalism, Gender and Other Seminal Acts', *Gender and History* 43 (1992): pp. 305–322.

Lal, B.V., 'Kunti's Cry: Indentured Women on Fiji Plantations', *Indian Economic & Social History Review* 22/1 (1985): pp. 55–71.

Lal, Brij (ed.), *Plantation Workers: Resistance and Accommodation* (Honolulu, HI, 1993).

Lal, Ruby, *Domesticity and Power in the Early Mughal World* (Cambridge, 2005).

Lal, Vinay, 'The Incident of the 'Crawling Lane': Women in the Punjab Disturbances of 1919', *Genders* 16 (1993): pp. 35–60.

Lambert, Michael C., 'From Citizenship to Negritude: "Making a Difference" in Elite Ideologies of Colonized Francophone West Africa', *Comparative Studies in Society and History* 35/2 (April 1993): pp. 239–62.

Landes, David S., *The Wealth and Poverty of Nations: Why Some are So Wealthy and Some So Poor* (New York, 1998).

Lang, James, *Portuguese Brazil: The King's Plantation* (New York, 1979).

Langer, Erick and Robert H. Jackson (eds), *The New Latin American Mission History* (Lincoln, NE, 1995).

Laqueur, Thomas, *Making Sex: Body and Gender from the Greeks to Freud* (Cambridge, 1990).

Latner, Richard B., *The Presidency of Andrew Jackson: White House Politics 1829–1837* (Athens, GA, 1979).

Latour, Bruno, *The Pasteurization of France* (Cambridge, MA, 1988).

— *Pandora's Hope: Essays on the Reality of Social Sciences* (London, 1998).

Laurence, K.O., *A Question of Labour: Indentured Immigration into Trinidad and British Guiana, 1875–1917* (Kingston, 1994).

Lawson, Philip, *The East India Company: A History* (London, 1993).

Leach, William, *Land of Desire: Merchants, Power, and the Rise of a New American Culture* (New York, 1993).

Leakey, L.S.B., *The Southern Kikuyu Before 1903* (London, 1977).

Lears, T. Jackson, *Fables of Abundance: A Cultural History of Advertising in America* (New York, 1994).

Leclerc, G.-L. Comte de Buffon, *Histoire naturelle: générale et particulière* (Paris, 1749–1804).

LeDonne, John, *The Russian Empire and the World, 1700–1917: The Geopolitics of Expansion and Containment* (New York, 1997).

Lee, C.H., *The British Economy since 1700: A Macroeconomic Perspective* (Cambridge, 1986).

Lee, Christopher J. (ed.), *Making a World after Empire: The Bandung Moment and its Political Afterlives* (Athens, OH, 2010).

Lee, Chulwoo, 'Modernity, Legality, and Power in Korea Under Japanese Rule', in Gi-Wook Shin and Michael Robinson (eds), *Colonial Modernity in Korea* (Cambridge, MA, 1999), pp. 21–51.

Lee, Robert H.G., *The Manchurian Frontier in Ch'ing History* (Cambridge, MA, 1970).

Lee, Sŏngsi and Jihŏn Im (eds), *Kuksa ŭi Sinhwa rul Nŏmŏsŏ* (Seoul, 2004).

Lefèvre, Corienne, 'Recovering a Missing Voice from Mughal India: The Imperial Discourse of Jahangir (r. 1605–1627)', *Journal of the Economic and Social History of the Orient* 50/4 (2007): pp. 452–89.

Leffler, Melvyn P., 'The Cold War: What Do "We Now Know"?' *American Historical Review* 104/2 (1999): pp. 501–524.

Lefroy, J.H., *Memorials of the Discovery and Early Settlement of the Bermudas or Somers Islands, 1515–1685: Compiled from the Colonial Records and other Original Sources* (London, 1877–79).

Lehning, James, *Peasant and French: Cultural Contact in Rural France During the Nineteenth Century* (Cambridge, 1995).

Leibsohn, Dana, *Script and Glyph: Prehistory, Colonial Bookmaking and Historia Toleteca-chichimoca* (Cambridge, MA, 2009).

Le Naour, Jean-Yves, *La Honte noire: L'Allemagne et les troupes coloniales françaises, 1914–1945* (Paris, 2004).

Lennon, Jane, 'Port Arthur, Norfolk Island, New Caledonia: Convict Prison Islands in the Antipodes', in William Logan and Keir Reeves (eds), *Places of Pain and Shame: Dealing with 'Difficult Heritage'* (London, 2009), pp. 165–81.

Lenin, V.I., *Imperialism, the Highest Stage of Capitalism* (Peking, 1964 [1916]).

Leonard, Karen, 'The "Great Firm" Theory of the Decline of the Mughal Empire', *Comparative Studies in Society and History* 21/1 (1979): pp. 151–67.

Lester, Alan, *Imperial Networks: Creating Identities in Nineteenth-Century South Africa and Britain* (London, 2001).

Le Sueur, James D. (ed.), *The Decolonization Reader* (New York, 2003).

Levine, Philippa, 'Battle Colors: Race, Sex, and Colonial Soldiery in World War I', *Journal of Women's History* 9/4 (1998): pp. 104–130.

— *Prostitution, Race and Politics: Policing Venereal Disease in the British Empire* (New York, 2003).

— 'Sexuality, Gender and Empire', in Philippa Levine (ed.), *Gender and Empire* (Oxford, 2004), pp. 134–55.

— (ed.), *Gender and Empire* (Oxford, 2004).

— 'States of Undress: Nakedness and the Colonial Imagination', *Victorian Studies* 50/2 (2008): pp. 189–219.

Levy, Avigdor (ed.), *The Jews of the Ottoman Empire* (Princeton, NJ, 1984).

Lewis, Bernard, *The Emergence of Modern Turkey* (Oxford, 1968).

— *Race and Slavery in the Middle East: A Historical Enquiry* (New York, 1990).

Lewis, Bernard *et al.* (eds), *Encyclopaedia of Islam* (Leiden, 1965)

Lewis, D.M., *Lighten their Darkness: The Evangelical Mission to Working-Class London, 1828–67* (New York, 1986).

Lewis, James R. and Olav Hammer (eds), *The Invention of Sacred Tradition* (Cambridge, 2007).

Lewis, Joanna, *Empire State-Building: War and Welfare in Kenya, 1925–52* (London, 2001).

Lewitter, L.R., 'The Partitions of Poland', in A. Goodwin (ed.), *The New Cambridge Modern History*: vol. 8, *The American and French Revolutions 1763–93* (Cambridge, 1965), pp. 333–59.

Li, Lillian M., *Fighting Famine in North China: State, Market, and Environmental Decline, 1690s-1990s* (Stanford, CA, 2007).

Liebowitz, Arnold, *Defining Status: A Comprehensive Analysis of United States Territorial Relations* (Dordrecht, 1989).

Lieven, Dominic, *Russia's Rulers under the Old Regime* (New Haven, CT, 1989).

— *Empire: The Russian Empire and its Rivals* (New Haven, CT, 2000).

Limerick, Patricia Nelson, *The Legacy of Conquest: The Unbroken Past of the American West* (New York, 1987).

Lin, Man-houng, *China Upside Down: Currency, Society, and Ideologies, 1808–1856* (Cambridge, MA, 2006).

Linebaugh, Peter and Marcus Rediker, *The Many Headed Hydra: Sailors, Slaves, Commoners, and the Hidden History of the Revolutionary Atlantic* (Boston, MA, 2000).

Linn, Brian McAllister, *Guardians of Empire: The US Army and the Pacific, 1902–1940* (Chapel Hill, NC, 1997)

Liu, Lydia H., 'Translingual Practice: The Discourse of Individualism between China and the West', in Tani S. Barlow (ed.), *Formations of Colonial Modernity in East Asia* (Durham, NC, 1997), pp. 83–112.

Livingstone, David and Charles, *Narrative of an Expedition to the Zambesi and its Tributaries: And of the Discovery of the Lakes Shirwa and Nyassa, 1858–1864* (New York, 1866).

Locher-Scholten, Elsbeth, *Women and the Colonial State: Essays on Gender and Modernity in the Netherlands Indies, 1900–1942* (Amsterdam, 2000).

— *Sumatran Sultanate and Colonial State: Jambi and the Rise of Dutch Imperialism 1839–1907* (Ithaca, NY, 2003).

— 'Morals, Harmony and National Identity: "Companionate Feminism" in Colonial Indonesia in the 1930s', *Journal of Women's History* 14/4 (2003): pp. 38–58.

— 'From Urn to Monument: Dutch Memories of World War II in the Pacific, 1945–1995', in Andrea L. Smith (ed.), *Europe's Invisible Migrants* (Amsterdam, 2003), pp. 115–20.

Locke, John, *Two Treatises of Government* (Cambridge, 1964).

Lockhart, James, *Men of Cajamarca: A Social and Biographical Study of the First Conquistadors of Peru* (Austin, TX, 1972).

— *Early Latin America: A History of Colonial Spanish America and Brazil* (Cambridge, 1983).

— 'Trunk Lines and Feeder Lines: The Spanish Reaction to American Resources', in Kenneth J. Andrien and Rolena Adorno (eds), *Transatlantic Encounters: Europeans and Andeans in the Sixteenth Century* (Berkeley, CA, 1991), pp. 90–120.

— and Stuart B. Schwartz, *Early Latin America: A History of Colonial Spanish America and Brazil* (New York, 1983).

Lockhart, P.D., *Denmark 1513–1660: The Rise and Decline of a Renaissance Monarchy* (Oxford, 2007).

Logan, Rayford W., *The Betrayal of the Negro: From Rutherford B. Hayes to Woodrow Wilson* (New York, 1965).

Lohr, Eric, *Nationalizing the Russian Empire: The Campaign Against Enemy Aliens During World War I* (Cambridge, MA, 2003).

Lombroso, Cesare, *Crime: Its Causes and Remedies*, trans. Henry P. Horton (Boston, MA, 1912).

Lone, Stewart, *Japan's First Modern War: Army and Society in the Conflict with China, 1894–95* (London, 1994).

Longworth, P., *Russia's Empires: Their Rise and Fall: From Prehistory to Putin* (London, 2005).

Loomba, Ania, *Colonialism/Postcolonialism* (London, 1998).

Lopes, Margaret Maria and Irina Podgorny, 'The Shaping of Latin American Museums of Natural History, 1850–1990', *Osiris* 15 (2000): pp. 108–118.

Lorcin, P.M., 'Imperialism, Colonial Identity, and Race in Algeria, 1830–1870: The Role of the French Medical Corps', *Isis* 90/4 (1999): pp. 652–79.

Lorenzen, David, 'Who Invented Hinduism?' *Comparative Studies in Society and History* 41/4 (1999): pp. 630–59.

Louis, Wm Roger, 'American Anti-Colonialism and the Dissolution of the British Empire', *International Affairs* 61/3 (1985): pp. 395–420.

— 'The Dissolution of the British Empire', in Judith M. Brown and Wm Roger Louis, *Oxford History of the British Empire: The Twentieth Century* (Oxford, 1999), pp. 329–56.

Love, Eric T.L., *Race over Empire: Racism and US Imperialism, 1865–1900* (Chapel Hill, NC, 2004).

— 'White is the Color of Empire: The Annexation of Hawaii in 1898', in James T. Campbell, Matthew Pratt Guterl and Robert G. Lee (eds), *Race, Nation and Empire in American History* (Chapel Hill, NC, 2007), pp. 75–102.

Lovejoy, Arthur O., *The Great Chain of Being: A Study of the History of an Idea* (Cambridge, 1936).

Lovejoy, Paul, *Transformations in Slavery: A History of Slavery in Africa* (Cambridge, 2000).

Lugard, Frederick, *The Dual Mandate in British Tropical Africa* (Edinburgh, 1922).

Luis-Brown, David, *Waves of Decolonization: Discourses of Race and Hemispheric Citizenship in Cuba, Mexico, and the United States* (Durham, NC, 2008).

Lundestad, Geir, 'Empire by Invitation', *Diplomatic History* 23 (1999): pp. 189–217.

Lunn, Joseph, '"Les Races Guerrières": Racial Preconceptions in the French Military about West African Soldiers during the First World War', *Journal of Contemporary History* 34/4 (1999): pp. 517–36.

Lynch, John, *Spain under the Habsburgs*, 2 vols (Oxford, 1968).

Maari, E., 'The Balokole Movement in Nyabushozi Country of Ankole', in A. Byaruhanga-Akiiki (ed.), *Occasional Research Papers*, vol. 22 (Kampala, 1974), n.p.

McAlister, Melani, *Epic Encounters: Culture, Media, and US Interests in the Middle East since 1945* (Berkeley, CA, 2005).

McCaa, Robert, 'Spanish and Nahuatl Views on Smallpox and Demographic Catastrophe in the Conquest of Mexico', *Journal of Interdisciplinary History* 25/3 (1995): pp. 397–431.

McCarthy, Angela, *A Global Clan: Scottish Migrant Networks and Identity since the Eighteenth Century* (New York, 2006).

McCarthy, Justin, *Death and Exile: The Ethnic Cleansing of Ottoman Muslims, 1821–1922* (Princeton, NJ, 1995).

— *The Ottoman Turks: A Introductory History to 1923* (Harlow, 1997).

— *The Ottoman Peoples and the End of Empire* (London, 2001).

McCaskie, T.C., 'Cultural Encounters: Britain and Africa in the Nineteenth Century', in Andrew Porter (ed.), *Oxford History of the British Empire*: vol. 3, *The Nineteenth Century* (Oxford, 1999).

McClellan, James, *Colonialism and Science: Saint Domingue in the Old Regime* (Baltimore, MD, 1992).

McClintock, Anne, 'The Angel of Progress: Pitfalls of the Term "Postcolonialism"', *Social Text* 31/32 (1992): pp. 84–98.

— *Imperial Leather: Race, Gender and Sexuality in the Colonial Contest* (New York, 1995).

McCook, Stuart, *States of Nature: Science, Agriculture, and Environment in the Spanish Caribbean, 1760–1940* (Austin, TX, 2002).

McCormick, Thomas J. and Walter LaFeber, *Behind the Throne: Servants of Power to Imperial Presidents, 1898–1968* (Madison, WI, 1993).

McCoy, Alfred, *A Question of Torture: CIA Interrogation for the Cold War to the War on Terror* (New York, 2006).

McCracken, Donal, *Gardens of Empire: Botanical Institutions of the Victorian British Empire* (Leicester, 1997).

McCulloch, Jock, *Black Peril, White Virtue: Sexual Crime in Southern Rhodesia, 1902–1935* (Bloomington, IN, 2000).

McCutcheon, Russell, *Manufacturing Religion* (New York, 1997).

— *The Discipline of Religion: Structure, Meaning, Rhetoric* (London, 2003).

MacDonald, Robert H., *Sons of the Empire: The Frontier and the Boy Scout Movement, 1890–1918* (Toronto, ON, 1993).

Macdonald, William, *The Conquest of the Desert* (London, 1913).

McFarlane, A., *The British in the Americas 1480–1815* (London, 1994).

McGovern, Charles F., *Sold American: Consumption and Citizenship, 1890–1945* (Chapel Hill, NC, 2006).

McGowan, Abigail, *Crafting the Nation in Colonial India* (New York, 2009).

McGowan, B., *Economic Life in Ottoman Europe: Taxation, Trade and the Struggle for Land, 1600–1800* (Cambridge, 1981).

McGrath, John T., *The French in Early Florida: In the Eye of the Hurricane* (Gainesville, FL, 2000).

McGurk, John, *The Elizabethan Conquest of Ireland* (Manchester, 1997).

McHugh, Paul, *The Maori Magna Carta: New Zealand Law and the Treaty of Waitangi* (Oxford, 1991).

McKay, Angus, *Spain in the Middle Ages: From Frontier to Empire, 1000–1500* (New York, 1977).

MacKenzie, John, *Propaganda and Empire: The Manipulation of British Public Opinion, 1880–1960* (Manchester, 1984).

— (ed.), *Imperialism and Popular Culture* (Manchester, 1987).

— *The Empire of Nature: Hunting, Conservation and British Imperialism* (Manchester, 1988).

— *Orientalism: History, Theory and the Arts* (Manchester, 1995).

— 'Empire and Metropolitan Cultures', in Andrew Porter (ed.), *Oxford History of the British Empire*: vol. 3, *The Nineteenth Century* (Oxford, 1999): pp. 270–94.

McKeown, Adam, 'Global Migration, 1846–1940', *Journal of World History* 15/2 (2004): pp. 155–89.

Mackie, J.A.C., *Bandung 1955: Non-Alignment and Afro-Asian Solidarity* (Singapore, 2005).

Mackinder, H.J., *Britain and the British Seas* (London, 1902).

Maclachan, Patricia L., *Consumer Politics in Postwar Japan* (Ithaca, NY, 2002).

Maclachan, Sheldon and Patricia L. Machlachan (eds), *The Ambivalent Consumer: Questioning Consumption in East Asia and the West* (Ithaca, NY, 2006).

Mclean, David, *War, Diplomacy and Informal Empire: Britain, France and Latin America, 1836–1852* (London, 1995).

MacLean, Ian, *White Aborigines: Identity Politics in Australian Art* (Cambridge, 1998).

MacLeod, Roy, 'On Visiting the "Moving Metropolis": Reflections on the Architecture of Imperial Science', *Historical Records of Australian Science* 5 (1982): pp. 1–16.

McLynn, Frank, *1759: The Year that Made Great Britain the Master of the World* (New York, 2004).

MacMaster, Neil, *Colonial Migrants and Racism: Algerians in France, 1900–62* (Basingstoke, 1997).

MacMunn, George Fletcher, *The Armies of India* (London, 1911).

— *The Martial Races of India* (London, 1933).

McNamara, Dennis L., *The Colonial Origins of Korean Enterprise, 1910–1945* (Cambridge, 1990).

McNeil, John Robert, *Atlantic Empires of France and Spain: Louisbourg and Havana* (Baltimore, MD, 1985).

McNeill, John, *Something New Under the Sun: An Environmental History of the Twentieth- Century World* (New York, 2000).

— 'Observations on the Nature and Culture of Environmental History', *History and Theory* 42 (2003): pp. 5–43.

— *The Boundaries of the Mediterranean World: An Environmental History* (Cambridge, 2003).

— and William H. McNeill, *The Human Web: A Bird's Eye View of World History* (New York, 2003).

McNeill, William H., *The Origins of Civilization* (New York, 1968).

— *Plagues and Peoples* (New York, 1976).

McPherson, Alan, *Yankee No! Anti-Americanism in US-Latin American Relations* (Cambridge, MA, 2003).

MacPherson, Robert, 'East African Revival', *Kikuyu News* 193 (September 1950).

Macqueen, Norrie, *The Decolonization of Portuguese Africa: Metropolitan Revolution and the Dissolution of Empire* (London, 1997).

McSherry, J. Patrice, *Predatory States: Operation Condor and Covert War in Latin America* (New York, 2005).

Madan, A.C., *An Outline Dictionary* (London, 1905).

Madra, Amandeep Singh and Parmjit Singh, *Warrior Saints: Three Centuries of The Sikh Military Tradition* (London, 1999).

Magee, Gary B. and Andrew S. Thompson, *Empire and Globalisation: Networks of People, Goods and Capital in the British World, c.1850–1914* (Cambridge, 2010).

Mahone, Sloan and Megan Vaughan (eds), *Psychiatry and Empire* (Basingstoke, 2007).

Maier, Charles, *Among Empires: American Ascendancy and Its Predecessors* (Cambridge, MA, 2006).

Maimbo, Samuel M. *et al.* (eds), *Migrant Labor Remittances in South Asia* (Washington, DC, 2005).

Makdisi, Ussama, *The Culture of Sectarianism: Community, History and Violence in Nineteenth Century Ottoman Lebanon* (Berkeley, CA, 2000).

Malik, Kenan, *The Meaning of Race: Race, History, and Culture in Western Society* (Houndmills, 1996).

Mamdani, Mahmood, *Citizen and Subject: Contemporary Africa and the Legacy of Late Colonialism* (Princeton, NJ, 1996).

— 'Historicizing Power and Responses to Power: Indirect Rule and Its Reform', *Social Research* 66/3 (1999), pp. 859–86.

— *When Victims Become Killers: Colonialism, Nativism, and the Genocide in Rwanda* (Princeton, NJ, 2001).

Mancall, Peter C. and James H. Merrell (eds), *American Encounters: Natives and Newcomers from European Contact to Indian Removal, 1500–1850*, 2nd edn (New York, 2007).

Mancke, Elizabeth, 'Negotiating an Empire: Britain and its Overseas Possessions', in Christine Daniels and Michael V. Kennedy (eds), *Negotiated Empires: Centers and Peripheries in the Americas, 1500–1820* (New York, 2002), pp. 235–66.

— and Carole Shammas (eds), *The Creation of the British Atlantic World* (Baltimore, MD, 2005).

Manderson, Lenore, *Sickness and the State: Health and Illness in Colonial Malaya, 1870–1940* (Cambridge, 1996).

Manela, Erez, *The Wilsonian Moment: Self-Determination and the International Origins of Anticolonial Nationalism* (Oxford, 2007).

Mani, Lata, *Contentious Traditions: The Debate on Sati in Colonial India* (Berkeley, CA, 1998).

Mann, Erick J., *Mikono ya damu: 'Hands of Blood': African Mercenaries and the Politics of Conflict in German East Africa, 1888–1904* (New York, 2002).

Mann, Gregory, *Native Sons: West African Veterans and France in the Twentieth Century* (Durham, NC, 2006).

Mann, Michael, 'Migration – Re-migration – Circulation: South Asian Kulis in the Indian Ocean and Beyond, 1840–1940', in Donna R. Gabaccia and Dirk Hoerder (eds), *Connecting Seas and Connected Ocean Rims. Indian, Atlantic, and Pacific Oceans and China Seas Migrations from the 1830s to the 1930s* (Leyden and Boston, MA, 2011), pp. 108–33.

Mantena, Karuna, 'Henry Maine and the Theoretical Origins of Indirect Rule', in Andrew Lewis and Michael Lobban (eds), *Law and History* (Oxford, 2004), pp. 159–88.

Mapp, Paul W., *The Elusive West and the Contest for Empire, 1713-1763* (Chapel Hill, NC, 2011).

Marco, G.J., *Silent Spring Revisited* (New York, 1987).

Marcovich, Anne, 'French Colonial Medicine and Colonial Rule: Algeria and Indochina', in Roy Macleod and Milton Lewis (eds), *Disease, Medicine and Empire: Perspectives on Western Medicine and the Experience of European Expansion* (London, 1988), pp. 103–118.

Marcus, Abraham, *The Middle East on the Eve of Modernity: Aleppo in the Eighteenth Century* (New York, 1989).

Marichal, Carlos, 'Mexican Cochineal and European Demand for American Dyes, 1550–1850', in Steven Topik, Carlos Marichal and Sephyr Frank (eds), *From Silver to Cocaine: Latin American Commodity Chains and the Building of the World Economy, 1500–2000* (Durham, NC, 2007), pp. 76–92.

Mark, Peter, *Portuguese Style and Luso-African Identity: Precolonial Senegambia, Sixteenth–Nineteenth Centuries* (Bloomington, IN, 2002).

Markovits, Claud, 'Indian Merchant Networks Outside India in the Nineteenth and Twentieth Centuries', *Modern Asian Studies* 33 (1999): pp. 883–911.

— *The Global World of Indian Merchants, 1750–1947: Traders of Sind from Bukhara to Panama* (Cambridge, 2000).

Marks, Robert B., *Tigers, Rice, Silk and Silt: Environment and Economy in Late Imperial South China* (New York, 1997).

Marks, Sally, 'Black Watch on the Rhine: A Study in Propaganda, Prejudice and Prurience', *European History Quarterly* 13/3 (1983): pp. 297–334.

Marks, Shula, *Reluctant Rebellion: The 1906–8 Disturbances in Natal* (Oxford, 1970).

— *The Ambiguities of Dependence in South Africa: Class, Nationalism and the State in Twentieth-Century Natal* (Baltimore, MD, 1986).

— 'What Is Colonial about Colonial Medicine? And What Has Happened to Imperialism and Health?', *Social History of Medicine* 10 (1997): pp. 205–219.

Marks, Steven G., *Road to Power: The Trans-Siberian Railroad and the Colonization of Asian Russia, 1850–1917* (Ithaca, NY, 1991).

Marr, David, *Vietnamese Anticolonialism, 1885–1925* (Berkeley, CA, 1971).

Marriott, John, *The Other Empire: Metropolis, India and Progress in the Colonial Imagination* (Manchester, 2003).

— and Bhaskar Mukhopadhyay (eds), *Britain in India, 1765–1905*, 6 vols (London, 2006).

Marsden, Ben and Crosbie Smith, *Engineering Empires: A Cultural History of Technology in Nineteenth-Century Britain* (New York, 2005).

Marseille, Jacques, *L'Âge d'or de la France coloniale* (Paris, 1986).

— *Empire colonial et capitalisme français: histoire d'un divorce* (Paris, 1989).

Marsh, George, *Man and Nature, or, Physical Geography as Modified by Human Action* (London, 1864).

— *The Earth as Modified by Human Action* (London, 1874).

Marshall, D.N., *Mughals in India: A Bibliographic Survey of Manuscripts* (London, 1985).

Marshall, P.J., 'Parliament and Property Rights in the Late Eighteenth-Century British Empire', in John Brewer and Susan Staves (eds), *Early Modern Conceptions of Property* (London, 1996), pp. 530–44.

— (ed.), *The Eighteenth Century in Indian History: Evolution or Revolution?* (Delhi, 2003).

— (ed.), *The Making and Unmaking of Empires: Britain, India and America, c.1750–1783* (Oxford, 2005).

— 'Empire and British Identity: The Maritime Dimension', in D. Cannadine (ed.), *Empire, The Sea and Global History: Britain's Maritime World, c. 1763–c. 1840* (London, 2007), pp. 41–59.

Marti, José, Letter to Manuel Mercado, 18 May 1895, in Robert H. Holden and Eric Zolov (eds), *Latin America and the United States: A Documentary History* (Oxford, 2000).

Martí, J. and C. Manzoni, *El Presidio Político en Cuba: Último Diario y Otros Textos* (Buenos Aires, 1995).

Marx, Anthony, *Making Race and Nation: A Comparison of South Africa, the United States, and Brazil* (Cambridge, 1998).

Marx, Karl, 'On the Jewish Question', in *Early Political Writings* (Cambridge, 1994), pp. 28–56.

— *The Communist Manifesto* (Harmondsworth, 2002).

— *Capital* (New York, 2007).

— and Friedrich Engels, *The German Ideology* (New York, 1970).

Maskiell, Michelle, 'Consuming Kashmir: Shawls and Empires, 1500–2000', *Journal of World History* 13/1 (2002): pp. 27–65.

Masters, Bruce, *The Origin of Western Economic Dominance in the Middle East: Mercantilism and the Islamic Economic in Aleppo 1600–1750* (New York, 1988).

— *Christians and Jews in the Ottoman Arab World: The Roots of Sectarianism* (Cambridge, 2001).

— 'Semi-autonomous Forces in the Arab Provinces', in Suraiya N. Faroqhi (ed.), *Cambridge History of Turkey*: vol. 3, *The Later Ottoman Empire 1603–1839* (Cambridge, 2006), pp. 186–208.

Masuzawa, Tomoko, *The Invention of World Religions: Or, How European Universalism was Preserved in the Language of Pluralism* (Chicago, IL, 2005).

Mathias, P. and P. O'Brien, 'Taxation in England and France, 1715–1810: A Comparison of the Social and Economic Incidence of Taxes Collected for the Central Governments', *Journal of European Economic History* 5 (1976): pp. 601–650.

Mathur, Saloni, 'Living Ethnological Exhibits: The Case of 1886', *Cultural Anthropology* 15/4 (2000): pp. 492–524.

— *India By Design: Colonial History and Cultural Display* (Berkeley, CA, 2007).

Matsuda, Matt, *Empire of Love: Histories of France and the Pacific* (New York, 2005).

Matsumoto, Takenori, *Chōsen'nōson no <Shokuminchikindai> keiken* (Tokyo, 2005), pp. 49–94.

Matthews, James K., 'World War I and the Rise of African Nationalism: Nigerian Veterans as Catalysts of Change', *Journal of Modern African Studies* 20/3 (1982): pp. 493–502.

Mauro, Frédéric, *Le Portugal et l'Atlantique au XVIIe siècle, 1570–1670: étude économique* (Paris, 1960).

Mayer, James H., 'Immigration, Return, and the Politics of Citizenship: Russian Muslims in the Ottoman Empire, 1860–1914', *International Journal of Middle East Studies* 39 (2007): pp. 15–32.

Mba, Nina Emma, *Nigerian Women Mobilized: Women's Political Activity in Southern Nigeria, 1900–1965* (Berkeley, CA, 1982).

Mbembe, Achille, *On the Postcolony* (Berkeley, CA 2001).

— 'On the Power of the False', trans. Judith Inggs, *Public Culture* 14 (2002): pp. 629–41.

Mbiti, John, *African Religions and Philosophy* (New York, 1969).

— *Introduction to African Religion* (Portsmouth, 1975).

Meek, Ronald L., *Social Science and the Ignoble Savage* (Cambridge, 1976).

Meggers, Betty J., *Amazonia: Man and Culture in a Counterfeit Paradise* (Chicago, IL, 1971).

Mehta, Uday, 'Liberal Strategies of Exclusion', *Politics and Society* 18 (1990): pp. 427–54.

— *Liberalism and Empire: A Study in Nineteenth-Century British Liberal Thought* (Chicago, IL, 1999).

Meisel, Seth, '"Fruits of Freedom": Slaves and Citizens in Early Republican Argentina', in Jane G. Landers and Barry M. Robinson (eds), *Slaves, Subjects, and Subversives: Blacks in Colonial Latin America* (Albuquerque, NM, 2006), pp. 273–305.

Mellanby, Kenneth, *Pesticides and Pollution* (London, 1967).

Melville, Elinor G.K., *A Plague of Sheep: Environmental Consequences of the Conquest of Mexico* (New York, 1994).

Memmi, Albert, *The Colonizer and the Colonized* (Boston, MA, 1967).

Mentz, Søren, 'The Commercial Culture of the Armenian Merchant: Diaspora and Social Behaviour', *Itinerario* 1 (2004): pp. 16–28.

— *The English Gentleman Merchant at Work: Madras and the City of London 1660–1740* (Copenhagen, 2005).

— 'European Private Trade in the Indian Ocean 1500–1800', in Om Prakash (ed.), *Trading World of the Indian Ocean 1500–1800* (Delhi, 2012), pp. 485–518.

Merchant, Carolyn, *The Death of Nature: Women, Ecology and the Scientific Revolution* (San Francisco, CA, 1982).

Merish, Lori, *Sentimental Materialism: Gender, Commodity Culture, and Nineteenth Century American Literature* (Durham, NC, 2000).

Merry, Sally Engle, *Colonizing Hawai'i: The Cultural Power of Law* (Princeton, NJ, 2000).

Metcalf, Alida, *Go Betweens and the Colonization of Brazil* (Austin, TX, 2005).

Metcalf, Thomas, *Imperial Connections: India and the Indian Ocean Arena, 1860–1920* (Berkeley, CA, 2007).

Meyer, Eric, 'Labour Circulation between Sri Lanka and South India in Historical Perspective', in Claude Markovits, Jaques Pouchepadass and Sanjay Subrahmanyam (eds), *Society in Circulation: Mobile People and Itinerant Cultures in South Asia, 1750–1950* (Delhi, 2003), pp. 55–88.

Meyer, Karl, *Tournament of Shadows: The Great Game and the Race for Empire in Central Asia* (Washington, DC, 1999).

Michasiw, Kim, 'Nine Revisionist Theories of the Picturesque', *Representations* 38 (1992): pp. 76–100.

Midgley, Clare, *Women Against Slavery: The British Campaigns, 1780–1870* (London, 1995).

— (ed.), *Gender and Imperialism* (Manchester, 1998).

— 'Gender and Imperialism: Mapping the Connections', in Clare Midgley (ed.), *Gender and Imperialism* (Manchester, 1998), pp. 1–21.

Mignolo, Walter D., *Local Histories/Global Designs: Essays on the Coloniality of Power, Subaltern Knowledges, and Border Thinking* (Princeton, NJ, 2000).

Mihesuah, Devon, *Cultivating the Rosebuds: The Education of Women at the Cherokee Female Seminary, 1851–1909* (Urbana, IL, 1998).

Mill, James, *The History of British India* (London, 1858 [1808]).

Miller, Aleksei, *Imperiia Romanovykh i natsionalizm: esse po metodologii istoricheskogo issledovaniia* (Moscow, 2006).

— 'Priobretenie neobkhodimoe, no ne vpolne udobnoe: transfer poniatiia *natsiia* v Rossiiu (nachalo xviii–seredina xix v.)', in Martin Aust, Ricarda Vulpius and Aleksei Miller (eds), *Imperium inter pares: rol' transferov v istorii rossiiskoi imperii (1700–1917): sbornik statei* (Moscow, 2010), pp. 42–66.

Miller, Gwenn A., *Kodiak Kreol: Communities of Empire in Early Russian America* (Ithaca, NY, 2010).

Miller, Joseph C., *Way of Death: Merchant Capitalism and the Angolan Slave Trade, 1730–1830* (Madison, WI, 1988).

Miller, Marjorie, 'Britain Illegally Expelled Chagos Islanders for US Base, Court Rules', *Los Angeles Times* (4 November 2000).

Miller, Rory, *Britain and Latin America in the Nineteenth and Twentieth Centuries* (London, 1993).

Miller, Ruth, 'The Ottoman and Islamic Substratum of Turkey's Swiss Civil Code', *Journal of Islamic Studies* 11/3 (2000): pp. 335–61.

Millett, Allan R., *Semper Fidelis: The History of the United States Marine Corps* (New York, 1980).

Milligan, Barry, *Pleasures and Pains: Opium and the Orient in Nineteenth Century British Culture* (London, 1995).

Milloy, John S., 'The Early Indian Acts: Developmental Strategy and Constitutional Change', in J.R. Miller (ed.), *Sweet Promises: A Reader on Indian-White Relations in Canada* (Toronto, ON, 1991), pp. 145–54.

Mills, Charles W., *The Racial Contract* (Ithaca, NY, 1997).

Mills, James H., *Cannabis Britannica: Empire, Trade, and Prohibition* (Oxford, 2003).

Mills, Sara, *Discourses of Difference: An Analysis of Women's Travel Writing and Colonialism* (London, 1991).

Minh-Ha, Trinh T., *Woman, Native, Other: Writing Postcoloniality and Feminism* (Bloomington, IN, 1989).

Mintz, Sidney, *Sweetness and Power: The Place of Sugar in Modern History* (New York, 1985).

'Minute Recorded in the General Department by Thomas Babington Macaulay, law member of the governor-general's council, dated 2 February 1835', in Lynn Zastoupil and Martin Moir (eds), *The Great Indian Education Debate: Documents Relating to the Orientalist-Anglicist Controversy, 1781–1843* (Richmond, Surrey, 1999).

Mironov, Boris, *Blagosostoianie naseleniia i revoliutsii v imperskoi Rossii* (Moscow, 2010).

Mitchell, Robert D. and Paul A. Groves, *North America: The Historical Geography of a Changing Continent* (Totowa, NJ, 1987).

Mitchell, T.C. (ed.), *The British Museum Yearbook*, vol. 3 (London, 1979).

Mitchell, Timothy, *Colonizing Egypt* (Berkeley, CA, 1988).

— 'The Stage of Modernity', in Mitchell (ed.), *Questions of Modernity* (Minneapolis, MN, 2000), pp. 1–34.

— *Rule of Experts: Egypt, Techno-Politics, Modernity* (Berkeley, CA, 2002).

Mitsui, Takashi, 'Chōsen', in Nihonshokuminchikenkyūkai (ed.), *Nihonshokumin chikenkyu no Genjō to Kadai* (Tokyo, 2008), pp. 92–119.

Mitter, Partha, *Art and Nationalism* (Oxford, 1994).

Miyajima, Hiroshi, 'Nihon ni okeru "kokushi" no seiritsu to kankokushi ninshiki – hōkenseiron wo chūshin ni', in Hiroshi Miyajima and Young-Deok Kim (eds), *Kindaikōryūshi to Sōgoninshiki I* (Tokyo, 2001), pp. 329–63.

— 'Nihonshi·chōsenshi kenkyu ni okeru 'hōkensei'ron – 1910–45 nen', in Hiroshi Miyajima and Young-Deok Kim (eds), *Kindaikōryūshi to Sōgoninshiki II* (Tokyo, 2005), pp. 283–312.

—, Sŏngsi Lee, Hae-dong Yun and Ji-hŏn Im (eds), *Shokuminchikindai no Shiza* (Tokyo, 2004).

Miyata, Setsuko, *Chōsenminshū to 'Kōminka' Seisaku* (Tokyo, 1985).

Mizutani, Satoshi, 'Hybridity and History: A Critical Reflection on Homi K. Bhabha's "Post-Historical" Thought', *Zinbun* 41 (2008): pp. 1–19.

Mohapatra, Prabhu P., 'Coolies and Colliers: A Study of the Agrarian Context of Labour Migration from Chota Nagpur, 1880–1920', *Studies in History* 1/2 (1985): pp. 247–303.

Mokyr, Joel, *The Lever of Riches: Technological Creativity and Economic Progress* (New York, 1990).

Molesworth, R., *An Account of Denmark as it Was in the Year 1692* (London, 1694).

Moon, David, 'Peasant Migration and the Settlement of Russia's Frontiers, 1550–1897', *Historical Journal* 40/4 (1997): pp. 859–93.

— *The Russian Peasantry, 1600–1930: The World the Peasants Made* (London, 1999).

Moore, Donald S., Anand Pandian and Jake Kosek (eds), *Race, Nature, and the Politics of Difference* (Durham, NC, 2003).

Moosvi, Shireen, *Economy of the Mughal Empire, c. 1595: A Statistical Study* (Delhi, 1987), pp. 214–19.

— *People, Taxation, and Trade in Mughal India* (New York, 2008).

Morgan, Edmund S., *American Slavery, American Freedom: The Ordeal of Colonial Virginia* (New York, 1975).

Morgan, G. and P. Rushton, *Eighteenth-Century Criminal Transportation: The Formation of the Criminal Atlantic* (New York, 2004).

Morgan, Jennifer, '"Some Could Suckle over Their Shoulder": Male Travelers, Female Bodies, and the Gendering of Racial Ideology, 1500–1770', *William and Mary Quarterly* 54/1, Third Series (1997): pp. 167–92.

— *Laboring Women: Reproduction and Gender in New World Slavery* (Philadelphia, PA, 2004).

Morgan, Philip D., 'Ending the Slave Trade: A Caribbean and Atlantic Context', in Derek R. Peterson (ed.), *Abolitionism and Imperialism in Britain, Africa, and the Atlantic* (Athens, OH, 2010), pp. 101–128.

Morris, H.F., 'How Nigeria got its Penal Code', *Journal of African Law* 14/3 (1970): pp. 137–54.

Morris-Suzuki, Tessa, 'Debating Racial Science in Wartime Japan', *Osiris*, 2nd Series, 13 (1998): pp. 354–75.

Morse, Richard M., *The Bandeirantes: The Historical Role of the Brazilian Pathfinders* (New York, 1965).

Morton, Patricia, *Hybrid Modernities: Architecture and Representation at the 1931 Colonial Exhibition, Paris* (Cambridge, MA, 2000).

Mosse, George L., *Toward the Final Solution: A History of European Racism* (New York, 1980).

— *Fallen Soldiers: Reshaping the Memory of the World Wars* (Oxford, 1990).

Mote, Frederick, 'The Growth of Chinese Despotism: A Critique of Wittfogel's Theory of Oriental Despotism as Applied to China', *Oriens Extremus* 8/1 (1961): pp. 1–41.

— and Denis Twitchett (eds), *The Cambridge History of China*, vol. 7: *The Ming Dynasty, 1368–1644* (Cambridge, 1988).

Mrázek, Rudolf, *Engineers of Happy Land: Technology and Nationalism in a Colony* (Princeton, NJ, 2002).

Muckle, Adrian, 'Kanak Experiences of WWI: New Caledonia's Tirailleurs, Auxiliaries and "Rebels"', *History Compass* 6/5 (2008): pp. 1325–45.

Mueller, Ferdinand von, *Australian Vegetation Indigenous or Introduced, Considered Especially in its Bearing on the Occupation of Territory* (Melbourne, 1867).

Mukhia, Harbans, *Mughals of India* (Malden, MA, 2004).

Mukund, K., 'New Social Elites and the Early Colonial State: Construction of Identity and Patronage in Madras', *Economic and Political Weekly* 38/27 (5 July 2003): pp. 2857–64.

Mullens, Joseph, *London and Calcutta, Compared in their Heathenism, their Privileges and their Prospects* (London, 1869).

Munholland, J. Kim, *Rock of Contention: Free French and Americans at War in New Caledonia, 1940–1945* (New York, 2005).

Muoria, Henry, *Writing for Kenya: The Life and Works of Henry Muoria*, ed. Wangari Muoria-Sal, B.F. Frederiksen, John Lonsdale and Derek R. Peterson (Leiden, 2009).

Murdoch, Steve and Andrew Mackillop (eds), *Fighting for Identity: Scottish Military Experience c. 1550–1900* (Leiden, 2002).

Murillo, Bianca, 'Ideal Homes and the Gender Politics of Consumerism in Postcolonial Ghana, 1960–1970', *Gender and History* 21/3 (2009): pp. 560–75.

Murphey, Rhoads, *Ottoman Warfare 1500–1700* (London, 1999).

Murphy, Gretchen, *Hemispheric Imaginings: The Monroe Doctrine and Narrative of US Empire* (Durham, NC, 2005).

Murray, Pauli, *States' Laws on Race and Color* (Athens, GA, 1997 [1950]).

Murtagh, Harman, 'Irish Soldiers Abroad, 1600–1800', in Thomas Bartlett and Keith Jeffery (eds), *A Military History of Ireland* (Cambridge, 1996).

Musselman, Elizabeth Green, 'Plant Knowledge at the Cape: A Study in African and European Collaboration', *International Journal of African Historical Studies* 36 (2003): pp. 367–92.

Myers, R.H., Mark R. Peattie and Qingqi Chen (eds), *The Japanese Colonial Empire, 1895–1945* (Princeton, NJ, 1984).

Namiki, Masahito, 'Sengonihon ni okeru Chōsenkindaishikenkyū no gendankai', *Rekishihyōron*, 482 (1990): pp. 21–6.

— 'Shokuminchikōkyōsei to Chōsenshakai – shokuminchikōhanki wo chūshin ni', in Choong-Seok Park and Hiroshi Watanabe (eds), *'Bunmei', 'Kaika', 'Heiwa': Nihon to Kankoku* (Tokyo, 2006), pp. 221–46.

Naquin, Susan, *Millenarian Rebellion in China: The Eight Trigrams Uprising of 1813* (New Haven, CT, 1976).

— and Evelyn Rawski, *Chinese Society in the Eighteenth Century* (New Haven, CT, 1987).

— and Chün-fang Yü (eds), *Pilgrims and Sacred Sites in China* (Berkeley, CA, 1992).

Narain, A.K., 'Dr Ambedkar, Buddhism and Social Change: A Reappraisal', in A.K. Narain and D.C. Ahir (eds), *Dr Ambedkar, Buddhism, and Social Change* (Delhi, 1994), pp. 77–98.

Nasson, Bill, 'War Opinion in South Africa, 1914', *Journal of Imperial and Commonwealth History* 23/2 (1995): pp. 248–76.

Nathan, Mirza, *Baharistan-i-Ghaybi: A History of the Mughal Wars in Assam, Cooch Behar, Bengal, Bihar and Orissa*, trans. M.I. Borah, 2 vols (Gauhati, 1936).

Nathans, Benjamin, *Beyond the Pale: The Jewish Encounter with Late Imperial Russia* (Berkeley, CA, 2002).

National Inquiry into the Separation of Aboriginal and Torres Strait Islander Children from their Families, *Bringing Them Home: Report of the National Inquiry into the Separation of Aboriginal and Torres Strait Islander Children and their Families* (Canberra, 1997).

Nead, Lynda, *Victorian Babylon: People, Streets and Images in Nineteenth-Century London* (New Haven, CT, 2000).

Nef, J.U., *The Conquest of the Material World* (Chicago, IL, 1964).

Nehru, Jawaharlal, *Discovery of India* (London, 1946).

Nelson, Keith, 'The "Black Horror on the Rhine": Race as a Factor in Post-World War I Diplomacy', *Journal of Modern History* 42/4 (1970): pp. 606–627.

Neptune, Harvey R., *Caliban and the Yankees: Trinidad and the United States Occupation* (Chapel Hill, NC, 2007).

Nevakivi, Jukka, *Britain, France and the Arab Middle East 1914–1920* (London, 1969).

Newitt, M.D.D., *Portugal in Africa: The Last Hundred Years* (London, 1981).

— *A History of Portuguese Overseas Expansion, 1400–1668* (London and New York, 2005).

Newman, Louise, *White Women's Rights: The Racial Origins of Feminism in the United States* (New York, 1999).

Newson, Linda A. and Susie Minchin, *From Capture to Sale: The Portuguese Slave Trade to Spanish America in the Early Seventeenth Century* (Leiden and Boston, MA, 2007).

Ngai, Mae, *Impossible Subjects: Illegal Aliens and the Making of Modern America* (Princeton, NJ, 2004).

Nhongo-Simbanegavi, Josephine, *For Better or Worse? Women and ZANLA in Zimbabwe's Liberation Struggle* (Harare, 2000).

Nichols, Roger L., *Indians in the United States and Canada* (Lincoln, NE, 1998).
Niezen, Ronald, 'Recognizing Indigenism: Canadian Unity and the International Movement of Indigenous Peoples', *Comparative Studies in Society and History* 42 (2000): pp. 119–48.
Nihonshokuminchikenkyūkai (ed.), *Nihonshokuminchikenkyu no Genjō to Kadai* (Tokyo, 2008).
Ninkovich, Frank, *The United States and Imperialism* (Oxford, 2001).
— 'The United States and Imperialism', in Robert D. Schulzinger (ed.), *A Companion to American Foreign Relations* (Malden, MA, 2006), pp. 79–102.
Nizami, Khaliq Ahmad, *Akbar and Religion* (Delhi, 1989).
Nkrumah, Kwame, *Neo-Colonialism: The Last Stage of Imperialism* (New York, 1965).
— *Consciencism: Philosophy and the Ideology for Decolonization* (New York, 1970).
Nochlin, Linda, *The Politics of Vision: Essays on Nineteenth-century Art and Society* (London, 1983).
Norris, Stephen M., *A War of Images: Russian Popular Prints, Wartime Culture, and National Identity* (DeKalb, IL, 2006).
Northrop, Douglas, *Veiled Empire: Gender and Power in Stalinist Central Asia* (Ithaca, NY, 2004).
Northrup, David, *Indentured Labor in the Age of Imperialism, 1834–1922* (Cambridge, 1995).
Norton, Marcy, 'Tasting Empire: Chocolate and the European Internalization of Mesoamerica', *American Historical Review* 111/3 (2006): pp. 660–91.
Nussbaum, Felicity, *Torrid Zones: Maternity, Sexuality, and Empire in Eighteenth-Century English Narratives* (Baltimore, MD, 1995).
Nyerere, Julius K., *Ujamaa: Essays on Socialism* (Oxford, 1968).
Nys, Ernest (ed.), *De Indis et De Iure Belli Relectiones being parts of Relectiones Theologicae XII by Franciscus de Victoria* (Washington, DC, 1917).
Nzongola-Ntalaja, Georges, *The Congo from Leopold to Kabila: A People's History* (London, 2002).
Obaid, Antonio H., Review of Raúl Prebisch, *Hacia una dinámica del desararollo para latinoamerica* (1963), *Hispanic American Historical Review* 44/3 (1964): pp. 400–401.
O'Brien, P., 'Inseparable Connections: Trade, Economy, Fiscal State and the Expansion of Empire, 1688–1815', in P.J. Marshall (ed.), *The Oxford History of the British Empire: The Eighteenth Century* (Oxford, 1998), pp. 53–77.
O'Brien, Thomas, *The Revolutionary Mission: American Enterprise in Latin America, 1900–1945* (Cambridge, 1996).
— *Making the Americas: The United States and Latin America from the Age of Revolutions to the Era of Globalization* (Albuquerque, NM, 2007).
Oddie, Geoffrey, *Imagined Hinduism: British Protestant Missionary Constructions of Hinduism, 1793–1900* (Thousand Oaks, CA, 2006).
Odhiambo, E.S. Atieno and John Lonsdale (eds), *Mau Mau and Nationhood: Arms, Authority & Narration* (Athens, OH, 2003).
Ōe, Shinobu *et al.* (eds), *Iwanamikōza: Kindainihon to Shokuminchi*, vols 1–8 (Tokyo, 1992–93).
Ogborn, Miles, *Spaces of Modernity: London's Geographies, 1680–1780* (New York, 1998).

Oguma, Eiji, <*Nihonjin*> *no Kyōkai* (Tokyo, 1998).

Oh, Sŏngch'ŏl, *Singminji Ch'odŭng Kyoyug ŭi Hyŏngsŏng* (Seoul, 2000).

O'Hanlon, Rosalind, 'Manliness and Imperial Service in Mughal North India', *Journal of the Economic and Social History of the Orient* 42/1 (1999): pp. 47–93.

— 'Kingdom, Household and Body: History, Gender and Imperial Service under Akbar', *Modern Asian Studies* 41/5 (2007): pp. 889–923.

Ohlmeyer, Jane, 'Seventeenth-Century Ireland and the New British and Atlantic Histories', *American Historical Review* 104/2 (1999): pp. 446–62.

Okabe, Makio, 'Teikokushugiron to shokuminchikenkyū', in Nihonshoku-minchikenkyūkai (ed.), *Nihonshokuminchikenkyu no Genjō to Kadai* (Tokyo, 2008), pp. 20–54.

Okamoto, Makiko, *Shokuminchikanryō no Seijishi* (Tokyo, 2008).

Ōkurashōkanrikyoku (ed.), *Nihonjin no Kaigaikatsudo ni kansuru Rekishitekichōsa 11* (Tokyo, 1950) [collected in vol. 5, the Korea Section (10) of the reprinted edition, 2000].

Olukoju, Ayodeji, 'The United Kingdom and the Political Economy of the Global-Oil Producing Nuts and Seeds during the 1930s', *Commodities of Empire Working Paper*, 5 (London, 2008).

Omissi, David, *The Sepoy and the Raj: The Indian Army, 1860–1940* (London, 1994).

— *Indian Voices of the Great War: Soldiers' Letters, 1914–18* (Basingstoke, 1999).

O'Neill, Kelly, 'Between Subversion and Submission: The Integration of the Crimean Khanate into the Russian Empire, 1783–1853', PhD dissertation, Harvard University, 2006.

Onuf, Peter S., *Jefferson's Empire: The Language of American Nationhood* (Charlottesville, VA, 2000).

Ooms, Emily Groszos, *Women and Millenarian Protest in Meiji Japan: Deguchi Nao and Omotokyo* (Ithaca, NY, 1993).

Osabu-Kle, Daniel Tetteh, *Compatible Cultural Democracy: The Key to Development in Africa* (Peterborough, 2000).

Osborne, Michael, *Nature, the Exotic and the Science of French Colonialism* (Bloomington, IN, 1994).

— 'Acclimatizing the World: A History of the Paradigmatic Colonial Science', *Osiris* 15 (2000): pp. 135–51.

— 'Science and the French Empire', *Isis* 96 (2005): pp. 80–87.

Os'kin, D., *Zapiski soldata* (Moscow, 1929).

Osorio, Jon Kamakawiwo'ole, *Dismembering Lahui: A History of the Hawai'ian Nation to 1887* (Honolulu, HI, 2002).

Outram, Dorinda, *Georges Cuvier: Vocation, Science and Authority in Post-revolutionary France* (Manchester, 1984).

Owen, Nicholas, *The British Left and India Metropolitan Anti-Imperialism, 1885–1947* (Oxford, 2007).

Owen, Norman G., *The Emergence of Modern Southeast Asia: A New History* (Honolulu, HI, 2005).

Owen, Roger, *The Middle East in the World Economy* (London, 1993).

— *Lord Cromer: Victorian Imperialist, Edwardian Proconsul* (New York, 2005).

Owensby, B., *Empire of Law and Indian Justice in Colonial Mexico* (Stanford, CA, 2008).

Oye, David Schimmelpennick van der and Bruce Menning (eds), *Reforming the Tsar's Army: Military Innovation in Imperial Russia from Peter the Great to the Revolution* (Washington, DC, 2004).

Padayachee, Vishnu and Robert Morrell, 'Indian Merchants and Dukawallahs in the Natal Economy, c. 1875–1914', *Journal of Southern African Studies* 17 (1991): pp. 71–102.

Pagden, Anthony, *Lords of All the World: Ideologies of Empire in Spain, Britain, and France c. 1500–c. 1800* (New Haven, CT, 1995).

Page, Melvin (ed.), *Africa and the First World War* (New York, 1987).

Paice, Edward, *Tip and Run: The Untold Tragedy of the Great War in Africa* (London, 2007).

Paisley, Fiona, 'Childhood and Race: Growing Up in the Empire', in Philippa Levine (ed.), *Gender and Empire* (Oxford, 2004), pp. 240–59.

Pak, Myŏnggyu, 'Singminji yŏksa-sahoehag ŭi sigonggangsŏng e taehayŏ', in Sŏk Hyŏnho and Yu Sŏkch'un (eds), *Hyŏndae Hanguk-sahoe Sŏngkyŏk-nonjaeng* (Seoul, 2001).

Pakenham, Thomas, *The Scramble for Africa, 1876–1912* (London, 1991).

Palat, Ravi A., *From World-Empire to World-Economy: Southeastern India and the Emergence of the Indian Ocean World-Economy (1350–1650)* (Ann Arbor, MI, 1988).

Pallot, J. and D. Shaw, *Landscape and Settlement in Romanov Russia* (Oxford, 1990).

Palumbo, Patrizia (ed.), *A Place in the Sun: Africa in Italian Colonial Culture from Post-Unification to the Present* (Berkeley, CA, 2003).

Pamuk, Sevket, *A Monetary History of the Ottoman Empire* (Cambridge, 2000).

— 'Institutional Change and the Longevity of the Ottoman Empire, 1600–1800', *Journal of Interdisciplinary History* 35/2 (2004): pp. 225–47.

Pandey, Gyanendra, *Routine Violence: Nations, Fragments, Histories* (Stanford, CA, 2005).

Pang, Alex Soojung-Kim, *Empire and the Sun: Victorian Solar Eclipse Expeditions* (Stanford, CA, 2002).

Papers Relating to the Foreign Relations of the United States 1895, vol. 1 (Washington, DC, 1896).

Paquette, Gabriel, *Enlightenment, Governance and Reform in Spain and its Empire, 1759–1808* (Basingstoke, 2008)

Paradis, James G., *T. H. Huxley: Man's Place in Nature* (Lincoln, NE, 1978).

— and George C. Williams (eds), *Evolution and Ethics: T.H. Huxley's Evolution and Ethics, With New Essays on Its Victorian and Sociobiological Context* (Princeton, NJ, 1989).

Parish, Susan Scott, 'Diasporic African Sources of Enlightenment Knowledge', in James Delbourgo and Nicholas Dew (eds), *Science and Empire in the Atlantic World* (New York and London, 2008), pp. 281–310.

Park, Soon-Won, 'Colonial Industrial Growth and the Emergence of the Korean Working Class', in Gi-Wook Shin and Michael Robinson (eds), *Colonial Modernity in Korea* (Cambridge, MA, 1999), pp. 128–60.

Parker, Geoffrey, 'Crisis and Catastrophe: The Global Crisis of the Seventeenth Century', *American Historical Review* 113/4 (2008): pp. 1053–1079.

Parry, J.H., *Europe and a Wider World, 1415–1715* (London, 1966).

— *The Spanish Seaborne Empire* (New York, 1966).

— *The Discovery of the Sea* (Berkeley, CA, 1981).

Parsons, Timothy H., '"Wakamba Warriors Are Soldiers of the Queen": The Evolution of the Kamba as a Martial Race, 1890–1970', *Ethnohistory* 46/4 (1999): pp. 671–701.

— *The African Rank and File: Social Implications of Colonial Military Service in the King's African Rifles, 1902–1964* (Oxford, 1999).

Pascoe, Peggy, *Relations of Rescue: The Search for Female Moral Authority in the American West, 1874–1939* (Oxford, 1990).

Pateman, Carole, *The Sexual Contract* (Cambridge, 1988).

Pati, Biswamoy (ed.), *The 1857 Rebellion* (New Delhi, 2007).

Patterson, Orlando, *Slavery and Social Death* (Cambridge, MA, 1982).

Peabody, Sue, *'There Are No Slaves in France': The Political Culture of Race and Slavery in the Ancien Régime* (New York, 1996).

Pearson, Jonathan, *Sir Anthony Eden and the Suez Crisis: Reluctant Gamble* (New York, 2003).

Pearson, M.N., *The New Cambridge History of India: The Portuguese in India* (New York, 1987).

— 'Shivaji and the Decline of the Mughal Empire', *Journal of Asian Studies* 35/2 (1976): pp. 221–35.

— 'Merchants and States', in J.D. Tracy (ed.), *The Political Economy of Merchant Empires: State Power and World Trade 1350–1750* (Cambridge, 1991).

Pedersen, Susan, 'National Bodies, Unspeakable Acts: The Sexual Politics of Colonial Policy-making', *Journal of Modern History* 63/4 (1991): pp. 647–80.

— 'The Maternalist Moment in British Colonial Policy: The Controversy over "Child Slavery" in Hong Kong 1917–1941', *Past and Present* 171/1 (2001): pp. 161–202.

Peers, Douglas M., *Between Mars and Mammon: Colonial Armies and the Garrison State in India, 1819–1835* (London, 1995).

— 'Martial Races and South Asian Military Culture in the Victorian Indian Army', in Daniel Marston and Chandar Sundaram (eds), *A Military History of Modern India* (New York, 2006), pp. 34–52.

Peifeng, Chen, *Dōka' no Dōshōimu: Nihontouchika Taiwan no Kokugokyōikushi Saikou* (Tokyo, 2001).

Peirce, Leslie, *The Imperial Harem* (New York, 1993).

— 'Changing Perceptions of the Ottomans: The Early Centuries', *Mediterranean Historical Review* 19/1 (2004): pp. 6–28.

Pels, Peter and Oscar Salmink (eds), *Colonial Subjects: Essays on the Practical History of Anthropology* (Ann Arbor, MI, 1999).

Pemberton, John, *On the Subject of 'Java'* (Ithaca, NY, 1994).

Penn, Donna, 'The Meanings of Lesbianism in Postwar America', in Barbara Melosh (ed.), *Gender and American History* (London, 1993).

Pennington, Brian, *The Invention of Hinduism: Britons, Indians, and the Construction of Religion in Colonial Bengal* (New York, 2005).

Penvenne, Jeanne Marie, *African Workers and Colonial Racism: Mozambican Strategies and Struggles in Lourenço Marques, 1877–1962* (Portsmouth, NH, 1995).

Perdue, Peter C., *Exhausting the Earth: State and Peasant in Hunan, 1500–1850* (Cambridge, MA, 1987).

— 'Empire and Nation in Comparative Perspective: Frontier Administration in Eighteenth Century China', *Journal of Early Modern History* 5/4 (2001): pp. 282–304.

— *China Marches West: The Qing Conquest of Central Eurasia* (Cambridge, MA, 2005).

— 'Commerce and Coercion on Two Chinese Frontiers', in Nicola Di Cosmo (ed.), *Military Culture in China* (Cambridge, MA, 2009), pp. 317–38.

Perdue, Theda and Michael D. Green, *The Cherokee Nation and the Trail of Tears* (New York, 2007).

Perez, Louis, *On Becoming Cuban: Identity, Nationality, and Culture* (Chapel Hill, NC, 1999).

Perkins, Kenneth P., 'Pressure and Persuasion in the Policies of the French Military in Colonial North Africa', *Military Affairs* 40/2 (1976): pp. 74–8.

Perry, Adele, *On the Edge of Empire: Gender, Race, and the Making of British Columbia, 1849–1871* (Toronto, ON, 2001).

Perry, Elizabeth J., *Rebels and Revolutionaries in North China, 1845–1945* (Stanford, CA, 1980).

Pestana, Carla Gardina, *The English Atlantic in an Age of Revolution, 1640–1661* (Cambridge, MA, 2004).

Peters, R., *Crime and Punishment in Islamic Law: Theory and Practice from the Sixteenth to the Twenty-First Century* (Cambridge, 2005).

Peterson, Derek R., '"Be Like Firm Soldiers to Develop the Country": Political Imagination and the Geography of Gikuyuland', *International Journal of African Historical Studies* 37 (2004): pp. 71–101.

— *Creative Writing: Translation, Bookkeeping and the Work of Imagination in Colonial Kenya* (Portsmouth, 2004).

— 'Culture and Chronology in African History', *Historical Journal* 50 (2007): pp. 483–97.

— (ed.), *Abolitionism and Imperialism in Britain, Africa, and the Atlantic* (Athens, OH, 2010).

— and Darren Walhof (eds), *The Invention of Religion: Rethinking Belief in Politics and History* (New Brunswick, NJ, 2002).

Peterson, Willard J. (ed.), *The Cambridge History of China*: vol. 9, *The Ch'ing Empire to 1800*, part 1 (Cambridge, 2002).

Petit, Jacques-Guy, 'La Colonizzazione Penale del Sistema Penitenziario Francese', in M. Da Passano (ed.), *Le Colonie Penali nell'Europa dell'Ottocento* (Rome, 2004), pp. 37–65.

Petrow, Stefan, 'Policing in a Penal Colony: Governor Arthur's Police System in Van Diemen's Land, 1826–1836', *Law and History Review* 18/2 (2000): pp. 351–95.

Pettit, Claire, *Dr Livingstone, I Presume? Missionaries, Journalists, Explorers and Empire* (Cambridge, 2007).

Pevsner, Nikolaus, *The Englishness of English Art* (New York, 1956).

Philipp, Thomas, *Acre: The Rise and Fall of a Palestinian City 1730–1831* (New York, 2001).

— and Ulrich Haarmann (eds), *The Mamluks in Egyptian Politics and Society* (Cambridge, 2007).

Phillips, Craig, *The Invention of Religion: Reason, Identity, and the Colonialist Imagination* (Basingstoke, 2003).

Picó, Fernando, *1898: la guerra despúes de la guerra* (Rio Piedras, 1987).

Pieterse, Jan Nederveen, *White on Black: Images of Africa and Blacks in Western Popular Culture* (New Haven, CT, 1998).

Pike, R., *Penal Servitude in Early Modern Spain* (Madison, WI, 1983).

Pilger, John, 'The Secret Files That Reveal How A Nation Was Deported', Z-Net (22 October 2004), www.zcommunications.org/the-secret-files-that-reveal-how-a-nation-was-deported-by-john-pilger. Accessed 4 August 2010.

Pimentel, Juan, 'The Iberian Vision: Science and Empire in the Framework of a Universal Monarchy, 1500–1800', *Osiris* 15 (2001): pp. 17–30.

Pinney, Christopher, *Camera Indica: The Social Life of Indian Photographs* (Chicago, IL, 1997).

— *The Coming of Photography in India* (London, 2008).

— 'The Material and Visual Culture of the British Empire', in Nandini Gooptu and Douglas Peers (eds), *Oxford Companion to the British Empire* (Oxford, forthcoming).

Pintner, Walter M., 'The Nobility and the Officer Corps in the Nineteenth Century', in Eric Lohr and Marshall Poe (eds), *The Military and Society in Russia 1450–1917* (Leiden, 2002), pp. 241–52.

Pioffet, Marie-Christine, *La Tentation de l'épopée dans les Relations des Jésuites* (Sillery, 1997).

Pitts, Jennifer, *A Turn to Empire: The Rise of Imperial Liberalism in Britain and France* (Princeton, NJ, 2005).

Platt, D.C.M., *Latin America and British Trade, 1806–1914* (London, 1972).

Plummer, Brenda Gayle, *Rising Wind: Black American and US Foreign Affairs, 1935–1960* (Chapel Hill, NC, 1996).

Pocock, J.G.A., *Barbarism and Religion* (Cambridge, 1999).

Poe, Marshall T., *The Russian Moment in World History* (Princeton, NJ, 2003).

Pogodin, M.P., 'Pis'mo k gosudariu tsarevichu, velikomu kniaziu Aleksandru Nikolaevichu v 1838 godu', in *Istoriko-politicheskie pis'ma i zapiski vprodolzhenii Krymskoi Voiny 1853–1856* (Moscow, 1874).

Poiger, Uta, *Jazz, Rock, and Rebels: Cold War Politics and American Culture in a Divided Germany* (Berkeley, CA, 2000).

Polachek, James M., *The Inner Opium War* (Cambridge, MA, 1992).

Pomeranz, Kenneth, *The Making of a Hinterland: State, Society, and Economy in Inland North China, 1853–1937* (Berkeley, CA, 1993).

— *The Great Divergence: China, Europe, and the Making of the Modern World Economy* (Princeton, NJ, 2000).

Pons, Frank Moya, *Española en el siglo XVI, 1493–1520* (Albuquerque, NM, 1973).

— *Después de Colón: Trabajo, sociedad, y política en la economia del oro* (Madrid, 1987).

Popkin, Jeremy D., *Facing Racial Revolution: Eyewitness Accounts of the Haitian Insurrection* (Chicago, IL, 2007).

Port, M.H., *Imperial London: Civil Government Building in London, 1850–1915* (New Haven, CT, 1995).

Porter, Andrew, *Religion versus Empire? British Protestant Missionaries and Overseas Expansion, 1700–1914* (Manchester, 2004).

Porter, Bernard, *The Lion's Share: A Short History of British Imperialism 1850–1995* (London, 1996).

— *The Absent-Minded Imperialists: Empire, Society, and Culture in Britain* (Oxford, 2004).

Prakash, Gyan, 'Post-colonial Criticism and Indian Historiography', *Social Text* 31/32 (1992): pp. 8–19.

— *Another Reason: Science and the Imagination of Modern India* (Princeton, NJ, 1999).

— 'Writing Post-Orientalist Histories of the Third World: Perspectives from Indian Historiography', in Vinayak Chaturvedi (ed.), *Mapping Subaltern Studies and the Postcolonial* (London, 2000), pp. 163–90.

— 'Can the Subaltern Ride? A Reply to O'Hanlon and Washbrook', in Vinayak Chaturvedi (ed.), *Mapping Subaltern Studies and the Postcolonial* (London, 2000), pp. 220–38.

Prakash, Om (ed.), *Trading World of the Indian Ocean, 1500-1800* (Delhi, 2012).

Pratt, Mary Louise, *Imperial Eyes: Travel Writing and Transculturation* (London, 1992).

Pratt, Stephanie, *American Indians in British Art, 1700–1840* (London, 2006).

Pravilova, Ekaterina, *Finansy imperii: dengi i vlast' v politike Rossii na natsional'nykh okrainakh, 1801–1917* (Moscow, 2006).

Prebisch, Raúl, *The Economic Development of Latin America and Its Principal Problems* (Lake Success, NY, 1950).

Prestholdt, Jeremy, *Domesticating the World: African Consumerism and the Geneologies of Globalization* (Berkeley, CA, 2008).

Prevost, Elizabeth, *The Communion of Women: Missions and Gender in Colonial Africa and the British Metropole* (Oxford, 2010).

Price, Richard, *Making Empire: Colonial Encounters and the Creation of Imperial Rule in Nineteenth-Century Africa* (Cambridge, 2008).

Prichard, James Cowles, *The Natural History of Man*, 2nd edn (London, 1845).

Pritchard, James, *In Search of Empire: The French in the Americas, 1670–1730* (Cambridge, 2004).

Procida, Mary, *Married to the Empire: Gender, Politics and Imperialisms in India, 1883–1947* (Manchester, 2002).

Proctor, Robert, *Racial Hygiene: Medicine Under the Nazis* (Cambridge, 1988).

Ptak, R., 'The Ryukyu Network in the Fifteenth and Early Sixteenth Centuries', in Om Prakash (ed.), *Trading World of the Indian Ocean 1500–1800* (Delhi, 2012), pp. 463-82.

Pugsley, Christopher, *The Anzac Experience: New Zealand, Australia and Empire in the First World War* (Auckland, 2004).

Pulsipher, J., *Subjects unto the Same King: Indians, English, and the Contest for Authority in Colonial New England* (Philadelphia, PA, 2005).

Purbrick, Louise (ed.), *The Great Exhibition of 1851: New Interdisciplinary Essays* (Manchester, 2001).

Putnam, Lara, *The Company They Kept: Migrants and the Politics of Gender in Caribbean Costa Rica, 1870–1960* (Chapel Hill, NC, 2002).

Putten, L.P. van, *Ideaal en werkelijkheid: Gouverneurs-generaal van Nederlands-Indië* (Rotterdam, 2003).

Pyenson, Lewis, *Cultural Imperialism and the Exact Sciences: German Expansion Overseas, 1900–1930* (New York, 1985).

— *Civilizing Mission: Exact Sciences and French Overseas Expansion, 1830–1940* (Baltimore, MD, 1993).

Quataert, Donald, *Manufacturing in the Ottoman Empire and Turkey, 1500–1950* (Albany, NY, 1994).

— (ed.), *Consumption Studies and the History of the Ottoman Empire, 1550–1922* (New York, 2000).

— *Ottoman Manufacturing in the Age of the Industrial Revolution* (Cambridge, 2002).

— 'The Massacres of Ottoman Armenians and the Writing of Ottoman History', *Journal of Interdisciplinary History* 37/2 (2006): pp. 249–59.

Queen, Christopher, 'Ambedkar, Modernity and the Hermeneutics of Buddhist Liberation', in A.K. Narain and D.C. Ahir (eds), *Dr Ambedkar, Buddhism, and Social Change* (Delhi, 1994), pp. 99–122.

Quesada, Miguel Angel Ladero, 'Spain, circa 1492: Social Values and Structures', in Stuart B. Schwartz (ed.), *Implicit Understandings: Observing, Reporting, and Reflecting on the Encounters between Europeans and Other Peoples in the Early Modern Era* (New York, 1994), pp. 96–133.

Qureshi, Sadiah, 'Displaying Sara Baartman, The 'Hottentot Venus', *History of Science* 42 (2004): pp. 233–57.

Quilley, Geoff, and John Bonehill (eds), *William Hodges 1744–1797: The Art of Exploration* (London, 2004).

— and Kay Dian Kriz (eds), *An Economy of Colour: Visual Culture and the Atlantic World, 1660–1830* (Manchester, 2003).

—, Tim Barringer and Douglas Fordham (eds), *Art and the British Empire* (Manchester, 2006).

Quinn, David B., *Set Fair for Roanoke: Voyages and Colonies, 1584–1606* (Chapel Hill, NC 1985).

Quinn, Frederick, *The French Overseas Empire* (Westport, CT, 2000).

Qureshi, Ishtiaq Husain, *Ulema in Politics: A Study Relating to the Political Activities of the Ulema in the South-Asian Subcontinent from 1556 to 1947* (Karachi, 1972).

Rabe, Stephen G., *The Most Dangerous Area in the World: John F. Kennedy Confronts Communist Revolution in Latin America* (Chapel Hill, NC, 1999).

Rabinow, Paul, *French Modern: Norms and Forms of the Social Environment* (Cambridge, MA, 1989).

Raeff, Marc, *Understanding Imperial Russia* (New York, 1984).

Rafael, Vicente, *White Love and Other Events in Filipino History* (Durham, NC, 2000).

Rafeq, Abdul-Karim, *The Province of Damascus 1723–1783* (Beirut, 1966).

Raj, Kapil, *Relocating Science: Circulation and the Construction of Knowledge in South Asia and Europe: Seventeenth to Nineteenth Centuries* (Delhi, 2006).

Rajan, Ravi, *Modernising Nature, Forestry and Imperial Eco-development* (Oxford, 2008).

Rall, Maureen, *Peaceable Warrior: The Life and Times of Sol T. Plaatje* (Kimberley, 2003).
Ralston, David B., *Importing the European Army: The Introduction of European Military Techniques and Institutions into the Extra-European World, 1600–1914* (Chicago, IL, 1990).
Ramamurthy, Anandi, *Imperial Persuaders: Images of Africa and Asia in British Advertising* (Manchester, 2003).
Ramaswamy, Sumathi, 'Conceit of the Globe in Mughal Visual Practice', *Comparative Studies in Society and History* 49/4 (2007): pp. 751–82.
Rangarajan, Mahesh, *Fencing the Forest* (Delhi, 1999).
Ranger, Terence, 'Race and Tribe in Southern Africa: European Ideas and African Acceptance', in Robert Ross (ed.), *Racism and Colonialism: Essays on Ideology and Social Structure* (The Hague, 1982), pp. 121–42.
— 'The Invention of Tradition Revisited: The Case of Colonial Africa', in Terence Ranger and Olufemi Vaughan (eds), *Legitimacy and the State in Twentieth-Century Africa: Essays in Honour of A.H.M. Kirk-Greene* (Basingstoke, 1993), pp. 62–111.
Rao, Prasada and V. Pala, *India–Pakistan: Partition Perspectives in Indo-English Novels* (New Delhi, 2004).
Rappaport, Erika, 'Art, Commerce or Empire? The Rebuilding of Regent Street, 1880–1927', *History Workshop Journal* 53 (2002): pp. 95–118.
— 'The Bombay Debt: Letter Writing, Domestic Economies and Family Conflict in Colonial India', *Gender and History* 16/2 (2004): pp. 233–60.
— 'Packaging China: Foreign Articles and Dangerous Tastes in the Mid-Victorian Tea Party', in Frank Trentmann (ed.), *The Making of the Consumer: Knowledge, Power and Identity in the Modern World* (London, 2006), pp. 125–46.
— 'Imperial Possessions, Cultural Histories, and the Material Turn', *Victorian Studies* 50/2 (Winter 2008): pp. 289–96.
Ratcliffe, Francis, *Flying Fox and Drifting Sand: The Adventures of a Biologist in Australia* (New York, 1938).
Ratekin, Mervyn, 'The Early Sugar Industry in Española', *Hispanic American Historical Review* 34/1 (1954): pp. 1–19.
Ray, Arthur, *Indians in the Fur Trade: Their Role as Hunters, Trappers and Middlemen* (Toronto, ON, 1974).
Ray, Romita and Angela Rosenthal, 'Britain and the World Beyond, c.1600–c.1900', in David Bindman (ed.), *History of British Art*, vol. 2 (London, 2008), pp. 86-115
Raychaudhuri, Tapan, 'The State and the Economy', in T. Raychudhuri and I. Habib (eds), *The Cambridge Economic History of India*, vol. 1 (Cambridge, 1982).
— and Irfan Habib (eds), *Cambridge Economic History of India*: vol. 1, c. 1200–1750 (Cambridge, 1982).
Raymond, André, *Cairo* (Cambridge, MA, 2000).
Reader, Ian and George Tanabe, *Practically Religious: Worldly Benefits and the Common Religion of Japan* (Honolulu, HI, 1998).
Reagin, Nancy Ruth, *Sweeping the German Nation: Domesticity and National Identity in Germany, 1870–1945* (New York, 2007).
Reeves-Ellington, Barbara, Connie Shemo and Kathryn Kish Sklar (eds), *Competing Kingdoms: Women, Mission, Nation, and Empire* (Durham, NC, 2010).

Reid, Mandy, 'Selling Shadows and Substance: Photographing Race in the United States, 1850–1870s' *Early Popular Visual Culture* 4 (2006): pp. 285–305.

Reilly, James, *A Small Town in Syria: Ottoman Hama in the Eighteenth and Nineteenth Century* (Oxford, 2002).

Reinders, Robert, 'Racialism on the Left: E.D. Morel and the "Black Horror on the Rhine"', *International Review of Social History* 13/1 (1968): pp. 1–28.

Rejali, Darius, *Torture and Democracy* (Princeton, NJ, 2007).

Renda, Mary A., *Taking Haiti: Military Occupation and the Culture of US Imperialism, 1915–1940* (Chapel Hill, NC, 2001).

— 'Practical Sovereignty: The Caribbean Region and the Rise of US Empire', in Thomas H. Holloway (ed.), *A Companion to Latin American History* (Malden, MA, 2008), pp. 307–329.

Renner, G.T., 'A Famine Zone in Africa: The Sudan', *Geographical Review* 16 (1926): pp. 583–96.

Restall, Matthew, 'Black Conquistadors: Armed Africans in Early Spanish America', *The Americas* 57/2 (2000): pp. 171–205.

Reynolds, Susan, 'Empires: A Problem of Comparative History', *Historical Research* 79/204 (2006): pp. 151–65.

Ribbentrop, Berthold von, *Forestry in the British Empire* (London, 1899).

Richards, G., *Race, Racism and Psychology* (London, 1997).

Richards, John F., 'The Imperial Crisis in the Deccan', *Journal of Asian Studies* 35/2 (1976): pp. 237–56.

— *Mughal Empire*: vol. 5, *The New Cambridge History of India*, part 1 (Cambridge, 1993).

Richards, Thomas, *Commodity Culture in Victorian England: Advertising and Spectacle, 1851–1914* (Stanford, CA, 1990).

Richardson, Peter, 'The Recruiting of Chinese Indentured Labour for the South African Gold-Mines, 1903–1908', *Journal of African History* 18/1 (1977): pp. 85–108.

Richter, Daniel K., *Facing East from Indian Country: A Native History of Early America* (Cambridge, MA, 2001).

Ricklefs, M.C., *A History of Modern Indonesia* (Bloomington, IN, 1981).

— *Polarizing Javanese Society: Islamic and Other Visions (c.1830–1930)* (Leiden, 2007).

Rieber, Alfred J., 'Persistent Factors in Russian Foreign Policy: An Interpretive Essay', in Hugh Ragsdale (ed.), *Imperial Russian Foreign Policy* (New York, 1993), pp. 315–59.

Ringrose, David, *Expansion and Global Interaction, 1200–1700* (New York, 2001).

Robb, Peter, *Ancient Rights and Future Comforts: Bihar, the Bengal Tenancy Act of 1885, and British Rule in India* (Richmond, 1997).

— (ed.), *The Concept of Race in South Asia* (New Delhi, 1997).

Roberts, J.A.G., *The Complete History of China* (London, 2006).

Roberts, Mary, *Intimate Outsiders: The Harem in Ottoman and Orientalist Art and Literature* (Durham, NC, 2005).

Roberts, Richard L., *Two Worlds of Cotton: Colonialism and the Regional Economy in the French Soudan, 1800–1946* (Stanford, CA, 1996).

Robertson, Esmonde, *Mussolini as Empire-Builder: Europe and Africa, 1932–36* (London, 1977).

Robinson, David, *Migration in Colonial Spanish America* (Cambridge, 1990).
— *Paths of Accommodation: Muslim Societies and French Colonial Authorities in Senegal and Mauritania, 1880–1920* (Athens, OH, 2000).
— *Bandits, Eunuchs, and the Son of Heaven: Rebellion and the Economy of Violence in Mid-Ming China* (Honolulu, HI, 2001).
Robinson, O.F., *The Criminal Law of Ancient Rome* (Baltimore, MD, 1995).
Robinson, Ronald and John Gallagher, *Africa and the Victorians: The Official Mind of Imperialism* (London, 1961).
Robinson-Dunn, Diane, *The Harem, Slavery and British Imperial Culture* (Manchester, 2006).
Robson, Brian (ed.), *Roberts in India: The Military Papers of Field Marshal Lord Roberts, 1876–1893* (Stroud, 1993).
Rochat, Giorgio, *Il colonialismo italiano* (Turin, 1973).
Rocher, Ludo (ed.), *Ezourvedam: A French Veda of the Eighteenth Century* (Philadelphia, PA, 1984).
Rodney, Walter, *How Europe Underdeveloped Africa* (Washington DC, 1972).
Rodríguez O., Jaime E., *The Independence of Spanish America* (New York, 1998).
Rodríguez, Moisés Enrique, 'The Spanish Habsburgs and their Irish Soldiers (1587–1700)', *Irish Migration Studies in Latin America* 5/2 (2007): pp. 125–30.
Rofel, Lisa, *Other Modernities: Gendered Yearnings in China after Socialism* (Berkeley, CA, 1999).
Rogan, Eugene, *Frontiers of the State in the Late Ottoman Empire: Transjordan 1850–1921* (Cambridge, 1999).
Rogin, Michael, *Fathers and Children: Andrew Jackson and the Subjugation of the American Indian* (New York, 1975).
Roman, Meredith, 'Racism in a "Raceless" Society: Racial Violence at the Stalingrad Giant of Socialist Industry and Images of Soviet Racial Equality, August 1930', *International Labor and Working-Class History* 71 (2007): pp. 185–203.
Romero, Patricia, *E. Sylvia Pankhurst: Portrait of a Radical* (New Haven, CT, 1987).
Roorda, Eric Paul, *The Dictator Next Door: The Good Neighbor Policy and the Trujillo Regime in the Dominican Republic, 1930–1945* (Durham, NC, 1998).
Rosen, Fred (ed.), *Empire and Dissent: The United States and Latin America* (Durham, NC, 2008).
Rosenberg, Emily S., *Spreading the American Dream: American Economic and Cultural Expansion, 1890–1945* (New York, 1982).
— *Financial Missionaries to the World: The Politics and Culture of Dollar Diplomacy, 1900–1930* (Cambridge, MA, 1999).
Rosenberg, William G., 'The Problems of Empire in Imperial Russia', *Ab Imperio* 3 (2005): pp. 453–69.
Rosenthal, Angela and A. Lugo-Ortiz (eds), *Invisible Subjects? Slave Portraiture in the Circum-Atlantic World, 1630–1890* (forthcoming)
Roseveare, H., *The Financial Revolution 1660–1760* (London, 1991).
Roshwald, Aviel, *Ethnic Nationalism and the Fall of Empires: Central Europe, Russia, and the Middle East, 1914–1924* (New York, 2001).

Rosier, Paul C., *Serving Their Country: American Indian Politics and Patriotism in the Twentieth Century* (Cambridge, MA, 2009).

Ross, R., *Beyond the Pale: Essays on the History of Colonial South Africa* (Hanover, NH, 1993), pp. 170–77.

Rothenberg, Gunther, *The Army of Francis Joseph* (West Lafayette, IN, 1998).

Rothman, Adam, *Slave Country: American Expansion and the Origins of the Deep South* (Cambridge, MA, 2005).

Rothschild, Emma, 'A Horrible Tragedy in the French Atlantic', *Past and Present* 192 (2006): pp. 67–108.

Routledge, David, *Matanitu: The Struggle for Power in Early Fiji* (Suva, 1985).

Roxburgh, David, *Prefacing the Image: Art History in Sixteenth-Century Iran* (Leiden, 2001).

Rudolph, Jennifer, *Negotiated Power in Late Imperial China: The Zongli Yamen and the Politics of Reform* (Ithaca, NY, 2008).

Ruiz, Vicki L., *Out of the Shadows: Mexican Women in Twentieth Century America* (Oxford, 1999).

Russell, Peter, *Prince Henry 'the Navigator': A Life* (New Haven, CT, 2000).

Russell-Wood, A.J.R., 'Centers and Peripheries in the Luso-Brazilian Work, 1500–1808', in Christine Daniels and Michael V. Kennedy (eds), *Negotiated Empires: Centers and Peripheries in the Americas, 1500–1820* (New York and London, 2002), pp. 105–142.

— 'The Portuguese Atlantic, 1415–1808', in Jack P. Greene and Phillip D. Morgan (eds), *Atlantic History: A Critical Appraisal* (Oxford, 2009), pp. 81–109.

Ryan, James R., *Picturing Empire: Photography and the Visualization of the British Empire* (Chicago, IL, 1997).

Rydell, Robert, *All the World's A Fair: Visions of Empire at American International Expositions, 1876–1916* (Chicago, IL, 1984).

Saada, Emmanuelle, 'Race and Sociological Reason in the Republic: Inquiries on the Métis in the French Empire (1908–37)', *International Sociology* 17/3 (2002): pp. 361–91.

— 'Empire of Law: Dignity, Prestige, and Domination in the "Colonial Situation"', *French Politics, Culture and Society* 20/2 (2002): pp. 98–120.

Saberwal, Vasant, *Pastoral Politics: Shepherds, Bureaucrats, and Conservation in the Western Himalaya* (Delhi, 1999).

Said, Edward, *Orientalism: Western Conceptions of the Orient* (New York, 1978).

— *Culture and Imperialism* (New York, 1993).

Saini, Muhammad Baqir Najm, *Advice on the Art of Governance, An Indo-Islamic Mirror for Princes: Mau''izah-i Jahangiri of Muhammad Baqir Najm-i Saini*, trans. Sajida Sultana Alvi (Albany, NY, 1989).

Saint, Ravikant and Tarun K. (eds), *Translating Partition: Stories by Attia Hosain et al* (New Delhi, 2001).

Saler, Beth, 'An Empire for Liberty, A State for Empire: The US National State before and after the Revolution of 1800', in James P. Horn, Peter S. Onuf and Jan Lewis (eds), *The Revolution of 1800: Democracy, Race, and the New Republic* (Charlottesville, VA, 2002), pp. 360–82.

Salesa, Damon, 'New Zealand's Pacific', in G. Byrnes (ed.), *The New Oxford History of New Zealand* (Oxford, 2009), pp. 149–72.

— *Racial Crossings: Victorian Britain, Colonial New Zealand and the Problem of the Races* (Oxford, 2011).

Salmond, Anne, *The Trial of the Cannibal Dog: The Remarkable Story of Captain Cook's Encounters in the South Seas* (New Haven, CT, 2003).

Sànchez, George J., *Becoming Mexican American: Ethnicity, Culture, and Identity in Chicano Los Angeles, 1900–1945* (Oxford, 1993).

Sanders, Edith R., 'The Hamitic Hypothesis: Its Origin and Functions in Time Perspective', *Journal of African History* 10/4 (1969): pp. 521–32.

Sandhu, K.S., *Indians in Malaya* (Cambridge, MA, 1969).

Sarkar, Jadunath, *India of Aurangzeb* (Calcutta, 1901).

— *History of Aurangzeb*, 5 vols (Calcutta, 1912–24).

Sarkar, Tanika, *Hindu Wife, Hindu Nation: Community, Religion, and Cultural Nationalism* (London, 2001).

Sassen, Saskia, *Guests and Aliens* (New York, 1999).

Satia, Priya, *Spies in Arabia: The Great War and the Cultural Foundations of Britain's Covert Empire in the Middle East* (Oxford, 2008).

Satre, Lowell J., *Chocolate on Trial: Slavery, Politics and the Ethics of Business* (Athens, OH, 2005).

Saunders, Kay (ed.), *Indentured Labour in the British Empire, 1834–1920* (London, 1984).

Savarkar, Vinayak Damoda, *Hindutva: Who is a Hindu?* 4th edn (Poona, 1949).

Savitt, Todd Lee, *Medicine and Slavery: The Diseases and Health Care of Blacks in Antebellum Virginia* (Urbana, IL, 1978).

Sayer, Derek, 'British Reaction to the Amritsar Massacre 1919–1920', *Past and Present* 131/1 (1991): pp. 130–64.

Schaffer, Simon, 'Enlightenment Brought Down to Earth', *History of Science* 41 (2003): pp. 257–68.

Schama, Simon, *Landscape and Memory* (New York, 1996).

Schatkowski-Schilcher, Linda, *Families in Politics: Damascene Families and Estates of the Eighteenth and Nineteenth Centuries* (Stuttgart, 1985).

Schiebinger, Londa, *Nature's Body: Gender in the Making of Modern Science* (Boston, MA, 1989).

— *Plants and Empire: Colonial Bioprospecting in the Atlantic World* (Cambridge, MA, 2004).

Schlesinger, Stephen and Stephen Kinzer, *Bitter Fruit: The Story of the American Coup in Guatemala* (Cambridge, MA, 1999).

Schmid, Andre, *Korea between Empires, 1895–1919* (New York, 2002).

Schmidt, Benjamin, 'The Dutch Atlantic: From Provincialism to Globalism', in Jack P. Greene and Philip D. Morgan (eds), *Atlantic History: A Critical Appraisal* (Oxford, 2008), pp. 166–71.

Schmidt, Hans, *Maverick Marine: General Smedley D. Butler and Contradictions of American Military History* (Lexington, KY, 1987).

Schmitz, David, *Thank God They're on Our Side* (Chapel Hill, NC, 1999).

Schmokel, Wolfe, *Dream of Empire: German Colonialism, 1919–1945* (New Haven, CT, 1964).

Schneer, Jonathan, *London 1900* (New Haven, CT, 1999).
— *The Balfour Declaration: The Origins of the Arab-Israeli Conflict* (New York, 2010).
Schneider, Alison, *Suffragists in an Imperial Age: US Expansion and the Woman Question, 1870–1929* (Oxford, 2008).
Schwab, Raymond, *The Oriental Renaissance* (New York, 1984).
Schwartz, Marie Jenkins, *Birthing a Slave: Motherhood and Medicine in the Antebellum South* (Cambridge, MA, 2006).
Schwartz, Stuart B., *Sugar Plantations in the Formation of Brazilian Society: Bahia, 1550–1835* (Cambridge, 1985).
— (ed.), *Tropical Babylons: Sugar and the Making of the Atlantic World, 1450–1680* (Chapel Hill, NC, 2004).
— *All Can Be Saved: Religious Tolerance and Salvation in the Iberian Atlantic World* (New Haven, CT, 2008).
Schwartzberg, Joseph E. (ed.), *A Historical Atlas of South Asia*, 2nd imp., with additional material (New York, 1992).
Sciortino, Rosalia, 'The Multifariousness of Nursing in the Netherlands Indies', in Peter Boomgaard, Rosalia Sciortino and Ines Smyth (eds), *Health Care in Java: Past and Present* (Leiden, 1996), pp. 23–50.
Scott, David, *Refashioning Futures: Criticism After Postcoloniality* (Princeton, NJ, 1999).
Scott, James C., *Seeing Like a State: How Certain Schemes to Improve the Human Condition Have Failed* (New Haven, CT, 1998).
— *The Art of Not Being Governed: An Anarchist History of Upland Southeast Asia* (New Haven, CT, 2009).
Scott, Joan, *Gender and the Politics of History* (New York, rev. edn, 1999).
Scully, Eileen P., 'Taking the Low Road in Sino-American Relations: "Open Door" Expansionists and the Two China Markets', in *Journal of American History* 82 (1995): pp. 62–83.
— *Bargaining with the State from Afar: American Citizenship in Treaty Port China, 1844–1942* (New York, 2001).
Seal, Graham, *Inventing Anzac: The Digger and National Mythology* (St Lucia, QLD, 2004).
Seat, Karen K., *Providence Has Freed Our Hands: Women's Missions and the American Encounter with Japan* (Syracuse, NY, 2008).
Secombe, L.J. and R.I. Lawless, 'Foreign Worker Dependence in the Gulf, and the International Oil Companies, 1910–1950', *International Migration Review* 20/3 (1986): pp. 548–74.
Seed, Patricia, *Ceremonies of Possession: Europe's Conquest of the New World, 1492–1640* (Cambridge, 1995).
— *American Pentimento: The Invention of Indians and the Pursuit of Riches* (Minneapolis, MN, 2001).
Segrè, Claudio, *Fourth Shore: The Italian Colonization of Libya* (Chicago, IL, 1974).
Segurado, E.M.S.C., '"Vagos, Ociosos y Malentretenidos": The Deportation of Mexicans to the Philippines in the Eighteenth Century', unpublished paper delivered at the American Historical Association Annual Meeting, Atlanta, GA, 5 January 2007.

Sekula, Allan, 'The Body and the Archive', in Richard Bolton (ed.), *The Contest of Meaning: Critical Histories of Photography* (Cambridge, MA, 1992), pp. 343–89.

Semmel, Bernard, *The Rise of Free Trade Imperialism: Classical Political Economy and the Empire of Free Trade Imperialism, 1750–1850* (Cambridge, 1970).

Sen, Amartya, *Poverty and Famines: An Essay on Entitlement and Deprivation* (Oxford, 1981).

Serulnikov, S., *Subverting Colonial Authority: Challenges to Spanish Rule in Eighteenth-Century Southern Andes* (Durham, NC, 2003).

Seshan, Radhika and Sushma J. Varma (eds), *Fractured Identities: The Indian Diaspora in Canada* (Jaipur, 2003).

Seth, Sanjay, *Subject Lessons: The Western Education of Colonial India* (Durham, NC, 2007).

Sharma, Sanjay, *Famine, Philanthropy and the Colonial State* (Delhi, 2001).

Sharma, Sri Ram, *Religious Policies of the Mughal Emperors* (London, 1940).

Sharpe, Pamela, *Women, Gender, and Labour Migration: Historical and Global Perspectives* (London, 2001).

Shaw, A.G.L., *Convicts and the Colonies: A Study of Penal Transportation from Great Britain and Ireland to Australia and Other Parts of the British Empire* (London, 1966).

Shaw, Stanford, *History of the Ottoman Empire and Turkey* 2 vols. (Cambridge, MA, 1976-77).

Shaw, Thurstan (ed.), *Discovering Nigeria's Past* (Ibadan, 1975).

Shechter, Relli (ed.), *Transitions in Domestic Consumption and Family Life in the Modern Middle East* (New York, 2003).

Sheehan, Bernard W., *Savagism and Civility: Indians and Englishmen in Colonial Virginia* (Cambridge, 1980).

Shell, Susan, 'Kant's Concept of a Human Race', in Sara Eigen and Mark Larrimor (eds), *The German Invention of Race* (New York, 2006), pp. 55–72.

Sheller, Mimi, 'Sword-Bearing Citizens: Militarism and Manhood in Nineteenth-Century Haiti', *Plantation Societies in the Americas* 4/2–3 (1997): pp. 233–88.

Shepard, Todd, *The Invention of Decolonization: The Algerian War and the Remaking of France* (Ithaca, NY, 2006).

Sheridan, Richard, *Doctors and Slaves: A Medical and Demographic History of Slavery in the British West Indies, 1680–1834* (Cambridge, 1985).

— *Sugar and Slavery: An Economic History of the British West Indies* (Kingston, 2000).

Sherry, Michael S., *The Rise of American Air Power: The Creation of Armageddon* (New Haven, CT, 1987).

Shin, Gi-Wook and Michael Robinson (eds), *Colonial Modernity in Korea* (Cambridge, MA, 1999).

— and Do-Hyun Han, 'Colonial Corporatism: The Rural Revitalization Campaign, 1932–1940', in Gi-Wook Shin and Michael Robinson (eds), *Colonial Modernity in Korea* (Cambridge, MA, 1999), pp. 70–96.

— and Michael Robinson, 'Introduction: Rethinking Colonial Korea', in Gi-Wook Shin and Michael Robinson (eds), *Colonial Modernity in Korea* (Cambridge, MA, 1999), pp. 1–20.

Shiraishi, Takashi, *An Age in Motion: Popular Radicalism in Java, 1912–1926* (Ithaca, NY, 1990).

Shoemaker, Nancy (ed.), *Negotiators of Change: Historical Perspectives on Native American Women* (New York, 1995).

Shohat, Ella, 'Notes on the Postcolonial', *Social Text* 31/32 (1992): pp. 99–113.

Shorto, Russell, *The Island at the Center of the World* (New York, 2004).

Showers, Kate, 'Themes in Environmental History, Method and Fieldwork', unpublished paper delivered at History and Sustainability Conference, Cambridge, 10 January 2009.

Shyllon, F.O., *Black People in Britain, 1555–1833* (London, 1977).

Siddle, Richard, *Race, Resistance and the Ainu of Japan* (Oxford, 1996).

Sigal, Pete (ed.), *Infamous Desire: Male Homosexuality in Colonial Latin America* (Chicago, IL, 2003).

Sikainga, Ahmad Alawad, *Slaves Into Workers: Emancipation and Labor in Colonial Sudan* (Austin, TX, 1996).

Silva, Noenoe K., *Aloha Betrayed: Native Hawaiian Resistance to American Colonialism* (Durham, NC, 2004).

Silver, Timothy, *A New Face on the Countryside: Indians, Colonists, and Slaves in the South Atlantic Forests* (Cambridge, 1990).

Singh, Bhagat, *Canadian Sikhs Through a Century (1897–1997)* (Delhi, 2001).

Singh, Chetan, 'Forests, Pastoralists and Agrarian Society in Mughal India', in David Arnold and Ramchandra Guha (eds), *Nature, Culture, Imperialism* (Delhi, 1995), pp. 21–48.

Singh, Kushwant, *Train to Pakistan* (New Delhi, 1988).

Singh, Nikhil Pal, 'Culture/Wars: Recoding Empire in an Age of Democracy', *American Quarterly* 50/3 (1998): pp. 471–522.

— *Black is a Country: Race and the Unfinished Struggle for Democracy* (Cambridge, MA, 2004).

Singha, Radhika, *A Despotism of Law: Crime and Justice in Early Colonial India* (Delhi, 1998).

— 'Settle, Mobilize, Verify: Identification Practices in Colonial India', *Studies in History* 16/2 (2000): pp. 151–98.

Sinha, Mrinalini, *Colonial Masculinity: The 'Manly Englishman' and the 'Effeminate Bengali' in the Late Nineteenth Century* (Manchester and New York, 1995).

— 'Britishness, Clubability and the Imperial Public Sphere: The Genealogy of an Imperial Institution in Colonial India', *Journal of British Studies* 40 (2001): pp. 481–529.

— *Specters of Mother India: The Global Restructuring of an Empire* (Durham, NC, 2006).

Sivaramakrishnan, K., *Modern Forests, State Making and Environmental Change in Eastern India* (Delhi, 1999).

Sivasundaram, Sujit, *Nature and the Godly Empire: Science and Evangelical Mission in the Pacific, 1795–1850* (Cambridge, 2005).

— '"A Christian Benares": Science, Orientalism and the Serampore Mission of Bengal', *Indian Economic and Social History Review* 44 (2007): pp. 111–45.

— 'Tales of the Land: British Geography and Kandyan Resistance in Sri Lanka, c. 1803–1850', *Modern Asian Studies* 41 (2007): pp. 925–61.

— (ed.), 'Global histories of science', *Isis*, 101 (2010), pp. 95-158.

Slatta, Richard W., *Comparing Cowboys and Frontiers: New Perspectives on the History of the Americas* (Norman, OK, 1997).

Slezkine, Yuri, *Arctic Mirrors: Russia and the Small Peoples of the North* (Ithaca, NY, 1994),

Slotkin, Richard, *Regeneration Through Violence: The Mythology of the American Frontier, 1600–1860* (Norman, OK, 1973).

Smellie, William, *The Philosophy of Natural History* (Edinburgh, 1790).

Smith, Adam, *An Inquiry into the Nature and Causes of the Wealth of Nations* (London, 1776).

Smith, Alison and Mary Bull (eds), *Margery Perham and British Rule in Africa* (London, 1991).

Smith, Bernard, *Place, Taste and Tradition: A Study of Australian Art since 1788* (London, 1945).

— *European Vision and the South Pacific, 1769–1850: A Study in the History of Ideas* (Oxford, 1960).

— *Imagining the Pacific* (New Haven, CT, 1992).

Smith, D. Woodruff, *The German Colonial Empire* (Chapel Hill, NC, 1978).

— *Consumption and the Making of Respectability, 1600–1800* (New York, 2002).

Smith, Jonathon Z., *Relating Religion: Essays in the Study of Religion* (Chicago, IL, 2004).

Smith, Neil, *American Empire: Roosevelt's Geographer and the Prelude to Globalization* (Berkeley, CA, 2003).

Smith, Pamela and Benjamin Schmidt (eds), *Making Knowledge in Early Modern Europe: Practices, Objects, and Texts, 1400–1800* (Chicago, IL, 2007).

Smith, Richard, *Jamaican Volunteers in the First World War: Race, Masculinity and the Development of National Consciousness* (Manchester, 2004).

Smith, Simon C., *Reassessing Suez 1956* (Farnham, 2008).

Smith, W.G. Clarence, *Islam and the Abolition of Slavery* (Oxford, 2006).

Smith, W. Tyler, 'Lectures on Parturition, and the Principles and Practice of Obstetrics', *The Lancet*, 50, no. 1264 (20 November 1847): pp 542–44.

Smoker, Dorothy, *Ambushed by Love: God's Triumph in Kenya's Terror* (Fort Washington, PA, 1994).

Sneider, Allison L., *Suffragists in an Imperial Age: US Expansion and the Woman Question, 1870–1929* (New York, 2008).

Snodgrass, Jeffrey, *Casting Kings: Bard and Indian Modernity* (New York, 2006).

Solkin, David, *Painting for Money: The Visual Arts and the Public Sphere in Eighteenth-Century England* (New Haven, CT, 1993).

Sorlin, Sverker and Paul Warde, 'The Problem of the Problem of Environmental History: A Re-reading of the Field', *Environmental History* 12/1 (2007): pp. 107–130.

Southard, Barbara, 'Colonial Politics and Women's Rights: Woman Suffrage Campaigns in Bengal, British India in the 1920s', *Modern Asian Studies* 27 (1993): pp. 397–439.

Spandounes, Theodōros, *On the Origins of the Ottoman State*, trans. and ed. Donald MacGillivray Nicol (Cambridge, 2009).

Spary, Emma, *Utopia's Garden: French Natural History from Old Regime to Revolution* (Chicago, IL, 2000).

Sparrow, Bartholomew H., *The Insular Cases and the Emergence of American Empire* (Lawrence, KS, 2006).

Spear, Percival, *Twilight of the Mughuls: Studies in Late Mughal Delhi* (Cambridge, 1951).

Spence, Jonathan D., *God's Chinese Son: The Taiping Heavenly Kingdom of Hong Xiuchuan* (New York, 1996).

— *The Search for Modern China* (New York, 1999).

— *Treason by the Book* (New York, 2001).

— and John E. Wills, Jr (eds), *From Ming to Ch'ing: Conquest, Region and Continuity in Seventeenth-Century China* (New Haven, CT, 1979).

Spenser, Daniela, *The Impossible Triangle: Mexico, Soviet Russia, and the United States in the 1920s* (Durham, NC, 1999).

Spieler, Miranda, 'The Legal Structure of Colonial Rule during the French Revolution', *William and Mary Quarterly* 66 (2009): pp. 365–408.

— *Empire and the Underworld: Captivity in French Guiana* (Cambridge, MA, 2012).

Spiers, Edward M., *The Scottish Soldier and Empire, 1854–1902* (Edinburgh, 2006).

Spitzer, Leo, *The Creoles of Sierra Leone: Responses to Colonialism, 1870–1945* (Madison, WI, 1974).

Spivak, Gayatri Chakravorty, 'Can the Subaltern Speak?', in Cary Nelson and Lawrence Grossberg (eds), *Marxism and the Interpretation of Culture* (Urbana, IL, 1988), pp. 271–313.

Springhall, John, *Decolonization Since 1945: The Collapse of European Overseas Empires* (New York, 2001).

Srivastava, Neelam, 'Anti-colonialism and the Italian Left', *Interventions: The International Journal of Postcolonial Studies* 8/3 (2006): pp. 413–29.

Stafford, Fiona, *The Last of the Race: The Growth of a Myth from Milton to Darwin* (Oxford, 1994).

Stamp, L.D., 'Notes on the Vegetation of Burma', *Geographical Journal* 43 (1924): pp. 231–3.

— 'The Aerial Survey of the Irrawady Delta Forests', *Journal of Ecology* 15 (1924): pp. 262–76.

— 'Burma: A Survey of a Monsoon Country', *Geographical Review* 20 (1930): pp. 86–109.

— 'The Irrawady River', *Geographical Journal* 95 (1940): pp. 329–56.

Stanley, Brian, *The Bible and the Flag: Protestant Mission and British Imperialism in the Nineteenth and Twentieth Centuries* (Nottingham, 1990).

Stasiulis, Daiva and Nira Yuval Davis, *Unsettling Settler Societies: Articulations of Gender, Race, Ethnicity and Class* (London, 1995).

Stearns, Peter N., *Gender in World History* (London and New York, 2000).

— *Consumerism in World History: The Global Transformation of Desire* (London, 2001).

Stebbing, E.P., *The Forests of India* (Edinburgh, 1922).

— *The Creeping Desert in the Sudan and Elsewhere in Africa: 15 to 13 Degrees Latitude* (Khartoum, 1953).

Steensgaard, Niels, *The Asian Trade Revolution of the Seventeenth Century: The East India Companies and the Decline of the Caravan Trade* (Chicago, IL and London, 1973).

— 'The Seventeenth-Century Crisis and the Unity of the Eurasian History', *Modern Asian Studies* 24/4 (1990): pp. 683–97.

— 'The Growth and Composition of the Long-distance Trade of England and the Dutch Republic before 1750', in J.D. Tracy (ed.), *The Rise of Merchant Empires: Long-distance Trade in the Early Modern World 1350–1750* (Cambridge, 1990), pp. 123–31.

Steijlen, Fridus (ed.), *Memories of 'The East': Abstracts of the Dutch Interviews about the Netherlands East Indies, Indonesia and New Guinea (1930–1962) in the Oral History Collection* (Leiden, 2002).

— and Erik Willems (eds), *Met ons alles goed: Brieven en films uit Nederlands-Indie van de familie Kuyck* (Zutphen, 2008).

Stein, Burton, 'Eighteenth-Century India: Another View', in P.J. Marshall (ed.), *The Eighteenth Century in Indian History: Evolution or Revolution?* (Oxford, 2005), pp. 62–89.

Stein, Stanley J. and Barbara H. Stein, *The Colonial Heritage of Latin America: Essays on Economic Dependence in Perspective* (Oxford, 1970).

Stepan, Nancy, *The Idea of Race in Science: Great Britain, 1800–1960* (Hamden, 1982).

— 'Race and Gender: The Role of Analogy in Science', *Isis* 77 (1986): pp. 261–77.

Stephanson, Anders, *Manifest Destiny: American Expansion and the Empire of Right* (New York, 1995).

— 'A Most Interesting Empire', in Lloyd C. Gardner and Marilyn B. Young (eds), *The New American Empire: A Twenty-First Century Teach-In on US Foreign Policy* (New York, 2005), pp. 253–75.

Stephens, Michelle Ann, *Black Empire: The Masculine Global Imaginary of Caribbean Intellectuals in the United States, 1914–1962* (Durham, NC, 2005).

Stern, Philip J., 'History and Historiography of the English East India Company: Past, Present, and Future', *History Compass* 7/4 (2009): pp. 1146–80.

Stetz, Margaret and Bonnie B.C. Oh (eds), *Legacies of the Comfort Women of World War II* (Amonk, NY, 2001).

Stevenson, Marion, *Karirikania* (Nyeri, 1924).

Stockel, H. Henrietta, *Salvation Through Slavery: Chiricahua Apaches and Priests on the Spanish Colonial Frontier* (Albuquerque, NM, 2008).

Stocking, Jr, George W., *Victorian Anthropology* (New York, 1987).

Stockwell, A.J., 'Imperialism and Nationalism in South-East Asia', in Judith M. Brown and Wm Roger Louis (eds), *The Oxford History of the British Empire*, vol. 4: *The Twentieth Century* (Oxford, 1999), pp. 465–98.

Stokes, Eric, *The English Utilitarians and India* (Oxford, 1959).

— *The Peasant and the Raj: Studies in Agrarian Society and Peasant Rebellion in Colonial India* (Cambridge, 1978).

Stolberg, Michael, 'A Woman Down to Her Bones: The Anatomy of Sexual Difference in the Sixteenth and Early Seventeenth Centuries', *Isis* 94 (2003): pp. 274–99.

Stoler, Ann Laura, *Race and the Education of Desire: Foucault's History of Sexuality and the Colonial Order of Things* (Durham, NC, 1995).

— *Carnal Knowledge and Imperial Power: Race and the Intimate in Colonial Rule* (Berkeley, CA, 2002).

— (ed.), *Haunted by Empire: Geographies of Intimacy in North American History* (Durham, NC, 2006).

— *Along the Archival Grain: Epistemic Anxieties and Colonial Common Sense* (Princeton, NJ, 2009).

— and Frederick Cooper, 'Between Metropole and Colony: Rethinking a Research Agenda', in Cooper and Ann Laura Stoler (eds), *Tensions of Empires: Colonial Cultures in a Bourgeois World* (Berkeley, CA, 1997), pp. 1–55.

— and Carole McGranahan, 'Introduction: Refiguring Imperial Terrains', in Ann L. Stoler, Carole McGranahan and Peter C. Perdue (eds), *Imperial Formations* (Santa Fe, NM, 2007), pp. 3–42.

Stovall, Tyler, 'Colour-blind France? Colonial Workers During the First World War', *Race and Class* 35/2 (1993): pp. 35–55.

Stowe, Steven, 'Obstetrics and the Work of Doctoring in the Mid-Nineteenth-Century American South', *Bulletin of the History of Medicine* 64/4 (1990): pp. 540–66.

Strasser, Susan, Charles McGovern and Matthias Judt (eds), *Getting and Spending: European and American Consumer Societies in the Twentieth Century* (Cambridge, 1998).

Streeby, Shelly, *American Sensations: Class, Empire, and the Production of Popular Culture* (Berkeley, CA, 2002).

Streets, Heather, *Martial Races: The Military, Race and Masculinity in British Imperial Culture, 1857–1914* (Manchester, 2004).

Streusand, Douglas E., *Formation of the Mughal Empire* (New York, 1989).

Striffler, Steve and Mark Moberg (eds), *Banana Wars: Power, Production, and History in the Americas* (Durham, NC, 2003).

Struve, Lynn A., *Voices from the Ming-Qing Cataclysm: China in Tigers' Jaws* (New Haven, CT, 1993).

Strzelecki, Paul, *Physical Description of New South Wales* (London, 1845).

Subrahmanyam, Sanjay, 'Persians, Pilgrims and Portuguese: The Travails of Masulipatnam Shipping in the Western Indian Ocean, 1590–1665', *Modern Asian Studies* 22/3 (1988): pp. 503–530.

— *The Political Economy of Commerce: Southern India, 1500–1650* (New York, 1990).

— 'Iranians Abroad: Intra-Asian Elite Migration and Early Modern State Formation', in Sanjay Subrahmanyam (ed.), *Merchant Networks in the Early Modern World* (London, 1996), pp. 72–95.

— 'Connected Histories: Notes toward a Reconfiguration of Early Modern Eurasia', *Modern Asian Studies* 31/3 (July 1997), pp. 735–62.

— *Explorations in Connected History*, 2 vols (New York, 2005).

— 'Holding the World in the Balance: The Connected Histories of the Iberian Overseas Empires, 1500–1640', *American Historical Review* 112/5 (2007): pp. 1329–58.

Summerskill, Michael, *China on the Western Front: Britain's Chinese Work Force in the First World War* (London, 1982).

Sunderland, Willard, *Taming the Wild Field: Colonization and Empire on the Russian Steppe* (Ithaca, NY, 2004).

— 'The Ministry of Asiatic Russia: The Colonial Office That Never Was But Might Have Been', *Slavic Review* 69/1 (2010): pp. 120–50.

Suny, Ronald Grigor and Terry Martin (eds), *A State of Nations: Empire and Nation-Making in the Age of Lenin and Stalin* (Oxford, 2001).

Swaminathan, P., 'Prison as Factory: A Study of Jail Manufactures in the Madras Presidency', *Studies in History* 11/1 (1995): pp. 77–100.

Szanton, David (ed.), *The Politics of Knowledge: Area Studies and the Disciplines* (Berkeley, CA, 2004).

Szonyi, Michael, *Practicing Kinship: Lineage and Descent in Late Imperial China* (Stanford, CA, 2002).

Taagepera, Rein, 'An Overview of the Growth of the Russian Empire', in Michael Rywkin (ed.), *Russian Colonial Expansion to 1917* (London and New York, 1988), pp. 1–7.

— 'Expansion and Contraction Patterns of Large Polities: Context for Russia', *International Studies Quarterly* 44 (1997): pp. 475–504.

Taube, Helene von (ed.), *Graf Alexander Keyserling: Ein Lebensbild aus seinen Briefen und Tagebüchern* (Berlin, 1902).

Tabili, Laura, *'We Ask For British Justice': Workers and Racial Difference in Late Imperial Britain* (Ithaca, NY, 1994).

Takaki, Ronald, *Hiroshima: Why America Dropped the Atomic Bomb* (Boston, MA, 1995).

Talbot, Ian, *Divided Cities: Partition and its Aftermath in Lahore and Amritsar, 1947–1957* (Karachi, 2006).

— and Shinder Thandi (eds), *People on the Move: Panjab Colonial and Post-Colonial Migration* (Karachi, 2004).

Tan, Seng and Amitav Acharya (eds), *Bandung Revisited: The Legacy of the 1955 Asian-African Conference for International Order* (Singapore, 2008).

Tanaka, Ryūichi, *Manshūkoku to Nihon no Teikokushihai* (Tokyo, 2007).

Tanaka, Stefan, *Japan's Orient: Rendering Pasts into History* (Berkeley, CA, 1993).

Tarling, Nicholas, '"Ah-Ah": Britain and the Bandung Conference of 1955', *Journal of Southeast Asian Studies* 23/1 (1992): pp. 74–111.

— *The Cambridge History of Southeast Asia* (Cambridge, 1993).

Tarlo, Emma, *Clothing Matters: Dress and Identity in India* (Chicago, IL, 1996).

Taussig, Michael, *Mimesis and Alterity: A Particular History of the Senses* (New York, 1993).

Tavakoli-Targhi, Mohamad, *Refashioning Iran: Orientalism, Occidentalism, and Historiography* (New York, 2001).

Taylor, A.J.P., *Germany's First Bid for Colonies, 1884–1885: A Move in Bismarck's European Policy* (London, 1938).

Taylor, Charles, 'Two Theories of Modernity', in Dilip P. Gaonkar (ed.), *Alternative Modernities* (Durham, NC, 2001), pp. 172–96.

Taylor, Jean Gelman, *The Social World of Batavia* (Madison, WI, 1983).

Taylor, Kim, *Chinese Medicine in Early Communist China, 1945–1963: A Medicine of Revolution* (London and New York, 2005).

Teng, Emma Jinhua, *Taiwan's Imagined Geography: Chinese Colonial Travel Writing and Pictures, 1683–1895* (Cambridge, MA, 2004).

Thal, Sarah, 'A Religion that was not a Religion: The Creation of Modern Shinto in Nineteenth-Century Japan', in Derek R. Peterson and Darren R. Walhof (eds), *The Invention of Religion: Rethinking Belief in Politics and History* (New Brunswick, NJ, 2002), pp. 100–114.

— *Rearranging the Landscape of the Gods: The Politics of a Pilgrimage Site in Japan, 1573–1912* (Chicago, IL, 2005).

Theodat, F. Gabriel Sagard, *Le Grand Voyage du Pays des Hurons* (Paris, 1865).

Thiong'o, Ngũgĩ wa, *Decolonising the Mind: The Politics of Language in African Literature* (London, 1986).

Thomas, Dominic, *Black France: Colonialism, Immigration, and Transnationalism* (Bloomington, IN, 2007).

Thomas, Kaiser, 'The Evil Empire? The Debate on Turkish Despotism in Eighteenth-Century French Political Culture', *Journal of Modern History* 72/1 (2000): pp. 6–34.

Thomas, Keith, *Man and the Natural World* (Oxford, 1984).

Thomas, Martin, 'Order Before Reform: The Spread of French Military Operations in Algeria, 1954–1958', in David Killingray and David Omissi (eds), *Guardians of Empire: The Armed Forces of the Colonial Powers c. 1700–1964* (Manchester, 1999), pp. 198–200.

Thomas, Nicola J., 'Embodying Imperial Spectacle: Dressing Lady Curzon, Vicereine of India, 1899–1905', *Cultural Geographies* 14/3 (2007): pp. 369–400.

Thomas, Nicholas, *Entangled Objects: Exchange, Material Culture and Colonialism in the Pacific* (Cambridge, MA, 1991).

— *Colonialism's Culture: Anthropology, Travel and Government* (Cambridge, 1994).

— *Possessions: Indigenous Art/Colonial Culture* (London, 1999).

— and Diane Losche (eds), *Double Vision: Art Histories and Colonial Histories in the Pacific* (London, 1999).

Thomas, William L. (ed.), *Man's Role in Changing the Face of the Earth* (Chicago, IL, 1956).

Thompson, Andrew, 'Empire and the British State', in Sarah Stockwell (ed.), *The British Empire: Themes and Perspectives* (Oxford, 2008), pp. 39–61.

Thompson, Leonard, *A History of South Africa* (New Haven, CT, 1990).

Thompson, T. Jack, 'Capturing the Image: African Missionary Photography as Enslavement and Liberation', Day Associates Lecture, 29 June 2007, Yale University Divinity School, New Haven, CT.

Thompson, Virginia and Richard Adloff, *The Malagasy Republic: Madagascar Today* (Stanford, CA, 1965).

Thomson, Alistair, *Anzac Memories: Living with the Legend* (Melbourne, 1994).

Thorne, Susan, *Congregational Missions and the Making of an Imperial Culture in Nineteenth-Century England* (Stanford, CA, 1999).

Thornton, John, *Africa and Africans in the Making of the Atlantic World, 1400–1800* (Cambridge, 1998).

— 'The Portuguese in Africa', in Francisco Béthencourt and Diogo Ramada Curto (eds), *Portuguese Oceanic Expansion, 1400–1800* (New York, 2007), pp. 138–60.

Thys-Şenocak, Lucienne, *Ottoman Women Builders: The Architectural Patronage of Hadice Turhan Sultan* (Aldershot, 2006).

Tilho, J., *Documents scientifiques de la Mission Tilho, 1906–1909* (Paris, 1910–11).

Tillotson, G.H.R., *The Artificial Landscape* (Aldershot, 1999).

Tilly, Charles, *Coercion, Capital, and European States, AD 990–1990* (Cambridge, MA, 1990).

Tilley, Helen, 'Global Histories, Vernacular Science and African Genealogies; or is the History of Science Ready for the World?', *Isis* 101 (2010): pp.110-19.

Tinker, Hugh, *A New System of Slavery: The Export of Indian Labour Overseas, 1830–1920* (Bombay, 1974).

— *Separate and Unequal: India and the Indians in the British Commonwealth, 1920–1950* (London, 1976).

Tobe, Hideaki, 'Post-colonialism to teikokushikenkyū', in Nihonshoku-minchikenkyūkai (ed.), *Nihonshokuminchikenkyu no Genjō to Kadai* (Tokyo, 2008), pp. 56–88.

Todorov, Tzvetan, *On Human Diversity: Nationalism, Racism and Exoticism in French Thought*, trans. Catherine Porter (Cambridge, 1993).

Toledano, Ehud, *Slavery and Abolition in the Ottoman Middle East* (Seattle, WA, 1998).

— *As if Silent and Absent: Bonds of Enslavement in the Islamic Middle East* (New Haven, CT, 2007).

Tomiyama, Ichiro, *Kindainihonshakai to 'Okinawajin'* (Tokyo, 1990).

Topik, Steven, Consuming Coffee in Central America, 1850–1930', *Diálogos: Revista Electrónica de Historia* 9 (2008), http://historia.fcs.ucr.ac.cr/dialogos.htm.

Toplin, Robert Brent, *The Abolition of Slavery in Brazil* (New York, 1972).

Toshio, Kuroda, 'Shinto in the History of Japanese Religion', *Journal of Japanese Studies* 7 (1981): pp. 1–21.

Toth, Stephen, 'The Lords of Discipline: The Penal Colony Guards of New Caledonia and Guyana', *Crime, Histoire & Sociétés / Crime, History & Societies* 7/2 (2004): pp. 41–60.

— *Beyond Papillon: The French Overseas Penal Colonies, 1854–1952* (Lincoln, NE, 2006).

Travers, Robert, *Ideology and Empire in Eighteenth Century India: The British in Bengal* (Cambridge, 2007).

Trentmann, Frank, 'The Modern Genealogy of the Consumer: Meanings, Identities and Political Synapses', in Frank Trentmann (ed.), *Consuming Cultures, Global Perspectives: Historical Trajectories, Transnational Exchanges* (Oxford, 2006), pp. 19–69.

— 'Knowing Consumers – Histories, Identities, Practices: An Introduction', in Frank Trentmann (ed.), *The Making of the Consumer: Knowledge, Power and Identity in the Modern World* (Oxford, 2006), pp. 1–29.

— *Free Trade Nation: Commerce, Consumption and Civil Society in Modern Britain* (Oxford, 2008).

Trocki, Carl A., *Opium, Empire and Political Economy: A Study of the Asian Opium Trade, 1750–1950* (London, 1999).

Troup, Freda, *South Africa: An Historical Introduction* (Harrmondsworth, 1975).

Troutt Powell, Eve M., *A Different Shade of Colonialism: Egypt, Great Britain and the Mastery of the Sudan* (Berkeley, CA, 2003).

— *Tell this is my Memory: Stories of Enslavement from Egypt, Sudan and the Ottoman Empire* (Stanford, CA, 2012).

Tryon, Thomas, *Friendly Advice to the Gentlemen-planters of the East and West Indies: In Three Parts by Philotheos Physiologus* (London, 1684).

Tsiunchuk, Rustem, 'Peoples, Regions, and Electoral Politics: The State Dumas and the Constitution of New National Elites', in Jane Burbank, Mark von Hagen and Anatolyi Remnev (eds), *Russian Empire: Space, People, Power, 1700–1930* (Bloomington, IN, 2007), pp. 366–97.

Tuck, Patrick, *French Catholic Missionaries and the Politics of Imperialism in Vietnam, 1857–1914: A Documentary Survey* (Liverpool, 1987).

Tucker, Richard P. and John F. Richards (eds), *Global Deforestation in the Nineteenth Century World Economy* (Durham, NC, 1983).

— *World Deforestation in the Twentieth Century* (Durham, NC, 1988).

Turnbull, David, 'Cook and Tupaia: A Tale of Cartographic Méconnaissance?' in Margarette Lincoln (ed.), *Science and Exploration in the Pacific: European Voyages to the Southern Oceans in the Eighteenth Century* (London, 1998), pp. 117–32.

Twitchett, Denis and Frederick W. Mote (eds), *The Cambridge History of China*, vol. 8, Part 2: *The Ming Dynasty, 1368–1644* (Cambridge, 1998).

Tyrrell, Ian, *Transnational Nation: United States History in Global Perspective since 1789* (New York, 2007).

Umland, Andreas, 'Zhirinovsky's *Last Thrust to the South* and the Definition of Fascism', *Russian Politics and Law* 46/4 (2008): pp. 31–46.

Urry, James, *Before Social Anthropology: Essays on the History of British Anthropology,* (Reading, 1993).

Vaidik, A., *Imperial Andamans: A Spatial History of an Island Colony* (Basingstoke, 2010).

Vail, Leroy (ed.), *The Creation of Tribalism in Southern Africa* (London, 1989).

Vaïsse, Maurice, *L'Armée française dans la guerre d'Indochine, 1946–1954: adaptation ou inadaptation* (Paris, 2000).

Valensi, Lucette, *The Birth of the Despot: Venice and the Sublime Porte* (Ithaca, NY, 1993).

Vallejo, Eduardo Aznar, 'The Conquest of the Canary Islands', in Stuart B. Schwartz (ed.), *Implicit Understandings: Observing, Reporting, and Reflecting on the Encounters between Europeans and Other Peoples in the Early Modern Era* (New York, 1994), pp. 134–56.

Vance, Jonathan F., *Death So Noble: Memory, Meaning, and the First World War* (Vancouver, BC, 1997).

Vaughan, Megan, *Curing Their Ills: Colonial Power and African Illness* (Cambridge, 1991).

Vaughan, Olufemi, 'Chieftaincy Politics and Communal Politics in Western Nigeria, 1893–1951', *Journal of Africa History* 44 (2003): pp. 283–302.

Veen, Ernst van, *Decay or Defeat: An Inquiry into the Portuguese Decline in Asia, 1580-1645* (Leiden, 2000).

Veidlinger, Jeffrey, *Jewish Public Culture in the Late Russian Empire* (Bloomington, IN, 2009).

Venkatachalapathy, A.R., '"In those Days there was no Coffee": Coffee Drinking and Middle-Class Culture in Colonial Tamilnadu', *Indian Economic and Social History Review* 39/2 (2002): pp. 301–316.

Verlinden, Charles, *The Beginnings of Modern Colonization* (Ithaca, NY, 1970).

Verma, Acharna B., *The Making of Little Punjab in Canada: Patterns of Immigration* (New Delhi, 2002).

Vernon, James, *Hunger: A Modern History* (Cambridge, 2007).

Vertovec, Steven, 'Caught in an Ethnic Quandary: Indo-Caribbean Hindus in London', in Roger Ballard (ed.), *Desh Pardesh: The South Asian Presence in Britain* (London 1994), pp. 272–90.
— *The Hindu Diaspora: Comparative Patterns* (London, 2000).
Vieira, Alberto, "Sugar Islands: The Sugar Economy of Madeira and the Canaries, 1450 to 1650," in Stuart B. Schwartz, ed., *Tropical Babylons: Sugar and the Making of the Atlantic World, 1450-1680* (Chapel Hill, NC, 2004).
Viswanathan, Gauri, *Outside the Fold: Conversion, Modernity, and Belief* (Princeton, NJ, 1998).
Vita-Finzi, Claudio, *The Mediterranean Valleys: Geological Changes in Historical Times* (Cambridge, 1969).
Voelz, Peter M., *Slave and Soldier: The Military Impact of Blacks in the Colonial Americas* (New York, 1993).
Wade, Bonnie C., *Imaging Sound: An Ethnomusicological Study of Music, Art, and Culture in Mughal India* (Chicago, IL, 1998).
Wagnleitner, Reinhold, *The Coca-colonization of Europe: The Cultural Mission of the United States in Austria after the Second World War* (Chapel Hill, NC, 1994).
Wakeman, Jr, Frederic, *Strangers at the Gate: Social Disorder in South China 1839–61* (Berkeley, CA, 1966).
Waldron, Arthur, *The Great Wall of China: From History to Myth* (Cambridge, 1990).
Waley-Cohen, J., *Exile in Mid-Qing China: Banishment to Xinjiang, 1758–1820* (New Haven, CT, 1991).
Walker, Timothy, 'Slaves or Soldiers?', in Indrani Chatterjee and Richard M. Eaton (eds), *Slavery and South Asian History* (Bloomington, IN, 2006), pp. 234–61.
Wallace, Elisabeth, *The British Caribbean from the Decline of Colonialism to the End of Federation* (Toronto, 1977).
Wallerstein, Immanuel, *The Modern World System*: vol. 1, *Capitalist Agriculture and the Origins of the World-Economy in the Sixteenth Century* (New York, 1974).
— *The Modern World-System*: vol. 2, *Mercantilism and the Consolidation of the European World-Economy, 1600–1750* (San Diego, CA, 1980).
— *World-Systems Analysis: An Introduction* (Durham, NC, 2004).
Wallis, Brian, 'Black Bodies, White Science: Louis Agassiz's Slave Daguerreotypes', *American Art* 9/2 (1995): pp. 39–61.
Walsh, Judith, *Domesticity in Colonial India: What Women Learnt When Men Gave Them Advice* (Lanham, 2004).
Ward, Alan D., *A Show of Justice* (Canberra, 1974).
Wark, Robert (ed.), *Discourses on Art* (New Haven, CT, 1981).
Washbrook, David, *The Emergence of Provincial Politics: The Madras Presidency, 1870–1920* (Cambridge, 1976).
— 'Progress and Problems: South Asian Economic and Social History, c. 1720–1860', *Modern Asian Studies* 22 (1988): pp. 57–96.
— 'South Asia, the World System and World Capitalism', in Sugata Bose (ed.), *South Asia and World Capitalism* (Delhi, 1990), pp. 40–84.
Waterson, James, *The Knights of Islam: The Wars of the Mamluks* (London, 2007).

Weaver, Karol, *Medical Revolutionaries: The Enslaved Healers of Eighteenth-Century Saint Domingue* (Urbana, IL, 2006).

Weber, Eugen, *Peasants into Frenchmen: The Modernization of Rural France, 1870–1914* (Stanford, CA, 1976).

Weber, Max, *The Theory of Social and Economic Organization*, trans. Talcott Parsons (New York, 1964).

Weeks, Theodore, 'Nationalities Policy', in Dominic Lieven (ed.), *The Cambridge History of Russia*: vol. 2, *Imperial Russia, 1689–1917* (New York, 2006), pp. 27–44.

Weeks, William Earl, *John Quincy Adams and American Global Empire* (Lexington, KY, 1992).

Wehler, Hans-Ulrich, 'Bismarck's Imperialism, 1862–1890', *Past and Present* 48/1 (1970): pp. 119–55.

Welch, Sidney, *Portuguese and Dutch in South Africa, 1641–1806* (Cape Town, 1951).

Wesseling, H.L., *The European Colonial Empires, 1815–1919* (Harlow, 2004).

West, Shearer (ed.), *The Victorians and Race* (London, 1996).

Westad, Odd Arne, *The Global Cold War: Third World Interventions and the Making of Our Times* (Cambridge, 2006).

Wexler, Laura, *Tender Violence: Domestic Visions in an Age of US Imperialism* (Chapel Hill, NC, 2000).

Wheatcroft, Andrew, *The Ottomans* (London, 1993).

Wheatley, Phillis, Preface to *Poems on Various Subjects, Religious and Moral* (London, 1773).

White, Luise, *The Comforts of Home: Prostitution in Colonial Nairobi* (Chicago, IL, 1990).

— *Speaking with Vampires: Rumor and History in Colonial Africa* (Berkeley, CA, 2000).

White, Jr, Lynn, *Medieval Technology and Social Change* (London, 1962).

White, Owen, *Children of the French Empire: Miscegenation and Colonial Society in French West Africa, 1895–1960* (Oxford, 1999).

White, Richard, *The Middle Ground: Indians, Empires, and Republics in the Great Lakes Region, 1650–1815* (Cambridge, 1991).

Wiener, Martin, *An Empire on Trial: Race, Murder, and Justice under British Rule, 1870–1935* (Cambridge, 2008).

Wieringa, Saskia, *The Politicization of Gender Relations in Indonesia: The Indonesian Women's Movement and Gerwani until the New Order State* (Amsterdam, 1995).

— *Sexual Politics in Indonesia* (Basingstoke, 2002).

—, Evelyn Blackwood and Abha Bhaiya (eds), *Women's Sexualities and Masculinities in Globalizing Asia* (New York, 2007).

Wigger, Iris, *Die 'Schwarze Schmach am Rhein': Rassistische Diskriminierung zwischen Geschlecht, Klasse, Nation und Rasse* (Münster, 2006).

Wildenthal, Lora, *German Women for Empire, 1884–1945* (Durham, NC, 2001).

Wilder, Gary, *The French Imperial Nation-State: Negritude and Colonial Humanism between the World Wars* (Chicago, IL, 2005).

Will, Pierre-Étienne, *Bureaucracy and Famine in Eighteenth-Century China* (Stanford, CA, 1990).

—, R. Bin Wong *et al.*, *Nourish the People: The State Civilian Granary System in China, 1650–1850* (Ann Arbor, MI, 1991).

Willan, Brian, 'The South African Native Labour Contingent, 1916–18', *Journal of African History* 10 (1978): pp. 61–86.
— *Sol Plaatje, South African Nationalist, 1876–1932* (Berkeley, CA, 1984).
Williams, Ann, *Britain and France in the Middle East and North Africa, 1914–1967* (London, 1968).
Williams, Brian Glyn, *The Crimean Tatars: The Diaspora Experience and the Forging of the Nation* (Leiden, 2001).
Williams, Jr, Robert A., *The American Indian in Western Legal Thought: The Discourses of Conquest* (Oxford, 1991).
Williams, William Appleman, *The Tragedy of American Diplomacy* (New York, 1959).
— *Empire as a Way of Life: An Essay on the Causes and Character of America's Present Predicament along with a Few Thoughts about an Alternative* (New York, 1980).
Willis, Deborah and Carla Williams, 'The Black Female Body in Photographs from World's Fairs and Expositions', *exposure* 33/1 and 2 (2000): pp. 11–20.
Wilson, Jon E., *The Domination of Strangers: Modern Governance in Eastern India, 1780–1835* (Basingstoke, 2008).
Wilson, Kathleen (ed.), *A New Imperial History: Culture, Identity, and Modernity in Britain and the Empire, 1660–1840* (Cambridge, 2004).
Winant, Howard, *The World is a Ghetto: Race and Democracy since World War II* (New York, 2001).
Wink, Andre, *Akbar* (Oxford, 2009).
Winter, Michael and Amalia Levanoni (eds), *Mamluks in Egyptian and Syrian Politics and Society* (Leiden, 2003).
Wiseman, Edith, *Kikuyu Martyrs* (London, 1958).
Wittkower, Rudolf, 'Marvels of the East: A Study in the History of Monsters', *Journal of the Warburg and Courtauld Institutes* 5 (1942): pp. 159–97.
Wolfe, Patrick, 'Land, Labor, and Difference: Elementary Structures of Race', *American Historical Review* 106 (2001): pp. 865–905.
— 'Can the Muslim Speak? An Indebted Critique', *History and Theory* 41 (2002): pp. 367–80.
Wolseley, Viscount, 'The Negro as a Soldier', *Fortnightly Review* 44/264 (1888): pp. 689–90.
Womack, Sarah, 'Ethnicity and Martial Races: The *Garde Indigène* of Cambodia in the 1880s and 1890s', in Karl Hack and Tobias Rettig (eds), *Colonial Armies in South East Asia* (London, 2006), pp. 100–118.
Wong, J.Y., *Deadly Dreams: Opium and the Arrow War in China* (Cambridge, 1998).
Wong, R. Bin, 'Relationship between the Political Economies of Maritime and Agrarian China, 1750–1850', in W. Gungwu and N. Chin-keong (eds), *Maritime China in Transition 1750–1850* (Wiesbaden, 2004).
Wood, Alan, *The Groundnut Affair* (London, 1950).
Wood, Ellen Meiksins, *Empire of Capital* (London, 2003).
Wood, John Cunningham, 'J.A. Hobson and British Imperialism', *American Journal of Economics and Sociology* 42/4 (1983): pp. 483–500.
Wood, Marcus, *Blind Memory: Visual Representations of Slavery in England and America* (Manchester, 2000).

Woodhead, Christine, 'Consolidation of the Ottoman Empire: New Works on Ottoman History, 1453–1839', *English Historical Review* 123/53 (2008): pp. 973–87.

Woollacott, Angela, *Gender and Empire* (Basingstoke, 2006).

Worster, Donald, *Dust Bowl: The Southern Plains in the 1930s* (New York, 1979).

— *Rivers of Empire: Water, Aridity, and the Growth of the American West* (New York, 1985).

— *Nature's Economy: A History of Ecological Ideas* (Oxford, 1985).Wortman, Richard S., *Scenarios of Power: Myth and Ceremony in Russian Monarchy* (Princeton, NJ, 1995).

— 'Ceremony and Power in the Evolution of Russian Monarchy', in Catherine Evtuhov *et al.* (eds), *Kazan, Moscow, St Petersburg: Multiple Faces of the Russian Empire* (Moscow, 1997).

Wrangell, Baron Wilhelm von, *Baron Wilhelm von Rossillon: Ein Lebensbild* (Dorpat, 1934).

Wright, Gwendolyn, *The Politics of Design in French Colonial Urbanism* (Chicago, IL, 1991).

Wright, Harrison M., *New Zealand, 1769–1840: Early Years of Western Contact* (Cambridge, MA, 1959).

Wright, Mary C., *The Last Stand of Chinese Conservatism: The T'ung-Chih Restoration, 1862–1874* (Stanford, CA, 1962).

— *China in Revolution: The First Phase, 1900–13* (New Haven, CT, 1968).

Yamamoto, Hiroshi, 'Manshū', in Nihonshokuminchikenkyūkai (ed.), *Nihonshoku-minchikenkyu no Genjō to Kadai* (Tokyo, 2008), pp. 218–48.

Yamamoto, Yūzō, *Nihon Shokuminchi Keizaishikenkyū* (Nagoya, 1992).

Yanagisawa, Asobu and Makio Okabe, 'Kaisetsu: Teikokushugi to shokuminchi', in Yanagisawa and Okabe (eds), *Tenbō Nihonrekishi 20: Teikokushugi to Shokuminchi* (Tokyo, 2001), pp. 1–12.

Yangwen, Zheng *The Social Life of Opium* (Cambridge, 2005).

Ye'or, Bat, *The Dhimmi: Jews and Christians Under Islam* (Rutherford, NJ, 1985).

Yoo, Theodore Jun, *The Politics of Gender in Colonial Korea: Education, Labor, and Health, 1910–1945* (Berkeley, CA, 2008).

Yoshiaki, Yoshimi, *Comfort Women: Sexual Slavery in the Japanese Military during World War II* (New York, 2000).

Youé, Chris, 'Mamdani's History', *Canadian Journal of African Studies* 34/2 (2000): pp. 397–408.

Young, Louise, *Japan's Total Empire: Manchuria and the Culture of Wartime Imperialism* (Berkeley, CA, 1999).

Young, Marilyn B., *The Vietnam Wars, 1945–1990* (New York, 1991).

Young, Paul, *Globalization and the Great Exhibition: The Victorian New World Order* (Basingstoke, 2009).

Young, Robert J.C., *Colonial Desire: Hybridity in Theory, Culture and Race* (London, 1995).

— *Postcolonialism: An Historical Introduction* (Oxford, 2001).

— 'Nihongoban eno jobun', in Robert Young, *Issatsu de wakaru: Post-colonialism*, trans. Tetsuya Motohashi (Tokyo, 2005).

Yu, Ji-Yeon, *Beyond the Shadow of Camptown: Korean Military Brides in America* (New York, 2002).

Yule, Henry and A.C. Burnell, *Hobson-Jobson: A Glossary of Colloquial Anglo-Indian Words and Phrases, and of Kindred Terms, Etymological, Historical and Discursive* (London 1889).

Yun, Hae-dong, 'Shokuminchininshiki no "gray zone"', *Gendaishisō* 30/6 (2002): pp. 132–47.

— *Singminji ŭi Hwoesaekjidae* (Seoul, 2003).

Zaionchkovskii, P.A., *Samoderzhavie i russkaia armiia na rubezhe xix–xx stoletii, 1881–1903* (Moscow, 1973).

Zaman, Naiz, *A Divided Legacy: The Partition in Selected Novels of India, Pakistan and Bangladesh* (Dhaka, 1999).

Zelin, Madeleine, *The Magistrate's Tael: Rationalizing Fiscal Reform in Eighteenth-Century Ch'ing China* (Berkeley, CA, 1984).

Zheng, Yangwen, *The Social Life of Opium in China* (Cambridge, 2005).

Ziegler, Norman P., 'Rajput Loyalties during the Mughal Period', in John F. Richards (ed.), *Kingship and Authority in South Asia* (New York, 1998), pp. 242–84.

Zika, Charles, 'Cannibalism and Witchcraft in Early Modern Europe: Reading the Visual Images', *History Workshop Journal* 44 (1997): pp. 77–105.

Zinoman, Peter, *The Colonial Bastille: A History of Imprisonment in Vietnam, 1862–1940* (Berkeley, CA, 2001).

Zubok, Vladislav M., *A Failed Empire: The Soviet Union in the Cold War from Stalin to Gorbachev* (Chapel Hill, NC, 2007).

Zürcher, Erik J., 'The Late Ottoman Empire as Laboratory of Demographic Engineering', unpublished paper, English translation.

— *The Unionist Factor: The Role of the Committee of Union and Progress in the Turkish National Movement* (Leiden, 1984).

— 'The Ottoman Conscription System, 1840–1914', *International Review of Social History* 43 (1998): pp. 437–49.

— 'Ottoman Labour Battalions in World War I', in Hans-Lukas Kieser and Dominik J. Schaller (eds), *Der Völkermord an den Armeniern und die Shoah: The Armenian Genocide and the Shoah* (Zürich, 2002), pp. 187–96.

— *Turkey: A Modern History*, 3rd edn (London, 2004).

Websites

www.eh.net/encyclopedia/article/carlos.lewis.furtrade

www.gallica.bnf.fr/ark:/12148/btv1b7702294z

www.h-net.org/~diplo/roundtables/PDF/Thomas-FrenchEmpire.pdf

www.h-net.org/reviews/showrev.php?id=13356

www.slavevoyages.org/tast/index.faces

Archives

Africa Inland Mission Archives (Nairobi)
Anglican Church of Kenya Archives
Archivo General de Indias, Seville
Archivo General de Simancas
Archivo Histórico Nacional, Madrid
Church Missionary Society Archive, University of Birmingham
Derzhavnyi arkhiv v Avtonomnii Respublitsi Krym
Edinburgh University Library Archives (Scotland)
Kenya National Archives (hereafter KNA)
London Mennonite Centre
Oriental and India Office Collections, British Library, London
Presbyterian Church of East Africa Archives (Nairobi, Kenya)
Sudan Archive, University of Durham
Tumutumu Church Archives, Karatina (Kenya)

Index